PACIFIC NORTHWEST
15TH EDITION

Where to Stay and Eat
for All Budgets

Must-See Sights
and Local Secrets

Ratings You Can Trust

Portions of this book appear in *Fodor's Alaska, Fodor's Oregon* and *Fodor's Seattle.*

Fodor's Travel Publications   New York, Toronto, London, Sydney, Auckland
www.fodors.com

FODOR'S PACIFIC NORTHWEST

Editors: Paul Eisenberg, Laura M. Kidder, Emmanuelle Morgen, Jane Onstott, William Travis

Editorial Production: David Downing

Editorial Contributors: Shelley Arenas, Gina Bacon, John Doerper, Zach Dundas, Julie Fay, John Gottberg, Susan Honthumb, Satu Hummasti, Sarah Kennedy, Sue Kernaghan, Vanessa Lazo Greaves, Chris McBeath, Janna Mock-Lopez, Donald S. Olson, Holly S. Smith, Lori Tobias

Maps: David Lindroth *cartographer;* Bob Blake and Rebecca Baer, *map editors*

Design: Fabrizio La Rocca, *creative director;* Guido Caroti, *art director;* Melanie Marin, *senior photo editor*

Production/Manufacturing: Colleen Ziemba

Cover Photo (Mt. Hood from Lost Lake, Oregon): J. A. Kraulis/Masterfile

Fifteenth Edition

ISBN 1-4000-1313-5

ISSN 1098-6774

SPECIAL SALES

This book is available for special discounts for bulk purchases for sales promotions or premiums. Special editions, including personalized covers, excerpts of existing books, and corporate imprints, can be created in large quantities for special needs. For more information, write to Special Markets/Premium Sales, 1745 Broadway, MD 6-2, New York, New York 10019 or e-mail specialmarkets@randomhouse.com. Inquiries from Canada should be directed to your local Canadian bookseller or sent to Random House of Canada, Ltd., Marketing Department, 2775 Matheson Boulevard East, Mississauga, Ontario L4W 4P7. Inquiries from the United Kingdom should be sent to Fodor's Travel Publications, 20 Vauxhall Bridge Road, London SW1V 2SA, England.

AN IMPORTANT TIP & AN INVITATION

Although all prices, opening times, and other details in this book are based on information supplied to us at press time, changes occur all the time in the travel world, and Fodor's cannot accept responsibility for facts that become outdated or for inadvertent errors or omissions. So **always confirm information when it matters**, especially if you're making a detour to visit a specific place. Your experiences—positive and negative—matter to us. If we have missed or misstated something, **please write to us**. We follow up on all suggestions. Contact the Pacific Northwest editor at editors@fodors.com or c/o Fodor's at 1745 Broadway, New York, New York 10019.

DESTINATION PACIFIC NORTHWEST

In this region, being rich is defined as living a clean, simple life. To understand people here, you must understand how the land and the climate combine to cast their spell. Regarding nature, there's always a mixture of respect and love, fear and admiration—all topped off with awe. Even in the cities, the wilderness is never far away. In Seattle, Mt. Rainier and the Olympics enchant commuters stuck in traffic; in Vancouver, British Columbia, the Coast Range juts out over downtown, keeping it in line; and in Portland, 5,000 acres of forestland north of the city center harbor deer, elk, and the odd bear and cougar. No matter how many planes Seattle's Boeing plant churns out, or how many chips come out of Oregon's high-tech Silicon Forest, or how many shares of stock change hands in the Vancouver Stock Exchange, the relationship with nature isn't altered. However you enjoy the landscape, you'll be in good company with the locals, who often seem more interested in day tripping than in day trading. Raft a river or kayak along the coast. Ski or snowboard the mountain slopes, or hike to the top of a butte. Have a fabulous trip!

Karen Cure, Editorial Director

CONTENTS

About this Book *F6*
On the Road with Fodor's *F8*
What's Where *F11*
When to Go *F13*
On the Calendar *F14*
Pleasures & Pastimes *F17*
Fodor's Choice *F19*
Smart Travel Tips *F27*

1 Portland   *1*

Exploring Portland *4*
Where to Eat *23*
Where to Stay *39*
Nightlife & the Arts *49*

Sports & the Outdoors *56*
Shopping *59*
Portland A to Z *64*

2 Oregon   *71*

The Oregon Coast *77*
The Willamette Valley &
   Wine Country *111*
The Columbia River Gorge &
   the Oregon Cascades *140*

Central Oregon *158*
Southern Oregon *173*
Eastern Oregon *191*
Oregon A to Z *218*

3 Seattle   *221*

Exploring Seattle *222*
Where to Eat *245*
Where to Stay *264*
Nightlife & the Arts *278*

Sports & the Outdoors *286*
Shopping *295*
Seattle A to Z *307*

4 Washington   *312*

Seattle Environs *314*
Northwestern Washington *350*
The San Juan Islands *385*
The Olympic Peninsula *402*

Southwestern Washington *439*
Yakima River Valley *467*
Eastern Washington *484*
Washington A to Z *514*

5 Vancouver & Victoria   *519*

Vancouver *521*
Victoria *544*

Vancouver Island *555*
Southern British Columbia *565*

Index   *575*

Maps

Pacific Northwest 10
Downtown, the Pearl District &
    Old Town/Chinatown 9
Nob Hill & Vicinity 16
Washington Park &
    Forest Park 18
East of the Willamette
    River 21
Where to Eat in Portland 26–27
Where to Stay in Portland 40–41
Oregon 78–79
The Oregon Coast 80
Willamette Valley &
    Wine Country 112
Salem 126
Eugene 134
Columbia River Gorge &
    the Cascades 143
Central Oregon 160
Bend 166
Southern Oregon 175
Crater Lake National Park 177
Eastern Oregon 195
Greater Seattle 226–227
Downtown Seattle &
    Environs 230–231
Capitol Hill &
    the U-District 236
North & West of
    Downtown 241
Where to Eat In & Around
    Downtown 246–247

Where to Eat North &
    East of Downtown 258
Where to Eat North &
    West of Downtown 262
Where to Stay In & Around
    Downtown 268–269
Where to Stay North &
    East of Downtown 275
Washington 318–319
Seattle Environs 321
Tacoma 329
The Northern Coast 355
Northwestern Washington 368
North Cascades
    National Park 371
San Juan Islands 388
Olympic Peninsula 408–409
Southwestern Washington 441
Mt. Rainier National
    Park 452–453
Yakima River Valley 470
Valley Wineries 474
Eastern Washington 487
Spokane 498
Southern British Columbia
    524–525
Downtown Vancouver 527
Stanley Park 531
Granville Island 533
Downtown Victoria 545
Salt Spring Island 568

ABOUT THIS BOOK

There's no doubt that the best source for travel advice is a like-minded friend who's just been where you're headed. But with or without that friend, you'll have a better trip with a Fodor's guide in hand. Once you've learned to find your way around its pages, you'll be in great shape to find your way around your destination.

SELECTION

Our goal is to cover the best properties, sights, and activities in their category, as well as the most interesting communities to visit. We make a point of including local food-lovers' hot spots as well as neighborhood options, and we avoid all that's touristy unless it's really worth your time. You can go on the assumption that everything you read about in this book is recommended wholeheartedly by our writers and editors. Flip to On the Road with Fodor's to learn more about who they are. It goes without saying that no property mentioned in the book has paid to be included.

RATINGS

Orange stars ★ denote sights and properties that our editors and writers consider the very best in the area covered by the entire book. These, the best of the best, are listed in the Fodor's Choice section in the front of the book. Black stars ★ highlight the sights and properties we deem Highly Recommended, the don't-miss sights within any region. Fodor's Choice options in each region are usually listed on the title page of the chapter covering that region. Use the index to find complete descriptions. In cities, sights pinpointed with numbered map bullets ❶ in the margins tend to be more important than those without bullets.

SPECIAL SPOTS

Pleasures & Pastimes focuses on types of experiences that reveal the spirit of the destination. Watch for Off the Beaten Path sights. Some are out of the way, some are quirky, and all are worth your while. If the munchies hit while you're exploring, look for Need a Break? suggestions.

TIME IT RIGHT

Wondering when to go? Check On the Calendar up front and chapters' Timing sections for weather and crowd overviews and best days and times to visit.

SEE IT ALL

Use Fodor's exclusive Great Itineraries as a model for your trip. (For a good overview of the entire destination, mix regional itineraries from several chapters.) In cities, Good Walks guide you to important sights in each neighborhood; ► indicates the starting points of walks and itineraries in the text and on the map.

BUDGET WELL

Hotel and restaurant price categories from ¢ to $$$$ are defined in the opening pages of each chapter—expect to find a balanced selection for every budget. For attractions, we always give standard adult admission fees; reductions are usually available for children, students, and senior citizens. Look in Discounts & Deals in Smart Travel Tips for information on destination-wide ticket schemes. Want to pay with plastic? AE, D, DC, MC, V following restaurant and hotel listings indicate whether American Express, Discover, Diner's Club, MasterCard, or Visa are accepted.

BASIC INFO

Tips lists travel essentials for the entire area covered by the book; city- and region-specific basics end each chapter. To find the best way to get around, see the transportation section; see individual modes of travel ("Car Travel," "Train Travel") for details. We assume you'll check Web sites or call for particulars.

ON THE MAPS Maps throughout the book show you what's where and help you find your way around. Black and orange numbered bullets ➊ ➊ in the text correlate to bullets on maps.

FIND IT FAST Within the book, chapters are arranged in a roughly south to north direction starting with Portland. Chapters are divided into small regions, within which towns are covered in logical geographical order; attractive routes and interesting places between towns are flagged as En Route. Heads at the top of each page help you find what you need within a chapter.

DON'T FORGET Restaurants are open for lunch and dinner daily unless we state otherwise; we mention dress only when there's a specific requirement and reservations only when they're essential or not accepted—it's always best to book ahead. Hotels have private baths, phone, TVs, and air-conditioning and operate on the European Plan (a.k.a. EP, meaning without meals). We always list facilities but not whether you'll be charged extra to use them, so when pricing accommodations, find out what's included.

SYMBOLS

Many Listings

★ Fodor's Choice

★ Highly recommended

⊠ Physical address

✛ Directions

⌖ Mailing address

☎ Telephone

🖶 Fax

⊕ On the Web

✉ E-mail

🎟 Admission fee

🕓 Open/closed times

► Start of walk/itinerary

Ⓜ Metro stations

▭ Credit cards

Outdoors

⛳ Golf

⛺ Camping

Hotels & Restaurants

🏨 Hotel

🛏 Number of rooms

⚒ Facilities

🍽 Meal plans

✕ Restaurant

🍴 Reservations

🏛 Dress code

🚭 Smoking

🍷 BYOB

✕🏨 Hotel with restaurant that warrants a visit

Other

☺ Family-friendly

🛈 Contact information

⇨ See also

⊠ Branch address

☞ Take note

ON THE ROAD WITH FODOR'S

A trip takes you out of yourself. Concerns of life at home completely disappear, driven away by more immediate thoughts—about, say, what marvels will beguile the next day, or where you'll have dinner. That's where Fodor's comes in. We make sure that you know all your options, so that you don't miss something that's around the next bend just because you didn't know it was there. Because the best memories of your trip might well have nothing to do with what you came to the Pacific Northwest to see, we guide you to sights large and small all over the region. You might set out to hike up or ski down a mountain, but back at home you find yourself unable to forget having a massage in a Seattle spa or the performance of *King Lear* during the Oregon Shakespeare Festival. With Fodor's at your side, serendipitous discoveries are never far away.

Our success in showing you every corner of the region is a credit to our extraordinary writers. Although there's no substitute for travel advice from a good friend who knows your style, our contributors are the next best thing—the kind of people you would poll for travel advice if you knew them.

Shelley Arenas is coauthor of *Lobster Kids Guide to Exploring Seattle* and has contributed to numerous guidebooks, including Fodor's *CityGuide Seattle, Away From It All, Pacific Northwest,* and *Great American Drives of the West.* She was born in Seattle, grew up in eastern Washington, and has lived in Seattle all her adult life.

Gina Bacon, who covered the state's southwestern reaches, is a Pacific Northwest native and freelance writer based in Camas, Washington, which is along the Lewis and Clark Trail. She has written for *Portland UpClose, Portrait of Puget Sound, Garden Showcase,* and *The Columbian* newspaper, among other publications.

Veteran writer and Washington resident **John Doerper,** who covered the state's northwestern reaches, has explored the Pacific Northwest for more than 25 years and has written extensively about this fascinating region. He is also the author of several guidebooks.

Zach Dundas has worked as a writer and editor in Montana and Oregon for seven years, and he has lived in the Pacific Northwest all his life. Since 1999, he's written for *Willamette Week,* the award-winning weekly newspaper in Portland, Oregon. He lives in North Portland.

A champion of great service, great food, and comfortable beds, freelance writer **Julie Fay** is a Seattle native who has been contributing to Fodor's since 1997. She also works as a development associate for the House of Dames Productions theater group and is on the board of directors for Cinema Seattle, which presents the Seattle International Film Festival.

Seattle-based writer **John Gottberg** loved covering Washington's Yakima River Valley and visiting its many great wineries. Once a news editor for the *Los Angeles Times* travel section and a journalist for both of Seattle's dailies, Gottberg is now a globetrotting freelancer who has penned articles for more than 50 publications and written more than a dozen books.

Born and raised in Boston, Yankee **Susan Honthumb** found her way to Eugene 20 years ago. For the last nine years, she has spent her weekdays at Eugene's daily newspaper, the *Register-Guard,* while on weekends she travels around the Northwest bowling competitively.

Sarah Kennedy lives in the Alberta Arts District of Northeast Portland. A former Harvard student, she has dabbled in the sundry working worlds of retail, restaurants, libraries, and amusement parks and has edited a guidebook of the American Southwest. She currently divides her time between writing, bicycling, waitressing, playing the oboe, and exploring the Northwest.

Vancouver-born freelance writer **Sue Kernaghan,** a fourth-generation British Columbian, has gathered historical insights and walked many city blocks, covered a lot of dirt roads, traversed open water, and contemplated in country pubs while researching the places covered in this book.

Vanessa Lazo Greaves, who updated the Seattle shopping section, fell in love with Seattle while on a trip for *W* magazine and soon became a resident. Now raising a son and restoring an old house with her husband, Vanessa writes about food for an online site, dispenses fashion advice, and often stops to help lost visitors.

After 25 years in the travel industy, freelance travel writer Chris McBeath knows what makes a great vacation experience. Whether routing through back country or discovering a hidden-away inn, Chris has combined history, insight, and anecdotes into her research for this book.

Janna Mock-Lopez is a freelance writer and public relations consultant residing in Beaverton. Her writing has appeared in numerous publications, including Portland's daily paper, the Oregonian.

After covering parts of Indonesia, Australia, Peru, and Oregon for Fodor's, Washington resident Holly S. Smith enjoyed working closer to home on Seattle, its environs, the San Juan Islands, and the Olympic Peninsula. Holly has written several books, including Aceh: Art & Culture and How to Bounce Back Quickly After Losing Your Job.

A journalist of 18 years, Lori Tobias calls the small town of Newport, on the central Oregon coast, home. When she's not on the beach walking her dogs, she writes for Ladies' Home Journal, Oregon Home, Oregon Coast Magazine, the Oregonian, and the Seattle Times, among other publications.

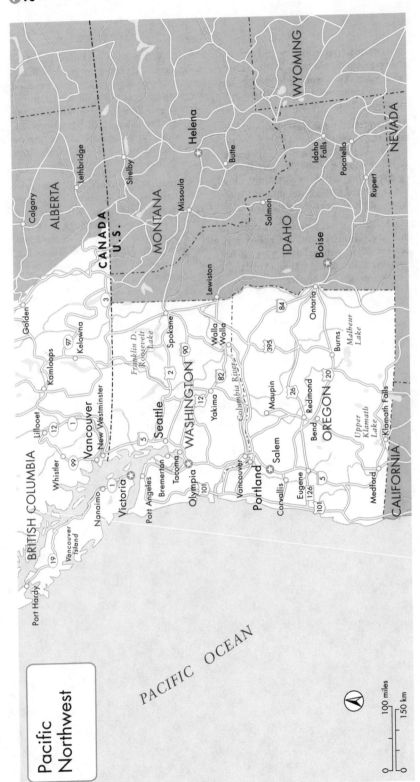

Pacific Northwest

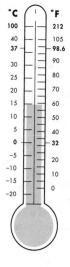

The Pacific Northwest's mild climate is best from June through September. Hotels in the major tourist destinations are often filled in July and August, so it's important to book reservations in advance. Spring and fall are also excellent times to visit. The weather usually remains quite good, and the prices for accommodations, transportation, and tours can be lower (and the crowds much smaller!) in the most popular destinations. In winter, snow is uncommon in the lowland areas but abundant in the nearby mountains, making the region a skier's dream.

Climate

Average daytime summer highs are in the 70s; winter temperatures are generally in the 40s. Rainfall varies greatly from one locale to another. In the coastal mountains, for example, 160 inches of rain falls annually, creating temperate rain forests. In eastern Oregon, Washington, and British Columbia, near-desert conditions prevail, with rainfall as low as 6 inches per year. Seattle has an average of only 36 inches of rainfall a year—less than New York, Chicago, or Miami. Throughout the Pacific Northwest, however, most rain falls during the winter months, when cloudy skies and drizzly weather persist. More than 75% of Seattle's annual precipitation occurs from October through March.

Forecasts Weather Channel Connection ⊕ www.weather.com.

The following are average daily maximum and minimum temperatures for major cities in the Pacific Northwest region.

PORTLAND

Jan.	44F	7C	May	67F	19C	Sept.	74F	23C
	33	1		46	8		51	10
Feb.	50F	10C	June	72F	22C	Oct.	63F	17C
	36	2		52	11		45	7
Mar.	54F	12C	July	79F	26C	Nov.	52F	11C
	37	3		55	13		39	4
Apr.	60F	15C	Aug.	78F	25C	Dec.	46F	8C
	41	5		55	13		35	2

SEATTLE

Jan.	45F	7C	May	66F	19C	Sept.	69F	20C
	35	2		47	8		52	11
Feb.	50F	10C	June	70F	21C	Oct.	62F	16C
	37	3		52	11		47	8
Mar.	53F	12C	July	76F	24C	Nov.	51F	10C
	38	3		56	13		40	4
Apr.	59F	13C	Aug.	75F	24C	Dec.	47F	8C
	42	5		55	13		37	3

VANCOUVER

Jan.	41F	5C	May	63F	17C	Sept.	64F	18C
	32	0		46	8		50	10
Feb.	46F	8C	June	66F	19C	Oct.	57F	14C
	34	1		52	11		43	6
Mar.	48F	9C	July	72F	22C	Nov.	48F	9C
	36	2		55	13		37	3
Apr.	55F	13C	Aug.	72F	22C	Dec.	45F	7C
	41	5		55	13		34	1

ON THE CALENDAR

WINTER	
Dec.	The Carol Ships, sailboats full of carolers and decorated with colored lights, ply the waters of the Vancouver, BC, harbor. New Year's Eve is famously celebrated at the Seattle Center's Space Needle, from where a spectacular fireworks show is staged at midnight. Village Lighting Festival in Leavenworth, WA, begins with the German-style village's tree-lighting ceremony and continues with holiday displays and activities through the New Year.
Jan.	Participating in the Polar Bear Swim on New Year's Day in Vancouver, BC, is said to bring good luck all year.
Feb.	Ashland's Oregon Shakespeare Festival, which starts in mid-February and runs through early November, presents classic and contemporary plays in repertory. The Lunar New Year is celebrated with parades, fireworks, and festivities in many Asian communities, particularly around Seattle.

SPRING	
Mar.	The Seattle Mariners' Opening Day sees a parade through Downtown, as well as stadium festivities celebrating the city's major-league baseball traditions. The Pacific Rim Whale Festival on Vancouver Island's west coast celebrates the spring migration of gray whales with guided tours by whale experts and accompanying music and dancing. Washington's Skagit Valley Tulip Festival showcases millions of colorful tulips and daffodils. The Seattle Cherry Blossom Festival celebrates Japanese arts and family traditions. Northwest vintages take center stage at BC's Vancouver International Wine Festival.
Apr.	Oregon's Hood River Valley Blossom Festival is a floral spectacle. The TerrifVic Jazz Party in Victoria, BC, presents top international Dixieland bands.
May	In late May, the Brookings Azalea Festival shows off the azaleas of Oregon's southern coast. Portland's Cinco de Mayo Festival is one of the largest such celebrations this side of Guadalajara. Lilacfest in Spokane, WA, celebrates the city's spectacular flowers with a parade, races, and family activities. Memorial Day weekend sees Seattle's Northwest Folklife Festival, one of the nation's largest folk-music celebrations.
	Riverfest in Cashmere, WA, shows off the area's river-running traditions with rafting demos, boat races, and kayaking "rodeos." Seattle's Pike Place Market Festival celebrates locally grown produce and locally made crafts; there's also free entertainment and children's activities. The Seattle International Children's Festival at the Seattle Center highlights international music, dance, and theater. The Seattle International Film Festival screens more than 200 films over three weeks, including many by local talents. Seattle's University District Street Fair has kitschy craft and food booths, a produce market, music stages, and children's activities The Viking Fest celebrates the Norwegian heritage of the folks in Poulsbo, WA.

SUMMER	
June	Britt Festivals, which runs from mid-June through early September, presents concerts, musical theater, and dance at an outdoor amphitheater in historic Jacksonville, OR. Canadian International Dragon Boat Festival in Vancouver, BC, includes entertainment, exotic foods, and the ancient "awakening the dragons" ritual of long, slender boats decorated with huge dragon heads. The Cannon Beach Sand Castle Contest—in Cannon Beach, OR—is the oldest such competition in the United States. The Edmonds Art Festival, north of Seattle, is one of the region's biggest arts events. The Fremont Street Fair celebrates the Seattle neighborhood's unique, unusual, and truly bizarre performance and visual artists.
	Ft. Vancouver Days in Vancouver, WA, includes a chili cook-off, musical events, and fireworks. Eugene's Oregon Bach Festival celebrates the works of the great composer. The Portland Rose Festival packs diverse events—an air show, three parades, auto racing, and a riverside carnival among them—into 25 days. Whistler Summer Festivals present daily street entertainment and music festivals at the renowned British Columbia ski and summer resort.
July	Canada Day inspires celebrations around the country in honor of Canada's birthday. In Vancouver, BC, Canada Place hosts an entire day of free outdoor concerts followed by a fireworks display in the inner harbor. Bite of Seattle, at the Seattle Center, is a huge event that shows off specialties from the city's finest restaurants. Bon Odori, celebrated in Seattle, is a festival of Japanese traditions with a parade, folk dancing, crafts, and food. Victoria, BC, stages the day-long Great Canadian Family Picnic in Beacon Hill Park. The event usually includes children's games, bands, food booths, and fireworks. Washington state's King County Fair has old-fashioned carnival rides, agricultural displays, country music, and children's activities. The two-day Northwest Festival of Jazz and Wine takes place at the fairgounds in Walla Walla, WA.
	The Oregon Brewer's Festival, a beer lover's delight, is held in Portland. The Oregon Coast Music Festival in Coos Bay, North Bend, and Charleston presents classical bluegrass, jazz, and other concerts. The Salem Art Fair and Festival, Oregon's biggest art fair, includes exhibits, food, entertainment, and tours of historic mansions. The Pacific Northwest Arts Fair, a juried show in Bellevue, WA, presents the works of several hundred artists. Seafair in Seattle begins with a torchlight parade and ends with a Blue Angels air show and hydroplane races. The Thurston County Fair near Olympia, WA, has exhibits of local farm animals and produce, plus music and carnival rides. The Vancouver Sea Festival celebrates the BC city's nautical heritage with the World Championship Bathtub Race, sailing regattas, and windsurfing races.
Aug.	Bumbershoot—The Seattle Arts Festival is a beloved showcase for music, dance, theater, comedy, and the visual and literary arts. Oregon's Mount Hood Jazz Festival brings nationally acclaimed jazz musicians to Gresham for performances in an outdoor setting. The Oregon State Fair takes place in Salem the 11 days before Labor Day. The

Pacific National Exhibition in Vancouver, BC, has parades, exhibits, sports, entertainment, and logging contests. The San Juan County Fair in Friday Harbor, WA, on San Juan Island celebrates the county's produce with open markets, contests, and hay rides. The Washington State International Kite Festival sends kites of all shapes and sizes flying above Long Beach.

FALL

Sept.

Cars speed through downtown Vancouver, BC, in the Molson Indy Formula. The Puyallup Fair brings top entertainment, animals, food, exhibits, and rides to the town of Puyallup, WA. The Rainier Mountain Festival in Ashford, WA, gathers some of the world's greatest climbers for storytelling and fun on the slopes. Spokane Interstate Fair celebrates eastern Washington's farming and creative traditions with a week of rodeos, livestock and produce shows, carnival rides, and other festivities.

Valleyfest in Spokane, WA, is a children's event with races, rides, and treats. The Washington State Apple Festival in Wenatchee celebrates the state's famous apple-growing traditions with horse rides, music, orchard tours—and lots of unique apple treats. The Wooden Boat Festival in Port Townsend, WA, includes historic boat displays, demonstrations, and a street fair.

Oct.

The Dungeness Crab and Seafood Festival in Port Angeles, WA, is a chance to sample some of the region's most delectable cuisine. Issaquah Salmon Days, in Issaquah, WA, honor the return of this fish to the area's waters with festivities, crafts booths, live entertainment, and lots of grilled salmon. Oktoberfest parties stretch over two weeks in Leavenworth, WA, when the town nearly overflows with polka music, sauerkraut and dill pickles, lederhosen, and beer. Washington's Skagit Festival of Family Farms celebrates the northern county's farming traditions with barn and field tours, equipment displays, children's activities, and lots of home-cooked samples.

Nov.

Seattle's glitzy Thanksgiving Day Parade kicks off the city's shopping season the Friday after Thanksgiving; the day is topped off by the Christmas tree lighting and fireworks at Westlake Center.

PLEASURES & PASTIMES

Beaches The coasts of Oregon, Washington, and British Columbia have long, sandy beaches that run for miles at a stretch. But the waters are generally too cold or treacherous for swimming. Even in summertime, beachgoers must be prepared to dress warmly. The most accessible ocean beaches in the Pacific Northwest are in Oregon, southern Washington, around the Olympic Peninsula, and tucked into Puget Sound, where frigid waters never deter swimmers, sunbathers, and boaters in summer.

Boating The area's swift rivers provide challenges to canoeists and kayakers, but many should only be attempted by those with experience. June through September are prime months for white-water rafting. You can sea kayak in the bays of Puget Sound, around Vancouver Island, or along the Pacific Northwest coast just about any time of year.

Cruising and deep-sea-fishing charters are available from many ports throughout the Pacific Northwest. Neah Bay and Port Angeles on Washington's Olympic Peninsula, Westport on the Long Beach Peninsula in southern Washington, and Depoe Bay in Oregon are leading ports.

The Columbia River, particularly at Hood River, Oregon, is one of the world's premier locations for windsurfing. Puget Sound and some of the inland lakes in Washington are other venues for the sport. Sailboard rentals and lessons are available from local specialty shops.

Climbing & Mountaineering The mountains of the Pacific Northwest have given many an adventurer quite a challenge. It is no coincidence that many members of the U.S. expedition teams to Mount Everest come from this region, where the challenges include Washington's Mt. Baker, Mt. Adams, and Mt. Rainier, as well as Oregon's Mt. Hood.

Dining Fresh-caught and just-picked Northwest seafood and produce are served in the best and most authentic local dining spots. You can't go wrong by ordering dishes based on salmon, crab, oysters, and other seafood delicacies, or with the hearty, tomato-based *cioppino* seafood stew so common here. Don't miss the summer's juicy berries and succulent fruits, or the plump apples and vegetables of autumn. There are fine Continental restaurants and tasty little ethnic cafés found in each neighborhood, as well as many waterfront restaurants with gorgeous views. In larger establishments with blended cuisines, Northwest chefs often use Asian ingredients and techniques to add unique flavorings. Casual but neat dress is expected at all of the restaurants reviewed; fancy attire is only required where noted.

Fishing The coastal regions and inland lakes and rivers of the Pacific Northwest are known for excellent fishing. Lodges, many of which are accessible only by seaplane, cater to anglers in search of the ultimate fishing experience. Visiting anglers must possess a nonresident license for the state or province in which they plan to fish. Licenses are easily obtainable at sporting-goods stores, bait shops, and other outlets in fishing areas.

Golf

The Northwest has many excellent golf courses, but not all of them are open to the public. Consequently, visitors may find it difficult to arrange a tee time at a popular course. If you are a member of a golf club at home, check to see if your club has a reciprocal playing arrangement with private clubs in the areas that you will be visiting.

Lodging

In the Pacific Northwest you can choose to stay in many settings: the city, along the beach, in the woods, or atop the snow-covered mountains. Accommodations include elegant, full-service downtown boutique hotels, simple chain hotels in the suburbs, luxury mountain retreats, ski chalets, national park cabins, and local motels. Bed-and-breakfasts are especially popular and are found throughout the region, with rooms in quaint, historic homes, farmhouses surrounded by grazing horses and llamas, sprawling log cabins amid the rain forest, and weathered cedar mansions beside the lake or bay.

Skiing

Moist air off the Pacific Ocean dumps snow on the coastal mountains, providing excellent skiing from November through the end of March and sometimes into April. Resort and lift-ticket prices tend to be less expensive here than at the internationally known ski destinations, but the slopes, especially on weekends, can be crowded. Winter driving in these high elevations usually requires a four-wheel-drive vehicle or tire chains.

Wildlife Viewing

Sea lions, seals, dolphins, and whales are a few of the marine mammals that can be observed in bays, near headlands, and along the coast. In the spring and summer thousands of gray whales pass by the British Columbia, Washington, and Oregon coasts on their seasonal migration from Alaska to Baja California in Mexico. One of the easiest and most exciting ways to see them is by taking a whale-watching boat excursion. In the forests and along coastal rivers and estuaries deer, bald eagles, herons, and egrets are commonly seen. The dedicated birders who annually trek to the Northwest find that their efforts are amply rewarded.

FODOR'S CHOICE

The sights, restaurants, hotels, and other travel experiences on these pages are our editors' top picks—our Fodor's Choices. They're the best of their type in the area covered by the book—not to be missed and always worth your time. In the destination chapters that follow, you will find all the details.

LODGING

$$$$	**Fairmont Château Whistler Resort,** Whistler, BC. This family-friendly fortress is a self-contained, ski-in, ski-out resort-within-a-resort, with its own shopping arcade, an impressive spa with exotic Asian and Ayurvedic treatments, and rooms with mountain views.
$$$$	**Fairmont Olympic Hotel,** Seattle. An estimable dame adorned with marble and draped with textiles.
$$$$	**Metolius River Resort,** Camp Sherman, OR. Flawless comfort and rustic elegance permeate the entire cabin experience. The sun on your face warms the soul while sounds of the gentle river gliding by soothe the senses.
$$$$	**Pan Pacific Hotel,** Vancouver. A centerpiece of the Canada Place complex, the luxurious Pan Pacific has a dramatic three-story atrium lobby and expansive views of the harbor and mountains.
$$$$	**Salish Lodge,** Snoqualmie, WA. Stare at the Snoqualmie River from a windowseat in your room, and pull that terrycloth robe more tightly around you. Contemplate a dinner of sea bass or beef tenderloin while shaking off the sleepiness that has set in after that late-afternoon massage.
$$$$	**Sooke Harbour House,** Sooke, BC. West of Victoria, this airy oceanfront inn looks like the home of a discerning but casual art collector. The restaurant is one of Canada's finest.
$$$$	**Sunriver Resort,** Sunriver, OR. A former military base near Bend has transformed into an almost self-contained resort village. Golf, great food, luxury rooms, and, above all, the high desert's sweeping sense of splendid isolation are the main draws here.
$$$$	**Wickaninnish Inn,** Tofino, BC. On a rocky promontory above Chesterman Beach, sits this cedar-sided inn where every room overlooks the ocean, including the glass-enclosed Pointe Restaurant.
$$$–$$$$	**Alexis Hotel,** Seattle. French and Italian fabrics? Free wine in the early evening? Why, it's a little bit of Europe in the middle of Seattle.
$$$–$$$$	**Inn at Langley,** Langley (Whidbey Island), WA. Sleek lines, modern furniture, and big windows allow your eyes to focus on what's really important: the sea and mountain views.
$$$–$$$$	**Inn at the Market,** Seattle. Just because the furniture is contemporary doesn't mean that such noble traditions as fresh flowers and free morning newspapers must become obsolete.
$$$–$$$$	**Spring Bay Inn,** Orcas Island, WA. What makes this B&B run by former park rangers so restful? Maybe it's being able to lounge before a roaring fire after kayaking along the coast. Or perhaps it's being able to collapse on a feather bed after a day on the trails.

$$$–$$$$	**Tu Tu' Tun Lodge,** near Gold Beach, OR. Tucked just far enough away from U.S. 101 to feel like a secret retreat, the Tu Tu' Tun Lodge on the banks of the Rogue River is pure class. Bed linens and room furnishings are designer quality, complementing (not competing with) the natural rustic mood. The spirit is relaxed and friendly.
$$$–$$$$	**WSeattle,** Seattle. The "W" stands for "welcoming," not to mention "wicked comfortable," and "way cool."
$$$	**Heathman Hotel,** Portland. Elegant rooms, beautifully restored public spaces, an exceptional restaurant, and superior service have earned this downtown hotel a reputation as one of the finest establishments in the city.
$$–$$$	**Colette's Bed & Breakfast,** near Port Angeles, WA. The excellent service is rivaled only by the Olympic Peninsula location and the way-cool amenities—CD and DVD players, Jacuzzis, fireplaces.
$$–$$$	**Inn at Harbor Steps,** Seattle. Public areas are low-key, guest rooms are commodious, and breakfast is a buffet.
$$–$$$	**Newport Belle B&B,** Newport, OR. With first-class views of the arcing Yaquina Bay Bridge and front seats to the bustling bay front, the triple-decker *Newport Belle* stern-wheeler, with staterooms and a woodstove-warmed salon, is one of the most unusual places on the coast to settle in for the night.
$$–$$$	**Under the Greenwood Tree,** Medford, OR. Luxurious rooms, stunning 10-acre gardens, and breakfasts cooked by the owner, a Cordon Bleu–trained chef, make a visit here memorable.
$–$$$$	**Flying M Ranch,** Yamhill, OR. "Daniel Boone eclectic" might be the best description of the furnishings at this great log lodge, the centerpiece of a 625-acre complex of cabins and riverside hotel units.
$–$$$	**Birchfield Manor,** Yakima, WA. A stay here puts you on a plateau in the middle of wine country. The restaurant is one of the region's best: all the entrées come with an exotic homemade bread of the day.
$–$$$	**Lara House Bed & Breakfast Inn,** Bend, OR. Across from Bend's Drake Park, the Deschutes River, and Mirror Pond, this brawny 1910 boarding house has become a stylish B&B; each room has its own bath, there's a hot tub, and breakfasts are dynamite. Downtown Bend is just a few blocks away.
$–$$$	**Steamboat Inn,** Steamboat, east of Roseburg, OR. A veritable Who's Who of the world's top fly fishermen have visited Oregon's most famous fishing lodge; others come simply to relax in the reading nooks or on the broad decks of the riverside cabins.
$–$$$$	**Timberline Lodge,** Mt. Hood, OR. A National Historic Landmark that is as much a quintessential sight as it is a place to stay, the lodge has withstood howling winter storms for more than six decades and warms its guests with hospitality, hearty food, and rustic rooms.

BUDGET LODGING

$$	**Lion and the Rose**, Portland. In a restored Victorian home in the city's Irvington neighborhood, this bed-and-breakfast, with friendly owners and fine food, is a luxurious historic inn.
$$	**Panacea Bed and Breakfast**, Friday Harbor, WA. It's a Craftsman bungalow where the living room is called the "parlor," guest rooms have garden motifs, and breakfast is served on Limoges.
$-$$	**Ann Starrett Mansion**, Port Townsend, WA. This 1889 mansion embodies what you picture when you hear "Victorian." Its many ells are covered with gingerbread and painted in contrasting colors. And, to reach that 70-foot-high cupola, you spiral up a flying staircase that seemingly defies the laws of physics.
$-$$	**Mattey House Bed & Breakfast**, McMinnville, OR. Whether you're a wine aficionado or just looking for a pleasurable stay in Yamhill County, this Victorian home is an immersion in comfort and the area's wine culture, thanks largely to the knowledgeable and welcoming owners.
$-$$	**McMenamins Edgefield**, Troutdale, OR. A McMenamins outpost just east of Portland, Edgefield combines a fabulously renovated lodge, several tiny bars, a vineyard, two restaurants, and a golf course, creating a fun, laid-back version of a resort at reasonable prices.
$-$$	**Shelburne Inn**, Seaview, WA. The state's oldest continuously run hotel is an 1896 Victorian with a rose garden and, of course, a white picket fence.
$	**Parker House**, Pendleton, OR. This beautiful B&B on a hill just north of downtown Pendleton has been preserved with the same French neoclassical and Italianate styles that it has had since 1917.
¢-$$	**Gaslight Inn**, Seattle. No two spaces are alike thanks to eclectic paint effects, fabrics, and fittings. You're as likely to find a glass chandelier as you are log furniture.
¢-$	**Union Hotel**, Union, OR. Just outside La Grande, this historic inn has restored a feeling of age-old elegance to an Old West town, with unique and beautifully furnished rooms.
¢	**Eagle Point Inn**, Beaver, WA. Aubergine settees, white linens, and lamps with fringed shades are juxtaposed with exposed log walls, a stone fireplace, and other bits of rusticity.
¢	**Vintage Inn**, Vancouver, WA. One guest room of this Craftsman house has a fireplace, another has a porch overlooking the herb garden. All rooms are filled with enough antiques to make a decorative-arts curator jealous.

RESTAURANTS

$$$$	**Hastings House**, Salt Spring Island, BC. Inside this regal Tudor-style manor, five-course prix-fixe dinners are served, which include local lamb, seafood, and herbs and produce from the inn's gardens.

$$$$	**Lampreia,** Seattle. The dishes, like the beige-and-gold color scheme, are classic with a little sparkle: pheasant is paired with apples, champagne, and sauerkraut; lamb is served with pesto.
$$$–$$$$	**C Restaurant,** Vancouver. The name and decor are minimalist, but the innovative seafood and the stunning location overlooking False Creek make this one of Vancouver's most exciting restaurants.
$$$–$$$$	**Christina's,** Eastsound (Orcas Island). The seafood is fresh and well prepared, and the sea views are fine.
$$$	**Tina's,** Dundee, OR. With fish, game, and desserts every bit as strong as the exemplary wine list, and service that can only come from people who love what they do, it's all good.
$$–$$$	**C'est Si Bon,** Port Angeles, WA. It's formal. It's French. *Et, alors,* the walls are red, the artwork European, the food terrific, the wine list superb.
$$–$$$	**Cork,** Bend, OR. This romantic candlelit restaurant and wine bar in downtown Bend infuses its Continental cuisine with Northwest freshness and bursts of Latin heat.
$$–$$$	**Dahlia Lounge,** Seattle. There's romance—think low lights and the color red. There's good food—think crab cakes, seared ahi tuna, and coconut-cream pie.
$$–$$$	**Duck Soup Inn,** San Juan Island, WA. Outside it's all about cedar shingles and flowering vines. Inside it's all about up-to-date dishes with a smidge of the Asian here and a dash of the Latin American there.
$$–$$$	**Higgins,** Portland. Pacific Northwest ingredients augment traditional French dishes with international flair at this sophisticated and popular spot near Portland's Art Museum and the Arlene Schnitzer Concert Hall.
$$–$$$	**Liliget Feast House,** Vancouver. Near English Bay is one of the few restaurants in the world where you can have original Northwest Coast First Nations cuisine. The longhouse setting is intimate.
$$–$$$	**Lonny's,** Port Townsend, WA. Contemporary American seafood and vegetarian dishes are given Italian touches. The results are sensual.
$$–$$$	**Mahle House,** Nanaimo. Innovative Pacific Northwest cuisine is served at this cozy 1904 farmhouse.
$$–$$$	**Merenda,** Bend. The cooking at this swaggering and confident spot backs up the large, loud room's verve, with hardy French and Italian influences brought to bear on Northwest ingredients.
$$–$$$	**Paley's Place,** Portland. French cuisine is served Pacific Northwest style at this charming Nob Hill bistro with porch seating.
$$–$$$	**Le Pichet,** Seattle. It's all French brasserie, from the earthenware wine vessels to the crusty baguettes for your ham and cheese, er, *jambon et fromage.*
$–$$$	**Oceanaire,** Seattle. This place is about retro. Your clams casino or oysters Rockefeller or baked Alaska is served in a room that evokes a supper club circa 1930.

$-$$$ | Red Agave, Eugene, OR. What inauspiciously used to be the site of a refuse dump couldn't distance itself further from its history; Mexican and Latino flavors inspire the menu, which includes a different flan according to the season.

BUDGET RESTAURANTS

$$ | Restaurant Zoë, Seattle. Is it only the inspired dishes that make the place so popular? After all, a charming waitstaff and a lively bar can be just as fetching as house-smoked hangar steak or pan-seared scallops on herbed rissotto.

$-$$ | The Ark, Nahcotta, WA. The oysters couldn't be fresher—they're raised in beds behind the restaurant.

$-$$ | Marco's Supper Club, Seattle. None of the flatware matches, which seems in keeping with the eclectic menu. When was the last time you had to choose between pork in a mole sauce and jerk chicken?

$ | Hing Loon, Seattle. Rumor has it that the city's Chinese chefs head here when they crave noodles.

¢-$ | Montage, Portland. Jambalaya, catfish, and Cajun mac and cheese are just a few of the specialties at this loud, festive, and sassy bistro on the east side.

¢-$ | Salumi, Seattle. It's a terrific, tiny, Italian lunch spot. The chef hands out samples while you wait for a table—prepare to sit with complete strangers.

MUSEUMS

Columbia Gorge Interpretive Center, near Stevenson, WA. The cliffs of the gorge rise behind it. Exhibits on the gorge—its explorers, inhabitants, and geology—fill the space within it.

Columbia River Maritime Museum, Astoria, OR. The observation tower of a World War II submarine and the personal belongings of the passengers of area shipwrecks are among the exhibits here.

Evergreen Aviation Museum, McMinnville, OR. Engrossing facts about aviation complement an awesome assortment of flying machines at this expansive repository best known as the address of Howard Hughes's "flying boat," the Spruce Goose, which has wingspan longer than a football field and its end zones.

High Desert Museum, Bend, OR. Evocative and intricate walk-through dioramas and an indoor-outdoor zoo with creatures great and tiny convey the High Desert's past and present in a delightfully airy and family-friendly space.

International Museum of Glass, Tacoma, WA. Breathtaking—often enormous—works by Dale Chihuly and other Pacific Northwest glass artisans fill this museum.

Maryhill Museum of Art, Goldendale, WA. A railroad baron built this chateau in the 1920s and filled it Native American artifacts and Rodin sculptures, among other things. It and the peacocks that stroll its grounds are the last things you expect to see on the Columbia Plateau.

Poulsbo Marine Science Center, Poulsbo, WA. The creatures of Puget Sound squirm, swim, and squirt. You can have a first-hand experience (excuse the pun) with some of them thanks to the center's "touch tanks."

Royal British Columbia Museum, Victoria. An authentic longhouse, a simulated submarine ride, a complete frontier town, and one of the province's leading collections of First Nations artifacts help trace several thousand years of British Columbian history at this impressive museum.

Seattle Asian Art Museum. Pick an Asian country—any Asian country—and you're likely to find art or artifacts from it here.

Wing Luke Museum, Seattle. Costumes, crafts, and photographs of immigrants from Asia and the Pacific islands all under one roof.

PARKS, GARDENS & NATURE

Dr. Sun Yat-Sen Classical Chinese Garden, Vancouver. The first authentic Ming Dynasty–style garden outside of China incorporates symbolism and design elements from centuries-old Chinese gardens.

Japanese Garden, Portland. Considered the most authentic Japanese garden outside Japan, this serene spot provides a peaceful retreat only minutes from city traffic, and a glimpse at an ever-changing landscape with plants and flowers blooming at all times of year.

Mt. Rainier National Park. This massive mountain is the centerpiece of a park filled with hiking and cross-country ski trails, lakes and rivers, woodlands and meadows.

Pacific Rim National Park Reserve, Vancouver Island. This park on Canada's far west coast has a 10-mi-long white-sand beach, a group of islands, and a demanding hiking trail with panoramic views of the sea and the rain forest.

Portland Classical Chinese Garden. A team of 60 artisans and designers from China literally left no stone unturned—500 tons of stone were brought here from Suzhou—in their efforts to create this walled Suzhou-style garden, the largest outside China. It occupies one city block in the Old Town/Chinatown area.

Stanley Park, Vancouver. An afternoon in this 1,000-acre wilderness park blocks from downtown can include beaches, the ocean, the harbor, Douglas fir and cedar forests, children's attractions and sculptures, and a good look at the North Shore mountains.

Valley of the Rogue State Park, Grants Pass, OR. If you're not quite intrepid enough to book a trip into the legendary river's wilderness heartland, you can wander its untamed banks on your own.

QUINTESSENTIAL PACIFIC NORTHWEST

Crystal Mountain Ski Area, near Mt. Rainier National Park, WA. Many swear that the state's biggest ski area is also one of its best.

Jacksonville Cemetery, Jacksonville, OR. With orange madrona branches tangling over tombstones dating back to the 1850s, this resting place provides a glimpse into this gold-rush town's frontier mores and culture.

Pike Place Market, Seattle. There's nothing quite like this market when it's in full swing. Try to visit on a Saturday afternoon for a robust experience.

Pioneer Square District, Seattle. A 24/7 district: shop and gallery hop by day, wine and dine by night.

Space Needle. It takes 42 seconds to ride the elevator up to the observation deck of this Seattle icon.

The Summit at Snoqualmie Pass, WA. Everything at this northern Cascades ski resort is in multiples: the peaks, the resorts, the downhill and Nordic trails, the lifts. There are also multiple ways to get down the slopes: on skis, on snowboards, or in inner tubes.

Underground, Pendleton, OR. Explore the scandalous and fascinating history of Pendleton on this guided tour of its brothels, saloons, and opium dens, as well as the living quarters of its Chinese laborers.

Vivace Roasteria, Seattle. It's easy to while away an afternoon or evening here, sipping what may well be the city's best espresso.

SHOPPING

Elliott Bay Book Company, Seattle. An enormous independent bookseller that keeps Seattle's literary heart beating clear and strong.

Granville Island Public Market, Vancouver. This small sandbar was a derelict factory district, but its industrial buildings and tin sheds, painted in primary colors, now house restaurants, a public market, marine activities, and artists' studios.

Portland Saturday Market. North America's largest open-air handicraft market transforms the area under and around the Burnside Bridge into a festive celebration of craft, food, and music every weekend.

Powell's City of Books, Portland. The largest independent bookstore in the world, with more than 1.5 million new and used books, is a delightful place to spend a few minutes or several hours.

Recreational Equipment, Inc., Seattle. It's so much more than just a sporting-goods store, and it has a 65-foot climbing wall to prove it.

Stonington Gallery, Seattle. This is *the* place to find contemporary works by members of Northwest Coast tribes.

Sur La Table, Seattle. If you like to cook, there are some 12,500 reasons to shop here.

Uwajimaya, Seattle. Do Shiseido and Hello Kitty have a place in your heart? What about Korean art, Vietnamese ceramics, Chinese pastries, or other foods and goods from Asia? This market has it all and then some.

VIEWS

Cove Palisades State Park, Madras, OR. Arid red-rock cliffs and the confluence of the Metolius, Deschutes, and Crooked rivers combine for a gleaming, refreshing destination, a favorite among boaters and anglers.

North Cascades Highway, North Cascades National Park, WA. It traverses the park, passing through pastures, woods, and orchards and switchbacking along ridges and rivers. An autumn drive along this highway (a.k.a. Route 20) is unforgettable.

Smith Rock State Park, Redmond, OR. Rock climbers from all over the world visit this vivid red-orange 550-foot slab of compressed volcanic ash. Even if you have no desire to assault Monkey Face, the Pleasure Palace, or any other piece of the Rock, the surrounding state park has miles of horizontal hiking.

Wonderland Trail, Mt. Rainier National Park. It's 93 mi long and takes in every possible type of mountain scenery. No other Rainier route can possibly compare.

SMART TRAVEL TIPS

Finding out about your destination before you leave home means you won't squander time organizing everyday minutiae once you've arrived. The organizations in this section can provide information to supplement this guide; contact them for up-to-the-minute details, and consult the A to Z sections that end each chapter for facts on the various topics as they relate to the Pacific Northwest's many regions. Happy landings!

AIR TRAVEL

BOOKING

When you book, look for nonstop flights and remember that "direct" flights stop at least once. Avoid connecting flights, which require a change of plane. Two airlines may operate a connecting flight jointly, so ask whether your airline operates every segment of the trip; you may find that the carrier you prefer flies only part of the way. To find more tips and to check prices and make reservations, log on to www.fodors.com.

CARRIERS

Many international carriers serve the region, including British Airways, Cathay Pacific, Japan Airlines, KLM, Lufthansa, and Qantas. Among the U.S. carriers are Continental, Delta, Northwest, and United. Alaska Airlines, America West, Big Sky, Frontier Airlines, Horizon Air, and United Express provide frequent service between cities in Washington, Oregon, Idaho, Montana, and California. The major regional carrier in western Canada is Air Canada, which has flights from Seattle and Portland to Vancouver and Victoria.

Helijet Airways provides jet helicopter service from Vancouver and Seattle's Boeing Field to Victoria. Kenmore Air has scheduled flights from Seattle's Lake Union to Victoria, the San Juan Islands, and the Gulf Islands of British Columbia. Air B.C. also has daily flights from Vancouver to Portland.

🛪 Major Airlines **Air Canada** 🕾 888/247-2262 ⊕ www.aircanada.com. **British Airways** 🕾 800/247-9297 ⊕ www.britishairways.com. **Cathay Pacific** 🕾 800/233-2742 in U.S., 800/268-6868 in Canada ⊕ www.cathaypacific.com. **Continental** 🕾 800/525-0280 ⊕ www.continental.com. **Delta** 🕾 800/221-1212 ⊕ www.delta-air.com. **Japan Airlines** 🕾 800/525-3663 ⊕ www.japanair.com. **Lufthansa** 🕾 800/645-3880 or 800/563-5954

Air Travel
Airports
Boat & Ferry Travel
Business Hours
Bus Travel
Cameras & Photography
Car Rental
Car Travel
Children in the Pacific Northwest
Consulates
Consumer Protection
Cruise Travel
Customs & Duties
Disabilities & Accessibility
Discounts & Deals
Eating & Drinking
Gay & Lesbian Travel
Guidebooks
Holidays
Insurance
Lodging
Mail & Shipping
Money Matters
National Parks
Packing
Passports & Visas
Senior-Citizen Travel
Sports & Outdoors
Students in the Pacific Northwest
Taxes
Telephones
Time
Tipping
Tours & Packages
Train Travel
Travel Agencies
Visitor Information
Web Sites

⊕ www.lufthansa.com. **Northwest/KLM** ☎ 800/225-2525 ⊕ www.nwa.com. **Qantas** ☎ 800/227-4500 ⊕ www.qantas.com. **United/United Express** ☎ 800/241-6522 ⊕ www.ual.com.

Smaller Airlines Air B.C. ☎ 800/776-3000. **Alaska Airlines** ☎ 800/252-7522 ⊕ www.alaskaair.com. **America West** ☎ 800/235-9292 ⊕ www.americawest.com. **Big Sky** ☎ 800/237-7788. **Frontier** ☎ 800/432-1359 ⊕ www.frontierairlines.com. **Helijet** ☎ 800/665-4354, 604/273-1414 in Vancouver ⊕ www.helijet.com. **Horizon Air** ☎ 800/547-9308 ⊕ www.alaskaairlines.com. **Kenmore Air** ☎ 800/543-9595 ⊕ www.kenmoreair.com.

CHECK-IN & BOARDING

Always **find out your carrier's check-in policy.** Plan to arrive at the airport about two hours before your scheduled departure time for domestic flights and 2½ to 3 hours before international flights. You may need to arrive earlier if you're flying from one of the busier airports or during peak air-traffic times. To avoid delays at airport-security checkpoints, try not to wear any metal. Jewelry, belt and other buckles, steel-toe shoes, barrettes, and underwire bras are among the items that can set off detectors.

Assuming that not everyone with a ticket will show up, airlines routinely overbook planes. When everyone does, airlines ask for volunteers to give up their seats. In return, these volunteers usually get a several-hundred-dollar flight voucher, which can be used toward the purchase of another ticket, and are rebooked on the next flight out. If there are not enough volunteers, the airline must choose who will be denied boarding. The first to get bumped are passengers who checked in late and those flying on discounted tickets, so get to the gate and check in as early as possible, especially during peak periods. Always **bring a government-issued photo I.D.** to the airport; even when it's not required, a passport is best.

CUTTING COSTS

The least expensive airfares to the Pacific Northwest are priced for round-trip travel and must usually be purchased in advance. Airlines generally allow you to change your return date for a fee; most low-fare tickets, however, are nonrefundable. Call a number of airlines and check the Internet; when you are quoted a good price, book it on the spot—the same fare may not be available the next day, or even the next hour. Check different routings and look into using alternate airports. Also, price off-peak flights, which may be significantly less expensive than others. Travel agents, especially low-fare specialists (⇨ Discounts and Deals), are helpful.

Consolidators are another good source. They buy tickets for scheduled flights at reduced rates from the airlines, then sell them at prices that beat the best fare available directly from the airlines. Sometimes you can even get your money back if you need to return the ticket. Carefully read the fine print detailing penalties for changes and cancellations, purchase the ticket with a credit card, and confirm your consolidator reservation with the airline.

Consolidators AirlineConsolidator.com ☎ 888/468-5385 ⊕ www.airlineconsolidator.com for international tickets. **Best Fares** ☎ 800/576-8255 or 800/576-1600 ⊕ www.bestfares.com, $59.90 annual membership. **Cheap Tickets** ☎ 800/377-1000 or 888/922-8849 ⊕ www.cheaptickets.com. **Expedia** ☎ 800/397-3342 or 404/728-8787 ⊕ www.expedia.com. **Hotwire** ☎ 866/468-9473 or 920/330-9418 ⊕ www.hotwire.com. **Now Voyager Travel** ✉ 45 W. 21st St., 5th fl., New York, NY 10010 ☎ 212/459-1616 🖷 212/243-2711 ⊕ www.nowvoyagertravel.com. **Onetravel.com** ⊕ www.onetravel.com. **Orbitz** ☎ 888/656-4546 ⊕ www.orbitz.com. **Priceline.com** ⊕ www.priceline.com. **Travelocity** ☎ 888/709-5983, 877/282-2925 in Canada, 0870/111-7060 in U.K. ⊕ www.travelocity.com.

ENJOYING THE FLIGHT

State your seat preference when purchasing your ticket, and then repeat it when you confirm and when you check in. For more legroom, you can request one of the few emergency-aisle seats at check-in, if you are capable of lifting at least 50 pounds—a Federal Aviation Administration requirement of passengers in these seats. Seats behind a bulkhead also offer more legroom, but they don't have under-seat storage. Don't sit in the row in front of the emergency aisle or in front of a bulkhead, where seats may not recline.

Ask the airline whether a snack or meal is served on the flight. If you have dietary concerns, request special meals when booking. These can be vegetarian, low-cholesterol, or kosher, for example. It's a good idea to pack some healthful snacks and a small (plastic) bottle of water in your carry-on bag. On long flights, try to maintain a normal routine, to help fight jet lag. At night, get some sleep. By day, eat light meals, drink water (not alcohol), and **move around the cabin** to stretch your legs. For additional jet-lag tips consult *Fodor's FYI: Travel Fit & Healthy* (available at bookstores everywhere).

Smoking policies vary from carrier to carrier. Many airlines prohibit smoking on all of their flights; others allow smoking only on certain routes or certain departures. Ask your carrier about its policy.

FLYING TIMES

It takes about 5 hours to fly nonstop to Seattle or Portland from New York, 4 hours from Chicago, and 2½ hours from Los Angeles. Flights from New York to Vancouver take about 6 hours nonstop; from Chicago, 4½ hours nonstop; and from Los Angeles, 3 hours nonstop.

HOW TO COMPLAIN

If your baggage goes astray or your flight goes awry, complain right away. Most carriers require that you **file a claim immediately.** The Aviation Consumer Protection Division of the Department of Transportation publishes *Fly-Rights,* which discusses airlines and consumer issues and is available on-line. You can also find articles and information on mytravelrights.com, the Web site of the nonprofit Consumer Travel Rights Center.

🔝 Airline Complaints **Aviation Consumer Protection Division** ⊠ U.S. Department of Transportation, C-75, Room 4107, 400 7th St. SW, Washington, DC 20590 ☎ 202/366-2220 ⊕ airconsumer.ost.dot.gov. **Federal Aviation Administration Consumer Hotline** ⊠ For inquiries: FAA, 800 Independence Ave. SW, Washington, DC 20591 ☎ 800/322-7873 ⊕ www.faa.gov.

RECONFIRMING

Check the status of your flight before you leave for the airport. You can do this on your carrier's Web site, by linking to a flight-status checker (many Web booking services offer these), or by calling your carrier or travel agent.

AIRPORTS

The main gateways to the Pacific Northwest are Portland International Airport (PDX), Sea-Tac International Airport

(SEA), and Vancouver International Airport (YVR).

🔝 Airport Information **Portland International Airport (PDX)** ⊠ N.E. Airport Way at I-205 ☎ 877/739-4636 ⊕ www.portlandairportpdx.com. **Sea-Tac International Airport (SEA)** ☎ 206/431-4444 ⊕ www.seatac.org. **Vancouver International Airport (YVR)** ☎ 604/207-7077 ⊕ www.yvr.ca.

BOAT & FERRY TRAVEL

Ferries play an important part in the transportation network of the Pacific Northwest. Some are the sole connection to islands in Puget Sound and to small towns and islands along the west coast of British Columbia. Each day ferries transport thousands of commuters to and from work in the coastal cities. Always comfortable, convenient, and surrounded by spectacular views, ferries are also one of the best ways for you to get a feel for the region and its ties to the sea.

The best times for travel are 9–3 and after 7 PM on weekdays. In July and August you may have to wait hours to take a car aboard one of the popular ferries, such as those to the San Juan Islands. Walk-on space is always available; if possible, leave your car behind. Reservations aren't taken for domestic routes.

WASHINGTON & OREGON

Washington State Ferries carries millions of passengers and vehicles each year on 10 routes between 20 points on Puget Sound, the San Juan Islands, and Sidney, British Columbia. Onboard services vary depending on the size of the ferry, but most ships have a cafeteria, vending machines, newspaper and tourist-information kiosks, arcade games, and rest rooms with family facilities. There are discounted fares in off-peak months, as well as monthly, passenger-only passes for those planning more than 16 round trips in 30 days.

Argosy cruising vessels make sightseeing, dinner, weekend brunch, and special event cruises around Elliott Bay, Lake Union, Lake Washington, the Ballard Locks, and other Seattle waterways. Black Ball Transport's MV *Coho* makes daily crossings year-round, from Port Angeles to Victoria. The *Coho* can carry 800 passengers and 100 cars across the Strait of Juan de Fuca in 1½ hours. Reservations aren't accepted. Clipper Navigation operates the passenger-only *Victoria Clipper* jet catamaran between Seattle, the San Juan Islands, and Victoria. The Puget Island Ferry crosses from Westport, Oregon, to Puget Island, near Cathlamet, Washington.

From Portland, the *Portland Spirit, Willamette Star,* and *Crystal Dolphin* make sightseeing and dinner cruises on the Willamette and Columbia Rivers. America West also uses paddle-wheel boats for overnight historic tours along the Columbia and Snake rivers. Departing from Cascade Locks, Oregon (45 minutes east of Portland), the sternwheeler *Columbia Gorge* cruises the Columbia Gorge and the Willamette River (December only). To view the rich wildlife along the western edge of the Columbia River, you can take an ecologically focused cruise or an estuary tour, both of which depart from Astoria, Oregon.

BRITISH COLUMBIA

British Columbia Ferries operates passenger and vehicle service between the mainland and Victoria and elsewhere. Most ferries take reservations.
Argosy Cruises ☎ 206/623-1445 or 800/642-7816 ⊕ www.argosycruises.com. **Black Ball Transport** ☎ 604/386-2202 in Victoria, 360/457-4491 in Port Angeles ⊕ www.cohoferry.com. **British Columbia Ferries** ☎ 250/386-3431 in Victoria, 888/223-3779 in Canada ⊕ www.bcferries.bc.ca. **Clipper Navigation** ☎ 250/382-8100 in Victoria, 206/448-5000 in Seattle, 800/888-2535 in U.S. ⊕ www.victoriaclipper.com. *Columbia Gorge* ☎ 541/374-8427 or 800/643-1354 ⊕ www.sternwheeler.com. *Portland Spirit* ☎ 503/224-3900 or 800/224-3901 ⊕ www.portlandspirit.com. **Puget Island Ferry** ☎ 360/795-3301 ⊕ www.cwcog.org/ferry. **Washington State Ferries** ☎ 206/464-6400, 800/843-3779 automated information line, 888/808-7977 in WA ⊕ www.wsdot.wa.gov/ferries.

BUSINESS HOURS

BANKS & OFFICES

Banks and offices are open weekdays from 9 to 5 or 6. Some bank branches are open Saturday mornings.

MUSEUMS & SIGHTS

Museum hours are generally 10 to 5 from Tuesday through Saturday and 12 to 5 on Sunday. Most parks and zoos are open daily. Some sights close on major holidays; sights in the mountains occasionally close for snow emergencies in winter.

SHOPS

Most department stores and shops in malls are open 10 to 9 weekdays and Saturday, 11 to 6 on Sunday. Freestanding boutiques are usually open from 10 to 6 weekdays and Saturday.

BUS TRAVEL

Greyhound and Northwestern Trailways buses travel to and within the region. Experience Oregon in Eugene operates charter bus services and scheduled sightseeing tours that last from a few hours to several days. People Mover travels on Route 26 between Bend and John Day. Greyhound serves most towns in British Columbia and provides frequent service on popular runs.

Gray Line, which operates from Portland, Seattle, Vancouver, and Victoria, schedules a variety of popular bus tours and overnight packages around the Pacific Northwest. The company also has daily service from Seattle to the Washington State Ferry terminal in Anacortes. Pacific Coach Lines runs multiple daily buses between Vancouver and Victoria, including a ferry ride across the Strait of Georgia. The company also has connections from Vancouver to Vancouver International Airport and the cruise ship terminal, and operates numerous package tours around British Columbia.

DISCOUNT PASSES

Greyhound's domestic and international Discovery Passes allow unlimited bus travel in North America—including Canada and Mexico—for periods of 4 to 60 days. Greyhound also offers several Ameripass and CanAm Pass options, which cover specific regions of North America.
Bus Companies Experience Oregon ☎ 541/342-2662 or 800/342-2662 ⊕ www.experience.oregon.com. **Gray Line** ☎ 503/285-9845, 800/422-7042 in Portland ⊕ www.grayline.com ☎ 206/624-5077, 800/426-7505 in Seattle ☎ 604/681-8687, 800/667-0882 in Vancouver ☎ 250/388-6539, 800/663-8390 in Victoria. **Greyhound Lines** ☎ 800/661-8747 in Canada, 800/231-2222 in U.S. ⊕ www.greyhound.com or www.greyhound.ca. **Northwest Trailways** ☎ 800/366-3830 ⊕ www.northwesttrailways.com. **Pacific Coach Lines** ☎ 800/661-1725 in U.S., 604/662-7575 in Vancouver ⊕ www.pacificcoach.com. **People Mover** ☎ 541/575-2370 or 800/527-2370.

CAMERAS & PHOTOGRAPHY

The *Kodak Guide to Shooting Great Travel Pictures* (available at bookstores everywhere) is loaded with tips.

F Photo Help **Kodak Information Center** ☎ 800/242-2424 ⊕ www.kodak.com.

EQUIPMENT PRECAUTIONS

Don't pack film or equipment in checked luggage, where it is much more susceptible to damage. X-ray machines used to view checked luggage are extremely powerful and therefore are likely to ruin your film. Try to ask for hand inspection of film, which becomes clouded after repeated exposure to airport X-ray machines, and keep videotapes and computer disks away from metal detectors. Always keep film, tape, and computer disks out of the sun. Carry an extra supply of batteries, and be prepared to turn on your camera, camcorder, or laptop to prove to airport security personnel that the device is real.

CAR RENTAL

In Washington, Seattle is the most expensive place for car rental, with rates that begin at $21 a day ($110 per week) for an economy car. This includes air-conditioning, automatic transmission, and unlimited mileage—but not the 18.5% tax. If possible, avoid renting a car at Sea-Tac Airport, where rates are higher still and an additional 10% airport tax is charged.

Rates in Portland begin at $35 a day and $145 a week, not including the 12.5% tax. Rates in Eugene begin at $19.95 a day and $125 a week, not including the 10% tax. Rates in Vancouver begin at about C$40 a day or C$230 a week, usually including unlimited mileage.

Car rentals in British Columbia also incur a 14.5% sales tax, a C$1.50-per-day social services tax, and a vehicle licensing fee of 91¢ per day. An additional 15.61% Concession Recovery Fee, charged by the airport authority for retail space in the terminal, is levied at airport locations. If you prefer a manual-transmission car, check whether the rental agency of your choice offers stick shifts; some companies, such as Avis, don't in Canada.

All the major agencies are represented in the region. If you're planning to cross the U.S.–Canadian border with your rental car, discuss it with the agency to see what's involved. See the A to Z sections throughout the chapters for local agency recommendations.

F Major Agencies **Alamo** ☎ 800/327-9633 ⊕ www.alamo.com. **Avis** ☎ 800/331-1212, 800/879-2847, 800/272-5871 in Canada, 0870/606-0100 in U.K., 02/9353-9000 in Australia, 09/526-2847 in New Zealand ⊕ www.avis.com. **Budget** ☎ 800/527-0700, 0870/156-5656 in U.K. ⊕ www.budget.com. **Dollar** ☎ 800/800-4000, 0124/622-0111 in U.K., where it's affiliated with Sixt, 02/9223-1444 in Australia ⊕ www.dollar.com. **Hertz** ☎ 800/654-3131, 800/263-0600 in Canada, 0870/844-8844 in U.K., 02/9669-2444 in Australia, 09/256-8690 in New Zealand ⊕ www.hertz.com. **National Car Rental** ☎ 800/227-7368, 0870/600-6666 in U.K. ⊕ www.nationalcar.com.

CUTTING COSTS

For a good deal, book through a travel agent who will shop around. Also, price local car-rental companies—whose prices may be lower still, although their service and maintenance may not be as good as those of major rental agencies—and research rates on the Internet. Remember to ask about deposits, cancellation penalties, and drop-off charges if you're planning to pick up the car in one city and leave it in another. If you're traveling during a holiday period, also make sure that a confirmed reservation guarantees you a car.

INSURANCE

When driving a rented car you are generally responsible for any damage to or loss of the vehicle. You also may be liable for any property damage or personal injury that you may cause while driving. Before you rent, see what coverage you already have under the terms of your personal auto-insurance policy and credit cards.

For about $9 to $25 a day, rental companies sell protection, known as a collision- or loss-damage waiver (CDW or LDW), that eliminates your liability for damage to the car; it's always optional and should never be automatically added to your bill. In most states you don't need a CDW if you have personal auto insurance or other liability insurance. However, **make sure you have enough coverage to pay for the car.** If you do not have auto insurance or an umbrella policy that covers damage to third parties, purchasing liability insurance and a CDW or LDW is highly recommended.

REQUIREMENTS & RESTRICTIONS

In the Pacific Northwest you must be 21 to rent a car. Car seats are compulsory for children under four years *and* 40 pounds; older children are required to sit in booster seats until they are eight years old *and* 80 pounds. (In British Columbia, children up to 40 pounds or 18 kilos in weight must use a child seat.) In the United States non-residents need a reservation voucher, passport, driver's license, and insurance for each driver.

SURCHARGES

Before you pick up a car in one city and leave it in another, ask about drop-off charges or one-way service fees, which can be substantial. Note, too, that some rental agencies charge extra if you return the car before the time specified in your contract. To avoid a hefty refueling fee, fill the tank just before you turn in the car, but be aware that gas stations near the rental outlet may overcharge. It's almost never a deal to buy the tank of gas that's in the car when you rent it; the understanding is that you'll return it empty, but some fuel usually remains. Surcharges may apply if you're under 25 or if you take the car outside the area approved by the rental agency. You'll pay extra for child seats (about $6 a day in the United States, C$8 in Canada) and usually for additional drivers (about $10 per day, C$5 in Canada).

CAR TRAVEL

Driver's licenses from other countries are valid in the United States and Canada. International driving permits (IDPs)—available from the American and Canadian automobile associations and, in the United Kingdom, from the Automobile Association and Royal Automobile Club—are a good idea. Valid only in conjunction with your regular driver's license, these permits are universally recognized; having one may save you a problem with local authorities.

At this writing unleaded gas averages about $1.89 a gallon. In Canada, gasoline sells for about 75.9¢ per liter. In Oregon, gasoline must be dispensed by a station attendant. Stations are plentiful. Most stay open late (24 hours along large highways and in big cities), except in rural areas, where Sunday hours are limited and where you may drive long stretches without a refueling opportunity.

Bookstores, gas stations, convenience stores, and rest stops sell maps (about $5) and multiregion road atlases (about $12). Along larger highways, roadside stops with rest rooms, fast-food restaurants, and sundries stores are well spaced. Police and tow trucks patrol major highways and lend assistance.

FROM THE U.S.

Drivers must carry owner registration and proof of insurance coverage, which is compulsory in Canada. The Canadian Non-Resident Inter-Provincial Motor Vehicle Liability Insurance Card, available from any U.S. insurance company, is accepted as evidence of financial responsibility in Canada. If you are driving a car that is not registered in your name, carry a letter from the owner that authorizes your use of the vehicle.

The main entry point into British Columbia from the United States by car is on I–5 at Blaine, Washington, 48 km (30 mi) south of Vancouver. Three highways enter British Columbia from the east: Highway 1, or the Trans-Canada Highway; Highway 3, or the Crowsnest Highway, which crosses southern British Columbia; and Highway 16, the Yellowhead Highway, which runs through northern British Columbia from the Rocky Mountains to Prince Rupert. From Alaska and the Yukon, take the Alaska Highway (from Fairbanks) or the Klondike Highway (from Skagway or Dawson City).

Border-crossing procedures are usually quick and simple. Every British Columbia border crossing is open 24 hours (except the one at Aldergrove, which is open from 8 AM to midnight). The I–5 border crossing at Blaine, Washington (also known as the Douglas, or Peace Arch, border crossing), is one of the busiest border crossings between the United States and Canada. Listen to local radio traffic reports for information about wait times.

ROAD CONDITIONS

Winter driving can present challenges. In coastal areas the mild, damp climate contributes to frequently wet roadways. Snowfalls generally occur only once or twice a year, but when it does fall, traffic grinds to a halt and roadways become treacherous and stay that way until the snow melts.

Tire chains, studs, or snow tires are essential equipment for winter travel in mountain areas. If you're planning to drive into high elevations, be sure to check the weather forecast beforehand. Even the main-highway mountain passes can close because of snow conditions. In winter state and provincial highway departments operate snow advisory telephone lines that give pass conditions.

RULES OF THE ROAD

The use of seat belts and child seats for infants is mandatory in Washington, Oregon, and British Columbia. The speed limit in Washington and Oregon on rural interstate highways is 65 mph. Elsewhere it's 55 mph unless otherwise posted. In British Columbia speed limits are usually within the 50–110 kph (30–66 mph) range outside the cities. Right turns are permitted on red signals.

CHILDREN IN THE REGION

Be sure to plan ahead and **involve your youngsters** as you outline your trip. When packing, include things to keep them busy en route. On sightseeing days try to schedule activities of special interest to your children. If you are renting a car, don't forget to **arrange for a car seat** when you reserve. For general advice about traveling with children, consult *Fodor's FYI: Travel with Your Baby* (available in bookstores everywhere).

FLYING

If your children are two or older, ask about children's airfares. As a general rule, infants under two not occupying a seat fly at greatly reduced fares or even for free. But if you want to guarantee a seat for an infant, you have to pay full fare. Consider flying during off-peak days and times; most airlines will grant an infant a seat without a ticket if there are available seats.

Experts agree that it's a good idea to use safety seats aloft for children weighing less than 40 pounds. Airlines set their own policies: if you use a safety seat, U.S. carriers usually require that the child be ticketed, even if he or she is young enough to ride free, because the seats must be strapped into regular seats. And even if you pay the full adult fare for the seat, it may be worth it, especially on longer trips.

Do **check your airline's policy about using safety seats during takeoff and landing.** Safety seats are not allowed everywhere in the plane, so get your seat assignments as early as possible.

When reserving, request children's meals or a freestanding bassinet (not available on all airlines) if you need them. But note that bulkhead seats, where you must sit to use a bassinet, may lack an overhead bin or storage space on the floor.

LODGING

Most hotels in the Pacific Northwest allow children under a certain age to stay in their parents' room at no extra charge, but others charge for them as extra adults; be sure to **find out the cutoff age for children's discounts.** You can get a second room for half-price (and sometimes free) at some Hyatt hotels. Cribs, cots, and extra beds are usually free or cost a nominal amount. Kids eat free at Holiday Inns and WestCoast properties. In many independent restaurants, young children can usually get half portions.

PRECAUTIONS

Keep hold of toddlers on ferries; although the space between bars on railings is too narrow to fall through, children might be tempted to climb the railings themselves. Ferries also have steep steps down which a toddler could easily tumble. What's more, vehicles parked closely together on car ferries create spaces where a wee one could get lost or stuck.

Caveat: If you plan to travel between the United States and Canada, be sure to bring documents that prove your children's identities and their relationships to you, including birth certificates, passports, and/or social security cards. Children under 18 crossing the border with only one parent, or with other relatives or friends, may need a notarized letter of permission from the other spouse or both parents.

SIGHTS & ATTRACTIONS

The Pacific Northwest is an ideal family destination, with its beaches, network of ferries, and fascinating museums, parks, and playgrounds. Skiing, climbing, kayaking, horseback riding, and hiking are always possibilities; many outfitters offer lessons geared to people of various ages and skill levels. Places that are especially appealing to children are indicated by a rubber-duckie icon (🦆) in the margin.

CONSULATES

🏛 **Australian Consulate** ✉ 888 Dunsmuir St., Suite 1225, Vancouver BC ☎ 604/684-1177. **British Consulate** ✉ 900 4th Ave., Suite 3001, Seattle, WA ☎ 206/622-9255 ⊕ www.britainusa.com/consular/seattle/seattle.asp ✉ 1111 Melville St., Suite 800, Vancouver, BC ☎ 604/683-4421. **Canadian Consulate** ✉ Plaza 600 Bldg., 6th Ave. and Stewart St., 4th fl., Seattle, WA ☎ 206/443-1777 ⊕ www.canada-seattle.org. **New Zealand Consulate** ✉ 10649 North Beach Rd., Bow, WA ☎ 360/766-8002 ⊕ www.nzemb.org/embassy/consulates.htm ✉ 888 Dunsmuir St., Suite 1200, Vancouver, BC ☎ 604/684-7388. **U.S. Consulate General** ✉ 1095 W. Pender St., 21st fl., Vancouver, BC ☎ 604/685-4311.

CONSUMER PROTECTION

Whether you're shopping for gifts or purchasing travel services, **pay with a major credit card** whenever possible, so you can cancel payment or get reimbursed if there's a problem (and you can provide documentation). If you're doing business with a company for the first time, contact your local Better Business Bureau and the attorney general's offices in your state and (for U.S. businesses) the company's home state. Have any complaints been filed? Finally, if you're buying a package or tour, always consider travel insurance that includes default coverage (⇨ Insurance).

🏛 BBBs **Council of Better Business Bureaus** ✉ 4200 Wilson Blvd., Suite 800, Arlington, VA 22203 ☎ 703/276-0100 🖷 703/525-8277 ⊕ www.bbb.org.

CRUISE TRAVEL

Seattle's cruise industry welcomes some of the world's largest ships to new docks on Elliott Bay. The city's strategic location along the west coast means that it's just a day's journey by water to Canada and California, and you can reach Alaska or Mexico in less than a week.

Of the large ships, Norwegian Cruise Line offers seven-day summer cruises from Seattle to Alaska, as well as five-day cruises from Los Angeles to Vancouver that stop in Seattle. Holland America Line, which has seven-day cruises to Alaska on the *MS Amsterdam*, and Princess Cruises, which offers seven-day Alaska cruises on

the *Star Princess,* also depart from Seattle and have a stop in Vancouver. Ships of the Radisson Seven Seas fleet also call at Victoria on the way from Vancouver to Seward (the port city for Anchorage).

Vancouver is the major embarkation point for Alaska cruises, and virtually all Alaska-bound cruise ships call there; some also call at Victoria and Prince Rupert. Once leaving Vancouver, however, most luxury liners make straight for Alaska, leaving the fjords and islands of British Columbia to smaller vessels and expedition ships. More than 30 ships, of all sizes, offer cruises to Alaska. You can sail the Inside Passage on a small ship carrying a handful of passengers or cross the Gulf of Alaska in the company of more than 1,000 other people.

The small, expedition-style ships operated by American Safari Cruises, Clipper Cruise Lines, and Cruise West explore the British Columbia coast on their way to Alaska. Bluewater Adventures has 7- to 10-day sailing cruises of the British Columbia coastline, including the Queen Charlotte Islands.

To get the best deal on a cruise, **consult a cruise-only travel agency.** To learn how to plan, choose, and book a cruise-ship voyage, check out Cruise How-to's on www.fodors.com and consult *Fodor's FYI: Plan & Enjoy Your Cruise* (available in bookstores everywhere).

🏛 Major Cruise Lines **Carnival Cruise Lines** ☎ 800/327-9501 ⊕ www.carnival.com. **Cruise Lines International Association** ☎ 212/921-0066. **Crystal Cruises** ☎ 310/785-9300 or 800/446-6620 ⊕ www.crystalcruises.com. **Celebrity Cruises** ☎ 800/437-3111 ⊕ www.celebritycruises.com. **Holland America** ☎ 206/281-3535 or 877/724-5425 ⊕ www.hollandamerica.com. **Norwegian Cruise Lines** ☎ 305/436-4000 or 800/327-7030 ⊕ www.ncl.com. **Princess Cruises** ☎ 661/753-0000 or 800/568-3262 ⊕ www.princess.com. **Radisson Seven Seas Cruises** ☎ 800/285-1835 ⊕ www.rssc.com. **Royal Caribbean** ☎ 800/327-6700 ⊕ www.royalcaribbean.com. **World Explorer Cruises** ☎ 415/820-9200 or 800/854-3835 ⊕ www.wecruise.com.

🏛 Local Cruise Lines **American Safari Cruises** ✉ 19101 36th Ave. W, Suite 201, Lynnwood, WA 98036 ☎ 425/776-4700 or 888/862-8881 ⊕ www.amsafari.com. **Bluewater Adventures** ✉ 3-252 E. 1st St., North Vancouver V7L 1B3 BC ☎ 604/980-3800 or 888/877-1770 ⊕ www.bluewateradventures.ca. **Clipper Cruise Lines** ✉ 11969 Westline Industrial

Dr., St. Louis, MO 63146-3220 ☎ 314/655-6700 or 800/325-0010 ⊕ www.clippercruise.com. **Cruise West** ✉ 2401 4th Ave., Suite 700, Seattle, WA 98121-1438 ☎ 206/441-8687 or 800/426-7202 ⊕ www.cruisewest.com.

CUSTOMS & DUTIES

When shopping abroad, keep receipts for all purchases. Upon reentering the country, **be ready to show customs officials what you've bought.** Pack purchases together in an easily accessible place. If you think a duty is incorrect, appeal the assessment. If you object to the way your clearance was handled, note the inspector's badge number. In either case, first ask to see a supervisor. If the problem isn't resolved, write to the appropriate authorities, beginning with the port director at your point of entry.

IN AUSTRALIA

Australian residents who are 18 or older may bring home A$400 worth of souvenirs and gifts (including jewelry), 250 cigarettes or 250 grams of cigars or other tobacco products, and 1,125 ml of alcohol (including wine, beer, and spirits). Residents under 18 may bring back A$200 worth of goods. Members of the same family traveling together may pool their allowances. Prohibited items include meat products. Seeds, plants, and fruits need to be declared upon arrival.
🇮 **Australian Customs Service** ⌖ Regional Director, Box 8, Sydney, NSW 2001 ☎ 02/9213-2000 or 1300/363263, 02/9364-7222 or 1800/803-006 quarantine-inquiry line ☎ 02/9213-4043 ⊕ www.customs.gov.au.

IN CANADA

Canadian residents who have been out of Canada for at least seven days may bring in C$750 worth of goods duty-free. If you've been away fewer than seven days but more than 48 hours, the duty-free allowance drops to C$200. If your trip lasts 24 to 48 hours, the allowance is C$50. You may not pool allowances with family members. Goods claimed under the C$750 exemption may follow you by mail; those claimed under the lesser exemptions must accompany you. Alcohol and tobacco products may be included in the seven-day and 48-hour exemptions but not in the 24-hour exemption. If you meet the age requirements of the province or territory through which you reenter Canada, you

may bring in, duty-free, 1.5 liters of wine *or* 1.14 liters (40 imperial ounces) of liquor *or* 24 12-ounce cans or bottles of beer or ale. Also, if you meet the local age requirement for tobacco products, you may bring in, duty-free, 200 cigarettes and 50 cigars. Check ahead of time with the Canada Customs and Revenue Agency or the Department of Agriculture for policies regarding meat products, seeds, plants, and fruits.

You may send an unlimited number of gifts (only one gift per recipient, however) worth up to C$60 each duty-free to Canada. Label the package UNSOLICITED GIFT—VALUE UNDER $60. Alcohol and tobacco are excluded.
🇮 **Canada Customs and Revenue Agency** ✉ 2265 St. Laurent Blvd., Ottawa, Ontario K1G 4K3 ☎ 800/461-9999, 204/983-3500, or 506/636-5064 ⊕ www.ccra.gc.ca.

IN NEW ZEALAND

All homeward-bound residents may bring back NZ$700 worth of souvenirs and gifts; passengers may not pool their allowances, and children can claim only the concession on goods intended for their own use. For those 17 or older, the duty-free allowance also includes 4.5 liters of wine or beer; one 1,125-ml bottle of spirits; and either 200 cigarettes, 250 grams of tobacco, 50 cigars, *or* a combination of the three up to 250 grams. Meat products, seeds, plants, and fruits must be declared upon arrival to the Agricultural Services Department.
🇮 **New Zealand Customs** ✉ Head office: The Customhouse, 17–21 Whitmore St., Box 2218, Wellington ☎ 09/300-5399 or 0800/428-786 ⊕ www.customs.govt.nz.

IN THE U.K.

From countries outside the European Union, including the United States and Canada, you may bring home, duty-free, 200 cigarettes or 50 cigars; 1 liter of spirits or 2 liters of fortified or sparkling wine or liqueurs; 2 liters of still table wine; 60 ml of perfume; 250 ml of toilet water; plus £145 worth of other goods, including gifts and souvenirs. Prohibited items include meat products, seeds, plants, and fruits.
🇮 **HM Customs and Excise** ✉ Portcullis House, 21 Cowbridge Rd. E, Cardiff CF11 9SS ☎ 0845/010-9000 or 0208/929-0152, 0208/929-6731 or 0208/910-3602 complaints ⊕ www.hmce.gov.uk.

IN THE U.S.

U.S. residents who have been out of the country for at least 48 hours may bring home, for personal use, $800 worth of foreign goods duty-free, as long as they haven't used the $800 allowance or any part of it in the past 30 days. This exemption may include 1 liter of alcohol (for travelers 21 and older), 200 cigarettes, and 100 non-Cuban cigars. Family members from the same household who are traveling together may pool their $800 personal exemptions. For fewer than 48 hours, the duty-free allowance drops to $200, which may include 50 cigarettes, 10 non-Cuban cigars, and 150 ml of alcohol (or 150 ml of perfume containing alcohol). The $200 allowance cannot be combined with other individuals' exemptions, and if you exceed it, the full value of all the goods will be taxed. Antiques, which the U.S. Bureau of Customs and Border Protection defines as objects more than 100 years old, enter duty-free, as do original works of art done entirely by hand, including paintings, drawings, and sculptures. This doesn't apply to folk art or handicrafts, which are in general dutiable.

You may also send packages home duty-free, with a limit of one parcel per addressee per day (except alcohol or tobacco products or perfume worth more than $5). You can mail up to $200 worth of goods for personal use; label the package PERSONAL USE and attach a list of its contents and their retail value. If the package contains your used personal belongings, mark it AMERICAN GOODS RETURNED to avoid paying duties. You may send up to $100 worth of goods as a gift; mark the package UNSOLICITED GIFT. Mailed items do not affect your duty-free allowance on your return.

To avoid paying duty on foreign-made high-ticket items you already own and will take on your trip, register them with Customs before you leave the country. Consider filing a Certificate of Registration for laptops, cameras, watches, and other digital devices identified with serial numbers or other permanent markings; you can keep the certificate for other trips. Otherwise, bring a sales receipt or insurance form to show that you owned the item before you left the United States.
🚩 **U.S. Bureau of Customs and Border Protection** ✉ For inquiries and equipment registration, 1300 Pennsylvania Ave. NW, Washington, DC 20229 ⊕ www.customs.gov ☎ 877/287-8667or 202/354-1000 ✉ For complaints, Customer Satisfaction Unit, 1300 Pennsylvania Ave. NW, Room 5.5D, Washington, DC 20229.

DISABILITIES & ACCESSIBILITY

The Easter Seal Society publishes *Access Seattle*, a free guide to the city's services for people with disabilities. Travelers with disabilities will find plenty of amenities in Oregon, especially in Portland, Eugene, and Salem. City buses have lifts. Most buildings have ramps or elevators. Based in Eugene, Mobility International runs exchange and development programs for people with disabilities worldwide. Adventures Without Limits and Big Bear Countree offer trips to people of all abilities.

Canadian legislation with respect to access and provision of services for people with disabilities is similar to that in the United States. Transportation facilities are largely accessible, and accessible restaurants and hotels are relatively easy to find, especially in the Vancouver area.

The British Columbia Paraplegic Association has information about touring in the province. The Government of Canada's Access to Travel Web site has information about travel in Canada for people with all manner of disabilities. You can also use this site to file a complaint about transportation obstacles in Canada.
🚩 **Local Resources Access to Travel** ⊕ www.accesstotravel.gc.ca. **Adventures Without Limits** ✉ 1341 Pacific Ave., Forest Grove, OR 97116 ☎ 503/359-2568. **Big Bear Countree** ✉ 17415 Panther Creek Rd., Carlton, OR ☎ 503/852-7926 ⊕ www.bigbearcountree.com. **British Columbia Paraplegic Association** ✉ 780 S.W. Marine Dr., Vancouver V6P 5Y7, BC ☎ 604/324-3611 or 877/324-3611 ⊕ www.canparaplegic.org/bc. **Easter Seal Society** ✉ 521 2nd Ave. W, Seattle, WA 98104 ☎ 206/281-5700. **Mobility International** ✉ 45 W. Broadway Eugene, OR 97401 ☎ 541/343-1284 [tel./TTY] ⊕ www.miusa.org.

LODGING

Despite disability legislation on both sides of the border, the definition of accessibility seems to differ from hotel to hotel. Some properties may be accessible for people with mobility problems but not for people with hearing or vision impairments, for example.

If you have mobility problems, ask for the lowest floor on which accessible services are offered. If you have a hearing impairment, check whether the hotel has devices to alert you visually to the ring of the telephone, a knock at the door, and a fire/emergency alarm. Some hotels provide these devices without charge. Discuss your needs with hotel personnel if this equipment isn't available, so that a staff member can personally alert you in the event of an emergency.

If you're bringing a guide dog, get authorization ahead of time and write down the name of the person with whom you spoke.

RESERVATIONS

When discussing accessibility with an operator or reservations agent, ask hard questions. Are there any stairs, inside *or* out? Are there grab bars next to the toilet *and* in the shower/tub? How wide is the doorway to the room? To the bathroom? For the most extensive facilities meeting the latest legal specifications, opt for newer accommodations. If you reserve through a toll-free number, consider also calling the hotel's local number to confirm the information from the central reservations office. Get confirmation in writing when you can.

SIGHTS & ATTRACTIONS

In compliance with the Americans with Disabilities Act, major attractions and zoos in Oregon and Washington are accessible to persons with disabilities via wheelchair ramps, elevators, and automatic doors. In Canada most major attractions—museums, churches, theaters—are equipped with ramps and lifts to handle wheelchairs. National and provincial institutions—parks, public monuments, and government buildings—almost always are accessible.

TRANSPORTATION

Portland's Tri-Met buses, streetcars, and MAX light-rail trains, Seattle's Metro buses, and Vancouver's BC Transit buses and SkyTrain rapid-transit trains all operate accessible public transit vehicles for persons with physical disabilities.
⚠ Complaints **Aviation Consumer Protection Division** (⇨ Air Travel) for airline-related problems. **Departmental Office of Civil Rights** ✉ For general inquiries, U.S. Department of Transportation, S-30, 400 7th St. SW, Room 10215, Washington, DC 20590 ☎ 202/366-4648 🖷 202/366-9371 ⊕ www.dot.

gov/ost/docr/index.htm. **Disability Rights Section** ✉ NYAV, U.S. Department of Justice, Civil Rights Division, 950 Pennsylvania Ave. NW, Washington, DC 20530 ☎ 202/514-0301 ADA information line, 800/514-0301, 202/514-0383 TTY, 800/514-0383 TTY ⊕ www.ada.gov. **U.S. Department of Transportation Hotline** ☎ 800/778-4838 for disability-related air-travel problems, 800/455-9880 TTY.

TRAVEL AGENCIES

In the United States, the Americans with Disabilities Act requires that travel firms serve the needs of all travelers. Some agencies specialize in working with people with disabilities.
⚠ Travelers with Mobility Problems **Access Adventures/B. Roberts Travel** ✉ 206 Chestnut Ridge Rd., Scottsville, NY 14624 ☎ 585/889-9096 ⊕ www.brobertstravel.com ✎ dltravel@prodigy.net, run by a former physical-rehabilitation counselor. **Accessible Vans of America** ✉ 9 Spielman Rd., Fairfield, NJ 07004 ☎ 877/282-8267, 888/282-8267, 973/808-9709 reservations 🖷 973/808-9713 ⊕ www.accessiblevans.com. **CareVacations** ✉ No. 5, 5110-50 Ave., Leduc, Alberta, Canada, T9E 6V4 ☎ 780/986-6404 or 877/478-7827 🖷 780/986-8332 ⊕ www.carevacations.com, for group tours and cruise vacations. **Flying Wheels Travel** ✉ 143 W. Bridge St., Box 382, Owatonna, MN 55060 ☎ 507/451-5005 🖷 507/451-1685 ⊕ www.flyingwheelstravel.com.
⚠ Travelers with Developmental Disabilities **New Directions** ✉ 5276 Hollister Ave., Suite 207, Santa Barbara, CA 93111 ☎ 805/967-2841 or 888/967-2841 🖷 805/964-7344 ⊕ www.newdirectionstravel.com.

DISCOUNTS & DEALS

Be a smart shopper and compare all your options before making decisions. A plane ticket bought with a promotional coupon from travel clubs, coupon books, and direct-mail offers or purchased on the Internet may not be cheaper than the least expensive fare from a discount ticket agency. And always keep in mind that what you get is just as important as what you save.

DISCOUNT RESERVATIONS

To save money, look into discount reservations services with Web sites and toll-free numbers, which use their buying power to get a better price on hotels, airline tickets (⇨ Air Travel), even car rentals. When booking a room, always **call the hotel's local toll-free number** (if one is available) rather than the central reservations number—you'll often get a better price. Always ask about special packages or corporate rates.

🛪 Airline Tickets **Air 4 Less** ☎ 800/AIR4LESS; low-fare specialist.

🛪 Hotel Rooms **Accommodations Express** ☎ 800/444-7666 or 800/277-1064 🌐 www. accommodationsexpress.com. **Hotels.com** ☎ 800/246-8357 🌐 www.hotels.com. **Quikbook** ☎ 800/789-9887 🌐 www.quikbook.com. **RMC Travel** ☎ 800/245-5738 🌐 www.rmcwebtravel.com. **Turbotrip.com** ☎ 800/473-7829 🌐 www.turbotrip.com.

PACKAGE DEALS

Don't confuse packages and guided tours. When you buy a package, you travel on your own, just as though you had planned the trip yourself. Fly–drive packages, which combine airfare and car rental, are often a good deal. In cities, ask the local visitor's bureau about hotel packages that include tickets to major museum exhibits or other special events.

EATING & DRINKING

You'll find almost any type of cuisine in Seattle, Portland, Vancouver, and Victoria. Pacific Northwest cuisine highlights regional seafood and locally grown produce, often prepared in styles that reflect an Asian influence. Seattle has several flourishing ethnic communities; its International District, for example, is a hub for Asian culture. Both Vancouver and Victoria have large Asian populations and many ethnic dining spots. All the region's major cities have top-rated, nationally renowned dining spots, as well as funky, inexpensive little eateries that are fun to experience.

No matter what the cuisine, however, the restaurants we list are the cream of the crop in each price category. For more information about these categories, *see* the price charts in individual chapters.

MEALTIMES

Unless otherwise noted, the restaurants listed in this guide are open daily for lunch and dinner.

RESERVATIONS & DRESS

Reservations are always a good idea; we mention them only when they're essential or not accepted. Book as far ahead as you can, and reconfirm as soon as you arrive. (Large parties should always call ahead to check the reservations policy.) We mention

dress only when men are required to wear a jacket or a jacket and tie.

WINE, BEER & SPIRITS

You must be 21 to buy alcohol in Washington, Oregon, and Alaska. The legal drinking age in British Columbia is 19.

GAY & LESBIAN TRAVEL

Seattle has a significant gay and lesbian population, particularly around Capitol Hill, Belltown, Fremont, Wallingford, and the University District. Gays and lesbians are accepted throughout western Washington, with active communities in Tacoma, Olympia, and Port Townsend. In smaller towns and settlements east of the Cascades, gay and lesbian behavior is less tolerated, so use discretion.

A majority of Oregon's gay bars are in Portland. During the third week of June, the Portland Pride Parade & Festival takes place at Tom McCall Waterfront Park. Also in June is the Eugene/Springfield Lesbian, Gay, Bisexual, and Transgender event and the Eugene Gay Pride Celebration. *Just Out* is an Oregon-based publication and Web site with expansive information for the gay and lesbian community. As a community resource, Portland has a hot line for gay and lesbian residents and travelers.

Canada is a tolerant country, and same-sex couples should face few problems in gay-friendly Victoria or Vancouver, where there's a large, visible, and active gay and lesbian community. The epicenter of Vancouver's gay scene is the stretch of Davie Street between Burrard and Jervis streets—a cluster of cafés, casual eating places, and shops offering designer T-shirts and sleek housewares. The city's lesbian community centers on Commercial Drive, a neighborhood shared with the Italian and Latin American community. Vancouver Pride Week, held in late July and early August, features parties, tea dances, and cruises and culminates in a parade on Sunday.

For details about the gay and lesbian scene in the United States, consult *Fodor's Gay Guide to the USA* (available in bookstores everywhere).

🛪 Community Resources **Greater Seattle Business Association** ☎ 206/363-9188. *Just Out* ☎ 503/236-1252 🌐 www.justout.com. **Portland Hotline** ☎ 800/777-2437. **Prideline B.C.** ☎ 800/

566-1170. *Seattle Gay News* ☏ 206/324-4297 ⊕ www.sgn.org. **Vancouver Lesbian Connection** ☏ 604/254-8458. *Xtra! West* ☏ 604/684-9696 in Vancouver ⊕ www.xtra.ca.
🔲 Gay- & Lesbian-Friendly Travel Agencies **Different Roads Travel** ✉ 8383 Wilshire Blvd., Suite 520, Beverly Hills, CA 90211 ☏ 323/651-5557 or 800/429-8747 (Ext. 14 for both) 🖷 323/651-3678 ✉ lgernert@tzell.com. **Kennedy Travel** ✉ 130 W. 42nd St., Suite 401, New York, NY 10036 ☏ 212/840-8659 or 800/237-7433 🖷 212/730-2269 ⊕ www. kennedytravel.com. **Now, Voyager** ✉ 4406 18th St., San Francisco, CA 94114 ☏ 415/626-1169 or 800/255-6951 🖷 415/626-8626 ⊕ www.nowvoyager. com. **Skylink Travel and Tour** ✉ 1455 N. Dutton Ave., Suite A, Santa Rosa, CA 95401 ☏ 707/546-9888 or 800/225-5759 🖷 707/636-0951, serving lesbian travelers.

HOLIDAYS

Major U.S. holidays are New Year's Day (Jan. 1); Martin Luther King Day (3rd Mon. in Jan.); Presidents' Day (3rd Mon. in Feb.); Memorial Day (last Mon. in May); Independence Day (July 4); Labor Day (1st Mon. in Sept.); Columbus Day (2nd Mon. in Oct.); Thanksgiving Day (4th Thurs. in Nov.); Christmas Eve and Christmas Day (Dec. 24 and 25); and New Year's Eve (Dec. 31).

Canadian national holidays are as follows: New Year's Day, Good Friday, Easter Monday, Victoria Day (May 24), Canada Day (July 1), Labour Day (Sept. 6), Thanksgiving (Oct. 11), Remembrance Day (Nov. 11), Christmas, and Boxing Day (Dec. 26). British Columbia Day (Aug. 2) is a provincial holiday.

INSURANCE

The most useful travel-insurance plan is a comprehensive policy that includes coverage for trip cancellation and interruption, default, trip delay, and medical expenses (with a waiver for preexisting conditions).

Without insurance you'll lose all or most of your money if you cancel your trip, regardless of the reason. Default insurance covers you if your tour operator, airline, or cruise line goes out of business. Trip-delay covers expenses that arise because of bad weather or mechanical delays. Study the fine print when comparing policies.

Britons and Australians need extra medical coverage when traveling overseas. U.K. residents can buy a travel-insurance policy valid for most vacations taken during the year in which it's purchased (but check preexisting-condition coverage).

Always **buy travel policies directly from the insurance company**; if you buy them from a cruise line, airline, or tour operator that goes out of business you probably won't be covered for the agency or operator's default, a major risk. Before making any purchase, review your existing health and home-owner's policies to find what they cover away from home.
🔲 Insurance Information In the U.K.: **Association of British Insurers** ✉ 51 Gresham St., London EC2V 7HQ ☏ 020/7600-3333 🖷 020/7696-8999 ⊕ www.abi.org.uk. In Australia: **Insurance Council of Australia** ✉ Insurance Enquiries and Complaints, Level 3, 56 Pitt St., Sydney, NSW 2000 ☏ 1300/363683 or 02/9251-4456 🖷 02/9251-4453 ⊕ www.iecltd.com.au. In Canada: **RBC Insurance** ✉ 6880 Financial Dr., Mississauga, Ontario L5N 7Y5 ☏ 800/565-3129 🖷 905/813-4704 ⊕ www. rbcinsurance.com. In New Zealand: **Insurance Council of New Zealand** ✉ Level 7, 111-115 Customhouse Quay, Box 474, Wellington ☏ 04/472-5230 🖷 04/473-3011 ⊕ www.icnz.org.nz.
🔲 Travel Insurers In the U.S.: **Access America** ✉ 6600 W. Broad St., Richmond, VA 23230 ☏ 800/284-8300 🖷 804/673-1491 or 800/346-9265 ⊕ www.accessamerica.com. **Travel Guard International** ✉ 1145 Clark St., Stevens Point, WI 54481 ☏ 715/345-0505 or 800/826-1300 🖷 800/955-8785 ⊕ www.travelguard.com.

LODGING

The lodgings we list are the cream of the crop in each price category. We always list the facilities that are available—but we don't specify whether they cost extra: when pricing accommodations, always ask what's included and what costs extra.

Assume that hotels operate on the European Plan (EP, with no meals) unless we specify that they use the Continental Plan (CP, with a Continental breakfast daily), Modified American Plan (MAP, with breakfast and dinner daily), or the Full American Plan (FAP, with all meals).

APARTMENT & HOUSE RENTALS

If you want a holiday base that's roomy enough for a family and comes with cooking facilities, **consider a furnished rental.** These can save you money, especially if you're traveling with a group. There are hundreds of apartments available for short-term rentals around the major

Northwest cities, as well as dozens of waterfront homes, island getaways, and cozy forest cabins for rent in the scenic areas. Contact a local agent with your specifications; he or she can work with you to find the best deals. Real-estate brokers, apartment management companies, and home-exchange services might also list rentals.

🏠 **International Agents Hideaways International** ✉ 767 Islington St., Portsmouth, NH 03801 ☎ 603/430-4433 or 800/843-4433 🖨 603/430-4444 ⊕ www.hideaways.com, membership $145. 🏠 **Portland Resource French Home Rentals** ☎ 503/219-9190. 🏠 **Seattle Resources Northwest Source Classifieds** ☎ 206/624-7355 or 800/628-8285 ⊕ http://classifieds.nwsource.com/classified/rent. **SeattleRentals.com** ☎ 206/284-2554 ⊕ www.seattlerentals.com. 🏠 **Vancouver & Victoria Resources Duttons & Co. Real Estate** ☎ 503/389-1011 or 800/574-7491 ⊕ www.duttons.com. **Oceanfront Victoria** ☎ 250/598-1551 ⊕ www.oceanfrontvictoria.com. **Vancouver Island Rentals** ☎ 604/683-7690 ⊕ www.vancouverislandrentals.com or www.aptrentals.net.

BED & BREAKFASTS

The Pacific Northwest is known for its vast range of bed-and-breakfast options, which are found everywhere from busy urban areas to casual country farms and coastal retreats. Many B&Bs here provide full gourmet breakfasts, and some have kitchens that guests can use. Other popular amenities to ask about are fireplaces, jetted bathtubs, outdoor hot tubs, and area activities.

The regional B&B organizations listed below can provide information on reputable establishments. Note that before leaving the United Kingdom, you can book a B&B through American Bed & Breakfast, Inter-Bed Network.

🏠 **B & B Organizations American Bed & Breakfast, Inter-Bed Network** ✉ 31 Ernest Rd., Colchester, Essex CO7 9LQ 🖨 0206/223162. **Best Canadian Bed & Breakfast Network** ✉ 1064 Balfour Ave., Vancouver, BC V6H 1X1 ☎ 604/738-7207. **Northwest Bed & Breakfast Reservation Service** ✉ 610 S.W. Broadway, Portland, OR 97205 ☎ 503/243-7616. **A Traveller's Reservation Service** ✉ 14716 26th Ave. NE, Seattle, WA 98155 ☎ 206/364-5900. 🏠 **Reservation Services British Columbia** ☎ 800/239-1141. **Oregon** ☎ 800/944-6196. **Washington** ☎ 800/647-2918.

CAMPING

Oregon, Washington, and British Columbia have excellent government-run campgrounds found throughout each state. A few accept advance camping reservations, but most do not. Privately operated campgrounds sometimes have extra amenities such as laundry rooms and swimming pools. For more information, contact the state or provincial tourism department.

HOME EXCHANGES

If you would like to exchange your home for someone else's, join a home-exchange organization, which will send you its updated listings of available exchanges for a year and will include your own listing in at least one of them. It's up to you to make specific arrangements.

🏠 **Exchange Clubs HomeLink International** 📫 Box 47747, Tampa, FL 33647 ☎ 813/975-9825 or 800/638-3841 🖨 813/910-8144 ⊕ www.homelink.org; $110 yearly for a listing, online access, and catalog; $70 without catalog. **Intervac U.S.** ✉ 30 Corte San Fernando, Tiburon, CA 94920 ☎ 800/756-4663 🖨 415/435-7440 ⊕ www.intervacus.com; $105 yearly for a listing, online access, and a catalog; $50 without catalog.

HOSTELS

No matter what your age, you can save on lodging costs by staying at hostels. In some 4,500 locations in more than 70 countries around the world. Hostelling International (HI), the umbrella group for a number of national youth-hostel associations, offers single-sex, dorm-style beds and, at many hostels, rooms for couples and family accommodations. Membership in any HI national hostel association, open to travelers of all ages, allows you to stay in HI-affiliated hostels at member rates; one-year membership is about $28 for adults (C$35 for a two-year minimum membership in Canada, £13.50 in the U.K., A$52 in Australia, and NZ$40 in New Zealand); hostels charge about $10–$30 per night. Members have priority if the hostel is full; they're also eligible for discounts around the world, even on rail and bus travel in some countries.

🏠 **Organizations Hostelling International–USA** ✉ 8401 Colesville Rd., Suite 600, Silver Spring, MD 20910 ☎ 301/495-1240 🖨 301/495-6697 ⊕ www.hiayh.org. **Hostelling International–Canada** ✉ 205 Catherine St., Suite 400, Ottawa, Ontario K2P 1C3 ☎ 613/237-7884 or 800/663-5777 🖨 613/237-7868 ⊕ www.hihostels.ca. **YHA England and**

Wales ✉ Trevelyan House, Dimple Rd., Matlock, Derbyshire DE4 3YH, U.K. ☎ 0870/870-8808, 0870/770-8868, or 0162/959-2700 🖷 0870/770-6127 ⊕ www.yha.org.uk. **YHA Australia** ✉ 422 Kent St., Sydney, NSW 2001 ☎ 02/9261-1111 🖷 02/9261-1969 ⊕ www.yha.com.au. **YHA New Zealand** ✉ Level 4, Torrens House, 195 Hereford St., Box 436, Christchurch ☎ 03/379-9970 or 0800/278-299 🖷 03/365-4476 ⊕ www.yha.org.nz.

HOTELS

When booking a room, always **call the hotel's local toll-free number** (if one is available) rather than the central reservations number—you'll often get a better price. Deals can often be found at hotel Web sites. Always ask about special packages or corporate rates. Many properties offer special weekend rates, sometimes up to 50% off regular prices. However, these deals are usually not extended during peak summer months, when hotels are normally full. All hotels listed have private bath unless otherwise noted.

🎫 **Toll-Free Numbers Best Western** ☎ 800/528-1234 ⊕ www.bestwestern.com. **Choice** ☎ 800/424-6423 ⊕ www.choicehotels.com. **Comfort Inn** ☎ 800/424-6423 ⊕ www.choicehotels.com. **Days Inn** ☎ 800/325-2525 ⊕ www.daysinn.com. **Doubletree Hotels** ☎ 800/222-8733 ⊕ www.doubletree.com. **Embassy Suites** ☎ 800/362-2779 ⊕ www.embassysuites.com. **Fairfield Inn** ☎ 800/228-2800 ⊕ www.marriott.com. **Hilton** ☎ 800/445-8667 ⊕ www.hilton.com. **Holiday Inn** ☎ 800/465-4329 ⊕ www.sixcontinentshotels.com. **Howard Johnson** ☎ 800/446-4656 ⊕ www.hojo.com. **Hyatt Hotels & Resorts** ☎ 800/233-1234 ⊕ www.hyatt.com. **La Quinta** ☎ 800/531-5900 ⊕ www.laquinta.com. **Marriott** ☎ 800/228-9290 ⊕ www.marriott.com. **Quality Inn** ☎ 800/424-6423 ⊕ www.choicehotels.com. **Radisson** ☎ 800/333-3333 ⊕ www.radisson.com. **Ramada** ☎ 800/228-2828, 800/854-7854 international reservations ⊕ www.ramada.com or www.ramadahotels.com. **Red Lion and WestCoast Hotels and Inns** ☎ 800/733-5466 ⊕ www.redlion.com. **Sheraton** ☎ 800/325-3535 ⊕ www.starwood.com/sheraton. **Sleep Inn** ☎ 800/424-6423 ⊕ www.choicehotels.com. **West Coast** ☎ 800/325-4000 ⊕ www.westcoasthotels.com. **Westin Hotels & Resorts** ☎ 800/228-3000 ⊕ www.starwood.com/westin.

MAIL & SHIPPING

IN CANADA

In British Columbia you can buy stamps at post offices, at many retail outlets, and at some newsstands. If you're sending mail to or within Canada, be sure to include the postal code (six digits and letters). Note that the suite number often appears before the street number in an address, followed by a hyphen. The postal abbreviation for British Columbia is BC.

Within Canada, postcards and letters up to 30 grams cost 48¢; between 31 grams and 50 grams, the cost is 77¢. Oversize letters up to 100 grams cost 96¢. Letters and postcards to the United States cost 65¢ for up to 30 grams, 90¢ for between 31 and 50 grams, and C$1.40 for 51 to 100 grams. Prices do not include GST (Goods and Services Tax).

International mail and postcards run C$1.25 for up to 30 grams, C$1.75 for 31 to 50 grams, and C$3 for 51 to 100 grams. Visitors may have mail sent to them c/o General Delivery in the town they are visiting, for pickup in person within 15 days, after which it will be returned to the sender.

IN THE UNITED STATES

You can buy stamps and aerograms and send letters and parcels in post offices. Stamp-dispensing machines can occasionally be found in airports, bus and train stations, office buildings, drugstores, and the like. You can also deposit mail in the stout, dark blue, steel bins at strategic locations everywhere and in the mail chutes of large buildings; pickup schedules are posted. You can deposit packages at public collection boxes as long as the parcels are affixed with proper postage and weigh less than one pound. Packages weighing 1 pound or more must be taken to a post office or handed to a postal carrier.

For mail sent within the United States, you need a 37¢ stamp for first-class letters weighing up to 1 ounce (23¢ for each additional ounce) and 23¢ for postcards. You pay 80¢ for 1-ounce airmail letters and 70¢ for airmail postcards to most other countries; to Canada and Mexico, you need a 60¢ stamp for a 1-ounce letter and 50¢ for a postcard. An aerogram—a single sheet of lightweight blue paper that folds into its own envelope, stamped for overseas airmail—costs 70¢.

To receive mail on the road, have it sent c/o General Delivery at your destination's main post office (use the correct five-digit

ZIP code). You must pick up mail in person within 30 days and show a driver's license or passport.

MONEY MATTERS

Prices for meals and accommodations in the Pacific Northwest are generally lower than in other major North American regions. Prices for first-class hotel rooms in major cities (Seattle, Portland, Vancouver, and Victoria) range from $100 to $200 a night, although you can still find some "value" hotel rooms for $65–$90 a night.

The dollar is the basic unit of U.S. currency. It has 100 cents. Coins are the copper penny (1¢); the silvery nickel (5¢), dime (10¢), quarter (25¢), and half-dollar (50¢); and the golden $1 coin, replacing a now-rare silver dollar. Bills are denominated $1, $5, $10, $20, $50, and $100, all mostly green and identical in size; designs vary. In addition, you may come across a $2 bill, but the chances are slim. U.S. dollars are accepted in much of Canada (especially in communities near the border), but you're better off exchanging currency and using Canadian dollars.

The units of currency in Canada are the Canadian dollar (C$) and the cent, in almost the same denominations as U.S. currency ($5, $10, $20, 1¢, 5¢, 10¢, 25¢, etc.). The C$1 and C$2 bill are no longer used; they have been replaced by C$1 and C$2 coins (known as a "loonie," because of the loon that appears on the coin, and a "toonie," respectively).

The exchange rates at this writing are as follows: one American dollar buys C$1.30; one Euro buys US$1.21 and C$1.59; one British pound buys US$1.73 and C$2.25; one Australian dollar buys US$0.73 and C$0.96; and one new Zealand dollar buys US$0.64 and C$0.84. Check with a bank or other financial institution for the current rate. A good way to be sure you're getting the best exchange rate is by using your credit card or ATM/debit card. The issuing bank will convert your bill at the current rate.

Prices throughout this guide are given for adults. Substantially reduced fees are almost always available for children, students, and senior citizens. For information on taxes, *see* Taxes.

ATMS
📘 ATM Locations **Plus** ☎ 800/843-7587.

CREDIT CARDS
Throughout this guide, the following abbreviations are used: **AE**, American Express; **D**, Discover; **DC**, Diners Club; **MC**, MasterCard; and **V**, Visa.
📘 Reporting Lost Cards **American Express** ☎ 800/441-0519. **Diners Club** ☎ 800/234-6377. **Discover** ☎ 800/347-2683. **MasterCard** ☎ 800/622-7747. **Visa** ☎ 800/ 847-2911.

NATIONAL PARKS

IN CANADA

If you plan to visit several national parks in Canada, you may be able to save money on park fees by buying a multipark pass. Parks Canada sells a National Parks of Canada pass, good for 12 months at most Canadian national parks, for C$38. You can buy passes at the parks covered by the pass. Contact the park you plan to visit for information. A National Historic Sites of Canada pass, offered by Parks Canada for C$30, is good for a year's admission to national historic sites. A Discovery package, which provides admission to national parks and national historic sites, is C$48 per year.

Most parks in British Columbia are provincial parks. Most are free, but 28 of the more popular parks on southern Vancouver Island and the lower mainland charge a C$3–C$5 per-vehicle parking fee for day users. The fee is included in the camping fee for campers. A C$75 Recreation Stewardship Annual Pass allows unlimited free parking in these parks, though you would need to visit frequently to make it worthwhile. The pass is available at provincial parks.
📘 **Parks Canada** national office ✉ 25 Eddy St., Hull, QC K1A 0M5 ☎ 888/773-8888 ⊕ www.parkscanada.gc.ca.

IN THE UNITED STATES
Look into discount passes to save money on park entrance fees. For $50, the National Parks Pass admits you (and any passengers in your private vehicle) to all national parks, monuments, and recreation areas, as well as other sites run by the National Park Service (NPS), for a year. (In parks that charge per person, the pass admits you, your spouse and children, and your parents, when you arrive to-

gether.) Camping and parking are extra. The $15 Golden Eagle Pass, a hologram you affix to your National Parks Pass, functions as an upgrade, granting entry to all sites run by the NPS, the U.S. Fish and Wildlife Service, the U.S. Forest Service, and the Bureau of Land Management. The upgrade, which expires with the parks pass, is sold by most national-park, Fish-and-Wildlife, and BLM fee stations. A percentage of the proceeds from pass sales funds National Parks projects.

Both the Golden Age Passport ($10), for U.S. citizens or permanent residents who are 62 and older, and the Golden Access Passport (free), for those with disabilities, entitle holders (and any passengers in their private vehicles) to lifetime free entry to all national parks, plus 50% off fees for the use of many park facilities and services. (The discount doesn't always apply to companions.) To obtain them, you must show proof of age and of U.S. citizenship or permanent residency—such as a U.S. passport, driver's license, or birth certificate—and, if requesting Golden Access, proof of disability. The Golden Age and Golden Access passes are available only at NPS-run sites that charge an entrance fee. The National Parks Pass is also available by mail and via the Internet.

🔳 **National Park Foundation** ⊠ 11 Dupont Circle NW, 6th fl., Washington, DC 20036 ☎ 202/238-4200 ⊕ www.nationalparks.org. **National Park Service** ⊠ National Park Service/Department of Interior, 1849 C St. NW, Washington, DC 20240 ☎ 202/208-6843 ⊕ www.nps.gov. **National Parks Conservation Association** ⊠ 1300 19th St. NW, Suite 300, Washington, DC 20036 ☎ 202/223-6722 ⊕ www.npca.org.

🔳 **Passes by Mail & On-Line National Park Foundation** ⊕ www.nationalparks.org. **National Parks Pass** Ⓓ Box 34108, Washington, DC 20043 ☎ 888/467-2757 ⊕ www.nationalparks.org; include a check or money order payable to the National Park Service, plus $3.95 for shipping and handling, or call for passes by phone.

PACKING

Residents of the Pacific Northwest are generally informal by nature and wear clothing that reflects their disposition. Locals tend to dress conservatively when going to the theater or symphony, but it's not uncommon to see some patrons wearing jeans. In other words, almost anything is acceptable for most occasions.

Summer days are warm, but evenings can cool off substantially. Your best bet is to **dress in layers**—sweatshirts, sweaters, and jackets are removed or put on as the day progresses. **Take comfortable walking shoes** if you'll be exploring the region's cities on foot, and **add insect repellent** if you'll be hiking along mountain trails or beaches. **Bring a collapsible umbrella and rain poncho** for unpredictable winter weather; towels are also handy when visiting any of the region's shores or waterways.

In your carry-on luggage, pack an extra pair of eyeglasses or contact lenses and enough of any medication you take to last a few days longer than the entire trip. You may also ask your doctor to write a spare prescription using the drug's generic name, as brand names may vary from country to country. In luggage to be checked, **never pack prescription drugs, valuables, or undeveloped film.** And don't forget to carry with you the addresses of offices that handle refunds of lost traveler's checks. Check *Fodor's How to Pack* (available at on-line retailers and bookstores everywhere) for more tips.

To avoid customs and security delays, carry medications in their original packaging. Don't pack any sharp objects in your carry-on luggage, including knives of any size or material, scissors, and corkscrews, or anything else that might arouse suspicion. To avoid having your checked luggage chosen for hand inspection, don't cram bags full. The U.S. Transportation Security Administration suggests packing shoes on top and placing personal items you on't want touched in clear plastic bags.

CHECKING LUGGAGE

You're allowed to carry aboard one bag and one personal article, such as a purse or a laptop computer. Make sure what you carry on fits under your seat or in the overhead bin. Get to the gate early, so you can board as soon as possible, before the overhead bins fill up.

Baggage allowances vary by carrier, destination, and ticket class. On international flights, you're usually allowed to check two bags weighing up to 70 pounds (32 kilograms) each, although a few airlines allow checked bags of up to 88 pounds (40 kilograms) in first class. Some international carriers don't allow more than 66 pounds (30 kilograms) per bag in business class and 44 pounds (20 kilograms) in economy. On domestic flights, the limit is usually 50 to 70 pounds (23 to 32 kilograms) per bag. In general, carry-on bags shouldn't exceed 40 pounds (18 kilograms). Most airlines won't accept bags that weigh more than 100 pounds (45 kilograms) on domestic or international flights. Check baggage restrictions with your carrier before you pack.

Airline liability for baggage is limited to $2,500 per person on flights within the United States. On international flights it amounts to $9.07 per pound or $20 per kilogram for checked baggage (roughly $640 per 70-pound bag), with a maximum of $634.90 per piece, and $400 per passenger for unchecked baggage. You can buy additional coverage at check-in for about $10 per $1,000 of coverage, but it often excludes a rather extensive list of items, shown on your airline ticket.

Before departure, itemize your bags' contents and their worth, and label the bags with your name, address, and phone number. (If you use your home address, cover it so potential thieves can't see it readily.) Include a label inside each bag and **pack a copy of your itinerary.** At check-in, make sure each bag is correctly tagged with the destination airport's three-letter code. Because some checked bags will be opened for hand inspection, the U.S. Transportation Security Administration recommends that you leave luggage unlocked or use the plastic locks offered at check-in. TSA screeners place an inspection notice inside searched bags, which are re-sealed with a special lock.

If your bag has been searched and contents are missing or damaged, file a claim with the TSA Consumer Response Center as soon as possible. If your bags arrive damaged or fail to arrive at all, file a written report with the airline before leaving the airport.

🔂 Complaints **U.S. Transportation Security Administration Consumer Response Center** ☎ 866/289-9673 ⊕ www.tsa.gov.

PASSPORTS & VISAS

When traveling internationally, carry your passport even if you don't need one (it's always the best form of I.D.) and **make two photocopies of the data page** (one for someone at home and another

for you, carried separately from your passport). If you lose your passport, promptly call the nearest embassy or consulate and the local police.

Visitor visas aren't necessary for Canadian or European Union citizens, or for citizens of Australia who are staying fewer than 90 days.

🔂 Australian Citizens **Passports Australia** ☎ 131-232 ⊕ www.passports.gov.au. **U.S. Consulate General** ✉ MLC Centre, Level 59, 19-29 Martin Pl., Sydney, NSW 2000 ☎ 02/9373-9200, 1902/941-641 fee-based visa-inquiry line ⊕ usembassy-australia.state.gov/sydney.

🔂 Canadian Citizens **Passport Office** ✉ to mail in applications: 200 Promenade du Portage, Hull, Québec J8X 4B7 ☎ 819/994-3500 or 800/567-6868,866/255-7655 TTY ⊕ www.ppt.gc.ca.

🔂 New Zealand Citizens **New Zealand Passports Office** ✉ For applications and information, Level 3, Boulcott House, 47 Boulcott St., Wellington ☎ 0800/22-5050 or 04/474-8100 ⊕ www.passports.govt.nz. **Embassy of the United States** ✉ 29 Fitzherbert Terr., Thorndon, Wellington ☎ 04/462-6000 ⊕ usembassy.org.nz. **U.S. Consulate General** ✉ Citibank Bldg., 3rd fl., 23 Customs St. E, Auckland ☎ 09/303-2724 ⊕ usembassy.org.nz.

🔂 U.K. Citizens **U.K. Passport Service** ☎ 0870/521-0410 ⊕ www.passport.gov.uk. **American Consulate General** ✉ Queen's House, 14 Queen St., Belfast, Northern Ireland BT1 6EQ ☎ 028/9032-8239 🖶 028/9024-8482 ⊕ www.usembassy.org.uk. **American Embassy** ✉ For visa and immigration information (enclose an SASE), Consular Information Unit, 24 Grosvenor Sq., London W1A 1AE ✉ to submit an application via mail, Visa Branch, 5 Upper Grosvenor St., London W1A 2JB ☎ 09068/200-290 recorded visa information, 09055/444-546 operator service, both with per-minute charges, 0207/499-9000 main switchboard ⊕ www.usembassy.org.uk.

SENIOR-CITIZEN TRAVEL

To qualify for age-related discounts, mention your senior-citizen status up front when booking hotel reservations (not when checking out) and before you're seated in restaurants (not when paying the bill). Be sure to have identification on hand. When renting a car, ask about promotional car-rental discounts, which can be cheaper than senior-citizen rates.

🔂 Educational Programs **Elderhostel** ✉ 11 Ave. de Lafayette, Boston, MA 02111-1746 ☎ 877/426-8056, 978/323-4141 international callers, 877/426-2167 TTY 🖶 877/426-2166 ⊕ www.elderhostel.org.

SPORTS & THE OUTDOORS

BICYCLING

British Columbia Information British Columbia Cycling Coalition ☎ 520/721-2800 ⊕ www.bccc. ca. **Canadian Cycling Association** ☎ 613/248-1353 ⊕ www.canadian-cycling.com. **Greater Victoria Cycling Coalition** ☎ 250/480-5155 ⊕ www.gvcc.bc.ca. **Vancouver Area Cycling Coalition** ☎ 604/878-8222 ⊕ www.vacc.bc.ca. **Vancouver Bicycle Club** ☎ No phone ⊕ www.vancouverbicycleclub.com.

Oregon Information Merry Cranksters of Salem ☎ 503/365-8914 ⊕ www.merrycranksters. org. **Portland Wheelmen Touring Club** ☎ 503/257-7982 ⊕ www.pwtc.org.

Washington Information Cascade Bicycle Club ☎ 206/522-3222 ⊕ www.cascade.org. **Olympic Peninsula Bicyclists** ☎ No phone ⊕ www.olypen. com/opb. **Seattle Bicycle Club** ☎ No phone ⊕ www.seattlebike.org. **Spokane Bicycle Club** ☎ 503/325-1171 ⊕ www.spokanebicycleclub.org.

CLIMBING–MOUNTAINEERING

British Columbia Information Alpine Club of Canada ☎ 403/678-3200 ⊕ www. alpineclubofcanada.com. **British Columbia Mountaineering Club** ☎ 604/268-9502 ⊕ www.bcmc.ca. **Oregon Information** Obsidians ⌂ Box 322, Eugene 97440 ⊕ www.obsidians.org. **Portland: Mazama Club** ☎ 503/227-2345 ⊕ www.mazamas. org. **Portland Mountain Rescue** ⌂ Box 5391, Portland 97228-5391 ☎ 503/972-7743 ⊕ www.pmru. org. **Salem: Chemeketans Outdoor Club** ⌂ Box 864, Salem 97308 ⊕ www.chemeketans.org. **Washington Information** The Mountaineers ☎ 206/284-6310 ⊕ www.mountaineers.org.

FISHING

Oregon Department of Fish and Wildlife ✉ Box 59, Portland, OR 97207 ☎ 503/872-5268 general information, 503/872-5275 license information ⊕ www.dfw.state.or.us. **Washington Department of Fish and Wildlife** ✉ 600 Capitol Way, Olympia, WA 98501-0091 ☎ 206/902-2500. For saltwater fishing: **Department of Fisheries and Oceans** ✉ 555 W. Hastings St., Suite 400, Vancouver, BC V6B 5G3 ☎ 604/666-0384. For freshwater fishing: **Ministry of Environment, Fish and Wildlife Information** ✉ Parliament Bldgs., Victoria, BC V8V 1X5 ☎ 604/387-9740.

HIKING

Washington Trails Association ✉ 1305 4th Ave., Suite 512, Seattle, WA 98101 ☎ 206/625-1367 ⊕ www.wta.org. **Federation of Mountain Clubs of British Columbia** ⌂ 47 W. Broadway, Vancouver, BC V5Y 1P1 ☎ 604/878-7007 ⊕ www.mountainclubs.bc. ca. **Nature of Oregon Information Center** ✉ 800 N.

E. Oregon St., Suite 177, Portland 97232 ☎ 503/872-2750, 503/872-2752 TDD ⊕ www.naturenw.org.

SKIING

Canada West Ski Areas Association ✉ 810 Waddington Dr., Vernon BC V1T 2M8 ☎ 250/542-9020. **Oregon Department of Transportation** ☎ 800/977-6368. **Oregon Nordic Club** ☎ 503/246-0616 ⊕ www.onc.org. **Washington Office of Winter Recreation, Parks and Recreation Commission** ✉ 7150 Cleanwater La., Olympia, WA 98504 ☎ 360/902-8500.

STUDENTS IN THE REGION

I.D.s & Services STA Travel ✉ 10 Downing St., New York, NY 10014 ☎ 212/627-3111, 800/777-0112 24-hr. service center ☏ 212/627-3387 ⊕ www.sta. com. **Travel Cuts** ✉ 187 College St., Toronto, Ontario M5T 1P7, Canada ☎ 800/592-2887 in U.S., 416/979-2406 or 866/246-9762 in Canada ☏ 416/979-8167 ⊕ www.travelcuts.com.

TAXES

Oregon has no sales tax, although many cities and counties levy a tax on lodging and services. Room taxes, for example, vary from 6%–9½%. The state sales tax in Washington is 8.6%, and there are also local taxes that can raise the total tax to 11.5%, depending on the goods or service and the municipality. A Goods and Services Tax (GST) of 7% applies on virtually every transaction in Canada except for the purchase of basic groceries.

In addition to the GST, British Columbia levies a sales tax of 7.5% on most items (although services, accommodation, groceries, children's clothes, and restaurant meals are exempt). Hotel rooms are subject to an 8% tax (in addition to the GST), and some municipalities levy an additional 2%. Wine, beer, and spirits purchased in bars and restaurants are subject to a 10% tax. Some restaurants build this into the price of the beverage, but others add it to the bill.

GST REFUNDS

You can **get a GST refund** on purchases taken out of the country and on short-term accommodations of less than one month, but not on food, drink, tobacco, car or motor-home rentals, or transportation; rebate forms, which must be submitted within a year of leaving Canada, may be obtained from certain retailers, duty-free shops, customs officials, or from the Canada Customs and Revenue Agency. Instant cash rebates up to a maximum of C$500 are provided by some duty-free shops when you leave Canada, and most provinces do not tax goods that are shipped directly by the vendor to the purchaser's home. Always **save your original receipts** from stores and hotels (not just credit-card receipts), and **be sure the name and address of the establishment are shown on the receipt.** Original receipts are not returned. For you to be eligible for a refund, your receipts must total at least C$200, and each individual receipt for goods must show a minimum purchase of C$50 before tax. Some agencies in Vancouver and Whistler offer on-the-spot cash GST refunds. Although they charge a commission of about 20%, some visitors may find it worth it for the convenience, especially as Canadian Government checks may be difficult to cash in some countries. See the shopping sections of individual chapters for locations.

🄵 **Canada Customs and Revenue Agency**
✉ Visitor Rebate Program, Summerside Tax Centre, 275 Pope Rd., Suite 104, Summerside, PE C1N 6C6
☎ 902/432-5608, 800/668-4748 in Canada
🌐 www.ccra-adrc.gc.ca.

TELEPHONES

All U.S. telephone numbers consist of a three-digit area code and a seven-digit local number. Within many local calling areas, you dial only the seven-digit number. Within some area codes, you must dial "1" first for calls outside the local area. To call between area-code regions, dial "1" then all 10 digits; the same goes for calls to numbers prefixed by "800," "888," "866," and "877"—all toll free. For calls to numbers preceded by "900" you must pay—usually dearly.

For international calls, dial "011" followed by the country code and the local number. For help, dial "0" and ask for an overseas operator. The country code is 61 for Australia, 64 for New Zealand, 44 for the United Kingdom. Calling Canada is the same as calling within the United States. Most local phone books list country codes and U.S. area codes. The country code for the United States is 1.

For operator assistance, dial "0." To obtain someone's phone number, call directory assistance at 555-1212 or occasionally 411 (free at many public phones). To have the person you're calling foot the bill, phone collect; dial "0" instead of "1" before the 10-digit number.

At pay phones, instructions often are posted. Usually you insert coins in a slot (usually 25¢–50¢ for local calls) and wait for a steady tone before dialing. When you call long-distance, the operator tells you how much to insert; prepaid phone cards, widely available in various denominations, are easier. Call the number on the back, punch in the card's personal identification number when prompted, then dial your number.

TIME

Washington, Oregon, and British Columbia are in the Pacific time zone. All observe daylight saving time from early April to late October.

TIPPING

Tips and service charges are usually not automatically added to a bill in the United States or Canada. If service is satisfactory, customers generally give waitstaff 15%–20% of the total bill. Hairdressers, taxi drivers, and other service specialists receive 10%–20%. Bellhops, doormen, and porters at airports and railway stations are generally tipped $1–$2 for each item of luggage.

TOURS & PACKAGES

Because everything is prearranged on a prepackaged tour or independent vacation, you spend less time planning—and often get it all at a good price.

BOOKING WITH AN AGENT

Travel agents are excellent resources. But it's a good idea to collect brochures from several agencies, as some agents' suggestions may be influenced by relationships with tour and package firms that reward them for volume sales. If you have a special interest, find an agent with expertise in that area; the American Society of Travel Agents (ASTA; ⇨ Travel Agencies) has a database of specialists worldwide. You can log on to the group's Web site to find an ASTA travel agent in your neighborhood.

Make sure your travel agent knows the accommodations and other services of the place being recommended. Ask about the hotel's location, room size, beds, and whether it has a pool, room service, or programs for children, if you care about these. Has your agent been there in person or sent others whom you can contact?

Do some homework on your own, too: local tourism boards can provide information about lesser-known and small-niche operators, some of which may sell only direct.

BUYER BEWARE

Each year consumers are stranded or lose their money when tour operators—even large ones with excellent reputations—go out of business. So check out the operator. Ask several travel agents about its reputation, and try to **book with a company that has a consumer-protection program.** (Look for information in the company's brochure.) In the United States, members of the National Tour Association and the United States Tour Operators Association are required to set aside funds to cover payments and travel arrangements in the event that the company defaults. It's also a good idea to choose a company that participates in the American Society of Travel Agents' Tour Operator Program; ASTA will act as mediator in any disputes between you and your tour operator.

Remember that the more your package or tour includes, the better you can predict the ultimate cost of your vacation. Make sure you know exactly what is covered, and beware of hidden costs. Are taxes, tips, and transfers included? Entertainment and excursions? These can add up.

🛈 Tour-Operator Recommendations **American Society of Travel Agents** (⇨ Travel Agencies). **National Tour Association** (NTA) ✉ 546 E. Main St., Lexington, KY 40508 ☎ 859/226–4444 or 800/682–8886 🖷 859/226–4404 ⊕ www.ntaonline.com. **United States Tour Operators Association** (USTOA) ✉ 275 Madison Ave., Suite 2014, New York, NY 10016 ☎ 212/599–6599 🖷 212/599–6744 ⊕ www.ustoa.com.

TRAIN TRAVEL

Amtrak, the U.S. passenger rail system, has daily service to the Pacific Northwest from the Midwest and California. The *Empire Builder* takes a northern route through Minnesota and Montana from Chicago to Spokane, from where separate legs continue to Seattle and Portland. The *Coast Starlight* begins in Los Angeles; makes stops throughout California, western Oregon, and Washington; and terminates in Seattle.

Canada's VIA Rail operates transcontinental routes on the *Canadian* from Toronto, via Edmonton and Jasper, Alberta, to Vancouver. The *Skeena* runs between Jasper and the northern British Columbia port city of Prince Rupert. The *Malahat* links Victoria with Courtenay, in north Vancouver Island.

WITHIN THE PACIFIC NORTHWEST

Amtrak's *Cascades* trains travel between Seattle and Vancouver and between Seattle, Portland, and Eugene. The *Empire Builder* travels between Portland and Spokane, with part of the route running through the Columbia River gorge.

On Vancouver Island, VIA Rail runs the *Malahat* from Victoria north to Courtenay. From May to September B.C. Rail operates the *Whistler Northwind* once a week from its north Vancouver terminal to the towns of Whistler and Prince George. At Prince George it's possible to connect with VIA Rail's *Skeena* service east to Jasper and Alberta or west to Prince Rupert.

The Great Canadian Railtour Co., Ltd. operates the *Rocky Mountaineer*, a two-day rail cruise between Vancouver and the Canadian Rockies that runs from April or May to October. There are two routes—one to Banff/Calgary and the other to Jasper—through landscapes considered to be the most spectacular in the world. An overnight hotel stop is made in Kamloops. The American Orient Express Railway Company operates several luxury trips, including a 10-day odyssey from Vancouver to Montreal, as well as eight-day journeys from Los Angeles or Salt Lake City to Seattle.

RAIL PASSES

Amtrak offers a 30-day North America Rail Pass good in the United States and Canada. Prices run $495 off-peak and $695 at peak travel times, with Internet discounts of 10% or more. The Canadian sections of the journey are operated by VIA Rail Canada. For nonresidents of Canada, VIA also offers a 30-day Canrailpass valid for a maximum 12 days of travel. System-wide passes cost C$448 off-peak and C$719 in peak season, and tickets can be purchased in advance from a travel agent or upon arrival in Canada.

🚂 Railway Companies **American Orient Express Railway Company** ☎ 800/320-4206 ⊕ www.americanorientexpress.com. **Amtrak** ☎ 800/872-7245 ⊕ www.amtrak.com. **Great Canadian Railtour Co., Ltd.** ☎ 800/665-7245 ⊕ www.rkymtnrail.com. **VIA Rail Canada** ☎ 604/383-4324 or 888/842-7245 ⊕ www.viarail.ca.

TRAVEL AGENCIES

A good travel agent puts your needs first. Look for an agency that has been in business at least five years, emphasizes customer service, and has someone on staff who specializes in your destination. In addition, **make sure the agency belongs to a professional trade organization.** The American Society of Travel Agents (ASTA)—the largest and most influential in the field with more than 20,000 members in some 140 countries—maintains and enforces a strict code of ethics and will step in to help mediate any agent-client disputes involving ASTA members if necessary. ASTA (whose motto is "Without a travel agent, you're on your own") also maintains a Web site that includes a directory of agents. (If a travel agency is also acting as your tour operator, *see* Buyer Beware *in* Tours and Packages.)

🚂 Local Agent Referrals **American Society of Travel Agents (ASTA)** ✉ 1101 King St., Suite 200, Alexandria, VA 22314 ☎ 703/739-2782, 800/965-2782 24-hr hotline 🖷 703/739-3268 ⊕ www.astanet.com. **Association of British Travel Agents** ✉ 68–71 Newman St., London W1T 3AH ☎ 020/7637-2444 🖷 020/7637-0713 ⊕ www.abta.com. **Association of Canadian Travel Agencies** ✉ 130 Albert St., Suite 1705, Ottawa, Ontario K1P 5G4 ☎ 613/237-3657 🖷 613/237-7052 ⊕ www.acta.ca. **Australian Federation of Travel Agents** ✉ Level 3, 309 Pitt St., Sydney, NSW 2000 ☎ 02/9264-3299 🖷 02/9264-1085 ⊕ www.afta.com.au. **Travel Agents' Association of New Zealand** ✉ Level 5, Tourism and Travel House, 79 Boulcott St., Box 1888, Wellington 6001 ☎ 04/499-0104 🖷 04/499-0786 ⊕ www.taanz.org.nz.

VISITOR INFORMATION

Learn more about foreign destinations by checking government-issued travel advisories and country information. For a broader picture, consider information from more than one country.

🚂 British Columbia **Canadian Tourism Commission** ☎ 613/946-1000 ⊕ www.canadatourism.com. **Hello B.C. (Tourism B.C.)** ☎ 800/435-5622 ⊕ www.hellobc.com. **Vancouver Tourist InfoCentre** ✉ Plaza Level, 200 Burrard St., Vancouver V6C 3L6 ☎ 604/683-2000 ⊕ www.tourismvancouver.com. 🚂 Oregon **Oregon Tourism Commission** ✉ 775 Summer St. NE, Salem 97310 ☎ 503/986-0000 or 800/547-7842 ⊕ www.traveloregon.com. 🚂 Washington **Visitors Information Center** ✉ 520 Pike St., Suite 1300, Seattle 98101 ☎ 206/461-5840 ⊕ www.seattleinsider.com. **Washington State Tourism** ✉ 101 General Administration Bldg., Olympia 98504 ☎ 800/544-1800 ⊕ www.tourism.wa.gov. 🚂 Government Advisories **Consular Affairs Bureau of Canada** ☎ 800/267-6788 or 613/944-6788 ⊕ www.voyage.gc.ca. **U.K. Foreign and Commonwealth Office** ✉ Travel Advice Unit, Consular Division, Old Admiralty Building, London SW1A 2PA ☎ 020/7008-0232 or 020/7008-0233 ⊕ www.fco.gov.uk/travel. **Australian Department of Foreign Affairs and Trade** ☎ 02/6261-1299 Consular Travel Advice Faxback Service ⊕ www.dfat.gov.au. **New Zealand Ministry of Foreign Affairs and Trade** ☎ 04/439-8000 ⊕ www.mft.govt.nz.

WEB SITES

Do check out the World Wide Web when planning your trip. You'll find everything from weather forecasts to virtual tours of famous cities. Be sure to visit Fodors.com (⊕ www.fodors.com), a complete travel-planning site. You can research prices and book plane tickets, hotel rooms, rental cars, vacation packages, and more. In addition, you can post your pressing questions in the Travel Talk section. Other planning tools include a currency converter and weather reports, and there are loads of links to travel resources.

PORTLAND

FODOR'S CHOICE

Heathman Hotel, *downtown*

Higgins, *downtown contemporary fare*

Japanese Garden, *landscaping in Washington Park*

Lion and the Rose, *B&B east of the Willamette*

Montage, *spicy Cajun east of the Willamette*

Paley's Place, *Nob Hill bistro*

Portland Classical Chinese Garden, *harmony in Old Town/ Chinatown*

Portland Saturday Market, *Old Town*

Powell's City of Books, *Pearl District*

By Donald S. Olson
Updated by Sarah Kennedy

PORTLAND IS LOADED WITH ENERGY. For decades this inland port on the Willamette River was the undiscovered gem of the West Coast, often overlooked by visitors seeking more sophisticated milieus. But in the past decade, people have begun flocking here in unprecedented numbers—to visit and to live. The city's proximity to mountains, ocean, and desert adds an element of natural grandeur to its urban character. Majestic Mt. Hood, about 70 mi to the east, acts as a kind of mascot, and on a clear day several peaks of the Cascade Range are visible, including Mt. St. Helens, which dusted the city with ash when it erupted in 1980. The west side of town is built on a series of forested hills that descend to the downtown area, the Willamette River, and the flatter east side. Filled with stately late-19th-century and modern architecture, linked by an effective transit system, and home to a vital arts scene, Portland is a place where there's much to do day or night, rain or shine.

The quality of life remains a constant priority here. As far back as 1852, Portland began setting aside city land as parks. Included among Portland's 250 parks, public gardens, and greenways are the nation's largest urban wilderness, the world's smallest park, and the only extinct volcano in the lower 48 states within a city's limits. A temperate climate and plenty of precipitation keep Portland green year-round. The City of Roses, as it's known, celebrates its favorite flower with a monthlong Rose Festival—a June extravaganza with auto and boat races, visiting navy ships, and a grand parade second in size only to Pasadena's Rose Parade. But the floral spectacle really starts three months earlier, when streets and gardens bloom with the colors of flowering trees, camellias, rhododendrons, and azaleas.

Portland, which began as an Indian clearing of about 1 square mi, has become a metropolis of more than 2 million people; within its 132-square-mi borders are 90 diverse and distinct neighborhoods. A center for sports and sportswear makers, the four-county metropolitan area, which includes the burgeoning city of Vancouver across the state line in Washington, contains the headquarters and factories of Jantzen, Nike, Columbia Sportswear, and Pendleton. The city's western suburbs of Beaverton and Hillsboro have been called the Silicon Forest because of their high concentration of high-tech manufacturing plants, including those of Intel, Tektronix, and Fujitsu. High-tech shipbuilding, furniture, fabricated metals, and other manufacturers have broadened the region's economic base even further. And its prime location at the confluence of the Columbia and Willamette rivers has helped Portland become the third-largest port on the West Coast.

The arts here flourish in unexpected places: there's artwork in police stations, office towers, banks, playgrounds, and on the sides of buildings. The brick-paved transit mall downtown is virtually an outdoor gallery of fountains and sculptures. As for the performing arts, Portland has several professional theater companies, the Oregon Symphony, the Portland Opera, and Chamber Music Northwest, to name a few. Those into nightlife will also find some of the best live-band and club action in the country. Families have plenty of kid-friendly attractions to enjoy, including the Oregon Zoo, Oaks Amusement Park, and Oregon Museum of Science and Industry.

Architectural preservation is a major preoccupation in Portland, particularly when it comes to the 1860s brick buildings with cast-iron columns and the 1890s ornate terra-cotta designs that grace areas like the Skidmore Old Town, Yamhill, and Glazed Terra-Cotta national historic districts. In the Pearl District, older industrial buildings are being given new life as residential lofts, restaurants, office space, galleries, and

Numbers in the text correspond to numbers in the margin and on the Downtown, the Pearl District & Old Town/Chinatown; Washington Park & Forest Park; and East of the Willamette River maps.

1

Spend the morning exploring downtown. Visit the Portland Art Museum or the Oregon History Center, stop by the historic First Congregational Church and Pioneer Courthouse Square, and take a stroll along the Park Blocks or Waterfront Park. Eat lunch and do a little shopping along Northwest 23rd Avenue in the early afternoon, and be sure to walk down a few side streets to get a look at the beautiful historic homes in Nob Hill. From there, drive up into the northwest hills by the Pittock Mansion, and finish off the afternoon at the Japanese Garden and the International Test Rose Garden in Washington Park. If you still have energy, head across the river for dinner on Hawthorne Boulevard; then drive up to Mt. Tabor Park for Portland's best view of sunset.

On your first day, follow the one-day itinerary above, exploring downtown, Nob Hill, and Washington Park, but stay on the west side for dinner, and take your evening stroll in Waterfront Park. On your second morning, visit the Portland Classical Chinese Garden in Old Town, and then head across the river to the Sellwood District for lunch and antiquing. Stop by the Crystal Springs Rhododendron Garden; then head up to Hawthorne District in the afternoon. Wander through the Hawthorne and Belmont neighborhoods for a couple hours, stop by Laurelhurst Park, and take a picnic dinner up to Mt. Tabor Park. In the evening, catch a movie at the Bagdad Theatre, or get a beer at one of the east side brewpubs. On Day 3, take a morning hike in Hoyt Arboretum or Forest Park; then spend your afternoon exploring the galleries in the Pearl District and on northeast Alberta Street. Drive out to the Grotto, and then eat dinner at the Kennedy School or one of the other McMenamins brewpubs.

With a whole week to enjoy the city, you can take a little more time to absorb it all. Spend your first day in downtown alone, devoting a few hours each to the Portland Art Museum and the Oregon History Center. Wander along the park blocks and through Riverfront Park, and stop into some of the historic buildings described in the walking tours, such as the Old Church and City Hall. On Day 2, spend the morning at the Portland Classical Chinese Garden, and take the early part of the afternoon to explore the galleries and shops in the trendy Pearl District. For a mid-afternoon break, stop by the Ecotrust building, get a cup of coffee at World Cup Coffee, and drink it while sitting on the "eco-roof," where you can get a good overview of the neighborhood; then stop by Powell's City of Books to browse for a little while. In the late afternoon drive out to Forest Park and take a hike in the country's largest urban wilderness.

On your third day, stop by Whole Foods Supermarket on West Burnside, pack a picnic lunch, and spend the day at Washington Park. Start out with a hike through the Hoyt Arboretum; then visit the Forest Discovery Center Museum and the Oregon Zoo. Spend the afternoon at the Japanese Garden and the International Test Rose Garden, and if you have time, take a tour of Pittock Mansion. Spend the first part of your fourth day exploring Northwest 23rd Avenue and Nob Hill. Visit some of the unique shops, take the walking tour of the neighborhood's historic homes, and drink a cup of coffee at one the area's myriad coffeehouses. In the afternoon drive to Mt. Tabor Park for a short walk.

Devote yourself to the east side of the river for the next two days. On Day 5, spend at least a few hours exploring the Hawthorne shopping district, stop by Laurelhurst Park for a scenic break in the action, and eat lunch on Hawthorne or Belmont Street. Head up to the northeast in the afternoon, winding your way through the streets of historic Irvington, just north of Broadway, to see some of the most beautiful Victorian homes in the city. Spend some time in the galleries and shops on Alberta Street, and, if you have time, head out to 82nd Avenue to see the Grotto. If you enjoyed your visit to Edgefield, stop by the Kennedy School to see another fascinating McMenamins renovation project; you can get dinner here, watch a movie in the evening, or get a drink at one of their bars. On Day 6, go to the Oregon Museum of Science and Industry (OMSI) in the morning; then keep heading south to Sellwood District for lunch and some antiques shopping. Take a walk at the Crystal Springs Rhodendron Garden and through Reed College campus. On your last day, you might want to see a little of the surrounding area of Portland. If so, you can take a drive along the Columbia River Gorge via I–84, or take a day trip to the coast on U.S. 26. If you're happy to stay closer to Portland, you might want to visit Sauvie Island to see some wildlife, pick berries, or walk along the beach. Or, you might want to revisit some of your favorite neighborhoods and explore them a little more fully.

boutiques. It has also become the center of the metro area's plan to more efficiently use available urban space by revitalizing existing neighborhoods. Not all Portlanders are happy with the results, which have brought increased traffic congestion and constant construction. But the new century also brought a renewed emphasis on mass transit. An extension of the MAX light-rail line to Portland International Airport opened in fall 2001, and the Portland Central City Streetcar began operation in summer 2001, connecting Portland State University, downtown, and the Pearl District and Nob Hill neighborhood. The city's farsighted approach to growth and its pitfalls means it reaps all of the benefits and few of the problems of its boom. As a result, Portland is better than ever, cultivating a new level of sophistication, building on enhanced prosperity, and bursting with fresh energy.

EXPLORING PORTLAND

The Willamette River is Portland's east–west dividing line. Burnside Street separates north from south. The city's 200-foot-long blocks make them easy to walk, but you can also explore the downtown core and Nob Hill by MAX light rail, the Central City Streetcar, or Tri-Met buses (⇨ Portland A to Z). Closer to the downtown core are the Pearl District and Old Town/Chinatown. Both the Old Town and Pearl District have a plethora of restaurants, specialty shops, and nightspots.

Downtown

Portland has one of the most attractive and inviting downtown urban cores in the United States. Clean, compact, and filled with parks, plazas, and fountains, it holds a mix of new and historic buildings. Hotels, shops, museums, restaurants, and entertainment can all be found here, and the entire downtown area is part of the Tri-Met transit system's Fareless Square, within which you can ride MAX, the Central City Streetcar, or any bus for free.

Numbers in the text correspond to numbers in the margin and on the Downtown, the Pearl District & Old Town/Chinatown map.

a good walk

Begin at Southwest Morrison Street and Southwest 6th Avenue at **Pioneer Courthouse Square** ❶ ▶. From the square, walk west on Yamhill for three blocks. Between Yamhill and Taylor streets on 10th Avenue is the **Central Library** ❷. Continue on 10th Avenue for two blocks and turn left on Main Street. Cross over the **South Park Blocks** and find the **Portland Center for the Performing Arts** ❸ between Park Avenue and Broadway. Back along the Park Blocks, the **First Congregational Church** ❹ will be on your left on the corner of Madison, followed by the **Oregon History Center** ❺, directly across the street, impossible to miss under the mural of Lewis and Clark and the Oregon Trail along the side of the building. West on Jefferson across the Park Blocks is the **Portland Art Museum** ❻. Walk west on Jefferson and south on 11th Avenue to reach the **Old Church** ❼. Loop back east to the South Park Blocks along Columbia Street and head south on Park Avenue to Market Street, where the campus of **Portland State University** ❽ begins.

Continue east on Market to 3rd Avenue to reach the **Keller Auditorium** ❾, which has a waterfall fountain. **KOIN Center** ❿, the most distinctive high-rise in downtown Portland, occupies the next block to the north. From here, head east on Clay Street to the waterfront and, crossing Naito Parkway, take a leisurely stroll through **Governor Tom McCall Waterfront Park** ⓫ past the **Salmon Street Fountain.** Heading back west along Taylor, you are now in the **Yamhill National Historic District** ⓬ of cast-iron and other buildings. Turn left on 2nd Avenue and proceed one block south toward the **World Trade Center** ⓭.

After wandering around the complex, continue west on Salmon Street. At the corner of Salmon and 3rd Avenue sits the **Mark O. Hatfield U.S. Courthouse** ⓮. The **State of Oregon Sports Hall of Fame** ⓯ sits nearby, between 3rd and 4th avenues on Salmon. Cross the street and find yourself in **Chapman and Lownsdale squares** ⓰, which abut the **Justice Center** ⓱, across 3rd Avenue. **Terry Schrunk Plaza** ⓲ sits one block south, and you can pass directly through the plaza into **City Hall** ⓳ across 4th Avenue. Walk through City Hall and exit onto 5th Avenue. Turn right and head north on 5th Avenue, stopping at the **Portland Building** ⓴ on the next block. Head one more block up 5th Avenue and turn left on Salmon Street, to find **Niketown** ㉑ at the corner of 6th and Salmon. Continue on 6th back past Pioneer Courthouse Square, and explore the area between Oak and Yamhill on 5th and 6th avenues. This is the heart of the **Glazed Terra-Cotta National Historic District** ㉒.

TIMING The entire downtown walk can be accomplished in about two hours. If you're planning to stop at the Oregon History Center or Portland Art Museum (both closed on Monday), add at least one to two hours for each. Allot 15 or 30 minutes for the Sports Hall of Fame, which is closed on Sunday.

What to See

❷ **Central Library.** The elegant central staircase and elaborate ceiling ornamentation make this no ordinary library. With a gallery space on the second floor, frequent musical performances in the spacious upper-floor lobbies, and a Starbuck's in the first-floor reading room, this building is well worth a walk around. ⊠ *801 S.W. 10th Ave., Downtown* ☎ *503/ 988–5123* 🎫 *Free* ⊙ *Tues.–Thurs. 9–9, Fri. and Sat. 9–6, Sun. 1–5.*

16 **Chapman and Lownsdale squares.** During the 1920s, these parks were seg- regated by sex: Chapman, between Madison and Main streets, was re- served for women, and Lownsdale, between Main and Salmon streets, was for men. The elk statue on Main Street, which separates the parks, was given to the city by former mayor David Thompson. It purportedly honors an elk that grazed here in the 1850s.

19 **City Hall.** Portland's four-story, granite-faced City Hall, which was com- pleted in 1895, is an example of the Renaissance Revival style popular in the late 19th century. Italian influences can be seen in the porch, the pink scagliola columns, the cornice embellishments, and other details. The building was renovated in the late 1990s. ⊠ *1220 S.W. 5th Ave., Downtown* ☎ *503/823–4000* ⊙ *Weekdays 8–5.*

4 **First Congregational Church.** This Venetian Gothic church, modeled after Boston's Old South Church, was completed in 1895, and you still can hear its original bell, purchased in 1871, ringing from its 175-foot tower. The church provided much of the land on which the Portland Center for the Performing Arts was built. ⊠ *1126 S.W. Park Ave., Downtown* ☎ *503/228–7219* 🎫 *Free.*

22 **Glazed Terra-Cotta National Historic District.** A century ago terra-cotta was often used in construction because of its availability and low cost; it could also be easily molded into the decorative details that were popular at the time. Elaborate lions' heads, griffins, floral displays, and other clas- sical motifs adorn the rooflines of the district's many buildings that date from the late 1890s to the mid-1910s. Public art lines 5th and 6th av- enues. On 5th is a sculpture that reflects light and changing colors, a nude woman made of bronze, a copper and redwood creation inspired by the Norse god Thor, and a large limestone cat in repose. Sixth Av- enue has a steel-and-concrete matrix, a granite-and-brick fountain, and an abstract modern depiction of an ancient Greek defending Crete. ⊠ *S.W. 5th and S.W. 6th Aves. between S.W. Oak and S.W. Yamhill Sts., Downtown.*

11 **Governor Tom McCall Waterfront Park.** The park named for a former gov- ernor of Oregon revered for his statewide land-use planning initiatives stretches north along the Willamette River for about a mile to Burnside Street. Broad and grassy, it yields what may be the finest ground-level view of downtown Portland's bridges and skyline. The park, on the site of a former expressway, hosts many events, among them the Rose Fes- tival, classical and blues concerts, and the Oregon Brewers Festival. The five-day **Cinco de Mayo Festival** (☎ 503/222–9807) in early May cel- ebrates Portland's sister-city relationship with Guadalajara, Mexico. Next to the Rose Festival, this is one of Portland's biggest get-togethers. Food and arts-and-crafts booths, stages with mariachi bands, and a carnival complete with a Ferris wheel line the riverfront for the event. Bikers, joggers, and roller and in-line skaters enjoy the area year-round. The arching jets of water at the **Salmon Street Fountain** change configura- tion every few hours and are a favorite cooling-off spot during the dog days of summer. ⊠ *S.W. Naito Pkwy. (Front Ave.) from south of Hawthorne Bridge to Burnside Bridge, Downtown.*

17 **Justice Center.** This modern building houses the county courts and sup- port offices and, on the 16th floor, the **Police Museum** (☎ 503/823–0019 🎫 Free ⊙ Mon.–Thurs. 10–3), which has uniforms, guns, and badges worn by the Portland Police Bureau. Thanks to a city ordinance requiring that 1% of the development costs of new buildings be allotted to the

1

Biking

Portland has been called the best city in the country for biking, and with bike lanes galore, mild weather year-round, and a beautiful waterfront to ride along, it's no wonder. With all this encouragement, cyclists in Portland have gotten creative: not only does cycling provide an excellent form of transportation around here, it also has evolved into a medium of progressive politics and public service. Riders gather at least once every month to ride en masse through the streets of the city in an event called Critical Mass to show solidarity as a powerful alternative to an auto-society, and they have been known to gather force for the purpose of political protest. In addition, several bike co-ops have sprung up throughout the city in the past several years, devoted to providing used bikes at decent prices to members of the community, as well as to teaching bike maintenance and the economic and environmental benefits of becoming a commuter on two wheels.

Brews and Views

Everyone knows that Oregon loves its microbrews and that good beer drinking makes for some of Oregon's favorite pastimes, but Portlanders have taken this a step further, creating a recreational venue fondly called the Brew and View; that is, a movie theater showing second-run, classic, or cult films for $2 or $3, where you can buy a pitcher of good locally brewed beer and a slice of pizza to enjoy while watching. The McMenamins brothers are largely to thank for this phenomenon, being the masterminds behind such popular spots as the Bagdad Theatre, the Mission Theatre, and the St. John's Pub, but unaffiliated establishments like the Laurelhurst Theatre manage to edge in on the action as well.

Bridges

With a river running through the center of the city, Portland has one of the most interesting urban landscapes in the country, due in no small part to the several unique bridges that span the width of the Willamette River. Five of the city's 10 bridges are drawbridges, frequently raised to let barges go through, and there is something awe-inspiring and anachronistic in watching a portion of a city's traffic and hubbub stand still for several minutes as a slow-moving vessel floats through still water. Each bridge is beautiful and different: the St. John's Bridge has elegant 400-foot towers, the Broadway Bridge is a rich red hue, the arches of the huge two-level Fremont Bridge span the river gracefully, and the Steel Bridge has a pedestrian walkway just 30 feet above the water, allowing walkers and bikers to get a fabulous view of the river.

---

arts, the center's hallways are lined with travertine sculptures, ceiling mosaics, stained-glass windows, and photographic murals. You're welcome to peruse the works of art. ⊠ *1111 S.W. 2nd Ave., Downtown.*

❾ **Keller Auditorium.** Home base for the Portland Opera, the former Civic Auditorium also hosts traveling musicals and other theatrical extravaganzas. The building itself, part of the Portland Center for the Performing Arts, is not particularly distinctive, but the **Ira Keller Fountain,** a series of 18-foot-high stone waterfalls across from the front entrance, is worth a look. ⊠ *S.W. 3rd Ave. and Clay St., Downtown* ☎ *503/274–6560* ⊕ *www.pcpa.com.*

⑩ KOIN Center. An instant landmark after its completion in 1984, this handsome tower with a tapering form and a pyramidal top takes its design cues from early art deco skyscrapers. Made of brick with limestone trim and a blue metal roof, the tower has offices (including those of the CBS-TV affiliate and a radio station), a multiplex cinema, and, on its top floors, some of the most expensive condominiums in Portland. ⊠ *S.W. Columbia St. and S.W. 3rd Ave., Downtown.*

⑭ Mark O. Hatfield U.S. Courthouse. The New York architectural firm Kohn Pedersen Fox designed this skyscraper, which was completed in 1997. The sophisticated exterior is clad in Indiana limestone, and the courtroom lobbies have expansive glass walls. Rooftop terraces yield grand city views but, due to heightened security, are not always open to the public; ask the security guards whether the roof is open. ⊠ *S.W. 3rd Ave. between Main and Salmon Sts., Downtown.*

need a break?

Stop at **Martinotti's** (⊠ 404 S.W. 10th Ave., Downtown ☎ 503/224–9028), on the Central City streetcar line, for a glass of wine and a deli sandwich. You can also shop for kitchen gadgets, bottled wines, and packaged snacks.

㉑ Niketown. This futuristic F. A. O. Schwarz for the athletically inclined is a showplace for Nike, the international sportswear giant headquartered in suburban Beaverton. A life-size plaster cast of Michael Jordan captured in mid-jump dangles from the ceiling near the basketball shoes. Autographed sports memorabilia, video monitors, and statuary compete for your attention with the many products for sale. But don't expect any bargains: prices are full retail, and the word "sale" is almost as taboo around here as the name Reebok. If you don't get your fill at this branch, there's an outpost at Portland International Airport. ⊠ *930 S.W. 6th Ave., Downtown* ☎ *503/221–6453* ⊕ *www.niketown.com* ◷ *Mon.–Thurs. and Sat. 10–7, Fri. 10–8, Sun. 11:30–6:30.*

❼ Old Church. This building erected in 1882 is a prime example of Carpenter Gothic architecture. Tall spires and original stained-glass windows enhance its exterior of rough-cut lumber. The acoustically resonant church hosts free classical concerts at noon each Wednesday. If you're lucky you'll get to hear one of the few operating Hook and Hastings tracker pipe organs. ⊠ *1422 S.W. 11th Ave., Downtown* ☎ *503/222–2031* ⊕ *www.oldchurch.org* ⊠ *Free* ◷ *Weekdays 11–3, Sat. by appointment.*

★ ❺ Oregon History Center. Impressive eight-story-high trompe l'oeil murals of Lewis and Clark and the Oregon Trail (the route the two pioneers took from the Midwest to the Oregon Territory) cover two sides of this downtown museum, which follows the state's story from prehistoric times to the present. Recent renovations include the construction of a new entrance and lobby space as well as several new spaces for large exhibits and public gatherings. Anticipated exhibits include "Oregon History A to Z," a comprehensive overview of the state's past; "Oregon Country"; and the "Lewis and Clark National Bicentennial Exhibition," showcasing the largest collection of artifacts from the expedition ever assembled. The center's research library is open to the public; its bookstore is a good source for maps and publications on Pacific Northwest history. ⊠ *1200 S.W. Park Ave., Downtown* ☎ *503/222–1741* ⊕ *www.lewisandclarktrail.com* ⊠ *$6* ◷ *Tues.–Sat. 10–5, Sun. noon–5.*

▶ ❶ Pioneer Courthouse Square. Downtown Portland's public heart and commercial soul are centered in this amphitheatrical brick piazza, whose design echoes the classic central plazas of European cities. Special events often take place in this premier people-watching venue, where the neatly

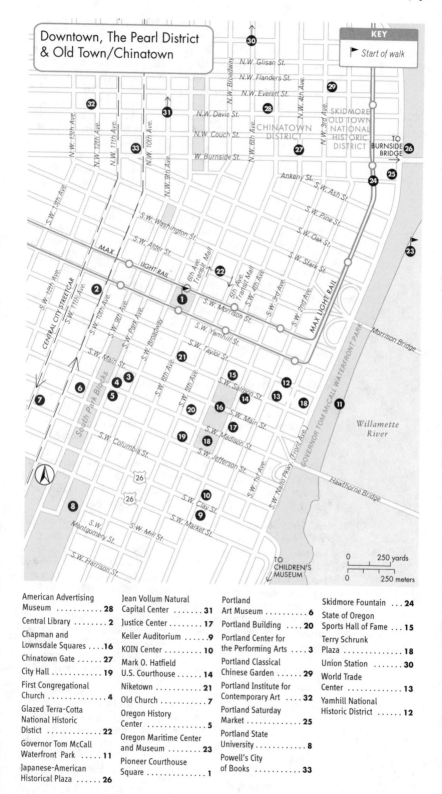

Downtown, The Pearl District & Old Town/Chinatown

KEY

► Start of walk

American Advertising
Museum **28**

Central Library **2**

Chapman and
Lownsdale Squares . . . **16**

Chinatown Gate **27**

City Hall **19**

First Congregational
Church **4**

Glazed Terra-Cotta
National Historic
Distict **22**

Governor Tom McCall
Waterfront Park . . . **11**

Japanese-American
Historical Plaza **26**

Jean Vollum Natural
Capital Center **31**

Justice Center **17**

Keller Auditorium **9**

KOIN Center **10**

Mark O. Hatfield
U.S. Courthouse **14**

Niketown **21**

Old Church **7**

Oregon History
Center **5**

Oregon Maritime Center
and Museum **23**

Pioneer Courthouse
Square **1**

Portland
Art Museum **6**

Portland Building **20**

Portland Center for
the Performing Arts **3**

Portland Classical
Chinese Garden **29**

Portland Institute for
Contemporary Art **32**

Portland Saturday
Market **25**

Portland State
University **8**

Powell's City
of Books **33**

Skidmore Fountain . . . **24**

State of Oregon
Sports Hall of Fame . . . **15**

Terry Schrunk
Plaza **18**

Union Station **30**

World Trade
Center **13**

Yamhill National
Historic District **12**

dressed office crowd mingles with some of the city's stranger elements. If you're here at noon on a day when all systems are operational, you might be lucky enough to see the goofy weather machine blast a fanfare and a shining sun, stormy dragon, or blue heron rise out of a misty cloud to confirm the day's weather. On Sunday, **vintage trolley** cars run from the MAX station here to Lloyd Center, with free service every half hour between noon and 6 PM. Call to check on the current schedule (☎ 503/323–7363). You can pick up maps and literature about the city and the state here at the **Portland/Oregon Visitors Association** (☎ 503/275–8355 ⊕ www.pova.com ⊙ weekdays 8:30–5:30, Sat. 10–4, Sun. 10–2). Directly across the street is one of downtown Portland's most familiar landmarks, the classically sedate **Pioneer Courthouse.** Built in 1869, it's the oldest public building in the Pacific Northwest. ⊠ *701 S. W. 6th Ave., Downtown.*

★ ❻ **Portland Art Museum.** The treasures at the Pacific Northwest's oldest visual- and media-arts facility span 35 centuries of Asian, European, and American art. A high point is the Center for Native American Art, with regional and contemporary art from more than 200 tribes. Keep an eye out for the large winter festival dish, the *potlatch,* and the transformation masks that really do transform. The film center presents the annual Portland International Film Festival in February and March and the Northwest Film Festival in early November. Also take a moment to linger in the peaceful outdoor sculpture garden. ⊠ *1219 S.W. Park Ave., Downtown* ☎ *503/226–2811, 503/221–1156 film schedule* ⊕ *www.pam.org* 🖭 *$10* ⊙ *Tues., Wed., and weekends 10–5, Thurs. and Fri. 10–8.*

❷⓿ **Portland Building.** *Portlandia,* the second-largest hammered-copper statue in the world, surpassed only by the Statue of Liberty, kneels on the second-story balcony of one of the first postmodern buildings in the United States. The building itself generates strong feelings; chances are you'll either love it or hate it. The controversial structure, architect Michael Graves's first major design commission, is buff-color, with brown-and-blue trim and exterior decorative touches. The interior spaces are dark and clumsily executed. A permanent exhibit of public art includes a huge fiberglass mold of Portlandia's face and original works by local artists. ⊠ *1120 S.W. 5th Ave., Downtown* 🖭 *Free* ⊙ *Weekdays 8–6.*

❸ **Portland Center for the Performing Arts.** The "old building" and the hub of activity here is the **Arlene Schnitzer Concert Hall,** host to the Oregon Symphony, musical events of many genres, and lectures. Across Main Street, but still part of the center, is the 292-seat **Delores Winningstad Theater,** used for plays and special performances. Its stage design and dimensions are based on those of an Elizabethan-era stage. The 916-seat **Newmark Theater,** which houses Portland Center Stage, a highly regarded resident theater company, is also part of the complex. The section of the street connecting the old and new buildings is sometimes blocked off for food fairs, art shows, and other events. ⊠ *S.W. Broadway and S.W. Main St., Downtown* ☎ *503/796–9293* ⊕ *www.pcpa.com* ⊙ *Free tours Wed. at 11 AM, Sat. every ½ hr 11–1, and 1st Thurs. of month at 6 PM.*

❽ **Portland State University.** The state's only university in a major metropolitan area takes advantage of downtown's South Park Blocks to provide trees and greenery for its 15,000 students. The compact campus, between Market Street and I–405, spreads west from the Park Blocks to 12th Avenue and east to 5th Avenue. Seven schools offer undergraduate, master's, and doctoral degrees. ⊠ *Park Ave. and Market St., Downtown* ☎ *503/725–3000* ⊕ *www.pdx.edu.*

⑮ State of Oregon Sports Hall of Fame. This museum has two multimedia theaters and sports memorabilia associated with prominent Oregonian athletes and organizations such as Heisman Trophy winner Terry Baker, the Portland Trail Blazers professional basketball team, and baseball player Mickey Lolich, who pitched for the Detroit Tigers in three World Series. ⊠ *321 S.W. Salmon St., Downtown* ☎ *503/227–7466* ⊕ *www.pova. com* ☞ *$4* ⊙ *Mon.–Sat. 10–5.*

⑱ Terry Schrunk Plaza. A terraced amphitheater of green lawn and brick, shaded by flowering cherry trees, the plaza is a popular lunch spot for the office crowd. ⊠ *Between S.W. 3rd and 4th Aves. and S.W. Madison and Jefferson Sts., Downtown.*

⑬ World Trade Center. The three sleek, handsome World Trade Center buildings, designed by the Portland architectural firm Zimmer Gunsel Frasca, are connected by sky bridges. Retail stores, a restaurant, coffee shops, banks, and travel agencies occupy the ground floors. ⊠ *Salmon St. between S.W. 2nd Ave. and S.W. Naito Pkwy., Downtown.*

⑫ Yamhill National Historic District. Many examples of 19th-century cast-iron architecture have been preserved within this district's six square blocks. Because the cast-iron facade helped support the main structure, these buildings traditionally did not need big, heavy walls to bear the weight; the interior spaces could therefore be larger and more open. North and west of this area, along 2nd Avenue, galleries exhibit fine art, ceramics, photography, and posters. On Southwest Naito Parkway at Taylor Street is **Mill Ends Park,** which sits in the middle of a traffic island. This patch of urban tranquillity, at 24 inches in diameter, has been recognized by *Guinness World Records* as the world's smallest official city park. ⊠ *Between S.W. Naito Pkwy. and S.W. 3rd Ave. and S.W. Morrison and S.W. Taylor Sts., Downtown.*

off the beaten path

LEWIS & CLARK COLLEGE – The college was founded by Presbyterian pioneers as Albany Collegiate Institute in 1867. The school moved to the former Lloyd Frank estate in Portland's southwest hills in 1942 and took the name Lewis & Clark College. The campus is in a wooded residential area 6 mi from downtown Portland. ⊠ *S.W. Palatine Hill Rd.* ☎ *503/768–7000* ⊕ *www.lclark.edu* ☞ *Free* ⊙ *Weekdays.*

Pearl District & Old Town/Chinatown

The Skidmore Old Town National Historic District, commonly called Old Town/Chinatown, is where Portland was born. The 20-square-block section, bounded by Oak Street to the south and Everett Street to the north, includes buildings of varying ages and architectural designs. Before it was renovated, this was skid row, and vestiges of that condition remain. One of Portland's newest attractions is here: the Portland Classical Chinese Garden, which opened in summer 2000. In addition to yielding many Chinese restaurants and gift shops, the area is home to several gay bars and restaurants. MAX serves the area with a stop at the Old Town/Chinatown station.

Bordering Old Town to the northwest is the Pearl District. Formerly a warehouse area along the railroad yards, the Pearl District is the fastest-growing part of Portland. Mid-rise residential lofts have sprouted on almost every block, and boutiques, galleries, and trendy restaurants line the streets. The new Central City streetcar line passes through here on its way from Nob Hill to downtown and Portland State University.

Numbers in the text correspond to numbers in the margin and on the Downtown, the Pearl District & Old Town/Chinatown map.

a good walk

Begin in Waterfront Park at the **Oregon Maritime Center and Museum** ㉓ ►. Cross Southwest Ash Street and walk north on Southwest 1st Avenue to **Skidmore Fountain** ㉔, which is the centerpiece of Ankeny Square. On Saturday and Sunday the area west of the fountain near 2nd Avenue is the site of the **Portland Saturday Market** ㉕. Go north one block on Naito Parkway past the Burnside Bridge to the **Japanese-American Historical Plaza** ㉖. Walk west on Burnside Street to Northwest 4th Avenue and the **Chinatown Gate** ㉗, the official entrance to the Chinatown District. Continue through the gate, down 4th Avenue to Davis Street, and turn left. Head west one block to the **American Advertising Museum** ㉘. Head down 5th Avenue to Everett Street and turn right; the **Portland Classical Chinese Garden** ㉙ is two blocks east.

Head back west along Everett and turn right on 6th Avenue. Walk about five blocks to its terminus at **Union Station** ㉚. Head back along 6th Avenue for two blocks, and turn right on Hoyt Street. Follow Hoyt Street to 9th Avenue, and look for the **Jean Vollum Natural Capital Center** ㉛ one block to your right, at the corner of 9th Avenue and Irving Street. Back on Hoyt Street, turn right and walk three blocks north. Turn left on 12th Avenue, and proceed three blocks to the **Portland Institute for Contemporary Art** ㉜. Walk two blocks farther on 12th Avenue and turn left on Burnside. Two blocks south on Burnside, at the corner of 10th Avenue, is **Powell's City of Books** ㉝.

TIMING   You can easily walk through Old Town/Chinatown and the Pearl District in an hour or two. However, a visit to the Portland Classical Chinese Garden is a must, so allow some extra time. If you also visit the American Advertising Museum or PICA, or plan on delving into the shelves at Powell's, allow a half day in the area.

What to See

㉘ **American Advertising Museum.** This museum is devoted exclusively to advertising. Exhibits celebrate memorable campaigns, print advertisements, radio and TV commercials, and novelty and specialty products. The museum also has the industry's most comprehensive collection of advertising and business artifacts. ⊠ *211 N.W. 5th Ave., Old Town/Chinatown* ☎ *503/226–0000* ⊕ *www.admuseum.com* ⊡ *$5* ⊙ *Thurs.–Sat. 11–5.*

㉗ **Chinatown Gate.** Recognizable by its five roofs, 64 dragons, and two huge lions, the Chinatown Gate is the official entrance to the **Chinatown District.** During the 1890s, Portland had the second-largest Chinese community in the United States. Today's Chinatown is compressed into several blocks with restaurants (though many locals prefer Chinese eateries outside the district), shops, and grocery stores. ⊠ *N.W. 4th Ave. and Burnside St., Old Town/Chinatown.*

㉖ **Japanese-American Historical Plaza.** Take a moment to study the evocative figures cast into the bronze columns at the plaza's entrance; they show Japanese-Americans before, during, and after World War II—living daily life, fighting in battle for the United States, and marching off to internment camps. More than 110,000 Japanese-Americans were interned by the American government during the war. This park was created to commemorate their experience and contributions. Simple blocks of granite carved with haiku poems describing the war experience powerfully evoke this dark episode in American history. ⊠ *East of Naito Pkwy. between W. Burnside and N.W. Davis Sts., Old Town/Chinatown.*

need a
break?

For a break from sightseeing and shopping, head back south under the Burnside Bridge into cool, dark **Kell's Irish Restaurant & Pub** (⊠ 112 S.W. 2nd Ave., between S.W. Ash and S.W. Pine Sts., Skidmore District ☎ 503/227–4057) for a pint of Guinness and authentic Irish pub fare—and be sure to ask the bartender how all those folded-up dollar bills got stuck to the ceiling.

③ **Jean Vollum Natural Capital Center.** Known to most locals simply as the Ecotrust Building, this building has a handful of environment-friendly businesses and organic-friendly retail spaces including Hot Lips Pizza, World Cup Coffee, and Patagonia (outdoor clothes). Originally built in 1895 and purchased by Ecotrust in 1998, the building has been significantly adapted to serve as a landmark in sustainable, "green" building practices. Take the self-guided tour of the building, which begins with the original "remnant wall" on the west side of the parking lot; proceeds throughout the building; and ends on the "eco-roof," a grassy rooftop used to provide temperature insulation, where you can get a great view of the Pearl District. ⊠ 721 N.W. 9th Ave., Pearl District ☎ 503/227–6225 ⊕ www.ecotrust.org 🖾 Free ⊗ Weekdays 9–5; ground-floor businesses also evenings and weekends.

👆 ☞ **②** **Oregon Maritime Center and Museum.** Local model makers created most of this museum's models of ships that plied the Columbia River. Contained entirely within the stern-wheeler steamship *Portland,* docked at the foot of Southwest Pine Street on the seawall in Tom McCall Waterfront Park, this small museum provides an excellent overview of Oregon's maritime history. ⊠ On steamship at the end of S.W. Pine St., in Waterfront Park, Skidmore District ☎ 503/224–7724 ⊕ www.oregonmaritimemuseum.org 🖾 $4 ⊗ Fri.–Sun. 11–4.

② FodorśChoice ★ **Portland Classical Chinese Garden.** In a twist on the Joni Mitchell song, the city of Portland and private donors took down a parking lot and unpaved paradise, as it were, when they created this wonderland abutting the Pearl District and Old Town/Chinatown. It's the largest Suzhou-style garden outside China, with a large lake, bridged and covered walkways, koi- and water lily-filled ponds, rocks, bamboo, statues, waterfalls, and courtyards. A team of 60 artisans and designers from China literally left no stone unturned—500 tons of stone were brought here from Suzhou—in their efforts to give the windows, roof tiles, gateways, including a "moongate," and other architectural aspects of the Garden some specific meaning or purpose. Also on the premises are a gift shop and a two-story teahouse overlooking the lake and garden. ⊠ N.W. 3rd Ave. and Everett St., Old Town/Chinatown ☎ 503/228–8131 ⊕ www.chinesegarden.org 🖾 $7 ⊗ Nov.–Mar., daily 10–5; Apr.–Oct., daily 9–6. Tours daily at noon and 1.

③ **Portland Institute for Contemporary Art (PICA).** Founded in 1995, PICA seeks to advance new ideas in art by bringing innovative artists working in all media (visual arts, dance, music, theater) to Portland to showcase their work. Exhibits and performances vary greatly throughout the year; call ahead or visit the Web site to find out what to expect. ⊠ 219 N.W. 12th Ave., Pearl District ☎ 503/242–1419 ⊕ www.pica.org 🖾 $3 ⊗ Wed.–Sat. noon–6.

② FodorśChoice ★ **Portland Saturday Market.** On weekends from March to Christmas, the west side of the Burnside Bridge and the Skidmore Fountain environs has North America's largest open-air handicraft market. This is not upscale shopping by any means, but if you're looking for crystals, yard goods, beaded hats, stained glass, birdhouses, jewelry, flags, wood and rubber stamps, or custom footwear and decorative boots, you stand a good chance of finding them. Entertainers and food and produce booths add to the festive feel. ⊠ *Under west end of Burnside Bridge, from S.W. Naito Pkwy. to Ankeny Sq., Skidmore/Old Town* ☎ *503/ 222–6072* ⊕ *www.saturdaymarket.org* ☉ *Mar.–Dec., Sat. 10–5, Sun. 11–4:30.*

㉝ Powell's City of Books. The largest independent bookstore in the world, with more than 1.5 million new and used books, Powell's is a Portland landmark that can easily consume you for several hours if you're not careful. Rooms and ample signs are helpfully color-coded according to the types of books, so you'll have a blueprint for wandering. Be sure to espy the pillar bearing signatures of prominent sci-fi authors who have passed through the store—the scrawls are protected by a jagged length of Plexiglas. At the very least, stop into Powell's for a peek just to say you've seen it, or grab a cup of coffee at the adjoining branch of World Cup Coffee. Should you miss the store or require another dose, there's a branch at Portland International Airport that's useful for whiling away an hour or two. ⊠ *1005 W. Burnside St., Pearl District* ☎ *503/ 228–4651* ⊕ *www.powells.com* ☉ *Daily 9 AM–11 PM.*

FodorśChoice
★

㉔ Skidmore Fountain. This unusually graceful fountain built in 1888 is the centerpiece of **Ankeny Square**, a plaza around which many community activities take place. Two nymphs uphold the brimming basin on top; citizens once quenched their thirst from the spouting lions' heads below, and horses drank from the granite troughs at the base of the fountain. ⊠ *S.W. Ankeny St. between S.W. Naito Pkwy. and 1st Ave., Skidmore District.*

㉚ Union Station. You can always find your way to Union Station by heading toward the huge neon GO BY TRAIN sign that looms high above the station. The vast lobby area, with high ceilings and marble floors, is particularly worth a brief visit if you hold any nostalgia for the heyday of train travel in the United States. It's a far cry from the Greyhound station next door. ⊠ *800 N.W. 6th Ave., Old Town/Chinatown* ☎ *503/ 273–4866.*

Nob Hill & Vicinity

The showiest example of Portland's urban chic is Northwest 23rd Avenue—sometimes referred to with varying degrees of affection as "trendy-third"—a 20-block thoroughfare that cuts north–south through the neighborhood known as Nob Hill. Fashionable since the 1880s and still filled with Victorian residential architecture, the neighborhood is a mixed-use cornucopia of old Portland charm and new Portland hip. With its cafés, restaurants, galleries, and boutiques, it's a delightful place to stroll, shop, and people-watch. More restaurants, shops, and nightspots can be found on Northwest 21st Avenue, a few blocks away. Finding parking in this neighborhood has become such a challenge that the city put in a streetcar line. The Central City streetcar line runs from Legacy Good Samaritan Hospital in Nob Hill, through the Pearl District on 10th and 11th avenues, connects with MAX light rail near Pioneer Courthouse Square downtown, and then continues on to Portland State University. The line will eventually extend to RiverPlace on the Willamette River.

Numbers in the text correspond to numbers in the margin and on the Nob Hill & Vicinity map.

a good
walk

Northwest 23rd Avenue between West Burnside Street and Northwest Lovejoy Street—the east–west-running streets are in alphabetical order—is the heart of Nob Hill. There's such a profusion of coffee bars and cafés along the avenue that some locals call it Latte-land Central. You don't need a map of the avenue, just cash or credit cards. Some of the shops and restaurants are in newly designed quarters, and others are tucked into restored Victorian and other century-old homes and buildings. As it continues north past Lovejoy Street, the avenue begins to quiet down. Between Overton and Pettygrove streets, a block of open-porch frame houses converted into shops typifies the alternative, new-age side of Portland. The **Pettygrove House** ㉞ ⌐, a Victorian gingerbread on the corner of 23rd Avenue and Pettygrove Street, was built by the man who gave Portland its name. Continue on 23rd Avenue past Pettygrove to Quimby Street to reach the **Clear Creek Distillery** ㉟.

There's much more to Nob Hill than Northwest 21st and 23rd avenues, something you'll discover if you walk among the neighborhood's Victorian residences. Most of the noteworthy structures are private residences and do not have identifying plaques, nor do they admit visitors. Begin at 23rd Avenue and Flanders Street, with the 1891 **Trevett-Nunn House** ㊱ ⌐, an excellent example of the Colonial Revival style. Continue east to the 1907 **Day Building** ㊲. Farther east is the Byzantine **Temple Beth Israel** ㊳, completed in 1928. At Flanders and 17th Avenue head north (to the left) to Irving Street. The **Campbell Townhouses** ㊴ are the only known example of brick row-house construction in Oregon. Continue west on Irving and north (to the right) on 18th Avenue to the **Ayer-Shea House** ㊵, an elegant Colonial Revival house.

Heading west on Johnson Street, you'll pass the Italianate-style Sprague-Marshall-Bowie House, built in 1882, and the 1893 Albert Tanner House, a rare Stick-style residence with a wraparound porch and richly decorated front gables. The 2½-story **Mary Smith House** ㊶ offers an unusual variation on the Colonial Revival style. At 22nd Avenue, turn south (left) to reach the **Nathan Loeb House** ㊷, a fine late-19th-century Queen Anne–style structure. Continue south on 22nd Avenue and turn east (left) on Hoyt Street to reach the Joseph Bergman House, a High Victorian Italianate-style home built in 1885. Head two blocks east to 20th Avenue and two blocks south (to the right) to reach the rare, Shingle-style **George Huesner House** ㊸.

TIMING Strolling along 23rd Avenue from Burnside Street to Pettygrove Street can take a half hour or half a day, depending on how many eateries or shops lure you in along the way. The tour of neighborhood Victorian residences can be done in about an hour.

What to See

㊵ **Ayer-Shea House.** This Colonial Revival house was built in 1892 by Whidden and Lewis, who also designed Portland's City Hall. ✉ *1809 N.W. Johnson St., Nob Hill.*

㊴ **Campbell Townhouses.** These six attached buildings with Queen Anne–style detailing, reminiscent of row houses in San Francisco and along the East Coast, have undergone virtually no structural modification since they were built in 1893. ✉ *1705–1719 N.W. Irving St., Nob Hill.*

㉟ **Clear Creek Distillery.** The distillery keeps such a low profile that it's practically invisible. But ring the bell and someone will unlock the wrought-iron gate and let you into a dim, quiet tasting room where you can sample Clear Creek's world-famous Oregon apple and pear brandies and grappas. ✉ *1430 N.W. 23rd Ave., near Quimby St., Nob Hill* ☎ *503/*

Ayer-Shea House **40**

Campbell Townhouses **39**

Clear Creek Distillery **35**

Day Building **37**

George Huesner House **43**

Mary Smith House **41**

Nathan Loeb House **42**

Pettygrove House **34**

Temple Beth Israel **38**

Trevett-Nunn House **36**

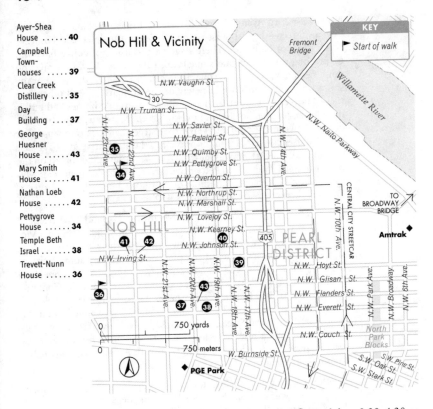

248–9470 ⊕ *www.clearcreekdistillery.com* ⊘ *Weekdays 8:30–4:30 or by appointment.*

need a break? You won't have any trouble finding a place to sit and caffeinate in this Northwest Portland neighborhood. **Coffee Time** (⊠ 710 N.W. 21st Ave., Nob Hill ☎ 503/497–1090) serves all the requisite brews and pastries. Inside, discover a surprising labyrinth of dark, cozy rooms with couches, small tables, and floor lamps. Retreat into its depths or sit outdoors at a sidewalk table.

③⑦ **Day Building.** Architecture buffs in particular might appreciate this 1907 Colonial Revival apartment house, fronted by 30 foot, fluted Corinthian columns. The building is on the National Register of Historic Places.

⊠ *2068 N.W. Flanders St., Nob Hill.*

④③ **George Huesner House.** Typical of the Shingle style that came into vogue in the 1890s, this home was designed by Edgar Lazarus, architect of landmarks such as Vista House in the Columbia River Gorge. ⊠ *333 N.W. 20th Ave., Nob Hill.*

④① **Mary Smith House.** Dating from 1906, this home has a central second-story bow window and a full-length veranda with a central bowed portico supported by Ionic columns. ⊠ *2256 N.W. Johnson St., Nob Hill.*

④② **Nathan Loeb House.** One of the most ornate Victorians in Portland, the Loeb House has turned-wood posts, wood arches with central pendants and sunburst spandrel patterns, and a projecting ground-floor section with an ornamental three-bay round-arch window. ⊠ *726 N.W. 22nd Ave., Nob Hill.*

⌐ ③④ **Pettygrove House.** Back in 1845, after he'd bought much of what is now downtown Portland for $50, Francis Pettygrove and his partner, Asa Lovejoy, flipped a coin to decide who would name the still unbuilt city. Pettygrove won and chose Portland, after a town in his native Maine. His beautifully restored Victorian gingerbread house was built in 1892. Inside, **Vivace** creperie and coffee house has several laid-back sitting areas with colorful walls and comfortable chairs spread among its rooms. ⊠ *2287 N.W. Pettygrove St., Nob Hill.*

③⑧ **Temple Beth Israel.** The imposing sandstone, brick, and stone structure with a massive domed roof and Byzantine styling was completed in 1928 and still serves a congregation first organized in 1858. ⊠ *1972 N.W. Flanders St., Nob Hill.*

⌐ ③⑥ **Trevett-Nunn House.** Built in 1891, this Colonial Revival home is the oldest extant residence designed by Whidden and Lewis, Portland's most distinguished late-19th-century architectural firm. ⊠ *2347 N.W. Flanders St., Nob Hill.*

Washington Park & Forest Park

Numbers in the text correspond to numbers in the margin and on the Washington Park & Forest Park map.

a good tour

The best way to get to Washington Park is via MAX light rail, which travels through a tunnel deep beneath the city's West Hills. Be sure to check out the Washington Park station, the deepest (260 feet) transit station in North America. Graphics on the walls depict life in the Portland area during the past 17 million years. There's also a core sample of the bedrock taken from the mountain displayed along the walls. If you're driving, head west of downtown on West Burnside Street and south (turn left) on Southwest Tichner Drive to reach 322-acre Washington Park, home to the **Hoyt Arboretum** ㊹ ⌐, the **International Rose Test Garden** ㊺, and the **Japanese Garden** ㊻. By car, the **Oregon Zoo** ㊼, **Forest Discovery Center Museum** ㊽, and **Children's Museum** ㊾ can best be reached by heading west on U.S. 26. North of the park is the opulent **Pittock Mansion** ㊿. Also north of Washington Park is **Forest Park** ㉛.

TIMING   You could easily spend a day at either Washington Park or Forest Park. Plan on at least two hours at the zoo; an hour or more at the arboretum, rose garden, and Japanese Garden; and an hour to tour the Pittock Mansion and its grounds.

What to See

☾ ㊾ **Children's Museum.** In summer 2001 this museum for kids 12 and under moved from downtown to Washington Park across from the Oregon Zoo. Hands-on play is the order of the day, with rotating exhibits, a clay shop, and a child-size grocery store. The zoo parking lot provides free parking. Take MAX light rail to Washington Park station. ⊠ *4015 S.W. Canyon Rd., Washington Park (U.S. 26, Zoo exit)* ☎ *503/223–6500* ⊠ *$5.50* ☉ *Tues.–Sun. 9–5.*

☾ ㊽ **Forest Discovery Center Museum.** The two-level center, across from the Oregon Zoo, takes its arboreal interests seriously—its spokesperson is a 70-foot-tall talking tree. Outside, a 1909 locomotive and antique logging equipment are displayed, and inside is the multi-image "Forests of the World," a collection of 100-year-old wood, and a gift shop. Take MAX to the Washington Park station. ⊠ *4033 S.W. Canyon Rd., Washington Park* ☎ *503/228–1367* ⊕ *www.worldforest.org* ⊠ *$5* ☉ *Daily 9–5.*

㉛ **Forest Park.** The nation's largest (5,000 acres) urban wilderness, this city-owned park, with more than 100 species of birds and 50 species of mam-

Children's
Museum **49**

Forest
Discovery
Center
Museum **48**

Forest Park .. **51**

Hoyt
Arboretum ... **44**

International
Rose
Test Garden .. **45**

Japanese
Garden **46**

Oregon Zoo .. **47**

Pittock
Mansion **50**

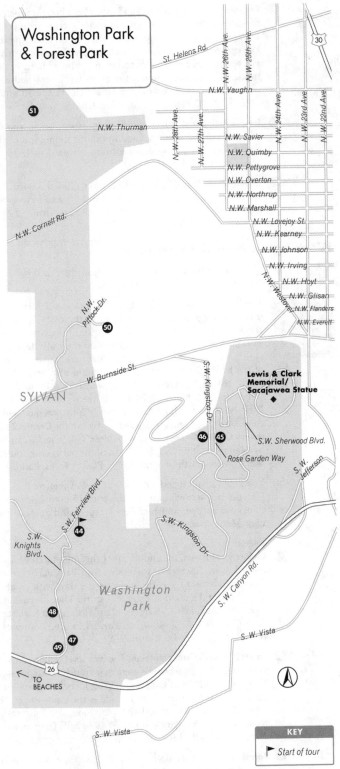

Washington Park
& Forest Park

SYLVAN

Washington
Park

Lewis & Clark
Memorial/
Sacajawea Statue
◆

KEY

▶ Start of tour

mals, has more than 50 mi of trails. The **Portland Audubon Society** (✉ 5151 N.W. Cornell Rd. ☎ 503/292–9453) supplies free maps and sponsors a bevy of bird-related activities in the heart of the only old-growth forest in a major U.S. city. Programs include guided bird-watching events, and there's a hospital for injured and orphaned birds as well as a gift shop stocked with books, feeders, and bird lovers' paraphernalia. ✛ *Take N.W. Lovejoy St. west to where it becomes Cornell Rd. and follow to the park, past Nob Hill in the Northwest* ☎ *503/823–7529* ✉ *Free* ☉ *Daily dawn–dusk.*

▶ ㊹ **Hoyt Arboretum.** Ten miles of trails wind through the arboretum, which has more than 800 species of plants and one of the nation's largest collections of coniferous trees; pick up trail maps at the visitor center. Also here are the Winter Garden and a memorial to veterans of the Vietnam War. ✉ *4000 S.W. Fairview Blvd., Washington Park* ☎ *503/228–8733* ⊕ *www.portlandparks.org* ✉ *Free* ☉ *Arboretum daily dawn–dusk, visitor center daily 9–4.*

★ ㊺ **International Rose Test Garden.** Despite the name, these grounds are not an experimental greenhouse laboratory but three terraced gardens, set on 4 acres, where 10,000 bushes and 400 varieties of roses grow. The flowers, many of them new varieties, are at their peak in June and July and September and October. From the gardens, you can see highly photogenic views of the downtown skyline and, on fine days, the Fuji-shape slopes of Mt. Hood, 50 mi to the east. Summer concerts take place in the garden's amphitheater. Take MAX light rail to Washington Park station and transfer to Bus No. 63. ✉ *400 S.W. Kingston Ave., Washington Park* ☎ *503/823–3636* ⊕ *www.portlandparks.com* ✉ *Free* ☉ *Daily dawn–dusk.*

㊻ **Japanese Garden.** The most authentic Japanese garden outside Japan is
Fodor's Choice   nestled among 5½ acres of Washington Park above the International Rose
★   Test Garden. This serene spot, designed by a Japanese landscape master and opened to the public in 1967, represents five separate garden styles: Strolling Pond Garden, Tea Garden, Natural Garden, Sand and Stone Garden, and Flat Garden. The Tea House was built in Japan and reconstructed here. The west side of the Pavilion has a majestic view of Portland and Mt. Hood. Take MAX light rail to Washington Park station and transfer to Bus No. 63. ✉ *611 S.W. Kingston Ave., Washington Park* ☎ *503/223–1321* ⊕ *www.japanesegarden.com* ✉ *$6.50* ☉ *Oct.–Mar., Mon. noon–4, Tues.–Sun. 10–4; Apr.–Sept., Mon. noon–7, Tues.–Sun. 10–7.*

★ ㉃ ㊼ **Oregon Zoo.** This beautiful animal park in the West Hills is famous for its Asian elephants. Major exhibits include an African section with rhinos, hippos, zebras, and giraffes. Steller Cove, a state-of-the-art aquatic exhibit, has two Steller sea lions and a family of sea otters. Other exhibits include polar bears, Siberian tigers, chimpanzees, an Alaska Tundra exhibit with wolves and grizzly bears, a penguinarium, and habitats for beavers, otters, and reptiles native to the west side of the Cascade Range. In summer a 4-mi round-trip narrow-gauge train operates from the zoo, chugging through the woods to a station near the International Rose Test Garden and the Japanese Garden. Take the MAX light rail to the Washington Park station. ✉ *4001 S.W. Canyon Rd., Washington Park* ☎ *503/226–7627* ⊕ *www.oregonzoo.org* ✉ *$8, free 2nd Tues. of month after 1 PM* ☉ *Oct.–Mar., daily 9–4, Apr.–Sept., daily 9–6.*

★ ㊿ **Pittock Mansion.** Henry Pittock, the founder and publisher of the *Oregonian* newspaper, built this 22-room mansion, which combines French Renaissance and Victorian styles. The opulent manor, built in 1914, is filled with art and antiques of the 1880s. The 46-acre grounds, north of Washington Park and 1,000 feet above the city, have superb views of the skyline, rivers, and the Cascade Range. There's a tea house and a small hiking trail. ⊠ *3229 N.W. Pittock Dr. (from W. Burnside St. heading west, turn right on N.W. Barnes Rd. and follow signs), north of Washington Park* ☎ *503/823–3624* ⊕ *www.portlandparks.org* ✉ *$5.25* ☉ *June–Aug., daily 11–4, Sept.–Dec. and Feb.–May, daily noon–4.*

East of the Willamette River

Portland is known as the City of Roses, but the 10 distinctive bridges spanning the Willamette River have also earned it the name Bridgetown. The older drawbridges, near downtown, open several times a day to allow passage of large cargo ships and freighters. You can easily spend a couple of days exploring the attractions and areas on the east side of the river.

Numbers in the text correspond to numbers in the margin and on the East of the Willamette River map.

a good tour

Most people visit Portland's east-side destinations separately, and by car rather than public transportation. At the western end of Hawthorne Boulevard, along the banks of the Willamette River, is the **Oregon Museum of Science and Industry** ⑫ ▶. After visiting OMSI head east on busy Hawthorne Boulevard through the **Hawthorne District** ⑬, where there are interesting shops and restaurants. Hawthorne runs into **Mt. Tabor Park** ⑭ at its eastern end. Park your car and hike up the mountain for a spectacular view of the city and surrounding mountains. Head back toward town and stop at **Laurelhurst Park** ⑮, a stately enclave. Head south to **Crystal Springs Rhododendron Garden** ⑯, and then make your way back toward the river and the shops of the **Sellwood District** ⑰. At river's edge stands **Oaks Amusement Park** ⑱, a good spot for kids; another option is to drive to **North Clackamas Aquatic Park** ⑲, where you can all unwind in the wave pool.

TIMING You could spend a pleasant hour or so in each of the parks, gardens, and neighborhoods here. Spend two to three hours each at either the Oregon Museum of Science and Industry or the amusement park.

What to See

⑯ **Crystal Springs Rhododendron Garden.** For much of the year this 7-acre retreat near Reed College is used by bird-watchers and those who want a restful stroll. But starting in April, thousands of rhododendron bushes and azaleas burst into flower. The peak blooming season for these woody shrubs is May; by late June the show is over. ⊠ *S.E. 28th Ave. (west side, 1 block north of Woodstock Blvd.), Sellwood/Woodstock area* ☎ *503/771–8386* ⊕ *www.portlandparks.org* ✉ *$3 Mar.–Labor Day, Thurs.–Mon. 10–6; otherwise free* ☉ *Daily dawn–dusk.*

need a break?

At the **Bagdad Theatre and Pub** (⊠ 3702 S.E. Hawthorne Blvd., Hawthorne District ☎ 503/230–0895) you can buy a pint of beer and a slice of pizza and watch a movie.

⑬ **Hawthorne District.** Though it has become more upscale in recent years, this neighborhood stretching from the foot of Mt. Tabor to 30th Avenue tends to attract a slightly younger, more "alternative" crowd than downtown or Nob Hill, and it is one of the most crowded and popular areas east of the Willamette. With many bookstores, coffeehouses, taverns, restaurants, antiques stores, used-CD shops, and boutiques filling the streetfront, it is easy to spend a few hours wandering the street. Finding a parking space can be a real challenge on Hawthorne; be pre-

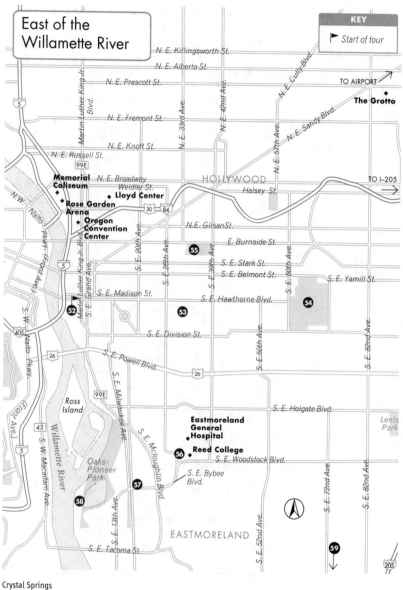

East of the
Willamette River

Crystal Springs
Rhododendron
Garden **56**

Hawthorne District **53**

Laurelhurst Park **55**

Mt. Tabor Park **54**

North Clackamas
Aquatic Park **59**

Oaks
Amusement Park **58**

Oregon Museum
of Science
and Industry **52**

Sellwood District **57**

pared to look on a few side streets. ✉ *S.E. Hawthorne Blvd. between 30th and 42nd Aves., Hawthorne District.*

⑤ Laurelhurst Park. Manicured lawns, stately trees, and a wildfowl pond make this 25-acre southeast Portland park a favorite urban hangout. Laurelhurst, one of the city's most beautiful neighborhoods, surrounds the park. ✉ *S.E. 39th Ave. between S.E. Ankeny and Oak Sts., Laurelhurst* ⊕ *www.portlandparks.org* ⊙ *Daily dawn–dusk.*

⑤ Mt. Tabor Park. Dirt trails and an asphalt road wind through forested hillsides and past good picnic areas to the top of Mt. Tabor, which provides a panoramic view of Portland's West Hills and Cascade mountain peak. Mt. Tabor is an extinct volcano; the buttes and conical hills east of the park are evidence of the gigantic eruptions that formed the Cascade Range millions of years ago. Said to be the best place in the city to watch the sunset, the park is also a popular place to bike, hike, picnic, or just throw a Frisbee. ✉ *S.E. 60th Ave. and Salmon St., just east of Hawthorne District* ☏ *503/823-7529* ⊕ *www.portlandparks.org.*

> **off the beaten path**

THE GROTTO – Owned by the Catholic Church, the National Sanctuary of Our Sorrowful Mother, as it's officially known, displays more than 100 statues and shrines in 62 acres of woods. The grotto was carved into the base of a 110-foot cliff and has a replica of Michelangelo's *Pietà*. The real treat is found after ascending the cliff face via elevator, as you enter a wonderland of gardens, sculptures and shrines, and a glass-walled cathedral with an awe-inspiring view of the Columbia River and the Cascades. There's a dazzling Festival of Lights at Christmastime (late November and December), with 250,000 lights, and holiday concerts in the 600-seat chapel. Sunday masses are held here, too. ✉ *Sandy Blvd. at N.E. 85th Ave., near airport* ☏ *503/254-7371* ⊕ *www.thegrotto.org* ✉ *Plaza level free; elevator to upper level $3* ⊙ *Mid-May–Labor Day, daily 9–7:30; Labor Day–late Nov., daily 9–5:30; late Nov.–Jan., daily 9–4:30; Feb.–mid-May, daily 9–5:30.*

⑤ North Clackamas Aquatic Park. If you're visiting Portland with kids any time of the year and are looking for a great way to cool off—especially on one of Portland's hot July or August days—check out this 45,000-square-foot, all-indoor attraction, whose main pool has 4-foot waves and three super slides. There's also a 25-yard-long lap pool, a wading pool, an adults-only hot whirlpool, and a café. Children under age 8 must be accompanied by someone 13 or older. ✉ *7300 S.E. Harmony Rd., Milwaukie* ☏ *503/557-7873* ⊕ *www.co.clackamas.or.us/ncap* ✉ *$9.50* ⊙ *Mon., Wed., and Fri. 4–8, weekends 11–8; no open swim weekends 3–4.*

Northeast Alberta Street. More than two dozen art galleries and studios, alongside coffeehouses, restaurants, and specialty shops, line this street in this quickly gentrifying neighborhood in northeast Portland. The neighborhood, which has undergone rapid transition since the mid-'90s, is a fascinating place to witness the intersection of cultures and lifestyles in a growing city. There are few other places in Portland with a Mexican grocery, a vintage-clothing store, a barbecue joint, and an art gallery on the same block. Galleries and businesses host the Art on Alberta sidewalk event on the last Thursday evening of each month. A street fair in September showcases the area with arts-and-crafts booths and food vendors. ✉ *Between Martin Luther King Jr. Blvd. and 30th Ave., Alberta District.*

NORTHWEST ALPACAS RANCH – The kids can pet the llamalike animals at this ranch southwest of Portland. A gift shop sells sweaters made from alpaca wool. ⊠ *11785 S.W. River Rd., Scholls* ☎ *503/ 628-3110* ⊕ *www.alpacas.com* ⊠ *Free* ⊙ *Fri.–Sun. 10–5.*

🕲 **58** **Oaks Amusement Park.** There's a small-town charm to this park, with thrill rides and miniature golf in summer and roller-skating year-round. In summer 1999 Oaks Park opened Acorn Acres, complete with a 360-degree loop roller coaster, carousel, and Ferris wheel. The skating rink, built in 1905, is the oldest continuously operating one in the United States. There are outdoor concerts in summer. Also in the park is the **Ladybug Theater** (☎ 503/232–2346), which presents shows for children. ⊠ *S. E. Spokane St. east of Willamette River, from east side of Sellwood Bridge, take Grand Ave. north and Spokane west, Sellwood* ☎ *503/233–5777* ⊕ *www.oakspark.com* ⊠ *Park free, 5-hr ride passes $8.50–$11, individual-ride tickets $1.25* ⊙ *Mid-June–Labor Day, weekends noon–7; late Mar.–mid-June and Labor Day–Oct., weekends noon–5.*

★ 🕲 ▶ **52** **Oregon Museum of Science and Industry** (OMSI). An Omnimax theater and planetarium are among the main attractions at the Northwest's largest astronomy educational facility, which also has a hands-on computer center, a space wing with a mission-control center, and many permanent and touring scientific exhibits. Moored in the Willamette as part of the museum is a 240-foot submarine, the USS *Blueback*. ⊠ *1945 S.E. Water Ave., south of Morrison Bridge, under Hawthorne Bridge* ☎ *503/797– 6674 or 800/955–6674* ⊕ *www.omsi.edu* ⊠ *Full package $16, museum $8, planetarium $3.50, Omnimax $7, submarine $3.50* ⊙ *Memorial Day–Labor Day, Fri.–Wed. 9:30–7, Thurs. 9:30–8; Labor Day–Memorial Day, Tues.–Sun. 9:30–5:30.*

57 **Sellwood District.** The browsable neighborhood that begins east of the Sellwood Bridge was once a separate town. Annexed by Portland in the 1890s, it retains a modest charm. On weekends the antiques stores along 13th Avenue do a brisk business. Each store is identified by a plaque that tells the date of construction and the original purpose of the building. More antiques stores, specialty shops, and restaurants are near the intersection of Milwaukie and Bybee. ⊠ *S.E. 13th Ave. between Malden and Clatsop Sts., Sellwood.*

WHERE TO EAT

First-time visitors to Portland are often surprised by how diverse and inexpensive many restaurants are. Lovers of ethnic foods can choose from restaurants serving Chinese, French, Indian, Italian, Japanese, Middle Eastern, Tex-Mex, Thai, and Vietnamese specialties. Pacific Northwest cuisine also dominates; Portlanders view salmon with passion, and likewise other regional seafood including halibut, crab, oysters, and mussels. Many restaurants are devoted to organic, locally grown produce such as wild mushrooms, hazelnuts, and berries, as well as free-range local beef and poultry.

Portland claims to have more restaurants per capita than any other city in the country, so while it is easy to stumble upon some great food, it is also worth doing a little research to find some of the out-of-the-way places that have much to offer. Many of the city's trendier restaurants are in Nob Hill and the Pearl District, and downtown is filled with many diverse, quality menus at some of the city's long-running old reliables. But an incredible smattering of cuisines can be found on the east side of town as well, near Hawthorne Boulevard and Alberta Street and tucked away in myriad neighborhoods in between.

Restaurants are arranged first by neighborhood and then by type of cuisine served.

	WHAT IT COSTS				
	$$$$	$$$	$$	$	¢
RESTAURANTS	over $30	$20–$30	$15–$20	$10–$15	under $10

Restaurant prices are per person for a main course at dinner.

Downtown

American

$–$$$ ✕ **Jake's Grill.** Not to be confused with the Jake's of seafood fame, this eatery in the Governor Hotel has more turf than surf. Steaks and the Sunday brunch are popular draws. Private booths with green velvet curtains make for a cozy, intimate dinner. The bar is famous for its Bloody Marys. ⌧ *611 S.W. 10th Ave., Downtown* ☎ *503/220–1850* ▭ *AE, D, DC, MC, V.*

$–$$$ ✕ **Red Star Tavern & Roast House.** Cooked in a wood-burning oven, smoker, rotisserie, or grill, the cuisine at Red Star can best be described as American comfort food inspired by the bounty of the Pacific Northwest. Spit-roasted chicken, maple-fired baby-back ribs with a brown-ale glaze, charred salmon, and crayfish étouffée are some of the better entrées. The wine list includes regional and international vintages, and 12 microbrews are on tap. The spacious restaurant, in the 5th Avenue Suites Hotel, has tufted leather booths, murals, and copper accents. ⌧ *503 S.W. Alder St., Downtown* ☎ *503/222–0005* ▭ *AE, D, DC, MC, V.*

¢–$$ ✕ **Mother's Bistro.** The menu is loaded with home-style favorites—macaroni and cheese with extra ingredients of the day, soups, pierogi, chicken and dumplings, pot roast, and meat loaf. For vegetarians there's a couscous stew. The high ceilings in the well-lit dining room lend an air of spaciousness, but the tables are a bit close together. The bar is open late Friday and Saturday. ⌧ *409 S.W. 2nd Ave., Downtown* ☎ *503/464–1122* ▭ *AE, D, DC, MC, V* ☽ *Closed Mon.*

¢–$$ ✕ **Rock Bottom Brewing Co.** Some locals might balk at the idea of a corporate brewpub in a city that prides itself on its outstanding local microbrews, but this slightly upscale establishment manages to do just fine and serves some tasty dinner options, including burgers, pasta, and salads. With a full bar, pool upstairs, and rustic decor, there is plenty to please the after-work crowd. Brewery tours are available. ⌧ *210 S.W. Morrison St.* ☎ *503/796–2739* ▭ *AE, D, MC, V.*

Chinese

$–$$$ ✕ **Mandarin Cove.** One of Portland's best Chinese restaurants has Hunan- and Szechuan-style beef, chicken, pork, seafood, and vegetarian dishes. There are almost two dozen seafood choices. Try the sautéed scallops simmered in spicy tomato sauce. ⌧ *111 S.W. Columbia St.,* ☎ *503/222–0006* ▭ *AE, DC, MC, V* ☽ *No lunch Sun.*

Contemporary

$$–$$$$ ✕ **Portland City Grill.** On the 30th floor of the US Bank Tower, Portland City Grill has one of the best views in town. You can sit at a window-side table and enjoy the Portland skyline while eating fine steak and seafood with an Asian flair; it's no wonder that this restaurant, opened in 2002, has quickly become a favorite hot spot for the city's jet-set. The adjoining bar and lounge has comfortable arm chairs all along its win-

dowed walls, which are the first to get snatched up during the extremely popular happy hour each day. ⊠ *111 S.W. 5th Ave., Downtown* ☎ *503/450–0030* ⊟ *AE, D, DC, MC, V* ⊘ *No lunch weekends.*

$$–$$$
Fodor'sChoice
★

✕ **Higgins.** Chef Greg Higgins, former executive chef at the Heathman Hotel, focuses on ingredients from the Pacific Northwest and on organically grown herbs and produce while incorporating traditional French cooking styles and other international influences into his menu. Start with a salad of warm beets, asparagus, and artichokes or the country-style terrine of venison, chicken, and pork with dried sour cherries and a roasted-garlic mustard. Main courses change seasonally and might include dishes made with Alaskan spot prawns, halibut, duck, or pork loin. Vegetarian items are available. A bistro menu is available in the adjoining bar, where comfortable leather booths and tables provide an alternative to the main dining room. ⊠ *1239 S.W. Broadway, Downtown* ☎ *503/222–9070* ⊟ *AE, MC, V* ⊘ *No lunch weekends.*

★ **$–$$$**
✕ **The Heathman.** Chef Philippe Boulot revels in fresh ingredients of the Pacific Northwest. His menu changes with the season and includes entrées made with grilled and braised fish, fowl, veal, lamb, and beef. Among the chef's Northwest specialties are a delightful Dungeness crab, mango, and avocado salad and a seafood paella made with mussels, clams, shrimp, scallops, and chorizo. Equally creative choices are available for breakfast and lunch. The dining room, scented with wood smoke and adorned with Andy Warhol prints, is a favorite for special occasions. ⊠ *Heathman Hotel, 1001 S.W. Broadway, Downtown* ☎ *503/790–7752* ⊟ *AE, D, DC, MC, V.*

¢–$
✕ **Bijou Cafe.** This spacious, sunny, high-ceiling restaurant has some of the best breakfasts in town: French-style crepes and oyster hash are a few popular favorites, along with fabulous pancakes and French toast. Breakfast is served all day, and at lunch there are burgers, sandwiches, and soups, as well as delectable daily specials. ⊠ *132 S.W. 3rd Ave., Downtown* ☎ *503/222–3187* ⊟ *MC, V* ⊘ *No dinner.*

Continental

$$$–$$$$
✕ **London Grill.** The plush, dimly lit dining room in the historic Benson Hotel serves classic dishes made with fresh, seasonal local ingredients with an Asian influence. Try the salmon glazed with sake and ginger. With one of the longest wine lists around and a good chance of live harp or piano music, this a place to truly indulge. Breakfast is also available. ⊠ *309 S.W. Broadway* ☎ *503/295–4110* ⛪ *Jacket required* ⊟ *AE, D, DC, MC, V.*

French

★ **$$$$**
✕ **Couvron.** Understated elegance defines this crown jewel for contemporary French cuisine. Chef Anthony Demes prepares prix-fixe menus—vegetarian, seasonal, and grand—each of which includes an appetizer, lobster or vegetable soup, and signature dishes such as honey-glaze Oregon duck breast with curry and anise, and scallops with braised short ribs ravioli. The full-service wine pairings to match each course are a special treat. ⊠ *1126 S.W. 18th Ave., Downtown* ☎ *503/225–1844* ⊱ *Reservations essential* ⊟ *AE, MC, V* ⊘ *Closed Sun. and Mon. No lunch.*

Italian

$$–$$$
✕ **Alessandro's.** This cozy eatery turns out Roman-style Italian pastas and entrées made with seafood, poultry, and veal. Try the cioppino, or filetti Rossini, two fillet medallions with Portobello mushrooms and pancetta bacon, laced with a red wine sauce. ⊠ *301 S.W. Morrison St.,* ☎ *503/222–3900* ⊟ *AE, DC, MC, V* ⊘ *Closed Sun.*

¢–$$$
✕ **Pazzo.** The aromas of roasted garlic and wood smoke greet patrons of the bustling, street-level dining room of the Hotel Vintage Plaza. Pazzo's

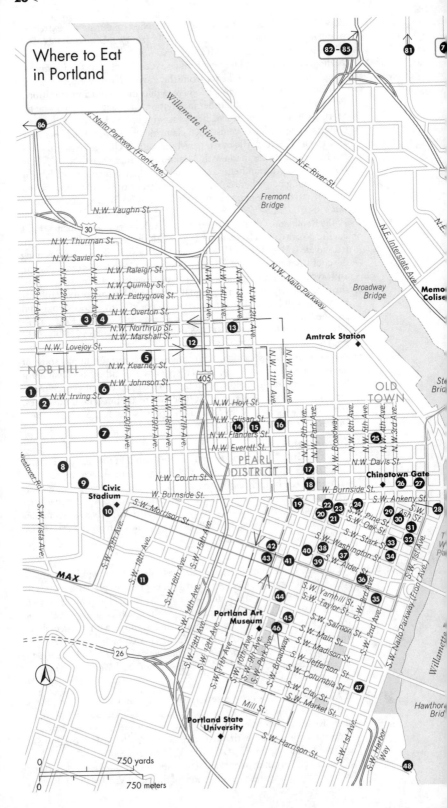

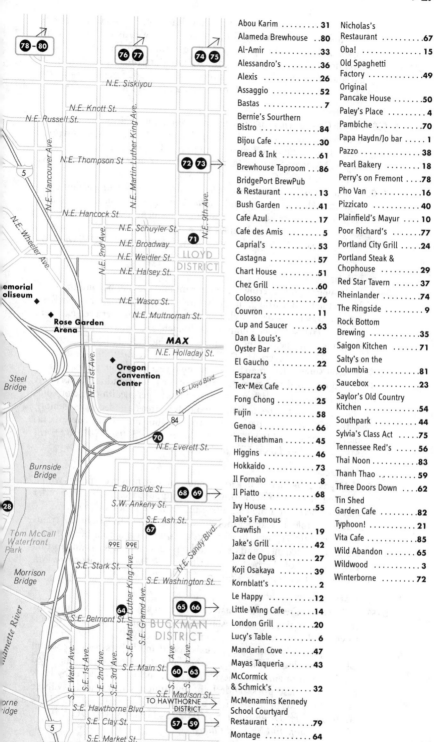

Abou Karim **31**
Alameda Brewhouse . . **80**
Al-Amir **33**
Alessandro's **36**
Alexis **26**
Assaggio **52**
Bastas **7**
Bernie's Sourthern
Bistro **84**
Bijou Cafe **30**
Bread & Ink **61**
Brewhouse Taproom . . . **86**
BridgePort BrewPub
& Restaurant **13**
Bush Garden **41**
Cafe Azul **17**
Cafe des Amis **5**
Caprial's **53**
Castagna **57**
Chart House **51**
Chez Grill **60**
Colosso **76**
Couvron **11**
Cup and Saucer **63**
Dan & Louis's
Oyster Bar **28**
El Gaucho **22**
Esparza's
Tex-Mex Cafe **69**
Fong Chong **25**
Fujin **58**
Genoa **66**
The Heathman **45**
Higgins **46**
Hokkaido **73**
Il Fornaio **8**
Il Piatto **68**
Ivy House **55**
Jake's Famous
Crawfish **19**
Jake's Grill **42**
Jazz de Opus **27**
Koji Osakaya **39**
Kornblatt's **2**
Le Happy **12**
Little Wing Cafe **14**
London Grill **20**
Lucy's Table **6**
Mandarin Cove **47**
Mayas Taqueria **43**
McCormick
& Schmick's **32**
McMenamins Kennedy
School Courtyard
Restaurant **79**
Montage **64**
Mother's Bistro **34**
Newport Bay at
RiverPlace **48**

Nicholas's
Restaurant **67**
Oba! **15**
Old Spaghetti
Factory **49**
Original
Pancake House **50**
Paley's Place **4**
Pambiche **70**
Papa Haydn/Jo bar **1**
Pazzo **38**
Pearl Bakery **18**
Perry's on Fremont . . . **78**
Pho Van **16**
Pizzicato **40**
Plainfield's Mayur **10**
Poor Richard's **77**
Portland City Grill **24**
Portland Steak &
Chophouse **29**
Red Star Tavern **37**
Rheinlander **74**
The Ringside **9**
Rock Bottom
Brewing **35**
Saigon Kitchen **71**
Salty's on the
Columbia **81**
Saucebox **23**
Saylor's Old Country
Kitchen **54**
Southpark **44**
Sylvia's Class Act **75**
Tennessee Red's **56**
Thai Noon **83**
Thanh Thao **59**
Three Doors Down . . . **62**
Tin Shed
Garden Cafe **82**
Typhoon! **21**
Vita Cafe **85**
Wild Abandon **65**
Wildwood **3**
Winterborne **72**

menu relies on deceptively simple new Italian cuisine—creative pastas, risottos, and grilled meats, fish, and poultry as well as antipasti and appetizers. All the baked goods are made in the Pazzoria Bakery & Cafe next door. The decor is a mix of dark wood, terra-cotta, and dangling garlands of garlic. Breakfast is served daily. ⊠ *627 S.W. Washington St., Downtown* ☎ *503/228–1515* ▤ *AE, D, DC, MC, V.*

Japanese

$–$$$ ✕ **Bush Garden.** This authentic Japanese restaurant, which opened in 1960, is known for its sashimi and sukiyaki but also offers traditional favorites such as udon noodles, bento, tempura, and teriyaki. There is karaoke singing Monday–Saturday. ⊠ *900 S.W. Morrison St.,* ☎ *503/226–7181* ▤ *AE, D, DC, MC, V* ☼ *No lunch Sun.*

¢–$ ✕ **Koji Osakaya.** Inside this little storefront, sushi and sashimi reign supreme. The *uni* (sea urchin), *hamachi* (yellowtail tuna), *saba* (mackerel), and *kasu* (cod) are all outstanding. The menu also includes teriyaki, tempura, and udon. Small tables and a sushi bar at the back fill the cozy, L-shape space. ⊠ *606 S.W. Broadway, Downtown* ☎ *503/294–1169* ▤ *AE, MC, V.*

Lebanese

$–$$ ✕ **Al-Amir.** Upon entering the restaurant and moving beyond the small bar in the front, through the elaborately large and ornate Middle Eastern gateway into a dark, stylish dining room, choose between excellent broiled kebabs, falafel, hummus, tabbouleh, and baba ghanouj. There's live music and belly dancing on the weekends. ⊠ *223 S.W. Stark St.,* ☎ *503/274–0010* ▤ *AE, D, DC, MC, V* ☼ *No lunch weekends.*

¢–$ ✕ **Abou Karim.** More than half the menu is vegetarian, but the leg of lamb served on a bed of rice with lentil soup or a full salad is a favorite. A special menu of meals low in saturated fats targets health-conscious diners. The laid-back restaurant's two dining areas are decorated simply, with white linen and dark wood. You can dine outside on sidewalk tables in summer. ⊠ *221 S.W. Pine St., Downtown* ☎ *503/223–5058* ▤ *AE, MC, V* ☼ *Closed Sun. No lunch Sat.*

Mexican

¢ ✕ **Mayas Taqueria.** Part of a local chain, this downtown outpost is within walking distance of many downtown shopping areas. Give your order cafeteria style, and then sit along the window inside or at one of the sidewalk tables in warmer months and watch the MAX light-rail trains and streetcars pass by. The delicious taco, with a generous heap of your choice of grilled meat and beans and served with fresh salsa and tortilla chips, is one of the best deals in town. ⊠ *1000 S.W. Morrison St., Downtown* ☎ *503/226–1946* ▤ *AE, D, DC, MC, V.*

Pan-Asian

$–$$ ✕ **Saucebox.** Creative pan-Asian cuisine and many creative cocktails draw the crowds to this popular restaurant and nightspot near the big downtown hotels. Inside the long and narrow space with closely spaced tables draped with white cloths, Alexis Rockman's impressive and colorful 24-foot painting *Evolution* spans the wall over your head, and mirrored walls meet your gaze at eye level. The menu includes Korean baby-back ribs, Vietnamese pork tenderloin, and Indonesian roasted Javanese salmon. An excellent late-night menu is served after 10 PM. ⊠ *214 S. W. Broadway, Downtown* ☎ *503/241–3393* ▤ *AE, DC, MC, V* ☼ *Closed Sun. and Mon. No lunch.*

Pizza

¢ ✕ **Pizzicato.** This local chain serves pies and slices topped by inventive combinations such as chanterelles, shiitakes, and Portobellos, or andouille sausage, shrimp, and smoked mozzarella. The menu includes large salads to share, antipasti, and panini. The restaurant interiors are clean, bright, and modern. Beer and wine are available. ⊠ *705 S.W. Alder St., Downtown* ☎ *503/226–1007* ⊠ *505 N.W. 23rd Ave., Nob Hill* ☎ *503/242–0023* ▭ *AE, D, DC, MC, V.*

Seafood

$–$$$ ✕ **Jake's Famous Crawfish.** Diners have been enjoying fresh Pacific Northwest seafood in Jake's warren of wood-panel dining rooms for more than a century. The back bar came around Cape Horn during the 1880s, and the chandeliers hanging from the high ceilings date from 1881. The restaurant gained a national reputation in 1920 when crawfish was added to the menu. White-coat waiters take your order from an almost endless sheet of daily seafood specials year-round, but try to come during crawfish season (May–September), when you can sample the tasty crustacean in pie, cooked Creole style, or in a Cajun-style stew over rice. ⊠ *401 S.W. 12th Ave., Downtown* ☎ *503/226–1419* ▭ *AE, D, DC, MC, V* ⊘ *No lunch weekends.*

$–$$$ ✕ **McCormick & Schmick's.** The seafood is flawless at this lively restaurant, where you can dine in a cozy, private wooden booth downstairs or upstairs overlooking the bar. Fresh Pacific Northwest oysters and Alaskan halibut are favorites; specialties include Dungeness crab cakes with roasted red-pepper sauce. A new menu is printed daily with a list of more than two dozen fresh seasonal choices. Oregon and California vineyards take center stage on the wine list. The popular bar has bargain happy-hour appetizers and a wide selection of top-shelf, single-malt scotches. ⊠ *235 S.W. 1st Ave., Downtown* ☎ *503/224–7522* ▭ *AE, D, DC, MC, V* ⊘ *No lunch Sun.*

$–$$$ ✕ **Newport Bay at RiverPlace.** When it comes to river, bridge, and city-skyline views, there's not a bad seat in this circular glass dining room, which floats on the Willamette River. The regional chain's menu includes seafood and chicken salads, seasonal specials, and creative seafood fare. The oven-roasted jumbo prawns are stuffed with crab, Brie, and roasted garlic and topped with béarnaise sauce. Upstairs, a comfortable lounge has a popular happy hour every day in the late afternoon and before closing. ⊠ *RiverPlace, 0425 S.W. Montgomery St., Downtown* ☎ *503/227–3474* ▭ *AE, D, DC, MC, V.*

$–$$ ✕ **Southpark Seafood Grill & Wine Bar.** Wood-fired seafood is served in this comfortable, art deco-tinged room with two bars. Chef Ronnie Mac-Quarrie's Mediterranean-influenced menu includes grilled grape-leaf-wrapped salmon with pomegranate and sherry glaze as well as tuna au poivre with mashed potatoes and red wine demi-glace. There's a wide selection of fresh Pacific Northwest oysters and fine regional wines available by the glass. Some of the desserts are baked to order. There is no smoking. ⊠ *901 S.W. Salmon St., Downtown* ☎ *503/326–1300* ▭ *AE, D, DC, MC, V.*

¢–$$ ✕ **Dan & Louis's Oyster Bar.** Oysters at this Portland landmark near the river come fried, stewed, or on the half shell. The clam chowder is tasty, but the crab stew is a rare treat. Combination dinners let you mix your fried favorites. The collection of steins, plates, and marine art has grown since the restaurant opened in 1907 to fill beams, nooks, crannies, and nearly every inch of wall. ⊠ *208 S.W. Ankeny St., Downtown* ☎ *503/227–5906* ▭ *AE, D, DC, MC, V.*

Steak

$$$–$$$$ ✕ **El Gaucho.** Three dimly lit dining rooms with blue walls and striped upholstery invite those with healthy pocketbooks. The specialty here is 28-day, dry-aged, certified Angus beef, but chops, ribs, and chicken entrées are also cooked in the open kitchen. The chateaubriand for two is carved tableside. Seafood lovers might want to try the tomato fennel bouillabaisse. Service is impeccable at this Seattle transplant in the elegant Benson Hotel. Each night live Latin guitar music serenades the dinner guests. ⊠ *319 S.W. Broadway, Downtown* ☎ *503/227–8794* ⊟ *AE, DC, MC, V* ☽ *No lunch.*

¢–$$$$ ✕ **Portland Steak & Chophouse.** Expensive cuts of steak and prime rib are the draw at this steak house in the Embassy Suites hotel. The menu includes wood-fired pizzas, pasta, and café meals. Surf lovers can choose the ahi chop, cioppino, or seafood linguine. Lunch is served until 4:30 weekdays, and brunch is served on weekends. The bar menu draws a loyal happy-hour crowd. ⊠ *121 S.W. 3rd Ave., Downtown* ☎ *503/223–6200* ⊟ *AE, D, MC, V.*

Thai

$–$$$ ✕ **Typhoon!** A Buddha statue with burning incense watches over diners at this popular restaurant in the Lucia Hotel. Come enjoy the excellent food in a large, modern dining room filled with colorful art and sleek red booths. The spicy chicken or shrimp with crispy basil, the curry and noodle dishes, and the vegetarian spring and salad rolls are standouts. If tea is your thing, 145 varieties are available, from $2 a pot to $55 for some of the world's rarest. ⊠ *400 S.W. Broadway, Downtown* ☎ *503/224–8285* ⊟ *AE, D, DC, MC, V.*

Pearl District & Old Town/Chinatown

American

$–$$$ ✕ **Jazz de Opus.** The draw here is live jazz, but this dark Old Town establishment, which centers on the bar and a small stage, also turns out decent seafood and prime rib. Panfried oysters and crab cakes are popular, and specialties include the jambalaya and the mesquite-grilled salmon Oscar, topped with fresh Dungeness crab and drizzled with béarnaise. ⊠ *33 N.W. 2nd Ave., Old Town* ☎ *503/222–6077* ⊟ *AE, MC, V* ☽ *No lunch.*

¢ ✕ **BridgePort BrewPub & Restaurant.** The hops- and ivy-covered, century-old industrial building seems out of place among its neighbors, but once inside you'll be clear about the business here: serving thick, hand-thrown pizza on sourdough crust to boisterous crowds, who wash it down with frothy pints of BridgePort's ale, brewed on the premises. The India Pale Ale is a specialty, but a treat for the indecisive is the seven glass sampler that might also include "Old Knucklehead," the brewery's barley wine–style ale. Handmade focaccia, sandwiches, including a tasty chicken almond salad sandwich, upscale pub snacks like figs marsala—baked figs with blue cheese—and salads are also available, and pizza is served by the pie, half pie, and the slice. In summer the flower-festooned loading dock is transformed into a beer garden. ⊠ *1313 N.W. Marshall St., Pearl District* ☎ *503/241–3612* ⊟ *MC, V.*

Cafés

¢–$$ ✕ **Little Wing Cafe.** In the heart of the Pearl District, the small and friendly Little Wing Cafe manages to be a refreshingly unpretentious place for simple lunches and elegant, quality dinners; evening entrées might include pork tenderloin with cherry sauce and apple-fennel relish or braised lamb shoulder with butternut-squash curry. Vegan and vegetarian dishes are available. ⊠ *529 N.W. 13th Ave., Pearl District* ☎ *503/228–3101* ⌕ *Reservations not accepted* ⊟ *AE, MC, V* ☽ *Closed Sun. No dinner Mon.*

¢ ✕ **Pearl Bakery.** A light breakfast or lunch can be had at this popular spot known for its excellent fresh breads, pastries, cakes, and sandwiches. The cakes, cookies, croissants, and Danish are some of the best in the city. ✉ *102 N.W. 9th Ave., Pearl District* ☎ *503/827–0910* ▭ *No credit cards* ⊘ *Closed Sun. No dinner.*

Chinese

¢–$ ✕ **Fong Chong.** Considered by some to be Chinatown's best Chinese restaurant, Fong Chong serves dim sum every day. The family-style eatery has dumplings filled with shrimp, pork, or vegetables, accompanied by plenty of different sauces. If you haven't eaten dim sum before, just take a seat: the food is brought to you on carts. Pick what you want as the food carts come by. The menu also lists traditional entrées. ✉ *301 N. W. 4th Ave., Chinatown* ☎ *503/220–0235* ▭ *MC, V.*

French

¢–$$ ✕ **Le Happy.** This tiny creperie just outside of the hubbub of the Pearl District can serve as a romantic dinner-date spot or just a cozy place to enjoy a drink and a snack. You can get sweet crepes with fruit, cheese, and cream or savory ones with meats and cheeses; in addition, the dinner menu is rounded out with steaks and salads. It's a classy joint, but not without a sense of humor: Le Trash Blanc is a bacon and cheddar crepe, served with a can of Pabst. ✉ *1011 N.W. 16th Ave., Pearl District* ☎ *503/226–1258* ⊘ *Closed Sun.*

Greek

$ ✕ **Alexis.** The Mediterranean furnishings here consist only of white walls and basic furnishings, but the authentic Greek flavor keeps the crowds coming for *kalamarakia* (deep-fried squid served with *tzatziki*, a yogurt dip), *horiatiki* (a Greek salad combination with feta cheese and kalamata olives), and other traditional dishes. If you have trouble making up your mind, the gigantic Alexis platter includes a little of everything. ✉ *215 W. Burnside St., Old Town* ☎ *503/224–8577* ▭ *AE, D, DC, MC, V* ⊘ *No lunch weekends.*

Latin

$–$$$ ✕ **Oba!** Many come to Oba! for the upscale bar scene, but this Pearl District salsa hangout also serves excellent Latin American cuisine, including coconut prawns, ahi tuna, roasted vegetable enchiladas and tamales, and other seafood, chicken, pork, and duck dishes. The bar is open late Friday and Saturday. ✉ *555 N.W. 12th Ave., Pearl District* ☎ *503/228–6161* ▭ *A, D, MC, V* ⊘ *No lunch.*

Mexican

$$–$$$ ✕ **Cafe Azul.** This busy restaurant retains the building's Pearl District industrial feel with a simple yet elegant brick-wall interior. The plates may seem pricey if you're accustomed to the other Mexican food offerings in the city, but these authentic and beautifully prepared dishes are nothing like most other Mexican food found nearby, and your palate won't be disappointed. Owner and chef Claire Archibald's menu includes innovative creations made with fish, chicken, lamb, beef, and pork. The complex sauces, such as the 28-ingredient Oaxacan mole, are spectacular. ✉ *112 N.W. 9th Ave., Pearl District* ☎ *503/525–4422* ▭ *D, MC, V* ⊘ *Closed Sun. and Mon. No lunch.*

Vietnamese

¢–$$ ✕ **Pho Van.** This spacious, minimalist restaurant is the newer and trendier of the two Pho Van locations in Portland—the other is on the far east side, on 82nd Avenue. A big bowl of pho noodle soup is delicious, enough to fill you up, and costs only $7 or $8. The friendly waitstaff will help you work your way through the menu and will make suggestions to give you the best sampling of Vietnamese cuisine. ✉ *1012 N.W. Glisan St., Pearl District* ☎ *503/248–2172* ▭ *MC, D, V* ⊘ *Closed Sun.* ✉ *1919 S.E. 82nd Ave.* ☎ *503/788–5244.*

Nob Hill & Vicinity

American

$$–$$$$ ✕ **The Ringside.** This Portland institution has been famous for its beef for more than 50 years. Dine in cozy booths on rib eye, prime rib, and New York strip, which come in regular- or king-size cuts. Seafood lovers will find plenty of choices: a Chilean platter with an 8-ounce lobster tail, Dungeness crab, oysters, jumbo prawns, and Oregon bay shrimp. The onion rings, made with Walla Walla sweets, are equally renowned. ⊠ *2165 N.W. Burnside St., close to Nob Hill* ☎ *503/223–1513* ▭ *AE, D, DC, MC, V* ☺ *No lunch.*

¢–$$$ ✕ **Papa Haydn/Jo Bar.** Many patrons come to this bistro just for the luscious desserts. Favorite dinner entrées include oven-roasted sea bass, fresh four-cheese ravioli, and pan-seared rib eye. Wood-fired, rotisserie-cooked meat, fish, and poultry dishes plus pasta and pizza are available next door at the jazzy **Jo Bar,** which also serves bar munchies and Sunday brunch (reservations essential). ⊠ *701 N.W. 23rd Ave., Nob Hill* ☎ *503/228–7317 Papa Haydn, 503/222–0048 Jo Bar* ▭ *AE, MC, V* ☺ *No dinner Sun.*

Contemporary

$$–$$$$ ✕ **Wildwood.** The busy center bar, stainless-steel open kitchen, and blond-wood chairs set the tone at this restaurant serving fresh Pacific Northwest cuisine. Chef Cory Schreiber's entrées include dishes made with lamb, pork loin, chicken, steak, and seafood. There's also a vegetarian selection. Wildwood also has a Sunday brunch and a family-style Sunday supper menu with selections for two or more people. ⊠ *1221 N.W. 21st Ave., Nob Hill* ☎ *503/248–9663* ▭ *AE, MC, V.*

$–$$$ ✕ **Lucy's Table.** Amid this corner bistro's regal purple and gold interior, chef Alex Pitts creates Northwest cuisine with a mix of Italian and French accents. The seasonal menu includes lamb, steak, pork, and seafood dishes. For dessert try the *boca negra,* chocolate cake with Frangelico whipped cream and cherries poached with port and walnut Florentine. Valet parking is available Wednesday–Saturday. ⊠ *706 N. W. 21st Ave., Nob Hill* ☎ *503/226–6126* ▭ *AE, MC, DC, V* ☺ *Closed Sun. No lunch.*

¢–$ ✕ **Brewhouse Taproom.** The copper beer-making equipment at the door tips you off to the specialty of the house—beer. The restaurant is part of a 27,000-square-foot MacTarnahan's brewery complex. Try the Mac-Tarnahan's fish-and-chips: the batter is made with the Brewhouse's signature ale. The haystack back ribs with garlic rosemary fries are popular. Asparagus-artichoke lasagne served with salad is a good vegetarian option. Eat it all on the patio overlooking the landscaped garden. ⊠ *2730 N.W. 31st Ave.,* ☎ *503/228–5269* ▭ *AE, MC, V.*

Delicatessen

¢ ✕ **Kornblatt's.** This kosher deli and bagel bakery evokes a 1950s diner. Thick sandwiches are made with fresh bread and lean fresh-cooked meats, and the tender home-smoked salmon and sablefish are simply mouthwatering. For breakfast try the poached eggs with spicy corned-beef hash. ⊠ *628 N.W. 23rd Ave., Nob Hill* ☎ *503/242–0055* ▭ *MC, V.*

French

$$–$$$ ✕ **Paley's Place.** This charming bistro serves French cuisine Pacific Northwest–style. Among the entrées are dishes with duck, New York steak, chicken, pork tenderloin, and halibut. A vegetarian selection is also available. There are two dining rooms and a classy bar. In warmer months there's outdoor seating on the front porch and back patio. ⊠ *1204 N.W. 21st Ave., Nob Hill* ☎ *503/243–2403* ▭ *AE, MC, V* ☺ *No lunch.*

Fodor'sChoice ★

$–$$$ ✕ **Cafe des Amis.** This established, romantic bistro in a small vine-covered brick building serves fine French provincial cuisine. The menu focuses on entrées with lamb, pork, beef, and duck. Seafood is limited primarily to the appetizer selections. French varieties dominate the wine list, which includes a dozen by the glass. ⊠ *1987 N.W. Kearney St., Nob Hill* ☎ *503/295–6487* ▭ *AE, MC, V* ⊙ *Closed Sun. No lunch.*

Indian

$$–$$$ ✕ **Plainfield's Mayur.** Portland's finest Indian cuisine is served in an elegant Victorian house. The tomato-coconut soup with fried curry leaves and the vegetarian and vegan dishes are highlights. Appetizers include the authentic Bombay *bhel* salad with tamarind dressing and the *dahi wadi* (crispy fried lentil croquettes in a spicy yogurt sauce). Meat and seafood specialties include lobster in brown onion sauce and tandoori chicken or lamb. ⊠ *852 S.W. 21st Ave., one block south of Burnside, close to Nob Hill* ☎ *503/223–2995* ▭ *AE, D, DC, MC, V* ⊙ *No lunch.*

Italian

$–$$$ ✕ **Il Fornaio.** This outpost of the San Francisco–based trattoria and bakery serves handmade pastas, pizzas, and sandwiches. For the first two weeks of every month, cuisine from a different region of Italy is highlighted in addition to the basic menu. Many dishes are cooked in a wood-burning pizza oven and rotisserie. An open kitchen, warm redbrick walls, and vines with baskets of grapes and garlic hanging from the ceiling contribute to the restaurant's festive and welcoming character. ⊠ *115 N.W. 22nd Ave.,* ☎ *503/248–9400* ▭ *AE, D, MC, V.*

$–$$ ✕ **Bastas.** In a funky converted Tastee-Freeze, this bistro serves dishes from all over Italy. The walls are painted with Italian earth tones, and a small side garden provides alfresco dining in good weather. The menu includes veal scaloppine, grilled chicken, lamb chops, and creative pasta dishes. ⊠ *410 N.W. 21st Ave., Nob Hill* ☎ *503/274–1572* ▭ *AE, MC, V* ⊙ *No lunch Sat.–Wed.*

East of the Willamette

American

¢–$$ ✕ **Poor Richard's.** With an old-fashioned menu of burgers, steak, fish-and-chips, and potpies, this home-style restaurant has stuck to the reliable, no-frills environment that has kept it in business since 1959. With comfortable booths, a large and casual dining room, and a smoking lounge, this is the place to go to if you've had enough of the hip, innovative menus that abound in the city and just want to find some comfort food. ⊠ *3907 N.E. Broadway, Hollywood District,* ☎ *503/288–5285* ▭ *AE, D, MC, V* ⊙ *No lunch Sat.*

American/Casual

¢–$$ ✕ **Alameda Brewhouse.** A spacious dining room and bar in a high-ceiling room with light wood and stainless steel gives this brewhouse a feeling of urban chic while still managing to remain friendly and casual. Many people come for the excellent microbrews made on premises, but the food must not be overlooked; this is no pub grub. With creative pasta dishes such as mushroom-artichoke linguine, salmon gyros, ahi tacos, and delicious burgers, it is clear that this restaurant has as much thought going into its menu and ingredients as it does into its brewing. ⊠ *4675 N.E. Fremont St., Alameda* ☎ *503/460–9025* ▭ *AE, MC, V.*

¢–$ ✕ **McMenamins Kennedy School Courtyard Restaurant.** Whether you are coming to the Kennedy School to stay overnight at the hotel, to watch a movie, or just to enjoy dinner and drinks, the Courtyard Restaurant can add to your evening. The huge restaurant, with additional outdoor seating in the courtyard, is a hopping place every night of the week, and you may have to wait for a table, but there is so much to do on the premises that it doesn't really matter. The food, ranging from burgers, salads, and pizzas to fish-and-chips, pasta, prime rib, and beef stew, can satisfy most any appetite. Several standard McMenamins microbrews are always available, in addition to seasonal specialty brews. ⊠ *5736 N.E. 33rd Ave., near Alberta District* ☎ *503/249–3983* ▤ *AE, D, DC, MC, V.*

Barbecue

¢–$ ✕ **Tennessee Red's.** The best barbecue is arguably found in raw, out-of-the-way places, and this spot fits the bill—a corner rib joint in a laid-back neighborhood. The portions, served with a choice of five sauces and corn bread, are more than generous. In addition to the requisite ribs and brisket, you can get chicken, sausage, and blackened catfish. All entrées come with a choice of two southern-style side dishes. ⊠ *2133 S. E. 11th Ave., near Ladd's Addition* ☎ *503/231–1710* ▤ *MC, V.*

Cafés

¢ ✕ **Cup and Saucer.** This casual diner-style restaurant is extremely popular with hip young locals and is always packed on the weekends, especially for breakfast and lunch. The long menu includes all-day-breakfast, quiches, burgers, sandwiches, soups, and salads, with plenty of vegetarian and vegan options. ⊠ *3566 S.E. Hawthorne Blvd., Hawthorne District* ☎ *503/236–6001* ⌨ *Reservations not accepted* ▤ *No credit cards.*

¢ ✕ **Tin Shed Garden Cafe.** This small restaurant has been a popular breakfast spot since opening in 2002, growing widely known for its shredded potato cakes, biscuits and gravy, sweet-potato cinnamon French toast, creative egg and tofu scrambles, and breakfast burritos. The lunch and dinner menu has creative items like a creamy artichoke sandwich, and a chicken sandwich with bacon, Gorgonzola and apple, in addition to burgers, salads, and soups. A comfortable outdoor patio doubles as a beer garden on warm spring and summer evenings, and the adjacent community garden rounds off the property with a peaceful sitting area. ⊠ *1438 N.E. Alberta St., Alberta District* ☎ *503/288–6966* ⌨ *Reservations not accepted* ▤ *MC, V* ☉ *Closed Tues. No dinner Sun. and Mon.*

Cajun/Creole

¢–$ ✕ **Montage.** Spicy Cajun is the jumping-off point for the chef at this sassy
Fodor'sChoice bistro under the Morrison Bridge on Portland's east side. Jambalayas,
★ blackened pork, chicken, and catfish, linguine, and old-fashioned macaroni dishes are served up from around noon until the wee hours in a spot that's loud, crowded, and casually hip. The wine list includes more than 100 varieties. ⊠ *301 S.E. Morrison St., between Martin Luther King Blvd. and Morrison Bridge* ☎ *503/234–1324* ⌨ *Reservations not accepted* ▤ *No credit cards* ☉ *No lunch weekends.*

Chinese

¢ ✕ **Fujin.** Although the place looks a bit tattered, this family-run neighborhood restaurant consistently serves good wok-cooked favorites at reasonable prices. The fried tofu dishes and sesame-crusted shrimp are tasty. ⊠ *3549 S.E. Hawthorne Blvd., Hawthorne District* ☎ *503/231–3753* ▤ *D, MC, V* ☉ *No lunch Sun.*

Contemporary

$$–$$$$ ✕ **Salty's on the Columbia.** Pacific Northwest salmon (choose blackened or grilled, a half or full pound) is what this comfortable restaurant overlooking the Columbia River is known for. Try the seafood pesto fettuccine with prawns, scallops, halibut, salmon, grape tomatoes, and pine nuts. The menu includes chicken and steak offerings. There is a heated, covered deck and an uncovered deck for open-air dining. ⊠ *3839 N.E. Marine Dr.,* ☎ *503/288–4444* ▤ *AE, D, DC, MC, V.*

$$$ ✕ **Castagna.** Enjoy the bouillabaisse or one of the inventive Mediterranean seafood entrées at this tranquil Hawthorne restaurant. The pan-seared scallops with mushrooms are the signature dish. Next door is the more casual **Cafe Castagna** (☎ 503/231–9959), a bistro and bar open nightly serving pizzas and other slightly less expensive, lighter fare. ✉ *1752 S. E. Hawthorne Blvd., Hawthorne District* ☎ *503/231–7373* ☐ *AE, MC, V* ☉ *Closed Sun. and Mon. No lunch.*

$$–$$$ ✕ **Caprial's.** PBS cooking-show star Caprial Pence serves Mediterranean-inspired creations at her bustling, brightly lit bistro with an open kitchen, full bar, and velvet armchairs. The dinner menu changes monthly and is limited to four or five choices, which have included pan-roasted salmon as well as smoked and grilled pork loin chop. The wine "wall" (you pick the bottle) has more than 200 varieties. ✉ *7015 S.E. Milwaukie Ave., Sellwood* ☎ *503/236–6457* ☐ *MC, V* ☉ *Closed Sun. and Mon.*

$–$$$ ✕ **Perry's on Fremont.** This diner, still famous for burgers, chicken pot-pies, and fish-and-chips, has gone a bit more upscale with the addition of pricier menu items such as steak and salmon. Eat outside on the large patio among the flowers, and don't pass up one of the desserts. ✉ *2401 N.E. Fremont St.* ☎ *503/287–3655* ☐ *AE, D, MC, V* ☉ *Closed Sun. No dinner Sat.*

$–$$ ✕ **Ivy House.** This restaurant combines the unlikely duo of an extremely kid-centric dining environment and carefully prepared, elegant entrées for the adults who accompany them. Grown-ups might gravitate toward the shiitake mushroom risotto with Portuguese goat cheese, or seared duck breast with oyster mushroom ragout, while the little ones will likely be itching to retire to one of two play areas. There is seating outside on the patio in the center of a blooming rose garden. ✉ *1605 S.E. Bybee Blvd.* ☎ *503/231–9528* ☐ *MC, V.*

¢–$$ ✕ **Bread and Ink.** The old-fashioned elegance will strike you as soon as you walk in, but the high-ceiling dining room, done in cream and forest green, is not trendy in any way, and it is partly this earnest no-frills dedication to quality food that has helped it gain its name as a neighborhood landmark. Breakfast is a specialty and might include brioche French toast and smoked fish. Lunch and dinner yield good choices, including burgers, poached salmon, and crab cakes. You can get the legendary blintzes at every meal. ✉ *3610 S.E. Hawthorne Blvd., Hawthorne District* ☎ *503/239–4756* ☐ *AE, D, MC, V.*

¢–$$ ✕ **Wild Abandon and the Red Velvet Lounge.** Inside this small, bohemian-looking building, chef Michael Cox creates an inventive Mediterranean-influenced menu that includes fresh seafood, pork, beef, and pasta entrées. Vegetarian selections might be ziti, panfried tofu, or polenta lasagna made with roasted eggplant, squash, and spinach. The popular Sunday brunch includes omelets, Benedict dishes, breakfast burritos, and sandwiches. ✉ *2411 S.E. Belmont St., near Hawthorne District* ☎ *503/232–4458* ☐ *AE, D, DC, MC, V* ☉ *Closed Tues. No lunch weekdays.*

Cuban

★ **¢–$** ✕ **Pambiche.** Locals know that you can drive by Pambiche any night of the week and find it packed. With traditional Cuban fare including plantains, roast port, mojitos, and Cuban espresso, it is no surprise why. If you have some time to wait for a table, you should stop by and make an evening of it at this hopping neighborhood hot spot. Don't miss out on the incredible dessert here; it is the sole reason why some people make the trip. ✉ *2811 N.E. Glisan St., near Laurelhurst* ☎ *503/233–0511* ☒ *Reservations not accepted* ☐ *MC, V.*

German

$–$$ ✕ **Rheinlander.** A strolling accordionist and singing servers entertain as patrons dine on authentic traditional German food, including sauerbraten, hasenpfeffer, schnitzel, sausage, and rotisserie chicken. **Gustav's**, the adjoining pub and grill, serves slightly less expensive entrées, including sausages, cabbage rolls, and German meatballs, in an equally festive, if slightly more raucous, environment. ⊠ *5035 N.E. Sandy Blvd.,* ☎ *503/288–5503* ▤ *AE, MC, V.*

Italian

★ **$$$$** ✕ **Genoa.** Widely regarded as the finest restaurant in Portland, Genoa serves a prix-fixe menu (seven courses on Friday and Saturday evenings, four courses on weekdays), focusing on authentic Italian cuisine, that changes every two weeks. In a space that evokes Tuscany, seating is limited to a few dozen diners, so service is excellent. Smoking is permitted in a separate sitting room. ⊠ *2822 S.E. Belmont St., near Hawthorne District* ☎ *503/238–1464* ⌚ *Reservations essential* ▤ *AE, D, DC, MC, V* ☟ *No lunch.*

★ **$$–$$$** ✕ **Three Doors Down.** Just half a block away from the busy shopping district around Hawthorne, this small Italian restaurant is known for quality Italian food, with exquisite seafood dishes, skillful pasta concoctions, and decadent desserts. Reservations aren't accepted, but the intimate restaurant's reputation brings people coming back again and again, even though they might have to wait on the sidewalk for close to an hour. ⊠ *1429 S.E. 37th Ave., Hawthorne District* ☎ *503/236–6886* ⌚ *Reservations not accepted* ▤ *A, D, DC, MC, V* ☟ *Closed Sun. and Mon. No lunch.*

$–$$ ✕ **Il Piatto.** On a quiet residential street, this laid-back trattoria and espresso house turns out inventive dishes and classic Italian favorites. A tasty sun-dried-tomato–pesto spread instead of butter accompanies the bread. Entrées include ahi tuna ravioli with roasted red peppers, capers, and dill in a lemon cream sauce with leeks. The vegetarian lasagna with grilled eggplant, zucchini, and yams is rich and satisfying. The extensive wine selection focuses on varieties from Tuscany. ⊠ *2348 Ankeny St., near Laurelhurst* ☎ *503/236–4997* ▤ *AE, MC, V* ☟ *No lunch Sat.–Mon.*

$–$$ ✕ **Sylvia's Class Act.** This combo restaurant–dinner theater offers multiple dining options: Dine in a private candlelit booth, family style, in a banquet-room setting, in the lounge away from the kids, or in the theater. The food is classic southern Italian. Try the spinach lasagne or fettuccine Ricardo, with strips of boneless chicken breast, zucchini, and onions tossed in an Alfredo sauce. ⊠ *5115 N.E. Sandy Blvd.,* ☎ *503/288–6828* ▤ *AE, D, DC, MC, V* ☟ *No lunch.*

$ ✕ **Assaggio.** In an age of canned music, it's pleasant to enter a restaurant and hear opera arias. But then, everything about this Sellwood trattoria is extraordinarily pleasant. Many dishes are available as family-style samplers, perfect for sharing. The pasta menu favors vegetarian entrées, but dishes made with chicken or pork sausages are served as well. An excellent wine cellar highlights Italian vintages. The interior, painted in a burnt-sienna shade and accented with classical architectural motifs, lovingly evokes Italy. ⊠ *7742 S.E. 13th Ave., Sellwood* ☎ *503/232–6151* ▤ *AE, D, MC, V* ☟ *Closed Sun. and Mon. No lunch.*

Japanese

¢–$ ✕ **Hokkaido.** The soothing sound of water flowing over a rock fountain into a pool with koi greets diners at this Zen-inspired restaurant with a sushi bar. It's better than many Asian restaurants between 42nd and 70th avenues. The large selection of sushi and sashimi is impeccably fresh. The menu includes teriyaki and tempura favorites as well as udon. ⊠ *6744 N.E. Sandy Blvd., near airport* ☎ *503/288–3731* ▤ *MC, V* ☟ *Closed Mon. No lunch Sun.*

Lebanese

★ ¢ ✕ **Nicholas' Restaurant.** In a small streetfront along an unimpressive stretch of Grand Avenue, this hidden gem serves some of the best Lebanese food in Portland, for prices that can't be beat. Everything from the fresh homemade pita to the hummus, falafel, baba ghanouj, and kebabs is delicious and comes in enormous portions. No alcohol is served here. ⊠ *318 S.E. Grand Ave., near Morrison Bridge* ☎ *503/235–5123* ⊟ *No credit cards.*

Mexican

¢–$ ✕ **Chez Grill.** Creative Mexican cuisine, including grilled mushroom fajitas, Baja grilled pork, prawn quesadillas, and lamb tacos, is prepared lovingly at this large, festive restaurant. The fun and unusual feel is created by the combination of disparate elements including exposed forest-green ceiling pipes, crystal chandeliers, sculpted metal handrails and doorways, and Mexican figurines. ⊠ *2229 S.E. Hawthorne Blvd., Hawthorne District* ☎ *503/239–4002* ⊟ *D, MC, V* ☉ *No lunch.*

Seafood

$$–$$$ ✕ **Winterborne.** French flourishes enliven seafood served at this intimate retreat. The baked or sautéed selections on the seasonal menu come with soup, fresh vegetables, and salad, which is served after the main course. Add reasonable prices and quality service, and a satisfying dining experience unfolds. ⊠ *3520 N.E. 42nd Ave., Beaumont* ☎ *503/249–8486* ⌁ *Reservations essential* ⊟ *AE, D, MC, V* ☉ *Closed Sun.–Tues. No lunch.*

Southern

$–$$$ ✕ **Bernie's Southern Bistro.** You definitely won't find finer soul food in Portland. At first glance, Bernie's may seem fairly expensive for the cuisine, but then, this food is in a different realm from that of your garden variety fried chicken. Restaurant specialties include crisp fried green tomatoes, crawfish, and catfish, in addition to delectable fried chicken, collard greens, and black-eyed peas. The inside of the restaurant is painted in warm oranges, and the outdoor patio is one of Portland's best. ⊠ *2904 N.E. Alberta St.* ☎ *503/282–9864* ⊟ *AE, D, MC, V* ☉ *Closed Sun. and Mon. No lunch.*

Southwestern

¢–$ ✕ **Esparza's Tex-Mex Cafe.** Be prepared for south-of-the-border craziness at this beloved local eatery. Wild West kitsch festoons the walls, but it isn't any wilder than some of the entrées that emerge from chef-owner Joe Esparza's kitchen. Look for such creations as lean smoked-sirloin tacos—Esparza's is renowned for its smoked meats—and, for the truly adventurous diner, ostrich enchiladas. ⊠ *2725 S.E. Ankeny St., at S.E. 28th Ave., near Laurelhurst* ☎ *503/234–7909* ⊟ *AE, D, MC, V* ☉ *Closed Sun. and Mon.*

Spanish

¢–$ ✕ **Colosso.** A dimly lit tapas bar and restaurant, Colosso is one of the most hip and romantic places to dine in northeast Portland. The best way to get the full experience of the place is to order a pitcher of sangria and split a few of the small tapas plates between you and your companions. In the evening the restaurant is usually crowded with folks drinking cocktails late into the night. ⊠ *1932 N.E. Broadway, Broadway District* ☎ *503/288–3333* ⊟ *MC, V* ☉ *No lunch.*

Steak

$–$$$ ✕ **Sayler's Old Country Kitchen.** Home of the massive 72-ounce steak (free if you can eat it in an hour), Sayler's complements its steak-focused menu with a few seafood and chicken dinners. With no pretense of being trendy or hip, this large family-style restaurant and lounge near Gresham has been around since 1946 and relies today on the same old-fashioned menu and quality it did back then. There's brunch on Sunday. ⊠ *10519 S.E. Stark St.,* ☎ *503/252–4171* ▭ *AE, D, MC, V* ☉ *No lunch.*

Thai

¢–$ ✕ **Thai Noon.** Opened in 2003 along the bustling stretch of Alberta's art and shopping district, Thai Noon is a popular spot that serves excellent traditional dishes including red, green, and yellow curry; stir fries; and noodle dishes in a simple, attractive dining room with only about 12 tables. You can choose the spiciness of your meal, but beware that although "medium" may be milder than "extra hot," it is still quite spicy. Try the fried banana split or the mango ice cream for dessert. ⊠ *2635 N.E. Alberta St., Alberta District* ☎ *503/282–2021* ▭ *MC, V.*

Vegetarian

¢ ✕ **Vita Cafe.** Vegan mac and cheese and vegetarian biscuits and gravy are but a few of the old favorites with a new spin. This trendy restaurant along Alberta Street has a large menu with American, Mexican, Asian, and Middle-Eastern-inspired entrées, and both herbivores and carnivores are sure to find something. There is plenty of free-range, organic meat to go around, in addition to the vegan and vegetarian options. Finish off your meal with a piece of decadent German chocolate cake or a peanut-butter fudge bar. ⊠ *3024 N.E. Alberta St., Alberta District* ☎ *503/335–8233* ▭ *No credit cards.*

Vietnamese

¢–$$ ✕ **Saigon Kitchen.** Consistently good Vietnamese-Thai food and friendly service have made this restaurant a citywide favorite. The interior is no-nonsense diner, but don't let that deter you. Huge portions of wok-cooked seafood, meat, and vegetable entrées join Thai coconut-milk soups and pad thai on the extensive menu. The healthy spring rolls (meat or tofu) served with peanut sauce are a must. ⊠ *835 N.E. Broadway, Lloyd District* ☎ *503/281–3669* ▭ *AE, D, MC, V.*

¢–$ ✕ **Thanh Thao.** This busy Asian diner in the heart of Portland's bohemian Hawthorne neighborhood has an extensive menu of Vietnamese stir-fries, noodles, soups, and Thai favorites. Be prepared to wait for *and* at your table: the place is almost always packed, and service is famously slow. But the food and generous portions are worth the wait. ⊠ *4005 S.E. Hawthorne Blvd., Hawthorne District* ☎ *503/238–6232* ▭ *D, MC, V.*

West of Downtown

American/Casual

¢–$ ✕ **Original Pancake House.** Not to be confused with any chain imitations, this pancake house is the real deal. Faithful customers have been coming for close to 50 years to wait for a table at this bustling, cabin-like local landmark, and you can expect to find a contented crowd of locals and tourists alike from the time the place opens at 7 AM until afternoon. With pancakes starting at $7, it's not the cheapest place to get a stack, but with 20 varieties and some of the best waffles and crepes around, it's worth the trip. ⊠ *8600 S.W. Barbur Blvd., Burlingame,* ☎ *503/246–9007* ▭ *No credit cards* ☉ *Closed Mon. and Tues. No dinner.*

Contemporary

$$–$$$ ✕ **Chart House.** On a hill high above the Willamette River, the Chart House has a stunning view of the city and the surrounding mountains from almost all of its tables. Prime rib is a specialty, but the seafood dishes, including coconut-crunchy shrimp deep-fried in tempura batter and the Cajun

spiced yellowfin ahi are just as tempting. ✉ *5700 S.W. Terwilliger Blvd.,* ☎ *503/246–6963* 🖃 *AE, D, DC, MC, V* ⊗ *No lunch weekends.*

Italian

¢–$ ✕ **Old Spaghetti Factory.** An old trolley car, oversize velvet chairs, dark wood, and fun antiques fill this huge restaurant overlooking the Willamette River. With a lounge upstairs, room for 500 diners, and a great view of the river, the flagship location of this nationwide restaurant chain is a great place for families, with basic pasta dishes and a kids' menu. ✉ *0715 S.W. Bancroft St.,* ☎ *503/222–5375* ⟳ *Reservations not accepted* 🖃 *AE, D, DC, MC, V.*

WHERE TO STAY

Many of the elegant hotels near the city center or on the riverfront appeal because of their proximity to the city's attractions. MAX light rail is within easy walking distance of most properties. Many downtown hotels cater to business travelers and offer special discounts on weekends. Additional accommodations clustered near the Convention Center and the airport are almost exclusively chain hotels and tend to be slightly less expensive than those found downtown. An alternative to the standard hotels in the city are the several beautiful B&Bs spread throughout residential neighborhoods in the northwest and northeast, where there are lovely homes, unique and luxurious guest rooms, deluxe home-cooked breakfasts, and friendly and knowledgeable innkeepers.

WHAT IT COSTS					
	$$$$	**$$$**	**$$**	**$**	**¢**
HOTELS	over $180	$140–$180	$100–$140	$60–$100	under $60

Hotel prices are for a standard double room, excluding room tax, which varies 6%–9½% depending on location.

Downtown

★ **$$$–$$$$** 🏨 **Governor Hotel.** With its mahogany walls and mural of Pacific Northwest Indians fishing in Celilo Falls, the clubby lobby of the distinctive Governor sets the overall tone for the hotel's 1920s Arts and Crafts style. Painted in soothing earth tones, the tastefully appointed guest rooms have large windows, honor bars, and bathrobes. Some have whirlpool tubs, fireplaces, and balconies. Jake's Grill is off the lobby, the streetcar runs right out front, and the hotel is one block from MAX. Guests may purchase a one-day pass to the adjoining independent health club for $8. ✉ *611 S.W. 10th Ave., Downtown, 97205* ☎ *503/224–3400 or 800/554–3456* 🖷 *503/241–2122* ⊕ *www.govhotel.com* ⇋ *68 rooms, 32 suites* ⟳ *Restaurant, room service, in-room data ports, minibars, video games, health club, bar, dry cleaning, laundry service, concierge, business services, meeting rooms, parking (fee), no-smoking rooms* 🖃 *AE, D, DC, MC, V.*

$$$–$$$$ 🏨 **Portland Marriott Downtown.** The large rooms at Marriott's 16-floor corporate-focused waterfront property are decorated in off-whites; the best ones face east with a view of the Willamette and the Cascades. All rooms have work desks, high-speed Internet access, and voice mail. Champions Lounge, filled with sports memorabilia, is a singles' hot spot on weekends. It's six blocks from MAX light rail. ✉ *1401 S.W. Naito Pkwy., Downtown, 97201* ☎ *503/226–7600 or 800/228–9290* 🖷 *503/221–1789* ⊕ *www.marriott.com* ⇋ *503 rooms, 6 suites* ⟳ *Restaurant, coffee shop, room service, in-room data ports, indoor pool, hot tub, health*

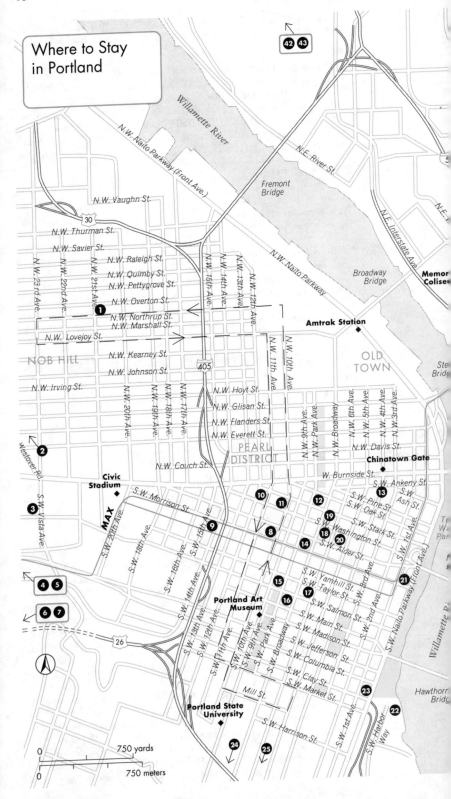

Where to Stay in Portland

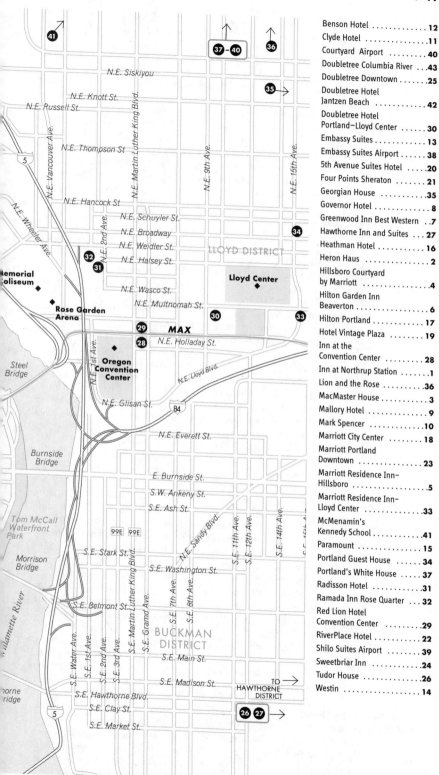

Benson Hotel **12**

Clyde Hotel **11**

Courtyard Airport **40**

Doubletree Columbia River . . **43**

Doubletree Downtown **25**

Doubletree Hotel
Jantzen Beach **42**

Doubletree Hotel
Portland–Lloyd Center **30**

Embassy Suites **13**

Embassy Suites Airport **38**

5th Avenue Suites Hotel **20**

Four Points Sheraton **21**

Georgian House **35**

Governor Hotel **8**

Greenwood Inn Best Western . . **7**

Hawthorne Inn and Suites . . . **27**

Heathman Hotel **16**

Heron Haus **2**

Hillsboro Courtyard
by Marriott **4**

Hilton Garden Inn
Beaverton **6**

Hilton Portland **17**

Hotel Vintage Plaza **19**

Inn at the
Convention Center **28**

Inn at Northrup Station **1**

Lion and the Rose **36**

MacMaster House **3**

Mallory Hotel **9**

Mark Spencer **10**

Marriott City Center **18**

Marriott Portland
Downtown **23**

Marriott Residence Inn–
Hillsboro **5**

Marriott Residence Inn–
Lloyd Center **33**

McMenamin's
Kennedy School **41**

Paramount **15**

Portland Guest House **34**

Portland's White House **37**

Radisson Hotel **31**

Ramada Inn Rose Quarter . . . **32**

Red Lion Hotel
Convention Center **29**

RiverPlace Hotel **22**

Shilo Suites Airport **39**

Sweetbriar Inn **24**

Tudor House **26**

Westin **14**

club, bar, shop, laundry facilities, dry cleaning, laundry service, concierge, business services, convention center, airport shuttle, meeting rooms, parking (fee), no-smoking rooms ⊟ *AE, D, DC, MC, V.*

★ **$$–$$$$** ⊞ **Benson Hotel.** Portland's grandest hotel was built in 1912. The hand-carved Russian Circassian walnut paneling and the Italian white-marble staircase are among the noteworthy design touches in the public areas. In the guest rooms expect to find small crystal chandeliers, inlaid mahogany doors, and the original ceilings. Extra touches include fully stocked private bars, bathrobes, and nightly turn-down service. ⊠ *309 S.W. Broadway, Downtown, 97205* ☎ *503/228–2000 or 800/549–9099* 🖶 *503/471–3920* ⊕ *www.bensonhotel.com* ⇄ *286 rooms* ⟁ *2 restaurants, coffee shop, room service, in-room data ports, minibars, cable TV with movies and video games, gym, bar, lobby lounge, laundry service, concierge, Internet, business services, meeting rooms, parking (fee)* ⊟ *AE, D, DC, MC, V.*

$$–$$$$ ⊞ **Paramount.** Inside this 15-story boutique-style property—two blocks from Pioneer Square, MAX, and the Portland Art Museum—earth tones, plush dark-wood furnishings, dried flowers, honor bars, and granite baths adorn the cozy rooms. Some have outdoor balconies and whirlpool tubs. The grand suites, which also have wet bars and gas fireplaces, have magnificent views of the city. ⊠ *808 S.W. Taylor St., Downtown, 97205* ☎ *503/223–9900* 🖶 *503/223–7900* ⊕ *www.paramounthotel.net* ⇄ *154 rooms* ⟁ *Restaurant, room service, in-room data ports, minibars, refrigerators, room TVs with video games, gym, dry cleaning, laundry service, business services, meeting rooms, concierge, parking (fee), no-smoking floors* ⊟ *AE, D, DC, MC, V.*

$$–$$$$ ⊞ **Westin.** Opened in 1999, this European-style boutique property combines luxury with convenience. Its tastefully appointed rooms include entertainment-center armoires, work desks, plush beds covered with layers of down, and granite bathrooms with separate showers and tubs. Pioneer Square and MAX are two blocks away. The Oritalia restaurant combines the best of Mediterranean and Asian cuisines. ⊠ *750 S.W. Alder St., Downtown, 97205* ☎ *503/294–9000 or 888/625–5144* 🖶 *503/241–9565* ⇄ *205 rooms* ⟁ *Restaurant, room service, in-room data ports, in-room safes, refrigerators, gym, bar, dry cleaning, laundry service, concierge, business services, meeting rooms, parking (fee)* ⊟ *AE, D, DC, MC, V.*

★ **$$$** ⊞ **5th Avenue Suites Hotel.** The 1912 Lipman Wolfe Department Store reopened as this boutique hotel in 1997. A tall vestibule with a marble mosaic floor leads to the art-filled lobby, where guests gather by the fireplace for an early-evening glass of wine or a cup of coffee. Warm fall colors, stripes, and floral prints adorn the 10-story property's 550-square-foot suites, divided by curtained sliding doors. Upholstered chairs, fringed ottomans, and other appointments in the sitting areas will make you feel right at home (or wish you had one like this). The large bathrooms are stocked with every amenity, including samplers of Aveda products—a nod to the Aveda Lifestyle Spa at the hotel. ⊠ *506 S.W. Washington St., Downtown, 97205* ☎ *503/222–0001 or 888/207–2201* 🖶 *503/222–0004* ⊕ *www.5thavenuesuites.com* ⇄ *82 rooms, 137 suites* ⟁ *Restaurant, room service, in-room data ports, minibars, room TVs with movies and video games, health club, massage, dry cleaning, laundry service, business services, meeting rooms, parking (fee), some pets allowed, no-smoking rooms* ⊟ *AE, D, DC, MC, V.*

$$$ ⊞ **Heathman Hotel.** Superior service, a renowned restaurant, a central downtown location (adjoining the Performing Arts Center), and swank public areas have earned the Heathman its reputation for quality. From the teak-panel lobby hung with Warhol prints to the rosewood elevators and marble fireplaces, this hotel exudes refinement. The earth-tone guest rooms are luxuriously comfortable, and the bathrooms have

Fodor's Choice
★

plenty of marble and mirrors. The second-floor mezzanine, with a small art gallery with works changing every several weeks and a small library (primarily filled with the works of notable Heathman guests), overlooks the high-ceiling Tea Court, a popular gathering spot in the evening. ⊠ *1009 S.W. Broadway, Downtown, 97205* ☎ *503/241–4100 or 800/ 551–0011* 🖷 *503/790–7110* ⊕ *www.heathmanhotel.com* ➲ *117 rooms, 33 suites* ⚖ *Restaurant, room service, in-room data ports, minibars, gym, bar, library, dry cleaning, laundry service, concierge, Internet, meeting rooms, parking (fee), no-smoking floors* ⊟ *AE, D, DC, MC, V.*

$$$ 🏨 **Hilton Portland.** Built in 1963, the Hilton became Oregon's largest hotel in 2002 when it opened its Executive Tower across the street, at the corner of 6th and Taylor. Together, the two buildings comprise a gargantuan complex of luxuriously contemporary bedrooms, meeting rooms, restaurants, and athletic facilities, including two indoor swimming pools. The property is within walking distance of the Performing Arts Center, Pioneer Courthouse Square, the Portland Art Museum, and MAX light rail. Alexander's restaurant offers a fantastic view of the Portland area from the 23rd floor. More than 60 restaurants are within a few blocks. ⊠ *921 S.W. 6th Ave., Downtown, 97204* ☎ *503/226– 1611 or 800/445–8667* 🖷 *503/220–2565* ⊕ *www.hilton.com* ➲ *773 rooms, 9 suites* ⚖ *3 restaurants, in-room data ports, room TVs with movies and video games, 2 indoor pools, gym, hot tub, massage, sauna, steam room, 2 bars, shop, Internet, business services, convention center, parking (fee), no-smoking rooms* ⊟ *AE, D, DC, MC, V.*

$$$ 🏨 **RiverPlace Hotel.** With its bright rooms, wing chairs, teak tables, and feather pillows, this hotel evokes a European setting, complete with landscaped courtyard. It has one of the best views in Portland, overlooking the river, the marina, and skyline. ⊠ *1510 S.W. Harbor Way, Downtown, 97201* ☎ *503/228–3233 or 800/227–1333* 🖷 *503/295–6161* ⊕ *www.riverplacehotel.com* ➲ *39 rooms, 45 suites* ⚖ *Restaurant, room service, in-room data ports, minibars, hot tub, sauna, concierge, business services, meeting rooms, parking (fee), no-smoking rooms* ⊟ *AE, D, DC, MC, V* ⦾| *CP.*

$$–$$$ 🏨 **Embassy Suites.** The grand lobby welcomes you at this Old Town property in the historic Multnomah Hotel building. The spacious accommodations in the all-suites property have large windows, sofa beds, and wet bars and come with terry bathrobes. The basement-level pool and exercise area is a special treat. A complimentary van will take you anywhere within a 2-mi radius. A full breakfast, cooked to order, and happy-hour cocktails are included in the room rate. The riverfront and MAX light rail are within walking distance. ⊠ *319 S.W. Pine St., Downtown, 97204* ☎ *503/279–9000 or 800/362–2779* 🖷 *503/497–9051* ⊕ *www.embassysuites.com* ➲ *276 suites* ⚖ *Restaurant, in-room data ports, microwaves, refrigerators, indoor pool, gym, hot tub, spa, steam room, bar, laundry service, concierge, business services, meeting room, parking (fee)* ⊟ *AE, D, DC, MC, V* ⦾| *BP.*

$$–$$$ 🏨 **Four Points Sheraton.** If you're concerned about location, consider this five-story hotel on the MAX light-rail line. Starwood Hotels converted the former Riverside into this boutique hotel in 1999. Some of the rooms have balconies; east-facing rooms offer views of the Willamette River and the Governor Tom McCall Waterfront Park. Guests have privileges at Bally's Total Fitness nearby. ⊠ *50 S.W. Morrison St., Downtown, 97204* ☎ *503/221–0711 or 800/899–0247* 🖷 *503/484–1417* ⊕ *www.fourpointsportlaned.com* ➲ *140 rooms* ⚖ *Restaurant, room service, room TVs with movies and video games, bar, dry cleaning, laundry service, business services, meeting rooms, parking (fee), some pets allowed, no-smoking floors* ⊟ *AE, D, DC, MC, V.*

$$–$$$ 🏨 **Hotel Vintage Plaza.** This historic landmark takes its theme from the area's vineyards. Guests can fall asleep counting stars in top-floor rooms, where skylights and wall-to-wall conservatory-style windows rate highly among the special details. Hospitality suites have extra-large rooms with a full living area, and the deluxe rooms have a bar. All are appointed in warm colors and have cherrywood furnishings; some rooms have hot tubs. Complimentary wine is served in the evening, and an extensive collection of Oregon vintages is displayed in the tasting room. Two-story town house suites are named after local wineries. ⊠ *422 S.W. Broadway, Downtown, 97205* ☎ *503/228–1212 or 800/243–0555* 🖷 *503/228–3598* ⊕ *www.vintageplaza.com* ⬦ *107 rooms, 21 suites* ♿ *Restaurant, room service, in-room data ports, minibars, gym, bar, concierge, business services, meeting room, parking (fee)* ⊟ *AE, D, DC, MC, V.*

$$–$$$ 🏨 **Mallory Hotel.** The years have been kind to this 1920s-vintage hotel eight blocks from the downtown core. Its gilt-ceiling lobby has fresh white paint and floral carpeting; crystal chandeliers and a leaded-glass skylight hark back to a more genteel era. The rooms are old-fashioned but clean and cheerful and have been refurbished; corner suites and rooms on the east side of the building have impressive skyline views. The hotel is a favorite with visiting singers, writers, and artists of every stripe. The staff is friendly and knowledgeable. ⊠ *729 S.W. 15th Ave., Downtown, 97205* ☎ *503/223–6311 or 800/228–8657* 🖷 *503/223–0522* ⊕ *www.malloryhotel.com* ⬦ *130 rooms* ♿ *Restaurant, in-room data ports, refrigerators, bar, free parking, some pets allowed (fee), no-smoking rooms* ⊟ *AE, D, DC, MC, V* ⊚ *CP.*

$$–$$$ 🏨 **Marriott City Center.** The lobby of this 20-story boutique property, in the heart of the downtown arts and dining area, is accented with a grand staircase, maple paneling, and marble floors. The plush rooms have voice mail, large work desks, and coffeemakers. The MAX light rail is two blocks away. ⊠ *520 S.W. Broadway, Downtown, 97205* ☎ *503/226–6300 or 800/228–9290* 🖷 *503/227–7515* ⊕ *www.marriott.com* ⬦ *249 rooms, 10 suites* ♿ *Restaurant, room service, in-room data ports, gym, hot tub, bar, laundry service, concierge, business services, meeting rooms, parking (fee)* ⊟ *AE, D, DC, MC, V.*

$–$$$ 🏨 **Clyde Hotel.** Built in 1902, this historic building has been restored to its original design. Today it operates as a limited-service historic hotel. Rooms have claw-foot tubs, and there are a few romantic suites. Don't expect all the amenities of the other downtown hotels here; the focus is on the historic charm, not luxury. Several shared-bath rooms are also available for slightly lower rates. ⊠ *1022 S.W. Stark St., 97205* ☎ *503/224–8000* 🖷 *503/224–9999* ⬦ *36 rooms* ♿ *Cable TV; no room phones* ⊟ *AE, D, MC, V* ⊚ *CP.*

$$ 🏨 **Doubletree Downtown.** Close to Portland State University and Oregon Health Sciences University, this hotel provides extremely comfortable and spacious accommodations for less money than many other downtown hotels. Close to the waterfront, it is in a convenient spot for walking to most downtown destinations. ⊠ *310 S.W. Lincoln, 97201* ☎ *503/221–0450* 🖷 *503/225–4303* ⊕ *www.doubletree.com* ⬦ *235 rooms* ♿ *Restaurant, in-room data ports, cable TV, pool, gym, laundry facilities, meeting rooms, parking (fee)* ⊟ *AE, D, DC, MC, V.*

$–$$ 🏨 **Mark Spencer.** Near Portland's gay bar district and Powell's City of Books, the Mark Spencer has one of the best values in town. The rooms are clean and comfortable, and all have full kitchens. Other amenities include free high-speed wireless Internet and a rooftop garden deck open to all guests. The hotels bills itself as a major supporter of the arts in the area and has acted as housing sponsor for the America Repertory Theatre, Portland Opera, and Center Stage. Special room-rate packages are available that include theater tickets to local performances. ⊠ *409*

S.W. 11th Ave., 97205 ☎ 503/224–3293 or 800/548–3934 🖷 503/
223–7848 ⊕ www.markspencer.com 🖙 101 rooms ⌂ In-room data
ports, kitchens, cable TV, laundry facilities, dry cleaning, meeting rooms,
some pets allowed (fee) ▭ AE, D, DC, MC, V ⊙ CP.

East of the Willamette

$$–$$$ 🏨 **Doubletree Hotel Portland—Lloyd Center.** This busy and business-ori-
ented hotel maintains a huge traffic in meetings and special events. The
public areas are a tasteful mix of marble, rose-and-green carpet, and an-
tique-style furnishings. The large rooms, many with balconies, have views
of the mountains or the city center. Lloyd Center and the MAX light-
rail line are across the street; the Oregon Convention Center is a five-
minute walk away. ⊠ 1000 N.E. Multnomah St., Lloyd District, 97232
☎ 503/281–6111 or 800/222–8733 🖷 503/284–8553 ⊕ www.doubletree.
com 🖙 476 rooms ⌂ 2 restaurants, coffee shop, room service, in-room
data ports, pool, gym, bar, dry cleaning, laundry service, concierge, business services, meeting rooms, parking (fee) ▭ AE, D, DC, MC, V.

★ $$–$$$ 🏨 **Portland's White House.** Hardwood floors with Oriental rugs, chan-
deliers, antiques, and fountains create a warm and romantic mood at
this elegant bed-and-breakfast inn in a Greek Revival mansion in the
historic Irvington District. The mansion, built in 1911 and on the National Register of Historic Landmarks, was remodeled in 1997. Rooms
have private baths and mahogany canopy or four-poster queen- and king-
size beds. The Garden Room overlooks a courtyard from its own portico. A full breakfast is included in the room rate, and the owners offer
vegetarian or low-fat options. Smoking and pets are not permitted.
⊠ 1914 N.E. 22nd Ave., Irvington, 97212 ☎ 503/287–7131 or 800/
272–7131 🖷 503/249–1641 ⊕ www.portlandswhitehouse.com 🖙 9
suites ⌂ Dining room, in-room data ports, library, free parking; no smoking ▭ AE, D, MC, V ⊙ BP.

$$ 🏨 **Lion and the Rose.** This 1906 Queen Anne–style mansion is one of Port-
FodorśChoice land's premier B&Bs and the city's only Victorian one. Oak and ma-
★ hogany floors, original light fixtures, antique silver, and the coffered
dining-room ceiling set a tone of formal elegance, while the wonderfully
friendly, accommodating, and knowledgeable innkeepers make sure
that you feel perfectly at home. A two-course breakfast and evening snacks
are served daily, and afternoon tea is available upon request. In a beau-
tiful residential neighborhood, you are just a block from the shops and
restaurants that fill northeast Broadway and within an easy walk of a
free MAX ride downtown. ⊠ 1810 N.E. 15th Ave., 97212 ☎ 503/287–
9245 or 800/955–1644 🖷 503/287–9247 ⊕ www.lionrose.com 🖙 6
rooms ⌂ In-room data ports, in-room VCRs, business services, free park-
ing; no kids under 7, no smoking ▭ AE, D, MC, V.

$$ 🏨 **Marriott Residence Inn—Lloyd Center.** With large, fully equipped suites
and a short walk both to the Lloyd Center and a MAX stop within Fare-
less Square, this three-level apartment-style complex is perfect for extended-
stay visitors or for tourists. Rooms come equipped with full kitchens and
ample seating space, and many have wood-burning fireplaces. There's a
large complimentary breakfast buffet each morning, and an hors d'oeuvres reception on weekday evenings. ⊠ 1710 N.E. Multnomah St., Lloyd
District, 97232 ☎ 503/288–1400 or 800/331–3131 🖷 503/288–0241
⊕ www.residenceinnportland.com 🖙 168 rooms ⌂ In-room data ports,
kitchens, microwaves, pool, outdoor hot tub, basketball, volleyball,
lobby lounge, laundry facilities, meeting rooms, business services, free
parking, some pets allowed (fee), no-smoking rooms ⊙ BP.

$$ 🏨 **Radisson Hotel.** This sleek, modern hotel is very close to the Rose Quar-
ter, the Coliseum, and the Convention Center and is within easy walk-

ing distance of Lloyd Center, the MAX line, and the Broadway Bridge leading to downtown. Between its attractive rooms and its ample facilities, it provides a reliable and convenient option for both business travelers and tourists. ⊠ *1441 N.E. 2nd Ave., 97232* ☎ *503/233–2401* 🖷 *503/238–7016* ⊕ *www.radisson.com* ⊃ *238 rooms* ⚐ *Restaurant, in-room data ports, cable TV, pool, gym, bar, business services, meeting rooms* ▭ *AE, D, DC, MC, V.*

$-$$ 🖾 **Georgian House.** This redbrick Georgian Colonial–style house with neoclassical columns is on a quiet, tree-lined street in the Irvington neighborhood. The gardens in back can be enjoyed from a solarium and from a vine-canopied deck and gazebo. The largest and sunniest of the guest rooms is the Lovejoy Suite, with a tile fireplace and brass canopy bed. ⊠ *1828 N.E. Siskiyou St., 97212* ☎ *503/281–2250 or 888/282–2250* 🖷 *503/281–3301* ⊕ *www.thegeorgianhouse.com* ⊃ *3 rooms, 2 with shared bath; 1 suite* ⚐ *No room phones, no TV in some rooms, no smoking* ▭ *MC, V* ⊙ *BP.*

$-$$ 🖾 **Inn at the Convention Center.** In 2002 this old Best Western changed hands and is now an independently run hotel with many of the same features. Directly across the street from the Convention Center, four blocks from Lloyd Center, and right along the MAX line, this no-frills hotel offers convenience as its main asset. Many of the simple and comfortable rooms at the six-story facility have refrigerators and/or minibars. ⊠ *420 N.E. Holladay St., Lloyd District/Convention Center, 97232* ☎ *503/233–6331* 🖷 *503/233–2677* ⊃ *97 rooms* ⚐ *Some minibars, some refrigerators, dry cleaning, laundry facilities, laundry service, free parking, no-smoking rooms* ▭ *AE, D, DC, MC, V.*

★ $-$$ 🖾 **McMenamins Kennedy School.** In a renovated elementary school in northeast Portland, the Kennedy School may well be one of the most unusual hotels you'll ever encounter. With all of the guest rooms occupying former classrooms, complete with the original chalkboards and cloakrooms, and with small bars known as Detention Bar (with cigars and the only television on site) and Honors Bar (with classical music and cocktails), the McMenamins brothers have created a multi-use facility that is both luxurious and fantastical. Room rates include breakfast for two, movie admission, and use of the outdoor soaking pool. ⊠ *5736 N.E. 33rd Ave., near Alberta District, 97211* ☎ *503/249–3983* ⊕ *www. kennedyschool.com* ⊃ *35 rooms* ⚐ *Restaurant, in-room data ports, outdoor hot tub, 4 bars, cinema, shop, meeting rooms, free parking; no room TVs, no smoking* ▭ *AE, D, DC, MC, V* ⊙ *BP.*

$-$$ 🖾 **Portland Guest House.** Inside a northeast Portland working-class Victorian home with a dusty-heather exterior paint job, this cozy B&B near the Lloyd Center contains rooms with antique walnut furniture, original Pacific Northwest artwork, and phones. The rates include a full breakfast. No smoking is permitted. ⊠ *1720 N.E. 15th St., Irvington, 97212* ☎ *503/282–1402* ⊕ *www.teleport.com/~pgh* ⊃ *7 rooms, 5 with bath* ⚐ *Free parking; no smoking* ▭ *AE, DC, MC, V* ⊙ *BP.*

$-$$ 🖾 **Red Lion Hotel Convention Center.** Across the street from the Convention Center and adjacent to the MAX, this hotel is as convenient as can be for both business travelers and tourists. Though a hotel has occupied this spot for quite some time, it became a Red Lion only in 2003, and the rooms and facilities were renovated during the transition. It provides a few more on-site amenities than some of the other hotels right by the Convention Center (Shilo Inn and Inn at the Convention Center are right across the street), which is reflected in its slightly higher rates. ⊠ *1021 N.E. Grand Ave., 97232* ☎ *503/235–2100 or 800/733–5466* 🖷 *503/238–0132* ⊕ *www.redlion.com* ⊃ *174 rooms* ⚐ *Restaurant, room service, in-room data ports, refrigerators, cable TV with movies and video games, gym, lounge, meeting rooms, business services, parking (fee).*

$–$$ ⊡ **Tudor House.** This 5,400-square-foot bed-and-breakfast, on extensive grounds with laurel bushes, hawthorne trees, and azaleas, resembles a Tudor manor. Antiques crowd the guest rooms and dining room, where breakfast is served. ⊠ *2321 N.E. 28th Ave., 97212* ☎ *503/287-9476* 🖷 *503/288-8363* ⊕ *www.tudor-house.com* ⇗ *3 double rooms, 1 suite* ⌕ *Cable TV; no smoking* ▤ *AE, D, MC, V* |◉| *BP.*

$ ⊡ **Ramada Inn Rose Quarter.** Remodeled in 1999, rooms at this Ramada have pastel walls, floral-print bedspreads, and mauve drapes. You're also only two blocks from the Rose Garden arena, Memorial Coliseum, the Oregon Convention Center, and MAX light rail. The Mucho Grande Restaurant and Lounge, adjoining the hotel, claims to be "Home of the World's Largest Margarita." ⊠ *10 N.E. Weidler St., Rose Quarter, 97227* ☎ *503/287-9900* 🖷 *503/287-3500* ⊕ *www.ramada.com* ⇗ *180 rooms* ⌕ *Restaurant, room service, in-room data ports, indoor pool, bar, dry cleaning, laundry service, business services, free parking, no-smoking floors* ▤ *AE, D, DC, MC, V.*

West of Downtown

$$–$$$$ ⊡ **Heron Haus.** This lovely, bright B&B is inside a stately, 100-year-old three-floor Tudor-style mansion near Forest Park. Special features include a tulip-shape bathtub in one room and a tile, seven-head antique shower in another. You can enjoy a relaxing afternoon in the secluded sitting garden. All rooms have phones, work desks, and fireplaces. Breakfast, included in the room rate, is a fancy Continental affair. ⊠ *2545 N.W. Westover Rd., Nob Hill, 97210* ☎ *503/274-1846* 🖷 *503/248-4055* ⊕ *www.heronhaus.com* ⇗ *6 rooms* ⌕ *In-room data ports, library, business services, free parking; no smoking* ▤ *MC, V* |◉| *CP.*

★ **$–$$$**   ⊡ **Inn @ Northrup Station.** Bright colors, original artwork, retro designs, and extremely luxurious suites fill this hotel in Nob Hill. Just moments from the shopping and dining on Northwest 21st Avenue, the inn looks like a stylish apartment building from the outside, with patios or balconies adjoining most of the suites, and a garden terrace for all guests to use. The striking colors and bold patterns found on bedspreads, armchairs, pillows, and throughout the halls and lobby manage to be charming, elegant, and fun, never falling into the kitschiness that plagues many places that strive for "retro" decor. All rooms have full kitchens, two TVs, three phones, and large sitting areas. ⊠ *2025 N.W. Northrup St., Nob Hill, 97209* ☎ *503/224-0543 or 800/224-1180* 🖷 *503/273-2102* ⊕ *www.northrupstation.com* ⇗ *70 suites* ⌕ *In-room data ports, kitchens, room TVs with movies and video games, free parking; no smoking* ▤ *AE, D, DC, MC, V* |◉| *CP.*

$$ ⊡ **Hilton Garden Inn Beaverton.** This four-level Hilton in suburban Beaverton brings a much-needed lodging option to Portland's west side. The property offers bright rooms with plush carpeting, work desks, and microwaves. It's right off U.S. 26. ⊠ *15520 N.W. Gateway Ct., Beaverton, 97006* ☎ *503/439-1717 or 800/445-8667* 🖷 *503/439-1818* ⊕ *www.hilton.com* ⇗ *150 rooms* ⌕ *Restaurant, room service, in-room data ports, microwaves, refrigerators, cable TV with movies, indoor pool, hot tub, exercise equipment, bar, business services, meeting rooms, free parking, no-smoking rooms* ▤ *AE, D, DC, MC, V.*

★ **$$**   ⊡ **MacMaster House.** On King's Hill, next to Washington Park's Japanese and rose gardens, this 17-room Colonial Revival mansion built in the 1890s is comfortable, funky, and fascinating. A hybrid assortment of Victorian furniture and antiques fills the parlors, and the guest rooms on the second and third floors are charming without being too cute. The two suites with large, private, old-fashioned baths are the ones to choose, especially the spacious Artist's Studio, tucked garretlike under the dormers, with a high brass bed and fireplace. A two-night minimum stay is required on the weekends. ⊠ *1041 S.W. Vista Ave., Washington Park area, 97205* ☎ *503/223–7362 or 800/774–9523* 🖶 *503/224–8808* ⊕ *www.macmaster.com* ⟳ *5 rooms with shared bath, 2 suites* 🗇 *Cable TV, free parking* ⊟ *AE, D, DC, MC, V* ⍟ *BP.*

$$ 🏨 **Marriott Residence Inn Hillsboro.** Near the west side's many high-tech offices and fabrication plants, this all-suites motel is popular with people relocating to Portland and perfect for extended stays. It's within walking distance of several restaurants, a shopping center, and a multiplex theater. The homey suites, some with fireplaces, have full kitchens. ⊠ *18855 N.W. Tanasbourne Dr., Hillsboro 97124* ☎ *503/531–3200 or 800/331–3131* 🖶 *503/645–1581* ⊕ *www.marriott.com* ⟳ *122 suites* 🗇 *In-room data ports, kitchens, cable TV, in-room VCRs, tennis court, pool, hot tub, gym, laundry facilities, laundry service, business services, meeting room, free parking, some pets allowed (fee), no-smoking rooms* ⊟ *AE, D, DC, MC, V* ⍟ *BP.*

$–$$ 🏨 **Hillsboro Courtyard by Marriott.** Next door to the Residence Inn, this hotel offers easy access to shopping and restaurants in Hillsboro, as well as quick access onto U.S. 26 toward Portland. With large, comfortable rooms, it is perfect for business travelers, or for tourists who don't mind being several miles from downtown Portland. ⊠ *3050 N.W. Stucki Pl., Hillsboro 97124* ☎ *503/690–1800 or 800/321–2211* 🖶 *503/690–0236* ⊕ *www.marriott.com* ⟳ *149 rooms, 6 suites* 🗇 *Restaurant, room service, in-room data ports, cable TV with movies, indoor pool, gym, hot tub, lounge, dry cleaning, laundry facilities, business services, meeting rooms, no-smoking rooms* ⊟ *AE, D, DC, MC, V.*

$ 🏨 **Sweetbrier Inn.** Set on landscaped grounds among fir and pine trees just off I–5 several miles south of Portland, this two-story manor-style property in Tualatin provides a peaceful lodging option for those who don't mind being a bit farther away from the action of the city. The majority of the bright, hardwood-furnished rooms in the L-shape complex are accessible via an outside walkway that winds around the complex, and many of them look out onto an inner courtyard. It's near golf courses, tennis courts, and a jogging track. ⊠ *7125 S.W. Nyberg Rd., Tualatin 97062* ☎ *503/692–5800 or 800/551–9167* 🖶 *503/692–3079* ⟳ *98 rooms, 32 suites* 🗇 *Restaurant, room service, in-room data ports, pool, gym, bar, playground, laundry service, meeting rooms, free parking* ⊟ *AE, D, DC, MC, V.*

Portland International Airport Area

$$$–$$$$ 🏨 **Embassy Suites Airport.** Suites in this eight-story atrium hotel have beige walls and blond-wood furnishings. The lobby has a waterfall and pond with koi. All suites come with separate bedrooms and living areas with sleeper sofas. A full breakfast is included, and cocktails are free at happy hour. It's on the new MAX airport line. ⊠ *7900 N.E. 82nd Ave., Airport, 97220* ☎ *503/460–3000* 🖶 *503/460–3030* ⟳ *251 suites* 🗇 *Restaurant, room service, in-room data ports, microwaves, refrigerators, minibars, cable TV, indoor pool, gym, hot tub, laundry service, concierge, meeting rooms, airport shuttle, business services, free parking* ⊟ *AE, D, DC, MC, V* ⍟ *BP.*

$–$$$ 🏨 **Doubletree Hotel Jantzen Beach.** The four-story Doubletree, on the Columbia River, has larger-than-average rooms, many with balconies and good views of the river and Vancouver, Washington. Public areas glitter with brass and bright lights that accentuate the greenery and the burgundy, green, and rose color scheme. The menu at Maxi's Seafood Restaurant highlights ingredients fresh from Pacific Northwest fields, farms, and waters. ✉ *909 N. Hayden Island Dr.,east of I–5's Jantzen Beach exit, Jantzen Beach, 97217* ☎ *503/283–4466 or 800/222–8733* 🖷 *503/283–4743* ⊕ *www.doubletree.com* ⇆ *320 rooms* ⚭ *2 restaurants, room service, in-room data ports, cable TV with movies, pool, tennis court, gym, hot tub, bar, laundry facilities, dry cleaning, business services, meeting room, no-smoking rooms* ▤ *AE, D, DC, MC, V.*

$$ ▦ **Courtyard Airport.** This six-story Marriott inn is designed for business travelers. Rooms are brightly decorated in earth tones and have sitting areas, work desks, and high-speed Internet access. It's ¾ mi east of I–205. ✉ *11550 N.E. Airport Way, Airport, 97220* ☎ *503/252–3200 or 800/321–2211* 🖷 *503/252–8921* ⊕ *www.courtyard.com* ⇆ *150 rooms, 10 suites* ⚭ *Restaurant, coffee shop, room service, in-room data ports, cable TV with movies, pool, gym, hot tub, bar, dry cleaning, laundry facilities, laundry service, business services, meeting rooms, free parking, no-smoking rooms* ▤ *AE, D, DC, MC, V.*

$$ ▦ **Shilo Suites Airport.** Each room in this large, four-level all-suites inn is bright, with floral-print bedspreads and drapes, and has a microwave, wet bar, and two oversize beds. The indoor pool and hot tub are open 24 hours. Local calls are free. ✉ *11707 N.E. Airport Way, Airport, 97220* ☎ *503/252–7500 or 800/222–2244* 🖷 *503/254–0794* ⊕ *www.shiloinns. com* ⇆ *200 rooms* ⚭ *Restaurant, room service, in-room data ports, microwaves, minibars, refrigerators, cable TV with movies, indoor pool, gym, hot tub, steam room, bar, dry cleaning, laundry facilities, laundry service, business services, meeting rooms, airport shuttle, free parking, no-smoking floor* ▤ *AE, D, DC, MC, V* ⏺⏺ *CP.*

$–$$ ▦ **Doubletree—Columbia River.** On Hayden Island between Portland and Vancouver, Washington, close to the Jantzen Beach shopping area, this Doubletree overlooks the Columbia River and is directly next to the Doubletree Jantzen Beach, its sister hotel. It is an easy drive to downtown and the airport, although nothing terribly interesting is within walking distance. Rooms are decorated in earth tones and many have riverfront views and balconies. ✉ *1401 N. Hayden Island Dr., 97217* ☎ *503/283–2111* 🖷 *503/283–4718* ⇆ *351 rooms* ⚭ *2 restaurants, room service, in-room data ports, cable TV with movies, putting green, pool, hair salon, business services, airport shuttle, some pets allowed (fee)* ▤ *AE, D, DC, MC, V.*

$ ▦ **Hawthorne Inn and Suites.** Although it is in Gresham, this hotel's proximity to I–205 makes for easy access to downtown, and it's just a short ride to the airport. Rooms are spacious and comfortable, and much of the hotel's interior has a woodsy flair that distinguishes it from many other chain hotels. Suites include kitchenettes, and a hot breakfast buffet is offered every morning. ✉ *2323 N.E. 181st Ave., Gresham, 97230* ☎ *503/492–4000* 🖷 *503/492–3271* ⇆ *71 rooms, 23 suites* ⚭ *In-room data ports, some kitchenettes, cable TV with movies, indoor pool, gym, hot tub, laundry facilities, meeting rooms, business services, free parking, some pets allowed, no-smoking rooms* ▤ *AE, D, DC, MC, V* ⏺⏺ *BP.*

NIGHTLIFE & THE ARTS

"A&E, The Arts and Entertainment Guide," published each Friday in the *Oregonian*, contains listings of performers, productions, events, and club entertainment. *Willamette Week,* published free each Wednesday and widely available throughout the metropolitan area, contains similar, but hipper, listings. *Just Out,* the city's gay and lesbian newspaper, is published bimonthly.

Nightlife

Portland's flourishing music scene encompasses everything from classical concerts to the latest permutations of rock and roll and hip-hop. The city has become something of a base for young rock bands, which perform in dance clubs scattered throughout the metropolitan area. Good jazz groups perform nightly in clubs and bars. Top-name musicians and performers in every genre regularly appear at the city's larger venues.

Bars & Lounges

DOWNTOWN Many of the best bars and lounges in Portland are found in its restaurants.

Brasserie Montmartre (⊠ 626 S.W. Park Ave., Downtown ☎ 503/224–5552) is a popular late-night spot with live jazz. At the elegant **Heathman Hotel** (⊠ 1001 S.W. Broadway, Downtown ☎ 503/241–4100) you can sit in the marble bar or the wood-panel Tea Court. **Huber's Cafe** (⊠411 S.W. 3rd Ave., Downtown ☎ 503/228–5686), the city's oldest restaurant, is noted for its Spanish coffee and old-fashioned feel. The young and eclectic crowd at the **Lotus Cardroom and Cafe** (⊠ 932 S.W. 3rd Ave., Downtown ☎ 503/227–6185) comes to drink, dance to modern sounds, and play pool. At **Oba!** (⊠ 555 N.W. 12th Ave., Pearl District ☎ 503/228–6161), plush tans and reds with lime-green backlit walls set a backdrop for South American salsa. The **Rialto** (⊠ 529 S.W. 4th Ave. ☎ 503/228–7605) is a large, dark bar with several pool tables and enthusiastic pool players as well as some of the best Bloody Marys in town. **Saucebox** (⊠214 S.W. Broadway, Downtown ☎ 503/241–3393) attracts a sophisticated crowd who enjoy colorful cocktails and trendy DJ music. At **Veritable Quandary** (⊠ 1220 S.W. 1st Ave., Downtown ☎ 503/228–5672), along the river, you can sit in the cozy tree-filled outdoor patio or in the glass atrium.

NOB HILL Boisterous **Gypsy** (⊠ 625 N.W. 21st Ave., Nob Hill ☎ 503/796–1859) has 1950s-like furnishings. Young hipsters pack **Muu-Muus** (⊠ 612 N.W. 21st Ave., Nob Hill ☎ 503/223–8169) on weekend nights. **21st Avenue Bar & Grill** (⊠ 721 N.W. 21st Ave., Nob Hill ☎ 503/222–4121) is open 'til 2:30 AM and has a patio and outdoor bar. The upscale martini set chills at **Wildwood** (⊠ 1221 N.W. 21st Ave., Nob Hill ☎ 503/248–9663).

EAST PORTLAND An artsy, hip east-side crowd, not to be mistaken for the downtown jetsetters, hangs and drinks martinis and wine at the minimalist **Aalto Lounge** (⊠ 3356 S.E. Belmont St. ☎ 503/239–4698). One of few bars on northeast Alberta Street, **Bink's** (⊠2715 N.E. Alberta St. ☎ 503/293–4430) is a small, friendly neighborhood spot with cozy seats around a fireplace, a pool table, and a good jukebox. It serves only beer and wine. **Colosso** (⊠ 1932 N.E. Broadway ☎ 503/288–3333), a popular tapas bar, draws a cocktail-sipping crowd of hipsters at night. A laid-back beer-drinking crowd fills the **Horse Brass Pub** (⊠ 4534 S.E. Belmont St. ☎ 503/232–2202), as good an English-style pub as you will find this side of the Atlantic, with nearly 50 beers on tap and air thick with smoke. **Noble Rot** (⊠ 2724 S.E. Ankeny St. ☎ 503/233–1999) is a chic east-side wine bar with excellent food and red leather booths.

Brewpubs, Brew Theaters & Microbreweries

Dozens of small breweries operating in the metropolitan area produce pale ales, bitters, bocks, barley wines, and stouts. Some have attached pub operations, where you can sample a foaming pint of house ale. "Brew theaters," former neighborhood movie houses, whose patrons enjoy food, suds, and recent theatrical releases, are part of the microbrewery phenomenon.

The **Bagdad Theatre and Pub** (✉ 3702 S.E. Hawthorne Blvd., Hawthorne District ☎ 503/225–5555 Ext. 8830) screens recent Hollywood films and serves microbrews. The first McMenamins brewpub, the **Barley Mill Pub** (✉ 1629 S.E. Hawthorne Blvd., Hawthorne District ☎ 503/231–1492), is filled with Grateful Dead memorabilia and concert posters and is a fun place for families. **BridgePort BrewPub & Restaurant** (✉ 1313 N. W. Marshall St., Pearl District ☎ 503/224–4400), Portland's oldest microbrewery, prepares hand-tossed pizza (⇨ Where to Eat) to accompany its ales. The **Mission Theater** (✉ 1624 N.W. Glisan St., Nob Hill ☎ 503/225–5555 Ext. 8830) was the first brew theater to show recent Hollywood offerings and serve locally brewed McMenamins ales. In an old church, the **St. John's Pub** (✉ 8203 N. Ivanhoe, St. John's ☎ 503/224–4400) is another McMenamins brewpub and includes a beer garden and a movie theater. **Tugboat Brewery** (✉ 711 S.W. Ankeny St., Downtown ☎ 503/226–2508) is a small, cozy brewpub with books and games, picnic tables, and experimental jazz several nights a week.

The McMenamins chain of microbreweries includes some pubs in restored historic buildings. **Ringlers** (✉ 1332 W. Burnside St., Downtown ☎ 503/225–0543) occupies the first floor of the building that houses the famous Crystal Ballroom (⇨ Dancing). **Ringlers Annex** (✉ 1223 S. W. Stark St., Downtown ☎ 503/525–0520), one block away from Ringlers, is a pie-shape corner pub where you can puff a cigar while drinking beer, port, or a single-malt scotch. **Widmer Brewing and Gasthaus** (✉ 955 N. Russell St., North Portland, near Fremont Bridge ☎ 503/281–3333) brews German-style beers and has a full menu; you can tour the adjacent brewery Monday–Saturday.

Coffeehouses & Teahouses

DOWNTOWN   Traditional English teas, complete with scones and Devonshire cream, are served with authentic English accents at the **British Tea Garden** (✉ 725 S.W. 10th Ave., Downtown ☎ 503/221–7817). **Three Lions Bakery** (✉ 1138 S.W. Morrison St., Downtown ☎ 503/224–3429) turns out excellent pastries as well as strong java; sandwiches, fresh-made quiches, and salads are also served.

NOB HILL &   **Anna Bannanas** (✉ 1214 N.W. 21st Ave., Nob Hill ☎ 503/274–2559)
VICINITY   serves great espresso and coffee, veggie sandwiches, soup, and smoothies; there's outdoor seating out front. **Coffee People** (✉ 533 N.W. 23rd Ave., Nob Hill ☎ 503/221–0235) is a local chain that draws crowds from early in the morning until late in the evening. **Torrefazione Italia** (✉ 838 N.W. 23rd Ave., Nob Hill ☎ 503/228–1255) has several locations in Portland and beyond but manages to feel like a real Italian espresso house, with the best cappuccino in town. One of the newer additions to the Portland coffee scene, **World Cup Coffee and Tea** (✉ 1740 N.W. Glisan St. ☎ 503/228–5503) sells excellent organic coffee and espresso in Nob Hill, as well as at its store in the Pearl District at the Ecotrust building and at Powell's City of Books on Burnside. **Village Coffee** (✉ 1037 N.W. 23rd St., Nob Hill ☎ 503/225–0746) is a sleek coffee shop right in the center of the shopping district on Northwest 23rd and offers free Internet to customers.

EAST PORTLAND   **Common Grounds** (✉ 4321 S.E. Hawthorne Blvd., East Portland ☎ 503/236–4835) has plush couches and serves desserts plus sandwiches and soup. **Palio Coffee and Dessert House** (✉ 1996 S.E. Ladd St., Ladd's Addition, near Hawthorne District ☎ 503/232–9412), in the middle of peaceful residential Ladd's Addition, has delicious desserts and espresso, and is open later than many coffee shops in the area. Twentysomething sippers lounge on sofas and overstuffed chairs at **Pied Cow** (✉ 3244 S.E. Belmont St., East Portland ☎ 503/230–4866), a laid-back alternative to more yuppified establishments. **Rimsky Korsakoffee House** (⊠ 707 S. E. 12th Ave., East Portland ☎ 503/232–2640), one of the city's first coffeehouses, is still one of the best, especially when it comes to desserts. **Torrefazione Italia** (⊠ 1403 N.E. Weidler St., East Portland ☎ 503/288–1608) is just off the Broadway strip in a busy area near Lloyd Center.

Dancing
McMenamins Crystal Ballroom (⊠ 1332 W. Burnside St., Downtown ☎ 503/225–0047) is a famous Portland dance hall that dates from 1914. Rudolph Valentino danced the tango here in 1923, and you may feel like doing the same once you step out onto the 7,500-square-foot "elastic" floor (it's built on ball bearings) and feel it bouncing beneath your feet. Bands perform everything from swing to hillbilly rock nightly except Monday. **Polly Esther's Culture Club** (⊠ 424 S.W. 4th Ave., Downtown ☎ 503/221–1970) is a dance bar with several levels and a DJ playing a '70s–'80s nostalgia mix.

Gay & Lesbian Clubs
Boxxes/Panorama (⊠ Stark St. between 10th and 11th Aves., Downtown ☎ 503/221–7262) is a bar-disco-restaurant complex with a video bar, poker machines, a pool table, late-night dancing Friday and Saturday in the cavernous Panorama, and outdoor seating at the Red Cap Café. **C. C. Slaughters** (⊠ 219 N.W. Davis Ave., Old Town ☎ 503/248–9135) is a male-oriented bar with a restaurant and a dance floor that's crowded on weekend nights; weeknights yield karaoke and country dancing. **Egyptian Room** (⊠ 3701 S.E. Division St., south of Hawthorne District ☎ 503/236–8689), Portland's lesbian bar-disco, has pool tables, video poker, and a medium-size dance floor. **Fox and Hounds** (⊠ 217 N.W. 2nd Ave., Old Town ☎ 503/243–5530) is popular with gay men and lesbians. A full menu is served in the evenings, and the place is packed for Sunday brunch. **Scandals** (⊠ 1038 S.W. Stark St., Downtown ☎ 503/227–5887) is low-key and has plate-glass windows with a view of Stark Street and the city's streetcars. The lower level has video poker and a pool table, and the adjoining Other Side bar serves light food.

Live Music
BLUES, FOLK & ROCK   The **Aladdin Theater** (⊠ 3017 S.E. Milwaukie St. ☎ 503/224–4400), in an old movie theater, is one of the best music venues in town and serves microbrews and pizza. The **B Complex** (⊠ 320 S.E. 2nd Ave., under Burnside Bridge ☎ 503/235–4424), in an industrial loft building with brick walls and exposed duct work, is a great venue for all kinds of live music, including jazz, hip-hop, and electronica. No alcohol is served.

Berbati's Pan (⊠ 10 S.W. 3rd Ave., Old Town ☎ 503/248–4579), on the edge of Old Town, has dancing and presents live music, everything from big band and swing to acid jazz, rock, and R&B. **Candlelight Room** (⊠ 2032 S.W. 5th Ave., Downtown ☎ 503/222–3378) presents blues nightly. **Dublin Pub** (⊠ 6821 S.W. Beaverton–Hillsdale Hwy., Beaverton ☎ 503/297–2889), on the west side, pours more than 100 beers on tap and hosts Irish bands and rock groups. **Kell's Irish Restaurant & Pub** (⊠ 112 S.W. 2nd Ave., Old Town ☎ 503/227–4057) serves terrific Irish food and presents Celtic music nightly. Locals crowd the **Laurelthirst Public House** (⊠ 2958 N.E. Glisan St., Laurelhurst ☎ 503/232–1504) to eat tasty food, sit in cozy red booths, and listen to folk, jazz, country, or bluegrass music on its tiny stage. There are pool tables in an adjoining room. **Meow Meow** (⊠ 527 S.E. Pine St., east side, near Burnside Bridge ☎ 503/230–2111) hosts punk-rock acts in a nonalcohol environment for all ages. **Produce Row Cafe** (⊠ 204 S.E. Oak St., east side, near Burnside Bridge and I–5 ☎ 503/232–8355) has a huge beer list, a great beer garden, a down-to-earth flavor, and live bluegrass, folk, and acoustic music most nights of the week. **Satyricon** (✉ 125 N.W. 6th Ave., Old Town ☎ 503/243–2380) is Portland's leading outlet for grunge, punk, and other alternative rock music.

During the Rose Festival–dominated month of June, **Beaverton SummerFest** (✉ Griffith Park, at intersection of Hwys. 10 and 217, Beaverton ☎ 503/644–0123) attracts big-name entertainers to a three-day bash in suburban Beaverton. A food pavilion presents Pacific Northwest specialties while the bands play on. The **North by Northwest Music Festival** (☎ 512/467–7979), an annual new music conference, spotlights hundreds of up-and-coming musicians from around the West in late September. The focus is on alternative rock, but other musical genres are represented as well. One admission price gets you into about two dozen downtown clubs during the three-day event. There are also panels, workshops, and a music trade show.

COUNTRY & WESTERN
The **Drum** (✉ 14601 S.E. Division St., close to Gresham ☎ 503/760–1400) books traditional country and contemporary country-rock performers. The Ponderosa Lounge at **Jubitz Truck Stop** (✉ 10210 N. Vancouver Way ☎ 503/283–1111) presents live country music and dancing nightly—not your ordinary truck stop.

JAZZ
Brasserie Montmartre (✉ 626 S.W. Park Ave., Downtown ☎ 503/224–5552) presents duos on weeknights and quartets and larger groups on weekends; its European-style bistro serves Pacific Northwest cuisine. **Jazz de Opus** (✉ 33 N.W. 2nd Ave., Old Town ☎ 503/222–6077) books local musicians with national reputations seven nights a week; its menu focuses on seafood and prime rib.

Since 1982 the **Mt. Hood Jazz Festival** (✉ 26000 S.E. Stark St., Gresham ☎ 503/224–4400 ⊕ www.mthoodjazz.com) has drawn big names as well as new talent to this three-day event in August. Past years have seen appearances by Ella Fitzgerald, Sarah Vaughan, and George Benson. The festival is held on the campus of Mount Hood Community College in suburban Gresham. Take MAX light rail to Gresham Transit Center and transfer to Bus 26.

The Arts

When it comes to public arts funding, Oregon ranks low compared with other states, yet Portland has a symphony orchestra, opera and dance companies, and a number of theater companies. Most Portland-based performing arts groups have their own box-office numbers; *see* individual listings. For tickets to most events, call **Ticketmaster** (☎ 503/224–4400) or **Fastixx** (☎ 503/224–8499).

During the summer half-price tickets for almost any event are available the day of the show at Ticket Central in the **Visitor Information and Services Center** (✉ Pioneer Courthouse Sq., Downtown ☎ 503/275–8358 after 10 AM), open Monday–Saturday 9–4:30. This is an outlet for tickets from Ticketmaster and Fastixx. Credit cards are accepted, but you must buy tickets in person.

Classical Music

CHAMBER MUSIC
Chamber Music Northwest (✉ 522 S.W. 5th Ave., Suite 725, Downtown ☎ 503/294–6400 ⊕ www.cnmw.org) presents some of the most sought-after soloists, chamber musicians, and recording artists from the Portland area and abroad for a five-week summer concert series; performances take place at Reed College and Catlin Gabel School.

OPERA   **Portland Opera** (✉ 222 S.W. Clay St. ☎ 503/241–1802 ⊕ www. portlandopera.org) and its orchestra and chorus stage five productions annually at the Keller Auditorium.

ORCHESTRAS   The **Oregon Symphony** (✉ 923 S.W. Washington ☎ 503/228–1353 or 800/228–7343 ⊕ www.orsymphony.org) presents more than 40 classical, pop, children's, and family concerts each year at the Arlene Schnitzer Concert Hall.

The **Portland Baroque Orchestra** (☎ 503/222–6000 ⊕ www.pbo.org) performs works on period instruments in a season that runs October–April. Performances are held at **Reed College's Kaul Auditorium** (✉ 3203 S.E. Woodstock Blvd., Reed/Woodstock) and downtown at **First Baptist Church** (✉ 1425 S.W. 20th Ave., Downtown).

Dance

Body Vox (☎ 503/229–0627 ⊕ www.bodyvox.com) performs energetic contemporary dance–theater works at several locations in Portland.

Do Jump! Extremely Physical Theatre (✉ 1515 S.E. 37th Ave. ☎ 503/231–1232 ⊕ www.dojump.org) showcases its creative acrobatic work at the Echo Theatre near Hawthorne.

Founded in 1982, the **Northwest Afrikan American Ballet** (✉ Box 11143, Portland 97211 ☎ 503/287–8852) was the first traditional African dance company in the Northwest United States, and it continues to offer excellent authentic and electrifying performances in and outside Portland.

Oregon Ballet Theatre (✉ 818 S.E. 6th Ave. ☎ 503/222–5538 or 888/922–5538 ⊕ www.obt.org) produces five classical and contemporary works a year, including a much-loved holiday *Nutcracker*. Most performances are at Keller Auditorium.

Film

Cinema 21 (✉ 616 N.W. 21st Ave., Nob Hill ☎ 503/223–4515) is an art-movie house in Nob Hill; it also hosts the annual gay and lesbian film festival in June.

Cinemagic (✉ 2021 S.E. Hawthorne Blvd., Hawthorne District ☎ 503/231–7919) shows progressive and cult films.

A 70-year-old landmark, the **Hollywood Theatre** (✉ 4122 N.E. Sandy Blvd., Hollywood District ☎ 503/281–4215) shows everything from obscure foreign art films to old American classics and second-run Hollywood hits.

For Hollywood blockbusters, new foreign films, and interesting low-budget sleepers, check out **KOIN Center Cinemas** (✉ 222 S.W. Columbia Blvd., Downtown ☎ 503/225–5555 Ext. 4608).

The **Laurelhurst Theatre** (✉ 2735 E. Burnside ☎ 503/232–5511) is a beautiful theater and pub showing excellent second-run features and cult classics for only $2–$3.

Not-to-be-missed Portland landmarks when it comes to movie-viewing, the **McMenamins theatres and brewpubs** offer beer, pizza, and inexpensive tickets to second-run blockbusters in uniquely renovated buildings that avoid any hint of corporate streamlining. Local favorites include the Bagdad Theatre (✉ 3702 S.E. Hawthorne Blvd. ☎ 503/225–5555 Ext. 8831), the Mission Theatre (✉ 1624 N.W. Glisan ☎ 503/225–5555 Ext. 8832), and the Kennedy School (✉ 5736 N.E. 33rd St. ☎ 503/225–5555 Ext. 8833), found in a renovated elementary school along with a bed-and-breakfast and a restaurant.

The **Northwest Film and Video Center** (✉ 1219 S.W. Park Ave., Downtown ☎ 503/221–1156), a branch of the Portland Art Museum, screens all manner of art films, documentaries, and independent features and presents the three-week Portland International Film Festival in February and March. Films are shown at the Whitsell Auditorium, next to the museum, and at the Guild Theatre (✉ 879 S.W. Park Ave.).

Performance Venues

The 2,776-seat **Arlene Schnitzer Concert Hall** (✉ Portland Center for the Performing Arts, S.W. Broadway and Main St., Downtown ☎ 503/796–9293), built in 1928 in Italian rococo revival style, hosts rock stars, choral groups, lectures, and concerts by the Oregon Symphony and others.

With 3,000 seats and outstanding acoustics, **Keller Auditorium** (✉ 222 S.W. Clay St., Downtown ☎ 503/796–9293) hosts performances by the Portland Opera and Portland Ballet as well as country and rock concerts and touring shows.

Memorial Coliseum (✉ 1 Center Ct., Rose Quarter, Lloyd Center District ☎ 503/235–8771), a 12,000-seat venue on the MAX light-rail line, books rock groups, touring shows, the Ringling Brothers circus, ice-skating extravaganzas, and sporting events.

Remodeled in 2001, **PGE Park** (✉ 1844 S.W. Morrison St., Downtown/ Nob Hill ☎ 503/553–5400 ⊕ www.pgepark.com) is home to the Portland Beavers Triple-A baseball team and the Portland Timbers soccer team. The 20,000-seat stadium also hosts concerts and other sporting events. No parking is available at the park; MAX light rail is the most convenient option. Your game ticket entitles you to a free round-trip.

Portland Center for the Performing Arts (✉ 1111 S.W. Broadway, Downtown ☎ 503/796–9293 ⊕ www.pcpa.com) hosts opera, ballet, rock shows, symphony performances, lectures, and Broadway musicals in its three venues (⇨ Downtown *in* Exploring Portland).

The 21,000-seat **Rose Garden** (✉ 1 Center Ct., Broadway and N. Interstate Ave., Lloyd Center District ☎ 503/235–8771) is home to the Portland Trail Blazers basketball team and the site of other sporting events and rock concerts. The arena is on the MAX light-rail line.

The **Roseland Theater** (✉ 8 N.W. 6th Ave., Old Town/Chinatown ☎ 503/224–2038), which holds 1,400 people, primarily stages rock and blues shows.

Theater

Artists Repertory Theatre (✉ 1516 S.W. Alder St., Downtown ☎ 503/241–1278 ⊕ www.artistrep.org) stages seven productions a year—regional premieres, occasional commissioned works, and selected classics.

Imago Theatre (✉ 17 S.E. 8th Ave. ☎ 503/231–9581 ⊕ www.imagotheatre. com) is considered by some to be Portland's most outstanding innovative theater company, specializing in movement-based work for both young and old.

Oregon Children's Theatre (☎ 503/228–9571 ⊕ www.octc.org) puts on three or four shows a year at major venues throughout the city for school groups and families.

Oregon Puppet Theater (☎ 503/236–4034) stages five children's productions a year at different locations in town.

Portland Center Stage (✉ 1111 S.W. Broadway, Downtown ☎ 503/274–6588) produces six contemporary and classical works between October and April in the 800-seat Newmark Theater.

Stark Raving Theatre (✉ 2257 N.W. Raleigh St. ☎ 503/232–7072 ⊕ www.starkravingtheatre.org) provides a forum for cutting-edge dramatic work, producing four shows a year at the CoHo Theatre in the Northwest.

SPORTS & THE OUTDOORS

Portlanders are definitely oriented to the outdoors. Hikers, joggers, and mountain bikers take to the city's hundreds of miles of parks, paths, and trails. The Willamette and Columbia rivers are used for boating and water sports; however, it's not easy to rent any kind of boat for casual use. Big-sports fervor is reserved for Trail Blazer games, held at the Rose Quarter arena on the east side. The Portland/Oregon Visitors Association (⇨ Visitor Information *in* Portland A to Z) provides information on sports events and outdoor activities in the city.

Participant Sports

Bicycling

Bicycling magazine has named Portland the number one cycling city in the United States, and you will soon find out why; aside from the sheer numbers of cyclists you are bound to see on every road and pathway, notable bike-friendly aspects of this city include well-marked bike lanes on many major streets, bike paths meandering through parks and along the shoreline of the Willamette River, street signs reminding motorists to yield to cyclists at many intersections, and bike racks on the front of all Tri-Met buses.

Despite the occasionally daunting hills and frequent wintertime rain, cycling remains one of the best ways to see some of what Portland has to offer. Bike paths on both the east and west sides of the Willamette River continue south of downtown, and you can easily make a several-mile loop by crossing bridges to get from one side to the other. (Most bridges, including the Broadway Bridge, the Steel Bridge, the Hawthorne Bridge, and the Sellwood Bridge, are accessible to cyclists.)

Forest Park's Leif Erikson Drive is an 11-mi ride through Northwest Portland's Forest Park, accessible from the west end of Northwest Thurman Street. Parts of this ride and other Forest Park trails are recommended only for mountain bikes. Bicycling on Sauvie Island is a rare treat, with a 12-mi loop around the island with plenty of spots for exploring. To get to Sauvie Island from Portland, you can brave the 10-mi ride in the bike lane of U.S. 30, or you can shuttle your bike there via Tri-Met bus 17. The Springwater Corridor, when combined with the Esplanade ride on the east side of the Willamette, can take you all the way from downtown to the far reaches of southeast Portland along a former railroad line. The trail heads east beginning near Sellwood, close to Johnson Creek Boulevard.

For more information on bike routes and resources in and around Portland, visit the **Department of Transportation** Web page (⊕ www.trans.ci.portlande.or.us/bicycles). Here, you can download maps, or order "Bike There," a glossy detailed bicycle map of the metropolitan area. Bikes can be rented at several places in the city. Rentals can run anywhere from $20 to $50 per day and commonly are available for cheaper weekly rates, running from $75 to $150 per week. Bike helmets are generally included in the cost of rental. Good hybrid bikes for city riding are available at

City Bikes Workers Cooperative (⊠ 714 S.E. Ankeny St., near Burnside and Martin Luther King Blvd. ☎ 503/222–2376) on the east side. For treks in Forest Park, mountain bikes can be rented at **Fat Tire Farm** (⊠ 2714 N.W. Thurman St., near Forest Park ☎ 503/222–3276). In the Northwest, rentals are offered at **Northwest Bicycles** (⊠ 916 N.W. 21st Ave., Nob Hill ☎ 503/248–9142). For jaunts along the Willamette, try **Waterfront Bicycle Rentals** (⊠ 36015 S.W. Montgomery St., Suite 3, Downtown ☎ 503/227–1719).

Fishing

The Columbia and Willamette rivers are major sportfishing streams with opportunities for angling virtually year-round. Though salmon can still be caught here, runs have been greatly reduced in both rivers in recent years, and the Willamette River is still plagued by pollution. Nevertheless, the Willamette still offers prime fishing for bass, channel catfish, sturgeon, crappies, perch, panfish, and crayfish. It is also a good winter steelhead stream. June is the top shad month, with some of the best fishing occurring below Willamette Falls at Oregon City. The Columbia River is known for its salmon, sturgeon, walleye, and smelt. The Sandy and Clackamas rivers, near Mt. Hood, are smaller waterways popular with local anglers.

OUTFITTERS Outfitters throughout Portland operate guide services. Few outfitters rent equipment, so bring your own or be prepared to buy. **Countrysport Limited** (⊠ 126 S.W. 1st Ave., Old Town ☎ 503/221–3964) specializes in all things fly-fishing, including tackle, rentals, and guided outings.

G.I. Joe's (⊠ 3900 S.E. 82nd Ave., near Powell Blvd. ☎ 503/283–0312) sells rods, reels, tackle, accessories, and fishing licenses. You can find a broad selection of fishing gear, including rods, reels, and fishing licenses, at **Stewart Fly Shop** (⊠ 23830 N.E. Halsey St., near Troutdale ☎ 503/666–2471).

REGULATIONS Local sport shops are the best sources of information on current fishing hot spots, which change from year to year. Detailed fishing regulations are available from the **Oregon Department of Fish and Wildlife** (⊠ 2501 S.W. 1st Ave., 97207 ☎ 503/872–5263).

Golf

Broadmoor Golf Course (⊠ 3509 N.E. Columbia Blvd., near airport, 97211 ☎ 503/281–1337) is an 18-hole, par-72 course where the greens fee runs $22–$26 and an optional cart costs $22.

At the 18-hole, par-70 **Colwood National Golf Club** (⊠ 7313 N.E. Columbia Blvd., near airport, 97218 ☎ 503/254–5515), the greens fee is $26–$28, plus $22 for an optional cart. On mornings and weekends, the $31 greens fee includes a cart.

Eastmoreland Golf Course (⊠ 2425 S.E. Bybee Blvd., Sellwood, 97202 ☎ 503/775–2900) has a highly regarded 18-hole, 72-par course close to the Rhododendron Gardens, Crystal Springs Lake, and Reed College. The greens fee is $21–$23.

Glendoveer Golf Course (⊠ 14015 N.E. Glisan St., near Gresham, 97230 ☎ 503/253–7507) has two 18-hole courses, one par-71 and one par-73, and a covered driving range. The greens fee is $17–$19; carts are $13 for 9 holes, $25 for 18 holes.

Heron Lakes Golf Course (⊠ 3500 N. Victory Blvd., west of airport, off N. Marine Dr., 97217 ☎ 503/289–1818) consists of two 18-hole, par-72 courses: the less-challenging Greenback and the Great Blue, generally acknowledged to be the most difficult links in the greater Portland area. The greens fee at the Green, as it is locally known, is $19–$21, while the fee at the Blue is $31 at all times. An optional cart at either course costs $24.

Pumpkin Ridge Golf Club (✉ 12930 N.W. Old Pumpkin Ridge Rd., Cornelius 97133 ☎ 503/647–4747 or 888/594–4653 ⊕ www.pumpkinridge.com) has 36 holes, with the 18-hole Ghost Creek par-71 course open to the public. According to *Golf Digest,* Ghost Creek is one of the best public courses in the nation. Pumpkin Ridge hosted the U.S. Women's Open in 1997 and will again in 2004. The greens fee is $40–$120; the cart fee is $15.

Rose City Golf Course (✉ 2200 N.E. 71st Ave., east of Hollywood District, 97213 ☎ 503/253–4744) has one 18-hole, par-72 course. Greens fees are $19–$21; carts are $13 for 9 holes, $25 for 18 holes.

Ice-Skating

Ice Chalet at Lloyd Center (✉ Multnomah St. and N.E. 9th Ave., Lloyd District ☎ 503/288–6073) has open skating and skate rentals ($9 admission includes skate rental). The indoor rinks are open year-round. You can skate year-round on the indoor rink at **Ice Chalet at Clackamas Town Center** (✉ 12000 S.E. 82nd Ave., Clackamas ☎ 503/786–6000). The $9 admission includes skate rental. The indoor rink is open year-round.

Skiing

Mountain Shop (✉ 628 N.E. Broadway, Lloyd District/Irvington, 97232 ☎ 503/288–6768) rents skis and equipment. **REI** (✉ 1798 Jantzen Beach Center, Jantzen Beach ☎ 503/283–1300) can fill all your ski-equipment rental needs.

Swimming & Sunbathing

Blue Lake Regional Park (✉ 20500 N.E. Marine Dr., Troutdale ☎ 503/797–1850) has a swimming beach that's packed on hot summer days. You can also fish and rent small boats here. This is a great place for a hike on the surrounding trails or for a picnic.

If you feel like tanning au naturel, drive about a half hour northwest of downtown to **Sauvie Island,** a wildlife refuge with a secluded beachfront that's popular (and legal) with nude sunbathers. If the sky is clear, you'll get a spectacular view from the riverbank of three Cascade mountains—Hood, St. Helens, and Adams. Huge oceangoing vessels cruise by on their way to and from the Port of Portland. To get here, take U.S. 30 north to Sauvie Island bridge, turn right, and follow Reeder Road until you hit gravel. Look for the Collins Beach signs. There's plenty of parking, but a permit is required. You can buy it ($3.50 for a one-day permit, $11 for an annual permit) at the Cracker Barrel country store just over the bridge on the left side of the road.

Tennis

Lake Oswego Indoor Tennis Center (✉ 2900 S.W. Diane Dr., Lake Oswego ☎ 503/635–5550) has four indoor tennis courts. **Portland Parks and Recreation** (☎ 503/823–7529) operates more than 100 outdoor tennis courts (many with night lighting) at Washington Park, Grant Park, and many other locations. The courts are open on a first-come, first-served basis year-round, but you can reserve one, starting in March, for play May–September. The **Portland Tennis Center** (✉ 324 N.E. 12th Ave., just south of I-84 ☎ 503/823–3189) operates four indoor courts and eight lighted outdoor courts. The **St. John's Racquet Center** (✉ 7519 N. Burlington Ave., St. John's ☎ 503/823–3629) has three indoor courts.

Spectator Sports

Auto Racing

Portland International Raceway (✉ West Delta Park, 1940 N. Victory Blvd., west of I–5, along the Columbia Slough ☎ 503/823–7223) presents bicycle and drag racing and motocross on weeknights and sports-car, motorcycle, and go-cart racing on weekends April–September.

Portland Speedway (✉ 9727 N. Martin Luther King Jr. Blvd., at I–5 along Columbia Slough ☎ 503/285–9511) hosts demolition derbies and NASCAR and stock-car races April–September. In June it hosts the Budweiser Indy Car World Series, a 200-mi race that lures the top names on the Indy Car circuit.

Baseball

The **Portland Beavers** (☎ 503/553–5555), Portland's Triple-A team, play at the downtown **PGE Park** (✉ 1844 S.W. Morrison St., Downtown ☎ 503/553–5400) April–September.

Basketball

The **Portland Trail Blazers** (✉ 1 Center Ct., Rose Quarter ☎ 503/797–9617) of the National Basketball Association play in the Rose Garden.

Dog Racing

Greyhounds race at the **Multnomah Greyhound Park** (✉ 944 N.E. 223rd Ave., Wood Village, Gresham, 97060 ☎ 503/667–7700) from early May to mid-October.

Horse Racing

Thoroughbred and quarter horses race, rain or shine October–April, at **Portland Meadows** (✉ 1001 N. Schmeer Rd., between I–5 and Martin Luther King Blvd., along Columbia Slough ☎ 503/285–9144 or 800/944–3127).

Ice Hockey

The **Portland Winter Hawks** (☎ 503/236–4295) of the Western Hockey League play home games September–March at **Memorial Coliseum** (✉ 300 N. Winning Way, Rose Quarter) and at the **Rose Garden** (✉ 1 Center Ct., Rose Quarter).

SHOPPING

Portland's main shopping area is **downtown,** between Southwest 2nd and 10th avenues and between Southwest Stark and Morrison streets. The major department stores are scattered over several blocks near Pioneer Courthouse Square. Northeast **Broadway** between 10th and 21st avenues is lined with boutiques and specialty shops. **Nob Hill,** north of downtown along Northwest 21st and 23rd avenues, is home to eclectic clothing, gift, book, and food shops. Most of the city's fine-art galleries are concentrated in the booming **Pearl District,** north from Burnside Street to Marshall Street between Northwest 8th and 15th avenues, along with furniture and design stores. **Sellwood,** 5 mi from the city center, south on Naito Parkway and east across the Sellwood Bridge, has more than 50 antiques and collectibles shops along southeast 13th Avenue, plus specialty shops and outlet stores for sporting goods. You'll find the largest concentration near the intersection of Milwaukie Boulevard and Bybee. **Hawthorne Boulevard** between 30th and 42nd avenues has an often countercultural grouping of bookstores, coffeehouses, antiques stores, and boutiques.

The open-air **Portland Saturday Market** (✉ Burnside Bridge, underneath west end, Old Town ☎ 503/222–6072), open on weekends, is a good place to find handcrafted items. *See* Old Town/Chinatown *in* Exploring Portland.

Portland merchants are generally open Monday–Saturday between 9 or 10 AM and 6 PM and on Sunday noon–6. Most shops in downtown's Pioneer Place, the east side's Lloyd Center, and the outlying malls are open until 9 Monday–Saturday and until 6 on Sunday.

Malls & Department Stores

Downtown/City Center

Meier & Frank (⊠ 621 S.W. 5th Ave., Downtown ☎ 503/223–0512), a Portland department store that dates from 1857, has 10 floors of general merchandise at its main location downtown.

Seattle-based **Nordstrom** (⊠ 701 S.W. Broadway, Downtown ☎ 503/224–6666) sells fine-quality apparel and accessories and has a large footwear department. Bargain lovers should head for the **Nordstrom Rack** (⊠ 401 S.W. Morrison St., Downtown ☎ 503/299–1815) outlet across from Pioneer Place mall.

Pioneer Place (⊠ 700 S.W. 5th Ave., Downtown ☎ 503/228–5800) has 70 upscale specialty shops (including Williams-Sonoma, Coach, J. Crew, Godiva, and Caswell-Massey) in a three-story, glass-roof atrium setting. You'll find good, inexpensive ethnic foods from more than a dozen vendors in the Cascades Food Court in the basement.

Saks Fifth Avenue (⊠ 850 S.W. 5th Ave., Downtown ☎ 503/226–3200) has two floors of men's and women's clothing, jewelry, and other merchandise.

Beyond Downtown

NORTHEAST PORTLAND **Lloyd Center** (⊠ N.E. Multnomah St. at N.E. 9th Ave., Northeast Portland ☎ 503/282–2511), which is on the MAX light-rail line, has more than 170 shops (including Nordstrom, Sears Roebuck, and Meier & Frank), an international food court, a multiscreen cinema, and an ice-skating pavilion. The mall is within walking distance of northeast Broadway, which has many specialty shops, boutiques, and restaurants.

SOUTHEAST PORTLAND **Clackamas Town Center** (⊠ Sunnyside Rd. at I–205's Exit 14, Southeast Portland ☎ 503/653–6913) has four major department stores, including Nordstrom and Meier & Frank; more than 180 shops; and an ice-skating rink. Discount stores are nearby.

SOUTHWEST PORTLAND **Washington Square** (⊠ 9585 S.W. Washington Square Rd., at S.W. Hall Blvd. and Hwy. 217, Tigard ☎ 503/639–8860) contains five major department stores, including Meier & Frank and Sears Roebuck; a food court; and 140 specialty shops. Discount and electronics stores are nearby.

The **Water Tower** (⊠ 5331 S.W. MacAdam Ave., Southwest Portland ☎ 503/242–0022), in the John's Landing neighborhood on the Willamette River, is a pleasant mall with more than 20 specialty shops and nine restaurants.

Specialty Stores

Antiques

Portland Antique Company (⊠ 2929 S.E. Powell, Pearl District ☎ 503/232–4001) spreads over 35,000 square feet. It has the Pacific Northwest's largest selection of European and English antiques.

Moreland House (⊠ 826 N.W. 23rd, Nob Hill ☎ 503/222–0197) has eclectic antiques and gifts, with a notable selection of dog collectibles, old printing-press type, and fresco tiles.

Shogun's Gallery (⊠ 1111 N.W. 23rd Ave., Nob Hill ☎ 503/224–0328) specializes in Japanese and Chinese furniture, especially the lightweight wooden Japanese cabinets known as *tansu*. Also here are chairs, tea tables, altar tables, armoires, ikebana baskets, and Chinese wooden picnic boxes, all of them at least 100 years old and at extremely reasonable prices. **Stars Antique Mall** (⊠ 7027 S.E. Milwaukie, Sellwood ☎ 503/239–0346), Portland's largest antiques mall, with three stores in the Sellwood neighborhood, rents its space to 300 antiques dealers; you might find anything from low-end 1950s kitsch to high-end treasures. The stores are within walking distance of each other.

Art Dealers & Galleries

Butters Gallery, Ltd. (⊠ 520 N.W. Davis, Pearl District ☎ 503/248–9378) has monthly exhibits of the works of nationally known and local artists in its Pearl District space.

Graystone Gallery (⊠ 3279 S.E. Hawthorne Blvd., Hawthorne District ☎ 503/238–0651) takes up two floors of a large house on Hawthorne and is filled with pottery and paintings, as well as some kitschy gift items and jewelry.

In Her Image Gallery (⊠ 3208 S.E. Hawthorne Blvd., Hawthorne ☎ 503/231–3726) specializes in statues, totems, and works of art dedicated to the great earth goddesses.

Margo Jacobsen Gallery (⊠ 1039 N.W. Glisan St., Pearl District ☎ 503/224–7287) exhibits works by local and nationally known artists and has a large selection of glass, ceramics, sculpture, paintings, and photography.

Our Dream Gallery (⊠ 2315 N.E. Alberta St., Alberta District ☎ 503/288–3024) displays contemporary works by local African-American artists.

Photographic Image Gallery (⊠ 240 S.W. 1st Ave., Old Town ☎ 503/224–3543) carries prints by nationally known nature photographers Christopher Burkett and Joseph Holmes, among others, and has a large supply of photography posters.

Pulliam/Deffenbaugh Gallery (⊠ 522 N.W. 12th Ave., Pearl District ☎ 503/228–6665) generally shows contemporary figurative and expressionistic works by Pacific Northwest artists.

Quintana's Galleries of Native American Art (⊠ 501 S.W. Broadway, Downtown ☎ 503/223–1729 or 800/321–1729) focuses on Pacific Northwest coast, Navajo, and Hopi art and jewelry, along with photogravures by Edward Curtis.

Talisman Gallery (⊠ 1476 N.E. Alberta St., Alberta District ☎ 503/284–8800) is a cooperative gallery formed in 1999 that showcases two artists each month, including local painters and sculptors.

Twist (⊠ 30 N.W. 23rd Pl., Nob Hill ☎ 503/224–0334 ⊠ Pioneer Place ☎ 503/222–3137) has a huge space in Nob Hill and a smaller shop downtown. In Nob Hill are contemporary American ceramics, glass, furniture, sculpture, and handcrafted jewelry; downtown carries an assortment of objects, often with a pop, whimsical touch.

Books

Broadway Books (⊠ 1714 N.E. Broadway, Broadway District ☎ 503/284–1726) is a fabulous independent bookstore with books on all subjects including Judaica literature and information on the Pacific Northwest.

In Other Words (⊠ 3734 S.E. Hawthorne Blvd., Hawthorne District ☎ 503/232–6003) is a nonprofit feminist bookstore that carries feminist literature, as well as acting as a community resource for feminist events and readings.

New Renaissance Bookshop (⊠ 1338 N.W. 23rd Ave., Nob Hill ☎ 503/224–4929), between Overton and Pettygrove, is dedicated to new-age and metaphysical books and tapes.

Powell's City of Books (⊠ 1005 W. Burnside St., Downtown ☎ 503/228–4651), the largest used- and new retail bookstore in the world (with more than 1.5 million volumes), covers an entire city block on the edge of the Pearl District. It also carries rare hard-to-find editions.

Powell's for Cooks and Gardeners (✉ 3747 Hawthorne Blvd., Hawthorne District ☎ 503/235–3802), on the east side, has a small adjoining grocery. There's also a small store in the Portland International Airport.

Twentythird Ave. Books (✉ 1015 N.W. 23rd Ave., Nob Hill ☎ 503/224–5097) is a cozy independent bookstore that makes for great browsing if you want to escape the bustle of 23rd Avenue.

Clothing

Clogs 'n' More (✉ 717 S.W. Alder, Downtown ☎ 503/279–9358 ✉ 3439 S.E. Hawthorne, Hawthorne District ☎ 503/232–7007), with locations both on the west and east sides of the city, carries quality clogs and other shoes.

Eight Women (✉ 3614 S.E. Hawthorne, Hawthorne District ☎ 503/236–8878) is a tiny boutique "for mother and child," with baby clothes, women's nightgowns, jewelry, and handbags.

Elizabeth Street and Zelda's Shoe Bar (✉ 635 N.W. 23rd Ave., Nob Hill ☎ 503/243–2456), two connected boutiques in Nob Hill, carry a sophisticated, highly eclectic line of women's clothes, accessories, and shoes.

Imelda's Designer Shoes (✉ 1431 S.E. 37th Ave., Hawthorne District ☎ 503/233–7476) is an upscale boutique with funky, fun shoes for women with flair.

Jane's Obsession (✉ 521 S.W. Broadway, Downtown ☎ 503/221–1490), a porch-level shop in one of Northwest 23rd Avenue's "house boutiques," sells luxurious French and Italian lingerie.

Mario's (✉ 921 S.W. Morrison St., Downtown ☎ 503/227–3477), Portland's best store for fine men's clothing, carries designer lines by Canali, Armani, Vestimenta, Donna Karan, and Calvin Klein, among others.

Mario's for Women (✉ 811 S.W. Morrison St., Downtown ☎ 503/241–8111) stocks Armani, Calvin Klein, and Vesti.

Mimi and Lena (✉ 823 N.W. 23rd Ave., Nob Hill ☎ 503/224–7736) is a small boutique with expensive but beautifully feminine and unique designer clothing.

Nob Hill Shoes and Repair (✉ 921 N.W. 23rd Ave., Nob Hill ☎ 503/224–8682), a tiny spot, sells men's and women's Naot sandals from Israel and Swedish Bastad clogs.

Norm Thompson Outfitters (✉ 1805 N.W. Thurman St., Nob Hill ☎ 503/221–0764) carries classic fashions for men and women, innovative footwear, and one-of-a-kind gifts.

Portland Outdoor Store (✉ 304 S.W. 3rd Ave., Downtown ☎ 503/222–1051) stubbornly resists all that is trendy, both in clothes and decor, but if you want authentic western gear—saddles, Stetsons, boots, or cowboy shirts—head here.

Portland Pendleton Shop (✉ S.W. 4th Ave. and Salmon St., Downtown ☎ 503/242–0037) stocks clothing by the famous local apparel maker.

M. Sellin, Ltd. (✉ 3556 S.E. Hawthorne Blvd., Hawthorne District ☎ 503/239–4605) has quality clothing for women as well as shoes and jewelry.

Tumbleweed (✉ 1804 N.E. Alberta St., Alberta District ☎ 503/335–3100) carries fun and stylish designer clothing you might describe as "country chic," for the woman who likes to wear flirty feminine dresses with cowboy boots. There is also unique baby and toddler clothing.

Gifts

Babik's (✉ 730 N.W. 23rd Ave., Nob Hill ☎ 503/248–1771) carries an enormous selection of hand-woven rugs from Turkey, all made from hand-spun wool and all-natural dyes.

The **Backyard Bird Shop** (✉ 3574 S.E. Hawthorne Blvd., Hawthorne District ☎ 503/230–9557) has everything for the bird lover: bird feeders, birdhouses, a huge supply of bird seed, and quality bird-theme gifts ranging from wind chimes to stuffed animals.

Christmas at the Zoo (⊠ 118 N.W. 23rd Ave., Nob Hill ☎ 503/223–4048 or 800/223–5886) is crammed year-round with decorated trees and has Portland's best selection of European hand-blown glass ornaments and plush animals.

Gai-Pied (⊠ 2544 N.E. Broadway, near Lloyd District ☎ 503/331–1125) carries periodicals, books, gifts, and videos of interest to the gay community.

Greg's (⊠ 3707 S.E. Hawthorne Blvd., Hawthorne District ☎ 503/235–1257) has the feel of an upscale vintage shop, with a fun poster art, postcards, '20s-style gifts, and artsy home furnishings.

Hawthorne Coffee Merchant (⊠ 3562 Hawthorne Blvd., Hawthorne District ☎ 503/230–1222) will lure you in with its aroma of coffee and candy, and once you're inside, you will find coffeepots and teapots, coffee and tea blends, espresso makers, and candy.

Heaven and Earth Home and Garden (⊠ 3206 S.E. Hawthorne Blvd., Hawthorne District ☎ 503/230–7033) is a lovely small store with gifts for home and garden as well as plants and flowers.

Kathmandu to You (⊠ 511 N.W. 21st Ave., Nob Hill ☎ 503/221–9986) sells clothing, incense, and Eastern religious artifacts and gifts.

La Bottega de Mamma Ro (⊠ 940 N.W. 23rd, Nob Hill ☎ 503/241–4960) carries Italian tabletop and home accessories, including a colorful line of dishes and cloth for tablecloths and napkins.

Made in Oregon (☎ 800/828–9673), which sells books, smoked salmon, local wines, Pendleton woolen goods, carvings made of myrtle wood, and other products made in the state, has shops at Portland International Airport, the Lloyd Center, the Galleria, Old Town, Washington Square, and Clackamas Town Center.

Moonstruck (⊠ 526 N.W. 23rd Ave., Nob Hill ☎ 503/542–3400), even without its nod from Oprah, is doing well for itself as a chocolatier extraordinaire. Just a couple of the rich confections might sustain you if you're nibbling—water is available for palate cleansing in between treats—but whether you're just grazing or boxing some up for the road, try The Ocumarian Truffle, chocolate laced with chili pepper; the unusual kick of sweetness and warmth is worth experiencing.

Pastaworks (⊠ 3735 S.E. Hawthorne Blvd., Southeast Portland ☎ 503/232–1010) sells cookware, fancy deli food, organic produce, beer, wine, and pasta.

At **Stella's on 21st** (⊠ 1108 N.W. 21st Ave., Nob Hill ☎ 503/295–5930), there are eccentric, colorful, and artsy items for the home, including lamps, candles, and decorations, as well as jewelry.

Jewelry

Carl Greve (⊠ 731 S.W. Morrison St., Downtown ☎ 503/223–7121), in business since 1922, carries exclusive designer lines of fine jewelry, such as Mikimoto pearls, and has the state's only Tiffany boutique. The second floor is reserved for china, stemware, and housewares.

Music

Artichoke Music (⊠ 3130 S.E. Hawthorne Blvd., Hawthorne District ☎ 503/232–8845) is a friendly family-owned business that sells guitars, banjos, mandolins, and other instruments that might come in handy for a bluegrass bands. Music lessons are led in two sound-proof practice rooms, and music performances and song-circles are held in the café in the back.

Classical Millennium (⊠ 3144 E. Burnside St., Laurelhurst ☎ 503/231–8909) has the best selection of classical CDs and tapes in Oregon.

Django Records (✉ 404 N.W. 10th Ave., Pearl District ☎ 503/227–4381) is a must for collectors of music and video. There is an extensive used-CD selection.

Music Millennium Northwest (✉ 801 N.W. 23rd Ave., Nob Hill ☎ 503/248–0163) stocks a huge selection of CDs and tapes in every possible musical category, from local punk to classical.

Outdoor Supplies

Andy and Bax (✉ 324 S.E. Grand Ave., near Morrison Bridge ☎ 503/234–7538) is an army-navy/outdoors store, with good prices on everything from camo-gear to rafting supplies.

Countrysport Limited (✉ 126 S.W. 1st Ave., Old Town ☎ 503/221–4545) is a fly-fishing specialty shop and a fascinating place to wander whether or not you're an angler.

Next Adventure Sports (✉ 426 S.E. Grand Ave., near Morrison Bridge ☎ 503/233–0706) carries new and used sporting goods, including camping gear, snowboards, kayaks, and mountaineering supplies.

Perfume

Aveda Lifestyle Store and Spa (✉ 500 S.W. 5th Ave., Downtown ☎ 503/248–0615) sells the flower-based Aveda line of scents and skin-care products.

Perfume House (✉ 3328 S.E. Hawthorne Blvd., Hawthorne District ☎ 503/234–5375) carries hundreds of brand-name fragrances for women and men.

Toys

Finnegan's Toys and Gifts (✉ 922 S.W. Yamhill St., Downtown ☎ 503/221–0306), downtown Portland's largest toy store, stocks artistic, creative, educational, and other types of toys.

Kids at Heart (✉ 3445 S.E. Hawthorne Blvd., Hawthorne District ☎ 503/231–2954) is a small, colorful toy store on Hawthorne with toys, models, and stuffed animals for kids of all ages.

PORTLAND A TO Z

To research prices, get advice from other travelers, and book travel arrangements, visit www.fodors.com.

ADDRESSES

The Willamette River and Burnside Street divide the metro area into four quarters. Addresses containing a northwest designation are north of Burnside and west of the river, southwest designations are south of Burnside and west of the river, and so forth. Downtown is in the southwest, and Hawthorne Boulevard is in the southeast. Numbered roads in Portland are avenues and run north–south, and named roads are streets, generally running east–west, with several exceptions, including Martin Luther King Blvd., Grand Avenue, S.W. Broadway, and S.W. Park. House numbers on east–west streets correspond to the numbered avenue on the closest cross street (for example, 601 Burnside would be on the corner of 6th Avenue and Burnside Street), and house numbers on north–south streets correspond to the number of blocks north or south of Burnside (for example, 500 S.W. 6th Ave. is five blocks south of Burnside). On the west side, the streets north of Ankeny are alphabetized: Ankeny, Burnside, Couch, Davis, etc., all the way to Thurman, Vaughn, and Wilson in the far northwest.

AIR TRAVEL

Portland International Airport (PDX) is a sleek, modern airport with service to many international destinations, as well as all over the United

States. It is easily accessible from downtown Portland and is easy to navigate once inside. Even if your final destination is in another city in Oregon, you may choose to fly into Portland and rent a car to get there, because all other airports in the state are small regional airports with limited service. It is possible, however, to get a connecting flight from Portland airport to smaller cities in Oregon. Portland Airport is served by all major airlines as well as by several smaller regional carriers.

🔸 Carriers **Air B.C.** ☎ 888/247-2262 ⊕ www.aircanada.ca. **Alaska Airlines** ☎ 800/252-7522 ⊕ www.alaskaairlines.com. **America West** ☎ 800/235-9292 ⊕ www.americawest.com **American** ☎ 800/433-7300 ⊕ www.im.aa.com. **Continental** ☎ 800/523-3273 ⊕ www.continental.com. **Delta** ☎ 800/221-1212 ⊕ www.delta.com. **Frontier Air** ☎ 800/432-1359 ⊕ www.frontierairlines.com. **Hawaiian** ☎ 800/367-5320 ⊕ www.hawaiianair.com. **Horizon** ☎ 800/547-9308 ⊕ www.alaskaairlines.com. **Lufthansa** ☎ 800/645-3880 ⊕ www.lufthansa-usa.com. **Mexicana** ☎ 800/531-7921. **Northwest** ☎ 800/225-2525 ⊕ www.nwa.com. **Southwest** ☎ 800/435-9792 ⊕ www.southwest.com. **Sky West** ☎ 800/453-9417 ⊕ www.skywest.com. **United/United Express** ☎ 800/241-6522 ⊕ www.ual.com

AIRPORTS

For flights departing from Portland International Airport (PDX), you should arrive at least an hour early for domestic flights and two hours early for international flights. Security lines can be long, and you will not necessarily get bumped to the front of the line just because you are running late.

🔸 Airport Information **Portland International Airport** ✉ N.E. Airport Way at I-205 ☎ 877/739-4636 ⊕ www.portlandairportpdx.com.

AIRPORT TRANSFERS Gray Line buses leave from the airport every 45 minutes and serve most major downtown hotels. The fare is $15 one-way. Tri-Met trains and buses also serve the airport (⇨ Bus Travel Within Portland).
🔸 **Gray Line** ☎ 503/285-9845 or 800/422-7042.

BUSINESS HOURS

BANKS & OFFICES Most banks are open weekdays 10 AM–4 PM. Many are open Saturday morning.

GAS STATIONS Stations are open seven days a week, and many are open 24 hours a day. Several are on northeast Broadway near the Rose Garden arena.

MUSEUMS & SIGHTS Most museums and attractions are open Tuesday–Sunday.

SHOPS Most retail businesses are open Monday–Saturday 10 AM–6 PM and Sunday noon–6 PM. Shopping centers are open Monday–Saturday until 9 PM and Sunday noon–6 PM.

BUS TRAVEL TO & FROM PORTLAND

Greyhound is a good way to get between destinations in Oregon for a reasonable price if you don't have a car at your disposal. It is cheaper than the train but often takes longer and makes frequent stops. Portland is the main hub for nearly all routes in the state, making it the most practical starting and ending point for most bus excursions. One route heads north on I–5 to Seattle and beyond, and south through Salem, Eugene, and Ashland. An east–west route follows I–84 through Pendleton, La Grande, and Ontario, and another route dips down to Bend and follows Route 97 to Klamath Falls. Finally, a coast route runs down to California on U.S. 101. Keep in mind that many small towns in Oregon may not be regularly accessible by bus and that there may be no public transportation or car rental locations in many towns you visit. Buses arrive at and depart from the Greyhound terminal next to the Amtrak station in Old Town. You can book tickets ahead of time by phone or online, but it is generally unnecessary. The only way to guarantee a seat on a given bus is to get there early enough and be on line before the bus fills up. Often, during peak travel times, Greyhound will send an additional bus if there are too many passengers for one vehicle.

🚌 Bus Depots **Greyhound Terminal** ✉ 550 N.W. 6th Ave., Old Town ☎ 503/243-2310 or 800/231-2222, 503/243-2337 baggage, 503/243-2361 customer service ☉ Daily 5 AM–11:30 PM and midnight–1 AM.

BUS TRAVEL WITHIN PORTLAND

Tri-Met operates an extensive system of buses, streetcars, and light-rail trains. The Central City streetcar line runs between Legacy Good Samaritan hospital in Nob Hill, the Pearl District, downtown, and Portland State University. To Nob Hill it travels along 10th Avenue and then on Northwest Northrup; from Nob Hill it runs along Northwest Lovejoy and then on 11th Avenue. Trains stop every few blocks. MAX light-rail trains run between downtown, the airport, and the western and eastern suburbs and stop at the zoo, the Rose Garden arena, PGE Park, and Lloyd Center.

A 5½-mi extension of the MAX light-rail system, running from the Gateway Transit Center (at the intersection of I–84 and I–205) directly to and from the airport, opened in fall 2001. Trains arrive at and depart from inside the passenger terminal near the south baggage-claim area. The trip takes about 35 minutes from downtown. Tri-Met Bus 12, which runs about every 15 minutes, also serves the airport. The fare to or from the airport on MAX or the bus is $1.25.

FARES & SCHEDULES Bus, MAX, and streetcar fare is $1.25 for one or two zones, which cover most places you will have cause to go, and $1.55 for three zones, which includes all of the outlying areas of the city. Ask the driver if you are uncertain whether you are traveling within Zones 1 and 2. A "fareless square" extends from downtown all the way to the Lloyd Center on the east side. If you are riding only within this area, your ride is free; just say "fareless" as you board the bus, and be sure to get off before you pass into a fare zone; drivers really do take note of who is riding for free, and may ask you to get off the bus. Day passes for unlimited system-wide travel cost $4. Three-day and monthly passes are available. As you board the bus, the driver will hand you a transfer ticket that is good for one to two hours, depending on the time of day, on all buses and MAX trains. Be sure to hold on to it whether you are transferring or not; it also serves as proof that you have paid for your ride. MAX trains run every 10 minutes Monday–Saturday before 8 PM and every 15 minutes after 8 PM and all day Sunday and holidays. Buses can operate as frequently as every five minutes or once an hour. Bikes are allowed on designated areas of MAX trains, and there are bike racks on the front of all buses that everyone is free to use.

🚌 Bus Information **Tri-Met/MAX** ✉ 6th Ave. and Morrison St., Downtown ☎ 503/238-7433 ⊕ www.tri-met.org, www.portlandstreetcar.org.

CAR RENTALS

Most major rental companies have rental offices in the Portland airport and downtown. (For rental-company 800 numbers, *see* Car Rentals *in* Smart Travel Tips).

🚗 Local Agencies, Portland Airport **Alamo** ☎ 503/249-4907 ⊕ www.alamo.com. **Avis** ☎ 503/249-4953 ⊕ www.avis.com. **Budget** ☎ 503/249-4556 ⊕ www.budget.com. **Dollar** ☎ 503/249-4792 ⊕ www.dollar.com. **Hertz** ☎ 503/249-8216 ⊕ www.hertz.com. **National** ☎ 503/249-4907 ⊕ www.nationalcar.com.

🚗 Local Agencies, Downtown **Enterprise** ☎ 503/252-1500 ⊕ www.enterprise.com. **Thrifty** ☎ 503/254-6563.

CAR TRAVEL

I–5 enters Portland from the north and south. I–84, the city's major eastern corridor, terminates in Portland. U.S. 26 and U.S. 30 are primary east–west thoroughfares. Bypass routes are I–205, which links I–5 and I–84 before crossing the Columbia River into Washington, and I–405, which arcs around western downtown. Most city-center streets are one-way only, and Southwest 5th and 6th avenues between Burnside and Southwest Madison streets are limited to bus traffic.

From the airport to downtown, take I–205 south to westbound I–84. Drive west over the Willamette River and take the City Center exit. If going to the airport, take I–84 east to I–205 north; follow I–205 to the airport exit.

EMERGENCY SERVICES **American Automobile Association** ☎ 503/222–6777 or 800/AAA–HELP. **Oregon State Police** ☎ 503/731–3030.

PARKING Most parking meters are patrolled Monday–Saturday 8 AM–6 PM. Meters, which accept credit cards, cost $1 an hour, emitting a transferrable parking sticker that you can affix to your car window. Many streets have parking time limits or prohibited parking during rush hour. To avoid the hassle of moving your car every two hours, consider one of the reasonably priced "Smart Park" parking garages downtown. Meter parking is free on Sunday and major holidays. The meters, representing one of Portland's many efforts to maintain sustainability, are solar powered.

TRAFFIC Traffic on I–5 north and south of downtown and on I–84 and I–205 east of downtown is heavy between 6 AM and 9 AM and between 4 and 8 PM. Four-lane U.S. 26 west of downtown can be bumper-to-bumper any time of the day going to or from downtown.

CHILDREN IN PORTLAND

Portland has green parks scattered throughout the city, making it a great place to travel with kids. Washington Park can provide a day's worth of outdoor fun, but the smaller parks found all over the east side of the city also provide endless opportunity for picnics, ball games, or just a short jaunt on a playground. Attractions specifically geared toward children include the Children's Museum, the Oregon Museum of Science and Industry, Oaks Amusement Park, and the Oregon Zoo.

CONSULATES

Belgium, Cyprus, Denmark, Germany, Italy, Japan, Mexico, the Netherlands, Sweden, Thailand, and the United Kingdom all have consulates in the Portland area.

Belgium ✉ 2812 N.W. Imperial Terr. ☎ 503/228–0465. **Cyprus** ✉ 1130 S.W. Morrison St., Suite 510 ☎ 503/248–0500. **Denmark** ✉ 888 S.W. 5th Ave. ☎ 503/802–2131. **Germany** ✉ 200 S.W. Market St. ☎ 503/222–0490. **Italy** ✉ 4507 S.E. Milwaukie Ave., Suite A ☎ 503/287–2578. **Japan** ✉ 1300 S.W. 5th Ave., Suite 2700 ☎ 503/221–1811. **Mexico** ✉ 1234 S.W. Morrison St. ☎ 503/274–1442. **Netherlands** ✉ 520 S.W. Yamhill St., Suite 600 ☎ 503/222–7957. **Sweden** ✉ 111 S.W. 5th Ave., Suite 2900 ☎ 503/227–0634. **Thailand** ✉ 121 S.W. Salmon St., Suite 1430 ☎ 503/221–0440. **United Kingdom** ✉ 520 S.W. Yamhill St., Suite 800 ☎ 503/227–5665.

DISABILITIES & ACCESSIBILITY

In many areas, Portland is exemplary for the measures it has taken to assist travelers and residents with disabilities. All Tri-Met buses and MAX trains are wheelchair accessible, and the Portland airport has received praise for the excellent access it provides for deaf and hearing-impaired travelers. Most restaurants and hotels are accessible for travelers who use wheelchairs, although several historical inns and B&Bs may not be. Independent Living Resources is an excellent source for people with disabilities living and traveling in the Portland area and has information on facilities, assistance, and basic rights for people with disabilities.

🔢 Local Resources **Independent Living Resources** ✉ 2410 S.E. 11th Ave. ☎ 503/232-7411.

DISCOUNTS & DEALS

The Portland Oregon Visitors Association is an excellent resource for information on discounts and promotional deals that may save you money on lodging, dining, and area attractions. The Big Deal is sponsored by POVA and is geared toward providing discounts for hotels, restaurants, and attractions between October and May, to promote tourism during the "off-season." Discounts vary in size from $1 off museum admission to as much as 50% off the advertised room rates for several lovely area hotels. Visit the POVA Web site or call to find out what establishments are participating. Ticket Central has half-price tickets every day for theater and musical performances to be held that night, depending on availability. Call after 10 AM to hear the day's offerings. You must go in person to purchase tickets. It's open weekdays 10–5, Saturday 10–2, and is closed Sunday.

🔢 **The Big Deal** ☎ 877/678-5263 ⊕ www.pova.com. **Ticket Central** ✉ In visitor center in Pioneer Sq. ☎ 503/275-8358.

EMERGENCIES

🔢 Doctors & Dentists **Tanasbourne Urgent Care** ✉ 1881 N.W. 185th Ave., Hillsboro ☎ 503/690-6818. **Willamette Dental Group PC** ✉ 1933 S.W. Jefferson St., Goose Hollow, near Downtown ☎ 503/644-3200.

🔢 Emergency Services **Ambulance, fire, police** ☎ 911.

🔢 Hospitals **Eastmoreland Hospital** ✉ 2900 S.E. Steele St., Eastmoreland ☎ 503/234-0411. **Legacy Emanuel Hospital and Health Center** ✉ 2801 N. Gantenbein Ave., North Portland, near Fremont Bridge ☎ 503/413-2200. **Legacy Good Samaritan Hospital & Medical Center** ✉ 1015 N.W. 22nd Ave., Nob Hill ☎ 503/413-7711. **Providence Portland Medical Center** ✉ 4805 N.E. Glisan St., near Laurelhurst ☎ 503/215-1111. **Providence St. Vincent Hospital** ✉ 9205 S.W. Barnes Rd., west of Downtown ☎ 503/216-1234.

🔢 Hotlines **Poison Center** ☎ 503/494-8968.

🔢 24-Hour Pharmacy **Walgreens** ✉ 940 S.E. 39th Ave., Hawthorne District ☎ 503/238-6053.

LODGING

While vacation rental homes and cabins abound in areas outside of Portland, around Mt. Hood, and on the coast, in the city you are mostly limited to fairly standard hotels, motels, and B&Bs. If you are planning a long-term stay, however, many hotels, such as the Marriott Residence Inn, offer weekly or monthly rates. If you intend to spend more than a month in the city, you might look into short-term rental options, such as sublets. You can peruse the options for independently arranged short-term rentals in the newspaper classifieds. The *Oregonian* and *Willamette Week* both make their classified ads available online. If you are looking for a standard hotel or motel, POVA runs a room reservation service that may be of assistance if you find yourself at a loss for where to stay; it's open weekdays 8:30–5.

🔢 Resources **The *Oregonian*** ⊕ www.oregonlive.com. **The *Willamette Week*** ⊕ www.wweek.com. **POVA** ✉ In Pioneer Courthouse Sq. ☎ 877/678-5263.

BED-AND-BREAKFASTS Bed-and-breakfasts abound in Portland, and most offer lovely, carefully tended rooms; full breakfast; and knowledgeable and helpful owners. It might be difficult to choose between them. The Oregon Bed & Breakfast Guild can provide detailed information to help you make up your mind, but it is not a reservation service; Northwest Bed & Breakfast Reservation Service can take you the whole way to booking a room.

🛈 Resources **Oregon Bed & Breakfast Guild** ☎ 541/201–0511 or 800/944–6196 🌐 www. obbg.org. **Northwest Bed & Breakfast Reservation Service** ✉ 610 S.W. Broadway, Portland ☎ 503/243–7616.

MAIL & SHIPPING

🛈 Post Offices **Central Station Post Office** ✉ 204 S.W. 5th Ave. ☎ 503/294–2564. **Pioneer Station** ✉ 520 S.W. 5th Ave., across from Pioneer Courthouse Sq. ☎ 503/294–2564. **Main Post Office** ✉ 715 N.W. Hoyt, Pearl District ☎ 800/275–8777. **University Station** ✉ 1505 S.W. 6th Ave.

MEDIA

NEWSPAPERS & MAGAZINES The *Oregonian* is Portland's daily newspaper. The *Portland Tribune* is distributed free Tuesday and Friday. *Willamette Week* is a free weekly published every Friday. *Just Out,* published twice monthly, is the city's gay newspaper. The *Skanner* is the city's African-American weekly.

RADIO & TELEVISION NBC: KGW Channel 8; ABC: KATU Channel 4; CBS: KOIN Channel 6; UPN: KPTV Channel 12; PBS: KOPB Channel 10; Fox: KPDX Channel 49; WB: KWBP Channel 32. NPR: KOPB-FM 91.5; News/talk: KXL-AM 750.

TAXIS

Taxi fare is $2.50 at flag drop plus $1.50 per mile. The first person pays by the meter, and each additional passenger pays $1. Cabs cruise the city streets, but it's better to phone for one. The major companies are Broadway Cab, New Rose City Cab, Portland Taxi Company, and Radio Cab. The trip between downtown Portland and the airport takes about 30 minutes by taxi. The fare is about $20.

🛈 Taxi Companies **Broadway Cab** ☎ 503/227–1234. **New Rose City Cab** ☎ 503/282–7707. **Portland Taxi Company** ☎ 503/256–5400. **Radio Cab** ☎ 503/227–1212.

TELEPHONES

AREA CODES The area codes for the Portland metro area are 503 and 971.

PHONE CARDS **AT&T** (☎ 800/321–0288). **MCI/Worldcom** (☎ 800/444–3333). **Sprint** (☎ 800/877–8000).

PUBLIC PHONES Local calls at most pay phones cost 50¢. Before making a long-distance call from a pay phone, check to see which long-distance provider is being used. Use a calling card if you have one.

TOURS

BIKE TOURS Rose City Bike Tours has regularly scheduled tours of the Portland area.

🛈 Tour Operator **Rose City Bike Tours** ✉ 2080 S.E. Caruthers St., south of Hawthorne District ☎ 503/241–0340.

BOAT TOURS Sternwheeler Riverboat Tours' *Columbia Gorge* departs year-round from Tom McCall Waterfront Park on two-hour excursions of the Willamette River; there are also Friday-night dinner cruises. During the summer the stern-wheeler travels up the Columbia River. Yachts-O-Fun Cruises operates dinner and Sunday-brunch cruises, Portland harbor excursions, and historical tours.

🛈 Tour Operator **Sternwheeler Riverboat Tours** ✉ S.W. Naito Pkwy. and Stark St., Riverfront Park ☎ 503/223–3928. **Yachts-O-Fun Cruises** ✉ S.E. Marion Street ☎ 503/234–6665.

BUS TOURS Gray Line operates city tours year-round and scheduled service to Chinook Winds Casino in Lincoln City; call for departure times.

🛈 Fees & Schedules **Gray Line** ☎ 503/285–9845.

TROLLEY TOURS The Willamette Shore Trolley company operates vintage double-decker electric trolleys that provide scenic round-trips between suburban Lake Oswego and downtown, along the west shore of the Willamette River. The 7-mi route, which the trolley traverses in 45 minutes, passes over trestles and through Elk Rock tunnel along one of the most scenic stretches of the river. The line, which opened in 1885, was electrified in 1914, and Southern Pacific Railway operated dozens of trips daily along this route in the 1920s. Passenger service ended in 1929, and the line was taken over by the Oregon Electric Railway Historical Society. Reservations are recommended. The trolley ($8 round-trip) departs Lake Oswego at noon and 2:30 PM and Portland at 1 and 3:15 on weekends from April through September. Charters are available.

🚋 **Willamette Shore Trolley** ✉ 311 N. State St., Lake Oswego ✉ South of RiverPlace Marina, at Sheridan and Moody Sts., Portland ☎ 503/222-2226.

WALKING TOURS The Portland Oregon Visitors Association (⇨ Visitor Information, which is open on weekdays 9–5 and Saturday 9–4, has brochures, maps, and guides to art galleries and select neighborhoods.

TRAIN TRAVEL

Amtrak serves Union Station. The *Coast Starlight* operates daily between Seattle, Portland, and Los Angeles. The *Empire Builder* travels between Portland and Chicago via Spokane and Minneapolis. The *Cascades,* modern European trains, operate daily between Eugene, Portland, Seattle, and Vancouver, B.C.

Metropolitan Area Express, or MAX, links the eastern and western Portland suburbs with downtown, Washington Park and the Oregon Zoo, the Lloyd Center district, the Convention Center, and the Rose Quarter. From downtown, trains operate daily 5:30 AM–1 AM, with a fare of $1.25 for travel through one or two zones, $1.55 for three zones, and $4 for an unlimited all-day ticket. A three-day visitor pass is also available for $10. Trains run about every 10 minutes Monday–Saturday and every 15 minutes on Sunday and holidays.

🚆 Train Information & Reservations **Amtrak** ✉ 800 N.W. 6th Ave., Old Town ☎ 800/872-7245. **MAX** ☎ 503/228-7246.

TRANSPORTATION AROUND PORTLAND

Tri-Met operates bus service throughout the greater Portland area. The fares are the same for buses and the MAX light-rail system, and tickets can be used on either system. Travel is free throughout the entire downtown "Fareless Square," whose borders are Northwest Irving Street to the north, I-405 to the west and south, and the Willamette River to the east. The Portland Central City Streetcar, which began operation in summer 2001, travels between Portland State University, the Pearl District, and the popular Nob Hill neighborhood northwest of downtown. The Tri-Met information office at Pioneer Courthouse Square is open weekdays 9–5.

🚍 **Tri-Met** ✉ 6th Ave. and Morrison St., Pioneer Courthouse Sq. ☎ 503/238-7433 ⊕ www.tri-met.org or www.portlandstreetcar.org.

VISITOR INFORMATION

🚹 Tourist Information **Portland Oregon Visitors Association** ✉ 1000 S.W. Broadway, Suite 2300, 97205 ☎ 800/962-3700 ⊕ www.pova.com.

Portland Oregon Visitors Association Information Center ✉ Pioneer Courthouse Sq. ☎ 503/275-8355 or 877/678-5263, is open weekdays 8:30–5:30, Saturday 10–4, Sunday 10–2.

OREGON

2

FODOR'S CHOICE

Columbia River Maritime Museum, *Astoria*

Cork, *contemporary fare in Bend*

Cove Palisades State Park, *Madras*

Evergreen Aviation Museum, *McMinnville*

High Desert Museum, *Bend*

Jacksonville Cemetery, *Jacksonville*

Lara House Bed & Breakfast Inn, *Bend*

Mattey House Bed & Breakfast, *McMinnville*

McMenamins Edgefield, *Troutdale B&B*

Merenda, *fine appetizers and wine in Bend*

Metolius River Resort, *Camp Sherman*

Newport Belle Bed & Breakfast, *Newport*

Parker House, *Pendleton B&B*

Red Agave, *southwestern fare in Eugene*

Smith Rock State Park, *Redmond*

Sunriver Resort, *Bend*

The Flying M Ranch, *Yamhill*

The Steamboat Inn, *Steamboat, east of Roseburg*

Timberline Lodge, *Mt. Hood*

Tina's, *country French food in Dundee*

Tu Tu' Tun Lodge, *near Gold Beach*

Under the Greenwood Tree, *Medford*

Underground, *old west tour in Pendleton*

Union Hotel, *Union*

Valley of the Rogue State Park, *Grants Pass*

NO MATTER WHAT you're looking for in a vacation, few other states offer more than Oregon. Within a 90-minute drive from Portland or Eugene you can lose yourself in the recreational landscape of your choice: un-crowded ocean beaches, snow-silvered mountain wilderness, or a mono-lith-studded desert that has served as the backdrop for many a Hollywood western. In the Willamette Valley wine country, scores of tasting rooms offer up the fruit of the vine. Food lovers find that Oregon produces some of the nation's best fruits, vegetables, and seafood, all of which can be enjoyed in fine restaurants throughout the state. Plenty of attractions keep the kids busy, too, from the Enchanted Forest near Salem to the exceptional Oregon Coast Aquarium in Newport. And shoppers take note—there's no sales tax in Oregon.

Although the state has a notorious reputation for being rainy, and win-ters can indeed be wet and dreary, the rest of the year more than makes up for it. Much of the state is actually a desert, and most of the pre-cipitation falls west of the Cascades. At its eastern end, Oregon begins in a high, sage-scented desert plateau that covers nearly two-thirds of the state's 96,000 square mi. As you move west, the landscape rises to 11,000-foot-high alpine peaks, meadows, and lakes; plunges to fertile farmland and forest; and ends at the cold, tumultuous Pacific.

Oregon's beneficent climate and landscape have supported human res-idents for a very long time. Evidence of Oregon's earliest Native Amer-ican inhabitants is tantalizingly rare, but what does exist suggests that tribes of nomadic hunter-gatherers established themselves throughout the region many centuries before the first white explorers and settlers arrived. In eastern Oregon, a pair of 9,000-year-old sagebrush sandals (now in the Oregon Museum of Natural History in Eugene) and nets woven from reeds have been discovered; on the coast, ancient shell middens indicate that even the earliest Oregonians feasted on seafood.

Although historians now suspect Sir Francis Drake secretly visited the Oregon coast in 1579, the first officially recorded visit came much later. In 1792, Robert Gray, an American trading captain, followed a trail of debris and muddy water inland and came upon the Columbia River. Shortly thereafter, British Army lieutenant William Broughton was dis-patched to investigate Gray's find, and he sailed as far upriver as the rapids-choked mouth of the Columbia River Gorge. Within a few years, a thriving seaborne fur trade sprang up, with American and British en-trepreneurs exchanging baubles, cloth, tools, weapons, and liquor with the native peoples for high-quality beaver and sea-otter pelts.

In 1805 American explorers Meriwether Lewis and William Clark reached the site of present-day Astoria after their epic overland jour-ney, spurring an influx of white pioneers—mostly fur trappers and traders sent by John Jacob Astor's Pacific Fur Company in 1811 to do business and claim the land for the United States. The English disputed American claims to the territory on the basis of Broughton's earlier ex-ploration, and after the War of 1812 began, they negotiated the pur-chase of Astoria from Astor's company. It wasn't until 1846, with the signing of the Oregon Treaty, that the British formally renounced their claims in the region.

Oregon Country, as it was called, grew tremendously between 1841 and 1860, as more than 50,000 settlers from the eastern United States made the journey westward over the plains in their covered wagons. There is a story, never confirmed, that early pioneers arriving at a crossroads of the Oregon Trail found a pile of gold quartz or pyrite pointing the way south to California. The way north was marked by a hand-lettered sign:

2

If you have
3 or 4
days

On your first day take U.S. 101 to the coastal resort town of Cannon Beach, and then continue south to Newport and visit the Oregon Coast Aquarium. On Day 2 drive east on U.S. 20, stopping briefly in Corvallis before continuing east on U.S. 20 and north on Interstate 5 (I–5) to Salem, the state capital. After touring Salem, visit one or more of the Willamette Valley vineyards around Forest Grove, Newberg, and Dundee before stopping in McMinnville for the night. On Day 3 take Highway 99 W north toward Portland and connect with I–5 heading north to I–84. The interstate winds eastward to the Columbia Gorge. At Troutdale, get on the Historic Columbia River Highway, which passes Multnomah Falls before rejoining I–84. Continue east to the Bonneville Dam and The Dalles. If you'll be staying in the area four days, spend night three in Hood River and swing down to Mount Hood the next morning.

If you have
7 or 8
days

Begin in Oregon's northwest, in Astoria, where the Columbia River meets the Pacific Ocean. From there, continue south on U.S. 101 to Cannon Beach. On Day 2 head south from Cannon Beach to Tillamook and the oceanfront parks on the Three Capes Loop. Continue south to Newport, where the Oregon Coast Aquarium is a must-see attraction. Spend the night south of Newport in the Florence area.

Drive south on Day 3 to Coos Bay and Bandon, then east on Highway 42 over the Coast Range to pick up I–5 heading south to Ashland. On Day 4 backtrack north on I–5 to Medford, where you can pick up Highway 62 heading north and then east to Crater Lake National Park. Spend the night at the park, or backtrack west on Highway 62 and pick up Highway 230 north to Highway 138 west to I–5, which leads north to Eugene. (If you're not going to stay at Crater Lake, you'll need to get an early start from Medford.)

If you've stayed at Crater Lake, on Day 5 take Highway 138 east from the north end of the park to U.S. 97, which travels north past the Newberry Volcanic National Monument to Bend. If you've spent the night in Eugene, travel east along the McKenzie River on Highway 126 to Highway 242 (closed in winter, in which case stay on 126) to U.S. 20. This route travels past the western-theme town of Sisters to Bend. On Day 6 head north on U.S. 97 and east on Highway 126 and U.S. 26 past the Ochoco National Forest and the John Day Fossil Beds National Monument. You have three options for lodgings, depending on how much time you spend at the fossil beds: Mitchell and John Day are both on U.S. 26; farther east on Highway 7 is Baker City. On Day 7, take scenic U.S. 30 north from Baker City to North Powder, and then continue north on I–84 to La Grande and Pendleton.

If you have the time, spend the night in Pendleton, and on Day 8 drive west on I–84 to the Columbia Gorge, stopping at the Bonneville Dam and Multnomah Falls.

TO OREGON, and Oregonians like to think that the more literate of the pioneers found their way here, while the fortune hunters continued south. As settlers capitalized on gold-rush San Francisco's need for provisions and other supplies, Oregon reaped its own riches, and the lawless frontier gradually acquired a semblance of civilization. Most white pioneers settled in the Willamette Valley, where the bulk of Oregon's 3.4 million residents still live. The territory's residents voted down the idea of statehood three times, but in 1859, Oregon became the 33rd U.S. state.

Tourism grows in importance every year, as visitors from all over the world discover the scenic and recreational treasures that so thrill Oregonians themselves. A sophisticated hospitality industry has appeared, making Oregon more accessible than ever before. You'll feel more than welcome here, but when you visit, expect a little ribbing if locals catch you mispronouncing the state's name: it's "Ore-ey-gun" not "Ore-uh-gone."

Exploring Oregon

Oregon's coastline stretches south from Astoria to the California border. Inland a bit, the fertile Willamette River valley also runs north–south. The mighty Columbia River travels west of the Cascade Range past the Mount Hood Wilderness Area to Astoria. The resort towns of Bend and Sisters are in Central Oregon, and the sparsely populated desert region is east of the Cascades.

Oregon tourist-information centers are marked with blue "I" signs from main roads. Opening and closing times vary, depending on the season and the individual office; call ahead for hours (⇨ Visitor Information *in* Oregon A to Z).

Numbers in the text correspond to numbers in the margin and on the maps.

About the Restaurants

Fresh foods grown, caught, and harvested in the Northwest are standard fare in gourmet restaurants throughout Oregon. Outside urban areas and resorts, most restaurants tend to be low-key and unpretentious, both in ambience and cuisine. On the coast, look for regional specialties—clam chowder, fresh fish (particularly salmon), sweet Dungeness crab, mussels, shrimp, and oysters. Elsewhere in the state fresh river fish, local lamb and beef, and seasonal game dishes appear on many menus, supplemented by Oregon hazelnuts and wines. Desserts made with local fruits such as huckleberries, raspberries, and marionberries are always worth trying.

About the Hotels

Luxury hotels, sophisticated resorts, historic lodges, Old West hotels, and rustic inns are among Oregon's diverse accommodations. Cozy bed-and-breakfasts, many of them in Victorian-era houses in small towns, are often real finds.

WHAT IT COSTS				
$$$$	**$$$**	**$$**	**$**	**¢**
RESTAURANTS over $30	$20–$30	$15–$20	$10–$15	under $10
HOTELS over $180	$140–$180	$100–$140	$60–$100	under $60

Restaurant prices are per person for a main course at dinner. Hotel prices are for a standard double room, excluding room tax, which varies 6%–9½% depending on location.

2

Beaches

Oregon has the most accessible shoreline in the Pacific Northwest. The long, sandy beaches run for miles at a stretch. But the waters are generally too cold or treacherous for swimming. Even in summertime, beach-goers must be prepared to dress warmly.

Biking & Hiking

For the past 20 years, Oregon has set aside 1% of its highway funds for the development and maintenance of bikeways throughout the state, resulting in one of the most extensive networks of bicycle trails in the country. The system of hiking trails through state-park and national-forest lands is equally comprehensive.

Boating, Canoeing & Rafting

Oregon's swift rivers provide challenges to boaters, canoeists, kayakers, and rafters. Many of these rivers should be attempted only by experienced boaters. Many companies operate boating and white-water rafting tours, or you can rent equipment and head out on your own. The Deschutes River north of Bend is a popular white-water rafting destination. Boating and rafting permits are required for the Rogue and lower Deschutes rivers. Recreational access to the Rogue is limited; a lottery for permits is held each February. For more information, contact the Rand Visitors Center in Galice. Permits for the Deschutes can be obtained at the Bureau of Land Management office in Prineville. June through September are prime months for white-water rafting.

Driving

While bicycling has a special place in the hearts of many Oregonians, motoring can be transformed from a utilitarian chore into a simple pleasure if you slow it down, drink in the scenery, and make liberal use of the state's many turnouts and overlooks. Driving along the coast is a singular pleasure, while taking the Columbia River Highway through the Columbia River Gorge is a historical and leisurely delight. McKenzie Pass, a scenic route in the Cascade Range that winds through the Mt. Washington Wilderness Area, is a challenging and indelible driving experience with its tight turns and birds-eye views. Hitting any road in Oregon at daybreak may heighten your driving experiences; you'll seemingly have the byways and pink and orange morning skies to yourself, at least for a while.

Fishing

The coastal regions and inland lakes and rivers of Oregon are known for excellent fishing. Depoe Bay is a leading port for cruising and deep-sea-fishing charters. Visiting anglers must possess a nonresident license for the state or province in which they plan to fish. Licenses are easily obtainable at sporting-goods stores, bait shops, and other outlets in fishing areas.

Golf

The Northwest has many excellent golf courses, but not all of them are open to the public. Consequently, visitors may find it difficult to arrange a tee time at a popular course. If you are a member of a golf club at home, check to see if your club has a reciprocal playing arrangement with private clubs in the areas that you will be visiting.

Hot-Air Ballooning

If you've ever wanted to float over a verdant landscape in the basket of a hot-air balloon, come to the Willamette Valley in the warmer months for an aerial view of Oregon's wine country.

Rockhounding

Rockhounding—searching for semiprecious or unusual rocks—is very popular in the Ochocos in central Oregon and Harney County and the Stinkingwater Mountains in eastern Oregon. Agate, obsidian, jasper, and thunder eggs are among the sought-after stones.

Sailboarding

The Columbia River, particularly at Hood River, is one of the world's premier locations for windsurfing. Sailboard rentals and lessons are available from local specialty shops.

Skiing

Most Oregon downhillers congregate around Mt. Hood and Mt. Bachelor, but there is also skiing to the south, at Willamette Pass and Mt. Ashland. The temperate Willamette Valley generally receives only a few inches of snow a year, but the Coast Range, the Cascade Range, and the Siskiyou Mountains are all Nordic skiers' paradises, crisscrossed by hundreds of miles of trails. Every major downhill ski resort in the state also has Nordic skiing, but don't rule out the many Forest Service trails and logging roads. Resort and lift-ticket prices tend to be less expensive in Oregon than at the internationally known ski destinations, but the slopes, especially on weekends, can be crowded.

Wildlife Viewing

Sea lions, seals, dolphins, and whales are a few of the marine mammals that can be observed in bays, near headlands, and along the coast. In spring and summer thousands of gray whales pass by the Oregon coast on their seasonal migration from Alaska to Baja California in Mexico. One of the easiest and most exciting ways to see them is by taking a whale-watching boat excursion. In the forests and along coastal rivers and estuaries deer, bald eagles, herons, and egrets are commonly seen. The dedicated birders who annually trek to the Northwest find that their efforts are amply rewarded.

Wine Tasting

The Willamette Valley is Oregon's main region for viticulture—many area wineries are open for tours, tastings, or both. Wineries near Forest Grove can be toured in an afternoon outing from Portland. South of the Willamette Valley are the Umpqua Valley and Rogue River wine-growing regions. The free Oregon winery guide published by the Oregon Wine Advisory Board (☎ 503/228–8336) provides profiles, detailed maps, and service information about most Oregon wineries that welcome visitors. It's available at many wine shops and visitor centers in the state.

Timing

Winters in western Oregon are usually mild, but they can be relentlessly rainy. To the east of the Cascade Range, winters are clearer, drier, and colder. December–April are the best months for whale-watching along the coast and February–May are best for bird-watching at the Malheur National Wildlife Refuge in southeastern Oregon. Spring weather is changeable on both sides of the Cascades, but the landscape is a Technicolor wonder of wildflowers, flowering fruit trees (in the Hood River valley), and gardens bursting with rhododendrons and azaleas.

Jacksonville and Eugene host world-class summer music festivals, and the theater season in Ashland lasts from February to October. July and August are the prime months for visiting Crater Lake National Park, which is often snowed in for the rest of the year. Those months are predictably dry east of the Cascades, where it can get downright hot, but you can make a quick escape to the coast, where even summer weather can be cool and foggy. If you're looking for clear days along the coast, however, late summer and early fall are your best bets; these are also the best times to visit the many wineries in the Willamette Valley. Fall is spectacular throughout the state, with leaves at their colorful peak in late October.

THE OREGON COAST

Updated by
Lori Tobias

Oregon has 300 mi of white-sand beaches, not a grain of which is privately owned. U.S. 101, called Highway 101 by most Oregonians (it sometimes appears this way in addresses as well), parallels the coast along the length of the state. It winds past sea-tortured rocks, brooding headlands, hidden beaches, historic lighthouses, and tiny ports, with the gleaming gun-metal-gray Pacific Ocean always in view. With its seaside hamlets and small hotels and resorts, the coast seems to have been created with pleasure in mind. South of Newport, the pace slows. The scenery and fishing and outdoor activities are just as rich as those in the towns to the north, but the area is less crowded and the commercialism less obvious.

Numbers in the text correspond to numbers in the margin and on the Oregon Coast map.

Astoria

❶ *96 mi northwest of Portland on U.S. 30.*

The mighty Columbia River meets the Pacific at Astoria, which was founded in 1811. The city was named for John Jacob Astor, then America's wealthiest man, who financed the original fur-trading colony here. Modern Astoria is a placid amalgamation of small town and hard-working port city. Settlers built sprawling Victorian houses on the flanks of **Coxcomb Hill.** Many of the homes have since been restored and are no less splendid as bed-and-breakfast inns. With so many museums, inns, and recreational offerings, Astoria should be one of the Northwest's prime tourist destinations. Yet the town remains relatively undiscovered, even by Portlanders.

Fodor'sChoice
★

The **Columbia River Maritime Museum,** on the downtown waterfront, explores the maritime history of the Pacific Northwest and is one of the two most interesting man-made tourist attractions on the Oregon coast (Newport's aquarium is the other). Beguiling exhibits include the personal belongings of some of the ill-fated passengers of the 2,000 ships that have foundered here since 1811. Also here are an observation tower of the World War II submarine USS *Rasher* (complete with working periscopes), the fully operational U.S. Coast Guard Lightship *Columbia,* and a 44-foot Coast Guard motor lifeboat. ⊠ *1792 Marine Dr., at 17th St.* ☎ *503/325–2323* ⊕ *www.crmm.org* ⊠ *$5* ☉ *Daily 9:30–5.*

The **Astoria Column,** a 125-foot monolith atop Coxcomb Hill that was patterned after Trajan's Column in Rome, rewards your 164-step, spiral-stair climb with views over Astoria, the Columbia River, the Coast

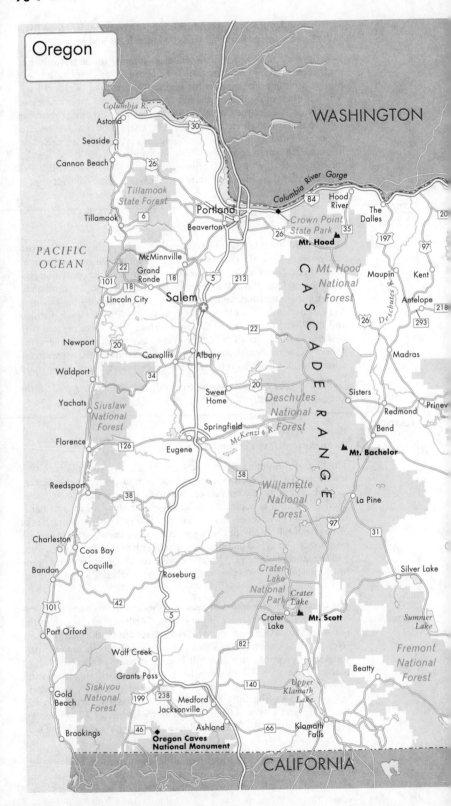

Oregon

WASHINGTON

Columbia R.

Astoria

Seaside

Cannon Beach

30

26

Tillamook
State Forest

Tillamook

6

Portland

Beaverton

Columbia River Gorge

84

Hood
River

The
Dalles

20

Crown Point
State Park

26

35

Mt. Hood

197

97

PACIFIC
OCEAN

McMinnville

22

Grand
Ronde

18

5

213

22

C
A
S
C
A
D
E

Mt. Hood
National
Forest

Maupin

Kent

Deschutes R.

Antelope

293

218

101

18

Lincoln City

Salem

Newport

20

Corvallis

Albany

22

Waldport

34

Sweet
Home

20

R
A
N
G
E

Deschutes
National
Forest

Sisters

Redmond

Prinev

Madras

Yachats

Siuslaw
National
Forest

Springfield

McKenzie R.

Bend

Florence

126

Eugene

Mt. Bachelor

Reedsport

58

Willamette
National
Forest

La Pine

38

97

31

Charleston

Coos Bay

Coquille

Roseburg

Crater
Lake
National
Park

Crater
Lake

Silver Lake

Bandon

42

Mt. Scott

Summer
Lake

Port Orford

5

82

Crater
Lake

Fremont
National
Forest

101

Wolf Creek

Grants Pass

140

Beatty

Gold
Beach

Siskiyou
National
Forest

199

238

Medford

Jacksonville

Upper
Klamath
Lake

Brookings

46

Ashland

66

Klamath
Falls

Oregon Caves
National Monument

CALIFORNIA

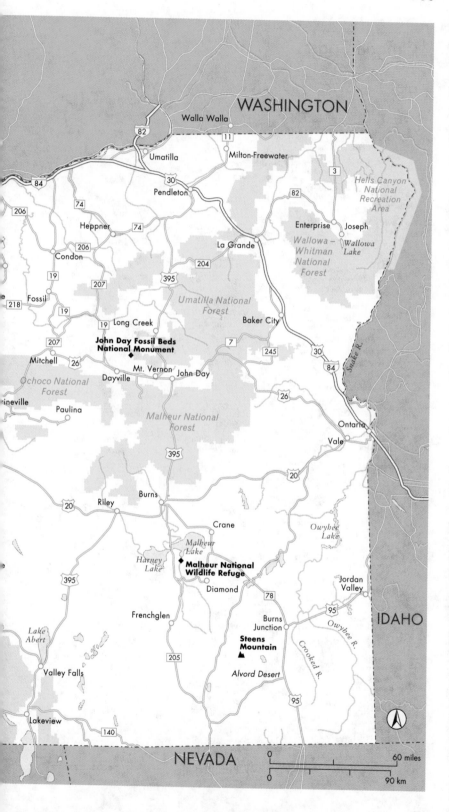

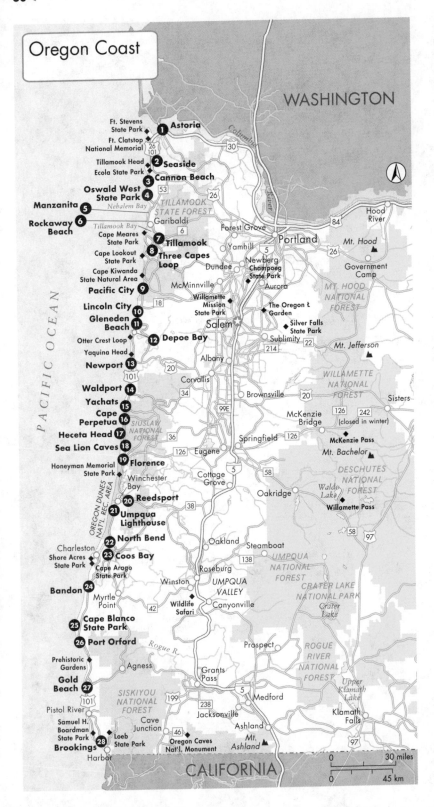

Oregon Coast

WASHINGTON

1 Astoria
Ft. Stevens State Park
Ft. Clatsop National Memorial
2 Seaside
Tillamook Head
Ecola State Park
3 Cannon Beach
4 Oswald West State Park
5 Manzanita
Nehalem Bay
6 Rockaway Beach
Tillamook Bay
Garibaldi
Cape Meares State Park
7 Tillamook
Cape Lookout State Park
8 Three Capes Loop
Cape Kiwanda State Natural Area
9 Pacific City
10 Lincoln City
11 Gleneden Beach
Otter Crest Loop
12 Depoe Bay
Yaquina Head
13 Newport
14 Waldport
15 Yachats
16 Cape Perpetua
17 Heceta Head
18 Sea Lion Caves
19 Florence
Honeyman Memorial State Park
Winchester Bay
20 Reedsport
21 Umpqua Lighthouse
22 North Bend
Charleston
Shore Acres State Park
23 Coos Bay
Cape Arago State Park
24 Bandon
Myrtle Point
25 Cape Blanco State Park
26 Port Orford
Prehistoric Gardens
27 Gold Beach
Pistol River
Samuel H. Boardman State Park
Loeb State Park
28 Brookings
Harbor

PACIFIC OCEAN

TILLAMOOK STATE FOREST

Forest Grove
Portland
Yamhill
Dundee
Newberg
Champoeg State Park
Aurora
McMinnville
Willamette Mission State Park
Salem
The Oregon Garden
Silver Falls State Park
Sublimity
Albany
Corvallis
Brownsville
SIUSLAW NATIONAL FOREST
McKenzie Bridge
Eugene
Springfield
Cottage Grove
Oakridge
Winchester Bay
OREGON DUNES NATL. REC. AREA
Oakland
Steamboat
UMPQUA NATIONAL FOREST
Roseburg
Winston
UMPQUA VALLEY
Wildlife Safari
Canyonville
Myrtle Point
Rogue R.
Agness
Grants Pass
ROGUE RIVER NATIONAL FOREST
Prospect
Crater Lake
CRATER LAKE NATIONAL PARK
SISKIYOU NATIONAL FOREST
Cave Junction
Oregon Caves Nat'l. Monument
Jacksonville
Ashland
Mt. Ashland
Medford
Grants Pass
Upper Klamath Lake
Klamath Falls

Hood River
84
Mt. Hood
Government Camp
MT. HOOD NATIONAL FOREST
Mt. Jefferson
WILLAMETTE NATIONAL FOREST
Sisters
McKenzie Pass (closed in winter)
McKenzie Pass
Mt. Bachelor
DESCHUTES NATIONAL FOREST
Waldo Lake
Willamette Pass

Columbia River

CALIFORNIA

0   30 miles
0   45 km

Range, and the Pacific. ✛ *From U.S. 30 downtown take 16th St. south 1 mi to the top of Coxcomb Hill* ✉ *Free* ☉ *Daily 9–dusk.*

The prim **Flavel House** was built between 1884 and 1886. Its Victorian-era furnishings, including six handcrafted fireplace mantels carved from different hardwoods and accented with tiles imported from Asia and Europe, yield insight into the lifestyle of a wealthy 19th-century shipping tycoon. Visits start in the Carriage House interpretive center. ✉ *441 8th St., at Duane St.* ☎ *503/325–2203* ⊕ *www.clatsophistoricalsociety.org* ✉ *$5* ☉ *May–Sept., daily 10–5; Oct.–Apr., daily 11–4.*

★ ℭ "Ocean in view! O! The joy!" recorded William Clark, standing on a spit of land south of present-day Astoria in the fall of 1805. **Fort Clatsop National Memorial** is a faithful replica of the log stockade depicted in Clark's journal. Park rangers, who dress in period garb during the summer and perform such early-19th-century tasks as making fire with flint and steel, lend an air of authenticity, as does the damp and lonely feel of the fort itself. ✉ *Fort Clatsop Loop Rd., 5 mi south of Astoria; from U.S. 101 cross Youngs Bay Bridge, turn east on Alt. U.S. 101, and follow signs* ☎ *503/861–2471* ⊕ *www.nps.gov.focl* ✉ *$5 per vehicle* ☉ *Mid-June–Labor Day, daily 8–6; Labor Day–mid-June, daily 8–5.*

ℭ The earthworks of 37-acre **Fort Stevens,** at Oregon's northwestern tip, were mounded up during the Civil War to guard the Columbia against a Confederate attack. No such event occurred, but during World War II, Fort Stevens became the only mainland U.S. military installation to come under enemy (Japanese submarine) fire since the War of 1812. The fort's abandoned gun mounts and eerie subterranean bunkers are a memorable destination. The corroded skeleton of the *Peter Iredale,* a century-old English four-master ship, protrudes from the sand just west of the campground, a stark testament to the temperamental nature of the Pacific. ✉ *Fort Stevens Hwy., (from Fort Clatsop, take Alt. U.S. 101 west past U.S. 101, turn north onto Main St.–Fort Stevens Hwy., and follow signs)* ☎ *503/861–2000* ⊕ *www.visitfortstevens.com* ✉ *$3 per vehicle, park tours in summer $2.50* ☉ *Mid-May–Sept., daily 10–6; Oct.–mid-May, daily 10–4.*

One of the Oregon coast's oldest commercial smokehouses, **Josephson's** uses alderwood for all processing and specializes in Pacific Northwest chinook and coho salmon. You can also buy smoked sturgeon, tuna, oysters, mussels, scallops, and prawns by the pound or in sealed gift packs. An exhibit of photos and magazine articles provides a history of the smokehouse. ✉ *106 Marine Dr., 97103* ☎ *503/325–2190* 🖨 *503/325–4075* ⊕ *www.josephsons.com* ✉ *Free* ☉ *Weekdays 9–5:30, Sat. 10–5:30, Sun. 10–5.*

In a 100-year-old Colonial Revival building originally used as the city hall, the **Heritage Museum** has two floors of exhibits detailing the history of the early pioneers, Native Americans, and logging and marine industries of Clatsop County, the oldest American settlement west of the Mississippi. The research library, where you may research local family and building history, is also open to the public. ✉ *1618 Exchange St.* ☎ *503/338–4849* ✉ *$3* ☉ *May–Labor Day, daily 10–5; Labor Day–Apr., daily 11–4.*

Old equipment, including hand-pulled and horse-drawn fire engines, and a collection of photos of some of Astoria's most notable fires make up the exhibits at **Uppertown Firefighters Museum.** Built in the late 1880s as a brewpub, the building was converted to a firehouse during prohibition in 1928. Plans are under way to add a children's museum, which will have educational safety and history programs. ✉ *2968 Marine Dr.* ☎ *503/325–0920* ✑ *$3* ☉ *Wed.–Sat. 11–2.*

The **The Astoria Riverfront Trolly,** also known as "Old 300," is a beautifully restored 1913 streetcar travels for 4 mi along Astoria's historic riverfront. Get a close-up look at the waterfront, from the Port of Astoria to the East Morring Basin; the Columbia River; and points of interest in between; while reliving the past through guided and narrated historical tours. ✉ *1095 Dwayne St.* ☎ *503/325–6311* ⊕ *www.oldoregon.com* ✑ *$1 per boarding, $2 all-day pass* ☉ *Memorial Day–Labor Day, weekdays 3–9, weekends noon–9; Labor Day–Memorial Day, weekends noon–dusk.*

Where to Stay & Eat

$–$$$ ✕ **Columbian Cafe.** Locals love this unpretentious diner with such tongue-in-cheek south-of-the-border decor as chili-pepper-shape Christmas lights. Simple food—crepes with broccoli, cheese, and homemade salsa for lunch; grilled salmon and pasta with a lemon-cream sauce for dinner—is served by a staff that usually includes the owner. Come early; this place always draws a crowd. ✉ *1114 Marine Dr.* ☎ *503/325–2233* ▭ *No credit cards* ☉ *No dinner Sun.–Tues.*

$–$$ ✕ **Cannery Cafe.** Original fir floors, windows, and hardware combine with expansive views of the Columbia River to give this restaurant in a renovated 1879 cannery an authentic nautical feel. Homemade breakfast fare, often with crab or salmon, comes with potato pancakes and buttermilk biscuits. Fresh salads, large sandwiches, clam chowder, and crab cakes are lunch staples. The dinner menu emphasizes seafood, including cioppino, an Italian fish stew, and homemade southern Italian pasta dishes. ✉ *1 6th St.* ☎ *503/325–8642* ▭ *AE, D, DC, MC, V.*

$–$$$ 🏨 **Benjamin Young Inn.** On the National Register of Historic Places, this handsome 5,500-square-foot Queen Anne–style inn is surrounded by century-old gardens. Among the ornate original details are faux graining on frames and molding, shutter-blinds in windows, and Povey stained glass. The spacious guest rooms mix antiques with contemporary pieces and have views of the Columbia River from their tall windows. City tennis courts are right next door. There's a two-night minimum on holiday and July and August weekends. ✉ *3652 Duane St., 97103* ☎ *503/325–6172 or 800/201–1286* ⊕ *www.benjaminyounginn.com* ↜ *4 rooms, 1 2-bedroom suite* ⚷ *Some in-room hot tubs; no a/c, no smoking, no TV in some rooms* ▭ *AE, D, MC, V* ⦿| *BP.*

$–$$ 🏨 **Franklin Street Station Bed & Breakfast.** Ticking grandfather clocks and mellow light filtering through leaded-glass windows set the tone at this velvet-upholstered Victorian built in 1900 on the slopes above downtown Astoria. Breakfasts are huge, hot, and satisfying, and there's always a plate of goodies and a pot of coffee in the kitchen. ✉ *1140 Franklin St., 97103* ☎ *503/325–4314 or 800/448–1098* ⊕ *www.franklin-st-station-bb.com* ↜ *6 rooms* ▭ *MC, V* ⦿| *BP.*

Seaside

❷ *12 mi south of Astoria on U.S. 101.*

The now busy resort town of Seaside has grown up around the spot where the Lewis and Clark expedition finally reached the Pacific Ocean. A bronze statue of the two explorers commemorates the end of their trail and faces the ocean at the center of Seaside's historic Promenade. The Prom was originally built in 1908 as a wooden walkway, and in 1920 it was extended to its current length, 1½ mi, with concrete sidewalks.

For years Seaside had a reputation as a garish arcade-filled town. But it cleaned up its act and now supports a bustling tourist trade with hotels, condominiums, and restaurants surrounding a long beach. Only 90 mi from Portland, Seaside is often crowded, so it's not the place to come if you crave solitude. Peak times include February, during the Trail's End Marathon; mid-March, when hordes of teenagers descend on the town during spring break; and July, when the annual Miss Oregon Pageant is in full swing.

Just south of town, waves draw surfers to the Cove, a spot jealously guarded by locals.

It's a 2½-mi hike from the parking lot of **Saddle Mountain State Park** to the summit of Saddle Mountain. It's much cooler at that elevation. The campground, which is 14 mi north of Seaside, has 10 primitive sites. ⊠ *Off U.S. 26* ☎ *503/861–1671 or 503/436–2844* ☞ *$3 per vehicle day-use fee* ☉ *Mar.–Nov., daily.*

Jellyfish, giant king crab, octopus, moray eels, wolf eels, and other sea life are swimming in 35 tanks at **Seaside Aquarium,** on the 1½ mi beachfront Promenade. You can feed the harbor seals. ⊠ *200 N. Promenade* ☎ *503/738–6211* ☞ *$6.50* ☉ *Daily 9–5.*

Where to Stay & Eat

$–$$$ ✕ **Breakers Restaurant and Lounge.** Inside the Best Western Ocean View Resort, this is a high-quality family restaurant, serving steaks, chicken, seafood, and pasta. Try the Oregon crab cakes or go way out to sea with the Alaskan salmon and halibut. Locals often come for the prime rib and the western steak (rib-eye coated in Creole seasoning). Save room for the Oregon blueberry white-chocolate cheesecake. ⊠ *414 N. Promenade, 97138* ☎ *503/738–3334 or 800/234–8439* 🖷 *503/738–5959* ☉ *No lunch* ▤ *AE, D, DC, MC, V.*

¢–$$ ✕ **Doogers.** The original branch of this Northwest chain is much loved by local families. The seafood is expertly prepared, and the creamy clam chowder may be the best on the coast. A collection of oil paintings by Oregon women artists colors the dining-room walls. ⊠ *505 Broadway* ☎ *503/738–3773* ⟁ *Reservations not accepted* ▤ *AE, D, MC, V.*

$ 🏨 **Hillcrest Inn.** The Hillcrest is only one block from both the beach and the convention center and three blocks from the downtown area and several restaurants and shops. The inn has been owned by the same family for more than two decades, and friendliness, cleanliness, and convenience are bywords here. You're welcome to use the picnic tables, lawn chairs, and even the barbecue on the grounds. ⊠ *118 N. Columbia St., 97138* ☎ *503/738–6273 or 800/270–7659* 🖷 *503/717–0266* ➶ *19 rooms, 4 suites, 3 2-bedroom cottages, 1 5-bedroom house* ⟁ *Picnic area, some in-room hot tubs, some kitchenettes, microwaves, refrigerators, cable TV, sauna, laundry facilities; no a/c in some rooms* ▤ *AE, DC, MC, V.*

$ 🏨 **Royale.** This small motel right in the center of downtown is on the Necanicum River, 3½ blocks from the beach and in very close walking distance to shopping and restaurants. Some rooms have river views. There's ample off-street parking. ⊠ *531 Ave. A, 97138* ☎ *503/738–9541* ➶ *26 rooms* ⟁ *No a/c* ▤ *D, DC, MC, V.*

en route A brisk 2-mi hike from U.S. 101 south of Seaside leads to the 1,100-foot-high viewing point atop **Tillamook Head.** The view from here takes in the **Tillamook Rock Light Station,** which stands a mile or so out to sea. The lonely beacon, built in 1881 on a straight-sided rock, towers 41 feet above the surrounding ocean. In 1957 the lighthouse was abandoned; it is now a columbarium. Eight miles south of

Seaside, U.S. 101 passes the entrance to **Ecola State Park,** a playground of sea-sculpted rocks, sandy shoreline, green headlands, and panoramic views. The park's main beach can be crowded in summer, but the **Indian Beach** area contains an often-deserted cove and explorable tidal pools. ☎ *800/551–6949* ⌑ *$3 per vehicle* ☉ *Daily sunrise–sunset.*

Cannon Beach

❸ *10 mi south of Seaside on U.S. 101, 80 mi west of Portland on U.S. 26.*

Cannon Beach is Seaside's refined, artistic alter ego, a more mellow yet trendy place (population 1,400) for Portlanders to take the sea air. One of the most charming hamlets on the coast, the town has beachfront homes and hotels and a weathered-cedar downtown shopping district. On the downside, the Carmel of the Oregon coast is expensive, crowded, and afflicted with a subtle, moneyed hauteur (such as the town's ban on vacation-home rentals) that may grate on more plebeian nerves.

The town got its name when a cannon from the wrecked schooner USS *Shark* washed ashore in 1846 (the piece is on display a mile east of town on U.S. 101). Towering over the broad, sandy beach is **Haystack Rock,** a 235-foot-high monolith that is supposedly the most-photographed feature of the Oregon coast. The rock is temptingly accessible during some low tides, but the coast guard regularly airlifts stranded climbers from its precipitous sides, and falls have claimed numerous lives over the years. Every May the town hosts the Cannon Beach Sandcastle Contest, for which thousands throng the beach to view imaginative and often startling works in this most transient of art forms.

Shops and galleries selling kites, upscale clothing, local art, wine, coffee, and food line **Hemlock Street,** Cannon Beach's main thoroughfare.

The road takes hair-raising curves as it climbs to 700 feet above the Pacific around the flank of 1,661-foot **Neahkahnie Mountain,** south of Cannon Beach. The views are dramatic. Carvings on nearby beach rocks and old Native American legends gave rise to a tale that a fortune in gold doubloons from a sunken Spanish galleon is buried somewhere on the mountainside. ⌑ *U.S. 101.*

Where to Stay & Eat

★ **$–$$$** ✕ **The Bistro.** Flowers, candlelight, and classical music convey romance at this 11-table restaurant. The menu includes imaginative Continental-influenced renditions of local seafood and pasta dishes as well as specialty salads. The signature dish is the fresh seafood stew. ⌑ *263 N. Hemlock St.* ☎ *503/436–2661* ▤ *MC, V* ☉ *Closed Tues. and Wed. Nov.–Jan. No lunch.*

★ **$$$–$$$$** ✕▥ **Stephanie Inn.** Superior service, luxurious rooms, and tastefully decorated public areas make this three-story inn the premier oceanfront hotel in Cannon Beach. Impeccably maintained, with country-style furnishings, fireplaces, large bathrooms with whirlpool tubs, and balconies commanding outstanding views of Haystack Rock, the rooms are so comfortable you may never want to leave—except perhaps to enjoy the four-course prix-fixe dinners of innovative Pacific Northwest cuisine. Generous country breakfasts are included in the room price, as are evening wine and hors d'oeuvres. ⌑ *2740 S. Pacific St., 97110* ☎ *503/436–2221 or 800/633–3466* ⌑ *503/436–9711* ⊕ *www.stephanie-inn.com* ⌑ *50 rooms* ⌑ *Dining room, in-room VCRs, minibars, refrigerators, massage, library* ▤ *AE, D, DC, MC, V.*

$$$$ 🔲 **Ocean Lodge.** Designed to capture the feel of a 1940s beach resort, this lodge is right on the beach. Most of the rooms have full oceanfront views, and all have open wood beams, simple but sophisticated furnishings, gas fireplaces, and balconies or decks. The lobby floor is reclaimed spruce wood, while stairs were fashioned from old stadium bleachers. A massive rock fireplace anchors the lobby, and there is a second fireplace in the second-floor library. Bungalows across the street do not have ocean views but are large and private. An expanded Continental breakfast is served in the second-floor breakfast room. ⊠ *2864 S. Pacific St., 97110* ☎*888/777–4047* 📠*503/436–2159* ⊕*www.theoceanlodge. com* 🛏*45 rooms* ⚭ *Some in-room hot tubs, kitchenettes, cable TV, some pets allowed (fee); no a/c in some rooms, no smoking* 🖃 *AE, D, MC, V.*

$ 🔲 **Grey Whale Inn.** This small, charming inn dates from 1948. It is in a very quiet residential neighborhood, a 5-minute walk to the beach or a 20-minute walk to Haystack Rock. All the rooms are individually decorated with original artwork, done either by the family or local artists. The rooms have shower facilities only. ⊠ *164 Kenai St., 97110* ☎ *503/ 436–2848* 🛏 *5 rooms* ⚭ *Some kitchenettes, cable TV, in-room VCRs; no a/c, no smoking* 🖃 *MC, V.*

en route   South of Cannon Beach, U.S. 101 climbs 700 feet above the Pacific, providing dramatic views and often hair-raising curves as it winds along the flank of **Neahkahnie Mountain.** Cryptic carvings on beach rocks near here and centuries-old Native American legends of shipwrecked Europeans gave rise to a tale that the survivors of a sunken Spanish galleon buried a fortune in doubloons somewhere on the side of the 1,661-foot-high mountain.

Oswald West State Park

❹ *10 mi south of Cannon Beach on U.S. 101.*

Adventurous travelers will enjoy a sojourn at one of the best-kept secrets on the Pacific coast, **Oswald West State Park,** at the base of Neahkahnie Mountain. Park in one of the two lots on U.S. 101 and use a park-provided wheelbarrow to trundle your camping gear down a ½-mi trail. An old-growth forest surrounds the 36 primitive campsites (reservations not accepted), and the spectacular beach contains caves and tidal pools.

The trail to the summit, on the left about 2 mi south of the parking lots for Oswald West State Park (marked only by a HIKERS sign), rewards the intrepid with unobstructed views over surf, sand, forest, and mountain. Come in December or March and you might spot pods of gray whales. ⊠ *Ecola Park Rd.* ☎ *503/368–5943 or 800/551–6949* ⊕ *www. oregonstateparks.org* 🗐 *Day use free, campsites $16* ☉ *Day use daily sunrise–sunset; camping Mar.–Oct., daily sunrise–sunset.*

en route   After passing through several small fishing, logging, and resort towns, U.S. 101 skirts around **Tillamook Bay,** where the Miami, Kilchis, Wilson, Trask, and Tillamook rivers enter the Pacific. The bay rewards sportfishing enthusiasts with quarry that includes sea-run cutthroat trout, bottom fish, and silver, chinook, and steelhead salmon, along with mussels, oysters, clams, and the delectable Dungeness crab. Charter-fishing services operate out of the **Garibaldi** fishing harbor 10 mi north of Tillamook. For some of the best rock fishing in the state, try Tillamook Bay's North Jetty.

Manzanita

⑤ *20 mi south of Cannon Beach on U.S. 101.*

Manzanita is a secluded seaside community with only 500 full-time residents. It's on a sandy peninsula peppered with tufts of grass on the northwestern side of Nehalem Bay. It is a tranquil small town, but its restaurants, galleries, and 18-hole golf course have increased its appeal to tourists. Manzanita and Nehalem Bay both have become popular windsurfing destinations.

Established in 1974, **Nehalem Bay Winery,** the sixth-oldest winery in Oregon, is known for its pinot chardonnay and blackberry and plum fruit wines. You can taste them here, in a building that was once the Mohler Cheese Factory, and enjoy the picnic area. The winery also has a busy schedule of events with concerts, barbecues, an occasional pig roast, children's activities, performances at the Theatre Au Vin, and a bluegrass festival the third week of August. ⊠ *34965 Hwy. 53, Nehalem 97131* ☎ *503/368-9463 or 888/368-9463* 🖷 *503/368-5300* ⊕ *www. nehalembaywinery.com* ♡ *Daily 9–6.*

Where to Stay & Eat

¢–$$$ ✕ **Blue Sky Cafe.** Stained glass, a jungle of plants, and funky furnishings lend a quirky air to this casual hole-in-the-wall café. Try the chive crepes with asparagus, leeks, and morel mushrooms; Thai peanut chicken with mint cilantro and fresh-picked cucumbers; or the prawn posole. Save room for one of the rich desserts. ⊠ *154 Laneda St., off U.S. 101* ☎*503/368-5712* ▭*No credit cards* ♡ *Closed Mon. and Tues. Oct.–June. No lunch.*

$$–$$$ 🏠 **Inn at Manzanita.** This 1987 Scandinavian structure, filled with light-color woods, beams, and glass, is half a block from the beach. Shore pines on the property give upper-floor patios a tree-house feel, all rooms have decks, and two have skylights. A nearby café serves breakfast, and area restaurants are nearby. In winter the inn is a great place for storm-watching. There's a two-day minimum stay on weekends. ⊠ *67 Laneda Ave.* 🖅 *Box 243, 97130* ☎ *503/368-6754* 🖷 *503/368-5941* ⊕ *www. innatmanzanita.com* 🖙 *13 rooms in 4 buildings* ♨ *In-room hot tubs, some kitchenettes, some microwaves, refrigerators, cable TV; no a/c in some rooms, no phones in some rooms, no smoking* ▭ *MC, V.*

🏕 **Nehalem Bay State Park.** Close enough to the ocean that you'll potentially be lulled to sleep by the waves, the park is on the edge of Nehalem Bay, which is popular for kayaking, crabbing, and fishing. ♨ *Flush toilets, partial hookups, dump station, drinking water, showers, fire pits, picnic tables, electricity, swimming (ocean)* 🖘 *267 electrical sites, 18 yurts, 17 sites with corrals* ▭ *MC, V* ⊠ *Off U.S. 101, 3 mi south of Manzanita Junction* ☎ *800/452-5687 reservations, 800/551-6949 information* ⊕ *www.oregonstateparks.org.* ♨ *Reservations essential* 🖃 *Electrical hookups $20, tent sites $17, horse camp $16, yurts $27.*

Rockaway Beach

⑥ *28 mi south of Cannon Beach on U.S. 101*

Rockaway Beach, a small community of just over 1,000 residents, sits between Nehalem Bay and the Manzanita area to the north and Tillamook Bay and Tillamook dairy-farming country to the south. Rockaway originated in the early 1900s as a summer-vacation destination for Portlanders, a role it now fills for visitors from elsewhere in the state and country.

Where to Stay & Eat

¢–$ ✕ **Beach Pancake and Dinner House.** This cozy restaurant's specialty is homemade chicken and dumplings; it has a children's menu, offers senior-citizen discounts, is wheelchair accessible, and serves breakfast—voted by locals the best in Tillamook County—all day. Authentic Mexican dishes add south-of-the-border zest to the down-home menu. ⊠ *202 N. U.S. 101, 97136* ☎ *503/355–2411* ▤ *MC, V.*

$$–$$$ ▥ **Silver Sands.** Each room in this beachfront motel has a balcony and view of the ocean. It's central to local shopping and restaurants and is right in the middle of town; it's also an easy and scenic drive from here to the northern coast. ⊠ *215 S. Pacific St., 97136* ☎ *503/355–2206 or 800/457–8972* ⎙ *503/355–9690* ▱ *64 rooms* ♿ *Some kitchenettes, refrigerators, cable TV, indoor pool, hot tub; no a/c* ▤ *AE, D, DC, MC, V.*

Tillamook

❼ *30 mi south of Oswald West State Park and Neahkahnie Mountain on U.S. 101.*

Tillamook County is something of a wet Wisconsin-on-the-Pacific. More than 100 inches of annual rainfall and the confluence of three rivers contribute to the lush green pastures around Tillamook, probably best known for its thriving dairy industry and cheese factory. The Tillamook County Cheese Factory ships about 40 million pounds of cheese around the world every year. Both Tillamook and the Blue Heron French Cheese Factory offer you a look at their cheese-making processes.

Just south of town is the largest wooden structure in the world, one of two gigantic buildings constructed in 1942 by the U.S. Navy to shelter blimps that patrolled the Pacific Coast during World War II. Hangar A was destroyed by fire in 1992, and Hangar B was subsequently converted to the Tillamook Naval Air Station Museum.

The Three Capes Loop over Cape Meares, Cape Lookout, and Cape Kiwanda offers spectacular views of the ocean and coastline. A lighthouse and an old Indian burial Sitka spruce, Octopus Tree, are worth the trip to Cape Meares, while Cape Lookout is one of the Northwest's best whale-watching viewpoints. Along the route from Tillamook's small resort area of Oceanside, take a look at Three Arch Rocks, a National Wildlife Refuge, with hundreds of sea lions and seals and nesting habitat for as many as 200,000 birds.

ⓒ The **Pioneer Museum** in Tillamook's 1905 county courthouse has an intriguing if old-fashioned hodgepodge of Native American, pioneer, logging, and natural-history exhibits, along with antique vehicles and military artifacts. ⊠ *2106 2nd St.* ☎ *503/842–4553* ▱ *$3* ☉ *May–Sept., Mon.–Sat. 8:30–5, Sun. 12:30–5.*

The **Latimer Quilt and Textile Center** is dedicated to the preservation, promotion, creation, and display of the fiber arts. Spinners, weavers, beaders, and quilters can be found working on projects in the Quilting Room and may engage you in hands-on demonstrations. Rotating exhibits range from costumes, cloth dolls, crocheted items from the 1940s and 1950s, exquisite historical quilts dating from the early to mid-1800s, basketry, and weavings. ⊠ *2105 Wilson River Loop Rd.* ☎ *503/842–8622* ▱ *$2.50* ☉ *Tues.–Sat. 10–4, Sun. noon–4.*

More than 750,000 visitors annually press their noses against the spotlessly clean windows at the **Tillamook County Creamery,** the largest cheese-making plant on the West Coast. Here the rich milk from the area's thousands of Holstein and brown Swiss cows becomes ice cream, butter, and cheddar and Monterey Jack cheeses. Exhibits at the visitor center, where free samples are dispensed, explain the cheese-making process. ✉ *4175 U.S. 101 N, 2 mi north of Tillamook* ☎ *503/815–1300* ⊕ *www. tillamookcheese.com* ✑ *Free* ☉ *Mid-Sept.–May, daily 8–6; June–mid-Sept., daily 8–8.*

The **Blue Heron French Cheese Company** specializes in French-style cheeses—Camembert, Brie, and others. There's a petting zoo for kids, a sit-down deli, wine and cheese tastings, and a gift shop that carries wines and jams, mustards, and other products from Oregon. ✉ *2001 Blue Heron Dr., watch for signs from U.S. 101* ☎ *503/842–8281* ✑ *Free* ☉ *Memorial Day–Labor Day, daily 8–8; Labor Day–Memorial Day, daily 8:30–5.*

In the world's largest wooden structure, a former blimp hangar south of town, the **Tillamook Naval Air Station Museum** displays one of the finest private collections of vintage aircraft from World War II, including a B-25 Mitchell and an ME-109 Messerschmidt. The 20-story building is big enough to hold half a dozen football fields. ✉ *6030 Hangar Rd., ½ mi south of Tillamook; head east from U.S. 101 on Long Prairie Rd. and follow signs* ☎ *503/842–1130* ✑ *$9.50* ☉ *Daily 10–5.*

Where to Stay & Eat

$–$$$ ✕ **Roseanna's.** Nine miles west of Tillamook in Oceanside, Roseanna's is in a rustic 1915 building on the beach opposite Three Arch Rock, so you might be able to watch sea lions and puffins while you eat. The calm of the beach is complemented in the evening by candlelight and fresh flowers. Have halibut or salmon half a dozen ways, or try the poached baked oysters or Gorgonzola seafood pasta. ✉ *1490 Pacific Ave., Oceanside 97134* ☎ *503/842–7351* ⟐ *Reservations not accepted* ▭ *MC, V.*

$–$$ ✕ **Artspace.** You'll be surrounded by artwork as you enjoy homemade creations at Artspace in Bay City, 6 mi north of Tillamook. The menu may include garlic-grilled oysters, vegetarian dishes, and other specials, all beautifully presented, often with edible flowers. And if you reserve in advance, you'll get a complimentary appetizer for your thoughtfulness. ✉ *9120 5th St., Bay City 97107* ☎ *503/377–2782* ⎙ *503/377–2010* ▭ *No credit cards* ☉ *Closed Mon.*

$$–$$$ ⊞ **Sandlake Country Inn.** Tucked into a bower of old roses on 2 acres, this intimate bed-and-breakfast is in a farmhouse built of timbers that washed ashore from a shipwreck in 1890. It is listed on the Oregon Historic Registry and filled with antiques. The Timbers Suite has a massive, king-size wood canopy bed and two-person jetted tub; the Starlight Suite occupies four rooms on the second floor and includes a canopy queen bed and double-sided fireplace. ✉ *8505 Galloway Rd., Sandlake 97112* ☎ *503/965–6745 or 877/726–3525* ⎙ *503/965–7425* ⊕ *www. sandlakecountryinn.com* ⤳ *4 rooms, 1 suite* ⟡ *Some kitchenettes, cable TV, in-room VCRs, hot tub; no a/c, no phones in some rooms, no smoking* ▭ *D, MC, V* ❙◎❙ *BP.*

$$ ⊞ **Hudson House.** The son of the original owner of this 1906 farmhouse was a photographer who captured the area's rough beauty on postcards. The larger suite is downstairs, with a parlor and private porch overlooking the Nestucca Valley. The more popular, upstairs suite has a bedroom in the house's turret. The two guest rooms are under the high-gabled roof. The house has a wraparound porch from which you can enjoy a view of the surrounding woods. ✉ *37700 U.S. 101 S, Cloverdale 97112* ☎ *503/ 392–3533 or 888/835–3533* ⊕ *www.hudsonhouse.com* ⤳ *2 rooms, 2 suites* ⟡ *Picnic area, some in-room data ports, hot tub, library; no kids under 12, no room phones, no room TVs, no smoking* ▭ *MC, V* ❙◎❙ *BP.*

Three Capes Loop

★ ❽ *Starts south of downtown Tillamook off 3rd St.*

The Three Capes Loop, a 35-mi byway off U.S. 101, is one of the coast's most thrilling driving experiences. The loop winds along the coast between Tillamook and Pacific City, passing three distinctive headlands—Cape Meares, Cape Lookout, and Cape Kiwanda. Bayocean Road heading west from Tillamook passes what was the thriving resort town of Bay Ocean. More than 30 years ago, Bay Ocean washed into the sea—houses, a bowling alley, everything—during a raging Pacific storm.

Nine miles west of Tillamook, trails from the parking lot at the end of Bay Ocean Spit lead through the dunes to a usually uncrowded and highly walkable white-sand beach.

Cape Meares State Park is on the northern tip of the Three Capes Loop. Cape Meares was named for English navigator John Meares, who voyaged along this coast in 1788. The restored **Cape Meares Lighthouse,** built in 1890 and open to the public May–September, provides a sweeping view over the cliff to the caves and sea-lion rookery on the rocks below. A many-trunked Sitka spruce known as the Octopus Tree grows near the lighthouse parking lot. ✥ *Three Capes Loop 10 mi west of Tillamook* ☎ *800/551–6949* ✉ *Free* ☉ *Park daily sunrise–sunset. Lighthouse May–Sept., daily 11–4; Mar., Apr., and Oct., weekends 11–4.*

Cape Lookout State Park lies south of the beach towns of Oceanside and Netarts. A fairly easy 2-mi trail—marked on the highway as WILDLIFE VIEWING AREA—leads through giant spruces, western red cedars, and hemlocks to views of Cascade Head to the south and Cape Meares to the north. Wildflowers, more than 150 species of birds, and migrating whales passing by in early April make this trail a favorite with nature lovers. The park has a picnic area overlooking the sea and a year-round campground. ✥ *Three Capes Loop 8 mi south of Cape Meares* ☎ *800/551–6949* ✉ *Day use $3, campsites $18–$22* ☉ *Daily sunrise–9 PM.*

Huge waves pound the jagged sandstone cliffs and caves at **Cape Kiwanda State Natural Area.** The much-photographed, 327-foot-high **Haystack Rock** juts out of Nestucca Bay just south of here. Surfers ride some of the longest waves on the coast, hang gliders soar above the shore, and beachcombers explore tidal pools and take in unparalleled ocean views. ✥ *Three Capes Loop 15 mi south of Cape Lookout* ☎ *800/551–6949* ✉ *Free* ☉ *Daily sunrise–sunset.*

Pacific City

❾ *1½ mi south of Cape Kiwanda on Three Capes Loop.*

The beach at Pacific City, the town visible from Cape Kiwanda, is one of the few places in the state where fishing dories (flat-bottom boats with high, flaring sides) are launched directly into the surf instead of from harbors or docks. During the commercial salmon season in late summer, it's possible to buy salmon directly from the fishermen.

A walk along the flat white-sand beach at **Robert Straub State Park** leads down to the mouth of the Nestucca River, considered by many to be the best fishing river on the north coast. ✉ *West from main intersection in downtown Pacific City across Nestucca River, follow signs* ☎ *800/551–6949* ✉ *Free* ☉ *Daily sunrise–sunset.*

off the beaten path

NATURE CONSERVANCY CASCADE HEAD TRAIL – The trail at one of the most unusual headlands on the Oregon coast winds through a rain forest where 250-year-old Sitka spruces and a dense green undergrowth of mosses and ferns is nourished by 100-inch annual rainfalls. After the forest comes grassy and treeless Cascade Head, a rare example of a maritime prairie. Magnificent views down to the Salmon River and west to the Coast Range open up as you continue along the headland, where black-tailed deer often graze and turkey vultures soar in the strong winds. You need to be in fairly good shape for the first and steepest part of the hike, which can be done in about an hour. The 270-acre area has been named a United Nations Biosphere Reserve. Coastal bluffs make this a popular hang-gliding and kite-flying area. A campground has 54 full hookups, 1 electrical and 191 tent sites, and 4 yurts. ⊠ *Savage Rd., 6 mi south of Neskowin off U.S. 101; turn west on Three Rocks Rd. and north on Savage* ☎ *503/230–1221* ⊠ *Free* ☉ *July–Dec., daily sunrise–sunset.*

The small 350-foot stretch of **Mugg Estuarine Park,** on the Nestucca River, is an ideal bird-watching vantage point. All facilities are accessible by people with disabilities. ✛ *2 blocks from center of town, across bridge* ☎ *503/965–6161.*

Where to Stay & Eat

¢–$$$ ✕ **Riverhouse.** Fresh seafood, sandwiches, and home-baked desserts are the specialties at this casual dining spot overlooking the Nestucca River. Original, all-natural salad dressings are a big hit with guests and available for sale in gift packs. ⊠ *34450 Brooten Rd.* ☎ *503/965–6722* 🖃 *MC, V.*

$$ 🏨 **Eagles View Bed and Breakfast.** This small inn was built in 1995 and is set amid tall trees overlooking the Nestucca Bay and River about 1 mi from town. Furnishings are themed around original and limited-edition art. All rooms have a view of either the forest or the bay. Children under 12 and pets are not permitted. ⊠ *37975 Brooten Rd., 97135* ☎ *503/965–7600 or 888/846–3292* ⊕ *eaglesviewbb.com* ⇌ *5 rooms* ⚬ *Some in-room hot tubs, outdoor hot tub; no kids under 12, no smoking* 🖃 *AE, D, MC, V* ⏐❂⏐ *BP.*

Lincoln City

⏺ *16 mi south of Pacific City on U.S. 101, 78 mi west of Portland on Hwy. 99 W and Hwy. 18.*

Once a series of small villages, Lincoln City is a sprawling, suburbanish town without a center. But the endless tourist amenities make up for whatever it lacks in charm. Clustered like barnacles on the offshore reefs are fast-food restaurants, gift shops, supermarkets, candy stores, antiques markets, dozens of motels and hotels, a factory-outlet mall, and a busy casino. Lincoln City is the most popular destination city on the Oregon coast, but its only real geographic claim to fame is the 445-foot-long **D River,** stretching from its source in Devil's Lake to the Pacific; *Guinness World Records* lists the D as the world's shortest river.

The only casino built directly on the beach in Oregon, **Chinook Winds** has slot machines, blackjack, poker, keno, and off-track betting. The entry atrium is accented with a two-story waterfall and natural rocks, trees, and plants to replicate the fishing ground of the Confederated Tribes of the Siletz, who own the casino. The Siletz Room has good food, and there is an all-you-can-eat buffet, a snack bar, and a lounge. An arcade will keep the kids busy while you are on the gambling floor. Big-name entertainers perform in the showroom. ⊠ *1777 N.W. 44th St., 97367* ☎ *541/996–5825 or 888/244–6665.*

The imaginative craftspeople at the **Alder House II** studio turn molten glass into vases and bowls, which are available for sale. It is the oldest glass-blowing studio in the state. ⊠ *611 Immonen Rd.* ☎ *541/996–2483* ⊕ *www.alderhouse.com* ⊠ *Free* ⊙ *Mid-Mar.–Nov., daily 10–5.*

Canoeing and kayaking are popular on the small lake at **Devil's Lake State Park,** which is in turn popular with coots, loons, ducks, cormorants, bald eagles, and grebes. It's the only Oregon-coast campground within the environs of a city. There are 32 full hookups, 55 tent sites, and 10 yurts. ⊠ *1452 N.E. 6th St.* ☎ *541/994–2002 or 800/551–6949* ⊠ *Free* ⊙ *Daily.*

The community performing arts center **Theatre West** showcases local talent in a year-round schedule of popular plays. ⊠ *3536 S.E. U.S. 101* ☎ *541/994–5663* ⊙ *Thurs.–Sat., call for hrs.*

Where to Stay & Eat

$–$$$ ✕ **Bay House.** Inside a charming bungalow, this restaurant serves meals to linger over while you enjoy views across sunset-gilded Siletz Bay. The seasonal Pacific Northwest cuisine includes Dungeness crab cakes with roasted-chili chutney, fresh halibut Parmesan, and roast duckling with cranberry compote. The wine list is extensive, the service impeccable. ⊠ *5911 S.W. U.S. 101, about 5 mi south of Lincoln City* ☎ *541/996–3222* ⊟ *AE, D, MC, V* ⊙ *Closed Mon. and Tues. Nov.–Apr. No lunch.*

$–$$ ✕ **Kyllo's.** Light-filled Kyllo's rests on stilts beside the D River. It's one of the best places in Lincoln City to enjoy casual but well-prepared seafood, pasta, and meat dishes. ⊠ *1110 N.W. 1st Ct.* ☎ *541/994–3179* ⊟ *AE, D, MC, V.*

¢–$$ ✕ **Dory Cove.** For more than 25 years, this spot has been serving up an extensive menu of seafood and steak. The clam chowder is remarkable. There's also a large selection of low-cholesterol dishes. Some booths have ocean views; nautical and aeronautical knickknacks accent wood-panel walls. ⊠ *5819 Logan Rd., 97367* ☎ *541/994–5180* ⊟ *AE, D, MC, V.*

$$$–$$$$ 🏨 **Inn at Spanish Head.** You'll find tidal pools right outside your door at this condominium resort set on a bluff. All of the bright, contemporary units have ocean views. Choose from one-bedroom suites, deluxe studios, or deluxe rooms. ⊠ *4009 S. U.S. 101, 93767* ☎ *541/996–2161 or 800/452–8127* 🖷 *541/996–4089* ⊕ *www.spanishhead.com* 🛏 *120 rooms, 25 suites* & *Restaurant, bar, room service, cable TV, pool, exercise equipment, hot tub, Ping-Pong, billiards, business services* ⊟ *AE, D, DC, MC, V.*

Gleneden Beach

❶ *7 mi south of Lincoln City on U.S. 101.*

Salishan, the most famous resort on the Oregon coast, perches high above placid Siletz Bay. This expensive collection of guest rooms, vacation homes, condominiums, restaurants, golf fairways, tennis courts, and covered walkways blends into a forest preserve; if not for the signs, you'd scarcely be able to find it.

The long-established **Gallery at Salishan** has a well-informed staff that will guide you through the collections of work by Northwest artists, including paintings (pastels, oils, and watercolors), glassworks, bronze and metal, furniture, and ceramics and porcelain. ⊠ *7755 N. U.S. 101, 97388* ☎ *541/764–2318 or 800/764–2318* ⊙ *Memorial Day–Labor Day, Mon.–Sat. 10–6, Sun. 10–5; Labor Day–Memorial Day, daily 10–5.*

Where to Stay & Eat

$$–$$$ ✕ **Sidedoor Cafe.** This dining room with a high ceiling, exposed beams, a fireplace, and many windows just under the eaves shares a former tile factory with the Eden Hall performance space. The menu changes constantly—fresh preparations have included mushroom-crusted rack of lamb and broiled swordfish with citrus-raspberry vinaigrette over coconut-ginger basmati rice. ⊠ *6675 Gleneden Beach Loop Rd., 97388* ☎ *541/764-3825* ▤ *MC, V* ☺ *Closed Tues. Sept.–Apr.*

★ $–$$$ ✕ **Dining Room at Salishan.** The Salishan resort's main dining room, a multilevel expanse of hushed waiters, hillside ocean views, and snow-white linen, serves Pacific Northwest cuisine. House specialties include fresh local fish, game, beef, and lamb. By all means make a selection from the wine cellar, which has more than 10,000 bottles. ⊠ *7760 N. U.S. 101* ☎ *541/764-2371* ⚑ *Reservations essential* ▤ *AE, D, DC, MC, V* ☺ *No lunch.*

$$$$ ▦ **Salishan Lodge and Golf Resort.** From the soothing, silvered cedar of its rooms, divided among eight units in a hillside forest preserve, to its wood-burning fireplaces, Salishan embodies a uniquely Oregonian elegance. Each of the quiet rooms has a balcony, and original works by Northwest artists. Given all this, plus fine food, you'll understand why the timeless lodge also carries one of the steepest price tags on the coast. ⊠ *7760 N. U.S. 101, 97388* ☎ *541/764-3600 or 800/452-2300* 🖷 *541/764-3681* ⊕ *www.salishan.com* ➲ *205 rooms* ⬧ *2 restaurants, room service, in-room data ports, minibars, driving range, 18-hole golf course, putting green, 4 tennis courts, indoor pool, gym, hair salon, massage, sauna, hiking, beach, bar, billiards, piano, library, baby-sitting, playground, dry cleaning, laundry service, concierge* ▤ *AE, D, DC, MC, V.*

Depoe Bay

⑫ *12 mi south of Lincoln City on U.S. 101.*

The small town of Depoe Bay was founded in the 1920s and named in honor of Charles DePoe, of the Siletz tribe, who in turn was named for his employment at a U.S. Army depot in the late 1800s. Depoe Bay calls itself the whale-watching capital of the world.

Depoe Bay Park. The park runs along the beach in front of the town's retail district. With a narrow channel and deep water, the tiny harbor is also one of the most protected on the coast. It supports a thriving fleet of commercial- and charter-fishing boats. The Spouting Horn, a natural cleft in the basalt cliffs on the waterfront, blasts seawater skyward during heavy weather. ⊠ *South on U.S. 101* ☎ *541/765-2889* ⊕ *www.stateoforegon.com/depoe_bay/chamber* ▧ *Free* ☺ *Daily.*

Fogarty Creek State Park. Bird-watching and viewing the tidal pools are the key draws here, but hiking and picnicking are also popular at this park 4 mi north of Depoe Bay on U.S. 101. Wooden footbridges arch through the forest. The beach is rimmed with cliffs. ⊠ *U.S. 101* ☎ *541/265-9278 or 800/551-6949* ⊕ *www.prd.state.or.us* ▧ *$3 per vehicle day-use fee* ☺ *Daily.*

Tradewinds. Every year a few of the gigantic gray whales migrating along the coast decide to linger in Depoe Bay, and for more than six decades, Tradewinds has operated whale-watching cruises. The skippers are all marine naturalists who give a running commentary, and the boats can accommodate from 6 to 40 passengers (daylight hours only). The ticket office is on U.S. 101 at the north end of Depoe Bay Bridge. ⊠ *U.S. 101 97341* ☎ *541/765-2345 or 800/445-8730* 🖷 *541/765-2282* ⊕ *www.tradewindscharters.com* ▧ *1 hr $15, 2 hrs $20.*

Where to Eat

$$–$$$ ✕ **Whale Cove Inn.** Known for its homemade jumbo cinnamon rolls, this little restaurant overlooking the cove from which it takes its name has pasta, seafood, steaks, ribs, and chowders. Every table and booth has an ocean view. The property came under new ownership in 2001 and has been completely remodeled. ⊠ *2345 S.W. U.S. 101* ☎ *541/765–2255* 🗀 *AE, D, MC, V.*

$–$$ ✕ **Sea Hag.** This friendly restaurant has been specializing in fresh seafood for more than 30 years. There's a seafood buffet on Friday night, while Saturday the focus is on prime rib with Yorkshire pudding. Several booths at the front of the restaurant have views of the "spouting horns" across the highway. The restaurant is kid friendly, and there's an adjoining grown-up–friendly bar. ⊠ *53 U.S. 101* ☎ *541/765–2734* 🗀 *AE, D, DC, MC, V.*

en route | Five miles south of Depoe Bay off U.S. 101 (watch for signs), the **Otter Crest Loop,** another scenic byway, winds along the cliff tops. Only parts of the loop are now open to vehicles, but you can drive to points midway from either end and turn around. The full loop is open to bikes and hiking. British explorer Captain James Cook named the 500-foot-high **Cape Foulweather,** at the south end of the loop, on a blustery March day in 1778. Backward-leaning shore pines lend mute witness to the 100-mph winds that still strafe this exposed spot. At the viewing point at the **Devil's Punchbowl,** 1 mi south of Cape Foulweather, you can peer down into a collapsed sandstone sea cave carved out by the powerful waters of the Pacific. About 100 feet to the north in the rocky tidal pools of the beach known as **Marine Gardens,** purple sea urchins and orange starfish can be seen at low tide. The Otter Crest Loop rejoins U.S. 101 about 4 mi south of Cape Foulweather near **Yaquina Head,** which has been designated an Outstanding Natural Area. Harbor seals, sea lions, cormorants, murres, puffins, and guillemots frolic in the water and on the rocks below **Yaquina Bay Lighthouse**—a gleaming white tower activated in 1873.

Newport

⓭ *12 mi south of Depoe Bay on U.S. 101, 114 mi from Portland, south on I–5 and west on Hwy. 34 and U.S. 20.*

Newport was transformed after Keiko, the orca star of the movie *Free Willy,* arrived at the Oregon Coast Aquarium in 1996. The small harbor and fishing town with about 8,000 residents became one of the most-visited places on the coast. The surge of tourists brought new prosperity to a town feeling the pinch of federally imposed fishing restrictions that had cut into its traditional economy. Keiko moved to Iceland in 1998, so the crowds have diminished, but thanks to its easily accessible beach, a lively Performing Arts Center, and the local laid-back attitude, Newport remains a favorite both with regional travelers looking for a weekend escape and those who come for longer stays.

Newport exists on two levels: the highway above, threading its way through the community's main business district, and the old **Bayfront** along Yaquina Bay below (watch for signs on U.S. 101). With its high-masted fishing fleet, well-worn buildings, seafood markets, and art galleries and shops, Newport's Bayfront is an ideal place for an afternoon stroll. So many male sea lions in Yaquina Bay loiter near crab pots and bark from the waterfront piers that locals call the area the Bachelor Club.

Visit the docks to buy fresh seafood or rent a small boat or kayak to explore Yaquina Bay.

Nye Beach, a neighborhood west of the highway, preserves a few remnants of Newport's crusty past—you can still get an idea of the simple beach architecture that once characterized most of the Oregon coast—but in the aftermath of a $2.5 million face-lift, many old cottages and other sites have been gentrified. One of the first beachside communities on the Oregon coast, Nye Beach once had a sanitarium with hot seawater baths and the popular Natatorium, a looming bluffside structure with an indoor saltwater-fed pool, dance floors, and miniature golf. Those old buildings are long gone, replaced today by the Yaquina Art Center, parking, and access to the beach. The graceful 3,280-foot **Yaquina Bay Bridge,** a Work Projects Administration structure completed in 1936, leads to Newport's southern section.

★ ☾ The **Oregon Coast Aquarium,** a 4½-acre complex, has re-creations of offshore and near-shore Pacific marine habitats, all teeming with life: playful sea otters, comical puffins, fragile jellyfish, and even a 60-pound octopus. There's a hands-on interactive area for children and North America's largest seabird aviary. For a few years the biggest attraction was Keiko, the 4-ton killer whale brought to the aquarium to be rehabilitated. Since 1998, when Keiko was moved, the aquarium has developed new attractions. Permanent exhibits include Passages of the Deep, a trio of tanks linked by a 200-foot underwater tunnel with 360-degree views of sharks, wolf eels, halibut, and other sea life. Large coho salmon and sturgeon can be viewed in a naturalistic setting through a window wall 9 feet high and 20 feet wide. Keiko's former home has been transformed into a deep-sea exhibit complete with a wrecked ship. ⊠ *2820 S.E. Ferry Slip Rd.;, Heading south from Newport, turn right at southern end of Yaquina Bay Bridge and follow signs* ☎ *541/867–3474* ⊕ *www.aquarium.org* ⚑ *$10.75* ☾ *Daily 10–5.*

☾ Interactive and interpretive exhibits at Oregon State University's **Hatfield Marine Science Center,** which is connected by a trail to the Oregon Coast Aquarium, explain current marine research from global, bird's-eye, eye-level, and microscopic perspectives. The star of the show is a large octopus in a touch tank near the entrance. She seems as interested in human visitors as they are in her; guided by a staff volunteer, you can sometimes reach in to stroke her suction-tipped tentacles. ⊠ *2030 S. Marine Science Dr.;, Heading south from Newport, cross Yaquina Bay Bridge on U.S. 101 S and follow signs* ☎ *541/867–0100* ⚑ *Suggested donation $4* ☾ *Memorial Day–Labor Day, daily 10–6; Labor Day–Memorial Day, Thurs.–Mon. 10–5.*

Mariner Square has several touristy attractions. **Ripley's Believe It or Not** (⚑ *call for prices* ☾ *Mid-June–mid-Sept., daily 9–9; mid-Sept. and Oct. and mid-Feb.–mid-June, daily 10–5; Nov.–mid-Feb. daily 11–4*) has strange but true exhibits. **Undersea Gardens** (⚑ *Call for prices* ☾ *Mid-June–mid-Sept., daily 9–9; mid-Sept. and Oct. and mid-Feb.–mid-June, daily 10–5; Nov.–mid-Feb. daily 11–4*) has scuba-diving shows, marine plants, and animal exhibits. **Wax Works** (⚑ *Call for prices* ☾ *Mid-June–mid-Sept., daily 9–9; mid-Sept. and Oct. and mid-Feb.–mid-June, daily 10–5; Nov.–mid-Feb., daily 11–4*) has wax-figure exhibits of famous people. ⊠ *250 S.W. Bay Blvd.* ☎ *541/265–2206.*

Marine Discovery Tours conducts narrated whale-watching cruises in the bay. The 65-foot excursion boat *Discovery,* with inside seating for 49 and two viewing levels, departs from the Newport bayfront in the morning and afternoon. You can also watch from outside. The best viewing is March–October, though tours run year-round except during storms. While they can't guarantee you'll see a whale, 95% of outings are successful. There is a resident population of gray whales that stays near Newport year-round, including young mothers with calves who feed less than 1 mi from shore. In summer they often come right up to the boat. *Discovery* is wheelchair accessible. ⊠ *345 S.W. Bay Blvd., Newport 97365* ☎ *800/903–2628* ⊠ *$25* ▤ *D, MC, V.*

Seven miles north of Newport, beachfront **Beverly Beach State Park** extends from Yaquina Head to the headlands of Otter Rock. It has a campground with 53 full hookups, 76 electrical and 136 tent sites, and 14 yurts. ⊠ *U.S. 101* ☎ *541/265–9278 or 800/551–6949* ⊕ *www.prd.state. or.us* ⊠ *Free* ⊗ *Daily.*

A rocky shoreline separates the day-use **Devil's Punch Bowl State Natural Area** from the surf. It's a popular whale-watching site just 9 mi north of Newport and has excellent tidal pools. ⊠ *U.S. 101* ☎ *541/265–9278* ⊠ *Free* ⊗ *Daily.*

The **Lincoln County Historical Society Museums** include a log cabin and an 1895 Victorian house. Exhibits focus on Native American, maritime, and coastal settlement history. ⊠ *579 S.W. 9th St.* ☎ *541/265–7509* ⊠ *Donations accepted* ⊗ *June–Sept., Tues.–Sun. 10–5; Oct.–May, Tues.–Sun. 11–4.*

The day-use **Ona Beach State Park** is a popular beachcombing and picnic spot, 5 mi south of Newport. ⊠ *U.S. 101 S* ☎ *541/867–7451* ⊠ *Free* ⊗ *Daily.*

Ray Kowalski invented the art of chain-saw sculpture. For years he displayed 300 of his sculptures of cowboys, Indians, trolls, gnomes, and other figures at a park here called **Sea Gulch**, 10 mi south of Newport. The park is gone now, fallen victim to flashier tourist attractions, but Ray still presides over the busy workshop where his sons turn out new figures, mostly of bears. You're welcome to come by, take a look at the workshop, and buy small wooden sculptures in a small shop. You'd do best to call ahead. ⊠ *U.S. 101 97376* ☎ *541/563–2727* ⊠ *Free.*

Fishing, crabbing, boating, windsurfing, hiking, and beachcombing are popular at **South Beach State Park.** A campground has 238 electrical and 6 primitive sites as well as 16 yurts. ⊠ *U.S. 101 S* ☎ *541/867–4715 or 541/867–7451* ⊠ *Free* ⊗ *Daily.*

At the north end of Yaquina Bay near its outlet to the Pacific, **Yaquina Bay State Park** has a historic lighthouse that in more recent years was used as a Coast Guard Lifeboat Station. It's been restored and is now open to the public. ⊠ *U.S. 101 S* ☎ *541/867–7451* ⊠ *Free* ⊗ *Daily.*

★ ☾ The tallest lighthouse on the Oregon Coast is the 93-foot **Yaquina Head Lighthouse,** which is on a rocky peninsula. Guided morning tours are limited to 15 people. ⊠ *4 mi north of bridge in Newport* ☎ *541/574–3100* ⊠ *Call for prices* ⊗ *Mid-June–mid-Sept., daily noon–4; in winter, call ahead.*

★ In addition to the Yaquina Head Lighthouse, the **Yaquina Head Outstanding Natural Area** is the site of man-made tidal pools universally accessible, as well as natural tidal pools, and Cobble Beach, a stretch of round basalt rocks believed to have originated from volcano eruptions 14 million years ago in the Columbia Gorge 300 mi away. Thousands of birds—cormorants, gulls, common murres, pigeon guillemots—make their home just beyond shore on Pinnacle and Colony Rocks, and nature trails wind through fields of sea-grass and wildflowers, leading to spectacular views.

There is also an interpretive center, where you can view a short video about the area, read old lighthouse log books and listen to the songs of seabirds and whales. It's a great place to pass a rainy day. ⊠ *750 N.W. Lighthouse Dr.* ☎ *541/574–3100* ⌦ *$5 per vehicle, 9 passengers or fewer* ⊗ *Daily sunrise–sunset.*

Where to Stay & Eat

$$ ✕ **Tables of Content.** The well-plotted prix-fixe menu at the restaurant of the outstanding Sylvia Beach Hotel changes nightly. Chances are the main dish will be fresh local seafood, perhaps a moist grilled salmon fillet in a sauce Dijonnaise, served with sautéed vegetables, fresh-baked breads, rice pilaf; a decadent dessert is also included. The interior is functional and unadorned, with family-size tables. Come for the food, not the furnishings. ⊠ *267 N.W. Cliff St., from U.S. 101 head west on 3rd St.* ☎ *541/ 265–5428* ⌂ *Reservations essential* ▤ *AE, MC, V* ⊗ *No lunch.*

¢–$$ ✕ **Canyon Way Restaurant and Bookstore.** Cod, Dungeness crab cakes, bouillabaisse, and Yaquina Bay oysters are among the specialties of this Newport dining spot up the hill from the center of the Bayfront. There's also a deli counter for takeout. The restaurant, which has an outdoor patio, is to one side of a well-stocked bookstore. The new Fast Eddie's Bar serves lighter fare and lunch sandwiches as well as light dinners. ⊠ *S. W. Canyon Way off Bay Front Blvd.* ☎ *541/265–8319* ▤ *AE, MC, V* ⊗ *Closed Sun.*

★ ¢ ✕ **Panini Bakery.** The young couple who operate this bakery and espresso bar—a local favorite after just a few years in existence—pride themselves on hearty and home-roasted meats, hand-cut breads, and friendly service. The coffee's organic, the eggs free range, the orange juice fresh squeezed, and just about everything is made from scratch. Take a seat inside, or, in good weather, streetside tables are a great place to view the Nye Beach scene. ⊠ *232 N.W. Coast Hwy.* ☎ *541/265–5033* ▤ *No credit cards* ⊗ *Closed Tues. and Wed.*

$$–$$$ ⊡ **Newport Belle Bed & Breakfast.** This fully operational stern-wheeler **Fodor'sChoice** stays permanently moored at the Newport Marina, where you have front-
★ row seats to all the boating activity in the bay. Five rooms have themes that run from the Australian Outback to Montana's West. The main salon is cozy, with hardwood floors, a woodstove, and comfortable furniture. Facilities, such as Internet access, TV and phones, not found in guest rooms, are all available in the salon. ⊠ *H Dock, Newport Marina, 97365* ☎ *541/867–6290 or 800/348–1922* ⎙ *541/867–6291* ⊕ *www. newportbelle.com* ⌦ *5 rooms* ⌂ *No a/c, no kids under 7, no room phones, no room TVs, no smoking* ▤ *AE, D, MC, V* ⦿ *BP.*

$–$$$ ⊡ **Sylvia Beach Hotel.** Make reservations far in advance for this 1913-vintage beachfront hotel, whose antiques-filled rooms are named for famous writers. A pendulum swings over the bed in the Poe room. The Christie, Twain, and Colette rooms are the most luxurious; all have fireplaces, decks, and great ocean views. A well-stocked split-level upstairs library has decks, a fireplace, slumbering cats, and too-comfortable chairs. Complimentary mulled wine is served here nightly at 10. ⊠ *267 N.W. Cliff St., 97365* ☎ *541/265–5428 or 888/795–8422* ⊕ *www. sylviabeachhotel.com* ⌦ *20 rooms* ⌂ *Restaurant, library; no room phones, no room TVs* ▤ *AE, MC, V* ⦿ *BP.*

Waldport

⑭ *15 mi south of Newport on U.S. 101, 67 mi west of Corvallis on Hwy. 34 and U.S. 20.*

Long ago the base of the Alsi Indians, Waldport later became a gold-rush town and a logging center. In the 1980s it garnered national attention when local residents fought the timber industry and stopped the spraying of dioxin-based defoliants in the Coast Range forests. Waldport attracts many retirees and those seeking an alternative to the expensive beach resorts nearby.

At **Alsea Bay Bridge Interpretive Center,** displays recount the construction of the Oregon Coast highway and its many graceful bridges through dioramas, bridge models, photography, and time lines. ✉ *620 N.W. Spring St., off U.S. 101 at south end of bridge* ☎ *541/563–2002* 💲 *Free* ⊙ *Daily 10–5.*

The **Drift Creek Wilderness** east of Waldport holds some of the rare old-growth forest that has triggered battles between the timber industry and environmentalists. Hemlocks hundreds of years old grow in parts of this 9-square-mi area. The 2-mi **Harris Ranch Trail** winds through these ancient giants—you may even spot a spotted owl. The Siuslaw National Forest–Waldport Ranger Station provides directions and maps. ✉ *Risely Creek Rd.,, From Waldport, take Hwy. 34 east for 7 mi to Alsea River crossing* ☎ *541/563–3211* ⊙ *Daily 8–4.*

Where to Stay

$$ 🏠 **Cliff House Bed-and-Breakfast.** The view from Yaquina John Point, on which this B&B sits, is magnificent. The house, which in livelier days was a bordello, is done in a mix of classic American antiques and comfortable overstuffed furniture. Plush rooms all have ocean views; three have balconies and wood-burning stoves. A glass-front terrace looking out over 8 mi of white-sand beach leads down to the garden. ✉ *1450 Adahi Rd., 1 block west of U.S. 101, 97394* ☎ *541/563–2506* 🖨 *541/ 563–3903* ⊕ *www.cliffhouseoregon.com* ⟿ *4 rooms* ᕱ *In-room VCRs, hot tub* ➡ *MC, V* ⦿ *BP.*

Yachats

🅕 *8 mi south of Waldport on U.S. 101.*

A tiny burg of 685 inhabitants, Yachats (pronounced "yah-*hots*") has acquired a reputation among Oregon beach lovers that is disproportionate to its size. The small town is at the mouth of the Yachats River, and from its rocky shoreline, which includes the highest point on the Oregon coast, trails lead to beaches and dozens of tidal pools. A relaxed alternative to the more touristy communities to the north, Yachats has all the coastal pleasures: B&Bs, good restaurants, deserted beaches, tidal pools, surf-pounded crags, fishing, and crabbing. The town's name is a Native American word meaning "foot of the mountain."

At **Neptune State Park** you can look for animals, watch the surf, or reflect on the view over Cumming Creek from the benches set on the cliff above the beach. It's also a great spot for whale watching. Low tide provides access to a natural cave and tidal pools. ✉ *U.S. 101 S* ☎ *800/551–6949* ⊕ *www.prd.state.or.us* 💲 *Free* ⊙ *Daily.*

Six miles south of Yachats, **Sea Rose** sells seashells from Oregon and around the world, plus gift items and souvenirs, and serves both casual collectors and serious shell aficionados. A free museum displays shells and sea life. There's an exhibit of glass fishing floats, but a favorite item is the giant clam. ✉ *95478 U.S. 101, 97498* ☎ *541/547–3005* 🖨 *541/ 547–5197* ⊙ *Memorial Day–Labor Day, daily 9:30–6; Labor Day–Memorial Day, daily 10–5.*

The oceanside **Tillicum Beach Campground** 3½ mi north of Yachats is so popular there is a 10-day-stay limit. Stairs provide access to the beach.

Open year-round, there are 61 sites. ⊠ *U.S. 101* ☏ *541/563–3211* ▩ *Day use free* ☉ *Daily.*

The Yachats River meets the Pacific Ocean at **Yachats Ocean Road State Recreation Area,** 1 mi from Yachats. Whale-watching is a popular activity. ⊠ *U.S. 101 to Yachats Ocean Rd.* ☏ *541/997–3851 or 800/551–6949* ⊕ *www.prd.state.or.us* ▩ *Free* ☉ *Daily.*

Where to Stay & Eat

$–$$$ ✕ **Adobe Restaurant.** The food at the dining room of the Adobe Hotel doesn't always measure up to the extraordinary ocean views, but if you stick to the seafood, you'll come away satisfied. The Baked Crab Pot is a rich, bubbling casserole filled with Dungeness crab and cheese in a shallot cream sauce; best of all is the Captain's Seafood Platter, heaped with prawns, scallops, grilled oysters, and razor clams. ⊠ *1555 U.S. 101* ☏ *541/547–3141* ▤ *AE, D, DC, MC, V.*

★ **$–$$$** ✕ **La Serre.** Don't be dismayed by the vaguely steak-and-salad-bar feel at this skylit, plant-filled restaurant—the chef's deft touch with fresh seafood attracts knowledgeable diners from as far away as Florence and Newport. Try the tender geoduck clam, breaded with Parmesan cheese and flash-fried in lemon-garlic butter. A reasonably priced wine list and mouthwatering desserts complete the package. ⊠ *2nd and Beach Sts.* ☏ *541/547–3420* ▤ *AE, MC, V* ☉ *Closed Jan. and Tues. No lunch.*

$$$ ▦ **Ziggurat.** You have to see this four-story cedar-and-glass pyramid 6½ mi south of Yachats to believe it. And you need to spend a night or two, serenaded by the wind and sea, to fully appreciate it. Odd angles, contemporary furnishings, and works of art gathered on the owners' world travels lend a discerning, sophisticated air. Two first-floor suites open out to grassy cliffs; the smaller, fourth-floor bedroom has two balconies and dramatic views. ⊠ *95320 U.S. 101, 97498* ☏ *541/547–3925* ⊕ *www.newportnet.com/ziggurat* ▭ *1 room, 2 suites* ♿ *No kids under 14, no smoking* ▤ *No credit cards* ⏣ *BP.*

Cape Perpetua

★ ⑯ *9 mi south of Yachats town on U.S. 101.*

With the highest lookout point on the Oregon coast, Cape Perpetua towers 800 feet above the rocky shoreline. Named by Captain Cook on St. Perpetua's Day in 1778, the cape is part of a 2,700-acre scenic area popular with hikers, campers, beachcombers, and naturalists. General information and a map of 10 trails are available at the **Cape Perpetua Visitors Center,** on the east side of the highway, 2 mi south of Devil's Churn. The easy 1-mi **Giant Spruce Trail** passes through a fern-filled rain forest to an enormous 500-year-old Sitka spruce. Easier still is the marked Auto Tour; it begins about 2 mi north of the visitor center and winds through Siuslaw National Forest to the ¼-mi **Whispering Spruce Trail.** Views from the rustic rock shelter here extend 150 mi north and south and 37 mi out to sea. The **Cape Perpetua Interpretive Center,** in the visitor center, has educational movies and exhibits about the natural forces that shaped Cape Perpetua. ⊠ *U.S. 101* ☏ *541/547–3289* ▩ *Visitor center free, interpretive center $3* ☉ *Memorial Day–Labor Day, daily 9–5; Labor Day–Memorial Day, weekends 10–4.*

Heceta Head

⑰ *10 mi south of Cape Perpetua on U.S. 101, 65 mi from Eugene, west on Hwy. 126 and north on U.S. 101.*

A ½-mi trail from the beachside parking lot at **Devil's Elbow State Park** leads to **Heceta Head Lighthouse,** whose beacon, visible for more than

21 mi, is the most powerful on the Oregon coast. The trail passes **Heceta House,** a pristine white structure said to be haunted by the wife of a lighthouse keeper whose child fell to her death from the cliffs shortly after the beacon was lit in 1894. The house is one of Oregon's most remarkable bed-and-breakfasts. ⊠ *U.S. 101* ☎ *541/997–3851* 🖾 *Day use $3, lighthouse tours free* ☉ *Lighthouse Mar.–Oct., daily noon–5; park daily sunrise–sunset.*

In 1880 a sea captain named Cox rowed a small skiff into a fissure in a 300-foot-high sea cliff. Inside, he was startled to discover a vaulted chamber in the rock, 125 feet high and 2 acres in area. Hundreds of massive sea lions—the largest bulls weighing 2,000 pounds or more—covered every available horizontal surface. Cox had no way of knowing it, but his discovery would eventually become one of the Oregon coast's premier tourist attractions, **Sea Lion Caves.** An elevator near the cliff-top ticket office descends to the floor of the cavern, near sea level, where Steller's and California sea lions and their fuzzy pups can be viewed from behind a wire fence. This is the only known hauling-out area and rookery for wild sea lions on the mainland in the Lower 48, and it's an awesome—if aromatic—sight and sound. In the spring and summer the mammals usually stay on the rocky ledges outside the cave; in fall and winter they move inside. You'll also see several species of sea birds here, including migratory pigeon guillemots, cormorants, and three varieties of gulls. Gray whales are visible during their northern and southern migrations, October–December and March–May. ⊠ *91560 U.S. 101, 1 mi south of Heceta Head* ☎ *541/547–3111* 🖾 *$7* ☉ *Opens at 9 AM daily; closing times vary.*

Where to Stay

$$-$$$$ 🏠 **Heceta House.** On a windswept promontory, this unusual B&B is surrounded by a white-picket fence. The late-Victorian house, owned by the U.S. Forest Service, is managed by Mike and Carol Korgan, certified executive chefs who prepare a seven-course breakfast (included in the room rate) each morning. The nicest of the simply furnished rooms is the Mariner's, with a private bath and an awe-inspiring view. Filled with period detailing and antiques, the common areas are warm and inviting. If you're lucky, you may hear Rue, the resident ghost, in the middle of the night. ⊠ *92072 U.S. 101 S, Yachats 97498* ☎ *541/547–3696* ⊕ *www. hecetalighthouse.com* 🛏 *3 rooms, 1 with bath* ▤ *MC, V* 🍽 *BP.*

en route

South of Heceta Head, U.S. 101 jogs inland, and the frowning headlands and cliffs of the north coast give way to the beaches, lakes, rivers, tidal estuaries, and rolling dunes of the south. Historic bridges span many of the famous fishing rivers that draw anglers from around the world. **Darlingtona Botanical Wayside** (⊠ Mercer Lake Rd. ☎ No phone), 6 mi south of Sea Lion Caves on the east side of U.S. 101, is an example of the rich plant life found in the marshy terrain near the coast. It's also a surefire child pleaser. A short paved nature trail leads through clumps of insect-catching cobra lilies, so named because they look like spotted cobras ready to strike. This wayside area is the most interesting in May, when the lilies are in bloom. Admission is free.

Florence

⑲ *12 mi south of Heceta Head on U.S. 101, 63 mi west of Eugene on Hwy. 126.*

Tourists and retirees have been flocking to Florence in ever greater numbers in recent years. Its restored waterfront Old Town has restaurants, antiques stores, fish markets, and other diversions. But what really makes the town so appealing is its proximity to remarkable stretches of coastline. Seventy-five creeks and rivers empty into the Pacific Ocean in and around Florence, and the Siuslaw River flows right through town. When the numerous nearby lakes are added to the mix, it makes for one of the richest fishing areas in Oregon. Salmon, rainbow trout, bass, perch, crabs, and clams are among the water's treasures. Fishing boats and pleasure craft moor in Florence's harbor, forming a pleasant backdrop for the town's restored buildings. South of town, miles of white-sand dunes lend themselves to everything from solitary hikes to rides aboard all-terrain vehicles.

★ ☾ Florence is the gateway to the **Oregon Dunes National Recreation Area,** a 41-mi swath of undulating camel-color sand. The dunes, formed by eroded sandstone pushed up from the sea floor millions of years ago, have forests growing on them, water running through them, and rivers that have been dammed by them to form lakes. **Honeyman Memorial State Park,** 522 acres within the recreation area, is a base camp for dune-buggy enthusiasts, mountain bikers, hikers, boaters, horseback riders, and dogsledders (the sandy hills are an excellent training ground). The dunes are a vast and exuberant playground for children, particularly the slopes surrounding cool **Cleawox Lake.** ⊠ *Oregon Dunes National Recreation Area office, 855 U.S. 101, Reedsport 97467* ☎ *541/271–3611* ✆ *Day use $5* ☉ *Daily sunrise–sunset.*

Ride year-round along the Oregon Dunes National Recreation Area at **C and M Stables,** spotting not only marine life—sea lions, whales, and all manner of coast bird—but also bald eagles, red-tailed fox, and deer. Choose a 10-minute corral ride or take a horse out for the day to explore the beach or dunes. Children must be at least eight years old for the beach ride or six years old for the dune trail rides. There are also six overnight RV spaces. ⊠ *90241 U.S. 101 N* ☎ *541/997–7540* ⊕ *www.touroregon.com/horses/index.html* ✆ *$25–$40 per hr* ☉ *Daily 10–sunset.*

---

need a break?

A small, homey business, **Siuslaw River Coffee Roasters** (⊠ 1240 Bay St. ☎ 541/997–3443) serves cups of drip-on-demand coffee—you select the roast and they grind and brew it on the spot. Beans are roasted on site, muffins and breads are freshly baked, and a view of the namesake river can be savored from the deck out back.

The focus at **Siuslaw Pioneer Museum,** formerly a Lutheran church, is on pioneer and Native American history. ⊠ *85294 U.S. 101 S* ☎ *541/997–7884* ✆ *$1 suggested donation* ☉ *Jan.–Nov., Tues.–Sun. 10–4.*

A trail from **Carl G. Washburne Memorial** park connects you to the Heceta Head trail, which you can use to reach the Heceta Head lighthouse. The campground has 58 full hookups, 2 tent sites, and 2 yurts. ⊠ *93111 U.S. 101 N* ☎ *541/547–3416* ⊕ *www.prd.state.or.us* ✆ *$3 per vehicle* ☉ *Daily.*

The Victorian ***Westward Ho!* Sternwheeler** leaves from the Old Town Docks and cruises the Siuslaw River past forests and the Oregon Dunes National Recreation Area. ⊠ *Bay and Maple Sts.* ☎ *541/997–9691* ⊕ *www.westward-ho.com* ✆ *$14, sunset dinner cruise $33* ☉ *Apr.–Oct., daily; call for schedules.*

Beginning at the Siltcoos Lake, where cottages float on calm waters, the ★ **Siltcoos River Canoe Trail** winds through thick rain forest, past towering sand dunes, emerging some 4 mi later at white-sand beaches and the blue waters of the Pacific, where seals and snowy plovers rest. The river is a Class I with no rapids, but there are a few trees to navigate and one very short portage around a small dam.

Where to Eat

$–$$$ ✕ **Bridgewater Seafood Restaurant.** Freshly caught seafood—25 to 30 choices nightly—is the mainstay of this creaky-floored Victorian-era restaurant in Florence's Old Town. The cooking is plain and not exactly inspired, but that may be part of its appeal. ⊠ *1297 Bay St.* ☎ *541/997–9405* ▤ *MC, V.*

$–$$$ ✕ **Clawson's Windward Inn.** One of the south coast's most elegant eateries, this tightly run ship prides itself on its vast seafood-heavy menu, master wine list, and fresh and fine desserts. The chinook salmon fillets poached in Riesling and the shrimp and scallops sautéed in white wine are delectable. ⊠ *3757 U.S. 101 N* ☎ *541/997–8243* ▤ *D, MC, V.*

¢–$$ ✕ **Mo's.** Going hand in hand at Mo's are clear bayfront views and a creamy bowl of clam chowder. This coastal institution has been around for more than 40 years, consistently providing fresh seafood and down-home service. ⊠ *1436 Bay St.* ☎ *541/997–2185* ▤ *D, MC, V.*

Reedsport

㉒ *20 mi south of Florence on U.S. 101, 90 mi west of Eugene on I–5 and Hwy. 38.*

The small town of Reedsport owes its existence to the Umpqua River, one of the state's great steelhead fishing streams. Exhibits at the **Umpqua Discovery Center** in the waterfront area give a good introduction to the Lower Umpqua estuary and surrounding region. The center's chief attraction is the *Hero,* the laboratory ship Admiral Byrd used on his expeditions to the Antarctic. ⊠ *409 Riverfront Way* ☎ *541/271–4816* ▦ *Museum $5, tour of ship $3* ☉ *May–Sept., daily 10–6; Oct.–Apr., daily 10–4.*

The natural forces that created the towering sand dunes along this section of the Oregon coast are explained in interpretive exhibits at the Reedsport **Oregon Dunes National Recreation Area Visitors Center.** The center, which also sells maps, books, and gifts, is a good place to pick up free literature on the area. ⊠ *855 Highway Ave., south side of Umpqua River Bridge* ☎ *541/271–3611* ▦ *Free* ☉ *Memorial Day–Labor Day, daily 8:30–5; hrs vary rest of year.*

A herd of wild Roosevelt elk, Oregon's largest land mammal, roams within sight of the **Dean Creek Elk Viewing Area.** Abundant forage and a mild winter climate enable the elk to remain at Dean Creek year-round. The best viewing times are early morning and just before dusk. ⊠ *Hwy. 38, 3 mi east of Reedsport, watch for signs* ▦ *Free* ☉ *Daily sunrise–sunset.*

Two miles south of Reedsport at the mouth of the Umpqua River, **Salmon Harbor** is one of the largest marinas on the Oregon coast. An RV park is near the county-operated facility. ⊠ *U.S. 101* ☎ *541/271–3407* ▦ *Free* ☉ *May–Sept., daily; Oct.–Apr., weekdays.*

On Eel Lake near the town of Lakeside, the little-known **William M. Tugman State Park** is surrounded by a dense forest of spruce, cedar, fir, and alder. Recreational activities include fishing, swimming, canoeing, and sailing. A campground has 115 electrical sites and 3 yurts. ⊠ *U.S. 101 S* ☎ *541/888–4902 or 800/551–6949* ⊕ *www.prd.state.or.us* ▦ *$3 per vehicle day-use fee* ☉ *Daily.*

en route A public pier at **Winchester Bay's Salmon Harbor,** 3¼ mi south of Reedsport, juts out over the bay and yields excellent results for crabbers and fishermen (especially those after rockfish). There's also a full-service marina with a fish market.

Where to Stay

$ 🏨 **Salbasgeon Inn of the Umpqua.** In the heart of fishing country, this inn takes its name from salmon, striped bass, and sturgeon. It overlooks the Umpqua River, and all rooms have river views. ⊠ *45209 Rte. 38, 97467* ☎ *541/271–2025* ⊕ *www.salbasgeon.com or www.umpquariver.com* ➯ *12 rooms* ⚷ *Picnic area, some kitchenettes, cable TV, putting green, some pets allowed (fee)* ⊟ *AE, D, DC, MC, V.*

¢–$ 🏨 **Anchor Bay Inn.** Right in the center of Reedsport, this motel has easy access to the dunes. Elk viewing is only 4 mi away. ⊠ *1821 Winchester Ave., 97467* ☎ *541/271–2149 or 800/767–1821* ⊟ *541/271–1802* ✉ *anchorbay@presys.com* ➯ *21 rooms* ⚷ *Some kitchenettes, some microwaves, some refrigerators, cable TV, pool, laundry facilities, business services, some pets allowed (fee)* ⊟ *AE, D, MC, V* ⭗ *CP.*

Umpqua Lighthouse Park

㉑ *6 mi south of Reedsport on U.S. 101.*

Some of the highest sand dunes in the country are found in the 50-acre Umpqua Lighthouse Park. The first **Umpqua River Lighthouse,** built on the dunes at the mouth of the Umpqua River in 1857, lasted only four years before it toppled over in a storm. It took local residents 33 years to build another one. The "new" lighthouse, built on a bluff overlooking the south side of Winchester Bay and operated by the U.S. Coast Guard, is still going strong, flashing a warning beacon out to sea every five seconds. The **Douglas County Coastal Visitors Center** adjacent to the lighthouse has a museum and can arrange lighthouse tours. ⊠ *Umpqua Hwy., west side of U.S. 101* ☎ *541/271–4118* ⊠ *Donations appreciated* ⊘ *Lighthouse May–Sept., Wed.–Sat. 10–4, Sun. 1–4.*

North Bend

㉒ *20 mi south of Reedsport on U.S. 101.*

Named by the town's founder, sea captain and shipbuilder Asa Simpson, for its location on the north bend of Coos Bay, this town continues a decades-long tradition by making its livelihood from forest products, fishing, agriculture, and tourism. North Bend and its neighbors Coos Bay and Charleston make up the Bay Area, the largest urban area on the Oregon coast; North Bend sits at the south end of the 41-mi-long Oregon Dunes National Recreation Area.

The highlight here at **Coos County Historical Society Museum** is a 1922 steam locomotive used in Coos County logging. On display are a formal 1900 parlor, a pioneer kitchen, and exhibits on Native American history, agriculture, and industry such as logging, shipping, and mining. ⊠ *1220 Sherman St.* ☎ *541/756–6320 or 541/756–4847* ⊠ *$2* ⊘ *Tues.–Sat. 10–4.*

The complex at **Mill Casino-Hotel** has a casino with 350 slots, blackjack, poker, and bingo. There's a waterfront restaurant and a showroom. ⊠ *3201 Tremont Ave., 97459* ☎ *541/756–8800 or 800/953–4800* ⊟ *541/756–0431* ⊕ *www.themillcasino.com* ⊠ *Free* ⊘ *Daily.*

Where to Eat

$–$$$ ✕ **Hilltop House.** A dining tradition on the coast for 40 years, Hilltop House offers specialties that include Bouillabaisse Marseillaise, Salmon

Neptune, rack of lamb, and lobster Newberg. Enjoy views of the bay, harbor, and sand while dining in the many-window dining room. ⊠ *166 N. Bay Dr., 97459* ☎ *541/756–4160* ⊟ *AE, MC, V.*

¢–$$ ✕ **Plank House.** The Plank House menu is designed to satisfy many tastes, whether with a simple home-style meat loaf, the local seafood catch of the day, or a tender cut of steak. All the baking, including chocolate decadence tortes and cheesecakes, is done right here. The restaurant, part of the Mill Casino-Hotel, serves breakfast, lunch, and dinner, and the outside deck, though not for eating, has a fantastic view of Coos Bay. ⊠ *3201 Tremont Ave., 97459* ☎ *541/756–8800 or 800/953–4800* 🖷 *541/756–0431* ⊟ *AE, D, MC, V.*

Coos Bay

❷❸ *27 mi south of Reedsport on U.S. 101, 116 mi southwest of Eugene, I–5 to Hwy. 38 to U.S. 101.*

The Coos Bay–Charleston–North Bend metropolitan area, collectively known as the Bay Area (population 25,000), is the gateway to rewarding recreational experiences. The town of Coos Bay lies next to the largest natural harbor between San Francisco Bay and Seattle's Puget Sound. A century ago vast quantities of lumber cut from the Coast Range were milled in Coos Bay and shipped around the world. Coos Bay still has a reputation as a rough-and-ready port city, but with mill closures and dwindling lumber reserves it has begun to look in other directions, such as tourism, for economic prosperity. One former mill has even been converted into a casino.

To see the best of the Bay Area head west from Coos Bay on Newmark Avenue for about 7 mi to **Charleston.** Though it's a Bay Area community, this quiet fishing village at the mouth of Coos Bay is a world unto itself. As it loops into town the road becomes the Cape Arago Highway and leads to several oceanfront parks.

At **Charleston Marina Complex** there's a launch ramp, a store with tackle and marine supplies, a 110-space RV park, a motel, restaurants, and gift shops. Fishing charters also set out from here. ⊠ *4535 Kingfisher Dr., Charleston 97420* ☎ *541/888–2548* ⊕ *www.charlestonmarina.com* 🖼 *Free* ☉ *Daily.*

A placid semicircular lagoon protected from the sea by overlapping fingers of rock and surrounded by reefs, **Sunset Bay State Park** is one of the few places along the Oregon coast where you can swim without worrying about the currents and undertows. Only the hardiest souls will want to brave the chilly water, however. ✛ *2 mi south of Charleston off Cape Arago Hwy.* ☎ *800/551–6949* 🖼 *Free* ☉ *Daily sunrise–sunset.*

At **Shore Acres State Park,** an observation building on a grassy bluff overlooking the Pacific marks the site that held the mansion of lumber baron Louis J. Simpson. The view over the rugged wave-smashed cliffs is splendid, but the real glory of Shore Acres lies a few hundred yards to the south, where an entrance gate leads into what was Simpson's private garden. Beautifully landscaped and meticulously maintained, the gardens incorporate formal English and Japanese designs. From March to mid-October the grounds are ablaze with blossoming daffodils, rhododendrons, azaleas, roses, and dahlias. In December the entire garden is decked out with a dazzling display of holiday lights. ⊠ *10965 Cape Arago Hwy., 1 mi south of Sunset Bay State Park* ☎ *800/551–6949* 🖼 *$3 per vehicle day-use fee* ☉ *Daily 8–sunset.*

The distant barking of sea lions echoes in the air at **Cape Arago State Park.** A trio of coves connected by short but steep trails, the park overlooks the **Oregon Islands National Wildlife Refuge,** where offshore rocks, beaches, islands, and reefs provide breeding grounds for seabirds and marine mammals. ⊠ *End of Cape Arago Hwy., 1 mi south of Shore Acres State Park* ☎ *800/551–6949* ☒ *Free* ☉ *Daily sunrise–sunset.*

On a rock island just 12 mi offshore south of Coos Bay, **Cape Arago Lighthouse** has had several iterations; the first lighthouse was built here in 1866, but it was destroyed by storms and erosion. A second, built in 1908, suffered the same fate. The current white tower, built in 1934, is 44 feet tall and towers 100 feet above the ocean. If you're here on a foggy day, listen for its unique foghorn. The lighthouse is connected to the mainland by a bridge. Neither is open to the public, but there's an excellent spot to view this lonely guardian and much of the coastline. From U.S. 101, take Cape Arago Highway to Gregory Point, where it ends at a turnaround, and follow the short trail.

The wreck of the *New Carissa* freighter in winter 1999 was considered a serious threat to the fragile ecosystem at **South Slough National Estuarine Research Reserve,** but not much leaking oil reached the slough. The mudflats and tidal estuaries of Coos Bay support everything from algae to bald eagles and black bears. More than 300 species of birds have been sighted at the reserve; an interpretive center, guided walks (summer only), and nature trails give you a chance to see things up close. ⊠ *Seven Devils Rd., 4 mi south of Charleston* ☎ *800/551–6949* ☒ *Free* ☉ *Trails daily sunrise–sunset, interpretive center daily 8:30–4:30.*

Both a gift shop and a factory, the **Oregon Connection** produces more than 200 myrtlewood items and sells Oregon food and wine, homemade fudge, Pendleton woolen clothes, and jewelry. You can take a free tour of the factory. ⊠ *1125 S. 1st St.* ☎ *541/267–7804 or 800/255–5318* ☒ *Free* ☉ *Daily 9–5.*

Where to Stay & Eat

$–$$ ✕ **Portside Restaurant.** The fish at this gem of a restaurant overlooking the Charleston boat basin comes straight to the kitchen from the dock outside. Try the steamed Dungeness crab with drawn butter. On Friday night come for the all-you-can-eat seafood buffet. The nautical furnishings—vintage bayside photos, boat lamps, navigational aids, coiled rope—reinforce the view of the harbor through the restaurant's picture windows. ⊠ *8001 Kingfisher Rd.,, Follow Cape Arago Hwy. from Coos Bay* ☎ *541/888–5544* ☐ *AE, DC, MC, V.*

★ **¢–$$** ✕ **Blue Heron Bistro.** You'll find subtle preparations of local seafood, chicken, and homemade pasta at this busy bistro. There are no flat spots on the far-ranging menu; even the innovative soups and desserts are excellent. The skylit tile-floor dining room seats about 70 amid natural wood and blue linen. The seating area outside has blue awnings and colorful Bavarian window boxes that add a festive touch. Espresso and 18 microbrewery beers are available. ⊠ *100 W. Commercial St.* ☎ *541/267–3933* ☐ *AE, D, MC, V* ☉ *Closed Sun. Oct.–May.*

$ 🏠 **Coos Bay Manor.** Built in 1912 on a quiet residential street in Coos Bay, this 15-room Colonial Revival manor is listed on the National Register of Historic Places. Hardwood floors, detailed woodwork, high ceilings, and antiques and period reproductions offset the red-and-gold-flecked wallpaper. An unusual open balcony on the second floor leads to the large rooms. Innkeeper Pam Bate serves a full breakfast (included in the rates) in the wainscoted dining room. ⊠ *955 S. 5th St., 97420* ☎ *541/269–1224 or 800/269–1224* 🖷 *541/269–1224* 🛏 *5 rooms, 3 with bath* ⚘ *Airport shuttle* ☐ *D, MC, V* ⏍ *BP.*

Bandon

24 *25 mi south of Coos Bay on U.S. 101.*

Referred to by some who cherish its romantic lure as Bandon-by-the-Sea, Bandon is both a harbor town and a popular vacation spot. Bandon is famous for its cranberry products and its cheese factory, as well as its artists' colony, complete with galleries and shops. Two National Wildlife Refuges, Oregon Islands and Bandon Marsh, are within the city limits. Newly developed on natural rolling dune land along the Pacific Ocean, the Bandon Dunes links-style course is attracting interest from golfers worldwide.

It may seem odd that tiny Bandon, built above a beach notable for its gallery of photogenic seastacks, bills itself as the cranberry capital of Oregon. But 10 mi north of town lie acres of bogs and irrigated fields where tons of the tart berries are harvested every year. Each October a Cranberry Festival, complete with a parade and a fair, takes place.

The town, almost entirely rebuilt after a devastating fire in 1936, has fine restaurants, resort hotels, and a busy boat basin on the Coquille River estuary. A few of the buildings in the Old Town area a block north of the boat basin hark back to the early 20th century, when Bandon was a booming port of call for passengers traveling from San Francisco to Seattle by steamship.

The **Bandon Historical Society Museum,** in the old City Hall building, documents the town's past through dioramas, historic photos, and artifacts, such as marine and logging equipment. ⊠ *270 Fillmore St.* ☎ *541/347–2164* ⊑ *$1* ☯ *May–Sept., Mon.–Sat. 10–4, Sun. noon–3.*

The tiny **Bandon Beach State Park,** along the Beach Loop Road 5 mi south of Bandon, has access to beaches, fishing, and hiking trails. ⊠ *Bradley Lake Rd.* ☎ *541/347–3501 or 800/551–6949* ⊕ *www.prd.state.or.us* ⊑ *Free* ☯ *Daily.*

The octagonal **Coquille Lighthouse** at **Bullards Beach State Park,** built in 1896 and no longer in use, stands lonely sentinel at the mouth of the Coquille River. From the highway the 2-mi drive to reach it passes through the Bandon Marsh, a prime bird-watching and picnicking area. The beach beside the lighthouse is a good place to search for jasper, agate, and driftwood. ⊠ *U.S. 101, 2 mi north of Bandon* ☎ *800/551–6949* ⊑ *Free* ☯ *Daily sunrise–sunset.*

In the old City Hall building, the **Coquille River Museum** documents Bandon's past with displays of pioneer furniture, glassware, and clothing, plus exhibits on the Bandon fire of 1936 and the local lumber, cranberry, creamery, and maritime industries. ⊠ *270 Fillmore St., 97411* ☎ *541/347–2164* ⊑ *$2* ☯ *Oct.–Memorial Day, Mon.–Sat. 10–4; Memorial Day–Sept., Mon.–Sat. 10–4, Sun. noon–3.*

The stone sculptures of **Face Rock Wayside,** formed only by wind and rain, have names such as Elephant Rock, Table Rock, and Face Rock. To reach them follow signs from Bandon south along Beach Loop Road; then walk down a stairway to the sand. ⊑ *Free* ☯ *Daily.*

The "walk-through safari" on 21 acres of **West Coast Game Park** has free-roaming wildlife: 450 animals and 75 species including lions, tigers, snow leopards, bears, chimps, cougars, and camels, make it one of the largest wild-animal petting parks in the United States. The big attractions here are the young animals: bear cubs, tiger cubs, whatever is suitable for actual handling. It is 7 mi south of Bandon on U.S. 101. ⊠ *U.S. 101*

☎ *541/347–3106* ⊕ *www.gameparksafari.com* ✉ *$11* ☉ *Mid-June–Labor Day, daily 9–7; spring and early fall, daily 9–5.*

Where to Stay & Eat

$–$$$ ✕ **Lord Bennett's.** His lordship has a lot going for him: a cliff-top setting, a comfortable and spacious dining area, sunsets visible through picture windows overlooking Face Rock Beach, and musical performers on weekends. The rich dishes include prawns sautéed with sherry and garlic and steaks topped with shiitake mushrooms. A Sunday brunch is served. ✉ *1695 Beach Loop Rd.* ☎ *541/347–3663* ▤ *AE, D, MC, V.*

$$–$$$$ ▦ **The Lighthouse.** Wide windows and a porch off the dining room of this 1980 cedar home on Bandon's waterfront, within walking distance of Old Town and restaurants, provide great views of the Coquille River Lighthouse across the estuary. The simple furnishings include antiques and plants. Three guest rooms have dramatic ocean and sunset views, and guests say the Gray Whale Room has the best view on the Oregon coast, right from the room's hot tub. ✉ *650 Jetty Rd., 97411* ☎ *541/347–9316* ⊕ *www.lighthouselodging.com* ⇖ *5 rooms* ♿ *Some in-room hot tubs; no kids under 12, no smoking, no TV in some rooms* ▤ *MC, V* ▮❍▮ *BP.*

Cape Blanco State Park

㉕ *27 mi south of Bandon on U.S. 101.*

Cape Blanco is the westernmost point in Oregon and perhaps the windiest—gusts clocked at speeds as high as 184 mph have twisted and battered the Sitka spruces along the 6-mi road from U.S. 101 to the **Cape Blanco Lighthouse.** The lighthouse, atop a 245-foot headland, has been in continuous use since 1870, longer than any other in Oregon. No one knows why the Spaniards sailing past these reddish bluffs in 1603 called them *blanco* (white). One theory is that the name refers to the fossilized shells that glint in the cliff face. Campsites at the 1,880-acre **Cape Blanco State Park** are available on a first-come, first-served basis. Saturday-evening tours are available in summer, with a donation suggested. ✉ *Cape Blanco Rd., follow signs from U.S. 101* ☎ *541/332–6774 state park, 541/332–2750 lighthouse* ✉ *Day use free, campsites $13–$18* ☉ *Park daily sunrise–sunset; lighthouse Apr.–Oct., Thurs.–Mon. 10–3:30.*

---

en route | U.S. 101 between Port Orford and Brookings, often referred to as the "fabulous fifty miles," soars up green headlands, some of them hundreds of feet high, and past a seascape of cliffs and seastacks. The ocean is bluer and clearer—though not appreciably warmer—than it is farther north, and the coastal countryside is dotted with farms, grazing cattle, and small rural communities. As you round a bend between Port Orford and Gold Beach you'll see one of those sights that make grown-ups groan and kids squeal with delight: a huge, open-jawed Tyrannosaurus rex, with a green brontosaurus peering out from the forest beside it.

☾ The **Prehistoric Gardens** (✉ *36848 U.S. 101* ☎ *541/332–4463*) are filled with life-size replicas of these primeval giants. The complex is open daily 9 AM–sunset. Admission is $7.

Port Orford

㉖ *27 mi south of Bandon on U.S. 101.*

The most westerly incorporated city in the contiguous United States, Port Orford is surrounded by forests, rivers, lakes, and beaches of the Pacific

Ocean. The jetty at Port Orford offers little protection from storms, so every night the fishing boats are lifted out and stored on the docks. Commercial fishing boats search for crab, tuna, snapper, and salmon in the waters out of Port Orford, and diving boats gather sea urchins for Japanese markets. The area is a favorite spot for sport divers because of the near-shore, protected reef and for whale watchers in fall and early spring.

Six miles south of Port Orford, **Humbug Mountain State Park** is especially popular with campers. The park usually has warm weather, thanks to the nearby mountains, which block the ocean breezes. Windsurfing and scuba diving are popular here. Hiking trails lead to the top of Humbug Mountain. The campground has 30 electrical and 78 tent sites. ⊠ *U.S. 101* ☎ *541/332–6774 or 800/551–6949* ⊕ *www.prd.state.or.us* ☜ *$3 per vehicle day-use fee* ☉ *Daily.*

Where to Stay

$$ ▦ **Floras Lake House by the Sea.** This cedar home rests beside freshwater Floras Lake, spring-fed and separated from the ocean by only a sand spit. The owners run a windsurfing school on the lake. The interior of the house is light, airy, and comfortable, with picture windows, exposed beams, contemporary couches, and a woodstove. Two rooms have fireplaces, and all have private deck entrances. Outside, there's a garden, with a sauna beside the lake. ⊠ *92870 Boice Cope Rd., Langlois 97450* ☎ *541/348–2573* ☐ *541/348–9912* ⊕ *www.floraslake.com* ☜ *4 rooms* ♨ *Lake, sauna; no room phones, no room TVs, no smoking* ▤ *D, MC, V* ☉ *Closed mid-Nov.–mid-Feb.* ¦○¦ *BP.*

$–$$ ▦ **Home by the Sea.** On a headland jutting into the Pacific is this 1985 three-story shingle house. A nearby path leads down to the beach. Both guest rooms have views of the ocean, as does the lower-level solarium and breakfast room, a great spot for watching whales (October–May is the best time) and winter storms. Both rooms have myrtlewood beds. ⊠ *444 Jackson St., 97465* ☎ *541/332–2855* ⊕ *www.homebythesea.com* ☜ *2 rooms* ♨ *Refrigerators, in-room data ports, cable TV, laundry facilities, Internet; no a/c, no smoking* ▤ *MC, V* ¦○¦ *BP.*

Gold Beach

❷❼ *35 mi south of Cape Blanco on U.S. 101.*

The fabled **Rogue River,** which empties into the Pacific at Gold Beach, has been luring anglers and outdoors enthusiasts for more than a century. Zane Grey, in such books as *Rogue River Feud,* was among the writers who helped establish the Rogue's reputation as a renowned chinook salmon and steelhead stream. Celebrities as diverse as Winston Churchill, Clark Gable, and Ginger Rogers, who had a home on the Rogue, have all fished here. It's one of the few U.S. rivers to merit Wild and Scenic status from the federal government.

From spring to late fall an estimated 50,000 visitors descend on the town to take one of the daily jet-boat excursions that roar upstream from Wedderburn, Gold Beach's sister city across the bay, into the Rogue River Wilderness Area. Some of the boats go to Agness, 32 mi upstream, where the riverside road ends and the Wild and Scenic portions of the Rogue begin. Other boats penetrate farther, to the white-knuckle rapids at Blossom Bar, 52 mi upstream. Black bears, otters, beavers, ospreys, egrets, and bald eagles are regularly seen on these trips. From Grave Creek to Watson Creek, along the 40-mi stretch classified as Wild, a National Recreation Trail grants access to this "vestige of primitive America."

Gold Beach is very much a seasonal town, thriving in the summer and nearly deserted the rest of the year. It marks the entrance to Oregon's banana belt, where mild, California-like temperatures take the sting out of winter and encourage a blossoming trade in lilies and daffodils.

The parking lots at **Cape Sebastian State Park** are more than 200 feet above sea level. At the south parking vista you can see up to 43 mi north to Humbug Mountain. Looking south, you can see nearly 50 mi toward Crescent City, California, and the Point Saint George Lighthouse. A deep forest of Sitka spruce covers most of the park. There's a 1½-mi walking trail. ⊠ *U.S. 101* ☎ *541/469–2021 or 800/551–6949* ⊕ *www.prd. state.or.us* ☞ *Free* ☉ *Daily.*

Area Native American baskets, historic photos, and documents fill the diminutive **Curry County Historical Museum** on the Curry County Fairgrounds. ⊠ *920 S. Ellensburg* ☎ *541/247–6113* ☞ *Free* ☉ *June–Sept., Tues.–Sat. noon–4; Oct.–May, Sat. 10–4.*

Where to Stay & Eat

$$–$$$$ ✕ **Nor'Wester Seafood Restaurant.** At the mouth of the Rogue River, this 24-year-old casual eatery has a cedar interior, fireplace, and waterfront views. Refined fare includes fresh-caught salmon, clam chowder, and fettuccine tapenade. Specialty salads, razor clams, and choice cut steaks are also menu favorites, and the wine list is varied and full. ⊠ *Port of Gold Beach* ☎ *541/247–2333* ⊟ *AE, MC, V* ☉ *No lunch.*

$$–$$$ ✕ **Chives.** With some of the finest dining on the southern coast, this spot has an ever-changing menu of eclectic regional seafood and meat dishes. Specials might include local Pistol River shiitake mushrooms in Madeira cream, swordfish, fresh Hawaiian ono, scallops, or King salmon purchased that day from the dock. The restaurant faces the ocean and has a 1,200-foot patio with fire pit. ⊠ *29212 U.S. 101* ☎ *541/247–4121* ⊟ *AE, D, MC, V* ☉ *Closed Mon. and Tues.*

$$$–$$$$ ⊡ **Tu Tu' Tun Lodge.** Pronounced "*too-too-*tin," this well-known fishing **Fodor'sChoice** resort is on the Rogue River, 7 mi upriver from Gold Beach. Salmon and ★ steelhead fishing made the Tu Tu' Tun's name, but jet-boat excursions, golf, and other outdoor activities are also draws. All the units in this small establishment are rustically elegant. Some have hot tubs, others have fireplaces, and a few have both; private decks overlook the river. Two deluxe rooms have tall picture windows, tile baths, and outdoor soaking tubs with river views. The dining room (closed November–April) serves breakfast, lunch, and dinner; the last, open to nonguests (though reservations are hard to come by), consists of a five-course prix-fixe meal that changes nightly. ⊠ *96550 N. Bank Rogue, 97444* ☎ *541/247–6664* ☐ *541/247–0672* ⊕ *www.tututun.com* ⇨ *18 rooms, 3-bedroom house* ⚘ *Restaurant, 4-hole golf course, pool, dock, boating, fishing, hiking, horseshoes, bar* ⊟ *D, MC, V.*

⬭ **en route**   Between Gold Beach and Brookings, you'll cross Thomas Creek Bridge, the highest span in Oregon. Take advantage of the off-road coastal viewing points along the 10-mi-long **Samuel H. Boardman State Park**—especially in summer, when highway traffic becomes heavy and rubbernecking can be dangerous.

Brookings

❷⓼   *27 mi south of Gold Beach on U.S. 101.*

The little town of Brookings, on the southern Oregon Coast just north of the California border, calls itself Oregon's banana belt and, in fact, is often noted for having the highest temperatures in the state. As a result, Brookings also bills itself as the home of winter flowers. The area supplies the majority of lilies in the United States. A botanical garden and an azalea park are among the town's prized assets.

A startling 90% of the pot lilies grown in the United States come from a 500-acre area inland from Brookings. Strangely enough, these white symbols of peace probably wouldn't be grown here in such abundance if not for the fact that in 1942 Brookings experienced the only wartime aerial bombing attack on the U.S. mainland. A Japanese air raid set trees ablaze and understandably panicked the local residents; the imminent ban on Japanese flowers set them to work cultivating the Easter lilies that appear in stores across the country every spring. Mild temperatures along this coastal plain provide ideal conditions for flowering plants of all kinds—even a few palm trees, a rare sight in Oregon.

The town is equally famous as a commercial and sportfishing port at the mouth of the turquoise-blue **Chetco River.** If anything, the Chetco is more highly esteemed among fishermen and wilderness lovers than is the Rogue. A short jetty, used by many local crabbers and fishermen, provides easy and productive access to the river's mouth; salmon and steelhead weighing 20 pounds or more swim here.

Brookings celebrates its horticultural munificence on Memorial Day weekend with an Azalea Festival in **Azalea Park** (⌂ N. Bank Rd. off U.S. 101 downtown) amid blossoming wild azaleas, some of them hundreds of years old. Take the kids to Kidtown to play on its wooden playground equipment.

The **Chetco Valley Historical Museum,** inside a mid-19th-century stagecoach stop and trading post, has some unusual items and is worth a brief visit. An iron casting that bears a likeness to Queen Elizabeth I has led to speculation that it was left during an undocumented landing on the Oregon coast by Sir Francis Drake. On a hill near the museum stands the **World Champion Cypress Tree,** 99 feet tall and with a 27-foot circumference. ⌂ *5461 Museum Rd.* ☎ *541/469–6651* ⌂ *$1* ☉ *Memorial Day–Labor Day, Wed.–Sun. noon–5; Labor Day–Memorial Day, Fri.–Sun. noon–5.*

Loeb State Park contains 53 riverside campsites and some fine hiking trails, including one that leads to a hidden redwood grove. There's also a grove of myrtlewood trees, which you'll find only in southwest Oregon and northern California. ✛ *North bank of Chetco River, 10 mi east of Brookings (follow signs from U.S. 101)* ☎ *541/469–2021* ⌂ *Reservations not accepted* ⌂ *Day use free, campsites $13–$16* ☉ *Daily sunrise–sunset.*

There is plenty to see and do at **Harris Beach State Park,** where you can watch the gray whales migrate in spring and winter. Bird Island, also called Goat Island, is a National Wildlife Sanctuary and a breeding site for rare birds. There is a campground with 34 full hookups, 52 electrical and 66 tent sites, and 4 yurts. ⌂ *U.S. 101* ☎ *541/469–2021 or 800/551–6949* ⊕ *www.prd.state.or.us* ⌂ *Free* ☉ *Daily.*

Where to Stay & Eat

$–$$$ ✕ **Smuggler's Cove.** Fishing vessels docked in the adjacent boat basin and picture windows looking out to the sea lend a salty feel to this low-key restaurant. The daily seafood specials—usually halibut and salmon—are the best bets. For lunch try the fish-and-chips or the crab melt, and for a real dinner treat, dive into the steak and lobster for $55.95. ⌂ *16011 Boat Basin Rd.* ☎ *541/469–6006* ▭ *MC, V.*

★ **$$–$$$** ⊟ **Chetco River Inn.** Forty acres of private forest surround this remote inn 17 mi from Brookings up the North Bank Road along the Chetco River. The house stands only 100 feet from one of the cleanest rivers in the country, so you can swim in summer and fish in fall and winter. Guests also come here to hike, hunt wild mushrooms, and relax in the library or in front of the fireplace. There's a lavender and herb garden, as well. The host cooks delicious dinners that sometimes star a nickel-bright salmon fresh from the stream. Rooms have thick comforters and panoramic river and forest views. A full breakfast is included. ⊠ *21202 High Prairie Rd., 97415* ☎ *541/670–1645 or 800/327–2688* 🖶 *541/ 469–4341* ⊕ *www.chetcoriverinn.com* ⇨ *5 rooms, 1 cottage* ⊛ *Picnic area, some in-room hot tubs, boating, fishing, library, laundry facilities; no a/c, no room phones, no smoking* ⊟ *MC, V* ⦿ *BP.*

The Oregon Coast A to Z

AIRPORTS
The North Bend Municipal Airport (OTH) is the only airport on the coast serviced by a major carrier; Horizon Air flies into North Bend from Portland four times daily. Regional service is provided at the Newport Municipal Airport (ONP) by two shuttle services, Sky Taxi and Central Oregon Coast Air Service.

🛈 **Airport Information Central Oregon Coast Air Service** ☎ 800/424-3655. **Horizon Air** ☎ 800/547-9308. **Newport Municipal Airport** ☎ 541/867-7422. **North Bend Municipal Airport** ☎ 541/756-8531. **Sky Taxi** ☎ 866/759-8294.

BUS TRAVEL
Greyhound serves Astoria (inside Mini Mart's Video City store), Brookings (inside Fiji Tanning), Coos Bay, Florence, Newport, and other coastal cities. Sunset Empire Transportation provides service on the north coast from Astoria to Cannon Beach, and Porter Stage lines connects the Coos Bay area with Eugene.

🛈 **Bus Depots Greyhound Astoria** ⊠ 95 W. Marine Dr. ☎ 503/325-4162. **Greyhound Brookings** ⊠ 66 Railroad ☎ 541/469-3326. **Greyhound Coos Bay** ⊠ 275 N. Broadway ☎ 541/267-4436. **Greyhound Gold Beach** ⊠ 29770 Colvin St. ☎ 541/247-7710. **Greyhound Newport** ⊠ 956 S.W. 10th St. ☎ 800/231-2222 or 541/265-2253.

🛈 **Bus Lines Greyhound** ☎ 800/231-2222. **Porter Stage Lines** ☎ 541/269-7183. **Sunset Empire Transportation** ☎ 503/325-6500.

CAR TRAVEL
U.S. 101 runs the length of the coast, sometimes turning inland for a few miles. The highway enters coastal Oregon from Washington State at Astoria and from California near Brookings. U.S. 30 heads west from Portland to Astoria. U.S. 20 travels west from Corvallis to Newport. Highway 126 winds west to the coast from Eugene. Highway 42 leads west from Roseburg toward Coos Bay.

VISITOR INFORMATION
🛈 **Tourist Information Astoria–Warrenton Area Chamber of Commerce** ⊠ 143 S. U.S. 101, Astoria 97103 ☎ 503/861-1031 or 800/875-6807 ⊕ www.oldoregon.com. **Bay Area Chamber of Commerce** ⊠ 50 E. Central St., Coos Bay 97420 ☎ 541/269-0215 or 800/ 824-8486 ⊕ www.oregonsbayareachamber.com. **Brookings Harbor Chamber of Commerce** ⊠ 16330 Lower Harbor Rd., 97415 ☎ 541/469-3181 or 800/535-9469 ⊕ www. brookingsoregon.com. **Cannon Beach Chamber of Commerce** ⊠ 2nd and Spruce Sts., 97110 ☎ 503/436-0910 ⊕ www.cannonbeach.org. **Florence Area Chamber of Commerce** ⊠ 270 U.S. 101, 97439 ☎ 541/997-3128 or 800/524-4864 ⊕ www.florencechamber. com. **Greater Newport Chamber of Commerce** ⊠ 555 S.W. Coast Hwy., 97365 ☎ 503/ 265-8801 or 800/262-7844 ⊕ www.newportchamber.org. **Lincoln City Visitors Center** ⊠ 801 S.W. U.S. 101, Suite 1, 97367 ☎ 541/994-8378 or 800/452-2151 ⊕ www. oregoncoast.org. **Seaside Visitors Bureau** ⊠ 7 N. Roosevelt Ave., 97138 ☎ 503/738- 6391 or 800/444-6740 ⊕ www.clatsop.com/seaside. **Tillamook Chamber of Commerce** ⊠ 3705 U.S. 101 N, 97141 ☎ 503/842-7525. **Yachats Area Chamber of Commerce** ⊠ U.S. 101 near 2nd St., 97498 ☎ 541/547-3530 ⊕ www.yachats.org.

THE WILLAMETTE VALLEY & WINE COUNTRY

Updated by
Susan
Honthumb

During the 1940s and 1950s, researchers at Oregon State University concluded that the Willamette Valley—the wet, temperate trough between the Coast Range to the west and the Cascade Range to the east—had an unsuitable climate for the propagation of varietal wine grapes. Evidently, they were wrong.

The faultiness of the researchers' techniques has been proven by the success of Oregon's burgeoning wine industry. More than 100 wineries dot the Willamette (pronounced "wil-*lam*-it") Valley, with the bulk of them in Yamhill County in the northern part of the state. Two dozen more wineries are scattered among the Umpqua and Rogue valleys (near Roseburg and Ashland, respectively) to the south. Their products—mainly cool-climate varietals like pinot noir, chardonnay, and Johannesberg Riesling—have won gold medals in blind tastings against the best wines of California and Europe.

Numbers in the margin correspond to points of interest on the Willamette Valley & Wine Country, Salem, and Eugene maps.

Forest Grove

❶ *24 mi west of Portland on Hwy. 8.*

Though it is named for a large grove of Oregon white oak trees situated on a knoll above the Tualatin Plains, Forest Grove is also surrounded by stands of Douglas firs and giant sequoia, including the largest giant sequoia in the state. Originally inhabited by the Tualatin tribe, the site was settled by pioneers in 1840, and the town was incorporated in 1872. To get there, take U.S. 26 west to Highway 6 and go west to Forest Grove. For the wineries, head south from Forest Grove on Highway 47 and watch for the blue road signs between Forest Grove, Gaston, and Yamhill.

With 1,800 students, **Pacific University** is on a shady campus that provides a respite from sightseeing. It was founded in 1849, making it one of the oldest educational institutions in the western United States. Concerts and special events are held in McCready Hall in the Taylor-Meade Performing Arts Center. The school also has a College of Optometry. ✉ *2043 College Way, 97116* ☎ *503/357–6151* ⊕ *www.pacificu.edu* 🎫 *Free* ☼ *Daily.*

In the wake of a forest fire, the Oregon Department of Forestry created **Forest Grove Educational Arboretum**, a facility on 364,000 acres that addresses how the environment can be salvaged following devastating natural disasters. ✉ *801 Gales Creek Rd., 97116-1199* ☎ *503/357–2191* ☼ *Tours on request.*

Just southeast of Forest Grove, **Fernhill Wetlands**, on 243 acres, is a haven for waterfowl. For a guided tour of the Fernhill Wetlands, or other wildlife areas, contact the **Tualatin Riverkeepers** (☎ *503/590–5813*) ☎ *503/357–5890 E. Viewing Shelter.*

A beautiful area in the Coast Range foothills, **Scoggin Valley Park and Henry Hagg Lake** has a 15-mi-long hiking trail that surrounds the lake. Bird-watching is best in spring. Recreational activities include fishing, boating, water-skiing, and picnicking, and a 10½-mi, well-marked bicycle lane parallels the park's perimeter road. ✉ *Scoggin Valley Rd.* ☎ *503/846–8715 or 503/359–5732* ⊕ *www.co.washington.or.us* 🎫 *$3* ☼ *Daily sunrise–sunset; facilities Mar.–Nov.*

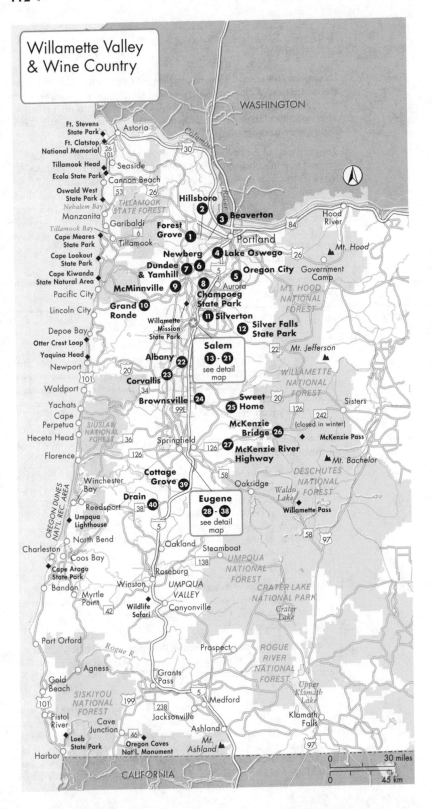

Willamette Valley
& Wine Country

WASHINGTON

Ft. Stevens
State Park
Ft. Clatstop
National Memorial
Tillamook Head
Ecola State Park
Oswald West
State Park
Nehalem Bay
Manzanita
Garibaldi
Cape Meares
State Park
Cape Lookout
State Park
Cape Kiwanda
State Natural Area
Pacific City
Lincoln City
Depoe Bay
Otter Crest Loop
Yaquina Head
Newport
Waldport
Yachats
Cape
Perpetua
Heceta Head
Florence
Winchester
Bay
Reedsport
Umpqua
Lighthouse
North Bend
Charleston
Coos Bay
Cape Arago
State Park
Bandon
Myrtle
Point
Port Orford
Agness
Gold
Beach
Pistol
River
Loeb
State Park
Harbor

Astoria
Seaside
Cannon Beach

TILLAMOOK
STATE FOREST

Tillamook Bay
Tillamook

Hillsboro **2**
Forest **1**
Grove
Newberg **4** Lake Oswego
Dundee **7** **6**
& Yamhill
McMinnville **9**
8
Grand **10**
Ronde
Willamette
Mission
State Park
Albany **22**
23
Corvallis
Brownsville **24**

Cottage **39**
Grove
Drain **40**

Beaverton **3**

Portland

Oregon City **5**
Aurora
Champoeg
State Park
11 Silverton
12
Salem
13 - **21**
see detail
map

Sweet
Home **25**
McKenzie
Bridge **26**
McKenzie River **27**
Highway

Eugene
28 - **38**
see detail
map

Oakland
Steamboat

Roseburg
Winston
UMPQUA
VALLEY
Wildlife
Safari
Canyonville

Prospect

Grants
Pass
Medford
Jacksonville
Ashland
Mt.
Ashland

Hood
River

Mt. Hood

Government
Camp

MT. HOOD
NATIONAL
FOREST

Silver Falls
State Park

Mt. Jefferson

WILLAMETTE
NATIONAL
FOREST

Sisters

McKenzie Pass
(closed in winter)

Mt. Bachelor

DESCHUTES
NATIONAL
FOREST

Waldo
Lake
Willamette Pass

UMPQUA
NATIONAL
FOREST

CRATER LAKE
NATIONAL PARK
Crater
Lake

ROGUE
RIVER
NATIONAL
FOREST

Upper
Klamath
Lake

Klamath
Falls

SIUSLAW
NATIONAL
FOREST

OREGON DUNES
NAT'L. REC. AREA

SISKIYOU
NATIONAL
FOREST

Cave
Junction
Oregon Caves
Nat'l. Monument

CALIFORNIA

Springfield

Columbia

Rogue R.

0   30 miles
0   45 km

Where to Stay & Eat

$–$$$ ✕ **Mothersheads.** Chef Eric Wayne makes a mean fettuccine with home-made sour cream, and if you're in the mood for something exotic, try the Forest Grove–raised buffalo. Seafood and Italian dishes round out the menu. Plush, comfy booths and a large stone fireplace lend warmth to the large dining room, which seats up to 120 people. ⊠ *1819 19th Ave.* ☎ *503/357–6623 or 877/303–0843* ▤ *AE, D, DC, MC, V* ☺ *Closed Mon.*

$–$$$$ ▦ **McMenamins Grand Lodge.** On 13 acres of pastoral countryside, this converted Masonic rest home has accommodations that run from bunk-bed rooms to a three-room fireplace suite. The lodge's sturdy 1922 brick buildings also include pubs that serve several McMenamins draft beers. Rooms are furnished with period antiques such as oak night stands and porcelain sinks. For those not staying in the bunkhouse, rates include use of the European-style soaking pool, Continental breakfast during the week, and a full breakfast on weekends. Bring your own food and ale to the Compass Room Theater, where feature films are screened nightly; kids accompanied by a guardian are permitted at the early show. ⊠ *3505 Pacific Ave., 97116* ☎ *503/992–9533 or 877/992–9533* ⊕ *www.thegrandlodge.com* ⨼ *77 rooms* ⟁ *Spa, library, 3 bars, meeting rooms* ▤ *AE, D, DC, MC, V.*

Hillsboro

❷ *18 mi west of Portland on Hwy. 8.*

East Tualatin Plains was the original name for Hillsboro, but it was re-named for early settler David Hill, elected territorial governor before Oregon became a state. As trappers, Tualatin Indians, and others settled, the town began to grow and prosper and was incorporated in 1876. Over the past 20 years Hillsboro has experienced rapid growth associ-ated with the Silicon Forest, where high-tech business found ample sprawl-ing room. The population has grown to nearly 75,000 residents. Several of Intel's industrial campuses are in Hillsboro, as are the facilities of other leading electronics manufacturers. Businesses related to its original agri-cultural roots remain a significant part of Hillsboro's culture and econ-omy. Alpaca ranches, nurseries, berry farms, nut and fruit orchards, and numerous wineries are among the area's most active agricultural businesses.

Every Saturday, from May through September, the **Hillsboro Saturday Mar-ket** sells fresh local produce—some from booths, some from the backs of trucks—as well as local arts and crafts. Live music is played through-out the day. ⊠ *Main St. between 1st and 2nd Aves., and along 2nd Ave. between Main and Lincoln Sts.* ☎ *503/844–6685* ⊕ *www.tuesdaymarketplace.com* ☺ *May–Sept., Sat. 8–1; Oct., Sat. 9–2.*

☾ The **County Museum** gives a glimpse of history through exhibits on early pioneers and the Tualatin Indians. Exhibits rotate, usually with a hands-on display geared toward children. ⊠ *17677 N.W. Springville Rd.* ☎ *503/645–5353* ⊡ *$2* ☺ *Mon.–Sat. 10–4:30.*

In 1938 Richard and Helen Rice began collecting beach agates. Over the years they developed one of the largest private mineral collections in the United States, which forms the foundation of the **Rice Northwest Museum of Rocks and Minerals.** The most popular item here is the Alma Rose Rhodochrosite, a 4-inch red crystal. The museum (in a ranch-style home) also has petrified wood from all over the world and a gallery of Northwest minerals, including specimens of rare crystallized gold. ⊠ *26385 N.W. Groveland Dr., 97124* ☎ *503/647–2418* 🖷 *503/647–5207* ⊕ *www.ricenwmuseum.org* ⊡ *$4.50* ☺ *Wed.–Sun. 1–5.*

Part of the Tualatin River floodplain, the 710-acre **Jackson Bottom Wetlands Preserve** has several miles of trails. ⊠ *2600 S.W. Hillsboro Hwy., 97123* ☎ *503/681–6424* 🖷 *503/681–6277 or 503/687–6026* ⊕ *www.jacksonbottom.org* ⊘ *Mon.–Sat. 10–4.*

.Comprised of 61 acres of forest, **Rood Bridge Park** has river frontage and canoe-launching facilities, as well as a conference center. ⊠ *4000 S.E. Rood Bridge Rd., From Hwy. 8 take River Rd. southeast to Rood Bridge Rd. Follow Rood Bridge Rd. south for a few blocks. Park is on east side of Rood Bridge Rd. just you cross river.*

A 13-acre grove of towering oak trees, **Shadywood Park** has a playground and a trail that winds through the park. ⊠ *N.E. 24th Ave. and Laura St.*

Where to Eat

★ ¢–$ ✕ **Mazatlan Mexican Restaurant.** Though it's hidden away in a small shopping mall, this spot feels like a small village inside, with stunning murals and ceramic wall furnishings. Try the Mazatlan Dinner, a house specialty with sirloin, a chile relleno, and an enchilada, or *arroz con camarones*, prawns sautéed with vegetables. Save room for the flan or the *sopapillas* (fried dough). The kids' menu is a good value. ⊠ *20413 S.W. TV Hwy., Aloha 97006* ☎ *503/591–9536* 🖃 *AE, D, MC, V.*

Beaverton

❸ *7 mi west of Portland on Hwy. 8.*

Named for its location in the midst of a large network of beaver dams, Beaverton has itself become a network of residential neighborhoods, shopping areas, and business parks spanning 15 square mi. Once a small town surrounded by thriving Washington County farm fields, Beaverton today has well over 60,000 residents and is the fifth-largest community in Oregon. At 7 mi from Portland, it is considered Portland's long-expanding, affluent suburb to the west. The roots of Oregon's Silicon Forest are in Beaverton, with some of the state's largest high-tech employers contributing to the town's popularity. Among Beaverton's high-profile employers are Adidas and Nike, whose famous world-headquarters campus is regularly visited by celebrities. The town has more than 100 parks spread over 1,000 acres. There is an extensive system of hiking trails and bike paths, as well as many numerous public and private golf courses and tennis courts.

In the heart of the Silicon Forest is **Tualatin Hills Nature Park,** a real forest with creeks, ponds, fir trees, and red cedars. The 195-acre urban wilderness has, appropriately, beavers, as well as great blue herons and dozens of other bird species. There are several trails, some with boardwalks. To reach the park, take the MAX light rail to the Merlo Road station. No dogs are allowed. ⊠ *15655 S.W. Millikan Blvd., 97005* ☎ *503/644–5595* ⊕ *www.thprd.com/facilities/nature* 🖃 *Free* ⊘ *Daily sunrise–sunset.*

Trails, a wetland area, and a 10-acre pond stocked for fishing are at **Bethany Lake Park.** ⊠ *N.W. 185th Ave. NW at West Union Rd.* ☎ *503/645–6433* 🖷 *503/690–9649.*

At 22 acres, **Commonwealth Lake Park** has athletic fields, play equipment for rent, trails, wetlands, and a 3-acre fishing lake. ⊠ *S.W. Huntington Ave., S.W. Butner Rd., S.W. Foothills Dr.* ☎ *503/645–6433* 🖷 *503/690–9649.*

Greenway Park is on 80 acres and has playing fields, playground equipment, a wetland area, and trails, as well as a barbecue area. ⊠ *S.W. Hall Blvd. to S.W. Scholls Ferry Rd.* ☎ *503/645–6433* 🖷 *503/690–9649.*

Wineries

Growing methods are a source of pride at **Cooper Mountain Vineyards** (✉ 9480 S.W. Grabhorn Rd., 97007 ☎ 503/649–0027 ⊕ www.coopermountainwine.com), whose wines are made from organic grapes. The novelty of this 105-acre vineyard is that it's situated on Cooper Mountain, an extinct volcano. The vineyard is open February–December, daily noon–5, and in January by appointment.

Founded in 1970, **Ponzi Vineyards** (✉ 14665 S.W. Winery La., Beaverton 97007 ☎ 503/628–1227 🖷 503/628–0354 ⊕ www.ponziwines.com) produces pinots and chardonnay, as well as Dolcetto and Arneis. The Ponzi family also launched the BridgePort Brewing Company in 1984 and run a wine bar and restaurant in Dundee (⇨ Dundee Bistro in Dundee). The winery is open daily 11–5.

Where to Eat

$$–$$$$ ✕ **Pavilion Trattoria.** Amid the garden surroundings is fine seasonal Pacific Northwest cuisine, such as the grilled salmon served on a warm beet salad with roasted shallot vinaigrette or the apple-wood-smoked prime rib served with sweet onion rings. Early-bird suppers and a kids' menu are available, and the Sunday brunch is especially popular. ✉ 10700 S.W. Allen Blvd., 97005 ☎ 503/626–4550 ▭ AE, DC, MC, V ☾ No lunch.

¢–$$$ ✕ **McCormick's Fish House & Bar.** The neighborhood feeling of this restaurant belies its association with the national chain. Try creative seasonal preparations such as macadamia-nut-crusted Alaskan halibut with mango–beurre blanc sauce or salmon baked on a cedar plank. Mounted fish are displayed on the ceiling of the rusty-brown main dining room. The restaurant is popular with local families. ✉ 9945 S.W. Beaverton–Hillsdale Hwy. ☎ 503/643–1322 ▭ AE, D, DC, MC, V ☾ No lunch Sun.

Lake Oswego

❹ *9 mi south of Portland*

Contrary to the intentions of its early founders, who built iron smelters in an effort to turn the area into "the Pittsburgh of the West," Lake Oswego is an affluent residential community immediately to the south of Portland, situated between the Willamette and Tualatin rivers. The Willamette Shore Trolley, operated by the Oregon Electric Railway Historical Society, carries passengers along the Willamette between downtown Lake Oswego and the Riverplace area at the south end of Portland's downtown.

Framed by an open fireplace on one end and a reflecting pond on the other, **Millennium Plaza Park** is the site of many community events as well as a Saturday farmer's market. ✉ 200 1st St., 97034 ☎ 503/675–3983 ☾ Mid-May–mid-Oct., Sat. 8–1.

Cooks Butte Park consists of 42 acres of informal pathways and undeveloped land. ✉ Delenka La. ☎ No phone.

A circular 7-mi route around Lake Oswego, **Lake Loop** is popular with joggers, walkers, or mere gazers of scenery.

Originally built in 1887, the **Willamette Shore Trolley**—one standard and one double-decker trolley, both of museum quality—carries passengers on a 45-minute ride to Portland along a scenic 7-mi route, which you can travel one-way or round-trip; you'll take in Mt. Hood and the wooded banks of the Willamette River. In summer, there are four departures daily from Lake Oswego. Reservations are recommended. In

December there are special Lights Along the River excursions. ✉ *311 State St., 97034* ☎ *503/697-7436* ⊕ *www.trainweb.org/oerhs/wst.htm* 🎫 *$9 round-trip* ⊙ *May 1–Memorial Day, weekends; Memorial Day–Labor Day, Thurs.–Sun.; Labor Day–end of Sept., Fri.–Sun.*

Where to Stay & Eat

$$–$$$ ✕ **Amadeus.** Reserve a table overlooking the river, select a bottle of wine from the extensive wine list—preferably an Oregon wine—and settle in for a sensuous experience. Winners are the Willapa Bay oysters, slightly panfried; the wilted spinach salad; and the pistachio-crusted salmon. ✉ *148 B Ave., 97034* ☎ *503/636-7500* 🖨 *503/636–6233* ▭ *AE, DC, MC, V.*

$ 🏨 **Phoenix Inn—Lake Oswego.** Three miles from the Washington Square Mall, this all-minisuites motel has spacious rooms with picturesque views of Lake Oswego and a patio for relaxing. ✉ *14905 S.W. Bangy Rd., 97034* ☎ *503/624-7400 or 800/824-9992* 🖨 *503/624-7405* 🛏 *62 suites* ♿ *In-room data ports, minibars, microwaves, refrigerators, cable TV, indoor pool, exercise equipment, hot tub, laundry facilities, business services* ▭ *AE, D, DC, MC, V* ❐ *CP.*

Oregon City

⑤ *6 mi southwest of Newberg on Hwy. 99 W.*

Many bits of western U.S. history converge in Oregon City. It was the first incorporated city west of the Rocky Mountains, the first capital of the Territorial government in 1848, site of the first Oregon legislative session, and site of the only federal and district court west of the Rockies in 1849, when the city of San Francisco was platted. (The plat, filed in 1850, is still in Oregon City.)

Oregon City was the destination for thousands of pioneer families, who traveled the Oregon Trail from St. Louis, Missouri, to the promised land on the western frontier. Several of Oregon's prominent early residents built homes in Oregon City on the Willamette River's east bank, where the river plunges 40 feet over a basaltic ridge at Willamette Falls. The official End of the Oregon Trail Interpretive Center in Oregon City debuted in 1993 to commemorate the 150-year anniversary of the Oregon Trail. Dozens of historic homes, churches, and other buildings have been restored and now offer tours into times past. More than 26,000 people live here today; the city is the seat of Clackamas County, one of three counties that make up the Portland metropolitan area.

Resembling three large covered wagons, the **End of the Oregon Trail Interpretive Center,** 19 mi south of Portland, is hard to miss. The history of the Oregon Trail is brought to life through theatrical shows, exhibits, and hands-on activities. Maps and guidebooks are available if you're charting a trip along the Oregon Trail from one end to the other. ✉ *1726 Washington St., Oregon City* ☎ *503/657-9336* ⊕ *www.endoftheoregontrail.org* 🎫 *Store free, show $5.50* ⊙ *Store Mon.–Sat. 9–5, Sun. 10–5. Shows Memorial Day–Labor Day, Mon.–Sat. 10–4, Sun. 10:45–4; Labor Day–Memorial Day, Wed.–Sat. 10–3:30, Sun. 11–3:30.*

Waterfowl are part-time residents at the ½-acre **John Inskeep Environmental Learning Center** on the Clackamas Community College campus. The property has a trail that circles two ponds at the headwaters of Newell Creek. ✉ *19600 S. Molalla* ☎ *503/657–6958 Ext. 2351* 🖨 *503/650–6669* ⊕ *www.clackamas.cc.or.us/elc* 🎫 *$2 donations accepted* ⊙ *Daily sunrise–sunset.*

Built in 1845, **Ermatinger House** was the first frame house built in Oregon City and the only two-story Federal-style house in the state with a flat roof. The McLoughlin Memorial Association moved the house to save it from development, and then in 1986 it was moved again to 6th and John Adams. For groups, hosts will present a Living History Tea. ⊠ *6th and John Adams* ☎ *503/656–1619, 503/557–9199 tours* ⊠ *$2* ⊙ *Fri.–Sun. 1–4.*

An officer for a fur-trading company, Dr. John McLoughlin lost his job when he forwarded supplies to needy Oregon Trail pioneers, but his presence and deeds in the area are remembered at **McLoughlin House National Historic Site,** the mansion he moved to with his family in 1846. The site is perhaps the key historic home in the city; another, owned by the McLoughlin Memorial Association, is **Rose Farm** (⊠ Holmes La. at Rilance St.). It is open March–October, daily 1–4; admission is $2. ⊠ *713 Center St.* ☎ *503/656–5146* ⊕ *www.mcloughlinhouse.org* ⊠ *$4* ⊙ *Feb.–Dec., Tues.–Sat. 10–4, Sun. 1–4.*

Stevens Crawford Heritage House celebrates the contributions of two Oregon City natives. Harley Stevens joined the Emigrant Escort Service to help protect pioneers on the Oregon Trail, and he went on to become the first telegraph operator in Oregon City. Mary Crawford was a important member of the Women's Christians Temperance Union. When the house was built in 1908, it was one of the first homes to have indoor plumbing and both gas and electric light fixtures. Special events such as tea and luncheon provide a living-history lesson as the hosts wear era-specific attire. ⊠ *603 6th St., 97045* ☎ *503/655–2866* ⊠ *$4* ⊙ *Wed.–Fri. noon–4, weekends 1–4.*

Artifacts dating back 10,000 years are on display at the **Museum of the Oregon Territory.** One such display examines the ways different tribes of the Northwest gathered to trade with the Chinooks; another exhibit takes up the history of wedding fashion. ⊠ *211 Tumwater Dr., 97045* ☎ *503/ 655–5574* ⊠ *503/655–0035* ⊙ *Weekdays 10–4, weekends noon–4.*

Along the Clackamas River and only 45 minutes from Portland, **Milo McIver State Park** is a popular rafting, canoeing, and kayaking area. An annual Civil War reenactment is staged here in April; 300 actors participate. A campground has 44 electrical and 9 primitive sites. ⊠ *Rte. 213 N to Rte. 212 and Rte. 211 SE* ☎ *503/630–7150 or 800/551–6949* ⊕ *www.prd.state.or.us* ⊠ *Day use $3 per vehicle* ⊙ *Daily, some areas Mar.–Nov.*

The Willamette Falls are created when the Willamette River at Oregon City spills 40 feet over a basaltic ridge. The **Willamette Falls Locks** were built in the early 1870s to move river traffic around the falls. ⊠ *On Willamette River, in West Linn* ☎ *503/656–3381* ⊙ *Daily. Information center Apr.–Oct., daily 9:30–8; Nov.–Mar., daily 7:30–6.*

Where to Stay & Eat

¢ ✕ **McMenamins Pub.** At this bustling family favorite you can order a Communication Breakdown Burger—Tillamook cheddar, onions, mushrooms, and peppers—among others, including a few meatless options. Couple your burger or sandwich with a creative ale like chocolaty Black Rabbit Porter or raspberry Ruby Ale. Kid-pleasing comfort foods include grilled cheese, corn dogs, and peanut butter and jelly. The pub becomes more of a bar scene after 10 PM. ⊠ *102 9th St., 97045* ☎ *503/ 655–8032* ⊟ *AE, D, MC, V.*

$ ⊞ **Tolle House Bed & Breakfast.** Though Viola Tolle has never had anything to do with the legendary Toll House cookies, she found that people expected the treats, which prompted her to give a cookie jar to every guest. Her complimentary breakfast might include blueberry pancakes and fresh fruit compote. One room has a rhapsody decor, another a French country flavor, and the third is a combination. Rooms will be outfitted with masculine or feminine furnishings at your request. ⊠ *15921 Hunter, 97045* ☎ *503/655–4325* 🛏 *3 rooms* 🚭 *No credit cards* ❄️ *BP.*

Newberg

6 *25 mi southwest of Portland on Hwys. 99 W and 18.*

Fertile fields of the Willamette Valley surround the community of Newberg, named by the first postmaster for his Bavarian hometown, Newburgh. Many of its early settlers were Quakers from the Midwest who founded the school that has become George Fox University, an accredited four-year institution. Newberg's most famous resident, likewise a Quaker, was Herbert Hoover, the 31st president of the United States. For about five years during his adolescence, he lived with an aunt and uncle at the Hoover-Minthorn House, now a museum listed on the National Register of Historic Places. In addition to numerous well-reputed wineries, the Newberg area also offers slightly more out-of-the-ordinary entertainment, with tours of nine llama ranches and the Pacific Northwest's largest hot-air balloon company. St. Paul, a historic town with a population of about 325, is about 8 mi south of Newberg and 20 mi north of Salem. Every July, St. Paul holds a professional rodeo.

Named by *U.S. News and World Report* one of America's Best Colleges, the small **George Fox College,** founded by the Quakers in 1884, is on a 75-acre shady campus in a residential neighborhood. Centennial Tower is surrounded by a campus quad and academic buildings, the library, and the student commons. Hess Creek Canyon cuts through the campus. ⊠ *414 N. Meridian* ☎ *503/538–8383 Ext. 222* ⊕ *www.georgefox. edu* 🎟 *Free* ☉ *Daily.*

The oldest and most significant of Newberg's original structures is the **Hoover-Minthorne House,** the boyhood home of President Herbert Hoover. Built in 1881, the preserved frame house still has many of the original furnishings. Outside is the woodshed that no doubt played an important role in shaping young "Bertie" Hoover's character. ⊠ *115 S. River St.* ☎ *503/538–6629* 🎟 *$2* ☉ *Mar.–Nov., Wed.–Sun. 1–4; Dec. and Feb., weekends 1–4.*

The drive-in is a perpetual novelty, and **99W Drive-in** is a good bet for a double feature. Ted Francis built this one in 1953 and operated it until his death at 98; the business is now run by his grandson. The first film begins at dusk. Kids 6–11 get in for $3, and children 5 and under are free. ⊠ *Hwy. 99 W (Portland Rd.), just west of Springbrook Rd. intersection* ☎ *503/538–2738* 🎟 *$6 per person, $9 minimum vehicle charge* ☉ *Fri.–Sun.*

Sports & the Outdoors

BALLOONING If you're intrigued by what it might feel like to have the Earth gently moving toward you, ride with **Vista Balloon Adventures** (⊠ 701 S.E. Sherk Pl., Sherwood 97140 ☎ 503/625–7385 or 800/622–2309 🖨 503/625–3845), which has several balloons taking off daily from Sportsman Airpark in Newberg. From April through October, FAA licensed pilots take the balloons about 1,500 feet over Yamhill County's wine country. Rates are $179 per person ($160 for a group of four or more).

Dundee & Yamhill

❼ *6 mi southwest of Newberg on Hwy. 99 W.*

William Reid traveled to Oregon from Dundee, Scotland. As he became interested in the railway business, he got support from his homeland to finance the Oregon Railway Co., Ltd. After the city was incorporated in 1895, Dundee was named after Reid's hometown in recognition of its support.

The lion's share (more than 90%) of the U.S. hazelnut crop is grown in Dundee, a haven of produce stands and tasting rooms. The 25 mi of Highway 18 between Dundee and Grande Ronde, in the Coast Range, roll through the heart of the Yamhill Valley wine country; wide shoulders and relatively light traffic earned the route a "most suitable" rating from the *Oregon Bicycling Guide*.

Wineries

Merlot, chardonnay, and gewürztraminer are among the wines emanating from **Duck Pond Cellars** (✉ 23145 Hwy. 99 W, 97115 ☎ 503/538–3199 or 800/437–3213 ⊕ www.duckpondcellars.com). Tasting is free and the tasting room also stocks goodies to buy. Picnicking in the outdoor seating area is encouraged. The winery is open November–April, daily 11–5 and May–October, daily 10–5.

Sokol Blosser (✉ 5000 Sokol Blosser La., 3 mi west of Dundee off Hwy. 99 W ☎ 503/864–2282 or 800/582–6668 ⊕ www.sokolblosser.com), one of Oregon's oldest and largest wineries, has a tasting room and walk-through vineyard with a self-guided tour that explains the grape varieties—pinot noir and chardonnay, among others. It's open daily 11–5.

Where to Stay & Eat

$$$ ✕ **Tina's.** Chef–proprietors Tina and David Bergen bring a powerful one-
Fodor's Choice two punch to this Dundee favorite that often lures Portlanders away from
★ their own restaurant scene. The couple shares cooking duties—Tina does the baking and is often on hand to greet you—and David brings his experience as a former caterer and employee of nearby Sokol Blosser Winery to the table, ensuring that you have the right glass of wine—and there are many—to match your course. Fish and game vie for attention on the country French menu—entrees might include grilled Oregon salmon or Alaskan halibut, or a double cut pork chop, rack of lamb, or rib-eye steak. Avail yourself of any special soups, particularly if there's corn chowder in the house. A lunch menu includes soup, sandwiches, and Tina's grilled hamburger, made with free range beef. Service is as intimate and laid-back as the interior. A double fireplace divides the dining room, with heavy glass brick shrouded by bushes on the highway side, so you're not bothered by the traffic on Highway 99. ✉ *760 Hwy. 99W* ☎ *503/ 538–8880* ▭ *AE, D, MC, V.*

$–$$$ ✕ **Dundee Bistro.** Opened in 1999, this 80-seat restaurant uses Northwest organic foods such as Draper Valley chicken and local produce. Vaulted ceilings provide an open feeling inside, warmed by abundant fresh flowers and the works of local Oregon artists. The bistro is one piece of what the winemaking Ponzi family describes as the state's first "culinary center;" also part of the property are Your Northwest, a specialty food market, and the Ponzi Wine Bar, which serves Oregon wines, most prominently those from the family's winery (⇨ Ponzi Vineyards in Beaverton). ✉ *100-A S.W. 7th St., Dundee 97115* ☎ *503/554–1650* ▭ *AE, DC, MC, V.*

$–$$$$ ▦ **The Flying M Ranch.** Rendered in a style best described as Daniel
Fodor's Choice Boone eclectic, a log lodge is the centerpiece of this 625-acre ranch, perched
★ above the steelhead-filled Yamhill River. Choose between somewhat aus-

tere cabins (the cozy, hot-tub-equipped Honeymoon Cabin is the nicest) and riverside hotel units. In keeping with the rustic tone, there are no TVs or telephones. Book ahead for a Flying M specialty: the Steak Fry Ride, on which you climb aboard your choice of a horse or a tractor-drawn wagon and ride into the mountains for a feast of barbecued steak with all the trimmings. ⊠ 23029 N.W. Flying M Rd.; from McMinnville, off Hwy. 99 W head north on North Baker Rd.—which becomes West Side Rd.—for 5 mi, head west on Meadowlake Rd., and follow signs, Yamhill 97148 ☎ 503/662–3222 ⓐ 503/662–3202 ⊕ www.flying-m-ranch.com ↪ 24 units, 7 cabins, more than 100 campsites ⚑ Restaurant, tennis court, fishing, basketball, hiking, horseback riding, horseshoes, bar ⊟ AE, D, DC, MC, V.

Champoeg State Park

8 9 mi from Newberg, south on Hwy. 219 and east on Champoeg Rd.

Pronounced "sham-poo-ee," this 615-acre state park on the south bank of the Willamette River is on the site of a Hudson's Bay Company trading post, granary, and warehouse that was built in 1813. This was the seat of the first provisional government in the Northwest. The settlement was abandoned after a catastrophic flood in 1861, then rebuilt and abandoned again after the flood of 1890. The park's wide-open spaces, groves of oak and fir, modern visitor center, museum, and historic buildings yield vivid insight into pioneer life. Tepees and wagons are also displayed here. There are 10 mi of hiking and cycle trails, and a campground has 48 electrical and 58 tent sites and 6 yurts.

Robert Newell was among the inaugural American settlers in the Willamette Valley and helped establish the town of Champoeg; a replica of his 1844 home, what is now the **Newell House Museum** (⊠ 8089 Champoeg Rd. NE, St. Paul 97137 ☎ 503/678–5537), was rebuilt inside the park grounds in 1959 and paid for by the Oregon State Society Daughters of the American Revolution. The first floor is furnished with 1860s antiques. Pioneer quilts and a collection of gowns worn by the wives of Oregon governors at inaugurations are displayed on the second floor. There's also a pioneer jail and schoolhouse. Admission is $2. It's open March through October, Friday–Sunday 1–5, Wednesday and Thursday by appointment. Also on park grounds is the historic **Pioneer Mother's Memorial Log Cabin** (⊠ 8035 Champoeg Rd. NE, St. Paul 97137 ☎ 503/633–2237), with pioneer artifacts from the Oregon Trail era. Admission is $2. It's open February through November, Monday–Saturday noon–5. ⊠ 8239 Champoeg Rd. NE, St. Paul 97137 ☎ 800/551–6949 ⊠ $3 per vehicle ⊙ Memorial Day–Labor Day, daily 10–6; Labor Day–Memorial Day, weekdays 8–4, weekends noon–4.

off the beaten path

OLD AURORA COLONY – A fascinating slice of Oregon's pioneer past, the colony was the only major 19th-century communal society in the Pacific Northwest. Created by Germans in 1856, this frontier society espoused a "Love thy neighbor" philosophy, shared labor and property, and was known for its hospitality. Aurora retains many white frame houses dating from the 1860s and 1870s. Several structures have been incorporated into the Old Aurora Colony Museum (2nd and Liberty Sts. 503/678–5754, $2), which provides an overview of the colony's way of life. Follow an easy self-guided tour of the historic district, or take the guided walking tour ($3.50) given during special events. The colony is open Tuesday–Saturday 10–4, Sunday noon–4.

✢ *About 14 mi from Champoeg State Park; take Champoeg Rd. east to Arndt Rd.; pass under I–5 and turn south onto Airport Rd., then east onto Ehlen Rd.* ⊕ *www.auroracolonymuseum.com.*

McMinnville

❾ *14 mi south of Newberg on Hwy. 99 W.*

The Yamhill County seat, McMinnville lies at the center of Oregon's burgeoning wine industry. There is a larger concentration of wineries in Yamhill County than in any other area of the state, and the vineyards in the McMinnville area, including some in the town of Dayton to the east, also produce the most award-winning wines. Among the varieties are chardonnay, pinot noir, and pinot gris. Most of the wineries in the area offer tours and tastings. McMinnville's downtown area, with a pleasantly disproportionate amount of bookstores and art galleries for its size, is well worth exploring; many of the historic district buildings, erected from 1890–1915, are still standing and are remarkably well-maintained.

Fodor'sChoice ★ The claim to fame of the **Evergreen Aviation Museum** is the Hughes (H-4) HK-1 Flying Boat, better known by its more sibilant nickname, the *Spruce Goose,* on permanent display here. The famous plane, which eccentric millionaire Howard Hughes flew only once—on November 2, 1947—was moved to Portland in 1992 from Long Beach, California, and eventually shipped to McMinnville in pieces. If you can take your eyes off the Spruce Goose there are also more than 45 historic planes and replicas here from the early years of flight and World War II, as well as the post war and modern eras. Among the aircraft are a Spitfire, a C-47 "Gooney Bird," a Messerschmitt Bf 109, and the sleek SR-71 Blackbird, which set both speed and high altitude records as "the world's fastest spy plane." Among the replicas are a Wright 1903—the craft the Wright brothers used for the first sustained powered flight flight. If you're curious to know which of these planes are still flyable, look for the telltale oil pan resting on the floor underneath the aircraft. There's a museum store and café—the Spruce Goose Café, of course—and there are ongoing educational programs and special events. ⊠ *365 N.E. Three Mile La.* ☎ *503/434–4206* ⊕ *www.sprucegoose.org* ☞ *$9.50* ☽ *Daily 9–5.*

A perennial football powerhouse in NCAA Division III, **Linfield College** is an outpost of brick and ivy amid McMinnville's farmers'-market bustle. The college, founded in 1849 and the second oldest in Oregon, hosts the **International Pinot Noir Celebration** (☎ 800/775–4762) at the end of July and beginning of August. ⊠ *Linfield Ave. east of Hwy. 18* ⊕ *www.linfield.edu.*

need a break? Try Tillamook Ice Cream on a waffle cone at **Serendipity Ice Cream** (⊠ 502 N.E. 3rd St. ☎ 503/474–9189), an old-fashioned ice cream parlor in the former Cook's Hotel; the building was constructed in 1886.

Wineries

Its original tasting area was the back of a 1952 Ford pick-up. Its Gamay noir label notes that the wine gives "more enjoyment to hamburgers fried chicken." And the winery's current architecture still includes a trailer affectionately referred to as the "mobile chateau," already on the property when winemaker Myron Redford purchased the winery in 1974. These modest and whimsical touches underscore what seems to be Red-
★ ford's philosophy for **Amity Vineyards** (⊠ 18150 Amity Vineyards Rd. SE, Amity 97101 ☎ 503/835–2362): take your winemaking a lot more

seriously than you take yourself. Taste the pinot blanc for Redford's take on the grape, and also linger in the tasting room to sample the pinot noir and the gewürztraminer, among other varieties. Chocolates made with Amity's pinot noir and other products are available for sale. Also drink in the impressive view of Yamhill County while you're here, and don't miss a chance to walk among the vines with Myron if he's available. Hours are daily noon–5, February–December.

In Dundee's Red Hills, **Domaine Serene** (⊠ 6555 N.E. Hilltop La., Dayton ☎ 503/864–4600 ⊕ www.domaineserene.com) is a world-class five-level winery and a well-regarded producer of Oregon pinot noir. It's open Memorial Day and Thanksgiving weekends and otherwise by appointment.

If Oregon presents the problem of so many wines, so little time, the **Oregon Wine Tasting Room and The Bellevue Market** (⊠ 19690 S.W. Hwy. 18, 97128 ☎ 503/843–3787) provides a handy one-stop tasting venue, with 150 wines from 70 Oregon wineries, some of which are only open to the public twice a year. There's also a gallery and deli on the premises.

Where to Stay & Eat

★ **$–$$$$** ✕ **Nick's Italian Cafe.** Modestly furnished but with a voluminous wine cellar, Nick's is a favorite of area wine makers. The food is spirited and simple, reflecting the owner's northern Italian heritage. The five-course prix-fixe menu changes nightly. À la carte options are also available. ⊠ 521 N.E. 3rd St. ☎ 503/434–4471 ⬛ 503/472–0440 ⬥ Reservations essential ⊟ AE, DC, MC, V ⊘ Closed Mon. No lunch.

$$–$$$ ✕ **Joel Palmer House.** Joel Palmer was an Oregon pioneer, and his 1857 home in Dayton is now on the National Register of Historic Places. There are three small dining rooms, each seating about 15 people. The chef here specializes in wild mushroom dishes; a popular starter is Heidi's three-mushroom tart. Entrées include rib eye au poivre, rack of lamb, breast of duckling, and coq au vin; desserts include apricot-walnut bread pudding and crème brûlée. ⊠ 600 Ferry St., Dayton 97114 ☎ 503/864–2995 ⬛ 503/864–3246 ⊟ AE, D, DC, MC, V ⊘ Closed Sun. and Mon. No lunch Sat.

$–$$ ▦ **Hotel Oregon.** Built in 1905, this historic facility—the former Elberton Hotel—was rescued from decay by the McMenamins chain, renovated in 1998, and reopened the following year. It's four stories of brick; rooms have tall ceilings and high windows. The hotel is outfitted in late Victorian furnishings, but its defining design element is its artwork: the hotel is whimsically decorated by McMenamins's half-dozen staff artists: around every corner, even in the elevator, you'll find art—sometimes serene, often times bizarre and haunting—as well as photos and sayings scribbled on the walls. The Oregon has a first-floor pub serving three meals a day, a rooftop bar with an impressive view of Yamhill County, and a cellar wine bar, resembling a dark speakeasy, that serves only area vintages. Breakfast is included in the room rate. ⊠ 310 N.E. Evans St., 97128 ☎ 503/472–8427 or 888/472–8427 ⊕ www.mcmenamins.com ⋩ 42 rooms ⬧ 2 bars, café, cinema, meeting rooms ⊟ AE, D, DC, MC, V.

$–$$ ▦ **Mattey House Bed & Breakfast.** Built in 1982 by English immigrant Joseph
Fodor'sChoice Mattey, a local butcher, this Queen Anne Victorian mansion—on the
★ National Register of Historic Places—has several cheerful areas that define it. Downstairs is a cozy living room jammed with antiques, dual dining areas—a parlor with white wicker and a dining room with elegant furniture—and a porch with a swing. The four upstairs rooms are whimsically named after locally grown grape varieties—Riesling, chardonnay, pinot noir, and Blanc de Blanc—and are decorated in keeping with

the character of those wines; the chardonnay room, for instance, has tall windows and crisp white furnishings, and pinot noir has dark-wood pieces and reddish wine accents. A small balcony off the upstairs landing is perfect for sipping a glass of wine on a cool Yamhill Valley evening. Proprietors Jack and Denise will ensure you're comfortably en-sconced, familiar with the local history, surrounding vineyards, and an-tiquing scene, and holding that glass of wine: in case you don't remember where you are, the house, on 10 acres, is bound by an orchard and its own vineyard, which the couple maintain. If you're fool enough to duck out before the fine full breakfast, which might include poached pears with raspberry sauce, frittatas, and Dutch-apple pancakes, Denise or Jack will have pastry and hot coffee available before you set off. A rule barring children under 10 is waived if you're renting the entire house. ✉ 10221 N.E. Mattey La., off Hwy. 99 W, ¼ mi south of Lafayette, 97128 ☎ 503/434–5058 🖷 503/434–6667 ⊕ www.matteyhouse.com 🛏 4 rooms ♿ No room phones, no room TVs, no smoking ▤ MC, V.

Grand Ronde

⑩ 24 mi southwest of McMinnville on Hwy. 18.

Grand Ronde is mostly a stopping place for people en route to the coast who want to spend time at the town's Indian-operated casino. In July and August, the Confederated Tribes of Grand Ronde hold powwows; the August event draws between 12,000 to 15,000 people.

On the campus of the Confederated Tribes of Grand Ronde, the **West Valley Veterans Memorial** pays tribute to all war veterans but in particu-lar is a marker for the 190,000 Native American veterans. Four flags sur-round the memorial wall: a U.S. flag, a Grand Ronde flag, an Oregon flag, and a POW-MIA flag. ✉ 9615 Grand Ronde Rd., 97347 ☎ 800/422–0232 or 503/879–5211 🖷 503/879–2117 ⊕ www.grandronde.org.

Where to Stay & Eat

$–$$$ ✕▧ **Spirit Mountain Casino and Lodge.** Its location on Highway 18, one of the main routes from Portland to the ocean, makes this casino (owned and operated by the Confederated Tribes of the Grande Ronde Com-munity of Oregon) a popular destination. Only 90 minutes from Port-land and 45 minutes from Salem, this is the biggest casino resort in Oregon. The 183,000-square-foot casino has more than a thousand slots, as well as poker and blackjack tables, roulette, craps, Pai Gow poker, keno, bingo, and off-track betting. Big-name comedians and rock and country mu-sicians perform in the 1,700-seat concert hall, and there's an arcade for the kids. Patrons can take advantage of complimentary shuttle service from Portland and Salem. Dining options include an all-you-can-eat buf-fet, a deli, and a café. Some rooms have Pacific Northwest and Native American themes, with carved wooden headboards and Pendleton Woolen Mills bedding. ✉ 27100 S.W. Hwy. 18, Grande Ronde 97396 ☎ 503/879–3764 or 888/668–7366 🖷 503/879–3938 ⊕ www.spirit-mountaincasino.com 🛏 100 rooms ♿ 4 restaurants, room service, lounge ▤ D, MC, V.

Silverton

⑪ 14 mi northeast of Salem on I–5.

Near the foothills of the Cascade Mountains, south of Portland and east of Salem, Silverton takes pride in the fact that it stands apart from the fast pace of urban life. Silverton remains an agricultural center, much as it was when it was established in the mid-1800s. The town is the largest producer in the world of the bearded iris. Passing these beautiful fields of flowers, which can be seen along I–5, can be quite distracting. Silverton is the gateway to Silver Falls State Park, the largest state park in Oregon.

At the **Country Museum/Restored Train Station,** photos and artifacts related to farming and logging in the Silverton area are displayed in a 1908 house and show how the community changed from 1854 forward with the advance of technology. The museum is a community effort, staffed by volunteers. ✉ *428 S. Water St.* ☎ *503/873–4766* 🖃 *$1* ☉ *Mar.–Dec., Thurs. and Sun. 1–4.*

Produce and crafts are available at the **Farmers Market.** Plant nurseries also bring some of their stock, and local musicians perform. ✉ *Town Square Park on corner of Main and Fiske Sts.* ☉ *Mid-May–mid-Oct., Sat. 9–2.*

Exhibits on colonial music and tools are highlights of the **Old Aurora Colony Museum,** opened in 1966 in a building that formerly served as a barn and truck depot. ✉ *Corner of 2nd and Liberty Sts., Aurora 97002* ☎ *503/678–5754* ⊕ *www.auroracolonymuseum.com* 🖃 *$3.50.*

★ Created in the mid-'90s on a 240-acre tract of serene oak foothills, the ambitious **The Oregon Garden** is a work in progress. A dozen horticultural theme gardens showcase indigenous and introduced plants alike, ranging from kitchen herbs to an extensive collection of North American conifers. There is also a restored Frank Lloyd Wright–designed home and a preserved oak-strewn meadow, which are open for tours. Most of the gardens are wheelchair accessible. ✉ *879 W. Main St., 1 mi south of Silverton on Sublimity Rd., Silverton 97381* ☎ *503/ 874–6005 or 877/674–2733* 🖃 *$7* ☉ *Mar.–Oct., daily 9–6, Nov.–Feb., daily 9–3.*

Where to Eat

$$–$$$ ✕ **Silver Grille.** Owner and chef Jeff Nizlek uses local ingredients, ensuring that the menu changes monthly and sometimes more often. Specialties include locally raised lamb and Kobe beef and dishes prepared with Bandon cheese, Oregon truffles, and seasonal produce. There's a four-course Chef's Choice for $35, which has a vegetarian option. ✉ *206 E. Main St.* ☎ *503/873–4035* 🖃 *AE, D, DC, MC, V* ☉ *Closed Mon. and Tues.*

¢ ✕ **O'Brien's Cafe.** Antiques, which are for sale, surround you as you eat a home-cooked meal. You won't find anything fancy on the menu: a stack of buttermilk pancakes or perhaps homemade biscuits and eggs can jumpstart your day; a locally named Silver Falls omelet of ham, linguiça, and cheddar cheese is good any time; or perhaps sink your teeth into a juicy hamburger or a specialty item, chicken strips. What it lacks in unusual cuisine is countered by a beautiful view of Silver Creek. ✉ *105 S. Water St.* ☎ *503/873–7554* 🖃 *MC, V* ☉ *No dinner, except 1st Fri. of month.*

Silver Falls State Park

★ ⑫ *26 mi east of Salem, Hwy. 22 to Hwy. 214.*

Hidden amid old-growth Douglas firs in the foothills of the Cascades, Silver Falls is the largest state park in Oregon (8,700 acres). South Falls, roaring over the lip of a mossy basalt bowl into a deep pool 177 feet below, is the main attraction here, but 13 other waterfalls—half of them more than 100 feet high—are accessible to hikers. The best time to visit is in the fall, when vine maples blaze with brilliant color, or early spring, when the forest floor is carpeted with trilliums and yellow violets. There are picnic facilities and a day lodge; during the winter you can cross-country ski. There are 14 cabins. ✉ *20024 Silver Falls Hwy.*

SE, Sublimity ☎ *800/551–6949 or 503/873–8681* 🖃 *$3 per vehicle* ☉ *Daily sunrise–sunset.*

Salem

⑬–㉑ *24 mi from McMinnville, south on Hwy. 99 W and east on Hwy. 22, 45 mi south of Portland on I–5.*

Salem has a rich pioneer history, but before that it was the home of the Calapooia Indians, who called it Chemeketa, which means "place of rest." Salem is said to have been renamed by missionaries. According to one story, the name is an Anglicized form of the Hebrew "shalom," or peace, while another story suggests it was named specifically for Salem, Massachusetts. Although trappers and farmers preceded them in the Willamette Valley, the Methodist missionaries had come in 1834 to minister to Native Americans, and they are credited with the founding of Salem. They also established the first academic institution west of the Rockies in 1842, now known as Willamette University.

Salem became the official capital when Oregon achieved statehood in 1859, replacing Oregon City as the capital of the Oregon Territory. Today, with a population of more than 135,000, Salem is the second largest city in Oregon and serves as the seat to Marion County as well as the home of the state fairgrounds. Because this is the state capital and county seat, government ranks as a major industry in the community, while the city's placement in the heart of the fertile Willamette Valley stimulates rich agricultural and food-processing industries. Extensive nearby farmlands are devoted to the cultivation of vegetables, berries, hops, and flowers, and at least 15 wineries are in or near Salem. The main attractions in Salem are west of I–5 in and around the Capitol Mall.

Numbers in the text correspond to numbers in the margin and on the Salem map.

a good walk

Begin at Court Street and the **Oregon Capitol** ⑮. Behind the Capitol, just across State Street, is **Willamette University** ⑯. Cross over 12th Street to the **Mission Mill Village** ⑰. From there, stroll down 12th Street to **Deepwood Estate** ⑱, south of Salem's downtown district. West of here is **Bush's Pasture Park** ⑲.

TIMING Without stopping for tours, this walk can be done in about two hours. Allot an additional half hour for a guided tour of the Capitol, two hours for a full tour of Mission Mill Village, and a half hour each for the house tours at Deepwood Estate and Bush's Pasture Park. If you're pressed for time, skip the Capitol and university and begin your tour at Mission Mill Village.

Sights to See

⑬ A. C. Gilbert's Discovery Village. In a Victorian house, this museum celebrates the inventions of A. C. Gilbert, including Erector sets and American Flyer trains. The first floor and grounds are wheelchair accessible. ✉ *116 Marion St., 97301-3437* ☎ *503/371–3631* ⊕ *www.acgilbert.org* 🖃 *$5* ☉ *Mon.–Sat. 10–5, Sun. noon–5.*

⑲ Bush's Pasture Park. These 105 acres of rolling lawn and formal English gardens include the remarkably well preserved **Bush House,** an 1878 Italianate mansion at the park's far western boundary. It has 10 marble fireplaces and virtually all of its original furnishings. The house and gardens are on the National Register of Historic Places. **Bush Barn Art Center,** behind the house, exhibits the work of Northwest artists and has a sales gallery. ✉ *600 Mission St. SE* ☎ *503/363–4714* ⊕ *www.*

A.C. Gilbert's
Discovery
Village **13**

Bush's
Pasture
Park **19**

Deepwood
Estate **18**

Elsinore
Theater **14**

Mission Mill
Village **17**

Mount Angel
Abbey **21**

Oregon
Capitol **15**

Willamette
Mission
State Park **20**

Willamette
University **16**

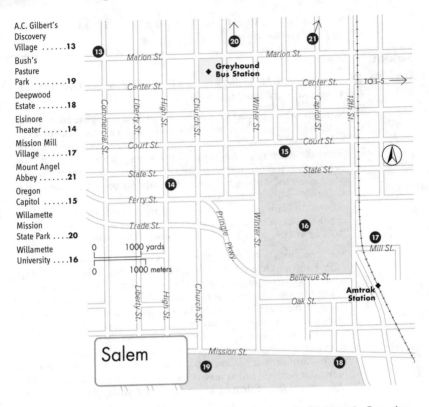

salemart.org ✉ *$4* ⊙ *May–Sept., Tues.–Sun. noon–5; Oct.–Apr.,*
Tues.–Sun. 2–5.

⑱ **Deepwood Estate.** This fanciful 1894 Queen Anne–style house has splendid interior woodwork and original stained glass. An ornate gazebo from
the 1905 Lewis and Clark expedition graces the fine gardens created in
1929 by landscape designers Elizabeth Lord and Edith Schryver. The
estate is on the National Register of Historic Places. ✉ *1116 Mission
St. SE* ☎ *503/363–1825* ✉ *$4* ⊙ *May–Sept., Sun.–Fri. noon–4:30;
Oct.–Apr., Tues.–Sat. noon–5.*

⑭ **Elsinore Theatre.** This flamboyant Tudor Gothic vaudeville house opened
on May 28, 1926, with Edgar Bergen in attendance. Clark Gable (who
lived in Silverton) and Gregory Peck performed on the stage. The theater was designed to look like a castle, with a false stone front, chandeliers, ironwork, and stained-glass windows. It's now a lively performing
arts center with a busy schedule of bookings, and there are concerts on
its Wurlitzer pipe organ. ✉ *170 High St. SE, 97301* ☎ *503/375–3574*
🖨 *503/375–0284* ⊕ *www.elsinoretheatre.com.*

⑰ **Mission Mill Village.** The **Thomas Kay Woolen Mill Museum** complex (circa
1889), complete with working water wheels and millstream, looks as if
the workers have just stepped away for a lunch break. Teasel gigging,
napper flock bins, and the patented Furber double-acting napper are but
a few of the machines and processes on display. The **Jason Lee House,**
the **John D. Boon Home,** and the **Methodist Parsonage** are also part of
the village. There is nothing grandiose about these early pioneer homes,
the oldest frame structures in the Northwest, but they reveal a great deal
about domestic life in the wilds of Oregon in the 1840s. The adjacent
Marion County Historical Society Museum (☎ *503/364–2128*) displays

pioneer and Calapooia Indian artifacts. ✉ *Museum complex, 1313 Mill St. SE* ☎ *503/585–7012* ⊕ *www.missionmill.org* 🎫 *$6, includes tour* ⊙ *Daily 10–4* ☞ *Guided tours of houses and woolen mill museum leave from mill's admission booth every hr on the hr.*

㉑ Mount Angel Abbey. On a 300-foot-high butte, this Benedictine monastery was founded in 1882. It's the site of one of two American buildings designed by Finnish architect Alvar Aalto. A masterpiece of serene and thoughtful design, Aalto's library opened its doors in 1970 and has become a place of pilgrimage for students and aficionados of modern architecture. ✛ *18 mi from Salem, east on Hwy. 213 and north on Hwy. 214* ☎ *503/845–3030* ⊕ *www.mountangel.org* 🎫 *Free.*

▶ **⑮ Oregon Capitol.** A brightly gilded bronze statue of the Oregon Pioneer stands atop the 140-foot-high Capitol dome, looking north across the Capitol Mall. Built in 1939 with blocks of gray Vermont marble, Oregon's Capitol has an elegant yet austere neoclassical feel. New east and west wings were added in 1978. Relief sculptures and deft historical murals soften the interior. Tours of the rotunda, the house and senate chambers, and the governor's office leave from the information center under the dome. ✉ *900 Court St.* ☎ *503/986–1388* 🎫 *Free* ⊙ *Weekdays 8–5, Sat. 9–4, Sun. noon–4. Guided tours Memorial Day–Labor Day, daily on the hr; rest of year by appointment.*

⑳ Willamette Mission State Park. Along pastoral lowlands by the Willamette River, this serene park holds the largest black cottonwood tree in the United States. A thick-barked behemoth by a small pond, the 265-year-old tree has upraised arms that bring to mind JRR Tolkien's fictional Ents. Site of Reverend Jason Lee's 1834 pioneer mission, the park also offers quiet strolling and picnicking amid an old orchard and along the river. The Wheatland ferry, at the north end of the park, began carrying covered wagons across the Willamette in 1844, using pulleys. ✛ *Wheatland Rd., 8 mi north of Salem, I–5 Exit 263* ☎ *503/393–1172 or 800/551–6949* ⊕ *www.oregonstateparks.org* 🎫 *Day use $3, or annual permit $25. Charcoal barbecue rental $25.* ⊙ *Daily 8 AM–sunset.*

⑯ Willamette University. Behind the Capitol, across State Street but half a world away, are the brick buildings and grounds of Willamette University, the oldest college in the West. Founded in 1842, Willamette has long been a breeding ground for aspiring politicians (former Oregon senators Mark O. Hatfield and Robert Packwood are alumni). **Hatfield Library,** built in 1986 on the banks of Mill Stream, is a handsome brick-and-glass building with a striking campanile; tall, prim **Waller Hall,** built in 1841, is one of the oldest buildings in the Pacific Northwest. ✉ *Information Desk, Putnam University Center, Mill St.* ☎ *503/370–6300* ⊙ *Weekdays 9–5.*

| off the beaten path | **SCHREINER'S IRIS GARDENS** – Some call the Willamette Valley near Salem the Bulb Basket of the Nation. Irises and tulips create fields of brilliant color in near-perfect growing conditions. Schreiner's Iris Gardens, established in 1925, ships bulbs all over the world; during the short spring growing season (mid-May–early June), the 10-acre display gardens blaze with fancifully named varieties such as Hello Darkness, Well Endowed, and Ringo. ✉ *3625 Quinaby Rd. NE, north from Salem take I–5 to Exit 263, head west on Brooklake Rd., south on River Rd., and east on Quinaby* ☎ *503/393–3232* ⊕ *www. schreinersgarden.com* 🎫 *Free* ⊙ *Daily 8 AM–dusk during blooming season only.* |

Where to Stay & Eat

$–$$$ ✕ **DaVinci.** Salem politicos flock to this two-story downtown restaurant for Italian-inspired dishes cooked in a wood-burning oven. No short-cuts are taken in the preparation, so don't come if you're in a rush. But if you're in the mood to linger over seafood and fresh pasta that's made on the premises, this may be your place. The wine list is one of the most extensive in the Northwest; the staff is courteous and extremely pro-fessional. ✉ *180 High St.* ☎ *503/399–1413* ▤ *AE, DC, MC, V* ⊘ *No lunch Sun.*

$ ✕▧ **A Creekside Inn, the Marquee House.** The guest rooms in this 1938 Mt. Vernon Colonial-style house are decorated with movie themes—Top-per, Auntie Mame, Blazing Saddles, and others—and there are movies and popcorn in the evening. Only nine blocks from the center of town, the house is on ½ acre of flower gardens bordering Mill Creek, a view that you can enjoy from the large porch out back. There's a two-night minimum during holidays and events at Willamette University. ✉ *333 Wyatt Ct. NE, 97301* ☎ *503/391–0837 or 800/949–0837* ▧ *503/391–1713* ⊕ *www.marqueehouse.com* ➥ *5 rooms* ⚐ *Picnic area, some in-room data ports; no phones in some rooms, no smoking* ▤ *D, DC, MC, V* ⋈ *BP.*

---

en route   South of Salem, the **Enchanted Forest** is the closest thing Oregon has to a major theme park. The park has several attractions in forest-like surroundings, including a Big Timber Log Ride. On it, you ride logs through flumes that pass through a lumber mill and the woods. The ride—the biggest log ride in the Northwest—has a 25-foot roller-coaster dip and a 40-foot drop at the end. Other attractions include the Ice Mountain Bobsled roller coaster, the Haunted House, English Village, Storybook Lane, the Fantasy Fountains Water Light Show, Fort Fearless, and the western town of Tofteville. The park is 7 mi south of Salem at Exit 248 off I–5. ✉ *8462 Enchanted Way SE, Turner 97392* ☎ *503/363–3060 or 503/371–4242* ⊕ *www. enchantedforest.com* ✉ *$7.95, some attractions extra* ⊘ *Mar. and May–Labor Day, daily 9:30–6; Apr. and Labor Day–end of Sept., weekends, 9:30–6.*

Albany

㉒ *46 mi south of Silver Falls State Park on I–5 and Hwy. 20, 20 mi from Salem, south on I–5 and west on U.S. 20.*

To see what a quintessential Willamette Valley river town looked like before the major highways were built, explore Albany, a former wheat and produce center in the heart of the valley. It is still so rich with agri-cultural crops that it is known as the grass-seed capital of the world. Named by Thomas and Walter Monteith after their hometown in New York State, Albany is believed to be home to one of the largest and most varied collections of historic buildings in Oregon. Some 700 historic build-ings, scattered over a 100-block area in three districts, include every major architectural style in the United States from 1850. The area is listed on the National Register of Historic Places. Eight covered bridges can also be seen on a half-hour drive from Albany. Pamphlets and maps for self-guided walking and driving tours are available from the **Albany Visitors Association** (✉ *300 S.W. 2nd Ave.* ☎ *541/928–0911 or 800/526–2256*), open weekdays 9–5.

In an 1887 Italianate building in the heart of historic downtown Albany is the **Albany Regional Museum.** The Rod and Marty Tripp Reference Room has many historical documents and provides ample room to spread books out and do research projects. ☒ *136 Lyons St. SW* ☎ *541/967–7122* ☒ *Free* ☉ *Mon.–Sat. noon–4.*

The first frame house in Albany was Monteith House, built in 1849. Now the **Monteith House Museum,** restored and filled with period furnishings and historic photos, it is widely thought to be the most authentic restoration of a Pacific Northwest pioneer-era home. ☒ *518 2nd Ave. SW, 97321* ☎ *800/526–2256* ☒ *541/926–1500* ⊕ *www.albanyvisitors. com* ☒ *Donation* ☉ *Mid-June–mid-Sept., Wed.–Sat. noon–4; mid-Sept.–mid-June, by appointment.*

Where to Eat

¢–$$$ ✕ **Buzz Saw.** Fresh seafood and prime rib are the most popular items at this riverside restaurant, along with steaks and pasta dishes. Window tables and raised booths all have a view of the river. The hottest club in town, with the same name, is right next door where a DJ keeps things moving five nights a week. There are pool tables, too. ☒ *421 Water St., 97321* ☎ *541/928–0642* ☒ *541/928–0644* ☒ *AE, DC, MC, V* ☉ *No lunch.*

★ $–$$ ✕ **Capriccio Ristorante.** Capriccio is *the* place for pasta in Albany. The house specialty is spinach ravioli in a cream sauce, but you might also choose from osso buco Orvieto, lemon chicken, or New York strip steak, and there's fresh fish every day. ☒ *442 W. 1st Ave. SW, 97321* ☎ *541/924–9932* ☒ *541/967–9454* ☒ *AE, D, DC, MC, V* ☉ *Closed Sun. and Mon. No lunch.*

Corvallis

㉓ *10 mi southwest of Albany on U.S. 20, 35 mi from Salem, south on I–5 and west on Hwy. 34.*

A compound construction of the Latin words for "heart of the valley," Corvallis is home to the Beavers and Oregon State University. But it also has more than 52,0000 residents. To some, Corvallis is a brief stopping place along the way to Salem or Portland. To others, it's a little town that gives you a chance to escape from the bigger cities. Driving the area's economy is a growing engineering and high-tech industry, including long-time Corvallis employer Hewlett Packard, a burgeoning wine industry, and more traditional local agricultural crops, such as grass and legume seeds. Corvallis offers plenty of outdoor activities as well as scenic attractions, from covered bridges to local wineries and gardens.

The **Osborn Aquatic Center** is not the site of your ordinary lap pool. There are water slides, a water channel, water cannons, and floor geysers. ☒ *1940 N.W. Highland Dr.* ☎ *541/766–7946* ☒ *$4.*

The pace quickens in Corvallis around the 500-acre campus of **Oregon State University,** west of the city center. Established as a land-grant institution in 1868, OSU has more than 15,000 students, many of them studying the agricultural sciences and engineering. ☒ *15th and Jefferson Sts.* ☎ *541/737–0123* ⊕ *oregonstate.edu.*

At 75-acres, **Avery Park** includes rose and rhododendron gardens, jogging trails, and picnic shelters. ☒ *South 15th St. and U.S. 20* ☎ *541/ 757–6918* ☒ *Free* ☉ *Weekdays.*

There are more than 20,000 pioneer and Native American artifacts on display at **Benton County Historical Museum.** There is also a cut-glass and porcelain collection, the reconstruction of a Victorian parlor, and a costume exhibit. ☒ *1101 Main St., Philomath* ☎ *541/929–6230* ☒ *Free* ☉ *Tues.–Sat. 10–4:30.*

A favorite of bird-watchers, **Finley National Wildlife Refuge** has large fields of grass and grain and a wetland area that attracts Canada geese, especially the dusky Canada goose, a threatened species because of its limited breeding area. You might also spot grouse, pheasants, quail, wood ducks, and other birds, as well as numerous deer. A herd of large Roosevelt elk also calls this area home. Also within the refuge is **Fiechter House** (☎ 541/929–6230 or 541/757–7236), one of Oregon's remaining examples of Classical Revival architecture, open Sunday in summer 10–4. ⊠ *26208 Finley Refuge Rd., 97333* ☎ *541/757–7236* 🖷 *541/757–4450* 🖃 *Free* ☉ *Daily sunrise–sunset.*

The highest point in the Coast Range, at 4,097 feet, Mary's Peak, within **Siuslaw National Forest,** offers panoramic views of the Cascades, Willamette Valley, and the rest of the Coast Range. On a clear day you can see as far as the Pacific Ocean. There are several picnicking areas, more than 10 mi of hiking trails, and a small campground. There are stands of noble fir and alpine meadows. The forest, which is 2 mi from Corvallis, includes the Oregon Dunes National Recreation Area, and the Cape Perpetua Interpretive Center. ⊠ *Rte. 34 at Hwy. 3024* ☎ *541/750–7000* ⊕ *www.fs.fed.us/r6/siuslaw* 🖃 *Free* ☉ *Daily sunrise–sunset.*

Where to Stay & Eat

$$$ ✕ **Michael's Landing.** In a former railroad depot overlooking the Willamette River, this restaurant is known for its large menu of steak, seafood, chicken, and pasta dishes. Try the Northwest salmon baked in a wine and butter sauce. There's a kids' menu. Sunday brunch includes omelets, quiche, and pancakes. ⊠ *603 N.W. 2nd St., 97330* ☎ *541/754–6141* 🖃 *AE, D, DC, MC, V.*

$–$$ 🏠 **Hanson Country Inn.** On a knoll overlooking the Willamette Valley, this 7,100-square-foot 1928 Dutch Colonial was once headquarters of a poultry-breeding business. Restored, it now has a massive fireplace in the living room, many sitting areas, tall windows, and a sunporch with stained-glass windows and rattan furniture. Rooms have views of either the English garden or the valley, and the largest has broad views from windows on three sides. The cottage is at the edge of the woods and has two bedrooms, a front porch, and a rear deck. ⊠ *795 S.W. Hanson St., 97333* ☎ *541/752–2919* 🛏 *3 suites, 1 cottage* ⚬ *Picnic area, in-room data ports, cable TV, laundry service; no kids under 13, no smoking* 🖃 *AE, D, DC, MC, V* ⦿ *BP.*

Brownsville

㉔ *27 mi south of Corvallis off I–5.*

Early settler James Blakely named this area on the banks of the Calapooia River "Brownsville" after his uncle, Hugh Brown. Blakely helped lay out the town, and in 1895 the communities of North Brownsville, Amelia, and Brownsville consolidated into the city of Brownsville. This Willamette Valley town has retained much of its original character and was a character itself in the film *Stand by Me.* The **Linn County Historical Museum,** in Brownsville's 1890 railroad depot, has some noteworthy pioneer-era exhibits, including a covered wagon that arrived in 1865 after a trek along the Oregon Trail from Missouri. ⊠ *101 Park Ave.* ☎ *541/466–3390* 🖃 *Free* ☉ *Mon.–Sat. 11–4, Sun. 1–5.*

John Moyer, a carpenter turned businessman, owned a lumber mill, banks, and other businesses in the state. His house, the **Moyer House,** built in 1881, has been turned into a museum. Most of the furniture is from the 1880s. There are original murals on the ceiling and over the bay windows, artist or artists unknown. ☒ *204 N. Main St.* ☎ *541/466–3070* ⊙ *Mon.–Sat. 11–4, Sun. 1–5.*

Sweet Home

㉕ *About 12 mi east of Brownsville.*

Situated on the south fork of the Santiam River near the foothills of the Cascades, Sweet Home has heritage as a timber town, but that has given way to thriving recreational activities afforded by the middle and south forks of the river. Its mild climate and ample rain and sun produce one of the state's most diversified farming areas, leading the nation in the production of common and perennial ryegrass. There are also many dairy and berry farms. Keep an eye out around town for colorful murals painted by local artists.

The trials and joys of pioneer life are graphically displayed at **East Linn Museum** with artifacts, pictures, and documents from the years 1850–1940. ☒ *746 Long St., 97386* ☎ *541/367–4580* 🖂 *Donations accepted* ⊙ *Memorial Day–Labor Day, Tues.–Sat. 11–4, Sun. 1–4; Labor Day–Memorial Day, Thurs.–Sat. 11–4, Sun. 1–4; or by appointment.*

Where to Stay & Eat

$–$$ ✕ **Mountain House Country Restaurant.** Filled with knotty pine, log beams, and a stone fireplace, this lodge is in the Willamette National Forest. You can choose among Black Angus steak, organic hamburgers, Cajun catfish, jambalaya, and other dishes, and then finish up with marionberry cobbler. ☒ *52855 Santiam Hwy. (Hwy. 20), 97329* ☎ *541/367–3074* ⊙ *Closed Jan.–Mar.* ⊟ *AE, MC, V.*

¢–$ 🏨 **Sweet Home Inn.** Some rooms here overlook a wooded creek while others have balconies, but all are large and comfortable. The inn is near lakes and golfing. ☒ *805 Long St., 97386* ☎ *541/367–5137* 🖷 *541/367–8859* ➴ *31 rooms* ⌂ *Some in-room hot tubs, microwaves, refrigerators, cable TV, hot tub, gym, laundry facilities* ⊟ *AE, MC, V.*

McKenzie Bridge

㉖ *58 mi east of Eugene on Hwy. 126.*

On the beautiful McKenzie River, the town of McKenzie Bridge is surrounded by lakes, waterfalls, covered bridges, and wilderness trails in the Cascades. Fishing, skiing, backpacking, and rafting are among the most popular activities in the area.

A 1,240-acre reservoir in the Willamette National Forest, **Blue River Dam and Lake** has miles of forested shoreline. From May through September, boats are launched from ramps at Saddle Dam and Lookout Creek. Recreational activities include fishing, swimming, water skiing, and camping at Mona Campground. ☒ *Forest Rd. 15 in Willamette National Forest* ☎ *541/937–2131* 🖂 *Free* ⊙ *Daily.*

Four miles outside of McKenzie Bridge is **Cougar Dam and Lake,** the highest embankment dam ever built by the Army Corps of Engineers— 452 feet above the stream bed. The resulting reservoir, on the South Fork McKenzie River, covers 1,280 acres. The public recreation areas are in the Willamette National Forest. A fish hatchery is in the vicinity. You can visit the dam year-round, but the campgrounds are open only from May to September. ☒ *Forest Rd. 19 in Willamette National Forest* ☎ *541/937–2131* 🖂 *Free* ⊙ *May–Sept., daily; most areas closed rest of yr.*

McKenzie River Highway

㉗ *East of Eugene on Hwy. 126*

Highway 126, as it heads east from Eugene, is known as the McKenzie River Highway. Following the curves of the river, it passes grazing lands, fruit and nut orchards, and the small riverside hamlets of the McKenzie Valley. From the highway you can glimpse the bouncing, bubbling, blue-green McKenzie River, one of Oregon's top fishing, boating, and white-water rafting spots, against a backdrop of densely forested mountains, splashing waterfalls, and jet-black lava beds. The small town of McKenzie Bridge marks the end of the McKenzie River Highway and the beginning of the 26-mi McKenzie River National Recreation Trail, which heads north through the Willamette National Forest along portions of the Old Santiam Wagon Road.

Where to Stay & Eat

★ $ ✕▥ **Log Cabin Inn.** On the banks of the wild, fish-filled McKenzie River, this inn is equally appropriate for a fishing vacation or a romantic weekend getaway. Antique furniture decorates log-cabin-style buildings; each room has a river view. Six riverfront tepees share a bath. Menu standouts at the delightful restaurant include wild boar, quail, salmon, a decadent homemade beer-cheese soup, and a locally famous marionberry cobbler. ⊠ *56483 McKenzie Hwy., 97413* ☎ *541/822–3432 or 800/355–3432* 🖶 *541/822–6173* ⊕ *www.logcabinin.com* 🛏 *8 cabins, 6 tepees* ⚐ *Restaurant, fishing, bar* ▤ *MC, V.*

---

off the beaten path

MCKENZIE PASS – Just beyond McKenzie Bridge, Highway 242 begins a steep, 22-mi eastward climb to McKenzie Pass in the Cascade Range. The scenic highway, which passes through the Mt. Washington Wilderness Area and continues to the town of Sisters (⇨ Central Oregon), is generally closed October–June because of heavy snow. Novice motorists take note, this is not a drive for the timid: it's a challenging exercise in negotiating tight curves at quickly fluctuating speeds, often slow speeds—the skid marks on virtually every turn attest to hasty braking—so take it slow, and don't be intimidated by cars on your tail itching to take the turns more quickly.

Eugene

㉘–㊳ *63 mi south of Corvallis on I–5.*

Eugene was founded in 1846 when Eugene Skinner staked the first federal land-grant claim for pioneers. Back then it was called Skinner's Mudhole. Wedged between two landmark buttes—Skinner and Spencer—along the Willamette River, Eugene is the culinary, cultural, sports, and intellectual hub of the central Willamette Valley. The home of the University of Oregon is consistently given high marks for its "livability." A large student and former-student population lends Oregon's second-largest city a youthful vitality and countercultural edge. Full of parks and oriented to the outdoors, Eugene is a place where bike paths are used, pedestrians *always* have the right-of-way, and joggers are so plentiful that the city is known as the running capital of the world.

Shopping and commercial streets surround the Eugene Hilton and the Hult Center for the Performing Arts, the two most prominent downtown buildings.

a good
walk

Numbers in the text correspond to numbers in the margin and on the Eugene map.

From downtown Eugene, walk north across the Willamette River on the Autzen Footbridge and stroll through **Alton Baker Park** ㊳. Head north to the entertaining **Science Factory** ㉘ science and technology museum, which is just outside the park to the west of Autzen Stadium. Or follow the path that leads west along the river. Walk back across the Willamette River via the Ferry Street Bridge to Gateway Park. Stay to the left at the end of the bridge and you'll eventually hit High Street. Head south on High to the **5th Street Public Market** ㉙ (which, despite its name, is on 5th Avenue). The market is a great place to have lunch, as you'll want to refuel before your next stop, **Skinner Butte Park** ㉜. From the market take 5th Avenue west and Lincoln Street north. If you're feeling hardy, you can climb to the top of Skinner Butte for a great view. The **George E. Owen Memorial Rose Garden** ㉝ is west of the park. Follow the bike path west from Skinner Butte Park along the Willamette River to the garden.

TIMING   This tour takes more than half a day unless you drive it. Plan to spend an hour or so at each stop, and add an extra hour if you visit the science center.

What to See

㊳ **Alton Baker Park.** Named after the community newspaper's publisher, the Alton Baker Park is a place of many community events. Live music is performed in summer. There's fine hiking and biking at Alton Baker, the largest of three adjoining riverside parks—Gateway and Skinner Butte are the other two—on the banks of the Willamette River. A footpath along the river runs the length of the park. Also worth seeing is the Whilamut Natural Area, an open space with 13 "talking stones," each with an inscription. ⊠ *Centennial Blvd. east of Ferry St. Bridge* ☎ *541/ 484–5307 or 541/682–2000* ☉ *Daily 6 AM–11 PM.*

㉚ **Eugene Saturday Market.** Every Saturday between April and November, local craftspeople, farmers, and chefs provide cheap eats and nifty arts and crafts at this outdoor market. ⊠ *8th Ave. and Oak St.* ☎ *541/686– 8885* ⊕ *www.eugenesaturdaymarket.org* ☒ *Free* ☉ *Sat. 10–5.*

★ ㉙ **5th Street Public Market.** A former chicken-processing plant is the site of this popular shopping mall, filled with small crafts, art, and gifts stores. Dining includes sit-down restaurants, decadent bakeries, and the international diversity of the second-floor food esplanade. ⊠ *5th Ave. and High St.* ☎ *541/484–0383* ☉ *Shops Sat.–Thurs. 10–6, Fri. 10–9; restaurants weekdays 7 AM–9 PM, weekends 7 AM–10 PM.*

㉝ **George E. Owen Memorial Rose Garden.** Three thousand roses bloom June–September at this 9-acre garden west of Skinner Butte Park, along the Willamette River. Magnolia, cherry, and oak trees dot the grounds. ⊠ *300 N. Jefferson St.* ☎ *541/682–4824* ☒ *Free* ☉ *Daily 6 AM–11 PM.*

㊱ **Hendricks Park.** This quiet park east of the University of Oregon is at its most glorious in May, when its towering rhododendrons and azaleas blossom in shades of pink, yellow, red, and purple. From the university's Franklin Boulevard gate, head south on Agate Street, east on 19th Avenue, south on Fairmont Boulevard, and east on Summit Avenue. ⊠ *Summit and Skyline Aves.*

㉛ **Hult Center for the Performing Arts.** This is the locus of Eugene's cultural life. Renowned for the quality of its acoustics, the center has two theaters that are home to Eugene's symphony and opera. ⊠ *1 Eugene*

Alton Baker
Park **38**

Eugene
Saturday
Market **30**

5th Street
Public
Market **29**

George E. Owen
Memorial Rose
Garden **33**

Hendricks
Park **36**

Hult Center
for the
Performing
Arts **31**

Lane County
Historical
Museum **34**

Maude Kerns
Art Center **37**

Science
Factory **28**

Skinner
Butte Park ...**32**

University
of Oregon **35**

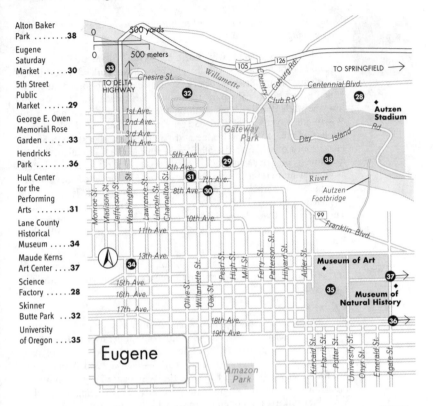

Eugene

Center, at 7th Ave. and Willamette St. ☎ 541/682–5087, 541/682–5000 tickets, 541/682–5746 24-hr event recording ☉ Call for hrs.

③④ Lane County Historical Museum. Collections dating from the 1840s to the present are in a 14,000-square-foot building. Exhibits include period rooms, vehicles, early trades, Oregon Trail and early settlement, historic photographs, and memorabilia from the 1920s and 1930s. ✉ 740 W. 13th Ave. ☎ 541/682–4242 💲$2 ☉ Wed.–Fri. 10–4, Sat. noon–4.

③⑦ Maude Kerns Art Center. The oldest church in Eugene, two blocks east of the University of Oregon, is the site of this arts facility, which exhibits contemporary fine arts and crafts. ✉ 1910 E. 15th Ave. ☎ 541/345–1571 💲 Free ☉ Mon.–Sat. 10–5, Sun. 1–5.

☺ ②⑧ Science Factory. Formerly the Willamette Science and Technology Center (WISTEC) and still known to locals by its former name, Eugene's imaginative, hands-on museum assembles rotating exhibits designed for curious young minds. The adjacent **planetarium,** one of the largest in the Pacific Northwest, presents star shows and entertainment events. ✉ 2300 Leo Harris Pkwy. ☎ 541/682–7888 museum, 541/461–8227 planetarium ⊕ www.sciencefactory.org 💲$4 ☉ Fri.–Sun. noon–4.

②② Skinner Butte Park. Eugene's parks and gardens are wonderfully diverse and add to the outdoor fabric of the city. Skinner Butte Park, rising from the south bank of the Willamette River, has the greatest historic cachet, since it was here that Eugene Skinner staked the claim that put Eugene on the map. Skinner Butte Loop leads to the top of Skinner Butte, from which **Spencer Butte,** 4 mi to the south, can be seen. The two main trails to the top of Skinner Butte traverse a sometimes difficult terrain through a mixed-conifer forest. ✉ 2nd Ave. and High St. ☎ 541/682–5521 💲 Free ☉ Daily 10 AM–midnight.

③⑤ **University of Oregon.** The true heart of Eugene lies southeast of the city center at its university. Several fine old buildings can be seen on the 250-acre campus; **Deady Hall,** built in 1876, is the oldest. More than 400 varieties of trees grace the bucolic grounds, along with outdoor sculptures that include *Pioneer* and *Pioneer Mother*. The two bronze figures by Alexander Phimster Proctor were dedicated to the men and women who settled the Oregon Territory and less than a generation later founded the university.

Eugene's two best museums are affiliated with the university. The collection of Asian art at the **University of Oregon Museum of Art** (⊠ 1430 Johnson La. ☎ 541/346–3027 ⊕ www.uoma.uoregon.edu), next to the library, includes examples of Chinese imperial tomb figures, textiles, and furniture. Relics of a more localized nature are on display at the **University of Oregon Museum of Natural History** (⊠ 1680 E. 15th Ave. ☎ 541/346–3024 ⊕ www.natural-history.uoregon.edu), devoted to Pacific Northwest anthropology and the natural sciences. Its highlights include the fossil collection of Thomas Condon, Oregon's first geologist, and a pair of 9,000-year-old sagebrush sandals.

On the west side of the campus, **Knight Library** (⊠ Kincaid St. and E. 15th Ave. ☎ 541/346–3054) is the main building in the university's library system, which has more than 2 million volumes. It's open daily, and admission is free. *University of Oregon main entrance ⊠ Agate St. and Franklin Blvd. ☞ $3 suggested donation for both museums ⊙ Art museum Wed. noon–8, Thurs.–Sun. noon–5; natural history museum Wed.–Fri. noon–5, weekends 11–5.*

Where to Stay & Eat

$$$–$$$$ ✕ **Sweetwaters.** The dining room at the Valley River Inn, which overlooks the Willamette at water level, has Pacific Northwest cuisine. Try the salmon with Szechuan peppercorn crust and cranberry vinaigrette or the grilled beef fillet with Oregon blue-cheese crust. There is a bar area outside as well as a deck for open-air dining. There's a kids' menu and a Sunday brunch. ⊠ *1000 Valley River Way* ☎ *541/687–0123* ▤ *AE, D, DC, MC, V.*

$–$$$ ✕ **Red Agave.** Two local women managed to establish this cozy ro-
Fodor's Choice   mantic restaurant in an old building that at one point was a refuse dump,
★   and the result is a hard-to-categorize winner that has Mexican and Latino influences. Items might include the sesame-crusted salmon with chipotle barbecue glaze, which you can consider washing down with a tamarind margarita. Flans, like much of the menu, are seasonal; try the Kahlua flan or the orange flan with chocolate in the middle. ⊠ *454 Willamette St.* ☎ *683/683–2206* ▤ *DC, MC, V ⊙ No lunch.*

★ **¢–$$** ✕ **Excelsior Café.** Its accomplished cuisine enhances the appealing European elegance of this restaurant, bar, and bistro-style café across from the University of Oregon. The chef uses only fresh local produce, some of it grown on the premises. The menu changes according to the season, but staples include delicious salads and soups, gnocchi, grilled chicken, broiled salmon, and sandwiches. The dining room, shaded by blossoming cherry trees in the spring, has a quiet, understated feel. There's outdoor seating on the front terrace or under a grape arbor in the back. ⊠ *754 E. 13th Ave.* ☎ *541/342–6963* ▤ *AE, D, DC, MC, V.*

★ **¢–$$** ✕ **Turtles Bar & Grill.** Parking around this spot is scarce and there aren't enough tables, but the food is worth the obstacles. The barbecue entrées, particularly the pulled-pork sandwich, are tasty, and the staff is quite friendly. ⊠ *2692 Willamette St.* ☎ *541/465–9038* ▤ *AE, D, DC, MC, V.*

★ **$$$–$$$$** ✕🏠 **Valley River Inn.** At this inn on the banks of the Willamette River, some rooms have an outdoor patio or balcony, some have river or pool views, and concierge rooms have access to a private lounge. All rooms have hair dryers, coffeemakers, and irons. Book the fishing package and the concierge will arrange a river or ocean fishing trip; when you get back the chef will prepare your catch just for you. The inn's restaurant is the popular Sweetwaters. ⊠ *1000 Valley River Way, 97401* ☎ *541/ 687–0123 or 800/543–8266* 🖷 *541/682–0289* ⊕ *www.valleyriverinn. com* 🛏 *257 rooms* ⚿ *Restaurant, pool, gym, hot tub, steam room, bicycles, bar, dry cleaning, laundry service, concierge, business services, meeting room, airport shuttle, free parking* ▭ *AE, D, DC, MC, V.*

$–$$$ 🏠 **Campbell House.** Built in 1892 on the east side of Skinner Butte, Campbell House is one of the oldest structures in Eugene. Restored with fastidious care, the luxurious B&B is surrounded by an acre of landscaped grounds. The parlor, library, and dining rooms have their original hardwood floors and curved-glass windows. Differing architectural details, building angles, and furnishings (a mixture of century-old antiques and reproductions) lend each of the rooms a distinctive personality. One suite has a whirlpool. The room rates include a breakfast of fresh-baked pastries and other items. ⊠ *252 Pearl St., 97401* ☎ *541/ 343–1119 or 800/264–2519* 🖷 *541/343–2258* ⊕ *www.campbellhouse. com* 🛏 *12 rooms, 6 suites* ⚿ *In-room VCRs, no-smoking room* ▭ *AE, D, MC, V.*

★ **$–$$$** 🏠 **Excelsior Inn.** This small hotel in a former frat house manifests a quiet sophistication more commonly found in Europe than in America. Crisply detailed, with cherrywood doors and moldings, it has rooms furnished in a refreshingly understated manner, each with a marble-and-tile bath. The rates include a delicious breakfast. The ground-level Excelsior Café is one of Eugene's best restaurants. ⊠ *754 E. 13th Ave., 97401* ☎ *541/ 342–6963 or 800/321–6963* 🖷 *541/342–1417* ⊕ *www.excelsiorinn.com* 🛏 *14 rooms* ⚿ *Restaurant, café, in-room data ports, in-room VCRs, bar, free parking, no-smoking rooms* ▭ *AE, D, DC, MC, V.*

Nightlife & the Arts

The **Hult Center For the Performing Arts** (⊠ 1 Eugene Center ☎ 541/ 682–5733 ⊕ www.hultcenter.org), a spacious building of glass and native wood, is the locus of Eugene's cultural life. Renowned for the quality of their acoustics, the center's two theaters are home base for Eugene's symphony and opera companies. Ballets, major performers, traveling Broadway shows, and rock bands appear regularly.

Conductor Helmuth Rilling leads the internationally known **Oregon Bach Festival** (☎ 541/346–5666 or 800/457–1486 ⊕ www.bachfest.uoregon. edu) every summer. Concerts, chamber music, and social events—held mainly in Eugene at the Hult Center and the University of Oregon School of Music but also in Corvallis and Florence—are part of this 17-day event. In May and August, the **Oregon Festival of American Music** (☎ 541/687–6526 or 800/248–1615 ⊕ www.ofam.org) presents concerts at the Hult Center and parks around Eugene. **Oregon Mozart Players** (☎ 541/345–6648), the state's premier professional chamber music orchestra, plays 20 concerts a year. The **Eugene Opera** (☎ 541/682–5000 ⊕ www.eugenopera.com) produces three fully staged operas per season. The **Eugene Symphony** (☎ 541/687–9487 ⊕ www.eugenesymphony. org) performs a full season of classical, family, and pops concerts.

Sports & the Outdoors

BASEBALL   The **Eugene Emeralds** (⊠ 2077 Willamette St. ☎ 541/342–5367 ⊕ www. go-ems.com), the Northwest League (Class A) affiliate of the San Diego Padres, play at Civic Stadium.

BASKETBALL | The **University of Oregon Ducks** (✉ 1601 University St. ☎ 800/932–3668) play at MacArthur Court.

BIKING & JOGGING | The **River Bank Bike Path,** originating in Alton Baker Park on the Willamette's north bank, is a level and leisurely introduction to Eugene's topography. It's one of 120 mi of trails in the area. **Prefontaine Trail,** used by area runners, travels through level fields and forests for 1½ mi. **Pedal Power** (✉ 535 High St. ☎ 541/687–1775) downtown rents bikes.

SKIING | **Willamette Pass** (✉ Hwy. 58, 69 mi southeast of Eugene ☎ 541/345–7669 or 800/444–5030), 6,666 feet high in the Cascades Range, packs an annual average snowfall of 300 inches atop 29 runs. The vertical drop is 1,563 feet. Four triple chairs and one double chair service the down-hill ski areas, and 13 mi of Nordic trails lace the pass. Facilities here include a ski shop; day care; a bar and a restaurant; and Nordic and downhill rentals, repairs, and instruction.

Shopping

Tourists coming to the Willamette Valley, especially to Eugene, can't escape without experiencing the 5th Street Public Market in downtown Eugene. There are plenty of small crafts shops and the food mall yields many cuisines, including vegetarian, pizza, and seafood. **Smith Family Bookstore** (✉ 768 E. 13th ☎ 541/345–1651 ✉ 525 Willamette ☎ 541/343–4717) is a wonderful resource for used books. **Valley River Center** (✉ Delta Hwy. and Valley River Dr., 97401 ☎ 541/683–5511) is the largest shopping center between Portland and San Francisco. There are five department stores, including Meier & Frank and JCPenney, plus 144 specialty shops and a food court.

> off the beaten path

WALDO LAKE – Nestled in old-growth forest, Waldo Lake is famed as a remarkably clean and pristine body of water. The lake is accessible only after a short hike, so bring comfortable shoes. ✛ *From Eugene take Hwy. 58 to Oakridge and continue toward Willamette Pass; follow signs north to Waldo Lake.*

Cottage Grove

39 *20 mi south of Eugene on I–5.*

With more than a half dozen historic "creek covers" close by, Cottage Grove's self-proclaimed title as the covered bridge capital of Oregon is well deserved. Of particular note is the Chambers Railroad Bridge, the only one of its kind west of the Mississippi River, built in 1925 to carry logs to mill. Cottage Grove's historic downtown, through which the Willamette River flows, has attracted moviemakers and light-industrial developers alike.

Formerly a mining area, **Brice Creek Trail** has been transformed into a path for hikers and bikers, though it is recommended for only intermediate and advanced riders. ✛ *Trailhead is 25 mi southeast of Cottage Grove. From Cottage Grove, I–5's Exit 174, go right on Brice Creek Rd. No. 2470 (19 mi)* ☎ *541/942–5591* ☺ *Daily.*

A mile outside Cottage Grove in the Coast Range foothills, **Chateau Lorane Winery** produces some unusual varieties including Grignolino, Durif, pinot meunier, and Baco noir. A 25-acre lake and picnic area make this a popular spot for picnics and large events. ✉ *27415 Siuslaw River Rd., Lorane 97451* ☎ *541/942–8028* 🖷 *541/942–5830* ⊕ *www. chateaulorane.com* ☺ *June–Sept., daily noon–5; Jan.–May and Oct.–Dec., weekends noon–5; also by appointment.*

Industrial, farm, mining, and household tools are at the **Cottage Grove Museum.** On display is a 19th-century octagonal church with its original stained-glass windows. ⊠ *147 H St.* ☎ *541/942-3963* ✉ *Free* ☉ *Mid-June–Labor Day, Wed.–Sun. 1–4; Labor Day–mid-June, weekends 1–4.*

Oregon has the largest collection of **covered bridges** in the western United States. The Willamette Valley has more than 34 of the wooden structures. There are six bridges on a loop drive just outside Cottage Grove. The widest bridge in the state is off Highway 58 near Lowell. Four others are nearby. ☎ *503/986-3514* ⊕ *www.odot.state.or.us/ eshtm/br.htm* ✉ *Free* ☉ *Daily.*

Three parks at **Dorena Lake,** a reservoir built in the 1940s, offer boating, swimming, sailing, fishing, and waterskiing. Schwartz Park, downstream from the dam, and Baker Bay Park, on the south side of the lake, have campgrounds. ⊠ *Row River Rd., at Exit 174 off I-5* ☎ *541/ 942-1418* ✉ *Free* ☉ *Daily.*

You can access the 15.6 mi **Row River Trail,** a scenic, flat, hiking and biking path, formerly a railroad track, by following the Row River 3 mi east of town at the Mosby Bridge. ☎ *541/942-2411.*

Where to Eat

¢–$$$ ✕ **Cottage.** Heat from a single wood-burning stove and the sun are the only energy sources at this environmentally friendly restaurant, with healthy cooking. Entrées include seafood, steak, and chicken. There's also a wide selection of sandwiches, soups, salads, and burgers as well as a kids' menu. ⊠ *2915 Row River Rd., 97424* ☎ *541/942-3091* ▤ *MC, V* ☉ *Closed Sun.*

Drain

40 *8 mi west of I-5, halfway between Roseburg and Eugene.*

Famous for its castle and covered bridge, this small timber town between Roseburg and Eugene has several Victorians and good antiques shops worth seeing. Other nearby attractions in Douglas County include Wildlife Safari and Crater Lake National Park. Drain is about 30 mi south of Eugene at the junction of Highways 99 and 38.

On the Coast Fork of the Willamette River, **Cottage Grove Lake,** a reservoir built in the 1940s, is 3 mi long. There are two parks and two campgrounds. Recreational activities include boating, swimming, waterskiing, fishing, and picnicking. The area has many birds (including bald eagles) and blacktail deer. ⊠ *75166 Cottage Grove Lake Rd., 97424* ☎ *541/ 942-8657 or 541/942-5631.*

Residents Charles and Anna Drain donated 60 acres of land to found the town of Drain. This Victorian, known as **Drain Castle,** was built in 1895 and is on the National Register of Historic Places. Today it serves as a school district administration office. ⊠ *500 S. Main St.* ☎ *541/ 836-2223.*

The only Oregon covered bridge within city limits is **Pass Creek Covered Bridge.** Built in the 1870s and rebuilt in 1925, Pass Creek bridge was moved to Drain City Park in the late 1980s. The 61-foot-long span carried cars until 1981. Today only pedestrians are welcome. ⊠ *Behind 205 W. A St.* ☎ *541/836-2417.*

Where to Stay & Eat

¢–$ ✕ **Road Kill Grill.** People drive from nearby cities for the home cooking at this popular barbecue restaurant, which looks like a 1950s throwback. There are hubcaps as light fixtures and tire marks on the floor with tinsel road kill. They don't serve skunk, but they do dish up great barbecued chicken, steaks, and—their specialty—ribs. ⊠ *306 Hwy. 38, 97135* ☎ *541/836–2156* ▤ *No credit cards* ⊘ *Closed Mon. No lunch.*

$$–$$$$ ▣ **Big K Guest Ranch.** A 12,000-square-foot log lodge, 4 mi south of Highway 38 and 20 mi from Drain, anchors this working ranch secluded in wooded surroundings on the Umpqua River. Fly-fishing is a staple here, as are rafting and swimming. ⊠ *20029 Hwy. 138 W, Elkton 97436* ☎ *541/584–2295 or 800/390–2445* ☖ *541/584–2395* ⊕ *www.big-k. com* ↴ *20 cabins* ⚲ *Restaurant, hiking, horseback riding, fishing, meeting room* ▤ *AE, D, DC, MC, V.*

Willamette Valley & Wine Country A to Z

AIR TRAVEL

You can fly into Portland's International Airport and begin your travels at the northern part of the Willamette Valley, or explore the southern end first by flying into Eugene's Mahlon Sweet Airport. The latter is served by America West, Horizon, Skywest, and United/United Express. Another option is to mix your itineraries and use both airports, as the flight from Portland to Eugene is a mere 40 minutes. There are also smaller airports scattered throughout the valley.

BUS TRAVEL

Between the local bus companies and the Greyhound bus system, the Willamette Valley is accessible by bus. Many of the Lane Transit District (LTD) buses will make a few stops to the outskirts of Lane County, such as to McKenzie Bridge, and buses come with bike racks so you can combine your means of transport; it's better for the environment and you can do more sightseeing by letting someone else do the driving.
🚌 Bus Depots **Cottage Grove Bus Terminal** ⊠ 1250 Gateway Blvd. ☎ 541/942-7331. **Eugene Greyhound Bus Terminal** ⊠ 987 Pearl St. ☎ 541/344-6265.
🚌 Bus Lines **Greyhound** ☎ 800/231-2222.
🚌 **Lane Transit District** ⊠ 1080 Willamette ☎ 541/687-5555 ⊕ www.ltd.org. **Salem Area Mass Transit District** ⊠ 555 Court St. NE, Suite 5230 ☎ 503/588-2424 ☖ 503/566-3933 ⊕ www.cherriots.org.

CAR TRAVEL

I–5 runs north–south the length of the Willamette. Many Willamette Valley attractions lie not too far east or west of I–5. Highway 22 travels west from the Willamette National Forest through Salem to the coast. Highway 99 travels parallel to I–5 through much of the Willamette Valley. Highway 34 leaves I–5 just south of Albany and heads west, past Corvallis and into the Coast Range, where it follows the Alsea River. Highway 126 heads east from Eugene toward the Willamette National Forest; it travels west from town to the coast.

VISITOR INFORMATION

🚌 Tourist Information **Beaverton Chamber of Commerce** ⊠ 4800 S.W. Griffith Dr., Suite 100, 97005 ☎ 503/644-0123 ☖ 503/526-0349 ⊕ www.beaverton.org. **Brownsville Chamber of Commerce** ⊡ Box 278, 97327 ☎ 541/466-5311 ☖ 541/466-5312. **Corvallis Convention and Visitors Bureau** ⊠ 420 N.W. 2nd St., 97330 ☎ 541/757-1544 or 800/334-8118 ⊕ www.visitcorvallis.com. **Cottage Grove Chamber of Commerce** ⊠ 700 E. Gibbs, Suite C, 97424 ☎ 541/942-2411 ☖ 541/431-7044 ⊕ www.cgchamber.com. **Eugene Convention & Visitors Bureau** ⊠ 115 W. 8th St., Suite 190, 97440 ☎ 541/484-5307 or 800/547-5445 ⊕ www.visitlanecounty.org. **Forest Grove Chamber of Commerce** ⊠ 2417 Pacific Ave., 97116 ☎ 503/357-3006 ☖ 503/357-2367 ⊕ www.fgchamber.org. **Greater Hillsboro Area Chamber of Commerce** ⊠ 334 S.E. 5th Ave., 97123 ☎ 503/648-1102 ☖ 503/681-0535 ⊕ www.hilchamber.org. **Lake Oswego Chamber of Commerce and Visitor's Center** ⊠ 242 B St., 97034 ⊕ www.lake-oswego.com. **Lane**

County Convention and Visitors Association ⊠ 115 W. 8th Ave., Suite 190, Eugene, 97401 ☎ 541/343-6335 or 800/547-5445 ⊕ www.visitlanecounty.org. **McMinnville Chamber of Commerce** ⊠ 417 N.W. Adams St., 97128 ☎ 503/472-6196 ⊕ www. mcminnville.org. **Newberg Area Chamber of Commerce** ⊠ 115 N. Washington St., 97132 ☎ 503/538-2014 🖶 503/538-2463 ⊕ www.newberg.org. **North Plains Area Chamber of Commerce** ✍ Box 152, North Plains 97133 ☎ 503/647-2207 🖶 503/647-2838 ⊕ www.northplains.org. **Oregon City Chamber of Commerce** ⊠ 1810 Washington St., 97045 ☎ 503/656-1619 or 800/424-3002 🖶 503/656-2274. **Philomath Area Chamber of Commerce** ✍ Box 606, Philomath 97370 ☎ 541/929-2454 🖶 541/929-4420 ⊕ www.philomathchamber.org. **Salem Convention & Visitors Center** ⊠ 1313 Mill St. SE, 97301 ☎ 503/581-4325 or 800/874-7012 ⊕ www.scva.org. **Sweet Home Chamber of Commerce** ⊠ 1575 Main St., 97386 ☎ 541/367-6186 ⊕ www.sweethomechamber. org. **Yamhill County Wineries Association** ✍ Box 25162, Portland 97298 ☎ 503/646-2985. **Yamhill Valley Visitors Association** ⊠ 417 N.W. Adams, 97128 ☎ 503/883-7770 🖶 503/472-6198 ⊕ www.oregonwinecountry.org.

THE COLUMBIA GORGE & THE CASCADES

Updated by
Janna Mock-
Lopez

Thousands of years interacting with nature's volcanoes, lava flows, Ice Age floodwaters, and glaciers left behind the Columbia River Gorge's dramatic landscape. Native Americans hunted and fished for many millenniums along the Columbia River, equally rich in history as it is in beauty, and a natural divide between Oregon and Washington. Only in the last few hundred years have pioneers, including Lewis and Clark, forged towards the west over the Cascades to discover the Columbia Gorge. Local Native American tribes still have exclusive fishing rights on many areas of the river.

A tour of the Columbia River Gorge and the Oregon Cascades rewards you with a combination of recreation and spectacular scenery. Sightseers, hikers, and skiers find contentment in this robust region and won't regret packing extra rolls of film for the never-ending views, particularly in spring, when dozens of accessible waterfalls are full. Out of the Columbia Gorge's 70-plus waterfalls, 11 cascade over 100 feet. In fall and spring, the drama of fast-moving mixtures of clouds and sun will likely be pierced by a rainbow arching across the sky.

Highlights of the Columbia River Gorge, where the mighty waterway is dwarfed by steep, basalt cliffs, include Multnomah Falls, Bonneville Dam, and the windsurfing hub and rich orchard land of Hood River. To the south of Hood River lie the skiing and other alpine attractions of the 11,239-foot-high Mt. Hood. From Portland, the Columbia Gorge–Mt. Hood Loop is the easiest way to see the gorge and the mountain. Take I–84 east to Troutdale and follow U.S. 26 to Bennett Pass (near Timberline), where Highway 35 heads north to Hood River; then follow I–84 back to Portland. Or make the loop in reverse.

Winter weather in the Columbia Gorge and the Mt. Hood area is much more severe than that in Portland and western Oregon. Even I–84 may be closed because of snow and ice. If you're planning a winter visit, be sure your car has chains and carry plenty of warm clothes. Travelers canvassing farther south over the 4,800-foot Santiam Pass of the Cascade Range, via the North Santiam Highway, will see a stark transition between the western Cascade's dominance of cedar and the eastern slopes of pine. Exploration leads to pristine lakes and a panorama of all-season snow-capped vistas. In early fall brilliant red and gold leaves burst from vine maple, tamarack and aspen. During winter, chains are a requirement for traveling over mountain passes.

Numbers in the margin correspond to points of interest on the Columbia River Gorge and Cascades map.

Gresham

❶ *10 mi east of Portland off I–84.*

Gresham was founded in the mid-1800s by westward-bound pioneers who cut a trail in the wilderness as they descended Mt. Hood. Today, it remains a well-traveled passageway between the Columbia River Gorge and the Mt. Hood recreation areas.

With a population of about 91,000, Gresham is Oregon's fourth-largest city and is recognized as Portland's largest suburb to the east, with light manufacturing, technology, and agriculture forming its employment infrastructure. Gresham calls itself the "city of music" for the festivals that have flourished in its midst. The first and most notable is the annual Mt. Hood Jazz Festival, hosted by Gresham and Mt. Hood Community College in early August.

Learn about this city's logging and agricultural roots at **Gresham History Museum**, in the beautiful former Carnegie Library building built in 1913. The English Tudor exterior is complemented by an artfully crafted interior with original clear lead-glass windows, finely-finished wood and trim. Authentic artifacts and an extensive gallery of more than 3,000 photos are on display. Even the bathroom has its own gallery. ⊠ *410 N. Main Ave.* ☎ *503/661–0347* ✉ *Free, donations accepted* ⊙ *Tues. and Thurs. 10–4, Sat. noon–4.*

> **need a break?**
>
> Pull into the Gresham Station Mall for the fresh handmade ice cream, at **Cold Stone Creamery** (⊠ 1044 N.W. Civic Dr., 97080 ☎ 503/491–5920). Base flavors are rolled on a frozen granite stone and combined with such swell mix-ins as peanut butter, fudge, or fruit. The waffle cones are baked fresh daily. Expect the crew to serenade you for a tip.

In downtown Gresham, **Main City Park** has more than 17 acres of tree-filled outdoor space for picnics, basketball, and other recreational activities. A 4½-mi stretch of the **Springwater Trail Corridor**, which runs through the park and connects to a regional 40-mi loop, is a beautiful spot for walking, biking, and horseback riding. The park is open from sunrise to sunset ⊠ *219 S. Main Ave.* ⊕ *www.parks.ci.portland.or.us.*

Where to Eat

$–$$$ ✕ **Persimmon Grille.** The Grille is at the Persimmon Country Club, tucked away in the hills 5 mi from Gresham. On the lower level of the hillside clubhouse, this light and airy room overlooks the golf course with a view of Mt. Hood in the background. Northwest touches accent the menu of Black Angus prime rib, charbroiled salmon, baked halibut, Dungeness crab, and shrimp salad, as well as a very special local dessert, marionberry cobbler. ⊠ *500 S.E. Butler Rd., 97080* ☎ *503/666–4797* 🖷 *503/667–3885* 🖃 *AE, D, MC, V* ⊙ *No dinner Mon. and Tues. Oct.–Mar.*

$ ✕ **Rose's Tea Room.** Take tea in this converted 1928 home while being serenaded in three-part harmony by Rose and her two daughters. Rose's specialty is a four-tier royal high tea with some contemporary twists. The first tier is seasonal soup served with scones and Devonshire cream; the second is fresh fruit, traditional tea sandwiches, and savories; the third has desserts that might include English sticky toffee pudding or tarts. Leave room for the final tier, a chocolate course, with truffles and cakes. The lunch menu also has a selection of other sandwiches, soups, and salads. ⊠ *155 S.E. Vista Ave.* ☎ *503/665–7215* ▤ *MC, V* ☯ *Closed Sun. and Mon. No dinner.*

Troutdale

❷ *13 mi east of Portland on I–84.*

An eastern suburb of Portland on the Columbia River, Troutdale was named by its founder for the fish ponds he built and stocked and is the gateway to the Columbia River Gorge. Upscale galleries, antiques stores, and specialty gift shops stretching ½ mi adorn this charming community. Extending into the gorge from Troutdale is the 22-mi-long **Historic Columbia River Highway**, U.S. 30 (also known as the Columbia River Scenic Highway and the Scenic Gorge Highway), which leaves I–84 and begins its climb to the forested riverside bluffs high above the interstate. Completed in 1915, the serpentine highway was the first paved road in the gorge built expressly for automotive sightseers.

❸ East of Troutdale, a few miles on U.S. 30 is **Crown Point State Park**, a 730-foot-high bluff with an unparalleled 30-mi view down the Columbia River Gorge. **Vista House,** the two-tier octagonal structure on the side of the cliff, opened its doors to visitors in 1918; the rotunda has displays about the gorge and the highway. ⊠ *U.S. 30* ☎ *503/695–2230* ⊕ *www.vistahouse.com* ✑ *Free* ☯ *Mid-Apr.–mid-Oct., daily 9–6.*

About 4 mi east of the Troutdale bridge, **Dabney State Park** has boating, hiking, and fishing. It's also a popular summer swimming hole. There's also an 18-hole disc golf course. A boat ramp is open from October through May—when no one is swimming. ⊠ *Rte. 30* ☎ *800/551–6949* ⊕ *www.oregonstateparks.org* ✑ *Day use $3 per vehicle* ☯ *Daily sunrise–sunset.*

The most famous beach lining the Columbia River, **Rooster Rock State Park** is below Crown Point; access is from the interstate only. Three miles of sandy beaches, panoramic cascades, and a large swimming area make this a popular spot. True naturists appreciate that one of Oregon's only two designated nude beaches is at Rooster Rock at the east end, not visible to conventional sunbathers. ⊠ *I–84, 7 mi east of Troutdale* ☎ *503/ 695–2261* ✑ *Day use $3 per vehicle* ☯ *Daily 7 AM–sunset.*

Where to Stay & Eat

$$$ ✕ **Black Rabbit.** At McMenamins Edgefield, this restaurant in the main lodge serves all day and offers northwestern cuisine, such as fresh green curry mussels steamed with green curry coconut milk, lime juice, and basil, and traditional favorites, such as New York steak. A kids' menu is also available. Dine indoors or in the outdoor courtyard. ⊠ *2126 S. W. Halsey St., 97060* ☎ *503/492–3086* ▤ *AE, D, MC, V.*

$–$$ **McMenamins Edgefield.** This European-style bed-and-breakfast hotel in
Fodor'sChoice a historic Georgian Revival–style manor is a tranquil getaway. Its 38
★ acres of gardens and vineyards include a winery, brewery, distillery, several small bars and gathering areas, an 18-hole pitch-and-putt golf course, gardens, and a movie theater. Relaxing and enjoying simple pleasures are the focus here. Rooms have no telephones, and most share separate men's and women's bathrooms. The only television on the grounds is found in the Ice House, a tiny cigar bar decorated with old sports memorabilia. There's also a wine-tasting room here. Massage service is available on site, and a full country breakfast is included. ⊠ *2126 S.W. Halsey St., Troutdale 97060* ☎ *503/669–8610 or 800/669–8610* ⇨ *103 rooms* ⚴ *2 restaurants, 18-hole golf course, massage, 4 bars, beer garden, pub, cinema, shop, meeting rooms, free parking; no smoking* ▤ *AE, DC, MC, V* ⚏ *BP.*

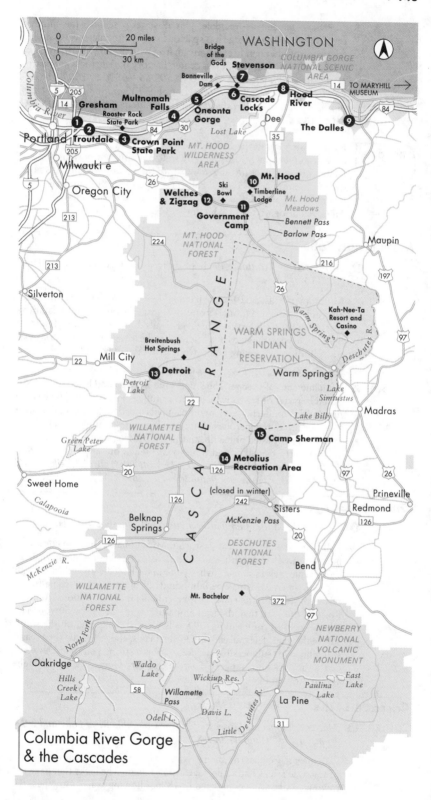

Columbia River Gorge & the Cascades

$ ▣ **Phoenix Inn Suites—Troutdale.** This all-suites hotel near the mouth of the Columbia River Gorge has spacious suites with microwaves and refrigerators. Other handy extras are an iron with ironing board, free local calls, and pool, spa, and fitness center. Factory outlet stores are nearby. ⊠ 477 N.W. Phoenix Dr., 97060 ☎ 503/669–6500 or 800/824–6824 ⊜ 503/669–3500 ⬡ 73 rooms ᗒ Cable TV, indoor pool, hot tub, business services, airport shuttle, some pets allowed (fee) ▭ AE, D, DC, MC, V ⧮ CP.

> **en route**
>
> From Crown Point, the Columbia River Highway heads downhill over graceful stone bridges built by Italian immigrant masons and winds through quiet forest glades. More than a dozen waterfalls pour over fern- and lichen-covered cliffs in a 10-mi stretch. Latourell, Bridal Veil, Wahkeena, and Horsetail falls are the most impressive. All have parking areas and hiking trails.

Multnomah Falls

❹ 20 mi east of Troutdale on I–84 or Historic Columbia River Hwy. (U.S. 30).

Multnomah Falls, a 620-foot-high double-decker torrent, the fifth-highest waterfall in the nation, is by far the most spectacular of the cataracts east of Troutdale. The scenic highway leads down to a parking lot; from there, a paved path winds to a bridge over the lower falls. A much steeper trail climbs to a viewing point overlooking the upper falls.

Where to Eat

★ **$–$$** ✕ **Multnomah Falls Lodge.** The lodge, built in 1925 and listed on the National Register of Historic Places, has vaulted ceilings and classic stone fireplaces. Wonderful service complements a wide selection of delicious food prepared in generous helpings such as a zesty apple-wood-grilled salmon, slow-roasted prime rib, and grilled flat-iron steak. Other favorites are blueberry pancakes and traditional French onion soup. ⊠ 50000 Historic Columbia River Hwy. (Exit 31 off I–84), Bridal Veil ☎ 503/695–2376 ⊕ www.multnomahfallslodge.com ▭ AE, D, MC, V.

Oneonta Gorge

❺ 2 mi east of Multnomah Falls on Historic Columbia River Hwy.

Following the old highway east from Multnomah Falls, you come to a narrow, mossy cleft with walls hundreds of feet high. Oneonta Gorge is most enjoyable in summer, when you can walk up the streambed through the cool green canyon, where hundreds of plant species—some found nowhere else—flourish under the perennially moist conditions. At other times of the year, take the trail along the west side of the canyon. The clearly marked trailhead is 100 yards west of the gorge, on the south side of the road. The trail ends at Oneonta Falls, about ½ mi up the stream. Bring boots or submersible sneakers—plus a strong pair of ankles—because the rocks are slippery. East of Oneonta Gorge, the scenic highway returns to I–84.

Cascade Locks

❻ 7 mi east of Oneonta Gorge on Historic Columbia River Hwy. and I–84, 30 mi east of Troutdale on I–84.

In pioneer days, boats needing to pass the bedeviling rapids near the town of Cascade Locks had to portage around them. The locks that gave the town its name were completed in 1896, allowing waterborne passage for the first time. Native Americans still use the locks for their traditional dip-net fishing.

The first federal dam to span the Columbia, **Bonneville Dam** was dedicated by President Franklin D. Roosevelt in 1937 and may be the state's most impressive man-made attraction. Its generators (visible from a balcony during self-guided powerhouse tours) have a capacity of nearly a million kilowatts, enough to supply power to more than 200,000 single-family homes. There is a modern visitor center on Bradford Island, complete with underwater windows for viewing migrating salmon as they struggle up fish ladders. The best viewing times are between April and October. In recent years the dwindling runs of wild Columbia salmon have made the dam a subject of much environmental controversy. ⊠ *From I–84 take Exit 40, head northeast, and follow signs 1 mi to visitor center* ☎ *541/374–8820* 📼 *Free* ☉ *Visitor center daily 9–5.*

Below Bonneville Dam, the ponds at the **Bonneville Fish Hatchery** teem with fingerling salmon, fat rainbow trout, and 6-foot-long sturgeon. The hatchery raises Chinook and coho salmon; from mid-October to late November, you can watch as staff members spawn the fish, beginning a new hatching cycle, or feed the trout with food pellets from a coin-operated machine. ✛ *From I–84 take Exit 40 and follow signs northeast 1 mi to hatchery* ☎ *541/374–8393* 📼 *Free* ☉ *Hatchery grounds daily sunrise–sunset, spawning room daily 7:30–4:30.*

Cascade Locks is the home port of the 600-passenger stern-wheeler *Columbia Gorge.* Between mid-June and early October the relic ship churns upriver, then back again, on two-hour excursions through some of the Columbia River Gorge's most impressive scenery. The ship's captain will talk about the gorge's fascinating 40-million-year geology and about pioneering spirits and legends, such as Lewis and Clark, who once triumphed over this very same river. ✛ *Cruises leave from Marine Park in Cascade Locks* ☎ *541/374–8427* ⊕ *www.sternwheeler.com* ⌖ *Reservations essential* 📼 *2-hr cruises (no meal) $12.95, longer cruises with meals $26–$36* ☉ *2-hr cruises June–Sept., daily at 10, 12:30, and 3; dinner cruise Fri. at 7 PM, Sat. at 6 PM; brunch cruise weekends at 12:30 PM* 🖃 *AE, MC, V.*

Where to Stay & Eat

¢–$$ ✕ **Salmon Row Pub.** A woodsy tavern with cedar-shake walls, historical photos, and a stone fireplace provides hearty servings of starters, salads, and main courses, including smoked salmon chowder and oven-roasted chicken accompanied by house-specialty horseradish. Sit outside in the adjacent courtyard and take in mountain and river views while sipping one of 11 featured microbrews. ⊠ *500 Wanapa St.* ☎ *541/374–9310* 🖃 *D, MC, V* ☉ *No lunch Mon. or Tues.*

¢ 🏨 **Bridge of the Gods Motel and RV Park.** One block from the historic Bridge of the Gods and within walking distance of Cascade Locks activities, this locally owned business offers clean, spacious rooms with modest furnishings, including microwaves. Some have kitchenettes, patios, and balconies. ⊠ *630 Wanapa, Box 278, 97014* ☎ *541/374–8628* 🖨 *541/374–9056* 📼 *15 rooms* ♿ *Some kitchenettes, microwaves, laundry facilities, some pets allowed (fee)* 🖃 *AE, D, MC, V.*

Stevenson, Washington

❼ *Across the river from Cascade Locks via the Bridge of the Gods and 4 mi east on Washington State Hwy. 14.*

For a magnificent vista from high above the Columbia, pay the 75¢ toll and take the truss bridge, called the **Bridge of the Gods**, above Cascade

Locks over to the Washington side. Slightly west of the bridge, hikers gain access to the Oregon-Washington link of the Mexico-to-Canada **Pacific Crest Trail.** Travel east on Highway 14 for about 10 minutes to reach the small town of Stevenson, with several antiques shops and good places to grab a bite.

★ For several hundreds years, 800-foot **Beacon Rock** was a landmark for river travelers, including Native Americans, who recognized this point as the last rapid of the Columbia River. Lewis and Clark were reportedly the first white men to see the volcanic remnant in 1805. Picnic atop old lava flows after hiking a 1-mi trail, steep but safe, which leads to tremendous views of the Columbia Gorge and river. A round-trip hike takes 45 minutes to one hour. The site is a few miles west of the Bridge of the Gods.

The **Columbia Gorge Interpretive Center,** below the dramatic basaltic cliffs on the north bank of the Columbia River Gorge, has exhibits that explain the volcanic forces that shaped the gorge landscape and the cultural history of the area. On display are a huge fish wheel and native dip nets used for salmon fishing, a Native American pit house, and artifacts pertaining to the explorers, missionaries, fur trappers, and soldiers who came through the gorge. ⊠ *990 S.W. Rock Creek Dr., Stevenson, WA, 1 mi east of Bridge of the Gods on Hwy. 14* ☎ *509/427–8211* ⊕ *www.columbiagorge.org* ⊠ *$6* ☉ *Daily 10–5.*

Where to Stay & Eat

★ **$–$$$** ✕ **The Cascade Room at Dolce Skamania Lodge.** Gaze at the perfect fusion of sky, river, and cliffscapes through the Cascade Room's expansive windows during an exquisite dining experience. Alder-plank potlatch salmon and oat-crusted trout stuffed with Northwest potatoes and herbs are signature dishes; also try the garlic sizzling shrimp and sautéed forest mushrooms. Melt-in-your-mouth chocolate soufflé and fresh mixed-berry cobbler are grand finales. Breakfast specialties include hazelnut pancakes and fresh berry crepes. The Gorge Harvest Buffet brunch is offered on Sunday, and the seafood, salads, sushi, and pasta draw patrons from miles around. ⊹ *Skamania Lodge Way north of Hwy. 14, 2 mi east of the Bridge of the Gods* ☎ *509/427–2508* ⌨ *Reservations essential* ⊟ *AE, D, DC, MC, V.*

$$$–$$$$ ▦ **Bonneville Hot Springs Resort.** The pampering at this 6,000-square-foot property has a history; local lore says that the same 97°F hot-springs ground waters being fed into present-day resort spa treatments, pools, and hot tubs were once used by Native American tribes seeking health and healing. The expansive three-story lobby has floor-to-ceiling windows overlooking lush forest and an equally tall two-sided river-rock fireplace. Impressive use of stone, fiber, and wood finishes throughout includes a 25-meter redwood-panel indoor lap pool and an outdoor patio garden with an 8-foot stone waterfall wall, soaking pool, and attractive stone sculptures. Massage, mineral and herbal baths, and wraps are administered by candlelight. Rooms are spacious with upscale furnishings. ⊹ *3 mi west of Bridge of the Gods on Hwy. 14, right on Hot Springs Way, right on E. Cascade Dr. follow for ½ mi* ⊠ *1252 E. Cascade Dr., North Bonneville, WA 98639* ☎ *509/427–9720 or 866/459–1678* ⊟ *509/427–7733* ⊕ *www.bonnevilleresort.com* ⇥ *78 rooms* ♨ *Restaurant, indoor pool, indoor and outdoor hot tubs, massage, bar* ⊟ *AE, D, MC, V.*

★ **$$$–$$$$** ▦ **Dolce Skamania Lodge.** Because this grand lodge is situated high on a forested knoll situated high on the Columbia River, the natural touches of endless windows, pine floors, and an immense river-rock fireplace leave an organic imprint. The rooms, many with fireplaces and gorgeous views, have lodge-style furniture covered with handwoven fabrics. Breathe in the surrounding beauty by walking one of the lodge's mile-plus wooded nature trails or replenish your spirit in the beautiful spa. Outstanding recreational facilities make this a premier resort on the Columbia. ⚓ *Skamania Lodge Way north of Hwy. 14, 1½ mi east of the Bridge of the Gods* ☎ *509/427–7700 or 800/221–7117* 🖷 *509/427–2547* ⊕ *www.dolce.com/skamania* ➳ *254 rooms* 🛆 *Restaurant, bar, 18-hole golf course, 2 tennis courts, indoor pool, gym, indoor and outdoor hot tubs, massage, sauna, hiking, volleyball, bicycles, cross-country skiing, library, business services, some pets allowed (fee)* ▭ *AE, D, DC, MC, V.*

Hood River

❽ *17 mi east of Cascade Locks on I–84.*

For years the incessant easterly winds at the town of Hood River, where the Columbia Gorge widens and the scenery changes to tawny, wheat-covered hills, were nothing but a nuisance. Then somebody bolted a sail to a surfboard, and a new recreational craze was born. A fortuitous combination of factors—mainly the reliable gale-force winds blowing against the current—has made Hood River the self-proclaimed boardsailing capital of the world. Especially in summer, this once-somnolent town swarms with colorful "boardheads," many of whom have journeyed from as far away as Europe and Australia. In winter, many of these same athletes stay in town but turn south to ski on mountain slopes that are only a short drive away. Other outdoor enthusiasts find the area's fishing, boating, swimming, and hiking venues the best in the region.

Hood River's rich pioneer past is reflected in its downtown historic district. The City of Hood River publishes a free, informative self-guided walking tour (available through the City of Hood River government office or the Hood River chamber of commerce) that takes you roughly 10 blocks to more than 40 civic and commercial buildings dating from 1893 to the 1930s, a handful of which are listed in the National Register of Historic Places.

Either by car or bicycle, tour Hood River valley's **Fruit Loop**, whose vast orchards surround the Hood River. You'll see apples, pears, cherries, and peaches fertilized by volcanic soil, pure glacier water, and a conducive harvesting climate. Along the 35 mi of farms are a host of delicious baked goods, wines, flowers, and nuts. Festive farm activities from April to November also give a taste of the agricultural life. While on the loop, consider stopping at the town of **Parkdale** to lunch, shop, and snap a photo of Mt. Hood's north face. There are well-marked signs on the entire 35-mi loop. ⊠ *Route begins on Hwy. 35* ⊕ *www.hoodriverfruitloop.com.*

The **Hutson Museum** exhibits Native American dolls, taxidermy, and a rare rock collection, which includes thousands of rough specimens, polished slabs, spheres and eggs. More than 2,500 arrow and spear points, stone bowls, mortars, grinding tools, and specialized tools are prized for their regional geological and historical value. The Mt. Hood excursion train terminates at the museum. ⊠ *4967 Baseline Dr., Parkdale* ☎ *541/352–6808* 🖾 *$1* ⊙ *Oct.–Apr., Wed.–Fri. 11–4; Sat. 11–6.*

On the river downtown, **Columbia Gorge Sailpark** has a boat basin, swimming beach, jogging trails, picnic tables, and rest rooms. ⊠ *Port Marina, Exit 64 off I–84* ☎ *541/386–1645.*

An efficient and relaxing way to survey Mt. Hood and the Hood River, the **Mt. Hood Scenic Railroad and Dinner Train** was established in 1906 as a passenger and freight line. Chug alongside the Hood River through vast fruit orchards before climbing up steep forested canyons, glimpsing Mt. Hood along the way. There are four trip options: a four-hour excursion (serves light concessions with two daily departures, morning and afternoon), dinner, brunch, and themed murder-mystery dinner. Choose from brunch fare such as quiche stuffed with mushrooms, caramelized onions, bacon, cottage and cheddar cheeses, or fresh berry crepes. Favorite dinner selections are the herbed fillet of salmon served with chardonnay-lime butter or roasted chicken breast filled with shallots, mushrooms, and spinach. Exceptional service is as impressive as the scenery. ⊠ *110 Railroad Ave.* ☎ *541/386–3556 or 800/872–4661* ⊕ *www.mthoodrr.com* ⊠ *Excursion $23, brunch $57, dinner $70, murder mystery dinner $80* ⊙ *Apr.–Dec., call for schedule.*

need a break? A glass-walled microbrewery with a windswept deck overlooking the Columbia, the **Full Sail Tasting Room and Pub** (⊠ 506 Columbia St. ☎ 541/386–2247) has won major awards at the Great American Beer Festival. Savory snack foods complement fresh ales.

An amalgam of education, history, and fun, **Oregon's International Museum of Carousel Art** has the world's largest and most comprehensive collection of antique carousel art. Admire, without touching, the master craftsmanship and beauty of 150 restored animals, including horses, tigers, and dragons. ⊠*304 Oak St.* ☎*541/387–4622* ⊠*$5* ⊙ *Wed.–Sun. 11–3.*

In the scenic Hood River valley, **Flerchinger Vineyards** has a 6-acre vineyard nearby where Riesling and chardonnay grapes are grown. ⊠ *4200 Post Canyon Dr.* ☎*541/386–2882 or 800/516–8710* ⊕*www.flerchinger. com* ⊠ *Free* ⊙ *Daily 11–5.*

Sauvignon blanc, cabernet sauvignon, and merlot are among the varieties produced at the 12-acre, family-owned **Hood River Vineyards,** which overlook the Columbia River Gorge and Hood River valley. Bottles are sold individually; best-sellers are the pinot noir and chardonnay. ⊠*4693 Westwood Dr.* ☎ *541/386–3772* ⊠ *Free* ⊙ *Mar.–Dec., daily 11–5.*

off the beaten path **LOST LAKE –** The waters of one of the most-photographed sights in the Pacific Northwest reflect towering Mt. Hood and the thick forests that line the lakeshore. Cabins are available for overnight stays, and because no motorboats are allowed on Lost Lake, the area is blissfully quiet. ⊠ *Lost Lake Rd., Take Hood River Hwy. south from Hood River to town of Dee and follow signs* ☎ *541/386–6366* ⊠ *Day use $5.*

Where to Stay & Eat

$–$$$ ✕ **Stonehedge Gardens.** Unique to this dinner-only spot is a five-level Italian stone terrace for outdoor summer dining. The 1898 house rests on 6½ acres of gardens and a wooded area. The interior is embellished by fine woodwork detail and stained-glass windows. The menu has a mix of Northwest and Continental dishes that includes locally raised organic beef filet mignon and seared ahi tuna. Complement your meal with a glass of wine from the extensive cellar. Listen to folk music or jazz on Wednesday nights during July and August. ⊠ *3405 Cascade St.,* ☎ *541/ 386–3940* ▤ *AE, MC, V.*

$$$ ✕▥ **Columbia Gorge Hotel.** One selling point of this grande dame of gorge hotels is the view of a 208-foot-high waterfall. Rooms with plenty of wood, brass, and antiques overlook the formal gardens. Rates include

a seven-course breakfast, dubbed the World Famous Farm Breakfast (nonguests pay $24.95). While watching the sun set on the Columbia River, you can dine in the hotel's restaurant, also open to nonguests, where selections might include breast of pheasant with pear wine, hazelnuts, and cream, as well as grilled venison, breast of duck, Columbia River salmon, or sturgeon. ⊠ *4000 Westcliff Dr., 97031, Off I–84 Exit 62* ☎ *541/386–5566 or 800/345–1921* 🖶 *541/387–5414* ⊕ *www. columbiagorgehotel.com* ⟳ *46 rooms* ⚲ *Restaurant, bar* ▤ *AE, D, DC, MC, V* ⦿ *BP.*

★ **$$–$$$** ⬚ **Lakecliff Bed & Breakfast.** Architect A. E. Doyle, who designed the Multnomah Falls Lodge, the Classical Revival public library, and Benson Hotel in Portland, also designed the summer home that's now a bed-and-breakfast inn. The 1908 house, built on a cliff overlooking the river, is a popular site for weddings and is beautifully maintained and exceptionally comfortable. A deck at the back of the house, fireplaces in three of the rooms, and top-notch service ensure a relaxing stay. For summer months, reservations are required at least three months in advance. ⊠ *3820 Westcliff Dr., head east from I–84 Exit 62, 97031* ☎ *541/386–7000* 🖶 *541/ 386–1803* ⊕ *www.lakecliffbnb.com* ⟳ *4 rooms* ▤ *MC, V.*

The Dalles

⑨ *20 mi east of Hood River on I–84.*

The Dalles lies on a crescent bend of the Columbia River where the river narrows and once spilled over a series of rapids, creating a flagstone effect. French voyagers christened it *dalle,* or "flagstone." The Dalles is the seat of Wasco County and the trading hub of north-central Oregon. It gained fame early in the region's history as the town where the Oregon Trail branched, with some pioneers departing to travel over Mt. Hood on Barlow Road and the others continuing down the Columbia River. This may account for the small-town Old West feeling that still permeates the area. Several historical Oregon moments as they relate to The Dalles's past are magnificently illustrated on eight murals painted by renowned Northwest artists. They're downtown within short walking distance of one another.

Outstanding exhibits at the 130-year-old **Wasco County Courthouse** illustrate the trials and tribulations of those who traveled the Oregon Trail. ⊠ *410 W. 2nd Pl.* ☎ *541/296–4798* 📷 *Free, donation suggested* ⊙ *Mon., Tues., Fri., and Sat. 10–4.*

The 1856-vintage Fort Dalles Surgeon's Quarters is the site of the **Fort Dalles Museum,** the oldest history museum in Oregon. On display in these authentic hand-hewn log buildings are the personal effects of some of the region's settlers and a collection of early automobiles. The entrance fee gains you admission to the **Anderson House** museum across the street, which also has pioneer artifacts. ⊠ *15th and Garrison Sts.* ☎ *541/296– 4547* 📷 *$3* ⊙ *Daily 10–5.*

A favorite of windsurfers, **Celilo Park** also has swimming, sailboarding, and fishing. It's 7 mi east of The Dalles. ⊠ *Exit 99 off I–84* ☎ *541/ 296–1181* 📷 *Free* ⊙ *Daily.*

Exhibits at **Columbia Gorge Discovery Center—Wasco County Historical Museum** highlight the geological history of the Columbia Gorge, back 40 million years when volcanoes, landslides, and floods carved out the area. The museum focuses on 10,000 years of Native American life and exploration of the region by white settlers. ⊠ *5000 Discovery Dr.* ☎ *541/ 296–8600* ⊕ *www.gorgediscovery.org* 📷 *$6.50* ⊙ *Daily 10–6.*

At **The Dalles Dam and Reservoir,** a hydroelectric dam just east of the Bonneville Dam, you can ride the free Dalles Dam Tour Train to the fish ladder and powerhouse. There's also a sturgeon pond at the visitor center. ⊠ *Exit 87 (in summer) or Exit 88 other times off I–84* ☎ *541/296–1181* 🖃 *Free* ☉ *Daily; tour train departs mid-Apr.–Labor Day, Wed.–Sun. 8–4; Labor Day–Memorial Day, daily 8–5.*

Built in 1897, **Old St. Peter's Landmark** is a Gothic brick church with brilliant stained glass, hand-carved pews, marble altars, and an immense pipe organ. Steamboat captains once used the steeple, which rises 176 feet, as a navigational benchmark. The landmark now functions as a nondenominational, nonprofit organization that makes the space available for tours, weddings, and other private functions. ⊠ *3rd and Lincoln Sts.* ☎ *541/296–5686* 🖃 *Free, donations accepted* ☉ *Feb.–Dec., Tues.–Fri. 11–3, weekends 1–3.*

View the lower part of **Mayer State Park** from the top of Rowena Crest. Recreational activities include swimming, boating, fishing, and picnicking. ⊠ *Exit 77 off I–84* ☎ *800/551–6949* ⊕ *www.prd.state.or.us* 🖃 *Day use $3 per vehicle* ☉ *Daily.*

Where to Stay & Eat

¢–$ ✕ **Cousin's Restaurant and Saloon.** Home cooking rules at this family restaurant with a frontier motif. Try the pot roast or turkey supper with all the trimmings. A kids' menu is available, as is a breakfast menu. ⊠ *2114 W. 6th St., 97058* ☎ *541/298–2771* ⊟ *AE, D, DC, MC, V.*

$ 🏠 **Columbia House.** A period feel lingers at this enormous late-1930s house on a cliff overlooking the Columbia. The rooms have king-size beds; two have river views. On a quiet wooded acre three blocks from downtown, the B&B has three decks out back, perfect for relaxing or, in good weather, enjoying the breakfast served up by the owner. ⊠ *525 E. 7th St., 97058* ☎ *541/298–4686 or 800/807–2668* 🛏 *4 rooms, 1 with shared bath* ⚓ *Airport shuttle* ⊟ *MC, V* 🍴 *BP.*

Mt. Hood

⑩ *About 60 mi east of Portland on I–84 and U.S. 26, 65 mi from The Dalles, west on I–84 and south on Hwy. 35 and U.S. 26.*

Majestically towering 11,235 feet above the Columbia River Gorge, Mt. Hood is what remains of the original north wall and rim of a volatile crater. Although the peak no longer spews ash or fire, active steam vents can be spotted high on the mountain. Native Americans in the area named it Wy'east, after a great chief who mystically became the mountain. In anger, Wy'east spouted flames and threw rocks toward the sky. The name was changed when in 1792 the British Royal Navy, the first recorded Caucasians sailing down the Columbia River, spotted the mountain and named it after the ship's admiral, Hood.

Mt. Hood offers the only year-round skiing in the lower 48 states, with three major ski areas and 26 lifts, as well as extensive areas for cross-country skiing and snowboarding. Many of the ski runs turn into mountain bike trails in summer. The mountain is also popular with climbers and hikers. In fact, some hikes follow parts of the Oregon Trail, and signs of the pioneers' passing are still evident.

The fourth-highest peak in the Cascades, towering at 11,000 feet and crowned by year-round snow, is a focal point of the 1.1-million-acre

★ **Mt. Hood National Forest,** an all-season playground attracting more than 7 million visitors annually. Twenty miles southeast of Portland, it extends south from the Columbia River Gorge for more than 60 mi and includes 189,200 acres of designated wilderness. These woods are perfect for hikers, horseback riders, mountain climbers, and cyclists. Within the forest are more than 80 campgrounds and 50 lakes stocked with brown, rainbow, cutthroat, brook, and steelhead trout. The Sandy, Salmon, and other rivers are known for their fishing, rafting, canoeing, and swimming. Both forest and mountain are crossed by an extensive trail system for hikers, cyclists, and horseback riders. The **Pacific Crest Trail,** which begins in British Columbia and ends in Mexico, crosses at the 4,157-foot-high Barlow Pass. As with most other mountain destinations within Oregon, weather can be temperamental, and snow and ice may affect driving conditions as early as October and as late as May. Bring tire chains and warm clothes as a precaution.

For a glimpse into the area's vivid history stop at the **Mt. Hood Information Center** (⊠ 65000 E. Hwy. 26, Welches 97067 ☎ 503/622–7674 or 503/622–3360) in the Mt. Hood Village RV park and pick up a copy of the *Barlow Road*. This is a great navigational map of the first emigrant road over the Cascades where pioneers traveled west via ancient Indian trails to avoid the dangers of the mighty Columbia River. Since this forest is close to the Portland metro area, campgrounds and trails are potentially crowded over the summer months, especially on weekends. If camping, contact the forest service desk while you're at the Mt. Hood Information Center. Prepare yourself by gathering information about the more than 80 campgrounds, including a string of neighboring campgrounds that rest on the south side of Mt. Hood: Trillium Lake, Still Creek, Timothy Lake, Little Crater Lake, Clackamas Lake, Summit Lake, Clear Lake and Frog Lake. Each varies in what it offers and in price. The mountain is overflowing with day-use areas, and passes can be obtained for $5. There are also Mt. Hood National Forest maps with details about well-marked trails. ⊠ *Information center 3 mi west of town of Zigzag on north side of U.S. 26* ☎ *503/622–7674* ⊕ *www.mthood.org* ⊠ *Day use free–$5, campsites $12–$14* ⊙ *Information center daily 8–6, most campgrounds open year-round.*

Where to Stay & Eat

★ **$$-$$$$** ✕ **Cascade Dining Room.** If the large windows in this room at Timberline Lodge aren't coated with snow, a clear day or night will yield a spectacular view of five mountain peaks, including the Three Sisters, Mt. Jefferson, and Broken Top. Inside, wooden beams and a wood-plank floor, handcrafted furniture, and a huge stone fireplace with a rendering of a forest scene create a warmth complemented by an attentive staff and a highly regarded wine list. Entrées lean toward game: you might choose free range bison, Kobe or Angus beef, or rack of lamb, and elk occasionally makes an appearance on the specials list. The grilled salmon is also worthy; finish up with the house crème brûlée. The lunch menu includes sandwiches, salads, and inventive starters. ⊠ *Timberline Rd., Timberline,* ☎ *503/622–0700 or 800/547–1406* ⊟ *503/727–3710* ⊟ *AE, D, MC, V.*

$-$$$$ ⊡ **Timberline Lodge.** Depression-era workers built it, FDR dedicated it,
Fodor'sChoice and howling winter storms and intermittent disrepair dogged it, but the
★ one question staffers answer several times a day is, "Was 'The Shining' filmed here?" (Yes, but only some exteriors.) And once you make the intimidating 6-mi drive midway up the slope of Mt. Hood and get a glimpse of the place, a Work Projects Administration structure and a National Historic Landmark, you'll understand why. At once awesome and formidable, the lodge is gargantuan: the buildings, especially the head house, were constructed to complement the size and majesty of the mountain it's on—the lodge itself is built from huge timbers and stone, and bannisters were crafted from old telephone poles. Once inside, no-

tions of whether Jack Nicholson will make an appearance give way to cozier thoughts. Much of what you see looks handcrafted, and is, from the massive beams and wooden chairs to the curtains, quilts, and rugs. Rooms incorporate different handmade pieces and artwork that hark back to the lodge's beginnings in 1937. Don't miss a peek at the low-ceiling Blue Ox Bar, with stained-glass murals of Paul Bunyan and fronted by a wrought-iron gate, and treat yourself to some exceptional cooking in the Cascade Dining Room. ⊠ *Timberline Rd., Timberline 97028, North from U.S. 26; follow signs* ☎ *503/231–5400 or 800/547–1406* 🖷 *503/727–3710* ⊕ *www.timberlinelodge.com* 🛏 *60 rooms* ⚭ *Restaurant, pool, outdoor hot tub, sauna, cross-country skiing, downhill skiing, bar* ▭ *AE, D, MC, V.*

Sports & the Outdoors

SKIING   One of the longest ski seasons in North America unfolds at **Timberline Lodge Ski Area** (⊠ Off U.S. 26, Timberline ☎ 503/272–3311). The U.S. ski team conducts summer training at this full-service ski area—the only ski area in the lower 48 states that's open year-round—which welcomes snowboarders. Timberline is famous for its Palmer chairlift, which takes skiers to a high glacier for summer skiing. There are five double chairs and two high-speed quad chairs. The top elevation is 8,500 feet, with a 3,600-foot vertical drop, and the longest run is 3 mi. Facilities include a day lodge with fast food and a ski shop; lessons and equipment rental and repair are available. Parking requires a Sno-Park permit. Lift tickets weekdays are $31, $34 on weekends. The area is open Sunday–Tuesday 9–5 and Wednesday–Saturday 9 AM–10 PM; the lift is open June–August, daily 7 AM–1:30 PM.

Government Camp

⓫ *45 mi from The Dalles, south on Hwy. 35 and west on U.S. 26, 54 mi east of Portland on I–84 and U.S. 26.*

Government Camp, an alpine resort village, has a fair amount of hotels and restaurants. It's a convenient drive from here to Mt. Hood's five ski resorts or to Welches, which has restaurants and a resort.

Where to Stay & Eat

¢–$ ✕ **Charlie's Mountainview.** Old and new skis plaster the walls, lift chairs now function as furniture, and photos of famous skiers and other memorabilia are as abundant as the menu selections. Steaks and hamburgers are worthy here, but house specialties include creamy mushroom soup and chicken Caesar salad with dressing made from scratch. Top it off with apple dumplings when they're in season. There's also a full bar, with live music on weekends year-round. ⊠ *88462 Government Camp Loop* ☎ *503/272–3333* ▭ *AE, D, MC, V.*

¢   ✕ **Huckleberry Inn.** Whether it's 2 AM or 2 PM, Huckleberry Inn welcomes you 24 hours a day with soups, milk shakes, burgers, sandwiches, and omelets. Well-known treats are made with huckleberries and include pie, pancakes, tea, jelly, and huckleberry-vinaigrette salad dressing. ⊠ *E. Government Camp Loop, 97028* ☎ *503/272–3325* ⊕ *www.huckleberry-inn.com* ▭ *MC, V.*

$–$$$ ▣ **Thunderhead Lodge.** Jaw-dropping mountain views and the night lights of the Mt. Hood Ski Bowl are among the sights at this fun and friendly condominium lodge. Room sizes and capacities vary according to your needs, and there's a rec room with foosball, a pool table, wet bar, and fireplace. The outdoor pool is heated. ⊠ *W. Government Camp Loop, 97028* ☎ *866/622–1142 or 503/272–3368* ⊕ *www.thunderheadlodge.com* 🛏 *10 units* ⚭ *Pool, laundry facilities* ▭ *MC, V.*

Sports & the Outdoors

DOWNHILL
SKIING

On the eastern slope of Mt. Hood, **Cooper Spur Ski and Recreation Area** (⊕ Follow signs from Hwy. 35 for 3½ mi to ski area ☎ 541/352–7803) caters to families and has two rope tows and a T-bar. The longest run is ⅔ mi, with a 500-foot vertical drop. Facilities and services include rentals, instruction, repairs, and a ski shop, day lodge, snack bar, and restaurant. Call for hours. Mt. Hood's largest resort, **Mt. Hood Meadows Ski Resort** (⊕ 10 mi east of Government Camp on Hwy. 35 ☎ 503/337–2222 or 800/754–4663) has more than 2,000 skiable acres, dozens of runs, seven double chairs, one triple chair, one quad chair, a top elevation of 7,300 feet, a vertical drop of 2,777 feet, and a longest run of 3 mi. Facilities include a day lodge, seven restaurants, two lounges, a ski school, and a ski shop; equipment rental and repair are also available. The ski area closest to Portland, **Mt. Hood Ski Bowl** (⊕ 53 mi east of Portland, across U.S. 26 from Government Camp ☎ 503/272–3206) has 63 trails serviced by four double chairs and five surface tows, a top elevation of 5,050 feet, a vertical drop of 1,500 feet, and a longest run of 3½ mi. Night skiing is a major activity here. You can take advantage of two day lodges, a mid-mountain warming hut, three restaurants, and two lounges. Sleigh rides are conducted, weather permitting. The longest run at the **Summit Ski Area** (⊕ Government Camp Loop Hwy., east end, Government Camp ☎ 503/272–0256) is ½ mi, with a 400-foot vertical drop; there's one chairlift and one rope tow. Facilities include instruction, a ski shop, a cafeteria, and a day lodge. Bike rentals are available in summer.

Welches & Zigzag

⑫ *14 mi west of Government Camp on U.S. 26, 40 mi east of Portland, I–84 to U.S. 26.*

Find restaurants and other services in these two small towns at the base of Mt. Hood. Drop by the **Mt. Hood Visitors Center** (⊠ 65000 E. Hwy. 26 ☎ 503/622–3017) in Welches for detailed information on all the Mt. Hood area attractions.

Where to Stay & Eat

$$$–$$$$ ✕ **Tartans Pub and Steakhouse.** Enjoy a view of the resort at the mountain's lush, green golf course and Mt. Hood foothills from your indoor or outdoor table. This classy-casual dining spot offers dishes such as the house-smoked barbecue baby-back ribs and smoked chicken with mushrooms, spinach, and Asiago cream sauce poured over penne pasta. There's an inexpensive kids' menu, and breakfast is also available. ⊠ *68010 E. Fairway Ave., Welches,* ☎ *503/622–3101 or 800/669–7666* ▤ *AE, D, DC, MC, V.*

$–$$ ✕▥ **Resort at the Mountain.** In the burly Cascade foothills, this sprawling golf and ski resort is the most complete in the Mt. Hood area. Outdoor activities are plentiful, including fly-fishing on the Salmon River, horseback riding, white-water rafting, and croquet. Accommodations run from double rooms to two-bedroom condos. Each of the tastefully decorated rooms has a deck or patio overlooking the forest, courtyard, or a fairway. The resort is about a one-hour drive east of Portland. ⊠ *68010 E. Fairway Ave.; follow signs south from U.S. 26 in Welches, 97067* ☎ *503/622–3101 or 800/669–7666* ▤ *503/622–2222* ⊕ *www. theresort.com* ➥ *160 rooms ⌂ 2 restaurants, picnic area, in-room data ports, some kitchenettes, 27-hole golf course, putting green, 4 tennis courts, pool, indoor hot tub, outdoor hot tub, health club, bicycles, horseback riding, 2 bars, laundry facilities, business services, meeting room* ▤ *AE, D, DC, MC, V.*

★ $ 🖼 **The Cabins Creekside at Welches.** Affordability, accessibility to recreational activities, and wonderful hosts make this a great lodging choice in the Mt. Hood area. Comfortable, large studio units have knotty-pine vaulted ceilings and log furnishings. As a bonus, full-size kitchens make cooking "at home" a breeze. Surrounding woods offer privacy. Patios on each unit face the seasonal creek, and each cabin has lock-storage units large enough to hold bikes, skis, or snowboards. ✉ 25086 E. Welches Rd., 97067 ☎ 503/622–4275 ⊕ mthoodcabins.com ⇆ 10 cabins ⚒ Kitchens, microwaves, refrigerators, ski storage, laundry facilities ☐ AE, D, MC, V.

The Oregon Cascades

Oregon's segment of the Cascade Range begins with Mt. Hood and pushes on south, covering millions of wilderness acres until Mt. McLoughlin in southern Oregon. Slightly below Mt. Hood in the Cascade Range are hundreds of tranquil campgrounds as well as trails friendly to all levels of hikers. In a relatively short west-to-east route over the range (which encompasses large pieces of two scenic byways, McKenzie-Santiam Pass and West Cascades Scenic Byways), you'll get a geographical sampling of the state. Just 47 mi east of Salem along the North Santiam River is the Detroit Lake Recreation Area, controlled by the Detroit Dam. Only 10 mi north of Detroit Lake, but a secluded world apart, is Breitenbush Hot Springs Retreat and Conference Center, a spiritual healing and renewal community surrounded by old-growth forest.

Other popular spots within this region are Hoodoo Ski Bowl near the crest of the Cascades at Santiam Pass, and over on the eastern slope within the Deschutes National Forest is the serenity of Suttle Lake. If you're looking to fly fish or relax by listening to stands of ponderosa pine whisper on a warm, lazy afternoon, consider the Metolius Recreation Area. The Metolius River, flowing through the small town of Camp Sherman, has biking and walking trails along its banks in addition to cabins and several other lodgings.

Detroit
⓫ 40 mi east of Salem on Hwy. 22.

A small town with fewer than 300 residents, Detroit was founded in the late 1800s during construction of the Oregon Pacific Railroad. Its name was chosen because many of the earlier settlers were from Detroit, Michigan. Because Detroit Lake is surrounded by tree-laden mountains and national and state forests, it will not grow much beyond its current size. It's also near a wealth of trails and creeks, many of which are more secluded and tranquil than those in the Mt. Hood area. Detroit's elevation is 1,573 feet, so getting here through winter snow likely won't be a problem. One waterway influencing the water level of Detroit Lake is **Detroit Dam** (☎ 503/897–2385 tours), which rises 463 feet above its foundation in the steep, narrow slopes of North Santiam Canyon. The dam creates 33 mi of shoreline along Detroit Lake conducive to boating, fishing, camping, and picnicking. Guided tours of the lake are available, though in winter the lake is lowered, so depending on snow pack, lake activities may be suspended. Three miles downstream from Detroit Dam, **Big Cliff Dam** rises 191 feet above its foundation into the canyon and also feeds Detroit Lake.

off the
beaten
path

CANYON LIFE MUSEUM – As you travel to or from Detroit Lake via Salem, stop at the yellow Southern Pacific train depot, site of this small but insightful repository in Mill City, about 10 mi west of Detroit. Lore, photos, and artifacts related to the bygone era of logging, mills, railroads, and farm life are on display. Visitors are welcome during scheduled hours or outside posted hours by appointment; call to schedule. ⊠ *143 Wall St. NE, Mill City* ☎ *503/897–4088 or 503/897–2877* ⚏ *Free, donations accepted* ☉ *Apr., May, and Sept., Thurs. and Fri. 1:30–4:30; June–Aug., Wed.–Fri. 1:30–4:30; Oct.–Mar., call for appointment.*

WHERE TO STAY &
EAT
¢–$

✕ **The Cedars Restaurant and Lounge.** The open dining room in this wood-panel, lodge-style spot complements the counter seating, lengthy booths, and lumberjack motif of painted rusty saw blades. Have healthy portions of buttery biscuits and gravy made from scratch, juicy burgers, or the owner-recommended seasoned pork chops. Toward the back is a dim lounge with a full bar, separated from the main dining area; country music hums from a jukebox while patrons shoot pool, throw darts, or watch a sporting event glowing from a big-screen TV. The heaping Nachos Supreme is the appetizer of choice for lounge patrons. ⊠ *200 Detroit Ave.,* ☎ *503/854–3636* ⊟ *MC, V.*

★ ¢ ✕ **KC's Espresso & Deli.** In this friendly deli and gift shop with locally handmade goodies, order such house specialties as homemade soup and potato salad, the meat-loaf sandwich, or the fresh mocha or strawberry shakes. Sit outside with your lunch and a large scoop of ice cream on hot summer days. The shop carries its own line of products, some seasonal, including huckleberry lotions, taffy, tea, and muffins. ⊠ *155 N. Detroit Ave.,* ☎ *503/854–3145* ⊕ *www.kcsespresso.com* ⊟ *MC, V.*

¢–$ ▦ **Breitenbush Hot Springs Retreat and Conference Center.** A cooperative community, tucked away on 150 acres that went uninhabited for 11,000 years, bonds to protect the forest, heal the soul, and provide solitude. Power sources throughout the facility are geo- and hydrothermal. Retreat prices include modest cabins, three vegetarian meals per day, well-being programs—including yoga, ancient forest walks, and meditation—and the use of 45 naturally occurring hot-springs pools. Bathing in the hot springs is clothing optional. ✛ *Just east of Detroit, turn north on Hwy. 46 off Hwy. 22; 10 mi past Cleator Bend Campground turn right onto single-lane bridge crossing Breitenbush River. Road is gravel after bridge and has three forks in its 1½-mi course. Go left at every fork until parking lot* ⊠ *Detroit 97342* ☎ *503/854–3314* ▦ *503/854–3819* ⊕ *www.breitenbush.com* ⇗ *42 cabins* ♨ *Massage, sauna, hiking* ⊟ *MC, V* ⦿ *FAP.*

Metolius Recreation Area

⓮ *9 mi northwest of Sisters, off Hwy. 22.*

On the eastern slope of the Cascades and within the 1.6-million-acre Deschutes National Forest, this bounty of recreational wilderness is drier and sunnier than the western side of the mountains, giving way to bountiful natural history, outdoor activities, and wildlife. Spectacular views of jagged, 10,000-foot snow-capped Cascade peaks—including Broken Top, Three Sisters, and Mt. Jefferson, the second-highest peak in Oregon—sprawl high above the basin of an expansive evergreen valley carpeted by pine.

At the base of **Black Butte,** a dark cinder cone about 5 mi south of Camp Sherman that rises at 6,400 feet, the **Metolius River** springs forth. Witness the birth of this "instant" river by walking a paved ¼-mi path embedded in ponderosa forest, eventually reaching a viewpoint with the dramatic snow-covered peak of **Mt. Jefferson** on the horizon. At this point, water gurgles to the ground's surface and pours into a wide-trickling creek cascading over a cloister of moss-covered rocks. Within feet it funnels outward, expanding its northerly flow; becomes a full size river; and meanders east alongside grassy banks and a dense pine forest to join the Deschutes River 35 mi downstream. Because the river is spring fed, the 48° flow of the water remains constant. In 1988 the 4,600-acre corridor of the Metolius was designated a National Wild and Scenic River. Within the area and along the river, there are ample resources for camping, hiking, biking, swimming, and boating. You'll also discover some of the best fly-fishing—for rainbow, brown, and bull trout—in the Cascades.

WHERE TO STAY & EAT

★ $–$$$

✕🏠 **Suttle Lake Resort and Marina.** On the eastern side of the 1½-mi shore of Suttle Lake is this superb dining, lodging, and outdoor experience. The 10,000-square-foot Cascadian log-style lodge has 11 elegant guest rooms, each with a fireplace and whirlpool. Lakefront cabins have picnic tables and fire pits outside the front door. Inhale the fresh pine mountain air as you stroll or bike around the lake on a 3.2-mi trail, or troll the waters at dawn and wait for trout to nibble. Paddleboats and canoes are also available. You'll have a lake view wherever you sit in the Boathouse restaurant. Aside from daily Northwest specials of wild game or fresh fish, the chef prepares a signature grilled pistachio chicken and wood-oven-roasted rack of lamb. Creative salads and vegetarian and lighter fare are also available. During summer months sit outside and sip a cold tropical drink; there's live entertainment on some weekends. ✉ *13300 Hwy. 20, 97759* ☎ *541/595-2628* ⊕ *www.suttlelake. com* 🛏 *11 rooms 14 cabins* ⚘ *Some kitchens, some microwaves, boating, marina, fishing, bicycles, bar* ☰ *MC, V* ☽ *Boathouse restaurant closed Mon. and Tues. Oct.–May.*

SKIING

On a 5,711-foot summit, **Hoodoo Ski Area** (✉ Hwy. 20, 20 mi west of Sisters ☎ 541/822–3799) has 806 acres of skiable terrain. With three quad lifts, one triple lift, one double lift, and 30 downhill runs, skiers of all levels will find suitable thrills. For tranquillity, upper and lower Nordic trails are surrounded by silence. At a 60,000-square-foot lodge at the mountain's base you can take in the view, grab bait, shop, or relax your weary feet. The ski area has kids' activities and child-care services available.

Camp Sherman

⑮ *10 mi northwest of Sisters on Hwy. 20, 5 mi north on Hwy. 14.*

Surrounded by groves of whispering yellow-bellied ponderosa pines, larch, fir and cedars, and miles of streamside forest trails, this small, peaceful resort community of 250 residents is part of a designated 86,000-acre conservation area. The area's beauty and natural resources are the big draw: the spring-fed Metolius River prominently glides through town. In the early 1900s Sherman County wheat farmers escaped the dry summer heat by migrating here to fish and rest in the cool river environment. To help guide fellow farmers to the spot, devotees nailed a shoebox top with the name CAMP SHERMAN to a tree at a fork in the road. Several original buildings still stand from the homesteader days, including some cabins, a schoolhouse, and a tiny chapel.

WHERE TO STAY & EAT

¢–$$$

✕ **Kokanee Cafe.** People from miles around come to this upscale yet casual spot. The juniper-smoked salmon is a winner; also try the free-range chicken rubbed with roasted garlic and fresh thyme or the pan-fried rainbow trout with spicy bacon, roasted corn hash, and chili orange butter. Ginger beef and spinach salad are also popular. ✉ *25545 S.W. Forest Service Rd. 1419, 97730* ☎ *541/595-6420* ☰ *MC, V* ☽ *Closed Nov.–Apr. and Mon. May–Oct.*

$$$$

Fodor'sChoice

★

🏠 **Metolius River Resort.** If you want a sense of what a 1930s alpine fishing village might have looked like, consider this upscale resort. Comfort and elegance merge in these bi-level riverside cedar-shake cabins.

Hand-painted bathroom tiles, custom lodgepole furniture, quilted bedding, and wrought-iron accessories complement predominantly knotty-pine interiors. Spacious kitchens are completely equipped. Sit by your cabin's oversized river-rock fireplace with a good book, or kick back on the large deck with the sounds of the nearby Metolius River to soothe you. ⊠ *25551 S. W. Forest Service Rd. 1419; take U.S. 20 northeast 10 mi from Sisters, turn north on Camp Sherman Rd. and east on Forest Service Rd. 1419, 97730* ☎ *800/818–7688* ⊕ *www. metoliusriverresort.com* ➫ *11 cabins* ♿ *Kitchens, microwaves, some in-room VCRs* ⊟ *MC, V.*

$–$$$ 🏠 **Metolius River Lodges.** Homespun cottages give you cozy river views, fireplaces, and woodsy interiors complemented by top-notch hospitality. Pick from studiolike four-plex lodges or free-standing lodges with kitchen and bedrooms. Big picture windows bring in the pine scenery and blue sky reflecting off the water. Of the cabins, the Salmonfly is the most popular, as its large front deck overhangs the current. Make reservations well in advance, especially for summer. ⊠ *12390 S. W. Forest Service Rd. 1419–700, 97730* ☎ *800/595–6290* ⊕ *www.metoliusriverlodges.com* ➫ *13 cabins* ♿ *Kitchens, microwaves* ⊟ *MC, V.*

The Columbia Gorge & the Cascades A to Z

BUS TRAVEL

Greyhound provides service from Portland to Hood River, The Dalles, and Government Camp. CARTS Canyon Connector offers public transportation from Salem to the North Santiam Canyon area, Monday through Friday, three times a day.

🚍 Bus Lines **CARTS Canyon Connector** ☎ 503/585–5197 or 800/422–7723. **Greyhound** ☎ 800/454–2487.

🚍 Bus Depots **The Dalles Depot** ⊠ 201 Federal St., The Dalles 97058 ☎ 541/296–2421. **Government Camp Depot** ⊠ Huckleberry Inn, Hwy. 26 Business Loop, Government Camp 97028 ☎ 503/272–3325. **Hood River Depot** ⊠ 600 E. Marina Way, Hood River 97031 ☎ 541/386–1212.

CAR TRAVEL

I–84 is the main east–west route into the Columbia River Gorge. U.S. 26, heading east from Portland and northwest from Prineville, is the main route into the Mt. Hood area. Portions of I–84 and U.S. 26 that pass through the mountains pose winter-travel difficulties, though the state plows these roadways regularly. The gorge is closed frequently during harsh winters due to ice and mud slides. Extreme winds can also make driving hazardous and potentially result in highway closures. The Historic Columbia River Highway (U.S. 30) from Troutdale, to just east of Oneonta Gorge, passes Crown Point State Park and Multnomah Falls. I–84/U.S. 30 continues on to The Dalles. Highway 35 heads south from The Dalles to the Mt. Hood area, intersecting with U.S. 26 at Government Camp.

VISITOR INFORMATION

🏛 Organizations **Columbia River Gorge Visitors Association** ⊠ 2149 W. Cascade, Suite 106A, Hood River 97031 ☎ 800/98–GORGE ⊕ www.crgva.org. **Detroit Lake Recreation Area Business Association** ⌂ Box 574, Detroit 97342 ⊕ www.detroitlakeoregon.org. **Hood River County Chamber of Commerce** ⊠ Port Marina Park, 97031 ☎ 541/386–2000 or 800/366–3530 ⊕ www.hoodriver.org. **Hoodoo Recreation Services** ⊠ Hwy. 20, Sisters 97759 ☎ 541/822–3799 ⊕ www.hoodoocom. **Metolius Recreation Area** ⌂ Box 64, Camp Sherman 97730 ☎ 541/595–6117 ⊕ www.Metoliusriver.com. **Mt. Hood Chamber of Commerce** ⊠ 65000 E. Hwy. 26, Welches 97067 ☎ 503/622–4822 or 888/622–4822 ⊕ www.mthood.org. **Mt. Hood Information Center** ⊠ 65000 E. Hwy. 26, Welches 97067 ☎ 503/622–7674 ✉ 70220 W. Hwy. 26, Zigzag 97049 ☎ 503/622–3191. **Mt.**

Hood National Forest Ranger Stations ✉ 6780 Hwy. 35, Mt. Hood 97041 ☎ 541/352–6002 ✉ Superintendent, 16400 Champion Way, off Hwy. 26, Sandy 97055 ☎ 503/668–1771. **Oregon Tourism Commission** ✉ 775 Summer St. NE, Salem 97301-1282 ☎ 503/986–0000 ⊕ www.traveloregon.com.

CENTRAL OREGON

Updated by
Zach Dundas

The arid landscape east of the Cascades differs dramatically from that on the lush, wet western side. Crossing the mountains, you enter a high-desert plateau with scrubby buttes, forests of ponderosa pine, and mile after mile of sun-bleached earth. The booming resort town of Bend is the most prominent playground in central Oregon, but within the region are dozens of other outdoor recreational hubs, many of them blissfully uncrowded.

Numbers in the text correspond to numbers in the margin and on the Central Oregon and Bend maps.

Warm Springs

❶ *115 mi southeast of Portland on U.S. 26.*

If, like the many visitors who begin their journey in Portland, you enter the Warm Springs Indian Reservation after traversing the frosty alpine skirt of Mt. Hood, you may feel you've been teleported from *The Sound of Music* into *A Fistful of Dollars.* This austere desert landscape is nothing short of stunning—a country of brooding solitary buttes, lonely pines, and untamed ravines, lorded over by the snow-capped spires of Mt. Jefferson and Mt. Hood. For a crash course in Oregon's thrilling contrasts, you could do no better. A singular museum and the popular desert resort of Kah-Nee-Ta provide cultural and economic bases for the three confederated tribes who live here.

★ ♥ The Confederated Tribes of the Warm Springs Reservation created the **Museum at Warm Springs** south of town to preserve their traditions and keep their legacy alive. On display are tribal heirlooms, beaded artifacts, baskets, historic photographs, ceramics, and traditional dwellings. This haul is the product of years of carefully planned collecting and curating and is seen as a model tribal-run cultural resource. The museum's buildings, with such unmistakable nods to tribal history as conical, teepee-like atriums and sleek modernist lines, received an award from the American Institute of Architects. The museum's gift shop sells Native American crafts. ✉ 2189 U.S. 26 ☎ 541/553–3331 ☜ $6 ☉ Daily 9–5.

Where to Stay & Eat

★ $$ ✕🏨 **Kah-Nee-Ta Resort and Casino.** Kah-Nee-Ta means "root digger" in one of the reservation's native tongues, but this modern destination resort doesn't really match that humble moniker. Built around hot mineral springs that feed huge open-air swimming pools, Kah-Nee-Ta has an isolated, exclusive feel that makes a tempting escape from bustling Portland or Bend. The casino, straight out of third-tier Vegas, strikes a depressing and tacky note with its windowless, stifling atmosphere and hordes of mostly unhappy would-be winners. But the rooms are comfortable, and the staff is friendly and helpful. Best of all, however, are the sweeping, sparse desert panoramas; restorative mineral pools; and pristine juniper-scented air, a form of aromatherapy in and of itself. (For those who want to address the health-beauty nexus in a more formal way, Spa Wanapine has massage, reflexology, facials and other new-age treatments.) The Juniper Room serves decent upscale food with a distinct regional inflection; a more affordable seafood buffet is also available. The Warm Springs, Wasco, and Paiute suites, which cost a little extra, have tile fireplaces and hot tubs, big-screen TVs, and king-size beds. An RV park and wood-frame, canvas-covered teepees, for those who don't mind packing their own bedrolls, form the "village" around the hot springs below the main lodge. Kah-Nee-Ta also has a water slide, kayak rentals, and maps to nearby hiking trails. ⊠ *6823 Hwy. 8, 11 mi north of Warm Springs, Hwy. 3 north of U.S. 26, follow signs, 97761* ☎ *541/553–6123 or 800/831–0100* 🖷 *541/553–6119* 🌐 *www.kahnee-taresort.com* ↪ *139 rooms, 21 tepees* ⚲ *2 restaurants, 2 pools, 18-hole golf course, tennis court, gym, hot tub, sauna, fishing, mountain bikes, hiking, horseback riding, bar, casino, convention center* ▤ *AE, D, DC, MC, V.*

¢ ✕**Deschutes Crossing.** Even if you're just passing through, this classic diner on the banks of the verdant Deschutes makes a worthy stop. Breakfast, served all day, includes basic eggs, hash browns, and toast configurations, along with pork chops, steak and eggs, and the heart-stopping Cowboy Breakfast of ground beef, eggs, hash browns, and toast. Check out the vintage photos as you consume. ⊠ *Hwy. 26 at Deschutes River* ☎ *541/553–1300* ▤ *MC, V.*

Sports & the Outdoors

Kah-Nee-Ta Resort makes a convenient base for different kinds of outdoor recreation in the dazzling surrounding desert. The resort's front desk provides free maps of nearby hiking trails. You can rent a kayak for an expedition on the Warm Springs River or book a guided horseback ride.

If you plan to camp on the Warm Springs reservation or fish stretches of the Deschutes or Warm Springs River within its borders, be sure your **tribal permits** (⊠ 1233 Veterans St., 97761 ☎ 541/553–3333 🖷 541/553–1924) are in order. You can buy permits at some area sporting-goods stores, even off the reservation, or inquire with the tribal government. Reservation officials can also fill you in on what exactly non-members are allowed to do within the tribes' sovereign territory, and it makes sense to check in with them, whatever your plans may be.

Madras

❷ *120 mi southeast of Portland on U.S. 26.*

Madras, a hard-scrabble community of about 5,000 just outside the Warm Springs Reservation's border, is the seat of Jefferson County. This crossroads town at the junction of Highways 26 and 97 has a "tri-cultural" population of Hispanics, Native Americans, and Anglos; thriving Mexican groceries, restaurants, and bakeries add splashes of color to its gritty streets. Though there's not much doing in town, in recent years Madras has become a popular launchpad for outdoors adventure. Fly-fishing and rafting on the Deschutes River attract river rats, while geology enthusiasts are drawn to the area's abundance of thunder eggs—egg-shape rocks with crystalline agate interiors. Nearby Cove Palisades, a well-maintained state park flanking the dramatic canyon banks of Lake Billy Chinook, lures about 500,000 boaters, anglers, hikers, and sightseers annually.

In the former city hall built in 1917, the tiny **Jefferson County Museum** has pioneer artifacts, with an emphasis on agricultural tools and memorabilia. ⊠ *34 S.E. D St., 97741* ☎ *541/475–3808* ⊡ *Free* ⊗ *June–Sept., Tues.–Fri. 1–5.*

Rent boats or fish at **Lake Simtustus RV Park,** 11 mi west of Madras, or swim, picnic, or camp here; it's quieter and less trafficked than Cove Palisades State Park. The park is open year-round, but fishing season

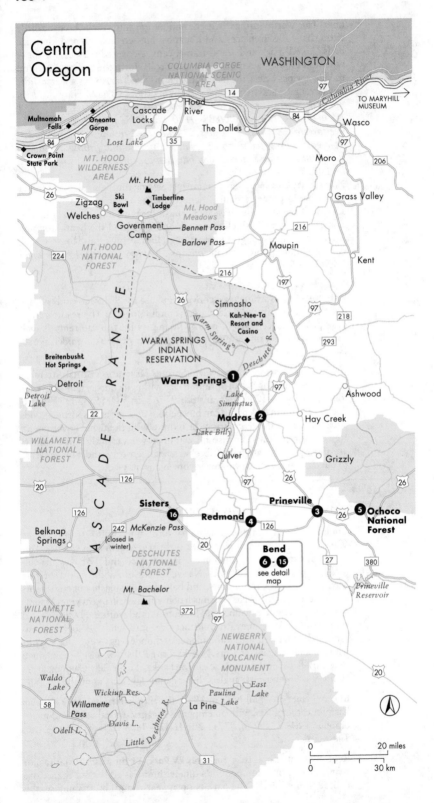

Central
Oregon

runs only from mid-April through October. ⊠ *2750 N.W. Pelton Dam Rd., 97741* ☎ *541/475–1085.*

need a break? Quick caffeine jolts, scoops of homemade hard ice cream, and pastries are plentiful at **Madras Coffee Station** (⊠ 118 S.W. 5th St. ☎ 541/475–6044), a small shop near the edge of downtown Madras.

Fifteen miles north of Madras, **Richardson's Recreational Ranch** has the largest concentration of thunder eggs in North America. You can also hunt for agates here. ⊠ *Off U.S. 97 N* ☎ *541/475–2680* 🎫 *Free* ☉ *Store daily 7–5; must arrive by 3 PM to dig; diggings dependent on weather, call for information.*

FodorsChoice ★ The Deschutes, Metolius, and Crooked rivers combine to form Lake Billy Chinook, a glittering stretch of water snaking through the **Cove Palisades State Park,** a mini–Grand Canyon of red-rock cliffs and gorges 14 mi west of Madras. On a clear day, a column of snow-capped Cascades peaks lines the horizon during the drive from town. The Crooked River Day Use Area is the most immediately accessible part of the park, a great place to cast a line into the water, launch a boat, or raid your picnic basket. In addition to 10 mi of hiking trails, a store, restaurant, and full-service marina, Cove Palisades has a driving loop around its craggy rim. A full-service campground has 87 full hookups, 91 electrical and 94 tent sites, houseboats, and cabins. ⊠ *Old Culver Hwy.* ☎ *541/546–3412 or 800/ 551–6949* ⊕ *www.prd.state.or.us* 🎫 *Day use $3 per vehicle* ☉ *Daily.*

Where to Stay & Eat

¢–$ ✕ **The Black Bear Diner.** Hordes of locals gather to wolf down this attractive family-style café's all-American burgers, sandwiches, and gargantuan Hungry Bear breakfasts. Western-theme knickknacks and whimsical menus printed to look like old newspapers enliven standard family restaurant surroundings. ⊠ *237 S.W. 4th St.* ☎ *541/475–6632* ▭ *AE, D, MC, V.*

¢–$ 🏨 **Madras Hotel/Motel.** A very Old West–looking establishment, the Madras includes both hotel rooms in a 1911 building and more modern, motel-style wings. Every room is different; some have a historical theme appropriate to the main building's vintage look. The hotel's convenient location, just off the highway and two blocks from the heart of downtown, puts it within easy walking distance of most shops and restaurants. ⊠ *171 S.W. C St., at 4th St.* ☎ *877/475–2345* 🛏 *40 rooms* ▭ *AE, D, MC, V.*

Prineville

❸ *52 mi east of Sisters on Hwy. 126, 35 mi northeast of Bend on Hwy. 126 and U.S. 97.*

Prineville is the oldest town in central Oregon and the only incorporated city in Crook County. Surrounded by verdant ranch lands and the purplish hills of the Ochoco National Forest, Prineville will likely interest you chiefly as a jumping-off point for some of the region's more secluded outdoor adventures. The area attracts thousands of anglers, boaters, sightseers, and rock hounds to its nearby streams, reservoirs, and mountains. Rimrocks nearly encircle Prineville, and geology nuts dig for free agates, limb casts, jasper, and thunder eggs on mining claims provided by the local chamber of commerce.

The town itself is dominated by a tire-distribution company owned by local magnate Les Schwab. The dusty streets of the state's unofficial "cowboy capital" have seen woolier days—the city grew up around a disreputable saloon, and range wars between cattlemen and sheep men claimed casualties among all involved species a century ago.

A tough little stone building (it was a bank once, and banks out here needed to be tough) is the site of the museum of the Crook County Historical Society, the **Bowman Museum.** The 1911 edifice is now on the National Register of Historic Places. Prominent are pioneer artifacts—chiefly agricultural implements and deadly weapons—that defined early Prineville. ⊠ *246 N. Main St.* ☎ *541/447–3715* ☒ *Free* ☉ *Mar.–Dec., weekdays 10–5, Sat. 11–4.*

Three stolid stories of gray stone anchor the **Crook County Courthouse.** A perpetual memorial flame maintained by the local American Legion burns in front of this stately 1909 building. ⊠ *300 N. 3rd St.* ☎ *541/ 447–6553.*

Mountain streams flow out of the Ochoco Mountains and join together to create the Crooked River, which is dammed near Prineville. Bowman Dam on the river forms **Prineville Reservoir State Park.** Recreational activities include boating, swimming, fishing, and hiking. A campground has 22 full hookups, 23 electrical and 25 tent sites, and 3 cabins. ⊠ *Juniper Canyon Rd.* ☎ *541/447–4363 or 800/452–5687* ⊕ *www.prd.state. or.us* ☒ *Day use $3 per vehicle* ☉ *Daily.*

About ½ mi west of Prineville, **Ochoco Viewpoint** is a scenic overlook that commands a sweeping view of the city and the hills, ridges and buttes beyond. ⊠ *½ mi west of Prineville on U.S. Hwy. 126* ☒ *Free* ☉ *Daily.*

Where to Stay & Eat

$–$$$ ✕ **Crooked River Railroad Company Dinner Train.** Dine aboard this excursion train as it winds through the rimrock-lined Crooked River valley between Redmond and Prineville. The ride and show are the draw here; the food is nothing special. Murder mysteries are played out on Saturday nights year-round and on Friday nights from June to September, while a simulated Jesse James train robbery keeps the Sunday champagne brunch hopping with live entertainment. Call for reservations and departure times. ⊠ *525 S.W. 6th St., Redmond* ☎ *541/548–8630* ▤ *AE, D, MC, V.*

¢ ▥ **Rustler's Inn.** From the old-style covered walkways to the large, antiques-furnished rooms, this motel is Old West all the way. Each room is decorated differently—if you call in advance, the managers will attempt to match your room furnishings to your personality. Some rooms have kitchenettes. The Rustler's allows pets to stay for a onetime $10 fee. ⊠ *960 W. 3rd St. (U.S. 26), 97754* ☎ *541/447–4185* ⊕ *www. majestyhotels.com/rustlers_inn.html* ☞ *20 rooms* ☖ *Some kitchenettes, some pets allowed (fee)* ▤ *AE, D, DC, MC, V.*

Redmond

❹ *40 mi east of Sisters on Hwy. 126, 15 mi northeast of Bend on U.S. 97.*

Redmond sits at the western end of Oregon's High Desert, 4 mi from the Deschutes River and within minutes of several lakes. As with Deschutes County, Redmond has experienced some of the most rapid growth in the state during the past 10 years, largely owing to a dry and mild climate and year-round downhill and cross-country skiing, fishing, hiking, mountain biking, and rock hounding. Still, this is no gentrified resort town à la Bend, as a stroll through downtown will attest. Smith Rock State Park, north of Redmond, attracts aggro rock climbers from around the world to hundreds of climbing routes and hiking trails. Wildlife is abundant in the park, which is a nesting area for birds of prey.

Picnicking and fishing are popular at **Cline Falls State Park,** a rest area commanding scenic views on the Deschutes River 5 mi west of Redmond. ⊠ *Rte. 126* ☎ *800/551–6949* ⊕ *www.prd.state.or.us* ☜ *Free* ☉ *Daily.*

During trout season, **Firemen's Pond** is jumping with fish. Only children and adults with disabilities are permitted to fish here. ⊠ *Lake Rd. and Sisters Ave.* ☎ *541/548–6068* ☜ *Free* ☉ *Daily.*

need a break? Hiding just off the lobby of the New Redmond Hotel, **Redmond Coffee Works** (⊠ 521 S. 6th St. ☎ 541/548–5964) is a pocket-size espresso bar with light fare. After cooling your heels here, take a peek at the lobby fixtures.

A local farmer created the 4-acre **Petersen's Rock Gardens** near Bend. All of the petrified wood, agate, jasper, lava, and obsidian came from within an 85-mi radius of the garden and was used to make miniature buildings and bridges, terraces and towers. Among the structures are a micro–Statue of Liberty and five little castles up to 6 feet tall. The attraction includes a small museum and picnic tables. ⊠ *7930 S.W. 77th St., 97756* ☎ *541/382–5574* ☜ *$3, suggested* ☉ *Daily 9–5.*

★ A small, scenic viewpoint, **Peter Skene Ogden Wayside** is at the top of a dizzyingly severe 300-foot-deep river canyon 10 mi north of Redmond. ⊠ *U.S. 97 N* ☎ *541/548–7501* ☜ *Free* ☉ *Daily.*

Fodor'sChoice ★ Eight miles north of Redmond, **Smith Rock State Park** is world-famous for rock climbing. You might spot golden eagles, prairie falcons, mule deer, river otters, and beavers. Due to the environmental sensitivity of the region, the animal leash law is strongly enforced. ⊠ *Off U.S. 97* ☎ *541/548–7501 or 800/551–6949* ⊕ *www.prd.state.or.us* ☜ *Day use $3 per vehicle* ☉ *Daily.*

Where to Stay & Eat

$ ✕ **Sully's Italian Restaurant.** The historic New Redmond Hotel building is also the site of this home-style Italian restaurant. Tuck into such classics as spaghetti and meatballs, manicotti, and eggplant Parmesan. ⊠ *521 S.W. 6th St.* ☎ *541/548–5483* ▭ *MC, V* ☉ *No lunch.*

$$–$$$ ▦ **Eagle Crest Resort.** Eagle Crest is 5 mi west of Redmond, above the canyon of the Deschutes River. In this high desert area, the grounds are covered with juniper and sagebrush. The rooms are in a single building on the landscaped grounds, and some of the suites have gas fireplaces. The resort is on nearly 1,700 acres. There are 10 mi of bike trails and a 2-mi hiking trail where you can fish in the river. ⊠ *1522 Cline Falls Hwy., 97756* ☎ *541/923–2453 or 800/682–4786* 🖷 *541/923–1720* ⊕ *www.eagle-crest.com* ⇦ *100 rooms, 45 suites, 75 town houses* ⚹ *Dining room, picnic area, some kitchenettes, some microwaves, cable TV, 4 18-hole golf courses, putting green, driving range, tennis court, pool, gym, hair salon, hot tub, hiking, horseback riding, bicycles, cross-country skiing, downhill skiing, bar, children's programs (ages 3–12), playground, laundry facilities, business services, airport shuttle* ▭ *AE, DC, MC, V.*

Ochoco National Forest

❺ *25 mi east of Prineville off U.S. 26.*

East of the flat, juniper-dotted countryside around Prineville the landscape changes to forested ridges covered with tall ponderosa pines and Douglas firs. Sheltered by the diminutive Ochoco Mountains and with only about a foot of rain each year, the **Ochoco National Forest,** established in 1906 by President Theodore Roosevelt, manages to lay a blanket of green across the dry, high desert of central Oregon. This arid landscape—marked by deep canyons, towering volcanic plugs, and sharp ridges—goes largely unnoticed except for the annual influx of hunters during the fall. The Ochoco, part of the old Blue Mountain Forest Reserve, is a great place for camping, hiking, biking, and fishing in relative solitude. In its three wilderness areas—Mill Creek, Bridge Creek, and Black Canyon—it's possible to see elk, wild horses, eagles, and even cougars. The **Ochoco Ranger Station** (✉ County Rd. 23 ☎ 541/416–6645) has trail maps and other information. It's open daily 7–4:30. ✉ *Ochoco National Forest Headquarters/Prineville Ranger Station, 3160 N.E. 3rd St. (U.S. 26)* ☎ *541/416–6500* ☉ *Forest year-round, some sections closed during bad weather, ranger station weekdays 7:30–4:30.*

A 43-mi scenic route, **Big Summit Prairie Loop** begins at the Ochoco Ranger Station and winds past Lookout Mountain, Round Mountain, Walton Lake, and Big Summit Prairie. The prairie abounds with trout-filled creeks and has one of the finest stands of ponderosa pines in the state; wild mustangs roam the area. The prairie can be glorious between late May and June, when wildflowers with evocative names like mules ear, wyethia, biscuit root, and yellow bells burst into bloom. ⊹ *Forest Service Rd. 22 east to Forest Service Rd. 30 (which turns into Forest Service Rd. 3010) south, to Forest Service Rd. 42 heading west, which loops back to Forest Service Rd. 22.*

Sports & the Outdoors

HIKING Pick up maps at the Prineville or Ochoco ranger station for the trails through the 5,400-acre **Bridge Creek Wilderness** and the demanding **Black Canyon Trail** (24 mi round-trip) in the Black Canyon Wilderness. The 1½-mi **Ponderosa Loop Trail** follows an old logging road through ponderosa pines growing on hills. In early summer, wildflowers take over the open meadows. The trailhead begins at Bandit Springs Rest Area, 22 mi east of Prineville on U.S. 26. A 2½-mi, one-way trail winds through old-growth forest and mountain meadows to **Steins Pillar,** a giant lava column with panoramic views; be prepared for a workout on the trail's poorly maintained second half, and allow at least three hours for the hike. To get to the trailhead drive east 9 mi from Prineville on U.S. 26, head north (to the left) for 6½ mi on Mill Creek Road (also signed as Forest Service Road 33), and head east (to the right) on Forest Service Road 500.

SKIING Two loops for cross-country skiers start at Bandit Springs Rest Area, 29 mi east of Prineville on U.S. 26. One loop is designed for beginners and the other for intermediate to advanced skiers. Both traverse the area near the Ochoco Divide and have great views. Ochoco National Forest headquarters has a handout on skiing trails and can provide the required Sno-Park permits, which are also available from the **Department of Motor Vehicles** (✉ Ochoco Plaza, 1595 E. 3rd St., Suite A-3, Prineville ☎ 541/ 447–7855).

Bend

⑥–⑮ *58 mi south of Warm Springs, U.S. 26 to U.S. 97, 160 mi from Portland, east and south on U.S. 26 and south on U.S. 97*

Bend, Oregon's largest city east of the Cascades, is a modern-day boom-town; in the '90s, it was the state's fastest-growing city, spurting to more than 55,000 residents (at last count) in the city, plus more in the sprawl outside its limits. The fuel for this bonanza isn't oil, gold, or timber—instead, Bend swells on the strength of its enviable climate, proximity to skiing, and its growing reputation as a playground and escape. Sadly, the growth has also propelled a soulless spread of chain stores and fast-food slingers along U.S. 20 outside of town, camouflaging Bend's attractiveness. On the other hand, stylish, highly walkable downtown Bend retains a small-city charm.

Nearby Mt. Bachelor, though hardly a giant among the Cascades at about 9,000 feet, gets snow before and keeps it after most other mountains by virtue of its location. Inland air collides with the Pacific's damp influence, creating skiing conditions immortalized in songs by local rock bands, raves in the ski press, and by excellent resort facilities. Like all other great ski hills, "the Batch" is as much a way of life as recreation for some; a strong ski-bum ethic injects Bend with a dose of hormonal postcollegiate buzz.

Alongside this outdoorsy counterculture, though, Bend has boutique shopping and upscale dining and lodging on par with anything else in the state, if not beyond. In recent years, despite Oregon's overall economic doldrums, downtown Bend has undergone a serious make-over, with flashy new restaurants and bars taking over one street corner after another.

<table>
<tr><td>

a good
tour

</td><td>

Numbers in the text correspond to numbers in the margin and on the Bend map.

</td></tr>
</table>

Start out by strolling through **Drake Park** ❻, on the banks of the Deschutes and the Mirror Pond. Then walk a few blocks east through the city's most historic residential neighborhood to the beautiful, airy 1998 **Bend Public Library** ❽. Just another block or so east, you'll find the **Deschutes Historical Museum** ❾; browse there to get a sense of Bend's history. A block north on Bond Street, you'll find yourself in the bustling thick of **downtown Bend** ❼, where jet-set sophistication rubs up against small-town charm. Once you've explored downtown, hop in your vehicle and head west out of town on **Century Drive** ❿, a.k.a. U.S. 46. The scenic 100-mi loop leads to **Mt. Bachelor** ⓫. Once the Century loop brings you back to town, take Highway 97 3½ mi south of town to check out the **High Desert Museum** ⓬. The same road takes you to **Newberry National Volcanic Monument** ⓮, from which you can take in **Lava Butte** ⓭. Finally, if covering all this ground makes you yearn for a wider perspective on things, swing east from Bend on Highway 20 for the **Pine Mountain Observatory** ⓯, where you can take in the cosmos.

TIMING   The tour outlined here is definitely an all-day affair—completing the Century Drive loop alone, for example, should take about two hours, not counting stops at scenic points along the way. You may want to split this itinerary into two days to allow more leisurely appreciation of the High Desert Museum and other linger-worthy sights. Keep in mind that challenging winter driving conditions between October and May might prolong this or any itinerary in and around Bend.

What to See

❽ **Bend Public Library.** You may feel like you're in Finland when you ascend this 1998 building's main staircase—Scandinavian-style blond wood and sharp modernist architectural lines abound, and light pours through a translucent wall by sculptor Maya Radoczy. Upstairs, the library's fine collection, national and international periodicals, and dozens of public Internet terminals bask in a light-flooded, vaulted space. ⊠ *601 N.W. Wall St.* ☎ *541/388–6679* ⊕ *www.dpls.lib.or.us* ☽ *Mon.–Thurs. 10–8, Fri. 10–6, Sat. 10–5, Sun. 1–5.*

❿ **Century Drive.** For 100 mi, this forest-highway loop beginning and ending in Bend meanders among dozens of high mountain lakes good for

Bend Public
Library **8**

Century
Drive **10**

Deschutes
Historical
Museum **9**

Downtown
Bend **7**

Drake Park **6**

High Desert
Museum **12**

Lava Butte and
Lava River
Cave **13**

Mt. Bachelor
Ski Area **11**

Newberry
National Volcanic
Monument . . . **14**

Pine Mountain
Observatory . . **15**

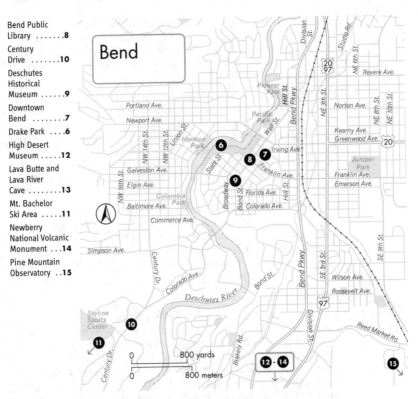

fishing, hiking, waterskiing, and camping. To find it take Highway 46 for the first two-thirds of the trip, and then take Highway 97 at LaPine to return to Bend.

Deschutes Historical Museum. A striking 1914 building constructed from locally quarried volcanic tuff has Indian artifacts, historical photos of the region, and a pioneer schoolroom. ✉ *129 N.W. Idaho, 97701* ☎ *541/389–1813* 🖾 *Free* ☉ *Tues.–Sat. 10–4:30.*

Deschutes National Forest. This 1.6-million-acre forest has 20 peaks higher than 7,000 feet, including three of Oregon's five highest mountains, more than 150 lakes, and 500 mi of streams. A pass is required for all day and overnight use of the trailhead facilities in 13 national forests in Oregon and Washington. ✉ *Cascades Lakes Hwy.* ☎ *541/388–2715* 🖶 *541/383–5531* ⊕ *www.fs.fed.us/r6/deschutes* 🖾 *Park pass required* ☉ *Daily.*

★ **Downtown Bend.** Bend's heart is an area of about six blocks, centered on Wall and Bond streets. Here you'll find boutique shops, fine restaurants, and lively nightlife establishments, as well as a few old-time pharmacies, taverns, and hardware stores keeping it real. ⊕ *www. downtownbend.com.*

Drake Park. Bend's first city park is also its most prominent and lovely. Eleven acres of exactly manicured greensward and trees snake along the banks of the Deschutes just a few blocks south of downtown. Running and walking trails lead to foot bridges to the opposite bank and decorous early-century neighborhoods. ✉ *Riverside Dr., south of downtown.*

need a break? A sleekly designed coffee shop with modernist blond-wood furnishings, **Bellatazza** (⊠ 869 N.W. Wall St., Suite 101 ☎ 541/318–0606) serves morning jolts and pastries on Bend's main street. Wireless Internet access is free.

⑫ High Desert Museum. The High Desert—embracing Idaho, southwest Montana, Nevada and Washington, as well as Oregon—has a rich history, and it's told from several perspectives here. Intricately crafted walk-through dioramas include a stone-age Indian campsite, a pioneer wagon camp, a mine (go ahead and ring the bell in the mine shaft), and part of an Old West town (complete with a brothel). Individual stores are also meticulously re-created; walk into a telegraph office and see the equipment used to send a wire, or browse in a general store where the sounds of mah-jongg playing—Chinese-speaking men and clacking tiles—emanate from a back room. Many of the displays capture the sights and even the smells of various historical periods. The Spirit of the West exhibit shows what life was like in different states at different times of day, including a look at an Oregon Trail campsite. There are outstanding exhibits on local Native American cultures as well. A bonus is that this museum is also a zoo: a "Desertarium" showcases smaller desert animals, including lizards and bats, and in an outdoor section, the spotlight is on birds of prey, including eagles, turkey vultures, and owls. Museum staff handle some of these raptors during demonstrations and there are touch exhibits where you can feel the wings and talons of various birds. Also wandering the grounds are fat porcupines, river otters, and turtles. ⊠ 59800 S. Hwy. 97, 3½ mi south of Bend ☎ 541/382–4754 ⊕ www.highdesert.org ☎ $8.50 ☉ Daily 9–5.

⑬ Lava Butte and Lava River Cave. Lava River Cave is a 1-mi-long lava tube, 10 mi south of Bend. The Lava Butte area has several large basalt lava flows as well as the 500-foot Lava Butte cinder cone. Enter by the visitor center. ⊠ 58201 S. U.S. 97, 97707 ☎ 541/593–2421 ☎ $5 per vehicle ☉ May–Sept., daily 9–5.

⑪ Mt. Bachelor Ski Area. There are five ski lodges with restaurants and bars at this ski resort 22 mi from Bend. The 9,000-foot mountain has a base at about 5,600 feet and a vertical drop of about 3,365 feet. There are lots of cross-country trails and 70 downhill runs. ⊠ Cascade Lakes Hwy. ☎ 541/382–2442 or 800/829–2442 ⊕ www.mtbachelor.com ☉ Nov.–July, daily 8–4.

⑭ Newberry National Volcanic Monument. The last time Newberry Volcano blew its top was about 13 centuries ago. Paulina Peak, up an unpaved road at the south end of the national monument, has the best view into the crater and its two lakes (Paulina and East). Lava Butte and Lava River Cave are at the north end of the monument near the visitor center. ⊠ Visitor center: U.S. 97, 10 mi south of Bend ☎ 541/383–5300 ☎ $5 per vehicle ☉ Memorial Day–Labor Day, daily 9:30–5; Labor Day–Memorial Day, Wed.–Sun. 9:30–5.

⑮ Pine Mountain Observatory. Three reflecting telescopes, with 15-inch-, 24-inch-, and 32-inch-diameter mirrors, each in its own domed building, monitor the universe from atop 6,500-foot Pine Mountain. Take a peek, 26 mi east of Bend. ⊠ U.S. 20, near Millican ☎ 541/382–8331 ⊕ www.pmo-sun.uoregon.edu ☎ $3 donation requested ☉ May–Sept., Fri. and Sat. evenings.

Where to Stay & Eat

$$-$$$ × **Cork.** This romantic, candlelight-washed restaurant and wine bar has
Fodor'sChoice the feel of a much older establishment, the sort of place that's hosted
★ countless prom dates, anniversary dinners, and convivial evening-long
conversations over wine. No doubt it will. The menu consists of a tra-
dition-minded mix of comforting standards—filet mignon, rack of pork,
cioppino—awakened with subtle, almost Latin bursts of flair. A huge
wine list complements the kitchen's inventive—but never gimmicky–verve.
☒ *150 N.W. Oregon Ave.* ☎ *541/383–6881* ⌾ *Reservations essential*
⊟ *MC, V.*

$$-$$$ × **Merenda.** Chef Jody Denton left San Francisco's go-go restaurant world
Fodor'sChoice to open this swaggering, big-city place. Her vivacious cooking draws
★ heavily on French and Italian influences, with a reliance on seasonal and
regional ingredients. You can eat tapas-style, assembling a meal from
the appetizer list; order a pizza or some pasta; or simply go for a small
gang of raw oysters, depending on your mood and pocketbook. An appetizer of roasted halibut cheeks aswim in a comforting, buttery sherry-
spiked broth is a must-try. A salad of apple, endive, walnuts, and
pungent Gorgonzola chunks is vibrant and fresh. Entrées, from meaty
spare ribs to Tuscan meat loaf, tend to be hearty. Merenda claims to
have the Northwest's longest list of wines by the glass. ☒ *900 N.W. Wall
St.* ☎ *541/330–2304* ⌾ *Reservations essential* ⊟ *AE, D, DC, MC, V.*

¢–$ × **Alpenglow Café.** Don't walk by this nondescript breakfast and lunch
spot, and if you do, locals will likely point you back to it. The mandate
for freshness dictates that no can openers are permitted in the kitchen,
and the yield is such delightfully hearty dishes as an overstuffed breakfast burrito, Eggs Benedict, and buttermilk pancakes. The good, strong
coffee and fresh-squeezed orange juice are worthy companions to any
meal. Order breakfast until closing (2 [am]) or pick from tasty sandwiches and burgers. ☒ *1040 N.W. Bond St.* ☎ *541/383–7676* ⊟ *MC,
V* ⊙ *No dinner.*

¢–$ × **Deschutes Brewery & Public House.** Try the admirable Black Butte
Porter, a local ale, at this brewpub which serves upscale Pacific Northwest cuisine. Gourmet burgers and sandwiches, such as smoked salmon
and a brewery-cured pastrami Reuben, dominate the menu. Vegetari-
ans can choose the smoked vegetable sandwich or the vegetarian black
bean chili. It's almost always bustling, so keep in mind that you might
have to while away a short wait over a pint. Dinner specials vary daily
(check the blackboard). Portions are large. ☒ *1044 N.W. Bond St., Downtown Bend* ☎ *541/382–9242* ⌾ *Reservations not accepted* ⊟ *MC, V.*

★ **$$$$** ▥ **Pine Ridge Inn.** Spacious and romantic suites with dark wood accents
and modern furnishings provide a nice respite after a day of exploring
Bend. Request a suite that has both a Jacuzzi tub (seven rooms do) and
an outdoor deck, a pleasure for taking in deliciously icy air day or night
as well as a view of the Deschutes River. If you're around in the afternoons, there's a wine tasting reception in the lobby, and mornings bring
hot entrées and cereals, included in the rate. The hotel has special packages that cater to couples and spa lovers as well as anglers, golfers, and
skiers. ☒ *1200 S.W. Century Dr., 97701* ☎ *541/389–6137 or 800/
600–4095* ⎙ *541/385–5669* ⊕ *www.pineridgeinn.com* ⇴ *20 rooms*
⌂ *In-room data ports, cable TV, in-room VCRs, some in-room hot tubs*
⊟ *AE, D, DC, MC, V* ⦿| *BP.*

$$$$ ▥ **Sunriver Resort.** When people refer to Bend as an "escape," this place
Fodor'sChoice is what they're talking about. Sunriver, one of Oregon's premier outdoor
★ resort destinations, provides a slew of facilities convenient to skiing at
Mt. Bachelor; Class IV white-water rafting on the Deschutes River (which
flows right through the complex); and high-desert hiking and mountain
biking. Horseback-riding trails, golf courses, and extensive walking trails

surround the resort. A former army base, this self-contained community has stores, restaurants, contemporary homes, condominiums, and even a private airstrip—all in a pine-scented desert landscape. You can rent condos, hotel rooms, or houses; shops rent a host of outdoorsy paraphernalia. *Box 3609, Sunriver 97707* ✛ *West of U.S. 97, 15 mi south of Bend* ☎ *541/593–1000 or 800/547–3922* ⊜ *541/593–5458* ⊕ *www.sunriver-resort.com* ⊠ *510 units* ⚬ *6 restaurants, 3 18-hole golf courses, 28 tennis courts, 2 pools, hot tub, sauna, boating, fishing, bicycles, horseback riding; no smoking* ☰ *AE, D, DC, MC, V.*

$–$$$$ 🏨 **Inn of the Seventh Mountain.** This resort in the Deschutes National Forest has hosted year-round outdoor activities and relaxation for 25 years. It's on the banks of the Deschutes River, so white-water rafting and fishing are right at your doorstep in summer. On the property are a host of recreational facilities, including a 65-foot water slide, canoeing, and an outdoor ice-skating rink. Five golf courses are within 15 minutes, and Mt. Bachelor, with great downhill skiing, is only 14 mi away. The inn is child-friendly: Kids Camp 7 has activities for children ages 4 to 11. Accommodations include standard bedrooms with a queen-size bed, deluxe bedrooms with an additional Murphy bed and private deck, and studios with fireplaces and full kitchens. There are also suites and lofts with extra amenities. ⊠ *18575 S.W. Century Dr., Deschutes National Forest, Bend 97702* ☎ *800/452–6810* ⊜ *541/382–3517* ⊕ *www.7thmtn. com* ⊠ *300 rooms* ⚬ *3 restaurants, grocery, 4 tennis courts, 2 pools, hot tub, fishing, horseback riding, ice-skating, bar, children's programs (ages 4–11), meeting rooms* ☰ *AE, D, DC, MC, V.*

$–$$$
Fodor'sChoice
★
🏨 **Lara House Bed & Breakfast Inn.** On a lot overlooking Drake Park and Mirror Pond, this huge, restored 1910 Craftsman home, once a boarding house, attracts vacationing "intuitive counselors" fresh from Sedona. The rooms, all on the second floor, have seating areas and private bathrooms, and the public areas are sunny and inviting. Breakfast is included. ⊠ *640 N.W. Congress St., west 1 mi on Franklin St. from U.S. 97, Bend Historical District, 97701* ☎⊜ *541/388–4064* ☎ *800/766–4064* ⊕ *www. larahouse.com* ⊠ *6 rooms* ⚬ *Outdoor hot tub; no smoking* ☰ *D, MC, V* ⦿ *BP.*

★ ¢–$$ 🏨 **Bend Riverside Motel.** Comfort and efficiency are the bywords at this nicely landscaped property only four blocks from downtown and within walking distance of shops and restaurants, including Deschutes Brewery & Public House. Every room has a balcony overlooking Pioneer Park along the river. ⊠ *1565 N.W. Hill St., 97701* ☎ *541/388–4000 or 800/ 284–2363* ⊜ *541/389–2363* ✉ *bendrive@teleport.com* ⊠ *200 rooms* ⚬ *Some kitchenettes, some microwaves, some refrigerators, cable TV, tennis court, indoor-outdoor pool, outdoor hot tub, laundry facilities, laundry service, business services* ☰ *AE, D, DC, MC, V.*

Nightlife & the Arts

Bend's take on a bumping urban-modern cocktail haven, **Astrolounge** (⊠ 163 N.W. Minnesota Ave. ☎ 541/389–2025) comes complete with matte-black-and-chrome industrial furnishings, a loft-style layout, and pounding hip-hop sound track. On weekend nights, Astrolounge is packed with the young, loud, and on-the-make. The bar connects to a bistro sharing the Space Age motif. The cavernous **Aviemore Arms** (⊠ 1020 N.W. Wall St. ☎ 541/385–8898) pub doesn't offer much in the way of across-the-pond authenticity. It does, however, have cheap pints of Guinness ($3.50) and very friendly, competent service. Competition around the two dart boards can be fierce, while a rockin' jukebox in the rear of the sprawling space is so loud, you might think they've booked a cover band for the evening. If the cultural shift under way in Bend hasn't sunk in yet, visit **Barcelona** (⊠ 920 N.W. Bond St.

☎ 541/383–8000), a slick tapas bar in the airy St. Claire's Place commercial development. With its glowing-red glass-top bar, jet-black walls, retro-Euro art, and foot-long list of specialty cocktails, Barcelona wouldn't be out of place in any major metropolitan area. This being Bend, however, you get gratitude in place of attitude from the black-clad waitstaff. Jazz duos and trios squeeze into a corner of this tiny rectangular space three or four nights a week. Oregon may be synonymous with microbrew ale and pinot noir, but until **Bendistillery Sampling Room and Martini Bar** (✉ 850 N.W. Brooks St. ☎ 541/388–6868) came along in 1995, hard stuff produced in-state usually ended up on the bottom shelves of low-end taverns. In a few short years, Bendistillery changed that, handcrafting small batches of spirits flavored with local herbs. Bend sits in the middle of one of the world's great juniper forests, so the gin is a particular treat. This slick little tasting room stirs up bracing martinis and highballs incorporating Bendistillery's products, making a perfect barcrawl kickoff or classy nightcap. Named for the Prineville tire tycoon, **Les Schwab Amphitheater** (✉ 344 S.W. Shevlin-Hixon Dr. ☎ 541/322–0168), an open-air venue in the Old Mill District, brings national music tours to Bend.

Sports & the Outdoors

BICYCLING **U.S. 97** north to the Crooked River gorge and Smith Rock provides bikers with memorable scenery and a good workout. **Sunriver** has 26 mi of paved bike paths.

CANOEING If you haven't taken a moment lately to listen to the silence of nature, a nighttime canoe ride with **Wanderlust Tours** (⌂ 143 S.W. Cleveland Ave. ☎ 541/389–8359 or 800/962–2862) is a palliative for the system and the soul. Owners Dave and Aleta Nissen, recognized for their dedication to ecotourism, lead trips from June to October on several of Central Oregon's smooth lakes, and depending on the season, also run other tours that include forest and volcano hikes, cave treks, and snowshoeing trips. Rates for the moonlight canoe rides are $50 per person and range from $30–$40 for most of the other trips.

SKIING Many Nordic trails—more than 165 mi of them—wind through the **Deschutes National Forest** (☎ 541/383–5300). Call for information about conditions.

Mount Bachelor Resort (✉ 22 mi southwest of Bend off U.S. 97 ☎ 541/382–7888 or 800/829–2442), the Northwest's largest facility, is one of the best in the United States—60% of the downhill runs are rated expert. One of the 11 lifts takes skiers all the way to the mountain's 9,065-foot summit. The vertical drop is 3,265 feet; the longest of the 70 runs is 2 mi. Facilities and services include equipment rental and repair, a ski school, ski shop, Nordic skiing, weekly races, and day care; you can enjoy restaurants, bars, and six lodges. The 36 mi of trails at the **Mount Bachelor Nordic Center,** most of them near the base of the mountain, are by and large intermediate.

Shopping

A superb and eminently civilized bookshop, **Antiquarian of Bend** (✉ 1002 N.W. Bond St. ☎ 541/322–9788) specializes in rarities and first editions, with a particular emphasis on regional history. Check out the envelope hand-addressed by George Washington, under glass behind the front desk. Kitschy keepsakes and an eclectic selection of gifts, from African-theme coffee mugs to windsocks, crowd the riotous little **Azila Nora** (✉ 1002 N.W. Wall St. ☎ 541/389–6552). A fun, flashy little shop, **Hot Box Betty** (✉ 740 N.W. Wall St. ☎ 541/383–0050) has high fashion for women. Kenneth Cole and Diane Von Furstenburg, among others, are on the racks, and old refrigerator doors guard the fitting rooms. An enthusiastic husband-and-wife team presides over **Millette's Kitchen Store** (⊠ 1052 N.W. Newport Ave., Suite 103 ☎ 541/617–0312), crammed to the ceiling with fine foods. Bend was once the site of one of the world's largest sawmill operations, a sprawling industrial complex along the banks of the Deschutes. In recent years, the abandoned shells of the old factory buildings of the **Old Mill District** (⊠ 545 S.W. Powerhouse Dr. ☎ 541/312–0131) have been transformed into an attractive shopping center, known as The Shops at the Old Mill District, a project honored with national environmental awards. Bend's main concentration of national chain retailers, including Gap, Banana Republic, and Victoria's Secret, can be found here, along with a multiplex movie house and the Les Schwab Amphitheater. As of this writing, an AmeriTel Inns hotel is due to open in the district. A friendly and attentive staff sells sleek modern outdoor gear and clothing at **Pandora's Backpack** (⊠ 920 N.W. Bond St., Suite 101 ☎ 541/382–6694). Looking more like a stylish downtown development than a mini-mall, **St. Claire Place** (⊠ 920 N.W. Bond St.) has an Aveda spa and lifestyle store, antiques shops, galleries, and the sleek Barcelona jazz club.

Sisters

16 *18 mi northwest of Bend on U.S. 20.*

Sisters derived its name from a group of three Cascade peaks (Faith, Hope, and Charity) that rise to the southwest. If you enter the central Oregon high-desert area from Santiam Pass or the McKenzie River Highway, Sisters appears to be a town out of the Old West. Rustic cabins border a llama ranch on the edge of town. Western storefronts give way to galleries. A bakery occupies the former general store, and the town blacksmith's home now has a flower shop. Although its population remains under 1,000, Sisters increasingly attracts visitors as well as urban refugees who appreciate its tranquillity and charm. The Metolius River in the Riverside area near Sisters is a special find for wildflower lovers, with extensive blooms from early spring to late summer.

Three and a half miles east of Sisters, **Hinterland Ranch** has been breeding llamas and Polish Arabian horses since 1965 and has one of the largest (250) and oldest llama herds in North America. This is a working ranch where you can observe the llamas and a small number of horses. ⊠ 67750 Hwy. 20 W ✎ Box 1839, 97759 ☎ 541/549–1215 📠 541/549–5262 ⊗ Mon.–Sat. 7:30–5.

need a break? In a rustic-looking former general store, **Sisters Bakery** (⊠ 251 E. Cascade St. ☎ 541/549–0361) turns out high-quality pastries, coffee, and doughnuts.

Where to Stay & Eat

¢–$$ ✕ **Bronco Billy's.** The most popular restaurant in Sisters first opened as a hotel in 1912. Broiled steaks, barbecued chicken and ribs, and Mexican dishes form the backbone of the extensive menu. The place looks like a saloon where Old West baddies might shoot it out, but the service is friendly. Outdoor dining on a covered deck is available. ⊠ 105 W. Cascade St. ☎ 541/549–7427 ⊟ AE, MC, V.

★ ¢ ✕ **Depot Deli & Cafe.** A railroad theme prevails at this main-street deli. A miniature train circles above as the kitchen dishes out excellent, inexpensive sandwiches and burgers. Sit inside, bounded by the roughwood walls, or out back on the deck. ⊠ 250 W. Cascade St. ☎ 541/549–2572 ⚠ Reservations not accepted.

¢ ✕ **Harvest Basket.** Healthy snacks, sandwiches, and ready-to-go salads can be had at this organic grocery, which also shares the space with a fishmonger. It may well be the only place in the region for specialty health foods. There really isn't a place to sit down and eat on premises, so plan to picnic elsewhere. ✉ *110 S. Spruce St.* ☎ *541/549–0598.*

$$–$$$ ⊡ **Black Butte Ranch.** Eight miles west of Sisters, Black Butte Ranch is a resort with gorgeous mountain views and landscaping to match, with biking and hiking paths meandering for miles around golf courses, ponds, and meadows. Ample windows in the hotel style rooms, condos, and homes, or in the Restaurant at the Lodge keep you in perpetual contact with the snowcapped mountains and pine forest that envelop the property. Horseback riding, swimming, and golf are dominant sports here, and the ranch is also convenient to Smith Rock State Park, the Deschutes River, Mt. Bachelor, and the Hoodoo Ski Bowl. ✉ *13653 Hawks Beard, 97759* ☎ *541/595–6211* ⊟ *541/595–1299* ⊕ *www.blackbutteranch.com* ⇝ *126 rooms* ⚲ *2 restaurants, some kitchens, 2 18-hole golf courses, 23 tennis courts, 4 pools, gym, hot tub, massage, fishing, bicycles, horseback riding, cross-country skiing, snowmobiling, lounge* ⊟ *AE, D, DC, MC, V.*

Shopping

More than a dozen Central Oregon artists have a cozy showcase at the **High Desert Gallery** (✉ 101 West Main St. ☎ 541/549–6250), a repository of affordable contemporary art that includes precious metal jewelry, clay jewelry, oil paintings, vases, and stained glass. Sisters is the site of the lavishly stocked **Lonesome Waters Books** (✉ 221C W. Cascade Ave. ☎ 541/549–2203), one of Oregon's great independent bookstores. You can find everything from $1 paperbacks to premium first editions here.

Central Oregon A to Z

BUS TRAVEL

Greyhound services Warm Springs, Madras, Prineville, Redmond, and Bend with one bus a day via Portland. CAC Transportation, a regional carrier, likewise runs one bus a day each way between Portland and Bend, with stops in Redmond, Madras, and Warm Springs. From Bend, you can also catch buses to other Oregon transportation hubs, including Medford, Salem, and The Dalles, but schedules are sporadic.

🚌 Bus Depots **Greyhound Bend** ✉ 63076 N. Hwy. 97 ☎ 800/231-2151.
🚌 Bus Lines **CAC Transportation** ☎ 800/847-0157. **Greyhound** ☎ 800/231-2222 ⊕ www.greyhound.com.

CAR TRAVEL

U.S. 20 heads west from Idaho and east from the coastal town of Newport into central Oregon. U.S. 26 goes southeast from Portland to Prineville, where it heads northeast into the Ochoco National Forest. U.S. 97 heads north from California and south from Washington to Bend. Highway 126 travels east from Eugene to Prineville; it connects with U.S. 20 heading south (to Bend) at Sisters. Roads throughout central Oregon are well maintained and open throughout the winter season, though it's always advisable to have tire chains in the car.

Rapid population growth in the Bend area has sparked traffic problems out of scale with the city's size. If you're trying to head out of or into town on a major highway during the morning or 5 PM rush, especially on 97 between Bend and Redmond, be advised that you may hit congestion. Parking in downtown Bend is free for the first two hours; you can park for free in the historic residential neighborhood just west of downtown. Free on-street parking is plentiful in all of central Oregon's other towns and cities.

VISITOR INFORMATION

The best one-stop source for information is the Central Oregon Visitors Association, a thorough umbrella agency serving the entire area. ▣ Tourist Information **Bend Chamber of Commerce** ⊠ 777 N.W. Wall St. Bend 97701 ☎ 541/382-3221 ⊕ www.bendchamber.org. **Bend Visitor & Convention Bureau** ⊠ 63085 N. Hwy. 97, Bend 97701 ☎ 877/245-8484 ⊕ www.visitbend.org. **Central Oregon Visitors Association** ⊠ 63085 N. Hwy. 97, Suite 104, Bend 97701 ☎ 541/389-8799 or 800/800-8334 ⊕ www.covisitors.com. **Confederated Tribes of Warm Springs** ⊠ Warm Springs 97761 ☎ 541/553-1161. **Deschutes National Forest** ⊠ 1645 Hwy. 20 E, Bend 97701 ☎ 541/383-5300. **Ochoco National Forest Headquarters and Prineville Ranger Station** ⊠ 3160 N.E. 3rd St., Prineville 07754 ☎ 541/416-6500. **Prineville/Crook County Chamber of Commerce** ⊠ 390 N. Fairview St., 97754 ☎ 541/447-6304 ⊕ www.prineville.org. **Sisters Chamber of Commerce** ⊠ 222 Hood Ave., 97759 ☎ 541/549-0251 ⊕ www.sisterschamber.com.

SOUTHERN OREGON

Updated by
Zach Dundas

Approached from the north, southern Oregon begins where the verdant lowlands of the Willamette Valley give way to a complex collision of mountains, rivers, and ravines. The intricate geography of the "Land of Umpqua," as the area around Roseburg is somewhat romantically known, signals that this is territory very distinct from neighboring regions to the north, east, and west. Wild rivers—the Rogue and the Umpqua are legendary for fishing and boating—and twisting mountain roads venture through the landscape that saw Oregon's most violent Indian wars and became the territory of a self-reliant breed. Don't-Tread-on-Me southern Oregonians see themselves as markedly different from fellow citizens of the Pacific Wonderland. In fact, several early-20th-century attempts to secede from Oregon and proclaim a "state of Jefferson" survive in local folklore and culture—the region's beloved public radio affiliate, for instance, is Jefferson Public Radio.

Some locals refer to this sun-kissed, sometimes blistering-hot landscape as the Mediterranean; others call it Oregon's banana belt. It's a climate built for slow-paced pursuits and a leisurely outlook on life. Folks like to chat down here, and the big cultural draws are Ashland's Oregon Shakespeare Festival and Jacksonville's open-air, picnic-friendly Britt Festivals concert series.

The centerpiece of the region is actually at the region's eastern edge: Crater Lake, created by the violent eruption of Mt. Mazama, is the deepest lake in the United States. Its dark blue clarity is mesmerizing on sunny days but equally stunning in winter, when its rim is covered with snow.

Numbers in the margin correspond to points of interest on the Southern Oregon map

Crater Lake National Park

★ ❶ *Route 62, 75 mi northeast of I–5 and 30 mi northwest of U.S. 97; Route 138, 87 mi east of I–5 and 15 mi west of U.S. 97.*

The pure, untrammeled blue of Crater Lake defies easy description but never fails to astound at first sight. The 21-square-mi lake was created 7,700 years ago after the eruption of Mt. Mazama. Rain and snowmelt filled the caldera, creating a sapphire lake so clear that sunlight penetrates to 400 feet (the lake is 1,943 feet deep). Crater is the clearest and deepest lake in the United States, and the world's seventh deepest. Aside from the breathtaking sight of the lake, the 183,224-acre park is a geologic marvel: the aftermath of geologic activity is everywhere, including huge cinder cones, pumice deserts, and old lava flows.

Prospectors discovered the lake in 1853. Pioneer photographer Peter Britt (for whom the Britt Festivals in Jacksonville are named) brought this natural wonder to national attention in the 1870s and '80s. After years of campaigning by pioneer–activist–journalist–jack-of-all-trades William Gladstone Steel, Crater Lake became Oregon's only national park, in 1902. Steel first heard of the lake when he was a Kansas farm boy in 1870. After a visit in 1885, he dedicated his life to preserving it, overcoming opposition from ranchers and timber interests.

All park and visitor facilities at Crater Lake are within a few miles of each other at Mazama Village near Route 62, at Steel Information Center, and at Rim Village and Crater Lake Lodge. Except for a few picnic areas and overlooks, the rest of the park is completely undeveloped. Entrance to the park costs $10 per vehicle; the pass is good for seven days.

Virtually everyone who comes to the park makes the 33-mi circle of the crater on Rim Drive, which is open roughly mid-July to mid-October. The road is narrow, winding, and hilly, so to take in the scenery it's imperative that you pull off at some of the 30 overlooks. Begin your circumnavigation of the crater's rim by heading northeast on Rim Drive, allowing an hour to stop at a few overlooks—be sure to check out the Phantom Ship rock formation in the lake below. As you continue around the lake, stop at the Watchman for a short but steep hike to this peak above the rim, which affords not only a splendid view of the lake but a broad vista of the surrounding southern Cascades. Wind up your visit at Crater Lake Lodge—allowing some time to wander through the lobby.

Technically, the park is open 24 hours a day year-round; however, snow and freezing temperatures close the park and most of its roadways from mid-October through mid-July. The rest of the year, snow closes all park roadways and entrances except Highway 62 and the access road to Rim Village from Mazama Village. Rim Drive is typically closed because of heavy snowfall from mid-October to mid-July, and icy conditions can be encountered any month of the year, particularly in early morning. Crater Lake receives more snowfall—an annual average of 44 feet—than any other national park except for Mt. Rainier. High season for the park is July and August. September and early October—which can have delightful weather—bring much smaller crowds. The road is kept open just to the rim in winter, except during severe weather.

The park's elk and deer are reclusive but can sometimes be seen at dusk and dawn feeding at forest's edge. Birds are more commonly seen in the summer in the pine and fir forests below the lake.

The highest road-access overlook on the Crater Lake rim, **Cloudcap Overlook** has a westward view across the lake to Wizard Island and an eastward view of Mt. Scott, the volcanic cone that is the park's highest point, just 2 mi from the overlook. ⊠ *2 mi off Rim Dr., 13 mi northeast of Steel Information Center.*

★ First built in 1915, the muscular log-and-stone **Crater Lake Lodge** is considered one of the country's most glorious national-park lodges. Lake views from the lodge perched right on the caldera rim are sensational. The original lodgepole pine pillars and beams and stone fireplaces and abutments remain. Its grand lobby has leather furniture, Pendleton wool throws, and rustic trimmings such as mounted animals. The lodge

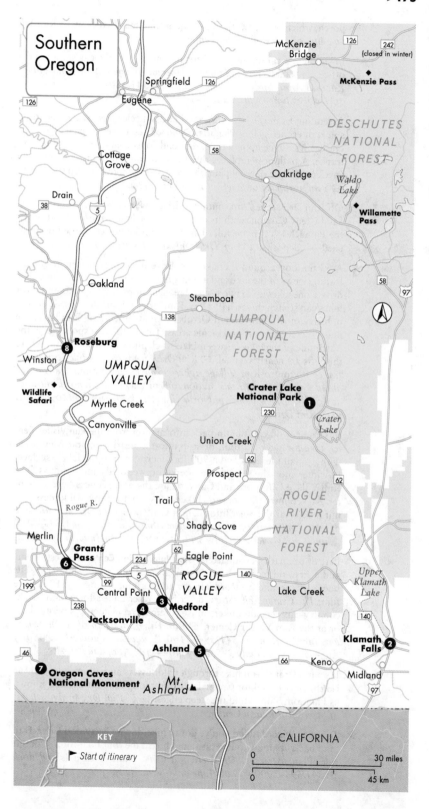

Southern Oregon

McKenzie Bridge
126 242 (closed in winter)
◆ McKenzie Pass

Springfield 126

Eugene 126

DESCHUTES NATIONAL FOREST

Cottage Grove

58

Oakridge *Waldo Lake*

Drain 38

I 5

◆ **Willamette Pass**

Oakland

58 97

Steamboat

138 *UMPQUA NATIONAL FOREST*

Roseburg 8

Winston *UMPQUA VALLEY*

Wildlife Safari ◆

Crater Lake National Park 1

230 *Crater Lake*

Myrtle Creek

Canyonville

Union Creek

62

Rogue R.

227 Prospect

ROGUE RIVER NATIONAL FOREST

62

Trail

Merlin Shady Cove

Grants Pass 6

234 62 Eagle Point

I 5 140

Upper Klamath Lake

199 99 *ROGUE VALLEY*

238 Central Point Lake Creek

Jacksonville 4 3 **Medford**

140

Klamath Falls 2

46 **Ashland** 5

140

7 **Oregon Caves National Monument** *Mt. Ashland* ▲ 66 Keno

Midland 97

KEY

▶ *Start of itinerary*

CALIFORNIA

0 ———————— 30 miles

0 ———————— 45 km

porch, which overlooks the lake, offers an unmatched view. ⊠ *Rim Village just east of Rim visitor center.*

In summer, a campground, motor inn, amphitheater, gas station, post office, and small store are open at **Mazama Village.** ⊠ *Mazama Village Rd. near Annie Spring entrance station* ☎ *541/830–8700* ⊕ *www.nps.gov/crla* ⊙ *June–Sept., daily 8–6.*

Ascending from the banks of Sand and Wheeler creeks, the unearthly spires of eroded ash at **Pinnacles Overlook** resemble the peaks of fairy-tale castles. Once upon a time, the road continued east to a former entrance. A path now replaces the old road and follows the rim of Sand Creek (and more views of pinnacles) to where the entrance arch still stands. ⊠ *5 mi northeast of Steel Information Center.*

Off Rim Drive, the 7-mi southeast drive of **Pinnacles Road** scoots along Sand Creek Canyon, with its exotic volcanic landscape, and ends up at the Pinnacles, a canyon full of spires and hoodoos composed of hardened ash deposits. ⊠ *Rim Dr., 9 mi east of Steel Information Center.*

★ A 33-mi loop around the lake, **Rim Drive** is the main scenic route, affording views of the lake and its cliffs from every conceivable angle. The drive alone takes up to two hours. Frequent stops at viewpoints and short hikes can stretch this to half a day. Rim Drive is typically closed because of heavy snowfall from mid-October to mid-July. Along Rim Drive are many scenic turnouts and picnic areas. Two of the best spots are on the north side of the lake, between Llao Rock and Cleetwood Cove, where the cliffs are nearly vertical. ⊠ *Rim Drive leads from Annie Springs entrance station to Rim Village, where drive circles around the rim; it's about 4½ mi from entrance station to Rim Village. From north entrance at Route 230, it's 10 mi on North Crater Lake access road to where it joins Rim Drive.*

In summer you can obtain park information from the **Rim Visitor Center,** take a ranger-led tour, or stop into the nearby Sinnott Memorial, with a small museum and a 900-foot view down to the lake's surface. In winter snowshoe walks are offered on weekends and holidays. The Rim Village Gift Store and Cafeteria are the only services open in winter. Backcountry campers and hikers must obtain a free wilderness permit here or at the Steel Information Center. ⊠ *Rim Dr. on south side of lake, 7 mi north of Annie Spring entrance station* ☎ *541/594–3100* ⊕ *www.nps.gov/crla* ⊙ *July–Sept., daily 9:30–5:30; June, daily 9:30–5.*

Part of the park headquarters, **Steel Information Center** has rest rooms and a first aid station. There's a small post office and shop that sells books, maps, and postcards. In the auditorium, an ongoing 18-minute film, *The Crater Lake Story,* describes Crater Lake's formation. Backcountry campers and hikers must obtain a free wilderness permit here or at the Rim Visitor Center. ⊠ *Rim Dr., 4 mi north of Annie Spring entrance station* ☎ *541/594–3100* ⊕ *www.nps.gov/crla* ⊙ *Early Apr.–early Nov., daily 9–5; early Nov.–early Apr., daily 10–4.*

It's a moderate ¼-mi hike through wildflowers and dry meadow to **Sun Notch,** an overlook of Crater Lake and the spooky little island known as Phantom Ship. Mind the steep edges. ⊠ *E. Rim Dr., 4 mi northeast of Steel Information Center.*

★ To get to **Wizard Island** you've got to hike down Cleetwood Cove Trail (and back up upon your return) and board the tour boat for a 1¾-hour ride. Plan to picnic. ⊠ *Cleetwood Cove Trail, Wizard Island dock* ☎ *541/594–3000* ⊙ *Late June–mid-Sept., daily.*

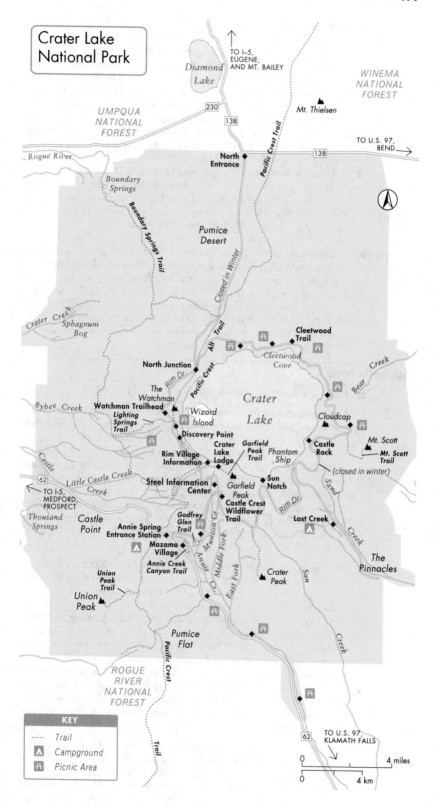

Crater Lake
National Park

Diamond
Lake

TO I–5,
EUGENE,
AND MT. BAILEY

WINEMA
NATIONAL
FOREST

UMPQUA
NATIONAL
FOREST

230

138

Mt. Thielsen

Rogue River

138

TO U.S. 97,
BEND

North
Entrance

Boundary
Springs

Pumice
Desert

Pacific Crest Trail

Closed in Winter

Boundary Springs Trail

Crater Creek

Sphagnum
Bog

Cleetwood
Trail

Bear Creek

All Trail

North Junction

Rim Dr.

Cleetwood
Cove

Pacific Crest

The
Watchman

Crater
Lake

Bybee Creek

Watchman Trailhead

Lighting
Springs
Trail

Wizard
Island

Cloudcap

Discovery Point

Rim Village
Information

Crater
Lake
Lodge

Garfield
Peak
Trail

Phantom
Ship

Castle
Rock

Mt. Scott

Mt. Scott
Trail

Castle

Little Castle Creek
Creek

62

TO I–5,
MEDFORD,
PROSPECT

Steel Information
Center

Garfield
Peak

Sun
Notch

(closed in winter)

Thousand
Springs

Castle
Point

Godfrey
Glen
Trail

Castle Crest
Wildflower
Trail

Lost Creek

Sand Creek

Annie Spring
Entrance Station

Munson Cr.

Rim Dr.

The
Pinnacles

Mazama
Village

Annie Creek
Canyon Trail

Annie Cr.

Middle Fork

East Fork

Crater
Peak

Sun Creek

Union
Peak
Trail

Union
Peak

Pumice
Flat

Pacific Crest

ROGUE
RIVER
NATIONAL
FOREST

Trail

Creek

62

TO U.S. 97,
KLAMATH FALLS

KEY

..... Trail

△ Campground

🏕 Picnic Area

0   4 miles

0   4 km

Where to Stay & Eat

$–$$$ ✕ **Dining Room at Crater Lake Lodge.** Virtually the only place where you can dine well once you're in the park, this spot serves ambitious fare in decidedly upscale surroundings. The room itself is magnificent, with a large stone fireplace and views out over the clear blue waters of Crater Lake. The evening menu usually includes fresh Pacific Northwest seafood, a pasta dish, pork medallions, and steak Oscar. The wines are from Oregon and Washington. Breakfast runs from standard two-eggs-with-bacon plates to specialty omelets and a salmon scramble. ⊠ *Crater Lake Lodge, Rim Village* ☎ *541/594–2255* ⚏ *Reservations essential* ▤ *MC, V* ☉ *Closed mid-Oct.–mid-May.*

$ ✕ **Watchman Restaurant.** Within Crater Lake Lodge, this casual alternative to the Dining Room also affords a view of the lake, but there's no menu—it's an all-you-can-eat buffet, with salads, soups, potato bar, taco bar, and entrées like salmon, Salisbury steak, and chicken. ⊠ *Crater Lake Lodge, Rim Village* ☎ *541/594–2255* ▤ *MC, V* ☉ *Closed mid-Sept.–mid-May. No lunch.*

$$–$$$ ▦ **Crater Lake Lodge.** The period feel of this 1915 lodge on the caldera's rim survived a much-needed mid-'90s renovation. Lodgepole pine columns, gleaming wood floors, and stone fireplaces grace the common areas, and modern couches and chairs blend in perfectly. The lodge has only two telephones, in the lobby area. ⊠ *1211 Ave. C, White City 97503* ☎ *541/830–8700* 🖷 *541/830–8514* ⊕ *www.crater-lake.com* ⇙ *71 rooms* ⚒ *Restaurant, no-smoking rooms; no room phones, no room TVs* ▤ *MC, V* ☉ *Closed mid-Oct.–mid-May.*

Klamath Falls

❷ *60 mi south of Crater Lake National Park on U.S. 97.*

Often overlooked by visitors to the region, the Klamath Falls area is one of the most beautiful parts of Oregon. The city of Klamath Falls stands at an elevation of 4,100 feet, on the southern shore of Upper Klamath Lake. The highest elevation in Klamath County is the peak of Mt. Scott, at 8,926 feet. The Klamath Basin, with its six national wildlife refuges, hosts the largest wintering concentration of bald eagles in the contiguous United States. Each February nature enthusiasts from around the world flock to Klamath Falls for the Bald Eagle Conference, the nation's oldest birding festival. There are more than 82 lakes and streams in Klamath County, including Upper Klamath Lake, which covers 133 square mi.

Many species of migratory birds congregate in the Klamath Basin, including the largest concentration of migratory waterfowl on the continent. The Nature Conservancy has called the basin a western Everglades because it is the largest wetland area west of the Mississippi. Humans have significantly damaged the ecosystem through farming and development. More than 25% of vertebrate species in the area are now endangered or threatened. Where 30 years ago about 6 million birds used the area every year, today that number is down to 2 to 3 million. Environmental organizations are working to reverse some of the damage. In 2000 and 2001, severe droughts led to bitter, borderline-violent fights over water use among Native Americans, farmers, environmentalists, and federal officials; it's worth keeping in mind that feelings inflamed by the issue linger.

A frontier military post was established in 1863 at the site of what is now **Fort Klamath Museum and Park** to protect pioneers from Indian attack. In 1973, 8 acres of the original post, including the original buildings, were dedicated as Klamath County Park. In 2001 the museum's main log-cabin building burned to the ground, taking some larger exhibits with it. The bulk of the museum's collection survived, however, and is now in a replica of the fort's original guard post. Actors in period military duds lead interpretive tours of the grounds. ✚ *44 mi north of Klamath Falls on Hwy. 62* ☎ *541/381–2230* 💲 *Donation requested* ⊙ *Late May–Sept., Wed.–Mon. 10–6.*

Almost 1 million waterfowl use the **Lower Klamath National Wildlife Refuge** during fall migration. In summer white pelicans, cormorants, herons, egrets, terns, white-faced ibis, grebes, and gulls congregate here. But the area's star is the bald eagle: the largest concentration of bald eagles in the lower 48 U.S. states, an estimated 1,000, winters here. ⊠ *8 mi south of Klamath Falls on U.S. 97* ☎ *530/667–2231.*

The anthropology, history, geology, and wildlife of the Klamath Basin are explained at **Klamath County Museum**, with special attention given to the hardships faced by early white settlers. ⊠ *1451 Main St., 97601* ☎ *541/883–4208* 💲 *$3* ⊙ *Tues.–Sat. 9–5.*

On 9 acres along the Williamson River, **Kla-Mo-Ya Casino**, 22 mi north of Klamath Falls, has 300 slot machines, poker, blackjack, and a buffet restaurant. The casino is owned by the Klamath, Modoc, and Yahooskin tribes. ⊠ *22 mi north of Klamath Falls on Hwy. 97 at Crater Lake Junction, Chiloquin 97417* ☎ *888/552–6692.*

Thirty miles north of Klamath Falls, **Collier Memorial State Park and Logging Museum** sits on land given to the State of Oregon by the locally born Collier brothers in honor of their parents. A historic log-cabin exhibit and antique logging equipment dating to the 1880s are among the displays. The park also has picnic areas and a campground. ⊠ *46000 Hwy. 97, Chiloquin 97624* ☎ *541/783–2471* ⊕ *www.collierloggingmuseum. org* 💲 *Free* ⊙ *May–Oct., daily 8–8; Nov.–Apr., daily 8–4.*

More than 100,000 Native American artifacts, the works of 300 major contemporary Western artists, and the largest miniature-gun collection in the world are on display at **Favell Museum of Western Art and Native American Artifacts** in a building made from local volcanic rock. ⊠ *125 W. Main St., 97601* ☎ *541/882–9996* 💲 *$4* ⊙ *Tues.–Sat. 9:30–5:30.*

Three miles north of Fort Klamath, **Jackson F. Kimball State Park** is at the headwaters of the Wood River, which has good fishing. A campground with 10 primitive sites is next to a spring-fed lagoon. ⊠ *U.S. 97* ☎ *541/ 783–2471 or 800/551–6949* ⊕ *www.prd.state.or.us* 💲 *Day use $3 per vehicle* ⊙ *Mid-Apr.–Oct., daily.*

The 800-seat **Ross Ragland Theater** hosts the 30-year-old Linkville Players theater group, as well as traveling and local plays and musical performances. ⊠ *218 N. 7th St., 97601* ☎ *541/884–0651.*

The history of the region is the focus of a guided tour and exhibits at **Senator George Baldwin Hotel Museum**, a former hotel that the turn-of-the-20th-century politico Baldwin ran and where President Theodore Roosevelt once stayed. Some of the photographs on display were part of Senator Baldwin's daughter Maud's own collection. In summer you can take a replica street trolley from here to the Klamath County Museum. ⊠ *31 Main St., 97601* ☎ *541/883–4207 or 541/883–4208* ⊕ *www.co.klamath.or.us* 💲 *$4* ⊙ *June–Sept., Tues.–Sat. 10–4.*

Twelve miles north of Klamath Falls, **Winema National Forest** covers 1.1 million acres on the eastern slopes of the Cascades. It borders Crater Lake National Park. Hiking, camping, fishing, and boating are popular. In winter snowmobiling and cross-country skiing are available.

⊠ *U.S. 97* ☎ *541/883–6714* ⊕ *www.fs.fed.us/r6/winema* ✑ *Day use $3 per vehicle* ☉ *Daily; campgrounds and picnic areas Memorial Day–Labor Day.*

Where to Stay & Eat

$$–$$$ ✕ **Chez Nous.** The dark-wood dining room in this 1920 house suggests more formal pleasures but encourages dining in a relaxed mood. A thoughtful French chef prepares duck in orange sauce, Chateaubriand, veal dishes, and the house specialty, rack of lamb. Fresh strawberry short-cake often appears on the menu, and there's a good wine list. ⊠ *3927 S. 6th St., 97603* ☎ *541/883–8719* 🖷 *541/883–3996* ⊟ *AE, MC, V* ☉ *Closed Sun. and Mon. No lunch.*

$$–$$$$ ⊡ **Running Y Ranch Resort.** Golfers rave about the Arnold Palmer–de-signed course here, which wends its way through a juniper-and-pon-derosa–shaded canyon overlooking Upper Klamath Lake. The resort consists of a main lodge and several town house complexes, with hik-ing, biking, horseback riding, sailing, fishing, and wildlife watching the prime activities. Rooms in the lodge are spacious and modern, if undis-tinguished; the two- to three-bedroom town houses have a plethora of amenities. ⊠ *5115 Running Y Rd., 5 mi north of Klamath Falls, 97601* ☎ *541/850–5500 or 888/850–0275* 🖷 *541/850–5593* ⊕ *www.runningy. com* ⮑ *83 rooms* ₺ *18-hole golf course, 4 tennis courts, hiking, horse-back riding, laundry service, meeting rooms* ⊟ *AE, D, DC, MC, V.*

Medford

❸ *88 mi south of Roseburg on I-5.*

Although Medford has only about 60,000 residents, the community is the professional, retail trade, and service center for eight counties in south-ern Oregon and northern California. As such, it offers more professional and cultural venues than might be expected for a city of its size. The town has four major shopping centers and the fruit marketing company Harry and David. Lodging and dining tend to be much cheaper in Med-ford than in nearby (and easily accessible) Ashland and Jacksonville. Near two major rivers and more than 30 lakes and streams, Medford is 71 mi southwest of Crater Lake and 80 mi southwest of the Oregon Caves, so it makes a good starting place for tours of both places.

An 1872 water-powered flour grist mill, **Butte Creek Mill** is listed in the National Historic Register and still produces whole-grain food prod-ucts, which you can buy at the country store here. There's also a mod-est display of antiques. ⊠ *402 Royal Ave. N, Eagle Point* ☎ *541/826–3531* ⊕ *www.buttecreekmill.com* ✑ *Free* ☉ *Mon.–Sat. 9–5.*

The late Hollywood star Ginger Rogers retired to this area, and the re-stored vaudeville house **Craterian Ginger Rogers Theater** presents concerts, ballets, theatrical works, and touring shows like the Vienna Boys Choir and Brazil Night. ⊠ *23 S. Central Ave., 97501* ☎ *541/779–3000* 🖷 *541/779–8175* ⊕ *www.craterian.org.*

> **need a break?**   Next door to the Craterian Theater, **Sonny's Downtown Cafe** (⊠ 210 E. Main St. ☎ 541/245–1616 ☉ Closed weekends. No dinner) is a friendly deli with inexpensive sandwiches, cinnamon rolls, and coffee.

Jackson County's natural history and collections of the Roxy Ann Gem and Mineral Society are on display at **Crater Rock Museum.** ⊠ *2002 Scenic Ave., Central Point* ☎ *541/664–6081* ✑ *Free* ☉ *Tues.–Sat. 10–4.*

Thirty-four miles from Medford, **Joseph H. Stewart State Park** overlooks Lost Creek Reservoir, where you can rent canoes. There are 8 mi of hiking trails. The campground has 151 electrical and 50 tent sites. ⊠ *Hwy. 62* ☎ *541/560–3334 or 800/551–6949* ☒ *Free* ⊙ *Mar.–Nov., daily.*

Covering 630,000 acres, **Rogue River National Forest** has fishing, swimming, hiking, and skiing. Motorized vehicles and equipment—even bicycles—are prohibited in the 113,000-acre Sky Lakes Wilderness, south of Crater Lake National Park. Its highest point is the 9,495-foot Mt. McLoughlin. Summers here are warm and dry, while winters are bitterly cold, with lots of snow. ⊠ *I–5 to Exit 39, Hwy. 62 to Rte. 140* ☎ *541/858–2200* ⊕ *www.fs.fed.us/r6/rogue* ☒ *Free for most of forest, some trailheads have fees, call for details* ⊙ *Daily.*

The focus at **Southern Oregon History Center** is on the Rogue Valley's past, with a research library augmenting rotating exhibits on pioneer history. ⊠ *106 N. Central Ave.* ☎ *541/773–6536* ⊕ *www.sohs.org* ☒ *Free* ⊙ *Weekdays 9–5, Sat. 1–5.*

A popular spot for weddings and picnics, **Tou Velle State Park** is a day-use park with beautiful hiking trails that wind through a wildlife viewing area. ⊠ *Off I–5 to Table Rock Rd.* ☎ *541/582–1118 or 800/551–6949* ⊕ *www.prd.state.or.us* ☒ *Day use $3 per vehicle* ⊙ *Daily.*

Where to Stay & Eat

¢ ✕ **C. K. Tiffins.** Healthy food is the focus of this downtown place. It serves poached eggs at breakfast, along with waffles, pancakes, and baked goods made fresh every morning on site. Try the popular chicken sesame salad or vegetarian lasagna at lunch; red meat is not served. The restaurant is on the site of a former early-20th-century men's clothier and displays the work of local artists. ⊠ *226 E. Main St., 97501* ☎ *541/779–0480* ▭ *AE, D, MC, V* ⊙ *No dinner.*

$$–$$$ 🏠 **Under the Greenwood Tree.** Regulars at this B&B between Medford
Fodor'sChoice and Ashland find themselves hard-pressed to decide what they like
★ most: the luxurious and romantic rooms, the stunning 10-acre farm, or the breakfasts cooked by the owner, a Cordon Bleu–trained chef. Gigantic old oaks hung with hammocks shade the inn, a 130-year-old farmhouse exuding genteel charm. There's a manicured 2-acre lawn and a creaky three-story barn for exploring; an outbuilding holds the buckboard wagon that brought the property's original homesteaders westward on the Oregon Trail. The interior is decorated in Renaissance splendor and all rooms have private baths. Afternoon tea is served. ⊠ *3045 Bellinger La., head west from I–5 Exit 27 on Barnett Rd., south briefly on Hwy. 99, west on Stewart Ave., south briefly on Hull Rd., and west on Bellinger, 97501* ☎ *541/776–0000or 800/766–8099* ⊕ *www.greenwoodtree.com* ➭ *5 rooms* ▭ *MC, V.*

$–$$ 🏠 **Rogue River Guest House.** The wide front porch of the 1890s farmhouse 12 mi north of town looks out to fir, catalpa, and holly trees. This is one of the few bed-and-breakfasts that welcomes children, and business travelers will find a small office at their disposal. One room overlooks the Rogue from a private deck, while a two-room suite is available for larger traveling parties. ⊠ *41 Rogue River Hwy., Gold Hill 97525* ☎ *541/855–4485 or 877/764–8322* ➭ *3 rooms* ⚲ *Some cable TV, business services, some pets allowed; no room phones* ▭ *No credit cards* ⧍ *BP.*

Jacksonville

❹ *5 mi west of Medford on Hwy. 238.*

A glimpse down Jacksonville's Wild West main drag, California Street, may inspire a brief flicker of panic: you forgot your six-shooter and have no idea how far behind the sheriff's posse may be. This perfectly preserved town founded in the frenzy of the 1851 gold rush has served as the backdrop to several western flicks. It's easy to see why. (J-Ville, as locals rather jauntily refer to it, is one of only eight towns anointed to the National Register of Historic Places lock, stock, and barrel.) These days, living-history exhibits offering a glimpse of pioneer life and the world-renowned Britt Festivals of classical, jazz and pop music are the draw, rather than gold. Trails winding up from the town's center lead to the Festival amphitheater, 150-year-old gardens, exotic madrona groves, and an intriguing pioneer cemetery.

For free maps and guides to Jacksonville's many historic structures, stop by the **Jacksonville Visitors Information Center** (⊠ 185 N. Oregon St. ☎ 541/899–8118).

History comes alive as actors dressed in costumes of the period portray the Beekman family at **Beekman House,** an 1875 house with original furnishings. The Beekman Bank, established in 1863, is also open to the public. ⊠ *352 E. California St.* ☎ *541/773–6536* ☎ *$2* ⊙ *Memorial Day–Labor Day, daily 1–5.*

ℭ In the 1920 Jackson County Jail, the **Children's Museum** has hands-on exhibits of pioneer life and a collection of antique toys. There's an Indian tepee and an old-fashioned store in which to play. A special display highlights local resident Pinto Colvig, the original Bozo the Clown, who co-composed "Who's Afraid of the Big Bad Wolf" and was the voice of a Munchkin, Goofy, both Sleepy and Grumpy, and many other animated film characters. The adjacent **Jacksonville Museum,** inside the old Jackson County Courthouse, has intriguing gold-rush-era artifacts. The "Jacksonville! Boomtown to Home Town" exhibit lays out the area's history. ⊠ *206 N. 5th St., 97530* ☎ *541/773–6536* 🖷 *541/776–7994* ⊕ *www.sohs.org* ☎ *$3, $7 pass for both museums* ⊙ *Wed.–Sat. 10–5, Sun. noon–5.*

Perched on a bench in the scenic Applegate Valley, **Valley View Vineyard** enjoys one of the best settings in all Oregon. The valley's especially sunny, warm climate produces rich chardonnay, merlot, and cabernet sauvignon vintages. First founded in the 1850s by pioneer Peter Britt, the vineyard was reestablished in 1972. A restored pole barn houses the winery and tasting room. Valley View also operates a tasting room and gift shop (⊠ *125 W. California St.* ☎ *541/899–1001*) in Jacksonville. ⊠ *1000 Upper Applegate Rd., 10 mi southwest of Jacksonville* ☎ *541/899–8468 or 800/781–9463* ⊕ *www.valleyviewwinery.com* ⊙ *Daily 11–5.*

ℭ Native Americans avoided the **Oregon Vortex Location of the House of Mystery,** referring to it as "forbidden ground." Birds and other wildlife appear to avoid it as well. In fact, tennis balls really do seem to roll uphill here, and brooms do stand on end in this 1-acre spherical area. It opened as a tourist attraction around 1930. ⊠ *4303 Sardine Creek Rd., Gold Hill 97525* ☎ *541/855–1543* ⊕ *www.oregonvortex.com* ☎ *$8* ⊙ *Mar.–May, Sept., and Oct., daily 9–5, last tour at 4:15; June–Aug., daily 9–6, last tour at 5:15.*

A trip up the winding road—or, better yet, a hike via the old cart-track Fodor'sChoice marked "Catholic access"—leads to the **Jacksonville Cemetery,** resting place ★ of the clans (the Britts, the Beekmans, and the Orths) that built Jacksonville. You'll also get a fascinating, if sometimes unattractive, view of the social dynamics of the Old West: older graves (the cemetery is still in use) are strictly segregated, Irish Catholics from Jews from Protestants. A somber granite plinth erected in the late '90s marks the Pauper's Field, where those who found themselves on the losing end of gold rush economics entered eternity anonymously. The cemetery closes at sundown. ⊠ *Oregon St.; follow posted direction signs from downtown.*

Where to Stay & Eat

$$–$$$ ✕ **Jacksonville Inn.** The Continental fare and 600-label wine cellar at this dining room in a gold-rush-era bed-and-breakfast are among the best in southern Oregon. Book well in advance, particularly between late June and August, during the Britt Festival. Try the fresh razor clams and veal dishes. There are tables on the patio for dining alfresco. Breakfast and a Sunday brunch, which tends to highlight seasonal and regional fruits, are also offered. ⊠ *175 E. California St.* ☎ *541/899–1900* ⌖ *Reservations essential* ▤ *AE, D, DC, MC, V* ⊘ *No lunch Mon.*

★ $–$$$$ ✕▦ **Jacksonville Inn.** The spotless period antiques and the host of well-chosen amenities at this 1861-vintage inn evoke what the Wild West might have been had Martha Stewart been in charge. In addition to the main building, the inn includes three larger and more luxurious cottages with fireplaces and saunas. The room rates include a full breakfast. One of the eight rooms in the main inn is named in honor of ubiquitous Jacksonville founding father Peter Britt, while another, the Blanchet Room, honors one of the area's earliest Catholic priests. Both have meticulous pioneer-period furnishings. The inn's Continental restaurant is among the best places to eat in the region. ⊠ *175 E. California St., 97530* ☎ *541/899–1900 or 800/321–9344* ☐ *541/899–1373* ⊕ *www.jacksonvilleinn.com* ↹ *8 rooms, 3 cottages* ⌂ *Restaurant, refrigerators* ▤ *AE, D, DC, MC, V.*

$–$$ ✕▦ **The McCully House Inn.** One of Jacksonville's six original homes, a gleaming white Gothic Revival mansion built in 1860, McCully House sits in the midst of a fragrant rose garden. The period-decorated rooms, one with a fireplace and all of them filled with antiques, are on the second floor and have private baths. One upstairs bedroom is furnished with the original bedstead that was shipped around Cape Horn. The room rates include a full breakfast. ⊠ *240 E. California St., 97530* ☎ *541/899–1942 or 800/367–1942* ☐ *541/899–1560* ↹ *3 rooms* ⌂ *Restaurant* ▤ *AE, MC, V.*

Nightlife & the Arts

Every summer some of the finest musicians in the world gather for the **Britt Festivals** (☎ 541/773–6077 or 800/882–7488), outdoor concerts and theater presentations lasting from mid-June to early September. Folk, country, pop, and classical performances are staged in an outdoor amphitheater on the estate of 19th-century photographer and painter Peter Britt. Tickets must be obtained well in advance for most performances, and those who wish the best spaces on the lawn near the stage should show up early.

Ashland

❺ *20 mi from Jacksonville, east on Hwy. 238 and southeast on I–5.*

As you walk Ashland's twisting hillside streets, it seems like every house is a restored Victorian operating as an upscale B&B, though that's not quite all that there is to this town: the Oregon Shakespeare Festival attracts about a quarter of a million theater lovers to the Rogue Valley every year, from mid-February to early November (though tourists don't start showing up en masse until June or so). That influx means Ashland is more geared toward the arts, more eccentric, and more expensive than its size might suggest. The mix of well-heeled theater tourists, bohemian students from southern Oregon University, and dramatic show folk imbues the town with some one-of-a-kind cultural frissons. The stage isn't the only show in town—skiing at Mt. Ashland and the town's reputation as a secluded getaway keep things hopping year-round.

At the Oregon Shakespeare Festival's **Exhibit Center** in the festival complex, theater fans can try on costumes and see displays that outline the history of the festival. A fascinating guided backstage tour includes peeks at production shops and the Angus Bowmer Theatre, and a walk to the very heavens above the Elizabethan Theatre's stage. ⊠ *S. Pioneer and Main Sts.* ☎ *541/482–4331* 🖷 *541/482–8045* 🖾 *Backstage tour $11 early June–early Oct.; $8.25 Feb.–early June and mid–late Oct., under 5 not admitted; exhibit center $2* ☉ *Tues.–Sun. 10–11:45.*

The Elizabethan Theatre overlooks **Lithia Park,** a 99-acre jewel that is Ashland's physical and psychological anchor. Whether thronged with colorful hippie folk and picnickers on a summer evening or buzzing with joggers and dog walkers in the morning, Lithia is a well-used, well-loved, and well-tended spot. An old-fashioned band shell, a duck pond, a children's playground, nature trails, and Ashland Creek make this a perfect spot for a pretheater picnic. On summer weekend mornings, the park plays host to a '60s-ish artisans' market. Each June the festival opens its outdoor season by hosting the Feast of Will in the park, with music, dancing, bagpipes, and food. Tickets (about $16) are available through the festival box office.

The **Schneider Museum of Art,** at the edge of the southern Oregon University campus, includes a spruce, light-filled gallery devoted to special exhibits by Oregon, West Coast, and international artists. Hallways and galleries throughout the rest of the 66,000-square-foot complex display many works by both students and faculty. ⊠ *250 Siskiyou Blvd.* ☎ *541/ 552–6245* ⊕ *www.sou.edu/sma* ☉ *Tues.–Sat. 10–4; extended hrs 1st Fri. of month.*

Mt. Ashland Ski Area. This winter sports playground in the Siskiyou Mountains is halfway between San Francisco and Portland. The ski runs get more than 300 inches of snow each year. There are 23 trails in addition to chute skiing in a glacial cirque called the bowl. The 6,350-foot mountain has a vertical drop of 1,150 feet. ⊠ *Exit 6 off I–5, access road to top* ☎ *541/482–2754 snow conditions, 541/482–2897* ⊕ *www. mtashland.com* ☉ *Nov.–Apr., daily 9–4.*

Where to Stay & Eat

The Oregon Shakespeare Festival has stimulated one of the most extensive networks of B&Bs in the country—more than 50 in all. High season for Ashland-area bed-and-breakfasts is between June and October. Expect to pay $90–$150 per night, which includes breakfast for two; during the off-season the rates are between $60 and $100. The **Ashland B&B Network** (☎ 800/944–0329 ⊕ www.abbnet.com) provides referrals to local inns. The **Southern Oregon Reservations** (☎ 541/488–1011 or 800/ 547–8052 ⊕ www.sorc.com) clearinghouse handles both hotel rooms and theater packages.

★ **$$–$$$** ✕ **Hong Kong Bar.** Hidden on the third floor of a Main Street building and accessed by elevator, this wood-panel, atmospheric Asian restaurant and lounge feels a little like a Shanghai speakeasy circa 1935. In the restaurant, Chinese flavors dominate a menu based on a three-course dinner, with the lemon halibut with fresh ginger perhaps the most distinctive entrée. Despite its discreet location, the bar draws an enthusiastic drinking crowd in the post-theater hours. ⊠ *24 N. Main St.* ☎ *541/488–5511* 🖃 *MC, V* ☉ *Closed Mon.*

★ **$–$$$** ✕ **Black Sheep.** In an 1879 downtown building, this pub is what many quasi-British bars want to be but aren't. Cluttered tables, gold stars on the black ceiling, and an authentic red phone booth lend it cultural credibility, while a rock sound track and funky servers chase away any hint of stodginess. The obligatory traditional fish-and-chips match up with creative dishes like venison with gin and juniper-berry sauce. The bread pudding is not to be missed. ✉ *51 N. Main St.,* ☎ *541/482–6414* ▤ *MC, V.*

★ **$–$$$** ✕ **Chateaulin.** One of southern Oregon's most romantic restaurants is in an ivy-covered storefront a block from the Oregon Shakespeare Festival exhibit center, where it dispenses French food, local wine, and impeccable service with equal facility. This might be Ashland's most iconic restaurant, the fixed point in a hopping dining scene, where Shakespeare pilgrims return religiously year after year. The bar is the center of the post-theater social scene. Try the pan-roasted rack of lamb with a white-wine demi-glace sauce of roasted garlic, fresh basil, black olives, and sun-dried tomatoes, accompanied by a bottle of Ken Wright Cellars Pinot Noir. ✉ *50 E. Main St.* ☎ *541/482–2264* ✍ *Reservations essential* ▤ *AE, D, MC, V* ☺ *Closed Mon. No lunch.*

¢ ✕ **Morning Glory.** Breakfast reaches new heights at this distinctive café across the street from southern Oregon University. In a blue Craftsman-style bungalow, the café has eclectic furnishings, and an attractive patio space bounded by arbors, that complement the food—omelets bursting with fillings such as mushrooms, apple-wood-smoked bacon, toasted walnuts, and fontina cheese; gingerbread waffles; and sourdough blueberry pancakes. ✉ *1149 Siskiyou Blvd.* ☎ *541/488–8636* ▤ *MC, V.*

★ **$$$–$$$$** ⌂ **Mt. Ashland Inn.** Close to the summit ski area on Mt. Ashland, 15 mi south of Ashland, this 5,500-square-foot lodge, hand-built of cedar logs, has magnificent views of Mt. Shasta and the rest of the Siskiyou Mountains; the Pacific Crest Trail runs through the parking lot. A large stone fireplace, antiques, hand-stitched quilts, and natural wood provide welcoming warmth. The room rates include a three-course breakfast that's wonderfully prepared and gracefully served, and the owners plan bike trips and provide snowshoes for guests. ✉ *550 Mt. Ashland Rd., 97520, Take Exit 6 from I–5 and follow signs west toward ski area to beyond Mile Post 5* ☎ *541/482–8707* ☎ *800/830–8707* ⇨ *5 rooms* ⚴ *Outdoor hot tub, sauna, hiking, mountain bikes, cross-country skiing* ▤ *D, MC, V.*

★ **$$–$$$$** ⌂ **Ashland Creek Inn.** Every one of the seven plush suites in this converted mill has a geographic theme—if it's Tuesday, this must be Normandy, while Moroccan and New Mexican motifs prevail next door. Each sitting room–bedroom combo has its own entrance and a deck just inches from burbling Ashland Creek. Privacy, space, high-concept elegance, and dynamite breakfast served in an understated central dining room make this well-run place an alternative to up-close-and-personal traditional B&Bs. Downtown shopping, Lithia Park, and the theaters are within an easy walk. ✉ *70 Water St.* ☎ *541/482–3315* ☎ *541/482–1092* ⊕ *www.ashlandcreekinn.com* ⇨ *7 suites* ⚴ *Kitchens; no smoking* ▤ *MC, V* ⎮◉⎮ *BP.*

Nightlife & the Arts

From mid-February to early November, more than 100,000 Bard-loving fans descend on Ashland for the **Oregon Shakespeare Festival** (✉ 15 S. Pioneer St., 97520 ☎ 541/482–4331 ☎ 541/482–8045 ⊕ www. osfashland.org), presented in three theaters. Its accomplished repertory company mounts some of the finest Shakespearean productions you're likely to see on this side of Stratford-upon-Avon—plus works by Ibsen, Williams, and contemporary playwrights. Between June and October, plays are staged in the 1,200-seat Elizabethan Theatre, an atmospheric re-creation of the Fortune Theatre in London, the 600-seat Angus

Bowmer Theatre, a state-of-the-art facility typically used for five different productions in a single season, and the 350-seat New Theater, which tends to host productions of new or experimental work. The festival generally operates close to capacity, so it's important to book ahead.

Ashland's after-theater crowd (including many of the actors) congregates in the wood-and-brick-lined bar at **Chateaulin** (✉ 50 E. Main St. ☎ 541/ 482–2264).

Q's Music Hall (✉ 140 Lithia Way ☎ 541/488–4880), a rock and jazz club that's literally down a back alley, books local and touring acts aimed at Ashland's sizeable youth culture.

Sports & the Outdoors

The **Adventure Center** (✉ 40 N. Main St., Ashland 97520 ☎ 541/488–2819 or 800/444–2819) books outdoor expeditions in the Ashland region, including white-water raft trips, fishing outings, and bike excursions.

SKIING **Mt. Ashland** (✉ Mt. Ashland Access Rd., 18 mi southwest of downtown Ashland; follow signs 9 mi from I–5 Exit 6 ☎ 541/482–2897 or 888/ 747–5496), a cone-shape, 7,523-foot Siskiyou peak, has some of the steepest runs in the state. Two triple and two double chairlifts accommodate a vertical drop of 1,150 feet; the longest of the 22 runs is 1 mi. Facilities include rentals, repairs, instruction, a ski shop, a restaurant, and a bar.

Grants Pass

❻ *30 mi northwest of Medford on I–5.*

"It's the Climate!" So says a confident neon sign of 1950s vintage presiding over the downtown of Josephine County's seat. Grants Pass bills itself as Oregon's white-water capital. The Rogue River, preserved by Congress in 1968 as a National Wild and Scenic River, runs right through town. Downtown Grants Pass is a National Historic District, a stately little enclave of 19th-century brick storefronts housing folksy businesses harking back to the 1950s. It's all that white water, however, that compels most visitors—and not a few moviemakers. If the river alone doesn't serve up enough natural drama, the sheer rock walls of nearby Hellgate Canyon rise 250 feet.

A city museum, **Grants Pass Museum of Art** in Riverside Park, displays classic and contemporary art, including the works of local artists. Sculpture and painting dominate, and the focus is on American and regional work. A first-Friday art night is a community rallying point. ✉ 229 S. W. G St. ☎ 541/479–3290 ⚏ Free ☉ Tues.–Sat. noon–4.

You'll see some of Oregon's most magnificent scenery on a tour of Hellgate Canyon, via **Hellgate Jetboat Excursions**, which depart from the Riverside Inn. The 36-mi round-trip from Grants Pass through Hellgate Canyon takes 2 hours. There is also a 5½-hour, 75-mi round-trip from Grants Pass to Grave Creek with a stop for a meal on an open-air deck (cost of meal not included). ✉ 966 S.W. 6th ☎ 541/479–7204 or 800/ 648–4874 ⊕ *www.hellgate.com* ⚏ *2-hr trip $27; 5½-hr trip $50; brunch cruises $40; lunch excursion $35; supper cruises $43; special rates for children* ☉ *May–Sept., daily; brunch cruises May–Sept., weekends 9:15; supper cruises May–Sept., weekends 4:15, 3:15 in Sept.*

In the Klamath Mountains and the Coast Range of southwestern Oregon, the 1.1-million-acre **Siskiyou National Forest** contains the 35-mi-long Wild and Scenic section of the Rogue River, which races through the Wild Rogue Wilderness Area, and the Illinois and Chetco Wild and Scenic Rivers, which run through the 180,000-acre Kalmiopsis Wilderness

Area. Activities include white-water rafting, camping, and hiking, but many hiking areas require trail-park passes. There are 25 campgrounds. ⊠ *Off U.S. 199* ☎ *541/471–6516* ⊕ *www.fs.fed.us/r6/siskiyou* ☜ *Park pass required* ☉ *Daily.*

Fodor'sChoice **Valley of the Rogue State Park** has a 1¼-mi hiking trail that follows the
★ Rogue River bank. A campground along 3 mi of shoreline has 97 full hookups, 49 electrical and 21 tent sites, and 6 yurts. There are picnic tables, walking trails, playgrounds, and rest rooms. ⊠ *Exit 45B off I–5* ☎ *541/582–1118 or 800/551–6949* ⊕ *www.prd.state.or.us* ☜ *Day use $3 per vehicle* ☉ *Daily.*

Where to Stay & Eat

¢–$$ ✕ **The Brewery.** No beer has been brewed in this 1886 building since Prohibition, but the name sounds good anyway. You can order Australian lobster tails (at the market price, more expensive than most of the entrées), steak, Caribbean jerk catfish, and other surf-and-turf dishes from the extensive menu. Dine under exposed beams between the original brick walls, which surround three dining rooms filled with booths and oak tables. Brunch is served on Sunday. ⊠ *509 S.W. G St., 97526* ☎ *541/479–9850* ☐ *AE, D, DC, MC, V* ☉ *No lunch Mon. or Sat.*

¢ ✕ **Grants Pass Pharmacy.** A classic, out-of-time soda fountain is besieged by cheesy souvenirs—ignore the ceramic dolls and concentrate on the root beer floats. Grants Pass may be the only town in America where teenagers still race into the soda fountain hollering "Gimme a phosphate!" These multiflavored little coolers are just 75¢. Solid sandwiches come for $5 or less, though an odd ordering routine requires you to order food and drink at separate counters. ⊠ *414 S.W. 6th St.* ☎ *541/476–4262* ☐ *MC, V* ☉ *Closed Sun.*

¢–$ ▦ **Ivy House.** In the Historic District, this 1908 English Arts and Crafts-style brick home was originally a restaurant and tea room. The restored interior is unfussy, but the guest rooms have eider down quilts and antiques, and there are two sitting rooms. From the porch, you can enjoy the rose bushes, which were planted in 1908. Restaurants, theaters, galleries, and the river are all within walking distance. The charming English owner observes a fine old tradition: you can have morning tea and biscuits in bed before your full English breakfast. There's a TV in the common area. ⊠ *139 S.W. I St., 97526* ☎ *541/474–7363* ☐ *541/474–7363* ✍ *ivyhousebb@msn.com* ➫ *5 rooms* ♨ *No smoking* ☐ *D, MC, V* ⧈ *BP.*

Oregon Caves National Monument

❼ *90 mi from Jacksonville, west on Hwy. 238, south on U.S. 199, and east on Hwy. 46.*

The town of Cave Junction is the turnoff point for the Oregon Caves National Monument. The "Marble Halls of Oregon," high in the verdant Siskiyou Mountains, have enchanted visitors since local hunter Elijah Davidson chased a bear into them in 1874. Huge stalagmites and stalactites, the Ghost Room, Paradise Lost, and the River Styx are part of a ½-mi subterranean tour that lasts about 75 minutes. The tour includes more than 200 stairs and is not recommended for anyone who experiences difficulty in walking or has respiratory or coronary problems. Children over six must be at least 42 inches tall and pass a safety and ability test, because they cannot be carried. ⊠ *Hwy. 46, 20 mi southeast of Cave Junction* ☎ *541/592–3400* ☜ *$7* ☉ *May–mid-June, daily 9–5; mid-June–Sept., daily 9–7; Oct.–Apr., daily 8:30–4.*

In the pine-oak foothills of Siskiyou Mountain, **Foris Vineyards,** where coastal and inland climates mingle, has earned a reputation for richly flavored varietal wines such as pinot noir, merlot, and cabernet sauvignon. ⊠ *654 Kendall Rd.* ☎ *800/843–6747* ⊕ *www.foriswine.com* ⊗ *Daily 11–5.*

Documenting area Native American and pioneer history, **Kerbyville Museum** is centered in an 1871 home on the National Register of Historic Places. You can investigate your pioneer and mining ancestors in the research library and see exhibits of taxidermy and antique dolls, as well as local Native American artifacts. ⊠ *24195 Redwood Hwy., 97531* ☎ *541/592–5252* 🎫 *$3* ⊗ *Mid-May–mid-Sept., Mon.–Sat. 10–5, Sun. noon–5; mid-Sept.–mid-May, by appointment only.*

Where to Stay & Eat

¢ ✕ **Wild River Pizza Company & Brewery.** Cool your heels at the communal redwood picnic tables in this pizza parlor on the north end of town. If you aren't in the mood for pizza, choose from fish-and-chips, chicken dishes, and sandwiches. There is also an all-you-can-eat buffet, and the restaurant's own seasonal brews are on tap. ⊠ *249 N. Redwood Hwy., 97523* ☎ *541/592–3556* ▭ *D, MC, V.*

$ ✕🏠 **Oregon Caves Lodge.** If you're looking for a quiet retreat in an unusual place, consider this lodge on the grounds of the national monument. Virtually unchanged since it was built in 1934, it has a rustic authenticity. Rooms, all with their original furnishings, have canyon or waterfall views. The dining room serves the best regional fare in the vicinity. ⊠ *20000 Caves Hwy., Cave Junction 97523* ☎ *541/592–3400* 🖷 *541/592–6654* ➲ *22 rooms, 3 suites* ⚭ *Restaurant, coffee shop, hiking* ⌖ *No smoking* ▭ *MC, V.*

★ $–$$$ 🏠 **Out N' About.** You sleep among the leaves in the tree houses of this extraordinary resort—the highest is 37 feet from the ground. One has an antique, claw-foot bath; another has separate kids' quarters connected to the main room by a swinging bridge. There is also an earthbound cabin with a view of the old-growth forest. There is a two-night minimum stay Memorial Day–Labor Day. ⊠ *300 Page Creek Rd.* ☎ *541/592–2208* ⊕*www.treehouses.com* ➲ *10 tree houses* ⚭ *Some kitchenettes, horseback riding; no a/c, no room phones, no room TVs* ▭ *AE, D, MC, V* 🍽 *CP.*

Roseburg

❽ *73 mi south of Eugene on I–5.*

Fishermen the world over hold the name Roseburg sacred. The timber town on the Umpqua River attracts anglers in search of a dozen popular fish species including bass, brown and brook trout, and chinook, coho and sockeye salmon. The native steelhead, which makes its run to the sea in the summer, is king of them all.

The seat of Douglas County is the old-economy Northwest in a nutshell—with 3 million acres of commercial forest land and the largest stand of old-growth timber in the world close at hand, the timber business dominates local enterprise, and knocks suffered in recent years hit Roseburg particularly hard. Suffice it to say the spotted owl is not a popular beast here, and environmental politics remain a tough sell.

The north and south branches of the Umpqua River meet up just north of Roseburg. The roads that run parallel to this river give spectacular views of the falls, and the North Umpqua route also provides access to trails, hot springs, and the Winchester fish ladder. White-water rafting, riverside hiking, horseback riding, mountain biking, snowmobiling, and skiing are available in the area.

Sixty miles due west of the northern gateway to Crater Lake National Park and in the Hundred Valleys of the Umpqua, Roseburg produces innovative, well-regarded wines. Wineries are sprouting up throughout the mild, gorgeous farm country around town, mostly within easy reach of I–5.

One of the best county museums in the state, **Douglas County Museum** surveys 8,000 years of human activity in the region. Its fossil collection is worth a stop. ⊠ *123 Museum Dr.* ☎ *541/957–7007* ⊕ *www.co.douglas. or.us/museum* 🖾 *$3.50* ⊙ *Weekdays 9–5, Sat. 10–5, Sun. noon–5.*

★ ☾ Come face to face with free-roaming animals at the 600-acre **Wildlife Safari,** a drive-through wildlife park. There's also a petting zoo, a miniature train, and elephant rides. The admission price includes two drive-throughs in the same day. From I–5 take Exit 119, follow Highway 42 west 3 mi to Lookingglass Road, and take a right on Safari Road. 🏠 *Box 1600, Winston 97496* ☎ *541/679–6761* ⊕ *www.wildlifesafari. org* 🖾 *$17.50* ⊙ *Daily 9–5.*

★ **Abacela Vineyards and Winery** (⊠ 12500 Lookingglass Rd., Roseburg; from I–5 Exit 119, head into Winston, take a right on Hwy. 42, a right on Brockway Rd., and a left on Lookingglass Rd. ☎ 541/679–6642 ⊕ www.abacela.com) derives its name from an archaic Spanish word meaning "to plant grapevines," and that's exactly what this winery's husband-wife team did not so very long ago. Abacela released its first wine in 1999, and quickly established itself as an innovator in the region. Hot-blooded Spanish Tempranillo is this place's pride and joy, though inky malbec and torrid Sangiovese also highlight a repertoire heavy on Mediterranean varietals. Admission is free. Hours are 11–5 daily.

Where to Stay & Eat

$–$$$ ✕ **Tolly's.** You can go formal or informal at this restaurant in Oakland, 18 mi north of Roseburg. Have an old-fashioned soda or malt downstairs in the Victorian ice cream parlor, or head upstairs to the oak- and antiques-filled dining room for expertly prepared beef, chicken, seafood, and lamb. Try the grilled salmon or the grilled flank steak marinated and served with fiery chipotle chilies. ⊠ *115 Locust St., Take I–5's Exit 138 and follow the road north from the exit for 4 mi, cross the railroad tracks, and turn west on Locust* ☎ *541/459–3796* ▭ *AE, D, MC, V* ⊙ *Closed Mon.*

¢–$$ ✕ **Casey's Family Dining.** Do they serve breakfast? "Honey, we always serve breakfast." Got it? This classic small-town diner—in a busy highwayside spot that doesn't feel exactly like Mayberry—dishes up massive omelets and crispy hash browns, along with other hearty items for lunch and dinner. ⊠ *326 N.W. Garden Valley Blvd.* ☎ *541/672–1512* ⚠ *Reservations not accepted* ▭ *AE, D, MC, V.*

$–$$$ ✕🔚 **The Steamboat Inn.** Every fall a Who's Who of the world's top fly
Fodor's Choice fishermen converges here, high in the Cascades above the emerald North
★ Umpqua River, in search of the 20-pound steelhead that haunt these waters; guide services are available, as are equipment rentals and sales. Others come simply to relax in the reading nooks or on the broad decks of the riverside guest cabins. Another renowned attraction is the nightly Fisherman's Dinner, a multicourse feast served around a massive 50-year-old sugar-pine dinner table. Lodging choices include riverside cabins, forest bungalows, and riverside suites; the bungalows and suites have kitchens. Make reservations well in advance, especially for a stay between July and October, the prime fishing months. ⊠ *42705 N. Umpqua Hwy., 38 mi*

east of Roseburg on Hwy. 138, near Steamboat Creek, Steamboat 97447 ☎ *541/498-2230* 🖶 *541/498-2411* ⊕ *www.thesteamboatinn.com* 🛏 *8 cabins, 5 bungalows, 2 suites* 🖎 *Restaurant, library, meeting room; no smoking* ☰ *MC, V* ⊘ *Closed Jan. and Feb.*

> **off the beaten path**
>
> **ROGUE RIVER VIEWS** – Nature lovers who want to see the Rogue Rive at its loveliest can take a side trip to the Avenue of the Boulders, Mill Creek Falls, and Barr Creek Falls, off Highway 62, near Prospect. Here the wild waters of the upper Rogue foam through volcanic boulders and the dense greenery of the Rogue River National Forest.

Southern Oregon A to Z

BUS TRAVEL

A half-dozen Greyhound buses a day connect Portland, Salem and other northern points on the I–5 corridor to Medford, southern Oregon's transportation hub. Direct Greyhound service from some other parts of the state can be harder to come by, though you can reach Medford from almost every major Oregon town by some combination of regional carriers. Most bus service to other southern Oregon cities from outside the region goes through Medford. Greyhound serves Klamath Falls and environs via Bend.

The Rogue Valley Transportation District is the area's major public transportation provider. RVTD provides a number of bus routes within Medford itself, service from Medford to Ashland every half-hour between 7 AM and 6:30 PM, and nine buses a day from Medford to Jacksonville. 🖪 Bus Information **Greyhound** ☎ 800/231-2222 ⊕ www.greyhound.com. **Rogue Valley Transportation District** ☎ 541/779-5821 ⊕ www.rvtd.org.

CAR TRAVEL

I–5 runs north–south the length of the Umpqua and Rogue River valleys, linking Roseburg, Grants Pass, Medford, and Ashland. Many regional attractions lie not too far east or west of I–5. Jacksonville is a short drive due west from Medford. Highway 138 winds along the Umpqua River, east of Roseburg to the back door of Crater Lake National Park. Highway 140 passes through Klamath Falls.

VISITOR INFORMATION

Ashland Chamber of Commerce and Visitors Information Center (✉ 110 E. Main St., 97520 ☎ 541/482-3486 ⊕ www.ashlandchamber.org). **Grants Pass Visitors & Convention Bureau** (✉ 1501 N.E. 6th St., 97526 ☎ 541/476-7717 or 800/547-5927 ⊕ www.visitgrantspass.org). **Illinois Valley Chamber of Commerce (Cave Junction and Oregon Caves National Monument)** (🖃 Box 312, Cave Junction 97523 ☎ 541/592-3326 ⊕ www.cavejunction.com). **Jacksonville Chamber of Commerce** (🖃 Box 33, 97530 ☎ 541/899-8118 ⊕ www.jacksonvilleoregon.org). **Klamath County Chamber of Commerce** (✉ 507 Main St., 97601 ☎ 541/884-5193 or 877/552-6284 ⊕ www.klamath.org). **Medford Visitors & Convention Bureau** (✉ 101 E. 8th St., 97501 ☎ 800/469-6307 or 541/779-4847 ⊕ www.visitmedford.org). **Roseburg Visitors & Convention Bureau** (✉ 410 S.E. Spruce St., 97470 ☎ 541/672-9731 or 800/444-9584 ⊕ www.visitroseburg.com). **Southern Oregon Visitors Association** (✉ 332 W. 6th St., Medford 97501 ☎ 541/779-4691 ⊕ www.sova.org).

EASTERN OREGON

Updated by
Sarah Kennedy

Travel east from The Dalles, Bend, or any of the foothill communities blossoming in the shade of the Cascades, and a very different side of Oregon makes its appearance. The air is drier, clearer, and often pungent with the smell of juniper. The vast landscape of sharply folded hills, wheat fields, and mountains shimmering in the distance evokes the Old West. There is a lonely grandeur in eastern Oregon, a plain-spoken, independent spirit that can startle, surprise, and entrance.

Much of eastern Oregon consists of national forest and wilderness, and the people who live here lead very down-to-earth lives. This is a world of ranches and rodeos, pickup trucks and country-western music. Some of the most important moments in Oregon's history took place in the towns of northeastern Oregon. The Oregon Trail passed through this corner of the state, winding through the Grande Ronde Valley between the Wallowa and Blue mountain ranges. The discovery of gold in the region in the 1860s sparked a second invasion of settlers and eventually led to the displacement of the Native American Nez Perce and Paiute tribes. Pendleton, La Grande, and Baker City were all beneficiaries of the gold fever that swept through the area. Signs of even earlier times survive, from the John Day Fossil Beds with its fragments of saber-toothed tigers, giant pigs, and three-toed horses to Native American writings and artifacts hidden within canyon walls in Malheur County's Leslie Gulch.

Numbers in the text correspond to numbers in the margin and on the Eastern Oregon map.

Umatilla

❶ *185 mi east of Portland on I–84 and Rte. 730; 36 mi northwest of Pendleton.*

Umatilla is at the confluence of the Umatilla and Columbia rivers. It was founded in the mid-1800s as a trade and shipping center during the gold rush, and today it is a center for fishing activities. Just east of Umatilla, Hat Rock State Park contains the unusual geological formation from which it gets its name. Farther upstream, McNary Dam generates extensive hydroelectric power and impounds a lake that extends from Umatilla to Richland, Washington, some 70 mi away.

On the south shore of Lake Wallula, **Hat Rock State Park** was the first major landmark that Lewis and Clark passed on their expedition down the Columbia. The rock itself stands tall amid rolling sagebrush hills and looks down upon the lake, which is a popular spot for jet skiing, swimming, boating, and fishing for walleye and sturgeon. In addition to water sports, the park provides scenic picnic spots and gorgeous views of the stark, desert-like landscape. Be aware, however, that it abuts an upscale lakeside housing development that's visible from some of the park, making it a little difficult to pretend you're in the days of Lewis and Clark. ⊠ *U.S. 730, 9 mi. east of Umatilla* ☎ *800/551–6949* ⊕ *www.prd.state.or.us* ☒ *Free* ☺ *Mid-Mar.–Oct., daily.*

On the Columbia River, the hydroelectric dam at **McNary Lock and Dam,** completed in 1954, impounds a lake that extends 70 mi upstream from Umatilla to Richland, Washington. Today the area surrounding the dam includes the McNary Wildlife Nature Area, two small parks and picnic areas, an elaborate visitor center with an exhibit and information about Pacific salmon, and a trail that follows the Columbia River bank for 3 mi to Hat Rock State Park. Above the dam, McNary Beach Park's picnic area overlooks a large swim beach, while Hat Rock Scenic Corridor also leads to Hat Rock State Park. ⊠ *U.S. 730* ☎ *541/ 922–4388* 🖃 *Free* ☾ *Daily; marinas June–Sept., daily.*

With a marina, a boat-launch, a small swimming area, and an RV campground with 26 full hookups, the unadorned **Umatilla Marina Park** provides great access to the Columbia, but if you're planning a relaxing afternoon of picnicking or lounging on land, go to Hat Rock State Park or one of the parks at McNary Dam. There's little in the way of scenery or greenery here. ⊠ *3rd Ave. on Columbia River* ☎ *541/922–3939* 🖃 *Day use free; full hookups $20, tent sites $12* ☾ *Marina daily 7–7.*

Stretching from west of Boardman to Irrigon, the 23,555-acre **Umatilla National Wildlife Refuge** includes marsh, woodland, and wetland habitats that make it vital to migrating waterfowl and bald eagles, in addition to myriad species of resident wildlife. Although there are numerous routes to access portions of the refuge, the best and easiest way to view wildlife in ponds and wetlands is to drive along the McCormick Auto Route, accessible from Paterson Ferry Road, off Route 730, 9 mi west of Umatilla. ⊠ *Stretches from Boardman, 20 mi west of Umatilla, to Irrigon, 9 mi west of Umatilla, north of I–84 along Columbia River* ☎ *503/922–3232* ⊕ *www.fws.gov* 🖃 *Free* ☾ *Daily sunrise–sunset on designated roadways only.*

Where to Stay & Eat

$–$$ ✕ **Desert River Inn.** With large booths and pastel walls, this casual and family-friendly spot—widely regarded as the best restaurant in either Umatilla or Hermiston—has no pretention of urban chic, but the large menu of prime rib, fresh pasta, and seafood, as well as the vegetarian entrées (a rare find in eastern Oregon), is bound to tempt most palates. A stop here is a satisfying finish to a day of exploring, boating, or golfing at the course next to the inn. ⊠ *705 Willamette Ave., 97882* ☎ *541/ 992–1000 or 877/922–1500* 🖃 *AE, D, DC, MC, V.*

$ 🏨 **Desert River Inn.** The largest and, by far, the most well-equipped hotel in Umatilla, the Desert River Inn acts as the centerpiece of the town, with its restaurant, golf course, and banquet rooms making it far more than a place to spend the night. The rooms are large and comfortable, even if the furnishings—brown shag carpet offset by blue bedspreads and curtains—are a bit dated. Some rooms have kitchenettes. ⊠ *705 Willamette Ave., 97882* ☎ *541/922–1000 or 877/922–1500* 🖶 *541/922– 1200* 🛏 *66 rooms* ♿ *Restaurant, room service, in-room data ports, some kitchenettes, microwaves, refrigerators, cable TV, 18-hole golf course, pool, gym, outdoor hot tub, horseshoes, bar, meeting rooms, free parking, some pets allowed (fee)* 🖃 *AE, D, DC, MC, V* ⛾ *CP.*

Hermiston

❷   *188 mi east of Portland on I–84, 28 mi northwest of Pendleton.*

Although its population is just over 10,000 residents, Hermiston is the urban service center for nearly three times that many people in the expansive and productive agricultural industry that surrounds it. Irrigated farmlands and ranch lands produce livestock and crops, including alfalfa, potatoes, corn, wheat, and the watermelons for which Hermiston is best known. The town was named for Robert Louis Stevenson's unfinished novel, *The Weir of Hermiston.* Hermiston contains more than 75 acres of city parks, with the Columbia River just 6 mi to the north and the Umatilla River and Blue Mountains nearby.

The railroad came to Hermiston in 1883, and some of the original tracks are still at **Maxwell Siding Railroad Display,** an outdoor exhibit of railroad cars and memorabilia. There is a 1910 rotary snowplow, a 1913 diner from the Oregon Short Line, a 1912 passenger car, a 1949 steam-powered snowplow (the last of its kind used in the United States), and two cabooses; if you like, you can arrange to get married in one of them. There are some unusual automobiles too, including a rare 1922 Buda. ⊠ *200 W. Highland Ave., across from Hermiston High School, 97838* ☎ *541/567–8532 or 541/567–3759* ✉ *Donation* ☉ *Sat. and by appointment.*

★ Ten miles south of Hermiston, just off I–84, the tiny town of **Echo,** site of Fort Henrietta, sits at the intersection of the Oregon Trail and the transcontinental railroad that arrived in 1881. With only a handful of streets comprising the center of town, a short walking tour will take about an hour. You'll pass several buildings erected in the town's heyday—in the late 19th and early 20th centuries—and you'll see the Chinese House/ON&R Railroad Museum, originally a bunkhouse for Chinese railroad crews, which now has railroad artifacts. From Echo, head back to Hermiston or along the scenic old Highway 30 to Pendleton (21 mi). ⊹ *1 mi south of I–84 at Exit 188.*

> **need a break?**
>
> After exploring historic Echo, grab a cup of coffee or an ice cream cone at **Little River Cafe** (⊠ 231 W. Main St., Echo ☎ 541/376–8573).

Where to Stay & Eat

$–$$$ ✕ **Hale's Restaurant and Lounge.** With rodeo artifacts on the walls, country music playing, a menu bound in soft brown leather, and dark red leather booths, Hale's manages to create a classy, upscale feel with an old West rodeo flair. A Hermiston institution since 1906, Hale's is a dependable choice for prime rib, steak, and pork chops. Open from 10 AM daily, it also serves a breakfast menu all day, including huge omelets and steak and eggs. ⊠ *174 E. Main St.* ☎ *541/567–7975* ▭ *AE, D, DC, MC, V.*

$–$$ ▦ **Oxford Suites.** Perhaps Hermiston's most luxurious hotel, this all-suites facility has lovely, spacious rooms in two buildings, all with large sitting areas with work desks and sofas. In addition to a complimentary breakfast buffet, an evening reception with free food and drinks is held daily in the lounge area. ⊠ *1050 N. 1st St., 97838* ☎ *514/564–8000 or 888/545–7848* 🖷 *514/564–0633* ⊕ *www.oxfordsuites.com* ⇌ *127 suites* ♿ *Dining room, in-room data ports, microwaves, refrigerators, cable TV with VCRs, indoor pool, gym, spa, shop, laundry facilities, business services, meeting rooms, free parking, no-smoking rooms* ▭ *AE, D, DC, MC, V* ⧖ *BP.*

$ ▦ **Oak Tree Inn.** Comfortable and well equipped, this hotel is directly behind Safeway Supermarket, minutes from Main Street. The newest addition to Hermiston's fleet of hotels, it has lovely rooms and useful amenities inside a surprisingly plain and understated exterior. Microwaves and refrigerators are available upon request. ⊠ *1110 S.E. 4th St., 97838* ☎ *503/567–2330 or 800/537–8483* ⇌ *62 rooms* ♿ *In-room data ports, cable TV, gym, hot tub, spa, laundry facilities, free parking; no smoking* ▭ *AE, D, DC, MC, V.*

Sports & the Outdoors

RODEO The **Farm City Pro Rodeo** (⊠ 495 E. Main St. ☎ 541/564–8500) is held for several days in August each year, in conjunction with the Umatilla County Fair.

Pendleton

3 *211 mi east of Portland, 129 mi east of The Dalles on I–84.*

At the foot of the Blue Mountains amid vast wheat fields and cattle ranches, Pendleton is a quintessential western town with a rip-snorting history. The herds of wild horses that once thundered across this rolling landscape were at the center of the area's early Native American cultures. Later, Pendleton became an important pioneer junction and home to a sizable Chinese community. Lacking a sheriff until 1912, Pendleton was a raw and wild frontier town filled with cowboys, cattle rustlers, saloons, and bordellos. The many century-old homes still standing vary in style from simple farmhouses to stately Queen Annes.

Given its raucous past, Pendleton, the largest city in eastern Oregon (population almost 17,000), looks unusually sedate. But all that changes in September when the **Pendleton Round-Up** (⇨ Sports & the Outdoors) draws thousands for a rodeo and related events. Motels fill up, schools close down, and everybody goes hog-wild for a few days.

Perhaps Pendleton's main source of name-recognition in the country today comes from the Pendleton Woolen Mills, home of the trademark wool plaid shirts and colorful woolen Indian blankets that are sold nationwide. Pendleton also produces a full line of men's and women's clothing, and although Pendleton headquarters has moved to Portland, the Pendleton mill is still operating and is available to tour.

The collection at the **Round-Up Hall of Fame Museum** spans the rodeo's history since 1910 with photographs—including some great ones of Rodeo Queens and the Happy Canyon Princesses (all Native American)—as well as saddles, guns, costumes, and even a stuffed championship bronco named War Paint. ⊠ *Round-Up Grounds, 1205 S.W. Court Ave., near S.W. 12th St.* ☎ *541/278–0815* ☕ *Free* ☾ *May–Oct., daily 10–4; other times, call for appointment.*

Fodor's Choice
★ The **Underground**, a 90-minute vividly guided tour, yields clues about life in Pendleton more than a century ago, when the town held 32 saloons and 18 brothels. The first half of the tour heads into a subterranean labyrinth that hid gambling rooms, an opium den, and other illegal businesses. Chinese laborers lived in a chilly jumble of underground rooms. The second half focuses on the life of Madame Stella Darby, the town's best-known madam, and includes a visit to her bordello. Tours operate year-round and leave throughout the day. Call for information; reservations are strongly recommended. ⊠ *37 S.W. Emigrant Ave.* ☎ *541/276–0730 or 800/226–6398* ⊕ *www.pendletonundergroundtours.com* ☕ *$10.*

need a break? A popular little laid-back spot across from the Underground Tours, the **Cookie Tree** (⊠ 39 S.W. Emigrant Ave. ☎ 514/278–0343) is good for a quick breakfast, sandwich, pastry, or fresh bread.

Displays and photographs at the **Umatilla County Historical Society Museum** outline Pendleton's story. The town's old railway depot houses the museum. ⊠ *108 S.W. Frazer Ave.* ☎ *541/276–0012* ☕ *$2* ☾ *Tues.–Sat. 10–4.*

The **Pendleton Chamber of Commerce** (⊠ 501 S. Main St. ☎ 541/276–7411 or 800/547–8911 ⊕ www.pendleton-oregon.org ☾ Weekdays 8–5), has information about the town and surrounding area, including the Umatilla National Forest and the Blue Mountains.

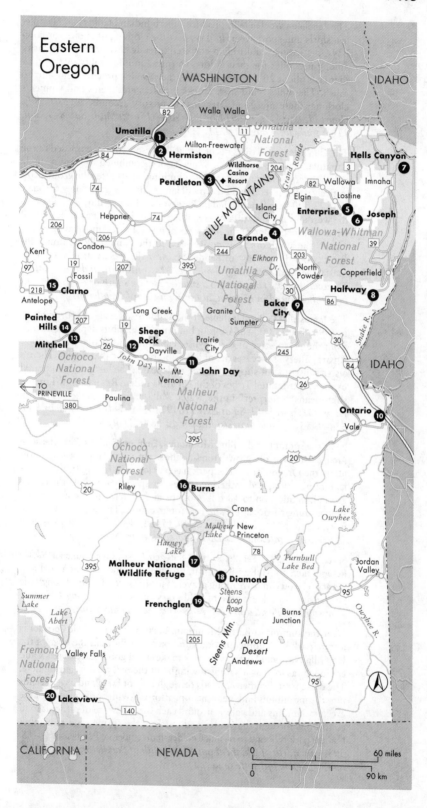

The **Pendleton Woolen Mills** produce superb Indian blankets and Pendleton shirts and sportswear. In days past the clothing of choice for cowboys, the western and Indian–inspired threads have gained popularity among urbanites for their colors, warmth, and durability. A free tour that lasts about 20 minutes describes the weaving process from start to finish. The mill's retail store stocks blankets and men's and women's clothing; there are good bargains on factory seconds. ⊠ *1307 S.E. Court Pl.* ☎ *541/276–6911 or 800/568–3156* ☉ *Mon.–Sat. 8–5, Sun. 11–3; tours weekdays at 9, 11, 1:30, and 3.*

The Confederated Tribes of the Umatilla Reservation, composed of the Umatilla, Cayuse, and Walla Walla Tribes, combined to form a single tribal government in 1949, nearly a hundred years after the groups collectively ceded several million acres of land to the U.S. government. Today, the 172,000-acre **Umatilla Indian Reservation,** bordered by Pendleton to the west and the Umatilla National Forest to the east, has about 2,000 tribal members. One of the major economic ventures undertaken by the tribe is the Wildhorse Casino Resort and the Tamastslikt Cultural Institute, found 6 mi east of Pendleton, near the Reservation's westernmost edge. ⊠ *Bounded by I–84, Rte. 11 (to Athena), and the Umatilla National Forest. There is also a smaller section south of I–84. Governing bodies found in Mission, about 6 mi east of Pendleton.*

The **Tamastslikt Cultural Institute** at the Wildhorse Casino Resort opened in 1998. The 45,000-square-foot building has exhibits depicting history from the perspective of the Cayuse, Umatilla, and Walla Walla tribes. An art gallery showcases art of local and regional tribal artists. There's also a museum gift shop, a theater, and a café. The institute is operated by the Confederated Tribes of the Umatilla Indian Reservation. Tamastslikt means "interpret" in the Walla Walla native language. ⊠ *72789 Hwy. 331, north of I–84 at Exit 216, 97801* ☎ *541/966–9748 or 800/ 654–9453* ⊕ *www.tamastslikt.com* 💲 *$6* ☉ *Daily 9–5.*

Near the summit of the Blue Mountains, **Emigrant Springs State Heritage Area,** a park in an old-growth forest, is the site of a popular pioneer stopover along the Oregon Trail. The park has picnic areas, hiking trails, historical information, and gathering spaces for special events. At the campground, in addition to 18 full hookups and 33 tent sites, you will find six charming rustic cabins and two totem cabins. There also is a six-site horse camp. ⊠ *Off I–84 at Exit 234* ☎ *541/983–2277 or 800/551–6949* ⊕ *www.prd.state.or.us* 💲 *Day use free* ☉ *Mar.–Nov., daily.*

Seven miles south of Pendleton, the 1,836-acre **McKay Creek National Wildlife Refuge,** next to McKay Reservoir, provides a home for waterfowl and plant life. You can drive along gravel roads for several miles through the enchantingly stark expanse of wild grass and sage. ⊠ *Along U.S. 395, 7 mi south of Pendleton* 💲 *Free* ☉ *Mar.–Sept., daily sunrise–sunset.*

Near the summit of Battle Mountain, **Battle Mountain Scenic Corridor** is a state park with gorgeous views and picnic facilities at the edge of the Umatilla National Forest. The park makes for a good place to relax and eat lunch (as long as it's not snowing), but the real treat is getting here. The drive from Pendleton winds through hills of farmland as it ascends into the mountains and, near the top, affords jaw-dropping views of the green mountains and valleys around each turn. Beware of difficult road conditions through the winter and much of the spring, and remember that the park is bound to be much colder than temperate Pendleton. ⊠ *U.S. 395, 9 mi north of Ukiah; about 40 mi south of Pendleton* ☎ *800/551– 6949* ⊕ *www.prd.state.or.us* 💲 *Free.*

The North Fork of the John Day River and Camas Creek, which flow through **Ukiah-Dale Forest State Park,** have excellent trout, steelhead, and salmon fishing. Three miles southwest of Ukiah, this park is quite a hike from Pendleton, but if you want to camp in the Umatilla National Forest, or are heading as far as Ukiah on a day of scenic driving, be sure to check it out. A campground has 27 primitive sites. ⊠ *U.S. 395, about 50 mi south of Pendleton* ☎ *541/983–2277 or 800/551–6949* ⊕ *www. prd.state.or.us* ⊠ *Free* ⊙ *Mid-Apr.–Nov., daily.*

The 1.4-million-acre **Umatilla National Forest** has three wilderness areas, as well as the Blue Mountain Scenic Byway and 22 campgrounds. In the Blue Mountains of northeastern Oregon and southeastern Washington, the diverse forest land is found both east and south of Pendleton and extends south almost as far as John Day, where it borders the Malheur National Forest. To the east, it is bordered by the Wallowa-Whitman National Forest. Major thoroughfares, including I–84, U.S. 395, and Routes 204 and 244, pass through portions of the forest. In the summer months, the Blue Mountain Scenic Byway provides a beautiful way to travel to Baker City from Ukiah or points farther west. A ski area in the Umatilla National Forest, **Spout Springs** (⊠ Summit of Hwy. 204 at Tollgate, Milepost 22 ☎ 541/566–0327 ⊙ Thurs. 5 PM–9 PM, Fri. 1 PM–9 PM, Sat. 9–9, Sun. 9–4) has an elevation of 4,950 feet at the base, 5,550 feet at the top, and a vertical drop of 550 feet. There are 11 runs and 21 km of Nordic trails. ☎ *541/278–3716* ⊙ *Some areas only in summer; call to confirm accessibility.*

Where to Stay & Eat

★ **$–$$$**   ✕ **Raphael's.** Chef Raphael Hoffman serves traditional steaks, seafood, and fettuccine dishes, but she also specializes in adventurous seasonal cuisine—venison, elk, rattlesnake, blackened Cajun alligator, and Indian salmon topped with huckleberries. This may be the only place in eastern Oregon to get a huckleberry daiquiri. Native American artwork figures prominently among the interior furnishings, and a garden out back is perfect for alfresco dining. ⊠ *233 S.E. 4th St.* ☎ *541/276–8500* ⊟ *AE, D, DC, MC, V* ⊙ *Closed Sun. and Mon. No lunch.*

¢   ✕ **Main St. Diner.** Pictures of Elvis and old movie posters fill the walls of this small, flashy retro diner. The black-and-white tile floors and teal vinyl booths might seem a little too self-consciously hip in a larger city, but here in Pendleton, it just feels earnestly fun and friendly. Stop in for an inexpensive breakfast of bacon and eggs, or a basic burger for lunch. ⊠ *349 S. Main St.* ☎ *541/278–1952* ⊟ *MC, V* ⊙ *No dinner.*

$ ▦ **Parker House.** Virtually unchanged since it was built in 1917, this handsome pink stucco home in Pendleton's North Hill neighborhood is a very grand reminder that the Old West had its share of wealth and worldly sophistication. A hybrid blend of French neoclassical and Italianate styles, Parker House is a rarity among B&Bs: it still has its original Chinese wallpaper, custom fittings, and woodwork, which is nothing less than astonishing. The rooms, furnished with period furniture, are quiet and comfortable. Four of the rooms share one bathroom, but once you see it you'll understand why the owner has chosen to preserve everything as it was rather than adding modern "improvements." Breakfasts are delicious and filling and might include eggs Benedict with smoked salmon or pecan-and-cranberry-stuffed French toast. ⊠ *311 N. Main St., 97801* ☎ *541/276–8581 or 800/700–8581* ⇥ *5 rooms, 1 with bath* ⊟ *AE, MC, V* ⦿| *BP.*

FodorsChoice
★

¢–$ ▦ **Working Girls Hotel.** In downtown Pendleton, this 1890s building served at different times as a boardinghouse and a bordello—hence its name— before it was restored and opened as a hotel in 1991. Today, it is owned and operated by the Underground Tours. The rooms, with 18-foot-high ceilings and exposed-brick walls, are individually furnished with antiques dating from the early 1900s to the 1950s, and a full kitchen and dining room are available to guests. ⊠ *17 S.W. Emigrant Ave., 97801* ☎ *541/ 276–0730 or 800/226–6398* ⊟ *541/276–0665* ⊅ *4 rooms share 1 bath, 1 suite* ♿ *No kids, no smoking* ⊟ *D, MC, V.*

Sports & the Outdoors

FISHING Oregon's largest full-service fly shop east of the Cascades, **Blue Mountain Anglers and Fly Shop** (⊠ 1847 Westgate ☎ 800/825–1548) also has a fishing school and information about angling in the area; the focus here is on fishing in the Umatilla River for steelhead, trout, and salmon.

RODEO The Blue Mountains may be the area's largest attraction, but the **Pendleton Round-Up** is certainly the biggest; more than 50,000 people roll into town for this overwhelming event, one of the oldest and most prominent rodeos in the United States. Held on the second full week of September, it attracts rodeo performers and fans for four days of rodeo events, wild-horse races, barbecues, parades, and milking contests. Vendors line the length of Court Avenue and Main Street, selling beadwork and western-style curios while country bands twang in the background. Tickets for the events—which include the Happy Canyon Pageant and Dance—cost between $6 and $12; make your reservations far in advance. ⊠ *Rodeo grounds and ticket office: 1205 S.W. Court Ave., at S.W. 12th St.* ⅅ *Box 609, Pendleton 97801* ☎ *541/276–2553 or 800/457–6336.*

Shopping

Claiming to be "Pendleton's Favorite Store," **Clough's on Main** (⊠ 216 S. Main St. ☎ 541/276–2227) has plenty of women's clothing, jewelry, gifts, leather goods and handcrafted wood products worth browsing, as long as you can endure the strong scents emanating from the adjoining nail and hair salon. The **Collector's Gallery** (⊠ 223 S.E. Court Ave. ☎ 541/276–6697) is a large, disorganized antiques store where you get the feeling there are always more fun treasures to be unearthed around the next corner. On-site craftspeople fashion hand-tooled saddles that are considered the best in the world at **Hamley & Co. Western Store & Custom Saddlery** (⊠ 30 S.E. Court Ave. ☎ 541/276–2321), which carries authentic cowboy and cowgirl gear and quality leather products. The only store in town that sells the women's line of Pendleton fashions is **Murphy House** (⊠ 1112 S.E. Emigrant Ave. ☎ 541/276–7020). Inside the Center for the Arts, **Pendleton Foundation Craft Gallery** (⊠ 214 N. Main St. ☎ 541/278–9201) sells the original artwork and crafts pieces of approximately 40 local artists. **Picket Fences** (⊠ 239 S.E. Court Ave. ☎ 541/276–9515) is a charming country store with home and garden gifts, as wells as some antiques.

La Grande

4 *56 mi southeast of Pendleton on I–84 at Rte. 82.*

La Grande started life in the late 1800s as a farming community. It grew slowly while most towns along the Blue Mountains were booming or busting in the violent throes of gold-fueled stampedes. When the railroad companies were deciding where to lay their tracks through the valley, a clever local farmer donated 150 acres to ensure that the iron horse would run through La Grande. With the power of steam fueling a new boom, the town quickly outgrew its neighbors, claimed the title of county seat from fading Union City, and now, with its population of 12,000, sits at the urban center of the valley. La Grande is also the site of the only four-year college in the region, Eastern Oregon State College. The town is a convenient stop if you're heading to the nearby Wallowa Mountains.

Stop by the **La Grande Visitor Center** for information and brochures. ⊠ *102 Elm St.* ☎ *541/963–8588 or 800/848–9969* ⊕ *www.visitlagrande.com.*

The **Wallowa Mountains** form a rugged U-shape fortress between Hells Canyon on the Idaho border and the Blue Mountains, west of the Grande Ronde Valley. Sometimes called the American Alps or Little Switzerland, the granite peaks in this range are between 5,000 and 9,000 feet in height. Dotted with crystalline alpine lakes and meadows, rushing rivers, and thickly forested valleys that fall between the mountain ridges, the Wallowas have a grandeur that can take your breath away. Bighorn sheep, elk, deer, and mountain goats populate the entire area. Nearly all the trails in the Wallowa Mountains are at least partially contained within the Eagle Cap Wilderness. The offices and visitor center for the mountains are in Enterprise. ✦ *From La Grande, Rtes. 82, 203, and 237 will all lead to parts of the Wallowa Mountains.*

> **need a break?** Don't visit **Joe and Sugar's** (⊠ 1119 Adams Ave. ☎ 514/975–5282) if you want to remain an anonymous tourist; you can't avoid being chatted up by the funny, friendly, and helpful owner of this sweet-smelling café and coffee shop. If you make it past the cookies and pastries that greet you at the front counter without filling up, you can look forward to some truly delicious homemade soup.

The 358,441-acre **Eagle Cap Wilderness,** the largest in Oregon, encompasses most of the Wallowa range and has 534 mi of trails for hardcore backpackers and horseback riders. Most of the popular trailheads are along the wilderness' northern edge, most accessible from Enterprise or Joseph, but you also can find several trailheads 20 to 30 mi southeast of La Grande along Route 203. For wilderness information, contact the Wallowa Mountains Visitor Center in Enterprise. To park at most trailheads, you must purchase a Northwest Forest Pass: $5 per day, $30 per year; to hike into the wilderness, you also must get a free permit that will alert rangers of your plans. Some areas of the wilderness are accessible year-round, while the high-elevation areas are accessible only for a few months in the summer. ⊠ *East of La Grande, via Rte. 82 and Rte. 203.*

Several miles southeast of La Grande, **Union's National Historic District** is a Victorian-era town that is working to restore many of its historic buildings along the several-block stretch of Main Street. In addition to the charming buildings lining Main Street, the main attractions are the **Union Hotel** (⊠ 326 N. Main St. ☎ 541/562–6135 ⊕ www. theunionhotel.com), a beautifully restored hotel with a restaurant and parlor, and the **Union County Museum** (⊠ 333 S. Main St. ☎ 541/562–6003 ☉ May–mid-Oct., Mon.–Sat. 10–4, Sun. 1–4, or by appointment), which has the Cowboy Heritage Collection. ⊠ *11 mi southeast of La Grande via Rte. 203.*

Where to Stay & Eat

★ ¢–$$$ ╳ **Foley Station.** Widely regarded as one of La Grande's finest places to eat, this local favorite has an open kitchen, exposed-brick walls, comfortable booths, and lovely outdoor seating. The rotating menu incorporates Northwest ingredients in innovative creations such as lamb chops grilled with fire-roasted Fuji apples and Jack Daniels jus, and Italian crespelle (like a crepe) with spinach, mushrooms, tomato, and cheese saffron risotto. At lunch look for anything from rock-shrimp gemellini to gyros, fish-and-chips, and burgers, and at breakfast choose from seven varieties of waffles (including lemon poppy seed and Cuban banana) or go all out for a frittata with scallops, bacon, asparagus, and smoked Gouda. ⊠ *1011 Adams Ave.* ☎ *541/963–7473* ⊟ *MC, V* ☉ *Closed Mon. and Tues. No dinner Sun. or Wed.*

¢–$$$ ✕ **Ten Depot St.** In a stylish historic brick building that has a VFW upstairs, Ten Depot St. has everything from burgers to beautifully prepared steak and seafood dishes. With dark wood throughout accented by plum tablecloths and teal plates and napkins, it's an elegant place to dine. Start off your evening with a drink at the adjoining bar. ⊠ *10 Depot St.* ☎ *514/963–8766* ⊟ *AE, D, DC, MC, V* ☉ *Closed Sun. No lunch.*

★ $–$$ ▣ **Stang Manor Bed and Breakfast.** Get a feel for the luxury of a bygone era at this 10,000-square-foot Georgian Revival mansion built in 1926 by a timber baron. The elegant and beautifully maintained guest rooms in this house, which has remained unmodified except for its wall coverings, include the Maid's Room, with seven doors and a balcony overlooking the rose garden, and the Fireplace Suite, with a queen canopy bed and sitting room with a fireplace. Breakfast is a lavish multicourse affair served in the formal dining room by the charming and witty hosts. ⊠ *1612 Walnut St., 97850* ☎ *541/963–2400* ⊜ *888/286–9463* ⊕ *www.stangmanor.com* ⇱ *3 rooms, 1 suite* ⊟ *MC, V.*

¢–$ ▣ **Union Hotel.** The lavish Union Hotel first opened in 1921 and, after
Fodor'sChoice a period of disrepair late in the century, was renovated and reopened in
★ 1996, providing the historic town of Union with a gorgeous and reasonably priced hotel. It's also a handy place if you're exploring the historic towns in the area or are just looking for a place to sleep between jaunts into the great outdoors. The accommodations run from spacious and romantic suites to far smaller and simpler bedrooms. The Northwest Room has antique timbers, a kitchenette, and Jacuzzi; the Davis Brothers Room has a walk-in wood-panel shower and western decor; and the Southwest Room has live cacti and handcrafted log furniture. ⊠ *326 N. Main St., Union 97883* ☎ *541/562–6135 or 888/441–8928* ⊕ *www.theunionhotel.com* ⇱ *13 rooms* ♻ *Restaurant, lounge, shop; no room phones, no room TVs* ⊟ *MC, V.*

> en route   Heading north from La Grande, Highway 82 passes through the small towns of Elgin and Minam before looping south toward Wallowa, Lostine, Enterprise, and Joseph en route to Wallowa Lake, where it dead-ends. Packed with RVs and cars during the summer, the road sprouts diners, motels, and plenty of antiques shops in every town it passes. If you have only limited time for browsing, save it for Joseph.

Enterprise

❺ *6 mi north of Joseph on Rte. 82.*

The seat of Oregon's northeasternmost county, Enterprise is surrounded by some of the region's most rugged natural beauty and is a locus for rugged outdoor activities in winter and summer. To the west lie the Eagle Cap Wilderness, the alpine Wallowa Mountains, and pristine Wallowa Lake, and to the east is the Hells Canyon National Recreation Area.

For information about the Eagle Cap Wilderness, stop in at the **Wallowa Mountains Visitors Center** outside Enterprise. It has videos of the area, pamphlets, and topographical maps. ⊠ *Hwy. 82, 1 mi west of Enterprise* ☎ *541/426–5546* ☉ *Memorial Day–Labor Day, Mon.–Sat. 8–5; Labor Day–Memorial Day, weekdays 8–5.*

Wallowa County Chamber of Commerce (✉ 936 W. North St. ☎ 541/426–4622 or 800/585–4121) has valuable information about the whole county, including lodging, dining, and sightseeing in Joseph, Enterprise, and around Wallowa Lake and Hells Canyon.

At the **Wallowa Valley Ranger District** headquarters (✉ 88401 Hwy. 82 ☎ 541/426–4978) you can find detailed information about the Wallowa-Whitman National Forest and its recreational possibilities.

Where to Stay & Eat

★ ¢–$ ✕ **Terminal Gravity Brew Pub.** Beer connoisseurs from across the state, and just about all the locals, rave about the India Pale Ale at this tiny microbrewery in a yellow house on the outskirts of downtown, but with kids and dogs lounging on the front porch and in the small upstairs dining room, it is clear that it's not just about the booze in this friendly local hangout. The menu is short and simple, with creative sandwiches and burgers. There's a rotating selection of the brews on tap. ✉ 803 School St. ☎ 541/426–0158 ▭ No credit cards ☉ Closed Mon. and Tues. No lunch. Limited hrs in winter, call ahead.

¢–$ ▣ **Cherokee Mingo Motel.** About 16 mi west of Enterprise, the tiny town of Wallowa has a main street, a couple of restaurants, and a few stores, as well as this small and friendly motel. Each room has a different theme, ranging from celestial bodies to sea life. Bedspreads, borders, and shower curtains all share a colorful pattern that gives each large room a unique flair; the furnishings aren't subtle, but they're fun, and the rooms stand out from the run-of-the-mill units to be found in other motels in the same price range. If you are headed into the Wallowa-Whitman National Forest, or are just seeking to avoid some of the summertime crowds in Enterprise and Joseph, consider spending a night at this little outpost of civilization. ✉ 102 N. Alder, Wallowa 97885 ☎ 541/886–2021 ⇥ 11 rooms ⚭ Refrigerators, cable TV ▭ D, MC, V.

Joseph

❻ *80 mi east of La Grande on Hwy. 82.*

The area around Wallowa Lake was the traditional home of the Nez Perce Indians—the town of Joseph is named for Chief Joseph, their famous leader. The peaks of the Wallowa Mountains, snow-covered until July, tower 5,000 feet above the town and Wallowa Lake, which are the regional tourist hubs.

☾ The **David and Lee Manuel Museum** has a superb collection of Nez Perce clothing and artifacts. The museum, which also has pioneer wagons, is one of the town's leading bronze foundries, with 14,000 square feet of facilities in separate buildings. There are also a children's museum and an exhibit of bronze sculptures. ✉ 400 N. Main St. ☎ 541/432–7235 ▣ $6 ☉ June–Oct., daily 8–5; Nov.–May, Mon.–Sat. 10–4; tours at 10:15 and 2:15.

need a
break?

Across from the David and Lee Manuel Museum, **Magnoni's Market Place** (✉ 403 N. Main St. ☎ 541/432–3663) has an Italian restaurant with pasta and salads, plus an espresso café, a beauty salon, and gift shops.

To tour the **Valley Bronze of Oregon** foundry facility, head to its showroom, the **Valley Bronze Gallery** (☎ 541/432–7445 ✉ 18 S. Main St.), which displays the bronze sculptures of many artists whose works are cast at the foundry, in addition to the work of other artists from around the world. The gallery is open Monday–Saturday 10–5, Sunday noon–5.

The foundry itself is just a ¼ mi away, and your tour guide will lead you there after you have gathered at the showroom. ✉ *307 W. Alder St.* ☎ *541/432-7551* ⊕ *www.valleybronze.com* 🖾 *$5* ⊙ *Two tours daily; call for times.*

The **Wallowa County Museum** in Joseph has a small but poignant collection of artifacts and photographs chronicling the Nez Perce Wars, a series of battles against the U.S. Army that took place in the late 1870s. The building, originally built as a bank in 1888, was robbed in 1896, an event that is reenacted with full pageantry every Wednesday at 1 PM in summer, complete with music, dancing girls, gunshots, and yelping. ✉ *110 S. Main St.* ☎ *541/432-6095* 🖾 *Free* ⊙ *Memorial Day–Sept., daily 10–5.*

From Joseph, Highway 82 continues south and ends at sparkling, blue-green **Wallowa Lake** (✉ Wallowa Lake Hwy.), the highest body of water in eastern Oregon (elevation 5,000 feet). Call the **Joseph Chamber of Commerce** (✉ 102 E. 1st St., 97846 ☎ 541/32-1015) for information about Wallowa Lake and its facilities.

Six miles south of Joseph, **Wallowa Lake State Recreation Park** is a campground surrounded on three sides by 9,000-foot-tall snowcapped mountains. It also serves as a gateway to Hells Canyon. It has 121 full hookups, 89 tent sites, and 2 yurts. Popular activities include fishing and boating as well as hiking on wilderness trails, horseback riding, and canoeing. There are also bumper boats and miniature golf. You can ride a tramway to the top of one of the mountains. ✉ *Rte. 82* ☎ *541/432-4185 or 800/551-6949* ⊕ *www.prd.state.or.us* 🖾 *Day use $3 per vehicle* ⊙ *Daily.*

★ The **Wallowa Lake Tramway,** the steepest gondola in North America, rises to the top of 8,150-foot Mt. Howard in 15 minutes. Vistas of mountain peaks, forest, and Wallowa Lake far below will dazzle you on the way up and at the summit. Two and a half miles of hiking trails await you at the top, and you can enjoy lunch at the Summit Grill and Alpine Patio before descending to Earth. ✉ *59919 Wallowa Lake Hwy.* ☎ *541/432-5331* 🖾 *$14.95* ⊙ *May, June, and Sept., daily 10–4; July and Aug., daily 10–5.*

Where to Stay & Eat

¢-$ ✕ **Stubborn Mule Saloon and Steakhouse.** With a dark red and green barnlike exterior behind large wooden columns, this restaurant and bar really does feel like an old saloon from the outside. Inside is a small no-frills dining room, where you seat yourself at simple wooden tables, and an adjoining tavern where locals drink beer and play pool. The family-friendly restaurant makes great burgers (nothing smaller than a half-pound), sandwiches, and steak, and there are plenty of beers on tap. ✉104 S. Main St. ☎ 541/432-6853 ▤ MC, V ⊙ Closed Mon.

★ ¢ ✕ **Summit Grill and Alpine Patio.** At an altitude of 8,200 feet on Mt. Howard, this is the Northwest's highest restaurant, reached by a 15-minute ride on the Wallowa Lake Tramway. The menu is limited to burgers, sandwiches, burritos, salads, chili, soups, and Oregon beers and wines, but the view of four bordering states is striking. ✉ *59919 Wallowa Lake Hwy.* ☎ *541/432-5331* 🖨 *541/432-1300* ▤ *No credit cards* ⊙ *Open Memorial Day–Labor Day, daily 10–4.*

$-$$$$ ✕▥ **Wallowa Lake Lodge.** At this friendly 1920s lodge, handmade replicas of the structure's original furniture fill a large common area with a massive fireplace. The lodge's rooms are simple yet appealing; the grandest have balconies facing the lake. The cabins, all with fireplaces and some with lake views, are small, old-fashioned havens of knotty pine.

The on-site restaurant serves standard American fare for breakfast, lunch, and dinner. ✉ *60060 Wallowa Lake Hwy., Wallowa Lake 97846* ☎ *541/432–9821* 🖶 *541/432–4885* ⊕ *www.wallowalake.com* ➥ *22 rooms, 8 cabins* ⚴ *Restaurant; no smoking, no room phones, no room TVs* ▭ *D, MC, V* ☉ *Lodge closed weekdays in winter.*

Sports & the Outdoors

Rainbow trout, kokanee, and mackinaw are among the species of fish in 300-foot-deep, 4½-mi-long Wallowa Lake. You can picnic on the water at several moored docks.

HIKING **BackCountry Outfitters** (✆ Box 137, 97846 ☎ 541/426–5908 or 800/966–8080) leads pack trips into the Eagle Cap Wilderness and Hells Canyon.

HORSEBACK **Eagle Cap Wilderness Pack Station** (✉ 59761 Wallowa Lake Hwy. ☎ 541/432–4145 or 800/681–6222), at the south end of Wallowa Lake, conducts guided rides and leads summer pack trips into the Eagle Cap Wilderness.

RAFTING & **Cooley River Expeditions** (✆ Box 1068, 97846 ☎ 541/432–0461 or 888/468–5998) leads white-water rafting and kayaking trips on the Deschutes, Grande Ronde, and John Day rivers. **Hells Canyon Adventures** (✉ 4200 Hells Canyon Dam Rd., Oxbow ☎ 541/785–3352 or 800/422–3568 ⊕ www.hellscanyonadventure.com) runs white-water rafting and jet-boat trips on the Snake River through Hells Canyon. **Wallowa Lake Marina Inc.** (✉ Wallowa Lake, south end ☎ 541/432–9115), open May to September, rents paddleboats, motorboats, rowboats, and canoes by the hour or by the day.

en route   The **Wallowa Mountain Loop** is a relatively easy way to take in the natural splendor of the Eagle Cap Wilderness and reach Baker City without backtracking to La Grande. The 3½-hour trip from Joseph to Baker City, designated the Hells Canyon Scenic Byway, winds through the national forest and part of Hells Canyon Recreation Area, passing over forested mountains, creeks, and rivers. Before you travel the loop, check with the Joseph Chamber of Commerce about road conditions; in winter always carry chains. ⊹ *From Joseph take Little Sheep Creek Hwy. east for 8 mi, turn south onto Forest Service Rd. 39, and continue until it meets Hwy. 86, which winds past town of Halfway to Baker City.*

Hells Canyon

★ ➐ *30 mi northeast of Joseph on Wallowa Mountain Loop.*

This remote place along the **Snake River** is the deepest river-carved gorge in North America (7,900 feet), with many rare and endangered animal species. There are three different routes from which to view and experience the canyon, though only one is accessible year-round.

Most travelers take a scenic peek from the overlook on the 45-mi **Wallowa Mountain Loop,** which follows Route 39 from just east of Halfway on Route 86 to just east of Joseph on Route 350. At the junction of Route 39 and Forest Road 3965, take the 6-mi round-trip loop to the 5,400-foot-high rim at Hells Canyon Overlook. This is the easiest way to get a glimpse of the canyon, but be aware that Route 39 is open only during the summer and early fall months. During the late fall, winter, and spring, the best way to experience Hells Canyon is to follow a slightly more out-of-the-way route along the **Snake River Segment** of the Wallowa Mountain Loop. Following Highway 86 north from Copperfield, the 60-mi round-trip route winds along the edge of Hells Canyon Reservoir, crosses the Snake River to Hells Canyon Dam on the border of Oregon and Idaho, and continues on to the Hells Canyon National Recreation Site, with a visitor center and hiking trails. The canyon is 10 mi wide in places. The trip is a memorable one, but be certain you have a full tank before starting out, as there are no gas stations anywhere along the route. If you are starting from Joseph, you also have the option of heading to the **Hat Point Overlook.** From Joseph, take Route 350 northeast to Imnaha, a tiny town along the Imnaha River. From there Forest Road 4240 leads southeast to Route 315, which in turn heads northeast up a steep gravel road to the overlook. This route is also open only during the summer. Be sure to have plenty of gas, as well as water for yourself and your car.

The **Hells Canyon National Recreation Area** is the site of one of the largest elk herds in the United States, plus 422 other species, including bald eagles, bighorn sheep, mule deer, white-tailed deer, black bears, bobcats, cougars, beavers, otters, and rattlesnakes. The peregrine falcon has also been reintroduced here. Part of the area was designated as Hells Canyon Wilderness, in parts of Oregon and Idaho, with the establishment of the Hells Canyon National Recreation Area in 1975. Additional acres were added as part of the Oregon Wilderness Act of 1984. There are now 219,006 acres and about 360 mi of trails in the wilderness area, and the trails are closed to all mechanized travel. If you want to visit the wilderness it must be on foot or horseback. Environmental groups have proposed the creation of Hells Canyon National Park to better manage the area's critical habitat. A wildlife-viewing guide is available from the Idaho Department of Fish and Game. ⊠ *88401 Hwy. 82, Enterprise, OR 97828* ☎ *541/426–4978* ☍ *Idaho Department of Fish and Game, Box 25, Boise, ID 83707.*

The **Wild and Scenic Snake River Corridor** consists of 67½ mi of river federally designated as part of the National Wild and Scenic Rivers System. Extending ¼ mi back from the high-water mark on each shore, the corridor is available for managed public use. Since the corridor itself is not designated wilderness and wilderness area regulations do not apply, there are developed campsites and man-made structures here, and some motorized equipment is allowed. In season, both powerboaters and rafters must make reservations and obtain permits for access to the river corridor. ☎ *509/758–1957 float reservations, 509/758–0270 powerboat reservations* ☉ *Daily Memorial Day–early Sept.*

Camping

⚠ **Imnaha River.** Hells Canyon National Scenic Byway runs through the Imnaha corridor, a critical habitat for the chinook salmon and bull trout. Access to the camping areas is via dirt and gravel roads that are generally not suitable for passenger cars. Some of the areas have toilets, RV hookups, picnic areas, swimming, and boat launches. Forest Road 46, or the Wellamotkin Drive area, has two developed campsites along the rim area within timbered groves north and west of Enterprise, permitting spectacular views of Hells Canyon. The Hat Point area begins at the Imnaha River and ends at Hat Point Lookout. Duck Lake and Twin Lakes campgrounds are in an alpine zone near the lakes for which they are named. ☍ *Wallowa-Whitman National Forest, Box 907, Baker City 97814 P 541/523–4476.*

Halfway

❽ *63 mi south of Joseph on Wallowa Mountain Loop.*

Halfway, the closest town to Hells Canyon, originally got its name because it was midway between the town of Pine and the gold mines of

Cornucopia, but in 2000, the official name of the town was changed to half.com, as a promotional venture between the town and a Philadelphia start-up Internet company. Halfway changed its name in exchange for cash, computers, and a little notoriety that residents hoped would draw some tourism. Don't worry: everyone still calls it Halfway, and its quiet, laid-back character reveals none of this kitschy ad-campaign. On the southern flanks of the Wallowas, it's a straightforward, unpretentious community with a Main Street and a quiet rural flavor.

Where to Stay & Eat

★ **$–$$$** ✕☐ **Pine Valley Lodge.** From the outside, this building on Main Street is styled like many others built in eastern Oregon during the timber boom of the late 1920s. Inside, the common area is artfully cluttered with a mixture of antique fishing gear, Native American artifacts, and paintings. Guest rooms, available in the main lodge, the Blue Dog house next door, and the Love Shack, have antiques and western memorabilia, as well as original artwork by the inn's owner, Babette Beatty, a cook who prepares a full breakfast for guests each morning. Her restaurant, the Halfway Supper Club, used to be open to the public but now serves as a private dining room for guests; Babette will prepare dinner upon request. ✉ *163 N. Main St., 97834* ☎ *541/742–2027* ⊕ *www.pvlodge. com* 🖙 *6 rooms, plus Love Shack* ⚘ *Dining room, coffee shop, meeting room, free parking, some pets allowed (fee); no room phones, no room TVs, no smoking* ▭ *No credit cards* ¶◎ *BP.*

$ ☐ **Clear Creek Farm Bed and Breakfast.** Amid 160 acres of orchards, woods, and fields on the southeastern flank of the Wallowa Mountains, this 1880s Craftsman-style farmhouse is a simple but comfortable rural retreat. The main house has four rooms. Two bunkhouses with ceilings but no windows are available May–October. Lakeview, with a balcony overlooking a small pond, is the better of the two. Breakfast, served in an outdoor kitchen in warm weather, includes eggs, buffalo sausage, Dutch babies (sweet, fluffy omelets), and homegrown raspberries and peaches in season. You can choose between paying a standard rate, which includes breakfast, and taking the Ranch Privileges Plan, in which, for $30 more, you get three meals a day, free use of bicycles, fishing, and several tour options. ✉ *4821 Clear Creek Rd., off Fish Lake Rd., 5½ mi north of Halfway, 97834* ☎ *541/742–2238 or 800/742–4992* 🖨 *541/742–5175* 🖙 *5 rooms in lodge, 2 2-room bunkhouses share 3 baths* ⚘ *Outdoor hot tub, laundry facilities, some pets allowed* ▭ *MC, V.*

Sports & the Outdoors

CAMPING **Hells Canyon Outdoor Supply** (✉ Pine Creek, 2 mi southwest of Oxbow on Hwy. 86 ☎ 800/785–3358), is the home office of Hells Canyon Shuttle and sells outdoor supplies, water, and some groceries. **Wallowa Llamas** (✉ Rte. 1 ⊕ Box 84, 97834 ☎ 541/742–4930) conducts guided tours into the Eagle Cap Wilderness. The llamas, which walk alongside the hikers, carry most of the gear necessary for a comfortable backpacking trip and are even-tempered and calm enough to be easily led by those with no previous experience, including children. The company provides tents, eating utensils, and all meals on three- to seven-day pack trips.

Baker City

❾ *53 mi west of Halfway on Hwy. 86, 44 mi south of La Grande on U.S. 30 off I–84.*

You'd never guess that quiet Baker City, positioned between the Wallowa Mountains and the Elkhorn Range of the Blue Mountains, was once bigger than Spokane and Boise. During the gold-rush era in the late 19th century, the town profited from the money that poured in from nearby mining towns. With the end of the gold rush, the city transformed itself into the logging and ranching town it is today. Remnants of its opulence are still visible in the many restored Victorian houses and downtown shops, but all this history seems minor when you consider the region's fascinating geography.

Oregon Trail pioneers first glimpsed the Oregon Territory from the Baker Valley. History buffs will be particularly interested in Baker City, now the location for the National Historic Oregon Trail Interpretive Center. At the same time, outdoor enthusiasts will appreciate the nearby venues for fishing, hunting, waterskiing, canoeing, hiking, cycling, and skiing. Baker City has received national recognition for its historic restoration efforts and success in attracting visitors to its out-of-the-mainstream location near the Eagle Cap and Wallowa Mountains.

The **Baker County Visitors and Convention Bureau** (⊠ 490 Campbell St. ☎ 541/523–3356 or 800/523–1235 ⊕ www.visitbaker.com) operates a small pioneer museum and has information on area attractions.

The **Oregon Trail Regional Museum** may seem rather staid after a turn through the National Historic Oregon Trail Interpretive Center, but the museum has an enormous butterfly collection and one of the most impressive rock collections in the West, including thunder eggs, glowing phosphorescent rocks, and a 950-pound hunk of quartz. A back room has a covered wagon, an old firefighting wagon, and pioneer tools. ⊠ 2480 Grove St., at Campbell St. ☎ 541/523–9308 ⊠ $3.50 ☉ Late Mar.–Oct., daily 9–5; off-season by appointment.

A small gold display just inside the entrance to **U.S. Bank** (⊠ Washington and Main Sts.) contains the 80.4-ounce Armstrong Nugget, found in 1913.

★ The **National Historic Oregon Trail Interpretive Center,** 5 mi east of Baker City, does a superb job of re-creating pioneer life in the mid-1800s. From 1841 to 1861 about 300,000 people made the 2,000-mi journey from western Missouri to the Columbia River and the Oregon coast, looking for agricultural land in the West. A simulated section of the Oregon Trail will give you a feel for camp life, the toll the trip took on marriages and families, and the settlers' impact on Native Americans; an indoor theater presents movies and plays. A 4-mi round-trip trail winds from the center to the actual ruts left by the wagons. ⊠ Hwy. 86 E, east of I–84 ☎ 541/523–1843 ⊠ $5 ☉ Apr.–Oct., daily 9–6; Nov.–Mar., daily 9–4.

In the tiny town of Haines, several miles north of Baker City, **Eastern Oregon Museum,** which almost resembles an antique store or flea market at first glance, has 10,000 household, farming, mining, and pioneer artifacts. On the grounds is the old Union Pacific depot, built in the 1880s and given to the museum when the railroad discontinued stops at Haines in 1962. ⊠ 610 3rd St., 4 blocks from Hwy. 30, Haines 97833 ☎ 541/856–3233 ⊠ Donations accepted ☉ Mid-Apr.–mid-Oct., daily 9–5, or by appointment off-season.

In the Wallowa-Whitman National Forest, **Anthony Lakes Ski Area** has a vertical drop of 900 feet and a top elevation of 8,000 feet. There are 21 trails, two lifts, and a 13-km cross-country route. Snowboards are permitted. ⊠ Exit 285 off I–84 to Anthony Lakes Rd., 19 mi west of North Powder ☎ 800/856–3277 ⊠ Lift tickets $28 ☉ Nov.–Apr., Thurs.–Sun. 9–4.

The scenic 106-mi loop of **Elkhorn Drive** winds from Baker City through the Elkhorn Range of the Blue Mountains. Only white-bark pine can survive on the range's sharp ridges and peaks, which top 8,000 feet; spruce, larch, Douglas fir, and ponderosa pine thrive on the lower slopes. The route is well marked; start on Highway 7 west of Baker City, turn onto County Road 24 toward Sumpter, pass Granite on Forest Service Road 73, and then return to Baker City along U.S. 30.

The original track of the **Sumpter Valley Railway** was scrapped in 1947. With an all-volunteer work force, the railroad has rebuilt more than 7 mi of track on the original right-of-way. Today it operates along a 5.1-mi route in Sumpter. Trains leave from the McEwen and Sumpter stations; call for departure information. ⊠ *On Hwy. 7, 22 mi west of Baker City* ☎ *800/523–1235* ⊕ *www.svry.com* ⊠ *$9* ⊘ *Memorial Day–Sept., weekends and holidays.*

The smell of juniper fills the air at the high-desert **Unity Lake State Park,** 26 mi southwest of Baker City on U.S. 245. The Burnt River runs through the park where Unity Dam created the small lake. There is a boat ramp, 35 electrical campsites, and two tepees. ⊠ *U.S. 245 at U.S. 26* ☎ *541/932–4453 or 800/551–6949* ⊕ *www.prd.state.or.us* ⊠ *Free* ⊘ *Apr.–Oct., daily* ⊠ *Hookups $12–$17, tepees $29.*

Wallowa-Whitman National Forest. The 2.3-million-acre forest, found both east and west of Baker City, ranges in elevation from 875 feet in the Hells Canyon Wilderness to 9,845 feet in the Eagle Cap Wilderness. There are two other wilderness areas: Monument Rock and North Fork John Day. ⊠ *Roads leading into and through the forest accessible via Rtes. 7 and 237, west of Baker City, as well as Rtes. 86 and 203 on east side* ☎ *541/523–6391* ⊕ *www.fs.fed.us/r6/w-w/index.htm* ⊠ *Free* ⊘ *Daily.*

Where to Stay & Eat

★ **$–$$** ✕ **Phone Company.** In the Victorian historic district, this suitably named restaurant operates out of an old Bell Telephone building. Staples are steak, chicken, salads, pasta, and seafood, especially salmon. The real specialty, though, is chicken *mamou,* a Cajun pasta dish with a spicy tomato sauce named after the small town in southeastern Louisiana from which it supposedly originated. You can order it mild, medium, hot, or nuclear. ⊠ *1926 1st St., 97814* ☎ *541/523–7997* ☰ *MC, V* ⊘ *Closed Sun. No lunch Sat.*

¢ ✕ **Front St. Cafe and Coffee Co.** Sit at one of the swiveling vinyl stools at the old soda-fountain counter or at one of the picnic tables that fill the rest of the café to enjoy a basic breakfast of eggs and hash browns, French toast or pancakes, or just a cup of joe. There is something to look at in every direction at this fun and friendly place; vintage advertisements, lunch boxes, and food tins crowd the brick walls and the shelves behind the counter. ⊠ *1840 Main St.* ☎ *541/523–0223* ☰ *MC, V* ⊘ *No dinner.*

★ **$–$$$$** ✕▥ **Geiser Grand Hotel.** Considered for many years the finest hotel between Portland and Salt Lake City, the Geiser Grand was built in 1889 during the height of the gold rush. The Italian Renaissance Revival gem reopened in 1997 after a meticulous restoration. The rooms, filled with period furnishings, have 18-foot ceilings, enormous windows (many overlooking the nearby mountains), and large bathrooms. The striking Palm Court, with a suspended stained-glass ceiling, dominates the first floor. The hotel's Swan dining room, serving steaks, prime rib, fresh fish, and pasta dishes, is Baker City's finest restaurant. ⊠ *1996 Main St., 97814* ☎ *541/523–1889 or 888/434–7374* ☐ *541/523–1800* ⊕ *www.geisergrand.com* ⟿ *30 rooms* ⚘ *Restaurant, room service, cable TV with VCRs and movies, hair salon, bar, library, laundry* *service, dry cleaning, meeting rooms, free parking, some pets allowed (fee), no-smoking floors* 🖃 *AE, D, MC, V.*

¢ 🖭 **Bridge Street Inn.** Right off Main Street, Bridge Street Inn is one of the least-expensive motels in town and in a much better location than some of the others in the same price range. With rooms that are clean and reliable, it is an excellent option if you're short on funds. Some rooms have microwaves and refrigerators, and a Continental breakfast is included. ⊠ *134 Bridge St., 97814* ☎ *541/523–6571 or 800/932–9220* 🖶 *541/523–9424* 🌐 *www.bridgestreetinn.com* 🛏 *40 rooms* ⚙ *Cable TV, some pets allowed (fee), no-smoking rooms* 🖃 *MC, V* 🍴 *CP.*

Ontario

🔟 *70 mi southeast of Baker City on I–84.*

At the far eastern edge of Oregon, less than 5 mi from the Idaho border, Ontario is the largest town in the state's second-largest county, Malheur. Its 10,000 residents make up more than one-third of the county's population. For the adventurous visitor, the Ontario area offers an abundance of outdoor recreation.

Ontario's multiethnic heritage is on display at the **Four Rivers Cultural Center and Museum.** Learn about the populations of Northern Paiute Indians, Japanese-Americans, Mexican-Americans, and people from the Basque country. Most interesting and moving is a reconstructed barracks from a Japanese-American WWII internment camp. A 645-seat theater presents music, drama, and other events, from local productions to the Oregon Symphony. ⊠ *676 S.W. 5th Ave., 97914* ☎ *541/889–8191 or 888/211–1222* 🖶 *541/889–7628* 🌐 *www.4rcc.com* 🖼 *Museum $4* 🕙 *Mon.–Sat. 10–5.*

On the Snake River's Brownlee Reservoir, **Farewell Bend State Park** includes historic markers and displays describing the relevance of this point on the Oregon Trail, where pioneers bid adieu to their route along the Snake River and headed inland. Recreational activities on the lake include fishing, waterskiing, swimming, and boating. A campground has 101 electrical and 30 tent sites, 4 tepees, 2 cabins, and 2 covered wagons. 🖼 *Day use $3. Hookups $17, tent sites $15, cabins $37.* ⊠ *Exit 353 off I–84* ☎ *541/ 869–2365 or 800/551–6949, 800/452–5687 reservations only* 🌐 *www. prd.state.or.us* 🕙 *Daily; only 10 sites open in winter.*

Boat, fish, swim, or picnic at **Ontario State Park,** on the west bank of the Snake River. ⊠ *Exit 374 off I–84* ☎ *541/869–2365* 🖼 *Free* 🕙 *Daily.*

Twenty-eight miles south of Ontario, **Lake Owyhee State Park** has picture-perfect views of the surrounding mountains. It is next to a 53-mi-long reservoir formed by the Owyhee Dam. The area has bighorn sheep, pronghorn antelope, golden eagles, coyotes, mule deer, wild horses, and a few cougars. A campground has 31 electrical, 8 tent sites, and 2 tepees. ⊠ *Off Rte. 201* ☎ *800/551–6949* 🌐 *www.prd.state.or.us* 🖼 *Day use $3 per vehicle. Hookups $12–$16, tent sites $10–$14* 🕙 *Mar.–Nov., daily.*

Where to Stay & Eat

$–$$$ ✗ **Nichols Steak House.** Paintings by local artists and antiques cover the walls of this steak house in nearby Fruitland, Idaho. It is known for prime rib and 22-ounce T-bone steak suppers. ⊠ *411 S.W. 3rd St., Fruitland, ID 83619* ☎ *208/452–3030* 🖃 *D, MC, V* 🕙 *Closed Mon. No lunch Sat.*

¢–$ ✗ **DJ's.** Chicken-fried steak is served for breakfast, lunch, and dinner at this place, which provides room service for the Holiday Motel next door. You can order a burger, steak, chicken potpie, or one of the popular breakfast cinnamon rolls at a table or at the coffee bar. ⌧ *625 E. Idaho Ave., 97914* ☎ *541/889–4386* ▤ *D, MC, V.*

¢–$ 🏨 **Carlile Motel.** Most of the rooms in this mom-and-pop motor lodge five blocks from downtown have kitchenettes, and some have full kitchens with stoves. With everything from standard rooms with one double bed to multiroom family suites with three beds and two bedrooms, the friendly owners here seem prepared for the needs of everyone from business travelers to large families. ⌧ *589 N. Oregon St., 97914* ☎ *541/889–8658* 🛏 *18 rooms* ⚭ *Some kitchens, some kitchenettes, cable TV, some pets allowed (fee); no smoking* ▤ *AE, D, DC, MC, V.*

¢–$ 🏨 **Sears & Roebuck Bed & Breakfast.** This 1900 Sears & Roebuck mail-order Victorian is the closest B&B to Ontario, 17 mi west of town in nearby Vale. The two-story inn has a wide front porch with a bird-cleaning room, dog kennels, and horse stables and hosts many pheasant hunters. The rooms are ornately furnished in period pieces, including brass and four-poster beds. ⌧ *484 N. 10th St., Vale 97918* ☎ *541/473–9636* 🛏 *5 rooms* ⚭ *No room phones* ▤ *AE, DC, MC, V* ﺃﴼ *BP.*

John Day

⓫ *80 mi west of Baker City on U.S. 26.*

More than $26 million in gold was mined in the John Day area. The town was founded shortly after gold was discovered there in 1862. Yet John Day is better known to contemporaries for the plentiful outdoor recreation it offers and for the nearby John Day Fossil Beds. The town is also a central location for trips to the Malheur National Wildlife Refuge and the towns of Burns, Frenchglen, and Diamond to the south.

As you drive west through the dry, shimmering heat of the John Day Valley on U.S. 26, it may be hard to imagine this area as a humid subtropical forest filled with lumbering 50-ton brontosauruses and 50-foot-long crocodiles. But so it was, and the eroded hills and sharp, barren-looking ridges contain the richest concentration of prehistoric plant and animal fossils in the world.

Two miles south of John Day, Canyon City is a small town that feels like it hasn't changed much since the Old West days. Memorabilia from the gold rush is on display at the small **Grant County Historical Museum** there, along with Native American artifacts and antique musical instruments. ⌧ *101 S. Canyon City Blvd., 2 mi south of John Day, Canyon City* ☎ *541/575–0362* 🎫 *$4* ⊗ *Mid-May–Sept., Mon.–Sat. 9–4:30.*

★ The **Kam Wah Chung & Co. Museum** was a trading post on The Dalles Military Road in 1866 and 1867. It later served as a general store, a Chinese labor exchange for the area's mines, a Chinese doctor's shop, and an opium den. The museum contains a completely stocked Chinese pharmacy, items that would have been sold at the general store, and re-created living quarters. Adjacent to the City Park, the museum is an extraordinary testament to the early Chinese community in Oregon. ⌧ *Ing-Hay Way off Canton St., adjacent to City Park* ☎ *541/575–0028* 🎫 *$3* ⊗ *May–Oct., Mon.–Thurs. 9–noon and 1–5, weekends 1–5.*

★ The geological formations that compose the **John Day Fossil Beds National Monument** cover hundreds of square miles and preserve a diverse record of plant and animal life spanning more than 40 million years of the Age of Mammals. The national monument itself is divided into three "units"— Sheep Rock, Painted Hills, and Clarno (⇨ Sheep Rock, Painted Hills, and Clarno sections)—each of which looks vastly different and tells a different part of the story of Oregon's prehistory. Each unit has picnic areas, rest rooms, visitor information, and hiking trails. The main visitor center is in the Sheep Rock Unit, though bear in mind that it's almost 40 mi northwest of John Day; and Painted Hills and Clarno are about 70 and 115 mi northwest of John Day, respectively. ☎ 541/987–2333 🎟 Free.

Where to Stay & Eat

¢–$$ ✕ **The Grubsteak Mining Co.** Breakfasts of bacon and eggs, potatoes, and silver-dollar pancakes are served until 4 PM daily in the simple, casual dining room of this neighborhood joint. For lunch and dinner, try the excellent burgers, steaks, and seafood. Locals can be found at all hours in the adjoining bar at the back of the house, where you can choose from the full menu, shoot a game of pool, and drink a few beers. ⊠ 149 E. Main St. ☎ 541/575–1970 ▭ MC, V.

★ ¢–$$ ✕ **The Outpost Pizza, Pub, and Grill.** Having moved in 2003 to a new building just a few doors down from its old one, the Outpost is now in one of the sleekest spaces in town, in a large building with a log-cabin exterior, a vast entry lobby, and a bright, spacious, high-ceiling dining room. They serve creative pizzas and have a lengthy menu of standard entrées including burgers, steak, seafood, salads, and quesadillas. Breakfast is also available. ⊠ 155 W. Main St. ☎ 541/575–0250 ▭ MC, V.

¢–$ 🛏 **Dreamers Lodge.** The outside of this hotel is quite dated and unglamorous, but the rooms themselves are a definite step up from the exterior, with comfortable armchairs as well as some appliances in all the rooms. For simple accommodations, they are well equipped and reliable. In addition, there are two apartment-style suites. ⊠ 144 N. Canyon Blvd. ☎ 541/575–0526 or 800/654–2849 📠 541/575–2733 🛏 25 rooms ⏃ Microwaves, refrigerators, cable TV, some pets allowed (fee) ▭ AE, D, DC, MC, V.

Sheep Rock

⑫ *40 mi from John Day, west 38 mi on U.S. 26 and north 2 mi on Hwy. 19.*

The visitor center at this unit of the John Day Fossil Beds serves as a small museum dedicated to the fossil beds, with fossils on display, in-depth informational panels, handouts, and an orientation movie. Two miles north of the visitor center on Highway 19 is the impressive **Blue Basin**, a badlands canyon with sinuous blue-green spires. Winding through this basin is the ½-mi **Island in Time Trail,** where trailside exhibits explain the area's 28-million-year-old fossils. The 3-mi **Blue Basin Overlook Trail** loops around the rim of the canyon, yielding some splendid views. ⊠ Visitor center on Hwy. 19, just north of the junction with U.S. 26 ☎ 541/987–2333 ☺ Memorial Day–Labor Day, daily 9–6; Mar.–Memorial Day and Labor Day–late Nov., daily 9–5; late Nov.–Feb., weekdays 9–5.

Where to Stay

★ ¢–$ 🛏 **Fish House Inn Bed and Breakfast and RV Park.** One of the only places to stay near the Sheep Rock fossil beds is found 9 mi east in the small town of Dayville. The piscatory touches at this lovely B&B includes fishing gear, nets, and framed prints of fish. The main house, built in 1908, has three bedrooms upstairs that share an outdoor deck and a separate entrance, and behind it is a cottage with a large bedroom and suite. The friendly hosts serve a huge country breakfast (on the lawn in good weather). Low-fat and vegetarian options are available as well. While you're in town, stop by the Dayville Mercantile, a century-old general store on U.S. 26. With one café, a bar, and a gas station, Dayville can fill most of your traveling needs and has the only services in the area.

⊠ *110 Franklin St., Dayville 97825* ☎ *541/987–2124 or 888/286–3474* 🛏 *5 rooms, 2 with shared bath* 🝂 *MC, V* 🍴 *BP.*

Mitchell

⑬ *37 mi east of Sheep Rock.*

Mitchell, an authentic homey desert town that has managed to avoid all corporate invasion, truly feels like a slice of the Old West. While you're passing through town for food or fuel, you will have the strange thrill of observing the town's main "attraction": a black bear named Henry that is kept in a cage next to the town's gas station. Henry's owner will occasionally play and wrestle with the bear, who luckily seems to be in remarkably good spirits despite its unusual captivity. Mitchell is the closest town to the Painted Hills unit of the John Day Fossil Beds, about 9 mi away. From Mitchell, U.S. 26 continues southwest for 48 mi through the Ochoco National Forest to Prineville.

Where to Stay & Eat

¢–$ ✕ **Bridgecreek Cafe.** A friendly glow envelops this sunny roadside café serving old standards: pancakes for breakfast, sandwiches for lunch, burgers and fried chicken with all the fixings for dinner. ⊠ *218 U.S. 26* ☎ *541/462–3434* 🝂 *No credit cards.*

¢ ✕ **Little Pine Cafe.** Orange vinyl chairs and an orange tile floor set the mood for this casual, down-to-earth café, which serves biscuits and gravy all day, and burgers, deli sandwiches, and some good old-fashioned milk shakes during lunch. A small collection of jewelry, gifts, and Native American art is for sale. ⊠ *100 E. Main St.* ☎ *541/462–3733* 🕙 *Closed Tues.–Thurs. No dinner.*

¢–$ 🏨 **Sky Hook Motel.** This carefully tended inn surrounded by flower and vegetable gardens is a welcome haven after a day's hike in the fossil beds. The owners are friendly and the rooms, two with kitchens, are homey and comfortably furnished. ⊠ *101 U.S. 26, 97750* ☎ *541/462–3569* 🛏 *6 rooms* ♿ *No room phones* 🝂 *MC, V.*

Painted Hills

⑭ *9 mi from Mitchell, head west on U.S. 26 and follow signs north.*

The fossils at Painted Hills, another unit of the John Day Fossil Beds National Monument, date back about 33 million years and reveal a climate that had become noticeably drier than that of Sheep Rock's era. The eroded buff-color hills reveal striking red and green striations created by minerals in the clay. Come at dusk or just after it rains, when the colors are most vivid. Take the steep ¾-mi **Carroll Rim Trail** for a commanding view of the hills or sneak a peek from the parking lot at the trailhead, about 2 mi beyond the picnic area. The unit is open daily and admission is free.

Clarno

⑮ *67 mi from Mitchell, north 25 mi on Hwy. 207, north 21 mi on Hwy. 19 (to Fossil), and west 20 mi on Hwy. 218.*

The 48-million-year-old fossil beds in this small section have yielded the oldest remains in the John Day Fossil Beds National Monument. The drive to the beds traverses forests of ponderosa pines and sparsely populated valleys along the John Day River before turning through a landscape filled with spires and outcroppings that attest to the region's volcanic past. A short trail that runs between the two parking lots contains fossilized evidence of an ancient subtropical forest. Another trail climbs ¼ mi from the second parking lot to the base of the **Palisades,** a series of abrupt, irregular cliffs created by ancient volcanic mud flows. The unit is open daily and admission is free.

Burns

16 *76 mi south of the town of John Day on U.S. 395.*

Named after poet Robert Burns, this town was the unofficial capital of the 19th-century cattle empires that staked claims to these southeastern Oregon high-plateau grasslands. Today Burns is a working-class town with only about 3,000 residents, surrounded by the 10,185 square mi of sagebrush, rimrock, and grassy plains that compose Harney County, the ninth-largest county in the United States. As the only place in the county with basic tourist amenities, Burns serves as a convenient stopover for many travelers, but its usefulness as a source of modern conveniences comes hand in hand with the sense that its Old West flavor has been largely lost, unlike in many of the region's smaller outposts. Think of it not as your final destination but as a jumping-off point for exploring the real poetry of the Malheur National Wildlife Refuge, Steens Mountain, and the Alvord Desert. Outdoor recreation at this gateway to the Steens Mountains includes fishing, backpacking, camping, boating, and hiking.

The Harney County Chamber of Commerce and the Bureau of Land Management office in Hines are good places to obtain information about the area.

You can cut through the 1.4-million-acre **Malheur National Forest** in the Blue Mountains as you drive from John Day to Burns on U.S. 395. It has alpine lakes, meadows, creeks, and grasslands. Black bears, bighorn sheep, elk, and wolverines inhabit thickly wooded stands of pine, fir, and cedar. Near Burns the trees dwindle in number and the landscape changes from mountainous forest to open areas covered with sagebrush and dotted with junipers. ⊠ *Between U.S. 26 and U.S. 20, accessible via U.S. 395* ☎ *Information from Bureau of Land Management Office in John Day at 541/575–3000* ⊠ *Free* ☉ *Daily.*

On the site of a former brewery, the **Harney County Historical Museum** keeps a photo collection documenting the area's history. There's also a display of handmade quilts and a turn-of-the-20th-century kitchen exhibit. ⊠ *18 W. D St., 97720* ☎ *541/573–5618* ⊠ *$4* ☉ *Apr.–Sept., Tues.–Sat. 9–5.*

need a break? Sip an espresso and browse through cards, gifts, and books at the **Book Parlor** (⊠ *181 N. Broadway* ☎ *541/573–2665*), in the center of town.

Where to Stay & Eat

$–$$$$ ✕ **Pine Room Cafe.** Paintings of Harney County scenery cover the walls of this old-fashioned but classy restaurant, which serves the finest food in Burns. The menu has steaks and seafood, and house specialties include chicken liver bordelaise and stuffed prawns. All dinners come with soup, salad, potatoes, and bread. ⊠ *543 W. Monroe St.* ☎ *541/573–6631* ⊟ *AE, D, DC, MC, V* ☉ *Closed Sun. and Mon. No lunch.*

¢   ▦ **Bontemps Motel.** The Bontemps is a throwback to the days when motels had personalities. The small rooms, which surround a courtyard in the center of the property, incorporate an eclectic mix of new and aging furnishings—a far cry from of the standard, streamlined approach of many chain motels. Don't expect any glamorous vintage luxury, however; the accommodations are very modest, and it feels like an inexpensive motel with reliable but basic rooms. Four rooms have kitchenettes. ⊠ *74 Monroe St., 97220* ☎ *541/573–2037 or 800/229–1394* 🖷 *541/573–2577* 🛏 *15 units* ♨ *Some kitchenettes, microwaves, refrigerators, cable TV* ⊟ *MC, V.*

Malheur National Wildlife Refuge

⑰ *32 mi southeast of Burns on Hwy. 205.*

Highway 205 slices south from Burns through one of the most unusual desert environments in the West. The squat, snow-covered summit of Steens Mountain is the only landmark in this area of alkali playas, buttes, scrubby meadows, and, most surprising of all, marshy lakes. The **Malheur National Wildlife Refuge,** bounded on the north by Malheur and Harney lakes, covers 193,000 acres. It's arid and scorchingly hot in summer, but in the spring and early summer more than 320 species of migrating birds descend on the refuge's wetlands for their annual nesting and mating rituals. Following an ancient migratory flyway, they've been coming here for nearly a million years. The species include sandhill cranes, snowy white egrets, trumpeter swans, numerous hawks, golden and bald eagles, and white-faced ibis. The number of bird-watchers who turn up for this annual display sometimes rivals the number of birds.

The 30-mi Central Patrol Road, which runs through the heart of the refuge, is your best bet for viewing birds. But first stop at the **Malheur National Wildlife Refuge Headquarters,** where you can pick up leaflets and a free map. The staff will tell you where you're most likely to see the refuge's winged inhabitants. The refuge is a short way from local petroglyphs (ask at the headquarters); a remarkable pioneer structure called the **Round Barn** (head east from the headquarters on Narrows–Princeton Road for 9 mi; road turns to gravel and then runs into Diamond Highway, a paved road that leads south 12 mi to the barn); and **Diamond Craters,** a series of volcanic domes, craters, and lava tubes (continue south from the barn 6 mi on Diamond Highway). *Malheur National Wildlife Refuge Headquarters* ⊠ *32 mi southeast of Burns on Hwy. 205; follow signs 26 mi south of Burns* ☎ *541/493–2612* 🎟 *Free* ⊗ *Park daily sunrise–sunset; headquarters Mon.–Thurs. 7–4:30, Fri. 7–3:30, also 8–3 weekends mid-Mar.–Oct.*

Diamond

⑱ *54 mi from Burns, south on Hwy. 205 and east on Diamond–Grand Camp Rd.*

Diamond claimed a population of two year-round residents in 2003, and you could probably do the census yourself as you take in the undisturbed cluster of a few houses and the lone Hotel Diamond in the midst of the vast scenery and wildlife found near the Malheur National Wildlife Refuge. During its heyday at the turn of the 20th century, Diamond had a population of about 50, including the McCoy family ranchers, who continue to run the town's hotel today.

Not far from town is the **Kiger Mustang Lookout,** a wild-horse viewing area run by the Bureau of Land Management. With their dun-color coats, zebra stripes on knees and hocks, and hooked ear tips, the Kiger mustangs are perhaps one of the purest herds of wild Spanish mustangs in the world today. Once thought to be the descendants of Barb horses brought by the Spanish to North America in the 16th century, the Kiger horses remain the most sought-after for adoption throughout the country. The viewing area is accessible to high-clearance vehicles only and is passable only in dry weather. The road to it descends from Happy

Valley Road 6 mi north of Diamond. ✛ *11 mi from Happy Valley Rd.*
☎ *541/573–4400* ✍ *Free* ☉ *Dry season, generally May–Oct., sunrise–sunset.*

Where to Stay & Eat

★ ¢–$ ✕ **Frazier's.** Adjoining and owned by the Hotel Diamond, Frazier's is a small pub-style restaurant in a renovated icehouse, the oldest building in Diamond. Burgers, steaks, salads, and sandwiches are served for lunch and dinner. Aside from the reservations-only dinners served in the hotel, this is the only place in town to buy a meal. And as the Bureau of Land Management firefighters can tell you, it's also the only place for many miles to play a game of pool. The unmarked restaurant is found around the back of the Hotel Diamond and often looks like it might not be open, but head on through the doors for some friendly service. ✉ *At Hotel Diamond, 10 Main St.* ☎ *541/493–1898* ▤ *MC, V.*

★ $ 🏨 **Hotel Diamond.** A hundred years ago the Hotel Diamond served the local population of ranchers, Basque sheepherders, and cowhands. Now it caters to the birders, naturalists, and high-desert lovers who flock to the Malheur refuge. The air-conditioned rooms are clean, comfortable, and pleasantly furnished with an eclectic mix of furniture including wicker chairs, old wooden desks, and four-poster beds. Family-style meals are served both to hotel guests and to the general public at 6:30 PM, by reservation only. The hotel, owned and operated by the fifth-generation ranch family who formerly ran the now defunct McCoy Creek Inn, is also the only place in town to buy gas or groceries. ✉ *10 Main St., 10 mi east of Hwy. 205, 97722* ☎ *541/493–1898* ⬔ *8 rooms, 5 with shared bath* ⚷ *Restaurant, dining room, no-smoking room* ▤ *MC, V* ⦿ *CP.*

Frenchglen

⑲ *61 mi south of Burns on Hwy. 205.*

Frenchglen, the tiny town near the base of Steens Mountain, has no more than a handful of residents and in the off-season offers no basic services to travelers. Don't go expecting groceries and fuel; instead, prepare yourself for a small outpost of civilization that is refreshingly untrammeled by the mundane conveniences of the 21st century.

Frenchglen is the gateway to **Steens Mountain.** Amid the flat landscape of eastern Oregon, the mountain is hard to miss, but the sight of its 9,700-foot summit is more remarkable from the east, where its sheer face rises from the flat basin of the desolate Alvord Desert, which stretches into Idaho and Nevada. On the western side, Steens Mountain slopes gently upward over a space of about 20 mi and is less astonishing. Steens is not your average mountain—it's a huge fault block created when the ancient lava that covered this area fractured. Except for groves of aspen, juniper, and a few mountain mahogany, Steens is almost entirely devoid of trees and resembles alpine tundra. But starting in June, the wildflower displays are nothing short of breathtaking, as are the views: on Steens you'll encounter some of the grandest scenery in the West.

The mountain is a great spot for hiking over untrammeled and unpopulated ground, but you can also see it by car (preferably one with four-wheel drive) on the rough but passable 52-mi **Steens Loop Road,** open mid-July–October. You need to take reasonable precautions; storms can whip up out of the blue, creating hazardous conditions.

On the drive up you might spot golden eagles, bighorn sheep, and deer. The view out over **Kiger Gorge,** on the southeastern rim of the mountain, includes a dramatic U-shape path carved out by a glacier. A few miles farther along the loop road, the equally stunning **East Rim viewpoint** is more than 5,000 feet above the valley floor. The view on a clear day takes in Alvord Desert. ✛ *Northern entrance to Steens Loop Rd. leaves Hwy. 205 at south end of Frenchglen and returns to Hwy. 205 about 9 mi south of Frenchglen.*

Frenchglen Mercantile, Frenchglen's only store, is packed with intriguing high-quality western merchandise, including Stetson hats, horsehair belts, antique housewares and horse bits, fossilized shark's teeth, silver and turquoise Native American jewelry, Navajo rugs, books, postcards, and maps. Cold drinks, film, sunscreen, good coffee, snacks, and canned goods are also for sale. The store is only open in the summer, and the dates may change each year; if you are counting on finding something there, be sure to call ahead to ensure it's open. ⊠ *Hwy. 205* ☎ *541/ 493–2738.*

Where to Stay & Eat

¢-$$ ✕ **Buckaroo Room.** In a region where the food is basic, this tiny restaurant adjoining the Frenchglen Mercantile serves sophisticated fare. The rustic but carefully furnished dining room has a sloping ceiling, rough-hewn timber walls, deer heads, period memorabilia, and kerosene lamps. Sandwiches only are served for lunch. Dinner entrées are few but expertly prepared: Basque chicken coated with olive oil and marinated in herbs and Greek wine, a succulent filet mignon, pasta, and (a rarity in meat-and-potato land) a vegetarian dish. There's a good selection of beer and wine, and the only full bar for miles around. It's closed fall through spring, and sometimes into early summer; call ahead to be on the safe side. ⊠ *Hwy. 205* ☎ *541/493–2738* ⌂ *Reservations essential* ⊟ *AE, D, MC, V.*

¢-$$ ▦ **Steens Mountain Resort.** Bordering the Malheur National Wildlife Refuge and overlooking vast prairie and mountain land, the Steens Mountain Resort has many lodging options for anyone who wants to fall asleep under the stars and wake up to an undisturbed Oregon sunrise. Small modular cabins and log cabins, RV sites, tent space, and a fully equipped "homestead" are all available. A small selection of groceries, beer, wine, and guidebooks are available for sale in the office. All the two-room cabins come with a fully equipped kitchen, but you must bring your own bedding. The homestead sleeps four adults and has two bathrooms, a kitchen, living room, and laundry facilities. ⊠ *North Loop Rd., 2 mi from Frenchglen, 97736* ☎ *541/493–2415 or 800/542–3765* ⊟ *541/493–2484* ⌂ *No room phones, no room TVs* ⊟ *AE, D, MC, V.*

$ ▦ **Frenchglen Hotel.** Past the large front porch of this simple white wooden house built in 1920 is a warm and comfortable inn filled with a community of people who appreciate the peaceful retreat that Frenchglen and the state-owned Frenchglen Hotel can provide. Every evening a family-style dinner (reservations essential) is served to guests and the public at the long wooden tables in the combination lobby-dining room; breakfast and lunch are also served. The small bedrooms, upstairs off a single hallway, share two bathrooms. ⊠ *Hwy. 205, 97736* ☎ *541/ 493–2825* ⇝ *8 rooms* ⌂ *Restaurant; no room phones, no room TVs, no smoking* ⊟ *D, MC, V* ⊘ *Closed mid-Nov.–mid-Mar.*

off the beaten path

ALVORD DESERT – With the eastern face of Steens Mountain in the background, the Alvord Desert conjures up Western-movie scenes of parched cowboys riding through the desert—though today you're more likely to see wind sailors scooting across these hard-packed alkali flats and glider pilots using the basin as a runway. But once the wind jockeys and flyboys go home, this desert is deserted. Snowmelt *from Steens Mountain can turn it into a shallow lake until as late as mid-July. ⊹ From Frenchglen take Hwy. 205 south for about 33 mi until road ends at T-junction near town of Fields; go left (north) to Alvord Desert and the tiny settlement of Andrews.*

Lakeview

㉒ *144 mi southwest of Burns on U.S. 395.*

At 4,800 feet, Lakeview is the highest town in Oregon. It is surrounded by such natural wonders as Old Perpetual Geyser (in Hunter's Hot Springs), which erupts every 90 seconds, consistently shooting 60 feet in the air. There's also Abert Rim, about 20 mi to the north of town, the best known of the numerous earthquake and volcano remnants. This earth fault is more than 2,000 feet deep and 30 mi long. The Lakeview area is considered one of the state's best for hang gliding, rockhounding, fishing, and enjoying winter sports.

It's possible to camp, picnic, boat, ski, or swim at **Drews Reservoir,** in the high desert of the Fremont National Forest. ⊠ *1300 S. G St., 97630* ☎ *541/947–2151* ⊕ *www.fs.fed.us/r6/fremont* 🎫 *Free* ☉ *Daily.*

The 1.2-million-acre **Fremont National Forest** is 2 mi north of Lakeview and supports small populations of cougars, bobcats, and black bears, as well as the bald eagle and the peregrine falcon. There are 600 mi of streams and many lakes and reservoirs scattered throughout the forest. Anglers will find that the largemouth bass, yellow perch, black and white crappie, bullhead, and trout are plentiful. The winter recreation season, which runs from December through March, provides downhill and cross-country skiing, snowmobiling, snowshoeing, and ice fishing. In summer there's backpacking and camping. ⊠ *Rte. 140* ☎ *541/947–2151* ⊕ *www.fs.fed.us/r6/fremont* 🎫 *Free* ☉ *Daily.*

★ Established in 1936 as a home for remaining antelope herds, the 270,000-acre **Hart Mountain National Antelope Refuge,** surrounding Hart Mountain, provides a haven for the fastest land animal in North America, as well as more than 300 other species, including myriad birds, bighorn sheep, and coyotes. Camping, biking, horseback riding, and fishing are all permitted in designated areas, and hiking is encouraged throughout the refuge. ⊹ *Northeast of Lakeview; take Rte. 140 east 28 mi to Adel, north 18 mi to Plush, and east to refuge headquarters* ☎ *541/947–3315* ⊕ *www.fws.gov* 🎫 *Free* ☉ *Daily.*

One mile north of Lakeview, on the grounds of Hunter's Hot Springs Resort, **Old Perpetual** is the only active geyser in the Far West. Although the immediately surrounding area is not particularly scenic, it is worth stopping by on your way into town to witness the geyser, which spouts every 90 seconds. ⊠ *U.S. 395, 1 mi north of town, 97630.*

People have lived in **Paisley,** 48 mi north of Lakeview, for as long as 10,000 years. Evidence of its earlier inhabitants has been found in caves and rock paintings in the region. Over the years, the Northern Paiute, Modac, and Klamath Indians settled here. Today Paisley itself is a tiny cowboy town with a general store and a restaurant. ⊠ *Rte. 31, 97636.*

Run by the Oregon chapter of the Daughters of the American Revolution, **Schminck Memorial Museum** has glassware, china, books, tools, toys, and dolls from pioneer Lake County families. ⊠ *128 S. E St.* ☎ *541/947–3134* 🎫 *$2* ☉ *Feb.–Nov., Tues.–Sat. 1–5; also by appointment.*

Next door to the Schminck Memorial Museum, the **Lake County Museum** is in a 1926 building and displays local artifacts. ⊠ *118 S. E St.* ☎ *541/*

947–2220 ☺ *June–Sept., Tues.–Sat. 1–4:30; Oct.–Dec., Mar., and Apr., Thurs.–Sat. 1–4:30.*

Where to Stay & Eat

★ ¢–$$ ✕ **Eagle's Nest.** Some of the finest food in the area is served here, including excellent steak, shrimp, and chicken dishes. If you're not up for a full entrée at dinner, which comes with soup, salad, potatoes, bread, and sorbet, try Eagle's Nest's other claim to fame: the Essie Cobb chicken salad, named after the Lakeview-born "inventor" of the Cobb salad. Breakfast is also served daily. ⊠ *117 N. E St.* ☎ *541/947–4824* ▭ *AE, D, DC, MC, V.*

¢ ✕ **Jumpin Java Espresso and More.** The menu is short at this small café, which looks like a simple coffee shop but offers an appealing bunch of inexpensive breakfast items including spicy breakfast burritos and waffles, and soups and burgers for lunch. It doubles as a cybercafé, with high-speed Internet available. ⊠ *16 N. F St.* ☎ *541/947–4855* ☺ *No dinner.*

¢–$ ▣ **Best Value Inn and Suites–Lakeview Lodge Motel.** Close to downtown, this basic motel has friendly owners, large rooms with ample seating, and several spacious suites. ⊠ *301 N. G St., 97630* ☎ *541/947–2181* 🖷 *541/947–2572* ⊕ *www.bestvalueinn.com* ↪ *40 rooms* ⌂ *Cable TV, microwaves, refrigerators, exercise equipment, hot tub, sauna, some pets allowed (fee)* ▭ *AE, D, DC, MC, V.*

Sports & the Outdoors

Lakeview is known as the hang gliding capital of the west, and many launch spots can be found in the Fremont National Forest.

HORSEBACK RIDING **Coop's Guiding and Packing** (🖃 Box 682, 97630 ☎ 541/947–4533) leads horseback trail rides and pack trips, among other excursions.

SKIING & SNOWBOARDING **Warner Mountain Ski Area** (⊠ 10 mi northwest of Lakeview ☎ 541/947–5001) is a local skiing and snowboarding destination with lift tickets for $20.

Eastern Oregon A to Z

BUS TRAVEL

The vast majority of travelers in eastern Oregon get around by car, but with a little planning, you'll discover that many of the cities in the region can be reached by Greyhound bus or by a smaller, regional bus line. The major Greyhound route in the area travels along I–84, passing through Pendleton, La Grande, Baker City (whose depot is only open 7–9:30 AM and 5–8 PM), and Ontario, with the Wallowa Valley Stage Lines operating a secondary route once daily, every day except Sunday, between La Grande and Joseph along Route 82. A north–south Greyhound route runs between Bend and Klamath Falls. One offshoot of this route, run by the People Mover bus line, goes just once a day, on weekends only, between Bend to John Day along U.S. 26. Another line, run by Red Ball Stage Lines, runs twice daily between Klamath Falls and Lakeview.

While you can get to many cities and towns by bus, bear in mind that once you get there you won't usually have public transportation available for getting around, and not all cities have car-rental outlets. Also, most area bus routes operate only once or twice a day, and some don't run on weekends; be sure to check schedules ahead of time.

🚹 Bus Lines **Greyhound** ☎ 800/231–2222. **People Mover** ☎ 541/575–2370. **Red Ball Stage Lines** ☎ 541/269–7183. **Wallowa Valley Stage Lines** ☎ 541/569–2284.

🚹 Depots **Baker City Station** ⊠ At Baker Truck Corral, 515 Campbell St. ☎ 541/523–5011. **Hermiston Station** ⊠ 650 S. U.S. 395 ☎ 541/564–6170. **La Grande Station**

✉ 2108 Cove Ave. ☎ 541/963-5165. **Ontario Station** ✉ At Pilot Travel Center, 653 E. Idaho Ave. ☎ 541/823-2567. **Pendleton Station** ✉ At Virginia Conrad, 320 S.W. Ct. ☎ 541/276-1511.

CAR TRAVEL

I–84 runs east along the Columbia River and dips down to Pendleton, La Grande, and Baker City. U.S. 26 heads east from Prineville through the Ochoco National Forest, passing the three units of the John Day Fossil Beds. U.S. 20 travels southeast from Bend in central Oregon to Burns. U.S. 20 and U.S. 26 both head west into Oregon from Idaho.

To reach Joseph take Highway 82 east from La Grande. Highway 86 loops down from Joseph to Baker City. From Baker City, Highway 7 heading west connects to U.S. 26 and leads to John Day. U.S. 395 runs south from John Day to Burns. Highway 205 heads south from Burns through the Malheur National Wildlife Refuge to Frenchglen, Steens Mountain, and the Alvord Desert (all accessed by local roads). In all these areas, equip yourself with chains for winter driving.

VISITOR INFORMATION

Visitor centers and chambers of commerce are always eager to furnish you with information on area attractions, dining, lodging, and shopping. They are generally open from 9 to 5 during the week, sometimes with slightly reduced hours on the weekends and in the off-season. In addition, eastern Oregon has several visitor centers and ranger stations geared toward the forests, wildlife areas, and recreation areas in the region.

🚹 Tourist Information **Baker County Visitors and Convention Bureau** ✉ 490 Campbell St., Baker City 97814 ☎ 541/523-3356 or 800/523-1235 ⊕ www.visitbaker.com. **Bureau of Land Management** ✉ Hwy. 20 W, Burns 97220 ☎ 541/573-5241. **Harney County Chamber of Commerce** ✉ 18 W. D St., Burns 97720 ☎ 541/573-2636 ⊕ www. harneycounty.com. **La Grande Chamber of Commerce** ✉ 1912 4th St., Suite 200, La Grande 97850 ☎ 541/963-8588 or 800/848-9969 ⊕ www.visitlagrande.com. **La Grande Visitors Center** ✉ 102 Elm St. ☎ 541/963-8588 or 800/848-9969 ⊕ www.visitlagrande. com. **Pendleton Chamber of Commerce** ✉ 501 S. Main St., 97801 ☎ 541/276-7411 or 800/547-8911 ⊕ www.pendleton-oregon.org.

OREGON A TO Z

To research prices, get advice from other travelers, and book arrangements, visit www.fodors.com.

AIRPORTS

The major airports in Oregon are Portland International Airport and Eugene Airport, also known as Mahlon Sweet Field. See the A to Z sections of the individual chapters for details about other airports.

🚹 Airport Information **Eugene Airport (EUG)** (Mahlon Sweet Field) ✉ 28855 Lockheed Dr. ☎ 541/682-5430 ⊕ www.eugeneairport.com. **Portland International Airport (PDX)** ✉ N.E. Airport Way at I-205 ☎ 877/739-4636 ⊕ www.portlandairportpdx.com or flypdx.com.

BUS TRAVEL

Experience Oregon in Eugene and Gray Line in Portland operate charter bus services and scheduled sightseeing tours that last from a few hours to several days. Greyhound Lines services Oregon with routes from elsewhere on the West Coast and from points east. People Mover travels on U.S. 26 between Bend and John Day.

🚹 Bus Companies **Experience Oregon** ✉ 1574 Coburg Rd., No. 123, Eugene ☎ 541/342-2662 or 800/342-2662 ⊕ www.experience.oregon.com. **Gray Line** ☎ 503/285-9845, 800/422-7042 in Portland ⊕ www.grayline.com. **Greyhound** ☎ 800/231-2222

⊕ www.greyhound.com. **People Mover** ✉ 229 N.E. Dayton St., John Day ☎ 541/575–2370 or 800/527–2370.

CAR TRAVEL

I–5 and U.S. 101 enter Oregon heading north from California and south from Washington. I–84 and U.S. 26 head west from the Idaho border to Portland.

ROAD CONDITIONS Winter driving in Oregon can sometimes present some real challenges. In coastal areas the mild, damp climate contributes to frequently wet roadways. Snowfalls generally occur only once or twice a year, but when they do, traffic grinds to a halt and the roadways become treacherous and stay that way until the snow melts.

Tire chains, studs, or snow tires are essential equipment for winter travel in mountain areas. If you're planning to drive into high elevations, be sure to check the weather forecast beforehand. Even the main-highway mountain passes can be forced to close because of snow conditions. During the winter months state and provincial highway departments operate snow-advisory telephone lines that give pass conditions.

🔋 **Road Conditions hotline** ☎ 503/588–2941, 800/977–6368 in Oregon.

EMERGENCIES

🔋 For **police, ambulance,** or **other emergencies** in Oregon, dial 911. **Oregon State Police** ☎ 800/452–7888.

SPORTS & THE OUTDOORS

BICYCLING According to the Oregon Department of Transportation, Oregon ranks first in the country for bikeability due in part to an act of the legislature in 1971 that decreed that 1% of Oregon's gasoline tax would be spent the construction of bike paths and on-street bike lanes. That plan has blossomed. Portland is ranked number one in the big-city category for providing safe venues for cyclists. Eugene's bikeway master plan has put the smaller community in the number one position for its size. There are also bike paths along the Willamette River and other areas throughout the state for commuters as well as recreational users. Buses have bike racks for easy transport.

The Oregon Bikeway Program has information about biking throughout the state. Call for a free bicycle map of the Coast/U.S. 101 route. Bicycle Paper is a great source on biking in the Pacific Northwest. Prominent bike-touring outfits include Mid-Valley Bicycle Club, the Portland Wheelmen Touring Club, and Rolling Pub Crawl Pacific Northwest Cycle Tours.

🔋 Bike Resources **Bicycle Paper** ✉ 68 S. Washington St., Seattle, WA 98104 ☎ 206/903–1333 ⊕ www.bicyclepaper.com. **Oregon Bikeway Program** ✉ Room 210, Transportation Bldg., 355 Capitol St. NE, Salem 97310 ☎ 503/986–3556 ⊕ www.odot.state.or.us.

🔋 Bike Tours **Mid-Valley Bicycle Club** ✉ Box 1373, Corvallis 97339. **Portland Wheelmen Touring Club** ☎ 503/257–7982 ⊕ www.pwtc.com. **Rolling Pub Crawl Pacific Northwest Cycle Tours** ✉ 818 S.W. 3rd Ave., No. 99, Portland 97204 ☎ 503/720–6984 ⊕ www.rollingpubcrawl.com.

CLIMBING 🔋 Climbing Information Eugene: **Obsidians** ✉ Box 322, Eugene 97440 ⊕ www.obsidians.org. Portland: **Mazama Club** ☎ 503/227–2345 ⊕ www.mazamas.org. **Portland Mountain Rescue** ✉ Box 5391, Portland 97228-5391 ☎ 503/972–7743 ⊕ www.pmru.org. Salem: **Chemeketans Outdoor Club** ✉ Box 864, Salem 97308 ⊕ www.chemeketans.org.

FISHING To fish in most areas of Oregon, out-of-state visitors need a yearly (about $48.50), seven-day ($34.75), or daily ($8) nonresident angler's license. Additional tags are required for those fishing for salmon or steelhead ($11), sturgeon ($6), or halibut ($6); these tags are available from any local sporting-goods store. For more information, contact the Sport Fishing Information Line.

🔢 Fishing Information **Oregon Department of Fish and Wildlife** ✉ Box 59, Portland, OR 97207 ☎ 503/872-5268 general information, 503/872-5275 license information ⊕ www.dfw.state.or.us. **Sport Fishing Information Line** ☎ 800/275-3474.

HIKING Many of Oregon's hiking trails are shared by horses, dogs, bikes, and pedestrians. Some hiking areas call for a trailhead parking permit, $5 a day or $30 for the season, available at a Forest Service office or at outdoor stores.

🔢 Hiking Information **Nature of Oregon Information Center** ✉ 800 N.E. Oregon St., Suite 177, Portland 97232 ☎ 503/872-2750, 503/872-2752 TDD ⊕ www.naturenw.org.

SKIING Sno-Park permits, distributed by the Oregon Department of Transportation, are required for parking at winter recreation areas from mid-November to April. The permits may be purchased for one day ($2), three days ($5), or a full season ($12) at DMV offices and retail agents—sporting-goods stores, markets and gas stations, usually near the areas—which sometimes charge slightly more than the listed price. Permits can often be purchased upon arrival at a ski area, but it's best to call ahead.

🔢 Skiing Information **Oregon Department of Transportation** ☎ 800/977-6368 or 503/986-3006.

TRAIN TRAVEL

Amtrak, the U.S. passenger rail system, has daily service to the Pacific Northwest from the Midwest and California. The *Empire Builder* takes a northern route through Minnesota and Montana from Chicago to Spokane, whence separate legs continue to Seattle and Portland. Part of the route to Portland runs through the Columbia River Gorge. The *Cascades* train travels once daily between Seattle and Vancouver and several times a day between Seattle, Portland, and Eugene. The *Coast Starlight,* which runs between Seattle and Los Angeles, passes through the Willamette Valley, serving Portland, Salem, Albany (near Corvallis), Eugene, and Klamath Falls.

🔢 Train Information **Amtrak** ☎ 800/872-7245 ⊕ www.amtrak.com.

VISITOR INFORMATION

Oregon tourist-information centers are marked with blue "i" signs on main roads. Opening and closing times vary, depending on the season and the individual office; call ahead for hours.

🔢 Tourist Information **Central Oregon Visitors Association** ✉ 572 S.W. Bluff Dr., Suite C, Bend 97702 ☎ 541/389-8799 or 800/800-8334 ⊕ www.visitcentraloregon.org. **National Park Service Pacific Northwest Regional Office** ☎ 206/220-4000. **Oregon State Park Information Center** ☎ 800/551-6949. **Oregon Tourism Commission** ✉ 775 Summer St. NE, Salem 97310 ☎ 503/986-0000 or 800/547-7842 ⊕ www.traveloregon.com. **U.S. Forest Service Recreation Information Center** ☎ 503/872-2750, 877/444-6777 campground reservations.

SEATTLE

3

FODOR'S CHOICE

Alexis Hotel, *Downtown*

Dahlia Lounge, *Downtown restaurant*

Elliott Bay Book Company, *Pioneer Square*

Fairmont Olympic Hotel, *Downtown*

Gaslight Inn, *Capitol Hill*

Hing Loon, *International District restaurant*

Inn at Harbor Steps, *Downtown*

Inn at the Market, *Downtown*

Lampreia, *Belltown restaurant*

Le Pichet, *Downtown restaurant*

Marco's Supper Club, *Belltown*

Oceanaire, *Downtown restaurant*

Pike Place Market, *Downtown*

Pioneer Square District

Recreational Equipment, Inc, *Downtown store*

Restaurant Zoë, *Belltown*

Salumi, *Pioneer Square restaurant*

Seattle Asian Art Museum, *Capitol Hill*

Space Needle, *Queen Anne*

Stonington Gallery, *Pioneer Square*

Sur La Table, *Downtown store*

Uwajimaya, *International District market*

Vivace Roasteria, *Capitol Hill coffeehouse*

Wing Luke Museum, *International District*

WSeattle, *Downtown hotel*

SEATTLE IS DEFINED BY WATER. There's no use denying the city's damp weather, or the fact that its skies are cloudy for much of the year. Seattleites don't tan, goes the joke, they rust. But Seattle is also defined by the rivers, lakes, and canals that bisect its steep green hills, creating distinctive micro-landscapes along the water's edge. Funky fishing boats, floating homes, swank yacht clubs, and waterfront restaurants exist side by side.

A city is defined by its people as well as its weather or geography, and the people of Seattle—a half-million or so within the city proper, another 2.5 million in the surrounding Puget Sound region—are a diversified bunch. Seattle has long had a vibrant Asian and Asian-American population, and well-established communities of Scandinavians, African-Americans, Jews, Native Americans, and Latinos live here, too. It's impossible to generalize about such a varied group, but the prototypical Seattleite was once pithily summed up by a *New Yorker* cartoon in which one arch-eyebrowed East Coast matron says to another, "They're back-packy, but nice."

Seattle's climate fosters an easygoing lifestyle. Overcast days and long winter nights have made the city a haven for moviegoers and book readers. Hollywood often tests new films here, and residents' per-capita book purchases are among North America's highest. Seattle has all the trappings of a metropolitan hub—two daily newspapers; a state-of-the-art convention center; professional sports teams; a diverse music club scene; and top-notch ballet, opera, symphony, and theater companies. A major seaport, the city is a vital link in Pacific Rim trade.

During the last few decades, the population has boomed, thanks to such corporate giants as Microsoft, Nintendo, Alaska Airlines, Boeing, and Weyerhauser, as well as a plenitude of start-up sporting companies, travel-based businesses, and dot-com operations. Seattle's expansion has led to the usual big-city problems: increases in crime, homelessness, and traffic congestion. Many residents have fled east and north to the ever-growing suburbs of Bellevue, Kirkland, Redmond, Issaquah, Shoreline, and Bothell, and south to Renton, Kent, and Federal Way—all of which have swollen from quiet communities into sizable cities. Despite all the growing pains, though, Seattleites have a great love for their community and its natural surroundings; hence their firm commitment to maintaining the area's reputation as one of the country's most livable places.

EXPLORING SEATTLE

Updated by
Holly S. Smith

Seattle, like Rome, is built on seven hills. As a visitor, you're likely to spend much of your time on only two of them (Capitol Hill and Queen Anne Hill), but the seven knobs are indeed the most definitive element of the city's natural and spiritual landscape. Years of largely thoughtful building practices have kept tall buildings from obscuring the lines of sight, maintaining vistas in most directions and around most every turn. The hills are lofty, privileged perches from which residents are constantly reminded of the beauty of the forests, mountains, and waters lying just beyond the city—that is, when it stops misting long enough to see your hand in front of your face.

To know Seattle is to know its distinctive neighborhoods. Because of the hills, comfortable walking shoes are a must. Downtown is bounded on the west by Elliot Bay, on the south by Pioneer Square (the city's oldest neighborhood) and the International District (I.D.), on the north by Belltown and the attractive residences lining the slopes of Queen Anne Hill, and by I–5 to the east. You can reach most points of interest by

Buy a CityPass ticket book for $37 and you'll get 50% off admission to the Space Needle, the Seattle Art Museum, the Seattle Aquarium, the Pacific Science Center, the Woodland Park Zoo, and other sights. The booklet, available at any of these attractions, is valid for nine consecutive days.

If you have 3 days

3

Get up with the sun and stroll to Pike Place Market. Take the steps down to the docks and visit the Odyssey Maritime Discovery Center or the Seattle Aquarium. In the afternoon take a cruise on Elliott Bay or shop in Downtown's cosmopolitan shops. Return to Pike Place Market for dinner. Top off the night with a concert, a play, or a little clubbing in Belltown.

On the second day, take the two-minute monorail ride from Downtown's Westlake Center mall to the Seattle Center. Head up the Space Needle for 360-degree city views. Afterward take in the Pacific Science Center, the Children's Museum, the Experience Music Project, or the Science Fiction Experience. Have lunch in Queen Anne or Belltown, and then walk southwest down Broadway to the water. Ride the trolley past the docks and through Pioneer Square to the International District. Tour the Wing Luke Museum. For dinner, head to Uwajimaya, the market with a Pan-Asian food court. See what's happening at the Nippon Kan Theater, or head east to Capitol Hill's shops and bars. Start the third day exploring galleries and shops in Pioneer Square. Wander through the Klondike Gold Rush National Historical Park, then grab a latte at the corner Starbucks before you take the Seattle Underground Tour. Have lunch at Elliott Bay Books' café, then browse the shelves. Take a bay cruise or visit the Washington Park Arboretum. Head to Capitol Hill or back south to Pioneer Square for dinner and some nightclubbing.

If you have 6 days

Follow the three-day itinerary. On the fourth day, grab a coffee (or carrot juice) at a Green Lake café, then stroll around the water. Round out the morning exploring the Woodland Park Zoo or Ballard Locks. Head to Fremont for lunch and a little shopping. Cross over to the University District and the University of Washington's Waterfront Activities Center, where you can rent a kayak. Try one of the U-District's ethnic restaurants for dinner, then spend the evening shopping at University Village or bar-hopping along the Avenue.

Day 5 is for culture: spend the morning at the Frye Art Museum, the Burke Museum of Natural History and Culture, the Henry Art Gallery, or the Museum of History & Industry. Afterward, drive northeast to the Woodinville vineyards. Take a Chateau Ste. Michelle Winery tour, then head across the street to the Columbia Winery to sample the vintages. Have lunch in one of the area's many restaurants, or wait to eat until after you've toured the Redhook Brewery. Head back through Kirkland, pausing to wander along the docks and the beach. End the day in Bellevue with dinner at a trendy restaurant.

On Day 6 head to Capitol Hill and set out on a late morning stroll through Volunteer Park. Then tour the Seattle Asian Art Museum and the conservatory. Have lunch on Broadway; do a little shopping here and along 12th Avenue. Drive to West Seattle's Alki Beach for the afternoon, and have dinner at a beachside restaurant.

foot, bus, or trolley, or the monorail that runs between the Seattle Center and the Westlake Center. Capitol Hill, northeast of Downtown on Pine Street, east of Interstate 5 (I–5), is the center of youth culture in this very young city. University District, or U-District, the area around the University of Washington, is north of Capitol Hill and Union Bay.

Ballard, home to Seattle's fishing industry and fun-to-tour locks, is at the mouth of Salmon Bay, northwest of Downtown. Fremont, Seattle's eccentric and artsy hamlet, is north of Lake Union and the Lake Washington Ship Canal, east of Ballard, west of Wallingford, and south of Woodland Park. Magnolia, known for its expensive homes, is at the northwestern edge of Elliot Bay, west of Queen Anne Hill.

Downtown, Belltown & Queen Anne

a good tour

Numbers in the text correspond to numbers in the margin and on the Downtown Seattle & Environs map.

Start your day with a walk to **Pike Place Market** ❶ ▶. Get there early as the vendors set up (9 AM weekdays and Saturday, or 10:30 AM Sunday), and before the crowds have arrived. If you enjoy innovative paintings and crafts both modern and old, stop next at the **Seattle Art Museum** ❷. Otherwise, after your market tour, take the Hillclimb steps down to the waterfront and spend a couple of hours at the **Seattle Aquarium** ❸. Next door is the **Seattle IMAX Dome Theater** ❹, which shows compelling nature-oriented films on an enormous screen. You can walk out on Piers 62 and 63 for a good view of Elliott Bay, then head north to the refurbished Bell Street Pier (66), a conference center and cruise ship docking area that contains several restaurants and **Odyssey Maritime Discovery Center** ❺. From here, head back toward the aquarium and then south along the waterfront to Yesler Way and Pioneer Square, with its many historic buildings, art galleries, boutiques, bookshops, and bars.

Walk north along Fourth and Fifth avenues to the Downtown shopping district. Most of the exciting stores are within a few blocks of Westlake Center, a huge mall at Fourth and Pine. From here, you can take the two-minute monorail ride to the Seattle Center, whose many sights include the **Space Needle** ❻. If you have kids in tow, head to the fascinating interactive exhibits at the **Pacific Science Center** ❼ or at the **The Children's Museum** ❽. The **Experience Music Project** ❾, which celebrates American popular music, is known worldwide for architect Frank Gehry's daring design. Don't miss the Science Fiction Experience museum, also housed within.

TIMING　To see all the sights on this tour you really need two days. If you're pressed for time, choose just a couple—say, Pike Place Market or the Seattle Center, which can easily fill an entire morning, plus one museum or neighborhood for the afternoon.

What to See

❽　**The Children's Museum.** Enter this colorful spacious museum off the Seattle Center food court through a Northwest wilderness setting, with winding trails, hollow logs, and a waterfall. From here, you can explore a global village where rooms with kid-friendly props show everyday life in Ghana, the Philippines, and Japan. Another neighborhood contains an American post office, a fire station, and a grocery store. Cog City is a giant game of pipes, pulleys, and balls; and kids can test their talent in a mock recording studio. There's a small play area for toddlers, and lots of crafts to help kids learn more about the exhibits. ⊠ *Seattle Center House, 305 Harrison St., Queen Anne* ☎ *206/441-1768* ⊕ *www.thechildrensmuseum.org* ⊠ *$6* ⊘ *Weekdays 10–5, weekends 10–6.*

3

All in the Family

There's no better place to find something for everyone in your family than at the Pike Place Market, overlooking Elliott Bay. On the bay itself are the Seattle Aquarium and the Maritime Discovery Center. Hands-on museums, IMAX theaters, the Space Needle, and the Woodland Park Zoo are also perfect for families. Waterfront activities centers offer the chance to kayak, sail, or cruise on Seattle's lakes and bays, and just about every neighborhood has a park with a playground.

The Art of the Matter

The best way to view the works in Seattle's museums and galleries is on the First Thursday art walk, when admission is free and artists are often out with their displays. Western Washington is particularly known for its excellent glass art, the red-hot molten glass more easily fashioned in the region's temperate climate. Books are also big, and most bookstores host readings and other events. Benaroya Hall, with its perfect acoustics, is home to Seattle's symphony orchestra, while the beautiful McCaw Hall at the Seattle Center houses the city's renowned opera and ballet companies. Many historic theaters run first-rate performances with local casts.

Life After Dark

Although Seattle was the birthplace of grunge rock, today a variety of music overshadows the rumpled memories of the '90s. Clubs showcase the passionate musical stylings of everything from tinny garage bands to the biggest international names in Top 40 rock, country, and jazz and blues. Key Arena at the Seattle Center and Downtown's Paramount Theater are the two top indoor concert sites; in summer, outdoor music echoes from parks and at Pier 62. If you want to dance, head to a club in Downtown, Belltown, Capitol Hill, or the U-District.

Playing It Up

The classy Seahawks Stadium is home to the Seattle Seahawks football team. A block or so away is Safeco Field, home to the Seattle Mariners baseball team. The Seattle Supersonics shoot their hoops at Key Arena. Also look for Seafair's summer hydroplane races on Lake Washington, horseracing at Emerald Downs, cycling at the Marymoor Park Velodrome, and boating and fishing in the Sound and on the lakes.

Savory Cuisine

A quick scan of Pike Place Market's stalls shows you what's on restaurant plates every season: strawberries in June, Walla Walla onions in July, wild blackberries in August, and apples in autumn. Such ingredients fused with European and Asian cooking techniques define the heart of Pacific Northwest cuisine. Seafood also stars: meaty grilled salmon; fresh shellfish; thick, milky clam chowder; *cioppino* (seafood stew in a tomato base). Ethnic restaurants—particularly in the International and University districts— serve up authentic dishes from countries on nearly every continent. Washington's wineries produce many award-winning labels, and local brews come in a range of flavors, which you can often try in sample sizes.

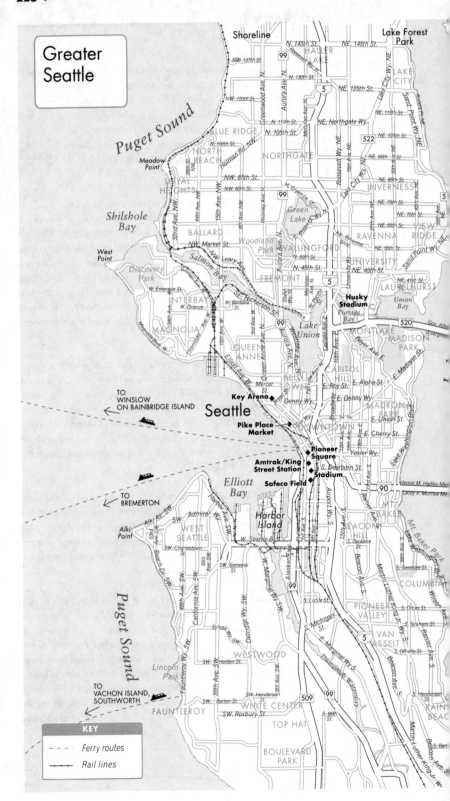

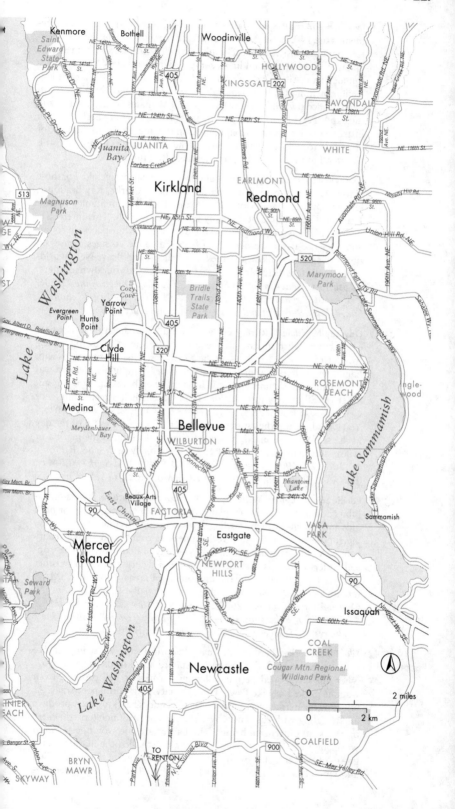

9 Experience Music Project. Seattle's most controversial architectural statement is the 140,000-square-foot interactive museum celebrating American popular music. Architect Frank Gehry drew inspiration from electric guitars to achieve the building's curvy design. Funded by Microsoft co-founder Paul Allen, it's a fitting backdrop for the world's largest collection of Jimi Hendrix memorabilia, which is flanked by a gallery of guitars once owned by Bob Dylan, Hank Williams, Kurt Cobain, and the bands Pearl Jam, Soundgarden, and the Kingsmen. Experiment with instruments and recording equipment in the interactive Sound Lab, or attend performances or workshops in the Sky Church concert hall, JBL Theater, Liquid Lounge bar, or Turntable Restaurant.

The **Science Fiction Experience** is another Paul Allen brainchild. For those who love sci-fi, the advisory board—Arthur C. Clarke, Ray Bradbury, Octavia Butler, Orson Scott Card, Syne Mitchell, Kim Stanley Robinson, and Greg Bear, among many others—says it all. This interactive multimedia museum truly takes you "out there" with spaceship rooms and a science-fiction heroes hall of fame. Fantastic Voyages focuses on time travel, Them! illustrates the fear of aliens, and Brave New Worlds explores the future. In Make Contact you can create your own journeys. ⊠ *5th Ave., between Broad St. and Thomas St., Queen Anne* 🖀 *206/ 770–2700* ⊕ *www.emplive.com* 🎫 *$19.95* 🕙 *May 23–Sept. 1 Sun.–Thurs. 9–6, Fri. and Sat. 9–9; otherwise daily 9–5.*

5 Odyssey Maritime Discovery Center. Cultural and educational maritime exhibits on Puget Sound and ocean trade are the focus of this waterfront attraction. Learn all about the Northwest's fishing traditions with hands-on exhibits that include kayaking over computer-generated waters, loading a container ship, and listening in on boats radioing one another on Elliott Bay just outside. The adjacent Bell Street Conference Center hosts major local events and press conferences; see what's on tap. You can also shop the on-site fish market, dine on the catch of the day at the seafood restaurant, or spy on boaters docking at the marina or cruise ships putting into port. ⊠ *2205 Alaskan Way, Pier 66, Belltown* 🖀 *206/374–4000* ⊕ *www.ody.org* 🎫 *$7* 🕙 *Mid-Sept.–mid-May, Tues.–Sat. 10–5, Sun. noon–5; otherwise Mon.–Sat. 10–5, Sun. noon–5.*

7 Pacific Science Center. With about 200 indoor and outdoor hands-on exhibits and a state-of-the-art planetarium, this is a great place for both kids and grown-ups. The startling dinosaur exhibit is complete with moving robotic creatures, while Tech Zones has robots and virtual-reality games. Machines analyze human physiology in Body Works. The tropical butterfly house is stocked with farm-raised chrysalises weekly; other creatures live in the woodland and tide pool areas. Next door, IMAX movies and rock music, laser light shows run daily. ⊠ *200 2nd Ave. N, Queen Anne* 🖀 *206/443–2001* ⊕ *www.pacsci.org* 🎫 *Center $9, IMAX $7.50–$8.50, light shows $5–$7.50* 🕙 *Labor Day–Memorial Day, weekdays 10–5, weekends 10–6; otherwise daily 10–6.*

1 Pike Place Market. Perhaps like many historical sites whose importance
FodorśChoice is taken for granted, this institution started small. It dates from 1907,
★ when the city issued permits allowing farmers to sell produce from wagons parked at Pike Place. Later the city built permanent stalls. At one time the market was a madhouse of vendors hawking their produce and haggling with customers over prices. Some fishmongers still carry on this kind of frenzied banter, but chances are you won't get them to waver on their prices. Urban renewal almost killed the market, but a group of residents, led by the late architect Victor Steinbrueck, rallied and voted it a historical asset in 1973. Many buildings have been re-

stored, and the complex is connected to the waterfront by stairs and elevators. Booths sell seafood—which can be packed in dry ice for your flight home—produce, cheese, wine, spices, tea, coffee, and crafts. There are also several restaurants.

Although wandering at will is fun, free maps of the venue are available at several locations throughout the market. The map distinguishes among the various types of shops and stalls. Farmers who come to the market from as far away as the Yakima Valley, east of the Cascade Mountains, have first dibs on the tables, known as "farmers' tables," where they display and sell their own vegetables, fruits, or flowers. Vendors in the so-called high stalls often have fruits and vegetables or crafts that they've purchased locally to sell here. The superb quality of the high-stall produce helps to set Seattle's dining standards.

The shopkeepers who rent stores in the market sell such things as packaged food items, art, curios, pets, and more. Because the market is along a bluff, the main arcade stretches down the cliff face for several stories; many shops are below street level. Other shops and restaurants are in buildings east of Pike Place and west of Western Avenue. ⊠ *Pike Pl. at Pike St., west of 1st Ave., Downtown* ☎ *206/682–7453* ⊕ *www. pikeplacemarket.org* ⊗ *Mon.–Sat. 9–6, Sun. 11–5.*

★ ☺ ❸ **Seattle Aquarium.** From its cylindrical tank, an octopus welcomes you to the aquarium, whose darkened rooms and large, lighted tanks brilliantly display Pacific Northwest marine life. The Tide Pool exhibit recreates Washington's rocky coast and sandy beaches, complete with a 6,000-gallon wave that sweeps in over the ecosystem. Huge glass windows provide underwater views of seals and sea otters; you can go up top to watch them play in their pools. Kids love the Discovery Lab, where they can touch starfish, sea urchins, and sponges, then peek through microscopes at baby barnacles and jellyfish. They can also don scuba gear and animal costumes, scramble through a play area with fake hollow trees, or wrap up in the rubbery arms of a life-size replica of the Puget Sound octopus, which, at 100 pounds, is the world's largest, with an armspan of more than 10 feet. ⊠ *Pier 59 off Alaskan Way, Downtown* ☎ *206/386–4320* ⊕ *www.seattleaquarium.org* ☒ *$8.50, $14 with IMAX admission* ⊗ *Memorial Day–Labor Day, daily 10–7; Labor Day–Memorial Day, daily 10–5.*

★ ❷ **Seattle Art Museum.** Postmodern architect Robert Venturi designed this five-story museum to be a work of art in itself: large-scale vertical fluting adorns the building's limestone exterior, accented by terra-cotta, cut granite, and marble. Sculptor Jonathan Borofsky's several-stories-high *Hammering Man* pounds away outside the front door. Inside, a large, airy, brightly lit hall is enlivened by two ancient Chinese stone camels. The pair once marked the entrance to the Asian Art Museum in Volunteer Park but had to be brought indoors because they weathered too rapidly in Seattle's moist clime. The museum's extensive collection surveys Asian, Native American, African, Oceanic, and pre-Columbian art. Among the highlights are the anonymous 14th-century Buddhist masterwork *Monk at the Moment of Enlightenment* and Jackson Pollock's *Sea Change*. The café behind the lobby is a terrific lunch spot, and the shop carries souvenirs as well as international arts and crafts publications. The entrance ticket includes a free visit to the Seattle Asian Art Museum if used within a week. A ticket to the latter is good for $3 off admission here if used within one week. ⊠ *100 University St., Downtown* ☎ *206/654–3255* ⊕ *www.seattleartmuseum.org* ☒ *$7, free 1st Thurs. of month* ⊗ *Tues.–Sun. 10–5, Thurs. until 9.*

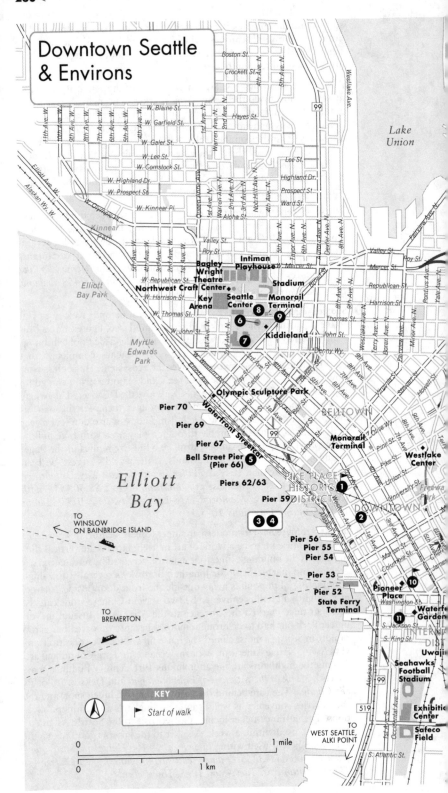

Downtown Seattle & Environs

Boston St.
Crockett St.
W. Blaine St.
Hayes St.
W. Garfield St.
W. Galer St.
Lee St.
W. Lee St.
W. Comstock St.
Highland Dr.
W. Highland Dr.
Prospect St.
W. Prospect St.
Ward St.
W. Kinnear Pl.
Aloha St.
Valley St.
Roy St.
Mercer St.
Republican St.
Harrison St.
Thomas St.
John St.
Denny Wy.

11th Ave. W.
9th Ave. W.
8th Ave. W.
7th Ave. W.
6th Ave. W.
5th Ave. W.
4th Ave. W.
3rd Ave. W.
2nd Ave. W.
1st Ave. W.
Warren Ave. N.
2nd Ave. N.
1st Ave. N.
Queen Anne Ave. N.
Nob Hill Ave. N.
4th Ave. N.
5th Ave. N.
Taylor Ave. N.
6th Ave. N.
Aurora Ave. N.
Dexter Ave. N.
8th Ave. N.

99

Elliott Ave. W.
Alaskan Wy. W.
W. Olympic Pl.

Lake Union

Kinnear Park

Elliott Bay Park

Myrtle Edwards Park

Bagley Wright Theatre
Intiman Playhouse
W. Republican St.
Northwest Craft Center
Stadium
Monorail Terminal
Key Arena
Seattle Center
W. Harrison St.
W. Thomas St.
6
8
9
W. John St.
7
Kiddieland

5th Ave. N.
4th Ave. N.
3rd Ave. N.
2nd Ave. N.
1st Ave. N.

Mercer St.
Republican St.
Harrison St.
Thomas St.
John St.

Roy St.
Valley St.

8th Ave. N.
9th Ave. N.
Westlake Ave. N.
Terry Ave. N.
Boren Ave. N.
Fairview Ave. N.
Minor Ave. N.

Clay St.
Vine St.
Wall St.
Battery St.
Bell St.
Blanchard St.
Lenora St.

Olympic Sculpture Park

BELLTOWN

Pier 70
Waterfront Streetcar
Pier 69
Pier 67
Monorail Terminal
Olive Wy.
Pine St.
Bell Street Pier (Pier 66)
5
Piers 62/63
99
Westlake Center
Pike St.
Union St.
University St.
PIKE PLACE HISTORIC DISTRICT
1
2
DOWNTOWN
Freeway Park

Pier 59
3 **4**
Western Ave.
Alaskan Wy.
1st Ave.
2nd Ave.
3rd Ave.

Elliott Bay

TO WINSLOW ON BAINBRIDGE ISLAND

Pier 56
Pier 55
Pier 54
Marion St.
Columbia St.

Pier 53

TO BREMERTON

Pier 52
State Ferry Terminal
Pioneer Place
10
Washington St.
11
S. Jackson St.
Waterfront Garden
INTERN'L DIST.
S. King St.
Uwaji

Seahawks Football Stadium
99

519
Exhibition Center

Safeco Field

TO WEST SEATTLE, ALKI POINT

Occidental Ave. S.
Alaskan Wy. S.

S. Atlantic St.

KEY
▶ *Start of walk*

N

0   1 mile

0   1 km

The Children's Museum **8**

Experience Music Project **9**

Frye Art Museum **14**

International District **12**

Klondike Gold Rush
National Historical Park **11**

Odyssey Maritime
Discovery Center **5**

Pacific Science Center **7**

Pike Place Market **1**

Pioneer Square District **10**

Seattle Aquarium **3**

Seattle Art Museum **2**

Seattle IMAX Dome Theater **4**

Space Needle **6**

Wing Luke Museum **13**

Seattle Center. The 74-acre Seattle Center complex was built for the 1962 World's Fair. A rolling green campus organized around the massive International Fountain, the center includes an amusement park, theaters, exhibition halls, museums, shops, restaurants, a skateboard park, Key Arena, the Pacific Science Center, the Children's Museum, Marion Oliver McCaw Hall performance center, and the Space Needle. Among the arts groups based here are the Seattle Repertory Theatre, Intiman Theatre, the Seattle Opera, and the Pacific Northwest Ballet. The center hosts several professional sports teams: the Seattle Supersonics (NBA basketball), Sounders (soccer), Seadogs (indoor soccer), and Thunderbirds (amateur hockey). It's a bit cramped, and parking can be a nightmare, but the Seattle Center is the undisputed hub of the city's leisure life. It's also the site of three of the area's largest summer festivals: the Northwest Folklife Festival, Bite of Seattle, and Bumbershoot. In addition, the city's monorail travels between here and Westlake Center, a mall that's about a mile away.

At the southeast corner stands a statue of Chief Seattle, of the Duwamish tribe. Seattle was among the first Native Americans to have contact with the white explorers who came to the region. He was viewed as a great leader and peacemaker by his fellow tribesmen and as a friendly contact by the white settlers. The sculpture was created by local artist James Wehn in 1912 and dedicated by the chief's great-great granddaughter, Myrtle Loughery, on Founder's Day, November 13, 1912. ✉ *Between 1st and 5th Aves. N and Denny Way and Mercer St., Queen Anne* ☎ *206/684–8582* ⊕ *www.seattlecenter.com.*

4 Seattle IMAX Dome Theater. The theater next to the aquarium shows 30- to 45-minute films on an enormous 180-degree curved screen several times a day, starting at 10 AM in summer. A big-deal Hexophonic sound system adds realism. Recent big-screen films have included *Extreme* sports action, *Bears*, and the *Living Sea. The Eruption of Mount St. Helens* is an awesome mainstay. A nice perk for weary-footed parents and their wee ones: kids under 5 are free. ✉ *Pier 59 off Alaskan Way, Downtown* ☎ *206/622–1869* ⊕ *www.seattleimaxdome.com* ✉ *$7, 2nd show same day $2, combination tickets including aquarium admission $14* ☉ *Daily 10–5.*

6 Space Needle. The distinctive exterior of the 520-foot-high Space Needle is visible throughout Downtown—but the view from the inside out is even better. A 42-second elevator ride up to the circular observation deck yields 360-degree vistas of Elliott Bay, Queen Anne Hill, the UW, and the Cascade Range. The Needle was built just in time for the World's Fair in 1962, but has since been refurbished with educational signs, interactive trivia game stations for kids, and the glass-enclosed SpaceBase store and Pavilion spiraling around the base of the tower. If you dine at the elite, top-floor SkyCity revolving restaurant, admission to the observation deck is free. Or, just enjoy views from the yummy coffee bar. ✉ *5th Ave. and Broad St., Queen Anne* ☎ *206/443–2111* *or 800/937–9582* ⊕ *www.spaceneedle.com* ✉ *$11* ☉ *Sun.–Thurs. 9 AM–11 PM, Fri. and Sat. 9 AM–midnight.*

FodorśChoice ★

South & East of Downtown

a good tour

Numbers in the text correspond to numbers in the margin and on the Downtown Seattle & Environs map.

Begin at Pioneer Place, at First Avenue and Yesler Way, in the **Pioneer Square District** ⑩ ▶. Explore the shops and historic buildings along First Avenue before heading to the **Klondike Gold Rush National Historical**

Park ⑪, on Main Street two blocks south and one block east of Pioneer Place. As you continue east along Main Street to the **International District** ⑫, a restful stop is Waterfall Garden park. Head south (right) on Second Avenue South and east (left) at South Jackson Street. You'll see Amtrak's King Street Station on your right as you head up South Jackson to Seventh Avenue, where the **Wing Luke Museum** ⑬ surveys the past and present of immigrants from Asia and the Pacific islands and their descendants. The museum has walking-tour maps of historic buildings and businesses. One intriguing stop is the Uwajimaya store at Sixth Avenue South and South Dearborn Street (head south four blocks on Seventh Avenue South and turn right on South Dearborn Street). You can return to the harbor on one of the vintage Waterfront Streetcar trolleys—the southern terminus is at Fifth Avenue South and Jackson Street. You can catch a bus to Downtown at the same corner.

A drive through the neighborhoods directly east of Downtown takes in several sights amid the compact condominiums and modest free-standing dwellings. Head east on Cherry Street to the corner of Terry Avenue, where a cylindrical tiled dome marks the **Frye Art Museum** ⑭.

TIMING   You could breeze through Pioneer Square and the I.D. in a couple of hours—but why? These are rich, historically and culturally intriguing areas with fascinating little shops, museums, and eateries, plus hidden green spaces and charming shaded spots to sit and take in the neighborhood. To wander through Pioneer Square's antiques stores, used bookshops, art galleries, and crafts boutiques—or to see all the wonders of the I.D., such as the herbal apothecaries, kitschy knickknack and housewares shops, Vietnamese noodle houses, Chinese dim sum restaurants, and Asian produce stalls—plan at least two hours for each. Add another two hours for an Underground Tour of Pioneer Square, which delves into Seattle's seedier history. Note that many Pioneer Square galleries, the Frye Art Museum, and the Wing Luke Museum are closed Monday.

What to See

⑭ **Frye Art Museum.** The tiled cylinder and adjacent museum were built in 1952 with funding from meat-packing millionaires. The permanent collection focuses on 19th- and 20th-century German, French, and American paintings and sculptures, including many European oils taken in trade for lard sold to bankrupt Germany after the Second World War. Temporary exhibits span Art Wolfe wildlife photos to exquisite Russian palace paintings. The museum also has drawing and ceramics studios; art, music, and craft classes; family activities; an auditorium; and a courtyard with a reflecting pool and waterfall. Nosh on light meals or sip coffee at the Gallery Café. Free tours run Sundays at 12:30 and 3. ✉ *704 Terry Ave., First Hill* ☎ *206/622–9250* ⊕ *www.fryeart.org* ☞ *Free* ⊙ *Tues.–Sat. 10–5, Thurs. until 9, Sun. noon–5.*

⟳ ⑫ **International District.** Bright welcome banners and 12-foot fiberglass dragons spinning in the wind capture the Asian spirit of the expanding International District (formerly called Chinatown). The I.D., as it's locally known, began as a haven for Chinese workers who came to the United States to work on the transcontinental railroad. The community has remained largely intact despite anti-Chinese riots and the forced eviction of Chinese residents during the 1880s and the internment of Japanese-Americans during World War II. About one-third of the residents are Chinese, one-third are Filipino, and another third come from elsewhere in Asia or the Pacific islands. Although today the main business anchor is the Uwajimaya Japanese superstore, there are also many small Asian restaurants, herbalists, acupuncturists, antiques shops, and private clubs for gambling and socializing. Look for the diamond-shape dragon signs in store windows—these establishments will give you a free-parking token. ⊠ *Between Yesler Way and S. Dearborn St. and 4th and 12th Aves.* ☎ *206/382–1197* ⊕ *www.internationaldistrict.org.*

⓫ Klondike Gold Rush National Historical Park. A redbrick building with wooden floors and soaring ceilings contains a small museum illustrating Seattle's role in the 1897–98 gold rush in northwestern Canada's Klondike region. Displays show antique mining equipment, and the walls are lined with photos of gold diggers, explorers, and the hopeful families who followed them. Film presentations, gold-panning demonstrations, and rotating exhibits are scheduled throughout the year. Other sectors of this park are in southeast Alaska. ⊠ *117 S. Main St., Pioneer Square* ☎ *206/553–7220* ⊕ *www.nps.gov/klse/index.htm* ⊡ *Free* ⊙ *Daily 9–5.*

off the beaten path

MUSEUM OF FLIGHT – Boeing, the world's largest builder of aircraft, was founded in Seattle in 1916. So it's not surprising that this facility at Boeing Field, south of the International District, is a great museum. It's especially fun for kids, who can climb in many of the aircrafts and pretend to fly, make flight-related crafts, or attend special programs. The Red Barn, Boeing's original airplane factory, houses an exhibit on the history of flight. The Great Gallery, a dramatic structure designed by Ibsen Nelson, contains more than 20 vintage airplanes. ⊠ *9404 E. Marginal Way S, take I–5 south to Exit 158, turn right on Marginal Way S, Renton* ☎ *206/764–5720* ⊕ *www.museumofflight.org* ⊡ *$9.50* ⊙ *Fri.–Wed. 10–5, Thurs. 10–9.*

⓾ Pioneer Square District. Seattle's oldest neighborhood is a round-the-clock hub of activity. Cafés, antiques shops, clothing boutiques, and art galleries fill elegantly renovated, turn-of-the-20th-century redbrick buildings lining the narrow streets that surround the historic central square. The district's most unique structure, the 42-story Smith Tower on Second Avenue and Yesler Way, was the tallest building west of the Mississippi when it was completed in 1914. By day, you'll see a mix of downtown workers and tourists strolling between the dining and arts spots, while darkness brings a frenzy of club-hoppers, plus late-night partyers spilling over from nearby festivals and stadium sports events. The ornate iron-and-glass pergola on First Avenue and Yesler Way marks the site where the pier and sawmill owned by Henry Yesler, one of Seattle's first businessmen, once operated. Actually, today's Yesler Way was the original "Skid Row," where in the 1880s timber was sent to the sawmill on a skid of small logs laid crossways and greased so that the cut trees would slide down to the mill. The area later grew into Seattle's first center of commerce. Many of the buildings you see today are replicas of the wood-frame structures destroyed by fire in 1889.

⓭ Wing Luke Museum. Named for the Northwest's first Asian-American elected official, this small, well-organized museum surveys the history and cultures of people from Asia and the Pacific islands who settled in the Pacific Northwest. The emphasis is on how immigrants and their descendants have transformed and been transformed by American culture. The permanent collection includes costumes, fabrics, crafts, basketry, photographs, and Chinese traditional medicines. ⊠ *407 7th Ave. S, International District* ☎ *206/623–5124* ⊕ *www.wingluke.org* ⊡ *$4* ⊙ *Tues.–Fri. 11–4:30, weekends noon–4.*

FodorsChoice ★ (Pioneer Square District)

FodorsChoice ★ (Wing Luke Museum)

Capitol Hill

a good tour

Numbers in the text correspond to numbers in the margin and on the Capitol Hill & the U-District map.

From Downtown, walk up Pine Street to Melrose Avenue and fortify yourself with a jolt of java (and perhaps an artsy new hardcover) at the Bauhaus. Continue east along the **Pike–Pine corridor** ⑮ ☞ on Pine Street to Broadway and turn left (but don't miss the art deco Egyptian Theater to the right). Passing Seattle Central Community College you'll cross Denny Way, the unofficial threshold of the **Broadway shopping district** ⑯. After six blocks, the road bears to the right, becoming 10th Avenue East.

You'll notice many beautiful homes on the side streets off 10th Avenue East in either direction as you continue north to Prospect Street. Turn right at Prospect Street and gird yourself for another hill. Continue on to 14th Avenue East and turn left (north) to enter **Volunteer Park** ⑰. After walking around a picturesque water tower (with a good view from the top), you'll see the Volunteer Park Conservatory straight ahead, the reservoir to your left, and the **Seattle Asian Art Museum** ⑱ to your right. Leave the park to the east via Galer Street. Walk north along 15th Avenue East to visit **Lakeview Cemetery** ⑲ (where Bruce Lee lies in repose), or turn right (south) and walk four blocks to shops and cafés. To return Downtown, continue walking south on 15th Avenue East and west on Pine Street (if you've had enough walking, catch Metro Bus 10 at this intersection; it heads toward Pike Place Market). At Broadway, cut one block south to Pike Street for the rest of the walk. The above tour is a good survey of Capitol Hill, but it's by no means complete. The **Washington Park Arboretum** ⑳, for example, is too far to walk; catch Metro Bus 11 heading northeast along East Madison Street, or drive.

TIMING Simply walking this tour requires four hours—two if you start and end in the Broadway shopping district. Allow at least two hours for shopping the Pike–Pine corridor and Broadway, an hour for the Asian Art Museum, and a half hour for the conservatory. The amount of time you spend at Bruce Lee's grave is between you and Mr. Lee. Allow two hours for the arboretum, where losing track of time is pretty much the point.

What to See

⑯ **Broadway Shopping District.** Seattle's youth-oriented culture, old money, and gay scene all converge on this lively, laid-back stretch of Broadway East between East Denny Way and East Roy Street. Complete with plenty of cafés, record shops, vintage clothing stores, and the obligatory art-house movie theater, Harvard Exit, it's great place to stroll, sip coffee, or have a brew. The avenue's appeal is that it's generally safe at all hours and has fascinating people-watching and a lot of cool stuff—specialty coffee, hand-made chocolates, sushi, salsa, boutique accessories, kitschy knickknacks.

Between Pine and Roy streets artist Jack Mackie inlaid seven sets of bronze dancing footprints demonstrating the steps for the tango, the waltz, the foxtrot, and others. Don't feel embarrassed about prancing out these ballroom dances. Even the most conservative Seattleites occasionally dance on this sidewalk. Look closely at the steps near Roy Street to see coffee beans in the concrete, a nod to the region's love affair with java. Near Pine Street is a dedication to the city's most worshiped rock-and-roll icon—Jimi Hendrix. His bronze effigy holds a guitar, and from the looks of things he hasn't just kissed the sky, he's made out with it. Buckled at the knees with his hand up, head thrown back, and eyes squeezed shut, Seattle's legendary son is frozen in the midst of what seems a par-

The Ave **21**

Broadway
Shopping
District **16**

Burke Museum of
Natural History
and Culture . .**24**

Henry Art
Gallery **23**

Lakeview
Cemetery **19**

Museum of
History &
Industry **25**

Pike--Pine
Corridor **15**

Seattle
Asian Art
Museum **18**

University of
Washington . .**22**

Volunteer
Park **17**

Washington
Park
Arboretum . . .**20**

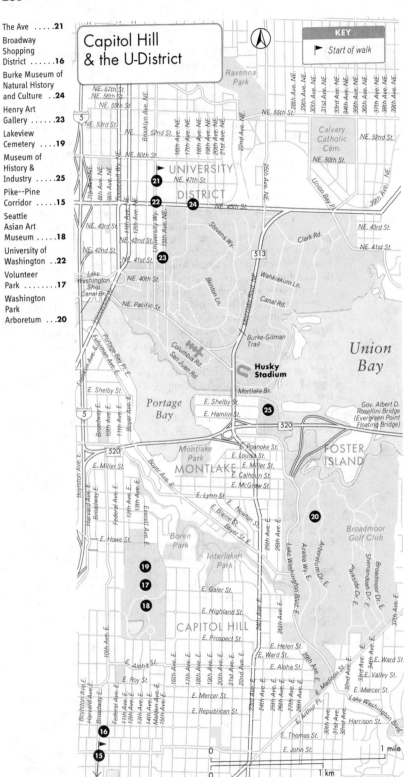

Capitol Hill
& the U-District

KEY

► Start of walk

ticularly ear-splitting riff. Frequently someone will leave an offering—a flower, a cigarette, or even a joint—in his outstretched fingers.

⑲ Lakeview Cemetery. One of the region's most beautiful cemeteries looks east toward Lake Washington from its elevated hillside directly north of Volunteer Park. Bruce Lee's grave and that of his son Brandon are the most visited sites. Several of Seattle's founding families are also interred here (their bodies were moved from a pioneer cemetery when Denny Hill was leveled to make room for the motels, car dealerships, and parking lots of the Denny Regrade south of Lake Union). Ask for a map at the cemetery office. ⊠ *1554 15th Ave. E, Capitol Hill* ☎ *206/322–1582* 🖃 *Free* ⊙ *Mon.–Sat. 9–4:30.*

⑮ Pike–Pine Corridor. An increasingly popular center of activity, this funky strip between Downtown and the south end of the Broadway shopping district contains galleries, thrift shops, designer retro furniture stores, and restaurants. Stop in for a drink at the famous Cha Cha Lounge, a dark hipster hangout decked out in south-of-the-border flair. On weekends the strip is hopping as club kids and drag performers flock to the alley entrance of Neighbors, Seattle's oldest gay bar, for disco dancing that lasts until 4 AM.

⑱ Seattle Asian Art Museum. This 1933 Art Moderne edifice fits surprisingly well with the stark plaza stretching from the front door to the edge of a bluff, and with the lush plants of Volunteer Park. The museum's collections include thousands of paintings, sculptures, pottery, and textiles from China, Japan, India, Korea, and several southeast Asian countries, many collected by the late Eugene Fuller, Seattle's most famous art collector. Children's crafts tables provide activities related to current exhibits, and free gallery tours are available by appointment. A ticket to the museum is good for $3 off admission to the Seattle Art Museum if used within one week and vice versa. ⊠ *Volunteer Park, 1400 E. Prospect St., Capitol Hill* ☎ *206/654–3100, 206/654–3123 gallery tours* ⊕ *www.seattleartmuseum.org* 🖃 *$3, free 1st Thurs. and Sat. of month* ⊙ *Tues.–Sun. 10–5, Thurs. until 9; call for tour schedule.*

FodorsChoice ★

⑰ Volunteer Park. High above the mansions of North Capitol Hill sits 45-acre Volunteer Park, a grassy expanse perfect for picnicking, sunbathing, reading, and strolling. You can tell this is one of the city's older parks by the size of the trees and the rhododendrons, many of which were planted more than a hundred years ago. The Olmsted Brothers, the premier landscape architects of the day, helped with the final design in 1904, and the park has changed surprisingly little since then. From a traffic circle at the park's south entrance, it's a mere 108 steps to some great views at the top of the 75-foot-high water tower, built circa 1906.

Beside the lake in the center of the park is the Seattle Asian Art Museum. Across from the museum is the romantic **Volunteer Park Conservatory** (☎ 206/684–4743). This Victorian-style greenhouse, completed in 1912, is one of only three conservatories remaining in the U.S. from the lavish golden age predating World War I (the other two are the W. W. Seymour Conservatory in Tacoma's Wright Park, and the Conservatory of Flowers in San Francisco's Golden Gate Park). The magnificent collection of tropical plants was accumulated largely by donation (like the artwork in the nearby museum). The extensive Anna Clise Orchid Collection, begun in 1919, is at its most spectacular in late fall and early winter, when most of the flowers are in full bloom. The conservatory also has some splendid palm trees, a well-stocked koi pond, and, almost incongruously, a magnificent collection of cacti and other succulents. A focal point of the park, at the western edge of the 445-foot-high hill and in front of the Asian Art

Museum, is Isamu Noguchi's sculpture *Black Sun,* carved from a 30-ton block of black granite. Many seem to enjoy taking photos of the Space Needle framed in the 9-foot, 9-inch hole of the "sun." ⊠ *Park entrance: 14th Ave. E at Prospect St., Capitol Hill* ⊕ *www.ci.seattle.wa.us/seattle/ parks/parkspaces/volpark.htm* ☏ *Free* ⊗ *Park: daily sunrise–sunset; Conservatory: May–mid-Sept., daily 10–7, otherwise 10–4.*

★ ☝ ⑳ **Washington Park Arboretum.** The 230-acre arboretum has more than 130 endangered plants, plus more than 40,000 native and exotic trees, shrubs, and vines. In warm winters, flowering cherries and plums bloom in its protected valleys as early as late February, while the flowering shrubs in Rhododendron Glen and Azalea Way are in full bloom March through June. In autumn, trees and shrubs glow in hues of crimson, pumpkin, and lemon; in winter, plantings chosen specially for their stark and colorful branches dominate the landscape. From March through October, visit the peaceful **Japanese Garden** (☎ 206/684–4725 ☏ $3), a compressed world of mountains, forests, rivers, lakes, and tablelands, open from 10 AM until sunset. The pond, lined with blooming water irises in spring, has turtles and brightly colored koi. An authentic Japanese tea house is reserved for tea ceremonies and instruction on the art of tea. The Graham Visitors Center at the park's north end has descriptions of the arboretum's flora and fauna, as well as brochures, a garden gift shop, and walking tour maps. ⊠ *2300 Arboretum Dr. E, Capitol Hill* ☎ *206/ 543–8800* ⊕ *depts.washington.edu/wpa* ☏ *Free* ⊗ *Park daily 7 AM–sunset; visitors center daily 10–4.*

University District

a good tour

Numbers in the text correspond to numbers in the margin and on the Capitol Hill & the U-District map.

Start at Northeast 45th Street and University Way Northeast. Proceed south on **The Ave** (University Way) ㉑ ⌐ through the heart of the district's many shopping and dining options. Turn left at Northeast Campus Parkway, stopping by the visitor center at the **University of Washington** ㉒. Straight ahead at the end of the block is the **Henry Art Gallery** ㉓. Continue east to Central Plaza, better known as Red Square. On clear days you'll be rewarded with views of Mt. Rainier to the southeast. Walk down Rainier Vista (past the Frosh Pond and fountain) to Stevens Way, turning left into Sylvan Grove, a gorgeous outdoor theater. Return via Rainier Vista to Red Square and strike out due north. A walk along shady Memorial Way past the commuter lot deposits you at the **Burke Museum of Natural History and Culture** ㉔. From the Burke step out onto Northeast 45th Street, walking two longish blocks to the left to return to University Way Northeast. If you want to continue farther afield, drive south over the Montlake Bridge to the **Museum of History & Industry** ㉕, where you can explore Seattle's growth and development through hands-on exhibits that trace its seafaring, gold-digging, timber-felling, neighborhood-melding traditions. Afterward, walk the marshy trail and watch the Canadian geese in adjacent McCurdy Park.

TIMING This walk takes about two hours, plus two hours to tour the Museum of History & Industry and another half-hour to explore McCurdy Park. You can easily spend an hour each in the Henry Art Gallery and Burke Museum and an additional hour (or two) on The Ave.

What to See

⌐ ㉑ **The Ave.** University Way Northeast, the hub of University of Washington social life, has all the activities you would expect to find in a student-oriented district—great coffeehouses, cinemas, clothing stores, bars, and cheap ethnic restaurants, along with panhandlers and pockets of grime. The major action along The Ave is between 42nd and 50th streets, though there are more shops and restaurants as University Way continues north to 58th Street and the entrance to Ravenna Park.

24 Burke Museum of Natural History and Culture. Totem poles mark the entrance to this museum, where exhibits survey the land and cultures of the Pacific Northwest. Highlights include memorabilia from Washington's 35 Native American tribes: costumes and masks, tools, baskets, blankets, and cookware, among many other items. You can also explore the surrounding terrain through dioramas and displays of archeological finds. For $1 more on the admission price, you get same-day admission to the Henry Art Gallery. ⊠ *University of Washington campus, 17th Ave. NE and NE 45th St., University District* ☎ *206/543–5590* ⊕ *www. washington.edu/burkemuseum* ☑ *$5.50* ⊙ *Daily 10–5, Thurs. until 8.*

23 Henry Art Gallery. The works by Northwest artists at this contemporary art gallery are culled from several genres and include photography, 19th- and 20th-century paintings, and textiles from the permanent collection. The Henry also hosts important touring multimedia exhibitions. One installation, *Volume: Bed of Sound,* encouraged visitors to listen rather than look—and lie upon a huge bed fitted with headphones while doing so. ⊠ *University of Washington campus, 15th Ave. NE and NE 41st St., University District* ☎ *206/543–2280* ⊕ *www.henryart.org* ☑ *$5* ⊙ *Tues.–Sun. 11–5, Thurs. until 8.*

25 Museum of History & Industry. Few places are better equipped to help you get a handle on the history of the Pacific Northwest. Since 1952 this museum has collected objects (some dating to 1780) that chronicle the region's economic, social, and cultural history. Factory and mining equipment, gramophones, clothing, newspapers, and everyday items from yesteryear are all on display, many along the re-created Seattle street from the 1880s. The interactive exhibits encourage kids to have fun and learn. On weekends look for educational presentations, family workshops, and historical walks. Students, teachers, and history buffs are always roaming the vast museum library. ⊠ *2700 24th Ave. E, across the Montlake Bridge from the University, on the south side of Union Bay, University District* ☎ *206/324–1126* ⊕ *www.seattlehistory.org* ☑ *$7, free 1st Thurs. of month* ⊙ *Daily 10–5; 1st Thurs. 10–8.*

22 University of Washington. The "U-Dub" is popular slang for this 35,000-student university founded in downtown Seattle in 1861. The campus moved to Denny Hall in 1895, and the Alaska-Yukon-Pacific Exposition hosted here in 1909 brought national attention to the Northwest. The UW is respected for its research and graduate programs in medicine, nursing, oceanography, Asian studies, drama, physiology, and social work, among many others. Its athletic teams—particularly football and women's basketball—have strong regional followings, and Red Square is the nerve center for student activity and politics. By the way, "red" refers to the square's brick paving, not to the students' political inclinations, though it's here that you'll see animal-rights, environmental, and other advocates attempting to rouse the masses.

North & West of Downtown

a good tour

Numbers in the text correspond to numbers in the margin and on the North & West of Downtown map.

Coming from downtown, you'll probably enter Fremont via the Fremont Bridge, one of the world's busiest drawbridges. **Fremont Center** 26 ▶ is tiny and easy to explore. Here's one strategy: proceed north on Fremont

Avenue North. Stop at the corner of North 34th Street to check out one of Fremont's "hysterical sites"—the *Waiting for the Interurban* sculpture. The life-size human statues may be draped with all manner of funky garb. Don't worry, it's not vandalism. It's tradition.

Continue up to North 35th Street and turn right. Walk two blocks to the Aurora Bridge (you'll be standing underneath it). Turn left and walk one block, but approach with care. The "Fremont Troll"—a whimsical concrete monster that lurks beneath the bridge—jealously guards his Volkswagen Beetle. Head back along North 36th Street, making a hard left at the statue of Lenin (seriously) at Fremont Place, the first street after you cross Fremont Avenue North. Walk a half block southeast, go right at the crosswalk, and then make a right on North 35th Street. At the end of the block is the 53-foot Fremont Rocket, "officially" designating the center of the universe. Walk straight ahead one long block to Phinney Avenue, then turn left and continue one block to the Ship Canal. On the right is Canal Park. Linger here, or turn left on North 34th Street and return to the Fremont Bridge.

Other area attractions are best reached by car, bus, or bike. The **Woodland Park Zoo** 27 is due north of Fremont via Fremont Avenue North (catch Bus 5 from the northeast corner of Fremont Avenue North and North 39th Street). **Green Lake** 28, with its park full of grassy hills, walkways, and sports courts, is northeast of the Woodland Park Zoo on Route 99 (Aurora Avenue North). **Gasworks Park** 29, on North Northlake Way, on Lake Union's north shore, is less than a 2-mi drive southeast of Fremont. The **Ballard Locks** 30 are west of Fremont (take Bus 28 from the corner of Fremont Avenue North and North 35th Street to Northwest Market Street and Eighth Avenue North and transfer to Bus 44 or, on weekdays only, Bus 46, heading west). A long block north of the Ballard Locks, on 32nd Avenue Northwest, is the **Nordic Heritage Museum** 31, which traces the immigration of Scandinavians to America and the Northwest, as well as their general history and culture. **Discovery Park** 32 is a walk of less than 1 mi from the south entrance to the Ballard Locks. Head west (right) on Commodore Way and south (left) on 40th Street.

TIMING   The walk around Fremont takes an hour at most, but the neighborhood is meant for strolling, browsing, sipping, and shopping. Plan to spend a full morning or a good part of an afternoon. You could easily spend two hours at the Ballard Locks or the Nordic Heritage Museum, and several hours at the Woodland Park Zoo, Green Lake, or Discovery Park.

What to See

★ ☺ 30 **Ballard Locks.** This passage in the 8-mi Lake Washington Ship Canal connects Puget Sound's saltwater Shilshole Bay to freshwater Lake Washington and Lake Union. Officially titled the Hiram M. Chittenden Locks and completed in 1917, the structure now services 100,000 boats yearly by raising and lowering water levels 6 feet to 26 feet. An estimated half million salmon and trout make the same journey from saltwater to fresh each year on the fish ladder, with waterline windows showing the 21 rising platforms where they migrate to their spawning grounds June through October. Along the south side of the locks is a 1,200-foot promenade with a footbridge, a fishing pier, and an observation deck. West are the 7-acre Carl English Jr. Botanic Gardens, with ornamental patches of native and exotic plants. Guided tours start at the nearby visitor center, where you'll find displays on the locks' history and operation, as well as several fanciful sculptures. From downtown, take Bus 15 or 18 to the stop at Northwest Market Street and 15th Avenue Northwest, then transfer to Bus 44 or (weekdays) 46 heading west on

Ballard
Locks **30**

Discovery
Park **32**

Fremont
Center **26**

Gasworks
Park **29**

Green Lake . . .**28**

Nordic
Heritage
Museum **31**

Woodland
Park Zoo **27**

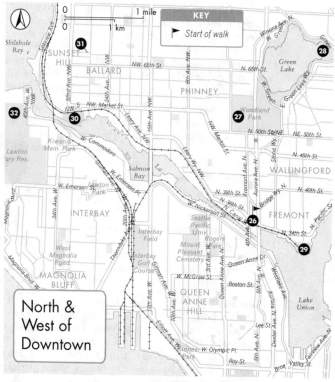

North &
West of
Downtown

Market Street. ✉ *3015 NW 54th St.; from Fremont, head north on Leary Way NW, west on NW Market St., and south on 54th St., Ballard* ☎ *206/783–7059* ⊕ *www.nws.usace.army.mil/opdiv/lwsc* ✎ *Free* ⊙ *Locks daily 7 AM–9 PM; visitor center mid-May to mid-Sept., daily 10–6; mid-Sept. to mid-May, Thurs.–Mon. 11–4; call for tour information.*

32 Discovery Park. At 534 acres, this former military base is a wildlife sanctuary and Seattle's largest park. You can hike through cool forests, explore saltwater beaches, or take in views of Puget Sound and Mt. Rainier. A 2.8-mi trail traverses this urban wilderness. ⊹ *From downtown Seattle take Elliott Avenue north until it becomes 15th Ave. NW, turn left on W. Emerson, right on Gilman Ave. W, left on W. Fort St., and right on E. Government Way* ✉ *3801 E. Government Way, Magnolia* ☎ *206/ 386–4236* ⊕ *www.ci.seattle.wa.us/parks/parkspaces/discovparkindex. htm* ✎ *Free* ⊙ *Park daily 6 AM–11 PM, visitor center daily 8:30–5.*

▶ 26 Fremont Center. The self-styled "Republic of Fremont" is a distinctive neighborhood. The center is an eclectic strip of Fremont Avenue stretching from the ship canal at the south end to North 36th Street, with shops and cafés two blocks on either side. The area also contains many lighthearted attractions.Beneath the Aurora Bridge lurks the gigantic, bearded *Fremont Troll* with a gleaming eye and a pouty lip. Eighteen feet tall and not so handsome, he clutches a real Volkswagen Beetle in his massive left hand. The gray giant watches over the neighborhood, and even allows people to crawl up on his shoulders for the obligatory photo. The troll appeared in 1991, commissioned by the Fremont Arts Council. The statue only looks frightening around Halloween, when, presiding over a wild parade, he has a bicycle-wheel rim as a nose ring and a giant spider crawling on his shoulder.

When Russian counterrevolutionaries knocked over a 7-ton **statue of Lenin** in 1989, they couldn't have known it would end up in Fremont. A man named Lewis Carpenter toted the striding bronze Red from Slovakia to Seattle in 1989, and when he died in 1994, the statue made its way to the neighborhood's Sunday flea market. Soon he was ousted from this den of capitalism, and today he sits in front of a burrito joint on North 36th Street, between Fremont and Evanston avenues.

Fremont's signature statue, *Waiting for the Interurban,* frequently fools those who drive by and wonder why this crowd looks so still and happy. It's a cast aluminum sculpture of five figures, one holding a small child. Residents enjoy dressing and ornamenting the figures for just about any joyful occasion. Look closely at the dog circling the legs of one figure and you'll see it wears the face of a bearded, ornery-looking man. As the story goes, the one-time honorary mayor of Fremont, Armen Stepanian, was upset with Richard Beyer for choosing himself as the artist to create the statue when no one else applied to the Fremont Arts Council for the job. Beyer had the final word in the brouhaha by putting Stepanian's face on the canine. The sculpture is on North 34th Street, just over the Fremont Bridge at Fremont Avenue. Walk another block to the corner of North 35th Street and Evanston Avenue, then look up to spot the 53-foot, Russian-built **Fremont Rocket.**

★ ☞ ㉙ **Gasworks Park.** Despite the hulking remains of an old gas plant here, the open, hilly, 20-acre park is actually easy on the eyes. Colorful kites soar in the air and bright-hued spinnakers bob offshore in Lake Union on summer days. Get a glimpse of downtown Seattle from the zodiac sculpture at the top of the hill, or feed the ducks on the lake. The sand-bottom playground has monkey bars, wooden platforms, and a spinning metal merry-go-round. Crowds throng to picnic and jam at the outdoor summer concerts, movies, and city-stopping Fourth of July fireworks display. ⊠ *North end of Lake Union, N. Northlake Way and Meridian Ave. N, Fremont* ⊙ *Daily 4 AM–11:30 PM.*

☞ ㉘ **Green Lake.** Cross beneath Route 99 (Aurora Avenue North) from the Woodland Park Zoo to a beautiful 342-acre park wrapped around a lovely lake. Take a boat out on the water; play basketball, tennis, baseball, or soccer on the nearby courts; or jog, blade, or bike the 3-mi lakeside trail. A first-rate play area includes a giant sandbox, swings, slides, and all the climbing equipment a child could ever dream of—plus lots of grassy areas and benches where adults can take a break. The park is generally packed (about 1 million people visit each year), especially on weekday evenings, when many Seattleites come to see and be seen. And you'd better love dogs; the canine to human ratio here is just about even. Surrounding the park are peaceful middle- and upper-class homes, plus a compact commercial district where you can grab a whole-wheat burrito and fresh carrot juice—or a full-fat latte and a chunk of chocolate cake. ⊠ *E. Green Lake Dr. N and W. Green Lake Dr. N, Green Lake.*

★ ☞ ㉛ **Nordic Heritage Museum.** The only educational institute in the country to focus solely on Nordic cultures, this museum in a 1900s schoolhouse traces Scandinavian art, artifacts, and heritage all the way from Viking times. Behind the redbrick walls, nine permanent galleries on three floors give an in-depth look at how immigrants from Denmark, Finland, Iceland, Norway, and Sweden came to America and settled in the Pacific Northwest. Among the finds are textiles, china, books, tools, and photographs. Delve into Nordic history in the library; learn a few phrases at the on-site Scandinavian Language Institute; or join in a class or children's program on Nordic arts and crafts. The temporary galleries display paintings, sculpture, and photography by contemporary artists.

✉ *3014 NW 67th St., Ballard* ☎ *206/789–5707* ⊕ *www.nordicmuseum. com* ✉ *$4* ⊘ *Tues.–Sat. 10–4, Sun. noon–4.*

★ ☉ ㉗ **Woodland Park Zoo.** Many of the 300 species of animals in this 92-acre botanical garden roam freely in habitat areas. A jaguar exhibit is the center of the Tropical Rain Forest area where rare cats, frogs, and birds evoke South American jungles. The Butterflies & Blooms exhibit ($1) shows off the amazing beauty and variety of the winged creatures and describes their relationship with local flora. With authentic thatch-roof buildings, the African Village has a replica school room overlooking animals roaming the savanna; the Asian Elephant Forest trail takes you through a Thai village; and the Northern Trail winds past rocky habitats where brown bears, wolves, mountain goats, and otters scramble and play. The terrain is mostly flat, making it easy for wheelchairs and strollers (which can be rented) to negotiate. Kids love the barnyard, bug house, and the adjacent wooded play yard with its rope spider web, giant gopher burrow, and otter slides. ✉ *5500 Phinney Ave. N, Phinney Ridge* ☎ *206/684–4800* ⊕ *www.zoo.org* ✉ *$9* ⊘ *Mid-Mar.–Apr. and mid-Sept.–mid-Oct., daily 9:30–5; May–mid-Sept., daily 9:30–6; mid-Oct.–mid-Mar., daily 9:30–4.*

The Eastside

On the far side of Lake Washington is East King County, the center of which is Bellevue. First across the floating bridge, though, is Mercer Island, a wooded, residential island. Continue over the bridge, hang a left, and you're in Bellevue, a fast-growing city. Top-name hotels, top-rated dining spots, renowned museums, a chic music and performance center, a professional theater, and numerous parks, gardens, and beaches have helped give Bellevue its own internationally spiced character. Its charming core is still evident, however, in the many early-20th-century buildings of the original town square and outlying residential areas.

North of Bellevue, Kirkland is on the eastern shores of Lake Washington. It's pedestrian-friendly, with shops, galleries, and restaurants along the water. North of Bellevue, Woodinville is best known for the Chateau Ste. Michelle and Columbia wineries; and the Redhook Brewery. Redmond, just east of Kirkland, has grown considerably since Microsoft chose the town for its headquarters. Redmond is also known as the "Bicycle Capital of the Northwest" because of its first-rate Velodrome at Marymoor Park.

Southeast of Bellevue, in the foothills at the south end of Lake Sammamish, Issaquah is a scenic bedroom community coming into its own with gatherings of upscale shops and gated neighborhoods of modern mansions. Yet salmon still run seasonally in local streams—an event celebrated with the Annual Salmon Days Festival. East of Issaquah lies the rural community of North Bend. A truck stop that was the setting for the TV serial *Twin Peaks,* the town gets its name from a bend in the Snoqualmie River, which here turns north. The surrounding scenery is beautiful, dominated by 4,167-foot Mt. Si (with many popular hiking trails), 4,420-foot Mt. Washington, and 4,788-foot Mt. Tenerife.

What to See

Bellevue Botanical Gardens. This beautiful, 36-acre public area in the middle of Wilburton Hill Park is encircled by spectacular perennial borders, brilliant rhododendron displays, and patches of alpine and rock gardens. A log cabin exhibits implements of pioneer life. The visitor center is open daily during park hours. ✉ *12001 Main St., Bellevue* ☎ *425/451–3755* ⊕ *www.bellevuebotanical.org* ✉ *Free* ⊘ *May–Sept., daily 10–6, Oct.–Apr., daily 10–4.*

🖑 **Burke-Gilman/Sammamish River Trail.** The 27-mi-long, paved Burke-Gilman Trail runs from Seattle's Gasworks Park, on Lake Union, east along an old railroad right-of-way along the ship canal and then north along Lake Washington's western shore. At Blyth Park in Bothell, the trail becomes the Sammamish River Trail and continues for 10 mi to Marymoor Park, in Redmond. Energetic Seattleites take the trail to Marymoor for the annual Heritage Festival and Fourth of July Fireworks. Except for a stretch of the Sammamish River Trail between Woodinville and Marymoor Park where horses are permitted on a parallel trail, the path is limited to walkers, runners, and bicyclists. ⊹ *Take I–90 east to north I–405, then Exit 23 east (S.R. 522) to Woodinville.*

Chateau Ste. Michelle Winery. One of the state's oldest wineries is 15 mi northeast of Seattle on 87 wooded acres. Once part of the estate of lumber baron Fred Stimson, it includes the original trout ponds, a carriage house, a caretaker's cottage, formal gardens, and the 1912 family manor house (which is on the National Register of Historic Places). Complimentary wine tastings and cellar tours run throughout the day. You're also invited to picnic and explore the grounds on your own; the wine shop sells delicatessen items. In summer Chateau Ste. Michelle hosts nationally known performers and arts events in its amphitheater. ⊹ *From downtown Seattle take I–90 east to north I–405; take Exit 23 east (S. R. 522) to Woodinville exit.* ⊠ *14111 NE 145th St., Woodinville* 🕾 *425/415–3300* ⊕ *www.ste-michelle.com* ⊠ *Free* ☉ *Daily 10:30–4:30.*

Columbia Winery. A group of University of Washington professors founded this winery in 1962, making it the state's oldest. Using only European vinifera-style grapes grown in eastern Washington, the founders' aim was to take advantage of the fact that the vineyards share the same latitude as the best wine-producing areas of France. Complimentary wine tastings are held daily; cellar tours are on weekends. The gift shop is open year-round and sells wines and wine-related merchandise. Columbia hosts special food-and-wine events throughout the year. It's also the final destination of the **Spirit of Washington Dinner Train** (🕾 *800/876–7245* ⊠ *$47–$69* ⊕ *www.spiritofwashingtondinnertrain.com*), which originates in Renton and makes the three-hour trip along the eastern shores of Lake Washington. ⊠ *14030 NE 145th St., Woodinville., From downtown Seattle take I–90 east to north I–405; take Exit 23 east (S.R. 522) to Woodinville exit, go right. Go right again on 175th St., and left on Rte. 202.* 🕾 *425/488–2776 or 800/488–2347* ⊕ *www.columbiawinery.com* ⊠ *Free* ☉ *Daily 10–7.*

🖑 **Cougar Mountain Zoo.** It's not just named for the mountain; this really is the place to see cougars up close. You'll also find reindeer and other Northwest creatures as well as parrots, macaws, and such endangered international species as lemurs and cheetahs. You can see everything in an hour, making this a good sight for young ones. ⊠ *19525 SE 54th St., Issaquah* 🕾 *425/391–5508* ⊕ *www.cougarmountainzoo.org* ⊠ *$8* ☉ *Mar.–Oct., Fri.–Sun. 10–5.*

★ 🖑 **Kelsey Creek Farm and Park.** With wide lawns, wood bridges curving over bubbling streams, and easy, paved walking paths through groomed gardens, this Bellevue park is a local favorite of families. Farm animals—which you can pet—roam the fields surrounding two enormous, white, Cape Dutch–style barns where smaller animals like rabbits and ducks are caged. The playground is most fun for children four and under, but big kids will get a kick out of spotting wildlife in the brooks and marshes. ⊠ *SE 4th Pl., Bellevue* 🕾 *425/455–7688* ⊠ *Free* ☉ *Daily 7–6.*

🔄 **Rosalie Whyel Museum of Doll Art.** Thousands of dolls span the ages and the world in this three-story museum. Displays include everything from antique porcelain models to state-of-the-art baby dolls that seem almost real. Related items such as detailed miniature houses, toys, clothing, strollers, and cribs show every aspect of a little girl's dream world—and yes, the ubiquitous Barbie is here. The gift shop stocks many unique items, but shop early or you'll compete with senior bus tour crowds picking up goodies for the grandkids. ✉ *1116 108th Ave. NE, Bellevue* ☎ *425/ 455–1116 or 800/440–3655* ⊕ *www.dollart.com* 🎫 *$6* 🕐 *Mon.–Sat. 10–5, Sun. 1–5.*

WHERE TO EAT

Updated by
Julie Fay

What was once a meat-and-potatoes town is now a culinary capital in its own right. It started with Chinese, Japanese, and French chefs who were inspired by the quality of local produce and seafood and able to cater to an upwardly mobile clientele spawned by the region's software industry. Young American chefs soon moved in and, applying lessons learned from their foreign-born mentors, raised the quality of local cookery even higher. Seattle's culinary revolution seems never-ending. Even long-established restaurants that once depended largely on exquisite views and expense-account clients have adjusted their menus to serve the increasingly sophisticated tastes of Seattle diners.

	WHAT IT COSTS				
	$$$$	$$$	$$	$	¢
AT DINNER	over $32	$24–$32	$16–$24	$8–$16	under $8

Prices are per person for a main course, excluding tax and tip.

Downtown

American

$$–$$$$ ✕ **13 Coins.** In Seattle's forward-looking food scene, this is the land that time forgot, circa 1967. Open 24 hours a day, 13 Coins is a longtime favorite of Seattle's nighthawk population. Menu benchmarks include liver and onions, jumbo shrimp on ice, and platters of steak and pasta big enough to stuff a logger. Breakfasts include such dinosaurs as Italian-sausage frittatas and eggs Benedict. Seafood dishes aren't quite up to Seattle's high standards, but the steamed clams and the baked king salmon fillet are decent. For dessert, the New York–style cheesecake comes with an "endless" cup of coffee. ✉ *1125 Boren Ave. N, Downtown* ☎ *206/682–2513* 🍴 *Reservations not accepted* ▭ *AE, D, MC, V.*

Contemporary

$$–$$$ ✕ **Dahlia Lounge.** Romantic Dahlia—with dimly lit valentine-red walls—
Fodor'sChoice worked its magic on Tom Hanks and Meg Ryan in *Sleepless in Seattle.*
★ It's cozy and then some, but the food plays its part, too. Crab cakes, served as an entrée or an appetizer, lead an ever-changing regionally oriented menu. Other standouts are seared ahi tuna, near-perfect gnocchi, and such desserts as coconut-cream pie and fresh fruit cobblers. Seattle's most energetic restaurateur, chef-owner Tom Douglas also owns Etta's Seafood in Pike Place Market, and the excellent Palace Kitchen on Fifth Avenue. But Dahlia is the one that makes your heart go pitter-pat. ✉ *2001 4th Ave., Downtown* ☎ *206/682–4142* 🍴 *Reservations essential* ▭ *AE, D, DC, MC, V* 🕐 *No lunch weekends.*

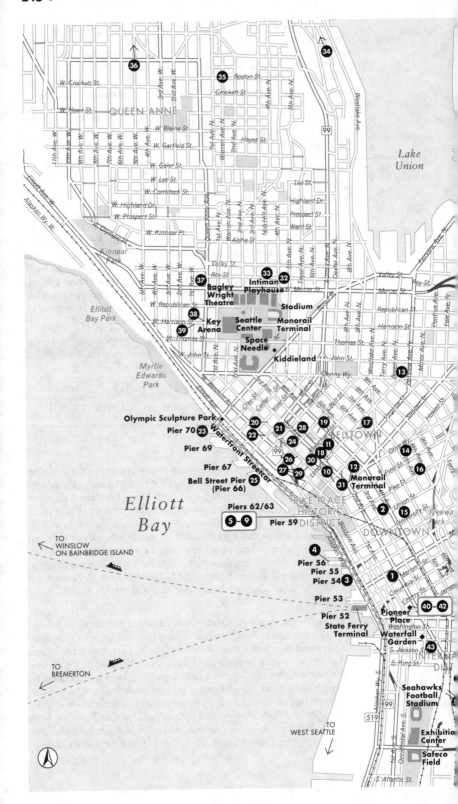

Where to Eat In & Around Downtown

Map labels:

Montlai... ...rk
E. Newton St.
E. Blaine St.
E. Garfield St.
E. Howe St.
Boren Park
Lakeview Cemetery
E. Garfield St.
E. Highland St.
Volunteer Park
CAPIT(
E. Prospect St.
Seattle Art Museum
E. Ward St.
E. Aloha St.
Broadway Shopping District
E. Thomas St.
E. Thomas S...
Seattle Central Community College
Broadway Playfield
E. John St.
E. John St.
E. Denny Wy.
E. Howell St.
Pike–Pine Corridor
E. Olive St.
E. Pine St.
E. Pike St.
Pike–Pine Corridor
Seattle University
E. Union St.
E. Spring St.
E. Marion St.
FIRST HILL
E. Columbia St.
E. Cherry St.
E. Jefferson St.
E. Spruce St.
E. Fir St.
CENTRAL AREA
Yester Wy.
Yester Wy.
Pratt Park
S. Main St.
S. Jackson St.
S. King St.
S. Weller St.
S. Lane St.
S. Dearborn St.
S. Charles St.
S. Plummer St.
S. Judkins St.
TO MUSEUM OF FLIGHT

Downtown ▼

Copacabana **7**
Crepe de Paris **15**
Dahlia Lounge **11**
Dragonfish **16**
Elliott's Oyster House ...**4**
Emmett Watson's Oyster Bar **9**
Fare Start **12**
Ivar's Acres of Clams **3**
Metropolitan Grill **1**
Oceanaire **14**
Le Pichet **10**
Pink Door **6**
Place Pigalle **5**
El Puerco Lloron **8**
13 Coins **13**
Wild Ginger **2**

Belltown ▼

Anthony's Pier 66 .....**25**
Brasa **31**
Cascadia **24**
Etta's Seafood **27**
Fandango **26**
Flying Fish **29**
Frontier Room **28**
El Gaucho **22**
Lampreia **21**
Marco's Supper Club ..**20**
Noodle Ranch **19**
Palace Kitchen **17**
Restaurant Zoë **30**
Saito's Japanese Café and Bar **18**
Waterfront Seafood Grill **23**

Queen Anne ▼

Bahn Thai **32**
Bamboo Garden **33**
Canlis **34**
Chinoise Café **35**
Chinook's **36**
Dick's Drive-In **38**
Kaspar's **39**
Peso's Kitchen & Lounge **37**

I.D. & Pioneer Square ▼

Bakeman's Restaurant **41**
Cafe Paloma **40**
Chinoise Café **50**
Hing Loon **49**
Linyen **47**
Malay Satay Hut **45**
Saigon Bistro **46**
Saigon Gourmet **51**
Salumi **43**
Takohachi **44**
Top Gun **48**
Trattoria Mitchelli **42**

$$–$$$ ✕ **Place Pigalle.** Large windows look out on Elliott Bay in this cozy spot tucked behind a meat vendor in Pike Place Market's main arcade. In nice weather, open windows let in the fresh salt breeze. Flowers brighten each table, and the staff is warm and welcoming. Despite its name, this is a very American restaurant. Go for the rich oyster stew, the Dungeness crab (in season), or the fish of the day. Local microbrews are usually on tap, and the wine list is thoughtfully compact. ⊠ *81 Pike Place Market, Downtown* ☎ *206/624–1756* ▱ *AE, MC, V* ☉ *Closed Sun.*

Eclectic

¢–$$ ✕ **Fare Start.** The homeless men and women who operate this café, a project of the FareStart job-training program, prepare an American-style lunch of sandwiches, burgers, and fries during the week. Reservations are essential for the $17 Thursday dinner, prepared by a guest chef from a restaurant such as Ray's Boathouse or the Metropolitan Grill. The cuisine changes with the chef. Whenever you go, you're assured a great meal for a great cause and a real taste of Seattle's community spirit. ⊠ *1902 2nd Ave., Downtown* ☎ *206/443–1233* ▱ *D, MC, V* ☉ *No lunch weekends. No dinner Fri.–Wed.*

French

$$–$$$
Fodor'sChoice
★

✕ **Le Pichet.** Slate tabletops, tile floor, and rolled-zinc bar transport you out of Downtown Seattle and into Paris, 1934. Blackboards spell out the specials. Wines are served from the earthenware *pichets* that inspired the brasserie's name. The menu is heartbreakingly French: at lunch there are rustic pâtés and *jambon et fromage* (ham and cheese) sandwiches on crusty baguettes; dinner sees homemade sausages, daily fish specials, and steak tartare. The roast chicken (for two) takes an hour to prepare and is worth every second you'll wait. It's enough to make you think the French invented soul food. Dinner reservations are essential. ⊠ *1933 1st Ave., Downtown* ☎ *206/256–1499* ▱ *MC, V.*

$ ✕ **Crepe de Paris.** Seattle's oldest French restaurant is still going strong, perhaps because it has bucked the trends, and serves up good, old-fashioned French fare. It has all the accoutrements to keep the Downtown crowd and visiting businesspeople happy: a full bar, happy hour, and, in warm weather, seating on the open-air terrace. In the evening, there's cabaret entertainment as well. ⊠ *1333 5th Ave., Downtown* ☎ *206/ 623–4111* ▱ *AE, D, DC, MC, V* ☉ *Closed Sun.*

Italian

$–$$ ✕ **Pink Door.** With its Post Alley entrance and meager signage, many enjoy the Pink Door's speak-easiness almost as much as the savory Italian food. In warm months patrons partake on the deck shaded by a grape arbor while enjoying the stunning view of Elliott Bay. The roasted garlic and tapenade are eminently sharable appetizers; spaghetti *alla puttanesca* (with anchovies, capers, and tomatoes), and cioppino are standout entrées. The whimsical bar is often crowded, the staff is saucy and irreverent, and cabaret acts regularly perform on a small corner stage. There's no place quite like it. ⊠ *1919 Post Alley, Downtown* ☎ *206/443–3241* ▱ *AE, MC, V* ☉ *Closed Sun. and Mon.*

Latin

$ ✕ **Copacabana.** Much of the strategy that preserved Pike Place Market in the 1960s was hatched at this small Bolivian café. Dishes include such tasty fare as spicy shrimp soup, *saltenas* (savory meat-and-vegetable pies), paella, and *pescado á la Español* (halibut in a saffron-tomato-onion sauce). Tasty food, cold beer, and great views are reasons to linger. ⊠ *1520 1st Ave., Downtown* ☎ *206/622–6359* ▱ *AE, D, MC, V* ⌂ *Reservations not accepted* ☉ *No dinner Sun. in summer.*

Mexican

★ ¢–$ ✕ **El Puerco Lloron.** This funky, cafeteria-style diner has some open-air terrace seating on the Pike Place Market Hillclimb, offering views of Elliott Bay on sunny days. It's also got some of Seattle's best and most authentic Mexican cooking—simple, tasty, and inexpensive. Even Mexican natives swear by it. More ambitious highlights include perfect *chiles rellenos* (mild green peppers that are breaded, stuffed with cheese, and fried) and a particularly flavorful guacamole. ⊠ *501 Western Ave., Downtown* ☎ *206/624–0541* ▤ *AE, MC, V.*

Pan-Asian

$$–$$$$ ✕ **Dragonfish.** From the pachinko machines around the bar to the colorful origami and rattan fans on the ceiling, kid-friendly Dragonfish is a freewheeling place that takes advantage of Seattleites' yen for Pan-Asian cuisine. The seafood and noodle specialties are worth investigating, but the small plates from the grill are the real stars. Try the Korean *bulgogi*, skirt steak marinated in soy, ginger, and *mirin* (a sweet rice wine), or the chicken wings in a caramel-ginger sauce. ⊠ *722 Pine St., Downtown* ☎ *206/467–7777* ▤ *AE, D, DC, MC, V.*

$–$$$ ✕ **Wild Ginger.** The seafood and Southeast Asian fare at this restaurant ranges from mild Cantonese to spicier Vietnamese, Thai, and Korean dishes. Specialties include *satay* (skewered and grilled chunks of beef, chicken, or vegetables with a spicy peanut sauce). In fact, the satay bar, where you can sip local brews and eat skewered tidbits until 2 AM, is a neighborhood hangout. The clubby dining room has high ceilings and lots of mahogany and Asian art. You might want to try the live crab cooked to order, sweetly flavored duck, wonderful soups, or one of the fine vegetarian options. ⊠ *1401 3rd Ave., Downtown* ☎ *206/623–4450* ▤ *AE, D, DC, MC, V* ☾ *No lunch Sun.*

Seafood

$$–$$$$ ✕ **Elliott's Oyster House.** No place in Seattle serves better Dungeness crab or oysters than Elliott's. You can't go wrong with the local rockfish or salmon. The dining room is bright, and there's a great view of Elliott Bay and of the harbor tour boats next door. On sunny days the place is packed with diners from all over the country who have come to learn what Seattle is all about. They've probably picked the right place. ⊠ *Pier 56, off Alaskan Way, Downtown* ☎ *206/623–4340* ▤ *AE, DC, MC, V.*

$–$$$ ✕ **Ivar's Acres of Clams.** A big restaurant on an old waterfront shipping pier, with windows overlooking Elliott Bay, this Seattle favorite has held its own against the influx of bright new restaurants. Look for seasonal dinners as well as local standbys such as fish-and-chips and Atlantic salmon. ⊠ *Pier 54, Downtown* ☎ *206/624–6852* ▤ *AE, MC, V.*

$–$$$ ✕ **Oceanaire.** For years Seattle restaurateurs have been trying to create
Fodor's Choice ★ the quintessential seafood restaurant, and wouldn't you know, a pair of midwestern businessmen have managed to pull it off. The stylish room is reminiscent of a 1930s supperclub, with plush booths and a circular oyster bar. Chef Kevin Davis has created a superbly fun retro menu complete with clams casino, oysters Rockefeller, up to 25 varieties of the freshest seafood, and a circa 1920s green goddess salad dressing. When is the last time you saw baked Alaska on a menu? Portions are huge, so plan to share. ⊠ *1700 7th Ave., Downtown* ☎ *206/267–2277* ▤ *AE, D, DC, MC, V* ☾ *No lunch weekends.*

¢ ✕ **Emmett Watson's Oyster Bar.** This unpretentious spot can be hard to find—it's in the back of Pike Place Market's Soames-Dunn Building, facing a small flower-bedecked courtyard. But for those who know their oysters, finding this place is worth the effort. Not only are the oysters very fresh and the beer icy cold, but both are inexpensive and available in any number of varieties. If you don't like oysters, try the salmon soup or the fish-and-chips—flaky pieces of fish with very little grease. ✉ *1916 Pike Pl., Downtown* ☎ *206/448–7721* ⌕ *Reservations not accepted* ▭ *No credit cards* ☺ *No dinner Sun.*

Steak

$$–$$$$ ✕ **Metropolitan Grill.** This favorite lunch spot of the white-collar crowd is not for timid eaters: custom-aged mesquite-broiled steaks are huge and come with baked potatoes or pasta. Even the veal chop is extra thick. Lamb, chicken, and seafood entrées are also on the menu. Onion rings and sautéed mushrooms are popular accompaniments. Among its many virtues, the Met Grill does one dish better than anyone else in Seattle: the exceptionally flavorful hamburger is about as delicious as grilled meat can get. ✉ *818 2nd Ave., Downtown* ☎ *206/624–3287* ▭ *AE, D, DC, MC, V* ☺ *No lunch weekends.*

Belltown

American

$–$$ ✕ **Frontier Room.** A bold makeover transformed this longtime Seattle resident from skid-row seedy to cowboy kitsch. The cowhide booths in the bar and original tongue-and-groove paneling discovered during the remodel set the proper carnivorous mood. Oysters Frontier brings together broiled oysters, arugula, and a punchy, bisquelike sauce with all the subtlety of a monster truck show. Barbecue offerings get an A for effort by focusing on the meat and the smoke, not the sauce. The St. Louis Ribs are flavorful, if a bit dry; the moist, tender pulled pork is better. It's very crowded on weekend nights. ✉ *2203 1st Ave., Belltown* ☎ *206/956–7427* ▭ *AE, D, MC, V* ☺ *Closed Sun. and Mon.*

Contemporary

$$$$ ✕ **Lampreia.** The beige-and-gold interior of this Belltown restaurant is
Fodor'sChoice the perfect backdrop for chef-owner Scott Carsberg's sophisticated cui-
★ sine. After an appetizer of cream of polenta soup with shiitake mushrooms, try one of the seasonal menu's second courses—perhaps squid-and-salmon-filled cannelloni—before moving on to a main course of pheasant with apple-champagne sauerkraut or lamb with pesto and whipped potatoes. The clear flavors of such desserts as lemon mousse with strawberry sauce are a soothing conclusion to an exciting experience. ✉ *2400 1st Ave., Belltown* ☎ *206/443–3301* ⌕ *Reservations essential* ▭ *AE, MC, V* ☺ *Closed Sun. and Mon. No lunch.*

$$$–$$$$ ✕ **El Gaucho.** Dress to impress here—you don't want to be outclassed by the waistcoated waitstaff that coolly navigates the packed floor of this retro steak house. For the complete show, order the items prepared table-side. From the flaming lamb shish kebab to the cool Caesar salad, the virtuoso presentation seems to make everything taste better. Ritzy yet comfortable, El Gaucho makes you relax no matter how stressful your day. ✉ *2505 1st Ave., Belltown* ☎ *206/728–1337* ⌕ *Reservations essential* ▭ *AE, MC, V* ☺ *No lunch.*

$$–$$$ ✕ **Cascadia.** Water flows over the "rain window," a 9-foot-long panel of glass, etched with a design of the Cascade mountain range, that separates the kitchen and the cherry-wood-paneled dining room. Chef Kerry Sears uses fresh regional produce, seafood, meat, and game to create memorable meals, which might include smoked Oregon Muscovy duck with pears and creamed collard greens, marinated sea bass with roasted potatoes and caviar dressing, or crab steak with chanterelles. Seven-course tasting menus ($55–$90) showcase the Northwest's culinary best. ✉ *2328 1st Ave., Belltown* ☎ *206/448–8884* ⌕ *Reservations essential* ▭ *AE, DC, MC, V* ☺ *Closed Sun. No lunch.*

$$ ✕ **Restaurant Zoë.** Reservations are sought after at this chic eatery on a
Fodor'sChoice high-trafficked corner. Its tall windows, lively bar scene, and charming
★ waitstaff add to the popularity, which comes mainly from its inspired
kitchen. The talents of chef-owner Scott Staples can be seen in his house-
smoked hanger steak served with mashed potatoes, parsnips, and veal
jus and his pan-seared sea scallops served over asparagus herb risotto
with smoked bacon and blood-orange vinaigrette. Ease into your meal
with an adventurous and expertly executed appetizer, remaining mind-
ful of the house-made desserts that await you. ⊠ *2137 2nd Ave., Bell-
town* 🕾 *206/256–2060* ▭ *AE, D, MC, V* ⊗ *No lunch.*

$–$$ ✕ **Flying Fish.** This joint is jumping, some might even think it noisy, but
rest assured, there's nothing noisy about the food. It is sublime. Chef
Christine Keff is a genius in the kitchen, and consistently produces innovative, high-quality dishes. Keff was among the first to introduce Seattleites to the joys of shared plates, and it's a pleasure—and sometimes
torture—to see servers walk by with large platters heaped high with steam-
ing clams or mussels, spicy crab cakes, or whole Dungeness crab, fried
oysters, crisp-fried calamari, or whole steamed rockfish. Her fish tacos
are delicious, as is her no-nonsense fried chicken. ⊠ *2234 1st Ave., Belltown* 🕾 *206/728–8595* ▭ *AE, D, MC, V* ⊗ *No lunch.*

Eclectic

$–$$$ ✕ **Palace Kitchen.** The star of this chic yet convivial Tom Douglas eatery
(he's also responsible for Dahlia Lounge and Etta's) may be the 45-foot
bar, but the real show takes place in the giant open kitchen at the back.
Sausages, sweet-pea ravioli, salmon carpaccio, and a nightly selection
of exotic cheeses vie for your attention on the ever-changing menu of
small plates. There are also always a few entrées, 10 fantastic desserts,
and a rotisserie special from the apple-wood grill. ⊠ *2030 5th Ave., Bell-
town* 🕾 *206/448–2001* ▭ *AE, D, DC, MC, V* ⊗ *No lunch.*

$–$$ ✕ **Marco's Supper Club.** Multiregional cuisine is the specialty of this
Fodor'sChoice family-owned restaurant with shrimp-color walls and mismatched flat-
★ ware. Marco's loyal following is a testament to the cooking. Start with
the fried sage-leaf appetizer with chipotle-garlic aioli and tomatillo
salsa, then move on to sesame-crusted ahi tuna, Jamaican jerk chicken,
or a pork porterhouse in an almond mole sauce. ⊠ *2510 1st Ave., Belltown* 🕾 *206/441–7801* ▭ *AE, MC, V* ⊗ *No lunch weekends.*

Japanese

$$–$$$ ✕ **Saito's Japanese Café and Bar.** Fusion won't fly at this Belltown restau-
rant, sushi bar, and lounge. Traditional appetizers include *kaarage* (mar-
inated, breaded, and deep-fried chicken), *gyoza* (steamed pork dumplings),
and *kakifry* (panfried oysters). Chef Yutaka Saito drapes elegant, enormous slices of the freshest fish over pillows of rice in his exquisite ni-
giri sushi. Aside from the gorgeous sushi and sashimi, consider the
unajyu (broiled freshwater eel with a tangy sweet sauce), *salmon mis-
ozuke* (brushed with red miso, baked slowly, and served with caramelized
turnips), and *tonkatsu* (breaded and fried pork cutlet). The full bar stocks
more than 30 different sakes. ⊠ *2122 2nd Ave., Belltown* 🕾 *206/728–
1333* ▭ *AE, D, DC, MC, V* ⊗ *Closed Sun. No lunch Sat.*

Latin

★ **$–$$** ✕ **Fandango.** Fandango is so much fun it should be called "*fun*dango,"
and so Latin it seems sunny even on a drizzly Seattle day. Aside from
the quality of food made by owner-chef Christine Keff, Fandango might
owe some of its popularity to its silent partners—Edgar Martinez, one
of the Seattle Mariners' hottest players, and Dave Valle, a TV baseball
commentator and former Mariners catcher. Specialties include Taras-
can bean-and-tomato soup; creamy walnut-and-chipotle soup; crisply
fried squid; Brazilian seafood stew; and suckling pig with zucchini,

poblano chiles, and onions. The bar, a favorite late-night hangout, has an enticing menu, plus 50 different tequilas. ☒ *2313 1st Ave., Belltown* ☎ *206/441–1188* ▣ *DC, MC, V* ⊘ *No lunch.*

Mediterranean

★ $$–$$$ ✕ **Brasa.** When famous Seattle chefs set out to open their own restaurants, the results are often spectacular. That's certainly true for Brasa, which has become a Seattle favorite since Tamara Murphy, formerly of Campagne, opened its Belltown doors. Locals go for such delectable dishes as Spanish fried squid, squid-ink risotto, braised short ribs with a red-wine glaze, and polenta cake. More traditional but equally toothsome and carefully prepared are the beef tenderloin and monkfish. ☒ *2107 3rd Ave., Belltown* ☎ *206/728–4220* ⌂ *Reservations essential* ▣ *AE, DC, MC, V* ⊘ *No lunch.*

Pan-Asian

$ ✕ **Noodle Ranch.** Tongue planted firmly in cheek, Noodle Ranch bills itself as a purveyor of "Pan-Asian vittles." Standouts on chef Nga Bui's menu include sugar-cane shrimp, Japanese eggplant in ginger, and a spicy basil stir-fry. The gentle sense of humor evident in the restaurant's name carries over to the design scheme. ☒ *2228 2nd Ave., Belltown* ☎ *206/ 728–0463* ▣ *AE, MC, V* ⊘ *Closed Sun.*

Seafood

$$–$$$$ ✕ **Anthony's Pier 66.** The straightforward preparations allow the seafood to speak for itself. The menu includes many items found elsewhere: raw oysters, steamed clams, mussels, and Dungeness crab, as well as the usual Northwest fish: halibut, rockfish, lingcod, and petrale sole. Everything is very good and very tasty and, in the true Northwest tradition, not at all pretentious. Best of all, the views are truly outstanding. ☒*2201 Alaskan Way (Bell St./Pier 66), Belltown* ☎ *206/448–6688* ▣ *AE, D, MC, V.*

★ $$–$$$$ ✕ **Waterfront Seafood Grill.** With its spectacular view, impeccable service, and inventively prepared seafood, Waterfront has all of the fine-dining bases covered. You can catch the sunset from the spacious bar, where cocktails and appetizers such as the salt-and-pepper prawns with lime vinaigrette and tuna tempura are served. The menu's largely Asian-influenced entrées might include sesame-seared sea bass with baby bok choy and coconut jasmine rice, or lobster risotto with butternut squash and snow peas. Although seafood is the focal point, the menu always includes a vegetarian dish as well as many meat dishes, such as rack of lamb with honey lavender demi-glace. ☒ *Pier 70, 2801 Alaskan Way, Belltown* ☎ *206/956–9171* ▣ *AE, DC, MC, V* ⊘ *No lunch.*

★ $–$$ ✕ **Etta's Seafood.** Tom Douglas's restaurant near Pike Place Market has a sleek and slightly whimsical design and views of Victor Steinbrueck Park. Try the Dungeness crab cakes in season or the various Washington oysters on the half shell. Brunch, served on weekends, always includes zesty seafood omelets, but the chef also does justice to French toast, eggs and bacon, and Mexican-influenced breakfast dishes. ☒ *2020 Western Ave., Belltown* ☎ *206/443–6000* ▣ *AE, D, DC, MC, V.*

Queen Anne

American

$$–$$$$ ✕ **Canlis.** Little has changed at this Seattle institution since the '50s, when steak served by kimono-clad waitresses represented the pinnacle of high living. The waitresses still wear kimonos, the view across Lake Union is as good as ever, and Canlis remains the only dining establishment in town with a dress code (no tennis shoes or blue jeans, and men must wear a jacket)—quite unusual for this casual town. Besides the famous steaks, there are equally famous Quilcene Bay oysters and fresh fish in

season. Every year since 1997 Canlis has been the recipient of *Wine Spectator* magazine's Grand Award for its wine list and service. ⊠ *2576 Aurora Ave. N, Queen Anne* ☎ *206/283–3313* ⌖ *Reservations essential* 𝔪 *Jacket required* ▤ *AE, DC, MC, V* ⊘ *Closed Sun. No lunch.*

Chinese

$–$$ ✕ **Bamboo Garden.** You can't tell that from the menu, but the Bamboo Garden serves some of the city's best vegetarian (and kosher) food. The Chinese dishes are listed by their traditional names even though all of the "meat"—including fish, chicken, pork, and beef—is made from gluten or other vegetarian substitutes. The dining room is simple, with the usual Oriental accoutrements. ⊠ *364 N. Roy St., Queen Anne* ☎ *206/282–6616* ▤ *AE, D, MC, V* ⊘ *No lunch weekends.*

Contemporary

$–$$$ ✕ **Kaspar's.** A decidedly unglamorous interior and a location amid Lower Queen Anne Hill's low-rise office buildings and light-industry warehouses focus diners' attention where it belongs—on chef-owner Kaspar Donier's finely wrought contemporary cuisine. Seafood, steak, and poultry options abound. The Muscovy duck with bosc pears, and the Hanoi-style sea bass with fennel and green onions are especially appealing. The five-course Northwest seafood dinner is a lifeline for the indecisive. Kaspar's proximity to Seattle Center makes it a natural destination before or after your evening's entertainment, but the food insists that you take your time. ⊠ *19 W. Harrison St., west of Queen Anne Ave. N, Queen Anne* ☎ *206/298–0123* ▤ *AE, MC, V* ⊘ *Closed Sun. and Mon. No lunch.*

Mexican

$–$$ ✕ **Peso's Kitchen & Lounge.** "Have a Margarita . . . at NOON!" proclaims the $3 happy hour menu at this "meet market" near the Seattle Center. There is no denying that the bar drives the show at this lively establishment that can best be described as Goth-Mex (think Madonna's "Like a Prayer" video). Nevertheless, the predictable Mexican menu delivers with above-average execution. The grilled prawns, carne asada, fish tacos, and Gulf-style crab cakes are winners. And, as you might imagine, the bartenders do have a special way with everyone's favorite tequila-and-lime cocktail. ⊠ *605 Queen Anne Ave. N, Queen Anne* ☎ *206/283–9353* ▤ *AE, MC, V.*

Pan-Asian

$ ✕ **Chinoise Café.** This small, very popular neighborhood café with tightly packed-in tables serves a number of simple Asian dishes, from sushi and *bento* boxes to seafood stir-fried with black-bean sauce, and Vietnamese spring rolls. Their successful formula is duplicated at the Madison Valley and I.D. locations. ⊠ *12 Boston St., Queen Anne* ☎ *206/284–6671* ⊠ *610 5th Ave. S, International District* ☎ *206/254–0413* ⊠ *2801 E. Madison, Madison Valley* ☎ *206/323–0171* ▤ *AE, D, DC, MC, V.*

Seafood

$–$$$ ✕ **Chinook's.** Large windows in this big, rather sterile family seafood house overlook fishing boats moored in Salmon Bay, one of the home ports of the Alaska salmon fleet. Not surprisingly, the restaurant is known for its king salmon and for the particularly pretty views from its patio. The wait for a table can be grueling on busy nights. Breakfast is available on weekends. ⊠ *1900 W. Nickerson, Queen Anne* ☎ *206/283–4665* ⌖ *Reservations not accepted* ▤ *AE, MC, V.*

Thai

¢–$ ✕ **Bahn Thai.** Because of the variety and high quality of its dishes, Bahn Thai, a pioneer in local Thai food, is still one of the city's best and most popular places, so it's a good idea to make a reservation. Start your meal with a skewer of tangy chicken or pork satay, or with the *tod mun goong* (spicy fish cake), and continue with hot and sour soup, and one of the many prawn or fish dishes. The deep-fried fish with garlic sauce is particularly good—and you can order it extra spicy. Evenings here are relaxed and romantic. ⊠ *409 Roy St., Queen Anne* ☎ *206/283–0444* ⊟ *AE, DC, MC, V* ☺ *No lunch weekends.*

International District & Pioneer Square

Café

¢–$ ✕ **Cafe Paloma.** You might swoon over the interior of this tiny café close to several art galleries, with its decorative bronze trays and big baskets full of glossy eggplants and tomatoes. Along with coffee service, there's light lunch and dinner fare with a Mediterranean/Turkish accent: handmade dolmas, hummus, and *baba ghanoush* (an eggplant puree made with yogurt—not tahini—in this case). The daily lunch specials can veer toward down-home American, though: a juicy pork tenderloin is frequently the centerpiece of the midday meal. ⊠ *93 Yesler Way, Pioneer Square* ☎ *206/405–1920* ⊟ *MC, V.*

Chinese

$–$$$ ✕ **Top Gun.** It brims with regulars devoted to the dim sum served daily from 10 until 3. Specialties include succulent *siu mai* (steamed pork dumplings), fried cubes of tofu with prawns, pork-filled *hum bao,* salt-and-pepper squid, and crisp *gai-lan* (Chinese broccoli) drizzled with a soy sauce–based dressing. Save room for the dessert cart: the buttery, bite-size egg tarts melt in your mouth, and the mango pudding turns many first-timers into repeat customers. ⊠ *668 S. King St., International District* ☎ *206/623–6606* ⊟ *MC, V.*

$ ✕ **Hing Loon.** Food magic happens in this eatery with bright fluorescent

Fodor'sChoice   lighting, shiny linoleum floors, and large round laminate tables. Although

★   many Chinese chefs may head to Linyen after hours, this is where they purportedly come for noodles. The walls are covered with menu specials handwritten (in Cantonese and English) on paper place mats. Employ the friendly waitstaff to help make your selections. Dishes of particular note are the stuffed eggplant, crispy fried chicken, *Funn* noodles, and any of the seafood offerings. ⊠ *628 S. Weller St., International District* ☎ *206/682–2828* ⊟ *MC, V.*

$ ✕ **Linyen.** If it weren't in the International District, you'd consider this elegant restaurant an upscale American café. But don't let the interior decoration fool you: the first-rate food is authentically Asian. This is the place where Chinese chefs come to eat late at night after they've closed their own kitchens. Favorite dishes include the honey walnut prawns and the Peking duck. ⊠ *424 7th Ave. S, International District* ☎ *206/ 622–8181* ⊟ *AE, MC, V.*

Delicatessen

¢ ✕ **Bakeman's Restaurant.** Low on frills but high on personality, this lunchery attracts business suits with its signature turkey and meat-loaf sandwiches, both served on fluffy white bread. Your window of opportunity is small: it's open weekdays from 10 to 3. Bakeman's is within easy striking distance of Pioneer Square, but the feel is far from touristy. ⊠ *122 Cherry St., Pioneer Square* ☎ *206/622–3375* ⊘ *Reservations not accepted* ⊟ *No credit cards* ☺ *Closed weekends. No dinner.*

Italian

$ ✕ **Trattoria Mitchelli.** Although the food is good, Trattoria Mitchelli is important for another reason: It's open until 4 AM most nights, and opens at 7 AM. Its Pioneer Square location may account for this, as many pub crawlers find "the Trat" a hospitable establishment for winding up an evening (and for getting some much-needed late-night/early-morning sustenance). The food is traditional—thin crust, applewood-fired pizzas; sizable pasta dishes; Caesar salads with anchovies (if you want them). ⊠ *84 Yesler Way, Pioneer Square* ☎ *206/623–3883* ⌖ *Reservations not accepted* ☰ *AE, MC, V.*

¢–$ ✕ **Salumi.** The kind chef-owner Armandino Batali (father of famed New York chef Mario Batali) doles out samples of his fabulous house-cured meats while you wait for a table (which you must be willing to share) at this postage-stamp of a place. Order a meatball, oxtail, sausage, or lamb sandwich—and get samples of your runners-up. Mainly this is a lunch spot, though every Friday Batali serves dinner to a lucky few (reservations are made as much as 12 months ahead). The house wine served at lunch is strong, inexpensive, and good. ⊠ *309 3rd Ave. S, Pioneer Square* ☎ *206/621–8772* ☰ *AE, D, DC, MC, V.*

FodorśChoice ★

Japanese

¢–$ ✕ **Takohachi.** Comfort food at a comfortable price is the name of the game at this popular little restaurant. The emphasis is on fried foods such as *tonkatsu* (breaded pork cutlet) and *kaarage* (breaded boneless chicken), but the *nabe* (cabbage soup) is also quite delicious. There are only two types of sushi on the menu—California roll and a *battera* (mackerel and sweet rice stuffed in a fried tofu pouch)—and neither is available at lunch. ⊠ *610 S. Jackson St., International District* ☎ *206/682–1828* ☰ *MC, V* ☺ *Closed Sun. No lunch Sat.*

Malaysian

¢–$ ✕ **Malay Satay Hut.** Grilled flat breads, called *roti canai* (unstuffed) and *roti relur* (stuffed with egg, green onion, and red pepper), are a specialty here. The roti are served with a curry dipping sauce studded with chunks of chicken and potato. Other menu favorites include Buddhist Yam Pot (scallops and prawns served in a ring of cooked shredded yam), Belachan string beans (string beans and prawns tossed in a spicy sauce), mango chicken, any of the curries, and the banana pancakes. ⊠ *212 12th Ave. S, International District* ☎ *206/324–4091* ☰ *MC, V.*

Vietnamese

¢–$ ✕ **Saigon Bistro.** Great values and weekend crowds are found at this bistro, the entrance of which is somewhat elusively located through the back parking lot of the Asian Plaza at 12th and Jackson. Noteworthy dishes include a turmeric-scented mung bean crepe filled with shrimp and scallops served on a cafeteria tray (we're not kidding) mounded with lettuce leaves and pungent herbs, fresh summer rolls stuffed with a filling of your choice (including green mango), traditional *pho* (noodle soups), and such savory dishes as lemongrass-marinated grilled skirt steak and deep-fried pork spring rolls. Parking is free. ⊠ *1032 S. Jackson St., International District* ☎ *206/329–4939* ☰ *MC, V.*

¢ ✕ **Saigon Gourmet.** This small café is about as plain as they get, but the food is superb and incredibly inexpensive. Aficionados make special trips for the Cambodian soup and the shrimp rolls, but don't overlook the unusual papaya with beef jerky. Parking can be a problem, but the food rewards your patience. ⊠ *502 S. King St., International District* ☎ *206/624–2611* ⌖ *Reservations not accepted* ☰ *MC, V* ☺ *Closed Mon.*

Capitol Hill & Environs

American

¢ ✕ **Dick's Drive-In.** This chain of orange hamburger stands has changed little since the 1950s. The fries are handcut, the shakes are hand dipped (i.e., made with hard ice cream), and the burgers are just handy. The top-of-the-line burger, Dick's Deluxe ($2.08), has two beef patties, American cheese, lettuce, onions and is slathered in their special tartar sauce. Many folks swear by the frill-free plain cheeseburger ($1.20). Open until 2 AM daily, these drive-ins are as popular with families and students as they are with folks girding themselves against hangovers after a night out on the town. ⊠ *1115 Broadway E, Capitol Hill* ☎ *206/323–1300* ⊟ *No credit cards* ⊠ *111 NE 45th St., Wallingford* ☎ *206/632–5125* ⊠ *500 Queen Anne Ave. N, Queen Anne* ☎ *206/285–5155* ⊟ *No credit cards.*

Contemporary

$–$$ ✕ **Coastal Kitchen.** Here's a chic yet casual place with a three-tiered menu. Local restaurant gurus Jeremy Hardy and Peter Levy hit on a sure-fire formula with their hearty diner-style dishes served alongside Southern-accented meals. The cooks also concoct a rotating menu with cuisines of such far-flung coastal places as Oaxaca, Vietnam, and Barcelona, to name a few. The experiments don't always work, but you can't knock their adventurous spirit. Besides, you can always fall back on the roast chicken with creamy mashed potatoes or the marinated pork chop. ⊠ *429 15th Ave. E, Capitol Hill* ☎ *206/322–1145* ⊟ *MC, V.*

★ **$–$$** ✕ **1200 Bistro and Lounge.** The interior glows at this comfortable bistro, which is half lounge, half restaurant. Both sides stay plenty busy due to the expertly prepared food and cocktails. Friendly servers make you feel like you're dining in the home of a dear friend—who also happens to be an excellent cook. Portions are generous, and the plates are artfully arranged. Menu favorites include the Muscovy duck served with roasted fingerling potatoes and green-peppercorn demi-glace; filet mignon with scalloped blue cheese potatoes; and a vegetable gratin with wilted spinach, caramelized onions, and feta cheese. ⊠ *1200 E. Pike St., Capitol Hill* ☎ *206/320–1200* ⊟ *AE, MC, V* ⊗ *No lunch.*

French

★ **$$$$** ✕ **Rover's.** The restaurant of Thierry Rautureau, one of the Northwest's most imaginative chefs, is an essential destination. Sea scallops, venison, squab, lobster, and rabbit are frequent offerings (vegetarian items are also available) on the prix-fixe menu. Traditional accoutrements such as foie gras and truffles pay homage to Rautereau's French roots, but bold combinations of local ingredients are evidence of his wanderlust. The service at Rover's is excellent—friendly but unobtrusive—the setting romantic, and the presentation stunning. ⊠ *2808 E. Madison St., Madison Valley* ☎ *206/325–7442* ⌦ *Reservations essential* ⊟ *AE, MC, V* ⊗ *Closed Sun. and Mon. No lunch.*

$$–$$$ ✕ **Cassis.** Everything served at candlelit Cassis is made on the premises by chef Charlie Durham or pastry chef Brandy Bassett, right down to the bread. In season a Yakima Valley farmer delivers a weekly truckload of freshly harvested produce grown exclusively for the Cassis kitchen. Specialties include panfried calves' liver, mussels *marinière* (with herbs and white wine), and fish soup topped with a rouille. A rotating selection of 10 wines are available by the glass, and three house wines are offered by the *pichet* (small pitcher). The menu changes monthly, and a prix-fixe menu is offered Sunday through Thursday before 7 PM. ⊠ *2359 10th Ave., Capitol Hill* ☎ *206/329–0580* ⌦ *Reservations essential* ⊟ *AE, MC, V.*

$$ ✕ **Madison Park Cafe.** Karen Binder's small, vaguely French neighborhood café is a local institution. Although this spot has been in the past widely known for its breakfast and lunch, recent years have brought a greater emphasis on the dinner service. Popular dishes on the ever-changing evening menu have included cassoulet, oysters in a Pernod cream sauce, pepper steak, and traditional rack of lamb. For warm-weather dining, there's a secluded cobblestone courtyard shaded by trees and scented by more than 12 species of lilies. In summer, foods cooked on an outdoor brick grill add to the delicious aromas wafting from the kitchen. ⊠ *1807 42nd Ave. E, Madison Park* ☎ *206/324–2626* ▤ *AE, MC, V* ☾ *No dinner Sun. and Mon.*

Italian

$–$$$ ✕ **Cafe Lago.** Hugely popular with locals, Cafe Lago specializes in wood-fired pizzas and light handmade pastas. The lasagna—ricotta, béchamel, and cherry-tomato sauce amid paper-thin pasta sheets—perfectly represents the menu's inclination toward the simply satisfying yet exquisitely prepared. ⊠ *2305 24th Ave. E, Capitol Hill* ☎ *206/329–8005* ▤ *D, DC, MC, V* ☾ *Closed Mon. No lunch.*

Southern

¢–$$ ✕ **Kingfish Cafe.** Good Southern cooking is such a novelty in Seattle that the three sisters who own and operate Kingfish are local celebrities. Here you can get a good po'boy with green tomatoes, fried chicken, pulled pork, scrumptious crab cakes, and, of course, sweet potato pie. The place is spare but elegant, with photographs culled from family albums. ⊠ *602 19th Ave. E, Capitol Hill* ☎ *206/320–8757* ⚐ *Reservations not accepted* ▤ *MC, V* ☾ *Closed Tues. No lunch weekends.*

Thai

$ ✕ **Siam.** Start your meal with satay or the city's best *tom kah gai*—a soup of coconut, lemongrass, chicken, and mushrooms. Entrées include curries, noodle dishes, and many prawn, chicken, and fish dishes. Specify one to five stars according to your tolerance for heat. ⊠ *616 Broadway, Capitol Hill* ☎ *206/324–0892* ▤ *AE, MC, V* ☾ *No lunch weekends.*

Vietnamese

★ ¢–$$ ✕ **Monsoon.** This elegant restaurant and wine bar sits unobtrusively on a Capitol Hill avenue, letting its classic Saigon cuisine make the splashy statements. Staff favorites include the caramelized gulf shrimp served with jasmine rice, the catfish claypot with chili-lime sauce, and the lemongrass tofu. Exotic homemade ice creams include jackfruit or lychee and muscat, but the restaurant's most famous dessert is the crème caramel. The wine cellar has more than 500 bottles of wine guaranteed to complement the sublime work of the chef. ⊠ *615 19th Ave. E, Capitol Hill* ☎ *206/325–2111* ▤ *MC, V* ☾ *Closed Mon.*

University District

American

$ ✕ **Portage Bay Cafe.** This casual, contemporary café is a favorite hang-out with the university crowd. Try the pot roast, pork chops, duck, and crab cakes. Breakfast is served, as is weekend brunch, and on nice days there is open-air dining. ⊠ *4130 Roosevelt Ave. NE, University District* ☎ *206/547–8230* ▤ *AE, D, MC, V.*

Brazilian

$–$$ ✕ **Tempero Do Brasil.** Folks come from far afield to this festive place for a taste of Brazil. The popular cod, prawn, and halibut dishes simmered in coconut-based sauces are complex and satisfying; entrées arrive with moist, chewy long-grain rice and delectable black beans. For a larger meal, try the charbroiled Argentine steak, *bife grelhado*. Finish with cold passionfruit mousse or tangy guava paste served with farmer's cheese, and strong dark coffee. The outstanding food, attention to detail, and earnest staff make dining here a pleasure. The airy patio is perfect for icy Brazilian cocktails in the summer. ⊠ *5628 University Way NE, University District* ☎ *206/523–6229* ▤ *AE, MC, DC, V* ☾ *Closed Mon.*

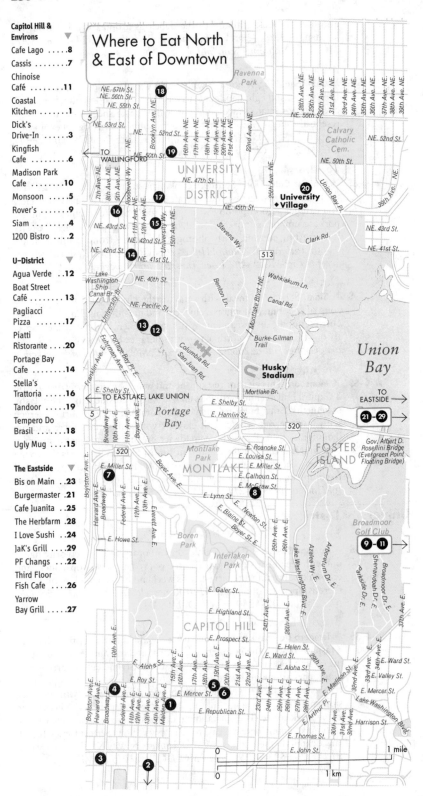

Where to Eat North & East of Downtown

Capitol Hill & Environs ▼

Cafe Lago **8**
Cassis **7**
Chinoise Café **11**
Coastal Kitchen **1**
Dick's Drive-In **3**
Kingfish Cafe **6**
Madison Park Cafe **10**
Monsoon **5**
Rover's **9**
Siam **4**
1200 Bistro **2**

U–District ▼

Agua Verde . . **12**
Boat Street Café **13**
Pagliacci Pizza **17**
Piatti Ristorante . . . **20**
Portage Bay Cafe **14**
Stella's Trattoria **16**
Tandoor **19**
Tempero Do Brasil **18**
Ugly Mug **15**

The Eastside ▼

Bis on Main . . **23**
Burgermaster . . **21**
Cafe Juanita . . **25**
The Herbfarm . . **28**
I Love Sushi . . **24**
JaK's Grill **29**
PF Changs . . . **22**
Third Floor Fish Cafe **26**
Yarrow Bay Grill **27**

Café

¢ ✕ **Ugly Mug.** Pleasantly worn couches, lamps on the tables, and jazz standards on the stereo recall the funky Seattle that once was. A sign at the cash register admonishes, FRIENDS DON'T LET FRIENDS GO TO STARBUCKS!. Indeed, the Ugly Mug doesn't aspire to be anything more than itself, with warming, inventive soups like garbanzo-cabbage or black bean cooked with wine and orange zest. The meat-loaf sandwich makes you want seconds. For breakfast, try the Belgian waffles with yogurt and fruit or the raspberry scone. ⊠ *1309 NE 43rd St., University District* ☎ *206/547–3219* ▤ *No credit cards.*

French

$–$$ ✕ **Boat Street Café.** A sunny day at the Boat Street Café is a treat for the senses. Open windows bring the scent of flowers and the clink of boats bobbing nearby as the kitchen sends enticing aromas to your table. The crab cakes evoke the Pacific Northwest; the chicken in tarragon cream sauce savors of France; and the fresh scallop ravioli might remind you of Italy. American touches are present in oven-roasted prawns, pork in blackberry sauce, and a sweet corn flan. The simple and spare interior has a rustic grace that belies the sophistication of the food. ⊠ *909 NE Boat St., University District* ☎ *206/632–4602* ▤ *No credit cards* ⊗ *Closed Mon. No dinner Sun.–Tues.*

Indian

$ ✕ **Tandoor.** The northern Indian menu focuses on tandoori (meat cooked in a clay oven, over charcoal) dishes, though it's the special naan (round leavened flat bread, in this case stuffed with chicken and nuts), lamb vindaloo (a spicy curry stew served over basmati rice), and curried meat and vegetable mulligatawny soup that really sing. The beer and wine, like the food, are bargain priced. ⊠ *5024 University Way NE, University District* ☎ *206/523–7477* ▤ *AE, D, DC, MC, V.*

Italian

$–$$ ✕ **Piatti Ristorante.** The staff is friendly, and everything about this place is casual. There's a fireside dining room; if it's warm you can sit on one of two patios. What more could you ask for? The rotisserie chicken is a favorite, as well as the chicken marsala. Or try the ravioli stuffed with arugula and ricotta. ⊠ *2800 NE University Village, University District* ☎ *206/524–9088* ▤ *AE, DC, MC, V.*

$ ✕ **Stella's Trattoria.** Paintings by local artists brighten the three dark, cavernlike dining rooms at this all-night trattoria. The food is standard Italian; try the melanzane parmigiana, which is eggplant browned in the pan and topped with marinara, mozzarella, and Parmesan, served with garlic pasta. There's open-air dining on the sidewalk out front. ⊠ *4500 9th Ave., University District* ☎ *206/633–1100* ▤ *AE, D, MC, V.*

Mexican

¢–$ ✕ **Agua Verde.** You can rent kayaks at Agua Verde, which is on a street bordering Portage Bay and surrounded by boat repair shops. The food here has been described as Baja California Mexican, which may refer as much to the bright, beachy colors as it does to the cuisine. Tacos aren't dripping with grease, cheese, or sour cream, and choices include fish and chili-chicken. With a nod to the U-District diet, there are lots of vegetarian items. Regulars swear by the black-bean cakes and *mangodillas*, quesadillas with mango and poblano chilis. Warning: The fresh-lime margaritas may hike your otherwise small bill. ⊠ *1303 NE Boat St., University District* ☎ *206/545–8570* ▤ *MC, V* ↻ *Sun. lunch takeout only.*

Pizza

$–$$ ✕ **Pagliacci Pizza.** These days, down-and-dirty pizza is hard to find. Pagliacci ascetically adheres to a thin-crust, no-nonsense ethic, which includes, yes, amazing, a cheese-and-tomato-sauce pie. That's all. Just pizza. It's almost zen. ⊠ *4529 University Way NE, University District* ☎ *206/632–0421* ▤ *AE, MC, V.*

The Eastside

American

¢–$ ✕ **Burgermaster.** Since 1952, carhops at this drive-in have been serving people at their car windows. The specialty, of course, is hamburgers, but the drive-in also serves fresh and savory fish sandwiches. ⊠ *10606 Northup Way, Bellevue* ☎ *425/827–9566* ▤ *AE, D, DC, MC, V.*

Chinese

¢–$ ✕ **PF Changs.** This upscale chain in The Lodge at Bellevue Square serves beautiful Chinese food in a lively dining room. The chicken in lettuce wraps are popular, the salt-and-pepper calamari pack a flavorful punch, and the Cantonese roasted duck served with steamed buns and hoisin sauce is a hearty choice. Upon request the kitchen will prepare Szechwan long beans and asparagus tossed together so you won't have to choose between the two. White and brown rice are available, and all dishes are served family style. ⊠ *525 Bellevue Sq., Bellevue* ☎ *425/637–3582* ▤ *AE, MC, V.*

Contemporary

$$$$ ✕ **The Herbfarm.** The sumptuous, nine-course, prix-fixe meals served at this restaurant 10 mi northeast of Kirkland are the paradigm for Pacific Northwest cuisine. The delectables you will encounter include goat cheese biscuits, green pickled walnuts, and salmon with a sauce of fresh herbs. ⊠ *14590 NE 145th St., Woodinville* ☎ *206/784–2222* ⌂ *Reservations essential* ☾ *No lunch* ▤ *AE, MC, V.*

Continental

★ $–$$ ✕ **Bis on Main.** The intimate, romantic dining room is given special flair from the rotating exhibits of modern art that adorn the walls. The most popular of the many scrumptious entrées are the crab cakes and the crispy garlic chicken, a free-range chicken deboned and marinated and then pan-seared, roasted, and served with horseradish mashed potatoes. ⊠ *10213 Main St., Bellevue* ☎ *425/455–2033* ▤ *AE, D, DC, MC, V* ☾ *No lunch on weekends.*

Italian

★ $$–$$$ ✕ **Cafe Juanita.** Under the direction of chef-owner Holly Smith, this romantic Eastside favorite focuses on traditional northern Italian recipes while allowing for exploration of other Italian cuisines. The menu changes daily as Smith uses the freshest ingredients available, many of which come from the restaurant's own garden. Favorites plates include a smoked trout served with pickled wild ramps; braised rabbit served over a chickpea-flour crepe; and a rich grilled rib-eye steak drizzled with red-wine syrup. ⊠ *9702 NE 120th Pl., Kirkland* ☎ *425/823–1505* ▤ *MC, V* ☾ *Closed Mon. No lunch.*

Japanese

$–$$ ✕ **I Love Sushi.** This is the Bellevue original of one of Seattle's most popular sushi bars. It's bigger and more bustling than its Lake Union offspring, and the food is every bit as good. The chefs occasionally bring in rare treats from around the world, but local specialties such as geoduck or salmon are available year-round. Start with some salty *edamame*—fresh green soybeans in the shell that you draw out with your teeth. ⊠ *11818 NE 8th St., Bellevue* ☎ *425/454–5706* ⌂ *Reservations essential* ▤ *MC, V* ☾ *No lunch Sun.* ⊠ *1001 Fairview Ave. N, Eastlake* ☎ *206/625–9604* ⌂ *Reservations essential* ▤ *MC, V* ☾ *No lunch Sun.*

Seafood

$$–$$$$ ✕ **Third Floor Fish Cafe.** This elegant restaurant with a great view (and an ugly name) is a popular Eastside dining spot. Chef Greg Campbell has a sure touch with Mediterranean-style fish, and he handles meats equally well. The menu focuses on fresh, preferably local, seafood (such as wild Pacific salmon or pan-seared scallops), but also includes chicken, lamb (as in cabernet-braised lamb shanks), and beef tenderloin. ⊠ *205 Lake St. S, Kirkland* ☎ *425/822–3553* ◬ *Reservations essential* ▤ *AE, D, MC, V* ⊗ *No lunch.*

★ $$–$$$$ ✕ **Yarrow Bay Grill.** This pleasant waterfront-view restaurant on Lake Union, south of Kirkland, always serves good food and has excellent service, making it one of the best restaurants east of Lake Washington. The Beach Cafe at Yarrow Bay, the Grill's informal downstairs offshoot, has tables closer to the water, the menu is less formal, and the prices are lower. ⊠ *1270 Carillon Point, off Lake Washington Blvd., Kirkland* ☎ *425/889–9052* ▤ *AE, DC, MC, V.*

Steak

$–$$$ ✕ **JaK's Grill.** The specialty is steak; people come from all around for it. The menu also includes seafood dishes and pastas. The large, open dining room is often boisterous. ⊠ *14 Front St., Issaquah* ☎ *425/837–8834* ▤ *DC, MC, V* ⊗ *No lunch.*

Fremont

Cuban

$ ✕ **Paseo.** The centerpiece of Lorenzo Lorenzo's slim Cuban-influenced menu is a highly secret sauce that was years in the making; word has it that Lorenzo even hides the recipe from his employees. The marinated pork sandwich, topped with sautéed onions, is doused with this sauce and keeps folks coming back for more. The entrées are also a bargain, from scallops with cilantro to prawns in red sauce. ⊠ *4225 Fremont Ave. N, Fremont* ☎ *206/545–7440* ▤ *No credit cards* ⊗ *No lunch Sun.*

Italian

★ $–$$ ✕ **Brad's Swingside Cafe.** You've probably dreamed of finding a place like this—funky, cramped, and dear to the heart of the owner. Lots of people share this dream, so you can expect to wait a while on weekends. Chef-owner Brad Inserra, who likes to come out and chat—so long as you don't dis the Pittsburgh Pirates—bills Swingside as Seattle's "best little Italian restaurant," but don't come expecting spaghetti and meatballs. You will find an imaginative lamb-and-venison stew with coconut milk, orange, and mango. Be sure to ask the server what wine Inserra recommends. He's always right. ⊠ *4212 Fremont Ave. N, Fremont* ☎ *206/633–4057* ▤ *MC, V* ⊗ *Closed Sun. No lunch.*

Mexican

★ ¢–$ ✕ **El Camino.** Loose, loud, and funky, this Fremont storefront restaurant gives its own irreverent Northwest interpretation of Mexican cuisine. Rock-shrimp quesadillas, chipotle-pepper and garlic sea bass, and duck with a spicy green sauce are typical of the kitchen's gentle spin. Even a green salad becomes transformed with toasted pumpkin seeds on crispy romaine with a cool garlic, lime juice, and cilantro dressing. You can eat until midnight, although there's no better place to chill on a summer afternoon than El Camino's deck. A tart margarita, served in a pint glass, makes the perfect accessory. ⊠ *607 N. 35th St., Fremont* ☎ *206/632–7303* ▤ *AE, DC, MC, V* ⊗ *No lunch weekdays.*

Seafood

$$–$$$ ✕ **Ponti.** Working in a placid canal-side location—and a villalike setting—chef Alvin Binuya builds culinary bridges between Northwest ingredi-

Fremont ▼

Brad's Swingside
Cafe 2

El Camino 3

Paseo 1

Ponti 4

**Green Lake &
Phinney** ▼

Le Gourmand ..6

Nell's 5

Ballard ▼

Anthony's
Homeport 12

Bait House ...13

Burk's Cafe ...10

Grapes Wine
Shop
and Bistro 9

Louie's 7

Market Street
Grill 8

Ray's
Boathouse ...11

Where to Eat
North & West
of Downtown

ents and Mediterranean and Asian techniques. Alaskan king crab legs with a chardonnay butter and herb mayonnaise manifest the kitchen's classic restraint; the grilled mahimahi with satsuma potato gratin and shallot jus walks on the wilder side. ⊠ *3014 3rd Ave. N, Fremont* ☎ *206/284–3000* ▤ *AE, DC, MC, V.*

Green Lake & Phinney

Contemporary

★ $$$–$$$$ ✕ **Le Gourmand.** Not every chef cares enough to grow the poppies that provide the seeds for his homemade crackers. Chef-owner Bruce Naftaly does. This man has routinely worked the line since taking the helm at this restaurant in the early 1980s. Bruce uses classic French techniques and locally grown ingredients to create stunning dishes such as his roast duckling with black currant sauce (using homemade cassis); or king salmon poached in champagne and gooseberry sauce. Pastry chef Sara Naftaly's dessert menu might include a flourless chocolate cake with raspberries and almond crème anglaise. ⊠ *425 NW Market St., Phinney* ☎ *206/ 784–3463* ⌂ *Reservations essential* ▤ *AE, MC, V.*

$$–$$$ ✕ **Nell's.** Nell's is a bright spot on the Seattle dining scene. Chef-owner Philip Mihalski's ever-changing menu focuses on coaxing maximum performance from the freshest of seasonal regional ingredients. Employing broadly European techniques, Mihalski creates such dishes as seared sea scallops with a curry cream sauce and shavings of black truffle over a puree of cauliflower, and poached halibut in kaffir lime broth with roasted spring onions. Suggested appetizers include a fantastic onion tart with hazelnut butter and Jerusalem artichoke chips, and seared foie gras in duck broth over a puree of turnips. ⊠ *6804 E. Greenlake Way N, Green Lake* ☎ *206/524–4044* ▤ *AE, MC, V* ☉ *No lunch.*

Ballard

American

¢ ✕ **Bait House.** It's no joke: In the summer fishermen stop here at 4 AM to pick up their bait (but the kitchen's closed then). You can come during a more reasonable hour for a deli sandwich, crab cocktail, the famous open-face crab-cheese melt, and definitely for the view. The patio and the small, crooked, rough-hewn dining room overlook boats gliding by on their way to the Ballard Locks. Take a peek behind the counter, too: All hot food is baked or warmed in little toaster ovens. Expect nautical charm. ⊠ *5517 Seaview Ave. NW, between Ballard Locks and train bridge overpass, Ballard* ☎ *206/297–9109* ▭ *MC, V* ☉ *Closed Mon. No dinner Sun. or Tues.*

Café

¢–$ ✕ **Grapes Wine Shop and Bistro.** Amid a number of tables and a comfy sofa, the wine-and-cheese merchant's counter is a jumble of paperwork and magazines. Piaf's voice might be resonating up to the rafters, though; a sea breeze from Shilshole Bay might be drifting in, and the grilled cheese sandwich of the day on rustic bread might be scrumptious raclette, a nutty, semifirm cheese similar to Gruyère. The large selection of wine by the glass and bottle is a veritable tour of Italy's wine regions. ⊠ *5424 Ballard Ave. NW, Ballard* ☎ *206/297–1460* ▭ *D, MC, V.*

Cajun/Creole

$–$$ ✕ **Burk's Cafe.** With homey wood floors, a tiny but comfortable bar, and plenty of light, immaculate Burk's is well versed in gumbos, jambalayas, and ribs, making it a godsend in a city with relatively few Creole restaurants. Big crocks of hot pickled okra sit on each table; servers are competent and even witty. The blackened rockfish is exceedingly tender inside, and the alder-wood-smoked sausages are made on the premises. Try the fetching sandwiches, which come on chewy rolls. Be warned: most dishes are extra spicy and can't be made milder. ⊠ *52411 Ballard Ave. NW, Ballard* ☎ *206/782–0091* ▭ *MC, V* ☉ *Closed Sun. and Mon.*

Chinese

¢–$ ✕ **Louie's.** Louie's looks straight out of a 1960s James Bond flick. Cavernous booths, mirror-paneled walls, and a huge banquet room make for a fun excursion. Besides the Cantonese/Szechuan fare, the menu includes dim sum and American chow like burgers and roast beef au jus sandwiches. Like many Chinese restaurants in town, it's open past midnight on weekends. ⊠ *5100 15th Ave. NW, just north of Ballard Bridge, Ballard* ☎ *206/782–8855* ▭ *AE, D, MC, V* ☉ *No lunch weekends.*

Contemporary

$–$$ ✕ **Market Street Grill.** In a space that mixes restrained, cool design elements with the warmth of candlelit tables, chef John Paul Kunselman oversees the Northwest menu. You can pair a number of attractive starters to make whole meals: warm lobster and artichoke salad, shrimp cakes with watercress mayonnaise, and foie gras with sweetbreads. The entrées, seasonally focused and equally appetizing, range from sea scallop potpie to grilled pork tenderloin with shaved Reggiano Parmigiano and porcini risotto cake. ⊠ *1744 NW Market St., Ballard* ☎ *206/789–6766* ▭ *AE, D, MC, V* ☉ *No lunch.*

Seafood

$$–$$$$ ✕ **Anthony's Homeport.** This is a comfortable waterfront restaurant where ample outside dining in protected nooks allows you a sea breeze and great views without getting blasted by gales. The seafood preparations are as good as those of the more upscale Ray's, next door. But this restaurant's true claim to fame rests on its annual Oyster Olympics, a

madcap oyster-shucking, oyster-judging, oyster-slurping event held in late March. ⊠ *6135 Seaview Ave. NW, at the Shilshole Marina, Ballard* ☎ *206/783–0780* ⊟ *AE, MC, V.*

★ **$$–$$$$** ✕ **Ray's Boathouse.** The view of Puget Sound might be the big draw here, but the seafood is also impeccably fresh and well prepared. Perennial favorites include broiled salmon, Kasu sake-marinated cod, Dungeness crab, and regional oysters on the half shell. Ray's has a split personality: there's a fancy dining room downstairs and a casual café and bar upstairs. In warm weather you can sit on the deck outside the café and watch the parade of fishing boats, tugs, and pleasure craft floating past, almost right below your table. ⊠ *6049 Seaview Ave. NW, Ballard* ☎ *206/789–3770* ⌔ *Reservations essential (dining room); reservations not accepted (café)* ⊟ *AE, DC, MC, V.*

WHERE TO STAY

Updated by
Julie Fay

Most of Seattle's hotels are Downtown, but there are good deals to be had in the outlying neighborhoods, and some places will transport you to and from Downtown for free. Both of the Marriotts at Lake Union, for example, offer a shuttle to the Pike Place Market, Westlake Center, the Space Needle, and Pier 70. Bed-and-breakfasts on Capitol Hill are a manageable walk from Downtown and are near boutiques, restaurants, bars, and movie theaters. Less expensive but still tasteful lodging options (rates often include parking) are available in the University District, which is well served by the city's buses and which has affordable restaurants, trendy shops, and lots of pubs. Both Belltown and Queen Anne attract a wealthier, more staid clientele.

WHAT IT COSTS				
$$$$	**$$$**	**$$**	**$**	**¢**
FOR 2 PEOPLE over $250	$200–$250	$150–$200	$100–$150	under $100

Price categories are assigned based on the range between the least and most expensive standard double rooms in high season. Tax (17%) is extra.

Downtown & Belltown

★ **$$$$** 🏨 **Elliott Grand Hyatt.** The Elliott was built as part of an expansion of the Washington State Convention Center. Both projects appear to have been designed to appeal to Seattleites in the high-tech industry. The hotel offers state-of-the-art Internet access (100Mb/s), Virtual Private Network technology, video conference rooms, and a 151-seat theater with data ports at every seat. Rooms on the upper floors have views of Elliott Bay, Lake Union, and the Cascade and Olympic Mountain ranges. Carrara marble floors, Vesuvio granite counters, and oversize soaking tubs are standard in all of the guest bathrooms. ⊠ *721 Pine St., Downtown, 98101* ☎ *206/774–1234* ⊟ *206/774–6311* ⊕ *www.hyatt.com* ⇆ *317 rooms, 108 suites* ⌂ *Restaurant, café, room service, in-room data ports, minibars, gym, bar, theater, laundry service, concierge, meeting rooms, parking (fee), no-smoking rooms* ⊟ *AE, D, DC, MC, V.*

$$$$ 🏨 **Fairmont Olympic Hotel.** This is the place to stay in town for incomparable elegance and service. The 1920s Renaissance Revival–style Olympic is the grande dame of Seattle hotels. Marble, wood paneling, thick rugs, and plush armchairs adorn the public spaces; graceful staircases lead to ballrooms. The Georgian (the hotel's premier dining room) and a gilded balcony overlook the lobby. Sizable guest rooms are done in soothing yellows, blues, and greens; each is furnished with a sofa and a desk. Amenities include chocolates on your pillow, complimentary shoe

Fodor'sChoice
★

shines, and the morning newspaper. ⊠ *411 University St., Downtown, 98101* ☎ *206/621–1700 or 800/223-8772* 🖷 *206/682–9633* ⊕ *www. fairmont.com* ⇌ *450 rooms* ♿ *3 restaurants, room service, in-room data ports, in-room safes, minibars, refrigerators, indoor pool, health club, lounge, children's programs (ages 0–17), laundry service, concierge, meeting rooms, parking (fee)* ☰ *AE, D, DC, MC, V.*

★ **$$$$** 🖃 **Hotel Monaco.** Goldfish in your room are among the fun touches at this luxury hotel in a former office building in the heart of the Financial District. The light and whimsical lobby has high ceilings and hand-painted nautical murals inspired by the fresco at the Palace of Knossos in Crete. A pleasing blend of bold and bright colors and patterns graces the spacious guest rooms. In-room amenities include voice mail, irons, hair dryers, coffeemakers, and stereos with CD players. The hotel really lays out the red carpet for pets. ⊠ *1101 4th Ave., Downtown, 98101* ☎ *206/621–1770 or 800/945–2240* 🖷 *206/621–7779* ⊕ *www.monaco-seattle.com* ⇌ *144 rooms, 45 suites* ♿ *Restaurant, room service, in-room data ports, in-room fax, gym, bar, dry cleaning, laundry service, concierge, business services, meeting rooms, airport shuttle, parking (fee), some pets allowed, no-smoking rooms* ☰ *AE, D, DC, MC, V.*

$$$$ 🖃 **Hotel Vintage Park.** Each guest room in this medium-size hotel is named for a Washington winery or vineyard. The theme extends to complimentary wine served each evening in the lobby while patrons relax on richly upholstered sofas and chairs facing a marble fireplace. Rooms—decorated in dark green, plum, deep red, taupe, and gold—have custom-made cherry furniture and original artwork. If you're literary-minded, hotel staff will deliver your choice of titles from the Seattle Public Library. The athletically inclined can have exercise equipment brought to their rooms. Tulio, the hotel restaurant, is a popular spot for rustic Italian fare. ⊠ *1100 5th Ave., Downtown, 98101* ☎ *206/624–8000 or 800/ 624–4433* 🖷 *206/623–0568* ⊕ *www.vintagepark.com* ⇌ *126 rooms* ♿ *Restaurant, room service, in-room data ports, minibars, refrigerators, spa, laundry service, concierge, meeting rooms, parking (fee), no-smoking floors* ☰ *AE, D, DC, MC, V.*

$$$$ 🖾 **Seattle Sheraton Hotel and Towers.** Business travelers are the primary patrons of this high-rise hotel close to shopping and the convention center. The busy lobby has a comfortable open lounge, which is ideal for people-watching and enjoying the notable collection of art glass produced by well-known Northwest artist Dale Chihuly. Guest rooms are plain, yet generously proportioned. Views here are mostly territorial, but you can get a glimpse Elliott Bay or Lake Union on or above the 20th floor. The rooms on the top five floors, larger and more elegant than those below, include concierge service and complimentary Continental breakfast. All rooms have two-line phones. ⊠ *1400 6th Ave., Downtown, 98101* ☎ *206/621–9000 or 800/325–3535* 🖷 *206/621–8441* ⊕ *www.sheraton.com/seattle* ⇌ *800 rooms, 40 suites* ♿ *3 restaurants, room service, in-room data ports, in-room safes, minibars, indoor pool, health club, 2 bars, laundry service, concierge, meeting rooms, parking (fee), no-smoking rooms* ☰ *AE, D, DC, MC, V.*

$$$–$$$$ 🖾 **Alexis Hotel.** The European-style Alexis occupies two restored buildings near the waterfront. Complimentary wine is served 5:30–6:30 in
Fodor'sChoice the lobby bar. Rooms, in subdued colors, are decorated in imported Italian and French fabrics, with antique and reproduction furniture. Some
★ suites have whirlpool tubs or wood-burning fireplaces, and some have marble fixtures. Unfortunately, views are limited, and rooms facing First Avenue can be noisy. Amenities include in-room cordless phones, shoe shines, the morning newspaper, and access to workout facilities. Pets are welcome. ⊠ *1007 1st Ave., Downtown, 98104* ☎ *206/624–4844 or 800/426–7033* 🖷 *206/621–9009* ⊕ *www.alexishotel.com*

🛏 *65 rooms, 44 suites* ♿ *Restaurant, room service, in-room data ports, minibars, refrigerators, gym, massage, steam room, bar, lobby lounge, laundry service, concierge, meeting rooms, parking (fee), no-smoking floors* ▤ *AE, D, DC, MC, V.*

$$$–$$$$ 🏨 **Edgewater.** The only hotel on a pier beside Elliott Bay, the Edgewater has spacious waterfront accommodations with balconies providing views of ferries, barges, and the Olympic Mountains. All rooms, including those facing Alaskan Way, have fireplaces and are decorated in rustic plaids and peeled-log furniture. From the lobby's comfortable sofas and chairs, you can sometimes watch sea lions frolicking in the bay. A courtesy van shuttles patrons to the Downtown area on a first-come, first-served basis. ✉ *Pier 67, 2411 Alaskan Way, Belltown, 98121* ☎ *206/728–7000 or 800/624–0670* 🖷 *206/441–4119* ⊕ *www.noblehousehotels.com* 🛏 *237 rooms* ♿ *Restaurant, room service, in-room data ports, minibars, gym, bicycles, bar, laundry service, concierge, meeting rooms, parking (fee), no-smoking rooms* ▤ *AE, D, DC, MC, V.*

$$$–$$$$ 🏨 **Westin Hotel.** The flagship of the Westin chain often hosts U.S. presidents and other visiting dignitaries. Northeast of Pike Place Market, Seattle's largest hotel is easily recognizable by its twin cylindrical towers. The innovative design gives all rooms terrific views of Puget Sound, Lake Union, the Space Needle, or the city. Airy guest rooms are furnished in a simple, high-quality style; some are equipped with speakerphones and modem hookups. ✉ *1900 5th Ave., Downtown, 98101* ☎ *206/728–1000 or 800/228–3000* 🖷 *206/727–5896* ⊕ *www.westin.com* 🛏 *822 rooms, 43 suites* ♿ *3 restaurants, room service, in-room data ports, some in-room faxes, in-room safes, minibars, indoor pool, gym, hair salon, massage, 2 bars, children's programs (ages 0–17), laundry service, concierge, business services, convention center, car rental, parking (fee), no-smoking floors* ▤ *AE, D, DC, MC, V.*

$$$–$$$$
Fodor'sChoice
★
🏨 **WSeattle.** Easily Seattle's coolest hotel, "the W" manages to maintain a welcoming and relaxed tone. Candlelight and custom-designed board games encourage lingering around the lobby fireplace on deep couches strewn with throw pillows. Nearby bookshelves hold art books, and rough-hewn wood bowls cradle shiny green apples. Decorated in black, brown, and French blue, guest rooms are almost austere, but beds are exceptionally comfortable with pillow-top mattresses and 100% goose-down pillows and comforters. Floor-to-ceiling windows maximize striking views of the Sound and the city. ✉ *1112 4th Ave., Downtown, 98101* ☎ *206/264–6000 or 877/946–8357* 🖷 *206/264–6100* ⊕ *www.whotels.com* 🛏 *419 rooms, 16 suites* ♿ *Restaurant, room service, in-room data ports, in-room safes, minibars, gym, bar, laundry service, concierge, business services, meeting rooms, parking (fee), no-smoking floors* ▤ *AE, D, DC, MC, V.*

★ **$$$** 🏨 **Marriott Waterfront.** Finally, another hotel takes advantage of Seattle's prime waterfront real estate. All rooms face the water (half have balconies) in this long narrow building overlooking the shoreline. For the best views, book the north tower. The elegant lobby has cascading Italian chandeliers, walnut detailing, glass-tile mosaic floors, and back-lit walls of fused onyx and glass. High tea is served in the gallery, a breeze-way that joins the lobby with Todd English's Fish Club Restaurant. Wireless Internet access is available in all of the hotel's public spaces. Irons, ironing boards, hair dryers, and a complimentary newspaper come with each room. ✉ *2100 Alaskan Way, between Piers 62/63 and Pier 66, Belltown 98121* ☎ *206/443–5000 or 800/228–9290* 🖷 *206/256–1100* ⊕ *www.gowestmarriott.com/seattlewaterfront* 🛏 *345 rooms, 13 suites* ♿ *Restaurant, café, room service, in-room data ports, indoor-outdoor pool, gym, bar, dry cleaning, laundry service, concierge, concierge floor, business services, meeting rooms, airport shuttle, parking (fee), no-smoking rooms* ▤ *AE, D, DC, MC, V.*

$$$ ☒ **Paramount Hotel.** The Paramount is a château-style hotel close to fine dining, shopping, and high-tech entertainment sites including Gameworks, Niketown, and a 16-screen multiplex theater. Inside, the comfortable lobby—with a fireplace, bookshelves, and period reproductions—looks like a country gentleman's smoking parlor. Decorated in hunter green and beige with gray accents, guest rooms are quiet but small. All have work areas, lounge chairs, and large bathrooms. ☒ *724 Pine St., Downtown, 98101* ☎ *206/292–9500 or 800/663–1144* ☐ *206/292–8610* ⊕ *www.paramounthotelseattle.com* ☜ *146 rooms, 2 suites ⚷ Restaurant, room service, in-room data ports, cable TV with movies and video games, gym, laundry service, concierge, meeting rooms, parking (fee), no-smoking rooms* ☐ *AE, D, DC, MC, V.*

$$$ ☒ **Seattle Hilton.** West of I–5, the Seattle Hilton is a popular site for meetings. The rooms, tasteful but nondescript, have soothing color schemes. Providing excellent views, the Top of the Hilton bar-restaurant serves well-prepared salmon dishes and other local specialties. An underground passage connects the Hilton with the Rainier Square shopping concourse, the 5th Avenue Theater, and the convention center. ☒ *1301 6th Ave., Downtown, 98101* ☎ *206/624–0500, 800/542–7700, or 800/426–0535* ☐ *206/682–9029* ⊕ *www.hilton.com* ☜ *237 rooms, 3 suites ⚷ 2 restaurants, room service, in-room data ports, minibars, gym, piano bar, laundry service, concierge, business services, meeting rooms, parking (fee), no-smoking floors* ☐ *AE, D, DC, MC, V.*

$$–$$$$
FodorśChoice
★
☒ **Inn at the Market.** This sophisticated yet unpretentious property up the street from Pike Place Market oozes personality. The good-size rooms have comfortable modern furniture and small touches such as fresh flowers and ceramic sculptures. Ask for a room with views of the Market and Elliott Bay. Coffee and the morning newspaper are complimentary. Comfortably furnished with Adirondack chairs, the fifth-floor deck overlooks the water and the Market. Restaurants include Campagne and the less formal yet equally romantic café Bacco, which serves tasty variations on breakfast classics. For a fee you have access to a health club and spa down the street. ☒ *86 Pine St., Downtown, 98101* ☎ *206/443–3600 or 800/446–4484* ☐ *206/448–0631* ⊕ *www.innatthemarket.com* ☜ *60 rooms, 10 suites ⚷ 3 restaurants, room service, in-room data ports, refrigerators, laundry service, concierge, meeting room, parking (fee), no-smoking rooms* ☐ *AE, D, DC, MC, V.*

$$–$$$
FodorśChoice
★
☒ **Inn at Harbor Steps.** On the lower floors of a high-rise residential building, this hotel is a departure for Four Sisters Inns, whose collection of small hotels focuses on quaint city and country properties. The entrance and corridors, in muted gray, tan, and sage, have something of a yuppie-dormitory feel, but guest rooms are large, with high ceilings, gas fireplaces, and tidy kitchenettes. Bathrooms accommodate large tubs (some of them whirlpools) and oversize glass-enclosed shower stalls. A tempting breakfast buffet is served in the dining room. Complimentary hors d'oeuvres, wine, and tea are served each afternoon in the library. ☒ *1221 1st Ave., Downtown, 98101* ☎ *206/748–0973 or 888/728–8910* ☐ *206/748–0533* ⊕ *www.foursisters.com* ☜ *30 rooms ⚷ In-room data ports, refrigerators, indoor pool, gym, sauna, basketball, laundry facilities, laundry service, concierge, meeting room, parking (fee)* ☐ *AE, MC, V* ○ *BP.*

$$–$$$ ☒ **Red Lion Hotel on 5th Avenue.** In the heart of Downtown, this former bank headquarters is a comfortable business-oriented hotel convenient to the shopping and financial districts. Service is warm and professional; the public spaces have high ceilings, tall windows, and dark-wood paneling. Lining the lobby are sitting areas with couches and overstuffed chairs upholstered in olive green and aubergine velvets and brocades. Guest rooms are mid-size and attractively appointed in a green and pink botanical theme.

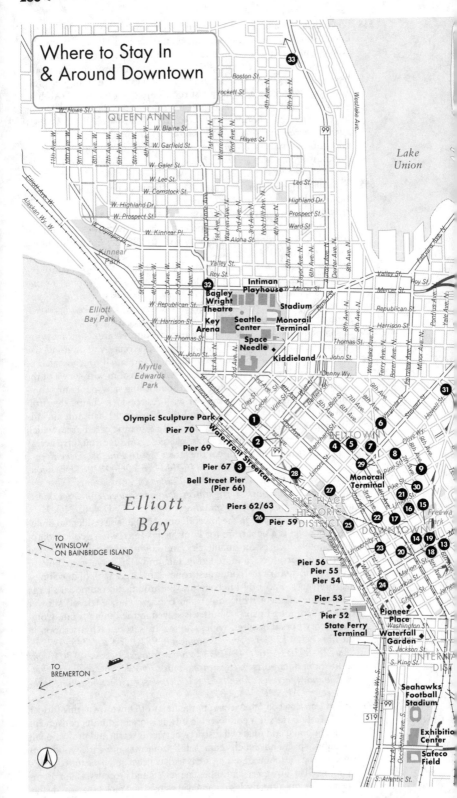

Where to Stay In
& Around Downtown

Downtown & Belltown ▼

Ace Hotel **2**
Alexis Hotel **24**
Claremont Hotel **5**
Crowne Plaza **15**
Edgewater **3**
Elliott Grand Hyatt **9**
Fairmont
Olympic Hotel **17**
Green Tortoise
Backpacker's Hotel **22**
Hostel International
Seattle **25**
Hotel Monaco **20**
Hotel Vintage Park **14**
Inn at Harbor Steps . . .**23**
Inn at the Market **26**
Madison
Renaissance **13**
Marriott Springhill
Suites **31**
Marriott Waterfront . . .**28**
Mayflower Park
Hotel **29**
Pacific Plaza **19**
Paramount Hotel **8**
Pensione Nichols **27**
Red Lion Hotel on
5th Avenue **21**
Seattle Hilton **16**
Seattle Sheraton
Hotel and Towers **30**
Vance Hotel **6**
Wall Street Inn **1**
Warwick Hotel **4**
WSeattle **18**
Westin Hotel **7**

International District &
Pioneer Square ▼
Amaranth Inn **11**
Panama Hotel **12**

First Hill ▼
Sorrento **10**

Fremont ▼
Chelsea Station **33**

Queen Anne ▼
MarQueen Hotel **32**

Seattle-Tacoma
International Airport ▼
Coast Gateway Hotel . . .**38**
Doubletree Hotel
Seattle Airport **35**
Hilton Seattle
Airport and
Conference Center **36**
Marriott Sea-Tac **34**
Wyndham Garden
Hotel **37**

Rooms on the Executive floors, 17–20, have exquisite views of Puget Sound or the city skyline. All rooms are equipped with coffeemakers, hair dryers, irons, and ironing boards. ✉ *1415 5th Ave., Downtown, 98101* ☎ *206/971–8000 or 800/325–4000* 🖷 *206/971–8100* 🌐 *www.redlion.com/5thave* *287 rooms, 10 suites* *Restaurant, room service, in-room data ports, gym, laundry service, concierge, business services, meeting rooms, parking (fee), no-smoking rooms* 💳 *AE, D, DC, MC, V.*

$$–$$$ **Warwick Hotel.** Service is friendly and leisurely (but not slow) at the Warwick, which is part of an international chain. The rooms are understated without being bland; most have small balconies providing Downtown views. Furnishings tend toward the traditional rather than the modern. Brasserie Margeaux, the hotel restaurant-lounge, is a welcome retreat after a day in this bustling neighborhood. The Warwick offers 24-hour courtesy transportation within Downtown. ✉ *401 Lenora St., Belltown, 98121* ☎ *206/443–4300 or 800/426–9280* 🖷 *206/448–1662* 🌐 *www.warwickhotels.com* *225 rooms, 4 suites* *Restaurant, room service, in-room data ports, indoor pool, gym, hot tub, sauna, bar, concierge, parking (fee), no-smoking rooms* 💳 *AE, D, DC, MC, V.*

$$ **Claremont Hotel.** The small lobby of this historic 1926 property has an understated beauty and lots of charm. The original marble wainscoting and fireplace have been affectionately preserved and are accented by a rich terra-cotta wall finish. Guest rooms run the gamut from cramped and viewless standards to spacious suites, some with kitchens. Many rooms have large walk-in closets; all of the bathrooms have been restored in keeping with their original style. The hotel's two-story ballroom is popular for weddings and other festivities. ✉ *2000 4th Ave., Downtown, 98121* ☎ *206/448–8600 or 800/448–8601* 🖷 *206/441–7140* 🌐 *www.claremonthotel.com* *30 rooms, 80 suites* *Restaurant, in-room data ports, gym, laundry service, meeting rooms, parking (fee), no-smoking rooms* 💳 *AE, D, DC, MC, V.*

$$ **Crowne Plaza.** A favorite of business travelers, the Crowne Plaza is directly off I–5, midway between First Hill and the financial district. The lobby is small and plainly appointed in teal and cream with brass accents and potted plants. Rooms are quiet and spacious, with lounge chairs and work areas. All have views of Harbor Island to the south and Elliott Bay, Seattle Center, and the Space Needle to the north. The relaxed and friendly staff is very attentive. ✉ *1113 6th Ave., Downtown, 98101* ☎ *206/464–1980 or 800/521–2762* 🖷 *206/340–1617* 🌐 *www.basshotels.com* *415 rooms, 28 suites* *Restaurant, room service, in-room data ports, health club, sauna, bar, laundry service, concierge, business services, meeting rooms, parking (fee), some pets allowed, no-smoking rooms* 💳 *AE, D, DC, MC, V.*

$$ **Madison Renaissance.** Rooms at this high-rise between Downtown and I–5 are decorated in deep green, burgundy, and brown, with metal accents and dark-wood furniture. Guests on the club-level floors get complimentary Continental breakfast and their own concierge. Amenities on all floors include free coffee, the morning newspaper, and shoe shines. The rooftop health club has a 40-foot pool. ✉ *515 Madison St., Downtown, 98104* ☎ *206/583–0300 or 800/278–4159* 🖷 *206/622–8635* 🌐 *www.renaissance.com* *466 rooms, 88 suites* *2 restaurants, room service, in-room data ports, minibars, pool, hot tub, bar, laundry service, concierge, meeting rooms, parking (fee)* 💳 *AE, D, DC, MC, V* 🍽 *CP.*

$–$$$ **Mayflower Park Hotel.** Brass fixtures, antiques, and lacquered screens give a muted Asian feel to the public and private spaces at this older property near the Westlake Center. Service is smooth and unobtrusive. Rooms are on the small side, but the Mayflower Park is so sturdily constructed that it's much quieter than many modern downtown hotels. You'll have privileges at a nearby health club. ✉ *405 Olive Way, Downtown,*

98101 ☎ *206/623–8700 or 800/426–5100* 🖨 *206/382–6997* ⊕ *www. mayflowerpark.com* 🛏 *159 rooms, 13 suites* ⚴ *Restaurant, room service, gym, bar, laundry service, business services, meeting rooms, parking (fee), no-smoking rooms* ▭ *AE, D, DC, MC, V.*

$–$$ 🏠 **Pensione Nichols.** One block from Pike Place Market, this B&B's location can't be beat. Some rooms have shared bath, but both of the second-floor suites have their own, as well as an enclosed balcony, full kitchen, separate bedroom, and large living room. Evidence of the owner's former life as an antiques collector and shop owner are apparent in the furnishings throughout. Each of the third-floor rooms is unique; most have skylights rather than windows. Breakfast consists of warm breads and fruit fresh from the market served in the natural-light-filled common area overlooking Elliott Bay. ⊠ *1923 1st Ave., Downtown, 98101* ☎ *206/441–7125 or 800/440–7125* 🛏 *10 rooms with shared bath, 2 suites with bath* ▭ *AE, D, DC, MC, V* ⦿ *CP.*

$ 🏠 **Marriott Springhill Suites.** Decorated in cheery yellows, the lobby is open and airy, with large windows, deep couches, a TV tuned to MSNBC, and stacks of *Wall Street Journals.* The all-suites accommodations have large desks, high-speed Internet access, and separate sleeping areas. Amenities include dual-line speakerphones, irons, ironing boards, and coffeemakers. A free shuttle takes you to one of three places Downtown. ⊠ *1800 Yale Ave., Downtown, 98101* ☎ *206/254–0500 or 888/287–9400* 🖨 *206/254–0990* ⊕ *www.springhillsuites.com* 🛏 *234 suites* ⚴ *Restaurant, in-room data ports, microwaves, refrigerators, indoor pool, exercise equipment, hot tub, lobby lounge, laundry facilities, business services, parking (fee), no-smoking rooms* ▭ *AE, D, DC, MC, V* ⦿ *CP.*

$ 🏠 **Wall Street Inn.** Built in the 1950s as a land base for merchant marines, this prime piece of Belltown real estate is now a homey land base for visitors. Guest rooms are comfortably furnished in an appealing mix of styles; some still have Murphy beds. A handful of rooms have kitchenettes, and seven have peek-a-boo views of Elliott Bay and the Olympic Mountains. Partake of the extensive Continental breakfast in front of the fire, on the patio, or back in your room. All rooms have hair dryers, robes, and slippers. ⊠ *2507 1st Ave., Belltown, 98121* ☎ *206/448–0125* 🖨 *206/448–2406* ⊕*www.wallstreetinn.com* 🛏*20 rooms* ⚴ *In-room data ports, some kitchenettes, refrigerators, business services, parking (fee)* ▭ *AE, MC, V* ⦿ *CP.*

★ ¢–$$ 🏠 **Ace Hotel.** "You are beautiful" is etched into every vanity mirror at this ultrahip, super-friendly hostelry in Belltown, and the color scheme is white on white, evoking the movie set for *Sleeper.* Offering the squeaky clean functionality of a Norwegian budget hotel, The Ace serves the nightclubbing public in the most modern of styles. Half the rooms sleep "one or two humans" and share bathrooms. Suites are larger and have full private bathrooms hidden behind rotating walls. Thoughtful amenities in these somewhat austere deluxe accommodations include condoms, *Kama Sutra* books, energy bars, and bottled water. ⊠ *2423 1st Ave., Belltown, 98121* ☎*206/448–4721* 🖨*206/374–0745* ⊕*www.theacehotel. com* 🛏 *24 rooms* ⚴ *Restaurant, room service, in-room data ports, parking (fee), no-smoking rooms* ▭ *AE, D, DC, MC, V.*

¢–$ 🏠 **Pacific Plaza.** Locally owned and independently operated, this 1929 property maintains a low profile. Its Fourth Avenue entrance is through a coffee shop, and its Spring Street entrance is marked only by a small awning. Location (across from the Rem Koolhaas library building), skilled management, and the fair price make this one of the best lodging bargains downtown. Guest beds have tan leather headboards and sage green spreads. The smallish rooms all have ceiling fans and city views. Irons, ironing boards, hair dryers, and coffeemakers are standard. ⊠ *400 Spring St., Downtown, 98104* ☎ *206/623–3900 or 800/426–*

1165 ☎ 206/623–2059 ⊕ www.pacificplazahotel.com ⇨ 159 rooms ⚭ Restaurant, coffee shop, pizzeria, concierge, parking (fee), no-smoking rooms ▤ AE, D, DC, MC, V.

¢–$ ▥ **Vance Hotel.** Close to shopping and the Convention Center, this historic hotel does a tidy little business keeping the budget traveler close to the major Downtown attractions. The small lobby is impressively elegant with its dark marble, original millwork, and deep blue walls. The guest rooms are clean and bright: pretty yellow fabrics were used to create a cheery effect. Rooms facing Stewart Street can get a little noisy during peak traffic times. ⊠ 620 Stewart St., Downtown, 98101 ☎ 206/441–4200 or 877/956–8500 ☎ 206/443–5754 ⊕ www.vancehotel.com ⇨ 169 rooms ⚭ Restaurant, concierge, laundry service, parking (fee), no-smoking floors ▤ AE, D, DC, MC, V.

¢   ▥ **Green Tortoise Backpacker's Hotel.** Kitchen privileges are included with the accommodations at this hostellike hotel one block from the Pike Place Market on a gritty stretch of Second Avenue. This facility is a bit grubby, and some of the front-desk staffers are terminally crabby, but the price is tough to beat. For $20 you can let a bed in a dorm room and spend your days fraternizing with the adventurous, young, international clientele that makes this place a vital travel hub. ⊠ 1525 2nd Ave., Downtown, 98101 ☎ 206/340–1222 ☎ 206/623–3207 ⊕ www.greentortoise.net ⇨ 7 private rooms, 30 dorm rooms all share bath ⚭ Laundry facilities ▤ MC, V.

¢   ▥ **Hostel International Seattle.** For about $20 a night you'll get a dorm-room bed at this hostel near Pike Place Market and the Seattle Art Museum. As is usual with youth hostels around the world, there's a dining room, and kitchen privileges are included in the price. June through August reservations with a credit card are essential. ⊠ 84 Union St., Downtown, 98101 ☎ 206/622–5443 or 888/622–5443 ⊕ www.hiseattle.org ⇨ 10 private rooms, 20 dorm rooms, all share bath ⚭ Library, laundry facilities ▤ AE, MC, V.

International District & Pioneer Square

¢–$ ▥ **Amaranth Inn.** An old Craftsman home just blocks from Chinatown has been converted into a sunny B&B. Common areas include a sunroom, a parlor, and a breakfast room. Guest rooms are done in creams and pale greens with touches of lace and brocades in bedspreads and window treatments; seven have private baths and gas fireplaces. The full breakfasts range from straightforward egg dishes with sausage or bacon to French toast with seasonal fruit, and always includes juice, pastries, coffee, and tea. ⊠ 1451 S. Main St., International District, 98144 ☎ 206/720–7161 or 800/720–7161 ☎ 206/323–0772 ⊕ www.amaranthinn.com ⇨ 8 rooms, 2 with shared bath ⚭ Dining room, free parking; no smoking ▤ AE, D, DC, MC, V ¶◎¶ BP.

★ ¢   ▥ **Panama Hotel.** From the unused traditional Japanese bathhouse in the basement to the lovingly restored teahouse and the unclaimed belongings of families interned during WWII, this 1910 three-story walk-up is almost a time capsule of Japanese culture in Seattle. Owner Pam Johnson sees to many distinctive touches throughout. Climb the steep creaky stairs to immaculate rooms featuring hand-embroidered cotton coverlets, kitschy Asian mementos, and armoires made from refrigerator crates during the 1940s. Rooms have sinks but share bathrooms. Rates include a teahouse breakfast of fresh doughnuts and hot beverages. ⊠ 605½ S. Main St., International District, 98104 ☎ 206/223–9242 ☎ 206/624–4947 ⊕ www.panamahotelseattle.com ⇨ 100 rooms share bath ⚭ Tea shop, laundry facilities, Internet; no room phones, no room TVs, no smoking ▤ AE, D, MC, V ¶◎¶ CP.

First Hill

★ $$$–$$$$ **Sorrento.** Built in 1909, the Sorrento was designed to look like an Italian villa, with a dramatic circular driveway surrounding a palm-fringed fountain. Sitting high on First Hill, the hotel overlooks Downtown and Elliott Bay. Rooms are quiet and comfortable, although some are quite small. The largest are the corner suites, which have spacious baths and some antique furnishings. In the lobby, the dark-panel Fireside Lounge is an inviting spot for coffee, tea, or cocktails; the Hunt Club serves Pacific Northwest dishes. Limousine service within the downtown area is complimentary, as are privileges at a nearby athletic club. ⊠ *900 Madison St., First Hill, 98104* ☎ *206/622–6400 or 800/426–1265* ☎ *206/343–6155* ⊕ *www.hotelsorrento.com* ⇆ *76 rooms, 42 suites ⚑ Restaurant, room service, in-room data ports, in-room fax, minibars, bar, dry cleaning, laundry service, concierge, business services, meeting rooms, parking (fee)* ☰ *AE, D, DC, MC, V.*

Fremont

$–$$ **Chelsea Station.** In a classic Seattle neighborhood across from the Woodland Park Zoo, this B&B offers warm hospitality in a quiet locale. The parlor and breakfast rooms are done in sage green and have Mission-style oak furniture, brocade upholstery, lace curtains, and works by local artists. Spacious guest rooms, each with a writing desk, have both antique and contemporary furnishings. The accommodations in front have views of the Cascades. One suite has a piano, another a kitchen. Several rooms have adjoining doors, useful for families or larger groups. Breakfast can be tailored to your dietary needs upon request. ⊠ *4915 Linden Ave. N, Fremont, 98103* ☎ *206/547–6077 or 800/400–6077* ☎ *206/632–5107* ⊕ *www.bandbseattle.com* ⇆ *2 rooms, 7 suites ⚑ In-room data ports* ☰ *AE, D, DC, MC, V* ⧫ *BP.*

Queen Anne

$$–$$$ **MarQueen Hotel.** A few blocks from the Seattle Center, the MarQueen is ideal for patrons of the opera, ballet, theater, or Key Arena sporting events. Formerly an apartment building, this 1918 brick hotel has a dark lobby with marble floors, overstuffed furniture, Asian-style lacquered screens, and a grand staircase overlooking a garden mural painted on a facing building. The spacious guest rooms, furnished with reproduction antiques, all have kitchens and sitting areas. A complimentary newspaper is left outside the door each morning. ⊠ *600 Queen Ave. N, Queen Anne, 98109* ☎ *206/282–7407 or 888/445–3076* ☎ *206/283–1499* ⊕ *www.marqueen.com* ⇆ *47 rooms, 4 suites ⚑ Room service, in-room data ports, kitchenettes, minibars, microwaves, refrigerators, cable TV, dry cleaning, laundry service, concierge, meeting room, parking (fee), no-smoking rooms* ☰ *AE, D, DC, MC, V.*

Seattle-Tacoma International Airport

★ $$ **Marriott Sea-Tac.** The luxurious Marriott has a five-story, 21,000-square-foot tropical atrium complete with a waterfall, a dining area, an indoor pool, and a lounge. In the guest rooms, greens and mauves compliment dark-wood and brass furnishings. If you must stay in the airport environs, this is your most comfortable option. ⊠ *3201 S. 176th St., Sea-Tac, 98188* ☎ *206/241–2000 or 800/643–5479* ☎ *206/248–0789* ⊕ *www.marriott.com* ⇆ *459 rooms ⚑ Restaurant, room service, in-room data ports, indoor pool, health club, hot tubs, sauna, lobby lounge, laundry service, concierge, meeting rooms, airport shuttle, free parking, no-smoking rooms* ☰ *AE, D, DC, MC, V.*

$ **Doubletree Hotel Seattle Airport.** The lobby of this large convention hotel has wood parquet floors and a fireplace; it's furnished in colors of autumn leaves. Five minutes from the airport and 10 minutes from Southcenter shopping mall, it serves its primarily corporate clientele well.

The orange, yellow, and burgundy color scheme of the lobby is carried into the spacious guest rooms. Some of the suites here are equipped with whirlpool tubs, and the Lakeside Suite—on one corner of the building—has a wraparound balcony overlooking Bow Lake. Irons, ironing boards, and hair dryers are standard equipment. ⊠ *18740 Pacific Hwy. S, Sea-Tac, 98188* ☎*206/246–8600* 🖷*206/431–8687* ⊕*www.doubletreehotels. com* ⇗ *837 rooms, 13 suites* ⚬ *3 restaurants, room service, in-room data ports, pool, gym, hair salon, 2 bars, laundry service, meeting rooms, airport shuttle, parking (fee)* 🚍 *AE, D, DC, MC, V.*

$ 🖻 **Hilton Seattle Airport and Conference Center.** Only a half-hour drive from Downtown, and directly across the street from Sea-Tac airport, this hotel and conference center were designed with the business traveler in mind. Rooms are spacious and cheery, decorated in pale yellows, greens, and burgundy. All come equipped with work desks, iron, ironing board, hair dryer, and robes. In addition to smaller meeting rooms, a full service conference center, which can accommodate up to 1,000 guests, is connected to the hotel by a breezeway. ⊠*17620 Pacific Hwy. S, Sea-Tac, 98188* ☎*206/ 244–4800* 🖷 *206/248–4499* ⊕ *www.hilton.com* ⇗ *175 rooms, 3 suites* ⚬ *Restaurant, room service, in-room data ports, minibars, refrigerators, cable TV, pool, gym, lounge, dry cleaning, laundry facilities, laundry service, concierge, business services, convention center, meeting rooms, airport shuttle, free parking, no-smoking rooms* 🚍 *AE, D, DC, MC, V.*

¢–$ 🖻 **Wyndham Garden Hotel.** The elegant lobby has a fireplace, a marble floor, and comfortable furniture. Rooms have large desks, overstuffed chairs, irons and boards, coffeemakers, and hair dryers. ⊠ *18118 Pacific Hwy. S, Sea-Tac, 98188* ☎ *206/244–6666* 🖷 *206/244–6679* ⊕ *www.wyndham.com* ⇗ *180 rooms, 24 suites* ⚬ *Restaurant, room service, in-room data ports, indoor pool, gym, lobby lounge, laundry facilities, laundry service, meeting rooms, airport shuttle, free parking, no-smoking floors* 🚍 *AE, D, DC, MC, V.*

¢ 🖻 **Coast Gateway Hotel.** You're allowed to play the baby grand piano in the lobby of this no-frills hotel. The subdued guest rooms are furnished in light wood and calming greens. Nintendo, WebTV, and HBO are all included in the price of the room. Irons, ironing boards, hair dryers, and coffeemakers are also standard. ⊠ *18415 Pacific Hwy. S, Sea-Tac, 98188* ☎ *206/248–8200 or 800/663–1144* 🖷 *206/244–1198* ⊕ *www.coasthotels.com* ⇗ *145 rooms* ⚬ *Room service, in-room data ports, gym, dry cleaning, meeting room, airport shuttle, free parking, no-smoking floors* 🚍 *AE, D, DC, MC, V* ⏀ *CP.*

Capitol Hill

$ 🖻 **Bed and Breakfast on Broadway.** Proprietors Don Fabian and Russel Lyons go out of their way to make you feel comfortable in their home. A Steinway grand piano dominates the music room, and antiques and art, including paintings by co-host Lyons, fill the living room. Queen-size beds with goose-down comforters are standard in the guest rooms, two of which have enclosed balconies. The inn is near restaurants, movie theaters, shops, and a bus stop. ⊠ *722 Broadway Ave. E, Capitol Hill, 98102* ☎ *206/329–8933 or 888/329–8933* 🖷 *206/726–0918* ⊕ *www.bbonbroadway.com* ⇗ *4 rooms* ⚬ *Free parking, no-smoking rooms* 🚍 *AE, D, DC, MC, V* ⏀ *CP.*

¢–$$ 🖻 **Bacon Mansion.** On a tree-lined street near Volunteer Park, this 1909 Tudor is surrounded by gardens. The first-floor living room is filled with comfortable furniture and lots of natural light. Each guest room is appointed with collectibles old and new. The Capitol Suite has a pine four-poster, a carved oak fireplace, and a view of the Space Needle; from the floral-themed Iris Room you can see Mt. Rainier. Several rooms have hideaway beds in addition to the queen-size beds that are the norm. The

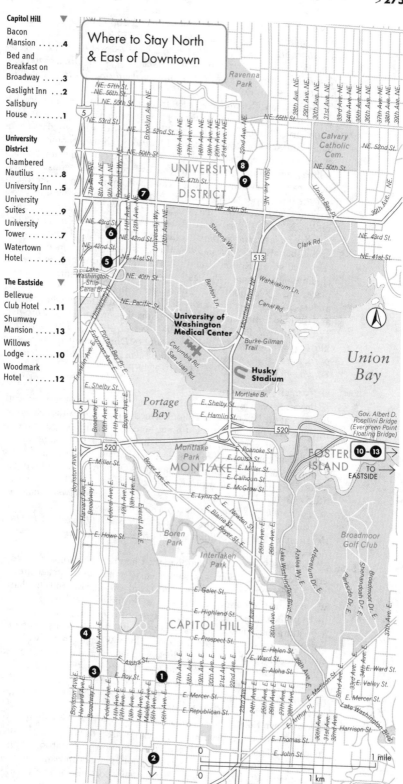

Capitol Hill ▼

Bacon
Mansion 4

Bed and
Breakfast on
Broadway 3

Gaslight Inn ...2

Salisbury
House 1

**University
District** ▼

Chambered
Nautilus 8

University Inn ..5

University
Suites 9

University
Tower 7

Watertown
Hotel 6

The Eastside ▼

Bellevue
Club Hotel ...11

Shumway
Mansion 13

Willows
Lodge 10

Woodmark
Hotel 12

Where to Stay North & East of Downtown

restored carriage house provides larger quarters; upstairs, the former chauffeur's quarters now serve as a cozy loft. ☒ *959 Broadway Ave. E, at E. Prospect St., Capitol Hill, 98102* ☏ *206/329–1864 or 800/240–1864* 🖷*206/860–9025* ⊕*www.baconmansion.com* ⇨*11 rooms, 2 share bath; 2 suites* ♿ *In-room data ports, some refrigerators, library; no a/c, no smoking* ☰ *AE, D, DC, MC, V* ⏐○⏐ *CP.*

¢–$$ 🛏 **Gaslight Inn.** Rooms here range from a crow's nest with peeled-log

Fodor'sChoice furniture and Navajo-print fabrics to suites with gas fireplaces and an-

★ tique carved beds. There's also an apartment with a blown-glass chandelier and views of Downtown and Elliott Bay. The large common areas evoke a gentlemen's club, with oak wainscoting, animal statuary, high ceilings, and hunter-green carpet. One owner's past career as a professional painter is evident in the impeccable custom-mixed finishes throughout the inn. Those staying in studios and suites receive free off-street parking. ☒ *1727 15th Ave., Capitol Hill, 98122* ☏ *206/325–3654* 🖷*206/328–4803* ⊕*www.gaslight-inn.com* ⇨*9 rooms, 7 suites* ♿ *Pool, laundry facilities, no-smoking rooms* ☰ *AE, MC, V* ⏐○⏐ *CP.*

¢–$ 🛏 **Salisbury House.** Built in 1904, this Craftsman house sits on a wide, tree-lined street. Rooms contain an eclectic collection of furniture, including some antiques. The basement suite has a private entrance, a fireplace, and a whirlpool bath. The Rose Room is filled with rose chintz and has a canopy bed, the Lavender Room is furnished in white wicker, and the Blue Room has a deck overlooking the garden. ☒ *750 16th Ave. E, Capitol Hill, 98112* ☏ *206/328–8682* 🖷 *206/720–1019* ⊕ *www. salisburyhouse.com* ⇨ *4 rooms, 1 suite* ♿ *Dining room, in-room data ports, business services; no a/c, no cable TV in some rooms, no kids under 12, no smoking* ☰ *AE, DC, MC, V* ⏐○⏐ *BP.*

University District

$–$$ 🛏 **University Inn.** This impeccable inn is mainly frequented by travelers with business at the UW or the surrounding medical facilities, although leisure travelers also find themselves at home here. The traditional guest rooms in the original wing, built in the 1960s, have smallish bathrooms, but on the plus side, many have balconies. A newer wing was built in the late 1980s; its junior suites have such amenities as microwaves and refrigerators. ☒*4140 Roosevelt Way NE, University District, 98105* ☏*206/632– 5055 or 800/733–3855* 🖷*206/547–4937* ⊕*www.universityinnseattle.com* ⇨*102 rooms* ♿ *Restaurant, in-room data ports, in-room safes, some microwaves, some refrigerators, outdoor pool, exercise equipment, hot tub, dry cleaning, laundry facilities, meeting rooms, free parking, no-smoking floors* ☰ *AE, D, DC, MC, V* ⏐○⏐ *CP.*

$–$$ 🛏 **University Suites.** A companion to the Chambered Nautilus, this property is a four-plex that was converted to suites with kitchenettes in 1998. Three of the units have separate bedrooms. The Ravenna has hardwood floors throughout, an antique cast-iron bed, and herb print tiles in the kitchen. The Cascades Suite has two bedrooms and, from the porch, a breathtaking view of its namesake mountains. Expertly prepared breakfasts are served at the B&B next door. Whereas they always include granola, perhaps you'll be lucky enough to try the owner's famed stuffed French toast. ☒ *5005 22nd Ave. NE, University District, 98105* ☏*206/522–2536* 🖷*206/528–0898* ⊕*www.chamberednautilus.com* ⇨*4 rooms* ♿ *Kitchenettes, microwaves, refrigerators, cable TV with movies; no smoking* ☰ *AE, MC, V* ⏐○⏐ *BP.*

★ $–$$ 🛏 **Watertown Hotel.** The developer of this property is a boater and an architect, and his predilection and profession are reflected in the exposed concrete and metal construction, porthole windows in bathroom doors, and the clean lines of the fountains and pools. Grasses and smooth river rock enhance the landscaping, while specially commissioned artworks add visual interest to the public areas. In the guest rooms, space-saving closets are accessible from two sides, big operable windows let in lots of light, and blackout curtains let you keep things dark. Rooms have full-length mirrors and come with irons, ironing boards, and coffeemakers. Free wine tastings nightly. ⊠ *4242 Roosevelt Way NE, University District, 98105* ☎ *206/826–4242 or 800/944–4242* 🖷 *206/ 315–4242* ⊕ *www.watertownseattle.com* 🗗 *155 rooms* ⚏ *Restaurant, in-room data ports, in-room safes, microwaves, refrigerators, exercise equipment, bicycles, laundry facilities, meeting rooms, free parking; no smoking* ⊟ *AE, D, DC, MC, V* ⦿ *CP.*

$ 🏠 **Chambered Nautilus.** You can't miss the bright red door of this Georgian Colonial Revival home near the University of Washington. Its big living room has Oriental rugs, a fireplace, and a sideboard stocked with cookies and coffee. Each guest room has a queen-size bed with down comforters, and many have private porches. Two have fireplaces. The Scallop Room has a wood-burning stove and is trimmed in khaki and green, while the larger Sunrise Room has yellow walls and crisp blue and white bedding. The noteworthy breakfasts might include roasted pears with caramel sauce or individual crustless quiches in ramekins. ⊠ *5005 22nd Ave. NE, University District, 98105* ☎ *206/522–2536* 🖷 *206/528–0898* ⊕ *www.chamberednautilus.com* 🗗 *6 rooms, 4 suites* ⚏ *Cable TV; no kids under 8, no smoking* ⊟ *AE, MC, V* ⦿ *BP.*

$ 🏨 **University Tower.** Within blocks of the University of Washington, this 1931 property (owned by the Best Western chain) has been restored to its original art deco elegance. Guest rooms are bathed in soothing shades of white with bright-red lounge chairs for bold contrast. The rooms, whose amenities include coffeemakers, hair dryers, and irons with ironing boards, have unparalleled views of the university, Mt. Rainier, Green Lake, or Lake Union. Rates include the morning newspaper and Continental breakfast. ⊠ *4507 Brooklyn Ave. NE, University District, 98105* ☎ *206/634–2000 or 800/899–0251* 🖷 *206/547–6029* ⊕ *www. meany.com* 🗗 *155 rooms* ⚏ *Restaurant, in-room data ports, gym, bar, laundry service, concierge, meeting rooms, free parking, no-smoking rooms* ⊟ *AE, D, DC, MC, V* ⦿ *CP.*

The Eastside

★ **$$$$** 🏨 **Willows Lodge.** A dramatically lit old growth Douglas Fir snag greets you at the entrance to this spa hotel. Timbers salvaged from a 19th-century warehouse lend rustic counterpoints to the lodge's sleek modern design. A stone fireplace dominates the lobby, and contemporary Native-American prints and sculptures by area artists adorn the walls and gardens. All guest rooms have fireplaces, oversize soaking tubs, and CD and DVD players. Bathrooms have a pair of freestanding stone sinks that resemble salad bowls and have industrial-looking spigots. The spa offers both beauty and rejuvenating treatments. ⊠ *14580 NE 145th St., Woodinville 98072* ☎ *425/424–3900 or 877/424–3930* 🖷 *425/424– 2585* ⊕ *www.willowslodge.com* 🗗 *83 rooms, 5 suites* ⚏ *Restaurant, room service, in-room data ports, in-room safes, minibars, refrigerators, pool, gym, spa, bar, laundry service, concierge, business services, meeting rooms, free parking* ⦿ *CP* ⊟ *AE, D, DC, MC, V.*

★ **$$$–$$$$** 🏨 **Bellevue Club Hotel.** This modern boutique hotel has won numerous design awards. Warm earthtones coupled with the clever use of lighting create the illusion of sunlight even when it's raining outside. Original oil paintings by Northwest artist Mark Rediske hang in each room. Pillows made from African Kuba textiles, Turkish area rugs, and *raku* pottery offset cherry furniture. All rooms have plush armchairs and large, spa-inspired, limestone-tile bathrooms with tubs and separate glass-enclosed showers. ⊠ *11200 SE 6th St., Bellevue 98004* ☎ *425/454–4424*

or 800/579–1110 🖷 *425/688–3101* ⊕ *www.bellevueclub.com/hotel.
htm* 🛏 *64 rooms, 3 suites* 🍴 *2 restaurants, room service, in-room data
ports, in-room safes, minibars, refrigerators, tennis court, pool, health
club, hot tub, spa, basketball, lounge, laundry service, concierge, business services, meeting rooms, parking (fee)* 🖃 *AE, DC, MC, V.*

★ **$$$–$$$$** ▦ **Woodmark Hotel.** The Woodmark is the only hotel on Lake Wash-
ington's shores. Its contemporary-style rooms—which face the water, a
courtyard, or the street—are done in shades of café au lait, taupe, and
ecru. Numerous amenities include terry bathrobes, coffeemakers, irons,
hair dryers, complimentary shoe shines, and the morning paper. A cir-
cular staircase, descending from the lobby to the Library Bar, passes a
huge bay window with a panoramic view of Lake Washington. Waters
Bistro serves Pacific Rim cuisine, with dishes such as lemongrass steamed
clams, and grilled halibut with roasted onion-ginger relish. ⊠ *1200 Car-
illon Pt., Kirkland 98033* ☎ *425/822–3700 or 800/822–3700* 🖷 *425/
822–3699* ⊕ *www.thewoodmark.com* 🛏 *79 rooms, 21 suites* 🍴 *Restau-
rant, room service, in-room data ports, in-room safes, minibars, refrig-
erators, gym, spa, bar, laundry service, concierge, business services,
meeting rooms, parking (fee)* 🖃 *AE, DC, MC, V.*

¢–$ ▦ **Shumway Mansion.** This B&B at Juanita Beach is close to downtown
Kirkland. Oriental carpets and a gas fireplace lend warmth to its par-
lor. Guest rooms are named after local towns: The Kirkland Suite has
a separate sitting area for reading, watching TV, or trying to catch a
glimpse of Lake Washington through the trees: a task more easily ac-
complished in the winter months. The Redmond offers a four-poster bed
and a sitting porch. A full breakfast is served each morning; there are
homemade cookies in the evening. ⊠ *11410 99th Pl. NE, Kirkland 98033*
☎ *425/823–2303* 🖷 *425/822–0421* ⊕ *www.shumwaymansion.com*
🛏 *8 rooms* 🍴 *In-room data ports, business services; no a/c, no kids under
12, no smoking* 🖃 *AE, MC, V* ⏺ *BP.*

NIGHTLIFE & THE ARTS

Nightlife

Updated by
Holly S. Smith

The Stranger and *Seattle Weekly* give detailed music, art, and nightlife
listings, as well as hot tips and suggestions for the week's events. Fri-
day editions of the *Seattle Times* and the *Seattle Post-Intelligencer* in-
clude weekend pullout sections detailing arts and entertainment events.
Shows usually begin around 9 PM, and cover charges range from $5 for
local acts and weeknight admissions to $20 for touring acts. The joint
cover charge of $10 gets you into up to 10 Pioneer Square blues, jazz,
and rock clubs. Bars and clubs stay open until 2 AM, with the rare ex-
ception of alcohol-free after-hours events.

Ticketmaster (☎ 206/628–0888 ⊕ www.ticketmaster.com) sells tickets
to most arts, entertainment, and sports events in the Seattle area. The
two locations of **Ticket/Ticket** (⊠ Broadway Market, 401 Broadway E,
2nd fl., Capitol Hill ☎ 206/324–2744 ⊠ Pike Place Information Booth,
1st Ave. and Pike St., Downtown ☎ 206/682–7453 Ext. 226) sell half-
price tickets to many events on the day of the show (or the previous day
for a matinee). Sales are cash and in-person only. The independent on-
line ticket company ⊕ www.ticketweb.com sells local-event tickets. For
movie show times and theater locations of current releases, call the *Seat-
tle Times* **InfoLine** (☎ 206/464–2000 Ext. 3456).

Bars

★ **Alibi Room** (⊠ 85 Post Alley, Downtown ☎ 206/623–3180), a wood-
paneled bar in Pike Place Market, is where well-dressed Seattle film-in-

dustry talents sip double martinis and hash out ideas while taking in views of Elliott Bay or studying the scripts, handbills, and movie posters that line the walls. It's an ever-cool yet low-key place. Stop by for a drink or a meal, or stay to catch a live band and dance.

Art Bar (✉ 1516 2nd Ave., Belltown ☎ 206/622–4344) has high ceilings, exposed-brick walls, and artfully arranged paintings and sculptures. Escape the crush of the main "gallery" by heading to the more subdued lounge, which has a pool table, in back. Entertainment could be a jazz ensemble, a DJ, or an author reading—it really depends on the night.

★ **Bada Lounge** (✉ 2230 1st Ave., Belltown ☎ 206/374–8717) is a sleek spot with a New York vibe, an Asian-inspired menu, and a Parisian-pretty crowd. Regulars on the club circuit slink up to the posh, crimson-lit alcove to sip pricey drinks and nibble on sushi. "Hypnotic," an open-mike showcase for actors, poets, singers, and storytellers happens the second and fourth Monday of each month.

Capitol Club (✉ 414 E. Pine St., Capitol Hill ☎ 206/325–2149) is a sumptuous escape where you can sprawl upon tasseled floor cushions to dish with your friends and dine on Middle Eastern treats. Peek into the private Blue Room, where the powerful and famous dine in peace—but even they can't smoke until after 10 PM.

Cha Cha Lounge (✉ 504 E. Pine St., Capitol Hill ☎ 206/329–1101) is a dark bohemian place, where up-and-comers congregate under the thatched roof of the crimson-walled main bar or at tables in the smoky back room. The sign on the door says it all: IF YOU ARE RACIST, SEXIST, HOMOPHOBIC, OR AN A - - - - - -, DON'T COME IN.

Lead Gallery Wine Bar (✉ 1022 1st Ave., Belltown ☎ 206/623–6240) lets you sip a savory Washington vintage while wandering through a gallery of contemporary art. After a couple of glasses you might just plunk down your credit card for a one-of-a-kind work.

Linda's Tavern (✉ 707 E. Pine St., Capitol Hill ☎ 206/325–1220), with its buffalo head and its wagon-wheel lights, is as western as a Montana cowboy bar, albeit one that's smack in the middle of the urbane Pike–Pine corridor. A neighborhood crowd gossips over a jukebox that beats out everything from lounge to punk.

Palomino (✉ 1420 5th Ave., Downtown ☎ 206/623–1300) is a classy place to stop for a drink after a shopping spree. Gleaming marble, wood, and glass accents surround the city's longest bar, and original paintings by the late Seattle artist Ambrose Patterson grace the walls. An adjacent lounge serves tapas and drinks.

Red Door (✉ 3401 Evanston Ave. N, Fremont ☎ 206/547–7521), a one-time biker dive nicknamed "Loud Door" for its weekend cacophony, has acquired considerable polish through the years. Fremont's diverse crowds mingle, sample microbrews, and slurp beer-steamed clams.

Sunset Tavern (✉ 5433 Ballard Ave. NW, Ballard ☎ 206/784–4880), a Chinese restaurant turned trendy bar, attracts everyone from college punks and sorority chicks to post-grad nomads and neighborhood old-timers. All come for the ever-changing music acts and Wednesday night karaoke backed by a live band.

Tini Bigs (✉ 100 Denny Way, Queen Anne ☎ 206/284–0931) attracts successful-looking couples, who drink martinis (there are 27 variations served here) and chat about each other through a thin, cigar-smoke haze. Black walls and shiny tables dimly lit with pink lights ensure the stylish a proper stage.

Virginia Inn (✉ 1937 1st Ave., Downtown ☎ 206/728–1937) blends the gaiety of the Pike Place Market district with the artsy vibe from neighboring Belltown. It's an institution, really; the kind of place where crowds spill out onto the patio on warm summer evenings.

Brewpubs

Big Time Brewery (✉ 4133 University Way NE, University District ☎ 206/545–4509) belongs more in yuppieville than the U-District, with its neat brick walls, polished wood floors, and vintage memorabilia. At least 10 beers—including pale ale, amber, and porter—are always on tap; tours of the adjacent brewery tell the whole story.

Dad Watson's (✉ 3601 Fremont Ave., Fremont ☎ 206/632–6505), which offers the same 17 brews as its sister operations, Six Ales and McMenamin's, is a popular stop on the Fremont Pub Crawl.

Elysian Brewing Company (✉ 1221 E. Pike St., Capitol Hill ☎ 206/860–1920), a large, industrial-looking space, lets you sample house concoctions at the copper-stamped upstairs bar or the downstairs lounge.

Elysian Tangle Town (✉ 2601 N. 55th St., Fremont ☎ 206/547–5929), owned by the same people as Capitol Hill's Elysian Brewing Company, is a snug, one-room, neighborhood bar that carries the same brews as its sister operation along with a few specialties of its own.

Hales Ales Brewery and Pub (✉ 4301 Leary Way NW, Fremont ☎ 206/782–0737) produces unique English-style ales and the nitrogen-conditioned Cream Ale, Special Bitter, and Stout. The pub's signature brews are its Pale Ale and Amber Ale.

McMenamin's (✉ 200 Roy St., Queen Anne ☎ 206/285–4722) is part of the same Portland-based brewpub chain as Six Ales, with the same brands on tap. It's a no-smoking spot that's a madhouse when Seattle Center events let out.

Pike Pub and Brewery (✉ 1415 1st Ave., Downtown ☎ 206/622–6044) is a cavernous bar and restaurant operated by the brewers of the renowned Pike Place Pale Ale. It also houses the Seattle Microbrewery Museum and an excellent shop with home-brewing supplies.

★ **Redhook Brewery** (✉ 14300 NE 145th St., Woodinville ☎ 425/483–3232) is a large complex with a pub, a beer garden, a gift shop, and brewing facilities. Tours ($1) run several times daily—enter sober, sample the half-dozen beers (with refills!), and totter your way back down to the bar.

Six Arms (✉ 300 E. Pike St., Capitol Hill ☎ 206/223–1698), named for its six-armed Indian dancer logo, is a spacious brewpub with 17 house and craft beers on tap. Two that stand out are the medium-bodied Hammerhead, and the dark Terminator Stout. As you head back to the rest rooms, note the fermenting tanks painted with amusing murals.

Coffeehouses

B&O Espresso (✉ 204 Belmont Ave. E, Capitol Hill ☎ 206/322–5028) is a cute, cozy neighborhood favorite—with one of the city's last indoor smoking sections. This was one of Seattle's earliest purveyors of the magical elixir known as the latte, and the drinks are still sheer perfection. The on-site bakery turns out gorgeous desserts.

Bauhaus (✉ 301 E. Pine St., Capitol Hill ☎ 206/625–1600) is a smart café in the heart of the Pike–Pine corridor where you can mingle with intellectuals on the rise. The bookshelf-lined walls are full of art and architecture books; the tables are full of punks and nerds.

Habitat Espresso (✉ 202 Broadway E, Capitol Hill ☎ 206/329–3087), a coffee collective, serves organic coffees and teas, baked goods, sandwiches, and soups. Profits from food and beverage sales go to charities as do those from the souvenirs that are also available.

Septième (✉ 214 Broadway E, Capitol Hill ☎ 206/860–8858) is like a French bistro, with its red-walled dining room, its banquettes, and tables draped in white cloths. But you won't find a supersize bowl of mocha (generously topped with whipped cream) in France. On summer nights you can sip your java to rumba and salsa music by the light of tiki torches.

FodorśChoice **Vivace Roasteria** (✉ 901 E. Denny Way, Capitol Hill ☎ 206/860–5869),
★ with its curving bar and checkerboard floor, is considered by many as

the home of Seattle's finest espresso. Carefully trained *baristas* "pull" espresso drinks made with the café's own blend. The neighboring **Espresso Vivace Sidewalk Bar** (⊠ 321 Broadway Ave. E., Capitol Hill ☏ No phone) has quick-as-a-flash service for take-away drinks. **Wit's End** (⊠ 4642 Fremont Ave. N, Fremont ☏ 206/547–2330) bookstore has a tearoom where you can sip world blends while perusing your purchases. What's more, the event stage brings folk-music jams (Friday), poetry readings (Sunday), acoustic gatherings (Tuesday), and openmike literary readings (first and third Wednesdays).

Gay & Lesbian Spots

aro.space (⊠ 925 E. Pike St., Capitol Hill ☏ 206/320–0424), a sprawling club, brought DJ culture to Seattle. Its turntable masters spin in a space that's reminiscent of the spaceship in Stanley Kubrick's *2001*. The mood is tongue-in-cheek at the weekly drag events, but when the music starts to pump, the dance floor gets serious.
Changes (⊠ 2103 N. 45th St., Wallingford ☏ 206/545–8363) is one of the few gay bars *not* on Capitol Hill. Locals make a night of it on karaoke Monday and Wednesday.
Cuff Complex (⊠ 1533 13th Ave., Capitol Hill ☏ 206/323–1525) strives to be a manly leather bar but attracts all shapes, sizes, and styles. The loud crowded dance floor is tucked away downstairs; the main-floor bar, with its patio, is the place to be on warm nights.
Man Ray (⊠ 514 E. Pine St., Capitol Hill ☏ 206/568–0750) takes you through a time portal to a sparkling-white future world with multiple video monitors bejeweling the circular bar. Try more than a couple of the 30-plus martinis. In summer, the upscale crowd likes to relax on the lanai, which is complete with a fountain.
Neighbors (⊠ 1509 Broadway, Capitol Hill ☏ 206/324–5358), with an entrance in an alley between Pike and Pine streets, isn't easy to find. But keep looking as this bar and dance club is a gay institution thanks in part to its drag shows, theme nights, and relaxed atmosphere.
Re-Bar (⊠ 1114 Howell St., Capitol Hill ☏ 206/233–9873) is a veteran gay bar with a loyal following that enjoys the cabaret shows and weekend stage performances. It's a great place to dance, and everyone has fun at the legendary Queer Disco party on Thursday—just dress the part.
Timberline Tavern (⊠ 2015 Boren Ave., Capitol Hill ☏ 206/622–6220), *the* place for honky-tonkin' and Seattle's only country and western dance club for gays and lesbians, is beloved. Come early Tuesday through Thursday evenings for beginning and advanced dancing lessons.
The Wildrose (⊠ 1021 E. Pike St., Capitol Hill ☏ 206/324–9210) is one of Seattle's few lesbian bars, so expect a mob nearly every night. The crowd at weeknight karaoke is fun and good-natured, cheering for pretty much anyone. Weekends are raucous, so grab a window table early and settle in for perpetual ladies' night.

Music Clubs

DANCE
★ **The Baltic Room** (⊠ 1207 E. Pine St., Capitol Hill ☏ 206/625–4444), a classy piano bar turned art deco cocktail club, has quietly become the favorite haunt of a sophisticated clientele. Dress up, but try to keep it comfortable. Top-quality, lesser-known rock, acid jazz, blues, and folk artists attract in-the-know music crowds as well as some celebs to a compact stage area.
Bohemian Reggae Club (⊠ 111 Yesler Way, Pioneer Square ☏ 206/447–1514), considered by many to be the city's best dance club, is where the hip-hop and reggae crowds chill to Nelly, Ja Rule, Eve, and others. National acts perform at the adjacent Bohemian Backstage, and two DJs spin a groove on weekends. Don't be put off by the metal detectors and brawny security guys—in Seattle, they're just for show.

Catwalk (⊠ 172 S. Washington St., Pioneer Square ☎ 206/622–1863), an ultrafashionable three-room haunt, is where *everyone* dresses as if they're out to strut the runway rather than simply to dance. Theme nights include costume balls, lesbian parties, and the monthly Utopia bash with trapeze artists, jugglers, fire-walkers, and other carnival acts. Stay for the after-hours party if you can't get enough.

★ **Century Ballroom** (⊠ 915 E. Pine St., 2nd fl., Capitol Hill ☎ 206/324–7263) is an elegant place for dinner and dancing, with a trendy restaurant and a polished, 2,000-square-foot dance floor. Salsa and swing events often include lessons in the cover charge. There's no smoking, it's 21 and over, and only leather-soled shoes are allowed on the floor.

The Last Supper Club (⊠ 124 S. Washington St., Pioneer Square ☎ 206/748–9975), a festive club in a hard-partying district, attracts the young and the trendy. House music and disco rock the walls, and the spacious dance floor is jammed on weekend drag nights.

Pampas Room (⊠ 2505 1st Ave., Belltown ☎ 206/728–1337), hidden beneath the top-rated El Gaucho restaurant, is a first-class, 1950s-style club. House band plays a mix of jazz, swing, and salsa into the wee hours. Weekends pack in the professional dancers; if you can't keep up, try blending into the mellower weeknight crowd. Dress way up, check your confidence, and step onto the dance floor.

Polly Esthers & Culture Club (⊠ 332 5th Ave. N, Queen Anne ☎ 206/279–1977) is a two-story retro dance club spinning '70s and '80s favorites beneath a disco ball. Bare walls, strobe lights, and worn carpet surround the post-college crowd. Weekends are a crush.

700 Club (⊠ 700 Virginia Ave., Downtown ☎ 206/343–7518) draws twentysomething singles to its dark basement rooms. Soft red light falls onto card tables surrounded by stackable chairs; patrons sit, smoke, drink, and listen to live or DJ-spun hip-hop, funk, and acid jazz. The dance floor undulates with highly individual moves.

The Vogue (⊠ 1516 11th Ave., Capitol Hill ☎ 206/324–5778), a spacious club on the Pike–Pine corridor, gets cozy fast as crowds squeeze in and groove to the latest alternative and industrial beats. Artful hair and piercings are all the rage on Saturday's New Wave night; bring your leather and props for Fetish Night on Sunday.

Washington Dance Club (⊠ 1017 Stewart St., Capitol Hill ☎ 206/628–8939) invites everyone to swoosh about the refurbished 1930s Avalon Ballroom, whose 3,000-square-foot maple wood dance floor is polished to perfection. Learn tango, swing, salsa, and ballroom moves with professional dancers, or drop in for a theme party.

JAZZ & R&B **Ballard Firehouse** (⊠ 5429 Russell St. NW, Ballard ☎ 206/784–3516), a Seattle music institution, books local and national blues, rock, and oldies bands nightly.

★ **Dimitriou's Jazz Alley** (⊠ 2037 6th Ave., Downtown ☎ 206/441–9729) is where Seattle's hip and groovy dress up to see nationally known jazz artists. The cabaret-style theater, where intimate tables for two surround the stage, runs smoke-free shows nightly except Monday. Those with reservations for cocktails or dinner, served during the first set, receive priority seating and $2 off the combined meal-and-show ticket.

★ **The Fenix** (⊠ 109 S. Washington St., Pioneer Square ☎ 206/405–4323), Seattle's legendary club, was demolished by a 2001 earthquake but reopened hotter than ever. The three-story behemoth has five circular neon-lit bars, three dance floors, a café, a pool room, and a stage. It's *the* place to jam with top local DJs and rockers.

J & M Café (⊠ 201 1st Ave. S, Pioneer Square ☎ 206/292–0663) crowds singles together at family-style tables. Blues bands jam here most weekends. Expect to party.

ROCK **The Breakroom** ($\boxtimes$ 1325 E. Madison, Capitol Hill $\textcircled{\small{2}}$ 206/860–5155) is *the* place to catch Seattle's alternative rock bands. There are pool and air-hockey tables in an area at the back of the space.

Crocodile Café ($\boxtimes$ 2200 2nd Ave., Belltown $\textcircled{\small{2}}$ 206/441–5611) books alternative music acts nightly except Monday. The main room is usually packed; the back bar is something of a getaway. Nonconcert nights still draw throngs to munch on Mexican and American fare.

Graceland ($\boxtimes$ 109 Eastlake E, Capitol Hill $\textcircled{\small{2}}$ 206/381–3094) is a dimly lit club that specializes in alternative rock. The low-ceiling performance area has the cramped feel of a ship's hold, but the raised seating at the rear offers excellent views of the rockin' on stage and the stompin' on the dance floor. All-ages events are also held here regularly.

Showbox ($\boxtimes$ 1426 1st Ave., Downtown $\textcircled{\small{2}}$ 206/628–3151), near Pike Place Market, presents locally and nationally acclaimed artists. Rave nights and guest DJ appearances are also popular in this one-time ballroom. The lounge area near the entrance is a quieter spot to enjoy the show.

The Sit & Spin ($\boxtimes$ 2219 4th Ave., Belltown $\textcircled{\small{2}}$ 206/441–9484) laundromat—which also houses a bar, nightclub, greasy spoon, and art gallery—is a fun neighborhood dive with nightly live music. It's the perfect spot for the multitasker.

The Arts

The high-tech boom provided an enthusiastic and philanthropic audience for Seattle's blossoming arts community. Benaroya Hall is now a national benchmark for acoustic design. Its main tenant is the Seattle Symphony, led by conductor Gerard Schwarz. At the Seattle Center, the ethereal Marion Oliver McCaw Hall combines Northwest hues and hanging screens in colorful light shows accompanying performances by the Seattle Opera and the Pacific Northwest Ballet.

The Seattle Repertory Theater, also at Seattle Center, hosts new and classical works, as well as preview runs of plays bound for Broadway. The celebrated Seattle Children's Theatre presents plays and musicals written for youths but polished and sophisticated enough for adults. Events for Bumbershoot, Seattle's Labor Day weekend arts festival, are held throughout the Seattle Center grounds.

Dance

Meany Hall for the Performing Arts ($\boxtimes$ 15th Ave. NE and 41st Ave. NE, University District $\textcircled{\small{2}}$ 206/685–2742 $\oplus$ www.meany.org), on the UW campus, hosts important national and international companies September through May. The emphasis is on modern and jazz dance.

On the Boards ($\boxtimes$ 100 W. Roy St., Queen Anne $\textcircled{\small{2}}$ 206/217–9888 $\oplus$ www.ontheboards.org) presents contemporary dance performances, as well as theater, music, and multimedia events. The main subscription series runs from October through May, but events are scheduled nearly every weekend year-round.

Pacific Northwest Ballet ($\boxtimes$ McCaw Hall at the Seattle Center, Mercer St. at 3rd Ave., Queen Anne $\textcircled{\small{2}}$ 206/441–2424 $\oplus$ www.pnb.org), the resident Seattle company and school, has an elegant home at the Seattle Center. The season, which runs September through June, always includes a mix of classic and international productions (think *Swan Lake* and *Carmina Burana*). *The Nutcracker,* with choreography by Kent Stowell and sets by Maurice Sendak, is a Christmastime tradition.

Film

★ **Cinerama** ($\boxtimes$ 2100 4th Ave., Belltown $\textcircled{\small{2}}$ 206/441–3080 $\oplus$ www. cinerama.com), a 1963 cinema scooped up and restored by billionaire Paul Allen, seamlessly blends the luxury of the theater with state-of-the-art technology. Behind the main, standard-size movie screen sits an enormous, 30-foot by 90-foot restored curved panel—one of only three in the world—used to screen old three-strip films like *How the West Was Won*, as well as 70-millimeter presentations of *2001: Space Odyssey*. The sight lines throughout are amazing. Rear-window captioning, assistive listening devices, audio narration, wheelchair access, and other amenities ensure that everyone has an outstanding experience.

Egyptian Theater (⊠ 801 E. Pine St., at Broadway, Capitol Hill ☎ 206/323–4978 theater, 206/324–9996 Seattle International Film Festival), an art deco movie palace that was formerly a Masonic temple, screens first-run films. It's also the prime venue of the wildly popular Seattle International Film Festival.

Grand Illusion Cinema (⊠ 1403 NE 50th St., at University Way, University District ☎ 206/523–3935), Seattle's longest-running independent movie house, was a tiny screening room in the 1930s. Now it's an outstanding home for independent and art films, one whose cozy, 70-seat space feels as comfortable as a home theater—albeit one without a bathroom (you can use the facilities at the coffee shop next door).

Harvard Exit (⊠ 807 E. Roy St., Capitol Hill ☎ 206/323–8986), a first-run and art-film house, is in the former home of the Women's Century Club, hence the quaint, antiques-filled lobby.

Little Theater (⊠ 608 19th Ave., Capitol Hill ☎ 206/675–2055), a former woodworking studio, is a hodgepodge of leftovers: the projector, sound system, 49 seats, and popcorn machine were donated by other neighborhood cinemas. The compact space shows offbeat art-house films, locally produced documentaries, and shorts. Look for special events (free chicken and mashed potatoes at the 7 PM Friday screenings in July) or hilarious stage productions that totally involve the audience.

Music

Northwest Chamber Orchestra (⊠ 1305 4th Ave., Suite 522, Downtown ☎ 206/343–0445 ⊕ www.nwco.org) performs everything from baroque to modern at the Illsley Nordstrom Recital Hall in Benaroya Hall and outdoors at the Seattle Asian Art Museum.

Seattle Opera (⊠ McCaw Hall at Seattle Center, Mercer St. at 3rd Ave., Queen Anne ☎ 206/389–7676 ⊕ www.seattleopera.org), whose home is the beautiful Marion Oliver McCaw Hall, stages such productions as *Carmine, Ariadne auf Naxos,* and *The Girl of the Golden West* from August through May. Evening event guests are treated to a light show from 30-foot hanging scrims above an outdoor piazza. Extra women's bathrooms and a soundproof baby "crying room" make the programs comfortable and family-friendly.

★ **Seattle Symphony** (⊠ Benaroya Hall, 1203 2nd Ave., at University St., Downtown ☎ 206/215–4747 ⊕ www.seattlesymphony.org) performs under the direction of Gerard Schwartz from September through June in stunning, acoustically superior Benaroya Hall. This exciting symphony has been nominated for numerous Grammy Awards and is well-regarded nationally and internationally.

Performance Venues

Benaroya Hall (⊠ 200 University St., Downtown ☎ 206/215–4800) is so state of the art that the acoustics are pure in every one of the main hall's 2,500 seats. This makes seeing the Seattle Symphony, which is based here, a requisite. The four-story lobby has a curved glass facade that makes intermissions almost as impressive as performances.

Cornish College of the Arts (⊠ 710 E. Roy St., Capitol Hill ☎ 206/323–1400 ⊕ www.cornish.edu/events) is headquarters for distinguished jazz, dance, and other groups. It also hosts solid student productions.

King Kat Theater (✉ 2130 6th Ave., Belltown ☎ 206/269–7444) is a large concert venue that books national folk, blues, and alternative rock acts. A former cinema, it affords great views from every seat, and the all-ages policy let families to enjoy a concert together.

★ **Marion Oliver McCaw Hall** (✉ Mercer St. at 3rd Ave., Queen Anne ☎ 206/389–7676 or 206/441–2424 ⊕ www.seattlecenter.org), home of the Seattle Opera and the Pacific Northwest Ballet, is an opulent, glass-enclosed structure reflecting the skies. Inside, walls are painted in the hues of sunsets and northern lights; outside, on the piazza, occasional evening light shows are projected onto 30-foot banners dangling above a pond. (Hint: If you're not here for a performance, head atop the parking garage across the street and catch the light show for free.)

Meydenbauer Center (✉ 11100 NE 6th St., Bellevue ☎ 425/637–1020 ⊕ www.meydenbauer.com) has state-of-the-art equipment and excellent acoustics. It hosts performances by children's theater troupes, the Ballet Bellevue, the Bellevue Civic Theater, and other groups.

Moore Theater (✉ 1932 2nd Ave., Downtown ☎ 206/443–1744 ⊕ www.themoore.com), built in 1907, is Seattle's oldest theater and still hosts off-Broadway performances and music events. A quick peek at the prominent marquee clues you in to what's happening: jazz concerts, instrumental duets, hard-rock bookings, pop-music shows. The venerable hall was featured in Pearl Jam's video, *Evenflow,* and many of the big grunge music acts of Seattle's early '90s rock heyday performed here.

Paradox Theater (✉ 1510 University Way NE, University District ☎ 206/524–7677) has punk, pop, and spoken word performances.

Paramount Theatre (✉ 907 Pine St., Downtown ☎ 206/682–1414 ⊕ www.theparamount.com), opened in 1928 as a vaudeville and silent film venue. Today its 2,800 cushy seats and opulent details make it a great place to see popular music acts, top comedians, and international dance troupes. Monday night brings silent movies accompanied by the original Publix organ.

Seattle Center (✉ 305 Harrison St., Queen Anne ☎ 206/684–8582 ⊕ www.seattlecenter.org) has several halls that present theater, opera, dance, music, and performance art. Live music, theme dances, and festivals are staged monthly in the Center House. The Seattle Center is also the site of Labor Day weekend's Bumbershoot Festival, which celebrates the arts.

Theaters

A Contemporary Theater (✉ 700 Union St., Downtown ☎ 206/292–7676) launches exciting works by emerging dramatists. Four staging areas include a theater-in-the-round and an intimate downstairs space for small shows. The April to November season highlight is *Late Night Catechism,* the long-running play dubbed the *Cats* of Seattle.

Empty Space Theater (✉ 3509 Fremont Ave., Fremont ☎ 206/547–7500) stages maverick productions November through June. The cozy theater has 150 tightly packed seats for viewing works by new writers and, occasionally, such famous names as David Mamet or Sam Shephard.

★ **5th Avenue Theater** (✉ 1308 5th Ave., Downtown ☎ 206/625–1418 ⊕ www.5thavenuetheatre.org) opened in 1926 as a silent movie house and vaudeville stage, complete with a giant pipe organ and ushers who dressed up as cowboys and pirates. Today the chinoiserie landmark has its own theater company, which stages lavish productions October through May. At other times it hosts concerts, lectures, and films.

Intiman Theater (✉ 201 Mercer St., Queen Anne ☎ 206/269–1901 ⊕ www.intiman.org), at the Seattle Center, presents important contemporary works and classics of the world stage from May through November in its 485-seat space.

Nippon Kan Theater (⊠ 409 7th Ave. S, International District ☎ 206/ 841–2521), a national historic landmark built in 1909, was once the gathering place for Japanese-Americans in Seattle. The building was boarded up in 1942, when all Japanese were moved to internment camps during World War II, but the beautiful interior was still intact when the theater reopened in 1981. Today, as a venue for concerts, plays, neighborhood events, and touring international performers, it's an integral part of Seattle's Asian-American community.

★ **Northwest Actors Studio** (⊠ 1100 E. Pike St., Capitol Hill ☎ 206/324– 6328), Seattle's oldest theater arts center, has a second-floor main stage and a third-floor cabaret space with an open bar. There's always something unique on the schedule, as the studio is home to such locally beloved troupes as the circus-style Bare; the UW student improvisational Collective; the free-form duo Improsia; the hilarious Jet City Improv comedy team; and Seattle's oldest improv group, Unexpected Productions.

Northwest Asian American Theater (⊠ 628 S. Washington St., International District ☎ 206/340–1445), below the Wing Luke Asian Museum, embraces innovative performances by artists in Seattle's Asian and Pacific Islander communities. Their Black Box season focuses on diverse, non-Asian productions, and the on-site RAW gallery exhibits Asian-American visual art. Catch international flicks here each fall here as part of the Seattle Asian-American Film Festival.

Northwest Puppet Center (⊠ 9125 15th Ave. NE, University District ☎ 206/523–2579) encourages kids to sprawl on the floor while folktales are told by marionettes. The troupe keeps the lively stories brief (45 minutes). Puppet workshops are available.

Open Circle Theater (⊠ 429 Boren Ave. N, Capitol Hill ☎ 206/382–4250) produces cutting-edge, very physical ensemble theater and one-person shows that address humanity through magical mythical stories.

Seattle Children's Theatre (⊠ Charlotte Martin Theatre at Seattle Center, 2nd Ave. N and Thomas St., Queen Anne ☎ 206/441–3322 ⊕ www. sct.org), stages top-notch productions of new works as well as adaptations from classic children's literature. After the show, actors come out to answer questions and explain how the tricks are done.

Seattle Repertory Theater (⊠ 155 Mercer St., Queen Anne ☎ 206/443– 2222 ⊕ www.seattlerep.org) brings nine new and classic plays to life split among Seattle Center's Bagley Wright and Leo K. theaters during its September through April season. Adoring fans flock to new takes on choice classics as well as those fresh from the New York stage. You can pre-order a boxed dinner from the Café at the Rep before the show, or linger afterward over coffee and dessert.

SPORTS & THE OUTDOORS

Arenas & Stadiums

Updated by
Shelley Arenas

Bank of America Arena at Hec Edmundson Pavilion. What's known locally as "Hec Ed" is where the UW's men's and women's basketball teams play. ⊠ 3870 Montlake Blvd. NE, University District ☎ 206/543– 2200 ⊕ gohuskies.ocsn.com.

Cheney Stadium. For some AAA Pacific Coast League baseball action and a fabulous view of Mt. Rainier, head south to this stadium, which is home to the Tacoma Rainiers, a Mariners' affiliate team. Take I–5 south to Exit 132, follow Route 16 west for 2 mi, get off at the South 19th Street East exit; take first right (Cheyenne St.), and follow the road to stadium parking lots. ⊠ 2502 S. Tyler, Tacoma ☎ 253/752–7707 ⊕ www. tacomarainiers.com.

Everett Memorial Stadium. The Everett Aquasox, an affiliate of the Seattle Mariners, play their games at this open ballpark, which is also a favorite of aficionados of old-fashioned baseball. ⊠ *3900 Broadway Ave., Exit 192 off I–5, Everett* ☎ *425/258–3673* ⊕ *www.aquasox.com.*

Husky Stadium. This U-shape stadium overlooks Lake Washington, so you can arrive by boat as well as by bike, bus, or car. The loud UW Husky fans are, however, noted for their ability to cause traffic jams on home game days. ⊠ *University of Washington, 3800 Montlake Blvd. NE, University District* ☎ *206/543–2200* ⊕ *gohuskies.ocsn.com.*

Key Arena. Seattle Center has its hands full not only with the Seattle SuperSonics (NBA) and the Seattle Storm (WNBA) but also with the Seattle Thunderbirds (a minor-league hockey club) and all the major concerts. The surrounding area has plenty to offer post-game, with restaurants to the north and south. Traffic is a major problem on game nights. ⊠ *Seattle Center, 1st Ave. N and Mercer St., Queen Anne* ☎ *206/283–3865, 800/4NBA–TIX Supersonics tickets, 206/217–9622 Seattle Storm information, 425/869–7825 or 206/448–7825 Seattle Thunderbirds information* ⊕ *www.seattlecenter.com.*

Safeco Field. It may sound cliché but there really isn't a bad seat in the house. When it rains, the retractable roof deflects most of the drops. When it's sunny, you can watch the sun set over the Olympics (the mountains!) from behind the Mariners' second base. One local sports columnist refers to the venue—the most expensive stadium in recorded history and $100 million over budget—as "the guilty pleasure." ⊠ *1st Ave. S and Atlantic St., Sodo* ☎ *206/346–4000* ⊕ *seattle.mariners.mlb.com.*

Seahawks Stadium. On the site of the former Kingdome and a block away from Safeco Field, this state-of-the-art stadium is home base for the Seattle Sounders soccer team as well as the Seahawks. The public paid $300 million of the facility's $430 million construction tab; Seahawks owner Paul Allen picked up the rest of the tab. ⊠ *800 Occidental Ave., Sodo* ☎ *425/827–9777* ⊕ *www.seahawks.com/stadium.*

Basketball

The men's NBA season runs from November to April. The Seattle SuperSonics play at Key Arena in the Seattle Center. You can buy tickets at the box office or by calling the NBA toll-free number.

After the demise of the Seattle Reign, the city's first pro women's team, hopes were immediately pinned on the WNBA to pick Seattle for an expansion team. The coach dribbled through Downtown for an entire day once to win supporters to the cause. Prayers were answered with the formation of the Seattle Storm, which plays its home games at Key Arena. The season is from mid-June to August.

The UW Huskies represent Seattle basketball in the Pac-10 Conference. The team has had less than its share of success. The tough women's team—which enjoys a very loyal (and loud) fan base—has, however, advanced to the NCAA tournament several times in recent years.

Beaches

With the Puget Sound to the west and 25-mi-long Lake Washington to the east, Seattle has miles of waterfront, much of it speckled with beaches. In addition smaller lakes, products of ancient glacial movements, spring forth throughout the city and the suburbs. You're never far from some body of water or another. Most Lake Washington beaches in Seattle, Kirkland, and Bellevue have lifeguards on duty in summer. Free swimming lessons are given at several Seattle beaches for ages 6 and up.

★ **Alki Beach** (✉ 1702 Alki Ave. SW, West Seattle ☎ 206/684–4075). In summer, cars inch along Alki Avenue, seeking a coveted parking space, all the passengers heading for this 2½-mi stretch of sand. It's something of a California beach scene (except for the water temperature), with in-line skaters, joggers, and cyclists sharing the walkway and sun-loving singles playing volleyball and flirting. Year-round, families come to build sand castles, beachcomb, and fly kites; in winter, storm-watchers come to see the crashing waves. Facilities include drinking water, grills, picnic tables, phones, and rest rooms; restaurants line the street across from the beach. To get here from Downtown, take either I–5 south or Route 99 south to the West Seattle Bridge and exit onto Harbor Avenue Southwest, turning right at the stoplight.

Golden Gardens Park (✉ 8498 Seaview Pl. NW, near NW 85th St., Ballard ☎ 206/684–4075). Puget Sound waters are bone-chilling cold, but that doesn't stop folks from jumping in. Besides brave swimmers, the park is packed with sunbathers in summer. In other seasons, beachcombers explore during low tide, and groups gather around bonfires to socialize and watch the sun go down. The park has drinking water, grills, picnic tables, phones, and rest rooms. It also has two wetlands, a short loop trail, and a rugged coast with breathtaking views. From Downtown, take Elliott Avenue North, which becomes 15th Avenue West, and cross the Ballard Bridge. Turn left to head west on Market Street and follow signs to the Ballard Locks; continue about another mile to the park.

Houghton Beach Park (✉ 5811 Lake Washington Blvd., Kirkland ☎ 425/828–1217). On hot days, sun-worshipers and swimmers flock to this beach south of downtown Kirkland on the Lake Washington waterfront. The rest of the year, the playground attracts families, and the fishing pier stays busy with anglers. Facilities include drinking water, picnic tables, phones, and rest rooms.

Juanita Beach Park (✉ 9703 Juanita Dr. NE, Kirkland ☎ 425/828–1217). Directly across Juanita Bay from wetlands, this beach hops: children playing in the sand, sunbathers on the dock, swimmers in the closed-in swimming area, and picnickers in the park. There are grills, picnic tables, phones, rest rooms, drinking water, and a snack bar.

Madison Park (✉ 2300 43rd Ave. E, Madison Park ☎ 206/684–4075). The sandy Lake Washington beach, with easy access to the water, the sloping lawn, the playgrounds, and the tennis courts fill quickly on warm days. There are coffee shops and other amenities nearby; the beach has drinking water, picnic tables, phones, rest rooms, and showers. From Downtown, go east on Madison Street for about 3 mi, turn right on East Howe Street and then turn left to head north on 43rd Avenue.

Madrona Park (✉ 853 Lake Washington Blvd., Madrona ☎ 206/684–4075). Several beach parks and green spaces front the lake along Lake Washington Boulevard; Madrona Park is one of the largest. Young swimmers stay in the roped-in area while teens and adults swim out to a floating raft with a diving board. Runners and in-line skaters follow the mile-long trail along the shore. Kids clamber about the sculpted-sand garden and climb on rocks and logs. Grassy areas encourage picnicking; there are grills, picnic tables, phones, rest rooms, and showers. A barbecue stand is open seasonally. From Downtown, go east on Yesler Way about 2 mi to 32nd Avenue. Turn left onto Lake Dell Avenue and then right; go to Lake Washington Boulevard and take a left.

★ **Matthews Beach Park** (✉ Sand Point Way NE and NE 93rd St., Sand Point ☎ 206/684–4075). On warm summer days, the parking lot and nearby streets overflow with people visiting Seattle's largest freshwater swimming beach. The Burke-Gilman Trail, popular with cyclists and runners, travels through the park. Picnic areas, basketball hoops, and a big playground round out the amenities. From Downtown, take I–5 north and get off at the Lake City Way Northeast exit. Stay on Lake City Way for about 1½ mi. Turn right on to Northeast 95th Street, right onto Sand Point Way Northeast, and left onto Northeast 93rd Street.

Newcastle Beach Park (⊠ 4400 Lake Washington Blvd. SE, off 112th SE Exit from I–405, Bellevue ☎ 425/452–6881 ⊕ www.ci.bellevue.wa. us/parks). On Lake Washington in Bellevue, this large park has a big swimming beach, a fishing dock, nature trails, volleyball nets, drinking water, phones, rest rooms, and a large grassy area with picnic tables. The playground is a favorite thanks to a train that tots can sit in and older kids can climb on and hop from car to car.

★ **Sand Point Magnuson Park** (⊠ Bordered by NE 65th and 74th Sts., Sand Point Way NE and Lake Washington, entrances at 65th St. and 74th St., Sand Point ☎ 206/684–4946). As it was once an airport, it's not surprising that this 200-acre park northeast of the University District is flat and open. The paved trails are wonderful for cycling and in-line skating. Many kids have learned to ride their two-wheelers here; quite a few more have spent time on the large playground. Leashed dogs are welcome on the trails; a large off-leash area includes one of the few public beaches where pooches can swim. Farther south, on the mile-long shore, there's a swimming beach, a seasonal wading pool, and a boat launch. The park also has tennis courts, sports fields, and a terrific kite-flying hill. Be sure to look for the unique public art: *The Fin Project: From Swords to Plowshares* uses submarine fins to depict a pod of orca whales. *No Appointment Necessary* has two bright red chairs extended into the sky. *The Sound Garden* (at the neighboring National Oceanic and Atmospheric Administration campus) has steel pipes that give off sounds when the wind blows for an art display that you can hear as well as see. From Downtown, take I–5 north to the Northeast 65th Street exit, turn right and continue east to Sand Point Way Northeast.

Bicycling

Gregg's Greenlake Cycle (⊠ 7007 Woodlawn Ave. NE, Green Lake ☎ 206/ 523–1822 ⊕ www.greggscycles.com). On Green Lake's northern end, this Seattle institution has been in business since 1932. It sells and rents mountain bikes, standard road touring bikes, and hybrids; helmets and locks are included with each rental. Gregg's is close to the Burke-Gilman Trail and across the street from the Green Lake Trail. Rental fees range from $15 to $30 for the day, $20 to $35 overnight, and $60 to $120 per week.

Marymoor Velodrome (⊠ 6046 W. Lake Sammamish Pkwy. NE, Redmond ⊕ www.marymoorvelodrome.org). When not used for competitive racing—National Championship meets, regional Olympic trials, the Goodwill Games—the banked oval here is open to the public. Granted, it's a bit of a haul from Seattle to Redmond, but for serious speedsters, there's no substitute. Since the Burke-Gilman Trail links up in Bothell with the Sammamish River Trail (which is connected to Marymoor Park), you can ride from Seattle to Marymoor, though you may not have anything left for the track once you get here. A free junior program for ages 5–8 introduces children to track cycling, with track bikes provided for free.

Boating & Sailing

Agua Verde Paddle Club and Cafe (⊠ 1303 NE Boat St., University District ☎ 206/545–8570 ⊕ www.aguaverde.com). If you hate to choose between your Mexican food and your kayaking, consider checking out Agua Verde. Start out by renting a kayak and paddling along either the Lake Union shoreline, with its hodgepodge of funky-to-fabulous houseboats and dramatic Downtown vistas, or Union Bay on Lake Washington, with its marshes and cattails. Afterward, take in the lakefront as you wash down a bite with a margarita. Kayaks are available March through October and are rented by the hour—$12 for singles, $16 for doubles, and $18 for triples. The third and fourth hours are free weekdays; fourth hours are free on weekends.

★ **Center for Wooden Boats** (⊠ 1010 Valley St., Lake Union ☎ 206/382–2628 ⊕ www.cwb.org). Seattle's free maritime heritage museum also rents classic wooden rowboats and sailboats. Rowboats are $12.50 or $15 an hour (depending on whether there's one person or two) on weekdays and $18 or $20 an hour on weekends. Sloops and catboats cost $15.75–$46 an hour, depending on the type and size of the vessel. There's a $5 skills-check fee. Free half-hour guided sails and steamboat rides are offered on Sunday from 2 to 3 (arrive an hour early).

Green Lake Boat Rental (⊠ 7351 W. Green Lake Way N, Green Lake ☎ 206/527–0171) is the source for canoes, paddleboats, sailboats, kayaks, sailboards, and rowboats to ply Green Lake's calm waters. On beautiful summer afternoons, however, be prepared to spend most of your time negotiating other traffic on the water as well as in the parking lot. Fees are $10 to $14 an hour.

Moss Bay Rowing and Kayak Center (⊠ 1001 Fairview Ave. N, Lake Union ☎ 206/682–2031 ⊕ www.mossbay.net). Moss Bay rents Whitehall pulling boats, wherries, and sliding-seat rowboats for $15 per hour. You can also rent a rowing shell or a sailboat. After a skills check (which costs $35), another $35 gets you an hour in a recreational or racing shell (single or double) or a sailboat. Single kayaks rent for $10 per hour, doubles go for $15. Also growing in popularity are dragon boats for up to 25 people and war canoes for up to 10 people. The cost is $10 per person per hour, and reservations are advised.

Northwest Outdoor Center (⊠ 2100 Westlake Ave. N, Lake Union ☎ 206/281–9694). This center on Lake Union's west side, rents one- or two-person kayaks (it also has a few triples) by the hour or day, including equipment and basic or advanced instruction. The hourly rate is $10 for a single and $15 for a double, with daily maximums of $50 and $70, respectively. Third and fourth hours are free during the week; a fourth hour is free weekends. If you want to find your own water, NWOC offers "to go" kayaks; the rate for a single is $50 first day, plus $25 each additional day. Doubles cost $70 the first day and $35 for each day thereafter. In summer, reserve least three days ahead. NWOC also runs guided sunset ($35 per person) and moonlight ($25 per person) trips. Day excursions are also possible, and every May, there are two overnight whale-watching trips to the San Juan Islands.

Waterfront Activities Center (⊠ 3800 Montlake Blvd. NE, University District ☎ 206/543–9433). This center behind UW's Husky Stadium rents three-person canoes and four-person rowboats for $7.50 an hour February through October. You can tour the Lake Washington shoreline or take the Montlake Cut portion of the ship canal and explore Lake Union. You can also row to nearby Foster Island and visit the Washington Park Arboretum.

Wind Works Sailing Center (⊠ 7001 Seaview Ave. NW, Ballard ☎ 206/784–9386 ⊕ www.windworkssailing.com). Although members are given first picks at Wind Works, which is on Shilshole Bay, nonmembers can arrange rentals. Experienced sailors are allowed to skipper their own boats after a brief qualifying process. Sailing a 25-foot Catalina will cost you $125 on weekdays and $167 on weekends; rates for a 43-foot Hunter are $321 on weekdays and $428 on weekends. In summer as many as 30 people can spring for a sunset cruise on a 61-foot, 1930s-era racing yacht, although only Wind Works staff can skipper it. The cruise runs 6 PM–10 PM and costs $935 weekdays, $1,080 weekends.

Yarrow Bay Marina (✉ 5207 Lake Washington Blvd. NE, Kirkland ☎ 425/822–6066 ⊕ www.yarrowbaymarina.com/rentals.htm). The marina rents 19- and 22-foot runabouts for $60 an hour on weekdays and $65 an hour on weekends. There's a two-hour minimum; weekly rentals are also an option.

Fishing

Adventure Charters (✉ 7001 Seaview Ave. NW, Ballard ☎ 206/789–8245 ⊕ www.seattlesalmoncharters.com) takes private groups out on six-person troll boats to fish for salmon, bottom fish, and crab—depending on the season. The guided trips last for six or seven hours. The price per person is $125 October–May and $135 June–September; a license, tackle, and bait are included, and your fish will be cleaned or filleted and bagged for free.

Fish Finders Private Charters (✉ 6019 Seaview Ave. NW, Ballard ☎ 206/632–2611 ⊕ www.fishingseattle.com) takes groups of four or more out on Puget Sound for guided salmon fishing trips. The cost is $135 per person plus $6 for a fishing license. Morning trips last about six hours; afternoon trips are about five hours. All gear, bait, cleaning, and bagging are included in the fee.

Fitness Clubs & Spas

All Star Fitness (✉ 330 2nd Ave. W, Queen Anne ☎ 206/282–5901 ⊕ www.allstarfitness.org). It's usually packed with 20- to 30-year-old urban professionals—maybe because it's one of the few gyms that has an indoor pool, plenty of Cybex machines, and a full schedule of classes (some only for women) that includes yoga, kickboxing, and step. There are lockers, towels, a sauna, a steam room, and a co-ed Jacuzzi. A day pass runs $10–$15, depending on the services you use, and includes classes. All Star Fitness has branches Downtown, in West Seattle, and in Woodinville, and it's affiliated with the Gateway Athletic Club.

Ballard Health Club (✉ 2208 NW Market St., Ballard ☎ 206/706–4882). Ballard is an anomaly among clubs. It's incredibly low-key and reasonably priced, with everything you need and nothing more: weights, cardio machines, many classes (including three kinds of yoga), a stretching room, and day care facility. Locker rooms have saunas; towels are available. A day pass costs $8 and includes access to classes.

Gateway Athletic Club (✉ 700 5th Ave., 14th fl., Downtown ☎ 206/343–4692 ⊕ www.allstarfitness.org). This member of the All Star Fitness chain is designed to impress with its striking views, tidy facilities, and attentive service. In addition to the usual lineup of free weights, weight machines, and cardio equipment, there are lots of classes, some of them unusual (ski conditioning, for example), as well as a squash court and a swimming pool. Day passes are $10–$15.

Gene Juarez Salon and Spa. Change into the signature kimono-style robe and sip a cinnamon tea while you wait for your trendy "stand-up haircut": you stand while the stylist snips away. Patrons also get a foot soak and have use of the eucalyptus steam chamber. Luxury treatments include wraps, massages, facials, waxing, manicures, and pedicures. ✉ 607 *Pine St., Downtown* ☎ *206/326–6000* ✉ *Bellevue Galleria, 550 106th Ave. NE, Bellevue* ☎ *425/455–5511* ⊕ *www.genejuarez.com* ✉ *Redmond Town Center, 16495 NE 74th St., Redmond* ☎ *425/882–9000.*

Habitude Salon, Day Spa & Gallery. Beamed ceilings, polished wood floors, plush furnishings, and tropical scents relax you the moment you enter. Indulge in a single treatment or in such packages as Beneath the Spring Thaw Falls (hydrating glow, massage, scalp treatment, sauna, and smoothie). Other offerings include the Hot Rocks detox sauna, Rainforest Steam Shower, delectable spa lunches, and door-to-door town car service. It's the state's only Aveda Lifestyle spa. ✉ *2801 NW Market St., Ballard* ☎ *206/782–2898* ⊕ *www.habitude.com.*

Pure Fitness (✉ 808 2nd Ave., Downtown ☎ 206/224–9000 ⊕ www.vaultfitness.com). This club, which is in a former bank, combines lots of equipment and classes with some unusual architectural features. The main floor has free weights; treadmills; and Cybex, Hammer Strength, and rowing machines. The loftlike second level contains a large aerobic studio and rows and rows of cardio machines facing a phalanx of TV monitors. Downstairs are saunas, steam rooms, and locker rooms. An enormous old vault door opens to the spa pool, which has an 8-foot waterfall that seems to flow from the corner of the ceiling. Classes on Qi Gong, an exercise combining movement with intellectual and emotional focus, are offered. Massage therapy costs $40–$90. The club also has tanning beds, nutrition counseling, personal trainers, and chiropractic services. Guest passes cost $10 a day.

Seattle Athletic Club (✉ 2020 Western Ave., Downtown ☎ 206/443–1111 ⊕ www.sacdt.com). Beyond this club's deceptively modest entrance, one block north of Pike Place Market, are more than 60,000-square-feet of free weights, Cybex machines, treadmills, Stairmasters, rowing machines, recumbent cycling machines, an indoor track, a full-size basketball court, racquetball and squash courts, and a pool. The club also offers a full slate of classes, from power cycling, step, and cardio to toning, Pilates, tai chi, and yoga. Massage therapy starts at $55 for a half-session for guests of affiliate hotels.

Spa Bellisima. Envelop yourself in a polar fleece robe, sink into a soft lounge chair, sip an herbal tea, and await simple luxury. Scented candles and soothing music surround you during your facial or massage, which use only certified organic botanicals, oils, and herbal essences. Custom-blended creams from ingredients such as honey, sesame seeds, and citrus are applied beneath diaphanous gauze "clouds." *Bellisima* (outrageously beautiful) is how you'll feel when you leave. ✉ *2620 2nd Ave., Belltown* ☎ *206/956–4156.*

Ummelina International Day Spa. Hand-carved Javanese doors open into this tranquil, luxurious, Asian-inspired spa. Relax beneath a warm waterfall, take a steamy, scented sauna, or submit to a mud wrap or smoothing body scrub. The three-hour Equator package for couples includes all this and more. Linger over the experience with a cup of delicately flavored tea. ✉ *1525 4th Ave., Downtown* ☎ *206/624–1370.*

Football

The Seattle Seahawks play in their $430 million stadium (which also hosts soccer matches), a tremendous improvement over the decrepit Kingdome that was imploded several years ago. The stadium is a civic project kick-started by Microsoft co-founder and billionaire Paul Allen, the Seahawks owner, who also built the Experience Music Project and saved the Cinerama movie theater from destruction.

People get more excited about the Huskies than the Seahawks, perhaps because so many UW students stay in town after graduating. Despite the litany of player scandals and the termination of Rick Neuheisel as coach in 2003 due to NCAA rules violations, the team has stayed strong, making it to the Rose Bowl (or close) several times in recent years.

Golf

Bellevue Municipal Golf Course (✉ 5500 140th Ave. NE, Bellevue ☎ 425/452–7250). Bellevue has a driving range and a short par-71 course with generous greens and few hazards. It's a very busy course; reservations are recommended, especially for weekends. Call on Monday for tee times. Greens fees are $29.50 Friday–Sunday and $25.50 Monday–Thursday; carts rent for $27.

Crossroads Par 3 Golf Course (✉ 15801 NE 8th St., Bellevue ☎ 425/452–4873). This course consists of 9 par-3 holes with small, flat greens throughout. Amenities are limited to a soda-vending machine and a putting green. Greens fees are $7 weekends and $6 weekdays, and tee times are first-come, first-served. You can play the course in about 90 minutes, and it's a great option for beginners.

Green Lake Pitch and Putt (✉ 5701 W. Green Lake Way N, at N. 57th St., Green Lake ☎ 206/632–2280). This 9-hole, par-3, pitch-and-putt course plays extremely short and easy. The cost is $4, and it's open 9 AM–dusk, March–October.

★ **Harbour Pointe Golf Club** (✉ 11817 Harbour Pointe Blvd., Mukilteo ☎ 800/233–3128 ⊕ www.harbourpt.com). If you're willing to spend some time and money, drive about 30 minutes north of Seattle to the town of Mukilteo and this club. Its challenging 18-hole championship layout—with 6,800 yards of hilly terrain and wonderful Puget Sound views—is one of Washington's best. Greens fees are $59 Friday through Sunday and $47 the rest of the week. Carts cost $15 per person. There's also a driving range where you can get 65 balls for $5. Reserve your tee time online, up to 21 days in advance. Inquire about early-bird, twilight, off-season, and junior discounts.

Interbay Family Golf Center (✉ 2501 15th Ave. W, Magnolia ☎ 206/285–2200 ⊕ www.interbaygolf.com). Interbay has a driving range ($5.50 for 50 balls, $9 for 100, $12 for 150), a 9-hole executive course ($15 weekends, $12.50 weekdays), and a miniature golf course ($7). The range and miniature golf course are open daily 7 AM–11 PM March–October and 7 AM–10 PM November–February; the executive course is open sunrise to sunset year-round.

Jackson Park (✉ 1000 NE 135th St., Olympic Hills ☎ 206/363–4747 ⊕ www.seattlegolf.com). There's an 18-hole course and a 9-hole executive course. Weekdays, greens fees are $25 and $12, respectively; on weekends expect to pay $30 and $12. Carts at the larger course cost $22; those on the smaller course are $14.

Jefferson Park (✉ 4101 Beacon Ave. S, Beacon Hill ☎ 206/762–4513 ⊕ www.seattlegolf.com). The 18-hole course has views of the city skyline *and* Mt. Rainier. The par-27, 9-hole course has a lit driving range with heated stalls that's open from dusk until midnight. Greens fees are $30 on weekends and $25 weekdays for the 18-hole course; you can play the 9-hole course for $12 daily. Carts are $22 and $14, and $2 buys you a bucket of 30 balls at the driving range.

West Seattle Golf Course (✉ 4470 35th Ave. SW, West Seattle ☎ 206/935–5187 ⊕ www.seattlegolf.com). This 18-hole course has a reputation for being tough but fair. Greens fees are $25 weekdays, $30 weekends. It's $22 for a cart.

Willows Run Golf Course (✉ 10402 Willows Rd. NE, Redmond ☎ 425/883–1200 ⊕ www.willowsrun.com). Willows has it all: an 18-hole, links-style course; a 9-hole, par-27 course; and a lit, 18-hole putting course that's open until 11 PM. Thanks to an improved drainage system, Willows plays reasonably dry even in typically moist Seattle-area weather. Greens fees for 9 holes are $11 weekdays, $13 Friday through Sunday; those for 18 holes are $41 or $55. Carts cost $18.50 per rider. There are also two pro shops and a driving range (75 balls cost $7, 35 balls cost $4).

The Horses

Take in Thoroughbred racing from April through September 15 at **Emerald Downs** (✉ 2300 Emerald Downs Dr., Auburn ☎ 253/288–7000 or 888/931–8400 ⊕ www.emeralddowns.com), a 166-acre track about 15 mi south of Downtown, east of I–5. Admission is $4. A few horseback-riding outfitters have guided treks through the surrounding hills. For most of the horses, you must weigh less than 250 pounds. Be sure to call ahead to schedule your ride.

Ez Times Outfitters (✉ 18703 Rte. 706, Elbe ☎ 360/569–2449). EZ Times has one- to three-hour guided horseback-riding trips on 20,000 acres of state forest trails near Mt. Rainier. Rates are $25 an hour. For a less strenuous outing, you can take a carriage ride, which will run you $50 an hour for two people and $10 per hour for each additional rider.

Tiger Mountain Outfitters (✉ 24508 SE 133rd St., Issaquah ☎ 425/392–5090). This Eastside outfitter leads three-hour, 10-mi rides to a lookout point on Tiger Mountain. The cost is $50 per person, and rides set out at 10 AM and 3 PM in summer and 1 PM in winter.

Rock Climbing

Recreational Equipment, Inc. (✉ 222 Yale Ave. N, Downtown ☎ 206/223–1944 Ext. 4086). Every day around 200 people have a go at REI's Pinnacle, a 65-foot indoor climbing rock. Climbing hours are Monday 10–6, Wednesday–Friday 10–9, weekends 10–7. The cost is $15 including equipment. Although reservations are a good idea, you can also schedule a climb in person. The wait can be anywhere from 30 minutes to four hours, but it's rare that you don't get to climb on the very day you sign up.

★ **Schurman Rock** (✉ Camp Long, 5200 35th Ave. SW, West Seattle ☎ 206/684–7434 ⊕ www.ci.seattle.wa.us/parks/environment/camplong.htm). The nation's first man-made climbing rock was designed in the 1930s by local climbing expert Clark Schurman. Generations of climbers have practiced here, from beginners to rescue teams to such legendary mountaineers as Jim Whittaker, the first American to conquer Mt. Everest. Years of use took their toll on Schurman Rock, and in 1999 it was closed. Fund-raising led by the Seattle Parks Foundation secured money to pay for restoration, and the rock was reopened in 2003. Rappelling classes for kids ($150 for 15 kids for two hours) are offered year-round at Camp Long, which is also the site of Seattle's only in-city campground, whose cabins rent for $35 a night.

Stone Gardens Rock Gym (✉ 2839 NW Market St., Ballard ☎ 206/781–9828 ⊕ www.stonegardens.com). Beyond the trying-it-out phase? Head here and take a stab at the bouldering routes and top-rope faces. Although there's plenty to challenge the advanced climber, the mellow vibe is a big plus for families, part-timers, and the aspiring novice-to-intermediate crowd. The cost is $14.

Vertical World (✉ 2123 W. Elmore St., Magnolia ☎ 206/283–4497). It opened in 1987 and claims to be nation's first indoor climbing gym. There are 14,000 square feet of climbable surface as well as a bouldering area and weight-lifting equipment. The top-rope routes max out at 32 feet, which can seem pretty darn high when you scramble up under your own power. Tuesday and Thursday nights are busiest, though rainy weekend days also breed lines. The cost is $15 a day, not including equipment rental. Vertical World has locations in Redmond and Bremerton, too.

SHOPPING

Downtown

Updated by
Vanessa Lazo
Greaves

Antiques & Collectibles

Big People Toys (✉ 90 Madison St., Downtown ☎ 206/749–9016) offers 18th- and 19th-century antiques from China, Mongolia, and Tibet. The lacquered trunks and small boxes are lovely, but what may arrest your attention is the stunning collection of insects under glass.

Glenn Richards (✉ Price–Asher Bldg., 964 Denny Way, Downtown ☎ 206/287–1877) gathers contemporary and antique tables, chests, screens, lamps, and other furnishings from all over Asia. Perhaps a handsome, carved-stone Japanese lantern is just what your garden needs.

★ **Great Jones Home** (✉ 1921 2nd Ave., Downtown ☎ 206/448–9405) takes inspirations from current fashion trends, filling this spacious skylit store with an eclectic mix of antiques, linens, and ornaments for your home. One wall is devoted to delectable imported textiles.

Pacific Galleries (✉ 2244 1st Ave. S, Downtown ☎ 206/264–9422 ✉ 241 S. Lander St., Downtown ☎ 206/292–3999) offers entirely different shopping experiences at its Downtown branches. The First Avenue store of the gallery with locations in Belltown and Greenlake sells high-end European antiques. The South Lander Street emporium has more than 200 reputable antiques dealers.

Porter Davis Antiques (✉ 103 University St., Downtown ☎ 206/622–5310) has 18th- and 19th-century European and American furniture accessorized with deluxe porcelain, silver, and Asian decorative arts.

Two Angels Antiques (✉ 1527 Western Ave., Downtown ☎ 206/340–6005) has European antiques from the 17th through the 20th centuries. There's also a 4,000-square-foot warehouse—chock-full of goodies—that's open by appointment.

Walker-Poinsett Antiques (✉ 411 University St., Downtown ☎ 206/624–4973) sells high-quality 17th- to 19th-century furniture, 16th-century brass candlesticks, and early-19th-century Sheffield plate.

Weatherford Gallery (✉ 1200 2nd Ave., Downtown ☎ 206/324–6514) specializes in 18th- and 19th-century European furniture and fine Asian porcelains. Note that Saturday, Sunday, and Monday are by appointment only. The main store on Capitol Hill has more goods on display.

Art Galleries

Foster/White Gallery (✉ 1331 5th Ave., Downtown ☎ 206/583–0100), in Rainier Square, is Washington's exclusive representative for glass artist Dale Chihuly, and exhibits works by Northwest masters such as Kenneth Callahan, Mark Tobey, and George Tsutakawa. There are also branches in Pioneer Square and Kirkland.

Kimzey Miller Gallery (✉ 1225 2nd Ave., Downtown ☎ 206/682–2339) has paintings, glass, and sculpture by contemporary Northwest and international artists.

The Legacy Ltd. (✉ 1003 1st Ave., Downtown ☎ 206/624–6340) is renowned for its stunning contemporary works and historic pieces by Northwest Coast Indian and Alaskan Eskimo artists, as well as for its friendly, knowledgeable staff.

Lisa Harris Gallery (✉ 1922 Pike Pl., Downtown ☎ 206/443–3315), in the Pike Place Market, represents Northwest and West Coast painters, sculptors, photographers, and printmakers.

Seattle Art Museum (✉ 100 University St., Downtown ☎ 206/654–3100) has a store that's packed with books, cards, and gifts relating to or complementing its superb permanent collection of art and artifacts from Asia, Africa, and the Pacific Northwest or its changing exhibits.

Vetri (✉ 1404 1st Ave., Downtown ☎ 206/667–9608), dedicated to the art of studio glass, has innovative pieces from emerging young artists, many from Washington's famous Pilchuck Glass School.

William Traver Gallery (✉ 110 Union St., Downtown ☎ 206/587–6501), mounts exhibitions of contemporary glass works, ceramics, paintings, and mixed-media installations in a theatrical, light-drenched space.

Woodside/Braseth Gallery (✉ 1533 9th Ave., Downtown ☎ 206/622–7243) specializes in works by such Northwest masters as Mark Tobey, William Ivey, George Tsutakawa, and William Cumming.

Books & Printed Material

Arundel Books (✉ 1113 1st Ave., Downtown ☎ 206/624–4442) carries new, used, and rare titles on architecture, the arts, and history.

Left Bank Books (✉ 92 Pike St., Downtown ☎ 206/622–0195) has poetry and titles on progressive politics and gay and lesbian issues.

M. Coy Books (✉ 117 Pine St., Downtown ☎ 206/623–5354) is not only pet-friendly, it's also beloved by those who enjoy contemporary literature. Grab something to peruse before taking a seat at the espresso bar.

Peter Miller Architecture and Design Books (✉ 1930 1st Ave., Downtown ☎ 206/441–4114) attracts Seattle's architects to a well-stocked bookstore that's every bit as cool and urbane as its owner. Portfolios and drawing tools are on hand for the discerning designer.

Read All About It International Newsstand (✉ 93 Pike St., Downtown ☎ 206/624–0140), in the Pike Place Market, carries more than 1,500 magazines and newspapers from around the world.

Clothing

Alexandra's (✉ 412 Olive Way, Downtown ☎ 206/623–1214) has thousands of women's designer-label pieces on consignment. Most seem to have hardly been worn. Look for Giorgio Armani, Calvin Klein, Donna Karan, and Richard Tyler, among others.

Alhambra (✉ 101 Pine St., Downtown ☎ 206/621–9571) is an exquisite women's clothing boutique. Look for fine fabrics and detailing.

Baby and Co. (✉ 1936 1st Ave., Downtown ☎ 206/448–4077), known for its dreamy window displays, dresses women in esoteric creations by Comme des Garçon and Yojhi Yamamoto.

Butch Blum (✉ 1408 5th Ave., Downtown ☎ 206/622–5760) dresses men in high-end apparel from Zegna, Barbera, Issey Miyake, and others. It's also the region's exclusive source for Armani's Black label. For women there are Schumacher—a youthful German sportswear line—and Armani jeans. A smaller store in University Village carries upscale casual wear for both sexes.

Escada (✉ 1302 5th Ave., Downtown ☎ 206/223–9433) offers classy, designer, ready-to-wear outfits, evening attire, sportswear, footwear, fragrances, and accessories in an ultrachic boutique.

Fini (✉ 86 Pine St., Downtown ☎ 206/443–0563) carries stylish jewelry, handbags, scarves, hats, and gloves—everything you need to help you finish your look.

Flora and Henri (✉ 717 Pine St., Downtown ☎ 206/749–9698) fashions muted cottons, linens, and silks into extraordinary children's garments. The lines are classic and the details hand stitched, yet nothing is too precious to play in. There's a second location in Capitol Hill.

Ian (✉ 1907 2nd Ave., Downtown ☎ 206/441–4055) is a fabulous place to shop if you're a trendy young man or woman with a healthy bank account. There's high-end street wear by Juicy Couture, Stüssy, and G-Star.

Isadora's Antique Clothing (✉ 1915 1st St., Downtown ☎ 206/441–7711) has elegant men's and women's garments that date from the 1900s to the 1950s.

Jeri Rice (✉ 421 University St., Downtown ☎ 206/624–4000) carries women's apparel by Lora Piana, Vera Wang, and Jean Paul Gaultier.

Kenneth Cole (✉ 520 Pike St., Downtown ☎ 206/382–1680) sells its sleek clothing, footwear, luggage, and accessories for men and women.

★ **Mario's of Seattle** (✉ 1513 6th Ave., Downtown ☎ 206/223–1461) has creations by Armani, Zegna, and Dolce & Gabbana. Ascend the ornate staircase to shop for women's designers. A free-standing Hugo Boss boutique sells suits, sportswear, and tuxedos.

Nancy Meyer (✉ 1318 5th Ave., Downtown ☎ 206/625–9200) has sexy European lingerie by Fernando Sanchez, La Perla, and others. The staff is adept at recommending styles and sizes for the best fit.

Olive (✉ 1633 6th Ave., Downtown ☎ 206/254–1310) is a boutique department store with bright trendy clothing and accessories for women; a wine merchant; a room dedicated to cosmetics and spa and bath products; and a café that sells Vietnamese spring rolls, French coffee, and bubble tea.

Quicksilver (✉ 409 Pike St., Downtown ☎ 206/625–9670) outfits young board riders—skate, surf, and snow—with cool fashions and seasonal hardware.

Sway and Cake (✉ 1631 6th Ave., Downtown ☎ 206/624–2699), where clothes are the Sway and shoes are the Cake, you can dress your girly self in the hottest styles from New York and Los Angeles.

Tulip (✉ 1201 1st Ave., Downtown ☎ 206/223–1791) is a high-end boutique with a "boyfriend couch," where your other half can cool his heels while you try on ethereal dresses or denim by Seven, Habitual, and Citizens of Humanity.

Zebraclub (✉ 1901 1st Ave., Downtown ☎ 206/448–8452), at Pike Place Market, has loads of fashion denim for men and women, including Diesel and Levi's vintage collection.

Department Stores

Bon-Macy's (✉ 3rd Ave. and Pine St., Downtown ☎ 206/506–6000), a Seattle landmark for 100+ years and the last of the true Downtown department stores, is a reliable source for clothing, housewares, cosmetics, furniture, and toys. Branch locations include Bellevue Square, Southcenter Mall, and Northgate Mall.

Nordstrom (✉ 500 Pine St., Downtown ☎ 206/628–2111), the local retail giant, sells clothing, accessories, cosmetics, jewelry, and lots of shoes—true to its roots in footwear—including many hard-to-find sizes. There are branches at Bellevue Square, Northgate Mall, and Southcenter Mall.

Gifts & Home Decor

Current (✉ 629 Western Ave., Downtown ☎ 206/622–2433) has European furniture and home accessories that are so enticing that design-conscious, bargain-hunting Seattleites live for the annual September sale.

Diva (✉ 1300 Western Ave., Downtown ☎ 206/287–9992), whose elegantly minimalist showroom is designed by Antonio Citterio, is the exclusive Northwest source for streamlined Italian furniture by B&B Italia, also designed by Citterio.

Found Objects (✉ 1406 1st Ave., Downtown ☎ 206/682–4324) combines contemporary jewelry, ceramics, and textiles—many handmade by local artisans—with good quality vintage housewares.

Inform (✉ 1220 Western Ave., Downtown ☎ 206/622–1608) sells sleek spare furniture in a modern, gallerylike setting.

McKinnon Furniture (✉ 1015 Western Ave., Downtown ☎ 206/622–6474) sells hand-crafted, made-to-order furniture made from non-threatened U.S. hardwoods.

★ **Peter Miller Details** (✉ 1924 1st Ave., Downtown ☎ 206/448–3436), carries a well-edited stock of indispensable *objets* for home and office. The emphasis is on contemporary Scandinavian design.

FodorśChoice ★ **Sur La Table** (✉ 84 Pine St., Downtown ☎ 206/448–2244), in the Pike Place Market, has been a culinary aficionado's haven since 1972. It's packed to the rafters with kitchen stuff—some 12,500 items, give or take, including an exclusive line of copper cookware. Check the schedule of in-store demonstrations. There's another branch is in Kirkland.

Twist (✉ 1503 5th Ave., Downtown ☎ 206/315–8080) carries theatrical jewelry, crafts, and furnishings—all handmade in America.

Watson Kennedy Fine Living (✉ 86 Pine St., Downtown ☎ 206/443–6281) is a jewel box of a shop that sells luxurious bath products. The sister store on First Avenue has tableware, fine food products, and fine linens.

Malls

City Centre (✉ 1420 5th Ave., Downtown ☎ 206/624–8800 ⊕ www.shopcitycentre.com) houses more than 20 retailers in a sleek structure adorned with spectacular art glass. Find the latest in upscale, urban fashion at Barneys New York. Discover why architects and design professionals love the wares at Design Concern. Romp through two floors of toys at FAO Schwarz.

Pacific Place (✉ 600 Pine St., Downtown ☎ 206/405–2655 ⊕ www.pacificplaceseattle.com) is an elegant atrium with about 30 retailers as well as a couple of restaurants and a top-notch cinema complex. Wow your sweetheart with jewelry from Cartier and Tiffany & Co. Find sexy sophisticated fashions from Bebe, MaxMara, Nicole Miller, and Club Monaco. Add to your domestic comforts at Pottery Barn, Restoration Hardware, and Williams-Sonoma Grande Cuisine. Or ponder the meaning of the "J" as you shop for casual clothing at J. Crew and J. Jill. A third-floor skybridge provides a sheltered route to Nordstrom.

Westlake Center (✉ 1601 5th Ave., Downtown ☎ 206/467–1600 ⊕ www.westlakecenter.com) is a busy place. Roughly 60 stores and food vendors draw crowds to a four-story glass pavilion that's also the Downtown link for the Monorail to Seattle Center. Fill a basket with locally produced specialty foods and crafts at Made in Washington, splurge on a fabulous writing instrument from Montblanc, or find quirky gifts and jewelry at Fireworks.

Market

Pike Place Market (✉ Pike Pl. at Pike St., west of 1st Ave., Downtown ☎ 206/682–7453 ⊕ www.pikeplacemarket.org) hums from the break of day, when the fish and produce arrive, until late at night, when the restaurants close. This exhilarating open-air market is where Seattleites shop for seasonal cut flowers; fruits and vegetables; wild salmon; and superb cheeses, breads, meats, wines, and pastries. Crafts vendors line the walkways, and singular stores are tucked into alleys, halls, and staircases. You could spend a whole day exploring and still not see it all. The market is open Monday–Saturday 9–6 and Sunday 11–5.

Outdoor Clothing & Equipment

Adidas (✉ 1501 5th Ave., Downtown ☎ 206/382–4317), the German sporting-goods giant, has two high-tech floors of athletic shoes, clothing, and accessories.

NikeTown (✉ 1500 6th Ave., Downtown ☎ 206/447–6453) does its part to promote shopping-as-theater with a cavernous space packed to the rafters with athletic shoes and sports apparel.

The North Face (✉ 1023 1st Ave., Downtown ☎ 206/622–4111) is a premium source for outdoor equipment, apparel, and footwear.

FodorsChoice ★ **Recreational Equipment, Inc.** (⊠ 222 Yale Ave. N, Downtown ☎ 206/223–1944), which everybody calls REI, has an incredible selection of outdoor gear at its enormous flagship store. You can try things out along the mountain-bike test trail, in the simulated rain booth, or on the 65-foot climbing wall. Branch locations are at Redmond Town Center and Southcenter Mall.

Belltown

Antiques & Collectibles

Pacific Galleries (⊠ 2121 3rd Ave., Belltown ☎ 206/441–9990) handles such an immense volume of Asian, European, and American antiques that the company holds auctions in this showroom *and* one in Greenlake. (Here they're held every five weeks, but you're welcome to drop in to browse or leave an absentee bid.) To shop for antiques head to the store or the emporium, both in Downtown.

Clothing

Darbury Stenderu (⊠ 2121 1st Ave., Belltown ☎ 206/448–2625) dazzles with hand-printed, natural-fiber creations for men and women.
Gian Decaro Sartoria (⊠ 2025 1st Ave., Belltown ☎ 206/448–2812) tailors professional and casual wardrobes for many well-heeled businessmen—including Microsoft's Bill Gates. Just remember, though, you don't have to be a billionaire to dress like one.
Karan Dannenberg Clothier (⊠ 2232 1st Ave., Belltown ☎ 206/441–3442) clothes women in opulent fabrics, many of which are wrinkle resistant.
Kuhlman (⊠ 2419 1st Ave., Belltown ☎ 206/441–1999) dresses both sexes in sophisticated urban designs often made with superb European and Japanese fabrics.
Margaret O'Leary (⊠ 2025 1st Ave., Belltown ☎ 206/441–6691) designs gorgeous hand-loomed cashmere knits for women, as well as fine cotton and linen apparel.
★ **Opus 204** (⊠ 2000 1st Ave., Belltown ☎ 206/728–7707) is a must-shop destination for locally designed women's clothes in luxurious fabrics and artistic silhouettes. The shop also has great raincoats.

Gifts & Home Decor

Egbert's (⊠ 2231 1st Ave., Belltown ☎ 206/728–5682) carries contemporary Italian and Scandinavian designs and is the U.S. headquarters for Erik Jørgensen furniture. Look for vases by Alvar Aalto, Murano glass signed by artist Carlo Moretti, and jubilant African art.
Riflessi (⊠ 2302 1st Ave., Belltown ☎ 206/728–5840) fills this vivid gallery with hand-painted majolica, glassware, and framed art from studios all over Italy.
Urban Ease (⊠ 2512 2nd Ave., Belltown ☎ 206/443–9546) showcases regionally designed contemporary furniture and housewares and is the exclusive Northwest source for high-style Italian modular kitchen, bedroom, and wall systems by Poliform.

Queen Anne

Antiques & Collectibles

Crane Gallery (⊠ 104 W. Roy St., Queen Anne ☎ 206/298–9425), at the foot of Queen Anne Hill, offers top-notch Japanese, Chinese, Korean, Tibetan, and Southeast Asian antiques and art objects, including bronzes, lacquer items, and porcelain pieces.
Galen Lowe Art & Antiques (⊠ 102 W. Roy St., Queen Anne ☎ 206/270–8888), at the foot of Queen Anne Hill, assembles a highly individualized and esoteric collection of Japanese art, furniture, textiles, outsider art and objets d'art in a small but stunning gallery.

Books, Printed Materials & Music

Easy Street Records (✉ 20 Mercer St., Queen Anne ☎ 206/691–3279), at the base of Queen Anne, is a large, lively independent music store with a terrific reputation for its cache of new releases, imports, and rare finds.

Queen Anne Avenue Books (✉ 1811 Queen Anne Ave. N, Queen Anne ☎ 206/283–5624) is a friendly neighborhood bookstore with a fine selection of children's literature.

Clothing

Adelita (✉ 1422 Queen Anne Ave. N, Queen Anne ☎ 206/285–0707), a boutique furnished like a romantic boudoir, caters to "the revolutionary fashionista" with strong yet feminine apparel as well as spa products and unique accessories. The fitting room is cushy.

La Femme (✉ 1622 Queene Ave. N, Queen Anne ☎ 206/285–2443) is a chic little shop that carries sexy, flirty, sophisticated clothing along with jeans from Paper Denim & Cloth, Lovetanjane lingerie, handmade shoes, and jewelry by local artists.

Queen Anne Mail & Dispatch/Undies & Outies (✉ 2212 Queen Anne Ave. N, Queen Anne ☎ 206/286–1024) feels like an old-fashioned general store. One side of the place has delectable Italian lingerie by Cosabella, an eclectic mix of women's casual clothing, and comfy, stylish shoes. The other side has a dandy mailing service with a long wooden counter and floor-to-ceiling wooden mail cubicles.

Gifts & Home Decor

Four Winds (✉ 1517 Queen Anne Ave. N, Queen Anne ☎ 206/282–0472) enchants you with exotic Tibetan, Nepali, and Indonesian crafts, jewelry, textiles, furniture, and candles. There are also more than 50 varieties of incense.

The Homing Instinct (✉ 1622 Queen Anne Ave. N, Queen Anne ☎ 206/281–9260) is a cottagelike boutique filled with such household items as fine linens, elegant tableware, and sumptuous bath products. The baby gifts are sweet as well.

Ravenna Gardens (✉ 2201 Queen Anne Ave. N, Queen Anne ☎ 206/283–7091) displays gear and gifts for genteel gardeners in a light, airy, corner store. You can find many more plants at the larger University Village location.

Stuhlbergs Fine Home Accessories (✉ 1805 Queen Anne Ave. N, Queen Anne ☎ 206/352–2351), in a cottage with a lovely shade garden in front, sells such things as fine Italian pewter and Petit Bateau baby clothes.

International District

Antiques & Collectibles

Eileen of China (✉ 624 S. Dearborn St., International District ☎ 206/624–0816) is the neighborhood's best-known antiques shop. The selection ranges from rosewood dining and living room sets, armoires, and cabinets to stone carvings and fine art.

Market

FodorsChoice ★ **Uwajimaya** (✉ 600 5th Ave. S, International District ☎ 206/624–6248 ⊕ www.uwajimaya.com) is one of West Coast's largest Japanese grocery and gift markets, though it also sells items from many other places in Asia. A 30-foot-long red Chinese dragon stretches above its piles of produce and aisles of packaged goods from Korea, Indonesia, the Philippines, India, Thailand, and more. Glass tanks teem with fish, crabs, lobster, prawns, and geoducks; the frozen-foods cases contain even more delicacies. A busy food court serves sushi, Japanese bento-box meals, Chinese stir-fry combos, Korean barbecue, Hawaiian dishes, Vietnamese spring rolls, and an assortment of jellied milk drinks and teas. The housewares section is well stocked with dishes, appliances, and decorations. There's also a card section, a Hello Kitty corner, a bank, and Yuriko's cosmetics, where you can find Shiseido products that are usually available only in Japan. Plan an extra hour to browse the attached Kinokuniya bookstore. The large parking lot is free for one hour with a minimum $5 purchase or two hours with a minimum $10 purchase (don't forget to have your ticket validated). The market is open Monday through Saturday 9 AM–11 PM and Sunday 9 AM–10 PM.

Pioneer Square

Antiques & Collectibles

Azuma Gallery (✉ 530 1st Ave. S, Pioneer Square ☎ 206/622–5599) specializes in traditional and contemporary Japanese prints, screens, baskets, and art objects.

Carolyn Staley Fine Japanese Prints (✉ 314 Occidental Ave. S, Pioneer Square ☎ 206/621–1888) deals in fine antique *ukiyo-e* (17th- to 19th-century paintings and prints depicting scenes from everyday life) and modern Japanese woodblock prints.

Chidori Asian Antiques (✉ 108 S. Jackson St., Pioneer Square ☎ 206/343–7736) sells high-quality Asian antiques; pre-Columbian and primitive art; and antiquities from all over the world.

★ **Elliott Bay Antiques** (✉ 165 S. Jackson St., Pioneer Square ☎ 206/340–0770) is a premier source for top-quality Chinese antique furniture and Buddhist sculptures.

Flury & Company (✉ 322 1st Ave. S, Pioneer Square ☎ 206/587–0260) has a fascinating vintage photographs by Edward Curtis, along with Native-American antiques, traditional carvings, baskets, jewelry, and tools.

Jean Williams Antiques (✉ 115 S. Jackson St., Pioneer Square ☎ 206/622–1110) stocks fine 18th- and 19th-century English, French, and Biedermeier furniture.

Kagedo Japanese Art and Antiques (✉ 520 1st Ave. S, Pioneer Square ☎ 206/467–9077) has Japanese antiques and works by modern masters. Among the treasures are intricately carved *okimono* (miniature figures rendered in wood, ivory, or bronze), stone garden ornaments, basketry, and textiles.

Laguna (✉ 116 S. Washington St., Pioneer Square ☎ 206/682–6162) carries collectible 20th-century American dinnerware, art pottery, vintage linens, tiles, and tile-topped tables.

Art Galleries

Bryan Ohno Gallery (✉ 115 S. Main St., Pioneer Square ☎ 206/667–9572) carries contemporary sculpture and Asian art and represents Northwest artists.

Davidson Galleries (✉ 313 Occidental Ave. S, Pioneer Square ☎ 206/624–7684) specializes in contemporary painting, sculpture, prints, and drawings as well as antique prints.

Foster/White Gallery (✉ 123 S. Jackson St., Pioneer Square ☎ 206/622–2833) showcases paintings and sculpture by Northwest masters and spectacular glass works by Dale Chihuly.

Greg Kucera Gallery (✉ 212 3rd Ave. S, Pioneer Square ☎ 206/624–0770) is a top venue for national and regional artists, with more than 4,000 square feet of exhibition space that include an outdoor sculpture deck.

Grover/Thurston Gallery (✉ 309 Occidental Ave. S, Pioneer Square ☎ 206/223–0816) specializes in contemporary figurative and narrative works, many by Northwest artists.

Kibo Galerie (✉ 323 Occidental Ave. S, Pioneer Square ☎ 206/442–2100) has a stunning collection of tribal masks and statuary from all over Africa.

Linda Hodges Gallery (✉ 316 1st Ave. S, Pioneer Square ☎ 206/624–3034) specializes in works by contemporary Northwest artists.

Stonington Gallery (✉ 119 S. Jackson St., Pioneer Square ☎ 206/405–4040) has contemporary masterworks by Northwest Coast tribal members as well as artists working in the native style.

Books, Printed Materials & Music

Bud's Jazz Records (✉ 102 S. Jackson St., Pioneer Square ☎ 206/628–0045) is a tightly packed underground store that sells all jazz and lots of it, including hard-to-find recordings.

David Ishii Bookseller (✉ 212 1st Ave. S, Pioneer Square ☎ 206/622–4719) is a small but mighty shop filled with a highly selective stock of used, out-of-print, and rare books. Many of the titles are dedicated to the owner's off-duty passions—baseball and fly-fishing.

Elliott Bay Book Company (✉ 101 S. Main St., Pioneer Square ☎ 206/624–6600), an enormous independent bookstore often held as Seattle's literary heart, stocks 150,000+ titles arranged on rustic wooden shelves in a labyrinth of rooms. The store hosts popular lectures and readings by local and international authors. A side room contains used books—about 22,000 of them—on all subjects; some are signed first editions.

Flora & Fauna Books (✉ 121 1st Ave. S, Pioneer Square ☎ 206/623–4727) attends to the natural world with new, used, and rare books on horticulture and birding.

Metsker Maps (✉ 702 1st Ave., Pioneer Square ☎ 206/623–8747) has the goods to guide you to where in the world you need go.

Seattle Mystery Bookshop (✉ 117 Cherry St., Pioneer Square ☎ 206/587–5737) thrills you with new, used, and collectible suspense novels.

Wessel & Lieberman (✉ 208 1st Ave. S, Pioneer Square ☎ 206/682–3545) specializes in first editions, Americana, book arts, and fine letterpress in a tidy shop with dark green walls and handsome wooden shelves. An extensive annex is on the underground level of Grand Central Arcade.

Clothing

Ebbets Field Flannels (✉ 404 Occidental Ave. S, Pioneer Square ☎ 206/262–0260) sells bits of baseball history with faithful reproduction team jackets, jerseys, and caps from the 1920s to '60s, focusing on the Negro Leagues, minor leagues, and the Pacific Coast League.

Ragazzi's Flying Shuttle (✉ 607 1st Ave., Pioneer Square ☎ 206/343–9762) sells exquisite, hand-woven clothing, textiles, and throws.

Gifts & Home Decor

Fireworks Fine Crafts Gallery (✉ 210 1st Ave. S, Pioneer Square ☎ 206/682–8707) sells whimsical hand-crafted jewelry, ceramics, and small items of furniture. It's just as fun to shop in the Bellevue Square, University Village, and Westlake Center branches.

Glass House Studio (✉ 311 Occidental Ave. S, Pioneer Square ☎ 206/682–9939), Seattle's oldest glassblowing studio and gallery, lets you watch fearless artisans at work in the "hot shop." Studio pieces and other works on display are for sale.

Northwest Fine Woodworking (✉ 101 S. Jackson St., Pioneer Square ☎ 206/625–0542) represents the work of more than 30 artist owner-members who value furniture craftsmanship and design. You can find almost anything in the showroom or have it handmade for you. Shipping is available.

Mall

Grand Central Arcade (✉ 214 1st Ave. S, Pioneer Square ☎ 206/623–7417) has an exposed-brick interior courtyard and an underground cache of fascinating shops. Locals linger at tables near a fireplace on damp Northwest days, sipping espresso and munching treats from Grand Central Bakery. You can sort through hundreds of rubber stamps at Paper Cat and peruse antiquarian books and images at David Ishii Books and Michael Maslin Historic Photographs. Go downstairs to see the wares at the Pottery School, sigh over the Japanese paper art at Tai Designs, or get an expert opinion at Grand Central Wine Merchant.

Capitol Hill

Antiques & Collectibles

Area 51 (✉ 401 E. Pine St., Capitol Hill ☎ 206/568–4782) is a 6,000-square-foot industrial space where anything of good modern design might materialize, especially if it's from the 1960s and '70s. Check out the Dwell bed linens with retro prints.

Chartreuse International (✉ 711 E. Pike St., Capitol Hill ☎ 206/328–4844) is a dependable source for authentic mid-century modern furniture and wares by Harry Bertoia, Arne Jacobsen, Isamu Noguchi, and others.

David Weatherford Antiques and Interiors (✉ 133 14th Ave. E, Capitol Hill ☎ 206/329–6533) sells handsome, 18th-century French and English furniture, artwork, and accessories in an 1894 mansion.

Honeychurch Antiques (✉ 1008 James St., Capitol Hill ☎ 206/622–1225), on the neighborhood's southwestern edge, has fine 19th-century Japanese and Chinese furniture. Read the informational tags as you wander through this serene shop to improve your Asian antiques IQ.

Standard Home (✉ 1108 Pike St., near Boren Ave., Capitol Hill ☎ 206/464–0850) is packed with mid-century modern furniture and housewares by such luminaries as George Nelson, Charles and Ray Eames, Russel Wright, and Hans Wegner. You can also find a few licensed reproductions in the mix.

Art Galleries

G. Gibson Gallery (✉ 514 E. Pike St., Capitol Hill ☎ 206/587–4033) focuses on vintage and contemporary photography and mixed-media works.

Martin-Zambito Fine Art (✉ 721 E. Pike St., Capitol Hill ☎ 206/726–9509) specializes in regional American artists, with an emphasis on WPA and Depression-era paintings and studio ceramics.

Books, Printed Materials & Music

Bailey/Coy Books (✉ 414 Broadway Ave. E, Capitol Hill ☎ 206/323–8842) is well-stocked with volumes on many topics. There's a substantial gay and lesbian section.

Confounded Books (✉ 315 E. Pine St., Capitol Hill ☎ 206/441–9880) specializes in underground, alternative, and European comics, independent 'zines, and small-press books.

Fillipi Book & Record Shop (✉ 1351 E. Olive Way, Capitol Hill ☎ 206/682–4266) stocks secondhand books and magazines plus collectible sheet music and 78-, 45-, and 33-rpm records.

Horizon Books (✉ 425 15th Ave. E, Capitol Hill ☎ 206/329–3586) has seven rooms of used, neatly organized books on all topics.

J & S Broadway News (✉ 204 Broadway Ave. E, Capitol Hill ☎ 206/324–7323) carries more than 1,500 international periodicals.

Twice Sold Tales (✉ 905 E. John St., Capitol Hill ☎ 206/324–2421) is an excellent source for gently used books. It stays open late on weekends—a bonus if you're ever sleepless in Seattle. Other locations in Fremont and the University District don't keep such late hours.

Wall of Sound (✉ 315 E. Pine St., Capitol Hill ☎ 206/441–9880) has world music, jazz, blues, and experimental works.

Clothing

Broadway Boutique (⊠ 113 Broadway St. E, Capitol Hill ☎ 206/325–0430) is the place to shop for something funky and cheap. Look for tropical-pattern halter tops, wide-leg pants, and platform shoes. Dress it all up with a zebra backpack or a feather boa.

Dumb Clothing (⊠ 413 E. Pine St., Capitol Hill ☎ 206/322–6630) is the brainchild of Paula Fletcher, who uses wild fabrics to create one-of-a-kind designs. She often gives her clothes quirky embellishments, too. Finish your look with jewelry made by local artists.

Le Frock (⊠ 317 E. Pine St., Capitol Hill ☎ 206/623–5339) sells a mix of good-quality men's and women's vintage clothing and gently used contemporary designer labels. Shop to the inspiring music of Billie Holiday and Sarah Vaughan.

Panache (⊠ 225 Broadway St. E, Capitol Hill ☎ 206/726–3300) carries floral slip dresses with slanted, ruffled edges; batik sarong skirts; and chic silk separates. It stocks the requisite accessories, too. The extensive men's section has dress clothes and shoes.

Red Light (⊠ 312 Broadway Ave. E, Capitol Hill ☎ 206/329–2200) lets you mix and match the decades with its miniskirts, feather boas, handbags, designer jeans, camp shirts, and darling tops. Time-warp toys, lunch boxes, underwear sets, and other cool kitsch are also available. If you're in the University District visit the sister store.

Vintage Chick (⊠ 303 E. Pine St., Capitol Hill ☎ 206/625–9800) carries men's and women's clothing and jewelry from the 1920s to the '70s—most of it funky and cute. Vintage bridal and evening wear is especially popular; expert alterations are available.

Gifts & Home Decor

Kobo (⊠ 814 E. Roy St., Capitol Hill ☎ 206/726–0704) carries hand-loomed textiles, studio ceramics, and figurines by Japanese and Northwest artisans.

Ragen & Associates (⊠ 517 E. Pike St., Capitol Hill ☎ 206/329–4737) imports dramatic garden accessories from Italy and Asia.

Mall

Broadway Market (⊠ 401 Broadway Ave. E, Capitol Hill ☎ 206/322–1610 ⊕ www.thebroadwaymarket.com) caters to the neighborhood's alternative aesthetic with cafés, hip clothing merchants, and art-house cinemas. Pick up an international newspaper at the Bulldog News kiosk and pretend to read it while you people-watch.

University District

Books, Printed Materials & Music

Bulldog News and Fast Espresso (⊠ 4208 University Way NE, University District ☎ 206/632–6397) has nearly 3,000 newspapers and magazines, both domestic and foreign. Just dash in, pick up a paper, a shot of espresso, and go. You can also hop online. The first five minutes are free with a coffee purchase; after that it's 50¢ per 10 minutes. The store also maintains a small but well-stocked kiosk at Broadway Market on Capitol Hill.

Cellophane Square (⊠ 4538 University Way NE, University District ☎ 206/634–2280), a store with an affinity for indie rock, punk, and garage bands, will buy, sell, and trade used CDs and vinyl. It also carries new releases, and it has classical and jazz sections on the second floor. From time to time there are in-store performances.

Cinema Books (⊠ 4753 Roosevelt Way NE, University District ☎ 206/547–7667) caters to film fans, TV junkies, and theater buffs with new and rare books, posters, and ephemera.

Half Price Books Records Magazines (✉ 4709 Roosevelt Way NE, University District ☎ 206/547–7859) has such great deals that you might well walk out with twice as much as you planned. The children's and history book sections are particularly notable.

University Book Store (✉ 4326 University Way NE, University District ☎ 206/634–3400), on the UW campus, is the nation's second-largest independent college bookstore. There's a well-stocked general book department, lots of university souvenirs, and author events all year long. The Downtown branch sells business and professional books.

Clothing

Buffalo Exchange (✉ 4530 University Way NE, University District ☎ 206/545–0175), a big, bright shop of new and recycled fashions, is always crowded—even on Saturday night—with UW girls looking for bargains. It takes time to browse the stuffed racks, but the trendy rewards are great: sequined jeans, leather jackets, vintage-style dresses.

Moksha (✉ 4542 University Way NE, University District ☎ 206/632–1190) sells hip little skirts and dresses fashioned out of old Indian saris and embellished with gossamer overlays and intricate beading. Or maybe you'd prefer cute girly T-shirts and trendy denim. It's all unique and affordable.

Red Light Clothing Exchange (✉ 4560 University Way NE, University District ☎ 206/545–4044) is filled with well-organized, good-quality vintage clothing from the 1940s to the '80s. Sample outfits from each era—complete with accessories—adorn the dressing rooms. There's plenty of denim, leather, and disco threads alongside cowboy boots and evening wear. There's also an equally well-stocked branch in Capitol Hill.

Pitaya (✉ 4520 University Way NE, University District ☎ 206/548–1001) is an unexpectedly chic boutique that's on top of the trends. The clothes are not only stylish and fun but also priced just right for college girls.

Gifts & Home Decor

Burke Museum of Natural History and Culture (✉ 17th Ave. NE and NE 45th St., University District ☎ 206/543–5590), on the UW campus, displays historic Northwest coast Native American works, and sells contemporary masks, plaques, rattles, and prints in its store.

La Tienda Folk Art Gallery (✉ 4138 University Way NE, University District ☎ 206/632–1796) has a colorful melange of handblown glass, pottery, jewelry, clothing, masks, toys, musical instruments, CDs, books, and games from different cultures. The sister store in Ballard is definitely worth a visit.

Snow Goose Associates (✉ 8806 Roosevelt Way NE, University District ☎ 206/523–6223), just north of UW, represents Alaskan Eskimo, Canadian Inuit, and Northwest Coast Native American artists.

Shopping Center

★ **University Village** (✉ NE 45th St. and 25th Ave. NE, University District ☎ 206/523–0622), northeast of the campus, is a pleasant outdoor shopping plaza with trees, fountains, whimsical sculptures, and other good-life adornments. Among the more than 80 upscale shops and restaurants are branches of Pottery Barn, Williams-Sonoma, Banana Republic, Smith & Hawken, Crate & Barrel, and Restoration Hardware. You can redo your kid's room at the Land of Nod, schedule your own makeover at Sephora, and sample divine delicacies from Fran's Chocolates. The whole place is kid-friendly, and there's ample free parking.

Fremont

Antiques & Collectibles

Deluxe Junk (✉ 3518 Fremont Pl. N, Fremont ☎ 206/634–2733) brings back the past with things that are flamboyant, retro, or chic. Some objects fall into all three categories.

Fremont Antique Mall (⊠ 3419 Fremont Pl. N, Fremont ☎ 206/548–9140) is an underground complex of 50 dealers who sell vintage clothing and items from popular American culture.

Books, Printed Materials & Music

J & S Fremont News (⊠ 3416 Fremont Ave. N, Fremont ☎ 206/633–0731) is well stocked with newspapers and magazines, and has a row of clocks that tell the time in Tokyo, Paris, New York, and—wouldn't you know it—Fremont. While browsing the foreign press, pick up a free copy of *The Walking Guide to Fremont.*

Sonic Boom (⊠ 3414 Fremont Ave. N, Fremont ☎ 206/547–2666) is in touch with the current music scene, especially the Northwest and independent labels. Browse for new and used records and CDs here and at the Capitol Hill and Ballard stores. Check local schedules for in-store performances and release parties.

Twice Sold Tales of Fremont (⊠ 3504 Fremont Ave. N, Fremont ☎ 206/ 632–3759) is a general-interest used bookstore with a soft spot for cats.

Clothing

Bellefleur (⊠ 720 N. 35th St., Fremont ☎ 206/545–0222) is a sensuous little shop fluttering with sexy European undies. It also has lotions and potions.

Enexile (⊠ 611 N. 35th St., Fremont ☎ 206/633–5771) outfits men and women in modern streetwear by Anna Sui, French Connection, and others.

Fritzi Ritz Vintage Clothing (⊠ 750 N. 34th St., Fremont ☎ 206/633–0929) is crammed with cool vintage apparel. Staffers label everything so it's easy to find clothes by era.

★ **Les Amis** (⊠ 3420 Evanston Ave. N, Fremont ☎ 206/632–2877) is all about luscious fabrics. Look for ultra-feminine dresses, gorgeous knits, and frothy lingerie from the best up-and-coming lines.

Private Screening (⊠ 3504 Fremont Pl. N, Fremont ☎ 206/548–0751) has classic clothing from the 1920s to the 1960s. Let the vintage Western wear bring out your inner cowpoke.

Gifts & Home Decor

Bitters Co. (⊠ 513 N. 36th St., Fremont ☎ 206/632–0886) is a general store with unusual textiles, linens, tableware, and jewelry. Look for hand-crafted furniture from Guatemala, Indonesia, and the Philippines as well as an in-house line of tables made from reclaimed Douglas fir.

Burnt Sugar (⊠ 601 N. 35th St., Fremont ☎ 206/545–0699), the store on the corner with the rocket on the roof, carries whimsical vintage furniture, hand-crafted photo albums, soaps, candles, jewelry, and other delights. Spend some quality time at the cosmetic bar sampling products by Susan Posnick, Body & Soul, and Somme Institute.

Dandelion Botanical Company (⊠ 708 N. 34th St., Fremont ☎ 206/545–8892) creates custom-scented candles and body products in a charming space that feels like an old-fashioned apothecary shop.

Essenza (⊠ 615 N. 35th St., Fremont ☎ 206/547–4895) is a refreshing, light-filled boutique that sells Italian bath items by Santa Maria Novella, the complete line of Fresh products, handmade bed linens, women's loungewear, delicate jewelry, and exquisite children's clothing.

Frank & Dunya (⊠ 3418 Fremont Ave. N, Fremont ☎ 206/547–6760), a shop named after the owners' dogs, sells colorful, locally crafted, functional art.

Portage Bay Goods (⊠ 706 N. 34th St., Fremont ☎ 206/547–5221) is a great source for crafts produced by local artisans using environmentally friendly methods.

SEATTLE A TO Z

Updated by
Holly S. Smith

To research prices, get advice from other travelers, and book travel arrangements, visit www.fodors.com.

AIR TRAVEL

Seattle is a hub for regional air service as well as service to Canada and Asia. It's also a convenient North American gateway for flights originating in Australia, New Zealand, and the South Pacific. But it's a long westbound flight to Seattle from Europe. Such flights usually stop in New York; Washington, D.C.; Boston; or Chicago after crossing the Atlantic. The major gateway is Seattle–Tacoma (Sea-Tac) International Airport.

AIRPORT   🔲 Airport Information **Seattle-Tacoma International Airport** ⊠ Pacific Hwy. S (Rte. 99) ☎ 206/431-4444 ⊕ www.portseattle.org/seatac.

AIRPORT
TRANSFERS
Sea-Tac is about 15 mi south of Downtown on I–5 (from the airport, follow the signs to I–5 north, and take the Seneca Street Exit for Downtown). Although it can take as little as 30 minutes to ride between Downtown and the airport, it's best to allow 1½ hours for the trip in case of traffic snarls.

Metered cabs cost $25–$30 between the airport and Downtown, though some taxi companies offer a flat rate to Sea-Tac from select Downtown hotels. Shuttle Express has the only 24-hour door-to-door service, a flat $20 from the airport to Downtown. You can make arrangements at the Shuttle Express counter upon arrival. For trips to the airport, make reservations at least 24 hours in advance. Express Car and Atlas Towncar have limo service to and from the airport. The fare is $45 to Downtown and can be shared by up to four passengers.

Gray Line Airport Express provides service to Downtown hotels for $8.50. Your least expensive transportation option ($2, cash only) is a Metro Transit city bus. You can catch one outside the baggage claim areas for the 45-minute ride into town. Take Express Tunnel Bus 194 or regular Buses 174 or 184.

🔲 Taxis & Shuttles **Atlas Towncar** ☎ 206/860-7777 or 888/646-0606 ⊕ www. atlastowncar.com. **Gray Line Airport Express** ☎ 206/626-6088 ⊕ www.graylineseattle. com. **Metro Transit** ☎ 206/553-3000. **Shuttle Express/Express Car** ☎ 206/622-1424, 800/487-7433 in WA ⊕ www.shuttleexpress.com.

BOAT & FERRY TRAVEL

Passenger-only speedboats depart from Seattle's Pier 50 weekdays on runs to Vashon Island. It's $7.40 from Seattle; the return trip is free. A $1 surcharge is collected in both directions on the Bremerton route. Late spring through fall, the Elliott Bay Water Taxi makes a quick, eight-minute journey from Pier 54 to Seacrest Park in West Seattle for $2 each way. Clipper Navigation operates the passenger-only *Victoria Clipper* jet catamaran service between Seattle, the San Juan Islands, and Victoria. The Washington State Ferry system—with vessels that take walk-on passengers only and those that take walk-ons as well as cars—serves the Puget Sound and San Juan Islands area.

🔲 Boat & Ferry Information **Clipper Navigation** ☎ 250/382-8100 in Victoria, 206/ 448-5000 in Seattle, 800/888-2535 in U.S. ⊕ www.victoriaclipper.com. **Elliott Bay Water Taxi** ⊠ Pier 54, Downtown ☎ 206/553-3000. **Washington State Ferries** ⊠ Colman Dock, Pier 52, Downtown ☎ 206/464-6400 or 888/808-7977, 800/843-3779 automated line in WA and BC ⊕ www.wsdot.wa.gov/ferries.

BUS TRAVEL

The Metropolitan Transit's transportation network is inexpensive and fairly comprehensive. Most buses, which are wheelchair accessible, run until around midnight or 1 AM; some run all night. The visitor center at the Washington State Convention and Trade Center has maps and schedules or you can call Metro Transit directly.

Between 6 AM and 7 PM, all public transportation is free within the Metro Bus Ride Free Area, bounded by Battery Street to the north, Sixth Avenue to the east (and over to Ninth Avenue near the convention center), South Jackson Street to the south, and the waterfront to the west; you'll pay as you disembark if you ride out of this area. Throughout King County, one-zone fares are $1.50; two-zone fares are $2. Onboard fare collection boxes have prices posted on them. The $5 King County Visitor Pass is a bargain if you're doing a lot of touring. Valid for one day, it includes rides on King, Pierce, and Snohomish county buses, the waterfront trolley, and the Elliott Bay Water Taxi. You can purchase passes online or at Metro offices.

Greyhound Lines and Northwest Trailways have regular service to points throughout the Pacific Northwest and the United States. The regional Greyhound/Trailways bus terminal at Ninth Avenue and Stewart Street is convenient to all Downtown destinations.

Bus Information Greyhound Lines ✉ 811 Stewart St., Downtown ☎ 800/231-2222 or 206/628-5526 ⊕ www.greyhound.com. **Metropolitan Transit** ☎ 206/553-3000, 206/287-8463 automated schedule line ⊕ transit.metrokc.gov/bus. **Northwest Trailways** ✉ 811 Stewart St., Downtown ☎ 800/366-3830 ⊕ www.trailways.com.

CAR TRAVEL

I–5, Seattle's major highway, runs right through the middle of the city and acts as the main north–south arterial. Route 99 (often referred to as Aurora Avenue) runs parallel to I–5 and is another main north–south throughway. Denny Way is an important east–west route within Seattle, especially for those trying to get from the waterfront or Lower Queen Anne to Capitol Hill. I–405 is the major highway that runs east of Lake Washington, beginning in South Center to connect Renton, Bellevue, Kirkland, and Woodinville.

I–90 is the major east–west state highway linking Seattle with south Bellevue, Issaquah, and cities east of the Cascades; Route 520 branches off from I–5 near Montlake and connects Seattle to north Bellevue and Redmond. The Lake Washington Floating Bridge (part of I–90) and the Evergreen Point Floating Bridge (part of Route 520) are the only routes across Lake Washington.

PARKING   Parking Downtown is scarce and expensive. Meters are $1 per hour and take quarters or dimes. On Sunday and after 6 PM street parking is free. Be vigilant during the day: parking enforcement officers are notoriously efficient. If you plan to be Downtown longer than two hours (the maximum time allowed on the street), you may find parking in a garage easier.

TRAFFIC   The I–5 corridor tends to be clogged with traffic heading into Downtown from both north and south from 7 to 9:30 each morning, and out again each evening from 4 to 6:30. It's not unusual for the heavy traffic pattern to continue throughout the day. There are two bridges heading east–west over Lake Washington, I–520 to the north of Downtown, and I–90 to the south. Traffic is usually better on one bridge than the other, so listen to local radio reports to make your choice about which one to use. On I–405, the north–south interstate highway on the east side of Lake Washington, the traffic is heavy during the traditional morning and evening rush hours.

EMERGENCIES

🔲 Doctors & Dentists **Dental Referral** ☎ 800/511-8663. **Doctor's Referral** ☎ 206/622-9933. **University of Washington Physicians Referral Service** ☎ 800/826-1121. 🔲 Emergency Services **Ambulance, Fire, and Police** ☎ 911.

MAIL & SHIPPING

There are post offices throughout Downtown Seattle and surrounding neighborhoods. They're generally well-staffed, and the lines move quickly. 🔲 Post Offices **Main Station** ✉ 301 Union St., Downtown ☎ 206/748-5417 or 800/275-8777. **Pioneer Square Station** ✉ 91 S. Jackson St., Pioneer Square ☎ 206/625-2293. **International District Station** ✉ 414 6th Ave. S, International District ☎ 206/625-2293. **Broadway Station** ✉ 101 E. Broadway, Capitol Hill ☎ 206/324-5474. 🔲 Overnight Services **Federal Express** ☎ 800/463-3339. **United Parcel Service** ☎ 800/742-5877. **United States Postal Service** ☎ 800/222-1811.

MONEY MATTERS

You generally need an account to cash a personal check at a specific bank. There are also check-cashing services (which charge a fee) throughout Seattle. However, it's best to use credit cards, cash machines, and traveler's checks while you're traveling. ATMs are *everywhere*. You can find them at banks, in grocery stores, convenience stores, many gas stations, restaurants, and bars. Most charge a 35¢ to $3 fee per transaction.

Bank of America, Seattle's largest American banking institution, has more than 50 area locations. Most are open weekdays 10–6 and some on Saturday 10–1. Key Bank has 40-plus branches. Hours are generally Monday–Thursday 9–5 and Friday 9–6. US Bank branches are open weekdays 9–5. Some are open Saturday 9–1. Washington Mutual's 40-plus branches have hours weekdays 9–6; some have hours Saturday 9–1. There are more than 30 branches of Wells Fargo; hours are weekdays 9–6. Some are open Saturday 9–2.

🔲 **Bank of America** ☎ 206/461-0800 ⊕ www.bankofamerica.com. **Key Bank** ☎ 206/447-5767 ⊕ www.keybank.com. **US Bank** ☎ 800/872-2657 ⊕ www.usbank.com. **Washington Mutual** ☎ 800/756-8000 ⊕ www.wamu.com. **Wells Fargo** ☎ 800/869-3557 ⊕ www.wellsfargo.com.

MONORAIL TRAVEL

Built for the 1962 World's Fair, the Seattle Monorail is a quick, convenient link between the Seattle Center and Downtown's Westlake Mall, located at Fourth Avenue and Pike Street. Making the 1-mi journey in just two minutes, the monorail departs both points every 10 minutes from 7:30 AM to 11 PM on weekdays and 9 AM to 11 PM weekends. The round-trip fare is $3; children 4 and under ride free. During weekends, Seattle Sonics basketball games, and the Folklife, Bite of Seattle, and Bumbershoot festivals—which all take place at the Seattle Center—you can park in the Bon-Macy's garage at Third Avenue and Stewart Street, take the monorail, and present your monorail ticket stub when you return for discounted parking rates of $5 on Friday and Saturday and $4 on Sunday and Monday.

A monorail for West Seattle, which would circle the California Avenue business core, is currently under construction.

🔲 **Seattle Center Monorail** ☎ 206/905-2600 ⊕ www.seattlemonorail.com.

STREETCAR TRAVEL

The Waterfront Streetcar line of vintage 1920s-era trolleys from Melbourne, Australia, runs 1.6 mi south along Alaska Way from Pier 70, past the Washington State Ferries terminal at Piers 50 and 52, turning inland on Main Street, and passing through Pioneer Square before ending on South Jackson Street in the International District. It runs at about 20-minute intervals daily from 7 AM to 9 or 10 PM (less often and for fewer hours in winter). The fare is $1.25 from 9 to 3 and after 6, $1.50 during peak commuting hours. The stations and streetcars are wheelchair accessible.

🚹 **Metropolitan Transit** ☎ 206/553-3000, 206/287-8463 automated schedule line ⊕ transit.metrokc.gov.

TAXIS

Rides generally run about $1.80 per mile, and it's usually easier to call for a taxi (no fee) than to flag down a ride on the street. There are no surcharges for late-night pickups. Taxis are readily available at most Downtown hotels. You can take an Atlas Towncar from the airport to your hotel for $45—or as far as Portland, Oregon, or Vancouver, British Columbia, for about $300. You can also hire a car and driver for the day; note that rates don't include the required 20% gratuity.

🚹 Taxi Companies **Atlas Towncar** ☎ 206/860-7777 or 888/646-0606 ⊕ www. atlastowncar.com. **Graytop Cab** ☎ 206/282-8222. **Orange Cab** ☎ 206/522-8800. **Yellow Cab** ☎ 206/622-6500.

TOURS

BALLOON Over the Rainbow offers balloon tours in Woodinville in spring and summer, weather permitting. The cost is between $135 and $165 and includes a morning champagne toast or a light supper at night.

BICYCLING Blazing Saddles rents bikes and runs tours of the Burke Gilman Trail, the Ballard Locks, and Bainbridge Island. Terrene Tours organizes private day trips for groups of up to five for $580, which includes bike rental, guide, support van, lunch, and drinks; you can also set up overnight tours here of the surrounding countryside and islands.

BOAT Argosy Cruises sails around Elliott Bay (one hour, from Pier 55, $16), the Ballard Locks (2½ hours, from Pier 56, $30), and other area waterways. Let's Go Sailing permits passengers to take the helm, trim the sails, or simply enjoy the ride aboard the *Obsession* or the SC70 *Neptune's Car*, both 70-foot ocean racers. Three 1½-hour excursions ($23) depart daily from Pier 54. A 2½-hour sunset cruise ($38) is also available. Passengers can bring their own food on board.

BUS TOURS Gray Line of Seattle operates bus and boat tours, including a six-hour Grand City Tour ($39), whichincludes many sights, lunch in Pike Place Market, and admission to the Space Needle observation deck.

CARRIAGE Sealth Horse Carriages narrated tours ($50 per half hour, $100 per hour) trot away from the waterfront and Westlake Center.

ORIENTATION For $36, Show Me Seattle takes up to 14 people in customized vans on day tours of the major sights, including the *Sleepless in Seattle* floating home, the Fremont Troll, and other offbeat stops. For the same price, Seattle Tours also has day tours of the city and its environs, with stops for picture taking. The Seattle Skyscrapers Tour visits all the major buildings of Downtown in about two hours for $12.

WALKING Chinatown Discovery Tours include four culinary excursions—from a light sampler to an eight-course banquet. The rates are $15 to $46, based on a minimum of four participants. Seattle Walking Tours creates customized, 2½-hour itineraries that cover specific areas of the city. These tours cost $15 per person for a minimum of three guests. Underground Seattle leads tours ($9) of the now-buried original storefronts and sidewalks of Pioneer Square are extremely popular. They offer an effective primer on early Seattle history, and it may be a good place to take cover if your aboveground tour starts to get soggy.

🚹 Tour Companies **Argosy Cruises** ☎ 206/623-4252 ⊕ www.argosycruises.com. **Blazing Saddles** ☎ 206/341-9994. **Chinatown Discovery Tours** ☎ 425/885-3085. **Gray**

Line of Seattle ☎ 206/626-5208 or 800/426-7505 ⊕ www.graylineofseattle.com.
Let's Go Sailing ☎ 206/624-3931. **Over the Rainbow** ☎ 206/364-0995 ⊕ www.
letsgoballooning.com/Seattle. **Sealth Horse Carriages** ☎ 425/277-8282 ⊕ www8.
bcity.com/heavyhorse. **Seattle Tours** ☎206/768-1234 ⊕www.seattlecitytours.com. **Seattle Skyscrapers Tour** ☎ 206/667-9184. **Seattle Walking Tours** ☎ 425/885-3173
⊕ www.seattlewalkingtours.com. **Show Me Seattle** ☎ 206/633-2489 ⊕ www.
showmeseattle.com. **Terrene Tours** ☎ 206/325-5569. **Underground Seattle** ☎ 206/
682-4646 ⊕ www.ohwy.com/wa/u/undertou.htm.

TRAIN TRAVEL

Amtrak, the U.S. passenger rail system, has daily service to Seattle from
the Midwest and California. The *Empire Builder* takes a northern route
from Chicago to Seattle. The *Coast Starlight* begins in Southern California, makes stops throughout western Oregon and Washington, and
terminates its route in Seattle. The once-daily *Mt. Baker International*
takes a highly scenic coastal route from Seattle to Vancouver. There is
not adequate train service in western Washington. The best regional train
service is offered to Oregon and Vancouver, B.C.

Sounder Trains (commuter rails) are still a new phenomenon in Seattle—and as such, you can only travel north to the city in the mornings
and south from Downtown during weekday evenings. Plans are in the
works to create more round-trips and to extend service to communities
north to Everett and from Lakewood to Tacoma. For now, trains leave
Tacoma at 6:15 AM and 6:45 AM, with stops in Puyallup, Sumner,
Auburn, Kent, and Tukwila prior to Seattle. Southbound trains leave
Seattle at 5:10 and 5:35 PM.

The cost is $2 for one zone, $3 for two zones, and $4 from endpoint to
endpoint; kids under six ride free. Tickets can be purchased at machines
inside the stations or by mail. One-week, two-week, and monthly passes
are also available. Transfers from Sounder Trains are accepted on buses
throughout the region. For more information, contact Metropolitan Transit or Pierce Transit.

🚆 Train Information **Amtrak** ✉ King Street Station, 303 S. Jackson St., International
District ☎ 206/382-4125 or 800/872-7245 ⊕ www.amtrak.com. **Metropolitan Transit**
☎ 206/553-3000, 206/287-8463 automated schedule line ⊕ transit.metrokc.gov.
Pierce Transit ☎ 253/581-8000 ⊕ www.ptbus.pierce.wa.us. **Sounder Trains** ☎ 888/
889-6368 ⊕ www.soundtransit.org.

VISITOR INFORMATION

🚆 Tourist Information **Seattle/King County Convention and Visitors Bureau** ✉ 520
Pike St., Suite 1300, Downtown, 98101 ☎ 206/461-5800 ⊕ www.seeseattle.org. **Seattle Visitor Center** ✉ Washington State Convention Center, 800 Convention Pl., Downtown, 98104 ☎ 206/461-5840. **Washington State Convention & Trade Center** ✉ 800
Convention Pl., Downtown, 98104 ☎ 206/447-5000 ⊕ www.wsctc.com. **Washington
Tourism Development Division** ✉ Box 42500, Olympia, WA 98504 ☎ 360/725-5050
⊕ www.tourism.wa.gov.

WASHINGTON

4

FODOR'S CHOICE

Ann Starrett Mansion, *Port Townsend B & B*

Birchfield Manor, *Yakima inn and restaurant*

C'est Si Bon, *Port Angeles restaurant*

Christina's, *Eastsound restaurant*

Colette's Bed & Breakfast, *Port Angeles*

Columbia Gorge Interpretive Center, *Stevenson*

Crystal Mountain Ski Area, *Crystal Mountain*

Duck Soup Inn, *Leavenworth restaurant*

Eagle Point Inn, *Beaver*

Inn at Langley, *Snoqualmie inn and restaurant*

International Museum of Glass, *Port Gamble*

Lonny's, *Port Townsend restaurant*

Maryhill Museum of Art, *Goldendale*

Mt. Rainier National Park, *Ashford*

North Cascades Highway, *North Cascades National Park*

Panacea Bed and Breakfast, *Friday Harbor*

Poulsbo Marine Science Center, *Poulsbo*

Salish Lodge, *Snoqualmie hotel and restaurant*

Shelburne Inn, *Seaview inn and restaurant*

Spring Bay Inn, *Olga*

The Ark, *Nahcotta restaurant*

The Summit at Snoqualmie, *Snoqualmie ski resort*

Vintage Inn, *Vancouver*

Wonderland Trail, *Mt. Rainier National Park*

LONG BEFORE OUTDOOR ADVENTURES WERE POPULAR in the rest of the country, they were a way of life for Washington residents—and still are. In this state, you're never far from natural attractions: saltwater sounds, windswept beaches, purling rivers, alpine peaks, majestic canyons, and rolling hills. The southern shore's sandy strands and calm bays contrast with the Olympic Peninsula's rugged sea cliffs. The coastal rain forests and the moist slopes of the Cascade Mountains are robed in moss and bedecked with ferns; the music of waterfalls and songbirds enlivens the deepest woods. East of the Cascades, mighty rivers flow through steep-walled coulees, while eagles and curlews drift above wildflowers and sagebrush, grasslands and wheat fields. Here ponds and lakes attract ducks, geese, and sandpipers; sandhill cranes stalk through irrigated fields bordering dry steppe.

The Salish Sea, a multifingered saltwater inlet, meanders inland, south to the state capital of Olympia and north to the Canadian waters of the Inland Passage. Large cities and busy ports—Seattle, Tacoma, Everett, and Bellingham—border these inland waters. The islands of southern Puget Sound, the Kitsap Peninsula, and the San Juan archipelago divide the Salish Sea into inlets and tidal passages. From these labyrinthine shores, where villages have sheltered moorages for pleasure boats, rise Mt. Rainier, the Olympic Mountains, Mt. Baker, and the North Cascades.

The mountains put on the most spectacular display of wildflowers in spring and summer. Flowering plums and cherries, dogwoods, rhodo-dendrons, azaleas, and peonies light up the landscape with the colors of an impressionist palette. In winter skiers rush to the area's slopes, from Mt. Baker in the north to White Pass in the south. Winthrop, Leav-enworth, and other small, friendly towns of the glaciated valleys east of the mountains are popular with cross-country skiers. Two great rivers, the Columbia and the Snake, flow through the arid steppes of the Columbia Plateau, greening a patchwork quilt of fields and fruit or-chards. The flow of these rivers is interrupted by dams, of which Grand Coulee Dam is the mightiest. The warm beaches of Lake Chelan, a deep inland fjord, draw Seattleites pining for the sun.

Bathed in constant radiance, vegetables and fruits thrive in the deep, fer-tile soils of the Yakima and Walla Walla valleys, beneath slopes covered with vineyards. Vast fields of wheat and barley gild the flanks of the Palouse and Horse Heaven Hills. Spokane, Washington's second-largest city, rules as the "Capital of the Inland Empire," a mountainous region of pastures and forests.

Exploring Washington

The Cascade Range divides Washington into western and eastern halves, which differ considerably in climate and topography. Western ecosys-tems vary from coastal areas to moist forests; eastern ecosystems range from pine woods to dry grass-and-brush steppes, from deep river val-leys to lakes and marshes. Curiously, the hot-summer "dry" east side has more wetlands and marshes than the cool-summer "wet" west side of the state. Both sections have alpine fells, which on the east side have two timberlines: one on the upper slopes (where forests are restricted by the heavy snows and frosts of an alpine climate), and another on the lower slopes (where tree growth is limited by lack of moisture).

About the Restaurants

Washington's abundant seafood shows up on menus throughout the state, and spicy yet subtle flavors testify to strong Asian influences. Tender halibut, sweet Dungeness crab, plump oysters, and delicate mussels are

314 <   **Washington**

as popular as the ubiquitous salmon. Coastal forests are rich in wild mushrooms, and the inland valleys are famed for their beef and lamb in addition to their wines. In autumn the mountains produce a bountiful harvest of wild berries; in fact, almost every region of the state grows great berries, as well as vegetables and apples. This bounty translates, in the hands of the state's many skilled chefs, into fine cuisine.

About the Hotels

There's a good mix of expensive and moderately priced properties throughout the state. Some of Washington's best lodgings are in bed-and-breakfasts (B&Bs) or small inns surrounded by breathtaking natural beauty. They're often equipped with hot tubs and in-room fireplaces that take the edge off the crisp coastal or wintry inland air. A vast B&B network is operated by the state tourism board, and you can request a brochure or research your options online. For budget travelers, there are youth hostels, inexpensive chain hotels, and campsites.

WHAT IT COSTS					
	$$$$	**$$$**	**$$**	**$**	**¢**
RESTAURANTS	over $32	$24–$32	$16–$24	$8–$16	under $8
HOTELS	over $250	$200–$250	$150–$200	$100–$150	under $100

Restaurant prices are per person, for a main course at dinner. Hotel prices are for two people in a standard double room in high season, excluding tax.

Timing

Summer is the best time for hiking mountain trails and enjoying coastal beaches. Skies are often clear and temperatures mild; July and August can be downright hot. Spring is often overcast and wet, but it's the time to catch the gorgeous Skagit Valley tulip fields in full bloom. Leavenworth and other mountain towns can be as busy in summer with hikers as they are with skiers in winter. Coastal towns are packed on summer weekends. Note that some inns and restaurants close from late fall through spring—be sure to call ahead. Washington's major cities, however, are lively year-round.

SEATTLE ENVIRONS

Updated by
Holly S. Smith

Seattle and its surrounding suburbs form a metropolis that stretches from Arlington in the north to Olympia in the south, and from Snoqualmie Falls in the east to the western edge of the Kitsap Peninsula. This 100-mi-long, 40-mi-wide, roughly formed megacity is fragmented into slim inlets and forested islands by Puget Sound. Only one span, the Tacoma Narrows suspension bridge, connects the mainland to the Kitsap Peninsula; car and passenger ferries are the alternative. The region is further subdivided by Lake Washington, which separates Seattle from the Eastside. You can cross it on the Evergreen Point and Mercer Island floating bridges. A third floating bridge crosses the Hood Canal near Port Gamble, connecting the Kitsap and Olympic peninsulas.

Many of western Washington's business, social, and cultural interests are in Seattle. A day's drive around the area makes it clear, however, that even such suburbs as Bainbridge and Vashon islands, Tacoma and Olympia, or Gig Harbor and Bremerton are very separate communities. Seals, sea lions, and gray whales patrol the Salish Sea; wild ducks and geese invade waterfront parks; and deer, black bears, and cougars wander through the woods.

If you have
4 days

Tour the northern section of the Olympic Peninsula, visit one of the coastal islands, and roam through a bit of the Cascade Range. On the first day, head from Seattle to Port Townsend, a seaside town with Victorian buildings. Explore shops and galleries, have lunch, and then take the ferry to Whidbey Island, passing through Deception Pass State Park en route to Anacortes. Take a late-afternoon ferry to the San Juan Islands, disembarking on hilly Orcas Island, the more touristy San Juan Island, or quiet Lopez Island. Whichever island you choose, you'll need two full days. On the fourth day, catch an early ferry back to the mainland and head—via Everett and Route 2—out on a loop through the North Cascades. Have lunch in Bavarian–style Leavenworth, before crossing Snoqualmie summit via Route 97 and I–90. Pass through Cle Elum, and consider stopping in the small, picturesque town of Roslyn for dinner. From here it's less than two hours back to Seattle.

4

If you have
7 days

Spend two days exploring the Seattle area, including an afternoon ferry trip to Bainbridge Island. On Day 3, drive southeast to Mt. Rainier National Park and spend the night. On Day 4 drive to Yakima, then make a long southeastern loop through Pasco and Walla Walla on your way to Spokane. Spend the night, then use Day 5 to look around the city. On Day 6, start out early for Moses Lake then travel northwest along Route 2 to explore the apple fields of Wenatchee and Lavenworth. Spend the night, then make a sidetrip north to Lake Chelan before returning to Seattle.

If you have
10 days

Take two days to look around Seattle, including a trip to Bainbridge Island, then make an early start on Day 3 and drive south to Tacoma. Have lunch, then head for Olympia to visit the state capitol, and drive to Mt. Rainier National Park for the night. On Day 4 head west on Route 12 around the Olympic Peninsula to the seaside town of Ocean Shores. Spend the night, then on Day 5 drive up Route 101 through the old-growth forests of Olympic National Park, taking a break at the Hoh River Rain Forest or on the Quinault Indian Reservation. Overnight in Port Angeles, then on Day 6 drive up 5,200-foot-high Hurricane Ridge before heading to Port Townsend for the night.

On Day 7 take the ferry to Whidbey Island to visit Ft. Casey, the old Admiralty Head Lighthouse, Ebey's Landing National Historic Reserve, and Coupeville. Next, head for Anacortes and take the San Juan Island ferry, spending the night and Day 8 on lively San Juan Island, relaxed Orcas Island, or quiet Lopez Island. On Day 9, catch the ferry back and then explore nearby Mt. Baker, heading out on scenic Route 542 to Glacier. Spend the night, then return to Seattle via Routes 9 and 20 and I–5.

Bainbridge Island

❶ *9 mi northwest of Seattle by ferry.*

The 35-minute ferry ride to Bainbridge Island from downtown Seattle provides superb views of the city skyline and surrounding hills. The inexpensive ferry trip lures tourists to cross Puget Sound; Bainbridge's small-town vibe and scenic countryside tempt them to stay a while. From the ferry terminal, take a walking tour of Winslow along its compact main street, Winslow Way, where it's easy to wander away an afternoon among the antiques shops, art galleries, bookstores, and cafés. Visitors are free to use the yellow bicycles around the ferry docks.

Pass the Winslow Way turnoff and head about ¼ mi north on Olympic to the **Bainbridge Island Vineyard and Winery** (⊠ 682 Rte. 305 ☎ 206/ 842–9463), open for tastings and tours Wednesday–Sunday noon–5. If you first grab lunch provisions, you can picnic on the pretty grounds.

★ The 150-acre **Bloedel Reserve** has fine Japanese gardens, a bird refuge, a moss garden, and other gardens planted with island flora. A French Renaissance–style mansion is surrounded by 2 mi of trails and ponds dotted with trumpeter swans. Dazzling rhododendrons and azaleas bloom in spring, and Japanese maples colorfully signal autumn's arrival. Reservations are essential, and picnicking is not permitted. ⊠ 7571 NE Dolphin Dr., 6 mi west of Winslow, via Rte. 305 ☎ 206/842–7631 ⊕ www.bloedelreserve.org ⊠ $6 ⊘ Wed.–Sun. 10–4.

Where to Stay & Eat

$–$$$ ✕ **Ruby's on Bainbridge.** Dark-wood accents, antique paintings, and a fireplace in this old Tudor manor surround linen-cloaked tables with views of Rich Passage. Brie with warm mango chutney or roasted beet salad precede such mouth-watering entrées as *Amatriciana* (sautéed bacon and kalamata olive sauce over angel-hair pasta) and chicken-stuffed ravioli in Riesling cream sauce. Vegetarian dishes include eggplant layered with mozzarella and tomatoes. ⊠ 4738 Lynnwood Center Rd., Winslow ☎ 206/780–9303 ☐ AE, MC, V.

$–$$ ✕ **Bistro Pleasant Beach.** The simple restaurant focuses on flavorful, beautifully presented cuisine. Fine choices are the roasted lamb with cabernet glaze or the linguine with crisp prawns, fresh spinach and feta; yet, even the straightforward seafood chowder has gourmet aspirations. The seasonal Vintner Series set dinners, limited to 60 guests, pair exquisite appetizers and entrées with traditional but versatile wines. ⊠241 Winslow Way W, Winslow ☎ 206/842–4347 ☐ AE, MC, V ⊘ Closed Mon.

$ ✕ **Harbor Public House.** An 1881 estate home overlooking Eagle Harbor was renovated to create this casual restaurant at Winslow's public marina. Seafood tacos, pub burgers, and grilled flatiron steak sandwiches are typical fare, as are key lime pie and root beer floats. This is where the pleasure-boating crowds come to dine in a relaxed, waterfront setting. Things get raucous during Tuesday-night open-mike sessions. ⊠ 231 Parfitt Way, Winslow ☎ 206/842–0969 ☐ AE, DC, MC, V.

$ ▦ **Island Country Inn.** One of a high-quality chain of Northwest hotels, the inn mixes contemporary styles with country comforts. Elegant rooms, done in the colors of the surrounding forest and sunsets, have such amenities as data ports and down pillows. Deluxe rooms some rooms also have gas fireplaces, VCRs, and CD players. ⊠ 920 Holdebrand La. NE, Bainbridge 98110 ☎ 206/842–6861 or 800/842–8429 ⊟ 206/842–9808 ⊕ www. nwcountryinns.com ➣ 31 rooms, 15 suites ♿ In-room data ports, some kitchenettes, some microwaves, some refrigerators, cable TV, some in-room VCRs, pool, hot tub, some pets allowed ☐ AE, D, DC, MC, V ⋈ CP.

★ **¢–$$** ▦ **Waterfall Gardens.** Waterfalls and spring-fed ponds are threaded throughout the wooded, 5-acre property. Luxury suites, each with private entrance, occupy two homes: one before a tumbling stream and magnificent cedars, the other surrounded by ponds and deep forest. The grounds have paths and quiet sitting areas. ⊠ 7269 NE Bergman Rd.,

Beaches

The southwestern coast's long, surf-tossed sands are popular with hikers, kite flyers, bird-watchers, and surfers; however, the waves are very rough and the water is cold—making swimming almost impossible for most people. In season, folks come here by the thousands to dig for tasty razor clams. The Olympic Peninsula's beaches are rocky, though there are a few sandy coves tucked between the headlands. The muddy shores of the Salish Sea are popular with clamdiggers probing for the hard-shelled mollusks. Sandy beaches are scarce, even in the San Juan Islands. More often than not, the glacier-cut rocks drop straight into the water. But tide pools teeming with sea slugs, crabs, anemones, and tiny fish hold a fascination all their own.

4

Bird-watching is great along all of the shores. California gray whales migrate close to the beaches of the outer shore and frequently visit the sheltered waters of the Salish Sea. The safest time for boating is from May to September, though storms can surprise boaters even in mid-summer. Sea kayaking is very popular, and most waterfront towns have kayak rentals.

Culture & History

Wooden blockhouses in Centralia, Tacoma, and on Whidbey Island survived the Indian wars of the turbulent mid-19th-century. There are remnants of old army forts at White Swan, near Yakima; at Ft. Spokane on Lake Roosevelt; at Port Townsend; and on Marrowstone and Whidbey Islands. Almost every town has a museum of local history. Seattle and Spokane have excellent art museums (Spokane's collection of Indian art and Seattle's Asian art exhibits are world renowned) and first-rate symphonies and opera companies. Many smaller towns have annual theater productions and host concerts, gallery shows, and other cultural and arts events.

Forests

Forests in western Washington are dense and overgrown with ferns, mosses, and other vegetation. This is true of the rain forests of the southwest coast and the Olympic Peninsula as well as the forests on the western slopes of the Cascades. Trees in the alpine areas are often gnarled and bent by snow and wind into fascinating shapes. Forests east of the Cascades are sunny and contain stands of ponderosa pine. In spring the forest floor is covered with wildflowers, as are the steppes of the Columbia Plateau. From the San Juan Islands south, and on the mainland from Tacoma south, prairies are dotted with stands of Oregon white oak and evergreens.

Lakes & Rivers

It's best to visit eastern Washington's lakes and coulees between April and mid-October, when the weather is at its best. Lake Chelan, Moses Lake, and the Columbia River Gorge are very popular during the height of the travel season. The scenic, central Okanogan highlands and the southeastern Blue Mountains are uncrowded year-round. The state's turbulent mountain streams and rivers are popular with rafters and white-water kayakers. The 160-mi Cascadia Marine Trail, which is completely navigable by kayak, traces part of a trading route used by early Native Americans to get from Olympia to Point Roberts on the Canadian border.

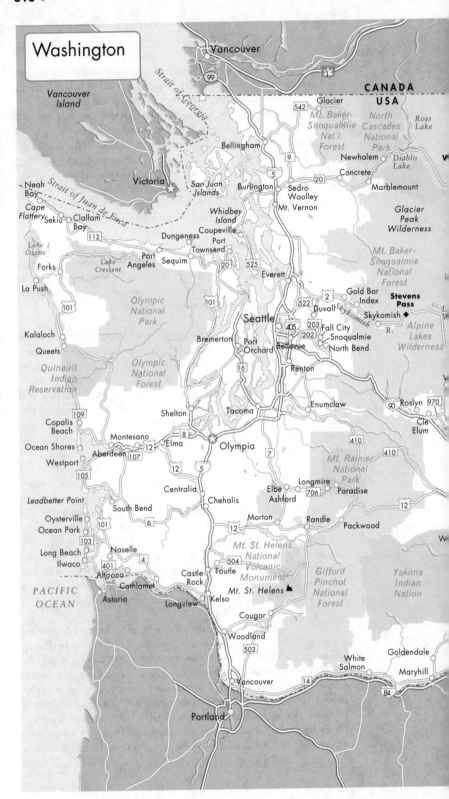

Washington

Vancouver

Strait of Georgia

99

CANADA
USA

Vancouver
Island

542   Glacier
   Mt. Baker-
   Snoqualmie
   Nat'l.   North
   Forest   Cascades   Ross
         National   Lake
Bellingham   Park

9   Newhalem   Diablo
5   Lake
Burlington   Sedro
         Woolley   20   Concrete
Mt. Vernon   Marblemount

Victoria   San Juan
         Islands   Glacier
                       Peak
Whidbey   Wilderness
Island
         Coupeville
Neah   Port
Bay   Cape   Dungeness   Townsend   Mt. Baker-
   Flattery Sekiu Clallam   Snoqualmie
         Bay   112   National
Lake   Sequim   20   525   Forest
Ozette   Port
      Angeles   Everett
                  2   Gold Bar
Forks   Lake   Index   Stevens
   Crescent   522   Duvall Skykomish   Pass
         101   Skykomish ◆
La Push   Seattle   203   Fall City   Alpine
   101   405   Snoqualmie   Lakes
Kalaloch   Bremerton   Port   202 North Bend   Wilderness
         Port   Orchard Bellevue
Queets   16   Renton
Quinault
Indian   Enumclaw
Reservation   Olympic   90   Roslyn 970
         National   Shelton   Tacoma
Copalis   Forest   Cle
Beach   Montesano   8   Elum
Ocean Shores   12 Elma   410
Westport   Aberdeen 107   Olympia   410
      105   12   7   Mt. Rainier
         12   5   National
         Centralia   Park
Leadbetter Point   Chehalis   Elbe Longmire
Oysterville   South Bend   Ashford 706 Paradise
Ocean Park   101   Morton   12
   103   6   Randle   Packwood
Long Beach   Naselle
Ilwaco   401   4   Castle   Toutle Mt. St. Helens   Gifford   Yakima
   Altoona   Rock   504 National   Pinchot   Indian
PACIFIC   Cathlamet   Volcanic   National   Nation
OCEAN   Astoria   Monument   Forest
      Longview Kelso Mt. St. Helens ▲
            Cougar

            Woodland
            503   Goldendale
                  White   Maryhill
                  Salmon
            Vancouver   14   84

      Portland

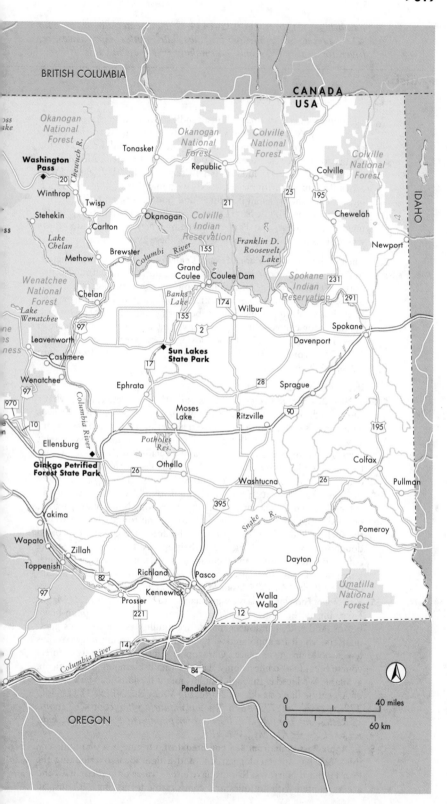

Bainbridge 98110 ☎ *206/842–1434* ⊕ *www.waterfall-gardens.com*
⊅ *4 suites* ⏥ *Some in-room hot tubs, kitchenettes, microwaves, re-frigerators, cable TV, ponds; no smoking* ⊟ *No credit cards.*

Poulsbo

❷ *12 mi northwest of Winslow.*

Velkommen til Poulsbo (*pauls*-bo), an endlessly charming village on lovely Liberty Bay. Soon after it was settled by Norwegians in the 1880s, shops and bakeries sprang up along Front Street, as did a cod-drying facility to produce the Norwegian delicacy called lutefisk. Although it's no longer made here, lutefisk is still served at holiday feasts. Front Street is crammed with authentic Norwegian bakeries, eclectic Scandinavian craft shops, small boutiques and bookstores, and art galleries. Norwegian flags flutter from the eaves of the town's chalet-style buildings. Grassy Liberty Bay Park is fronted by a network of slender docks where seals and otters pop in and out of the waves.

The excellent **Poulsbo Marine Science Center** is a wonderful introduction to Puget Sound's undersea life. A two-story mural at the entrance transports you below the ocean, and numerous "touch tanks" let you see and caress all sorts of saltwater creatures. Children will delight at patting starfish and playing games with tube worms. Be wary when you pick up the razor clams—they squirt! Anything dangerous or delicate is housed safely in glass tanks. The kid-loving docents are very knowledgable. ⊠ *18743 Front St. NE* ☎ *360/779–5549* ⊕ *www.poulsbomsc.org* ⊠ *$4* ⊘ *Daily 11–5.*

FodorsChoice
★

Where to Stay & Eat

¢–$ ✕ **New Day Seafood Eatery.** The restaurant's own crew catches what's cooked in the kitchen, fitting for a restaurant set right over the bay. Crowds gather in this rustic, nautical spot from lunchtime on for cold beer, water views, and lots of neighborly teasing. The inexpensive, tasty choices aren't surprising: grilled and fried fish, steamed shellfish, fish-and-chips, and burgers, salads, and sandwiches. You can't miss with the clam chowder. ⊠ *325 NE Hosmark St.* ☎ *360/697–3183* ⊟ *AE, MC, V.*

¢ ✕ **Sluys.** Pronounce it "Slews" and you'll sound like a local when you enter the town's most famous bakery. Gorgeous Norwegian pastries, braided bread, and *lefse* (traditional Norwegian round, flat bread) line the shelves. Kids often beg for one of the decorated cookies or frosted doughnuts, which are displayed at their eye level. There's only strong coffee and milk to drink, and there are no seats, but you can grab a bench along busy Front Street or take your goodies to the waterfront at Liberty Bay Park. ⊠ *18924 Front St.* ☎ *360/779–2798* ⊟ *MC, V.*

$–$$ ✕🏠 **Manor Farm Inn.** A classic white clapboard home built in 1886, Manor Farm Inn is the heart of a 25-acre farm. White walls, rough-hewn beams, and wide windows generate tranquillity in the spacious guest quarters, which are appointed with French country antiques. Two rooms have wood-burning fireplaces. Christopher's at the Inn ($$) serves a three-course breakfast to guests only. The seasonally changing dinner menu, available Wednesday through Sunday, might list Jamaican jerk chicken or Argentine flank steaks. ⊠ *26069 Big Valley Rd. NE, 98370* ☎ *360/779–4628* 🖷 *360/779–4876* ⊕ *www.manorfarminn.com* ⊅ *7 rooms* ⏥ *Restaurant, hot tub, bicycles; no room phones, no room TVs, no kids, no smoking* ⊟ *AE, MC, V* ❄⃝ *BP.*

¢–$ 🏠 **Agate Pass Waterfront Bed and Breakfast.** Originally a plant nursery, this B&B has spectacular gardens and a lighthouse overlooking the Port Orchard Narrows. Rooms have either water or garden views and are appointed with antiques and comfortable furnishings. It's just 50

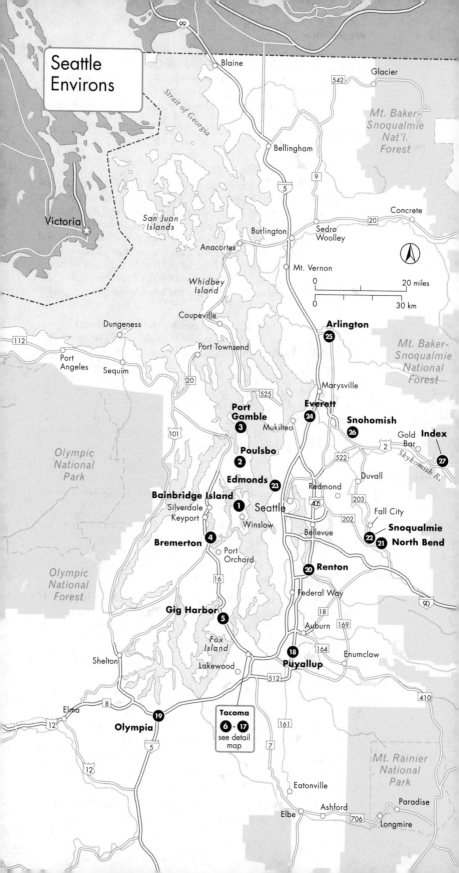

feet to the beach, and a minute's drive to the Agate Pass Bridge and Bain-bridge Island. ⊠ *16045 Rte. 305, Poulsbo, 98370* ☎ *206/842–1632 or 800/869–1632* ✍ *beds@agatepass.com* ➫ *3 rooms* ⚭ *Kitchenettes, microwaves, refrigerators, cable TV, in-room VCRs, beach; no smoking* ☰ *AE, D, DC, MC, V* ⦿ *BP.*

Port Gamble

❸ *6 mi northeast of Poulsbo.*

Residents from the opposite side of America founded Port Gamble around a sawmill in 1853; hence its New England–style architecture mimicking founder Capt. William Talbot's hometown of East Machias, Maine. Its setting amid the Kitsap Peninsula's tall stands of timber brought in great profits, but the mill was later destroyed by fire, and much of the forest has disappeared. Today many of the houses in this quiet town are on the National Register of Historic Places. A walk will take you past the 1870 St. Paul's Episcopal Church as well as the Thompson House, thought to be the state's oldest continuously lived-in home.

🖐 Behind the General Store, the **Port Gamble Historic Museum** takes you through original home and hotel rooms from the town's heyday. Highlights include artifacts from the Pope and Talbot Timber Company, which built the town, and realistic ship's quarters. Above the General Store, the **Of Sea and Shore Museum** houses more than 25,000 shells. Kids love the weird bug exhibit. Stop at the kitschy General Store for a cheap souvenir and a huge ice cream cone. ⊠ *1 Rainier Ave.* ☎ *360/297–8074* ⊕ *www.ptgamble.com* 💲 *$2.50* ⊗ *Historic museum: May–Oct., daily 10:30–5; Mar., Apr., and Nov., weekdays by appointment. Shell museum: Memorial Day to Labor Day, daily 10–4.*

Bremerton

❹ *18 mi southwest of Seattle by ferry, 68 mi southwest of Seattle by road, 25 mi southwest of Port Gamble by road.*

Nearly surrounded by water, and with one of the largest navy bases on the West Coast, Bremerton is a green city of colorful residential homes fronted by a wide bay full of war ships. Ten miles to the north, Keyport is a center for torpedo research, and nearby Bangor is home to a fleet of nuclear submarines.

From Bremerton you can make a quick trip to Port Orchard on the 1817 MV *Carlisle II* passenger ferry, one of the last of the famed Mosquito Fleet. When you arrive, head to Bay Street, crammed with antiques shops, craft stores, and galleries, or to the Saturday morning farmers' market, which bustles from April through October. Picnic at the marine park, then walk uphill along Sidney Avenue to view the memorabilia at the Log Cabin Museum. Meander along the Beach Drive waterfront to Manchester, where you'll have a gorgeous view of the Seattle skyline.

You can walk or picnic at the **Bremerton Marina** while watching the boats come and go. You'll see a host of birds and marine life around the docks and sunny waterfront park. ⊠ *Off Washington Ave.*

The **Bremerton Naval Museum** is in the ferry terminal. It has ship models, historic displays, and American and Japanese war artifacts. ⊠ *408 Pacific Ave.* ☎ *360/479–7447* 💲 *Free* ⊗ *Mon.–Sat. 10–4, Sun. 1–4.*

🖐 The **USS *Turner Joy*** Navy destroyer is open for self-guided tours. Walk through the narrow passages to view the cafeteria, medical office, barbershop, prison cell, cramped bunk rooms, and captain's quarters. Wear skid-resistant shoes and be wary of low doorways and hanging pipes. ✉ *300 Washington Beach Ave.* ☎ *360/792–2457* 🖙 *$7* ⊘ *Daily 10–4.*

The small **Kitsap County Historical Society Museum** has pioneers' artifacts, nautical items, and a collection of old photographs. ✉ *280 4th St.* ☎ *360/479–6226* ⊕ *www.waynes.net/kchsm* 🖙 *$2, free 1st Fri. of month* ⊘ *Tues.–Sat. 9–5.*

☝ In front of the **Naval Undersea Museum** is the 88-ton *Trieste II* submarine, which dove to the deepest spot in the ocean (the Marianas Trench) in 1960. In the main building are torpedoes, diving equipment, model submarines, and mines. ✉ *610 Dowell St., Keyport* ☎ *360/396–4148* ⊕ *num.kpt.nuwc.navy.mil* 🖙 *Free* ⊘ *June–Sept., daily 10–4; closed Tues. Oct.–May.*

Where to Stay & Eat

$–$$ ✕ **Boat Shed.** At this deliberately rustic waterfront restaurant diners share a casual, seaside camaraderie as they slurp up clam chowder, steamed clams, and mussels. Sailors, who enjoy free boat moorage, arrive early for the famed Sunday brunch. ✉ *101 Shore Dr., Bremerton* ☎ *360/377–2600* ☰ *AE, MC, V.*

$–$$ ✕ **Yacht Club Broiler.** With lovely views of Dyes Inlet (where gray whales are occasionally spotted), this simple but elegant family restaurant specializes in fresh, flavorful seafood. For those who prefer meat, the prime Nebraska steak is a good bet. In warm weather you can dine outside on the deck or on an adjacent grassy knoll. ✉ *9226 Bayshore Dr., Silverdale* ☎ *360/698–1601* ☰ *AE, D, MC, V.*

$–$$ ✕🖫 **Illahee Manor Bed and Breakfast.** Six acres of woods, orchards, and gardens surround this 1920s bayfront manor with its own beach. Some rooms have fireplaces and balconies; those in the turret have wraparound windows looking out onto grounds roamed by llamas and miniature deer. The Beach House has floor-to-ceiling windows, and the 1918 Cottage has rustic charm. The light- and plant-filled conservatory is a fine place to enjoy breakfast. ✉ *6680 Illahee Rd. NE, Bremerton 98311* ☎ *360/ 698–7555 or 800/693–6680* 🖷 *360/698–0688* ⊕ *www.illaheemanor. com* 🛏 *5 rooms, 2 cabins* ⚿ *Restaurant, room service, in-room hot tubs, some microwaves, refrigerators, cable TV, in-room VCRs, pond, some pets allowed* ☰ *AE, D, MC, V* ⦿ *BP.*

¢ ✕🖫 **Oyster Bay Inn.** This hotel sits at the lower curve of Oyster Bay, just outside of Bremerton but seemingly on an isle of its own. Panoramic views of the water are the highlight of the comfortable rooms, and you can see the bay up close on a stroll through the surrounding gardens and woods. The elegant restaurant is a lively spot to feast on seafood, steaks, and fancy pastas. Afterward head to the adjacent lounge, which has a piano bar. ✉ *4412 Kitsap Way, 98312* ☎ *360/377–5510 or 800/ 393–3862* ⊕ *www.oysterbayinn.com* 🛏 *62 rooms, 10 suites, 1 chalet* ⚿ *Restaurant, some kitchenettes, microwaves, refrigerators, cable TV, lounge, piano bar, some pets allowed (fee)* ☰ *AE, D, DC, MC, V* ⦿ *CP.*

¢–$$ 🖫 **Howard Johnson Plaza Hotel.** This chain hotel near Bremerton's naval base is a good choice for families. Rooms, although generic, have comfortable, upscale furnishings—and most have glorious views of the water and mountains. When winter rains render a walk along the waterfront park impossible, head to the indoor pool or hot tub. ✉ *5640 Kitsap Way, Bremerton 98312* ☎ *360/373–9900* 🖷 *360/377–8529* ⊕ *www.hojo.com* 🛏 *145 rooms* ⚿ *Restaurant, room service, in-room safes, some in-room hot tubs, cable TV, indoor pool, gym, hot tub, laundry service, concierge, meeting rooms, no-smoking rooms* ☰ *AE, D, DC, MC, V.*

¢ ▦ **Flagship Inn.** Although it's a budget spot, rooms here have private balconies overlooking Oyster Bay and the Olympic Mountains. It's close to everything, your room is stocked with amenities, and there's even a free video library for rainy evenings. Free tea, coffee, fruit, and cookies are available all day. ⊠ *4320 Kitsap Way, 98312* ☎ *360/479–6566 or 800/447–9396* 🖷 *360/479–6745* ⊕ *www.flagship-inn.com* ↩ *29 rooms* ⌂ *In-room data ports, kitchenettes, microwaves, refrigerators, cable TV, in-room VCRs, pool, business services* ▭ *AE, D, DC, MC, V* ⎁ *CP.*

Gig Harbor

❺ *23 mi southeast of Bremerton.*

One of the most picturesque and accessible waterfront cities on Puget Sound, Gig Harbor has a neat, circular bay dotted with sailboats and fronted by hills of evergreens pocketed with million-dollar homes. Expect spectacular views all along the town's winding 2-mi, bayside walkway, which is intermittently lined by boat docks, kitschy shops, cozy cafés, and broad expanses of open water.

The bay was a storm refuge for the 1841 survey team of Captain Charles Wilkes, who named the area after his small gig (boat). A decade later Croation and Scandinavian immigrants put their fishing, lumber, and boat-building skills to profitable use, and the town still has strong seafaring traditions. By the 1880s, steamboats carried passengers and goods between the harbor and Tacoma, and auto ferries plied the narrows between the cities by 1917.

The town winds around the waterfront, centering at the crossroads of Harborview Drive and Pioneer Way, where shops, art galleries, and restaurants often attract more foot traffic than vehicles. From here, Harborview makes a long, gentle curve around the bay toward the renovated Finholm Market building, which has shops, docks, a restaurant, kayak rentals, and more views. A Gig Harbor Historical Society self-guided walk brochure covers 49 sights.

Along the waterfront is **Jersich Park,** where the Fisherman's Memorial statue commemorates the town's sea-loving founders. A long walkway slopes right out into the bay, toward a sunny sitting spot where you can watch pleasure boats sliding in and out of the docks and kayakers practicing their paddling.

The **Gig Harbor Museum** has exhibits describing the city's maritime history, photo archives, and a research library. News clippings and videos about "Galloping Gertie," the original bridge, are particularly eerie. (⊠ 4218 Harborview Dr. ☎ 253/858–6722 ⎅ $2 ⊙ Tues.–Sat. 10–4)

Surrounding Gig Harbor, pine forests and open woods alternate with rolling pastures; it's enjoyable scenery (even on rainy days) during the 10-minute drive to **Fox Island.** Crossing the Fox Island Bridge over Echo Bay, you'll see stunning views of the Olympic Mountains to the right and the Tanglewood Lighthouse—against a backdrop of Mt. Rainier—to the left. At low tide, the rocky beach next to the bridge is scattered with stranded saltwater creatures. **Tanglewood Island,** the small drop of forest on which the Tanglewood lighthouse sits, was once an Indian burial grounds known as Grave Island.

The **Fox Island Historical Museum** displays island pioneer memorabilia in an authentic log cabin. Pioneer-days children's activities, such as dancing around the maypole dance and making old-fashioned Valentines, are scheduled the first Saturday of every month. ⊠ 1017 9th Ave. ☎ 253/549–2461 ⎅ $1 ⊙ Mon. and Sat. 1–4, Wed. 1–3.

Kopachuk State Park, a 10-minute drive from Gig Harbor, is a wonderful beachcombing area at low tide. Indian tribes once fished and clammed here, and you can still see people trolling the shallow waters or digging deep for razor clams in season. Children and dogs alike delight in discovering huge Dungeness crabs, sea stars, and sand dollars. Picnic tables and walking trails are interspersed throughout the steep, forested hills, and the campground is always full in summer. ⊠ *11101 56th St. NW* ☎ *253/265–3606* 🕮 *$5 per car* ⊗ *Daily 6 AM–10 PM.*

Where to Stay & Eat

$$–$$$ ✕ **Anthony's HomePort.** Here you're encircled by wide windows overlooking boats slipping through sapphire waters. Fine Northwest wines match: alder-planked salmon; red-broth cioppino; and ginger soy tuna with homemade pineapple chutney. Dine downstairs in the more casual Shoreline Room and you'll get the same pretty views without the wait (although the menu is lighter). In warm weather you can eat outside on the deck, and boat moorage is free. ⊠ *8827 N. Harborview Dr.* ☎ *253/853–6353* ▭ *AE, D, DC, MC, V* ⊗ *No lunch* ⊠ *Point Defiance Park, 5910 N. Waterfront Dr., Tacoma* ☎ *253/752–9700.*

$$ ✕ **Green Turtle.** The unassuming exterior belies a dining room surrounded by a mural of an azure underwater world, one that includes a huge sea turtle. Wraparound windows show off the bayside setting, as does the front deck. Eclectic Northwest cuisine is beautifully presented in such dishes as saffron rice with rare yellowfin ahi coated in black peppercorns and topped with roasted garlic and ginger glaze. It's difficult to leave without succumbing to crepes suzette topped with vanilla ice cream and warm orange liqueur. ⊠ *2905 Harborview Dr.* ☎ *206/851–3167* ▭ *AE, MC, V* ⊗ *No lunch Sun.*

$–$$$ ✕ **Beach House.** A weathered wood exterior gives this roadhouse-style restaurant at the edge of Henderson Bay a comfortable, summertime feel. Inside, though, the seafood dishes are nothing less than spectacular. Water views and a smart waitstaff make eating here a first-class experience, and you don't have to dress to the nines to have it, either. ⊠ *13802 Purdy Dr. NW* ☎ *253/858–9900* ▭ *AE, D, DC, MC, V.*

$–$$ ✕ **Marco's.** Step beneath the grapevine-entwined trellises and you're transported to Italy. Forest-green walls surround country-style furniture and old wooden wine cartons; candles cast a romantic glow. Homemade pastas and rich sauces bring texture and authentic flavors to classic seafood marinara, spinach fettuccine with tiger prawns, and half-duck with spicy plum sauce served over fettuccine. Excellent Italian, French, Californian, and Northwest wines are on hand. ⊠ *7707 Pioneer Way* ☎ *253/858–2899* ▭ *AE, MC, V* ⊗ *Closed Sun. and Mon. No lunch.*

¢–$ ✕ **El Pueblito.** The mariachi music, cilantro and chili pepper scents from the kitchen, and a waitstaff that chats in Spanish are reminiscent of a compact cantina south of the border. Huge portions of better-than-average Mexican dishes and frothy margaritas are served amid much gaiety. Located across the street from Jersich Park, the restaurant gets busy in the evenings. ⊠ *4120 Harborview Dr.* ☎ *253/851–1033* ▭ *MC, V.*

¢–$ ✕ **Judson Street Café.** Tucked inside the Gig Harbor Rexall drugstore, what started as a little 1950s-style soda fountain has expanded into an elegant café with booths and a grill-side counter. Heaping sandwiches and homemade soups draw crowds at lunchtime; locals come earlier on weekends for enormous Belgian waffles and steaming lattes. ⊠ *3114 Judson St. NW* ☎ *253/853–3877* ▭ *AE, MC, V.*

¢–$ ✕ **Le Bistro.** A charming, long-time local favorite, this cozy two-story former home has creaky wooden floors, close-set tables, and a porch with the best bay view in town. Chalkboard specials include mixed salads, hearty soups, and stacked sandwiches or wraps, all freshly made. Or order a hot drink and dig into a rich torte or slice of carrot cake. ⊠ *4120 Harborview Dr.* ☎ *253/851–1033* ▤ *MC, V.*

$–$$ ⌂ **Inn at Gig Harbor.** The largest hotel this side of the Narrows Bridge has a multicolor exterior that makes it seem more like a mansion than a member of the Heritage chain. Upstairs from the lodgelike foyer and handsome restaurant are the elegantly decorated rooms, many with Mt. Rainier views. All suites have fireplaces. Many of the guests are traveling on business, as the hotel is within easy driving distance of Seattle, Tacoma, and Bremerton. ⊠ *3211 56th St. NW* ☎ *253/858–1111 or 800/ 795–9980* 🖷 *253/851–5402* ⊕ *www.innatgigharbor.com* ➶ *52 rooms, 12 suites* ⌂ *Restaurant, room service, in-room data ports, some in-room hot tubs, minibars, cable TV, gym, outdoor hot tub, massage, shop, laundry service, business services, meeting rooms, airport shuttle, car rental* ▤ *AE, D, DC, MC, V* ⦿⎮ *CP.*

$ ⌂ **Beachside Bed & Breakfast.** You're right on the beach, surrounded by blossoming gardens, at this waterfront gem on Fox Island. The sunny suite's feminine touches—lacy curtains, floral couches, and frilly bedspread—are tempered by the masculinity of the beamed ceiling, enormous brick fireplace, and bold maritime accents. Step onto the deck and you're inspired to stroll on the pebbled sand, dip into the hot tub, or take a boat cruise from the deep-water moorage. A basket of homemade goodies awaits you each morning. ⊠ *679 Kamus Dr.* 🖷🖷 *253/549–2524* ⊕ *www.beachsidebb.com* ➶ *1 suite* ⌂ *Kitchen, microwave, refrigerator, cable TV, in-room VCR, hot tub, beach, boating; no smoking* ▤ *No credit cards* ⦿⎮ *CP.*

¢–$ ⌂ **Maritime Inn.** On a hill across from Jersich Park and the docks, this boutique hotel combines class and comfort with water views. Individually decorated and themed rooms include the Captain's Room, the Canterwood Golf Room, and the Victorian Room. All have fireplaces, and several have decks. Cottages along the back of the hill afford privacy and quiet; streetside rooms are noisy but have excellent views. ⊠ *3112 Harborview Dr.* ☎ *253/858–1818* ⊕ *www.maritimeinn.com* ➶ *15 rooms* ⌂ *In-room data ports, minibars, cable TV; no smoking* ▤ *AE, D, DC, MC, V.*

¢–$ ⌂ **Rose of Gig Harbor.** Sitting pretty right along the bayside road in downtown Gig Harbor, this 1917 landmark Craftsman home is fronted by a lovely garden and a brick porch where high tea is often served. Rooms have pastel walls, antiques, and many original fixtures. The elegant rooms have private baths; two have sitting rooms above the gardens. The bedand-breakfast also hosts club meetings, quilting bees, bridal and baby showers, and girls' birthday parties complete with princess dress-up attire and tea. ⊠ *3202 Harborview Dr.* ☎ *253/853–7990 or 877/640– 7673* ⊕ *www.gigharborrose.com* ➶ *1 room, 2 suites* ⌂ *Dining room* ▤ *AE, D, MC, V* ⦿⎮ *BP.*

Nightlife

BARS & LOUNGES **Art and Soul** (⊠ 3210 Harborview Dr. ☎ 253/851–3277), a pottery painting shop, is fronted by a coffee room that hosts acoustic guitar players in the evenings. It's a dive, but the unheated bar and wide deck at the **Hy-Iu-Hee-Hee** (⊠ 4309 Burnham Dr. ☎ 253/851–7885) tavern are packed nightly with locals wanting cheap drinks, dart and pool games, and big portions of bar food. The legendary **Tide's Tavern** (⊠ 2925 Harborview Dr. ☎ 253/858–3982), right on the water in a weather-worn building that housed the town's original general store, has been the local hot spot for drinks, darts, and live music since the 1930s.

Sports & the Outdoors

SAILING & **Arabella's Landing** (⊠ Harborview Dr. at Dororitch La., just past the
BOATING Bayview Dock ☎ 253/851–1793) provides moorage for those coming

by boat into Gig Harbor. **Charter Options** (⊠ 4316 N. Foxglove Dr. NW ☎ 253/851–4316) hires out its 65-foot sailboat. **Gig Harbor Rent-a-Boat** (⊠ 8829 N. Harborview Dr. ☎ 253/858–7341) has power boats, kayaks, pedal boats, and a 22-foot sailboat for hire. **Gig Harbor Sailing Club and School** (⊠ 3226 Harborview Dr. ☎ 253/858–3626) offers classes. **Gig Harbor Kayak Center** (⊠ 8809 N. Harborview Dr. ☎ 253/851–7987 or 888/429–2548) rents kayaks and leads trips.

SCUBA DIVING   The largest artificial reef in the world is beneath the Tacoma Narrows Bridge, where the original span collapsed in 1940. Sunrise Beach and the Fox Island bridge are other popular cold-water dive spots. **Tagert's Dive and Surf** (⊠ 4021 Harborview Dr. ☎ 253/857–3660) organizes trips, rents equipment, and offers dive lessons; kite-boarding equipment and classes are also available.

Tacoma

6–**17** *25 mi southeast of Gig Harbor, 34 mi southwest of Seattle.*

Tacoma is coming into its own, having in the last decade blossomed into a very livable city that has good museums, an edgy arts scene, and attractive old suburbs. It's a broad, hilly city whose clean-cut waterfront stretches west from the busy port, past the city and Puget Sound islands to the cliff-lined Tacoma Narrows. Renovated 18th-century homes, pretty beaches, and parks pocket the outskirts, and a young population gives the city a spirited character. The Tacoma Dome, that wooden, blue-and-gray half-sphere stadium visible along I–5, hosts international expos, sporting events, and famous entertainers in its 28,000-seat arena. The city's convenient setting provides easy access to Seattle and Canada to the north; the small town of Auburn to the northeast; Mt. Rainier to the east; Olympia to the south; and the Kitsap and Olympic peninsulas to the west.

Tacoma was the first Puget Sound port connected by train to the East, and its economy was once based on the railroad. Old photos show tall-masted windjammers loading at the City Waterway, whose storage sheds were promoted by local boosters as the "longest warehouse under one continuous roof in the world." The city's shipping industry certainly weathered the tests of time, as Tacoma is the largest container port in the Northwest.

Exploring

a good tour

Begin your tour early at **Union Station 6**, with its sapphire-blue chandelier and other colorful glass pieces created by world-famous artist (and homeboy) Dale Chihuly. Linked by a courtyard to the station is the state-of-the-art **Washington State History Museum 7**, connected to the **International Museum of Glass 8** by the beautiful Chihuly Bridge of Glass. Have lunch downtown, then head north on Pacific Avenue to the **Tacoma Art Museum 9**, where you'll see more Chihuly works amid the paintings and sculptures. Go west on 11th Street to Broadway, then walk north past the **Broadway Center for the Performing Arts 10** and the compact **Children's Museum of Tacoma 11**. At Ninth Street begins **Antique Row**, a collection of shops. From here, continue north on Broadway and turn left on South 3rd Street until the intersection with G Street, which marks the entrance to **Wright Park 12**. Stroll through the gardens and conservatory, then head across the street to the **Karpeles Manuscript Library Museum 13**. Return to Broadway and walk north to North 3rd Street, where you can wander through the **Stadium Historic District 14** neighborhood. You'll need a car to reach the **Tacoma Nature Center 15**, a cabin in the woods where kids can see local wildlife. From this point, aim for the sweeping afternoon views of Puget Sound and the Tacoma Narrows from **Point Defiance Park** ⑯, which includes the Point Defiance Zoo and Aquarium. Along Five Mile Drive, take a gander at the **Tacoma Narrows Bridge** ⑰ spanning the deep chasm over the water; it's the only way to reach the Kitsap Peninsula from here. Follow Five Mile Drive back to the ferry landing, then drive southeast down the Ruston Way waterfront to end your tour at the restaurants and nightspots along Commencement Bay.

TIMING   Wander Union Station for half an hour, then spend an hour or more in the history and art museums; add an hour for the Museum of Glass. If you're kidless, skip the Children's Museum; otherwise, take an hour to breeze through the exhibits. Antique Row and Wright Park are half-hour stops at most, although the former might make shoppers dawdle and the latter makes a nice picnic spot. The Karpeles Manuscript Library Museum will take an hour. You'll need a half hour to view the Tacoma Nature Centers interpretive displays, and another half hour to walk the trails. Spend the afternoon at Point Defiance Park, or pick a highlight (the zoo, Owen Beach, the Rhododendron Gardens); each can be visited in an hour or less.

WHAT TO SEE   **Broadway Center for the Performing Arts.** Cultural activity in Tacoma cen-
⑩   ters on this complex of performance spaces. The famous theater architect B. Marcus Pritica designed the **Pantages** (✉ 901 Broadway ☎ 253/591–5890), a 1918 Greco-Roman–influenced music hall with classical figures, ornate columns, arches, and reliefs. W. C. Fields, Mae West, Charlie Chaplin, Bob Hope, and Stan Laurel all performed here. The Tacoma Symphony and BalleTacoma perform at the Pantages, which also presents touring shows. Adjacent to the Pantages, the contemporary **Theatre on the Square** (✉ Broadway between 10th and 11th Sts. ☎ 253/591–5890) is the home of the Tacoma Actors Guild, one of Washington's largest professional theater companies. In its early days, the **Rialto Theater** (✉ 301 S. 9th St. ☎ 253/591–5890) presented vaudeville performances and silent films. The Tacoma Youth Symphony now performs in the 1918 structure.

🖐 ⑪   **Children's Museum of Tacoma.** This narrow, somewhat dark, meandering space has fun activities for little ones: sand and water play, cut-and-paste crafts, and dress-up and puppet stages, among others. It's best for those under age 8; older children tend to get bored. Families get in free on the first Friday of the month. ✉ 936 Broadway ☎ 253/627–6031 ⊕ www.childrensmuseumoftacoma.org ⊠ $3 adults, $4 children 1–12 ☉ Tues.–Sat. 10–5, Sun. noon–5.

⑧   **International Museum of Glass.** The showpiece of this spectacular, 2-acre
Fodor'sChoice   combination of exhibit spaces and shops is the 500-foot-long Chihuly
★   Bridge of Glass, a tunnel of glorious color and light that stretches above I–705. Wander among the glittering waterfront galleries, and watch glass-blowing artists at work at the Hot Shop. You'll also find a souvenir shop and café; Howard Ben Tré's lovely Water Forest glass sculpture is in the garden. ✉ 1801 Dock St. ☎ 253/284–4750 ⊕ www.museumofglass. org ⊠ $10 ☉ Mon.–Wed., Fri., and Sat. 11–5, Thurs. 11–8, Sun. noon–5.

⑬   **Karpeles Manuscript Library Museum.** Housed in the former Carnegie Library and across from Wright Park, the museum exhibits letters and documents by those who have shaped history. This unusual collection includes rare and unpublished literary works and documents from around the world. ✉ 407 S. G St. ☎ 253/383–2575 ⊕ www.rain. org~karpeles ⊠ Free ☉ Tues.–Sat. 10–4.

Broadway Center
for the
Performing
Arts **10**

Children's
Museum of
Tacoma **11**

International
Museum
of Glass **8**

Karpeles
Manuscript
Library
Museum **13**

Point
Defiance
Park **16**

Stadium
Historic
District **14**

Tacoma Art
Museum **9**

Tacoma
Narrows
Bridge **17**

Tacoma Nature
Center at
Snake Lake **15**

Union Station **6**

Washington
State History
Museum **7**

Wright Park ...**12**

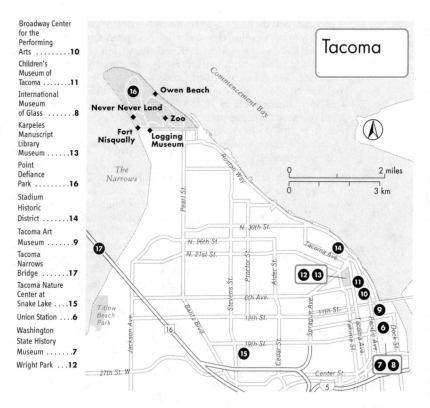

★ ☺ ⑯ **Point Defiance Park.** Jutting into Commencement Bay, this hilly, 698-acre
park surrounds Five Mile Drive with lush picnicking fields and patches
of forest. Hiking trails, bike paths, and numerous gardens draw crowds
year-round, particularly during summer festivals such as the Taste of
Tacoma, in June. The park begins at the north end of Pearl Street as you
drive toward the Point Defiance Ferry Terminal, where vehicles depart
for Vashon Island just across the Sound. A one-way road branches off
the ferry lane, past a lake and picnic area, a rose garden, and a Japanese garden, finally winding down to the beach.

One of the Northwest's finest collections of regional and international
species, **Point Defiance Zoo and Aquarium** displays animals—including elephants, polar bears, otters, and wolves—in natural-looking habitats. Hilly walkways and a petting farm are great fun for children, as is
the aquarium—with its floor-to-ceiling shark tank and state-of-the-art
sea horse exhibit, among other things. Special events include a costumed
Halloween trick-or-treat, and a nightly Zoolights Christmas light display in December. ⊠ *Point Defiance Park: 5400 N. Pearl St.* ☎ *253/
305–1000* ⊕ *www.pdza.org* ⊠ *Park free, zoo $7.75* ☉ *Park daily,
sunrise–sunset; zoo daily, Apr.–Memorial Day, 9–5; Memorial Day–Labor
Day, 9–6; Labor Day–1st weekend Nov., 9–5; 1st weekend Nov.–Apr.,
9:30–4.*

On Five Mile Drive, the **Rhododendron Species Botanical Garden** is a
22-acre expanse of more than 10,000 plants—some 2,000 varieties of
450 species—which bloom in succession. It's one of the finest rhododendron collections in the world. ⊠ *2525 S. 336 St.* ☎ *253/927–6960*
🖶 *253/838–4686* ⊠ *$4, free Nov.–Feb.* ☉ *Mar.–May, Mon.–Wed. and
Fri.–Sun. 10–4; June–Feb., Sat.–Wed. 11–4.*

A half-mile past the gardens is **Owen Beach,** a driftwood-strewn stretch of pebbly sand near the ferry docks and a wonderful place for beach-combing and sailboat-watching. Kayak rentals and concessions are available in summer.Continue around the looping drive, which offers occasional views of the narrows. Cruise slowly to take in the scenes—and watch out for joggers and bikers. Near the drive's end, the 15-acre **Camp Six Logging Museum** (☎ 253/752–0047) has restored bunkhouses, hand tools, and other equipment illustrating the history of steam logging from 1880 to 1950. From here, you can take a short ride through the woods on a steam train. The fare is $4, and the train runs weekends from noon until 4.

West of the Camp Six Logging Museum is **Ft. Nisqually** (☎ 253/591–5339), a restored Hudson's Bay Trading Post. A British outpost on the Nisqually Delta in the 1830s, it was moved to Point Defiance in 1935. The compound houses a trading post, granary, blacksmith's shop, bakery, and officers' quarters. Docents dress in 1850s attire and demonstrate pioneer skills like weaving and loading a rifle. Queen Victoria's birthday in August is a big event, and eerie candlelight tours run throughout October. It's open daily 11 to 6 Memorial Day–Labor Day, and Wednesday to Sunday 11–4 the rest of the year; admission is $3. **Never Never Land** (☎ 253/591–6117), a children's fantasy world of sculptured storybook characters, is across the parking lot from Ft. Nisqually.

⑭ Stadium Historic District. Several of the Victorian homes in this charming neighborhood, high on a hill overlooking Commencement Bay, have been converted to bed-and-breakfast inns. Stadium High School at 111 North E Street is in an elaborate château-style structure built in 1891 as a luxury hotel for the Northern Pacific Railroad. The building was converted into a high school after a 1906 fire.

⑨ Tacoma Art Museum. Adorned in glass and steel, this Antoine Predock masterpiece wraps around a beautiful garden. Inside you'll find paintings, ceramics, sculptures, and other creations dating from the 18th century to the present. Look for the many glass sculptures by Dale Chihuly—especially the magnificent, flame-colored *Mille Fiori* (Thousand Flowers) glass garden. ✉ *1701 Pacific Ave.* ☎ *253/272–4258* ⊕ *www.tacomaartmuseum.org* 🎫 *$6.50, free on 3rd Thurs. of month* ☉ *Mon.–Wed., Fri., and Sat. 10–5, Thurs. 10–8, Sun. noon–5. Sept.–Memorial Day, closed Mon.*

⑰ Tacoma Narrows Bridge. This delicately spun, mint-green suspension bridge stretches more than a mile over the treacherous narrows, a strait cutting a deep chasm between the Tacoma hills and the bluffs of the Kitsap Peninsula. The bridge's wind-buffeted predecessor, "Galloping Gertie," famously twisted itself to death and broke in half during a storm in 1940—only four months after completion. Underwater, the old bridge now comprises the world's largest man-made reef and is a popular dive site. ✉ *Part of Rte. 16.*

☜ ⑮ Tacoma Nature Center at Snake Lake. Fifty-four acres of marshland, evergreen forest, and shallow lake break up the urban sprawl of west Tacoma and shelter 25 species of mammals and more than 100 species of birds. The lake has nesting pairs of wood ducks, rare elsewhere in western Washington, and the interpretive center is a fun place for kids to look at small creatures, take walks and nature quizzes, and dress up in animal costumes. ✉ *1919 S. Tyler St.* ☎ *253/591–6439* 🖷 *253/593–4152* ⊕ *www. tacomaparks.com* 🎫 *Free* ☉ *Daily.*

⑥ Union Station. This heirloom dates from 1911, when Tacoma was the western terminus of the Northern Pacific Railroad. Built by Reed and

Stem, architects of New York City's Grand Central Terminal, the copper-domed, Beaux Arts–style depot shows the influence of the Roman Pantheon and Italian baroque style. The station houses federal district courts; its rotunda (open to the public weekdays from 8 to 5) contains a gorgeous exhibit of glass sculptures by Dale Chihuly. ⊠ *1717 Pacific Ave.* ☎ *253/931–7884* ⊠ *Free* ⊙ *Weekdays 8–5.*

❼ Washington State History Museum. Adjacent to Union Station, and with the same opulent architecture, Washington's official history museum presents interactive exhibits and multimedia installations about the exploration and settlement of the state. Some rooms are filled with Native American, Eskimo, and pioneer artifacts, while others display logging and railroad memorabilia. The upstairs gallery has rotating exhibits, and summer programs are staged in the outdoor amphitheater. ⊠ *1911 Pacific Ave.* ☎ *253/272–3500* ⊕ *www.whsh.org* ⊠ *$7* ⊙ *Tues., Wed., and Fri. 10–5, Thurs. 10–8, Sun. 1–5.*

⓬ Wright Park. The chief attraction at this 28-acre park, which is on the National Register of Historic Places, is the glass-dome **W. W. Seymour Botanical Conservatory** (⊠ 4th and S. G Sts. ☎ 253/591–5330), a Victorian-style greenhouse (one of only three such structures on the West Coast) with exotic flora. ⊠ *Between 6th and Division Sts., Yakima and Tacoma Aves.* ☎ *253/591–5331* ⊠ *Free* ⊙ *Park daily sunrise–sunset, conservatory daily 8:30–4:20.*

Where to Eat

$$–$$$ ✕ **Altezzo.** Fabulous views of Puget Sound, Commencement Bay, and Mt. Rainier surround this refined restaurant on the top floor of the Sheraton Tacoma Hotel. The setting evokes an Italian trattoria, complete with high, pale walls hung with local paintings, authentic Tuscan fare served at dark wood tables, and the aroma of homemade pastas and breads. Expertly prepared daily specials include pumpkin ravioli and saffron risotto with mahi-mahi. The decorative theme of lush grape vines hints at the extraordinary selection of Northwest and Italian labels on hand. ⊠ *1320 Broadway Plaza* ☎ *253/572–3200* ⊟ *AE, D, DC, MC, V* ⊙ *No lunch.*

$$–$$$ ✕ **Cliff House.** The ocean panorama from the Rainier Room is most spectacular when there's a full moon. Comfortable, curved banquettes with floral upholstery provide the best positioning, but the cozier tables tucked in between offer more intimacy. When the succulent steaks, seafood, and wild game are served, your attention is turned away from the views. Memorable entrées include oven-roasted New Zealand lamb rack and jumbo prawns stuffed with Dungeness crabmeat. The casual bistro Guido's Downstairs has the same scenery, but a lighter menu. ⊠ *6300 Marine View Dr.* ☎ *253/927–0400* ⊟ *AE, D, DC, MC, V.*

$$–$$$ ✕ **Johnny's Dock.** It opened a half-century ago, and has since survived two moves, a fire, and an ejection by the Port of Tacoma. Today's incarnation of this restaurant is in Fife—an eastern suburb of Tacoma—and has a casual, seaside character that makes meals fun. The menu brims with fresh meat and seafood choices like scallop and prawn sauté over linguine and fire-roasted sweet-red-pepper pork chops. You can dine on the deck any time, as heaters are set out to combat the winter chill. ⊠ *1900 East D St.* ☎ *253/627–3186* ⊟ *AE, D, DC, MC, V* ⊠ *5211 20th St. E, Fife* ☎ *253/922–6686.*

$–$$$ ✕ **Lobster Shop.** Built on stilts above the Dash Point tide flats, this former grocery store and beachside soda fountain is now an elite, two-story seafood spot with panoramic bay views. Start with a house martini (always a double) or a taste of Washington wine, and perhaps coconut–macadamia nut prawns or lobster bisque. Move on to crab cakes, potato-crusted ling cod, or pasta with wild mushroom cream sauce. Finish with white-chocolate banana-bread pudding—or the Ghiradelli's chocolate brownie tower. Twilight meals, served before 5:30, provide a mix of courses at a reduced price. ⊠ *6912 Soundview Dr. NE, off Dash Point Rd.* ☎ *253/927–1513* ▤ *AE, DC, MC, V* ◷ *No lunch* ⊠ *4013 Ruston Way* ☎ *253/759–2165* ▤ *AE, DC, MC, V* ◷ *No lunch.*

$–$$ ✕ **Engine House No. 9.** The 1907 building once housed the horse-drawn fire-engine brigade, and today the structure is on the National Register of Historic Places. It's now a pub-style restaurant that's filled with firehouse memorabilia. The hearty, offbeat, Americanized ethnic fare (Thai chicken, soft tacos, pizza, and pasta) made it a hit. The brewery next door, which has a dozen microbrews and regional wines, is packed on weekends. ⊠ *611 N. Pine St.* ☎ *253/272–3435* ▤ *AE, MC, V.*

$–$$ ✕ **Old House Café.** Its location in the heart of the Proctor District shopping area makes this upstairs café an especially convenient place for lunch. Antique fixtures include a stained-glass window from Yakima and ornamental, 19th-century bank lamps. The kitchen specializes in Northwest fare; highlights include a warm scallop salad and king salmon baked in phyllo dough. ⊠ *2717 N. Proctor St.* ☎ *253/759–7336* ▤ *AE, MC, V* ◷ *Closed Sun. No dinner Mon.*

¢–$ ✕ **Pastrami's.** East Coast transplants love this New York–style deli in Tacoma's theater district. A meeting place for much of the city's workforce, Pastrami's serves kosher and vegetarian items, French onion soup, and hot pastrami on rye. You can build your own sandwich or just order an espresso drink at the dark, curving bar. ⊠ *Rhodes Bldg., 950 Broadway* ☎ *253/779–0645* ⌒ *Reservations not accepted* ▤ *AE, MC, V* ◷ *Closed Sun. No dinner.*

¢–$ ✕ **Sar's.** Don't be put off by the plain-Jane building next to a gas station on the way to Point Defiance Park. This is where you'll find Cambodian and Vietnamese families feasting on fiery dishes. The friendly owners treat repeat customers like royalty and hand out lollipops to the kids. If you're spice-shy, go with the *pho* (beef noodle soup), the chopped beef salad, or a mild *pad Thai* (stir-fried noodle mix); otherwise, dare to try the milky red or green curries, the pepper beef, the garlic chicken. ⊠ *4612 N. Pearl St.* ☎ *253/761–2727* ▤ *No credit cards* ◷ *Closed Sun.*

Where to Stay

$$$ ▦ **Thornewood Castle Inn and Gardens Bed & Breakfast.** Spread over four lush acres along beautiful American Lake, this massive, Gothic Tudor–style mansion built in 1908 has hosted two American presidents: William Howard Taft and Theodore Roosevelt. Among the exquisite details inside are medieval stained-glass windows, gleaming wood floors, large mirrors, antiques, fireplaces, and hot tubs. From the lakeside patio and sunken garden you can meditate on the spectacular sunsets. The inn is 12 mi south of Tacoma. ⊠ *8601 N. Thorne La. SW, Lakewood, 98498* ☎ *253/589–9052* ⊟ *253/584–4497* ⊕ *www.thornewoodcastle.com* ◿ *4 rooms, 6 suites* ⌂ *Dining room, some in-room hot tubs, microwaves, refrigerators, cable TV, in-room VCRs, beach, library; no kids under 12, no smoking* ▤ *AE, D, MC, V* ◉ *BP.*

$$–$$$$ ▦ **Sheraton Tacoma Hotel.** This elegant hotel has cozy, beautifully decorated rooms. Most have an early-19th-century look, with striped pastel wallpaper and bold geometric or floral patterned carpets, curtains, and bedspreads. Suites have views of Commencement Bay, Mt. Rainier, or both; some also have dining areas, marble Jacuzzis, and two bathrooms. Club Level guests have access to a concierge and receive a complimentary Continental breakfast and evening hors d'oeuvres. There's no pool, but for $5 you get a pass to the modern YMCA across the street. ⊠ *1320 Broadway Plaza, 98402* ☎ *253/572–3200 or 800/845–9466*

🖷 253/591–4105 ⊕ *www.sheratontacoma.com* ⬎ *295 rooms, 24 suites ⟆ Restaurant, grill, room service, in-room data ports, some in-room hot tubs, minibars, cable TV, hot tub, sauna, 2 bars, piano bar, shop, laundry service, dry cleaning, concierge, Internet, business services, meeting rooms, parking (fee), some pets allowed* ▱ *AE, DC, MC, V.*

$–$$ 🖷 **Chinaberry Hill.** Original fixtures and stained-glass windows are among the grace notes in this 1889 Queen Anne–style B&B in the Stadium Historic District. Rooms have shining wood floors, antique feather beds dressed in fine-quality linens, and ornate desks; three have whirlpool tubs. The two-story Catchpenny Cottage carriage house, which sleeps six, has a claw-foot tub and memorabilia from its horse-and-buggy days. A guest kitchen stocks complimentary drinks, cookies, and popcorn. ✉ *302 N. Tacoma Ave., 98403,* 🕾 *253/272–1282* 🖷 *253/272–1335* ⊕ *www.chinaberryhill.com* ⬎ *4 suites, 1 cottage ⟆ Dining room, some in-room hot tubs, in-room VCRs, library* ▱ *AE, D, MC, V* ⦿ *BP.*

$–$$ 🖷 **The Villa.** The grand foyer of this Italianate mansion is surrounded by Palladian windows public areas are painted in soft hues of lime, fuschia, and coral. A wood staircase framed by white collonaded archways leads to the guest suites, all of which have bay or mountain views; three have fireplaces. Subdued paintings, glass art, and international textiles adorn the walls. Garden rooms invite laziness with Adirondack chairs and hammocks; romance brews around the Salon Piazza's fountain and gardens. ✉ *705 N. 5th St., 98403* 🕾 *253/572–1157* 🖷 *253/572–1805* ⊕ *www.villabb.com* ⬎ *4 rooms ⟆ Dining room, fans, hot tub, library, business services* ▱ *AE, MC, V* ⦿ *BP.*

$ 🖷 **DeVoe Mansion Bed and Breakfast.** On 1½ beautiful acres, this 1911 colonial-style mansion fronted tall white columns is a national and state historic site. Rooms, which are named after suffragettes, have such an antiques as an oak sleigh bed with claw feet. ✉ *208 E. 133rd St., 98445* 🕾 *253/539–3991 or 888/539–3991* 🖷 *253/539–8539* ⊕ *www.devoemansion.com* ⬎ *4 rooms ⟆ Dining room, in-room VCRs, outdoor hot tub; no kids under 12, no smoking* ▱ *MC, V* ⦿ *BP.*

$ 🖷 **Green Cape Cod Bed & Breakfast.** Built in 1929, this house stands in a residential neighborhood only blocks from the historic Proctor shopping district. Three rooms with frilly linens and beautiful antiques provide the full scale of pampering with down comforters, soft robes, and bedside Almond Roca candy, a Northwest specialty. Guests receive passes to the downtown YMCA. ✉ *2711 N. Warner, 98407* 🕾 *253/752–1977 or 888/752–1977* 🖷 *253/756–9886* ⊕ *www.greencapecod.com* ⬎ *3 rooms ⟆ Dining room, in-room data ports, cable TV, dry cleaning, laundry service, business services; no room phones, no kids under 10, no smoking* ▱ *AE, MC, V* ⦿ *BP.*

¢ 🖷 **Austrian Bed and Breakfast Suites.** Rustic Austrian antiques, some more than 250 years old, fill this 1891 home. Furnishings hide such modern amenities as TVs and telephones; Austrian folk art, paintings, and pottery hang from the walls and occupy the shelves. Rooms have private entrances, full kitchens, and beautiful antiques, such as the canopy bed in the Johann Strauss Suite. Despite all the breakables, children are welcomed—and they might just pick up a few German words from their hosts. ✉ *723 N. Cushman St., 98403* 🕾 *253/383–2216 or 800/495–4293* ⊕ *www.austrianbb.com* ⬎ *4 suites ⟆ Dining room, kitchenettes, microwaves, refrigerators, cable TV; no smoking* ▱ *MC, V* ⦿ *BP.*

Nightlife

BARS & LOUNGES Head to **Houston's Bar Grill** (✉ 2611 Pacific Ave. 🕾 253/272–5403) for country music and dancing. On the Ruston Way waterfront, the enormous **Ram Grill & Big Horn Brewery** (✉ 3001 Ruston Way 🕾 253/756–7886)—a wood-paneled restaurant, bar, and brewery complex—is a fun, loud, ever-packed nightspot popular with the post-college crowds. On weekends, live jazz and blues heighten the Cajun atmosphere at **Roof-n-Doof's New Orleans Cafe** (⊠ 754 Pacific Ave. ☎ 253/572–5113).

Dark, intimate **Shenanigans** (⊠ 3017 Ruston Way ☎ 253/752–8811), with gorgeous waterfront views, has a chic bar, excellent Northwest cuisine, and a line of sleek, cozy window booths. The **Swiss** (⊠ 1904 S. Jefferson Ave. ☎ 253/572–2821) has microbrews on tap, pool tables, and weekend jazz. The music varies from night to night at the **Vault** (⊠ 1025 Pacific Ave. ☎ 253/572–3145), a downtown Tacoma restaurant and dance club.

CASINOS Housed in an authentic paddle-wheel riverboat, the **Emerald Queen Casino** (⊠ 2102 Alexander Ave. ☎ 888/831–7655) has slot machines and gaming tables plus a restaurant, bar, dance club, and live music nightly. In addition to its casino (open 4 PM to 4 AM), with blackjack, poker, and Spanish 21, **Luciano's** (⊠ 3327 Ruston Way ☎ 253/756–5611) has a piano bar, lounge, and terrific southern Italian cuisine served by singing waiters. The extremely popular **Muckelshoot Casino** (⊠ 2402 Auburn Way S., Auburn ☎ 800/804–4944), on the Muckelshoot Indian reservation, has more than 2,000 slot machines, 65 gaming tables, five restaurants, and a stage for entertainers.

CONCERTS **White River Amphitheater** (⊠ 40601 Auburn Enumclaw Rd., on the Muckleshoot Indian Reservation, Auburn ☎ 360/825–6200), with snowy Mt. Rainier as a gorgeous backdrop, hosts acts like Aerosmith, Beck, Fleetwood Mac, and Neil Young.

Sports & the Outdoors

AMUSEMENT PARKS **Enchanted Village,** the only amusement park near Seattle, has huge, looping roller coasters that rank with those in California. A tamer section is geared for younger kids, and there are prizes to be won at games galore. From Thanksgiving through New Year's the park shimmers with a nightly drive-through holiday light show. The **Wild Waves Water Park,** part of Enchanted Village, is the Northwest's largest water park, with giant slides, a 24,000-square-foot wave pool, and "Splash Central," for younger children. The one-day price is hefty, but you can often get discount coupons at local grocery and drugstores. ⊠ 36201 Enchanted Pkwy. S ☎ 253/661–8000 or 253/925–8000 🖶 253/661–8065 ⊕ www.wildwaves.com 🎫 Enchanted Village: $15. Wild Waves: $30 🕙 Enchanted Village: daily 10–7. Wild Waves: Apr.–mid-Sept., daily 10–8.

BASEBALL The **Tacoma Rainiers,** the Class AAA affiliate of the Seattle Mariners baseball team, play at **Cheney Stadium** (⊠ 2502 S. Tyler St. ☎ 253/752–7707).

HORSE RACING **Emerald Downs** is a thoroughbred horse-racing stadium, with music, festivals, and picnics staged on summer weekends. Tours are available. ⊠ 2300 Emerald Downs Dr., Auburn ☎ 253/288–7000 or 888/931–8400 🖶 253/288–7733 ⊕ www.emeralddowns.com 🎫 $3 🕙 Mid-Apr.–mid-Sept., Wed.–Fri. 6 PM first post; weekends 1 PM first post.

HOCKEY The **Tacoma Rockets** (☎ 360/627–3653) of the Western Hockey League play their home games at the **Tacoma Dome** (⊠ 2727 E. D St. ☎ 253/272–3663).

SCUBA DIVING **Tacoma Lighthouse Diving Center** (⊠ 2502 Pacific Ave. ☎ 800/777–3843) is a full-service dive operation with lessons, equipment, and regional trips. **Tacoma Underwater Sports** (⊠ 9606 40th St. SW ☎ 253/588–6634 or 800/252–7177), the area's largest scuba center, sells and rents gear, plans trips, and has branches and repair facilities throughout Puget Sound.

Shopping

Antique Row (✉ Broadway and St. Helen's St. between 7th and 9th Sts.) contains upscale antiques stores and boutiques selling collectibles and 1950s paraphernalia. A farmers' market is held here every Thursday in summer. **Freighthouse Square Public Market** (✉ 25th and D Sts. ☎ 253/305–0678) is a former railroad warehouse filled with gift shops, offbeat boutiques, and ethnic food stalls. In the Proctor District, the **Pacific Northwest Shop** (✉ 2702 N. Proctor St. ☎ 253/752–2242) sells apparel, books, pottery, and regional food and wine. Look for Lionel model trains at **Tacoma Trains and Hobbies** (✉ 2525 N. Proctor ☎ 253/756–7517). **Teaching Toys** (✉ 2624 N. Proctor ☎ 253/759–9853) has educational toys and games from all over the world. **Tacoma Mall** (✉ Tacoma Mall Blvd. off I–5 ☎ 253/475–4565), 1½ mi south of the Tacoma Dome, contains department stores, specialty shops, and restaurants.

Puyallup

⑱ *10 mi southeast of Tacoma.*

Set before the towering forests and snowfields of Mt. Rainier is Puyallup (pyoo-*al*-lup), one of western Washington's oldest towns. Founder Ezra Meeker came west on the Oregon Trail in 1806–07, and he returned East at age 76 in hopes of prodding President Theodore Roosevelt to mark the trail before its route was forgotten. He caused quite a stir when he rode his ox-drawn covered wagon down Broadway in New York City, but he continued on to the White House and received the president's endorsement.

Today, the Puyallup Fair attracts all of western Washington to its carnival rides, performers, produce, and animals. The Spring Fair and Daffodil Festival (known as "The Little Puyallup") is another beloved event that takes place each April. The town itself is centered around Pioneer Park, which has a wading pool, play area, and an amphitheater for summer concerts. The popular Puyallup Farmers' Market (May–September on Saturdays, 9–2) sets up next to the park.

Another early pioneer settlement is Enumclaw (*ee*-num-claw), 14 mi southeast, which was founded in the 1850s and through stages grew as a railroad, lumber, and dairy town. The name is taken from a nearby peak, which—depending on which legend you believe—means either "Thundering Mountain" or "Abode of Evil Spirits" in the Salish language. The town is the site of the annual King County Fair, which has amusement rides, rodeos, and logging shows.

The **Ezra Meeker Mansion,** a showy, Italianate palace built in 1891, was a fitting place for the richest man in the Northwest. Meeker, known locally as the "Hop King" for his beer empire, sunk much of his profits into such elegant touches as inlaid fireplaces, ceiling murals, and stained-glass windows. Listed on the National Register of Historic Sites, the home is completely furnished in the style of its heyday. ✉ *312 Spring St.* ☎ *253/848–1770* ⊕ *www.meekermansion.org* 🎟 *$4* ☉ *Mar.–mid-Dec., Wed.–Sun. 1–4.*

★ ☾ The **Pioneer Farm Museum and Ohop Indian Village,** 23 mi south of Puyallup, provides a look at pioneer and Native American life. Kids can learn how to hunt and fish in a realistic Indian village, grind grain, milk a cow, churn butter, and do other old-fashioned chores. A trading post shows the commodities of earlier eras. One-hour pioneer farm tours ($6.50) take place 11:15 to 4; Ohop Indian Village tours ($6) are at 1 and 2:30 from Memorial Day to Labor Day. ✉ *Rte. 7 off Ohop Valley Rd.* ☎ *360/832–6300* ⊕ *www.pioneerfarmmuseum.org* 🎟 *$6–$6.50*

⊙ *Mid-Mar.–Father's Day and Labor Day–mid–Nov., weekends 11:15–4; Father's Day–Labor Day, daily 11:15–4.*

★ ♻ **Northwest Trek** is a spectacular wildlife park 35 mi south of Puyallup. It's devoted to native creatures of the Pacific Northwest. Walking paths wind through natural surroundings—so natural that in 1998 a cougar entered the park and started snacking on the deer (it was finally trapped and relocated to the North Cascades). See beavers, otters, and wolverines; get close to wolves, foxes, coyotes; and observe several species of big cats and bears in wild environments. Admission includes a 55-minute tram ride through fields of wandering moose, elk, bison, and mountain goats. ⊠ *11610 Trek Dr. E, Eatonville* ☎ *360/832–6117* ⊕ *www.nwtrek.org* ☚ *$8.75* ⊙ *Call for hrs.*

Federation Forest State Park, 18 mi south of Enumclaw, preserves parts of the Naches Trail over the Cascades. **Green River Gorge,** 12 mi northeast of Enumclaw, is a 12-mi-long canyon with sheer rock walls—some 300 feet high—adorned with so many wildflowers and ferns that it's known as the "Hanging Gardens." Along the Green River is **Flaming Geyser State Park,** a favorite kayaking and tubing spot named for two extinct geysers. One of the highest earthen dams in the world is 430-foot **Mud Mountain,** 7 mi southeast of Enumclaw.

Where to Stay & Eat

¢–$ ✕ **Powerhouse Brewery and Restaurant.** The interior of what was once a railroad powerhouse is adorned with glass insulators and high-voltage signs. A dozen brews are served—six brewed on the premises and six from a sister brewery. The pub fare includes salads, pizzas, burgers, sandwiches, and pastas. ⊠ *454 E. Main Ave.* ☎ *253/845–1370* ⊟ *MC, V.*

¢–$$ ▦ **Best Western Park Plaza.** The plushly carpeted rooms in this nicely appointed, conveniently located business travelers and family motel have reclining wingback chairs and traditional cherrywood furnishings; some have four-poster canopy beds and hot tubs. ⊠ *620 S. Hill Park Dr.* ☎ *253/848–1500* ⊟ *253/848–1511* ⇆ *100 rooms* ⚲ *Restaurant, some in-room hot tubs, pool, gym, outdoor hot tub, no-smoking rooms* ⊟ *AE, D, DC, MC, V* ⧖⧖ *CP.*

Olympia

⑲ *33 mi southwest of Puyallup.*

Olympia has been the capital of Washington since 1853, the beginning of city and state. It is small for the capital city of a major state, but that makes it all the more pleasant to visit. Old and charming, downtown is compact and easy on the feet. You can walk almost anywhere within minutes—from the state capitol to the downtown shops and restaurants at the foot of the hill, to Capitol Lake, which borders downtown to the west, and to the harbor at Budd Inlet, to the north. You don't see much salt water from downtown, unless you stroll the harborside boardwalk, because bluffs, trees, and buildings block the view.

The imposing state capitol, finished in 1928, seems almost too big for such a small town. Like a fortress, it occupies the crest of a hill. Its height is further emphasized by a skirt of granite steps. The monumental 287-foot-high dome is the fourth largest masonry dome in the world (only St. Peter's in Rome, St. Paul's in London, and the national capitol in the other Washington are larger). Surrounding the capitol and other government buildings is a park much visited by walkers and joggers. In spring the grounds are fragrant with lilacs and white with cherry blossoms.

Olympia retains a relaxed small-town air even when the state legislature is in session (starting on the second Monday in January and running for 30 or 60 days, depending on whether it's an even-numbered year or an odd-numbered one). When the legislators are away, the mood can be downright drowsy. The main attractions are the structures of the **Capitol Campus,** on a bluff high above Capitol Lake. The handsome neo-classical legislative building was finished in 1928. Visitors' galleries provide glimpses of state senators and representatives in action. The surrounding grounds contain memorials, monuments, rose gardens, and Japanese cherry trees (usually in bloom by March). The 1939 conservatory is open year-round on weekdays from 8 to 3 and also on weekends in summer. Directly behind the legislative building, the modern state library has exhibits devoted to Washington's history. At this writing, the legislative building is closed for renovations. You can still explore the campus grounds and many of the structures on your own or as part of a free 45-minute campus tour. There are also special tours just of the executive mansion, among other things. ⊠ *Capitol Way between 10th and 14th Aves.* ☎ *306/586–3460 State Capitol Visitor Center, 360/586–8687 tour information* ☎ *Free* ⊙ *Campus tours daily on the hr, 10–3.*

Capitol Lake was formed in 1951 by damming the Deschutes River at the mouth. The former mud flats are now covered with some 30 feet of water; salmon can be seen ascending the fish ladders in autumn. Surrounded by parks, the lake serves as a magnificent reflecting pool for the capitol building.

The 1920s mansion of a banker houses the **State Capitol Museum.** Exhibits survey local art, history, and natural history. The permanent collection includes rare Native American baskets. ⊠ *211 W. 21st St., off Capitol Way, 7 blocks south of the Legislative Bldg.* ☎ *360/753–2580* ☎ *Donations accepted* ⊙ *Tues.–Sun. 10–4.*

The **Japanese Garden,** a symbol of the sister-city relationship of Olympia and Yashiro, Japan, opened in 1989. Within it are a waterfall, a bamboo grove, a koi pond, and stone lanterns. ⊠ *Union and Plum Sts., east of Capitol Campus* ☎ *No phone* ☎ *Free* ⊙ *Daily sunrise–sunset.*

The 335-acre **Millersylvania State Park** has a deep lake as well as camping, picnicking, and boating facilities. The site was first settled by General John Mueller, who married a daughter of Austrian Emperor Franz Josef I without official permission. As a result of this misalliance, he and his wife were exiled. ⊠ *Exit 95 off I–5* ☎ *360/753–1519* ⊕ *www. parks.wa.gov* ☎ *Free, camping $12–$17* ⊙ *Daily 8–sunset.*

☺ **Wolf Haven International** is an 80-acre sanctuary dedicated to wolf conservation. One-hour guided walking tours show how wolves are raised, rehabilitated, and released into the wild. In summer, the facility hosts a so-called Howl-In (reservations essential), with tours, musicians performing around a campfire, and howling with the wolves. On the first Thursday of the month there's "Dinner at Dusk" with the wolves, and you can spend the final hour on your own in the sanctuary every last Sunday. ⊠ *3111 Offut Lake Rd., Tenino, from Olympia, take I–5 south to Exit 99 and follow signs east for 7 mi* ☎ *800/448–9653* ⊕ *www.wolfhaven.org* ☎ *Daily tours $6, Howl-Ins $10* ⊙ *May–Sept., Wed.–Mon. 10–5; Apr. and Oct., Wed.–Mon. 10–4, Nov.–Mar., weekends 10–4.*

Tumwater Falls Park. This long, narrow park south of Olympia follows the rapids and cascades of the Tumwater River to Capitol Lake. It's particularly pretty in spring, when the rhododendrons bloom along the river and the cherry trees bloom on the lakeshore. In fall, salmon ascend the rapids and fish ladders. ⊠ *Deschutes Way and C St., Tumwater* ☎ *360/943–2550* ☎ *Free* ⊙ *Daily.*

Tumwater Historical Park. This pleasant riverfront park marks the site of the first American settlement on Puget Sound, in 1845. It has a picnic area and a boat launch. ⊠ *777 Simmons Rd. SW* ☎ *360/754–4160* 🖷 *360/754–4166* ⊕ *www.olywa.net/tumwater* 🎟 *Free* ☉ *Daily sunrise–sunset.*

Where to Stay & Eat

$$$ ✕ **La Petite Maison.** A converted 1890 farmhouse (now near the center of the expanding city) houses an intimate restaurant serving great French-inspired food. Highlights include fresh local oysters (including the hard-to-find tiny Olympias), crab cakes, and rack of lamb marinated in rosemary, garlic, and Dijon mustard. Leave room for the excellent desserts. ⊠ *101 Division NW* ☎ *360/943–8812* 🖃 *MC, V* ☉ *Closed Sun. No lunch Sat.–Mon.*

★ **$$** ✕ **Alice's Restaurant.** A rural farmhouse adjacent to the Johnson Creek Winery in the Skookumchuck Valley is home to this charming, Norman Rockwell–style restaurant. The winery's vintages accompany five-course meals that are sophisticated variations on classic American cuisine. More than a dozen choices include pasta, catfish, ham, scallops, quail, and venison—all served with cream of peanut soup, fresh-baked bread, green salad with hot bacon dressing, homemade rice pilaf, and fresh carrots. ⊠ *19248 Johnson Creek Rd. E, from Olympia, follow Capitol Blvd. south, head east at Rte. 507 in Tenino for 5 mi, and turn right onto Johnson Creek Rd. for 5 mi* ☎ *360/264–2887* 🍴 *Reservations essential* 🖃 *AE, MC, V* ☉ *Closed Mon.–Thurs. No lunch.*

$–$$$ ✕ **Falls Terrace.** An elegant, multilevel restaurant in front of the Olympia Brewery, Falls Terrace offers unobstructed views of Tumwater Falls. Steaks, burgers, and seafood are as fancy as the food gets. There is dining on the deck, but you have to be over 21. Inside is the place to be for a family Sunday brunch. ⊠ *106 S. Deschutes Way* ☎ *360/943–7830* 🖃 *AE, D, DC, MC, V.*

$–$$ ✕ **Xinh's Clam and Oyster House.** This popular seafood restaurant is 22 mi northwest of Olympia, in the 1920s lumber town of Shelton. The dishes here have intriguing Asian touches. Consider trying the mussels in tamarind sauce or the fantastically hearty hot and spicy soup. If you prefer Continental fare, the creamy seafood fettuccine is a good bet. The waitstaff is attentive. Children are welcome; smoking is not. ⊠ *221 W. Railroad Ave., Suite D, Shelton* ☎ *360/427–8709* 🖃 *MC, V* ☉ *Closed Sun. and Mon. No lunch.*

¢ ✕ **Wagner's European Bakery & Café.** The delicious aromas unfurling from the restaurant seem to draw the whole neighborhood here at mealtimes. The specialties of this landmark are the sumptuous pastries—flaky glazed donuts, thick cookies, and beautifully iced cakes—that melt in your mouth. Lunchtime brings hot soups and delectable sandwiches served on fresh-baked breads. Come early, or be prepared to stand in line— the wait is worth it. ⊠ *1013 Capitol Way* ☎ *360/357–7268* 🖃 *MC, V* ☉ *Closed Sun. No dinner.*

¢–$$ 🏨 **Holiday Inn Select.** Views of Capitol Lake, the capitol dome, and the surrounding hills are highlights of this familiar chain hotel from which you can walk to many local sights. Spacious rooms are modern and comfortable; those facing the water are especially appealing. ⊠ *2300 Evergreen Park Dr., 98502* ☎ *360/943–4000* 🖷 *360/357–6604* ⊕ *www.holidayinn.com* 🛏 *177 rooms* ♿ *2 restaurants, room service, cable TV, pool, hot tub, bar, no-smoking rooms* 🖃 *AE, D, MC, V* ⧖◯ *CP.*

¢–$$ 🏨 **Ramada Inn–Governor House.** Overlooking Capitol Lake and Sylvester Park, this relaxed, eight-story hotel is a favorite of lobbyists. You can walk to all the important sights, then de-stress at day's end with a dip in the hot tub or pool. ⊠ *621 S. Capital Way, 98501* ☎ *360/352–7700*

🖳 360/943–9349 ⊕ *www.ramada.com* 🖙 *125 rooms* ⚐ *Restaurant, in-room data ports, refrigerators, cable TV, pool, exercise equipment, hot tub, bar, dry cleaning, laundry facilities, Internet, business services, meeting rooms; no smoking* 🖃 *AE, D, DC, MC, V.*

¢–$ 🏠 **Swantown Inn.** Antiques and lace ornament every room of this stylish Victorian inn, built as a mansion in 1893, then used as a boarding house (and later, perhaps, a brothel). Above gardens and landscaped lawns, rooms have views of the capitol. The Astoria suite has a four-poster bed and a two-person Jacuzzi tub; the smaller Columbia room has a claw-foot tub. Such treats as New Orleans French toast and German pancakes are on the breakfast menu. ⊠ *1431 11th Ave. SE, 98501* 🖀 *360/753–9123* ⊕ *www.olywa.net/swantown* 🖙 *3 rooms, 1 suite* ⚐ *Dining room, some in-room hot tubs, massage, piano, recreation room; no room phones, no kids under 9, no smoking* 🖃 *MC, V* 🍽 *BP.*

Renton

⑳ *52 mi northeast of Olympia, 14 mi southeast of Seattle.*

The industrial city of Renton, at the southern end of Lake Washington, has an old, refurbished downtown and a public library dramatically built on a bridge across the Cedar River. However, according to Seattle writer Bill Speidel, the city has always received the short end of the stick when it comes to regional development: "You sort of hesitate to suggest that Renton is always the bridesmaid and never the bride, but the fact is that she's been used and re-used by some of the stars of the show for the last century or more." One of the incidents Speidel cites is that Seattleites got Renton to agree to the ship canal connecting Lake Washington and Puget Sound by telling residents they'd get a seaport in return. Instead, the canal caused the lake's level to drop by 9 feet and all Renton got was mudflats. Now those mudflats are home to the Renton Airport, the Will Rogers–Wiley Post Seaplane Base, and the huge Boeing aircraft manufacturing plant, which together provide Renton with far more income than a port would have. A pleasant beach park runs along the shore north of the Boeing plant.

The simple marker of the **Jimi Hendrix Grave Site,** where the famed guitarist has rested since his death in 1970, is in Greenwood Memorial Park. At this writing refurbishments are in the works. Plans include a memorial with a domed roof, granite columns, a waterfall, and a life-size bronze sculpture depicting Hendrix striking a stance at his 1969 Woodstock performance. ⊠ *3rd and Monroe Sts.* 🖀 *425/255–1511* ⊕ *www. jimihendrixmemorial.com* 🕙 *Daily until sunset.*

Renton Historical Museum. Exhibits illustrate the history of the city, which began as a Duwamish Indian encampment. Later, it went through stages as a coal-mining center and a logging town. ⊠ *235 Mill Ave. S* 🖀 *425/ 255–2330* 🎫 *$3* 🕙 *Tues. 9–4, Wed.–Sun. 1–4.*

Where to Stay & Eat

★ $$$$ ✕ **Spirit of Washington** Dinner Train. Speed past splendid views of Lake Washington, Mercer Island, and Mt. Rainier on a train pulled by a 1935 diesel engine during this unique dining experience. The 3½-hour journey includes a stop at the Columbia Winery for a wine tasting and tour. As for the meal, entrées include prime rib, roasted salmon, stuffed chicken, crab crêpes, and vegetarian choices. Murder Mystery tours and Christmas journeys are also scheduled. ⊠ *625 S. 4th St.* 🖀 *425/227–7245 or 800/876–7245* ⊕ *www.spiritofwashingtondinnertrain.com* ⚐ *Reservations essential* 🖃 *AE, MC, V* 🕙 *No lunch weekdays.*

$ 🏨 **Holiday Inn Select.** The upscale lobby, which overlooks the pool, contains a large fireplace, cherry paneling, and marble details. Standard rooms have well-maintained if generic furnishings, but everything is always spicand-span and family-friendly. ⊠ *1 South Grady Way, 98055* ☏ *425/ 226–7700 or 800/521–1412* 🖷 *425/271–2315* ⊕ *www.holiday-inn. com/rentonwa* 🛏 *226 rooms* ♨ *Restaurant, room service, in-room data ports, refrigerators, cable TV, pool, gym, hot tub, bar, business services, airport shuttle* ▭ *AE, D, DC, MC, V.*

North Bend

㉑ *30 mi east of Renton.*

This truck stop gets its name from a bend in the Snoqualmie River, which here turns toward Canada. The gorgeous surrounding scenery is dominated by 4,420-foot Mt. Washington, 4,788-foot Mt. Tenerife, and 4,167-foot Mt. Si. Named for early settler Josiah "Si" Merrit, Mt. Si has a steep, four-hour trail that in summer provides views of the Cascade and Olympic peaks down to Puget Sound and Seattle. In winter, however, these mountains corner the rains: North Bend is one of the wettest places in western Washington, with an annual precipitation often exceeding 100 inches.

Scenes from the TV show *Twin Peaks*—notably the stunning opening waterfall sequence—were shot in North Bend, though most of the work was done in studios in Seattle. This is the last town on I–90 for gassing up before Snoqualmie Pass. The **Snoqualmie Valley Historical Museum** focuses on life centuries ago, with Native American tools, crafts, and attire as well as pioneer artifacts. The timber industry is another focus. ⊠ *320 S. Bendego Blvd.* ☏ *425/888–3200* ⊕ *www. snoqualmievalleymuseum.org* 🎟 *$1* ☉ *Apr.–Oct. and 1st 2 wks of Dec., Thurs.–Sun. 1–5; Nov.–Mar. by appointment.*

Where to Stay & Eat

$–$$$ ✕ **Gordy's Steak & BBQ Smokehouse.** "Wimpy eaters need not apply," says the menu at this former golf clubhouse of the elite Cascade links. Windows surrounding the simple dining room and bar let in light and views of the golf course and mountains. Premium cuts of strip steak, sirloin, prime rib, and filet mignon reign at dinner, while it's steak and eggs for breakfast, and lighter soups and salads for lunch. No nitrates or artificial flavorings are used in the pork and beef ribs. ⊠ *Exit 32 off I–90, 14303 436th Ave. SE* ☏ *425/831–2433* ▭ *MC, V.*

$ ✕ **Robertiello's.** Pictures of Venice add a European touch to the intimate dining room of the McGrath Hotel, built in 1922. Tastes are true to Italy: try the *carciofi* (artichoke hearts sautéed with capers), or penne *sovietiche* (pasta and prawns in a spicy *mascarpone*-cream-cheese sauce). For dessert there's homemade tiramisu and several types of cheesecake. On Tuesday nights specialty wines are just $10, and the flower-bedecked patio is perfect for summertime meals. The bar in the firelit McGrath Room is backed by a fresco from the building's early years. ⊠ *101 North Bend Way* ☏ *425/888–1803* ☉ *Closed Mon.* ▭ *MC, V.*

$ 🏨 **Roaring River Bed & Breakfast.** Tucked amid 2½ acres above the Snoqualmie River, this secluded B&B has unbeatable mountain and wilderness views. Rooms with wainscoting and fireplaces have private entrances and decks. The Mountain View Room has a whirlpool tub; the Bear-Iris Room has a feather bed and a two-person Japanese soaking tub. Herb's Place is a hunting cabin with a kitchen and loft, and the Rock and Rose Room has its own sauna—inside a giant boulder. Homemade goodies are delivered to your room each morning. ⊠ *46715 SE 129th St., 98045* ☏ *425/888–4834 or 877/627–4647* ⊕ *www.theroaringriver.*

com 🔊 *4 rooms* ♿ *Some in-room hot tubs, cable TV; no a/c, no room phones, no kids under 12, no smoking* ▭ *AE, D, MC, V* ⏐◯⏐ *BP.*

Snoqualmie

🔢 *3 mi northwest of North Bend.*

Spring and summer snowmelt turn the Snoqualmie (sno-*qual*-mie) River into a thundering torrent at Snoqualmie Falls, the sweeping cascades that provided the backdrop for the *Twin Peaks* opening montage. The water pours over a 268-foot rock ledge (100 feet higher than Niagara Falls) to a 65-foot-deep pool. These cascades, considered sacred by the Native Americans, are Snoqualmie's biggest attraction. A 2-acre park and observation platform affords views of the falls and the surrounding area. The 3-mi round-trip River Trail winds through trees and over open slopes to the base of the cascade.

🐾 The vintage cars of the **Snoqualmie Valley Railroad,** built in the mid-1910s for the Spokane, Portland, and Seattle Railroad, travel between the landmark 1890 Snoqualmie Depot and North Bend. The 50-minute (round-trip) excursion passes through woods and farmland. Inside the Snoqualmie depot, the Northwest Railway Museum displays memorabilia and has a bookstore. Crowds of families pack the midsummer and Santa Train journeys. If the weather's iffy, bring rain gear to prevent a soaking through the open windows. ✉ *Snoqualmie Depot: 38625 SE King St., at Rte. 202,* ☎ *425/888–3030 in Snoqualmie, 206/746–4025 in Seattle* 🎫 *$7* ⊙ *Trains May–Sept., weekends; Oct., Sun. only; on the hr 11–4 from Snoqualmie and on the ½ hr 11:30–3:30 from North Bend. Museum, depot, and bookstore Thurs.–Mon. 10–5.*

Where to Stay & Eat

¢ ✕ **Snoqualmie Falls Candy Factory.** An Old West–style storefront leads to this combination candy store, gift shop, and soda fountain serving quick-cooked American burgers and hot dogs. Homemade caramel corn, saltwater taffy, and nut brittles in pretty packages make great treats and souvenirs. ✉ *8102 Railroad Ave. SE* ☎ *425/888–0439 or 800/636–CANDY* ▭ *AE, MC, V.*

$$$–$$$$
Fodor'sChoice
★
✕▨ **Salish Lodge.** The stunning, chalet-style lodge sits right over Snoqualmie Falls. Eight rooms have gorgeous views of the cascades, while others have a river panorama. All the luxurious quarters have feather beds, fireplaces, whirlpool baths, terrycloth robes, and window seats or balconies. The world-famous spa offers relaxing and purifying treatments after a day of kayaking, golfing, or hiking. Favorites at the Dining Room restaurant (jacket and tie required, reservations essential) include lamb pot-au-feu, pan-seared bass, and grilled beef tenderloin; weekend brunches are elaborate. In the more casual Attic restaurant, you can still sample fine Northwest wines and views of the falls. ✉ *6501 Railroad Ave. SE, 98065* ☎ *206/888–2556 or 800/826–6124* 🖨 *425/888–2420* ⊕ *www.salishlodge.com* 🔊 *87 rooms, 4 suites* ♿ *2 restaurants, room service, some in-room hot tubs, minibars, cable TV with movies, some in-room VCRs, health club, hot tub, sauna, spa, bar, shops, dry cleaning, laundry service, concierge, Internet, business services, meeting room, travel services* ▭ *AE, D, DC, MC, V.*

¢–$$
✕▨ **Honey Farm Inn.** A brick fireplace, lots of books, and train-station antiques bring elegance to the common areas of this yellow inn with white trim. White and off-white fabrics, lace curtains, and wood furnishings decorate the Victorian-style guest rooms. Wildflower Restaurant ($–$$) serves dinner Wednesday through Sunday. Delicacies include Dungeness crab and Chilean shrimp over cappellini pasta; Angus beef steaks; and duck in fig sauce with toasted fennel. ✉ *9058 384th Ave. SE, 98065*

☎ 206/888–9399 🖷 425/888–8880 ⊕ *www.myenchantedmoments. com* 🗫 *9 rooms, 1 suite* ⚘ *Restaurant, some in-room hot tubs* ▤ *AE, D, DC, MC, V.*

¢–$$ 🏠 **Kimball Creek Inn.** This estate is on four acres of rolling meadows bisected by Kimball Creek. Homey rooms, some with fireplaces and whirlpool tubs, are filled with antique furniture and decorated with many collectibles. Splendid views of Mt. Si are right outside the door, and it's just 1 mi to Snoqualmie Falls. ⊠ *9050 384th Ave. SE, 98065* ☎ *425/ 888–9399* 🗫 *10 rooms* ⚘ *Restaurant, some pets allowed; no a/c, no room phones, no room TVs, no smoking* ▤ *MC, V* ⦿⦿ *CP.*

The Arts

Snoqualmie Falls Forest Theater, the state's only outdoor dinner theater, presents two or three summer melodramas in a 250-seat amphitheater. Shows staged by acting students and community performers play Friday through Sunday evenings in July and August. Tickets are $13; for another $12 you can enjoy a salmon or steak barbecue after the matinee or before the evening performance. Reservations are required for dinner. ✛ *From I–90 take Exit 22 and go 4 mi; take a right on David Powell Rd. and follow signs* ☎ *425/222–7044* ⊕ *www.foresttheater.org.*

Sports & the Outdoors

🆂 **The Summit at Snoqualmie,** 53 mi east of Seattle, combines the Alpental, FodorsChoice Summit West, Summit East, and Summit Central ski areas along Sno- ★ qualmie Pass. Spread over nearly 2,000 acres at elevations of up to 5,400 feet, the facilities include 65 ski trails, 22 chairlifts, and two half-pipes. Those seeking tamer pursuits can head to the Summit Nordic Center, with groomed trails and a tubing area. Shops, restaurants, lodges, and ski schools are connected by shuttle vans; there's even child care. For a different take on the mountains, head up to the pass after dinner; this is the world's largest night-skiing area. Tickets, which let you ski and play at any of the above areas, are $37 on weekends. Inner tube rentals, including lighted rope tows, are $10. ✛ *From Seattle, take I–90 east to Alpental Rd.* ☎ *425/434–6112, 425/236–1600 snow conditions* ⊕ *www. summit-at-snoqualmie.com* ⊙ *Oct.–Apr.*

Edmonds

㉓ *45 mi northwest of Snoqualmie, 15 mi north of Seattle.*

Charming Edmonds has a waterfront lined by more than a mile of chic shops and restaurants, beach-casual businesses, and several notable marine attractions. Just beyond is the small but lively downtown area. The Third Thursday Art Walk shows off the work of local artists, and a host of events and festivals takes place year-round. On the east side of Puget Sound, Edmonds is also the gateway to the Kitsap Peninsula, as ferries from here connect with Kingston.

The lower level of the **Edmonds Historical Museum** is the place to find out about local legends and traditions; temporary exhibits upstairs often have a patriotic theme. The museum's Summer Garden Market sells handmade and hand-grown items on Saturday from 9 to 4 from July through September. ⊠ *118 5th Ave. N* ☎ *425/774–0900* ⊕ *www.historicedmonds. org* 🖾 *$2* ⊙ *Wed.–Sun. 1–4.*

The **Olympic Beach** fishing pier attracts anglers all year. Today the park is dedicated to such Olympic athletes and champions as figure skater Roslyn Summers, and it's an excellent spot to watch the sun set behind Whidbey Island and the Olympic Mountains. ⊠ *Railroad Ave. at Dayton St.* ☎ *425/776–6711.*

The **Edmonds Underwater Park** (☎ 425/771–0230), perhaps the best known dive site in Puget Sound besides the Narrows Bridge, has 27 acres of sunken structures and developed dive trails. It's located immediately north of the ferry landing at the foot of Main Street. The adjacent Brackett's Landing Park has trails, picnic areas, and rest rooms.

Where to Stay & Eat

$–$$ ✕ **Arnie's in Edmonds.** Sitting directly across from the sound, the dining room has views of the water. The restaurant's specialty, seafood, means that the menu is constantly changing according to what's in season. One especially popular dish is Prawns Undecided, which consists of prawns prepared in three different ways—stuffed with crab, roasted with garlic, or coated in a beer batter and fried. ⊠ *300 Admiral Way* ☎ *425/771–5688* ▤ *AE, MC, V.*

¢–$ ▥ **Edmonds Harbor Inn.** In the midst of downtown Edmonds, this luxurious, country-style inn has comfortable mint-and-mauve rooms with such homey touches as natural soaps and feather pillows. Some rooms have a fireplace, kitchen, and oversize bathtub. The hotel's proximity to the waterfront, 1½ blocks from the Kingston ferry terminal, makes amends for the lack of beach views. A day pass to the adjacent health club costs just $5. ⊠ *130 W. Dayton St., 98020* ☎ *425/771–5021 or 800/441–8033* ▤ *425/672–2880* ⊕ *www.nwcountryinns.com/harbor* ⇥ *92 rooms* ⚫ *Dining room, some kitchens, some microwaves, some refrigerators, laundry facilities, laundry service, Internet, business services, meeting rooms, some pets allowed (fee), no-smoking rooms* ▤ *MC, V* ⵙ *CP.*

¢–$ ▥ **Edmonds Inn Bed & Breakfast.** Elegance is defined by this carefully preserved downtown Craftsman home whose five unique suites are named for influential African-Americans. The Ellington is the largest; the Hughes has an arched ceiling and leaded-glass window. Formal afternoon tea is complimentary. ⊠ *202 3rd Ave. S, 98020* ☎ *425/774–1134 or 888/770–7170* ▤ *425/774–1194* ⊕ *www.edmondsinn.com* ⇥ *5 suites* ⚫ *Dining room, Internet* ▤ *AE, DC, MC, V* ⵙ *BP.*

Everett

㉔ *19 mi north of Edmonds.*

Everett is the county seat of Snohomish County. Much of this industrial town sits high on a bluff above Port Gardner Bay and the Snohomish River. The waterfront was once lined by so many lumber, pulp, and shingle mills that Everett proudly called itself "the city of smokestacks." Downtown Everett has many elegant old commercial buildings dating from the period when John D. Rockefeller heavily invested in the fledgling town, hoping to profit from the nearby Monte Cristo mines—which turned out to be a flop. Another scheme failed when James J. Hill made Everett the western terminus of the Great Northern Railroad, hoping to turn it into Puget Sound's most important port. Everett is best known for the Boeing Aircraft plant and for having the second-largest Puget Sound port (Seattle has the largest). The naval station here is home to the U.S.S. *Abraham Lincoln* aircraft carrier and a support flotilla of destroyers and frigates.

The pleasant waterfront suburb of Mukilteo, about 5 mi southeast of Everett, is the main departure point for ferries to Clinton, on Whidbey Island. The old lighthouse and waterfront park are fun to explore. An important Indian treaty was signed in 1855 at nearby Point Elliott.

Marysville, 6 mi north of Everett, was set up as a trading post in 1877. Pioneers exchanged goods with the Snohomish Indians who once occupied southeastern Whidbey Island and the lower Snohomish Valley. Settlers drained and diked the lowlands, raised dairy cows, planted strawberry fields, cleared the forests, and in no time a thriving community was established. Marysville kept to itself for a century, until the I–5 freeway was built; today it's a thriving community and the home of the popular Tulalip (Too-*lay*-lip) Casino.

Snohomish Indians still live on the waterfront reservation at **Tulalip,** which means "almost land-locked bay." British explorer George Vancouver landed here on June 4, 1792, the birthday of King George III, to take possession of the region for England. A traditional cedar canoe, which can hold 20 people and carry more than a ton of cargo, is stored in the tribe's carving shed. The **Tulalip Museum** (✉ I–5, Exit 199 ☎ 360/651–4000 ⌨ Free ☉ Weekdays 8–4:30) has artifacts and exhibits describing tribal traditions.

★ The 11-story, 62-acre **Boeing Everett Facility,** where Boeing 747s and 767s are built, is one of the world's largest buildings. It's second only to Canada's West Edmonton Mall—and so big that it often creates its own weather system inside. You can watch planes in production on one-hour tours introduced by a short video. Tours are extremely popular—and you can't make reservations (except for groups), so get there early, as the wait time can be several hours. Three-hour bus tours from Seattle ($40) are operated daily by Gray Line. Note that there are no bathroom breaks on the tour, and no purses, cameras, videos, or children under 50 inches tall are permitted. ✉ *Rte. 526 W* ☎ *206/544–1264 or 800/ 464–1476* ⊕ *www.boeing.com* ⌨ *$5* ☉ *Tours weekdays at 9 and 1; also at 10, 11, 2, and 3 in summer.*

The **Museum of Flight Restoration Center** is where vintage planes are restored. You can wander among the mix of delicate and behemoth aircraft on a leisurely, self-guided tour at Paine Field. ✉ *100th St. SW, Building C-72* ☎ *425/745–5150* ⊕ *www.museumofflight.org* ⌨ *$2* ☉ *Tues.–Sat. 9–5.*

☾ The **Snohomish County Children's Museum** is on a pioneer homestead built in the 1800s. Interactive exhibits and crafts are part of the fun; wee ones will love the magic school bus as well. ✉ *3013 Colby St.* ☎ *425/ 258–1006* ⌨ *$3* ☉ *Mon.–Sat. 10–3.*

The **Snohomish County Historic Museum** displays Indian artifacts and a collection of old photos. Fascinating changing exhibits focus on Northwest topics; books on regional history are available at the shop. ✉ *1913 Hewitt Ave.* ☎ *425/259–2022* ⊕ *www.snocomuseum.org* ⌨ *Donations accepted* ☉ *Wed.–Sat. 1–4.*

Where to Stay & Eat

$–$$ ✕ **Alligator Soul.** The Louisiana cooking is straight from the bayou, and always receives rave reviews. Exposed brick walls and Mardi Gras beads set the tone for this fun, noisy place where plates come piled high with thick smoked ribs, shrimp-packed gumbo, or fried catfish. Spicy corn relish and hot barbecue sauce let you rachet up the heat. ✉ *2013½ Hewitt Ave.* ☎ *425/259–6311* ⊟ *MC, V.*

$–$$ ✕ **Anthony's Homeport.** Tucked into chic Marina Village, this elegant waterfront restaurant has large windows opening to a panorama of Port Gardner Bay. In summer, sunsets appear to ooze into the water. Meaty Dungeness crab, wild Chinook salmon, and other sea creatures are caught or flown in fresh daily. Desserts are fabulous, especially in summer, when many are made from Washington's succulent berries and fruits. ✉ *1726 W. Marine View Dr.* ☎ *425/252–3333* ⊟ *AE, MC, V.*

¢ ✕ **The Sisters.** This funky breakfast and lunch café in Everett Public Market is as popular now as it was a decade ago. Perhaps that's because the blueberry or pecan hot cakes, rich soups, and overflowing sandwiches are as good as ever. Eye-opening espresso drinks start the morning; homemade ice cream is a perfect end to the afternoon. ⊠ *2804 Grand St.* ☎ *425/252–0480* ⊙ *No dinner* ⊟ *MC, V.*

¢–$ ▦ **Gaylord House.** Down a lane lined by shady maples, this Craftsman welcomes visitors to relax in the creaky rockers on its wide front porch. Themed rooms, filled with antiques and original art, include the Sunrise Mediterranean room; the nautical Commodore's Quarters; and the Victorian-style Lady Anne's Chamber. An exquisite breakfast is included, and you can book ahead for equally exquisite high teas or dinners, when the table is set with fine china, sterling silverware, and crystal stemware. ⊠ *3301 Grand Ave., 98201* ☎ *425/339–9153 or 888/507–7177* ⊟ *425/303–9713* ⊕ *www.gaylordhouse.com* ⇆ *5 rooms* ⚘ *Dining room, in-room data ports, in-room hot tubs, cable TV, in-room VCRs, library; no smoking* ⊟ *AE, D, MC, V* �'◯' *BP.*

¢–$ ▦ **Harbor Hill Inn.** The 1910 Blackman Mansion has been turned into a luxury B&B with spectacular sound and mountain vistas. The Captain's Room has the best views, and the Northwest Room has a private entrance and a patio, but all guest quarters have antique furnishings, handmade quilts, exposed beams, and fir paneling. Modern facilities include a heated pool. ⊠ *2208 Rucker Ave., 98201* ☎ *425/259–3925 or 888/572–3925* ⊟ *425/259–6265* ⊕ *www.harborhillinn.com* ⇆ *4 rooms, 1 suite* ⚘ *Dining room, pool, gym, outdoor hot tub, Internet; no room phones, no smoking* ⊟ *MC, V* '◯' *BP.*

¢–$ ▦ **Marina Village Inn.** Surrounded by Marina Village and right at the head of Port Gardener Bay, this little gem has one of the best locations in town. Telescopes help you spot wildlife through the bay windows in the suave, modern rooms, each with a wet bar. ⊠ *1728 W. Marine View Dr., 98201* ☎ *425/259–4040 or 800/281–7037* ⊟ *425/252–8419* ⊕ *www.gtesupersite.com/marinavilinn* ⇆ *26 rooms, 16 suites* ⚘ *Dining room, some in-room hot tubs, minibars, refrigerators, laundry service, Internet, business services, meeting rooms* ⊟ *AE, D, DC, MC, V* '◯' *CP.*

¢ ▦ **Best Western Cambridge Inn.** Minutes from the Boeing factory, this all-suites hotel is a step up from the rest of the chains in town. Rooms in a modern style have living areas and full kitchens. Complimentary admission to a full-service health club with a hot tub and pool is included. ⊠ *10210 Evergreen Way, 98201* ☎ *425/347–2555 or 877/488–0510* ⊟ *425/347–2554* ⊕ *www.bestwestern.com/cambridgeinn* ⇆ *76 suites* ⚘ *In-room data ports, kitchens, microwaves, refrigerators, cable TV, laundry facilities, business services, no-smoking rooms; no kids under 12* ⊟ *AE, D, DC, MC, V* '◯' *CP.*

Arlington

㉕ *20 mi northeast of Everett.*

Adorable Arlington, as picturesque as early Americana can be, is surrounded by pastures, woods, and the rich farmlands of the Stillaguamish River plain. On sunny days the skies above the local airfield are filled with all sorts of odd-looking experimental planes. The world's largest pleasure boat manufacturer, Bayliner, is just outside town. In early spring the woods are white with trillium, and the pastures have splendid stands of the big yellow candles of skunk cabbage.

Volunteers run the **Air Station Flying Museum** out of a World War II hangar. The seven planes on display represent aviation in this country through several wars. Look for a Fiesler Storch as well as a German observation plane. ✉ *18008 59th Dr. NE* ☎ *360/403–9352* ⌖ *Donation suggested* ⊙ *Sat. 10–4.*

The beautiful, lakeside **Stillaguamish Valley Pioneer Museum** is an enormous, three-story building housing artifacts from Indian, pioneer, logging, and farming days. Exhibit oddities include a foot-powered milking machine, a moonshine still, and a saddle from the Berlin Olympics. Other collections—of model railroad equipment, World War I uniforms, and historic photos—make this museum an intriguing spot to learn about the region. ✉ *20722 67th Ave. NE* ☎ *360/465–7289* ⌖ *$2* ⊙ *Wed. and weekends 1–4.*

Where to Stay & Eat

$$–$$$$ ✕ **Bistro.** One of the most romantic spots in town, the Bistro sometimes hosts a harpist who sets the mood amid candlelit tables. Organic produces graces each plate, alongside fish, steak, or pasta. Try the sesame-encrusted oysters with hoisin-chili sauce. ✉ *231 N. Olympic* ☎ *360/403–9341* ▭ *AE, MC, V* ⊙ *Closed Sun. and Mon.*

★ **¢–$** ▥ **Mt. Higgins House.** Seventy acres of majestic mountain scenery surround this Western-style cedar A-frame, part of a Stillaguamish River valley horse farm. A river-rock fireplace is the living room's centerpiece; the opposite wall of windows overlooks a pond. Bedroom windows have views of towering peaks; inside, wood furniture adds rustic color. Fish for trout in the pond, hike through the woods, or fly-fish in the river. ✉ *29805 State Rte. 530 NE, 98223* ☎ *360/435–9757 or 888/296–3777* 🖷 *360/435–9757* ⊕ *www.snohomish.org/accom/MtHigginsHouse.htm* ⊟ *2 rooms* ⌕ *Dining room, pond, fishing, hiking, piano, library; no a/c, no room phones, no kids under 15, no smoking* ▭ *AE, MC, V* �井 *BP.*

Snohomish

㉖   *21 mi south of Arlington, 10 mi southeast of Everett.*

Snohomish arose in 1859 in typical Northwest fashion: around a shack in the woods. When E. C. Ferguson transported his Steilacoom mansion here, through the Sound and upriver, it was reassembled as the town's first store and hotel. More settlers arrived to construct a gathering of architecturally mismatched but stylish homes, and Snohomish soon became both the county seat and a major riverboat landing. However, the town lost the seat to Everett in 1896, and life slowed further when Everett's became the region's major port and industrial center.

Today, Snohomish is an undeniably quaint and quiet residential town. First Street is the center of the historic district, where elegant 19th-century buildings now house shops, restaurants, and small inns. Dutch-colonial–style homes, English-style cottages, and gingerbread Queen Annes are close-set along the narrow lanes. Not surprisingly, the town is the self-proclaimed "Antique Capital of the Northwest," with more than 400 stores, shops, and vendors selling old treasures.

A string of former logging and mining towns lines Route 2 southeast of Snohomish. Sultan, at the confluence of the Sultan and Skykomish rivers, was founded as a gold-mining settlement and some folks still pan the river. Gold Bar, a rough mining camp in the 1800s, is now a quiet resort town. Follow signs on First Street to the 2-mi trail winding uphill to 250-foot Wallace Falls, one of the highest waterfalls in the North Cascades. East of Skykomish, U.S. 2 crosses the Cascade crest along 4,061-foot-high Stevens Pass; farther east is the faux-Bavarian village of Leavenworth. Wenatchee, the orchard-filled apple capital of Washington, sits even closer to the sunrise in a valley at the confluence of the Wenatchee and Columbia rivers.

Blackman's House Museum, in an 1878 Victorian mansion, is filled with the odds and ends of local history—the kinds of furnishings, everyday objects, toys, and tools that make antiques collectors' hearts skip a beat. ⊠ *118 Ave. B* ☎ *360/568–5235* ⊡ *$1* ☉ *Thurs.–Sun. noon–4.*

Old Snohomish Village is a gathering of six authentic log cabins, including a blacksmith shop and a general store with items from a century ago on the shelves. ⊠ *2nd St. at Pine St.* ☎ *360/568–5235* ⊡ *$2* ☉ *Memorial Day–Labor Day, Wed.–Sun. noon–4.*

Where to Stay

$ 🏨 **Inn at Snohomish.** It may be plain on the outside, but this modern, mountain-view hotel provides all the basic comforts and more. Fresh flowers and jetted tubs await in rooms decorated in floral fabrics and lace. Guests have privileges at the local lap pool. ⊠ *323 2nd St., 98290* ☎ *360/568–2208 or 800/548–9993* ⊕ *www.snohomishinn.com* ➽ *22 rooms* ♿ *Kitchens, some pets allowed* ▤ *AE, MC, V* ⓧ *CP.*

¢ 🏨 **Pillows and Platters.** This beautifully restored Victorian, surrounded by a picket fence, has leaded-glass windows, hardwood floors, and period antiques. Themed guest quarters are "country cozy," Victorian, and "angelic," with touches of lace and gilded wood. An adjacent children's room is available for $50 per night. Breakfast might include stuffed French toast, crab quiche, or farmer's scrambled eggs. ⊠ *502 Ave. C, 98296* ☎ *206/819–3339* 🖷 *800/214–1305* ⊕ *www.pillowsandplatters.com* ➽ *3 rooms, 1 with bath* ♿ *Dining room; no room phones, no room TVs, no kids under 5* ▤ *MC, V* ⓧ *BP.*

Sports & the Outdoors

Following a former mountain train route, the **Centennial Trail** (⊠ Pine St. at Maple Ave.) is a paved, 8-mi, walking, blading, biking, and horseback riding path that leads all the way to Lake Stevens. A very snowy ski area (with avalanche danger and periodic closures in winter), **Stevens Pass** ranges in elevation from 3,800 feet to 5,800 feet; the vertical drop is 1,800 feet. There are 10 chair lifts. This popular ski area has limited parking, so arrive early or risk being turned away. ⊠ *Rte. 2 at the pass* ☎ *360/973–2441* ⊕ *www.stevenspass.com* ⊡ *$44* ☉ *Nov.–mid-Mar., daily 9 AM–10 PM; mid-Mar.–Apr., daily 9–4.*

Shopping

The **Star Antique Center Mall** (⊠ 829 2nd St. ☎ 360/568–2131 ⊕ www. antiquesnw.com/starcenter.html) gathers more than 200 vendors selling and appraising antiques from around the world. It's highly regarded as one of the best places in Washington to pick up true antiques.

Index

㉗ *29 mi southeast of Snohomish.*

Index, which has fewer than 200 residents, illustrates one of the anomalies of western Washington geography; the village lies only 500 feet above sea level yet looks like a remote alpine settlement. That's because as you drive deeper into the mountains of western Washington, the river valleys become deeply glaciated and crowded by jagged ridges and tall peaks. Rising above Index are 5,979-foot-tall Mt. Index and 6,125-foot-tall Mt. Baring. Besides logging, granite quarrying was once a major local industry. The nearby Cascades Tunnel was built to protect trains from the mountains' devastating avalanches.

Index Town Wall locally dubbed "The Wall," is the mammoth granite face that towers over this tiny community. It's a favorite rock-climbing spot. If the thought of dangling 400 feet above the hard ground doesn't pump you up, you can hike the steep dirt path to the top instead.

The century-old mountain and railroad village of **Skykomish**, 15 mi southeast of Index at the western end of the Cascades Tunnel, has a dramatic setting next to a roaring river and beneath jagged peaks to the south and north. Prospectors and miners rushed to build the settlement in 1888, when the Great Northern surveyed a route across the mountains. Skykomish has not changed much since the tunnel was completed in the 1920s, but today it's a gateway to the North Cascades and Alpine Lakes Wilderness. Rte. 2 crosses the Cascade crest on Stevens Pass east of the village.

Where to Stay & Eat

¢ ✕⊞ **Bush House Country Inn.** This carefully restored 1898 mansion has a memorable setting in front of the humongous rock face towering above Index. The inn's buckled wooden floors, odd nooks, and hidden crannies lend it a rustic charm. Fine antiques fill the rooms. Tables in the restaurant ($–$$) surround a stone fireplace, and windows have views of the beautiful gardens. Hearty favorites include prime rib and pot pie, which you can enjoy on the back patio. Ski crowds devour the gourmet Sunday brunch. ⊠ *300 5th St., 98256* ☎ *360/793–2312* ⤴ *11 rooms* △ *Restaurant, bar; no room phones, no room TVs, no smoking* ⊟ *AE, DC, MC, V* ⋆⃝ *CP.*

Seattle Environs A to Z

AIR TRAVEL

Seattle-Tacoma International Airport (Sea-Tac), 15 mi south of Seattle, is the hub for the Seattle Environs. Regional airports include Bellingham International Airport, the hub between northwestern Washington and Canada; Friday Harbor, the San Juan Islands airport; Oak Harbor, Whidbey Island's flight center; and Fairchild International in Port Angeles, serving the Olympic Peninsula and Vancouver Island. The Tacoma Narrows Airport in Gig Harbor connects the Kitsap Peninsula with Sea-Tac.

TRANSFERS Shuttle Express provides service from Sea-Tac Airport south to Tacoma ($20) and north to Everett ($36). Bremerton–Kitsap Airporter shuttles passengers from Sea-Tac to points in Bremerton, Port Orchard, and Gig Harbor ($11–$15). The Capital Aeroporter connects Sea-Tac with Olympia ($26 one-way, $45 round-trip). Olympic Bus Lines and Pennco have shuttles from Port Angeles and the Olympic Peninsula to Sea-Tac. The Bellair Airporter makes 10 round-trips daily between Sea-Tac and Bellingham ($55), with stops in Blaine, the Alaska Ferry, Marysville, Arlington, Mount Vernon, LaConner, Anacortes, San Juan Ferries, and Whidbey Island; the shuttle also runs east from Sea-Tac through Cle Elum and Ellensburg on the way to Yakima ($70). Quick as Air Coachlines takes passengers to Canada.

🛈 Airport Information **Bellingham International** ☎ 360/671-5674 ⊕ www. portofbellingham.com. **Fairchild International** ⊠ 1402 Airport Rd., Port Angeles ☎ 360/457-1138 ⊕ www.portofpa.com/airport. **Friday Harbor** ⊠ San Juan Island ☎ 360/378-4724 ⊕ www.portofpa.com/airport. **Oak Harbor** ⊠ Whidbey Island ☎ 800/ 359-3220. **Sea-Tac** ⊠ Pacific Hwy. S (Rte. 99) ☎ 206/431-4444 ⊕ www.seatac.org. **Tacoma Narrows Airport** ⊠ 1302 26th Ave., Gig Harbor ☎ 253/853-7742 or 866/724-8514.

🛈 Transfer Information **Bellair Airporter** ☎ 866/235-5247 ⊕ www.airporter.com. **Bremerton–Kitsap Airporter** ☎ 800/562-7948 ⊕ www.kitsapairporter.com. **Capital Aeroporter** ☎ 360/754-7113 ⊕ www.capair.com. **Olympic Bus Lines** ☎ 360/417-0700 or 800/457-4492 ⊕ www.olympicbuslines. **Pennco** ☎ 360/452-5104 or 888/673-6626. **Quick as Air** ☎ 800/665-2122, 604/244-3744 in Canada ⊕ www.quickcoach.com. **Shuttle Express** ☎ 425/487-7433 ⊕ www.shuttleexpress.com.

CARRIERS   Horizon Air flies between Bellingham, Port Angeles, and Sea-Tac airports. United Express also connects Bellingham with Sea-Tac. West Isle Air flies between Bellingham, Anacortes, and San Juan, Orcas, and Lopez islands.
🛈 Airlines **Horizon Air** ☎ 800/547-9308 ⊕ www.horizonair.com. **United Express** ☎ 800/241-6522 ⊕ www.ual.com. **West Isle Air** ☎ 800/874-4434 ⊕ www.westisleair. com.

BOAT & FERRY TRAVEL

Washington State Ferries ply Puget Sound, including from Seattle to Bainbridge Island, Port Orchard (via Vashon Island), and Bremerton; between Edmonds and Kingston on the Key Peninsula, between Mukilteo and Clinton, on Whidbey Island, and between Port Townsend and Keystone, also on Whidbey. You can get updated ferry information on the Web site.
🛈 Boat & Ferry Information **Washington State Ferries** ☎ 206/464-6400 or 888/808-7977, 800/843-3779 automated line in WA and BC ⊕ www.wsdot.wa.gov/ferries.

BUS TRAVEL

Greyhound Lines and Northwestern Trailways cover Washington and the Pacific Northwest. From Seattle, Greyhound connects Tacoma (45 minutes, $5), Olympia (1 hour and 45 minutes, $7.75), and Everett (1 hour and 45 minutes, $6). Northwestern Trailways also has daily buses from Seattle south through Tacoma ($6) and north through Everett ($6). Olympic Bus Lines stops at towns around the Olympic Peninsula. Pierce Transit provides bus service around Tacoma.
🛈 Bus Information **Greyhound Lines** ☎ 800/366-3830 ⊕ www.greyhound.com. **Northwestern Trailways** ☎ 800/366-3830 ⊕ www.northwesterntrailways.com. **Olympic Bus Lines** ☎ 800/457-4492 ⊕ www.olympicbuslines.com. **Pierce County Transit** ☎ 253/581-8000 ⊕ www.ptbus.pierce.wa.us.

CAR RENTAL

🛈 Local Agencies **Fine Family** ✉ 7821 Martin Way E., Olympia ☎ 360/923-0309. **Sears Auto Rental** ✉ 12415 Rte. 99, Everett ☎ 425/355-8349 ✉ 10002 Lakeview Ave. SW, Lakewood (Tacoma) ☎ 253/582-0697 ✉ 18th St. NW and W. Stewart Ave., Puyallup ☎ 253/841-1135. **U-Save** ✉ 5626 Evergreen Way S, Everett ☎ 425/438-1775 or 877/728-7283 ✉ 13512 47th Ave. Ct. NW, Tacoma ☎ 253/539-0405.

CAR TRAVEL

Interstate 5 runs south from the Canadian border through Seattle, Tacoma, and Olympia to Oregon and California. Interstate 90 begins in Seattle and runs east through North Bend all the way to Idaho. Route 2 meanders east, parallel to I–90, from Everett to Spokane. Routes 7 and 167 connect the Tacoma area with the Puyallup suburbs and towns around Mt. Rainier. Route 101 begins northwest of Olympia and traces the coast of the Olympic Peninsula.

EMERGENCIES

🛈 Hospitals **Providence Medical Center** ✉ 1321 Colby Ave., Everett ☎ 425/258-7123. **Providence St. Peter Hospital** ✉ 413 Lilly Rd. NE, Olympia ☎ 360/491-9480. **Mary Bridge Children's Hospital** ✉ 317 Martin Luther King Jr. Way, Tacoma ☎ 253/552-1400. **Tacoma General Hospital** ✉ 315 Martin Luther King Jr. Way, Tacoma ☎ 253/403-1000.
🛈 Pharmacies **Bartell Drugs** ⊕ www.bartelldrugs.com. **Rite Aid** ⊕ www.riteaid. com. **Walgreens** ⊕ www.walgreens.com.

MONEY MATTERS

Bank of America, Key Bank, Wells Fargo, and Washington Mutual are among the major banks outside of Seattle. All have multiple branches and ATM machines in cities throughout Puget Sound.
🛈 ATM Locations **Cirrus** ☎ 800/424-7787. **Plus** ☎ 800/843-7587.

🏧 Banks **Bank of America** ☎ 800/642-9855 ⊕ www.bankofamerica.com. **Key Bank** ☎ 206/447-5767 ⊕ www.keybank.com. **US Bank** ☎ 800/872-2657 ⊕ www.usbank.com. **Washington Mutual** ☎ 800/756-8000 ⊕ www.wamu.com. **Wells Fargo** ☎ 800/869-3557 ⊕ www.wellsfargo.com.

TOURS

Tours of Bremerton Harbor are operated in summer by Kitsap Harbor Tours. The *Captain Cook VII* is a 111-foot luxury dining ship serving gourmet brunches ($40) and dinners ($75) while cruising the Everett waterfront and the Snohomish River. Argosy Cruises operates daily trips from Seattle to Tacoma. The Tacoma Architectural Foundation conducts Saturday walking tours ($5) of the city that begin at the Washington State History Museum. Wavetrek organizes white-water rafting, kayaking, and climbing trips, and children's adventure activities in the North Cascades.

🏧 Tour-Operators **Argosy Cruises** ✉ Pier 55, Seattle ☎ 206/623-4252. **Captain Cook VII** ✉ Everett ☎ 425/259-5010. **Kitsap Harbor Tours** ✉ Bremerton ☎ 360/377-8924. **Tacoma Architectural Foundation** ✉ 1911 Pacific Ave., Tacoma ☎ 253/594-7839. **Wavetrek** ✉ Box 236, Index ☎ 360/793-1705 or 800/543-7971 ⊕ www.wavetrek.com

TRAIN TRAVEL

Amtrak has service within Washington and to Canada, Oregon, California, and the East. Sounder Trains (commuters) leave Tacoma at 6:15 AM and 6:45 AM, with stops in Puyallup, Sumner, Auburn, Kent, and Tukwila on the way to Seattle. Southbound trains leave Seattle for the reverse route at 5:10 and 5:35 PM. Cost is $2–$4.

🏧 **Amtrak** ☎ 800/872-7245 ⊕ www.amtrak.com. **Sounder Trains** ☎ 888/889-6368 ⊕ www.soundtransit.org.

VISITOR INFORMATION

🏧 Tourist Information **Bainbridge Island Chamber of Commerce** ✉ 590 Winslow Way ☎ 206/842-3700 ⊕ www.bainbridgechamber.com. **Bremerton Area Chamber of Commerce** ✉ 301 Pacific Ave., Bremerton ☎ 360/479-3579 ⊕ www.bremertonchamber.org. **Chamber of East Pierce County** ✉ 322 2nd St. SW, Puyallup ☎ 253/845-6755 ⊕ www.puyallupchamber.com. **Edmonds Chamber of Commerce** ✉ 125 5th Ave. N, Edmonds ☎ 425/776-6711 ⊕ edmondswa.com. **Everett Area Chamber of Commerce** ✉ 909 SE Everett Mall Way, Suite C30, Everett ☎ 425/438-1487 ⊕ snobiz.org. **Gig Harbor Chamber of Commerce** ✉ 3302 Harborview Dr., Gig Harbor ☎ 360/435-3708 ⊕ www.gigharborchamber.com. **Greater Arlington Chamber of Commerce** ✉ 120 N. Olympic Ave., Arlington ☎ 360/435-3708 ⊕ www.arlington-chamber.com. **Greater Poulsbo Chamber of Commerce** ✉ 19168 Jenson Way, Poulsbo ☎ 360/779-4848 or 877/768-5726 ⊕ www.poulsbochamber.com. **Greater Renton Chamber of Commerce** ✉ 300 Rainier Ave. N, Renton ☎ 425/226-4560 ⊕ www.renton-chamber.com. **Kitsap Peninsula Visitor and Convention Bureau** ✉ 2 Rainier Ave., Port Gamble ☎ 800/416-5615 ⊕ www.visitkitsap.com. **Marysville/Tulalip Visitor Information Center** ✉ Off I-5, Exit 199, Marysville ☎ 360/653-2634 ⊕ snohomish.org **Snohomish Chamber of Commerce** ✉ 127 Ave. A, Snohomish ☎ 360/568-2526 ⊕ www.cityofsnohomish.com. **Snohomish County Tourism Bureau/VIC** ✉ 101 128th St. SE, Suite 5000, Everett ☎ 888/338-0976 ⊕ www.snohomish.org **State Capitol Visitor Information Center** ✉ 14th St. and S. Capitol Way, Olympia ☎ 360/586-3460 ⊕ www.ci.olympia.wa.us/. **Tacoma-Pierce County Visitor and Convention Bureau** ✉ 1001 Pacific Ave., Suite 400, Tacoma ☎ 253/627-2836 or 800/272-2662 ⊕ www.tpctourism.org.

NORTHWESTERN WASHINGTON

Updated by
John Doerper

In the northwestern lowlands between the Snohomish River and the Canadian border, you're never far from saltwater or from the mountains. Three rivers lazily wind through lowland valleys covered in meadows and woods: the Stillaguamish, the Skagit, and the Nooksack. Rocky hills, which once were islands, have been joined to the mainland by the alluvial deposits of the streams, making for a rather flat landscape in places. Such former islands rise as hills above Burlington, La Conner, and Mount Vernon. A few rocky islands still rise offshore, though their proximity to the land almost makes them peninsulas: Fidalgo Island is separated from the mainland by a slough; Guemes and Lummi Island by a narrow passage. Despite its name, Samish Island is a peninsula.

All of this makes for a varied and beautiful landscape, especially since the flats are a patchwork of green pastures and vegetable fields highlighted in spring by acres of colorful tulips, and the moraine uplands and rocky outcroppings are covered with evergreen forest. White-water creeks gush from the mountains, and placid streams meander through the lowlands, providing havens for ducks, geese, and blue herons. In winter the low-lying flats are white with snow geese and swans.

Most of the towns and villages of this region are built along saltwater bays or on the banks of navigable rivers, because the swampy terrain, overgrown by tall trees, meant travel for the first settlers was feasible only by water. Today, with logging in decline, dairy and berry farming are the mainstays of local economies, though Bellingham and Mount Vernon also have some light industry. But increasingly the small towns and villages of western Washington have begun to market their real asset: the region's natural beauty.

The North Cascades look like a different world, and they are. Some geologists believe that they once were a Pacific Ocean island that drifted eastward and bumped into the North American continent, or, as geologists like to say, "docked," since the experts don't consider these attachments permanent.

Rising from valley floors that are only a few feet above sea level, 4,000-, 6,000-, even 7,000-foot peaks crowd out the sky. Farther east the peaks top 9,000 feet. Some, like Mt. Shuksan, glow with blue glacial ice; others are marked by white streaks of cascading creeks. In summer the hanging valleys are densely covered with wildflowers; in autumn they glow red and yellow with the fall foliage of huckleberry, mountain ash, and aspen. In winter, these mountains have the greatest measured snowfall on earth—more than 80 feet in the high places of the western slopes. Because of the depth of the glaciated valleys, these mountains are uncommonly accessible by roads and short, albeit steep, hiking trails. Passes are low, in the 3,000- to 5,000-foot range, making crossing feasible even at the height of winter.

While the Cascade Range in general is of volcanic origin, the North Cascades have only two prominent volcanic peaks, both more than 10,000 feet tall. Glacier Peak is almost hidden amid tall nonvolcanic mountains, but Mt. Baker, to the north, stands west of the main range and can be seen from far out to sea. This is the ultimate hiking and backpacking country, but it also has good fishing, quiet streams and lakes for boating, and shady trails for taking refreshing strolls.

Whidbey Island

❶ *The ferry makes a 3 mi trip from Mukilteo (5 mi south of Everett) across Possession Sound to Clinton, on Whidbey Island.*

On a nice day a pleasant excursion is a ferry trip across Possession Sound to Whidbey Island, 30 mi northwest of Seattle. It's a great way to watch gulls, terns, sailboats, and the occasional orca or bald eagle—not to mention the surrounding scenery, which takes in Camano Island and the North Cascades. Or you can drive across from the mainland on Route 20 at the island's northern end. (The island is also connected to Port Townsend on the Olympic Peninsula by a Washington State ferry that crosses several times a day from Keystone, a couple of miles west of Coupeville.) Sixty miles long and 8 mi wide, Whidbey is the second-longest island in the contiguous United States; only Long Island in New York stretches farther.

From the air, Whidbey Island looks like a languid dragon, with Fidalgo Island to the north as its head. Whidbey is a blend of low pastoral hills, evergreen and oak forests, meadows of wildflowers, sandy beaches, and dramatic (though unstable) bluffs. It's a great place for taking slow drives or bicycle rides, for viewing sunsets over the water, and for boating or kayaking along the protected shorelines of Saratoga Passage, Holmes Harbor, Penn Cove, and Skagit Bay.

The best beaches are on the west side, where wooded and wildflower-bedecked bluffs drop steeply to sand or surf—which can cover the beaches at high tide and can be rough on this exposed shore. Both beaches and bluffs have great views of the shipping lanes and the Olympic Mountains. Maxwelton Beach, with its sand, driftwood, and great views across Admiralty Inlet to the Olympic Mountains, is popular with the locals. Possession Point includes a park, a beach, and a boat launch. West of Coupeville, Ft. Ebey State Park has a sandy spread; West Beach is a stormy patch north of the fort with mounds of driftwood.

Langley
7 mi north of Clinton.

The village of Langley is above a 50-foot-high bluff overlooking Saratoga Passage, which separates Whidbey from Camano Island. A grassy terrace just above the beach is a great place for viewing birds that are on the water or in the air. On a clear day you can see Mt. Baker in the distance. Upscale boutiques selling art, glass, jewelry, and clothing line First and Second streets in the heart of town. The **South Whidbey Historical Museum** (⊠ 312 2nd St. ☎ 360/579–4696), open on weekends 1–4 in a former one-room schoolhouse, displays Victrolas, farm tools, kitchen utensils, and antique toys. A donation is requested.

WHERE TO ✕ **Star Bistro.** This 1980s-vintage bistro atop the Star Store feels like some-
STAY & EAT one's comfortable dining room. The seasonal menu changes weekly. Lunch
$–$$$ might include duck confit with wild mushroom salad, grilled figs, and seasonal greens. Dinner might bring cioppino; penne pasta with grilled eggplant, goat cheese, rosemary, and warm herb vinaigrette; a house-smoked pork chop with fire-roasted peppers and corn relish; or risotto with king salmon. Less adventurous eaters can opt for fish-and-chips or a burger. Popular for lunch, the dining room remains crowded well into late afternoon and evening. ⊠ 201½ 1st St. ☎ 360/221–2627 ⊕ *www.star-bistro.com* ⌣ *Reservations not accepted* ⊟ AE, MC, V ⊙ *No dinner Mon.*

$–$$ ✕ **Garibyan Brothers Café Langley.** Terra-cotta tile floors, antique oak tables, and the aroma of garlic, basil, and oregano set the mood at this Mediterranean restaurant with Northwest touches. The tables are small but not too close together. Exotic dishes include rich hummus and baba ghanoush, eggplant moussaka, stuffed grape leaves, Mediterranean seafood stew, and lamb or chicken shish kabob. For Northwest fare, try the Dungeness crab cakes, Penn Cove mussels, or a seafood salad. Green or Greek salads accompany all entrées. The staff is friendly, professional, and helpful. ⊠ 113 1st St. ☎ 360/221–3090 ⊟ MC, V ⊙ *Closed Tues. Jan.–Mar. No lunch Tues.*

¢–$ ✕ **Dog House Backdoor Restaurant.** A friendly and relaxed waterfront tavern and family restaurant, the Dog House is filled with collectibles that include a 1923 nickelodeon. This is the town's most popular restaurant, both for the quality and for the low prices of its tacos, burritos, juicy burgers, creative pizzas, and homemade chili. For vegetarians there are tempura vegetables, a fresh vegetable platter, and sweet-potato fries. Listed on the National Register of Historic Places, the restaurant has a fine view of the Langley waterfront and Saratoga Passage and, on a clear day, the snow-capped volcanic cone of distant Mount Baker. ⊠ *230 1st St.* ☎ *360/221–9996* ⌂ *Reservations not accepted* ▭ *No credit cards.*

$$$–$$$$ ✕▦ **Inn at Langley.** Langley's most elegant inn, the concrete-and-wood
FodorsChoice Frank Lloyd Wright–inspired structure perches on a bluff above the beach.
★ Asian-style guest rooms, all with fireplaces and balconies, have dramatic marine and mountain views. Stark yet comfortable rooms contrast beautifully with the lush landscape, which might be overpowering against a more baroque backdrop. Island Thyme Restaurant ($$$$, reservations essential) serves innovative prix-fixe, five-course seasonal dinners Friday and Saturday nights only, and Sunday supper in summer. For guests, the complimentary Continental breakfast includes the chef's own muesli, seasonal fruit, and fresh muffins. ⊠ *400 1st St., 98260* ☎ *360/ 221–3033* ⊕ *www.innatlangley.com* ⏎ *24 rooms* ⌂ *Restaurant, in-room hot tubs, spa* ▭ *MC, V* ⧉ *CP.*

$–$$ ▦ **Country Cottage of Langley.** On two landscaped acres, this 1927 Craftsman farmhouse overlooks downtown Langley, the water, and the Cascade Mountains. Dormer windows and a gabled entrance are some of the charming architectural details, complemented by the interior's stone fireplace and white-washed wainscoting. Other distinctive features include the dining room's murals, which depict the four seasons. Rooms are appointed according to their themes; some have fireplaces and views of the mountains or water. ⊠ *215 6th St., 98260* ☎ *360/221–8709 or 800/713–3860* ⊕ *www.acountrycottage.com* ⏎ *5 rooms, 1 cottage* ⌂ *In-room hot tubs, fans, refrigerators, cable TV, in-room VCRs, microwaves; no smoking* ▭ *AE, MC, V* ⧉ *BP.*

$–$$ ▦ **Saratoga Inn.** This inn—formerly known as Harrison House—sits at the edge of Langley, a short walk from the town's shops and restaurants. Wood-shingle siding, gabled roofs, and wraparound porches lend the inn a Pacific Northwest authenticity. This theme extends to the interior, with wood floors and fireplaces. The carriage house, which has a deck as well as a bedroom with a king-size bed, a bathroom with a claw-foot tub, and a sitting area with a sleep sofa, offers more privacy. Included in the price is afternoon tea with hors d'oeuvres. ⊠ *201 Cascade Ave., 98260* ☎ *360/221–5801 or 800/698–2910* ☒ *360/221–5804* ⊕ *www. foursisters.com* ⏎ *15 rooms, 1 carriage house* ⌂ *Cable TV, business services, meeting room; no a/c, no smoking* ▭ *AE, D, MC, V* ⧉ *BP.*

$ ▦ **Lone Lake Cottage and Breakfast.** Here you can stay in a cottage, a lakeside suite, or a houseboat. The boat has a queen-size loft bed and tiny galley; the cottages have rattan and soapstone-inlaid furniture, Oriental screens, and covered decks. ⊠ *5206 S. Bayview Rd., 98260* ☎☒ *360/ 321–5325* ⊕ *www.lonelake.com* ⏎ *1 houseboat, 1 suite, 2 cottages* ⌂ *In-room hot tubs, kitchenettes, microwaves, refrigerators, cable TV, in-room VCRs, boating, fishing, bicycles; no smoking* ▭ *No credit cards* ⧉ *CP.*

¢–$ ▦ **Eagle's Nest.** Views of the Saratoga Passage and Cascade Mountains abound at this hilltop inn. The octagonal shape of the contemporary building allows for maximum privacy in the rooms, each of which has a private balcony. The living room's enormous brick fireplace is flanked by elongated octagonal windows in clear and peach-color glass. ⊠ *4680 Saratoga Rd., 98260* ☎☒ *360/221–5331* ⊕ *www.eaglesnestinn.com* ⏎ *4* *rooms, 1 cottage* ⚪ *Cable TV, in-room VCRs, hot tub, hiking; no room phones, no kids under 12, no smoking* ☰ *D, MC, V* ⦿ *BP.*

SPORTS & THE OUTDOORS In the Bayview area of Whidbey Island, off Route 525 near Langley, **Pedaler Velocity Bikes** (✉ 5603½ S. Bayview Rd. ☎ 360/321–5040) rents bikes year-round. Langley's small **boat harbor** (☎ 360/221–6765) provides moorage for 35 boats, plus utilities and a 160-foot fishing pier, all protected by a timber-pile breakwater.

SHOPPING At **Blackfish Gallerio** (✉ 5075 S. Langley Rd. ☎ 360/221–1274) you can see pieces by Kathleen Miller, who produces enamel jewelry and hand-painted clothing and accessories; and Donald Miller, whose photographs depict the land and people of the Northwest as well as works by other regional artists. The **Cottage** (✉ 210 1st St. ☎ 360/221–4747) stocks vintage and imported men's and women's clothing. **Gaskill/Olson Gallery** (✉ 302 1st St. ☎ 360/221–2978) exhibits and sells paintings, jewelry, pottery, and sculpture by established and emerging artists in a variety of media. Exhibits change on the first Saturday of the month.

Meet glass and jewelry artist Gwenn Knight at her gallery, the **Glass Knight** (✉ 214 1st St. ☎ 360/221–6283), which also exhibits work by other Northwest artists. The **Museo** (✉ 215 1st St. ☎ 360/221–7737), a gallery and gift shop, carries contemporary art by recognized and emerging artists.

Freeland
7 mi west of Langley.

The sprawling, unincorporated village of Freeland is home to two parks. You'll find picnic spots and a sandy beach at Freeland Park on Holmes Harbor. Bush Point Lighthouse and the beach are the main attractions at South Whidbey State Park, which has hiking, camping, and swimming.

Greenbank
11 mi north of Freeland.

About halfway up Whidbey Island is the hamlet of Greenbank, home to the 125-acre **Greenbank Farm,** a loganberry farm and former winery that Island County purchased in late 1997. Volunteers now farm the berries, but the winery has closed. Local wines are, however, sold in a small wine shop, which also sells richly flavored jam. A small café next door sells pies. The 1904 barn, which once housed the winery, now serves as a community center.

The farm has a pond and walking trails with panoramic views of Admiralty Inlet, Saratoga Passage, and the Olympic and Cascade Mountains. A herd of alpacas is being raised on the farm by the Whidbey Island Alpacas company for their soft, spinnable hair and for sale as pets. The farm is also the site of several community events, including a Loganberry Festival each July, and a Sunday farmers' market held in summer. Picnic tables are scattered throughout the farm. ✉ *657 Wonn Rd.* ☎ *360/678–7700* ⊕ *www.greenbankfarm.com* ☞ *Free* ☉ *Daily 10–5.*

The 53-acre **Meerkerk Rhododendron Gardens** contain 1,500 native and hybrid species of rhododendrons and more than 100,000 spring bulbs on 10 acres of display gardens with numerous walking trails and ponds. The flowers are in full bloom in April and May. Summer flowers and fall color provide interest later in the year. The 43 remaining acres are kept wild as a nature preserve. ✉ *Resort Rd.* ☎ *360/678–1912* ⊕ *www. meerkerkgardens.org* ☞ *$3* ☉ *Daily 9–4.*

WHERE TO STAY
★ $$–$$$$ 🏠 **Guest House Cottages.** The very private log cabins here, surrounded by 25 forested acres, have feather beds, whirlpool tubs, country antiques,

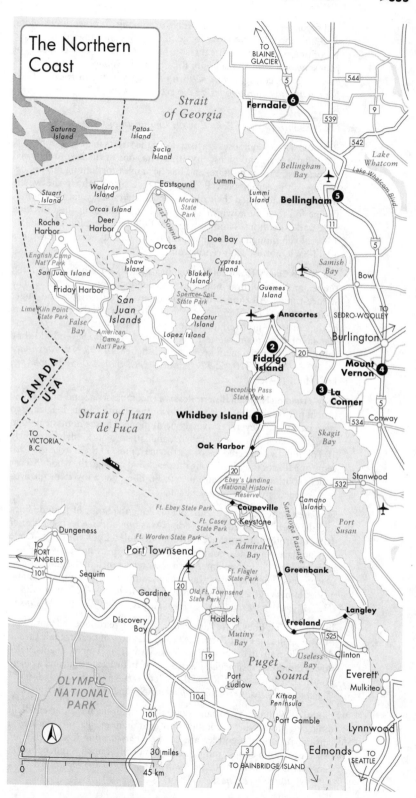

The Northern Coast

Strait of Georgia

Saturna Island

Patos Island

Sucia Island

TO BLAINE GLACIER

Ferndale ❻

544

539

9

542

Lake Whatcom

Lake Whatcom Blvd

Stuart Island

Waldron Island

Eastsound

Lummi

Bellingham Bay

Lummi Island

Bellingham ❺

Orcas Island

Deer Harbor

Moran State Park

East Sound

11

Roche Harbor

English Camp Nat'l Park

San Juan Island

Orcas

Shaw Island

Doe Bay

Blakely Island

Cypress Island

Samish Bay

Bow

5

Spencer Spit State Park

Guemes Island

TO SEDRO-WOOLLEY

Friday Harbor

San Juan Islands

Decatur Island

Anacortes

Lime Kiln Point State Park

False Bay

American Camp Nat'l Park

Lopez Island

❷ **Fidalgo Island**

Burlington

20

Mount Vernon ❹

❸ **La Conner**

5

Whidbey Island ❶

534

Conway

Strait of Juan de Fuca

Deception Pass State Park

Oak Harbor

Skagit Bay

CANADA USA

TO VICTORIA, B.C.

20

Ebey's Landing National Historic Reserve

Stanwood

532

Camano Island

Port Susan

Dungeness

TO PORT ANGELES

101

Sequim

Ft. Ebey State Park

Coupeville

Ft. Casey State Park

Keystone

Port Townsend

Ft. Worden State Park

Admiralty Bay

Saratoga Passage

Gardiner

20

Old Ft. Townsend State Park

Ft. Flagler State Park

Greenbank

Discovery Bay

Hadlock

Freeland

Langley

525

Clinton

19

Mutiny Bay

Useless Bay

OLYMPIC NATIONAL PARK

Port Ludlow

Puget Sound

Everett

Mulkiteo

104

Kitsap Peninsula

101

Port Gamble

Lynnwood

30 miles

45 km

Edmonds

TO SEATTLE

3

TO BAINBRIDGE ISLAND

and fireplaces. Fresh flowers and robes are among the other draws, along with an enormous two-story lodge filled with collectibles that include a working pump organ. Breakfast is included for the first two days of your stay. ⊠ *835 E. Christianson Rd., 98253* ☎ *360/678–3115* ⊕ *www. guesthouselogcottages.com* ⟳ *6 units* ⚭ *Kitchens, in-room VCRs, pool, gym; no room phones* ⊟ *No credit cards.*

Coupeville

★ *On the south shore of Penn Cove, 15 mi north of Greenbank.*

Restored Victorian houses grace many of the streets in quiet Coupeville, Washington's second oldest city. It also has one of the largest national historic districts in the state, and has been used for filming movies depicting 19th-century New England villages. Stores above the waterfront have maintained their old-fashioned character. Captain Thomas Coupe founded the town in 1852. His house was built the following year, and other houses and commercial buildings were built in the late 1800s. Even though Coupeville is the Island County seat, the town has a laid-back, almost 19th-century air.

☝ The **Island County Historical Museum** has exhibits on Whidbey's fishing, timber, and agricultural industries, and conducts tours and walks. The square-timber **Alexander Blockhouse** outside dates from the Puget Sound Indian War of 1855. Note the squared logs and dove-tailed joints of the corners—no overlapping log ends. This construction technique was favored by many western Washington pioneers. Several old-time canoes are exhibited in an open, roofed shelter. ⊠ *908 NW Alexander St.* ☎ *360/678–3310* 🎫 *$2* ☉ *May–Oct., daily 10–5; Nov.–Apr., Fri.–Mon. 11–4.*

☝ **Ebey's Landing National Historic Reserve** encompasses a sand-and-cobble beach, bluffs with dramatic views down the Strait of Juan de Fuca, two state parks, and several (privately held) pioneer farms homesteaded in the early 1850s. The reserve, the first and largest of its kind, holds nearly 100 nationally registered historic structures, most of them from the 19th century. Miles of trails lead along the beach and through the woods. Cedar Gulch, south of the main entrance to Ft. Ebey, has a lovely picnic area in a wooded ravine above the beach.

Ft. Casey State Park, on a bluff overlooking the Strait of Juan de Fuca and the Port Townsend ferry landing, was one of three forts built after 1890 to protect the entrance to Admiralty Inlet. Look for the concrete gun emplacement and a couple of 8-inch "disappearing" guns. The Admiralty Head Lighthouse Interpretive Center is north of the gunnery emplacements. There are also grassy picnic sites, rocky fishing spots, and a boat launch. ⊠ *2 mi west of Rte. 20* ☎ *360/678–4519 or 800/233–0321* ⊕ *www.parks.wa.gov* 🎫 *Free. Parking $5* ☉ *Daily 8 AM–sunset.*

In late May **Ft. Ebey State Park** blazes with native rhododendrons. West of Coupeville on Point Partridge, it has 22 acres of beach, campsites in the woods, trails to the headlands, World War II gun emplacements, wildflower meadows, spectacular views down Juan de Fuca Strait, and a boggy pond. ⊠ *3 mi west of Rte. 20* ☎ *360/678–4636 or 800/233–0321* ⊕ *www.parks.wa.gov* 🎫 *Free, parking $5* ☉ *Daily sunrise–sunset.*

WHERE TO ✕ **Rosi's.** Within a Victorian home, this restaurant has three candlelit
STAY & EAT dining rooms serving a combination of Italian and Pacific Northwest
$$$ cuisine. Among the entrées are chicken *mascarpone* (cream cheese), osso buco, lamb chops, and Penn Cove mussels. Lunch is much less expensive than dinner. ⊠ *602 N. Main St.* ☎ *360/678–3989* ⊟ *AE, MC, V* ☉ *No lunch weekends.*

$–$$ ✕ **Christopher's Front Street Cafe.** This eclectically furnished restaurant—whose tables are set with linens, fresh flowers, and candles—is warm and casual. The new American menu features local oysters and mussels, and such flavorful fare as raspberry barbecued salmon, bacon-wrapped pork tenderloin with mushrooms, lamb stew, and grilled ahi tuna—all prepared with a light touch. The wine list is extensive. ⊠ *23 Front St.* ☎ *360/678–5480* ▤ *AE, MC, V.*

¢–$$$ 🏨 **Captain Whidbey Inn.** Almost a century old, this venerable madrona lodge on a wooded promontory offers a special kind of hospitality and charm now rarely found. The lodge rooms, furnished with antiques, tend to be small, but they are well appointed with modern amenities; rooms on the north side have splendid views of Penn Cove. There are additional rooms in a separate modern motel overlook a quiet saltwater lagoon. Gracefully aged, surrounded by native shrubs and trees, the Captain Whidbey is the perfect hideout for those who want to escape the stress of the modern age. ⊠ *2073 Captain Whidbey Inn Rd., off Madrona Way, 98239* ☎ *360/678–4097 or 800/366–4097* ⊕ *www.captainwhidbey.com* 🛏 *25 rooms ⚐ Restaurant, bar, library* ▤ *AE, MC, V.*

¢–$ 🏨 **Anchorage Inn.** The exterior of this reproduction Victorian has fanciful details such as gables, dormer windows, and a tower. Inside, hardwood floors, reproduction furniture, and antiques harmonize with the Victorian theme. There are splendid views of the harbor from each room. ⊠ *807 N. Main St., 98239* ☎ *360/678–5581 or 877/230–1313* ⊕ *www.anchorage-inn.com* 🛏 *6 rooms, 1 suite ⚐ In-room data ports, cable TV with movies, in-room VCRs, bicycles; no kids under 5, no smoking* ▤ *D, MC, V* ⦿ *BP.*

¢–$ 🏨 **Colonel Crockett Farm.** The farmhouse, amid three acres of lawn and flower gardens, was built by a relative of Davy Crockett in 1855. Among the architectural details of the interior are stained- and leaded-glass windows, red oak paneling, and a slate fireplace. Antiques fill the guest rooms, some of which have views of the harbor and meadows. ⊠ *1012 S. Ft. Casey Rd., 98239* ☎ *360/678–3711* 📠 *360/678–3707* ⊕ *www.crockettfarm.com* 🛏 *5 rooms ⚐ Library; no a/c, no room phones, no room TVs, no kids under 14, no smoking* ▤ *MC, V* ⦿ *BP.*

¢–$ 🏨 **Ft. Casey Inn.** The inn comprises nine Georgian revival duplexes built in 1907 to house U.S. Army artillery officers and their families. Stationed here until the 1940s, the officers manned coastal batteries designed to defend Puget Sound and the U.S. naval base at Bremerton. The duplexes stand on a hillside overlooking the former parade grounds. Each has a fireplace, two bedrooms, a living room, and a kitchen (with breakfast fixings on hand). Owners Gordon and Victoria Hoenig restored the tin ceilings and decorated the units with rag rugs, old quilts, hand-painted furniture, and sundry Colonial touches. ⊠ *1124 S. Engle Rd., 98239* ☎ *360/678–8792 or 866/661–6604* ⊕ *www.fortcaseyinn.com* 🛏 *9 units ⚐ Kitchens, bicycles* ▤ *AE, MC, V.*

¢–$ 🏨 **Inn at Penn Cove.** This inn is composed of two stately Victorian homes standing side-by-side in the center of Coupeville's historic district. Fir floors, reproduction Victorian wallpaper, an antique pump organ, and a Victorian music box give special charm to Kineth House's parlor. The rooms in the Coupe-Gillespie House, though less ornate, are equally comfortable and have stenciled wall trim and Victorian bedsteads. ⊠ *702 N. Main St., 98239* ☎ *360/678–8000 or 800/688–2683* ⊕ *www.whidbey.net/penncove* 🛏 *6 rooms, 4 with bath ⚐ No a/c in some rooms, no room phones* ▤ *AE, D, MC, V* ⦿ *BP.*

¢ 🏨 **Compass Rose Bed and Breakfast.** Inside this 1890 Queen Anne Victorian, a veritable museum of art, artifacts, and antiques awaits you. The proprietor's naval career carried him and his wife to all corners of the globe, from which they have collected the inn's unique adornments.

The innkeepers' friendliness will make your stay all the more enjoyable and interesting. ⊠ *508 S. Main St., 98239* ☎ *360/678–5318* ☎ *800/ 237–3881* ⊕ *www.compassrosebandb.com* ⤴ *2 rooms* ⚲ *Cable TV; no smoking* ⊟ *No credit cards* ﺤ *BP.*

Oak Harbor
10 mi north of Coupeville.

Oak Harbor gets its name from the majestic Oregon oaks that grow above the bay. Dutch and Irish immigrants settled the town in the mid-1800s; several windmills in town were built by descendants of the Dutch as symbols of their heritage. Themarina, at the east side of the bay, has a picnic area with views of Saratoga Passage and the entrance of Penn Cove.

★ ⚲ **Deception Pass State Park** has 19 mi of rocky shore and beaches, three freshwater lakes, and more than 38 mi of forest and meadow trails. The park occupies the northernmost point of Whidbey Island and the southernmost tip of Fidalgo Island, on both sides of the Deception Pass Bridge. Park on Canoe Island and walk across the bridge for views of two dramatic saltwater gorges, whose tidal whirlpools have been known to swallow large logs. ⊠ *Rte. 20, 7 mi north of Oak Harbor* ☎ *360/ 675–2417* ⤳ *Park free, campsite fees vary* ⊗ *Apr.–Sept., daily 6:30 AM–dusk; Oct.–Mar., daily 8 AM–dusk.*

WHERE TO ✕ **Island Grill.** This friendly roadside café in the woods south of Deception
STAY & EAT Pass serves fresh and flavorful American fare such as salads, burgers,
$–$$ and fish-and-chips. You can enjoy your meal in the comfortable dining room, or pick up food from the take-out window for a picnic on the waterfront at adjacent Deception Pass State Park. ⊠ *41020 Rte. 20* ☎ *360/679–3194* ⊟ *MC, V.*

¢–$$ ⊞ **Coachman Inn.** This motel caters to families and each room is individually decorated. The place is uncommonly friendly and comfortable for a chain motel. ⊠ *32959 Rte. 20, 98277* ☎ *360/675–0727 or 800/ 635–0043* ☎ *360/675–1419* ⊕ *www.thecoachmaninn.com* ⤴ *100 rooms* ⚲ *Picnic area, some kitchenettes, refrigerators, cable TV, pool, gym, hot tub, playground, laundry facilities, business services* ⊟ *AE, D, DC, MC, V* ﺤ *CP.*

¢–$ ⊞ **Best Western Harbor Plaza.** This three-story motel, 1 mi from the city beachfront recreation area, is tucked into the edge of the woods off the main highway and is surprisingly comfortable and quiet. ⊠ *33175 Rte. 20, 98277* ☎ *360/679–4567* ☎ *360/675–2543* ⊕ *www.bestwestern.com/ harborplaza* ⤴ *80 rooms* ⚲ *In-room data ports, microwaves, refrigerators, cable TV, pool, gym, hot tub, lounge, business services, free parking, some pets allowed (fee)* ⊟ *AE, D, DC, MC, V* ﺤ *CP.*

¢ ⊞ **Inn at the Bay Bed and Breakfast.** This one-suite B&B on a hillside overlooking the bay has steep gabled roofs and a stained-wood exterior that give it the appearance of an Alpine home. The suite has a sitting room, deck, and balcony. Views across Oak Harbor and Saratoga Passage are great and the place is very comfortable. With luck, you can watch a bald eagle cruise by. ⊠ *5129 N. Alto La., 98277* ☎ *360/679–8320* ⊕ *www. innatbay.com* ⤴ *1 suite* ⚲ *Cable TV, in-room VCR; no smoking* ⊟ *No credit cards* ﺤ *BP.*

Fidalgo Island

❷ *15 mi north of Oak Harbor.*

The Deception Pass Bridge links Whidbey to Fidalgo (fee-*dal*-go) Island. From the bridge it's just a short drive to Anacortes, Fidalgo's main town and the terminus for ferries to the San Juan Islands. Anacortes has some well-preserved brick buildings along the waterfront, several well-maintained old commercial edifices downtown, and many beautiful older homes off the main drag.

The frequently changing exhibits at the **Anacortes Historical Museum** (⊠ 1305 8th St., Anacortes ☎ 360/293–1915) focus on the cultural heritage of Fidalgo and nearby Guemes Island.

West of Anacortes, near the ferry landing, **Washington Park** has dense forests, sunny meadows, trails, and a boat launch. A narrow loop road winds through woods to overlooks with views of islands and saltwater. You can picnic or camp under tall trees near the shore. ⊠ *12th St. and Oakes Ave.* ☎ *360/293–1927* 🎫 *Free, camping $12–$15* ⊙ *Daily sunrise–sunset.*

Shopping

Compass Wines (⊠ 1405 Commercial Ave., Anacortes ☎ 360/293–6500) is one of the state's premier wine shops, with lots of hard-to-find vintages from small wineries whose annual releases sell out quickly. Besides wines, Compass purveys artisan cheeses, provisions yachts and charter boats, and assembles delectable lunch baskets.

La Conner

❸ *14 mi southeast of Anacortes, 68 mi north of Seattle.*

Morris Graves, Kenneth Callahan, Guy Anderson, Mark Tobey, and other painters set up shop in La Conner in the 1940s, and the village on the Swinomish Channel (Slough) has been a haven for artists ever since. In recent years the community has become increasingly popular as a weekend escape for Seattle residents because it can be reached after a short drive but seems far away.

La Conner has several historic buildings near the waterfront or a short walk up the hill—use the stairs leading up the bluff, or go around and walk up one of the sloping streets—as well as several good shops and restaurants. In summer the village becomes congested with people and cars, and parking can be hard to find. The flat land around La Conner makes for easy bicycling along levees and through the tulip fields.

The **Museum of Northwest Art** presents the works of regional artists past and present. ⊠ *121 S. 1st St.* ☎ *360/466–4446* ⊕ *www.museumofnwart. org* 🎫 *$4* ⊙ *Daily 10–5.*

☝ The **Volunteer Fireman's Museum** contains turn-of-the-20th-century equipment that you can see from the street through the building's large windows. (It's not open to the public.) ⊠ *611 S. 1st St.* ☎ *No phone.*

Historic furnishings are on display at the Victorian **Gaches Mansion**. ⊠ *2nd and Calhoun Sts.* ☎ *360/466–4288* 🎫 *$4* ⊙ *Wed.–Sat. 11–4; Sun. noon–4.*

The **Skagit County Historical Museum** surveys domestic life in early Skagit County and Northwest Coastal Indian history. ⊠ *501 4th St.* ☎ *360/466–3365* 🎫 *$2* ⊙ *Tues.–Sun. 11–5.*

Roozengaarde is one of the largest growers of tulips, daffodils, and irises in the United States—200 or so varieties in all. It's open daily during the blooming season. ⊠ *1587 Beaver Marsh Rd.* ☎ *360/424–8531* ⊕ *www. tulips.com* 🎫 *Free* ⊙ *Mar.–May, daily 9–5; June–Mar., Mon.–Sat. 9–5.*

Where to Stay & Eat

$–$$$ ✕**Kerstin's.** The intimate dining room overlooks the channel. The menu, which changes seasonally, includes portobello mushrooms roasted with pesto, pan-braised fresh king salmon, pork tenderloin, rib eye steak with Indonesian spices, halibut, and lamb shank with port wine sauce. The oysters baked in garlic-cilantro butter and finished with Parmesan are particularly popular. ⊠ *505 S. 1st St.* ☎ *360/466–9111* ▤ *AE, DC, MC, V* ☯ *Closed Tues.*

¢–$ ✕ **Calico Cupboard.** This storefront bakery–café turns out some of the best pastries in Skagit County. It's very popular for breakfast and lunch and can become uncomfortably crowded on summer weekends (in which case you can buy the goodies at the take-out counter for a picnic in the park). ⊠ *720 S. 1st St.* ☎ *360/466–4451* ▤ *No credit cards* ☯ *No dinner.*

$–$$ ✕▥ **Wild Iris.** Next to the slightly less expensive Heron, this B&B is a sprawling, modern (1992) Victorian-style inn. Most of the rooms are suites, and these have CD players, robes, fireplaces, whirlpool spa tubs, and private decks or balconies. The small (24-seat) restaurant, Le Jardin ($$–$$$), serves dinners made with local ingredients. Dishes include wild salmon with seasonal herbs, seared beef fillet with a black-currant demi-glace, and wild mushroom polenta. There's a six-course tasting menu for $69 ($49 without wine). ⊠ *121 Maple Ave., 98257* ☎ *360/466–1400* ⊕ *www.wildiris.com* ⇴ *4 rooms, 12 suites* ♿ *Restaurant, cable TV, in-room data ports; no a/c* ▤ *AE, MC, V* ▯ *BP.*

$–$$$ ▥ **La Conner Channel Lodge.** La Conner's only waterfront hotel is an understated modern facility overlooking the narrow Swinomish Channel. Each room has a private balcony and a gas fireplace and is decorated in subdued gray tones with wooden trim; 12 rooms have whirlpool baths. ⊠ *205 N. 1st St., 98257* ☎ *360/466–1500* ▤ *360/466–5902* ⊕ *www. laconnerlodging.com* ⇴ *29 rooms, 12 suites* ♿ *Business services, meeting room* ▤ *AE, D, DC, MC, V* ▯ *CP.*

¢–$ ▥ **Heron.** This B&B, in a Victorian house, has a stone fireplace in the parlor. The rooms are spacious, and the homemade breads and muffins served with breakfast in the formal dining room are scrumptious. The on-site Watergrass Day Spa offers organic skin-care treatments and massage therapies that are simultanously simple and luxurious. ⊠ *117 Maple Ave., 98257* ☎ *360/466–4626* ▤ *360/466–3254* ⊕ *www. theheron.com* ⇴ *9 rooms, 3 suites* ♿ *Hot tub, spa, some pets allowed (fee); no a/c* ▤ *AE, MC, V* ▯ *BP.*

¢–$ ▥ **Hotel Planter.** This renovated hotel, the oldest in La Conner, is on the National Register of Historic Places. Homey rooms, which have fine views of the hill or the waterfront, are furnished with handmade country-style furniture; the TVs are hidden in armoires. A shaded courtyard enhanced by garden sculptures is the place to linger in serenity. ⊠ *715 1st St., 98257* ☎ *360/466–4710 or 800/488–5409* ▤ *360/466–1320* ⊕ *www. hotelplanter.com* ⇴ *12 rooms* ♿ *Hot tub; no smoking* ▤ *AE, MC, V* ▯ *EP.*

¢–$ ▥ **Rainbow Inn.** A white picket fence surrounds this stately three-story, century-old country house outside town. Large rooms are furnished with antiques; one room has a whirlpool tub. The hot tub is tucked in the gazebo behind the house, from which Mt. Baker can be seen. Breakfast is served on an enclosed porch with views of farmland. ⊠ *1075 Chilberg Rd., 98257* ☎ *360/466–4578 or 800/888–8879* ▤ *360/466–3844* ⊕ *www.rainbowinnbandb.com* ⇴ *8 rooms, 5 with bath* ♿ *Hot tub; no smoking* ▤ *MC, V* ▯ *BP.*

Mount Vernon

❹ *11 mi northwest of La Conner.*

This attractive riverfront town is the county seat of Skagit County and was founded in 1871. After a giant log jam on the lower Skagit was cleared, steamers began churning up the river, and Mount Vernon soon became the major commercial center of the Skagit Valley, a position it has never relinquished. More recently, Mount Vernon was named Best Small City in the U.S. by *The New Rating Guide to Life in America's Small Cities.*

The city is surrounded by dairy pastures, vegetable fields, and bulb farms, and is famous for its annual Tulip Festival in April, when thousands of people visit to admire the floral exuberance. Rising above downtown and the river, 972-foot-high Little Mountain is a city park with a view. It used to be an island until the mudflats were filled in by Skagit River silt. Glacial striations in rocks near the top of the mountain, dating from the last continental glaciation (10,000–20,000 years ago), were made when the mountain (and all of the Puget Sound region) was covered by some 3,500 feet of ice.

Atop Little Mountain at the southeastern edge of town, 490-acre **Little Mountain Park** has great views of the Skagit Valley (especially in March and April, when the daffodils and tulips are in full bloom), of the river, the San Juan Islands, and the distant Olympic Mountains. ⊠ *Blackburn Rd. W* ☎ *360/336–6213* ⊠ *Free* ☉ *Daily sunrise–sunset.*

Pleasant **Hillcrest Park,** in the shadow of Little Mountain, has a small Asian garden, picnic tables, a playground, and tennis and basketball courts. There is also a small, grassy park on the left bank of the Skagit River just north of downtown reached by taking Freeway Drive north of Division St. ⊠ *13th St. and Blackburn Rd.* ☎ *360/336–6213* ⊠ *Free* ☉ *Daily sunrise–sunset.*

Adjoining the small waterfront community of the same name, **Bay View State Park** has a campground in the woods and picnic tables on the low grassy bluff above the bay. If you do any boating here (including canoeing and kayaking), watch the tides. Padilla Bay runs almost dry at low tide, when water is restricted to a few creek-like tidal channels. It's no fun to sit on the mudflats for an hour or two until the water returns—and don't even think about wading through the soft mud. ⊠ *10905 Bay View-Edison Rd.* ☎ *360/757–0227 or 800/452–5687* ⊕ *www.parks. wa.gov* ⊠ *$5* ☉ *Daily 8 AM–sunset.*

At the **Padilla Bay National Estuarine Reserve,** the Breazeale Interpretive Center has great birding: there are black brant geese, raptors, peregrine falcons, and bald eagles. Trails lead into the woods and to a rocky beach, with more good bird-watching opportunities. The Padilla Bay Trail starts at the south end of Bayview; look for signs directing you to the parking area, which is away from the water off the east side of the road. ⊠ *10441 Bayview-Edison Rd.* ☎ *360/428–1558* ⊕ *www.imletgeol.sc. edu/PDB/home.html* ⊠ *Free* ☉ *Wed.–Sun. 10–5.*

Where to Stay & Eat

¢–$ ✕**Skagit River Brewing Company.** A former produce warehouse now houses one of western Washington's best microbreweries, along with a pub serving better-than-average food. Highlights include wood-fired pizzas, a half-pound pub burger, and a big bean burrito. Hewn-wood tables and comfortable couches make lounging inviting. There's a barbecue grill right outside, where the chef will prepare your ribs or chicken wings. ⊠ *404 S. 3rd St.* ☎ *360/336–2884* ⊟ *AE, MC, V.*

¢ ▦**White Swan Guest House.** This B&B is in an 1898 Queen Anne farm house on Fir Island in the Skagit River delta (near the tulip fields). Although built in the late 19th century, it's been thoroughly renovated and brought up to modern standards. The house is surrounded by lovely English-style gardens, which have been featured in national garden magazines. ⊠ *15872 Moore Rd., 98723* ☎ *360/445–6805* ⊕ *www.*

thewhiteswan.com 🛏 *3 rooms without bath, 1 cottage* 🍴 *Kitchenettes; no a/c, no room phones, no smoking* ▤ *MC, V* 🍴 *CP.*

Bellingham

5 *29 mi northeast of Mount Vernon.*

The fishing port and college community of Bellingham is transforming itself from a grungy blue-collar area to the arts, retirement, and pleasure-boating capital of Washington's northwest corner. Downtown has cafés, specialty shops, and galleries, and the waterfront, once dominated by lumber mills and shipyards, is slowly being converted into a string of parks with connecting trails. College students and professors from Western Washington University make up a sizable part of the town's population and contribute to its laid-back intellectual climate. The lushly green bayfront, creeks meandering through town, and Lakes Whatcom and Padden attract wildlife like deer, raccoons, river otters, beavers, ducks, geese, herons, bald eagles, and the occasional cougar.

The four-building **Whatcom Museum of History and Art** has as its centerpiece Bellingham's 1892 former city hall, a redbrick structure converted into a museum in 1940. Victorian clothing, toys, games, and clocks are on display, and there are art exhibits as well. The other buildings in the complex include a natural-history gallery (with a stuffed-bird collection) and a children's museum. ✉ *121 Prospect St.* ☎ *360/676–6981* 🎫 *Free, children's museum $2* ☉ *Tues.–Sun. noon–5.*

Stairs behind the Whatcom Museum of History and Art lead down into **Maritime Heritage Park,** which pays tribute to Bellingham's fishing industry. On self-guided tours at the Marine Heritage Center you can learn about hatcheries and salmon life cycles, see salmon-rearing tanks and fish ladders, and watch salmon spawning. A pretty waterfall is just upstream, below the post office. Bellingham was founded in 1852 at the foot of these falls. ✉ *1600 C St.* ☎ *360/676–6806* 🎫 *Free* ☉ *Weekdays 9–5.*

A good place to fish, lounge, picnic, or walk is the **Squalicum Harbor Marina,** which holds more than 1,900 commercial and pleasure boats. Pete Zuanich Park, at the end of the spit, has a telescope for close-up views of the water and a marine-life center with touch tanks. ✉ *Roeder Ave. and Coho Way.*

Western Washington University, high up on tree-clad Sehome Hill, overlooks the waterfront, Bellingham Bay, and Lummi Island. The visitor center has maps and an audio tour of the nearly two dozen outdoor sculptures scattered about campus. Take Garden Street to get to the university from the north, or Bill McDonald Parkway if you're coming from the south (Samish Way Exit from I–5). ✉ *Visitor Center: S. College Dr. off Bill McDonald Pkwy.* ☎ *360/650–3000.*

Above Western Washington University, **Sehome Hill Arboretum,** with its native trees, shrubs, and other plants, has good views of Bellingham Bay and Lummi Island. ✉ *25th St. and McDonald Pkwy.* ☎ *360/676–6985* 🎫 *Free* ☉ *Daily.*

On upper Whatcom Creek **Whatcom Falls Park** (reached via Lakeway, east from I–5), is increasingly encroached upon by housing developments (the ruffed grouse living here 20 years ago are now gone). The creek has a number of pretty waterfalls; one has the local high school kids' swimming hole, although the water is very cold. Trails lead down creek and up the creek to Scudder Pond and Bloedel Donovan Park. ✉ *1401 Electric Ave.* ☎ *360/676–6985* 🎫 *Free* ☉ *Daily sunrise–sunset.*

The only public access in Bellingham to 14-mi-long Lake Whatcom is at its north end, in **Bloedel Donovan Park.** Locals swim in the sheltered waters of a cove, but you might find the water too cold. If so, spend some time trying to spot beavers, river otters, ducks, great blue herons, and yellow pond lilies at Scudder Pond, which is another 100 feet west (reached by trail from a parking area at Northshore and Alabama). ⊠ *2214 Electric Ave.* ☎ *360/676–6985* ⊠ *Parking $3* ☼ *Daily sunrise–sunset.*

Fairhaven, the historic district just shy of 3 mi south of Bellingham and at the beginning of Chuckanut Drive (Route 11), was an independent city until 1903 and still retains its distinct identity as an intellectual and artistic center. The beautifully restored 1890s redbrick buildings of the Old Fairhaven District, especially on Harris Avenue between 10th and 12th streets, house restaurants, galleries, and specialty boutiques.

There's public access to the waterfront at the foot of the hill at the **Bellingham Cruise Terminal** (⊠ *355 Harris Ave.* ☎ *360/676–2500*). Here ferries leave daily for the San Juan Islands and Victoria, British Columbia, and an Alaska ferry docks every Friday. The ferry dock and adjacent shore are a great place to spot wildlife, from sea lions and an occasional gray whale to great blue herons, cormorants, and harlequin ducks. A couple of blocks south, at the foot of Harris Street, the small, sandy beach at **Marine Park** is a great place for launching sea kayaks. An unmarked (and unofficial) trail runs south from the park along the railroad tracks to shingle beaches and rocky headlands. Here you'll find clams and blackberries in season and splendid sunsets and views of Lummi Island year-round.

Route 11, also known as **Chuckanut Drive,** was once the only highway heading south from Bellingham. The drive begins in Fairhaven, reaches the flat farmlands of the Samish Valley near the village of Bow, and joins up with I–5 at Burlington, in Skagit County; the full loop can be made in a couple of hours. For a dozen miles this 23-mi road winds along the cliffs above beautiful Chuckanut and Samish bays. It twists its way past the sheer sandstone face of Chuckanut Mountain and crosses creeks with waterfalls. Turnouts are framed by gnarled madrona trees and pines and offer great views of the San Juan Islands. Bald eagles cruise along the cliffs or hang out on top of tall firs. Drive carefully: the cliffs are so steep in places that rock slides are common; note that the road washes out once or twice each winter.

Larrabee State Park, south of Chuckanut Bay along the Whatcom–Skagit county line, is one of the state's most scenic and popular parks. It straddles a rocky shore that has quiet, sandy coves and runs high up along the slopes of Chuckanut Mountain. Even though the mountain has been logged repeatedly, some of it is still wilderness. Miles of trails lead through ferny fir and maple forests to hidden lakes, caves, and cliff-top lookouts from which you can see all the way to the San Juan Islands. At the shore there's a sheltered boat launch; you can go crabbing here or watch the birds—and the occasional harbor seal—that perch on the offshore rocks. The area west of Chuckanut Drive has picnic tables as well as tent and RV sites with hookups, which are open all year. ⊠ *245 Chuckanut Dr.* ☎ *360/676–2093* ⊠ *$5* ☼ *Daily sunrise–sunset.*

Where to Stay & Eat

★ **$$–$$$$** ✕ **Oyster Bar.** Above the shore on a steep, wooded bluff, this intimate restaurant in the village of Bow is regionally famous for what is probably the best marine view from any Washington restaurant. People come here to dine and watch the sun set over the islands to the west or to watch the full moon reflect off the waters of Samish Bay. The menu changes regularly so it's hard to predict what you might find, but the seafood dishes never disappoint—neither does the restaurant's selection of wines. ☒ 240 *Chuckanut Dr., Bow* ☎ 360/766–6185 ▭ *AE, MC, V.*

$–$$$ ✕ **Chuckanut Manor.** The old-fashioned, glassed-in dining room and bar overlook the mouth of the Samish River, Samish Bay, and the mudflats, where great blue herons hang out. It's a popular spot for sunset and bird-watching: bird feeders outside the bar's picture windows attract finches, chickadees, redwinged blackbirds, and other songbirds. Occasionally bald eagles can be seen gliding past. Besides the view, folks come here for traditional American fare with an emphasis on steak and fresh seafood. ☒ 302 *Chuckanut Dr., Bow* ☎ 360/766–6191 ▭ *AE, DC, MC, V* ☉ *Closed Mon.*

$–$$ ✕ **Mambo Italiano.** This intimate Italian café in downtown Fairhaven has quickly become a local favorite for its garlicky antipasto platter, hearty pastas, and wood-fired pizzas. ☒ 1303 *12th St.* ☎ 360/734–7677 ▭ *MC, V.*

$–$$ ✕ **Wild Garlic.** Tucked into a tiny space across the street from the Whatcom Museum of History and Art, this small, elegant restaurant serves American food. Walls are painted in subdued colors, and the narrow dining room, with booths along one side, offers the kind of intimate setting all too rare in Bellingham. Dishes include garlic shrimp linguine, roast garlic fettuccine, roast chicken, and sautéed fresh fish and prawns. The service is friendly and professional; the wine list is respectable. ☒ 114 *Prospect St.* ☎ 360/671–1955 ▭ *MC, V* ☉ *Closed Sun. No lunch Sat.*

$$ ✕▥ **Chrysalis Inn and Spa at the Pier.** The facade, which rises above the waterfront, is gray and stark, but in the lobby warm wood predominates. On sunny days you can see far across Bellingham Bay; on cloudy days, you can stare into the blaze of the big main fireplace. Rooms also have fireplaces, as well as window seats and such amenities as coffeemakers, irons, hair dryers, and CD players. Artwork enlivens the walls of the modern Fino Wine Bar ($–$$$), and picture windows frame the bay. You can sample European and Pacific Northwestern wines at the long back bar or dine on Mediterranean-inspired fare at white-linen-clad tables. ☒ 804 *10th St., 98225* ☎ 360/756–1005 *or* 888/808–0005 ⊕ *www.thechrysalisinn.com* ⇆ 34 *rooms, 9 suites* ☖ *Restaurant, refrigerators, spa, wine bar* ▭ *AE, D, DC, MC, V* ⦿ *CP.*

★ $–$$$ ▥ **Hotel Bellwether.** Bellingham's first waterfront hotel overlooks the entrance to bustling Squalicum Harbor. Its luxuriously appointed rooms are augmented by a lighthouse suite ensconced in its own tower. Rooms have gas fireplaces and private balconies for lounging and dining. The pleasant Harborside Bistro and comfortable bar have grand views across Bellingham Bay to Lummi Island. ☒ 1 *Bellwether Way, Squalicum Harbor Marina, 98225* ☎ 360/392–3100 *or* 877/411–1200 ☐ 360/392–3101 ⊕ *www.hotelbellwether.com* ⇆ 54 *rooms, 13 suites, 1 lighthouse suite* ☖ *Restaurant, gym, bar; no smoking* ▭ *AE, D, DC, MC, V.*

$–$$$ ▥ **Schnauzer Crossing.** Meticulously maintained gardens surround this contemporary B&B in a peaceful residential neighborhood overlooking Lake Whatcom. The original 1920s house was extended in the 1970s; the modern living room has extremely high ceilings. The guest room has a lake view, while the large suite has a glass-enclosed atrium and fireplace. A cottage unit, whose cost may leave you expecting something more lavish, has a kitchen and a gas fireplace. Friendly owners Donna and Vermont McAllister serve such ample, unusual breakfast dishes as triple-sec French toast. ☒ 4421 *Lakeway Dr., 98226* ☎ 360/733–0055 *or* 800/562–2808 ☐ 360/734–2808 ⊕ *www.schnauzercrossing.com* ⇆ 1 *room, 1 suite, 1 cottage* ☖ *Some in-room hot tubs, outdoor hot tub, boating* ▭ *MC, V* ⦿ *BP.*

$-$$ ⊞ **Fairhaven Village Inn.** High on a bluff between the Fairhaven Village Green and the Port of Bellingham's south terminal, the inn overlooks Bellingham Bay; on a clear day the eye ranges all the way to the San Juans. Hair dryers, coffeemakers, and robes are provided; the bayview rooms have balconies and gas fireplaces. It's only a short walk to Fairhaven's shops, bookstores, galleries, pubs, and restaurants, and a trail running from downtown Bellingham to the waterfront and Padden Creek passes in front of the inn. ⊠ *1200 10th St., 98225* ☎ *360/ 733–1311 or 877/733–1100* 🖷 *360/756–2797* ⊕ *www.nwcountryinns. com/bellingham.html* ⇌ *22 rooms* ♻ *Cable TV, in-room data ports; no smoking* ⊟ *MC, V* ⦿ *BP.*

$-$$ ⊞ **Stratford Manor Bed-and-Breakfast.** Once a private school, this large and sumptuously furnished B&B sits on 30 landscaped acres 7 mi east of Bellingham. Among the common areas are a solarium, a living room with fireplace, a library, and two decks. Each of the three spacious rooms has oak furnishings, a gas fireplace, and a sitting area. A fourth room is available during the summer. ⊠ *4566 Andersen Way, 98226* ☎ *360/715–8441 or 800/240–6779* 🖷 *360/671–0840* ⊕ *www. stratfordmanor.com* ⇌ *3 rooms* ♻ *In-room hot tubs, some in-room VCRs, putting green, gym, outdoor hot tub, library; no room phones, no room TVs, no kids under 15, no smoking* ⊟ *MC, V* ⦿ *BP.*

¢–$ ⊞ **Fairhaven Bed and Breakfast.** This Victorian mansion—with stained-glass windows and a large deck—is filled with antiques and is great for a romantic getaway. Walking trails to the waterfront and up Padden Creek start just outside the grounds. ⊠ *1714 12th St., 98225* ☎ *360/734–7243 or 888/734–7243* 🖷 *360/738–1571* ⊕ *www.fairhavenbandb.com* ⇌ *2 rooms* ♻ *Dining room* ⊟ *D, MC, V* ⦿ *BP.*

¢–$ ⊞ **North Garden Inn.** A noteworthy Queen Anne–style mansion, the North Garden Inn is on the National Register of Historic Places. Near Western Washington University, the B&B has views of Bellingham Bay from some rooms; all guest quarters have antique furnishings and plenty of character. The Steinway grand piano in the entryway is occasionally used for concerts; guests may play it, too. ⊠ *1014 N. Garden St., 98225* ☎ *360/671–7828 or 800/922–6414* 🖷 *360/671–8790* ⇌ *10 rooms* ⊟ *MC, V* ⦿ *BP.*

¢ ⊞ **DeCann House Bed and Breakfast.** This Victorian house sits in a residential neighborhood above the Squalicum Harbor waterfront. The antique pool table is the main attraction in the common area, whose walls are lined with hardwood shelves. Quilts, heirlooms, and antiques give character to both guest rooms. ⊠ *2610 Eldridge Ave., 98225* 🖷🖷 *360/ 734–9172* ⊕ *www.decannhouse.com* ⇌ *2 rooms* ♻ *No a/c, no smoking* ⊟ *No credit cards* ⦿ *BP.*

Nightlife & the Arts

Boundary Bay Brewery & Bistro (⊠ 1107 Railroad Ave. ☎ 360/647–5593), a warehouse turned classy brewery, pours five beers, serves some of Bellingham's best food, and displays eclectic local art. **Mt. Baker Theatre** (⊠ 104 N. Commercial St. ☎ 360/734–6080), a restored vaudeville-era theater, has a 110-foot-tall Moorish tower and a lobby fashioned after a Spanish galleon. Home to the Whatcom Symphony Orchestra, it's also a venue for movies and touring performers. The mellowest place in Bellingham for a beer is the **Up and Up** (⊠ 1234 N. State St. ☎ 360/ 733–9739). **Western Washington University** (⊠ 516 High St. ☎ 360/650– 6146) presents classical music concerts and theatrical productions. The **Whatcom Museum of History and Art** (⊠ 121 Prospect St. ☎ 360/ 676–6981) sponsors downtown gallery walks several times a year; call for information.

Sports & the Outdoors

CLIMBING The **American Alpine Institute** (⊠ 1515 12th St. ☎ 360/671–1505) is a prestigious mountain- and rock-climbing school.

WHALE-WATCHING **Island Mariner Cruises** (⊠ 5 Harbor Esplanade ☎ 360/734–8866) conducts whale-watching and nature cruises to the Queen Charlotte Islands and Alaska, and sunset cruises around Bellingham Bay. **San Juan Islands Shuttle Express** (⊠ Alaska Ferry Terminal, 355 Harris Ave., at the railroad tracks ☎ 360/671–1137) operates summer whale-watching trips from Bellingham to the San Juans. **Victoria/San Juan Cruises** (⊠ 355 Harris Ave., inside the Bellingham Cruise Terminal ☎ 360/738–8099 or 800/443–4552) sails to Victoria, British Columbia, and the San Juan Islands on daylong or overnight trips. Under the right conditions, the views of whales and sunsets cannot be beat.

Shopping

Along lower Holly Street in Bellingham's Old Town you'll find antiques shops, secondhand stores, and suppliers of outdoor-recreation equipment. Try the **Old Town Antique Mall** (⊠ 427 W. Holly St. ☎ 360/671–3301) for antiques and collectibles.

Ferndale

❻ *10 mi north of Bellingham.*

On the Nooksack River and amid dairy farms, Ferndale is a pleasant town that has burst its seams in recent years as urban sprawl arrived. It has the best views of Mt. Baker in the county.

In **Pioneer Park** you can wander through log buildings from the 1870s—including Whatcom County's first church—that have been restored and converted into museums. Note the beautifully "squared" cedar logs, a western Washington pioneer building technique. ⊠ *1st and Cherry Sts.* ☎ *360/384–6461* 🎫 *Free* ⊙ *May–Sept., Tues.–Sun. 11:30–4:30.*

☙ **Hovander Homestead Park,** a pioneer farm, is now a national historic site with a Victorian-era farmhouse, barnyard animals, a water tower, vegetable gardens, and antique farm equipment. Surrounding it are 60 acres of walking trails and picnic grounds, and there's access to fishing in the Nooksack River. ⊠ *5299 Nielsen Rd.* ☎ *360/384–3444* 🎫 *Free* ⊙ *Daily sunrise–sunset.*

The **Tennant Lake Natural History Interpretive Center,** within the Nielsen House, an early homestead, has exhibits and information about nature walks. An observation tower allows for bird-watching from an eagle's perspective. The lake is part of a 200-acre marshy habitat where bald eagles, ducks, beavers, muskrats, and other wildlife can be seen. The unusual Fragrance Garden—with herbs and flowers—is designed for the visually impaired and can be explored by following Braille signs. ⊠ *5236 Nielsen Rd.* ☎ *360/384–3444* 🎫 *Free* ⊙ *Daily sunrise–sunset.*

Many species of waterfowl live within the 11,000-acre **Lake Terrell Wildlife Preserve.** This is a great place for watching birds, but stay away in fall, when the reserve is open to hunting. You can try to catch perch, catfish, bass, and cutthroat. ⊠ *5975 Lake Terrell Rd.* ☎ *360/384–4723* 🎫 *Free* ⊙ *Daily sunrise–sunset.*

Glacier

❼ *41 mi northeast of Ferndale.*

The canyon village of Glacier, just outside the Mt. Baker–Snoqualmie National Forest boundary, has a few shops, cafés, and lodgings. Route

542 winds east from Glacier into the forest through an increasingly steep-walled canyon. It passes 170-foot-high Nooksack Falls, about 5 mi east of Glacier, and travels up the north fork of the Nooksack River and the slopes of Mt. Baker to a ski area, which is bright with huckleberry patches and wildflowers in summer.

Mt. Baker–Snoqualmie National Forest is a vast area including much of the mountain and forest land encircling (or abutting, depending on whether you talk to someone from the parks service or the forest service) North Cascades National Park. The region has many hiking trails, but because the snowline is quite low in Washington State, the upper part of the ridges and mountains is covered by snow for much of the year, making for a short hiking season, usually from mid-July to mid-September or October. The wildflower season is also short but spectacular; expect fall color by late August and early September. The 10,778-foot-high, snow-covered volcanic dome of **Mt. Baker** is visible from much of Whatcom County and from as far north as Vancouver and as far south as Seattle. It's particularly exciting to watch when it smokes, which it does occasionally. ⊠ *Rte. 542* ☎ *360/599–2714* ⊕ *www.fs.fed.us/r6/mbs* ☞ *$5, $30 annual Northwest Forest Pass* ☉ *Daily 24 hrs.*

Where to Stay

¢ 🏠 **The Logs Resort.** This rustic, comfortable resort is a great place for viewing eagles, deer, and other wildlife. All the cabins have rock fireplaces (and lots of free, chopped wood), and fully equipped kitchens and bathrooms. ⊠ *9002 Mt. Baker Hwy., 98244* ☎ *360/599–2711* ⊕ *www.thelogs.com* ☞ *5 cabins* ⚐ *Outdoor pool* ☰ *No credit cards.*

Sports & the Outdoors

At the **Mt. Baker Ski Area** you can snowboard and ski downhill or cross-country from roughly November to the end of April. The area set a world snowfall record in winter 1998–99. Ski and snowboard equipment are available to rent. ⊠ *Rte. 542, Mt. Baker* ☎ *360/734–6771, 360/671–0211 snow reports* ⊕ *www.mtbakerskiarea.com* ☞ *Lift ticket Mon.–Wed. $24, Thurs. and Fri. $26, weekends and holidays $34.*

Sedro-Woolley

❽ *42 mi southwest of Glacier; 9 mi northeast of Mount Vernon.*

On its way east from I–5, Route 20 skirts Burlington and Sedro-Woolley (seedro wooley), a former mill and logging town. It has a bit of an old downtown and a smattering of Tar Heel culture, as it was settled by pioneer loggers and farmers from North Carolina. It also has an institute that arranges trips into the North Cascades National Park and a nearby park headquarters. That said, you're better off making Mount Vernon or Bellingham a hub for park exploration: Sedro-Woolley's hotels and restaurants reflect the fact that the town is in something of a slump.

North Cascades National Park Headquarters, the major administrative center, is a good place to pick up passes and permits, as well as to obtain information about current conditions. ⊠ *810 Rte. 20* ☎ *360/856–5700* ⊕ *www.nps.gov/noca* ☉ *Mid-Oct.–mid-May, weekdays 8–4:30; late May–mid-Oct., daily 8–4:30.*

The **North Cascades Institute** (NCI) offers classes, field trips, and wilderness adventures such as backpack trips to hot springs within the Cascades. Contact them for information about these events or for a comprehensive catalog of books, guides, maps, and other materials. Especially popular are hiking guides such as *Best Easy Day Hikes in the North Cascades* and *100 Hikes in the North Cascades.* ⊠ *810 Rte. 20* ☎ *360/856–5700 Ext. 209, 291, or 515* ⊕ *www.ncascades.org or www.nwpubliclands.com.*

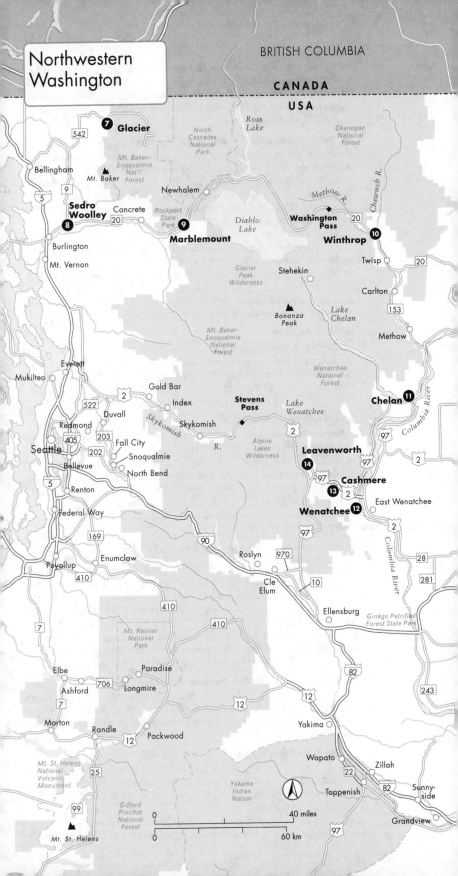

Public murals and carved log statues outside shops along the main streets give testament to the town's logging past, as does the **Sedro-Woolley Museum.** ⊠ *725 Murdock St.* ☎ *360/855–2390* ✉ *Free* ☉ *Sat. 9–4, Sun. 1:30–4:30.*

Eleven miles north of Sedro-Woolley, you can take a short ride through the woods on the steam-powered **Lake Whatcom Railway.** ⊠ *Rte. 9, in Wickersham* ☎ *360/595–2218* ✉ *$10* ☉ *Call for hrs.*

Marblemount

❾ *40 mi east of Sedro-Woolley.*

Like Sedro-Woolley, Marblemount is a former logging town now depending on outdoor recreation for its fortunes. Anglers, campers, hikers, bird-watchers, and hunters come and go from the town's collection of motels, cafes, and stores. It's also a good base for exploring North Cascades National Park.

Where to Eat

$-$$$ ✕ **Buffalo Run Restaurant.** This restaurant just west of the park specializes in nontraditional meats such as buffalo, venison, elk, and ostrich—though the menu also has a few vegetarian dishes. Buffalo heads and Old West memorabilia hang from the dining room's walls; a patio provides seating next to a garden outside. ⊠ *60084 Rte. 20* ☎ *360/873–2461* ▭ *AE, D, MC, V.*

North Cascades National Park

Park's west entrance, on Rte. 20 (North Cascades Hwy.), is 65 mi from I–5.

Countless snow-clad mountain spires dwarf glacial valleys and lowland, old-growth forests in one of America's least-developed national parks. Considered by some the most spectacular mountain scenery in the lower 48 states, the untrammeled expanse covers 505,000 acres of rugged mountain land. Only Route 20 (North Cascades Highway) traverses the park, and it's closed by snow at Diablo Lake half the year. Furthermore, it's within the Ross Lake National Recreation Area and Okanogan National Forest and never touches the park itself, which is almost entirely roadless. The exception is the Cascade River Road, a narrow two-lane, mostly gravel route that provides access from Marblemount to the Cascade Pass trailhead to the southeast. Most of the region's attractions are actually in the adjacent national recreation areas (administered by the park).

Grizzly bears and wolves are believed to inhabit the North Cascades, along with other endemic wildlife. Bald eagles are present year-round along the Skagit River and the various lakes. In December, they flock by the hundreds to the Skagit to feed on a rare winter salmon run, remaining through January. Black bears are often seen in spring and early summer along the road in the high country, feeding on new green growth. Deer and elk can often be seen in early morning and late evening, grazing and browsing at forest's edge.

The park never closes, though access is limited by winter snows. Summer is peak season—and up here, summer begins in July and ends around Labor Day—especially along the alpine stretches of the North Cascades Highway. Wildflowers paint the mountain meadows, hummingbirds and songbirds pepper the forest air, and even the high ridges are pleasantly warm. Although the views are best this time of year—when the usual spate of Pacific storms moderates—valleys can still start the day shrouded in fog. For the best chance to enjoy the scenery, it's best to drive the North Cascades Highway in the afternoon if you're traveling east from Sedro-Woolley, Concrete, or Marblemount, and in the morning if you're heading from Winthrop, Twisp, or Chelan.

Autumn brings crisp nights and many cool, sunny days. The North Cascades Highway is a popular drive in September and October, when the changing leaves—on larch, the only conifer that sheds its leaves, as well as aspen, vine maple, huckleberry, and cottonwood—make a colorful show. You can visit the lowland forests, such as those around the town of Newhalem, almost any time of year. They're quite peaceful in early spring or late autumn on mild, rainy days, when you can experience the weather that makes old-growth forest possible. Snow closes the North Cascades Highway by November, and the road doesn't fully reopen until late April.

Visitors centers—with pay phones, bathrooms, park information, nature walks, lectures, and children's programs—are found along the North Cascades Highway in Sedro-Woolley, in Marblemount, Newhalem, and Winthrop, and in Stehekin (accessible only by boat, plane, or on foot) at the head of Lake Chelan. Several trails are also accessible along this route, including Sterling Munro, River Loop, and Rock Shelter, three short trails into lowland old-growth forest, all at Mile 120 near Newhalem; and the Happy Creek Forest Trail at Mile 134. Campgrounds aside, there are no lodging facilities in the park; for a hotel or restaurant you'll have to head to a nearby town.

A Northwest Forest Pass, $5 per day or $30 annual, is required for hiking in North Cascades National Park, Ross Lake National Recreation Area, and most of Mt. Baker-Snoqualmie National Forest. A free wilderness permit is required for overnight backcountry activities; you can acquire one—in person only—at the Wilderness Information Center in Marblemount or at park ranger stations.

Fodor'sChoice ★ From Sedro-Woolley, **North Cascades Highway** (Route 20) winds through the green pastures and woods of the slowly narrowing upper Skagit Valley. As the mountains close in on the river and the highway, the road climbs only imperceptibly. Skagit Valley, like other valleys of the North Cascades, was cut below sea level by the glaciers of the last ice age, some 15,000 years ago. Close to sea level, the largely flat valley floor was created when the gash was filled in with alluvial deposit carried down from the mountains by the rivers. Beyond Concrete, a former cement-manufacturing town, the road begins to climb into the mountains, to Ross and Diablo dams.

East of Ross Lake, several turnouts offer great views of the lake and the snow-capped peaks surrounding it. The whitish rocks in the road cuts are limestone and marble. Meadows along this stretch of the highway are covered with wildflowers from June to September; nearby slopes are golden and red with fall foliage from late September through October. The pinnacle point of this stretch is 5,477-foot-high Washington Pass, east of which the road drops down along Early Winters Creek to the Methow Valley in a series of dramatic switchbacks (with vista turnouts).

From the Methow Valley, Route 153 takes the scenic route down the Methow River, with its apple, nectarine, and peach orchards, to Pateros on the Columbia River. From here, you can continue east to Grand Coulee or south to Lake Chelan.

The **North Cascades Visitor Center** has an extensive series of displays on the natural features of the surrounding landscape. You can learn about

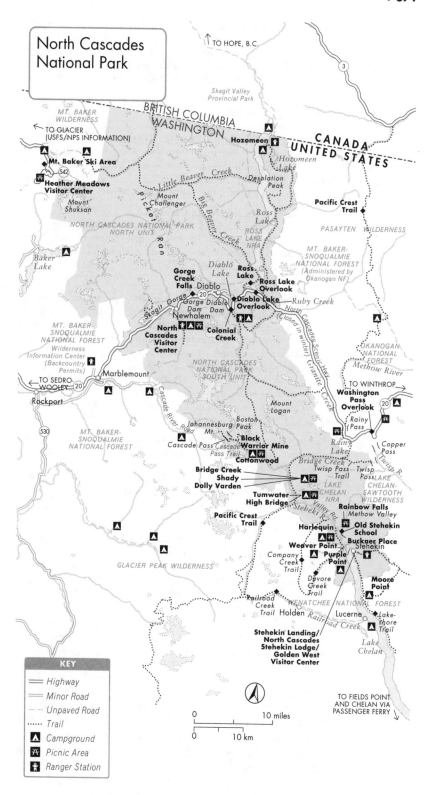

North Cascades National Park

↑ TO HOPE, B.C.

3

Skagit Valley Provincial Park

BRITISH COLUMBIA
WASHINGTON

CANADA
UNITED STATES

MT. BAKER WILDERNESS

← TO GLACIER (USFS/NPS INFORMATION)

Hozomeen

Hozomeen Lake

Mt. Baker Ski Area
542

Heather Meadows Visitor Center

Mount Shuksan

Mount Challenger

Little Beaver Creek

Desolation Peak

Big Beaver Creek

Ross Lake

Pacific Crest Trail

PASAYTEN WILDERNESS

NORTH CASCADES NATIONAL PARK NORTH UNIT

Picket Range

ROSS LAKE NRA

Baker Lake

MT. BAKER-SNOQUALMIE NATIONAL FOREST (Administered by Okanogan NF)

Gorge Creek Falls

Diablo Lake

Ross Lake

Ross Lake Overlook

Diablo

Skagit Gorge

Gorge Diablo Dam Dam

Newhalem

Diablo Lake Overlook

Ruby Creek

North Cascades Visitor Center

Colonial Creek

North Cascades Scenic Hwy (Closed in winter)

OKANOGAN NATIONAL FOREST

Methow River

MT. BAKER-SNOQUALMIE NATIONAL FOREST

Wilderness Information Center (Backcountry Permits)

Marblemount

NORTH CASCADES NATIONAL PARK SOUTH UNIT

Granite Creek

← TO SEDRO-WOOLLEY 20

Rockport

530

MT. BAKER-SNOQUALMIE NATIONAL FOREST

Cascade River Road

Mount Logan

Johannesburg Mt.

Boston Peak

Cascade Pass *Cascade Pass Trail*

Black Warrior Mine

Cottonwood

Bridge Creek

Bridge Creek
Shady
Dolly Varden

Tumwater High Bridge

Stehekin R.

Pacific Crest Trail

GLACIER PEAK WILDERNESS

TO WINTHROP

Washington Pass Overlook
20

Rainy Pass

Rainy Lake

Copper Pass

Twisp R.

Twisp Pass Trail *Twisp Pass*

LAKE CHELAN NRA

LAKE CHELAN-SAWTOOTH WILDERNESS

Rainbow Falls
Methow Valley

Harlequin

Old Stehekin School

Buckner Place

Stehekin

Weaver Point

Purple Point

Company Creek Trail

Moore Point

Devore Creek Trail

Railroad Creek Trail Holden *Railroad Creek*

Lucerne

Lake-shore Trail

Stehekin Landing/ North Cascades Stehekin Lodge/ Golden West Visitor Center

WENATCHEE NATIONAL FOREST

Lake Chelan

TO FIELDS POINT AND CHELAN VIA PASSENGER FERRY ↓

KEY	
═══	*Highway*
═══	*Minor Road*
---	*Unpaved Road*
⋯⋯	*Trail*
▲	*Campground*
⛱	*Picnic Area*
⚎	*Ranger Station*

0 _____ 10 miles
0 _____ 10 km

the history and value of old-growth trees, the many creatures that depend on the temperate rain-forest ecology, and the effects of human activity. Park rangers frequently conduct programs; check bulletin boards for schedules. ✉ *Rte. 20, Newhalem* ☎ *206/386–4495 Ext. 11* ⊙ *Memorial Day–Labor Day, daily 9–4:30; Labor Day–Memorial Day, weekends 9–4:30.*

Where to Stay & Eat

Developed picnic areas at Rainy Pass (Route 20, 38 mi east of the park visitor center) and Washington Pass (42 mi east) each have a half-dozen picnic tables, drinking water, and pit toilets. The vistas of surrounding peaks are sensational at these two overlooks. There are also picnic facilities near the visitor center in Newhalem, and at Colonial Creek Campground 10 mi east of the visitor center on Route 20.

There are no hotels inside North Cascades National Park, though the National Forest Service operates several area campgrounds, ranging from small, fairly primitive spots at the end of gravel access roads to larger facilities along state highways. Reservations aren't accepted at the campgrounds; reservations at Stehekin Valley lodgings, at the head of Lake Chelan, are imperative.

CAMPING
FACILITIES
🏕 **Newhalem Creek Campground.** With three loops, a small amphitheater, a playground, and a slate of ranger programs in summer, Newhalem Creek is the main North Cascades campground. Above the Skagit River in old-growth forest, it's adjacent to the visitor center, and close to trails that access the river and the surrounding second-growth forest. ♿ *Flush toilets, dump station, drinking water, fire grates, picnic tables, public telephone, ranger station* ⊃ *111 RV sites* ✉ *Rte. 20, along the access road to the park's main visitor center* ☎ *360/873–4590 Ext. 17, or 16 for Marblemount Ranger Station* ⊕ *www.nps.gov/noca/pphtml/camping. html* 🖃 *$12* ▱ *No credit cards* ⊙ *Mid-Oct.–mid-Apr.*

🏕 **Rockport State Park.** The park's camping area, in an old-growth Douglas fir grove, has 5 mi of hiking trails. ♿ *Flush toilets, dump station, drinking water, showers, fire grates* ⊃ *8 tent sites, 50 RV sites with full hookups* ✉ *Rte. 20, 25 mi west of Newhalem* ☎☎ *360/853–8461* ☎ *800/452–5687* ⊕ *www.parks.wa.gov* 🖃 *$20, $6 per additional vehicle* ▱ *MC, V* ⊙ *Mid-Oct.–mid-Apr.*

Sports & the Outdoors

HIKING
Dozens of trails wind their way from the lowland valleys into old-growth forest and then up into the national park highlands. Though trails are very steep, and some have switchbacks, views are virtually unmatched in the continental United States—at times literally dozens of snow-capped crags are visible. Note that group treks are limited to 12 persons.

★ **Cascade Pass.** Perhaps the most popular park hike, this much-traveled, moderate, switchbacked, 3⅔-mi trail leads to a divide from which dozens of peaks can be seen. The meadows here are covered with alpine wildflowers in July and early August. A Northwest Forest Pass is needed. On sunny summer weekends and holidays, the trailhead parking lot can fill up; it's best to arrive before noon. The trip up and back will take the average hiker less than four hours, but allow plenty of extra time at the summit for admiring the wildflowers and gawking at the surrounding peaks. ✉ *End of Cascade River Rd., 14 mi from Marblemount.*

Rainy Pass. An easy and accessible 1-mi paved trail leads to Rainy Lake, a waterfall, and glacier-view platform. ✉ *Rte. 20, 38 mi east of visitor center at Newhalem.*

★ **Skagit River Loop.** One of the most notable hikes in the park, this 1⅕-mi disability-accessible trail loops through stands of huge, old-growth firs and cedars, dipping down to the Skagit River and out onto a riverside gravel bar. ⊠ *Near North Cascades visitor center.*

Thornton Lakes Trail. A 5-mi climb into an alpine basin with two pretty lakes, this steep and strenuous hike takes about 5–6 hours round-trip. Northwest Forest Pass needed. ⊠ *Rte. 20, 3 mi west of Newhalem.*

★ **Trail of the Cedars.** Only ½ mi long, this trail winds its way through one of the finest surviving stands of old-growth Western red cedar in Washington. Some of the trees on the path are more than 1,000 years old. ⊠ *Near North Cascades visitor center.*

Winthrop

🔟 *87 mi east of Marblemount, 128 mi east of Sedro-Woolley.*

Before the cowboys came, the Methow Valley was a favorite gathering place for Indian tribes, who dug the plentiful and nutritious bulbs and hunted deer while their horses fattened on the tall native grasses. On hot summer days, the cool, glacier-fed river provides welcome relief; at night, its burbling lulls travelers to sleep.

A couple of decades ago, the small river town of Winthrop, in the heart of the Methow Valley, decided to adopt a false-front "Western" theme for its business district. That wasn't at all hard to do, since many old buildings survive from the 19th century, when cattle was king. Among the most famous visitors of that period was Owen Wister, whose novel *The Virginian* drew its literary portraits from some of the valley's local characters.

Where to Stay & Eat

$-$$$ ✕ **Duck Brand Cantina, Bakery and Hotel.** This modern roadhouse was built to resemble a frontier-style hotel—and it works. It serves good, square meals at reasonable prices, ranging from omelets at breakfast to burritos and pasta dishes at lunch, and chicken, stir-fries, and steaks at dinner. The freshly baked cinnamon rolls and berry pies are excellent. ⊠ *248 Riverside Ave.* ☎ *509/996–2192* ▤ *AE, D, DC, MC, V.*

★ $$-$$$$ ✕▦ **Sun Mountain Lodge.** This hilltop lodge has great views of the surrounding Cascade Mountains and Methow Valley. Some guest rooms have views of Mt. Gardner or Mt. Robinson. The cabins are located 1½ mi below on the Patterson lakefront. Every table in the restaurant ($$–$$$$) offers great scenery. The good food, although sometimes overly ambitious, centers around seafood and meat dishes, with an emphasis on fresh local ingredients. If you want to accompany your reveries with a glass of wine, you can choose from more than 3,000 bottles in the lodge's cellar. Breakfast is also served. ⊠ *Patterson Lake Rd., 98862* ☎ *509/996–2211 or 800/572–0493* 🖷 *509/996–3133* ⊕ *www. sunmountainlodge.com* ⇨ *102 rooms, 13 cabins* ♿ *Restaurant, picnic area, room service, some kitchenettes, some refrigerators, tennis court, 2 pools, exercise equipment, 2 hot tubs, spa, bicycles, hiking, horseback riding, cross-country skiing, bar, children's programs (ages 4–10), playground, business services* ▤ *AE, DC, MC, V.*

$-$$$ ▦ **Freestone Inn.** More than 2 million acres of forest surround this resort 15 mi northwest of Winthrop. Rough-hewn logs and rocks form the major building components of the inn and cabins. Guest rooms have fireplaces and decks that overlook Freestone Lake. ⊠ *17798 Rte. 20, Mazama 98833* ☎ *509/996–3906 or 800/639–3809* 🖷 *509/996–3907* ⊕ *www.freestoneinn.com* ⇨ *21 rooms, 15 cabins, 2 cottages* ♿ *Restaurant, some kitchenettes, some microwaves, some refrigerators, lake,* *fishing, bicycles, hiking, shops; no a/c in some rooms, no smoking* ⊟ *AE, D, DC, MC, V.*

¢ ✕▥ **Virginian Resort.** Though it's on the highway, this log lodge is comfortable and tranquil. Request a room overlooking the river, so at night you'll hear water purling over rocks rather than cars and trucks. The restaurant (¢–$$), which serves steaks, burgers, pastas, and salads, has seating on a deck under umbrellas, or inside the main building. ⊠ *808 North Cascades Hwy., 98862* ☎ *800/854-2834* 🖷 *509/996-2483* ⊕ *www.virginianresort.com* ⇨ *37 rooms* ⟁ *Restaurant, pool, hot tub, some pets allowed, no-smoking rooms* ⊟ *MC, V* ⊙ *Closed Oct.–Apr.*

Chelan

🔟 *61 mi south of Winthrop.*

Long before the first American settlers arrived at the long, narrow lake, Chelan (sha-*lan*) was the site of a Chelan Indian winter village. The Indians would range far and wide on their horses in spring and summer, following the newly sprouting grass from the river bottoms into the mountains; in winter they converged in permanent villages to feast, perform sacred rituals, and wait out the cold weather and snow. During the winter 1879–80, Chelan served briefly as an army post, but the troops were soon transferred to Ft. Spokane. American settlers arrived in the 1880s.

Today, Chelan serves as the favorite beach resort of western Washingtonians. In summer Lake Chelan is one of the hottest places in Washington, with temperatures often soaring above 100°F. The mountains surrounding the 55-mi-long fjordlike lake rise from a height of about 4,000 feet near Chelan to 8,000 and 9,000 feet near the town of Stehekin, at the head of the lake. There is no road circumventing the lake, so the only way to see the whole thing is by boat or floatplane. Several resorts line the lake's eastern (and warmer) shore. It's northwestern end, at Stehekin, just penetrates North Cascades National Park. South of the lake, 9,511-foot Bonanza Peak is the tallest nonvolcanic peak in Washington.

Lake Chelan State Park, right on the lake and 9 mi west of Chelan on the opposite (less crowded) shore, is a favorite hangout for folks from the cool west side of the Cascades who want to soak up some sun. There are docks, a boat ramp, RV sites with full hookups, and lots of campsites for those who prefer a less "citified" approach to camping. ⊠ *U.S. 97 west to South Shore Dr. or Navarre Coulee Rd.* ☎ *800/452-5687* ⊕ *www.parks.wa.gov* ⊞ *$5* ⊙ *Memorial Day–Labor Day, daily 6:30 AM–10 PM; Labor Day–Memorial Day, weekends 8–5.*

Directly north of Lake Chelan State Park, **Twenty-Five Mile Creek State Park** also abuts the lake's eastern shore. It has many of the same facilities as the park in Chelan, as well as a swimming pool. Because it's the more remote of the two, it's often less crowded. ⊠ *South Shore Dr.* ☎ *509/ 687-3610 or 800/452-5687* ⊕ *www.parks.wa.gov* ⊞ *$5* ⊙ *Apr.–Sept., daily sunrise–sunset.*

The **Lady of the Lake Boat Company** operates the vessel *Lady of the Lake II,* which makes one daily trip from Chelan to Stehekin and back, with stops at Manson, Fields Point, Prince Creek, Lucerne (Port of Holden), and Moore Point. The company also operates the faster *Lady Express* between Chelan and Stehekin (one trip daily) and the high-speed *Lady Cat* catamaran (two trips daily). Fares run $26–$90 per person roundtrip, and cruises last from two to four or five hours. ⊠ *1418 W. Woodin Ave.* ☎ *509/682-2224* ⊕ *www.ladyofthelake.com.*

In one of the most beautiful and secluded valleys in the Pacific Northwest, **Stehekin** was homesteaded by hardy souls in the late 19th century. It's not really a town but rather a small community at the north end of Lake Chelan. There's no road; access is by boat or floatplane or on foot. A few facilities serve about 200 summer visitors. Year-round residents enjoy a wilderness lifestyle—there are barely two dozen cars in the whole valley, outside communication is iffy, especially in winter, and supplies arrive once or twice a week by boat.

Buckner Homestead, founded in 1912, is a pioneer farm with an apple orchard, a farmhouse, a barn, and many ranch buildings that are slowly being restored by the National Park Service. ⊠ *Stehekin Valley Rd., 3½ mi from Stehekin Landing, Stehekin* ☎ *360/856–5700 Ext. 340 then press 14* ☉ *June–Sept., daily 9–5.*

Rangers at the **Purple Point Information Center** offer guidance on hiking, camping, and about the national parks and recreation areas. This is a good place to pick up permits and passes. Maps and concise displays explain the complicated ecology of the valley, which encompasses in its length virtually every ecosystem in the Northwest. Hours vary in spring and fall. ⊠ *Stehekin Valley Rd., ¼ mi north of Stehekin Landing, Stehekin* ☎ *360/856–5700 Ext. 340 then press 14* ☉ *Mid-Mar.–mid-Oct., daily 8:30–5.*

Where to Stay & Eat

$–$$ ✕ **Caper's Fine Dining.** This white-tablecloth restaurant is in downtown Chelan. As in many of the region's kitchens, meat is king. Preparations range from calf liver to loin of venison, from pork medallions to filet mignon and rack of lamb. The house dessert is pear poached in pinot noir wine. The dining room is comfortable; the staff is friendly and professional. ⊠ *127 E. Johnson Ave.* ☎ *509/682–1611* ▤ *MC, V.*

¢ ✕ **Ship 'n Shore Drive/Boat In.** It's a very casual, no frills drive-in: the "dining room" consists of dockside picnic tables shaded by awnings. The big hamburgers and taco salads are local favorites. On hot days, kids line up for ice cream. ⊠ *1230 W. Woodin Ave.* ☎ *509/682–5125.*

¢ ✕ **Stehekin Pastry Company.** Stehekin Pastry Company is one of the most popular valley attractions, offering fresh-baked muffins, rolls, pastries, and breads all morning until 1 PM. ⊠ *Stehekin Valley Rd., about 2 mi from Stehekin Landing, Stehekin* ☎ *509/682–4677* ▤ *No credit cards* ☉ *Closed Oct.–June.*

$$–$$$$ ✕▦ **Campbell's Resort.** This lakefront resort in Chelan has been receiving guests since the turn of the last century. Old hardwood walls give the café ($–$$), which is popular with locals, a nautical feel. The menu has a good selection of seafood, steak, chicken, and pasta dishes. Reservations are essential. ⊠ *104 W. Woodin Ave., 98816* ☎ *509/682–2561, 800/553–8225 WA* 🖷 *509/682–2177* ⊕ *www.campbellsresort.com* ➪ *172 rooms, 2 cottages* ⚅ *Café, in-room data ports, some kitchenettes, some minibars, refrigerators, cable TV, 2 pools, 2 hot tubs, beach, dock, cross-country skiing, bar, business services* ▤ *AE, MC, V.*

¢ ✕▦ **Stehekin Valley Ranch.** Nestled along pretty meadows at the edge of pine forest, this classic guest ranch has tent cabins with bunk beds and kerosene lamps—how much more genuine can you get? There are also five cabins with baths. Horseback riding, hiking, river rafting and other activities pass the time in the blissfully peaceful valley. Nonguests are welcome for meals at the restaurant ($–$$); hearty breakfasts include omelets, hash browns, and pancakes; dinners are buffet style, and include steak, ribs, hamburgers, salad, beans, and dessert. Shuttles provide transportation to and from Stehekin Landing, June through early October. ⊠ *Stehekin Valley Rd., 9 mi from Stehekin Landing, Stehekin*

98852 ☎ 509/682–4677 or 800/536–0745 ⊕ *www.courtneycountry. com* ⟲ *25 tent cabins, 5 cabins* ⚬ *Restaurant, hiking, horseback riding* ▤ *No credit cards* ⊘ *Closed Oct.–May* ¶◯┤ *FAP.*

$–$$$ ▦ **Silver Bay Inn.** A charming inn perched on a private little slip of land at the head of Lake Chelan, Silver Bay has two cabins and a guest house that can house up to six people. Aside from hiking, canoeing and swimming are available—or you can just sit in a lawn chair by the lake, reading. ⊠ *Silver Bay Rd.* ⚲ *Box 85, Stehekin 98852* ☎ *509/682–2212 or 800/555–7781* ⊕ *www.silverbayinn.com* ⟲ *2 cabins, 1 2-bedroom house* ⚬ *Boating, hiking* ▤ *AE, MC, V.*

¢–$ ▦ **North Cascades Stehekin Lodge.** A classic log lodge with functional but not upscale rooms, this place has a lobby with fireplace and a porch overlooking the lake. Some of the bigger, lake-view rooms have kitchenettes and sleep up to six people. The dining room here is one of two dinner-service facilities in the valley. ⊠ *Stehekin Landing, Stehekin 98852* ☎ *509/682–4494* ⊕ *www.stehekin.com* ⟲ *38 rooms* ⚬ *Restaurant, some kitchenettes, laundry facilities* ▤ *D, MC, V.*

¢–$ ▦ **Quail's Roost Inn.** This Queen Anne Victorian from 1902 perches on North Hill overlooking the city, lake, and mountains. Rooms have a handsome collection of period antiques and collectibles. The Sewing Room, for instance, has antique oak furniture, an antique sewing machine, and a vintage wedding dress. From the B&B's wraparound veranda and landscaped yard you can sit and enjoy the wonderful lake views. ⊠ *121 E. Highland Ave., 98816* ☎ *509/682–2892 or 800/681–2892* ⊕ *www. aquailsroostinn.com* ⟲ *3 rooms* ⚬ *No room phones, no kids under 12, no smoking* ▤ *MC, V* ¶◯┤ *BP.*

Sports & the Outdoors

On a scenic half-day raft trip, you can traverse the lower section of the Stehekin River, which winds through cottonwood and pine forest, from Yawning Glacier on the slopes of Magic Mountain southeast to Lake Chelan. From June through September guided trips on Class III waters leave from the **Stehekin Valley Ranch** (⊠ Stehekin Valley Rd., 3½ mi from Stehekin Landing, Stehekin ☎ 509/682–4677 or 800/536–0745). Trip prices are $35–$75.

Wenatchee

⑫ *39 mi southwest of Chelan.*

Wenatchee (we-*nat*-chee), the county seat of Chelan County, is an attractive city in a shallow valley at the confluence of the Wenatchee and Columbia rivers. Surrounded by orchards, Wenatchee is known as the "Apple Capital of Washington." Downtown has many old commercial buildings as well as apple-packing houses where visitors can buy locally grown apples by the case (at about half the price charged in supermarkets). The paved Apple Valley Recreation Loop Trail runs on both sides of the Columbia River. It crosses the river on bridges at the northern and southern ends of town and connects several riverfront parks. The Wenatchee section is lit until midnight.

The town was built on an ancient Wenatchi Indian village, which may have been occupied as long ago as 11,000 years, as recent archaeological finds of Clovis hunter artifacts suggest. (The Clovis hunters, also known as Paleo-Indians, were members of the oldest tribes known to have inhabited North America.)

The **North Central Washington Museum** has displays of local Indian and pioneer artifacts, as well as a working antique apple sorter. ⊠ *127 S. Mission St.* ☎ *509/664–3340* 🖷 *509/664–3356* 🖃 *$3* ⊘ *Mon.–Sat. 10–4.*

One of the most delightful gardens in the Northwest, this lush green oasis sprawling high atop bluffs near the confluence of the Columbia and Wenatchee rivers makes for a splendidly cool retreat on a hot day. A blend of native rocks, ferns, mosses, waterfalls, rock gardens, and conifers makes **Ohme Gardens** one of America's most acclaimed. ⊠ *North of Wenatchee near the junction of Rtes. 2 and 97A, 3327 Ohme Rd.* ☎ *509/662–5785* ⊕ *www.ohmegardens.com* ⊠ *$6* ⊙ *Mid-Apr.–mid-Oct., daily 9–7; Nov.–March, daily 9–6.*

Rocky Reach Dam has picnic tables and elaborately landscaped grounds. The Gallery of the Columbia has the pilothouse of the late-19th-century Columbia River steamer *Bridgeport,* as well as replicas of Indian dwellings, and Indian, logger, and railroad workers' tools. The Gallery of Electricity has exhibits explaining why dams are good for you. ⊠ *U.S. 97A N, about 10 mi north of Wenatchee* ☎ *509/663–7522 or 509/663–8121* ⊠ *Free* ⊙ *Mid-Feb.–Dec., daily sunrise–sunset.*

Okanogan-Wenatchee National Forest, a pine forest, covers 2.2 million acres, from the eastern slopes of the Cascades to the crest of the Wenatchee Mountains and north to Lake Chelan. Camping, hiking, boating, fishing, hunting, and picnicking are popular activities. ⊠ *215 Melody La., Wenatchee* ☎ *509/662–4335* ⊕ *www.fs.fed.us/r6/wenatchee* ⊠ *$5 daily parking pass, or $30 Northwest Forest Pass* ⊙ *Daily 24 hrs.*

Where to Stay & Eat

$–$$$ ✕ **The Windmill.** One of the Pacific Northwest's best-known steak houses opened in 1937. Although seafood is given fair play (try the charbroiled salmon coated with apple brandy barbecue sauce), this rustic, knotty-pine establishment is about steak—and justly so. Favorites include whiskey pepper steak (pepper-coated New York strip sautéed, flamed with whiskey, and finished with mushrooms in a rich demi-glace) and the marinated tenderloin chunks. Pies are baked every morning—in fact everything here is made from scratch—and the wine list has a small regional selection. ⊠ *1501 N. Wenatchee Ave.* ☎ *509/665–9529* ⌂ *Reservations not accepted* ⊟ *AE, DC, MC, V* ⊙ *Closed Sun.*

¢–$$ ✕ **Carriage House of Prime Rib.** Just behind the John Horan Steak and Seafood House is this slightly more casual eatery. The menu contains a variety of steak and seafood options prepared with less fanfare than at the restaurant next door. You may dine on a patio overlooking the gardens and lawns. ⊠ *2 Horan Rd.* ☎ *509/663–0018* ⊟ *D, DC, MC, V* ⊙ *No lunch.*

¢–$ ✕ **Casa Tapatia.** This small, unpretentious café on the dusty road to the airport pleases the local Mexican community with its authentic quesadillas, chiles rellenos, and tamales. The tortilla soup is also excellent. There's nothing special about the atmosphere except for the delightful aromas wafting from the kitchen and the often intense discussion of the food and of the day's affairs—in Spanish, of course. ⊠ *1650 Grant Rd., East Wenatchee* ☎ *509/886–1910* ⊟ *MC, V.*

¢–$ ▥ **Coast Wenatchee Center Hotel.** A skywalk links this hotel to a convention center. Although it tends to attract business travelers, the Coast Wenatchee has enough facilities and amenities to appeal to vacationing families. You can walk from the hotel to the riverfront park and downtown. ⊠ *201 N. Wenatchee Ave., 98801* ☎ *509/662–1234* ⊟ *509/662–0782* ⊕ *www.coasthotels.com* ⌂ *147 rooms* ⌂ *Restaurant, cable TV, indoor-outdoor pool, exercise equipment, hot tub, downhill skiing, bar, business services, airport shuttle, some pets allowed (fee)* ⊟ *AE, D, DC, MC, V.*

¢–$ ▥ **Mickey O'Reilly's Inn at the River.** This resort motel on the Columbia River offers views of the Cascade and Wenatchee Mountains. There's easy access to the Apple Valley Loop Trail and to the river; it's also close to the Wenatchee Valley Mall. Each room has a coffeemaker and blow dryer. ⊠ *580 Valley Mall Pkwy., East Wenatchee, 98802* ☎ *509/ 884–1474 or 800/922–3199* 🖷 *509/884–9179* 🖎 *55 rooms* ⚬ *Restaurant, cable TV, pool, hot tub, bar, business services* ▭ *AE, D, DC, MC, V* ⎟◉⎟ *CP.*

¢–$ ▦ **Warm Springs Inn Bed & Breakfast.** Roses planted along the driveway lead you to this 1917 mansion amid 10 acres of gardens and trees. The rooms are filled with a tasteful selection of art and antiques and overlook the gardens and lawns. ⊠ *1611 Love La., 98801* ☎ *509/662–8365 or 800/543–3645* 🖷 *509/663–5997* ⊕ *www.warmspringsinn.com* 🖎 *5 rooms* ⚬ *Cable TV, hot tub, some pets allowed; no room phones, no smoking* ▭ *AE, D, MC, V* ⎟◉⎟ *BP.*

Sports & the Outdoors

Four lifts, 33 downhill runs, powder snow, and some 30 mi of marked cross-country trails make **Mission Ridge Ski Area** one of Washington's most popular ski areas. There's a 2,100-foot vertical drop. Snowboarding is allowed. (Hey, this is a prime snowboarding state!) Lift tickets cost $37 per day. ⊠ *7500 Mission Ridge Rd.* ☎ *509/663–6543, 800/ 374–1693 snow conditions* ⊕ *www.missionridge.com* ⊙ *Dec.–Apr., Thurs.–Mon. 9–4.*

Cashmere

⑬ *11 mi northwest of Wenatchee.*

Surrounded by snow-capped mountain peaks, Cashmere is one of Washington's oldest towns, founded by Oblate missionaries back in 1853, when the Wenatchi and their vast herds of horses still roamed free over the bunch grasslands of the region. Some of the great Wenatchi leaders are buried in the mission cemetery. Today, Cashmere is the apple, apricot, and pear capital of the Wenatchee Valley.

Aplets and Cotlets/Liberty Orchards Co., Inc. was founded by two Armenian brothers who escaped the massacres of Armenians by Turks early in the 20th century, settled in this peaceful valley, and became orchardists. When a marketing crisis hit the orchards in the 1920s, the brothers remembered a dried-fruit confections from their homeland, recreated them, and named them aplets (made from apples) and cotlets (made from apricots). Sales took off almost immediately, and today aplets and cotlets are known as the combination that made Cashmere famous. Get free samples when you tour the plant. ⊠ *117 Mission St.* ☎ *509/ 782–2191* ⊕ *www.libertyorchards.com* 🖭 *Free* ⊙ *Jan.–Mar., weekdays 8:30–4:30; Apr.–Dec., weekdays 8–5:30, weekends 10–4.*

The **Chelan County Historical Society's Museum and Pioneer Village** has an excellent collection of Indian artifacts, as well as 18 pre-1900 Chelan County buildings that were reassembled here and furnished with period furniture and other historic objects. ⊠ *600 Cotlets Way* ☎ *509/782– 3230* 🖭 *$4* ⊙ *Mar. 1–Dec. 15, daily 9:30–5.*

Where to Stay

¢   ▦ **Wedge Mountain Inn.** All the brightly colored rooms at this quiet inn have private decks with views of the surrounding scenery. It is 7 mi west of Cashmere and close to area skiing. ⊠ *7335 U.S. 2* ☎ *509/548–6694 or 800/666–9664* ⊕ *www.wedgemountaininn.com* 🖎 *28 rooms* ⚬ *Cable TV, pool, laundry facilities, no-smoking rooms* ▭ *AE, D, MC, V.*

Leavenworth

⑭ *11 mi northwest of Cashmere, 134 mi east of Seattle.*

Leavenworth is one of Seattle's favorite weekend getaways and it's easy to see why: The charming (if occasionally *too* cute) Bavarian-style village, home to good restaurants and attractive lodgings, is a hub for some of the Northwest's best skiing, hiking, rock climbing, rafting, canoeing, and snowshoeing.

Leavenworth was a railroad and mining center for many years, but by the 1960s it had fallen on hard times. Civic leaders, looking for ways to capitalize on the town's setting in the heart of the Central Cascade Range, convinced shopkeepers and other businesspeople to maintain a gingerbread-Bavarian architectural style in their buildings—even the Safeway supermarket and the Chevron gas station carry out the theme. Restaurants prepare Bavarian-influenced dishes, candy shops sell Swiss-style chocolates, and stores and boutiques stock music boxes, dollhouses, and other Bavarian items.

The **Marlin Handbell Ringers** (☎ 509/548–5807) keep alive an 18th-century English tradition that evolved into a musical form. Twelve ringers play 107 bells covering 5½ chromatic octaves. The bells are rung as part of the town's Christmas festivities and also in early May.

Also noteworthy is the **Nutcracker Museum** (✉ 735 Front St. ☎ 509/548–4708), which contains more than 2,500 different kinds of antique and modern nutcrackers. The museum is open May–October, daily 2–5.

Icicle Junction is an amusement arcade in the wilderness replete with bumper car rides, miniature golf, and other activities. ✉ *Rte. 2 at Icicle Rd.* ☎ *509/548–2400* ☉ *Mon. noon–6, Sat. 10–9, Sun. 10–5.*

At the **National Fish Hatchery** salmon and trout hatched are released into the river in the hope they will return someday to spawn and keep the species alive while still providing fish for fishermen to catch. ✉ *12790 Fish Hatchery Rd.* ☎ *509/548–7641* ✉ *Free* ☉ *Daily 8–4.*

Where to Stay & Eat

★ **$$–$$$** ✕ **Restaurant Osterreich.** Chef Leopold Haas, who hails from Austria, prepares such authentic dishes as Wiener schnitzel, pork chops with apple sauce, crawfish strudel, venison topped with chanterelle mushrooms, red cabbage salad, potato salad, and apple strudel. The menu changes daily. The atmosphere is infinitely more casual than the food. ✉ *Tyrolean Ritz Hotel, 633A Front St.* ☎ *509/548–4031* ▭ *MC, V* ☉ *Closed Mon.*

★ **$$** ✕ **Cafe Mozart.** This café looks like the upstairs apartments of a central European town house: it's captured the essence of gemütlichkeit (cozy) in the way the small dining rooms are decorated and the curtains are cut as well as with the authentic aromas that drift from the kitchen. The food is superb, with ingredients blending together beautifully. Menu highlights include slow-roasted duck with pear and raspberry confiture, pork medallions accompanied by flavorful red cabbage, and chicken breast topped with Black Forest ham and melted Gouda cheese. A harpist plays during weekend dinners. ✉ *829 Front St.* ☎ *509/548–0600* ▭ *AE, D, MC, V.*

¢–$$ ✕ **Baren Haus.** The cuisine at this spacious, noisy, and often crowded beer hall–style room may not be haute, or even particularly interesting, but the generous servings and low prices will appeal to those traveling on a budget. Fill up on generous servings of basic American fare, like burgers and fries, sandwiches, and salads. ✉ *208 9th St.* ☎ *509/548–4535* ▭ *MC, V.*

¢–$ ✕**Home Fires Bakery.** This homey bakery, with a German wood-fired oven, turns out several absolutely delicious breads, as well as muffins, cinnamon rolls, and other baked goods. It's take-out only, but on a sunny day you can sit outside at a picnic table and enjoy the alpine view while sipping coffee and munching on goodies. ⊠ *13013 Bayne Rd.* ☎ *509/548–7362* ▭ *D, MC, V* ⊘ *Closed Tues. and Wed.*

★ $$$ ▣ **Run of the River.** This intimate, relaxed mountain inn stands on the banks of the Icicle River near Leavenworth, placing the modern rooms close to nature. The largest of them, the Tumwater Suite, has two wood stoves, a loft, and a private deck overlooking the river's cascading torrents. Other rooms have views of the Pinnacles (a dramatic rock formation), an aspen grove, meadows (where deer browse), or Icicle and Tumwater canyons. Cushy bathrobes are among the amenities at this luxury accommodation; breakfast is served in an enormous dining room on the main floor. ⊠ *9308 E. Leavenworth Rd., 98826* ☎ *509/548–7171 or 800/288–6491* ▤ *509/548–7547* ⊕ *www.runoftheriver.com* ⇩ *6 rooms* ⚘ *Dining room* ▭ *AE, D, MC, V* ❑ *BP.*

$ ▣ **Mountain Home Lodge.** This contemporary cedar and redwood inn sits in the middle of a 20-acre alpine meadow atop a mountain (3 mi south of Leavenworth), where breathtaking views of the Cascade Mountains abound. Peeled-pine and vine maple furniture fill the rooms, which also contain handmade quilts, binoculars, robes, and port wine. Rates in the winter are twice the normal price, and include Sno-Cat transportation from a parking area at the foot of the mountain, breakfast, lunch, and dinner. ⊠ *Mountain Home Rd., 98826* ☎ *509/548–7077 or 800/414–2378* ▤ *509/548–5008* ⊕ *www.mthome.com* ⇩ *10 rooms, 2 cabins* ⚘ *Tennis courts, pool, hot tub, cross-country skiing; no room phones, no room TVs, no kids under 16, no smoking* ▭ *D, MC, V* ❑ *BP.*

¢–$$ ▣ **Haus Rohrbach.** Unobstructed views at this alpine-style B&B take in the village and the valley. Some rooms have king-size beds, balconies, and separate sitting areas. Two suites also have coffeemakers and other amenities. The full breakfast typically includes Dutch babies (a sweet, fluffy omelet) or sourdough pancakes and sausage. ⊠ *12882 Ranger Rd., 98826* ☎ *509/548–7024 or 800/548–4477* ▤ *509/548–5038* ⊕ *www.hausrohrbach.com* ⇩ *7 rooms, 5 with bath, 3 suites* ⚘ *Some in-room hot tubs, some microwaves, some refrigerators, pool, hot tub* ▭ *AE, D, DC, MC, V* ❑ *BP.*

¢–$ ▣ **Evergreen Inn.** Popular with hikers and skiers, the Evergreen was built in the 1930s, and it still has much of the charm of the roadside inn it once was. Furnished in typical motel style, some of the rooms have king-size beds, gas fireplaces, and wet bars. The staff is very friendly. ⊠ *1117 Front St., 98826* ☎ *509/548–5515 or 800/327–7212* ▤ *509/548–6556* ⊕ *www.evergreeninn.com* ⇩ *39 rooms* ⚘ *Some in-room hot tubs* ▭ *AE, D, DC, MC, V* ❑ *CP.*

¢–$ ▣ **Haus Lorelei.** This rambling lodge-style house, built in 1903 by the town's largest lumber company, sits just two blocks from Leavenworth's center, and yet perches above the Wenatchee River amid the seclusion of evergreens and lovely mountain views. All the rooms have antiques; some have four-poster canopy beds with lace hangings. Three rooms upstairs have more space and are appropriate for families. ⊠ *347 Division St., 98826* ☎ *509/548–5726 or 800/514–8868* ▤ *509/548–6548* ⇩ *10 rooms* ⚘ *Tennis court, hot tub, bicycles, basketball, hiking; no a/c in some rooms, no room phones, no smoking* ▭ *No credit cards* ❑ *BP.*

¢–$ ▣ **Pension Anna.** Rooms and suites at this family-run Austrian-style pension in the heart of the village are decorated with sturdy antique pine furniture and fresh flowers; the beds have cozy comforters. A solid Continental breakfast of coffee, fruit, cereal, and rich pastries is served in a room decorated in traditional European style, with crisp linens, pine decor, dark green curtains, and a cuckoo clock. ⊠ *926 Commercial St., 98826* ☎ *509/548–6273 or 800/509–2662* 🖨 *509/548–4656* ⊕ *www. pensionanna.com* ⇆ *12 rooms, 3 suites* ♨ *Some in-room hot tubs* ⊟ *AE, D, MC, V* ⫯◎⫯ *CP.*

Sports & the Outdoors

FISHING   Trout are plentiful in many streams and lakes around Lake Wenatchee. **Leavenworth Ranger Station** (☎ 509/782–1413) issues permits for the Enchantment Lakes and Alpine Lake Wilderness area.

GOLF   **Leavenworth Golf Club** (⊠ 9101 Icicle Rd. ☎ 509/548–7267) has an 18-hole, par-71 course. The greens fee is $20, plus $20 for an optional cart.

HIKING   The Leavenworth Ranger District has more than 320 mi of scenic trails, among them Hatchery Creek, Icicle Ridge, the Enchantments, Tumwater Canyon, Fourth of July Creek, Snow Lake, Stuart Lake, and Chatter Creek. Both of the following sell the Northwest Forest pass ($5 day pass; $30 annual pass), which is required year-round for parking at trailheads and for camping in the upper Chiwawa Valley. The **Lake Wenatchee Ranger Station** (⊠ 22976 Rte. 207 ☎ 509/763–3101) provides updates on trails and fire closures. Contact the **Leavenworth Ranger District** (⊠ 600 Sherburne St. ☎ 509/782–1413) for information on area hikes.

HORSEBACK RIDING   Rent horses by the hour, or take daylong rides (including lunch) or overnight pack trips ($26–$100) at **Eagle Creek Ranch** (⊠ 7951 Eagle Creek Rd. ☎ 509/548–7798). **Icicle Outfitters & Guides** (⊠ 7373 Icicle Rd. ☎ 800/497–3912 ⊕ www.icicleoutfitters.com) has 2- to 4-mi trail rides ($20–$40 per person), daylong rides ($120), and overnight pack trips ($175).**Mountain Springs Lodge** (⊠ 19115 Chiwawa Loop Rd. ☎ 509/763–2713 or 800/858–2276 ⊕ www.mtsprings.com) offers horseback rides from 40 minutes to all day ($16–$150) long, as well as daytime sleigh rides ($16), moonlight dinner sleigh rides ($45), and snowmobile tours one to four hours long ($55–$150).

SKIING   More than 20 mi of cross-country ski trails lace the Leavenworth area. In winter, enjoy a Nordic ski jump, snowboarding, tubing, and really great downhill and cross-country skiing at **Leavenworth Ski Hill** (⊠ Ski Hill Dr. ☎ 509/548–5807 ⊕ www.skileavenworth.com). In summer enjoy the wildflowers or view the Leavenworth Summer Theatre's production of "The Sound of Music." The ski hill is 1 mi north of downtown Leavenworth. The Play All Day Pass is $12; there's also a Nordic Day Pass ($8), an Alpine Day Pass ($10), and a Tubing Pass ($7).

Stevens Pass (⊠ Summit Stevens Pass, Rte. 2, Skykomish ☎ 360/973–2441 or 360/634–1645 ⊕ www.stevenspass.com) has snowboarding and cross-country skiing as well as 36 major downhill runs and slopes for skiers of every level. Lift tickets cost $44.

WHITE-WATER RAFTING   Rafting is popular from March to July; the prime high-country runoff occurs in May and June. The Wenatchee River, which runs through Leavenworth, is considered one of the best white-water rivers in the state—a Class III on the International Canoeing Association scale.

Alpine Adventures (☎ 509/548–4159 or 800/926–7238) conducts challenging white-water and relaxing river floats through spectacular scenery. An all-day Wenatchee River drift costs $75 (lunch included); a half day drift is $50 (no lunch). The Methow River drift is $80. **Osprey Rafting Co.** (⊠ Icicle Rd. ☎ 509/548–6800 ⊕ www.shoottherapids.com) offers 4½-hour trips on the Wenatchee River for $65, which includes wet suits and booties, transportation, and lunch; a $50, two-hour trip includes gear and transportation but no lunch.

Northwestern Washington A to Z

AIR TRAVEL

In this part of the state there are too few flights going to too few places. Of the region's many airports, only Pangborn Memorial in East Wenatchee and Bellingham International have commercial flights (on Horizon Air); the rest only serve charter planes. Thanks to this limited service—as well as to prohibitive fares—fly into Seattle and rent a car to get here and get around.

AIRPORTS & TRANSFERS

🛪 Airports **Anacortes Airport** ✉ 4000 Airport Rd., Anacortes ☎ 360/293–3134. **Bellingham International Airport** ✉ 4255 Mitchell Way, Bakerview Exit off I–5, Bellingham ☎ 360/671–5674. **Lake Chelan Airport** ✉ 32 Airport Way, Chelan ☎ 509/682–5976. **Pangborn Memorial Airport** ✉ 1 Pangborn Dr., East Wenatchee ☎ 509/884–4912. **Skagit Regional Airport** ✉ 15400 Airport Dr., Burlington ☎ 360/757–0011.

🛪 Taxis & Shuttles **A Cab N Courier** ✉ Wenatchee ☎ 509/886–4222. **Airporter** ✉ Bellingham ☎ 866/235–5247 ⊕ www.airporter.com. **Taxi Services** ✉ Bellingham ☎ 360/733–8294.

CARRIERS

Horizon Air has service to Bellingham International Airport and Wenatchee's Pangborn Memorial Airport. Kenmore Air can arrange charter floatplanes to Whidbey Island from Seattle. On-demand (and very expensive) service between Chelan and Stehekin is available by charter floatplane through Chelan Airways; the scenic flight takes about 45 minutes.

🛪 Airlines **Chelan Airways** ☎ 509/682–5555 ⊕ www.chelanairways.com. **Horizon Air** ☎ 800/547–9308 ⊕ www.horizonair.com. **Kenmore Air** ☎ 206/486–1257 or 800/543–9595 ⊕ www.kenmoreair.com.

BOAT & FERRY TRAVEL

Washington State Ferries connect Mukilteo (20 mi north of Seattle off I–5 at Exit 189) with Clinton, at the south end of Whidbey Island. Walk-on passengers pay only for the westward leg of the trip. Ferries leave roughly every half hour, more erratically off-season. Ferries also run from Port Townsend, at the tip of the Olympic Peninsula, to Keystone, at Whidbey's midpoint. The ride is 20 minutes one-way.

🛪 Boat & Ferry Information **Washington State Ferries** ☎ 206/464–6400 ⊕ www.wsdot.wa.gov/ferries.

BUS TRAVEL

Greyhound has daily service to Mount Vernon and Bellingham from Seattle and Vancouver. It also serves Stevens Pass, Leavenworth, Cashmere, and Wenatchee from Everett and Spokane. (Note, though, that you can't buy tickets at Cashmere and Stevens Pass.) Valley Shuttles vans provide access to Stehekin Valley Road. In mid-May there's service to the lower Stehekin Valley; come June you can get a lift to the upper valley. In July the shuttles serve Cascade Pass's east trailhead (near Marblehead) and other destinations within 20 mi of the Stehekin boat dock. Reservations are strongly recommended.

Many communities throughout the region have bus service. Island Transit buses on Whidbey Island are free. Link Transit buses in the Wenatchee area cost 50¢ to $1 (payable in cash), depending on how far you travel. Rates also vary in Whatcom County. To ride buses in Skagit County you have to buy a pass (available at local stores); four trips will cost you $2; $5 buys 10 trips.

🛪 Bus Information **Greyhound** ☎ 360/733–5251 or 800/231–2222 ⊕ www.greyhound.com. **Island Transit** ☎ 800/240–8747 ⊕ www.islandtransit.org. **Link Transit** ☎ 509/662–1155 ⊕ www.linktransit.com. **Skagit Transit** ☎ 360/757–4433 or 360/299–2424

⊕ www.skat.org. **Valley Shuttles** ☎ 360/856–5700 Ext. 340, then press 14 ⊕ www. nps.gov/noca/focus/focus.htm. **WTA/Whatcom Transportation Authority** ☎ 360/376–7433 ⊕ www.ridewta.com.

CAR TRAVEL

You can reach Whidbey Island by heading north from Seattle or south from the Canadian border on I–5, west on Route 20 onto Fidalgo Island, and south across Deception Pass Bridge. Interstate 5 is the main north–south route through western Whatcom and Skagit counties. Route 542 winds east from Bellingham to Mt. Baker. Route 20 heads east from Burlington to Sedro-Woolley and continues on through the North Cascades to the Methow and Okanogan valleys, and across the northeastern mountains to the Idaho state line near Newport.

Most routes have two lanes and are paved; the busier ones have occasional passing lanes. A few remote mountain roads have gravel or dirt surfaces, which makes driving interesting during the November–April rainy season. Rains can be sufficiently heavy in fall, winter, and spring to make driving dangerous, even on the interstate.

Snow falls in the mountains from October or November until as late as May and makes driving extremely hazardous. Route 20 is usually closed (because of avalanche danger) from November through April. Stevens Pass faces intermittent closures for avalanche control (the avalanches are dislodged with howitzer shells; snow sliding onto the highway is cleared by plows). Every few winters it snows in the lowlands as well. Although the snow never lasts for more than a few days, snow tires and even chains may be required for driving even on I–5. If snow melt (which can occur at any time during the winter) coincides with heavy rain, lowland roads may flood. If the highways are closed for more than a few hours, local shelters aid stranded motorists.

A traffic hazard unique to western Washington is called a "sun-slow-down." A motorist slows way down when faced by the spectacle of the heavenly orb popping into his or her line of vision. These peculiar events are even mentioned on regional radio road reports.

GASOLINE   Gas stations are usually plentiful, except for along the mountain road (Route 20) between Marblemount and Winthrop, which has no services for 74 mi. Most filling stations are open between 6 AM and 10 PM. A few are open longer; fewer still are open 24 hours. Most are self-serve and have automated pay stations; a few keep no cash after dark. Gas prices skyrocket by as much as 50¢ away from major cities. Bellingham, which is near major refineries, consistently has the region's highest prices. No one seems to know why.

PARKING   Parking is rarely a problem in this region, and though time limits may apply, most of it is free—both on the streets and in lots. Some downtown areas have meters that take nickels, dimes, and quarters; in other places meters take only quarters.

EMERGENCIES

🏥 Hospitals **Central Washington Hospital** ⊠ 1201 S. Miller St., Wenatchee ☎ 509/665-6046. **Island Hospital** ⊠ 1211 24th St., Anacortes ☎ 360/468-3185. **Lake Chelan Community Hospital** ⊠ 137 Chelan Manson Hwy., Chelan ☎ 509/682-2531. **Skagit Valley Hospital** ⊠ 1415 Kincaid St., Mount Vernon ☎ 360/424-4111. **St. Joseph's Hospital** ⊠ 2901 Squalicum Pkwy., Bellingham ☎ 360/734-5400. **United General Hospital** ⊠ 2000 Hospital Dr., Sedro-Woolley ☎ 360/856-6021. **Whidbey General Hospital** ⊠ 101 N. Main St., Coupeville ☎ 360/321-5151.

🏥 24-Hour Pharmacies **Walgreens** ⊠ 909 17th St., Anacortes ☎ 360/299-2816 ⊠ 4090 Meridian St., Bellingham ☎ 360/734-0229.

MAIL & SHIPPING

⊞ Post Offices Bellingham ✉ 315 Prospect St. ☎ 360/752-9822. **Chelan** ✉ 144 E. Johnson Ave. ☎ 509/682-2625. **Leavenworth** ✉ 960 Rte. 2 ☎ 509/548-7212. **Sedro-Woolley** ✉ 111 Woodworth St. ☎ 360/855-0545. **Wenatchee** ✉ 301 Yakima St. ☎ 509/663-5069.

⊞ Overnight Services Federal Express ✉ 4167 Mitchell Way, Bellingham ☎ 800/463-3339 ✉ 200 Airport Way, East Wenatchee ☎ 800/463-3339. **UPS** ✉ 4152 Meridian St., Bellingham ☎ 800/742-5877.

MONEY MATTERS

Bank of America is the region's predominant institution. Check its Web site or call the toll-free number for the nearest location. Although banking hours vary, most branches are open Monday through Saturday from 10 or 11 to 4. All banks have 24-hour ATMs.

⊞ Banks Bank of America ☎ 800/642-9855 ⊕ www.bankofamerica.com. **Farmers State Bank** ✉ 159 Riverside Ave., Winthrop ☎ 509/996-2243. **Whidbey Island Bank** ✉ 401 N. Main St., Coupeville ☎ 360/678-4555 ✉ 221 2nd St., Langley ☎ 360/221-0203.

TOURS

Apple Country Tours has farm tours, and the Cascade Foothills Farmland Association has mapped out a driving tour of local orchards and vineyards. The Lady of the Lake Boat Company takes you up the lake on narrated cruises. Upper Lake Chelan tours are arranged by the *Lady of the Lake II* folks; options include a Stehekin Valley bike tour and a bus trip (including lunch) to Rainbow Falls and the High Bridge Gorge.

On Rainbow Falls tours, operators use an old school bus to take you 3½ mi upvalley to the 312-foot cascade. There are also stops at an old schoolhouse and a bakery. The driver, who narrates the tour, is an inexhaustible source of local lore. Tours are offered year-round—even in winter when the falls are frozen.

⊞ Tour-Operators Apple Country Tours ☎ 866/459-9614 ⊕ www.washingtonapplecountry.com. **Cascade Foothills Farmland Association** ✉ 125 Easy St. Wenatchee ☎ 509/663-5159 ⊕ www.visitwashingtonfarms.com. **Lake Chelan Tour Boat** ✉ Chelan ☎ 509/682-8287. **Upper Lake Chelan Tours** ✉ Chelan ☎ 509/682-4584 ⊕ www.ladyofthelake.com.

TRAIN TRAVEL

Train service in the region is far from comprehensive. Amtrak's *Empire Builder*, which runs from Chicago to Seattle, stops in Wenatchee. The company's *Cascades* train, which runs from Seattle to Vancouver, BC, stops in Mount Vernon and Bellingham.

⊞ Amtrak ☎ 1-800-USA-RAIL ⊕ www.amtrak.com.

VISITOR INFORMATION

⊞ Tourist Information Anacortes Chamber of Commerce ✉ 819 Commercial Ave., Suite G, Anacortes ☎ 360/293-7911. **BABS (Bed and Breakfast Service)** ☎ 360/733-8642. **Bellingham/Whatcom County Convention and Visitors Bureau** ✉ 904 Potter St., Bellingham 98227 ☎ 360/671-3990 or 800/487-2032 ⊕ www.bellingham.org. **Cashmere Chamber of Commerce** ✉ 101 Cottage Ave., Cashmere ☎ 509/782-7404 ⊕ www.visitcashmere.com. **Central Whidbey Chamber of Commerce** ✉ 5 S. Main St., Coupeville ☎ 360/678-5434 ⊕ www.centralcoupevillechamber.com. **Greater Oak Harbor Chamber of Commerce** ✉ 32630 Rte. 20, Oak Harbor ☎ 360/675-3535 ⊕ www.oakharborchamber.org. **La Conner Chamber of Commerce** ✉ Lime Dock, 109 N. 1st St., La Conner ☎ 360/466-4778. **Lake Chelan Chamber of Commerce** ✉ 102 E. Johnson, Chelan ☎ 800/424-3526 ⊕ www.lakechelan.com. **Langley Chamber of Commerce** ✉ 124½ 2nd St., Langley ☎ 360/221-6765. **Leavenworth Chamber of Commerce** ✉ 894 Rte. 2, Leavenworth ☎ 509/548-5807 ⊕ www.leavenworth.org. **Mount Vernon Chamber of Commerce** ✉ 117 N. 1st St., Mount Vernon ☎ 360/428-8547. **North Cascades Chamber of Commerce** ✉ 59831 Rte. 20, Marblemount ☎ 360/873-2106 or 877/875-2448 ⊕ www.marblemount.com. **North Cascades National Park** ✉ 2105 Rte. 20, Sedro-Woolley ☎ 360/856-5700. **Sedro-Woolley Chamber of Commerce** ✉ 714-B Metcalf St., Sedro-Woolley ☎ 360/835-1582 or 888/225-8365 ⊕ www.sedro-woolley.com. **Wenatchee Chamber of Commerce** ✉ 2 South Chelan Ave., Wenatchee ☎ 509/663-2116 or 800/572-7753 ⊕ www.wenatcheevalley.org. **Winthrop Chamber of Commerce** ✉ 202 Rte. 20, Winthrop ☎ 888/464-8469 ⊕ methownet.com

THE SAN JUAN ISLANDS

Updated by
Holly S. Smith

The coastal waters of the Pacific Northwest, between mainland Washington and Vancouver Island, contain hundreds of islands, some little more than sandbars, others rising 3,000 feet. Among these, the San Juans are considered by many to be the loveliest. There are 176 named islands in the San Juan archipelago, although these and large rocks around them amount to 743 at low tide and 428 at high tide. Sixty are populated (though most have only a house or two) and 10 are state marine parks, some of which are accessible only to kayakers navigating the Cascadia Marine Trail.

This small archipelago of rock and glacial till derives its singular beauty from dramatic cliffs, lush seaside meadows, gnarled trees, and multi-colored wildflowers clinging to seemingly barren rock. The islands have valleys and mountains where eagles soar, and forests and leafy glens where the tiny island deer browse. Even a species of prickly pear cactus (*Opuntia fragilis*) grows here. Beaches can be of sand or shingle, but all are scenic and invite beachcombers and kayakers to explore them. The islands are visited by ducks and swans, herons and hawks, otters and whales. Offshore, seals haul out on sandbanks and orcas patrol the deep channels. Since the late 1990s, gray whales have begun to summer here, instead of heading north to their arctic breeding grounds; an occasional minke or humpback whale can also be seen frolicking in the kelp.

Ferries stop at the four largest islands: Lopez, Shaw, Orcas, and San Juan; others, many privately owned, can be reached by commuter ferries from Bellingham and Port Townsend. Seaplanes owned by local airlines regularly splash down near the public waterfronts and resort bays around San Juan, Orcas, and Lopez, while charters touch down in private waters away from the crowds. Lopez, Orcas, and San Juan support a little fishing and farming, but tourism generates by far the largest revenues. Serene, well-appointed inns cater to visitors, and creative chefs operate small restaurants, serving food as contemporary as anything in Seattle. Each island maintains a distinct character, though all share in the archipelago's blessings of serene farmlands, unspoiled coves, blue-green or gray tidal waters, and radiant light. The area receives approximately 250 days of sunshine a year. Nevertheless, the islands stay cool in summer (around 70°F) and get outright cold in winter, when temperatures can hover at the freezing point.

Lopez Island

❶ *45 minutes by ferry from Anacortes.*

Quiet and relatively flat Lopez, the island closest to the mainland, has gentle, sloping roads, pebbly beaches, and peaceful trails through the woods. Of the three San Juan islands with facilities to accommodate overnight visitors, Lopez has the smallest population (approximately 1,800), and with its old orchards, weathered barns, and rolling green pastures, it's the most rustic. Lopez Village, the only settlement, has a market, a few shops and galleries, a couple of restaurants, and a post office.

The **Lopez Island Historical Museum** has relics from the region's Native American tribes and early settlers, including some impressive ship and small-boat models and maps of local landmarks. ⊠ *28 Washburn Pl., Lopez Village* ☎ *360/468–2049* 🕮 *Donations accepted* ⊙ *July and Aug., Wed.–Sun. noon–4; May, June, and Sept., Fri.–Sun. noon–4.*

🐾 **Spencer Spit State Park** is on former Native American clamming, crabbing, and fishing grounds. The spit is a stop along the Cascadia Marine Trail for kayakers, and it's a good place for summer camping. It's also one of the few Washington beaches onto which cars are allowed to drive. ⊕ *2 mi northeast of Lopez Village via Port Stanley Rd.* ☎ *360/468–2251* 🕮 *Free* ⊙ *Mar.–Oct., daily 8–dusk.*

🐾 **Odlin County Park** has a mile of sandy shoreline—a rarity on the shores of the Salish Sea. The park also has a pier, a floating dock, mooring buoys, ballparks, a covered cooking shack, and 30 campsites on 80 wooded acres. ⊠ *Off Ferry Rd., 1 mi south of the ferry landing* ☎ *360/468–2496* 🕮 *Free* ⊙ *Daily.*

A quiet forest trail along beautiful **Shark Reef** leads to an isolated headland jutting out above the bay. The sounds of raucous barks and squeals mean you're nearly there, and eventually you may see throngs of seals and seagulls on the rocky islets across from the point. Bring binoculars to spot bald eagles in the trees as you walk, and to view sea otters frolicking in the waves near the shore. The trail starts at the Shark Reef Road parking lot south of Lopez Village, and it's a 15-minute walk to the headland. ⊠ *Off Shark Reef Rd., 2 mi south of Lopez Island Airport* ☎ *360/856–3500 or 800/527–3305* 🕮 *Free* ⊙ *Daily.*

Lopez Island Vineyard is spread over 6 acres about 1 mi north of Lopez Village. The winery produces chardonnay, merlot, and cabernet sauvignon–merlot blends, as well as sweeter wines, such as those made from raspberries, blackberries, and other local fruits. The tasting room is open Memorial Day through Labor Day, Wednesday through Sunday, from noon to 5 PM or by appointment in other seasons. ⊠ *Fisherman Bay Rd., north of Cross Rd.* ☎ *360/468–3644* ⊕ *www.lopezislandvineyards.com* 🕮 *Free* ⊙ *Daily.*

Where to Stay & Eat

$$–$$$ ✕ **Bay Café.** Boats dock right outside this pretty waterside mansion at the entrance to Fisherman Bay. In winter sunlight streams into the window-framed dining room; in summer you can relax on the wraparound porch before a gorgeous sunset panorama. Seafood tapas, such as basil- and goat-cheese-stuffed prawns with saffron rice, or sea scallops with sun-dried tomatoes, delightfully tickle the palate. Homemade sorbet and a fine crème caramel are among the desserts. Weekend breakfasts draw huge crowds. ⊠ *Lopez Village* ☎ *360/468–3700* ▭ *MC, V* ⊙ *Closed Sun.–Thurs. Oct.–May. No lunch.*

$–$$ 🏠 **Edenwild.** This large Victorian-style farmhouse, surrounded by gardens and framed by Fisherman's Bay, looks as if it's at least a century old, but it actually dates from 1988. Large rooms, each painted or papered in different pastel shades, are furnished with simple antiques; some have claw-foot tubs and brick fireplaces. The sunny dining room is a cheery breakfast spot. In summer you can sip tea on the wraparound ground-floor veranda or relax with a book on the garden patio. ⊠ *132 Lopez Village Rd., Lopez Village 98261* ☎ *360/468–3238 or 800/606–0662* 🖷 *360/468–4080* ⊕ *www.edenwildinn.com* ⇗ *6 rooms, 2 suites* ⚘ *Dining room; no kids under 13* ▭ *AE, D, MC, V* ⫶◯⫶ *BP.*

★ $ 🏠 **Mackaye Harbor Inn.** This white former sea captain's house, built in 1904, rises two stories above the beach and rocks at the southern end of Lopez

Island. Rooms have golden-oak and brass details and wicker furniture; three have views of Mackaye Harbor. Breakfast includes Scandinavian specialties like Finnish pancakes; tea, coffee, and chocolates are served in the evening. Rooms are simple, with colorful coverlets. The Rose Room is done all in pink. The Harbor Suite has a private bath, deck, and fireplace. Kayaks are available for rent, and mountain bikes are complimentary. ⊠ *949 McKaye Harbor Rd., 98261* ☎ *360/468–2253 or 888/314–6140* 🖨 *360/468–3293* ⊕ *www.mackayeharborinn.com* ➪ *4 rooms, 2 with bath, 1 suite* ⟐ *Dining room, some kitchens, beach, boating, bicycles; no smoking* ⊟ *MC, V* ⊠◎⊠ *BP.*

¢–$ 🏠 **Inn at Swifts Bay.** Bay windows in the living and dining areas of this Tudor-style house overlook well-kept gardens, and a crackling fire warms the parlor on winter evenings. Small guest rooms on the main floor have heavy floral drapes, elaborate bedding, and shared baths. Suites have fireplaces and private baths, and the downstairs suite has a private entrance. Breakfast includes such creative specialties as pumpkin eggnog muffins. It's a four-minute walk to the private beach. ⊠ *856 Port Stanley Rd.* ⊕ *Box 3402, 98261* ☎ *360/468–3636 or 800/903–9536* 🖨 *360/468–3637* ⊕ *www.swiftsbay.com* ➪ *2 rooms without bath, 3 suites* ⟐ *Dining room, in-room VCRs, gym, hot tub, sauna, beach, library; no kids under 16* ⊟ *AE, D, MC, V* ⊠◎⊠ *BP.*

Sports & the Outdoors

BICYCLING Mountain bike rental rates start at around $5 an hour and $25 a day; tandem, recumbent, and electric bikes are $13 to $20 an hour or $42 to $65 per day. Helmets are $1 extra. Children's bike trailers and additional equipment are usually available. Reservations are recommended, particularly in summer.

The Bike Shop on Lopez (⊠ Lopez Village ☎ 360/468–3497) makes free deliveries to the ferry docks or your hotel. **Cycle San Juans** (⊠ Rte. 1 ☎ 360/468–3251) offers rentals and tours under the slogan "Cycle with bald Lopezian to discover island curiosities." **Lopez Bicycle Works** (⊠ 2847 Fisherman Bay Rd. ☎ 360/468–2847 ⊕ www.lopezbicycleworks.com) can bring bicycles to your door or the ferry.

BOATING & **Harmony Charters** (☎ 360/468–3310 ⊕ www.interisland.net/countess) SAILING maintains a 63-foot, two-cabin motorboat, for lunch ($65) and dinner ($75) cruises, as well as for trips to British Columbia and Alaska ($200 per person per day). Prices include crew, food, sports equipment, utensils, and linens. **Kismet Sailing Charters** (☎ 360/468–2435 ⊕ www.rockisland.com/~sailkismet) makes eight-hour cruises ($450 per person), three-day cruises ($145 per person per day), and custom charter trips in a skippered 36-foot yacht.

MARINA **Islands Marine Center** (⊠ 2792 Fisherman Bay Rd. ☎ 360/468–3377 ⊕ www.islandsmarinecenter.com) has standard marina amenities, repair facilities, and transient moorage.

SEA KAYAKING **Elakah! Expeditions** (☎ 360/734–7270 or 800/434–7270 ⊕ www.elakah.com), a family-run sea-kayaking company, leads kayaking clinics on Lopez and two- to five-day trips ($225 to $495) around the San Juans. Specialty trips, such as those for women only, are also organized. **Lopez Kayaks** (☎ 360/468–2847 ⊕ www.lopezkayaks.com), open May to October at Fisherman Bay, offers a four-hour tour of the southern end of Lopez for $75 and a two-hour sunset tour for $35. Kayak rentals start at $12 an hour or $40 per day, and the company can deliver kayaks to any point on the island.

Shopping

The **Chimera Gallery** (✉ Village Rd. ☎ 360/468–3265), a local artists' cooperative, exhibits and sells crafts, jewelry, and fine art. **Fish Bay Mercantile** (✉ Lopez Rd. ☎ 360/468–2126) is a fun, quirky gallery full of handcarved wooden masks and furnishings, handwoven shawls and blankets, handmade jewelry, and scenic paintings by island artists—plus quirky international stuff like the Hindu lunchbox collection. **Grayling Gallery** (✉ 3630 Hummel Lake Rd. ☎ 360/468–2779) displays the paintings, prints, sculptures, and pottery works of nearly a dozen Lopez Island artists. **Islehaven Books** (✉ Village Rd. ☎ 360/468–2132), which is supervised in part by the owner's pack of five Russian wolfhounds, is stocked with publications on San Juan Islands history and activities, as well as books about the Pacific Northwest. There's also a good selection of mysteries, literary novels, children's books, and craft kits, plus greeting cards, art prints, and maps. Many of the items sold here are the works of local writers, artists, and photographers. **Tsunami Books** (✉ Village Rd. ☎ 360/468–3763), in the Watertower, carries out-of-print, antiquarian, and used books, as well as music. You can even swap the bestseller you just finished for another book or perhaps a tape of '70s tunes.

Shaw Island

② *20 minutes by ferry from Lopez, 65 minutes by ferry from Anacortes.*

Tiny Shaw Island sits in the center of the San Juan archipelago, an approximately 8-square-mi speck of land covered with forests and orchards. Residents fiercely protect their privacy—there's just one little store by the ferry docks and a few public spots where you're permitted to land a kayak, but no restaurants or lodgings.

Few passengers disembark the ferry here, and those who do are treated to the sight of nuns, wearing traditional habits, manning the dock. Two Catholic groups are based here, the Franciscan Sisters of the Eucharist who run the docks, and Our Lady of the Rock Priory, home of the "spinning nuns" famous for their delicately knitted creations.

The little **Shaw Island Historical Museum,** built with planks from the island's original post office, exhibits pioneer furnishings and clothing, 19th-century fishing and farming equipment, and lots of old photos. Also on display are arrowheads and pestles used by local Native American tribes. The adjacent library was designed by Malcolm Cameron, a Shaw Island architect and artist. Readings by local authors are occasionally presented here. ⊠ *Hoffman Cove Rd. at Blind Bay Rd.* ☎ *360/468–4068* ☉ *Tues. 2–4, Thurs. 11–1, Sat. 10–noon and 2–4.*

Across the street from the museum, the **Little Red Schoolhouse** is where local children have been attending school since 1875. The main building was placed on the National Register of Historic Places in 1973. More recent additions include a computer room. ⊠ *Hoffman Cove at Neck Point Cove Rd.* ☎ ☉ *Sept.–May, weekdays 7:30–3:30.*

Orcas Island

❸ *10 minutes by ferry from Shaw Island, 75 minutes by ferry from Anacortes.*

Roads on flower-blossom–shape Orcas Island, the largest of the San Juans, sweep through wide valleys and rise to gorgeous hilltop views. Spanish explorers set foot here in 1791, and the island is named for their ship—not for the black-and-white whales that frolic in the surrounding waters. The island was also the home of Native American tribes, whose history is reflected in such places as Pole Pass, where the Lummi people used kelp and cedar-bark nets to catch ducks, and Massacre Bay, where in 1858 a tribe from southeast Alaska attacked a Lummi fishing village.

Today, farmers, anglers, artists, retirees, and summer-home owners make up the population of about 4,000. Houses are spaced far apart, and towns typically have just one major road running through them. Resorts dotting the island's edges are evidence of the thriving local tourism industry. Orcas is a favorite place for weekend getaways from the Seattle area any time of the year, as well as one of the state's top settings for summer weddings.

Eastsound, the main town, lies at the head of the East Sound channel, which nearly divides the island in two. Small shops here sell jewelry, pottery, and crafts by local artisans. Along Prune Alley are a handful of stores and restaurants.

The Funhouse is a huge, nonprofit activity center and museum for families. Interactive exhibits on age, hearing, kinetics, video production, among other subjects, are all educational. Kids can explore an arts and crafts yurt, a climbing wall, a library, Internet stations, and a big metal "Jupiter" tree fort. Sports activities include indoor pitching cages and games, as well as an outdoor playground. Kids and adults can also take classes on music, theater, digital film, and poetry. There are free programs for pre-teens and teenagers on Friday and Saturday nights (hint to mom and dad, who might want to enjoy dinner alone on this romantic island). ⊠ *30 Pea Patch La., Eastsound* ☎ *360/376-7177* ⊕ *www. thefunhouse.org* ⊠ *$5* ☉ *Sept.–June, weekdays 3–5:30, Sat. 11–3; July and Aug., Mon.–Sat. 11–5.*

The simple yet stately **Emmanuel Church,** built in 1886 next to the bay, resembles an English countryside chapel. The white-painted wood building has a large round stained-glass window and is topped by a white cross. A white picket fence winds around the front. From July through August, free noontime concerts are held each Thursday on the wide lawn. Prayer groups meet Saturdays at 9:30. ⊠ *218 Main St., Eastsound* ☎ *360/376–2352.*

★ **Moran State Park** comprises 5,000 acres of hilly, old-growth forests dotted with sparkling lakes, in the middle of which rises 2,400-foot-high Mt. Constitution, the tallest peak in the San Juans. A drive to the summit affords exhilarating views of the islands, the Cascades, the Olympics, and Vancouver Island. You can explore the terrain along 14 hiking trails and choose from among 151 campsites if you'd like to stay longer. ⊠ *Star Rte. 22, Head northeast from Eastsound on Horseshoe Hwy. and follow signs* ✆ *Box 22, Eastsound 98245* ☎ *360/376–2326, 800/452–5678 reservations* ⊠ *Camping $11 fee, plus $6 per night.*

Where to Stay & Eat

$$$–$$$$ ✕ **Christina's.** Copper-top tables and paintings by island artists enhance
Fodor'sChoice this cozy bayside spot. The seasonal menu focuses on local seafood, prepared with fresh herbs and served with vegetables. Look for delicacies
★ like spring greens with fennel and Samish Bay cheese; roast chicken with mushroom bread pudding; and curry coconut fish stew. Fine views of the East Sound make for a romantic dinner on the rooftop terrace or the enclosed porch. An excellent wine list and a bevy of rich desserts complement every meal. This is a place to propose. ⊠ *310 N. Beach Rd., Eastsound* ☎ *360/376–4904* ⊟ *AE, DC, MC, V* ☺ *Closed Tues. Oct.–mid-June. No lunch.*

¢–$ ✕ **Bilbo's Festivo.** Stucco walls, colorful tiles, and wood benches reflect this restaurant's Tex-Mex inclinations. And believe it or not, the food here is healthy. The fresh, delectable burritos, enchiladas and chalupas are lard-free. There's also fabulous homemade guacamole and locally-grown organic salad greens. Margaritas are served in the courtyard in summer, and you can warm your hands around the patio firepit on cool autumn evenings. Kids dash immediately to the outdoor play area. ⊠ *N. Beach Rd. and A St., Eastsound* ☎ *360/376–4728* ⚙ *Reservations not accepted* ⊟ *AE, MC, V* ☺ *No lunch Oct.–May.*

$$$–$$$$ 🏨 **Rosario Spa & Resort.** Shipbuilding magnate Robert Moran built this Mediterranean-style mansion on Cascade Bay in 1906. It's now on the National Register of Historic Places and worth a visit even if you're not staying here. The house has retained its original Mission-style furniture and numerous antiques; its centerpiece, an Aeolian organ with 1,972 pipes, is used for summer concerts in the ballroom. Some of the rooms are compact and basic; others are luxurious suites with outdoor decks, Jacuzzis, gas fireplaces, and kitchens. You can hike, kayak, and scuba dive nearby or stay in for a day of pampering in the downstairs Avanyu Spa. From your room you can watch seaplanes splash down in the bay and fishing and sailboat charters come into the the marina. With prior notice, a Rosario shuttle will meet you at the ferry dock and take you to the hotel. ⊠ *1 Rosario Way, Eastsound 98245* ☎ *360/376–2222 or 800/562–8820* ⊕ *www.rosario.rockresorts.com* ➷ *111 rooms, 4 suites* △ *2 restaurants, cable TV, some in-room hot tubs, some kitchens, 2 tennis courts, 3 pools (1 indoor), fitness classes, gym, hot tub, sauna, spa, dock, boating, fishing, boccie, croquet, hiking, horseshoes, shuffleboard, volleyball, lounge, concert hall, shop, children's program (ages 5–13), concierge, Internet, business services, meeting rooms* ⊟ *AE, DC, MC, V.*

$$$–$$$$ 🏨 **Spring Bay Inn.** Two former park rangers run this woodland bed-and-
Fodor'sChoice breakfast at the edge of private Spring Bay. All rooms have water views,
★ wood-burning fireplaces, feather beds, and sitting areas; one room has
an outdoor hot tub. Mornings begin with coffee, muffins, and croissants
outside your door—fortification for the free, two-hour kayaking trip
around the island's craggy edges, or for hiking the trails that meander
through the property. Afterward, there's an enormous complimentary
brunch. One of the owners is also a minister who can perform marriage
ceremonies along the inn's forested bluffs. ⊠ *Obstruction Pass Trail-
head Rd. off Obstruction Pass Rd., Olga 98279* 🕾 *360/376–5531*
🖷 *360/376–2193* ⊕ *www.springbayinn.com* ⇨ *5 rooms* ☖ *Dining
room, refrigerators, outdoor hot tub, beach, dock, boating, hiking, In-
ternet* ☰ *D, MC, V* ¶⊙¶ *BP.*

$$$ 🏨 **Resort at Deer Harbor.** The hillside cottages that make up this resort
were built in the 1930s as housing for apple-pickers. Renovated deluxe
cabins each have a fireplace, a porch with a hot tub, and serene water
views. Smaller cottages have woodstoves and showers. The units are close-
set, so friends and families can enjoy camaraderie at any hour. ⊠ *Deer
Harbor Rd., Deer Harbor 98243* 🕾 *360/376–4420 or 888/376–4480*
🖷 *360/376–5523* ⊕ *www.deerharbor.com* ⇨ *12 suites, 14 cottages*
☖ *Restaurant, in-room data ports, in-room hot tubs, kitchenettes, microwaves, refrigerators, cable TV, in-room VCRs, pool, hot tubs, massage; no a/c, no smoking* ☰ *AE, D, MC, V* ¶⊙¶ *CP.*

¢–$$$ 🏨 **Turtleback Farm Inn.** Eighty acres of meadow, forest, and farmland in
the shadow of Turtleback Mountain surround this forest-green inn.
Rooms are divided between the carefully restored late-19th-century
green-clapboard farmhouse and the newer cedar Orchard House. All
are well-lit, with hardwood floors, wood trim, and colorful curtains and
quilts, some of which are made from the fleece of resident sheep. The
inn is a favorite place for local weddings. Breakfast is in the dining room
or on the deck overlooking the valley. The Elopement package includes
a minister, flowers, champagne, photos, and more. ⊠ *1981 Crow Val-
ley Rd., Eastsound 98245* 🕾 *360/376–3914 or 800/376–4914* 🖷 *360/
376–5329* ⊕ *www.turtlebackinn.com* ⇨ *11 rooms* ☖ *Dining room, bar*
☰ *MC, V* ¶⊙¶ *BP.*

$ 🏨 **Deer Harbor Inn.** The 1915 log building here, on a knoll overlooking
Deer Harbor, was the island's first resort. A larger, newer lodge has eight
wood-paneled rooms, each with a balcony and peeled-log furniture. Four
cottages—including one with three bedrooms—and the Harborview
Suite have whirlpool tubs and propane fireplaces; two full-scale houses
have kitchens and laundry facilities. The original lodge is now the inn's
dining room. The century-old apple orchard is a favorite spot for wed-
dings, and the inn can arrange complete packages. ✛ *5½ mi southwest
of West Sound via Deer Harbor Rd.* ⬧ *Box 142, Deer Harbor 98243*
🕾 *360/376–4110 or 877/377–4110* 🖷 *360/376–2237* ⊕ *www.
deerharborinn.com* ⇨ *8 rooms, 1 suite, 4 cottages, 2 houses* ☖ *Restau-
rant, some in-room hot tubs, some kitchens, hot tub, boating, fishing,
laundry facilities* ☰ *AE, MC, V* ¶⊙¶ *CP.*

¢–$ 🏨 **Doe Bay Village Resort & Retreat.** Neohippies and outdoorsy types flock
to this commune and hostel, formerly a nudist colony, at the eastern tip
of Orcas. Patchwork accommodations include tent and RV sites, yurts
and geodomes, and cabins. The hostel has one private room for cou-
ples and another room with six beds. The window-lined, wood-floored
Café Doe Bay, which faces the ocean, is open daily for self-serve break-
fasts at $1 per item; dinners are served two or three times per week, de-
pending on the number of resort guests and the cook's whim. The small
beach is perfect for kayak launches. Cabin guests have free access to the

resort's mineral baths and sauna ($4 for others). ✉ *Star Rte. 86 off Pt. Lawrence Rd. near Olga* ✑ *Box 437, Olga 98279* ☎ *360/376–2291* 🖷 *360/376–4755* ⊕ *www.doebay.com* ↩ *30 cabins, 7 yurts, 3 geodomes, 15 campsites, 2 RV sites, 1 house, 2 rooms, 1 6-bed dorm* ⌁ *Café, hot tub, massage, sauna, beach, volleyball* ▤ *AE, MC, V.*

Sports & the Outdoors

BICYCLES & MOPEDS Mountain bikes rent for about $30 per day or $100 per week, including a helmet; tandem, recumbent, and electric bikes rent for about $50 per day. Most biking centers also rent strollers, children's bikes, and child trailers. Mopeds rent for $20 to $30 per hour or $60 to $70 per day. It's recommended that you reserve bikes and mopeds, especially in summer.

The Boardwalk (✉ Orcas Village ☎ 360/376–2791 ⊕ www.orcasislandboardwalk.com), at the ferry landing, rents road and mountain bikes. **Dolphin Bay Bicycles** (✉ Orcas Village ☎ 360/376–3093 ⊕ www.rockisland.com/~dolphin), at the Orcas ferry landing, rents road, mountain, and BMX bicycles for children and adults. They also organize guided bike tours of the San Juan Islands. **Key Moped Rental** (✉ Eastsound ☎ 360/376–2474) rents mopeds May through October. **Susie's Mopeds** (✉ Eastsound ☎ 360/376–5266 or 800/532–0087) rents mopeds June through September. **Wildlife Cycles** (✉ Eastsound ☎ 360/376–4708 ⊕ www.wildlifecycles.com) rents bikes and can recommend routes all over the island.

BOATING & SAILING **Amante Sail Tours** (✉ Deer Harbor ☎ 360/376–4231) offers half-day sailing trips for up to six people for $35 per person. **Deer Harbor Charters** (✉ Deer Harbor ☎ 360/376–5989 ⊕ www.deerharborcharters.com) has several small sailboats making half-day cruises around the San Juans for $45 to $75 per person. Outboards and skiffs are also available, as is fishing gear. **Lieber Haven Marina Resort** (✉ Obstruction Pass ☎ 360/376–2472 ⊕ www.lieberhavenresort.com) rents sailboats, motorboats, and kayaks June through September. **Orcas Boat Rentals** (✉ Deer Harbor ☎ 360/376–7616 ⊕ www.orcasboats.com) has sailboats, outboards, and skiffs for full- and half-day trips. **Northwest Classic Day Sails** (✉ Deer Harbor ☎ 360/376–5581) uses a 33-foot, 1940s-built cedar sloop for chartered and scheduled half-day trips from Deer Harbor for $50 per person. **Sharon L. Charters** (✉ West Sound ☎ 360/376–4305) has a 28-foot wooden vessel for six that costs $50 per person per day. **West Beach Resort** (✛ 3 mi west of Eastsound ☎ 360/376–2240 or 800/937–8224 ⊕ www.westbeachresort.com) rents motorized boats, kayaks and canoes, and fishing gear.

FISHING Three lakes at **Moran State Park** (✉ Star Rte. 22, northeast of Eastbound ☎ 360/376–2326) are open for fishing from late April to October. Fishing gear is available for rent at all the main boat rental agencies and marinas.

HORSEBACK RIDING **Walking Horse Country Farm** (☎ 360/376–3037 ⊕ www.walkinghorsefarm.com) is the place to rent Tennessee walking horses ($50 an hour) for exploring island trails.

MARINAS **Deer Harbor Resort & Marina** (☎ 360/376–3037) provides full-service moorage and repair facilities. **Island Petroleum** (✉ Orcas ☎ 360/376–3883) has docks, plus gas and diesel at the ferry landing. **Rosario Resort** (✉ Eastsound ☎ 360/376–2222) has moorage and a protected anchorage for small boats and larger vessels. **West Sound Marina** (☎ 360/376–2240), near West Sound, has moorage, fuel, a boat repair shop, a marine chandlery, and visitor facilities, such as showers.

SEA KAYAKING All equipment is usually included in a rental package or tour. One-hour trips cost around $25; three-hour tours, about $45; day tours, $95 to $120; and multiday tours, about $100 per day.

Crescent Beach Kayaks (⊠ Eastsound ☎ 360/376–2464) caters to families with free instruction and kayak rentals. **Orcas Outdoors Sea Kayak Tours** (⊠ Orcas Village ☎ 360/376–2222 ⊕ www.orcasoutdoors.com) has one- and three-hour journeys, as well as day trips and rentals; a second branch is based at the Outlook Inn in Eastsound. **Osprey Tours** (⊠ Eastsound ☎ 360/376–3677 or 800/529–2567 ⊕ www.fidalgo. net/~kayak) uses handcrafted wooden Aleutian-style kayaks for half-day, full-day, and overnight tours of the islands. **Shearwater Adventures** (⊠ Eastsound ☎ 360/376–4699 ⊕ www.shearwaterkayaks.com) holds kayaking classes and runs three-hour, day, and overnight tours from Rosario, Deer Harbor, and Doe Bay resorts. **West Beach Kayaks** (⊠ West Beach ☎ 360/376–2240 or 877/937–8224) has half-day guided tours of the island in summer.

SCUBA DIVING **Island Dive & Water Sports** (⊠ Rosario Resort, Eastsound ☎ 360/376–7615 ⊕ www.divesanjuan.com) has a dive shop with rentals and offers a complete program of services, including instruction, airfills, and charter trips. Two custom dive boats make two-tank dives for $75 with gear; resort packages are available. **West Beach Resort** (⊠ West Beach ☎ 360/376–2240 or 877/937–8224) is a popular dive spot where you can fill your own tanks.

WHALE-
WATCHING Cruises, which run about four hours, are scheduled daily in summer and once or twice weekly at other times. The cost is around $50 per person, and boats hold 20 to 40 people. Wear warm clothing, bring a snack, and have your camera ready to catch unexpected orca jumps and passes.

Deer Harbor Charters (☎ 360/376–5989 or 800/544–5758) has whale-watching cruises around the island straits. **Eclipse Charters** (☎ 360/376–4663 or 800/376–6566 ⊕ www.orcasislandwhales.com) searches around Orcas Island for whale pods and other wildlife. **Whale Spirit Adventures** (⊠ West Sound Marina ☎ 360/376–5052 or 800/376–8018 ⊕ www. whalespirit.com) offers whale-sighting tours to the accompaniment of new-age chanting or flutes.

Shopping
Crow Valley Pottery (⊠ 2274 Orcas Rd., Eastsound ☎ 360/376–2351 or 800/684–4297 ⊕ www.crowvalley.com) carries ceramics, metalworks, blown glass, and sculptures. **Darvill's Rare Print Shop** (⊠ Eastsound ☎ 360/376–2351) specializes in maps and unique bird and floral prints. **Orcas Island Artworks** (⊠ Main St., Olga ☎ 360/376–4408 ⊕ www.orcasisland.com/artworks) displays pottery, sculpture, jewelry, art glass, paintings, and quilts by resident artists.

San Juan Island

❹ *45 minutes by ferry from Orcas Island, 75 minutes by ferry from Anacortes.*

Lummi Indians were the first settlers on San Juan, with encampments along the north end of the island. North-end beaches were especially busy during the annual salmon migration, when hundreds of tribal members would gather along the shoreline to fish, cook, and exchange news. Many of the Lummi tribe were killed by smallpox and other imported diseases in the 18th and 19th centuries. Smallpox Bay was where tribal members plunged into the icy water to cool the fevers that came with the disease.

The 18th century brought explorers from England and Spain, but the island remained sparsely populated until the mid-1800s. From the 1880s Friday Harbor and its newspaper were controlled by lime-company owner and Republican bigwig John S. McMillin, who virtually ran San Juan Island as a personal fiefdom from 1886 until his death in 1936. The town's main street, rising from the harbor and ferry landing up the slopes of a modest hill, hasn't changed much in the past few decades, though the cafés and shops are snazzier now than they were in the 1960s and '70s. San Juan is the most convenient Pacific Northwest island to visit, since you can take the ferry here and explore the entire island by public transportation or bicycle.

You'll recognize the **Whale Museum** by the mural painted on its exterior. Models of whales and whale skeletons, recordings of whale sounds, and videos of whales are the attractions. Workshops survey marine-mammal life and San Juan ecology. ⊠ *62 1st St. N* ☎ *360/378–4710* ⊕ *www.whale-museum.org* ⊠ *$6* ⊙ *June–Sept., daily 10–5; Oct.–May, daily 11–4.*

The **San Juan Historical Museum,** in an old farmhouse, presents island life at the turn of the 20th century through historic photography, documents, and buildings. ⊠ *405 Price St.* ☎ *360/378–405* ⊕ *www.sjmuseum.org* ⊠ *$3* ⊙ *Oct.–Apr., Tues. and Thurs. 10–2; May–Sept., Thurs.–Sat. 1–4.*

★ To watch whales cavorting in Haro Strait, head to **Lime Kiln Point State Park,** on San Juan's western side just 6 mi from Friday Harbor. The little white 1914 lighthouse is a landmark for boats cruising these waters. The best period for sighting whales is from the end of April through August, but a resident pod of orcas regularly cruises past the point. ⊠ *6158 Lighthouse Rd.* ☎ *360/378–2044* ⊠ *Free* ⊙ *Daily 8 AM–10 PM.*

★ **San Juan Island National Historic Park** commemorates the Pig War, in which the United States and Great Britain nearly went to war over their respective claims on the San Juan Islands. The dispute began in 1859 when an American settler killed a British soldier's pig, and escalated until roughly 500 American soldiers and 2,200 British soldiers with five warships were poised for battle. Fortunately, no blood was spilled and the disagreement was finally settled in 1872 in the Americans' favor, with Emperor William I of Germany as arbitrator.

The park comprises two separate areas on opposite sides of the island. English Camp, in a sheltered cove of Garrison Bay on the northern end, includes a blockhouse, a commissary, and barracks. American Camp, on the southern end, has a visitor center and the remains of fortifications. From June to August you can take guided hikes and see reenactments of 1860s-era military life. ⊠ *American Camp 6 mi southeast of Friday Harbor; English Camp 9 mi northwest of Friday Harbor; Park Headquarters, 125 Spring St., Friday Harbor* ☎ *360/468–3663* ⊕ *www. nps.gov/sajh.*

★ The **San Juan Center for Art & Nature** is essentially a 19-acre open-air art gallery within the spectacular Westcott Bay Reserve. You can stroll along winding trails to view more than 80 sculptures spread amid freshwater and saltwater wetlands, open woods, blossoming fields, and rugged terrain. The park is also a haven for birds; more than 120 species nest and breed here. Art workshops and events are scheduled throughout the year in the tented area. ⊠ *Westcott Dr. off Roche Harbor Rd.* ☎ *360/370–5050* ⊕ *www.wbay.org.*

It's hard to believe that fashionable **Roche Harbor** at the northern end of San Juan Island was once the most important producer of builder's lime on the West Coast. In 1882 John S. McMillin gained control of the lime company and expanded production. But even in its heyday as a limestone quarrying village, Roche Harbor was known for abundant flowers and welcoming accommodations. McMillin transformed a bunkhouse into private lodgings for his invited guests, who included such notables as Teddy Roosevelt. The guest house is now the Hotel de Haro, which displays period photographs and artifacts in its lobby. The staff has maps of the old quarry, kilns, and the Mausoleum, an eerie Greek-inspired memorial to McMillin.

McMillin's heirs operated the quarries and plant until 1956, when they sold the company to the Tarte family. Although the old lime kilns still stand below the bluff, the company town has become a resort. Locals say it took two years for the limestone dust to wash off the trees around the harbor. McMillin's former home is now a restaurant, and workers' cottages have been transformed into comfortable visitors' lodgings. With its rose gardens, cobblestone waterfront, and well-manicured lawns, Roche Harbor retains the flavor of its days as a hangout for McMillin's powerful friends—especially since the sheltered harbor is very popular with well-to-do pleasure boaters.

At **Pelindaba Lavender Farm,** a spectacular 20-acre valley is smothered with endless rows of fragrant purple-and-gold lavender blossoms. The oils of these organically grown flowers are distilled for use in therapeutic, botanical, and household products, all created on site. The blossoms are also woven into gorgeous craft items and decorations, including holiday wreaths and ornaments, all sold on site. You can even buy tea, baked goods, and pet care products made with lavender extracts. ⊠ *33 Hawthorn La., Friday Harbor* ☎ *360/378–4248 or 866/819–1911* ⊕ *www.pelindaba.com* ⊠ *Free* ⊗ *Feb.–Apr., Nov., and Dec., Wed.–Sun. 9–5; May–Oct., daily 9–5.*

Where to Stay & Eat

$$–$$$ ✕ **Duck Soup Inn.** Blossoming vines thread over the cedar-shingled walls
Fodor'sChoice of this restaurant. Inside, island-inspired paintings and a flagstone fire-
★ place are the background for creative meals served at comfortable booths. Everything is made from scratch daily, including sourdough bruschetta and ice cream. You might start with Thai-style prawn roll-ups, made with peanuts, scallions, coconut, hot chilies, lime, and fresh mint; or perhaps applewood-smoked Westcott Bay oysters. For a second course, you might have grilled quail or chile rellenos. Vegetarian options and child portions are available. Northwest, California, and European wines are also on hand. ⊠ *50 Duck Soup La.* ☎ *360/378–4878* ▤ *MC, V* ⊗ *Closed Nov.–Mar. and Mon.and Tues. No lunch.*

$$–$$$ ✕ **Friday Harbor House Restaurant.** Soft lighting, widely spaced tables, parchment-color walls, and views of the Friday Harbor marina set the tone in this elegant, art gallery–style dining room. The menu, which changes seasonally, emphasizes fresh local seafood and produce. Grilled Oregon beef, served with horseradish mashed potatoes, and wild Alaskan king salmon, served with a caper-herb sauce and beluga lentils, are flawless in taste and appearance. Classic Northwest, European, and Australian wines are available to complement any season and style of meal. ⊠ *130 West St., Friday Harbor* ☎ *360/378–8453* ▤ *AE, MC, V* ⊗ *No lunch.*

$–$$$ ✕ **Downrigger.** You can watch ferries gliding across the bay from the dining room of this restaurant. You can't go wrong with fresh grilled or fried seafood. A good choice in summer is the chicken–gorgonzola salad, which you can eat on the deck in warm weather. Weekend breakfasts are popular for the stacked pancakes and stuffed omelettes. ⊠ *10 Front St., Friday Harbor* ☎ *360/378–2700* ▤ *AE, MC, V.*

$–$$ ✕ **The Place Next to the San Juan Ferry Landing Café.** A relaxed, harborside setting is the draw of this lunch spot next to the ferry dock. Paintings by local artists adorn the walls and menu covers, and candlelight and wildflowers add graceful touches to the simple, chic deck and dining room. Entrées like filet mignon and bouillabaisse are complemented by fresh-baked bread and locally grown herbs, berries, and vegetables. The signature dish (and local favorite) is linguine with San Juan Island clams. ⊠ *1 Spring St., Friday Harbor* ☎ *360/378–8707* ▱ *MC, V* ☺ *No dinner.*

¢–$ ✕ **Front Street Ale House.** This dark, woodsy English-style ale house serves traditional pub fare: bangers and mash (sausages and mashed potatoes), bubble and squeak (grilled cabbage and mashed potatoes), and a terrific shepherd's pie. A draught from the adjacent San Juan Brewing Company is the perfect accompaniment—try the Pig War Stout or Royal Marine Pale Ale. If you can't decide what to drink, choose the beer sampler, which comes with five types of draughts served in shot glasses. On Thursdays in winter, the bar hosts adults-only trivia tournaments, during which local contestants win kooky, white elephant–style prizes. The second-floor Top Side area has a dance floor and great harbor views. ⊠ *1 Front St., Friday Harbor* ☎ *360/378–2337* ⌂ *Reservations not accepted* ▱ *AE, MC, V.*

★ **$$$–$$$$** ▥ **Friday Harbor House.** This contemporary hotel takes advantage of its bluff-top location with floor-to-ceiling windows that overlook the marina, ferry landing, and San Juan Channel below. Sleek, modern, wood furnishings and fabrics in beige hues fill the rooms, all of which have fireplaces, deep jetted tubs, and at least partial views of the water. The elegant restaurant serves seasonal meals and special wine-tasting dinners, often to a backdrop of glowing sunsets in summer. ⊠ *130 West St., Friday Harbor 98250* ☎ *360/378–8455* ▱ *360/378–8453* ⊕ *www.fridayharborhouse.com* ⇥ *20 rooms* ⌂ *Restaurant, in-room data ports, in-room hot tubs, refrigerators, cable TV; no smoking* ▱ *MC, V* ⍣ *CP.*

$$$ ▥ **Harrison House Suites.** An abundance of plants and an artful rock garden surround this posh, renovated 1905 Craftsman cottage. Lovely, self-contained suites have fully stocked kitchens, private indoor or outdoor Jacuzzis, and vast harbor views. Local antiques, Persian carpets, and graceful art pieces decorate each space. The adjacent 1930s cottage has a fireplace and a sun porch facing a garden of wildflowers and winter annuals. You can take the house kayaks for a paddle in the bay or the mountain bikes into one of the nearby parks. The café, which doubles as a meeting room, serves breakfast and occasional dinners. ⊠ *253 C St., Friday Harbor 98250* ☎ *360/378–3587 or 800/407–7933* ▱ *360/378–2270* ⊕ *www.san-juan-lodging.com* ⇥ *3 suites, 1 cottage* ⌂ *Café, dining room, in-room hot tubs, kitchens, boating, mountain bikes* ▱ *AE, MC, V* ⍣ *BP.*

$$ ▥ **Panacea Bed and Breakfast.** Steel magnate Peter Kirk had this Craftsman bungalow built as a summer home in 1907. Rooms are all differently decorated: the Garden Room has a botanical motif, the sunny Trellis Room is done in peach hues, and the Arbor Room has French doors leading out to the garden. You may take breakfast in the parlor—or have it in bed, served on antique Limoges china. Bountiful wicker-basket picnics, with all the trimmings, can be prepared for a day's excursion. ⊠ *595 Park St., Friday Harbor 98250* ☎ *360/378–3757 or 800/639–2762* ▱ *360/378–8543* ⊕ *www.panacea-inn.com* ⇥ *4 rooms* ⌂ *Dining room, picnic area, some in-room hot tubs, cable TV, airport shuttle; no a/c, no room phones, no kids, no smoking* ▱ *MC, V* ⍣ *BP.*

FodorśChoice ★

$–$$ ▥ **Trumpeter Inn Bed & Breakfast.** Ten acres of rose gardens and pond-dotted meadows surround this attractive B&B. Each room is different—for example, Yarrow evokes spring with its lemony color and wildflower-embroidered comforter. King suites have fireplaces and private entrances, and one suite is wheelchair-accessible. ✉ *318 Trumpeter Way, Friday Harbor 98250* ☎ *360/378–3884 or 800/826–7926* 🖷 *360/ 378–8235* ⊕ *www.trumpeterinn.com* ↘ *5 rooms* ⟁ *Dining room, pond, hot tub, massage, fishing; no room phones, no kids under 12, no smoking* ⊟ *AE, D, MC, V* ⏣ *BP.*

¢–$$ 🏛 **Friday's Historic Inn.** One of the first hotels in the San Juan Islands, this 1891 bunkhouse is now a comfortable, boutique-style B&B. Rooms are individually decorated with a mix of antique furnishings and modern amenities, and styles range from simple economy spaces to deluxe suites. Some budget rooms even have a vaulted ceiling, balcony or patio, and water views, while suites might have a fireplace, wet bar, two-person jetted tub, or private outdoor hot tub. ✉ *35 1st St., Friday Harbor 98250* ☎ *360/378–5848 or 800/352–2632* 🖷 *360/378–2881* ⊕ *www. friday-harbor.com* ↘ *7 rooms, 4 with bath, 8 suites* ⟁ *Dining room, some in-room hot tubs, some kitchenettes, some microwaves, some refrigerators, cable TV, some in-room VCRs, Internet, airport shuttle; no a/c, no room phones, no smoking* ⊟ *MC, V* ⏣ *CP.*

¢–$$ 🏛 **Hillside House.** This split-level house less than a mile from Friday Harbor has views of the waterfront and Mt. Baker from a large deck. Some of the modern, well-furnished rooms have window seats overlooking the inn's private, full-flight aviary filled with exotic birds. On the deck, a pair of mounted 200 millimeter binoculars let you observe local birds, including bald and golden eagles. The inn's penthouse is a popular honeymoon retreat. ✉ *365 Carter Ave., Friday Harbor 98250* ☎ *360/ 378–4730 or 800/232–4730* 🖷 *360/378–4715* ⊕ *www.hillsidehouse. com* ↘ *6 rooms, 1 suite* ⟁ *Dining room* ⊟ *AE, D, MC, V* ⏣ *BP.*

¢ 🏛 **Roche Harbor Resort.** First a log trading post built in 1845, and later an 1880s lime-industry complex, including hotel, homes, and offices, this sprawling resort is still centered around the lime deposits that made John S. McMillan his fortune in the late 19th century. Rooms are filled with notable antiques, like the claw-foot tub where actor John Wayne used to soak. Luxury suites in the separate McMillan House have fireplaces, heated bathroom floors, and panoramic water views from a private veranda. The beachside Company Town Cottages, once the homes of lime company employees, have rustic exteriors but modern interiors. Elsewhere are contemporary condos with fireplaces; some have lofts and water views. Walking trails thread through the resplendent gardens and the old lime quarries. The resort is a very popular boating base, as it's an official entry point to Canada, just 15 mi to the north. ✉ *4950 Reuben Memorial Dr., Roche Harbor 98250, 10 mi northwest of Friday Harbor off Roche Harbor Rd.* ☎ *360/378–2155 or 800/451–8910* 🖷 *360/ 378–6809* ⊕ *www.rocheharbor.com* ↘ *16 rooms without bath, 14 suites, 9 cottages, 20 condos* ⟁ *Restaurant, café, coffee shop, grill, grocery, some kitchens, some minibars, some microwaves, some refrigerators, cable TV in some rooms, some in-room VCRs, tennis court, pool, dock, boating, marina, shops, playground, airstrip, travel services; no TVs in some rooms* ⊟ *AE, MC, V.*

¢ 🏛 **San Juan Inn.** Rooms in this restored 1873 inn less than a block from the ferry landing are small but serviceable. Muffins, coffee, and juice are served each morning in a parlor overlooking the harbor. The apartment-size Garden and Posey suites each have a VCR, full kitchen, and fireplace. In summer you can soak in the garden hot tub. ✉ *50 Spring St.* ⬚ *Box 776, Friday Harbor 98250* ☎ *360/378–2070 or 800/742– 8210* 🖷 *360/378–6437* ⊕ *www.sanjuaninn.com* ↘ *9 rooms, 4 with bath, 2 suites* ⟁ *Some kitchens, some in-room VCRs, outdoor hot tub; no TV in some rooms* ⊟ *MC, V* ⏣ *CP.*

Sports & the Outdoors

BEACHES **American Camp** (⊠ 6 mi southeast of Friday Harbor ☎ 360/468–3663), part of San Jaun Island National Historical Park, has 6 mi of public beach on the southern end of the island. **San Juan County Park** (⊠ 380 Westside Rd. N, Friday Harbor ☎ 360/378–2992) has a wide gravel beachfront where orcas often frolic in summer, plus grassy lawns with picnic tables and a small campground.

BICYCLES & You can rent classic, mountain, and BMX bikes for $30 per day or $100
MOPEDS per week. Prices include a helmet, although fits aren't always exact. Tandem, recumbent, and electric bikes rent for about $50 per day. Strollers, children's bikes, and child trailers are usually available as well. You can rent mopeds for $20 to $30 per hour or $60 to $70 per day. Make sure to reserve bikes and mopeds a few days ahead in summer.

Island Bicycles (⊠ 380 Argyle St., Friday Harbor ☎ 360/378–4941) is a full-service shop that rents bikes. **Island Scooter & Bike Rental** (⊠ Friday Harbor ☎ 360/378–8811) has bicycles and scooters for rent. **Susie's Mopeds** (⊠ Friday Harbor ☎ 360/378–5244 or 800/532–0087 ⊠ Roche Harbor) rents mopeds July through Labor Day at Roche Harbor and March through October in Friday Harbor.

BOATING Fees for moorage at private docks are $8 per night for boats under 26 feet long and $11 per night for larger vessels. Moorage buoys are $5 a night. Fees are paid in cash on site, while annual permits ($50–$80) are available from shops in Friday Harbor. At public docks, high-season moorage rates cost 70¢–$1.35 per foot (of vessel) per night.

Port of Friday Harbor (☎ 360/378–2688) provides marina services including guest moorage, vessel assistance and repair, bareboat and skippered charters; overnight accommodations; and whale-watching and wildlife cruises. **Roche Harbor Resort** (☎ 360/378–2155) can accommodate vessels of all sizes. A pump-out station is available, and a fuel dock provides gasoline and diesel fuel. **Snug Harbor Resort Marina** (☎ 360/378–4762) provides marina services and van service to and from Friday Harbor, including ferry and airport shuttle service, and rents small powerboats.

CHARTERS Charter sailboat cruises start at about $225 per day and run up to $400 per day for deluxe vessels. Charter powerboat trips start at about $150 per day. Extra costs for overnight cruises may include skipper fees ($150–$175), meals ($10–$15 per person daily), preboarding fees ($50–$100), spinnaker hire ($80–$100 per week), crab traps ($4–$6 each), sleeping bags ($13–$17), blanket sets ($15–$25), and towels ($6–$10).

Amante Sail Tours (☎ 360/376–4321) leads morning and afternoon sails for two to six guests. **Charters Northwest** (☎ 360/378–7196) offers three-day and week-long full-service sailboat and powerboat charters. **Harmony Sailing Charters** (☎ 360/468–3310) conducts day-long and multiday sailboat charters throughout the San Juan Islands and the Pacific Northwest. **Kismet Sailing Charters** (☎ 360/468–2435) leads overnight excursions through the San Juans and southwest Canada on a 36-foot-long customized yacht.

FISHING You can fish year-round for bass and trout at **Egg and Sportsman lakes,** both north of Friday Harbor off Roche Harbor Road.

Buffalo Works (☎ 360/378–4612) arranges saltwater fishing trips.

HORSEBACK **Saddle Up Trail Riding** (☎ 360/378–4244 or 800/722–2939) organizes
RIDING guided tours of San Juan Island on horseback. Prices begin at $49 for a two-hour tour.

SCUBA DIVING **Island Dive & Water Sports** (✉ Friday Harbor ☎ 360/378–2772), at the waterfront, is a full-service dive shop with classes, equipment, airfills, and charters. Single-tank dives cost $55 and two-tank dives cost $75, with gear included. Overnight adventure packages with two days of diving start at $200.

SEA KAYAKING Many kayakers bring their own vessels to the San Juans. If you're a beginner or didn't bring a kayak, you'll find rentals in Friday Harbor, as well as outfitters providing classes and tours. Be sure to make reservations for service in summer. One-hour trips start at $25, three-hour tours run about $45, day tours cost $90–$125, and overnight tours cost $80–$100 per day with meals. Equipment is always included.

Crystal Seas Kayaking (☎ 360/378–7899 or 888/625–7245) combines sea kayaking and sailing trips. **Doe Bay Resort** (☎ 360/376–2291) conducts guided kayak tours. **A Leisure Kayak Rentals** (☎ 360/378–5992 or 800/836–8224) will shuttle you from the ferry to the start of your kayaking class; hourly, daily, and overnight tours are also scheduled. **San Juan Kayak Expeditions** (☎ 360/378–4436) runs kayaking and camping tours in two-person kayaks. **Sea Quest** (☎ 360/378–5767 or 888/589–4253) conducts kayak ecotours.

WHALE-WATCHING Tour companies have offices near the docks at Friday Harbor or in Roche Harbor, and hotels can help you with bookings. Whale-watching expeditions run three to four hours and cost around $50 per person. **Salish Sea Charters** (☎ 360/378–8555 or 877/560–5711) has three tours per day from April through September that get you right up next to the orcas. **San Juan Excursions** (☎ 360/378–6636 or 800/809–4253) makes whale-watching cruises around the islands. **Western Prince Cruises** (☎ 360/378–5315 or 800/757–6722) operates a four-hour narrated whale-watching tour.

Shopping

Boardwalk Bookstore (✉ 5 Spring St., Friday Harbor ☎ 360/378–2787) has a good collection of popular and classic literature. **Dan Levin** (✉ 50 1st St., Friday Harbor ☎ 360/378–2051) stocks original jewelry. **Napier Sculpture Gallery** (✉ 232 A St., Friday Harbor ☎ 360/378–2221) exhibits metal sculptures. **Rainshadow Arts** (✉ 20 1st St., Friday Harbor ☎ 360/378–0988 ⊕ www.rainshadow-arts.com) displays Pacific Northwest arts and crafts: baskets, pottery, watercolors, sculpture, and photographs. **Waterworks Gallery** (✉ 315 Argyle St., Friday Harbor ☎ 360/378–3060) represents eclectic contemporary artists.

Near Friday Harbor, the **San Juan Vineyards** (✉ 2000 Roche Harbor Rd. ☎ 360/378–9463 or 888/983–9463), 3 mi north of Friday Harbor, has a winery, tasting room, and gift shop, and organizes such events as May barrel tastings, "Bottling Day" in July, volunteer grape-harvesting in October, and winter wine classes and tastings. Visit **Westcott Bay Sea Farms** (✉ 904 Westcott Dr., off Roche Harbor Rd. ☎ 360/378–2489), a rustic oyster farm tucked into a small bay 2 mi south of Roche Harbor, for some of the tasty oysters, especially November through April.

The San Juan Islands A to Z

AIR TRAVEL

AIRPORTS & TRANSFERS Port of Friday Harbor is the main San Juan Islands airport, although there are also small airports on Lopez, Shaw, and Orcas islands. Seaplanes land on the waterfront at Friday Harbor and Roche Harbor on San Juan Island, Rosario Resort and West Sound on Orcas Island, and Fisherman Bay on Lopez Island. San Juan Islands flights are linked with mainland airports at Anacortes, Bellingham, Port Angeles, and Seattle-Tacoma International (Sea-Tac).

There are taxis on Lopez, Orcas, and San Juan islands. Most hotels and B&Bs have complimentary airport pick-up and drop-off services.

🖪 Airport Information **Port of Friday Harbor Airport** ⊠ 72 Airport Circle Dr., San Juan Island ☎ 360/378-4724 ⊕ www.portfridayharbor.org/airport.

🖪 Transfer Information **A. Lopez Cab** ⊠ Lopez Island ☎ 360/468-2227. **Bob's Taxi & Tours** ⊠ San Juan Island ☎ 360/378-6777 or 877/4-TAXI-BOB. **Orcas Taxi** ⊠ Orcas Island ☎ 360/376-TAXI ⊕ www.portofpa.com/airport. **San Juan Taxi** ⊠ San Juan Island ☎ 360/378-3550.

CARRIERS The small propeller jets and seaplanes of Island Air and San Juan Airlines hop between the San Juans. Kenmore Air has seaplane flights from Seattle to all the main islands. Northwest Seaplanes has seaplane service from Renton to San Juan, Orcas, and Lopez islands. Sound Flight also connects the islands with Renton. West Isle Air flies to the main islands from Sea-Tac and Bellingham airports. Rose Air takes passengers from Portland, Oregon to the San Juans. All these airlines have charter and sightseeing flights.

🖪 **Island Air** ☎ 360/378-2376 or 888/378-2376 ⊕ www.rockisland.com/~islandair. **Kenmore Air** ☎ 206/486-1257 or 800/543-9595 ⊕ www.kenmoreair.com. **Northwest Seaplanes** ☎ 425/277-1590 or 800/690-0086 ⊕ www.rockisland.com/~islandair. **Rose Air** ☎ 503/675-7673 ⊕ www.roseair.com. **San Juan Airlines** ☎ 800/690-0086. **Sound Flight** ☎ 425/255-6500 or 800/825-0722 ⊕ www.soundflight.com. **West Isle Air** ☎ 360/293-4691 or 800/874-4434 ⊕ www.westisleair.com.

BOAT & FERRY TRAVEL

Washington State ferries depart from Anacortes, about 76 mi north of Seattle, to the San Juan Islands. Sunny weekends and summer months mean long lines of cars at ferry terminals all around the San Juan Islands. No reservations are accepted (except for the Sidney–Anacortes run from mid-May through September). Passengers and bicycles load first, and loading stops two minutes before sailing time.

The Mosquito Fleet connects Everett to Friday Harbor daily from early July through Labor Day, Thursday through Sunday in September, and weekends in October for $39.50. Humpback Hauling makes runs between the islands in summer for $95. The *San Juan Islands Shuttle Express* takes passengers from Bellingham to Orcas Island and Friday Harbor for $65 one-way. The *San Juan Island Commuter* has daily scheduled service for $35 one-way to 16 islands in the San Juans, including four islands that are state parks. The ferry also carries kayaks, bicycles, and camping equipment. April through October, the *P.S. Express* passenger-only ferry cruises daily from Port Townsend to Friday Harbor for $53 one-way. You can reach Victoria, British Columbia, from Seattle via Friday Harbor on the *Victoria Clipper* for $73 round-trip.

🖪 **Mosquito Fleet** ☎ 425/252-6800 or 800/325-6722 ⊕ www.whalewatching.com. **P.S. Express** ☎ 360/385-5288 ⊕ www.pugetsoundexpress.com. **San Juan Island Commuter** ⊠ Bellingham Cruise Terminal, 355 Harris Ave., No. 104, Bellingham ☎ 360/734-8180 or 888/734-8180. **San Juan Islands Shuttle Express** ⊠ Bellingham Cruise Terminal (a.k.a. Alaska Ferry Terminal), 355 Harris Ave., No. 105, Bellingham ☎ 360/671-1137 or 888/373-8522. **Victoria Clipper** ☎ 206/448-5000 or 800/888-2535 ⊕ www.victoriaclipper.com. **Washington State Ferries** ☎ 206/464-6400, 800/843-3779 in WA ⊕ www.wsdot.wa.gov/ferries.

CAR RENTAL

There are few car rental agencies on the islands. Angie's is the only office on Lopez. M&W is the only agency on Orcas, and they also have an office on San Juan Island. Island Petroleum Services rents cars on Orcas from June through September. Susan's Mopeds rents cars and mopeds on Orcas Island from June through September, as well as on San Juan Island at Friday Harbor from March through October and at Roche Harbor from July through Labor Day. Summer rates run $50 to $70 per day.

🚗 Local Agencies **Angie's Cab Courier** ✉ Lopez Island ☎ 360/468-2227. **Island Petroleum Services** ✉ Orcas Island ☎ 360/376-3883. **M&W Rental cars** ✉ San Juan Island ☎ 360/378-2794 or 800/323-6037 ⊕ www.interisland.net/mandw. **Susan's Mopeds** ✉ San Juan Island ☎ 360/378-5244 or 800/532-0087.

CAR TRAVEL

Island roads have one or two lanes, and all carry two-way traffic. Slow down and hug the shoulder when passing another car on a one-lane road. Expect rough patches, potholes, fallen branches, wildlife, and other hazards—plus the distractions of sweeping water views. Carry food and water, since you may want to stop frequently to explore.

To reach the San Juan Islands from Seattle, drive north on I–5 to Exit 230. From here, head west on Route 20 and follow signs to Anacortes, the mainland terminal for ferry travel to the islands. You may have to wait in long lines to take your car on the ferry. You can avoid the lines by leaving your car on the mainland and arranging for pick-up service at the island ferry terminal. Most B&B owners provide this service with prior arrangement.

EMERGENCIES

Medical clinics on San Juan, Orcas, and Lopez have several doctors on hand every weekday and Saturdays. The closest hospitals are in Anacortes or Victoria.

🚑 Fire, Medical, Police ☎ 911.

🚑 Doctors & Dentists **Inter-Island Medical Clinic** ✉ 550 Spring St., Friday Harbor, San Juan Island ☎ 360/378-2141. **Lopez Island Medical Clinic** ✉ 10 Washburn La. ☎ 360/468-2245. **Orcas Island Medical Clinic** ✉ 1269 Dove La. ☎ 360/376-2561.

🚑 Pharmacies **Friday Harbor Drug** ✉ 210 Spring St. ☎ 360/378-4421. **Lopez Island Pharmacy** ✉ Lopez Village ☎ 360/4680-2616. **Ray's Pharmacy** ✉ Eastsound, Orcas Island ☎ 360/376-2230 or 360/376-3693.

MAIL & SHIPPING

Post office hours on the San Juans are generally 8 to 4:30 or 5 on weekdays, sometimes with a 12:30–1:30 lunch break. The Orcas village and Olga offices are also open from 8 to 11 on Saturday. Mail is transported to the mainland Monday through Saturday.

📮 Post Offices **Deer Harbor Post Office** ✉ Deer Harbor Resort, Orcas Island 98243 ☎ 360/376-2548. **Eastsound Post Office** ✉ A St., Eastsound, Orcas Island 98245 ☎ 360/376-4121. **Friday Harbor Office** ✉ 220 Blair Ave., Friday Harbor, San Juan Island 98250 ☎ 360/3780-4511. **Lopez Village Post Office** ✉ 209 Weeks Rd., Lopez Village, Lopez Island 98261 ☎ 360/468-2282. **Olga Post Office** ✉ Orcas Island, 98279 ☎ 360/376-4236. **Orcas Village Post Office** ✉ 121 Killebrew Lake Rd., Orcas Island 98280 ☎ 360/376-4254. **Roche Harbor Post Office** ✉ 295 Reuben Memorial Dr., Roche Harbor, Orcas Island 98243 ☎ 360/370-7709.

MONEY MATTERS

The major bank in the San Juans is Islanders Bank, found on San Juan, Orcas, and Lopez islands. Key Bank is also on San Juan and Orcas, and Washington Federal is on Orcas as well. There are ATMs in major town shopping areas and grocery stores, including those in Friday Harbor and Roche Harbor on San Juan Island; on Orcas Island at the Orcas Island Market, the Orcas Village Store, and Ray's Pharmacy in Eastsound; and at the Village Market on Lopez Island.

🏦 Banks **Islanders Bank** ✉ 225 Blair Ave., Friday Harbor, San Juan Island ☎ 360/378-2265 ⊕ www.islanders-bank.com ✉ 475 Fern St. Eastsound, Orcas Island ☎ 360/

376-2265 ✉ 45 Weeks Rd., Lopez Village ☎ 360/468-2295. **Key Bank** ✉ 95 2nd St. S., Friday Harbor, San Juan Island ☎ 360/378-2111 ⊕ www.keybank.com ✉ 210 Main St., Eastsound, Orcas Island ☎ 360/376-2211. **Pacific Northwest Bank** ✉ 305 Argyle Ave., Friday Harbor, San Juan Island ☎ 360/378-2128 ⊕ www.pnwbank.com. **Washington Federal** ✉ Eastsound Sq., Eastsound, Orcas Island ☎ 360/376-2218.

TOURS

Numerous travel and tour agencies operate in the San Juan Islands. Walking tours of Friday Harbor, local parks, and island wineries are offered in addition to outdoor adventure and nature tours. Popular tours are those by air, speedboat, sea kayak, bicycle, and trail.

Krystal Acres Alpaca Farm can arrange tours of their scenic farm and the largest llama herd in the San Juans. The San Juan Nature Institute, Skylark, and Wescott Bay have nature tours on San Juan and other islands. Tortas & Hare covers Orcas Island. Bob's and San Juan Sightseeing can show you San Juan Island, while Island Girl has one-hour walking tours of Friday Harbor, and Soul of the San Juans offers historic tours.

🚩 Tour Operators **Bob's Taxi & Tours** ✉ 398 Spring St., San Juan Island ☎ 360/378-6777 or 877/481-94171. **Krystal Acres Alpaca Farm** ✉ 152 Blazing Tree Rd., Friday Harbor, San Juan Island ☎ 360/378-6125 ⊕ www.krystalacres.com. **San Juan Nature Institute** ✆ Box 3110, San Juan Island 98250 ☎ 360/378-3646. **San Juan Sightseeing** ✆ Box 2809, Friday Harbor, San Juan Island 98250 ☎ 360/378-8887 or 800/887-8387. **Skylark Nature Tours** ✉ 5163 Roche Harbor Rd., San Juan Island ☎ 360/378-3068. **Soul of the San Juans** ✉ San Juan Island ☎ 360/378-2942 or 800/874-4434. **Tortas & Hare Escursions** ✉ Orcas Island ☎ 360/376-2464.

VISITOR INFORMATION

🚩 **Lopez Island Chamber of Commerce** ✉ Box 102, Washington 98261 ☎ 360/468-4664 ⊕ www.lopezisland.com. **Orcas Island Chamber of Commerce** ✉ Box 252, Eastsound 98245 ☎ 360/376-2273 ⊕ www.orcasisland.org. **San Juan Island Chamber of Commerce** ✆ Box 98, Friday Harbor 98250 ☎ 360/378-5240 ⊕ www.sanjuanisland.org. **San Juan Islands Visitors Bureau** ✆ Box 98, Friday Harbor 98250 ☎ 360/468-3748 ⊕ www.sanjuanislander.com.

THE OLYMPIC PENINSULA

Updated by
Holly S. Smith

Wilderness covers much of the rugged Olympic Peninsula, the westernmost corner of the continental United States. Its heart of craggy mountains and a 60-mi strech of its ocean shore are safeguarded in Olympic National Park, 95% of which is designated wilderness land. Several thousand acres more are protected in Olympic National Forest, five wilderness areas, and seven Indian reservations.

This is a landscape whose primeval ecosystem has remained in large part intact, and it's a land of almost incredible variety. The rain forest of the western river valleys soaks up 140 to 167 inches of precipitation per year, while the dry slopes of the northeastern peninsula, in the so-called "rain shadow" of the mountains, generally receive fewer than 16 inches. With some of the wettest and driest climates in the coastal Pacific Northwest, the peninsula supports a great diversity of plants and animals.

At its southwestern corner, the peninsula is defined by Grays Harbor, Washington's second largest estuary and one of only eight natural harbors between Mexico and Canada. The harbor is named for discoverer and fur trader Robert Gray, who in 1792 became the first European-American to enter the harbor. Two long, forested sand spits separate and protect Grays Harbor from the fury of the Pacific Ocean.

Although rugged terrain and a lack of roads make much of the Olympic Peninsula's interior accessible only to backpackers, the 300-mi-long outer loop of U.S. 101 provides fabulous views over ocean, rain forest, and mountains. Side roads provide excellent opportunities for exploring remote villages, beaches, and valleys. The following section describes a clockwise journey, primarily via U.S. 101, beginning and ending in Olympia.

Montesano

❶ *30 mi west of Olympia.*

Montesano was settled in 1852 at the confluence of the Chehalis, Satsop, and Wynoochee rivers. Steamboats churned through the river passages from 1859 until railroad tracks arrived in 1885. When the town was incorporated in 1870, its population had reached about 1,500. You can still pick up a copy of the town newspaper, the *Vidette*, which published its first issue in 1883. Montesano became the Grays Harbor County seat in 1886. The town has a historic district with several buildings dating from the late 19th and early 20th centuries, including the Mission Revival–style Montesano City Hall, built in 1914.

In 1900 Frederick Weyerhaeuser and 15 partners began the Weyerhaeuser timber company with 900,000 acres of Washington forestland. Forty years later, the company purchased 200,000 acres near Montesano and established the Clemons Tree Farm, the world's first. Today the Weyerhaeuser Company ships paper and lumber worldwide and is one of Washington's most profitable firms, and Montesano dubs itself the "Home of the Tree Farm."

The enormous, sandstone **Grays Harbor County courthouse** seems exceptionally grand for such a small town, but it was entirely appropriate at the time it was built, between 1909 and 1912, when Montesano was a prosperous railroad boomtown. Its clock tower soars above the classical, pillared entrance. The lobby has a marble staircase flanked by murals depicting Robert Gray in 1792, discovering the harbor that bears his name, and Territorial Governor Isaac Stevens negotiating with Native Americans at Cosmopolis in 1855. The murals inaccurately depict native people wearing feather headdresses and standing in front of tepees (neither was used by the local Chehalis). ✉ *102 W. Broadway* ☎ *360/249–3441* 🎟 *Free* 🕐 *Weekdays 8–5.*

Where to Stay & Eat

¢ ✕ **Savory Faire.** Homemade sandwiches, salads, soups, and quiches are on order in the French-style café. The home-baked breads and desserts, including gooey cinnamon rolls and amaretto bread pudding, are famous around the peninsula. Breakfasts are hearty and home-style. ✉ *135 S. Main St.* ☎ *360/249–3701* ▱ *AE, D, MC, V* 🕐 *No dinner.*

¢ ▦ **Abel House.** This 1908 white-stucco-and-stone manor house, now a B&B, is surrounded by a lovely English garden. Pastel walls, wood trim, and handmade quilts distinguish the country-style rooms, one of which has a private bath. You can relax in the sitting room before the fireplace, pick out tunes on the piano, or shoot pool in the game room. ✉ *117 Fleet St. S, 98563* ☎ *360/249–6002 or 800/235–2245* ⊕ *www. abelhouse.com* ⇗ *5 rooms, 1 with bath* ♨ *Dining room, billiards, piano, recreation room, meeting room; no room phones, no room TVs, no smoking* ▱ *AE, D, MC, V* ⦿❙ *BP.*

Aberdeen

❷ *6 mi west of Montesano.*

The pretty town of Aberdeen, on Grays Harbor at the mouth of the Chehalis River, was settled in 1867 by farmers. Some of the earliest residents were Scottish immigrants who suggested the site be named Aberdeen after the city in Scotland also on a harbor at the mouth of a river. Growth and prosperity came to the town after Scotsman George R. Hume started a salmon cannery here in 1878 and the town's first sawmill was built in 1884. Soon tall ships crowded the narrow harbor to load lumber, and waterfront bars were busy with sailors and lumberjacks.

Early homesteaders found the cleared forest land too soggy from the heavy, year-round rains to support most crops; however, one product did do well—cranberries, planted in the bogs, thrived (and still do today). Other farmers turned to cultivating oysters in the shallow harbor bays. In 1903 most of Aberdeen's buildings, made of wood and surrounded by streets of sawdust, burned down during a dry spell. These were replaced with stone and brick buildings, many of which still stand in the downtown area.

Aberdeen is known for its lovely harbor and forest backdrop. You can tour and even sail on the *Lady Washington*, a replica 18th-century brig used in the 2003 Disney film *Pirates of the Caribbean*. And you can wander the streets in the footsteps of the late Kurt Cobain, who lived in Aberdeen prior to his fame as lead singer for the 1990s Seattle grunge group Nirvana.

The small **Aberdeen Museum of History** has canoes from local tribes, as well as photographs that document Aberdeen's logging and shipping industries. ⊠ *111 E. 3rd St.* ☎ *360/533–1976* 🖃 *Donations accepted* ⊘ *June–Labor Day, Wed.–Sun. 11–4; Labor Day–May, weekends noon–4.*

Strolling along the 1½-mi-long, paved **Morrison Riverfront Park Walk** is one of the most pleasant ways to see Aberdeen and the Wishkah and Chehalis rivers. Along the way, look for the 40-foot-wide **Compass Rose**, a giant compass in the ground at the rivers' confluence. ⊠ *Heron St. at the Wishkah River* ☎ *No phone* 🖃 *Free* ⊘ *Daily.*

Tall, billowing white sails in the harbor mark the presence of the *Lady Washington*, a replica of Robert Gray's wooden 90-ton brig *Columbia*, which sailed to the northwestern United States in 1792. The replica was converted into a multimasted sloop renamed the *HMS Interceptor* for the 2002 Disney movie *Pirates of the Caribbean*. You can tour the ship from deck to bunks, take a three-hour cruise, or even volunteer as a deckhand for one of the boat's frequent multiday trips around western Washington waters. Check the schedule before visiting, as the ship may be in another Puget Sound or Columbia River port. ⊠ *712 Hagara St.* ☎ *360/200–5239* ⊕ *www.ladywashington.org* 🖃 *Tours free 3-hr sails $40* ⊘ *Hrs vary.*

Where to Stay & Eat

$–$$$ ✕ **Bridges.** This café takes its name not from its location between the Wishkah and Chehalis river spans but from owner Sonny Bridges, who's been running local restaurants for more than 30 years. This is a classy, pastel-hue place with excellent seafood and huge steaks. ⊠ *112 N. G St.* ☎ *360/532–6563* ☐ *AE, D, DC, MC, V* ⊘ *No lunch weekends.*

$–$$$ ✕ **Parma.** This storefront restaurant serves Italian cuisine. Everything tastes authentic, from the spinach gnocchi to the wild boar with polenta.

Seafood complements the fresh pasta, made right on the premises. Grilled specialties include steaks, chops, and sausages. ✉ *116 W. Heron St.* ☎ *360/532–3166* ⊟ *AE, D, MC, V* ⊘ *Closed Sun. and Mon.*

$–$$ ✕ **Billy's.** This bar and grill used to be the most popular saloon and brothel in town, and the restaurant has a collection of prints recalling those bawdy days. Even the establishment's name was taken from the saloon's notorious owner, Billy Ghol. It's said his ghost haunts the premises. Standard fare includes burgers and salads, but you can go exotic with grilled yak. ✉ *322 E. Heron St.* ☎ *360/533–7144* ⊟ *AE, DC, MC, V.*

¢–$ ▦ **Aberdeen Mansion.** Surrounded by an acre of landscaped lawns and gardens, this 1905 turretted mansion was originally the home of Edward Hulbert, who made a fortune in the lumber industry. Wood floors, antiques, and nautical memorabilia accent the comfortable rooms, the largest of which is 500 square feet. Two rooms share a bath the carriage house out back is perfect for groups. ✉ *807 N. M St., 98520* ☎ *360/533–7079* 🖨 *360/537–9607* ⊕ *www.aberdeenmansion.com* ➟ *5 rooms, 3 with bath* ⟁ *Dining room, cable TV, in-room VCRs, library, free parking; no a/c, no room phones, no kids under 12, no smoking* ⊟ *AE, D, MC, V* �ΟΙ *BP.*

¢–$ ▦ **Guest House International Suites and Inn.** Three stories high and overlooking the Wishkah River, this white, peaked-roof inn looks more like a mansion than a chain hotel. Rooms, which all have VCRs and kitchenettes, are roomy and bright, with shades of cream and blue. Larger suites have fireplaces and Jacuzzis. The Wishkah Mall and the city center are just steps away. ✉ *701 E. Heron St., 98520* ☎ *360/537–7460 or 800/214–8378* 🖨 *360/537–7462* ⊕ *www.guesthouse.net* ➟ *87 rooms, 12 suites* ⟁ *In-room data ports, kitchenettes, microwaves, refrigerators, cable TV, in-room VCRs, pool, gym, hot tub, dry cleaning, laundry facilities, laundry service, business services, meeting rooms, some pets allowed (fee)* ⊟ *AE, D, MC, V* ΟΙ *CP.*

¢ ▦ **A Harbor View Inn.** You can see the harbor from every room in this 1905 Victorian mansion. Hand-stenciled walls surround the elegant parlors, where three fireplaces warm the air on cool autumn evenings. Sun rooms bring in the light to help a variety of plants flourish. Take the ballroom staircase to the old-fashioned rooms, where handmade quilts cover the antique beds. ✉ *11 W. 11th St., 98520* ☎ *360/533–7996 or 877/533–7996* 🖨 *360/533–0433* ⊕ *www.aharborview.com* ➟ *4 rooms* ⟁ *Dining room, cable TV; no a/c, no room phones, no kids under 8, no smoking* ⊟ *AE, MC, V* ΟΙ *BP.*

Westport

❸ *15 mi southwest of Aberdeen.*

Westport is a bayfront fishing village on the southern spit that helps protect the entrance to Grays Harbor from the fury of the Pacific Ocean. Numerous charter companies based here offer salmon, lingcod, rockfish, and albacore fishing trips, as well as whale-watching tours. If you're not taking a cruise, you can stand on Westport's beach to look for gray whales migrating southbound in November and December, toward their breeding grounds in Baja California, and northbound in April and May, toward their feeding grounds in the Bering Sea. Some swim quite close to the beach to dig for clams in the shallows. The serene beach is perfect for walking, surfing, or kite-flying—although it's too dangerous for swimming and too cold for sunbathing. In winter it's one of the best spots on the coast to watch oncoming storms.

⟲ Westport Aquarium has exhibits of local marine life, including a wolf eel, an octopus, and a dog shark. Touch tanks let you feel shells, starfish, anemones, and other sea creatures. You can even hand-feed two live seals. ⊠ *321 Harbor St.* ☎ *360/268–0471* ⊕ ☜ *$4* ☉ *Apr.–Oct., daily 10–5; Nov.–Mar. weekends 10–5.*

In a former Coast Guard station, the **Westport Maritime Museum** displays historic photos, equipment, clothing, and other relics from the life-saving service and such local industries as fishing, logging, and cranberry farming. Among the exhibits is a collection of sea mammal bones, and the 17-foot-tall Destruction Island Lens, a lighthouse beacon that was built in 1888 and weighs almost six tons. ⊠ *2201 Westhaven Dr.* ☎ *360/268–0078* ☎ *360/438–3224* ⊕ *www.westportwa.com/museum* ☜ *$2* ☉ *Memorial Day–Labor Day, daily 10–4; Labor Day–Memorial Day, Thurs.–Mon. noon–4.*

At 107 feet (123 feet above the water), the octagonal **Grays Harbor Lighthouse,** built in 1898, is the tallest on the Washington coast. It stands on Coast Guard–owned land, adjacent to Westport Light State Park, a day-use park with picnic tables and a beach. The interior is closed to the public. ⊠ *Ocean Ave.* ☎ *360/268–0078* ☜ *Free* ☉ *Daily sunrise–sunset.*

Westport's **Harbor Walkway** is a 2-mi-long paved promenade that winds along the sandy beach. ⊠ *Ocean Ave. between Grays Harbor Lighthouse and West Haven State Park.*

Where to Stay & Eat

$ ✕ **The Diner.** Only a few steps from the lighthouse, this eatery is a favorite of beach strollers. Fresh clam chowder and fish—much of it caught just offshore—are menu highlights. Home-baked pastries, some made with local cranberries, are the perfect endings. ⊠ *389 W. Ocean Ave.* ☎ *360/268–6097* ▤ *D, MC, V* ☉ *No dinner Sun.–Wed.*

¢ 🏨 **Chateau Westport Motel.** This big motel sits near the dunes and is perfect for families who want a base near the beach. Rooms are large and have contemporary furniture; some have fireplaces and kitchenettes. ⊠ *710 Hancock, 98595* ☎ *360/268–9101 or 800/255–9101* ☎ *360/ 268–1646* ⊕ *www.chateauwestport.com* ➫ *108 rooms, 2 suites* ☖ *In-room data ports, cable TV, some kitchenettes, indoor pool, hot tub, volleyball, playground, meeting rooms; no smoking* ▤ *AE, D, DC, MC, V* ⱺ *CP.*

¢ 🏨 **Harbor Resort.** Right next to the water, this two-story hotel offers prime views of seals, seabirds, and even whales. Cottages, all overlooking the bay, have soaring cathedral ceilings, plus fans, full kitchens, and bay windows with water views. Even the standard rooms have kitchenettes and decks looking out to sea. ⊠ *Float 20, 98595* ☎ *360/268–0169* ☎ *360/ 268–0338* ⊕ *www.harborresort.com* ➫ *7 rooms, 7 cottages* ☖ *Some kitchens or kitchenettes, some microwaves, some refrigerators, cable TV, some pets allowed (fee)* ▤ *AE, D, MC, V.*

Hoquiam

❹ *10 mi west of Aberdeen.*

Hoquiam (pronounced *hoh*-quee-ahm) is a historic lumber town near Aberdeen and the mouth of the Hoquiam River. Both river and town were named for the Chehalis word meaning "hungry for wood." The town was settled in the mid 19th century, around the same time as Aberdeen, and is now a major Grays Harbor port for cargo and fishing vessels. Its industries include canneries and manufacturers of wood products and machine tools.

In fall and spring, **Grays Harbor National Wildlife Refuge** is a perfect place to observe the multitude of migrating shorebirds that visit Grays Harbor. Keep your binoculars handy as you stroll along the 1,800-foot-long boardwalk. To get there from Hoquiam, drive west on Route 109 to Pawlson Road, then turn left and continue to Airport Way, where you make a right toward the refuge. ⊠ *Airport Way* ☎ *360/753–9467* ⌨ *Free* ☉ *Daily sunrise–sunset.*

The Polson Museum, in a 26-room mansion built in 1924, is filled with artifacts and mementos relating to Grays Harbor's past. You can walk through the remodeled dining room, kitchen, and living room, where an exhibit traces the history of tall ships in the Pacific Northwest. Upstairs is the logging exhibit, with a replica Little Hoquiam Railroad; a period-costume room; and the Polson children's room and doll house. Outside you can wander the riverside grounds, which have exotic trees and a rose garden. ⊠ *1611 Riverside Ave.* ☎🖨 *360/533–5862* ⊕ *www. polsonmuseum.org* ⌨ *$2* ☉ *June–Aug., Wed.–Sun. 11–4; Sept.–May, weekends noon–4.*

Where to Stay & Eat

$ ✕ **Duffy's Number Three.** The Duffy's name is so popular in nearby Aberdeen that the owners expanded their reach with this third branch. Steaks, chops, burgers, and salmon are great standbys. If you want to branch out, try the Swedish pancakes. The perfect finish is a slice of wild-blackberry pie. Come for breakfast to get in on the town's gossip. ⊠ *825 Simpson Ave.* ☎ *360/532–1519* ▱ *AE, D, DC, MC, V.*

$ ▦ **Hoquiam's Castle Bed & Breakfast.** A registered National Historic Site, this imposing, 10,000-square-foot Victorian mansion was built in 1887 by lumber baron Robert Lytle. Three floors and 28 rooms are filled with exquisite antique and reproduction furnishings, including crystal chandeliers, Tiffany-style lamps, stained-glass windows, and canopy beds. The charming bedrooms overlook the town and harbor. Nonguests can take a tour, scheduled on the hour from 11 to 3 daily, for $4. ⊠ *515 Chenault Ave., 98550* ☎ *360/533–2005* ⊕ *www.hoquiamscastle.com* ☞ *5 rooms* ⚒ *Dining room, recreation room; no a/c, no room phones, no room TVs, no kids under 12, no smoking* ▱ *AE, D, MC, V* ⦿| *BP.*

¢–$ ▦ **Lytle House.** Lumber lord Joseph Lytle built this Queen Anne mansion around 1900 next door to his brother Robert's home, Hoquiam Castle. Today you can see much of the house's original woodwork and furnishings in the guest rooms, two of which share a bath. Two parlors separate a quiet reading area from a more social TV room. Children can frolic outside with the dog, cats, and rabbit. Family-style breakfasts are enormous, with eggs, fruit, and fresh baked goods. ⊠ *509 Chenault Ave., 98550* ☎ *360/533–2320 or 800/677–2320* 🖨 *360/533–4025* ☞ *8 rooms, 6 with bath* ⚒ *Dining room, hot tub, business services; no a/c, no room phones, no room TVs* ▱ *AE, DC, MC, V* ⦿| *BP.*

Ocean Shores

❺ *18 mi west of Hoquiam, 4 mi northwest of Westport.*

Ocean Shores, on the northern spit that encloses Grays Harbor, differs from other communities along the North Beach stretch of the county in that it was deliberately organized by housing developers in the 1960s after sand carried in by the ocean widened the spit. This natural process has reversed itself in recent years, however, and residents are scrambling to save their homes and condominiums from the encroaching surf. As long as the land is there, this seaside resort town offers wide beaches, a gorgeous golf course, canals with boat moorage, lively restaurants, and comfortable, quality hotels.

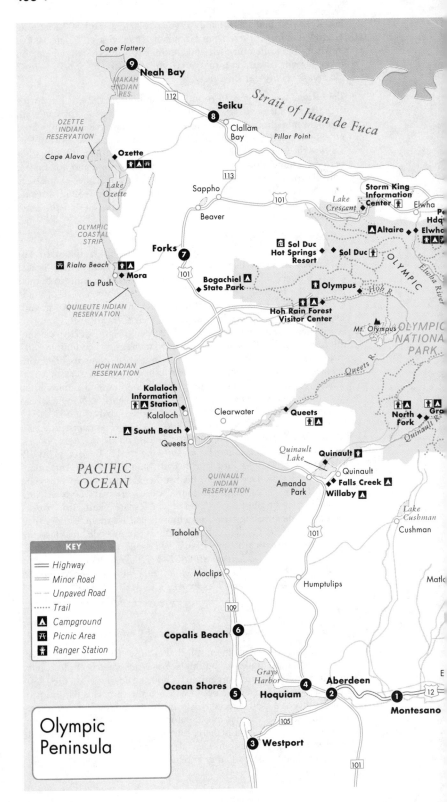

Cape Flattery

9 Neah Bay

MAKAH INDIAN RES.

112

8 Seiku

Clallam Bay

Strait of Juan de Fuca

Pillar Point

OZETTE INDIAN RESERVATION

Cape Alava

Ozette

Lake Ozette

Sappho

113

101

Beaver

Lake Crescent

Storm King Information Center

Elwha

P Hdq

Altaire

Elwha

OLYMPIC COASTAL STRIP

Forks 7

Rialto Beach

La Push

Mora

101

QUILEUTE INDIAN RESERVATION

Sol Duc Hot Springs Resort

Sol Duc

Bogachiel State Park

Olympus

Hoh Rain Forest Visitor Center

Hoh R.

OLYMPIC

Elwha River

HOH INDIAN RESERVATION

Mt. Olympus

OLYMPIC NATIONAL PARK

Queets R.

Kalaloch Information Station

Kalaloch

Clearwater

Queets

North Fork

Gra

Quinault R.

South Beach

Queets

Quinault Lake

Quinault

PACIFIC OCEAN

QUINAULT INDIAN RESERVATION

Amanda Park

Quinault

Falls Creek

Willaby

Lake Cushman

Cushman

Taholah

101

Moclips

Humptulips

Matl

109

Copalis Beach 6

Grays Harbor

Ocean Shores 5

Hoquiam

4

Aberdeen

2

1

12

Montesano

105

3 Westport

101

KEY

— Highway
═ Minor Road
--- Unpaved Road
···· Trail
▲ Campground
🎋 Picnic Area
👤 Ranger Station

Olympic Peninsula

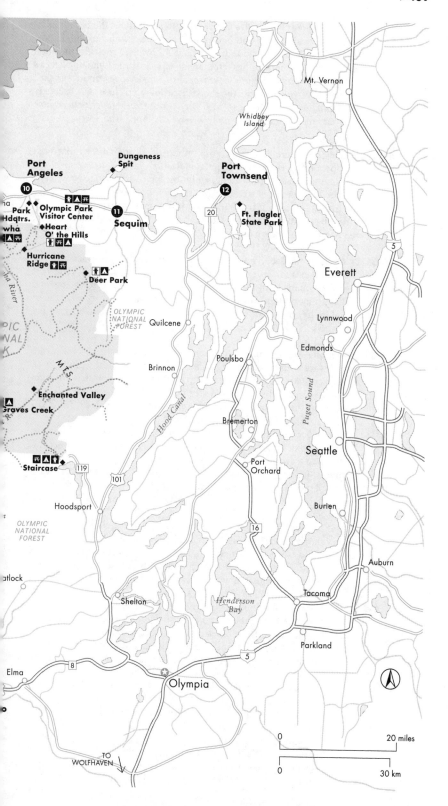

Mt. Vernon

Whidbey
Island

**Port
Angeles**

**Dungeness
Spit**

**Port
Townsend**

10

12

na

**Park
Hdqtrs.**

**Olympic Park
Visitor Center**

11

20

Sequim

**Ft. Flagler
State Park**

wha

**Heart
O' the Hills**

**Hurricane
Ridge**

Deer Park

Everett

Olympic River

OLYMPIC
NATIONAL
FOREST

Quilcene

Lynnwood

PIC
NAL
K

M T S.

Brinnon

Poulsbo

Edmonds

Puget Sound

Enchanted Valley

Graves Creek

Hood Canal

Bremerton

Seattle

Staircase

119

Port
Orchard

101

Hoodsport

16

Burien

OLYMPIC
NATIONAL
FOREST

Auburn

atlock

Shelton

*Henderson
Bay*

Tacoma

Elma

8

5

Parkland

Olympia

TO
WOLFHAVEN

0   20 miles

0   30 km

At **Ocean Shores Interpretive Center** you can learn about the seaside environment, local history, and Native American traditions through hands-on exhibits. Displays include dried local wildflowers, a rock identification table, Native American basketry, and a model of the Quinault River's Chow Chow Bridge. Reproduction seabirds, whale bones, and a vast shell collection let you examine the shoreline wildlife up close. ☒ *Discovery and Catala Aves.* ☎ *360/289–4617* ⊕ *www.oceanshoresinterpretivecenter. com* ☒ *Free* ☉ *May–Sept., daily 11–4; Oct.–Apr., Wed.–Mon. 1–4.*

Where to Stay & Eat

$–$$$ ✕ **Emily's Restaurant.** Warm colors, subdued lighting, and wraparound windows bring elegance to Quinault Resort's largest dining spot. Tables line tiers facing the Pacific, and most have spectacular views. The Northwest-theme menu emphasizes seasonal seafood and produce, like the melt-in-your-mouth salmon with honey–cider glaze, and the Dungeness Bay crab pot, stocked with crab claws, shrimp, and hunks of fish, red potatoes, and corn on the cob. ☒ *78 Rte. 115, 98569* ☎ *360/289–9466 or 888/461–2214* ▭ *AE, D, DC, MC, V.*

$–$$ ✕ **Alec's by the Sea.** This popular restaurant conveniently set between town and beach serves some of the region's best seafood. The best dishes are made with locally caught seafood, such as razor clams and Willapa Bay oysters. For a light meal, try the garlic bread served with bouillabaise, or one of the salads. Steaks and burgers are also on the menu. ☒ *131 E. Chance a la Mer Blvd.* ☎ *360/289–4026* ▭ *AE, D, DC, MC, V.*

¢–$$ ✕ **Mariah's Restaurant.** You can walk to this restaurant at the Polynesian Resort from the adjacent beach. The focus is on local seafood, with appetizers like Dungeness crab dip spread on baguettes, and main courses like grilled salmon and steamed shellfish. The prime rib is as popular as the seafood. ☒ *615 Ocean Shores Blvd. NW* ☎ *360/289–3315* ▭ *AE, D, DC, MC, V* ☉ *No lunch.*

★ $–$$ ✕ **Mike's Seafood.** Here you can wander through the seafood shop to see what's cooking before you sit down in the adjacent restaurant. Everything served is fresh-caught that day, and salmon is smoked on the premises. Italian specialties round out the menu—one of the best ways to sample is all is in the tomato-based cioppino. ☒ *830 Point Brown Ave.* ☎ *360/289–0532* ▭ *AE, D, MC, V* ☉ *Closed Mon.–Thurs. Dec.–Apr.*

¢–$ ✕ **Galway Bay.** With gray skies outside this authentic-looking pub, and savory shepherd's pie or Irish stew steaming before you, it seems as though the Emerald Isle is closer than you thought. Even breakfast is done in traditional fashion, with porridge and eggs, bangers, and soda bread. There's live Celtic music on weekend nights. ☒ *676 Ocean Shores Blvd. NW, Suite 3* ☎ *360/298–2300* ▭ *AE, MC, V.*

¢–$ ✕ **Our Place.** Home-cooked comfort food warms bellies at this little café. If you're on the run in the morning, grab a gooey pastry and coffee. If you can linger, dig into an omelette with a side of home fries or corned beef hash. Stacked sandwiches, juicy burgers, and combination salads are lunchtime highlights. ☒ *676 Ocean Shores Blvd. NW* ☎ *360/289–8783* ▭ *MC, V* ☉ *No dinner.*

★ $–$$ ⛉ **Quinault Beach Resort & Casino.** A half-mile of dunes and wild beach grasses separate this enormous resort from the crowds. Shades of green, grey, and gold appear throughout the rooms, which all have 9-foot ceilings, gas fireplaces, twin bathroom sinks, and large-screen TVs. The full-service spa has private sauna and Jacuzzi rooms and an oceanview patio. Surrounded by 200 acres of protected wetlands, there's plenty of room to swim, hike, and watch for wildlife. ☒ *78 Rte. 115, 98569* ☎ *360/289–9466 or 888/461–2214* ⊕ *www.quinaultbchresort.com* ⮂ *150* *rooms, 9 suites* ♁ *Restaurant, coffee shop, room service, some in-room hot tubs, in-room data ports, some kitchenettes, minibars, microwaves, refrigerators, cable TV, in-room VCRs, pool, hot tub, massage, sauna, spa, beach, billiards, lounge, cabaret, casino, dance club, shops, dry cleaning, laundry service, Internet, business services, meeting rooms* ▭ *AE, D, DC, MC, V.*

$ **Grey Gull.** This post-modern beach resort is within walking distance of all of the town's restaurants and shops. Rooms range from efficiencies to one- and two-bedroom units and a penthouse; all have kitchens, fireplaces, waterfront patios, and ocean views. Trails from the hotel lead to the beach. ✉ *651 Ocean Shores Blvd., 98569* ☎ *360/289–3381 or 800/562–9712* 🖷 *360/289–3673* 🌐 *www.thegreygull.com* *24 rooms, 6 1-bedroom units, 6 2-bedroom units, 1 penthouse* ♁ *In-room data ports, kitchenettes, refrigerators, cable TV, pool, hot tub, sauna, laundry facilities, business services, some pets allowed (fee), no-smoking rooms; no a/c* ▭ *AE, D, DC, MC, V.*

$ **Polynesian Resort.** You're only a short stroll through the dunes from the ocean at this resort, replete with modern amenities. Rooms, done in hues of beige and pearl, have fireplaces, kitchens, and private balconies; those on the upper floors have views of the water. When they're not on the sand, kids of every age hang out at the pool and in the game room. The adjacent park has basketball and volleyball courts and a picnic area. A Continental breakfast is included on weekdays. ✉ *615 Ocean Shores, 98569* ☎ *360/289–3361 or 800/562–4836* 🌐 *www.thepolynesian.com* *71 rooms* ♁ *Restaurant, picnic area, kitchenettes, microwaves, refrigerators, cable TV, pool, hot tub, sauna, beach, basketball, volleyball, recreation room, some pets allowed, no-smoking rooms* ▭ *AE, D, DC, MC, V.*

¢–$ **Discovery Inn Condos.** The connected apartments that make up this complex overlook either the ocean or the property's private dock. Studios have modern furnishings and most have kitchenettes and pull-out sofas. One-bedroom units have fireplaces and full kitchens. In the center of the complex are a pool, game room, and glassed-in hot tub with water views. The beach, Damon Point bird sanctuary, and Westport ferry dock are all within walking distance. ✉ *1031 Discovery Ave. SE, 98569* ☎ *360/289–3371 or 800/882–8821* 🌐 *www.oceanshores.com/discovery* *16 studios, 8 1-bedroom units* ♁ *Some kitchens, some kitchenettes, cable TV, pool, hot tub, dock, boating, fishing, Ping-Pong, recreation room, some pets allowed (fee)* ▭ *AE, DC, MC, V.*

¢–$ **Silver Waves Inn Bed & Breakfast.** This pretty white house, surrounded by a white picket fence and fronted by a fountain, stands next to the Grand Canal. The foyer opens into the Grand Lobby, warmed by a fireplace, and a few steps farther is a waterside sunroom. Each guest room is individually decorated. The Captain's Room has a deck, while the Queen Anne Room has two twin-size trundle beds and canal views. Those with pets can stay in the cottage behind the house. ✉ *982 Point Brown Ave. SE, 98569* ☎ *360/289–2490 or 888/257–0894* 🖷 *360/289–9291* 🌐 *www.silverwavesbandb.com* *4 rooms, 1 cottage* ♁ *Cable TV, some pets allowed (fee); no a/c, no room phones, no smoking* ▭ *AE, MC, V* 🍽 *BP.*

Copalis Beach

❻ *3 mi north of Ocean Shores.*

A Native American village for several thousand years, this small coastal town at the mouth of the Copalis (pronounced coh-*pah*-liss) River was settled by European-Americans in the 1890s. The beach here is known locally for its innumerable razor clams, which can be gathered by the thousands each summer, and for its watchtowers, built between 1870 and 1903 to spot and stalk sea otters—the animals are now protected by Washington state law. The first oil well in the state was dug here in 1901, but it proved to be unproductive. However, some geologists still claim that the continental shelf off the Olympic Peninsula holds major oil reserves.

You can hike or ride horses at **Griffiths-Priday Ocean State Park,** a 364-acre marine park stretching more than a mile along both the Pacific Ocean and the Copalis River. A boardwalk crosses low dunes to the broad, flat beach. The Copalis Spit section of the park is a designated wildlife refuge for thousands of snowy plover and other bird life. ⊠ *3119 Rte. 109* ☎ *360/902–8500 or 800/233–0321* ⊙ *Daily sunrise–sunset.*

Pacific Beach State Park, between Copalis Beach and the town of Moclips, is a lovely spot for walking, surf-perch fishing, and razor-clam digging. There's also excellent fishing for sea-run cutthroat trout in the Moclips River—but be careful not to trespass onto Indian land, as the Quinault Reservation starts north of the river. The park has developed tent and RV sites, as well as a few primitive beachfront campsites. ⊠ *Rte. 109 S, 5 mi north of Copalis Beach* ☎ *360/289-3553* ⊠ *Free* ⊙ *Daily sunrise–sunset.*

Moclips, 8 mi north of Copalis Beach, is a small, windswept beach town at the edge of the Quinault Reservation. Storm watchers, beachcombers, clammers, and surfers head to the string of magnificent, surf-tossed sands that begin here and run north along Route 109. The highway ends 8 mi north of Moclips at Taholah in the reservation; note that only tribal members are allowed to leave the main road. Non-members must contact the tribal office for permission to go onto Quinault land, including the beach.

Museum of the North Beach houses artifacts and mementos, such as turn-of-the-20th-century newspaper clippings and an old gas pump, from the communities of Copalis Beach, Ocean Shores, and Moclips, among others, as well as crafts from the nearby Quinault Indian Nation. ⊠ *4658 Rte. 109* ☎ *360/276-4441* ⊕ *www.moclips.org/museum.php* ⊠ *Free* ⊙ *May–Sept., Fri.–Mon. 10–4; Oct.–Apr., weekends 11–4.*

The **Quinault Pride Fish House,** famous for its environmentally conscious practices, harvests seafood from Quinault tribal lands. Goods include fresh, canned, and smoked salmon and steelhead, plus Quinault arts and crafts. If you're overwhelmed with the choices, get one of the gift packs, which combine a range of ocean delicacies. Sales proceeds benefit the Quinault Indian Nation. ⊠ *100 Quinault, Taholah* ☎ *360/276-4431 or 888/821-8650.*

Where to Stay & Eat

¢ ✕ **Green Lantern Tavern.** The Copalis River flows beside this high-energy local favorite, in business since the 1930s. Huge picture windows show off pristine views and the outdoor beer garden attracts beachgoers in summer. Although clams are the specialty—witness the 10-foot-long clam-digging shovel in the corner—BLTs, grilled cheese, and fried or grilled fish are also on the menu. Breakfast also is served. You must be 21 to enter. ⊠ *3119 Rte. 109* ☎ *360/289-2297* ⊟ *No credit cards.*

¢–$ ✕⊡ **Ocean Crest Resort.** On a 100-foot-high bluff, this casual, weathered hotel overlooks a stunning stretch of the coast. Accommodations in six buildings range from single, viewless rooms to large studios with good views and fireplaces to family cottages with complete kitchens. Beach access is down a maze of steps. Moss-covered trees frame the ocean views from the restaurant ($–$$$), where local seafood is served with rich sauces.

Steak, lamb, pasta, and huge breakfasts are also available. ✉ *4651 Rte. 109, Moclips 98562* ☎ *360/276–4465* 📠 *360/276–4149* ⊕ *www. oceancrestresort.com* 🛏 *32 rooms, 13 cottages* ♿ *Restaurant, cable TV, indoor pool, health club, hot tub, massage, sauna, bar, shop, meeting rooms, some pets allowed (fee); no smoking* ▭ *AE, D, MC, V.*

¢–$ 🖼 **Iron Springs Resort.** Simple cottages on the beach and in the forest make up this rustic vacation spot. Newer units are bright and comfortable, but older ones can be dimly lit and have a hodgepodge of retro furniture. There are units for 2 to 10 people, and all have kitchens and fireplaces. You can rent a television at the small shop, which also cooks up fresh cinnamon rolls and clam chowder. ✉ *3707 Rte. 109, 3 mi north of Copalis Beach, 98535* ☎ *360/276–4230* 📠 *360/276–4365* ⊕ *www. ironspringsresort.com* 🛏 *25 units* ♿ *Kitchens, indoor pool, beach, badminton, shop, some pets allowed (fee); no room phones, no room TVs* ▭ *AE, MC, V.*

¢–$ 🖼 **Sandpiper Beach Resort.** This resort is on a secluded beach 3 mi south of Moclips. The clean, contemporary studios and one-, two-, and three-bedroom suites each have a fireplace, a kitchen, exposed wood ceilings, and sliding glass doors leading to a porch overlooking the ocean. Little extras include heated towel bars. Housekeeping service is every third day. You can get coffee and do a little shopping at the on-site Espresso Bar and Gift Gallery. ✉ *4159 Rte. 109, Pacific Beach 98571* ☎ *360/ 276–4580 or 800/567–4737* 📠 ⊕ *www.sandpiper-resort.com* 🛏 *31 suites* ♿ *Coffee shop, some in-room hot tubs, kitchenettes, microwaves, refrigerators, shop, some pets allowed (fee); no a/c, no room phones, no room TVs, no smoking* ▭ *MC, V.*

¢ 🖼 **Echoes of the Sea.** This basic, one-story motel stands on 8 acres of wooded land just north of Copalis and is a ¾-mi walk from the beach. One- and two-bedroom units have living areas, kitchens, and queen-size beds. A common room provides space to watch TV, cook for a group, or play games. Several camping and RV sites are also on property. ✉ *3208 Rte. 109, 98535* ☎ *360/289–3358 or 800/578–3246* ⊕ *www. wa-accommodations.com/nw/echoes* 🛏 *8 rooms, 40 tent sites, 24 RV sites* ♿ *Picnic area, kitchens, cable TV, billiards, hiking, Ping-Pong, recreation room, shop, some pets allowed (fee); no a/c, no smoking* ▭ *AE, D, MC, V.*

en route **Ruby Beach,** named for the rosy fragments of garnet that color its sands, is one of the peninsula's most beautiful stretches of coastline. A short trail leads to the wave-beaten sands, where sea stacks, caves, ★ tidal pools, and bony driftwood make it a favorite place of beachcombers, artists, and photographers. It's 15 mi south of Forks, off U.S. 101.

Forks

❼ *99 mi north of Copalis Beach.*

The former logging town of Forks is named for two nearby river junctions: the Bogachiel and Calawah rivers merge west of town, and a few miles farther they are joined by the Soleduck to form the Quileute River, which empties into the Pacific at the Native American village of La Push. Forks is a small, quiet gateway town for Olympic National Park's Hoh River valley unit. The surrounding countryside is exceptionally green, with an annual precipitation of more than 100 inches.

The **Big Cedar,** thought to be the world's largest cedar tree, stands 178 feet tall and is 19 feet 5 inches in diameter. Area loggers left it standing when they realized just how enormous it really was. The tree is off Nolan

Creek Road. From U.S. 101, turn right onto Route N1000 for 1.3 mi, then turn right onto N1100 for 2.4 mi. Turn right again onto N1112 for 0.4 mi, and then turn right once more for 0.1 mi.

off the beaten path

LA PUSH – This tiny coastal town, 15 mi west of Forks on Route 110, is the tribal center of the Quileute Indians. The town's name is thought to be a variation of the French *la bouche* (the mouth), and indeed it's at the mouth of the Quileute River. Here the coastline is dotted with offshore rock spires, known as sea stacks, and you might catch a glimpse of bald eagles nesting in the nearby cliffs. During low tide, the tide pools on nearby Second and Third beaches brim with life, and you can walk out to some of the sea stacks. Gray whales play offshore during their annual migrations, and most of the year the cold waves are great for surfing and kayaking—if you bring a wet suit.

Where to Stay & Eat

$–$$ ✕ **Smoke House Restaurant.** Rough-panel walls give a rustic appeal to the dining room of this two-story Forks favorite. Successful surf-and-turf specials remain unchanged since the place opened as a smokehouse in 1975. Smoked salmon is a top-seller, but the steaks and prime rib are also delicious. Burgers, fries, and milk shakes will please the kids. ⊠ 193161 U.S. 101 ☎ 360/374–6258 ▭ D, MC, V ⊙ *No lunch weekends.*

$ ✕ **Forks Coffee Shop.** This modest restaurant on the highway in downtown Forks serves terrific, home-style, classic American fare. From 5 AM onward you can dig into giant pancakes and Sol Duc scrambles (eggs, sausage, hash browns, and veggies all scrambled together). At lunch, there's a choice of soups, salads, and hot and cold sandwiches, which you can get to go if you're on the run. Dinner specials come with free trips to the salad bar and may include entrées like baked ham, baby-back ribs, grilled Hood Canal oysters, and spaghetti. If you have room for dessert, try one of the flaky-crust pies made with locally grown marionberries, blueberries, strawberries, cherries, or apples. ⊠ *U.S. 101* ☎ *360/374–6769* ▭ *MC, V.*

¢–$$ ▦ **Miller Tree Inn Bed and Breakfast.** Built as a farmhouse in 1916, this pale yellow B&B is still bordered on two sides by pastures. Numerous windows make the rooms bright, cheerful places to relax amid antiques, knickknacks, and quilts. Premier rooms have king-size beds, gas fireplaces, hot tubs for two, and VCRs. A separate apartment has a private entrance and kitchenette. One parlor has a library and piano, the other has games. In summer, lemonade and cookies are served on the lawn or the wide front porch. From October through April, nearby rivers offer prime salmon and steelhead fishing. ⊠ *654 E. Division St., 98331* ☎ *360/374–6806 or 800/943–6563* ᐃ *360/374–6807* ⊕ *www. millertreeinn.com* ⇆ *6 rooms, 1 apartment* ♨ *Dining room, some in-room hot tubs, some in-room VCRs, kitchenette, hot tub, fishing, recreation room, library, some pets allowed (fee); no a/c, no room phones, no TV in some rooms, no kids under 7, no smoking* ▭ *MC, V* ⦿⦿ *BP.*

¢ ▦ **Eagle Point Inn.** Beside the Soleduck River and surrounded by forest land, this beautiful log lodge is the picture of a peaceful country retreat. Inside, exposed-log walls are the background for antique and reproduction finery, including polished-wood furnishings, crocheted white tablecloths, and Tiffany lamps. Spare, elegant bedrooms have antique fringed lamps; one bath has a black claw-foot tub. Downstairs, a great stone fireplace makes the living room an inviting spot to spend the evening. In summer, you can cook in the outdoor kitchen by the river, or gather round a bonfire on crisp autumn nights. The B&B is about 10 mi north of Forks off U.S. 101. ⊠ *202 Stormin' Norman Rd., Beaver 98305* ☎ *360/ 327–3236* ⊕ *www.eaglepointinn.com* ⇆ *3 rooms* ♨ *Dining room,*

FodorsChoice
★

kitchen, outdoor hot tub, fishing, hiking; no room phones, no room TVs, no kids under 12, no smoking ⊟ No credit cards ⵔⵔ BP.

¢ 🏠 **Hoh Humm Ranch Bed and Breakfast.** This 200-acre former ranch is surrounded by rolling fields where tame llamas, deer, goats, and other animals roam. Simple, comfortable rooms overlook the valley and river below, where you can cast for salmon, trout, and steelhead. Hikers can head 6 mi south to Ruby Beach or 7 mi north to the Hoh River rain forest. The ranch is 20 mi south of Forks. ✉ *171763 U.S. 101, near milepost 172, 98331* 📠 *360/374–5337* 🖨 *360/374–5344* ⊕ *www. olypen.com/hohhumm* 🛏 *4 rooms without bath* ♿ *Dining room, fishing, some pets allowed; no a/c, no room phones, no room TVs, no smoking* ⊟ No credit cards ⵔⵔ BP.

¢ 🏠 **Pacific Inn Motel.** This two-story motel in the center of town has spacious rooms with modern, standard furnishings, plus kitchenettes. Air-conditioning and an on-site laundromat make it a favorite summer spot for families. Other pluses are wheelchair-accessible units, free local calls, and fax service. ✉ *352 Forks Ave. (U.S. 101), 98331* 📠 *360/374–9400 or 800/235–7344* 🖨 *360/374–9402* ⊕ *www.pacificinnmotel.com* 🛏 *34 rooms* ♿ *Kitchenettes, microwaves, refrigerators, cable TV, laundry facilities, no-smoking rooms* ⊟ AE, D, DC, MC, V.

CAMPGROUNDS   🏕 **Cycle Campground.** Designed for bicyclists, this camp is set in the Sol Duc valley between Forks and La Push. Firewood, coffee, and apple cider are free. The fee includes one support vehicle per site. There's a group fire ring and a hot tub. ✉ *101 Mora Rd.* 📠 *360/374–8665* 🛏 *10 tent sites, 4 tent cabins, 3 tepees* ♿ *Flush toilets, full hookups, drinking water, grills, picnic tables, electricity, public telephone* 🏕 *Tents $10, tepee or tent cabin (2 people) $40* ⊟ MC, V ⊘ *Closed Nov.–Apr.*

🏕 **Lonesome Creek RV Park.** A mile of sandy beach abuts this shoreside park in La Push. The on-site store sells Native American arts. ✉ *490 Ocean Dr., La Push* 📠 *360/374–4338* 🛏 *41 sites, 40 with full hookups* ♿ *Flush toilets, drinking water, showers, grills, picnic tables, electricity, public telephone, general store* 🏕 *Tents $15, RVs $20–$30* ⊟ MC, V.

Sports & the Outdoors

FISHING   The **Quillayute River Guide Service** (🏠 Box 71, La Push 📠 360/374–2660 ⊕ www.forks-web.com/jim) focuses on steelhead fishing on the Quillayute and Hoh rivers. **Jim Leons Outdoor Adventures** (✉ 382 Elk Valley Rd., Forks 📠 360/374–3157 ⊕ www.fishingnorthwest.com/jimleons) conducts fishing and hunting trips around the Olympic Peninsula. **Mike Schmitz Olympic Peninsula Fishing Guides** (🏠 Box 2688, Forks 📠 360/364–2602 or 888/577–4656 ⊕ www.forks-web.com/mschmitz) runs fishing trips on the Hoh, Sol Duc, and other rivers.

Sekiu

❽ *18 mi northwest of Forks.*

The village of Sekiu (pronounced *seek*-you) rests on the peninsula's northern shore, an area inhabited by the Makah, Ozette, and S'Klallum tribes for centuries. White settlers moved to Sekiu after a salmon cannery opened near the fishing grounds in 1870. Logging became the mainstay of the local economy in the early 1900s. Both industries shut down when resources became overexploited, and now Sekiu is a scenic vacation town known for excellent fishing and scuba diving. Although salmon are scarce, the Sekiu River still has fall runs of cutthroat trout and steelhead, and the jetty attracts sports divers.

On the former site of an Indian fishing village, the 33-acre **Clallam Bay Spit** brings beachcombers, fishers, and divers. The 4-acre Pillar Point Fishing Camp to the east has campsites and a boat ramp. Dress warmly: Pysht Bay takes its name from a S'Klallam term meaning "where the wind blows from all directions." ⊠ *Off Rte. 112 at Clallum Bay and Pysht Bay* ⊙ *Daily.*

Where to Stay & Eat

$–$$ ✕ **Breakwater Restaurant.** This restaurant above the Strait of San Juan de Fuca claims to be the most northwesterly dining establishment in the continental United States. Look for seafood, of course, served by a friendly and accommodating staff. Chicken dishes, burgers, steaks, and breakfasts fill out the menu. ⊠ *Rte. 112, Clallam Bay* ☎ *360/963–2428* ▤ *MC, V.*

¢–$ ▥ **Winter Summer Inn.** The late-1800s home is the community's oldest, and its walls are appropriately adorned with American antiques and works by local artists. The master suite has a Jacuzzi, while a separate studio has a private deck, fireplace, and billiard table. You can see panoramas of Clallam Bay from all around the inn. ⊠ *16651 Rte. 112, Clallam Bay 98326* ☎ *360/963–2264* ⊕ *www.northolympic.com/winters* ➷ *3 rooms* ⚴ *Dining room, some in-room hot tubs, some kitchenettes, some microwaves, some refrigerators, library; no a/c, no TV in some rooms, no smoking* ▤ *No credit cards* ⍾ *BP.*

Neah Bay

❾ *15 mi northwest of Sekiu.*

One of the oldest villages in Washington, Neah (pronounced *nee*-ah) Bay is surrounded by the Makah Indian Reservation at the northwestern tip of the Olympic Peninsula. Standing on the rocky beach and looking toward the sunset, you can view Cape Flattery, the northwesternmost point in the contiguous United States. Explorer James Cook named the cape in 1778 when his ship missed the fog-smothered Strait of Juan de Fuca and landed here instead. In 1792 Spanish mariners established a short-lived fort here, which was the first European settlement in what is now Washington State. The local Makah tribe is more closely related to the Nootka of Vancouver Island than to any Washington tribe. Like their ancestors, they embark on whale hunts by canoe, so you might find both whales and protesters on a local beach during your visit.

The outstanding **Makah Cultural and Research Center** displays thousands of artifacts found in Ozette Village at Cape Alava, which was destroyed by a mud slide hundreds of years ago. You'll also find Makah art and a reconstructed cedar longhouse. ⊠ *1880 Bayview Ave.* ☎ *360/645–2711* ⊕ *www.makah.com* ▨ *$3* ⊙ *May–Sept., daily 10–5; Nov.–Apr., Wed.–Sun. 10–5.*

At the **Makah National Fish Hatchery** you can view Chinook salmon as they make their way over fish ladders to the hatchery's spawning area. Spawning months are October and November, and the salmon are released on February 1. Smaller numbers of coho and chum salmon and steelhead trout also populate the hatchery. From Neah Bay, follow signs south for 7 mi. ⊠ *1 Fish Hatchery Rd.* ☎ *360/645–2521* ▨ *Free* ⊙ *Daily 7:30–4.*

Where to Stay & Eat

★ $–$$ ✕ **Makah Maiden Café.** Freshly caught fish and shellfish, sautéed or fried, are the specialties of this popular waterfront café. On a sunny day, you might sit at the outdoor picnic tables. If you'll be in town during the weekend, call to find out if the restaurant will be hosting one of its occasional salmon bakes, when the fish is prepared in a fire pit on cedar sticks. Breakfast is also available. ⊠ *1471 Bay View Ave.* ☎ *360/645–2924* ⊟ *MC, V.*

¢ ⊞ **Silver Salmon Resort Motel.** In the center of Neah Bay and across from the marina, this motel is just a block from the beach. Restaurants and shopping are also just steps away. Sparse but clean rooms are appointed with simple furnishings, and most have kitchenettes. ⊠ *1280 Bayview Ave., 98357* ☎ *360/645–2388 or 888/713–6477* ⊕ *www.silversalmonresort.com* ➟ *11 rooms* ⟁ *Picnic area, some kitchenettes, some microwaves, some refrigerators, shop, some pets allowed (fee); no a/c, no room phones, no room TVs* ⊟ *D, MC, V* ⊘ *Closed Dec.–Feb.*

Port Angeles

❿ *65 mi west of Neah Bay.*

First settled by the Hoh, Makah, Quileute, Quinault, and S'Klallam tribes, the northeastern coast of the Olympic Peninsula remained untouched by explorers until the 17th century. In 1610 a Greek pilot named Apostolos Valerianus—a.k.a. Juan de Fuca—sailed into the strait that now bears his name. In 1791 Spanish explorer Juan Francisco de Eliza followed him and named the Puerto de Nuestra Señora de Los Angeles, or Port of Our Lady of the Angels. George Vancouver shortened to the name to Port Angeles in 1792, and the site was settled by pioneers in 1856.

In the century that followed Port Angeles became a timber-mill town, a military base, and a key regional fishing port. With a population of about 19,000, the town is the largest on the Olympic Peninsula and a major gateway to Olympic National Park. Sprawling along the hills above the Strait of San Juan de Fuca, Port Angeles is also a main sea-transport link for car and passenger ferries sailing to Victoria, British Columbia.

The city of Port Angeles and Peninsula College operate the modest aquarium at the **Arthur D. Feiro Marine Laboratory.** You can take a self-guided tour through the touch and display tanks to see sea life, including octopus, scallops, rockfish, and anemones. Volunteers are on hand to answer questions. ⊠ *Port Angeles City Pier* ☎ *360/452–9277 Ext. 264* ⊠ *$3* ⊘ *June–Aug., daily 10–8; Sept.–May, weekends noon–4.*

The **Clallam County Historical Museum** preserves a handsome 1914 Georgian Revival former courthouse. You can visit the original courtroom and even sit in the judge's chair. Historic photos and artifacts illustrate the lifestyles and history of the town's Native American and Anglo communities. ⊠ *223 E. 4th St.* ☎ *360/417–2364* ⊠ *Donations accepted* ⊘ *June–Aug., Mon.–Sat. 10–4; Sept.–May, weekdays 10–4.*

Ediz Hook, at the western end of Port Angeles, is a long natural sand spit that protects the harbor from big waves and storms. The Hook is a fine place to take a walk along the water and watch shore and sea birds, and to spot the occasional seal, orca, or gray whale. From downtown, take Front Street west and follow it as it meanders past the shuttered lumber mill.

> **need a break?**
>
> For morning start or a midday pick-me-up, follow the aromas of fresh-baked muffins, scones, and coffee cakes into **First Street Haven** (⊠ 107 E. 1st St. ☎ 360/457–0352). The storefront café serves blended espresso drinks from morning through mid-afternoon, and breakfast is served all day on Sunday.

The small, sophisticated **Port Angeles Fine Arts Center** is inside the former home of the late artist and publisher Esther Barrows Webster, one of Port Angeles's most energetic and cultured citizens. Outdoor sculpture and trees surround the center, which has panoramas of the city and harbor. Exhibitions emphasize the works in various media of emerging and well-established Pacific Northwest artists. ⊠ *1203 W. Lauridsen Blvd.* ☎ *360/457–3532* ⊕ *www.portangelesfineartscenter.com* ☒ *Free* ⊘ *Thurs.–Sun. 11–5 and by appointment.*

Where to Stay & Eat

$$–$$$ ✕ **C'est Si Bon.** Far more formal and more French than is typical on the
Fodor'sChoice Olympic Peninsula, this first-rate restaurant stands out for its setting.
★ Tables cloaked in white linen are set above views of a rose garden, and ornate chandeliers illuminate European oil paintings on bold red walls. The menu—think onion soup, Cornish hen, filet mignon, and lobster tail—is written by the French expatriate owners. The wine list is superb, with French, Australian, and American choices, including Washington wines. ⊠ *2300 U.S. 101E, 4 mi east of Port Angeles* ☎ *360/452–8888* ⚑ *Reservations essential* ▤ *AE, DC, MC, V* ⊘ *Closed Mon. No lunch.*

$$–$$$ ✕ **Toga's International.** The European-inspired cuisine at this classy restaurant, in a former home, melds world flavors and cooking styles with the best local ingredients. Mountain views from the dining room and patio harken images of the chef-owner's former home in Germany's Black Forest. For an unusual treat, have your meal cooked on a *Jagerstein* (hunting stone) right at your table. This is one of the few places west of Seattle where you can order cheese, meat, or seafood fondue (with a day's notice). ⊠ *122 W. Lauridsen Blvd.* ☎ *360/452–1952* ⚑ *Reservations essential* ▤ *MC, V* ⊘ *Closed Sun. and Mon. and Sept. and Jan.*

$–$$ ✕ **Bella Italia.** Beneath a local health food store, the restaurant appropriately cooks up wholesome meals with lots of fresh, organic local produce. Northwest seafood and Italian seasonings blend perfectly in the cioppino, and the flash-fried calamari, with olives, artichoke, tomato, and roasted garlic on polenta, is a signature dish. Other good choices include the gnocchi and the simple pizzas. Locals flock here for Sunday brunch. ⊠ *117–B E. 1st St.* ☎ *360/457–5442* ▤ *AE, MC, V* ⊘ *No lunch.*

$–$$ ✕ **The Bushwhacker.** More than two decades of excellent steaks keep the locals coming back to this surf-and-turf restaurant. It's a big, friendly place where families gather to dig into huge, perfect cuts of meat or seafood dishes. It's tempting to fill up at the salad and soup bar, which comes with every meal, but save room for your main course—and the amazing desserts. ⊠ *115 E. Railroad Ave.* ☎ *360/457–6768* ▤ *AE, MC, V.*

$–$$ ✕ **Crab House.** This first-class waterfront restaurant, linked to the Red Lion Inn in front of the Port Angeles Pier, is one of the region's most famous spots for fresh local seafood. Crab is the specialty, of course, and it shows up in a tasty variety of dishes, including crab hash, crab bisque, crab cakes, and crab-stuffed fish specials. Windows surrounding the elegant dining room let you view the serene gray waters where much of what's on the menu is caught daily. This is where well-to-do locals splurge on black-tie events. ⊠ *221 N. Lincoln St.* ☎ *360/457–0424* ▤ *AE, D, DC, MC, V.*

★ **$–$$** ✕ **Dupuis Restaurant.** Flower-filled gardens surround this old-time seafood spot on U.S. 101 between Port Angeles and Sequim. One of the dining rooms was a tavern in the 1920s. Close-set tables in the elegant main dining room are lit by small chandeliers overhead. Windows frame views of the well-tended gardens. Grilled local fish, steamed crabs and oysters, seafood sautés, and a selection of Continental choices, like cheese-topped French onion soup, round out the menu. ⊠ *256861 U.S. 101* ☎ *360/457–8033* ▤ *AE, MC, V* ⊘ *No lunch.*

$$–$$$ **Colette's Bed & Breakfast.** A contemporary mansion curving around
Fodor'sChoice 10 acres of gorgeous waterfront property, this B&B offers space, ser-
★ vice, and luxury equaled by no other property in the area. Leather sofas
and chairs and a river-rock fireplace make the great front room a lovely
spot to watch the water through expansive 20-foot windows. The
suites—with names like Iris, Azalea, and Cedar—also overlook the
water and have fireplaces, balconies, CD and DVD players, and two-
person Jacuzzis. A specially made outdoor fireplace means you can
enjoy the deck even in winter. Multicourse breakfasts include espresso-
based drinks and fresh fruit. ☒ *339 Finn Hall Rd., 10 mi east of Port
Angeles, 98362* ☎ *360/457–9197 or 888/457–9777* ☐ *360/452–0711*
⊕ *www.colettes.com* ☞ *5 suites* ⚹ *Dining room, in-room data ports,
in-room hot tubs, refrigerators, cable TV, in-room VCRs; no kids under
18, no smoking* ☰ *MC, V* ⦿ *BP.*

$$–$$$ **Domaine Madeleine.** The owners of this luxury B&B on a bluff above
the Strait of Juan de Fuca love to pamper their guests. Rooms, which have
private entrances, are decorated with either Impressionist or Asian accents
and overlook water and mountain views. Gas fireplaces, designer robes,
two-person whirlpool tubs, CD players, and VCRs are more en-suite
bonuses. The living room, set aside for private use with bookings of the
Renoir Room, has a 14-foot-tall basalt fireplace, antique Asian furnishings, and a harpsichord. For breakfast expect a five-course gourmet affair with fresh baguettes, chicken crepes, and seafood omelets. ☒ *146
Wildflower La., 8 mi east of Port Angeles, 98362* ☎ *360/457–4174 or
888/811–8376* ☐ *360/457–3037* ⊕ *www.domainemadeleine.com* ☞ *4
rooms* ⚹ *Dining room, some refrigerators, in-room VCRs, library, meeting rooms; no kids under 12, no smoking* ☰ *AE, D, DC, MC, V* ⦿ *BP.*

★ **$–$$$** **BJ's Garden Gate.** A gingerbread-style porch fronts this waterfront
Victorian home on three acres of landscaped grounds. Exquisitely ap-
pointed guest rooms include Victoria's Repose, which has a finely carved
half-tester English oak bed and a balcony with a private two-person hot
tub. All rooms have fireplaces, Jacuzzis, CD players and VCRs, plus
panoramic water views. Antiques are artfully arranged throughout the
living and dining rooms, which have expansive views of the strait. Gor-
geous flower gardens, which have been featured in national commer-
cials, help make this an ideal romantic getaway. ☒ *397 Monterra Dr.,
98362* ☎ *360/452–2322 or 800/880–1332* ⊕ *www.bjgarden.com* ☞ *5
rooms* ⚹ *Dining room, in-room data ports, in-room hot tubs, cable TV,
in-room VCRs; no kids, no smoking* ☰ *AE, MC, V* ⦿ *BP.*

$ **Red Lion Port Angeles.** One block from the harbor and ferry landing,
this big hotel makes a good base for exploring the Olympic Peninsula
and Vancouver Island, Canada. Modern rooms have plush carpets and
wood-framed furnishings; some have views and kitchen facilities. The
adjacent Crab House restaurant is a local favorite. ☒ *221 N. Lincoln,
98362* ☎ *360/452–9215* ☐ *360/452–4734* ⊕ *www.redlionportangeles.
com* ☞ *185 rooms, 2 suites* ⚹ *Restaurant, room service, in-room data
ports, some kitchenettes, some microwaves, some refrigerators, cable
TV, pool, hot tub, laundry facilities, business services, meeting rooms,
some pets allowed; no a/c* ☰ *AE, D, DC, MC, V.*

★ **¢–$** **Five Sea Suns Bed & Breakfast.** The clever name of this cozy 1926 inn
refers to its rooms, each elegantly appointed in the theme of a time of
year: the four seasons plus an Indian summer. If you stay in Lente
(spring), you can enjoy a breezy balcony. Na Zomer (Indian summer)
is in a separate carriage house. The B&B overlooks the mountains and
the bay, which you can view from the pondside pergola and landscaped
gardens. When you arrive, coffee is served in a silver tea set in your room.
☒ *1006 S. Lincoln, 98362* ☎ *360/452–8248 or 800/708–0777* ☐ *360/
417–0465* ⊕ *www.seasuns.com* ☞ *5 rooms* ⚹ *Dining room, picnic area,*

pond, travel services, airport shuttle; no a/c, no room phones, no kids under 12, no smoking ⊟ AE, MC, V ⦾ BP.

¢–$ ⊡ **Tudor Inn.** This 1910 Tudor-style B&B stands behind a white picket fence in a residential neighborhood. Several gathering spots throughout the house—a piano parlor, an antiques-filled sitting room, a front porch, and a back deck—encourage mingling. Guest rooms, all with views of the water or Hurricane Ridge, have themes like Country, Wedgewood, and Oriental. Yours might have a fireplace, balcony, or claw-foot bathtub. Candlelight breakfast and afternoon tea are included. ⊠ *1108 S. Oak St., 98362* ☎ *360/452–3138 or 866/286–2224* ⊕ *www.tudorinn. com* ⦆ *5 rooms* �ⅾ *Dining room, piano, library; no kids under 12, no smoking* ⊟ MC, V ⦾ BP.

¢ ⊡ **Port Angeles Inn.** Blue-and-white-striped awnings and lattice woodwork give this simple motel a cheerful look. The inn is in the middle of town, and some rooms on the upper floor have good views of the harbor. Rooms are done in warm colors; the four King Rooms have balconies and two also have kitchenettes. ⊠ *111 E. 2nd St., 98362* ☎ *360/452–9285 or 800/421–0706* 🖷 *360/452–7935* ⊕ *www.portangelesinn. com* ⦆ *22 rooms, 2 suites* �ⅾ *In-room data ports, some kitchenettes, some microwaves, some refrigerators, cable TV* ⊟ D, MC, V ⦾ CP.

CAMPGROUNDS ⚠ **Conestoga Quarters RV Park Campground.** Off U.S. 101, partly surrounded by a fir forest, this compact RV park provides a shuttle van to take you into Port Angeles and to the ferry dock. All of the sites have full hookups; eight sites have phones. ⊠ *40 Sieberts Creek Rd.* ☎ *360/452–4637 or 800/808–4637* ⦆ *8 tent sites, 34 RV sites* �ⅾ *Flush toilets, full hookups, drinking water, showers, grills, picnic tables, electricity, public telephone, play area* 🖾 *Tents $14, RVs $21* ⊟ D, MC, V ⊘ *Closed Nov.–Mar.*

⚠ **Salt Creek RV Park.** Adjacent to a golf course, this large park offers every conceivable campground amenity, including nightly security patrols and an on-site store. Quiet hours are 10 PM to 8 AM, and fireworks and firearms are strictly prohibited. ⊠ *53802 Rte. 122 W* ☎ *360/928–2488* ⦆ *51 sites* �ⅾ *Flush toilets, full hookups, drinking water, guest laundry, showers, grills, picnic tables, electricity, public telephone, play area* 🖾 *$20 RVs* ⊟ AE, MC, V.

⚠ **Salt Creek and Tongue Point Recreation Area.** Swimming in fresh and salt water, fishing, hiking, and beachcombing provide bountiful activity at this Clallam County park along a creek. There are no hookups. ⊠ *13 mi west of Port Angeles on Rte. 112, 3 mi north on Hayden Creek Rd.* ☎ *360/928–3441* ⦆ *90 sites* ⅾ *Flush toilets, drinking water, showers, grills, picnic tables, public telephone, play area, swimming (river, ocean)* 🖾 *$10* ⊟ *No credit cards* ⊘ *Closed Nov.–Mar.*

Shopping
Brown's Outdoor (⊠ 112 Front St. ☎ 360/457–4150) has an extensive collection of camping gear, including cookware and stoves, backpacks, tents, clothing, and the latest North Face sleeping bags. The staff can offer solid trip advice for the region.

Sports & the Outdoors
FISHING **Diamond Back Guide Service** (⊠ 140 Dolan Ave., Port Angeles ☎ 360/452–9966) leads fishing trips and scenic boat excursions around the peninsula.

Olympic National Park

U.S. 101, 89 mi west of I–5 at Exit 88 or 121 mi north of I–5 at Exit 104.

One of the largest, most remote, and least-developed protected areas in the United States, Olympic National Park preserves 922,651 acres of the peninsula's magnificent, mountainous interior and wave-stung shoreline. South and east of U.S. 101, the interior's thick forests of spruce, fir, and cedar spread out, supporting a thriving population of black bears, cougars, deer, elk, and numerous small animals. In the center rises a crown of glacier-topped peaks, almost as difficult to traverse now as it was a century ago. West of U.S. 101 the park claims 65 mi of wild coastline, where bald eagles, osprey, blue herons, and hawks soar the skies, and migrating whales, sea lions, sea otters, and seals swim off-shore.

Every year the park draws about 3.5 million visitors, more than Yellowstone and Yosemite, but even in the most congested spots you're still surrounded by endless forest or beaches and quite likely to see some wildlife. Wherever you go in the park, you'll find that this land is little changed from what was seen by the first European settlers, who arrived here 150 years ago.

Olympic's most popular panoramas, such as the view from atop Hurricane Ridge north to Vancouver Island, or the seascape at Ruby Beach, are best viewed during the clear-sky, sunny months of July, August, and September. Misty, rain-splashed days, however, add indelible atmosphere to the rain forest valleys and the Pacific coastline; and they are truer representations the area's character, even if they obscure distant views. Rain is possible any time of year, but it's most common from November through April.

U.S. 101 encircles most of the park's interior, and numerous smaller roads branch inward toward the mountains and outward toward the beaches. Even though few roads penetrate very far into the park, you can still see many of Olympic's larger wild animals by roadsides and at meadow edges at sunrise and sunset. Bears are most commonly seen in May and June, and in fall when they prowl berry patches. Elk spend the summer in the high country and return to lowland valleys in autumn. Keep in mind that all wild animals are just that—wild—and both people and animals benefit by keeping their distance.

The park's six entrances are open 24 hours year-round, and most gate stations are staffed daily from 9 to 4. The vehicle admission fee is $5. Parking at Ozette, the trailhead for one of the park's most popular hikes, is $1 per day. June through September are peak months, when the park receives 75% of its annual visitors. Its most popular sites, such as Hurricane Ridge, can approach capacity by 10 AM. May and October are much less crowded and have generally favorable weather. Winter brings persistent cloudiness, frequent rain, and chilly temperatures; crowds are almost nonexistent from Thanksgiving to Easter. When it snows the slopes draw skiers and snowshoers, although Hurricane Ridge Road is closed from Monday to Thursday, November through March.

At the **Olympic National Park Visitor Center,** park rangers provide advice on where to go and how to maximize your time, as well as information on campgrounds, wildlife movement in the park, programs, weather forecasts, and almost anything else you might want to know. You can pick up free road and trail maps, information pamphlets, and the park's newspaper, the *Bugler,* as well as buy books, postcards, and souvenirs. Ranger talks, guest programs, children's events, and other activities are scheduled throughout the year. ⊠ *600 E. Park Ave., Port Angeles 98362* ☎ *360/ 565–3130* ⊕ *www.nps.gov/olym.*

The **Olympic Park Institute** runs seminars on various aspects of park ecology, history, Native American culture, and arts such as writing, painting, and photography. It also organizes one- to five-day guided backpacking trips in summer and fall, as well as whale- and bird-watching trips in spring. Classes are led by wildlife experts, local artists, and park rangers. ⊠ *111 Barnes Point Rd., Port Angeles* ☎ *360/928–3720 or 800/775–3720* ☉ *Weekdays 8:30–4:30.*

★ The park's premier scenic drive is from the Port Angeles visitor center to **Hurricane Ridge.** The road climbs steeply to 5,242 feet, from the thick fir forest in the foothills to alpine meadow at the top of the ridge. As you drive upward, you may notice marmots and goats ambling along the roadsides. Meanwhile, ever-larger panoramas reveal spectacular views on all sides. From the Hurricane Ridge visitor center at the top, you can see the heart of the mountains to the south and Canada to the north, across the Strait of Juan de Fuca. Trails on Hurricane Ridge take you through alpine meadows covered with wildflowers in spring and summer. In winter, the area has miles of cross-country ski and snow-shoeing routes, and even a modest downhill-ski operation. ⊠ *Hurricane Ridge Rd,, 17 mi south of Port Angeles* ☎ *360/565–3130, 360/452–0329 snow conditions* ☉ *Visitor centers daily 10–5.*

Lake Crescent. Almost everyone who visits the park sees Lake Crescent, as U.S. 101 winds along its southern shore, giving way to gorgeous views of azure waters rippling in a basin formed by Tuscan-like hills. In the evening, low bands of clouds caught between the surrounding mountains often linger over its reflective surface. Along the lake's 12-mi perimeter are campgrounds, resorts, trails, and places to canoe and fish. ⊠ *U.S. 101, 16 mi west of Port Angeles and 28 mi east of Forks* ☎ *360/928–3380.*

The Sol Duc Valley is one of those magical, serene places where all the Northwest's virtues seem at hand—lush lowland forest, a sparkling river, salmon runs, and quiet hiking trails. Native Americans dipped into the soothing waters of **Sol Duc Hot Springs** for generations. Today visitors come from all areas to soak in the three hot sulfuric pools, ranging in temperature from 98°F to 104°F. Sol Duc Hot Springs Resort, built in 1910, has simple cabins for overnight visitors, plus a restaurant and hamburger stand. You need not patronize the resort to use the hot springs. ⊠ *Soleduck Rd. on Lake Crescent, 12 mi south of Fairholm* ☎ *360/327–3583* 💲 *$10* ☉ *Apr.–mid-May and Oct., daily 9–5; mid-May–Sept., daily 9–9.*

★ **Lake Ozette,** the third largest glacial impoundment in Washington, anchors the coastal strip of Olympic National Park at its north end. The small town of Ozette, home of a coastal tribe, is the trailhead for two of the park's better one-day hikes. Three-mile trails lead over board-walks through swampy wetland and coastal old-growth forest to the ocean shore and uncrowded beach. The northernmost trail reaches shore at Cape Alava, westernmost point in the continental United States. Wet weather makes the boardwalks slippery, so watch your step. ⊠ *At the end of Hoko-Ozette Rd., 26 mi southwest of Rte. 112 near Sekiu* ☎ *360/963–2725.*

An 18-mi spur road winds from U.S. 101 to the **Hoh River Rain Forest,** where spruce and hemlock trees soar to heights of more than 200 feet. Alders and big-leaf maples are so densely covered with mosses they look more like shaggy prehistoric animals than trees. Look for elk browsing in shaded glens. And be prepared for rain: the region receives 140 inches or more a year (that's 12 feet and up). The Hoh Visitor Center, near the campground and the trailheads, has maps and information. The 18-mi Hoh River Trail, one of the most popular in the park, follows the Hoh River to the base of Mt. Olympus, which rises 7,965 feet above the forest floor. Two other much shorter trails lead through the forestland around the visitor center. Naturalist-led campfire programs and walks are conducted almost daily in July and August. ✉ *From U.S. 101, about 20 mi north of Kalaloch, take Upper Hoh Rd. 18 mi east to Hoh Rain Forest Visitor Center* ☎ *360/374–6925.*

Lake Quinault, 4½ mi long and 300 feet deep, is partly in Olympic National Park, partly in Olympic National Forest, and partly on the Quinault reservation. The glimmering lake is the first landmark you reach when driving the west-side loop of U.S. 101. The rain forest is at its densest and wettest here, with moss-draped maples and alders, and towering spruces, firs, and hemlocks. Enchanted Valley, high up near the Quinault River's source, is a deeply glaciated valley that's closer to the Hood Canal than to the Pacific Ocean. A scenic loop drive circles the lake and travels around a section of the Quinault River. Quinault Lodge is on the southeast side of the lake, while several public and private campgrounds border the northwest side. ✉ *U.S. 101, 38 mi north of Hoquiam* ☎ *360/288–2444* ☉ *Ranger station May–Sept., daily 8–5.*

Where to Stay & Eat

$–$$$ ✕⬛ **Kalaloch Lodge.** A two-story cedar lodge overlooking the Pacific, Kalaloch has 20 cabins and five lodge rooms with sea views. Log cabins have either fireplaces or woodstoves, knotty pine furnishings, earth-tone fabrics, and kitchenettes; the ones on the waterfront also have deep couches looking seaward out of a picture window. To suit the rustic ambience, no phones or TVs are in the rooms, but there's a common area where guests gather for entertainment. The restaurant's menu changes seasonally, but usually includes local oysters, crab, and salmon. Dinner is served in the main dining room and in the upstairs cocktail lounge—which, like the restaurant, has unobstructed ocean views. ✉ *157151 U.S. 101* ⬚ *HC 80, Box 1100, Forks 98331* ☎ *360/962–2271 or 866/525–2562* 🖶 *360/962–3391* ⊕ *www.visitkalaloch.com* ⬚ *10 rooms, 44 cabins* ⬚ *Restaurant, grocery, kitchenettes, bar, shop, library, some pets allowed (fee); no room phones, no room TVs* ⊟ *AE, MC, V.*

$–$$ ✕⬛ **Lake Quinault Lodge.** On a lovely glacial lake in Olympic National Forest, this beautiful early-20th-century lodge complex is within walking distance of the lakeshore and hiking trails in the spectacular old-growth forest. A towering brick fireplace is the centerpiece of the great room, where antique wicker furnishings sit beneath ceiling beams painted with Native American designs. In the rooms, modern gadgets are traded in for old-fashioned comforts, such as claw-foot tubs and fireplaces. The lively bar is a good place to unwind after a day spent outdoors. The restaurant serves upscale seafood entrés like baked salmon with capers and onions. ✉ *S. Shore Rd.* ⬚ *Box 7, Quinault 98575* ☎ *360/288–2900 or 800/562–6672* 🖶 *360/288–2901* ⊕ *www.visitlakequinault.com* ⬚ *92 rooms* ⬚ *Restaurant, some in-room VCRs, putting green, indoor pool, lake, hot tub, sauna, dock, boating, fishing, hiking, bar, recreation room, some pets allowed (fee), no-smoking rooms; no room phones, no TV in some rooms* ⊟ *MC, V.*

¢–$ ✕⬛ **Lake Crescent Lodge.** Deep in the forest at the foot of Mt. Storm King, this comfortable farmhouse-style lodge, built in 1916, has a wraparound veranda and picture windows framing the lake's sapphire waters. Rooms in the rustic Roosevelt Cottage have polished wood floors, stone fireplaces, and lake views, while Tavern Cottage quarters resemble modern motel rooms. Second-floor rooms in the historic lodge, a former pub, have shared baths. The lodge's fir-paneled dining room ($–$$$) overlooks the lake, and the adjacent lounge is often crowded with campers. Seafood dishes like grilled salmon or steamed Quilcene oysters, as well as classic American fare, highlight the restaurant menu. ✉ *416 Lake Crescent Rd., Port Angeles 98363* ☎ *360/928–3211* 🖶 *360/928–3253* ⊕ *www.lakecrescentlodge.com* ⬚ *30 motel rooms, 17 cabins, 5 lodge* *rooms with shared bath ⚤ Restaurant, dining room, lake, dock, boating, fishing, hiking, lounge; no room phones, no room TVs* ▤ *AE, DC, MC, V* ⊗ *Closed Nov.–Apr.*

$ ✕▦ **Sol Duc Hot Springs Resort.** Deep in the brooding forest along the Sol Duc River, this remote 1910 resort is surrounded by 5,000-foot-tall mountains. Bubbling, steaming sulfur springs fill the three large outdoor pools, and the swimming pool is filled with slightly warmed glacial runoff. Some forest cabins have kitchens, but all are spartan; however, after a day's hike, a dip, and dinner at The Spring restaurant ($–$$), you'll hardly notice. The attractive fir-and-cedar-paneled dining room serves unpretentious meals all day, drawing on top Northwest seafood and produce. ⊠ *Soleduck Rd.* ✆ *Box 2168, Port Angeles 98362* ☎ *360/327–3583* 🖷 *360/327–3398* ⊕ *www.solduchotsprings.com* ✍ *32 rooms, 6 cabins* ⚤ *Restaurant, grocery, some kitchenettes, pool, hiking, bar, shop* ▤ *MC, V* ⊗ *Closed mid-Oct.–mid-May.*

CAMPGROUNDS Campgrounds in Olympic National Park range from primitive backcountry sites to paved trailer parks with nightly naturalist programs. Each designated site usually has a picnic table and grill or fire pit, and most campgrounds have water, toilets, and garbage containers. Park campgrounds have no hookups, showers, or laundry facilities. Firewood is available from camp concessions, but if there's no store you can collect dead wood within 1 mi of your campsite. Dogs are allowed in campgrounds but not on trails or in the backcountry. Trailers should be 21 feet long or less (15 feet or less at Queets Campground). There's a camping limit of two weeks.

Intrepid hikers can camp virtually anywhere along the park's shoreline or in its forested areas. The required overnight wilderness-use permit costs $5, plus $2 per person per night. Passes are available at visitor centers and ranger stations. Note that when you camp in the backcountry, you must choose a site at least ½ mi inside the park boundary.

⚠ **Altaire Campground.** This small campground sits amid an old-growth forest by the river in the narrow Elwha River valley. A popular trail leads downstream from the campground. ⊠ *Elwha River Rd., 8 mi south of U.S. 101, Olympic National Park* ☎ *No phone* ✍ *30 sites* ⚤ *Flush toilets, drinking water, fire grates* 🕮 *$10* ▤ *No credit cards* ⊗ *Closed Nov.–Mar.*

⚠ **Dosewallips Campground.** Popular with hikers, and hunters in the fall, this small, remote campground lies beneath Mt. Constance, one of the most conspicuous peaks in the park. The campground is in old-growth forest along the river. The long gravel access road is not suitable for RVs. ⊠ *Dosewallips River Rd., 15 mi west of Brinnon, Olympic National Park* ☎ *No phone* ✍ *30 sites* ⚤ *Pit toilets, drinking water, fire grates* 🕮 *$10* ▤ *MC, V* ⊗ *Closed Nov.–Apr.*

⚠ **Elwha Campground.** The larger of the Elwha Valley's two campgrounds, this is one of Olympic's year-round facilities, with two campsite loops in an old-growth forest. ⊠ *Elwha River Rd., 7 mi south of U.S. 101, Olympic National Park* ☎ *No phone* ✍ *41 sites* ⚤ *Flush toilets, drinking water, fire grates, public telephone, ranger station* 🕮 *$10* ▤ *MC, V.*

⚠ **Heart O' the Hills Campground.** At the foot of Hurricane Ridge in a grove of tall firs, this popular, sometimes crowded campground offers a regular slate of programs in summer. The price is a distinct lack of the peace and calm most people expect in a national park. ⊠ *Hurricane Ridge Rd., Olympic National Park* ☎ *No phone* ✍ *105 sites* ⚤ *Flush toilets, drinking water, fire grates, public telephone, ranger station* 🕮 *$10* ▤ *MC, V.*

△ **Hoh Campground.** Crowds flock to this rain forest campground under a canopy of moss-draped maples, towering spruce trees, and morning mist. ⊠ *Hoh River Rd., 17 mi east of U.S. 101, Olympic National Park* ☎ *No phone* ⇔ *89 sites* ⚹ *Flush toilets, dump station, drinking water, fire grates, public telephone, ranger station* ⚏ *$10* ⊟ *MC, V.*

△ **Hoh River Resort Campground.** Spruce trees shade this all-around sportsman's hangout along the Hoh River. Fishing and hiking are nearby. ⊠ *175443 U.S. 101, 20 mi south of Forks* ☎ *360/374–5566* ⇔ *13 sites with hookups, 7 tent sites* ⚹ *Flush toilets, full hook-ups, drinking water, showers, grills, picnic tables, electricity, public telephone, general store* ⚏ *RVs and tents $10* ⊟ *MC, V.*

△ **Kalaloch Campground.** Kalaloch is the biggest and most popular Olympic campground. Its vantage of the Pacific is duplicated nowhere on the park's coastal stretch, although the campsites themselves are set back in the spruce fringe. ⊠ *U.S. 101, ½ mi north of the Kalaloch Information Station, Olympic National Park* ☎ *No phone* ⇔ *177 sites* ⚹ *Flush toilets, dump station, drinking water, fire grates, public telephone, ranger station* ⚏ *$12* ⊟ *MC, V.*

△ **Lake Quinault Rain Forest Resort Village Campground.** Sprawled on the south shore of Lake Quinault, this campground has ample recreation facilities, including beaches, canoes, ball fields, and horseshoes. ⊠ *3½ mi east of U.S. 101, S. Shore Rd., Lake Quinault* ☎ *360/288–2535* ⇔ *30 sites* ⚹ *Flush toilets, full hookups, drinking water, showers, grills, picnic tables, electricity, public telephone, general store* ⚏ *RVs and tents $16* ⊟ *MC, V* ⊙ *Closed Nov.–Mar.*

△ **Ozette Campground.** Hikers heading to Cape Alava, a scenic promontory that's the westernmost point in the lower 48 states, use this lakeshore campground as a jumping-off point. There's a boat launch and a small beach. ⊠ *Hoko-Ozette Rd., 26 mi south of Rte. 112, Olympic National Park* ☎ *No phone* ⇔ *15 sites* ⚹ *Pit toilets, fire grates, ranger station* ⚏ *$10* ⊟ *MC, V.*

△ **Queets Campground.** Amid lush old-growth forests in the southwestern corner of the park, near the park's largest Douglas fir tree, this campground is not suitable for trailers or RVs. There's no water. ⊠ *Queets River Rd., 12 mi east of U.S. 101, Olympic National Park* ☎ *No phone* ⇔ *20 sites* ⚹ *Pit toilets, fire grates, ranger station* ⚏ *$8* ⊟ *No credit cards.*

△ **Sol Duc Campground.** Sol Duc resembles virtually all Olympic campgrounds except for one distinguishing feature—the famed hot springs are a short walk away. The nearby Sol Duc River has several spots where visitors can watch spawning salmon work their way upstream. ⊠ *Sol Duc Rd., 11 mi south of U.S. 101, Olympic National Park* ☎ *No phone* ⇔ *80 sites* ⚹ *Flush toilets, dump station, drinking water, fire grates, public telephone, ranger station, swimming (hot springs)* ⚏ *$12* ⊟ *No credit cards* ⊙ *Closed Nov.–Mar.*

△ **South Beach Campground.** The first campground travelers reach as they enter the park's coastal stretch from the south, this is basically an overflow campground for the more popular and better-equipped Kalaloch a few miles north. Campsites are set in the spruce fringe, just back from the beach. There is no water. ⊠ *2 mi south of the Kalaloch information station at the southern boundary of the park, U.S. 101* ☎ *No phone* ⇔ *50 sites* ⚹ *Pit toilets, fire grates* ⚏ *$8* ⊟ *No credit cards* ⊙ *Closed Nov.–Mar.*

Sports & the Outdoors

BEACHCOMBING Walking on the sand, observing tidepools, listening to the surf, and keeping your eyes peeled for sea otters, seals, and eagles are some of the simplest pleasures of a visit to the northern Pacific coast. Watch for wave-rolled logs and the rare but hazardous rogue wave, which can be two or three times as large as waves that precede and follow it. The best and most easily accessible nonwilderness beaches are Rialto; Ruby; First and Second near Mora and La Push; and beaches No. 2 and No. 4 in the Kalaloch stretch.

BICYCLING The Quinault Valley, Queets River, Hoh River, and Sol Duc River roads have bike paths through old-growth forest. U.S. 101, which carries heavy truck and RV traffic, is not recommended for leisure bicycling. **Sound Bike & Kayak** (⊠ 120 E. Front St., Port Angeles ☎ 360/457–1240) rents and sells biking equipment, and has a nice selection of gear and books.

BOATING Serene **Lake Crescent,** surrounded by the Olympic mountain forests, is one of the park's most popular places to boat. Besides canoeing and kayaking, you can drive motorboats and waterski here. Speedboats are not permitted around the designated swimming area at the west end of the lake. Rangers lead 75-minute tours of the lake aboard the *Storm King,* in cooperation with **Mosquito Fleet Enterprises** (☎ 425/252–6800 or 800/325–6722 ⊕ www.whalewatching.com), from late May through September. You can buy tickets at the Olympic National Park Visitor Center in Port Angeles.

Fairholm General Store (⊠ U.S. 101, Fairholm ☎ 360/928–3020) rents rowboats and canoes for $10 to $45 on Lake Crescent. The store is at the lake's west end, 27 mi west of Port Angeles. It's open May through September, daily 9 to 6. **Lake Crescent Lodge** (⊠ 416 Lake Crescent Rd. ☎ 360/928–3211) rents rowboats for $8.50 per hour and $35 per day. **Log Cabin Resort** (⊠ Piedmont Road, off U.S. 101 ☎ 360/928–3325), 17 mi west of Port Angeles, has boat rentals for $10 to $30. The dock makes it easy to access Lake Crescent's northeast section. It's on the lake's east arm and is open May through September, daily 9 to 6.

Lake Quinault has boating access from a gravel ramp on the north shore. From Route 101, take a right on North Shore Road, another right on Hemlock Way, and a left on Lakeview Drive. There are also plank ramps at Falls Creek and Willoughby campgrounds on South Shore Drive, ⅒ mi and 1.2 mi past the Quinault Ranger Station, respectively. Since there's only one access road to **Lake Ozette,** it's a good place for overnight trips. Only experienced canoe and kayak handlers should travel far from the put-in, since fierce storms occasionally strike, even in summer.

CLIMBING **Mt. Olympus** and other peaks in the park are very popular with climbers, partly because they are rugged and quite challenging, but not overly high. Olympus, the tallest, tops out at 7,965 feet. Get expert advice from rangers before setting out. The mountains are steep, the landscape is broken up by escarpments and ridges, and there are bridgeless creeks and rivers to cross. It's easy to take a fall or to get lost (which happens every year to inexperienced hikers and climbers). All climbers are asked to register with park officials and purchase wilderness permits before setting out.

Olympic Mountaineering (⊠ 140 W. Front St., Port Angeles ☎ 360/452–0240 ⊕ www.olymtn.com) organizes climbs and hikes in Olympic National Park. Climbing classes at an indoor gym and outdoor adventure clinics are also offered. **Olympic Mountain Outdoors** (⊡ Box 1468, Port Townsend ☎ 360/379–5336 ⊕ www.olympicguides.com) offers guided hiking, camping, skiing, snowshoeing, and wildlife-watching trips.

FISHING Rainbow and cutthroat trout are found in the park's streams and lakes, and salmon ply the rivers and shores. You don't need a state fishing license to fish in the park; however, anglers must acquire a salmon–steelhead punch card when fishing for those species. The Bogachiel, Hoh,

Quinault, Skokomish, and Dosewallips rivers are world-famous steelhead streams. Ocean fishing and shellfish and seaweed harvesting require licenses, which are available at sporting goods and outdoor supply stores. Fishing regulations vary throughout the park; check regulations for each location.

HIKING Wilderness beaches provide the park's most unusual hiking experience: an opportunity to explore an essentially unaltered Pacific coastline. Raccoons waddle from the forest to pluck dinner from the tide pools; bald eagles stoop over tangles of driftwood, the bones of ancient forests. Entry points are at La Push, Rialto Beach, and Cape Alava. Be sure to read the tide tables before starting out on beach trails. Plan your route carefully or you risk being trapped by the ocean. Park rangers and volunteers at the visitor centers can show you how to read the tide tables and warn you of any dangerous areas.

In the interior, trails embedded in forested river valleys provide perfect warm-ups for the intense climbs into alpine country. The Elwha, Dosewallips, Skokomish, Quinault, Hoh, and Sol Duc valleys all have developed trails that wend upstream, finally climbing into high passes and a glacier-rimmed alpine basin where they link up with each other. Although hikes of up to two weeks are possible, short exploratory walks also abound; every campground and road-end has both established and relatively easy trails suitable for day hikes. A wilderness permit ($5 per group of up to 12 people, plus $2 per person per night) is required for all overnight backcountry visits.

Boulder Creek Trail. The 5-mi round-trip walk up Boulder Creek leads to the Olympic hot springs, a half-dozen pools of varying temperatures; some are clothing-optional. ⊠ *End of the Elwha River Rd., 4 mi south of Altaire Campground.*

★ **Cape Alva Trail.** Beginning at Ozette, this 3-mi trail leads from forest to wave-tossed headlands. Be careful on the often-slippery boardwalks. ⊠ *End of the Hoko-Ozette Rd., 26 mi south of Rte. 112, west of Sekiu.*

Graves Creek Trail. This 6-mi-long moderately strenuous trail climbs from lowland rain forest to alpine territory at Sundown Pass. Due to spring floods, a fjord halfway up is often impassable in May and June. ⊠ *End of south Quinault Valley Rd., 23 mi east of U.S. 101.*

★ **Hoh Valley Trail.** Leaving from the Hoh Visitor Center, this rain forest jaunt takes you into the Hoh Valley, wending its way alongside the river, through moss-draped maple and alder trees, and past open meadows where elk roam in winter. ⊠ *Hoh Visitor Center, 18 mi east of U.S. 101.*

Hurricane Ridge Trail. A ¼-mi alpine loop, most of it wheelchair-accessible, leads through wildflower meadows overlooking numerous vistas of the interior Olympic peaks to the south and the Strait of Juan de Fuca panorama to the north. ⊠ *Hurricane Ridge visitor center, Hurricane Ridge Road, 17 mi south of Port Angeles.*

★ **Sol Duc Trail.** This easy, 1½-mi gravel path off Sol Duc Road winds through thick Douglas fir forests toward the thundering, three-chute Sol Duc Falls. Just ¹⁄₁₀ mi from the road, below a wooden platform over the Sol Duc River, you come across the 70-foot Salmon Cascades. In late summer and autumn, thousands of salmon negotiate 50 mi or more of treacherous waters to reach the cascades and the tamer pools near Sol Duc Hot Springs. The popular 6-mi **Lovers Lane loop Trail** links the Sol Duc falls with the hot springs. You can continue up from the falls 5 mi to the **Appleton Pass Trail**, at 3,100 feet. From there you can hike on to the 8½-mi mark, where views at the High Divide are from 5,050 feet. ⊠ *Sol Duc Rd., 11 mi south of U.S. 101.*

SKIING & SNOWSHOEING Snow is most likely to fall from mid-December through late March on the Olympic Peninsula. For recorded road and weather information from November through April, call 360/565–3131. **Hurricane Ridge** is the area to head to for downhill and cross-country skiing. The most popular route for day mushers is the 1½-mi Hurricane Hill Road, west of the visitor center parking area. A marked snow-play area with trails and gentle hills has been set aside near the visitor center for cross-country skiers, snowshoers, and inner tubers. There's a weekend and holiday ski lift that runs from 10 to 4, plus two rope tows and a ski school. Cross-country trails start next to the downhill area and Hurricane Ridge Lodge. Free guided snowshoe walks take place Friday through Sunday at 2, with signups at the lodge an hour beforehand. There's also a supervised tubing area, open Friday through Sunday, ¼ mi before the parking area on the right side of the road, as well as a children's tubing area across from the lodge. Ski and snowshoe rentals cost $12 to $35 at the Hurricane Ridge visitor center.

Sequim

⓫ *17 mi east of Port Angeles on U.S. 101.*

Sequim (pronounced *skwim*), incorporated in 1913, is a pleasant farming and mill town between the northern foothills of the Olympic Mountains and the southeastern stretch of the Strait of Juan de Fuca. With neat, quiet blocks and lovely views, it's also a popular place to retire. A few miles to the north is the shallow and fertile Dungeness Valley, which has some of the lowest rainfall in western Washington. Lavender flourishes in the warm weather and is raised commercially in local fields.

The 200-acre **Olympic Game Farm**—part petting zoo, part safari—is unique among exotic-animal habitats. For years the farm's exclusive client was Walt Disney Studios, and many of the bears and tigers here are former movie stars. On the drive-through tour, be prepared to see large animals like buffalo surround your car (and lick your windows). You'll view leopards, pumas, and small indigenous animals on the walk-through. Facilities also include an aquarium, a studio barn with movie sets, a snack kiosk, and a gift shop. You can drive through the park all year, and take guided walking tours from June through September. ⊠ *1423 Ward Rd.* ☎ *360/683–4295 or 800/778–4295* ⊕ *www. olygamefarm.com* ⊠ *Drive-through tour $9, walking tour $10, combined tour $15* ⊗ *Weekdays 9–5, weekends 9–6.*

In 1977 12,000-year-old mastodon remains were discovered near Sequim. You can view the bones of these ice-age creatures, plus a beautiful wall mural, at the **Sequim-Dungeness Museum.** There are also exhibits on Captain Vancouver's explorations, the early Klallam Indians, and the area's pioneer towns. Temporary exhibits examine regional topics like earthquakes. ⊠ *175 W. Cedar St.* ☎ *360/683–8110* ⊕ *www. sequimmuseum.org* ⊠ *Free* ⊗ *Tues.–Sun. 8–4, 1st Fri. of month 8–7:30.*

Jamestown S'Klallam Village, on the beach near the mouth of the Dungeness River, has been occupied by the S'Klallam tribe for thousands of years. The tribe, whose name means "strong people," was driven to the Skokomish Reservation on Hood Canal after the signing of the Treaty of Point No Point in 1855. However, in 1874, tribal leader James Balch and some 130 S'Klallam together purchased 210 acres where the town is today. S'Klallam members have lived here ever since. A gallery sells locally made artwork. ⊠ *Off U.S. 101, 7 mi east of Sequim.*

★ **Dungeness Spit,** curving 5½ mi into the Straight of San Jaun de Fuca, is the longest natural sand spit in the United States and a wild, beautiful section of shoreline. At high tide this thread of white sand may be only 50 feet wide, and occasionally it is completely covered when storms brew up turbulent waters. More than 30,000 migratory waterfowl stop here each spring and fall, but you'll see plenty of bird life any time of year. The entire spit is part of the Dungeness National Wildlife Refuge. At the end of the Dungeness Spit is the tall, white **Dungeness Lighthouse** (☎ 360/683–9166 ⊕ www.newdungenesslighthouse.com), in operation since 1867 and saved from closure in 1994. Tours are available, but access is limited to those who can hike the 5 mi out to the end of the spit, or boats that can pull up to the beach. Volunteers staff the lighthouse around the clock. ⊠ *Kitchen Rd., 3 mi north from U.S. 101, 4 mi west of Sequim* ☎ *360/457–8451 wildlife refuge, 360/683–5847 campground* ☞ *$3* ☉ *Wildlife refuge daily sunrise–sunset.*

Sequim Bay State Park, an inlet 4 mi southwest of Sequim, is protected by a sand spit. The woodsy park has picnic tables, campsites, hiking trails, tennis courts, and a boat ramp. ⊠ *Off U.S. 101* ☎ *360/683–4235* ⊕ *www.parks.wa.gov* ☞ *Free, camping $12–$17* ☉ *Daily 8–sunset.*

Where to Stay & Eat

$–$$$ ✕ **Marina Restaurant.** This large family restaurant overlooks a great view of John Wayne Marina and Sequim Bay. The menu emphasizes red meat—especially prime rib, served every Saturday night—although seafood, pasta, and salads are also available. ⊠ *2577 W. Sequim Bay Rd.* ☎ *360/681–0577* ☰ *AE, D, MC, V.*

★ $$ ✕ **Petals Garden Café.** This restaurant at Cedarbrook Herb farm, overlooking Sequim and the Strait of Juan de Fuca, draws much of its inspiration from local produce. Soups, salads, and sandwiches are on the lunch menu, while entrées such as pan-seared duck breast with thyme-infused honey fill out the dinner menu. ⊠ *1345 S. Sequim Ave.* ☎ *360/683–4541* ☰ *MC, V* ☉ *No dinner Sun.–Tues.*

¢–$ ✕ **Oak Table Café.** Pancakes, waffles, and omelets are made using creative techniques at this breakfast and lunch restaurant. Eggs Nicole, for instance, is a medley of sautéed mushrooms, onions, spinach, and scrambled eggs served over an open-face croissant and covered with hollandaise sauce. You can get breakfast all day, or opt for the lunch menu, which includes burgers, salads, and sandwiches. ⊠ *292 W. Bell St.* ☎ *360/683–2179* ☰ *AE, D, MC, V* ☉ *No dinner.*

★ ¢–$$ ▥ **Greywolf Inn.** On a hill overlooking the town and bay, this country retreat among the trees is right on the Olympic Discovery Trail. A gazebo, Japanese-style hot tub, and warm front room encourage convivial gatherings. Berry bushes and occasionally elk dot the five acres of wild grounds. Room themes are inspired by diverse places and cultures—the south of France, the African savanna, Bavaria. One room has a fireplace, another has a featherbed, and two have magnificent views. The glass-enclosed dining room and deck overlook a meadow. ⊠ *395 Keeler Rd., 98392* ☎ *360/683–5889 or 800/914–9653* ᤟ *360/683–1487* ⊕ *www.greywolfinn.com* ⊋ *5 rooms* ♨ *Dining room, outdoor hot tub, hiking, library, recreation room, business services; no smoking* ☰ *AE, D, MC, V* ⓞ *BP.*

¢–$$ ▥ **Toad Hall Bed and Breakfast.** Kenneth Grahame's *Wind in the Willows* inspired the decorations in this B&B. Suites have mahogany furnishings and views of the garden and mountains. You may take your afternoon tea in the lounge or on the wraparound porch. Aromatherapy products are left in the bathrooms, and you are welcome to pick a bouquet from the fragrant lavender plants in the garden. ⊠ *12 Jesslyn La., 98382* ☎ *360/681–2534* ⊋ *3 suites* ♨ *Dining room, some in-room hot tubs, refrig-*

erators, cable TV, in-room VCRs, pond, hot tub; no room phones, no kids, no smoking ☰ *MC, V* ¶⊙∣ *BP.*

¢–$ ⌂ **Dungeness Panorama Bed and Breakfast.** As you would expect from its name, this B&B is surrounded by unbeatable views of the bay and the Olympic Mountains. Custom furnishings in the main house and a separate cottage follow a French-provincial theme, reflecting the background of the proprietors. Suites, one blue with a lighthouse view and one green with a bay scene, have fireplaces, kitchenettes, and decks overlooking the water. The spit is only a short walk from the backyard. ✉ *630 Marine Dr., 98382* 📠 *360/683–4503* ⊕ *www.awaterview.com* 🛌 *2 suites, 1 cottage* ⚒ *Room service, kitchenettes, microwaves, refrigerators, in-room VCRs; no kids under 12, no smoking* ☰ *No credit cards* ¶⊙∣ *BP.*

Nightlife

The Jamestown S'Klallam tribe's enormous **7 Cedars Casino** (✉ 270756 U.S. 101 ☎ 360/683–7777) has blackjack, roulette, and slots. One end of the casino is devoted to bingo. The tribe also runs an excellent art gallery and gift shop.

Port Townsend

⑫ *31 mi east of Sequim.*

A Victorian-era city with a restored waterfront historic district, Port Townsend is the most picturesque gateway to the Olympic Peninsula. You could easily spend a weekend exploring its art galleries, shops, and trendy restaurants.

Settled in 1851, and fondly dubbed the "City of Dreams," Port Townsend was laid out with two separate urban quarters: Watertown, on the waterfront, catered to sailors, while uptown, on the plateau above the bluffs, was where Watertown merchants and other permanent citizens lived and raised their families. Today the city has a strong community of writers, musicians, painters, and other artists, and the waterfront is where you find the chicest stores and seafood restaurants. Many businesses are housed in the handsome restored brick buildings—constructed during the 1888–90 railroad boom—that line the streets at the waterfront. The many impressive yachts docked here attest to the town's status as one of the Salish Sea's premier sailing spots.

Look up at the **Lewis Building** (✉ Madison and Water Sts.) to see the "Genuine Bull Durham Smoking Tobacco" advertisement, one of the many relics harking back to the town's glory days as a customs port. The **bell tower** on Jefferson Street, at the top of the Tyler Street stairs, is the last of its kind in the country. Built in 1890, it was used to call volunteer firemen to duty. Inside are artifacts from the city museum, including a 19th-century horse-drawn hearse.

Built in 1858 by a local merchant, **Rothschild House** is furnished with 19th-century household goods and surrounded by herb and flower gardens. ✉ *Jefferson and Taylor Sts.* ☎ *360/385–2722* ⊕ *www.ptguide.com* 🎫 *$2* ⊙ *Apr.–mid-Oct., Wed.–Sun. 10–5; mid-Oct.–Apr., weekends 10–3.*

> **need a break?**
>
> Stop at the **Elevated Ice Cream Company** (✉ 627 and 631 Water St. ☎ 360/385–1156) for coffee, pastries, candy, or a scoop of ice cream. The proprietors first served their homemade ice cream from an antique Victorian elevator cage in 1977.

The 1892 City Hall building, where Jack London briefly languished in jail on his way to the Klondike, contains the **Jefferson County Historical Mu-**

seum. Here you'll find four floors of Native American artifacts, photos of the Olympic Peninsula, and exhibits chronicling Port Townsend's past. ⊠ *210 Madison St.* ☎ *360/385–1003* ⌸ *$2* ⊗ *Mon.–Sat. 11–4, Sun. 1–4.*

The neatly manicured grounds of 443-acre **Fort Worden State Park** include a row of restored Victorian officers' houses, a World War II balloon hangar, and a sandy beach that leads to the Point Wilson Lighthouse. The fort, which was built on Point Wilson in 1896, 17 years after the lighthouse, now hosts art events. A science center on site has aquariums and touch tanks where you can reach in and feel sea creatures like crabs and anemones. ⊠ *200 Battery Way* ☎ *360/385–4730* ⊕ *www. olympus.net/ftworden* ⌸ *Park free, science center $2* ⊗ *Park daily sunrise–sunset, science center Tues.–Sun. noon–6.*

off the
beaten
path

FORT FLAGLER STATE PARK – A 15- to 20-minute drive south and east of town leads to the tip of Marrowstone Island and this state park. Built in the 1890s, Fort Flagler was a military training center through the World Wars, and still has old gun placements overlooking its beaches. This fort, along with Fort Worden in Port Townsend and Fort Casey on Whidbey Island, was constructed as part of an "Iron Triangle" of defense for Puget Sound. Today the park has campgrounds and 7 mi of wooded and oceanfront hiking trails—remnants of old army roads. The inlets of the island are great for paddling around; you can rent canoes, kayaks, and pedal boats from Nordland General Store (☎ 360/385–0777), near the park entrance. ⊠ *10341 Flagler Rd., Nordland* ☎ *360/385–1259* ⌸ *Day use free, campground $10–$16* ⊗ *Daily sunrise–sunset.*

A gazebo is all that remains of the original fort, but 377 acres of forest and meadow land makes **Old Fort Townsend State Park** a lovely place for hiking, picnicking, and camping. ⊠ *1370 Old Ft. Townsend Rd.* ☎ *360/ 385–3595 or 800/233–0321* ⌸ *Free* ⊗ *Mid-Apr.–Sept., 6:30–sunset.*

Where to Stay & Eat

$$–$$$ ✕ **Lanza's Ristorante.** This uptown restaurant has been serving family recipes, like Grandma Gloria's meatballs, since 1985. Fettuccine with smoked salmon in feta-cream sauce, and pizzas, are other specialties. You might hear live piano music on weekends. ⊠ *1020 Lawrence St.* ☎ *360/379–1900* ⊟ *MC, V* ⊗ *Closed Sun.*

$$–$$$ ✕ **Lonny's.** Chef-owner Lonny Ritter aims to provide a sensual dining
Fodor'sChoice experience here. Handsome wood furnishings and ochre walls provide
★ the background for fresh, delicious meals. The cuisine is American with Italian influences and the focus is fresh, local seafood, such as Dungeness crab and Dabob Bay oyster stew laced with butter. Vegetarian dishes like grilled eggplant with fresh mozzarella and basil are also served. The staff is professional and the wine list extensive. ⊠ *2330 Washington St.* ☎ *360/385–0700* ⊟ *MC, V* ⊗ *Closed Tues.*

$–$$ ✕ **Ajax Café.** Every table overlooks the harbor at this restaurant. You check in at the front desk fashioned like a 1965 Cadillac then, if you like, you can try on a hat or tie from the restaurant's collection of vintage accessories. The menu includes wild salmon, mahi-mahi, snapper, and halibut, as well as pastas and steaks. A cast-iron stove warms the dining room in winter, and there's live music Thursday through Sunday. ⊠ *271 Water St., Port Hadlock* ☎ *360/385–3450* ⊟ *MC, V* ⊗ *Closed Mon. No lunch.*

$–$$ ✕ **Fountain Café.** This funky, art- and knickknack-filled café is a town favorite. Although it's known for sumptuous vegetarian dishes and delicate warm salads, you'll also find tender steaks, baked apple chicken, and other hearty choices on the rotating menu. Expect the occasional wait, or call to get your name on the list. ⊠ *920 Washington St.* ☎ *360/ 385–1364* ▤ *MC, V* ☉ *Closed Tues. and mid-Dec.–mid-Feb.*

★ **$–$$** ✕ **Khu Larb Thai.** Port Townsend's only Thai restaurant is the best on the Olympic Peninsula. Fresh herbs and spices are infused in such dishes as green-curry chicken, pad thai, and the Spicy Seafood Combination (stir-fried prawns, scallops, calamari, and clams in homemade curry paste). Knickknacks and art from Southeast Asia bring a tropical feel to the room, and candlelight enhances the intimate dinner setting. ⊠ *225 Adams St.* ☎ *360/385–5023* ▤ *MC, V* ☉ *Closed Mon.*

$–$$ ✕ **Silverwater Cafe.** On the first floor of the historic Elks' Lodge building, Silverwater matches its elegant surroundings with a sophisticated menu. Signature dishes include artichoke pâté, sauteed fresh oysters, and seafood pasta. Fresh fish, chicken, lamb, and Angus beef are also served. The lemon poppy seed cake has become a local legend. ⊠ *237 Taylor St.* ☎ *360/385–6448* ▤ *MC, V.*

$ ✕ **Salal Café.** Informal and bright, this restaurant is especially beloved for its ample, all-day Sunday breakfasts (you can get breakfast the rest of the week, too). The lunch menu mixes sandwiches and soups with fresh salads and vegetarian options—with Port Townsend's top-rated Elevated Ice Cream as the perfect dessert. Try to get a table in the glassed-in back room, which faces a plant-filled courtyard. ⊠ *634 Water St.* ☎ *360/385–6532* ⌔ *Reservations not accepted* ▤ *No credit cards* ☉ *No dinner Tues. and Wed.*

¢–$ ✕▥ **Manresa Castle.** An immense imposing stone structure, this mansion was built in 1892 for Port Townsend businessman and mayor Charles Eisenbeis and his wife Kate. Later tenants included Jesuit priests, who named the castle after the town in Spain where their order was founded. A hotel since the late 1960s, the castle retains its Victorian character, although it's been renovated to offer modern amenities. Rooms have wood trim and furniture, patterned wallpaper, and lace curtains covering tall windows. The austere, period dining room ($–$$) serves rack of lamb, beef tournedos, and osso buco. Make time for a round in the Edwardian-style cocktail lounge, set around the bar from San Francisco's old Savoy Hotel. ⊠ *7th and Sheridan Sts., 98368* ☎ *360/385– 5750 or 800/732–1281* ▤ *360/385–5883* ⊕ *www.manresacastle.com* ⬂ *37 rooms, 3 suites* ⌔ *Restaurant, some in-room hot tubs, cable TV, bar, business services; no a/c* ▤ *D, MC, V* ⦿| *CP.*

★ **$$** ▥ **Old Church Inn.** The chance to sleep in a National Historic Landmark church, complete with belltower, steeple, and Puget Sound panorama, is the draw of this simple, charming inn. The exterior remains much the same as it was a century ago inside, the pews have been removed to make room for living, kitchen, and dining areas. Wood floors, fir wainscoting, and pastel fabrics provide a gracious ambience. Upstairs are two bedrooms with large windows. The large backyard and barbecue area make this a favorite group gathering place. The inn is 10 mi south of Port Townsend. ⊠ *130 Randolph St., Port Hadlock 98339* ☎ *360/732– 7552* ⊕ *www.olypen.com/inn* ⬂ *1 house* ⌔ *Dining room, kitchen, refrigerator, croquet, laundry facilities* ▤ *AE, D, DC, MC, V.*

$–$$$ ▥ **James House.** This white three-story Victorian, built in 1889, occupies a prime position on the bluff overlooking Port Townsend's waterfront. Cozy top-floor rooms beneath the eaves have wonderful views but small baths. The second floor has spacious rooms and the splendid Bridal Suite. On the ground floor are two more spacious suites, and behind the house is the original Gardener's Cottage. Rooms have dark cherry, oak, or wicker furnishings, colorful rugs, and plush armchairs. Breakfasts are served in the formal dining room, as are fresh-baked cookies and complimentary sherry in the evening. The adjacent Bungalow on a Bluff, a contemporary-style, free-standing home, has a wood-burning fireplace, Jacuzzi, and sweeping bay views. ⊠ *1238 Washington St., 98368* ☎ *360/385–1238 or 800/385–1238* 🖷 *360/379–5551* ⊕ *www. jameshouse.com* ⇝ *7 rooms, 3 suites, 1 cottage, 1 bungalow* ⚘ *Dining room, in-room data ports, some in-room hot tubs* ⊟ *MC, V* ⭠⃘ *BP.*

$–$$ 🏠 **Ann Starrett Mansion.** Gables, turrets, and gingerbread trim decorate
Fodor'sChoice this glorious 1889 mansion, a gift from a wealthy contractor to his young
★ bride. You can climb the three-tiered hanging spiral staircase to a 70-
foot-high cupola tower, where outdoor murals and red stained-glass windows catch the first light of each changing season. Each guest room is unique and beautifully decorated with American antiques. Two separate cottages have more modern furnishings and facilities. ⊠ *744 Clay St., 98368* ☎ *360/385–3205 or 800/321–0644* 🖷 *360/385–2976* ⊕ *www.starrettmansion.com* ⇝ *9 rooms, 2 cottages* ⚘ *Dining room, some kitchens, cable TV in some rooms, business services; no a/c, no kids under 11, no smoking* ⊟ *AE, D, MC, V* ⭠⃘ *BP.*

$–$$ 🏠 **Bishop Victorian Guest Suites.** Once an office building and warehouse, this inn offers English-style accommodations in one- and two-bedroom suites, all with fireplaces, sleeping sofas, and kitchenettes. Take time to explore the art gallery, gorgeous Victorian gardens, and elegant lounges. A breakfast basket and passes to a nearby athletic club are included. ⊠ *714 Washington St., 98368* ☎ *360/385–6122, 800/824–4738 reservations* 🖷 *360/379–1840* ⊕ *www.bishopvictorian.com* ⇝ *16 suites* ⚘ *In-room data ports, kitchenettes, some microwaves, refrigerators, cable TV, business services, meeting rooms, some pets allowed (fee); no a/c, no smoking* ⊟ *AE, D, MC, V* ⭠⃘ *CP.*

★ **$–$$**   🏠 **Chanticleer Inn.** This Victorian house, built in 1876 on a bluff above town, has clean lines and a few well-chosen antiques rather than a lot of frills. Rooms have wood and wicker furniture, feather beds, plush robes, and complimentary French bath items. The Beach Haven has a Jacuzzi; the Bay View has a private deck; and Meg's Room has a king-size bed and private entrance. A family suite has a living room, fireplace, full kitchen, and canopy bed. Gourmet snack baskets appear every day. ⊠ *1208 Franklin St., 98304* ☎ *360/385–6239 or 800/858–9421* 🖷 *360/ 385–3377* ⊕ *www.northolympic.com/chanticleer* ⇝ *4 rooms, 1 cottage* ⚘ *Dining room, some in-room hot tubs, some in-room VCRs, kitchen; no room phones, no smoking* ⊟ *MC, V* ⭠⃘ *BP.*

$ 🏠 **Captain John Quincy Adams House Bed and Breakfast.** The great-great-grandson of John Quincy Adams built this house in 1887. Red accents on the windows and roof complement the Victorian architecture. Rooms have patterned wallpaper, hand-carved antiques, fireplaces, and claw-foot bathtubs. In one of the many common areas, a Victorian pool table provides turn-of-the-20th-century entertainment. ⊠ *1028 Tyler St., 98368* ☎ *360/379–8832* ⇝ *3 rooms, 1 suite* ⚘ *Dining room, hot tub, massage, billiards; no a/c, no room phones, no room TVs, no kids under 12, no smoking* ⊟ *MC, V* ⭠⃘ *BP.*

¢–$$$ 🏠 **Tides Inn.** Resembling an old-fashioned seaside motel, this condo-style inn is at the edge of the beach. The older building has small, simple, and inexpensive rooms, while the newer building has spacious, completely up-to-date, upscale rooms, some with private decks that extend over the water's edge. Note to movie buffs: scenes from *An Officer and a Gentleman* were filmed here. ⊠ *1807 Water St., 98368* ☎ *360/385–0595 or 800/822–8696* 🖷 *360/385–7370* ⊕ *www.tides-inn.com* ⇝ *21 rooms, 1 suite* ⚘ *Picnic grounds, some in-room hot tubs, some kitchens, some microwaves, some refrigerators, cable TV, beach, hot tub, meeting rooms; no smoking* ⊟ *AE, D, DC, MC, V* ⭠⃘ *CP.*

¢–$ 🏠 **Beach Cottages on Marrowstone.** Eight basic four-person cottages on 10 acres of waterfront land abutted by a wildlife sanctuary assure total seclusion. Each has a woodstove, deck, and complete kitchen. Bring jackets, good walking shoes, binoculars, and boats or bicycles, as the area is teeming with Northwest wildlife and you can explore it by land or water. Marrowstone Island is about a 20-minute drive southeast of Port Townsend. Note that property rules stipulate quiet after dark. ⊠ *10 Beach Dr., Nordland, Marrowstone Island 98358* ☎ *360/385–3077 or 800/871–3077* 🖶 *360/385–1181* ⊕ *www.ecologicplace.com* ➫ *8 cottages* ⚲ *Kitchens, microwaves, refrigerators, beach, boating, hiking; no smoking* ▭ *MC, V.*

★ ¢–$ 🏨 **Fort Worden Accommodations.** There's sleeping room for more than 600 people throughout this beautiful historical park. The elegant Victorian-style, 1930s officer's homes have fireplaces and kitchens. Madrona Vista is a former World War I barracks building with two large dining rooms, a huge kitchen, a deck with lovely views, and bedding for 23. The Olympic Hostel has private and family rooms and a common kitchen, and serves all-you-can-eat pancakes, but it's closed between 9:30 AM and 5 PM. Three dormitories with a combination of bunk rooms and private quarters sleep up to 365 people. Rates include three dining-hall meals per day, served family- or buffet-style. Campsites are also available. ⊠ *272 Battery Way, 98368* ☎ *360/344–4434 park, 360/385–0655 hostel* ⊕ *www.olympus.net/ftworden/accommod.html* ➫ *33 houses, 392 dorm beds, 6 rooms, 80 campsites* ⚲ *Cafeteria, kitchens, refrigerators, hiking; no room TVs, no smoking* ▭ *MC, V.*

¢–$ 🏨 **Palace Hotel.** This former bordello on the town's main street has an exposed-brick-wall lobby. The rooms, named for the ladies who used to work here, have 14-foot ceilings and worn antiques. Miss Ruby has graceful, arched windows and a kitchenette; Miss Rose has a whirlpool tub; and Miss Marie is a corner suite with a fireplace. A Continental breakfast is delivered to your room from October through April. ⊠ *1004 Water St., 98368* ☎ *360/385–0773 or 800/962–0741* 🖶 *360/946–5287* ⊕ *www.palacehotelpt.com* ➫ *15 rooms, 12 with bath* ⚲ *Some microwaves, some refrigerators, conference room* ▭ *AE, D, MC, V.*

¢–$ 🏨 **Quimper Inn.** The stately, white, colonnaded 1888 Georgian-style home is a retreat for those who love books. Suites are stuffed with tomes, including the favorite Library Room, which has a rolling ladder so you can reach the top shelves. Two rooms share a bath; two others have clawfoot tubs. A broad walking porch overlooks Admiralty Inlet. You'll find candlelight and music in the dining room, and a fireplace in the living room. ⊠ *1306 Franklin St., 98368* ☎ *360/385–1060 or 800/557–1060* 🖶 *360/385–2688* ⊕ *www.quimperinn.com* ➫ *5 rooms, 3 with bath* ⚲ *Dining room, piano; no room phones, no room TVs, no kids under 12, no smoking* ▭ *MC, V* ❘⊙❘ *BP.*

Nightlife & the Arts

NIGHTLIFE **Back Alley** (⊠ 923 Washington St. ☎ 360/385–2914), a favorite with locals, hosts rock-and-roll bands on weekends. Secluded **Sirens** (⊠ 832 Water St. ☎ 360/379–0776) overlooks the water from the third floor and books rock, blues, and jazz acts on weekends. The large old **Town Tavern** (⊠ 639 Water St. ☎ 360/385–4706) has live music—from jazz to blues to rock—on weekends.

Centrum (⌂ Box 1158, 98368 ☎ 360/385–3102 or 800/733–3608), Port Townsend's well-respected performing-arts organization, presents performances, workshops, and conferences throughout the year at Fort Worden State Park. The Centrum Summer Arts Festival runs from June to September.

Sports & the Outdoors

BICYCLING **P. T. Cyclery** (⊠ 100 Tyler St. ☎ 360/385–6470) rents mountain bikes and can advise you on where to start your journey. The nearest place to go riding is Fort Worden State Park, but you can range as far afield as Fort Flagler, the lower Dungeness trails (no bikes are allowed on the spit itself), or across the water to Whidbey Island.

BOAT CRUISE **Captain Jack's Sea Charters** (☎ 360/379–4033 or 877/278–5225 ⊕ www.cpt-jack.com) operates four- to five-hour narrated whale-watching tours around Port Townsend and the San Juan Islands. Tours cost $50 and operate from April to October, departing at 9:15 daily and also at 2:30 in July and August. Bring a jacket, binoculars, and lunch (although snacks and a $6.50 box lunch are available on board). If you don't see whales, the trip is free. **P. S. Express** (✉ 431 Water St. ☎ 360/385–5288 ⊕ www.pugetsoundexpress.com) has run summer speedboat connections between Port Townsend and Friday Harbor for more than 20 years. The round trips costs $52.50. May through September, boats depart Port Townsend at 8:30, arriving in Friday Harbor at noon; the return trip departs Friday Harbor at 3:30 and arrives back in Port Townsend at 5:30. Whale-watching trips from Friday Harbor depart at 12:15 and cost $25.

KAYAKING **Kayak Port Townsend** (✉ 435 Water St. ☎ 360/385–6240) conducts guided kayak tours from April to September. Tours cost $40 for three hours or $80 for a full day with lunch. You can also rent single and double kayaks for $15 and $25 per hour, respectively. **PT Outdoors** (✉ 10178 Water St. ☎ 360/379–3608 or 888/754–8598) offers kayaking classes and guided trips. Waterfront tours are $35; two- to three-hour early-bird tours, sunset tours, and half-day tours are $40; full-day tours are $70. Single kayaks and rowboats rent for $15 per hour; double kayaks rent for $25 per hour.

SCUBA DIVING The **Port Townsend Dive Shop** (✉ 2200 Washington St. ☎ 360/379–3635 ⊕ www.ptdive.com) makes seasonal charter trips to river and ocean sites around the peninsula. South of Port Townsend, the waterfront **Hood Sport 'n Dive** (✉ 27001 U.S. 101, Hoodsport ☎ 360/877–6818) has scuba equipment rentals and sales—and you can test your gear before you buy it. **Mike's Diving Center** (✉ 22270 U.S. 101, Shelton ☎ 360/877–9568) rents and sells gear for Hood Canal trips.

Shopping

Port Townsend is packed with art galleries, New Age-y book and gift shops, and pseudo-hippie clothing boutiques, especially along Water Street and its offshoots. More stores are uptown on Lawrence Street near an enclave of Victorian houses.

North by Northwest Gallery (✉ 18 Water St. ☎ 360/385–0955) specializes in Eskimo and Native American art, artifacts, jewelry, and clothing. **Russell Jaqua Gallery** (✉ 21 Taylor St. ☎ 360/385–5262) exhibits metalworks. **William James Bookseller** (✉ 829 Water St. ☎ 360/385–7313) stocks used and out-of-print books in all fields, with an emphasis on nautical, regional history, and theology titles.

Three dozen dealers at the two-story **Port Townsend Antique Mall** (✉ 802 Washington St. ☎ 360/385–2590) sell merchandise ranging from pricey Victorian collectors' items to cheap flea-market kitsch.

Sport Townsend (✉ 1044 Water St. ☎ 360/379–9711) is stocked with high-quality outdoor gear, including backpacks, hiking boots, camping supplies, and boating and fishing equipment. Winter sports gear is also sold here, including downhill and cross-country ski accessories, cold-weather clothing, and snowshoes.

The Olympic Peninsula A to Z

AIR TRAVEL

Port Angeles is the major northern gateway to the Olympic Peninsula, while Olympia is the major entry point in the south. San Juan Airlines connects Port Angeles with Boeing Field, near Seattle, from where passengers make the 15-minute trip to Sea-Tac Airport via a free shuttle bus. Big Sky Airlines connects Olympia with Spokane.

AIRPORTS & TRANSFERS
Fairchild International Airport, the largest on the Olympic Peninsula, is 6 mi southwest of Port Angeles off U.S. 101 (take Airport Rd. north from U.S. 101). Jefferson County Airport, a small charter-flight base, is 4 mi southwest of Port Townsend off Route 19.

Olympic Bus Lines, a Greyhound affiliate, transports passengers twice daily from Port Angeles and Sequim to Sea-Tac Airport ($43) and downtown Seattle ($29). Pennco also has service from the Olympic Peninsula to Seattle.

🛪 Airports **Fairchild International Airport** ✉ 1404 Fairchild International Airport Rd. ☎ 360/457-1138. **Jefferson County International Airport** ✉ 310 Airport Rd. ☎ 360/385-0656.

🛪 Transfers **Olympic** ☎ 360/417-0700 or 800/457-4492 ⊕ www.olympicbuslines. **Pennco** ☎ 360/452-5104 or 888/673-6626.

CARRIERS
🛪 Local Airlines **Big Sky Airlines** ☎ 800/237-7788. **San Juan Airlines** ☎ 425/277-1590 or 800/874-4434.

BOAT & FERRY TRAVEL

Washington State Ferries charge $9.50 per vehicle from Port Townsend to Keystone; it's $2.08 each way if you walk on. From Port Angeles, you can reach Victoria, BC on the *Victoria Express* passenger ferry, which makes the one-hour trip ($25) twice daily from mid-May to mid-October. Or, take your car on the M.V. *Coho*, operated by Black Ball Transport, which makes the 1½-hour crossing four times daily from mid-May through mid-October and twice daily the rest of the year (except when it's docked for maintenance, from mid-January through mid-March). Rates are $33 per car and driver, $8.50 per passenger, and $3.75 per bike. On both lines, discounts apply to senior citizens, youngsters and students; those under 5 ride free. The *Victoria Express* departs from the Landing Mall terminal, while the *Coho* departs from the ferry terminal at the foot of Laurel Street.

🚢 Boat & Ferry Information **Black Ball Transport** ☎ 360/457-4491 in Port Angeles, 250/386-2202 in Victoria ⊕ www.cohoferry.com. **Victoria/San Juan Cruises** ☎ 800/443-4552 ⊕ www.whales.com. **Washington State Ferries** ✉ Colman Dock, Pier 52, Downtown, Seattle ☎ 206/464-6400 or 888/808-7977, 800/843-3779 automated line in WA and BC ⊕ www.wsdot.wa.gov/ferries.

BUS TRAVEL

Traveling by bus is slow going on the Olympic Peninsula. Clallam Transit covers the northeastern side of the peninsula, including Port Angeles to Sequim, Forks, and La Push. Jefferson Transit makes connections between Port Angeles, Bremerton, Silverdale, Poulbo, and Seattle. Olympic Bus Lines connects Seattle, Sea-Tac Airport, and Edmonds with Port Angeles, Sequim, Port Townsend, and the Hood Canal Bridge.

🚌 **Clallam Transit** ☎ 360/452-4511 or 800/858-3747 ⊕ www.clallamtransit.com. **Jefferson Transit** ☎ 360/452-1397 or 800/436-3950 ⊕ www.jeffersontransit.com. **Olympic Bus Lines** ☎ 360/417-0700 or 800/457-4492 ⊕ www.olympicbuslines.com.

CAR RENTAL

Budget and Enterprise are the national car rental agencies on the Olympic Peninsula. Many local agencies also have reliable vehicles and competitive rates. Compact cars rent for about $25 per day sedans rent for $40 per day, and SUVs cost about $50 per day.

🛈 Major Agencies **Budget** ✉ 111 E. Front St., Port Angeles ☎ 360/452-4774 ✉ 518 Logan St., Port Townsend ☎ 360/385-7766. **Enterprise** ✉ 716 W. Market St., Aberdeen ☎ 360/533-1094 ✉ 902 E. 1st St., Port Angeles ☎ 360/417-3083.

🛈 Local Agencies **Gary's** ✉ 1510 W. Sims Way, Port Townsend ☎ 360/379-4739. **Evergreen** ✉ 808 E. Front St., Port Angeles ☎ 360/452-8001. **U-Save** ✉ 2959 Rte. 105, Grayland ☎ 360/247-1105.

CAR TRAVEL

U.S. 101, the main thoroughfare around the Olympic Peninsula, is a two-lane, well-paved highway. Rural backroads are blacktop or gravel, and tend to have potholes and get washed out during rains. In winter, landslides and wet weather frequently close roads.

EMERGENCIES

Pharmacies are generally open weekdays 9 to 7, Saturday 9 to 5, and Sunday noon to 5.

🛈 Hospitals **Forks Community Hospital** ✉ 520 Bogachiel Way, Forks ☎ 360/374-6271 ⊕ www.forkshospital.org. **Grays Harbor Community Hospital** ✉ 915 Anderson Dr., Aberdeen ☎ 360/537-5000. **Jefferson General Hospital** ✉ 834 Sheridan St., Port Townsend ☎ 360/385-2200 or 800/244-9912 ⊕ www.jgh.org. **Mason General Hospital** ✉ 901 Mt. View Dr., Bldg. 1, Shelton ☎ 360/426-1611. **Olympic Memorial Hospital** ✉ 929 Caroline St., Port Angeles ☎ 360/417-7000 ⊕ www.olympicmedical.org.

🛈 Pharmacies **Rite Aid** ✉ 110 Port Angeles Plaza, Port Angeles ☎ 360/457-3456 ✉ 680 W. Washington, Sequim ☎ 360/681-0129.

MAIL & SHIPPING

Post offices on the Olympic Peninsula are generally open weekdays 8 to 5 and Saturday 9 to noon.

🛈 Post Offices **Forks Post Office** ✉ 61 S. Spartan Ave., Forks 98331 ☎ 360/374-6303. **Neah Bay Post Office** ✉ 190 Buchanan St., Neah Bay 98357 ☎ 360/645-2325. **Ocean Shores Post Office** ✉ 689 Dolphin Ave., Ocean Shores 98569 ☎ 360/289-3665. **Port Angeles Post Office** ✉ 424 E. 1st St., Port Angeles 98362 ☎ 360/417-4920. **Port Townsend Post Office** ✉ 1322 Washington St., Port Townsend 9836 ☎ 360/379-2996.

MONEY MATTERS

Most banks have branches and ATMs in Port Angeles, Port Townsend, and Aberdeen. Ocean Shores and towns around the north and west Olympic coastline have only ATMs.

🛈 Banks **Bank of America** ☎ 800/642-9855 ⊕ www.bankofamerica.com ✉ 101 E. Market St., Aberdeen ☎ 360/532-8040 ✉ 5th St. and Bogachiel Ave., Clallam Bay ☎ 360/963-2208 ✉ 481 S. Forks Ave. (U.S. 101), Forks ☎ 360/374-2261 ✉ 102 E. Front St., Port Angeles ☎ 260/457-2737 ✉ 134 W. 8th St., Port Angeles ☎ 360/457-2747 ✉ 734 Water St., Port Townsend ☎ 360/385-1885 ✉ 114 S. Sequim Ave., Sequim ☎ 360/683-1988 ✉ 620 N. Monteseno Ave., Westport ☎ 360/268-9155 **Key Bank** ☎ 206/447-5767 ⊕ www.keybank.com ✉ 100 N. Broadway St., Aberdeen ☎ 360/533-1000 ✉ 1633 E. 1st St., Port Angeles ☎ 360/452-4554 ✉ 120 N. Dunlap Ave., Sequim ☎ 360/683-7924 ✉ 410 W. Railroad Ave., Shelton ☎ 360/426-8234. **US Bank** ☎ 800/872-2657 ⊕ www.usbank.com ✉ 777 Simpson Ave., Hoquiam ☎ 360/532-3480 ✉ 14890 Center Rd., Quilcene ☎ 360/765-3361 ✉ 134 E. 7th St., Port Angeles ☎ 360/457-1183 ✉ 1239 Water St., Port Townsend ☎ 360/385-2274 ✉ 101 W. Washington St., Sequim ☎ 360/683-3366. **Washington Mutual** ☎ 800/756-8000 ⊕ www.wamu.com ✉ 101 W. Front St., Port Angeles ☎ 360/452-8981 ✉ 419 Kearney St., Port Angeles ☎ 360/385-0425 ✉ 680 W. Washington St., Sequim ☎ 360/683-7242. **Wells Fargo** ☎ 800/869-3557 ⊕ www.usbank.com ✉ 221 W. Heron St. (in Safeway), Aberdeen ☎ 360/532-3428.

TOURS & TRIPS

BOATING, DIVING
& KAYAKING
TOURS

Kayak tours generally run for two to three hours and cost $30 to $40; full-day excursions with lunch cost between $70 and $100. Boat tours and whale-watching tours usually last three to five hours and cost $30 to $60. Scuba-diving tours, including equipment, are in the $50 to $75 range for a two-tank dive.

Curley's Resort & Dive Center in Sekiu is the region's top scuba shop and offers group tours to popular diving sites around the peninsula. Also in Sekiu, Puffin Adventures organizes boating, kayaking, fishing, and scuba diving trips in the region. Extreme Adventures runs two-hour and overnight float trips on the Hoh River. Olympic Adventures runs kayak trips on the Port Townsend waterfront and around the Strait of San Juan de Fuca. Olympic Raft & Kayak conducts white-water and scenic float trips on the Hoh and Elwha rivers. Sound Dive Center has scuba certification classes, dive equipment, and tours around the region.

🔳 **Curley's Resort & Dive Center** ✉ 291 Front St., Sekiu ☎ 360/963-2281 or 800/542-9680 ⊕ www.curleysresort.com. **Extreme Adventures** ⊕ Box 1991, Forks ☎ 360/374-8747. **Olympic Adventures** ✉1001 Water St., Port Townsend ☎360/379-7611. **Olympic Outdoor** ✉ 773 Pt. Brown Ave. NW, Port Townsend ☎ 360/289-3736. **Olympic Raft & Kayak** ✉ 123 Lake Aldwell Rd., Port Angeles ☎ 360/452-1443 ⊕ www.raftandkayak.com. **Puffin Adventures** ⊕ Box 157, Sekiu ☎ 360/963-2744 or 888/305-2437 ⊕ www.olypen.com/puffinadventures. **Sound Dive Center** ✉625 E. Front St., Port Angeles ☎360/457-3749 ⊕ www.sounddive.com.

HIKING &
WALKING TOURS

Guided Historical Tours conducts two- to three-hour walking tours of Port Townsend for $10 to $20. Olympic Van Tours and Bus Lines, based in Port Angeles, offers guided day and multiday tours of Olympic National Park and shuttle service for backpackers to all national park trail heads. Van tours of Olympic National Park and the surrounding area range from a half-day to full-day trips; costs range from $40 to $75. John Monk's Guide Service leads hiking and fishing tours around Washington's coastal rivers. Peak Six Tours, in Forks, provides gear and information for hiking, biking, camping, climbing, and sightseeing on the Olympic Peninsula. Guided hikes cost about $50 per day.

🔳 **Guided Historical Tours** ✉820 Tyler St., Port Townsend ☎360/385-1967. **John Monk's Guide Service** ⊕ Box 1012, Forks ☎ 360/374-5817. **Olympic Van Tours and Bus Lines** ☎360/452-3858 or 888/457-3500. **Peak Six Tours** ✉4883 Upper Hoh Rd., Forks ☎360/374-5254.

VISITOR INFORMATION

🔳 **Clallam Bay/Sekiu Chamber of Commerce** ⊕ Box 355, Clallam Bay 98326 ☎ 360/963-2339 ⊕ www.sekiu.com. **Forks Chamber of Commerce** ✉ 1411 S. Forks Ave., Forks 98331 ☎ 800/443-6757 ⊕ www.forkswa.com. **Grays Harbor Chamber of Commerce** ✉ 506 Duffy St., Aberdeen 98520 ☎ 360/532-1924 ⊕ www.graysharbor.org. **Montesano Chamber of Commerce** ✉ 128 Brumfield Ave., Montesano 98563 ☎ 360/249-5522 or 888/294-0483 ⊕ www.montesano-wa.com. **North Olympic Peninsula Visitor and Convention Bureau** ⊕ Box 670, Port Angeles 98362 ☎ 360/452-8552 or 800/942-4042 ⊕ www.olympicpeninsula.org. **Northwest Interpretive Association** ✉ 3002 Mt. Angeles Rd., Port Angeles ☎ 360/565-3195 ⊕ www.nwpubliclands.com. **Ocean Shores Chamber of Commerce** ✉ 120 Chance a la Mer, Ocean Shores 98569 ☎ 800/762-3224 ⊕ www.oceanshores.org. **Olympic National Forest** ✉ 1835 Blacklake Blvd., Olympia 98512 ☎ 360/956-2400. **Olympic National Park** ✉ 1835 Blacklake Blvd., Olympia 98512 ☎ 360/956-4501. **Port Angeles Chamber of Commerce** ✉ 121 E. Railroad Ave., 98362 ☎ 360/452-2363. **Port Townsend Chamber of Commerce and Visitor Information Center** ✉ 2437 Sims Way, Port Townsend 98368 ☎ 360/385-7869 or 888/365-6978 ⊕ www.ptguide.com. **Sequim-Dungeness Valley Chamber of Commerce** ⊕ Box 907, Sequim 98382 ☎ 360/683-6197 or 800/737-8462 ⊕ www.cityofsequim.com. **Washington Coast Chamber of Commerce** ✉ 2272 Rte. 109, Box 562, Ocean City

98569 ☎ 360/289-4552 ⊕ www.washingtoncoastchamber.org. **Westport-Grayland Chamber of Commerce** ✉ 2985 S. Montesano, Westport 98595 ☎ 360/268-9422 or 800/345-6223 ⊕ www.westportgrayland-chamber.org.

SOUTHWESTERN WASHINGTON

Updated by
Gina Bacon

With volcanic peaks to the northeast, the Columbia River Gorge to the southeast, and sandy beaches along the Pacific shore, southwestern Washington offers ample opportunity for exploration and adventure. It's also home to one of the most famous sections of the Lewis and Clark Trail: it was near Long Beach, after making their way west through the Columbia River Gorge, that Meriwether Lewis and William Clark first saw the Pacific Ocean.

Along much of Washington's southern coast, mountains are separated from ocean by wide beaches and broad inlets, which, in turn, are protected by sandy spits. The exception is Cape Disappointment at the mouth of the Columbia River. There are depressions in the sand that hold bogs, many of which are planted with cranberries. The mainland margins of the inlets and the banks of the lower Columbia are swampy and cut by channels into marshy islands. This area is as close to Louisiana bayou country as the Northwest comes. A few islands even have their own breed of swamp dwellers—fishermen and oyster growers, who live on house barges tied to the shore. This part of the coast is also very wet, and several of the lowland rivers are bordered by rain forest.

A long, sandy spit known as the Long Beach Peninsula stretches north from the rocky knobs at Cape Disappointment, shielding Willapa Bay, Washington's southernmost estuary, from the ocean's fury and creating an ideal stretch of sand for the peninsula's resort communities. One of every six U.S. oysters is grown in Willapa Bay. When you add the oysters grown in Grays Harbor, the Hood Canal, Samish Bay, and southern Puget Sound, you'll understand why Washington is the number one oyster-producing state. Follow the signs for a scenic drive around the peninsula. The trip along Route 100 follows headlands for the only panoramic views along the otherwise flat peninsula.

The Cascade Mountains south of Snoqualmie Pass are heavily eroded than those to the north and generally not as high. But a few peaks do top 7,000 feet, and two volcanic peaks are taller than any of the state's northern mountains. Mt. Adams is more than 12,000 feet high, and Mt. Rainier rises to more than 14,000 feet. The third of the southern peaks, Mt. St. Helens, blew its top in 1980, and is now little more than 8,000 feet tall.

The southern lowlands are part of a long trough that runs from the Georgia Strait in southern British Columbia to Oregon's southern Willamette Valley. The area is bordered in the west by the low hills of the coast ranges, to the east by the foothills of the Cascades, to the north by Puget Sound, and to the south by the Columbia. The region is bisected by two rivers: the Chehalis in the north, and the Cowlitz, which flows west from the southern slopes of Mt. Rainier, then turns south to the Columbia.

Vancouver, Washington, just across the Columbia River from Portland, Oregon, is the state's fourth largest city and by far the region's most populated area. The city has experienced a renaissance and has a large farmers' market; several waterfront restaurants, and an urban park surrounded by shops, eateries, and condominiums.

Cut thousands of feet deep, the Columbia River Gorge travels through the basalt ridges of the Cascades. West of the Cascade crest, there's one timberline; east of the crest there's an upper timberline in the alpine zone, like that of western Washington's mountains, and a lower timberline, where the land becomes too dry to support trees and grasses or steppe scrub take over. This is most visible as you follow the Columbia River east through the gorge and rain forests give way to the Columbia Plateau.

The rushing waters of the untamed, wild Columbia River encountered by American and British explorers gave their name to the bordering mountains. The Native Americans of the Pacific Northwest knew the wild river and its cascades well and came here to harvest salmon, to trade, and to socialize. The river was dammed long ago, but even in this captive state it's still exceptionally beautiful.

Long Beach Peninsula

❶ *Town of Ilwaco is 169 mi southwest of Seattle, 106 mi northwest of Portland, Oregon.*

The seas are so turbulent beneath the cliffs of Cape Disappointment, where the mighty Columbia River meets the stormy waters of the Pacific Ocean, that several explorers, from James Cook to George Vancouver, mistook the river's mouth for surf breaking on a wild shore. Many ships have crossed (and many have come to grief) here since American sea captain Robert Gray sailed into the river on May 11, 1792, and named it after his ship.

Long Beach Peninsula stretches north from Cape Disappointment, protecting Willapa Bay from the ocean. The peninsula has vast stretches of sand dunes, friendly beach towns, dank cranberry bogs, and forests and meadows. Willapa Bay was once known as Shoalwater Bay because it runs almost dry at low tide. It's a prime oyster habitat, producing more of the creatures than any other estuary in the country.

The 28-mi-long, uninterrupted stretch of sand that runs along the peninsula's ocean shore is a great place to beachcomb. Don't even think about swimming here, however. Though surfers in wetsuits brave the waves in some areas, the water is too cold and the surf too rough for most people; hypothermia, shifting sands underfoot, and tremendous undertows account for several drownings each year.

The peninsula is a great place to hike, bike, and bird-watch. Lakes and marshes attract migrating birds, among them trumpeter swans. Long Island, in southeastern Willapa Bay, has a stand of old-growth red cedar trees, home to spotted owls, marbled murrelets (a western seabird), elks, and black bears. The island is accessible only by private boat (the boat ramp is on the bay's eastern shore).

Chinook

172 mi southwest of Seattle, 99 mi northwest of Portland, OR.

The pleasant Columbia River fishing village of Chinook (*shi*-nook) takes its name from the local tribe that once controlled the river from its mouth to Celilo Falls. The same group encountered Lewis and Clark during their stay on the Pacific coast. Chinook is a great base from which to explore the lower Columbia River by boat.

★ **Ft. Columbia State Park and Interpretive Center** blends so well into a rocky knob above the river that it's all but invisible from land or water (Route 101 passes underneath, via tunnel). The 1902 bastions offer great views of the river's mouth and of the river flowing past the foot of the cliff. In spring the slopes are fragrant with wildflowers. The interpretive center has displays on barracks life and Chinook Indian culture. Two historic buildings on the property are available for vacation rental. ✉ *Rte.*

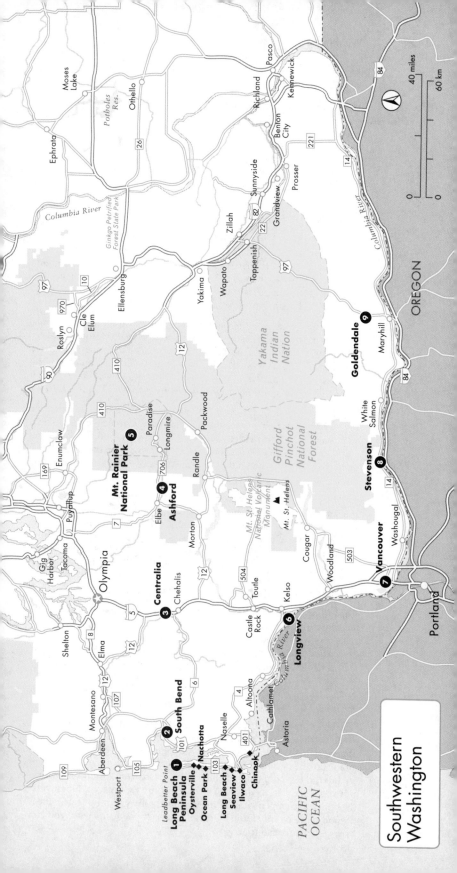

Southwestern Washington

PACIFIC OCEAN

OREGON

Portland

Long Beach Peninsula 1
Oysterville
Ocean Park
Long Beach 2
Seaview
Ilwaco
Chinook
Leadbetter Point

Westport
Aberdeen
Montesano
Shelton
Elma
Gig Harbor
Tacoma
Puyallup
Enumclaw
Olympia
Centralia 3
Chehalis
South Bend 2
Nachotta
Naselle
Altoona
Cathlamet
Astoria
Longview 6
Kelso
Castle Rock
Toutle
Woodland
Cougar
Morton
Randle
Packwood
Ashford 4
Elbe
Longmire
Paradise
Mt. Rainier National Park 5
Mt. St. Helens
Mt. St. Helens National Volcanic Monument
Gifford Pinchot National Forest
Vancouver 7
Washougal
Stevenson 8
White Salmon
Goldendale 9
Maryhill

Columbia River

Cle Elum
Roslyn
Ellensburg
Yakima
Wapato
Toppenish
Zillah
Yakama Indian Nation
Sunnyside
Grandview
Prosser
Benton City
Richland
Kennewick
Pasco
Ginkgo Petrified Forest State Park

Ephrata
Moses Lake
Potholes Res.
Othello

40 miles
60 km

101, 2 mi east of Chinook ☎ 360/642–3078 or 888/226–7688 ☞ Free
☉ Memorial Day–Sept., Wed.–Sun. 10–5.

WHERE TO EAT
★ $–$$$ ✕ **The Sanctuary.** Soft lighting, stained-glass windows, and contempo-
rary cuisine make this a very popular restaurant. The fare runs from local
seafood and well-aged beef to Scandinavian specialties such as Swedish
meatballs, pork loin stuffed with prunes, and lox wrapped in *lefse* (thin
bread). Regional labels and a few foreign vintages appear on the wine
list. ⊠ 794 Rte. 101 ☎ 360/777–8380 ⌂ *Reservations essential* ☰ AE,
D, MC, V ☉ Closed Mon. and Tues. No lunch.

Ilwaco
13 mi west of Chinook.

Ilwaco (ill-*wah*-co) has been a fishing port for thousands of years, first
as a Native American village and later as an American settlement. A 3-
mi scenic loop winds past Ft. Canby State Park to North Head Light-
house and through the town. The colorful harbor is a great place for
watching gulls and boats. Lewis and Clark camped here before moving
their winter base to the Oregon coast at Ft. Clatsop.

The dioramas and miniatures of Long Beach towns at the **Ilwaco Heritage
Museum** illustrate the history of southwestern Washington. Displays
cover Native Americans; the influx of traders, missionaries, and pioneers;
and the contemporary workers of the fishing, agriculture, and forest in-
dustries. ⊠ 115 SE Lake St., off Rte. 101 ☎ 360/642–3446 ☞ $3
☉ May–Aug., Mon.–Sat. 9–5, Sun. noon–4; Sept.–Apr., Mon.–Sat. 10–4.

★ ☙ The 1,700-acre **Ft. Canby State Park** was an active military installation
until 1957. Emplacements for the guns that once guarded the Columbia's
mouth remain, some of them hidden by dense vegetation. Trails lead to
stunning beaches. Be on the lookout for deer eagles on the cliffs. All of
the park's 250 campsites have stoves and tables; some have water, sewer,
and electric hookups.

Exhibits at the park's **Lewis & Clark Interpretive Center** tell the tale of
the duo's 8,000-mi round-trip expedition. Displays include artwork, jour-
nal entries, and other items that elaborate on the Corps of Discovery,
which left Wood River, Illinois, in 1803; arrived at Cape Disappoint-
ment in 1805; and got back to Illinois in 1807. ⊠ Robert Gray Dr., 2½
mi southwest of Ilwaco off Rte. 101 ☎ 360/642–3029 or 360/642–3078
⊕ www.parks.wa.gov ☞ Park and interpretive center free, campsites
$11–$16 ☉ Park: daily sunrise–sunset. Interpretive center: daily 10–5.

Cape Disappointment was named in 1788 by Captain John Meares, an
English fur trader who had been unable to find the Northwest Passage.
This rocky cape and treacherous sandbar—the so-called graveyard of
the Pacific—has been the scourge of sailors since the 1800s. More than
250 ships have sunk after running aground on its ever-shifting sands.
A ½-mi-long path from the Lewis & Clark Interpretive Center in Ft. Canby
State Park leads to the Cape Disappointment Lighthouse. Built in 1856,
it's the oldest lighthouse on the west coast still in use.

The **U.S. Coast Guard Station Cape Disappointment** (☎ 360/642–2384)
is the northwest coast's largest search-and-rescue station. The rough con-
ditions of the Columbia River provide plenty of lessons for the students
of the on-site National Motor Life Boat School. The only institution of
its kind, the school teaches elite rescue crews from around the world
advanced skills in navigation, mechanics, fire fighting, and lifesaving.
The observation platform on the north jetty in Ft. Canby State Park is
a good place to watch the motor lifeboats. If you call ahead, you can
arrange an informal tour.

★ **North Head Lighthouse** was built in 1899 to help skippers sailing from the north who couldn't see the Cape Disappointment Lighthouse. Stand high on a bluff above the pounding surf here, amid the windswept trees, for superb views of the Long Beach Peninsula. ⊠ *From Cape Disappointment follow the Spur 100 Rd. for 2 mi* ☎ *360/642–3078* 🖾 *$1* ☽ *Apr.–Sept., daily 10–5; Oct.–Mar., weekends only, hrs subject to volunteer availability.*

WHERE TO
STAY & EAT

✕ **Joan's Portside Café and Pizzeria.** This local favorite, two blocks from the dock and boat launch, is known for its breakfasts and its lunches

¢–$ of biscuits and gravy, soups, and pies—all of them homemade. There's also pizza on the menu, and delivery is free anywhere on the peninsula. ⊠ *303 Main St.* ☎ *360/642–3477* ☱ *MC, V.*

★ **$$–$$$** 🏨 **China Beach Retreat.** Between the port of Ilwaco and Ft. Canby State Park, this secluded B&B is surrounded by wetlands and has wonderful views of Baker's Bay and the mouth of the Columbia River. Each of the three rooms has antiques and original art. ⊠ *222 Robert Gray Dr., 98624* ☎ *360/642–5660* ⊕ *www.chinabeachretreat.com* 🛏 *3 rooms* ♨ *In-room hot tubs; no a/c, no room phones, no room TVs, no kids under 16, no smoking* ☱ *AE, MC, V* ◯ *BP.*

$$–$$$ 🏨 **Eagle's Nest Resort.** Its cedar cabins and cottages are on 94 acres of woodland ½ mi west of Ilwaco. All the accommodations are simple, though cottages have full kitchens. RV sites are also available. ⊠ *700 W. North Head Rd., 98624* ☎ *360/642–8351* 🖶 *360/642–8402* 🛏 *11 cottages, 3 cabins* ♨ *Some kitchens, microwaves, refrigerators, cable TV, miniature golf, pool, hot tub, basketball, volleyball, shops, playground; no a/c* ☱ *D, MC, V.*

¢–$$ 🏨 **Inn at Ilwaco.** All but two of this B&B's cozily furnished guest rooms are upstairs, in the former Sunday school of a 1928 New England–style church on a knoll overlooking the port. Breakfast is served on the altar stage in the sanctuary. ⊠ *120 Williams St. NE, 98624* ☎ *360/642–8686* 🖶 *360/642–8686* ⊕ *www.longbeachlodging.com* 🛏 *10 rooms, 7 with bath* ♨ *Business services; no a/c, no room phones, no smoking* ☱ *MC, V* ◯ *BP.*

SPORTS & THE
OUTDOORS

Gray whales pass the Long Beach Peninsula twice a year: December–February, on their migration from the Arctic to their winter breeding grounds in Californian and Mexican waters, and March–May, on the return trip north. The view from the North Head Lighthouse is spectacular. The best time for sightings is in the morning, when the water is calm and overcast conditions reduce the glare. Look on the horizon for a whale blow—the vapor, water, or condensation that spouts into the air when the whale exhales. If you spot one blow, you're likely to see others: whales often make several shorter, shallow dives before a longer dive that can last as long as 10 minutes.

The fish that swim in the waters near Ilwaco include salmon, rock cod, lingcod, flounder, perch, sea bass, and sturgeon. Record salmon runs keep the charter business bustling. Charters generally cost from $70 to $200 per person. Free fishing and charter guides are available from the **Port of Ilwaco** (☎ 360/642–3145 ⊕ www.portofilwaco.com).

Seaview
3 mi north of Ilwaco.

Seaview, an unincorporated town, has 750 year-round residents and several homes that date from the 1800s. The Shelburne Inn, built in 1896, is on the National Register of Historic Places. In 1892 U.S. Senator Henry Winslow Corbett built what's now the Sou'wester Lodge.

WHERE TO
STAY & EAT
★ $–$$

✗ **42nd Street Cafe.** Chef Cheri Walker's fare is inspired, original, and reasonably priced. Oysters are baked with spinach, Parmesan cheese, cream, bacon, brandy, fennel, and cracker crumbs; charbroiled albacore tuna is served with hoisin sauce and sesame guacamole; and baked spice-rubbed sturgeon comes with a salad of wild rice, dried cranberries, apples, and carrots with a bacon vinaigrette. The excellent wine list has Pacific Northwest labels. ⊠ *Rte. 103 and 42nd Pl.* ☎ *360/642–2323* ▭ *MC, V.*

$–$$
Fodor'sChoice
★

✗▣ **Shelburne Inn.** A white picket fence surrounds rose and other gardens as well as an 1896 Victorian that's home to Washington's oldest continuously run hotel. Fresh flowers, antiques, fine-art prints, and original works adorn guest rooms, a few of which have decks or balconies. The Shoalwater Restaurant ($$$–$$$$) has a dark wooden interior and a contemporary American menu dominated by seafood dishes. Ann Kischner, a master pastry chef, creates exquisite desserts. The cozy Heron & Beaver Pub serves lighter fare. ⊠ *Rte. 103 and N. 45th St., 98644* ☎ *360/642–2442* 🖶 *360/642–8904* ⊕ *www.theshelburneinn.com* 🛏 *15 rooms* ⚹ *Restaurant, bar; no a/c, no room phones, no room TVs, no smoking* ▭ *AE, D, DC, MC, V* †⦾† *BP.*

$–$$

▣ **Sou'wester Lodge.** A stay at the Sou'wester is a bohemian experience. Proprietors Len and Miriam Atkins came to Seaview from South Africa, by way of Israel and Chicago, and they're always up for a stimulating conversation. The lodge was built in 1892 as the summer retreat for Henry Winslow Corbett, a Portland banker, timber baron, shipping and railroad magnate, and U.S. senator. Soirees and chamber music concerts sometimes occur in the parlor. Guest rooms are eclectic. Beach cottages and the classic mobile-home units just behind the beach have cooking facilities; you're also welcome to make breakfast in the homey kitchen. ⊠ *Beach Access Rd.* ☎ *Box 102, 98644* ☎ *360/642–2542* ⊕ *www. souwesterlodge.com* 🛏 *3 rooms without bath, 6 suites, 4 cottages, 10 trailers* ⚹ *Beach* ▭ *D, MC, V.*

Long Beach
½ mi north of Seaview.

Long Beach bears a striking resemblance to Coney Island in the 1950s. Along its main drag, which stretches southwest from 10th Street to Bolstadt Street, you'll find everything from cotton candy and hot dogs to

★ ☾ go-carts and bumper cars.The ½-mi-long **Long Beach Boardwalk** runs through the dunes parallel to the beach and is a great place for strolling, bird-watching, or just sitting and listening to the wind and the roar of the surf. It's ¼ mi west of downtown.

Created to memorialize Lewis and Clark's explorations here in 1805–06,

★ ☾ the **Discovery Trail** traces the explorers' moccasin steps from Ilwaco to Long Beach. At this writing two segments are complete: from Long Beach several miles along the dunes, and from Ilwaco to the ocean at Beard's Hollow. ☎ *800/451–2542* ⊕ *www.funbeach.com.*

Each August Long Beach hosts the Washington State International Kite Festival; the community is also home to the Northwest Stunt Kite Championships, a competition held each June. At the **World Kite Museum and Hall of Fame,** you can view an array of kites and learn about kite making and history. ⊠ *Rte. 103 at 3rd St. N* ☎ *360/642–4020* 🎟 *$1.50* ⊙ *June–Aug., daily 11–5; Oct.–May, weekdays 11–5.*

WHERE TO
STAY & EAT
$–$$$

✗ **Doogers.** Locals will urge you to eat here—listen to them. The place serves seafood from 11 AM to 10 PM. The ample portions come with potatoes, shrimp-topped salad, and garlic toast. ⊠ *900 Rte. 103* ☎ *360/642–4224* ▭ *AE, D, MC, V.*

$ ✕ **Crab Pot.** If all that salt air has you thinking about seafood, stop at this restaurant/lounge/market, which opened in 1946. It's not only the perfect place to savor freshly caught fish, but also to down a pint. Must-tries include steamers, chowder, fish-and-chips, and the famous whole-crab dinner. ⊠ *1917 Rte.103* ☎ *360/642–8870* ▤ *MC, V.*

¢–$$$ ⊡ **Breakers Motel and Condominiums.** Each of the contemporary one- and two-bedroom condominiums has a private balcony or patio. Many also have fireplaces and exceptional views of the dunes and the surf. Some units have kitchenettes. ⊠ *26th St. and Rte. 103, 98631* ☎ *360/642–4414 or 800/219–9833* ᵬ *360/642–8772* ⊕ *www.breakerslongbeach. com* ⥯ *114 rooms* ⚷ *In-room hot tubs, some kitchenettes, cable TV, some in-room VCRs, indoor pool, spa, playground, laundry facilities; no a/c* ▤ *AE, D, MC, V.*

★ $ ⊡ **Boreas Bed and Breakfast.** A private path leads from this vintage 1920s beach house through the dunes to the shore. Antiques are scattered throughout the B&B, and there's a good selection of books. Rooms have balconies and ocean views. Breakfasts are extravagant, and there's full concierge service. ⊠ *607 N. Ocean Beach Blvd., 98631* ☎ *360/642–8069* ᵬ *360/642–5353* ⊕ *www.boreasinn.com* ⥯ *5 suites, 3 with shower only* ⚷ *Some in-room hot tubs; no a/c, no room phones, no smoking* ▤ *MC, V* ⦿| *BP.*

$ ⊡ **Rendezvous Place Bed and Breakfast.** Innkeepers David and Myong Haines spare no expense when it comes to ensuring their guests get a good night's sleep. Every bed has a comfy 3-inch-thick mattress pad. Guest rooms are named and decorated for flowers in the garden. Other thoughtful touches include homemade picnic lunches. ⊠ *1610 California St., 98631* ☎ *360/642–8877 or 866/642–8877* ᵬ *360/642–8877* ⊕ *www.rendezvousplace.com* ⥯ *4 rooms, 1 with shower only, 1 suite* ⚷ *Some in-room hot tubs, room TVs with movies, hot tub, sauna, library, recreation room, business services; no a/c, no room phones, no kids under 12, no smoking* ▤ *MC, V* ⦿| *BP.*

☾ ¢–$ ⊡ **Anchorage Cottages.** All the cottages have fireplaces, free firewood, and unobstructed views of the dunes and the ocean. Kitchens are stocked with cooking and dining essentials, but don't forget to do your dishes—there's a $25 fee if you don't. ⊠ *2209 Boulevard North* ☎ *360/642–2351 or 800/646–2351* ⊕ *www.theanchoragecottages.com* ⥯ *10 rooms* ⚷ *Kitchens, cable TV, basketball, volleyball, playground, some pets allowed (fee); no a/c* ▤ *AE, D, MC, V.*

¢–$ ⊡ **Edgewater Inn Motel.** The Edgewater is at the main entrance to the public beach. The rooms are standard motel-style, but are clean and comfortable. ⊠ *409 Sid Snyder Dr. SW, 98631* ☎ *360/642–2311 or 800/561–2456* ᵬ *360/642–8018* ⥯ *84 rooms* ⚷ *Restaurant, bar, cable TV, beach, some pets allowed (fee)* ▤ *AE, D, DC, MC, V.*

¢ ⊡ **Our Place at the Beach.** It's small, somewhat kitschy, and fronted by dunes. The beach, restaurants, and shops are a short walk away. ⊠ *1309 S. Ocean Beach Blvd., 98631* ☎ *360/642–3793 or 800/538–5107* ᵬ *360/642–3896* ⥯ *25 rooms* ⚷ *Picnic area, some kitchenettes, refrigerators, gym, 2 hot tubs, sauna, business services, some pets allowed (fee)* ▤ *AE, D, MC, V.*

¢ ⊡ **Shaman.** Some of the rooms at this plain but comfortable motel have fireplaces and some have kitchenettes. Half of the rooms face town and half face the ocean. ⊠ *115 3rd St. SW, 98631* ☎ *360/642–3714 or 800/753–3750* ᵬ *360/642–8599* ⊕ *www.shamanmotel.com* ⥯ *42 rooms* ⚷ *Some kitchenettes, some refrigerators, cable TV, pool, business services, some pets allowed (fee); no a/c* ▤ *AE, D, DC, MC, V.*

¢ ⊡ **Super 8.** This is a comfortable chain motel with nicely appointed rooms and a friendly and knowledgeable staff. It's within easy walking distance of shops, restaurants, and the boardwalk. The Continental breakfast includes fresh donuts and coffee cake from the popular Cottage Bakery. ✉ *500 Ocean Beach Blvd., 98631* ☎ *360/642–8988 or 888/478–3297* 🖷 *360/642–8986* ⊕ *www.longbeachsuper8.com* ➦ *50 rooms* ⚁ *Cable TV with movies, laundry facilities, business services, some pets allowed (fee); no a/c* ▤ *AE, D, DC, MC, V* ❜⊙❜ *CP.*

SPORTS & THE OUTDOORS **Back Country Horse Rides** (✉ 10th St. next to Edgewater Inn ☎ 360/642–2576) offers one-hour horseback rides for $15 and two-hour rides for $25. **Our Wonderful World (O.W.W.) Inc.** (✉ 1st Place Shopping Center, 106 Sid Snyder Dr. SW ☎ 360/642–4260) rents bikes for $7 per hour. The **Peninsula Golf Course** (✉ 9604 Pacific Hwy. ☎ 360/642–2828) consists of two 9-hole, par-33 courses on Long Beach's northern edge. Greens fees are $11 for 9 holes and $17 for 18 holes.

SHOPPING ★ ☙ **Long Beach Kites** (✉ 115 Pacific Ave. S ☎ 360/642–2202) stocks box, dragon, and many other kites. **Rainy Day Gallery** (✉ 600 S. Pacific Hwy. ☎ 360/484–3681) is a funky little shop stuffed with antiques, collectibles, art, and unique apparel.

Ocean Park
9 mi north of Long Beach.

Ocean Park is the commercial center of the peninsula's quieter north end. It was founded as a camp for the Methodist Episcopal Church of Portland in 1883. Although the law that prohibited the establishment of saloons and gambling houses no longer exists, the deeds for some homes still state that the properties will be forfeited if alcohol is bought on the premises. The **Taylor Hotel**, built in 1892 on Bay Avenue and N Place, houses retail businesses and is the only structure from the early days that's open to the public.

WHERE TO STAY ★ $$–$$$ 🛏 **Caswell's on the Bay B&B.** From the outside, this B&B with a wraparound porch looks like an old Victorian house. But inside it's clearly a modern creation, with high ceilings and enormous windows looking onto Willapa Bay and the Long Island wildlife sanctuary. Antiques-furnished guest rooms have sitting areas and waterside or garden views. Feather beds, robes, pressed linens, and full concierge service are among the indulgences. ✉ *25204 Sandridge Rd., 98640* ☎ *360/665–6535* 🖷 *360/665–6500* ⊕ *www.caswellsinn.com* ➦ *5 rooms* ⚁ *Room TVs with movies; no a/c, no room phones, no smoking* ▤ *MC, V* ❜⊙❜ *BP.*

★ $ 🛏 **Klipsan Beach Cottages.** Built in the 1940s, this row of waterfront cottages is a favorite for family getaways. An adjacent A-frame house is available for large groups. The cottages face the sea, and a trail makes short work of getting to the beach. Full kitchens and fireplaces or woodstoves—as well as plenty of (free) firewood—are among the amenities. ✉ *22617 Rte. 102, 98640* ☎ *360/665–4888* 🖷 *360/665–3580* ⊕ *www.klipsanbeachcottages.com* ➦ *8 cottages, 1 house* ⚁ *Kitchens, refrigerators, cable TV; no a/c, no room phones* ▤ *D, MC, V.*

SPORTS & THE OUTDOORS The **Surfside Golf and Country Club** (✉ 31508 Jay Pl., behind the Surfside Inn ☎ 360/665–4148), 2 mi north of Ocean Park, has a 9-hole, par-36 course. The greens fee is $12.

Nahcotta
3 mi east of Ocean Park.

Nahcotta (*nuh*-caw-ta), on the peninsula's bay side, has an active oyster industry. Named for a Native American chief who invited oystermen to settle on the peninsula, Nahcotta was the northernmost point on the peninsula's defunct narrow-gauge railway; the schedule is still posted in the Nahcotta Post Office. The town's waterfront is a good place from which to view the bay and Long Island. Clamming is a popular pastime here; the season varies depending on the supply.

WHERE TO EAT
$–$$
Fodor'sChoice
★ ✕ **The Ark.** This rambling restaurant has views of the oyster beds and cordgrass meadows that line Willapa Bay. Seafood, meat, and vegetarian entrées are given Northwestern twists. Baked goods and desserts are prepared on the premises; there's even a takeout bakery in front. You can also have light fare in the Willapa Cafe. Try the salmon that's glazed with scotch and orange juice and then lightly pan-fried. ✉ *273 Sandridge Rd.* ☎ *360/665–4133* ▭ *AE, MC, V* ⊘ *Closed Mon.*

Oysterville
6 mi north of Nahcotta.

Oysterville is a 19th-century waterfront village, with houses set in gardens or surrounded by greenswards. Signs posted on the fence of each building tell when it was built and who lived in it. You can tour the restored Oysterville Church (pick up a free historical map here), a schoolhouse, a tannery, and the home of the mayor. The town, established in 1854, got out of the oyster business after a decline in the late 19th century. Although the native shellfish were harvested to extinction, they have been successfully replaced with the Pacific oyster, a Japanese variety that has become thoroughly naturalized.

Three miles north of Oysterville (take Sandridge Road to the left and follow the signs) is **Leadbetter State Park,** a wildlife refuge at Long Beach Peninsula's northernmost tip and a great spot for bird-watching. Black brants, sandpipers, turnstones, yellowlegs, sanderlings, and knots are among the 100 species biologists have recorded here. The dune area at the very end of the point is closed from April to August to protect the nesting snowy plover. From the parking lot, a ½-mi-long paved wheelchair-accessible path leads to the ocean and a 2½-mi loop trail winds through the dunes along the ocean and Willapa Bay. Several trails along the loop lead to isolated patches of coast. These trails flood in winter, often becoming impassable swamps, so pay attention to the warning signs. ✉ *Off Stackpole Rd.* ☎ *360/642–3078* ▭ *Free* ⊘ *Apr.–mid-Oct., daily 6:30 AM–sunset; mid-Oct.–Mar., daily 8 AM–sunset.*

South Bend

❷ *57 mi northeast of Oysterville.*

The word "funky" is often used to describe odd little towns and villages, but it fits the Willapa River town of South Bend perfectly. The community has an eclectic riverfront, with restaurants and other buildings on pilings above the banks, and with parks that allow access to the water. But what you may notice most are the piles and piles of oyster shells, for this is the self-styled "Oyster Capital of the World." You can buy oysters—in the shell, shucked, or smoked—everywhere, even at gas stations.

The downtown business district, crowded onto a narrow shelf between the river and a hill, has many shops in false-front 19th- and early 20th-century buildings; the steep slopes above the river are densely packed with houses and cottages. The stately Pacific County Courthouse (1910–11) towers above all this with its colorful glass dome.

At the **Pacific County Historical Society Museum** the history of the region, its logging and fishing industry, early settler communities, and Native American habitation are illustrated with interpretive displays. Collections include more than 15,000 photographs and 1,500 artifacts. The museum is at Mile Post 54 on Route 101. ✉ *1008 W. Robert Bush Dr.* ☎ *360/875–5224* ▭ *Free* ⊘ *Daily 11–4.*

Where to Stay

¢ 🖼 **Maring's Courthouse Bed and Breakfast.** Above the Willapa River, five blocks from Route 101, this B&B was built as a Baptist church in 1892. The rooms are large and each has a beautiful view either of the river or the gardens. Antique furnishings fill the rooms. ⊠ 602 W. 2nd St., 98586 ☎ 360/875–6519 or 800/875–6519 �🖨 360/875–5808 ⊕ willapabay.org/~maringbb ➷ 3 rooms ⚬ Cable TV; no smoking ⊟ AE, MC, V ⭗ BP.

Centralia

❸ *60 mi east of South Bend.*

Centralia (sen-*trail*-ya) was founded by George Washington, a freed slave from Virginia, who faced serious discrimination in several states and territories before settling here in 1852. The town has a well-maintained historic business district. In a park just off I–5 stands the Borst Blockhouse (built during the 1855–56 Indian Wars) and the elegant Borst farmhouse. Centralia is an antiques-hunter's paradise, with 350 dealers in 11 malls. It's also know for its 17 murals depicting the region's history. Pick up a brochure about the murals at the Centralia Train Depot. Six miles to the south is the sister city of Chehalis (sha-*hay*-liss), where there's a historical museum and the Chehalis–Centralia Steam Train.

Constructed during the Indian Wars, **Ft. Borst** was later used for grain storage. Standing within a 100-acre park, the Borst Home is a Greek-revival mansion, built in 1857. ⊠ Borst Park, 2500 Bryden Ave. W ☎ 360/330–7688 ⊑ $2 ⊙ Thanksgiving–Christmas and Memorial Day–Labor Day, weekends 1–4.

The small **Lewis County Historical Museum** has regional pioneer memorabilia, some Chehalis Indian art, and a collection of children's dolls and toys. ⊠ 599 NW Front Way, Chehalis ☎ 360/748–0831 ⊑ $2 ⊙ Tues.–Sat. 9–5, Sun. 1–5.

⚘ Through scenic landscapes and over covered bridges, the authentic engines of the **Chehalis–Centralia Steam Train Ride** will carry you on rails originally laid for logging. The line runs through farmland and rolling hills, and crosses several wooden bridges. The 12-mi round-trip ride (departing at 11 and 3 on weekends) costs $8; the 18-mi ride (departing at 5 PM on Saturday) is $11. ⊠ 1945 S. Market Blvd., Chehalis ☎ 360/748–9593 ⊙ Memorial Day–Labor Day, weekends.

⚘ The wooded, 125-acre **Rainbow Falls State Park** is en route to the coast. Along the way several shallow waterfalls cascading down shelves of rock. The park, which opened in 1935, has towering old-growth forest and 3,400 feet of freshwater shoreline along the Chehalis River. Another popular feature is the fuchsia garden, with 40 varieties of the blooming shrubs. ⊠ Rte. 6, Chehalis ☎ 360/291–3767 or 800/233–0321 ⊕ www.parks. wa.gov ⊑ $7 parking fee ⊙ Daily sunrise–sunset.

Where to Stay & Eat

¢–$$ ✕ **Mary McCrank's Dinner House.** It's an elegant yet cozy farmhouse restaurant that opened in 1928. There are armchairs in the waiting parlor and fireplaces in some of the dining rooms. The chicken and dumplings are sublime; so are the dessert pies. You can buy the restaurant's signature jams, syrups, and sauces. ⊠ 2923 Jackson Hwy. ☎ 360/748–3662 ⊟ D, MC, V ⊙ Closed Mon.

¢–$ ✕ **Kit Carson.** The whole family will feel at home at this casual eatery, which serves salads, steaks, seafood, and pasta dishes. Grilled Dungeness crab sandwiches are as much a specialty here as the giant cinnamon rolls.

⊠ *107 SE Interstate Ave., Chehalis* ☎ *360/740–1084* ☰ *AE, D, DC, MC, V.*

★ ¢–$ ✕ **Olympic Club.** When it opened in 1908, the Olympic Club was an exclusive gentlemen's resort. It's now owned by the Portland, Oregon, microbrewery moguls, the Mcmennamin brothers, and it houses a restaurant, a bar, and a pool hall. The Tiffany chandeliers, the card room, and various signs (one reading WOMEN'S PATRONAGE NOT SOLICITED hangs above the entrance) remain almost as they were when the club first opened. The menu includes burgers, sandwiches, pastas, steak, and fish. The club not only brews its own beer but also bottles its own wine and distills its own spirits. ⊠ *112 N. Tower Ave.* ☎ *360/736–5164* ☰ *AE, D, MC, V.*

¢ ▥ **Ferryman's Inn.** Just off I–5 at Exit 82, this two-story motel is between Riverside Park, behind which the Skookumchuk River flows, and Borst Park, adjacent to the Chehalis River. Try for an upstairs room. ⊠ *1003 Eckerson Rd., 98532* ☎ *360/330–2094* ☐ *360/330–5049* ➪ *84 rooms* ☁ *Cable TV, pool, spa, laundry facilities, some pets allowed, no-smoking rooms* ☰ *AE, D, DC, MC, V* ▯⊙▮ *CP.*

¢ ▥ **Inn at Centralia.** It's only steps from factory outlet stores and antiques malls and it's conveniently close to I–5, less than two blocks from Exit 82. Rooms are modern and well maintained. ⊠ *702 Harrison Ave., 98531* ☎ *360/736–2875 or 800/459–0035* ☐ *360/736–2651* ➪ *88 rooms* ☁ *Picnic area, in-room hot tubs, some refrigerators, cable TV, pool, some pets allowed (fee)* ☰ *AE, D, DC, MC, V* ▯⊙▮ *CP.*

Ashford

❹ *70 mi northwest of Centralia.*

Ashford sits astride an ancient trans-Cascades trail used by the Yakama Indians to trade with the people of western Washington. The town began as a logging railway terminal; today, the village provides access to the Nisqually (Longmire) entrance to Mt. Rainier National Park, and caters to 2 million annual visitors with lodges, restaurants, groceries, and gift shops along Route 706.

★ ☺ Beginning at Elbe, 11 mi west of Ashford, **Mt. Rainier Scenic Railroad** trains will take you through lush forests and across scenic bridges. The railway covers 14 mi of incomparable beauty on two-hour runs. Trains leave at 11, 1:15, and 3:30. ⊠ *Rte. 7, Elbe* ☎ *360/569–2599 or 888/783–2611* ▱ *$12.50* ⊙ *Memorial Day–July 4, weekends; July 4–Labor Day, daily; Labor Day–end of Sept. and Dec., weekends.*

Where to Stay & Eat

☺ ¢ ✕ **Scaleburgers.** What started as a state weigh station in 1939 has been converted into a popular restaurant serving hamburgers, fries, milkshakes, and ice cream made from only the finest ingredients. You eat outside on tables overlooking the hills and scenic railroad. The restaurant is 11 mi west of Ashford. ⊠ *54109 Mountain Hwy. E, Elbe* ☎ *360/569–2247* ☰ *No credit cards.*

★ $–$$ ✕▥ **Alexander's Country Inn.** Serving guests since 1912, Alexander's offers premier lodging just a mile from Mt. Rainier. Antiques and fine linens lend the main building romance. There are also two adjacent guest houses. Rates include a hearty breakfast and evening wine. The cozy restaurant ($–$$; closed weekdays in winter), the best place in town for lunch or dinner, serves fresh fish and pasta dishes; bread and desserts are baked on the premises. Box lunches are available for picnics. ⊠ *37515 Rte. 706 E, 4 mi east of Ashford, Ashford 98304,* ☎ *360/569–2300 or 800/654–7615* ☐ *360/569–2323 or 800/654–7615* ⊕ *www.alexanderscountryinn.com* ➪ *12 rooms, 2 3-bedroom houses* ☁ *Restaurant, hot tub* ☰ *MC, V* ▯⊙▮ *BP.*

$–$$ 🏠 **Mountain Meadows Inn Bed and Breakfast.** Antiques, Native American baskets, and John Muir memorabilia adorn the living room of this homey inn, 6 mi southwest of Mt. Rainier National Park. The modern cottage has three units, each with its own entrance and kitchen. ⊠ *28912 State Rte. 706 E, 98304* ☎ *360/569–2788* ⊕ *www.mt-rainier.net* ⇨ *6 rooms, 3 efficiencies* ⚲ *Some kitchens, pond, hot tub; no a/c, no room phones, no room TVs, no children under 4, no smoking* ⊟ *MC, V* ⌶◉ *BP.*

★ ¢–$ 🏠 **Wellspring.** Accommodations here include tastefully designed log cabins, a tree house, and a room in a greenhouse. All guest quarters are individually decorated. There's a queen-size feather bed suspended by ropes beneath a skylight in the Nest Room; the Tatoosh Room has a huge stone fireplace and can house up to 10 people. Also available are a variety of spa facilities, as befits a property created by a massage therapist. ⊠ *54922 Kernehan Rd., 98304* ☎ *360/569–2514* ⇨ *9 units* ⚲ *Some kitchenettes, some microwaves, some refrigerators, pond, hot tubs, outdoor hot tub, massage, saunas, spa, hiking; no room phones, no room TVs, no smoking* ⊟ *MC, V.*

¢–$ 🏠 **Whittaker's Bunkhouse.** This 1912 motel once housed loggers and mill-workers. In those days it was referred to as "the place to stop on the way to the top." In the early 1990s famed climber Lou Whittaker bought and renovated the facility. Today it's a comfortable hostelry, with inexpensive bunk rooms as well as large private rooms. ⊠ *30205 S.R. 706 E, Ashford* ☎ *360/569–2439* ⚲ *Restaurant, hot tub* ⇨ *20 rooms* ⊟ *MC, V.*

¢ 🏠 **Nisqually Lodge.** Fires in the grand stone fireplace of this hotel a few miles west of Mt. Rainier National Park lend the Great Room warmth and cheer. Guest rooms are comfortable and have standard motel decor. ⊠ *31609 State Rd. 706 E 98304* ☎ *360/569–8804* 🖷 *360/569–2435 or 888/674–3554* ⊕ *www.escapetothemountains.com* ⇨ *24 rooms* ⚲ *Cable TV, hot tub, playground, laundry facilities, business services; no smoking* ⊟ *AE, MC, V* ⌶◉ *CP.*

Mt. Rainier National Park

FodorsChoice ★ *Nisqually (Longmire) entrance: Rte. 706, 14 mi east of Rte 7. Ohanapecosh (Stevens Canyon) entrance: Rte. 123, 5 mi north of U.S. 12. White River entrance: Rte. 410, 3 mi north of Chinook and Cayuse passes.*

Rainier is so massive that its summit is often obscured by its own shoulders. When the summit *is* visible—from up-close vantage points—the views are breathtaking. The impressive volcanic peak stands at an elevation of 14,411 feet, making it the fifth highest in the lower 48 states. More than 2 million visitors a year return home with a lifelong memory of its image. Its 235,612 acres were preserved by President McKinley in 1899, when he made it the nation's fifth national park. Douglas fir, western hemlock, and western red cedar—some more than 1,000 years old—stand in cathedral-like groves. Dozens of thundering waterfalls are accessible from the road or by a short hike.

Rainier is an episodically active volcano, showing off every thousand years or so, and steam vents are still active at its summit. With more than two dozen major glaciers, the mountain holds the largest glacial system in the continental United States. The winter tempests so much resemble those of the Himalayas that Everest expeditions train here. But that's on the mountain's face above 10,000 feet; most visitors see a much more benign place with an unmatched spirit.

Wildflower season in the meadows at and above the timberline is mid-July through August, depending on the exposure (southern earlier, northern later) and the preceding winter's snowfall. Most of the park's higher-elevation trails aren't snow-free until late June. You're not as likely to see Rainier's wildlife—deer, elk, black bears, cougars, and other creatures—as often as you might at other parks, such as Olympic. As always, the best times are at sunrise and sunset, when animals can often be spotted at forest's edge. Fawns are born to the park's does in May, and the bugling of bull elk on the high ridges can be heard in late September and October, especially on the park's eastern side.

The major roads to Mt. Rainier National Park—Routes 410, 706 and 123—are paved and well-maintained state highways. They eventually, however, become mountain roads and wind up and down many steep slopes. Drive with caution. Vehicles hauling large loads should gear down, especially on downhill sections. Even drivers of passenger cars should take care not to overheat brakes by constant use. Storms can cause delays at any time of year, and you can expect to encounter road-work several times if you are circumnavigating the mountain in summer. Side roads that wind into the park's western slope are all narrow, unpaved, and subject to frequent flooding and washouts.

All but Carbon River Road and Route 706 to Paradise are closed by snow in winter. During this time Carbon River Road is subject to frequent flooding near the park boundary. (Route 410 is open to the Crystal Mountain access road entrance.) Cayuse Pass usually opens in late April; Westside Road, Paradise Valley Road, and Stevens Canyon Road usually open in May; Chinook Pass, Mowich Lake Road, and White River Road, open in late May, and Sunrise Road in late June. All these dates are subject to weather fluctuations.

Crowds are heaviest in July, August, and September, when the parking lots often fill before noon. During this period campsites are reserved several months in advance, and other lodgings are reserved as much as a year ahead. Washington's rare periods of clear winter weather bring lots of residents up for cross-country skiing.

Mt. Rainier is open 24 hours a day but with limited access in winter. Gates at Nisqually (Longmire) are staffed in daylight hours year-round. Facilities at Paradise and Ohanapecosh are open daily from late-May to mid-October, and Sunrise is open July to early-October. Access to the park in winter is limited to the Nisqually entrance. The Jackson Memorial Visitor Center at Paradise is open on weekends and holidays in winter.

During off-hours you can buy passes at the gates from machines that accept credit and debit cards. The entrance fee is $10 per vehicle, which covers everyone in the vehicle for seven days. Motorcycles and bicycles pay $5. Annual passes are available for $30. Climbing permits are $30 per person per climb or glacier trek. Wilderness camping permits, which must be obtained for all backcountry trips, are free, but advance reservations are highly recommended and cost $20 per party.

There are public phones and rest rooms at all park visitor centers as well as at the National Park Inn in Longmire and the Paradise Inn at Paradise. The only fully accessible trail in the park is Kautz Creek Trail, a ½-mile boardwalk that leads to a splendid view of the mountain. Parts of the Trail of the Shadows at Longmire and the Grove of the Patriarchs at Ohanapecosh are accessible. The campgrounds at Cougar Rock, Ohanapecosh, and Sunshine Point have several accessible sites. All off-road vehicle use—4X4 vehicles, ATVs, motorcycles, snowmobiles—is prohibited in the park.

★ ☾ The town of Longmire, east of the Nisqually entrance, is the main southern gateway to Mt. Rainier National Park. Glass cases in the **Longmire Museum** contain plants and animals from the park, including a large,

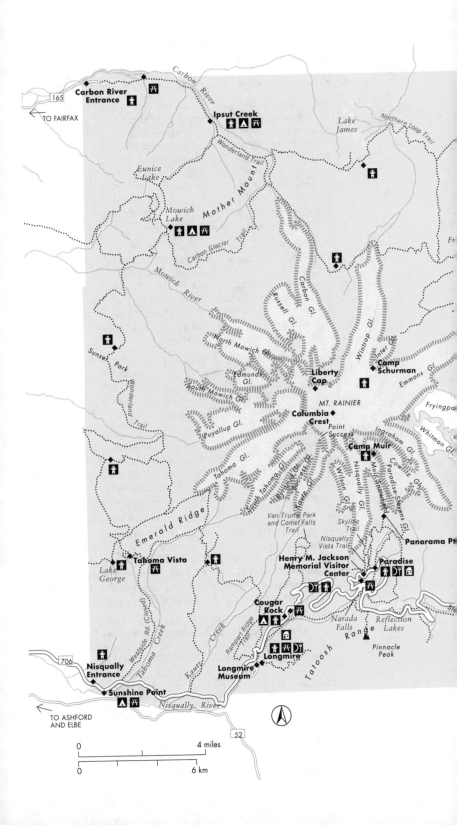

165

Carbon River Entrance

← TO FAIRFAX

Carbon River

Ipsut Creek

Lake James

Northern Loop Trail

Eunice Lake

Wonderland Trail

Mowich Lake

Mother Mount

Carbon Glacier Trail

Mowich River

Carbon Gl.

Russell Gl.

Winthrop Gl.

Inter Gl.

Camp Schurman

North Mowich Gl.

Sunset Park

Edmunds Gl.

Liberty Cap

Emmons Gl.

Fr

Wonderland Trail

South Mowich Gl.

MT. RAINIER

Columbia Crest

Fryingpa

Whitman Gl

Puyallup Gl.

Point Success

Ingraham Gl.

Camp Muir

Tahoma Gl.

South Tahoma Gl.

Success Gl.

Pyramid Gl.

Kautz Gl.

Wilson Gl.

Nisqually Gl.

Muir Snowfield

Paradise-Stevens Gl.

Cowlitz Gl.

Emerald Ridge

Van Trump Park and Comet Falls Trail

Skyline Trail

Nisqually Vista Trail

Panorama Pt

Tahoma Vista

Lake George

Henry M. Jackson Memorial Visitor Center

Paradise

Westside Rd. (Closed)

Tahoma Creek

Kautz Creek

Rampart Ridge Trail

Cougar Rock

Narada Falls

Reflection Lakes

Range

Tatoosh

Pinnacle Peak

706

Nisqually Entrance

Longmire

Longmire Museum

Sunshine Point

Nisqually River

← TO ASHFORD AND ELBE

52

St

0   4 miles

0   6 km

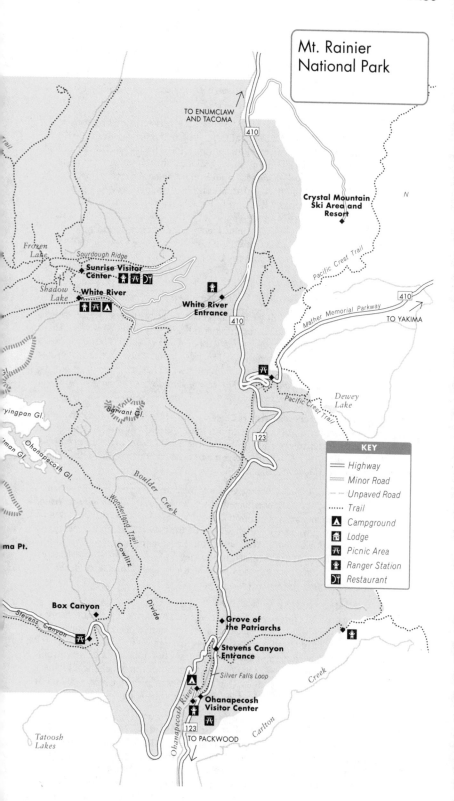

Mt. Rainier National Park

TO ENUMCLAW
AND TACOMA

410

Crystal Mountain
Ski Area and
Resort

N

Pacific Crest Trail

Frozen
Lake

Sourdough Ridge

**Sunrise Visitor
Center**

Shadow
Lake

White River

410

**White River
Entrance**

Mather Memorial Parkway

410

TO YAKIMA

Dewey
Lake

Pacific Crest Trail

123

yingpan Gl.

Sarvant Gl.

Ohanapecosh Gl.

man Gl.

Boulder Creek

Wonderland Trail

Cowlitz

ma Pt.

Divide

Box Canyon

Stevens Canyon

**Grove of
the Patriarchs**

**Stevens Canyon
Entrance**

Silver Falls Loop

Carlton Creek

**Ohanapecosh
Visitor Center**

Ohanapecosh River

Tatoosh
Lakes

123

TO PACKWOOD

KEY	
══	Highway
══	Minor Road
– –	Unpaved Road
····	Trail
▲	Campground
🏠	Lodge
⛩	Picnic Area
🧍	Ranger Station
🍴	Restaurant

friendly looking stuffed cougar. Photographs and geographical displays provide an overview of the park's history. The visitors center, next to the museum, has some perfunctory exhibits on the surrounding forest and its inhabitants, as well as information about park activities. ⊠ *Rte. 706, 17 mi east of Ashford and 6 mi east of Nisqually entrance* ☎ *360/569–2211 Ext. 3314* ⊞ *Free with park admission* ⊙ *July–Labor Day, daily 9–5; Labor Day–June, daily 9–4:15.*

Fantastic mountain views, alpine meadows crisscrossed by nature trails, a welcoming lodge and restaurant, and an excellent visitor center combine to make Paradise the first stop for most visitors to Mount Rainier National Park. There's a ranger station, visitor services, and lodging at 5,400 feet. The **Jackson Memorial Visitor Center at Paradise** has 360-degree views of the park, information, displays, and seasonal programs. The Stevens Canyon Road from Paradise east to Ohanapecosh is truly spectacular, with close-up views of the mountain, wildflowers, and the red and yellow fall foliage of huckleberry, mountain ash, and alpine dwarf willow. It's accessible from the Nisqually entrance at the park's southwest corner and from Stevens Canyon entrance at the park's southeast corner (summer only). ⊠ *Rte. 706, 9 mi east of Longmire* ☎ *360/569–2211 Ext. 2357* ⊞ *360/569–2170* ⊕ *www.nps.gov/mora* ⊠ *Free* ⊙ *May–mid-Oct., daily 9–6; mid-Oct.–Apr., weekends 10–5.*

★ ☚ As it's on an island in the Ohanapecosh River, the **Grove of the Patriarchs** is protected from the fires that periodically sweep the area. This small grove of 1,000-year-old trees is one of Mt. Rainier National Park's most memorable attractions. A 1½-mi loop trail heads over a small bridge through Douglas fir, cedar, and hemlock. ⊠ *Rte. 123, just north of the Stevens Canyon entrance, 20 mi east of Paradise on Stevens Canyon Rd., 13 mi north of Packwood via Rte. 123 and U.S. 12.*

At the **Ohanapecosh Visitors Center,** south of the Grove of the Patriarchs, you can learn about the region's dense old-growth forests through interpretive displays and videos. ⊠ *Rte. 123, 11 mi north of Packwood, 1½ mi south of Stevens Canyon entrance* ☎ *360/569–2211 Ext. 6046* ⊙ *Late May–Oct., daily 9–6.*

As you head north from the Grove of the Patriarchs you'll reach the White River and the park entrance that's named after it. At the **Sunrise Visitor Center,** to the east, you can watch the alpenglow fade from Rainier's domed summit. You can also view exhibits on the region's alpine and subalpine ecology. Nearby loop trails lead you through alpine meadows and forest to overlooks that afford broad views of the Cascades and Rainier. ⊠ *Sunrise Rd., 15 mi east of White River park entrance* ☎ *360/663–2425* ⊙ *July 4–Oct. 1, daily 9–6.*

Where to Stay & Eat

The area is bereft of quality lodging, which may be a result of its proximity to Seattle or the fact that accommodations here have never had to work hard to reach full occupancy in summer. The two national park lodges are well maintained and attractive but unless you've made summer reservations a year in advance, getting a room is a challenge. There are dozens of motels and cabin complexes near the park entrances, but most are plain, overpriced, or downright dilapidated.

The park's picnic areas are open from July through September only. Carbon River Picnic Ground, just east of the Carbon River entrance, has a half-dozen tables in the woods, near the park's northwest boundary. The main attraction at Paradise Picnic Area are great views. From here you can take an easy hike to numerous waterfalls—Sluiskin, Myrtle, and Narada, to name a few. In an alpine meadow, with wildflowers in July and August, Sunrise Picnic Area provides expansive views of the mountain and surrounding ranges in good weather. Sunshine Point Picnic Area, at the Sunshine Point Campground, has picnic tables in an open meadow along the burbling Nisqually River.

★ ¢–$ ✕🏠 **National Park Inn.** A large stone fireplace takes pride of place in the common room of this otherwise generic country inn, the only one of the park's two lodgings that's open year-round. Such rustic details as wrought-iron lamps and antique bentwood headboards adorn the rooms. The fare in the restaurant ($–$$) here is simple American. For breakfast, don't miss the home-baked cinnamon rolls. For lunch there's hamburgers, soups, and sandwiches. Dinner entrées include maple hazelnut chicken and grilled red snapper with black bean sauce and corn relish. The inn is operated as a B&B from October through April. ⊠ *Longmire Visitor Complex, Rte. 706, 10 mi east of Nisqually entrance, Longmire 98304* ☎ *360/569–2275* 🖷 *360/569–2770* ⊕ *www.guestservices.com/rainier* ↬ *25 rooms, 18 with bath* ⚒ *Restaurant, shop; no a/c, no room phones* ▤ *MC, V* ⦿❙ *BP (in winter).*

★ ¢–$ ✕🏠 **Paradise Inn.** With its hand-carved Alaskan cedar logs, burnished parquet floors, stone fireplaces, Indian rugs, and glorious mountain views, this 1917 inn is a sterling example of national park lodge architecture. German architect Hans Fraehnke designed the decorative woodwork. In addition to the full-service dining room, there's a small snack bar and a snug lounge. Lunches are simple and healthful: grilled salmon, salads, and the like. For dinner, you might find the signature bourbon buffalo meat loaf, Mediterranean chicken, and poached salmon with blackberry sauce. Summer sees leisurely Sunday brunches. ⊠ *Rte. 706, Paradise* ⑪ *C/o Mount Rainier Guest Services, Box 108, Star Rte., Ashford 98304* ☎ *360/569–2275* 🖷 *360/569–2770* ⊕ *www.guestservices.com/rainier* ↬ *127 rooms, 96 with bath* ⚒ *Restaurant, bar, snack bar; no room phones, no room TVs* ▤ *MC, V* ⦿ *Closed Nov.–mid-May.*

CAMPING FACILITIES
There are five drive-in campgrounds in the park—Cougar Rock, Ipsut Creek, Ohanapecosh, Sunshine Point, and White River—with almost 700 sites for tents and RVs. None of the park campgrounds has hot water or RV hookups; showers are available at Jackson Memorial Visitor Center.

For backcountry camping you must obtain a free wilderness permit at a visitor center. Primitive sites are spaced at 7- or 8-mi intervals along the Wonderland Trail. A copy of *Wilderness Trip Planner: A Hiker's Guide to the Wilderness of Mount Rainier National Park,* available from any of the park's visitor centers or through the superintendent's office, is an invaluable guide if you're planning backcountry stays. Reservations are available for specific wilderness campsites, from May 1 to September 30, for $20. For details, call the Wilderness Information Center at 360/569–4453.

★ ⛺ **Cougar Rock Campground.** This secluded, heavily wooded campground with an amphitheater is one of the first to fill up. You can reserve group sites for $3 per person, per night, with a minimum of 12 people per group. Reservations are accepted for summer only. ⊠ *2½ mi north of Longmire* ☎ *301/722–1257 or 800/365–2267* ⊕ *reservations.nps.gov* ↬ *173 sites* ⚒ *Flush toilets, dump station, drinking water, fire grates, ranger station* ▣ *$15* ⦿ *Closed mid-Oct.–late May.*

⛺ **Ipsut Creek Campground.** The quietest park campground is also the most difficult to reach. It's in the park's northwest corner, amid a wet, green, and rugged wilderness; many self-guided trails are nearby. The campground is theoretically open year-round, though the gravel Carbon River Road that leads to it is subject to flooding and potential closure at any time. Reservations aren't accepted here. ⊠ *Carbon River Rd., 4 mi east* *of the Carbon River entrance* ☎ *360/569–2211* ⌨ *31 sites* ♿ *Running water (non-potable), fire grates* 🏷 *$9 summer, winter free.*

★ ⛰ **Mowich Lake Campground.** This is Rainier's only lakeside campground. It's at 4,959 feet and is, by national park standards, peaceful and secluded. It's accessible only by 5 mi of convoluted gravel roads, which are subject to weather damage and potential closure at any time. ✉ *Mowich Lake Rd., 6 mi east of the park boundary* ☎ *360/568–2211* ⌨ *30 sites* ♿ *Pit toilets, running water (non-potable), fire grates, picnic tables, ranger station* 🏷 *Free* 🏕 *Reservations not accepted* ⊙ *Closed Nov.–mid July.*

⛰ **Mounthaven Resort.** Amid tall firs, this small, RV-only campground resort is just west of the national park boundary. Recreation includes volleyball, badminton, and horseshoes. ✉ *Rte. 706, Ashford 98304* ☎ *800/456–9380* ⊕ *www.mounthaven.com* ⌨ *19 sites* ♿ *Flush toilets, full hookups, drinking water, laundry facilities, showers, fire pits, grills, picnic tables, electricity, public telephone* 🏷 *$20* 🖃 *MC, V.*

⛰ **Packwood RV Park.** This large complex in Packwood provides grassy sites in the foothills of Mt. Rainier. ✉ *Rte. 12, Packwood 98361* ☎ *360/494–5145* ⌨ *88 sites, 77 with hookups* ♿ *Flush toilets, full hookups, drinking water, showers, grills, picnic tables, electricity, public telephone* 🏷 *$20 RVs* 🖃 *MC, V.*

★ ⛰ **Ohanapecosh Campground.** In the park's southeast corner, this lush, green campground has a visitor center, amphitheater, and self-guided trail. It's one of the first campgrounds to open. Reservations are accepted for summer only. ✉ *Ohanapecosh Visitor Center, Rte. 123, 1½ mi north of park boundary* ☎ *800/365–2267 or 301/722–1257* ⊕ *reservations. nps.gov* ⌨ *189 sites* ♿ *Flush toilets, dump station, drinking water, fire grates, ranger station* 🏷 *$12* ⊙ *Closed late-Oct.–May.*

⛰ **Sunshine Point Campground.** This is a pleasant, partly wooded campground near the river, and one of the first to fill up. ✉ *5 mi past the Nisqually entrance* ☎ *360/569–2211* ⌨ *18 sites* ♿ *Drinking water, fire grates* 🏷 *$10* 🏕 *Reservations not accepted.*

⛰ **White River Campground.** At an elevation of 4,400 feet, White River is one of the park's highest and least-wooded campgrounds. Here you can enjoy campfire programs, self-guided trails, and partial views of Mt. Rainier's summit. ✉ *5 mi past White River entrance* ☎ *360/569–2211* ⌨ *112 sites* ♿ *Flush toilets, drinking water, fire grates, ranger station* 🏷 *$10* 🏕 *Reservations not accepted* ⊙ *Closed mid-Sept.–late June.*

★ ⛰ **La Wis Wis Campground** Along a small creek in Gifford Pinchot National Forest, this forest service campground is a few miles from the Ohanapecosh gateway to Rainier. ✉ *Off Rte. 12, 7 mi northeast of Packwood then ½ mi west on Forest Service Rd. 1272* ☎ *360/494–5515* ⌨ *100 sites* ♿ *Drinking water, grills, picnic tables* 🏷 *$12* 🖃 *No credit cards* ⊙ *Closed mid-Sept.–late June.*

Sports & the Outdoors

BIRD-WATCHING Watch for kestrels, red-tailed hawks, and, occasionally, golden eagles on snags in lowland forests. Although they're rarely seen, you might catch a glimpse of great horned owls, spotted owls, and screech owls. Iridescent rufous hummingbirds flit from blossom to blossom in the lowlands on drowsy summer days, and sprightly water ouzels flutter in the many forest creeks. Raucous Steller's jays and gray jays scold you from trees, often darting boldly down to steal morsels from picnic tables. At higher elevations, look for the pure white plumage of the white-tailed ptarmigan as it hunts for seeds and insects in winter. Waxwings, vireos, nuthatches, sapsuckers, warblers, flycatchers, larks, thrushes, siskins, tanagers, and finches are common throughout the park in every season but winter.

HIKING It's almost impossible to experience the blissful beauty of the alpine environment or the hushed serenity of the old-growth forest without getting out of your car and walking. The numerous trails in and around Mt. Rainier range from low-key one-hour strolls to weeks-long traverses around the mountain. Although the mountain seems benign on calm summer days, each year dozens of hikers and trekkers lose their way and must be rescued. Weather that approaches cyclonic levels can appear quite suddenly, any month of the year. With the possible exception of the short loop hikes listed below, you should carry day-packs with warm clothing, food, and other emergency supplies on all treks.

Nisqually Vista Trail. This gradually sloping, 1¼-mi round-trip trail is popular with hikers in summer and cross-country skiers in winter. It heads out through subalpine meadows to point overlooking Nisqually Glacier. In summer, listen for the shrill alarm calls of the area's marmots. ⊠ *Jackson Memorial Visitor Center, Rte. 123, 1 mi north of Ohanapecosh, at the high point of Rte. 706.*

Skyline Trail. This 5-mi loop, one of the park's highest, beckons day-trippers with a cinemagraphic vista of alpine ridges and, in summer, meadows filled with brilliant flowers and birds. At 6,800 feet, Panorama Point, the spine of the Cascade Range, spreads away to the east, and Nisqually Glacier grumbles its way downslope. ⊠ *Jackson Memorial Visitor Center, Rte. 123, 1 mi north of Ohanapecosh at the high point of Rte. 706.*

Sourdough Ridge Self-Guiding Trail. The mile-long loop of this easy trail takes you through delicate subalpine meadows. A gradual climb to the ridge top yields magnificent views of Mt. Rainier and the more distant volcanic cones of Mounts Baker, Adams, Glacier, and Hood. ⊠ *Sunrise Visitor Center, Sunrise Rd., 15 mi from the White River park entrance.*

Trail of the Shadows. This ½-mi trek is notable for its glimpses of meadowland ecology, its colorful soda springs (don't drink the water), James Longmire's old homestead cabin, and the foundation of the old Longmire Springs Hotel, which was destroyed around 1900. ⊠ *Rte. 706, 10 mi east of Nisqually entrance.*

Van Trump Park Trail. You gain an exhilarating 2,200 feet while hiking through a vast expanse of meadow with views of southern Puget Sound. The 5-mi-long trail provides good footing, and the average hiker can make it up in three to four hours. ⊠ *Rte. 706 at Christine Falls, 4⁴⁄₁₀ mi east of Longmire.*

Fodor'sChoice **Wonderland Trail.** All other Mt. Rainier hikes pale in comparison to this
★ stunning 93-mi hike, which completely encircles the mountain. The trail passes through everything from the old-growth forests of the lowlands to the wildflower-studded alpine meadows of the highlands. Be sure to pick up a mountain goat sighting card from a ranger station or information center to help in the park's ongoing effort to learn more about the park's goat population. Wonderland is a rugged trail; elevation gains and losses totaling 3,500 feet are common in a day's hike, which averages 8 mi. Most hikers start from either Longmire or Sunrise and take 10–14 days to cover the route. Wilderness permits are required and reservations are strongly recommended. ⊠ *Longmire Wilderness Information Center, Rte. 706, 17 mi from Ashford; Sunrise Visitor Center, Sunrise Rd., 15 mi from the White River park entrance.*

MOUNTAIN Climbing Mt. Rainier is not for amateurs. That said, if you're experi-
CLIMBING enced in technical, high-elevation snow, rock, and icefield adventuring, climbing Mt. Rainier can be memorable. Experienced climbers can fill out a self-registration climbing card at the Longmire, Paradise, White River, or Carbon River ranger stations and lead their own groups of two or more. In winter, the Paradise Climbing Ranger Station has self-reg-

istration available 24 hours a day, 7 days a week; Jackson Visitor Center in Paradise is open 10–5 on weekends and holidays only; and the Longmire Museum is open 9–4 daily. You must register with a ranger before leaving and check out upon return. There's a $30 annual climbing fee no matter how many climbs are made per year. This applies to anyone venturing above 10,000 feet or onto one of Rainier's glaciers.

Rainier Mountaineering Inc., a highly regarded concessionaire, cofounded by Himalayan adventurer Lou Whittaker, makes climbing the Queen of the Cascades an adventure open to anyone in good health and physical condition. The company teaches the fundamentals of mountaineering at one-day classes held during climbing season, from late May through early September. Participants are evaluated on their fitness for the climb; they must be able to withstand a 16-mi round-trip with a 9,000-foot gain in elevation. Winter ski programs are also offered. Costs run $100–$200 for the guide's Glacier Hike, one-day climbing school, and crevasse rescue school. The two-day summit climb package is $771, including classes. ⊠ *Jackson Memorial Visitor Center, Rte. 123, 1 mi north of Ohanapecosh, at the high point of Rte. 706* ☎ *888/892–5462* ⊕ *www.rmguides.com.*

SKIING Mt. Rainier is a major Nordic ski center. Although trails aren't groomed, those around Paradise are extremely popular. If you want to ski with fewer people, try the trails in and around the Ohanapecosh–Stevens Canyon area, which are just as beautiful and, because of their more-easterly exposure, slightly less subject to the rains that can douse the Longmire side, even in the dead of winter. You should never ski on the plowed main roads, especially in the Paradise area—the snowplow operator can't see you. It's fine to ski or snowshoe along east-side routes 123 and 410, which aren't plowed. Be prepared to share these routes with snowmobilers, though. No rentals are available on the eastern side of the park.

Fodor'sChoice **Crystal Mountain Ski Area.** The state's biggest and best-known area is open in summer for chairlift rides ($15) that afford sensational views of Rainier and the Cascades. In winter, daily lift rates are $44. Crystal Mountain has 1,300 acres of serviced lift area and 1,000 acres of backcountry. ⊠ *Crystal Mountain Blvd. off Rte. 410, Crystal Mountain* ☎ *360/663-2265* ⊕ *www.crystalmt.com* ⊙ *June–Sept., summer chairlift daily 10–4; mid-Nov.–Apr., weekdays 9–4, weekends 8:30–4.*

Longmire Ski Touring Center. Adjacent to the National Park Inn, Longmire rents cross-country ski equipment and provides lessons from mid-December through Easter, depending on snow conditions. A set of skis, poles and boots is $15 per day. Snowshoe rental is $12 per day. Lessons range from $16 for a two-hour group lesson to $20 for a four-hour guided tour. ⊠ *Rte. 706, 10 mi east of Nisqually entrance, Longmire* ☎ *360/569-2411, 360-569-2271 mid-week* ⊙ *Thanksgiving–Easter, daily 9–5.*

Paradise Ski Area. Here you can cross-country ski or, in the Snowplay Area north of the upper parking lot at Paradise, sled using inner tubes and soft platters from December to April. Check with rangers for any restrictions that may apply. Ranger-led snowshoe walks begin here and several cross-country ski trails, from novice to advanced, lead from Paradise. ⊠ *Accessible from Nisqually entrance at park's southwest corner and from Stevens Canyon entrance at park's southeast corner (summer only)* ☎ *360/569-2211* ⊕ *www.nps.gov/mora* ⊙ *May–mid-Oct., daily, sunrise–sunset.; mid-Oct.–Apr., weekends sunrise–sunset.*

White Pass Village. This ski area has 54 privately owned condominiums and is about 10 mi east of the Stevens Canyon entrance. White Pass summit is about 6,000 feet high. There are 18 trails, including a Nordic network. A beginner lift allows novice skiers to stand for the 70-foot ride up the hill. An all-day lift ticket is $37, and Nordic passes are $16 per day. ⊠ *On U.S. 12* ☎ *509/672–3101* ⊕ *www.skiwhitepass.com* ⊙ *Nov.–Apr., 8:45–4.*

SNOWSHOEING Deep snows make Mt. Rainier a snowshoeing capital. The network of trails in the Paradise area is popular with snowshoers. The park's east-side roads, Route 123 and Route 410, are unplowed and provide another good snowshoeing venue, although you must share the main parts of the road with snowmobilers. Snowshoe rentals are available at the **Longmire Ski Touring Center** for $12 per day. From December through April, park rangers lead free twice-daily snowshoe walks that start at the visitor center at Paradise and cover 1¼ mi in about two hours. ⊠ *Rte. 706, 10 mi east of Nisqually entrance, Longmire* ☎ *360/569–2411* ⊙ *Thanksgiving–Easter, daily 9–5.*

Packwood

13 mi southwest of Mt. Rainier National Park's Stevens Canyon entrance.

Packwood is a pretty mountain village on U.S. 12, below White Pass. It's a great base for exploring wilderness areas, since it's between Mt. Rainier and Mt. St. Helens. From Randle to the west, a road runs through national forest land to the east side of Mt. St. Helens and the Windy Ridge Viewpoint, the best place from which to view the destruction wrought by the 1980 eruption and the dramatic renewal of the natural landscape.

★ **Goat Rocks Wilderness,** the crags in Gifford Pinchot National Forest, south of Mt. Rainier, are aptly named: you often see mountain goats in this 105,600-acre alpine area, especially when you hike into the backcountry. Goat Lake is a particularly good spot for viewing these elusive beasts. You can see the goats without backpacking by traveling along certain Forest Roads; ask for exact routes and directions in Packwood or ask a forest ranger. ⊠ *Forest Headquarters: 10600 NE 51st Circle, Vancouver* ☎ *360/891–5000* ⊕ *www.fs.fed.us/gpnf.*

Where to Stay

¢–$ 🏨 **Inn of Packwood.** Mount Rainier and the Cascade Mountains tower above this inn surrounded by lawns at the center of Packwood. Pine paneling and furniture lend the rooms rustic charm. You can swim in an indoor heated pool beneath skylights or picnic beneath a weeping willow. ⊠ *13032 Rte. 12, Packwood 98361* ☎ *360/494–5500* 🖷 *360/494–5503* ⊕ *www.innofpackwood.com* 🛏 *34 rooms* ⚘ *Picnic area, some kitchenettes, some microwaves, some refrigerators, cable TV, pool, spa* ▤ *MC, V* ⍥ *CP.*

¢ 🏨 **Cowlitz River Lodge.** You can't beat the location of this comfortable two-story family motel: it's just off the highway in Packwood, the gateway to Mt. Rainier National Park *and* the Mt. St. Helens National Volcanic Monument. A lodgelike construction and a large stone fireplace in the great room add some character—a good thing as guest rooms have standard motel furniture and bedding. ⊠ *13069 U.S. 12, Packwood 98361* ☎ *360/494–4444 or 888/305–2185* 🖷 *360/494–2075* ⊕ *www.escapetothemountains.com* 🛏 *32 rooms* ⚘ *Cable TV, hot tub, conference room, laundry facilities* ▤ *AE, DC, MC, V* ⍥ *CP.*

Mt. St. Helens

★ ⍟ *51 mi southwest of Packwood.*

It was once a premier camping destination, with a Mt. Fuji–like cone and pristine forest. But the May 18, 1980, eruption blew off its top and stripped its slopes of forest. The 8,365-foot-high mountain, formerly 9,665 feet high, is one of a string of volcanic Cascade Range peaks that runs from British Columbia's Mt. Garibaldi south to California's Mt. Lassen. The string includes such notable peaks as Mt. Baker and Mt. Rainier to the north, Mt. Adams to the east, Mt. Hood in Oregon, and Mt. Shasta in California. Most people travel to Mt. St. Helens via the Spirit Lake Memorial Highway (Route 504), whose predecessor was destroyed in a matter of minutes in 1980. This highway has unparalleled views of the mountain and the Toutle River Valley.

The U.S. Forest Service operates the Mt. St. Helens National Volcanic Monument. The user fee is $3 per day per visitor center within the monument or $6 per day for a multicenter pass. Monument passes are available at visitor centers, Ape's Headquarters, and Cascade Peaks Restaurant and Gift Shop on Forest Road 99. You'll also need a Northwest Forest Pass to park at trailheads, visitor centers, and other forest facilities. The pass costs $5 per vehicle per day.

Climbing is limited to the south side of the mountain. Permits are required; the fee is $15 per person. On the east side of the mountain are two bare-bones visitor centers, Windy Ridge and Ape Cave. On the south side of the mountain there's a center at Lava Canyon. The three centers along Route 504 on the forest's west side—Mt. St. Helens Visitor Center (at Silver Lake), Coldwater Ridge Visitor Center Complex, and Johnston Ridge Observatory—are open daily in summer. Johnston Ridge closes from October until May; the other centers remain open daily. Silver Lake has hours from 9 to 6, and Coldwater and Johnson Ridge operate from 10 to 6; hours may be slightly different in winter.

Castle Rock's location on I–5 at the Spirit Lake Highway makes it a major point of entry for the Mt. St. Helens National Monument. The site takes its name from a tree-covered knob that once stood on the banks of the Cowlitz River and served as a landmark for Hudson's Bay Company trappers and traders. The landscape changed dramatically when the 1980 eruption filled the Toutle and Cowlitz Rivers with volcanic mush. A local **visitors center** (⊠ Rte. 504, Castle Rock ☎ 360/274–2100) has an exhibit hall portraying the history of Castle Rock and Mt. St. Helens. *The Eruption of Mount St. Helens,* a 30-minute giant-screen film, plays every 45 minutes from 9 AM to 6 PM at the **Cinedome Theater** (⊠ Exit 49 off I–5, Castle Rock ☎ 360/274–9844). Admission is $6.

The **Mount St. Helens Visitors Center** (⊠ Rte. 504, 5 mi east of I–5, Silver Lake ☎ 360/274–2100) doesn't have great views of the mountain, but it has a walk-through volcano and exhibits documenting the eruption. **Weyerhauser/Hoffstadt Bluff Visitors Center** (⊠ Rte. 504, 27 mi east of I–5 ☎ 360/274–7750), run by Cowlitz County, contains the only full-service restaurant along Route 504. The center also has picnic areas; a helicopter-tour operator; hiking trails; and the Memorial Grove, which honors the 57 people who lost their lives during the 1980 eruption. Admission is free.

Exhibits at the **Coldwater Ridge Visitors Center** (⊠ Rte. 504, 43 mi east of I–5 ☎ 360/274–2131) document the great blast and its effects on the surrounding 150,000 acres—which were devastated but are going through a remarkable recovery. The center has a small concession area, and a ¼-mi-long trail that leads to Coldwater Lake. The **Johnston Ridge Observatory** (⊠ Rte. 504, 53 mi east of I–5 ☎ 360/274–2140) in the heart of the blast zone has spectacular views of the crater and lava dome. Exhibits here interpret the geology of Mt. St. Helens and explain how scientists monitor an active volcano.

Longview

❻ *12 mi south of Castle Rock.*

Longview, which was founded on the site of an 1805 Lewis and Clark encampment, is the largest planned community in the United States after Washington, D.C., but it's so well put together that it looks anything but planned. For one thing, the city isn't laid out on the familiar grid system, but has a roundabout where the civic center is located, surrounded by curving streets that are crossed by diagonal roads (which creates a somewhat out-of-kilter grid). To top it off, there's Lake Sacajawea, a former oxbow of the Cowlitz, that's part of a city park that encircles about one-third of downtown. Downtown itself is cut off from the Columbia River by a rather grungy industrial district and port. A 1,200-foot-long, 195-foot-high bridge, built in 1950, crosses from here to the Oregon side of the river.

Nutty Narrows isn't a traditional bridge: it's only for squirrels and serves as a safe passage for the animals across Olympia Way, between the Public Library and Civic Center. ⊠ *Olympia Way.*

Where to Stay & Eat

$–$$$ ✕ **Henri's.** This large but comfortable restaurant is the local businessmen's lunch hangout, but dinner is also popular for such hearty fare as good seafood bisque, rack of lamb, and steaks. ⊠ *4545 Ocean Beach Hwy.* ☎ *360/425–7970* ▤ *AE, D, MC, V* ⊗ *Closed Sun. No lunch Sat.*

★ ¢ ✕▥ **Rutherglen Mansion.** On the crest of a hill in the middle of 30 wooded acres, this 1926 Colonial revival enjoys a stupendous view of town. Rooms have fireplaces and tile baths. At the center of the dining room is a huge stone hearth flanked by a tile mural depicting a scene from the nearby forests. In the restaurant ($–$$), chef James Hill prepares traditional Northwest favorites; especially popular are cedar plank salmon and Jack Daniel's New York steak. Friday and Saturday nights are prime rib nights. ⊠ *420 Rutherglen Rd., 98632* ☎ *360/425–5816* 🖷 *360/636–3655* ⊕ *www.rutherglenmansion.com* ➷ *2 rooms* ♿ *Restaurant; no a/c, no room TVs, no smoking* ▤ *AE, MC, V* ⊙*| BP.*

¢ ▥ **Ramada Inn and Suites.** The lobby's many antiques make this quiet hotel, 3 mi from the highway, homey. There are standard rooms, minisuites, and a full suite with a hot tub. ⊠ *723 7th Ave., 98632* ☎ *360/414–1000* 🖷 *360/414–1076* ⊕ *www.the.ramada.com* ➷ *50 rooms* ♿ *Pool, hot tub, some pets allowed (fee), no-smoking rooms* ▤ *AE, D, DC, MC, V* ⊙*| CP.*

Vancouver

❼ *39 mi south of Longview.*

This sprawling river town started as a Hudson's Bay Company fort and trading depot in 1824 and soon became *the* frontier metropolis of the Pacific Northwest. The U.S. Army built a fort on the bluff above the Hudson's Bay post in 1846. Today the National Park Service maintains and runs the reconstructed Ft. Vancouver, and the fort as well as the Officers' Row complex are part of the larger Ft. Vancouver National Historic Reserve.

Downtown Vancouver has several historic buildings, and Esther Short Park, in the center of town, is surrounded by shops and restaurants and has gardens, a playground, fountains, and an amphitheater. On summer weekends the park hosts concerts. The nearby Vancouver Farmer's Market is the region's largest. The Columbia River waterfront district is another hot spot for dining, shopping, and strolling, along the paved Rennaisance Trail.

The 10 officers' houses and duplexes of **Officers' Row** line former parade grounds and were built between 1867 and 1906. Ulysses S. Grant lived in the 1849 log building now bearing his name when he was quartermaster of Vancouver Barracks from 1852 to 1853. Today, the Grant House is home to a folk art center and gift shop that sells crafts made by local artisans. All the homes along the main boulevard have been restored and and are part of the Ft. Vancouver National Historic Reserve. Picnic areas line the parade grounds. ⊠ *750 Anderson St.* ☎ *360/693–3103* ✉ *Free* ☉ *Daily 9–5.*

★ ☾ The fort of the **Ft. Vancouver National Historic Site**—with squared-log buildings, an encircling palisade, and corner bastions—was established here by the Hudson's Bay Company in 1825. In summer, rangers dress in period costume and demonstrate pioneer skills. ⊠ *1501 E. Evergreen Blvd.* ☎ *360/696–7655* ⊕ *www.nps.gov* ✉ *Free* ☉ *Daily 9:30–4.*

☾ The **Pearson Air Museum** has vintage aircraft in working order. Planes include a 1937 Rearwing Sportster, a Curtiss-type biplane replica, and a 1941 Boeing Stearman. Kids love the hands-on displays (and the gift shop). Pearson is the West's oldest continuously operating airfield. ⊠ *1115 E. 5th St.* ☎ *360/694–7026* ⊕ *www.pearsonairmuseum.org* ✉ *$5* ☉ *Tues.–Sun. 10–5.*

★ ☾ Bike, skate, jog, or stroll the 4-mi **Columbia Waterfront Renaissance Trail** that follows the Columbia River, passing restaurants and shops along the way. Visit the old apple tree, which was planted in 1826, and stop to enjoy the vistas. The trail passes by the Captain (George) Vancouver Monument and a plaza dedicated to Ilchee, a Chinook Indian chief's daughter. ⊠ *115 Columbia Way* ☎ *360/619–1111.*

Gifford Pinchot National Forest, stretching from Mt. St. Helens east to Mt. Adams and north to Mt. Rainier, is one of Washington's oldest forests. It's named for the first chief of the forest service. ⊠ *Forest Headquarters: 10600 NE 51st Circle, accessible via Rte. 14, Rte. 25, or Rte. 503* ✉ *Free.*

Where to Stay & Eat

★ ¢–$$ ✕ **Beaches Restaurant.** This restaurant is on the water and has gorgeous views up and down the river. The menu includes pastas, fresh fish, wood-fired-oven pizzas, steak, and salads. In summer the restaurant gets really lively, with antique-car cruise-ins and beach volleyball matches. ⊠ *1919 SE Columbia River Dr.* ☎ *360/699–1592 or 503/222–9947* ⊟ *AE, D, DC, MC, V.*

¢–$ ✕ **Puffin Cafe.** Just 16 mi east of Vancouver is a funky little restaurant hidden among the docks of the Port of Camas–Washougal Marina. Locals flock here for festive open-air dining or a quick bite after they haul in their pleasure boats. Coconut shrimp, zesty fish tacos, and other Caribbean-style offerings are served in ample portions. ⊠ *14 S. A St., Washougal* ☎ *360/335–1522* ⊟ *MC, V.*

★ ¢–$ ✕▥ **Heathman Lodge.** Amenities and facilities here—from the ultra-comfortable mattresses to the outstanding food in Hudson's Bar & Grill ($–$$)—make you feel spoiled. The alpine-style lodge, with massive hand-hewn logs, is central—just five minutes from Westfield Shoppingtown, Vancouver's only mall—yet seems very secluded. Oven-roasted venison and Dungeness crab–stuffed halibut with organic greens are among the offerings at Hudsons, where chef Mark Hosak is in charge. ⊠ *7801 NW Greenwood Dr., 98662* ☎ *360/254–3100 or 888/475–3100* ⊟ *360/254–6100* ⊕ *www.heathmanlodge.com* ⇆ *121 rooms, 22 suites*

♭ *Restaurant, room service, in-room data ports, in-room hot tubs, microwaves, refrigerators, cable TV, in-room VCRs, indoor pool, gym, hot tub, sauna* ⊟ *AE, D, DC, MC, V.*

$–$$ ⊞ **Homewood Suites by Hilton Portland-Vancouver.** Not only is this hotel near the banks of the Columbia River, but it's also close to Route 14 and Vancouver's waterfront Renaissance Trail. The picnic area, with its barbecue grills, is a great place to relax. There are lots of other amenities as well. ⊠ *701 SE Columbia Shores Blvd., 98661* ☎ *360/750–1100 or 800/225–5466* ⊟ *360/750–4899* ⊕ *www.homewood-suites.com* ⊅ *104 rooms* ♭ *Picnic area, in-room data ports, kitchenettes, microwaves, refrigerators, cable TV, tennis court, pool, gym, hot tub, basketball, shop, laundry service, business services, some pets allowed* ⊟ *AE, D, DC, MC, V* ⦿ *BP.*

¢–$ ⊞ **Red Lion Inn at the Quay.** This hotel overlooks the Columbia River and is close to downtown, Ft. Vancouver, and the airport in Portland, Oregon. There's a paved waterfront trail just outside the door. ⊠ *100 Columbia St., 98660* ☎ *360/694–8341* ⊟ *360/694–2023* ⊕ *www. westcoasthotels.com* ⊅ *160 rooms* ♭ *Restaurant, room service, in-room data ports, cable TV, pool, bar, business services, airport shuttle, free parking* ⊟ *AE, D, DC, MC, V.*

¢ ⊞ **Vintage Inn.** This 1903 Craftsman-style house is in the heart of downtown, close to the Vancouver National Historic Reserve and many restaurants. Antiques fill the rooms of the inn to the extent that some refer to it as a small museum. A working fireplace occupies one room; in another French doors lead to a sleeping porch overlooking an herb garden. ⊠ *310 W. 11th St., 98660* ☎ *360/693–6635 or 888/693–6635* ⊕ *www.vintage-inn.com* ⊅ *4 rooms* ♭ *No room phones, no smoking* ⊟ *MC, V* ⦿ *BP.*

Fodor'sChoice
★

Stevenson

❽ *49 mi west of Vancouver.*

The Skamania County seat, Stevenson is a hillside village overlooking the Columbia River Gorge. An interpretive center in town has interesting displays of Native American artifacts, as well the replica of a fish wheel, a mechanical contraption that automatically scooped salmon from the river (they were outlawed in 1935 because they were too efficient and took too many fish).

The rock in **Beacon Rock State Park** was named by Lewis and Clark and is actually the core of an ancient volcano. At this landmark along the Columbia River, the explorers first noticed tidal influences in the river. The 4,650-acre park has camping and a lengthy shoreline. You can climb the rock via a steep trail for amazing views of the Columbia River Gorge. Trails lead from the campground to stunning waterfalls and the top of Hamilton Mountain. ⊠ *Rte. 14, 35 mi east of Vancouver* ☎ *360/ 902–8608* ⊕ *www.parks.wa.gov* ⊠ *Free* ⊙ *May–Sept., daily 8 AM–10 PM; Oct.–Apr., daily 8–5.*

The **Columbia Gorge Interpretive Center** is dwarfed by the dramatic basalt cliffs that rise behind it. It's on the north bank of the Columbia River Gorge, 1 mi east of Bridge of the Gods on Route 14. Exhibits illustrate the region's geology and history. Among the many artifacts are a Native American pit house, a fish wheel, and dip nets used for hunting salmon. Other items pertain to Lewis and Clark and other explorers, missionaries, pioneers, and soldiers who have passed through the gorge. ⊠ *990 SW Rock Creek Dr.* ☎ *509/427–8211 or 800/991–2338* ⊠ *$6* ⊙ *Daily 10–5.*

Fodor'sChoice
★

Where to Stay & Eat

★ **$$–$$$** ✕▣ **Dolce Skamania Lodge.** Framed rubbings of petroglyphs ornament rooms, which are appointed with lodge-style furniture covered with hand-woven fabrics. Views are of the Columbia River and the surrounding landscape. Wood ceilings, booths, and floors give the dining room ($–$$$) a warm glow. Salmon, crab cakes, rack of lamb, and prime rib are some of the dishes cooked in the wood-burning oven. On Friday night the Gorge Harvest Seafood Buffet draws people from miles around. On Saturday, steak and lobster steal the spotlight. ⊠ *Skamania Lodge Way, 98648* ☎ *509/427–7700 or 800/221–7117* 🖷 *509/427–2548* ⊕ *www. dolce.com* ⇆ *254 rooms* ⚐ *Restaurant, in-room data ports, minibars, cable TV, 18-hole golf course, 2 tennis courts, indoor pool, gym, hot tubs, massage, sauna, bicycles, hiking, volleyball, cross-country skiing, bar, library, business services* ▭ *AE, D, DC, MC, V.*

Goldendale

9 *78 mi northwest of Stevenson.*

The seat of Klickitat County and a commercial center for ranchers and farmers, Goldendale was settled in 1872 and is a down-to-earth town with many old clapboard houses. Goldendale Observatory State Park, 1½ mi north of town via Columbus Avenue, has the nation's largest public telescope.

The **Klickitat County Historical Museum** is small but delightful, thanks to its local Native American and pioneer artifacts. ⊠ *127 W. Broadway* ☎ *509/ 773–4303* 🖾 *$3* ⊙ *Apr.–Oct., daily 9–5; Nov.–Mar., by appointment.*

The 12,276-foot-tall **Mt. Adams,** northwest of Goldendale, is enclosed by a wilderness area and by the Yakama Indian Reservation. Camping and hiking is permitted in the latter only by permission of the tribe. Call the tribe's Forestry Development Program or the Mt. Adams Ranger Station for information. ⊠ *Between Yakima Valley and Columbia Gorge* ☎ *509/395–2501 Ranger Station, 509/865–5121 Ext. 657 Forestry Development Program* 🖾 *$5* ⊙ *July–Sept., sunrise–sunset.*

🌣 **Goldendale Observatory,** the nation's largest public observatory, has a 24½-inch reflecting telescope. The night sky here is gorgeous, unaffected by light pollution. ⊠ *1602 Observatory Dr.* ☎ *509/773–3141* ⊕ *www. perr.com/gosp* 🖾 *Free* ⊙ *Apr.–Sept., Wed.–Sun. 2–5 and 8–midnight; Oct.–Mar., call for schedule.*

Fodor'sChoice **Maryhill Museum of Art.** Rising from the bare hills of the Columbia
★ Plateau, castle-like Maryhill is an oddity. A Flemish château–style museum built in the 1920s by railroad magnate Sam Hill. In 1926 Hill invited Queen Marie of Romania to dedicate the museum, which was still unfinished. The queen, who was grateful for Hill's generous aid to Romania after World War I, agreed and arrived to enthusiastic crowds who came for the dedication. The museum houses, among other objects, Rodin sculptures, Native American artifacts, and an extensive collection of chess sets. Peacocks stroll the manicured grounds, which overlook the Columbia River. ⊠ *35 Maryhill Museum Dr.* ☎ *509/773–3733* ⊕ *www. maryhillmuseum.org* 🖾 *$7* ⊙ *Mid-Mar.–mid-Nov., daily 9–5.*

You can fish, hike, windsurf, and rock climb at **Horsethief Lake State Park,** about 20 mi southwest of Goldendale. It's famous for its petroglyphs; there are tours of them from April to October, Friday and Saturday at 10 AM. You must make reservations. ⊠ *Rte. 14* ☎ *509/767–1159* 🖾 *Free* ⊙ *Daily 6:30–sunset.*

Where to Stay

¢ ⊡ **Ponderosa Motel.** This two-story motel is in the heart of town, just ¼ mi north of Route 97. Restaurants and shops are all within easy walking distance. Some suites and four of the rooms have kitchens. ⊠ *775 E. Broadway St., 98620* ☎ *509/773–5842* ⎙ *509/773–4049* ⌐ *28 rooms ⌂ Some kitchens, cable TV, business services, some pets allowed (fee)* ▭ *AE, D, DC, MC, V.*

Southwestern Washington A to Z

AIR TRAVEL

Getting to the northern and southern portions of southwestern Washington by air is no problem, but traveling to the mountains, coast, and Columbia River Gorge requires considerable road travel.

AIRPORTS &TRANSFERS — If you're planning to visit the Long Beach Peninsula, Mt. St. Helens National Volcanic Monument, and places near the Columbia River Gorge, you're better off flying into Portland International Airport (PDX) in Oregon, just 10 mi south of Vancouver, Washington. For visits to Mt. Rainier National Park, it's best to fly into Seattle-Tacoma International Airport (Sea-Tac), a larger airport with more carriers.

Driving is the best way to get from the airports to your southwestern Washington destination. At Portland's airport, car rental agencies are on the first floor of the parking garage. At Sea-Tac, the agencies have counters in the baggage claim area.

🛪 Airport Information **Portland International Airport** ⊠ NE Airport Way at I-205 ☎ 877/739–4636 ⊕ www.portlandairportpdx.com. **Sea-Tac International Airport** ⊠ International Blvd. and Pacific Hwy. S ☎ 206/431–4444 ⊕ www.seatac.org.

CARRIERS — Many national and international carriers serve Portland and Seattle. Leading regional carriers are Horizon Air and United Express.

🛪 Airlines **Horizon Air** ☎ 800/547–9308 ⊕ www.alaskaair.com. **United Express/Skywest** ☎ 800/241–6522 ⊕ www.skywest.com.

BUS TRAVEL

Greyhound and Gray Line offer limited service to points along major thoroughfares. Gray Line of Seattle has regular tours to Mt. Rainier National Park. Rainier Shuttle offers daily service from Sea-Tac to Ashford or Paradise from May 3 to October 10. The Ashford Mountain Center offers shuttle service from June through September to and from Sea-Tac and destinations within the park.

🚌 Bus Information **Ashford Mountain Center Shuttle** ☎ 360/569–2604 ⊕ www.ashfordmountaincenter.com. **Gray Line** ☎ 503/285–9845 or 800/422–7042 in Portland, 206/624–5077 or 800/426–7505 in Seattle ⊕ www.grayline.com. **Greyhound** ☎ 800/231–2222 ⊕ www.greyhound.com. **Rainier Shuttle** ☎ 360/569–2604.

CAR TRAVEL

Much of southwestern Washington is rural, with very little traffic congestion. The exceptions are Vancouver, due to its proximity to Portland, Oregon, and Mt. Rainier National Park, which experiences heavy summer traffic at the main visitor centers. You can avoid traffic problems by traveling to Rainier on weekdays and staying off the roads around Vancouver during morning and evening rush hours. Note, though, that that there are bound to be traffic jams along I–5 any night there's a concert at the amphitheater just north of Vancouver.

Route 101 curves around the southern part of the Long Beach Peninsula. Route 103 travels north through the peninsula. From I–5 north of Kelso, take Route 4 west through Longview to Route 401. Turn south if you're going to Chinook or Ilwaco, or continue on Route 4 to 101 if you're going to Seaview, Long Beach, and points north. The stretch of 101 along Willapa Bay's rocky eastern shore, south of the Naselle River estuary, is scenic. From Olympia, take 101 west; continue west on Route 8 and Route 12. At Montesano turn south onto Route 107, which will take you to 101; turn left (south) onto 101 at the junction.

Most visitors arrive at the Mt. Rainier National Park's Nisqually entrance, the closest entrance to I–5, via Route 706. Route 410 enters the park from the east. Route 123 enters from the southeast. Routes 410 and 123 are usually closed in winter. Route 165 leads to Ipsut Creek Campground through the Carbon River entrance to Mowich Lake, in the park's northwest corner.

Route 504 is the main road through the Mt. St. Helens National Volcanic Monument. The Castle Rock Exit (No. 49) of I–5 is just outside the monument's western entrance. Follow 504 into the park. You can access the park from the north by taking Forest Service Road 25 south from U.S. 12 at the town of Randle. Forest Service Road 25 connects with Forest Service Road 90, which heads north from the town of Cougar. These two roads are closed by snow in winter.

Route 14 through the Columbia River Gorge is a narrow, winding two-lane road that skirts steep drop-offs and overlooks as you head east to Goldendale. As it's the only east–west route on the Washington side of the river, backups behind slow trucks and RVs are common. Travel through the gorge in winter can be particularly treacherous owing to strong winds and icy conditions.

🚩 **Mt. Rainier National Park Road Conditions** ☎ Call 360/569-5211.

EMERGENCIES

🚩 Doctors & Dentists **Clark County Dental Society** ⊕ www.clarkdentists.org ☎ no phone. **Clark County Medical Society** ☎ 360/576-0987.
🚩 Hospitals **Ocean Beach Hospital and Clinics** ✉ 174 1st Ave., Ilwaco ☎ 360/642-3181. **St. John Medical Center** ✉ 1615 Delaware St., Longview ☎ 360/414-2000 or 800/438-7562. **Southwest Washington Medical Center** ✉ 400 NE Mother Joseph Pl., Vancouver ☎ 360/256-2000.

MAIL & SHIPPING

🚩 Post Offices **Ashford** ✉ 30312 Date Rd., 98304 ☎ 360/569-2346. **Long Beach** ✉ 101 Oregon Ave. N, 98631 ☎ 360/642-3984. **Longview** ✉ 1603 Larch St., 98632 ☎ 360/636-8593. **Vancouver** ✉ 2700 Caples Ave., 98661 ☎ 360/992-5000.
🚩 Overnight Services **UPS** ✉ 1701 Broadway St., Vancouver 98663 ☎ 360/693-8543. **FedEx** ✉ Seaview One Stop (drop box), 4105 Pacific Dr., Long Beach 98631 ✉ 1044 15th Ave., Longview 98632 ☎ 360/423-5399.

MONEY MATTERS

Just about every community in southwest Washington has a bank with an ATM machine. Many grocery stores and convenience stores also have ATMs. Major bank branches include Washington Mutual (no ATM fee), KeyBank, and Cowlitz Bank.
🚩 Banks **Cowlitz Bank** ✉ 927 Commerce Ave., Longview ☎ 360/423-9800. **KeyBank** ✉ 200 Bolstad Ave. E, Long Beach ☎ 360/642-2377. **Washington Mutual** ✉ 1205 Broadway St., Vancouver ☎ 360/750-3010.

TOURS

Gray Line of Seattle offers 10-hour bus tours from Seattle to Mt. Rainier National Park from May to September. The cost is $54. Lunch isn't included.
🚩 Tour-Operators **Gray Line of Seattle** ✉ 4500 W. Marginal Way SW, Seattle ☎ 800/426-7505.

VISITOR INFORMATION

Destination Packwood Association ⌖ Box 64, Packwood 98361 ☎ 360/494–2223 ⊕ www.destinationpackwood.com. **Greater Goldendale Area Chamber of Commerce** ✉ 131 W. Court St., Goldendale 98620 ☎ 509/773–3400 ⊕ www.goldendalechamber. org. **Greater Vancouver Chamber of Commerce** ✉ 1101 Broadway St., Suite 120, Vancouver 98663 ☎ 360/694–2588 ⊕ www.vancouverusa.com. **Long Beach Peninsula Visitors Bureau** ✉ Rte. 101 and Rte. 103 ⌖ Box 562, 98631 ☎ 360/642–2400 or 800/451–2542 ⊕ www.funbeach.com. **Longview Area Chamber of Commerce** ✉ 1563 Olympia Way, Longview 98632 ☎ 360/423–8400 ⊕ www.kelsolongviewchamber.com. **Mt. Rainier Business Association** ⌖ Box 214, Ashford 98304 ☎ 360/569–0910 or 877/617–9950 ⊕ www.mt-rainier.com. **Mt. Rainier National Park** ✉ Tahoma Woods, Star Rte., Ashford 98304 ☎ 360/569–2211 ⊕ www.nps.gov/mora. **Mt. St. Helens National Volcanic Monument** ☎ 360/449–7800 ⊕ www.fs.fed.us/gpnf/mshnvm. **Skamania County Chamber of Commerce** ✉ 167 NW 2nd St., Stevenson 98648 ☎ 800/989–9178 ⊕ www.skamania.org. **Southwest Washington Visitor and Convention Bureau** ✉ 605 Esther St., Vancouver 98663 ☎ 360/750–1553 or 800/600–0800 ⊕ www. southwestwashington.com. **Tourism Lewis County** ✉ 500 NW Chamber of Commerce Way, Chehalis 98532 ☎ 800/525–3323 ⊕ www.chamberway.com.

YAKIMA RIVER VALLEY

Updated by
John Anderson

The Yakima River binds a region of great contrasts. Snow-capped volcanic peaks and golden hills overlook a natural grass steppe turned green by irrigation. Famed throughout the world for its apples and cherries, its wine and hops, this fertile landscape is also the ancestral home of the Yakama people from whom it takes its name.

The river flows southeasterly from its source in the Cascade Mountains near Snoqualmie Pass. Between the college town of Ellensburg, at the heart of the Kittitas Valley, and Yakima, the region's largest city, the river cuts steep canyons through serried, sagebrush-covered ridges before merging with the Naches River. Then it breaks through Union Gap to enter its fecund namesake, the broad Yakima Valley. Some 200 mi from its birthplace, the river makes one final bend around vineyard-rich Red Mountain before joining the Columbia at the Tri-Cities.

Mount Rainier, Washington's tallest summit, stands west of the Cascade crest but is often more readiliy seen by those living east of the mountains, where the air is clear and clouds are few. South of Rainier is the broad-shouldered Mt. Adams, the sacred mountain of the Yakama people. The 12,276-foot-tall mountain marks the western boundary of their reservation, second largest in the Pacific Northwest. Here wild horses run free through the Horse Heaven Hills, as they have for centuries. Deer and elk roam the evergreen forests, eagles and curlews soar overhead.

Orchards and vineyards dominate Yakima Valley's agricultural landscape. Cattle and sheep ranching initially drove the economy; apples and other produce came with the first irrigation schemes in the 1890s. The annual asparagus harvest begins in April, followed by spring cherries; apricots and peaches ripen in early to mid-summer. Exported throughout the world for the brewing of beer, hops are ready by late August; travelers may see the bushy vines spiraling up fields of twine. The apple harvest runs from late summer through October.

The valley's real fame rests on its wines, however, which have a growing reputation as among the best in the world. Concord grapes were first planted here in the 1960s, and they still take up large tracts of land. But *vinifera* grapes, the noble grapes of Europe, now dominate the local wine industry. Merlot and white burgundies helped the region establish its reputation, and syrah is often regarded as the grape of the future. There are fine cabernets, grenaches, Rieslings, chardonnays, gewürztraminers, sémillons, sauvignon blancs, chenin blancs, and muscats, as well as such lesser known varietals as sangioveses, nebbiolos, and lembergers.

Yakima Valley wineries range in size from small backyard cellars to large commercial operations. Barrels are tapped and the main wine-tasting season begins in late April and runs to the end of the fall harvest in November. Most wineries are easily reached from I-82. Winery hours vary in winter, when you should call ahead before visiting. The Yakima Valley Winery Association (www.yakimavalleywine.com) publishes a map-brochure that lists wineries with tasting-room hours. Most are owned and managed by unpretentious enthusiasts, and their cellar masters are often on hand to answer questions.

Cle Elum

❶ *86 mi southeast of Seattle.*

A former railroad, coal, and logging town, Cle Elum (pronounced "klee *ell*-um") now caters to travelers stopping for a breath of air before or after tackling Snoqualmie Pass. The **Cle Elum Bakery** (⊠ 501 E. 1st St. ☎ 509/674–2233) has been doing business from the very same spot since 1906. Across from the bakery is **Owens Meats** (⊠ 502 E. 1st St. ☎ 509/674–2530), a marvelous smokehouse run by the same family for more than six decades.

Cle Elum was the last municipality in the United States to change from switchboard to rotary dialing. On display at the **Cle Elum Telephone Museum** are the switchboards and related equipment used until 1966. ⊠ 221 E. 1st St. ☎ 509/674–5702 ⊕ www.geocities.com/nkchs ✉ $2 ☉ Memorial Day–Labor Day, weekends noon–4.

The **Carpenter House Museum** displays the work of area artists in a three-story 1914 banker's home. ⊠ 302 W. 3rd St. ☎ 509/674–5939 ✉ Free ☉ Fri.–Sun. noon–4.

Roslyn, a former coal-mining town just 3 mi northwest of Cle Elum, is famous as the stand-in for the Alaskan village of Cicely on the 1990s TV program *Northern Exposure*. A map locating sites associated with filming is available from the city offices at First Street and Pennsylvania Avenue. Roslyn is also notable for its 28 ethnic cemeteries. Established by communities of miners in the late 19th and early 20th centuries, they are clustered on a hillside west of town.

Where to Stay & Eat

$–$$ ✕ **MaMa Vallone's Steak House and Inn.** Pasta dishes, the tomato-based *fagioli* (soup with vegetables and beans), and *bagna calda* (a bath of olive oil, garlic, anchovies, and butter for dredging vegetables and meat) are worthy dishes at this cozy and informal restaurant. The inn was built in 1906 as a boardinghouse for unmarried miners. ⊠ 302 W. 1st St. ☎ 509/674–5174 ☐ AE, DC, MC, V ☉ No lunch.

¢–$$ ✕ **Sunset Café and Loose Wolf Lounge.** Since 1936 this restaurant has been serving breakfast and such lunch and dinner favorites as homemade ravioli to the Cle Elum community. Italian dishes share the menu with traditional American favorites such as hamburgers and fried chicken. ⊠ 318 E. 1st St. ☎ 509/674–2241 ☐ AE, D, DC, MC, V.

¢–$ 🏠 **Iron Horse Inn Bed and Breakfast.** What was once a boarding house for rail workers (1909–74) is now a comfortable country inn owned by the daughter and son-in-law of a one-time lodger. Rooms are named for former crewmen and are full of railroad memorabilia. Three adjacent cabooses have been transformed into guest quarters complete with microwaves and refrigerators. ⊠ *526 Marie Ave. South Cle Elum, 98943* ☎ *509/674–5939, 800/228–9246 WA and OR only* ⊕ *www.ironhorseinnbb.com* ⇌ *12 rooms, 4 with shared bath* ⬦ *Dining room, some microwaves, some refrigerators, outdoor hot tub; no room phones, no TV in some rooms, no kids, no smoking* ▭ *MC, V* ⫝ *BP.*

¢ ⊞ **Aster Inn.** A quirky, circa-1918 antiques shop doubles as the office for this charming motel, which wraps around a central garden and picnic area. Grapevines drape the doors to each of the cozy rooms, some of which have brass beds and claw-foot tubs. ⊠ *521 E. 1st St., 98922* ☎ *509/674–2551 or 800/616–9722* ⇌ *10 rooms* ⬦ *Some in-room hot tubs, kitchenettes, microwaves, refrigerators, cable TV; no smoking* ▭ *AE, D, MC, V.*

¢ ⊞ **Cascade Mountain Inn.** Decor is simple at this well-kept two-story motel east of downtown. But the rooms are huge and, with the many amenities, give a home-away-from-home comfort. ⊠ *906 E. 1st St., 98922* ☎ *509/674–2380 or 888/674–3975* ⊟ *509/674–7099* ⇌ *43 rooms* ⬦ *Some in-room hot tubs, some microwaves, some refrigerators, cable TV, some pets allowed, no-smoking rooms* ▭ *AE, D, DC, MC, V* ⫝ *CP.*

Ellensburg

❷ *24 mi southeast of Cle Elum.*

This university and college town is one of the state's friendliest and most easygoing places. "Modern" Ellensburg had its origin in a Fourth of July fire that engulfed the original city in 1889. Almost overnight, Victorian brick buildings rose from the ashes; many still stand, though their functions have changed. Stroll downtown to discover art galleries, comfortable cafés, secondhand book and record stores, an old-fashioned hardware store, and one antiques shop after another.

Central Washington's single biggest event is the Ellensburg Rodeo, held Labor Day weekend. On the national circuit since the 1920s, the rodeo has a year-round headquarters on Main Street where you can buy tickets and souvenirs. You can also get a bird's-eye view of the rodeo grounds from Reed Park, in the 500 block of North Alder Street.

★ The 8,000 students of **Central Washington University** enjoy a pleasant, tree-shaded campus marked by tasteful redbrick architecture. Its 8th Avenue facade has several handsome buildings dating from its founding in 1891 as the State Normal School. Near the center of campus is a serene Japanese garden. ⊠ *400 E. 8th Ave.* ☎ *509/963–1111* ⊕ *www.cwu.edu* ▱ *Free* ☉ *Tours weekdays 10–2.*

The **Chimpanzee and Human Communication Institute** is a world-famous research center where chimps communicate with people through sign language. Every weekend the university hosts hour-long Chimposiums where visitors interact with the primates through large windows. ⊠ *Nicholson Blvd. (14th Ave.) and D St.* ☎ *509/963–2244* ⊕ *www.cwu.edu/~cwuchci* ▱ *$10* ☉ *Mar.–Nov., Sat. 9:15 and 10:45, Sun. 12:30 and 2.*

Rotating exhibits at **Sarah Spurgeon Art Gallery,** in Randall Hall, feature the work of regional and national artists as well as students and faculty. ⊠ *Nicholson Blvd.* ☎ *509/963–2665* ▱ *Free* ☉ *Sept.–June, weekdays 8:30–4:30.*

★ The **Clymer Museum of Art** has the largest collection of works by painter John Clymer (1907–89). The Ellensburg native was one of the most widely published illustrators of the American West, focusing his oils

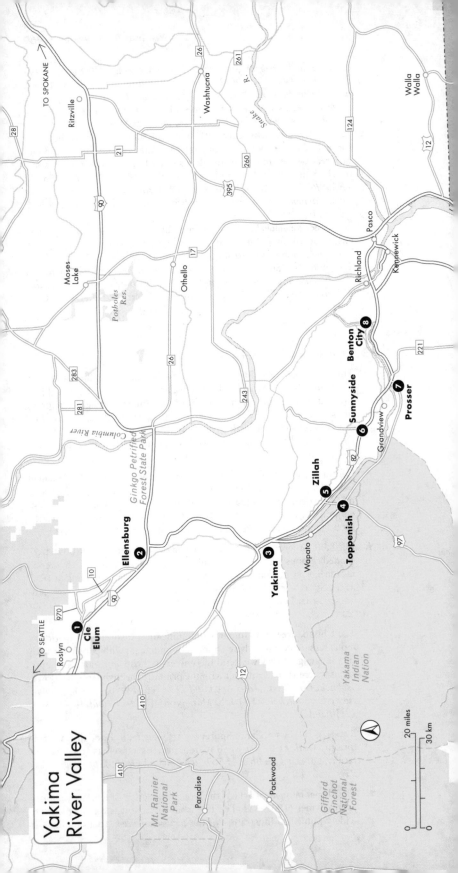

Yakima River Valley

and watercolors on wildlife and traditional lifestyles. ⊠ *416 N. Pearl St.* ☏ *509/962–6416* ⊕ *www.clymermuseum.com* ⬚ *Free* ☉ *Weekdays 10–5, weekends noon–5.*

Newly expanded **Gallery I,** in the 1889 Stewart Building, is a community art center with rotating shows by regional artists, a fine gift shop, and art classes. ⊠ *408 N. Pearl St.* ☏ *509/925–2670* ⬚ *Free* ☉ *Mon.–Sat. 11–5.*

The six-room **Kittitas County Museum** has one of the state's better pioneer artifact collections, ranging from Indian basketry to early-20th-century carriages. ⊠ *114 E. 3rd Ave.* ☏ *509/925–3778* ⬚ *Free* ☉ *Mon.–Sat. 10–4.*

☝ **Dick and Jane's Spot,** nestled in suburbia, is the area's most peculiar attraction. The home of artists Dick Elliott and Jane Orleman is a continuously growing whimsical sculpture, a collage of 20,000 bottle caps, 1,500 bicycle reflectors, and other bits. Their masterpiece stands on private property near downtown, but it's still possible to see the recycled creation from several angles; sign the guestbook mounted on the surrounding fence. ⊠ *101 N. Pearl St.* ☏ *509/925–3224.*

Olmstead Place State Park is an original pioneer farm built in 1875. A 0.7-mi interpretive trail links eight buildings, including a barn and schoolhouse, on a 217-acre working farm. ⊠ *N. Ferguson Rd., ½ mi south of Kittitas Hwy., 4 mi east of Ellensburg* ☏ *509/925–1943* ⊕ *www.parks.wa.gov* ⬚ *Free, parking $10* ☉ *Apr.–Oct., 6:30 AM–sunset; Nov.–Mar., 8 AM–sunset.*

Ginkgo and Wanapum State Parks, 28 mi east of Ellensburg on the Columbia River, are separated by I–90. Ginkgo Petrified Forest State Park preserves a fossil forest of ginkgos and other trees. A 3-mi-long trail leads from the interpretive center. Wanapum State Park, 3 mi south, has camping and river access for boaters. ⊠ *I–90 east to Exit 136, Vantage* ☏ *509/856–2700* ⊕ *www.parks.wa.gov* ⬚ *Free; parking $10, camping $17* ☉ *Apr.–Sept., 6:30 AM–sunset, Oct.–Mar., 8 AM–sunset.*

Indian and pioneer artifacts are exhibited at **Wanapum Dam Visitor Center,** which also has displays on modern hydroelectric power. ⊠ *Rte. 243 S.* ☏ *509/754–3541 Ext. 2571* ⬚ *Free* ☉ *Weekdays 8:30–4:30, weekends 9–5.*

Where to Stay & Eat

$–$$ ✕ **Pearl's on Pearl.** A smoke-free wine bar and bistro in the 1889 Geddis Building, Pearl's has live jazz on weekends. The menu changes every few months on the whim of chef Cinda Kohler. Expect anything from Mediterranean to Caribbean, French Provincial to Cajun. ⊠ *311 N. Pearl St.* ☏ *509/962–8899* ▤ *AE, MC, V* ☉ *No lunch weekdays.*

$–$$ ✕ **Starlight Lounge & Dining Room.** Like a speakeasy with flair, the Starlight is really three separate establishments: a fine restaurant, a college pool hall, and a martini-and-cigar bar. All nestle within Ellensburg's most prominent structure, the turreted 1889 Davidson Building. Chef Johnny Tremaine presents creative home cooking in dishes like meat loaf with a wild-mushroom demi-glace, and crab cakes with chili-lime aioli. ⊠ *402 N. Pearl St.* ☏ *509/962–6100* ▤ *AE, D, MC, V.*

★ **$–$$** ✕ **Valley Cafe.** Meals at this vintage art deco eatery consist of Mediterranean bistro-style salads, pastas, and other plates. Featured dinner entrées include rack of lamb, seared ahi tuna, and chicken Marsala. An impressive wine list offers dozens of Yakima Valley options. ⊠ *105 W. 3rd Ave.* ☏ *509/925–3050* ▤ *AE, D, DC, MC, V.*

¢–$ ✕ **Casa De Blanca.** This plain café serves up delectable Mexican and American fare, but the main attractions are steak and prime rib. Good beef cookery can be hard to find; the owners have been doing it right since 1975. ⊠ *1318 S. Canyon Rd.* ☎ *509/925–1693* ▭ *D, MC, V.*

¢–$ ✕ **Ellensburg Pasta Co.** Noodle lovers can't go wrong at this casual college-area café. Spaghetti, fettuccine, lasagna, and ravioli are presented with classic red and white sauces in the jazzy dining room or out on the patio. ⊠ *600 N. Main St.* ☎ *509/933–3330* ▭ *AE, D, MC, V* ☉ *Closed Sun. No lunch.*

¢–$ ✕ **Yellow Church Café.** Built in 1923 as a Lutheran church, this house of culinary worship now offers seating in the nave or choir loft. Soups, salads, sandwiches, pastas, and home-baked goods are served, as well as dinner specials. Breakfast is popular on weekends. ⊠ *111 S. Pearl St.* ☎ *509/933–2233* ⊕ *www.yellowchurchcafe.com* ▭ *AE, MC, V.*

$ ▥ **Best Western Lincoln Inn and Suites.** A spacious new hostelry one block off Ellensburg's main north–south arterial, the Lincoln Inn offers travelers plenty of elbow room, minimal noise, and lots of amenities and services. ⊠ *211 W. Umptanum Rd., 98926* ☎ *509/925–4244 or 866/925–4288* 🖷 *509/925–4211* ⊕ *www.bestwestern.com* ⇲ *55 rooms* ⚘ *In-room data ports, some in-room hot tubs, some kitchenettes, microwaves, refrigerators, cable TV, indoor pool, exercise equipment, hot tub, video game room, laundry facilities, Internet, business services, some pets allowed (fee), no-smoking rooms* ▭ *AE, D, DC, MC, V* ⦿❙ *CP.*

¢–$ ▥ **Inn at Goose Creek.** Each room of this modern house—spare from the outside, elegant within—has its own theme. The Homespun Room contains an assortment of black Shaker-style furniture, plain walls, and (like all the rooms) a handmade rug. The Timber Creek Lodge Room appeals to fishing enthusiasts. ⊠ *1720 Canyon Rd., 98926* ☎ *509/962–8030 or 800/533–0822* 🖷 *509/962–8031* ⊕ *www.innatgoosecreek.com* ⇲ *10 rooms* ⚘ *In-room data ports, in-room hot tubs, refrigerators, cable TV, in-room VCRs; no smoking.* ▭ *AE, MC, V* ⦿❙ *CP.*

¢ ▥ **Ellensburg Inn.** It's rodeo time year-round at this comfortable, full-service motel just off I-90 (Exit 109). From the covered wagon in the lobby to the country-and-western music in the lounge and the guest room decor, the Old West is alive and well here. ⊠ *1700 Canyon Rd., 98926* ☎ *509/925–9801 or 800/321–8791* 🖷 *509/925–2093* ⊕ *www.ellensburginn.com* ⇲ *105 rooms* ⚘ *Restaurant, room service, in-room data ports, refrigerators, cable TV, indoor pool, wading pool, exercise equipment, hot tub, lounge, business services, some pets allowed (fee), no-smoking rooms* ▭ *AE, D, MC, V.*

Yakima

❸ *38 mi south of Ellensburg.*

The gateway to Washington wine country is sunny Yakima (pronounced *yak*-imah), with about 72,000 people. Spread along the west bank of the Yakima River just south of its confluence with the Naches, it's a bustling community with lovely parklands and a downtown on the cusp of revitalization.

The town was settled in the late 1850s as a ranching center where Ahtanum Creek joins the Yakima River, on the site of earlier Yakama tribal villages at present-day Union Gap. When the North Pacific Railroad established its terminal 4 mi north in 1884, most of the town picked up and moved.

Yakima's mission-style Northern Pacific Depot (1912), the highlight of its historic North Front Street, houses one of America's oldest brewpubs. Other old buildings face the depot; behind it, colorful Track 29 Mall is in old rail cars. Four blocks east is the ornate Capitol Theatre, built in 1920. The former vaudeville and silent-movie hall is now a performing arts center. Opposite is Millennium Plaza, a public art installation that celebrates the importance of water to the Yakima Valley.

Downtown is home to a tasting room for **Yakima Cellars** (⊠ 32 N. 2nd St. ☎ 509/577–0461), whose sangiovese is earning wide acclaim. The winery itself is a few blocks east. On the east side of I–90, **Washington's Fruit Place Visitor Center** (⊠ 105 S. 18th St. ☎ 509/576–3090) presents exhibits on orchard management from bloom to harvest.

★ ☺ The **Yakima Valley Museum** documents Yakama, pioneer, and 20th-century history in exhibits ranging from horse-drawn vehicles to a "neon garden" of street signs. Highlights include a fully operating 1930s soda fountain and a model of Yakima native and Supreme Court Justice William O. Douglas's Washington D.C. office. ⊠ *2105 Tieton Dr.* ☎ *509/ 248–0747* ⊕ *www.yakimavalleymuseum.org* ⊠ *$3* ☺ *Tues.–Sun. 11–5.*

☺ The **Yakima Electronic Railway Museum** (⊠ 3rd Ave. and W. Pine St. ☎ 509/575–1700 ⊕ www.yakimavalleytrolleys.org) offers summer weekend rides on early-20th-century trolley cars. The fare is $4. The ☺ **McAllister Museum of Aviation** (⊠ 2008 S. 16th Ave. ☎ 509/457–4933 ⊕ www.mcallistermuseum.org) is on the site of a pioneering flight school. The museum is open Tuesday through Friday 10–4 and Saturday 9–4. Donations are accepted.

Central Washington Agricultural Museum in Fullbright Park displays antique farm machinery in 20 large buildings and on adjacent acreage. ⊠ *4508 Main St., Union Gap* ☎ *509/457–8735* ⊠ *Free* ☺ *Daily 9–5.*

The **Yakima Area Arboretum,** on the west bank of the Yakima River at Route 24 and I–82, adjoins the 10-mi-long Yakima Greenway, a paved path that links a series of riverfront parks. A Japanese garden and a wetland trail are the arboretum's highlights. ⊠ *1401 Arboretum Dr., off Nob Hill Blvd.* ☎ *509/248–7337* ⊕ *www.ahtrees.org* ⊠ *Free* ☺ *Daily sunrise–sunset.*

The Catholic **Ahtanum Mission** was established in 1847; U.S. soldiers burned it in 1855 when a powder keg was found buried in the yard, but it was rebuilt in 1867. The chapel and surrounding grounds are about 15 mi southwest of Yakima. ⊠ *17740 Ahtanum Rd.* ☎ *509/966–0865* ⊠ *$1* ☺ *May–Sept., daily 9–7.*

Sagelands Vineyard, 7 mi southeast of Yakima, produces cabernet sauvignon, merlot, and sémillon. The main building has a huge stone fireplace and a commanding view of the upper valley. ⊠ *71 Gangl Rd., Exit 40 off I–82, Wapato* ☎ *509/877–2112* ☺ *Mar.–Oct., daily 11–5:30; Nov.–Feb., daily noon–5.*

Where to Stay & Eat

$$–$$$$ ✕ **Gasperetti's.** John Gasperetti's restaurant keeps an elegant low profile in a high-traffic area north of downtown. Moderately priced pasta dishes share the menu with a short list of special weekly dinners—meat or seafood entrées with organically grown local produce. The cellar has an excellent selection of wines, including Italian varietals. ⊠ *1013 N. 1st St.* ☎ *509/248–0628* ▭ *AE, D, DC, MC, V* ☺ *Closed Sun. and Mon. No lunch Sat.*

$$–$$$ ✕ **Greystone Restaurant.** The 1899 Lund Building has come a long way since its days as a sheep ranchers' hotel, saloon, and brothel. Beneath the pressed-tin ceiling and between the gray stone walls, the same creative steak-and-seafood menu is served in the no-smoking dining room and bistro bar. ⊠ *5 N. Front St. at Yakima Ave.* ☎ *509/248–9801* ⊕ *www.greystonerestaurant.com* ▭ *AE, MC, V* ☺ *Closed &Sun. and Mon. No lunch.*

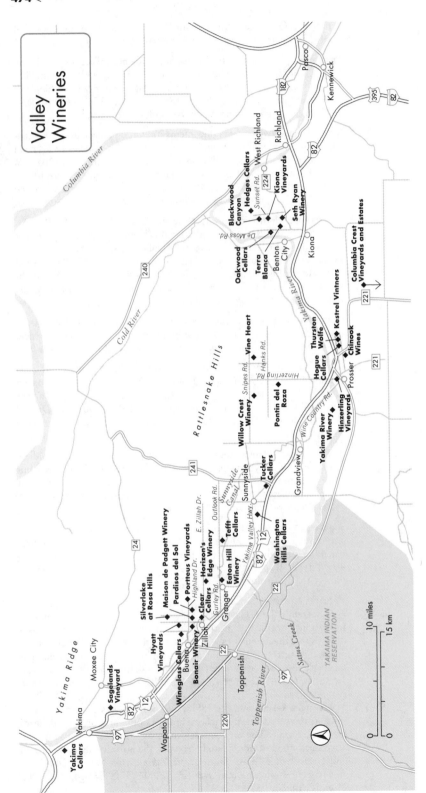

Valley Wineries

Columbia River

Yakima Ridge

Moxee City

Yakima

Wapato

Toppenish

Toppenish River

Satus Creek

YAKAMA INDIAN RESERVATION

Yakima Cellars

Sagelands Vineyard

Hyatt Vineyards

Wineglass Cellars

Bonair Winery

Buena

Zillah

Granger

Silverlake at Rosa Hills

Maison de Padgett Winery

Pardisos del Sol

Porteus Vineyards

Highland Dr.

Clear Cellars

Horizon's Edge Winery

Gurley Rd.

E. Zillah Dr.

Eaton Hill Winery

Tefft Cellars

Outlook Rd.

Washington Hills Cellars

Sunnyside

Sunnyside Canal

Yakima Valley Hwy.

Grandview

Tucker Cellars

Willow Crest Winery

Snipes Rd.

Pontin del Roza

Vine Heart

Hanks Rd.

Wine Country Rd.

Yakima River Winery

Hinzerling Vineyards

Hinzerling Rd.

Prosser

Hogue Cellars

Thurston Wolfe

Kestrel Vintners

Chinook Wines

Columbia Crest Vineyards and Estates

Ratlesnake Hills

Cold River

Oakwood Cellars

Terra Blanca

De Moss Rd.

Benton City

Kiona

Yakima River

Blackwood Canyon

Hedges Cellars

Sunset Rd.

Kiona Vineyards

Seth Ryan Winery

West Richland

Richland

Pasco

Kennewick

10 miles

15 km

$$ ✕ **Cafe Mélange.** This popular eatery has upscale white-tablecloth service, but the waitstaffers remain friendly. Smoked salmon ravioli and duck with a huckleberry and port wine sauce are favorites. Beer and wine are the only alcohol served, and it's no-smoking. ⊠ *7 N. Front St.* ☎ *509/453–0571* ⊟ *AE, D, MC, V* ☾ *Closed Sun. No lunch.*

$–$$ ✕ **Barrel House.** A former miners' tavern one block east of the depot, Barrel House is now Yakima's leading wine bar. Big John Caudill's creative menu ranges from vegetarian entrées to salads, burgers, steaks, and chops. ⊠ *22 N. 1st St.* ☎ *509/453–3769* ⊕ *www.localtoolbox.com/restaurant* ⊟ *AE, MC, V* ☾ *No lunch Sun.*

★ ¢–$$ ✕ **Santiago's.** Elegant and charming, Jar and Deb Arcand's skylit establishment puts a new spin on Mexican dishes. For chili verde, chunks of pork loin are slow-cooked in jalapeno sauce; the Yakima apple pork *mole* is prepared with chocolate and cinnamon. ⊠ *111 E. Yakima Ave.* ☎ *509/453–1644* ⊕ *www.santiagos.org* ⌖ *Reservations not accepted* ⊟ *MC, V* ☾ *Closed Sun. No lunch Sat.*

★ ¢–$ ✕ **Grant's Brewery Pub.** Bert Grant's place (in the old Northern Pacific station) is a Yakima institution. British-style pub fare shares the menu with Reubens, burgers, and salads. On weekends, live jazz accompanies the hand-crafted suds. ⊠ *32 N. Front St.* ☎ *509/575–2922* ⌖ *Reservations not accepted* ⊟ *MC, V.*

¢–$ ✕ **Rinconcito Salvadoreño.** The food of El Salvador has subtle variations from that of Mexico, and visitors here are lucky to be able to enjoy it. This casual café offers dishes like *pupusas* (stuffed tortillas) and *pastelitos* (corn turnovers), and serves them with imported Salvadoran beers. ⊠ *1006 S. 3rd Ave.* ☎ *509/248–5210* ⌖ *Reservations not accepted* ⊟ *No credit cards* ☾ *Closed Mon.*

¢ ✕ **Museum Soda Fountain.** Soda jerks at the Yakima Valley Museum's café make shakes and sundaes plus soups, hot dogs, and other sandwiches while a period Wurlitzer spins 1930s big band records. ⊠ *2105 Tieton Dr.* ☎ *509/248–0747* ⌖ *Reservations not accepted* ⊟ *No credit cards* ☾ *Closed Mon. No dinner Sept.–mid-June.*

$–$$$ ✕⊞ **Birchfield Manor.** The valley's only luxury accommodation is on a
plateau just outside Yakima surrounded by corn and cattle. The Old Manor House contains the restaurant and five upstairs rooms. Rooms in a newer cottage are more private and have such amenities as steam-sauna showers and gas fireplaces. Chef-owner Brad Masset oversees the Continental-style restaurant ($$$–$$$$, no lunch; one seating Thurs.–Fri., two seatings Sat.; reservations essential), often assisted by his father Will, a European-trained chef who established the inn in 1978, and his brother Greg, a local vintner. The limited prix-fixe menu changes seasonally. The wine cellar has an excellent selection of local and imported vintages. ⊠ *2018 Birchfield Rd., just south of Rte. 24, 98901* ☎ *509/452–1960 or 800/375–3420* ⊠ *509/452–2334* ⊕ *www.birchfieldmanor.com* ⊃ *11 rooms* ⌖ *Restaurant, some in-room hot tubs, some in-room VCRs, pool; no phones in some rooms, no TV in some rooms, no smoking* ⊟ *AE, DC, MC, V* ⊠| *BP.*

★ ¢–$ ✕⊞ **A Touch of Europe Bed & Breakfast Inn.** The many charms of this gracious 1889 Queen Anne have been preserved—the box-beam ceiling, extensive millwork, and stained-glass windows. But the real treasure here is Erika Cenci, who owns the house with her husband of over 40 years, Jim. Erika, raised and trained as a chef in Berlin, prepares multicourse prix-fixe dinners ($$$$; reservations essential); wild game is her specialty, but she's also been known to prepare Italian and east Indian dishes. Guests furnish their own wine. ⊠ *220 N. 16th Ave., 98902* ☎ *509/454–9775 or 888/438–7073* ⊠ *509/452–1303* ⊕ *www.winesnw.com/toucheuropeb&b.htm* ⊃ *3 rooms* ⌖ *Restaurant; no phones in some rooms, no room TVs, no kids under 17, no smoking* ⊟ *AE, MC, V* ⊠| *BP.*

🐚 **$**   ⊞ **DoubleTree Hotel Yakima Valley.** Sprawling around a broad central lawn with an extensive pool deck, this hotel on the north side of town is one of Yakima's best. A variety of recreational diversions serve business travelers and vacationing families alike. ⊠ *1507 N. 1st St., 98901* ☎ *509/248–7850 or 800/222–8733* 🖷 *509/575–1694* ⊕ *www.doubletree.com* ➴ *208 rooms* ⚑ *Restaurant, coffee shop, room service, in-room data ports, some in-room hot tubs, some refrigerators, cable TV with movies and video games, putting green, pool, hot tub, exercise equipment, billiards, lounge, video game room, playground, laundry service, business services, airport shuttle, some pets allowed (fee), no-smoking rooms* ▭ *AE, D, DC, MC, V.*

¢–**$**   ⊞ **Oxford Inn & Oxford Suites.** Overlooking the Yakima Greenway and its ancient cottonwoods, these adjacent properties give scant clue that they lie just off the freeway. All the suites, which are in a contemporary white-adobe building, have patios or riverview balconies. About half the rooms in the Oxford Inn, which is surrounded by evergreens, have balconies, too. ⊠ *1603 Terrace Heights Dr., 98901* ☎ *509/457–4444 or 800/521–3050 Inn, 509/457–9000 or 800/404–7848 Suites* 🖷 *509/453–7593* ⊕ *www.oxfordsuites.com* ➴ *96 rooms, 107 suites* ⚑ *Some in-room data ports, some kitchenettes, some microwaves, refrigerators, cable TV, pool, exercise room, hot tub, laundry facilities, laundry service, business services, airport shuttle, no-smoking rooms* ▭ *AE, D, DC, MC, V* ⧖ *CP.*

¢   ⊞ **Orchard Inn Bed and Breakfast.** Seven miles west of downtown Yakima, the inn is secluded in a cherry orchard that beckons guests to take strolls. The contemporary house is appointed with a refined country theme; each room has a private entrance. Breakfast is served in the orchard. ⊠ *1207 Pecks Canyon Rd., 98908* ☎ *509/966–1283 or 888/858–8284* ⊕ *www.orchardinnbb.com* ➴ *4 rooms* ⚑ *In-room hot tubs, laundry facilities, Internet, business services; no smoking* ▭ *AE, D, MC, V* ⧖ *BP.*

Sports & the Outdoors

Yakima folks enjoy several sports franchises. There also are minor-league pro basketball (Yakima SunKings) and soccer (Yakima Reds) clubs.

The **Yakima Bears** (⊠ Yakima County Stadium, 1301 S. Fair Ave. ☎ 509/457–5151), an Arizona Diamondbacks affiliate, play in the Class A Northwest League from June to August. The **Apple Tree Golf Course** (⊠ 8804 Occidental Rd. ☎ 509/966–5877) is rated as one of the state's top 10. The signature hole on the 18-hole, par-72 course is Number 17, shaped like a giant apple floating in a lake. Greens fees run $35–$50.

White Pass Village, a full-service ski area 50 mi west of Yakima toward Mt. Rainier, is the home mountain of former Olympic medalists Phil and Steve Mahre. Five lifts serve a vertical drop of 1,500 feet from the 6,000-foot summit. Here you'll find condominiums, a gas station, grocery store, and snack bar. Open woods are popular with cross-country skiers and summer hikers. ⊠ *48935 Rte. 12* ☎ *509/672–3101* ⊕ *www. skiwhitepass.com.*

Shopping

Congdon Orchards (⊠ 1117 S. 64th Ave. ☎ 509/966–4440) welcomes you into their apple and cherry warehouses. **Johnson Orchards** (⊠ 4906 Summitview Ave. ☎ 509/966–7479) has been growing fruit—including cherries, peaches, apples and pears—since 1904.

Central Washington's largest shopping center, **Valley Mall** (⊠ 2529 Main St., Union Gap ☎ 509/453–8233) has two major department stores: Sears and Gottschalks. Produce vendors gather in downtown Yakima every

Sunday, June through October, for the **Yakima Farmers Market.** At other times, roadside stands and farms welcome visitors.

Toppenish

❹ *17 mi southeast of Yakima.*

An intriguing small town with a rustic Old West sensibility, Toppenish—which lies within the Yakama Indian Reservation—blends history and culture, art and agriculture. You can't miss the 63 colorful murals that adorn the facades and exterior walls of businesses and homes: commissioned since 1989 by the Toppenish Mural Association, done in a variety of styles by regional artists, they commemorate the town's history and Western spirit. Tours in a horse-drawn covered wagon leave from the association's office on Toppenish Avenue.

★ ☺ The Yakima Valley grows 75% of the nation's hops and 25% of the world's. The industry's story is well told at the **American Hop Museum** (✉ 22 S. B St. ☎ 509/865–4677 ⊕ www.americanhopmuseum.com). Exhibits describe the history, growing process and unique biology of the plant, a primary ingredient in beer. It's open daily 10 to 4 from early May until late September. Admission is free, though donations are appreciated.

★ The **Yakama Nation Cultural Center** (✉ Buster Dr. at Rte. 97 ☎ 509/865–2800) has a fascinating museum of tribal history and culture, including costumes, basketry, beadwork, and reconstructions of traditional lodges. Tribal dances and other cultural events are often staged in the Heritage Theater; the six-building complex also includes a gift shop, library, and restaurant. The center is open daily, 8–5 year-round; admission is $4.

Ft. Simcoe Historical State Park. The residential quarters of an 1856 army fort 30 mi west of Toppenish look like a Victorian summer retreat. Exhibits focus on relations between the Yakama tribe—in the heart of whose reservation the fort stands—and American settlers. ✉ *5150 Ft. Simcoe Rd.* ☎ *509/874–2372* ⊕ *www.parks.wa.gov* ✉ *Free* ☼ *Apr.–Sept., daily sunrise–sunset; Oct.–Mar., weekends sunrise–sunset.*

Zillah

❺ *5 mi northeast of Toppenish.*

The south-facing slopes above Zillah, a tiny town named after the daughter of a railroad manager, are covered with orchards and vineyards. Several wineries are in or near the community; more are near Granger, 6 mi southeast.

Bonair Winery is run by the Puryear family, who after years of amateur wine making in California began commercial production in their native Yakima Valley. They make cabernets, chardonnays, and Riesling as well as medieval-style mead. ✉ *500 S. Bonair Rd.* ☎ *509/829–6027* ⊕ *www.bonairwine.com* ☼ *Mar.–Nov., daily 10–5; Dec.–Feb., Fri.–Sun. 10–4:30.*

Claar Cellars has one of the highest visitor rates of any Yakima Valley winery by virtue of its location: right off I–82 at Exit 52. The family-owned estate produces merlot, cabernet, chardonnay, sauvignon blanc, and dessert wines from vineyards in the White Bluffs region. ✉ *1001 Vintage Valley Pkwy.* ☎ *509/829–6810* ⊕ *www.claarcellars.com* ☼ *Apr.–Nov., daily 10–5; Dec.–Mar., daily 11–4.*

The **Teapot Dome,** a quirky gas station ½ mi east of I–82 from Exit 54 of the Yakima Valley Highway, is, indeed, shaped like a teapot—its white-shingle walls topped by a red lid. It was built in 1928 and its name and shape are in reference to the oil scandal that involved the Harding Administration. The station is now on the National Register of Historic Places.

Eaton Hill Winery, in the restored Rinehold Cannery building, produces cabernet, merlot, chardonnay, Riesling, sémillon and various sweeter and fortified wines. ⊠ *530 Gurley Rd., off Yakima Valley Hwy., Granger* ☎ *509/854–2220* ☉ *Mar.–Nov., Fri.–Wed. 10–5; Dec.–Feb., usually Fri.–Wed. noon–4.*

Horizon's Edge Winery takes its name from its tasting room's view of the Yakima Valley, Mt. Adams, and Mt. Rainier. The winery makes sparkling wine, chardonnay, pinot noir, merlot, cabernet sauvignon, and muscat canelli. ⊠ *4530 E. Zillah Dr., east of Yakima Valley Hwy.* ☎ *509/829–6401* ☉ *Mar.–Nov., Thurs.–Mon. 11–5.*

An estate vineyard on 97 acres, **Hyatt Vineyards** specializes in chardonnay, fume blanc, merlot, syrah, cabernet, and late-harvest Riesling. ⊠ *2020 Gilbert Rd., off Bonair Rd.* ☎ *509/829–6333* ⊕ *www. hyattvineyards.com* ☉ *Apr.–Nov., daily 11–5; Dec. and Feb.–Mar., daily 11–4:30.*

European-style gardens adjoin the **Maison de Padgett Winery,** a small, family operation producing hand-crafted wines. ⊠ *2231 Roza Dr., at Highland Dr.* ☎ *509/829–6794* ☉ *Mar.–Nov., Thurs.–Mon. 11–5; Dec.–Feb., by appointment.*

Paradisos del Sol is another family-owned winery, a labor of love for industry veteran Paul Vandenberg. Specialties are gewürztraminer, Riesling, cabernet, and a lemberger-cabernet blend designed especially for pizza. ⊠ *3230 Highland Dr.* ☎ *509/829–9000* ⊕ *www.paradisosdelsol. com* ☉ *Daily 11–5.*

Portteus Vineyards are beloved by red-wine drinkers. Production is limited to cabernet sauvignon and franc, merlot, syrah, zinfandel, and port—as well as a robust chardonnay. Grapes are grown at 1,440-foot elevation on 47 acres above Zillah. ⊠ *5201 Highland Dr.* ☎ *509/829–6970* ⊕ *www.portteus.com* ☉ *Mid-Feb.–Nov., weekdays 10–5, Sat. 11–5, Sun. noon–4:30; Dec.–mid-Feb., by appointment.*

★ On the expansive grounds at **SilverLake at Roza Hills,** bands serenade picnickers on summer weekends. Large windows afford views of the cabernets, merlots, chardonnays, Rieslings, and other vintages in production. ⊠ *1500 Vintage Rd., off Highland Dr.* ☎ *509/829–6235* ⊕ *www.silverlakewinery.com* ☉ *Apr.–Nov., daily 10–5; Dec.–Mar., Thurs.–Mon. 11–4.*

Tefft Cellars was an old Concord grape vineyard replanted in the late 1980s with *vinifera*. Today it produces cabernet, merlot, syrah, sangiovese, pinot grigio, pinot meunier, and late-harvest dessert wines. The owners' original three-bedroom house, adjacent to the winery, is now the Outlook Inn. ⊠ *1320 Independence Rd. via Gurley Rd., Outlook* ☎ *509/837–7651* ⊕ *www.tefftcellars.com* ☉ *Feb.–Dec., daily 10–5; Jan. by appointment.*

An unusual collection of antique wine glasses has given its name to **Wineglass Cellars.** The winery produces limited lots of merlot, cabernet sauvignon, zinfandel, chardonnay and port. ⊠ *206 N. Bonair Rd.* ☎ *509/829–3011* ⊕ *www.wineglasscellars.com* ☉ *Mid-Feb.–Nov., Fri.–Mon. 10:30–5.*

Where to Stay & Eat

$–$$ ✕ **Squeeze Inn Restaurant.** Family-operated since 1932, the Squeeze Inn looks as timeworn as the surrounding structures on Zillah's main street.

Prime rib and steaks are the big draws, but you'll also find deep-fried seafood. Local vintners and grape growers delight in the hearty breakfasts. ⊠ *611 E. 1st Ave.* ☎ *509/829–6226* ▤ *MC, V* ⊘ *Closed Sun.*

¢–$ ✕ **El Ranchito.** The food is tasty and inexpensive at this Mexican restaurant, tortilla factory, deli, bakery, and import shop. ⊠ *1319 E. 1st Ave.* ☎ *509/829–5880* ⊜ *Reservations not accepted* ▤ *MC, V.*

¢–$ 🏨 **Comfort Inn–Zillah.** Just a few steps from Claar Cellars off I–82, this clean and modern hotel is a favorite of winery visitors. Kids love the free cookies and milk served each evening. ⊠ *911 Vintage Valley Pkwy., 98953* ☎ *509/829–3399 or 800/501–5433* ⊟ *509/829–3428* ⊕ *www. choicehotels.com* ⇌ *40 rooms* ⇧ *In-room data ports, cable TV, indoor pool, exercise equipment, hot tub, laundry facilities, some pets allowed (fee), no-smoking rooms* ▤ *AE, D, MC, V* ℺ *CP.*

Sunnyside

❻ *14 mi southeast of Zillah.*

The largest community in the lower Yakima Valley, Sunnyside runs along the sunny southern slopes of the Rattlesnake Hills. Two notable wineries are on opposite ends of town.

Tucker Cellars adjoins a fruit and produce market just off the Yakima Valley Highway, about 4 mi east of Sunnyside. It produces gewürztraminer, chenin blanc, Riesling, chardonnay, and pinot noir. ⊠ *70 Ray Rd.* ☎ *509/837–8701* ⊕ *www.tuckercellars.com* ⊘ *May–Oct., daily 9–5; Nov.–Apr., daily 10–4.*

Washington Hills Cellars, in a handsome art deco building about a mile west of Sunnyside, offers winemaker Brian Carter's award-winning reds and whites on the Washington Hills, S. B. Bridgman, and premium Apex labels. ⊠ *111 E. Lincoln Ave. at S. 1st St.* ☎ *509/839–9463* ⊕ *www.washingtonhills.com* ⊘ *Daily 9–5.*

♻ South of I–82, the **Darigold Dairy Fair** allows self-guided tours of its large automated cheesemaking factory. There's also an expansive gift shop, and an ice-cream bar and deli. (⊠ *400 Alexander Rd.* ☎ *509/837–4321* ⊘ *Apr.–Oct., Mon.–Sat. 8–6 and Sun. 10–6; Nov.–Mar., Mon.–Sat. 8–7 and Sun. 10–7)*

Where to Stay & Eat

★ $–$$ ✕ **Dykstra House.** In a wine valley with few upscale restaurants, this 1914 Craftsman house in quiet Grandview (6 mi southeast of Sunnyside) has held its own for nearly two decades. Breads are made from hand-ground wheat grown locally. Lunch, which is quite a bit less expensive than dinner, features salads, sandwiches, and daily specials. Casual Friday night dinners are Italian; grand Saturday night dinners revolve around chicken, beef, or fish. ⊠ *114 Birch Ave., Grandview* ☎ *509/882–2082* ⊜ *Reservations essential* ▤ *AE, D, DC, MC, V* ⊘ *Closed Sun., Mon. No dinner Tues.–Thurs.*

¢–$$ ✕ **Snipes Mountain Microbrewery & Restaurant.** In an imposing log structure that resembles a hunting or ski lodge, the lower valley's sole brewpub is a grand restaurant whose fare ranges from burgers and wood-fired pizzas to pasta dishes, fresh king salmon, prime rib, and rack of lamb. ⊠ *905 Yakima Valley Hwy.* ☎ *509/837–2739* ⊕ *www.snipesmountain. com* ▤ *AE, MC, V.*

¢–$ ✕ **El Conquistador.** The menu ranges from burritos, fajitas, and enchiladas mole to shrimp sautéed with green peppers and onions and served with a tangy salsa. Hand-crafted clay masks on the walls add a festive flair. ⊠ *612 E. Edison Ave.* ☎ *509/839–2880* ▤ *AE, D, DC, MC, V.*

¢–$ ☺ **Sunnyside Inn Bed & Breakfast.** Built in 1919 as a doctor's residence and office, this two-house inn is larger than the usual B&B. The popular Lola Room still has the original fixtures. Eight rooms have whirlpool tubs; several have small sunrooms and/or four-poster beds. Breakfast consists of breads, pastries, meats, and a griddle entrée. Families are welcome. ⊠ *800–804 E. Edison Ave., 98944* ☎ *509/839–5557 or 800/221–4195* 🖷 *509/839–5350* ⊕ *www.sunnysideinn.com* 💭 *13 rooms* *Some in-room hot tubs, cable TV* ⊟ *AE, MC, V* *BP.*

Prosser

❼ *13 mi southeast of Sunnyside.*

On the south bank of the Yakima River, Prosser feels like small-town America of the 1950s. The seat of Benton County since 1905, it has a 1926 courthouse and a charming museum in City Park.

Chinook Wines, a small house winery, is run by Kay Simon and Clay Mackey, vintners known for their merlot, chardonnay, and sauvignon blanc. ⊠ *Wittkopf Loop at Wine Country Rd.* ☎ *509/786–2725* ☉ *May–Oct., weekends noon–5.*

★ **Hinzerling Vineyards** specializes in estate-grown cabernet and late-harvest gewürztraminer and Rieslings. Vintner Mike Wallace is one of the state's wine pioneers: he planted his first Prosser-area vines in 1972 and established the small winery in 1976. ⊠ *1520 Sheridan Rd. at Wine Country Rd.* ☎ *509/786–2163* ⊕ *www.hinzerling.com* ☉ *Apr.–Dec. 24, Mon.–Sat. 11–5, Sun. 11–4; Dec. 26–Mar., Mon.–Sat. 11–4.*

Hogue Cellars is a large commercial winery. The gift shop carries the winery's famous pickled beans and asparagus as well as cabernet sauvignon, merlot, chenin blanc, and pinot grigio, among other wines. ⊠ *2800 Lee Rd., in Prosser Wine and Food Park* ☎ *509/786–4557* ⊕ *www. hoguecellars.com* ☉ *Daily 10–5.*

Kestrel Vintners is one of Washington's newer wineries (1999), but its 145-acre vineyard is among the oldest, having been planted in 1973. Winemaker Ray Sandidge focuses on red wines, but also produces a superb old-vine chardonnay and an estate viognier. ⊠ *2890 Lee Rd., in Prosser Wine and Food Park* ☎ *509/786–2675* ⊕ *www.kestrelwines. com* ☉ *Daily 10–5.*

Pontin del Roza is named for its owners, the Pontin family, and the grape-friendly slopes irrigated by the Roza Canal. Here you'll find Italian-style sangioveses and pinot grigios as well as Rieslings, chenin blancs, chardonnays, sauvignon blancs, and cabernet sauvignons. ⊠ *35502 N. Hinzerling Rd., 3½ mi north of Prosser* ☎ *509/786–4449* ☉ *Daily 10–5.*

At **Thurston Wolfe,** look for Wade Wolfe's unusual blends—a white pinot gris-viognier, for instance, and a red mix of zinfandel, syrah, lemberger, and turiga. The zinfandel is excellent. ⊠ *2880 Lee Rd., in Prosser Wine and Food Park* ☎ *509/786–3313* ☉ *Apr.–early Dec., Thurs.–Sun. 11–5.*

VineHeart is a boutique winery that offers a buttery Riesling, a raspberry-toned sémillon, a lemberger, and a sangiovese. ⊠ *44209 N. McDonald Rd., 7 mi northeast of Prosser* ☎ *509/973–2993* ⊕ *www.vineheart.com* ☉ *Thurs.–Mon. 10–5.*

David Minick's tiny **Willow Crest Winery**—which indeed has a draping willow tree at its entrance—produces award-winning syrah as well as cabernet franc and pinot gris. ⊠ *135701 Snipes Rd., 6 mi north of Prosser*

☎ *509/786–7999* ⊕ *www.willowcrestwinery.com* ⊙ *Apr.–Nov., week-ends 10–5.*

Yakima River Winery, specializing in barrel-aged reds and a memorable port, was established by John and Louise Rauner in 1977. ✉ *143302 N. River Rd., 1½ mi south of Wine Country Rd.* ☎ *509/786–2805* ⊙ *Daily 9–5.*

Where to Stay & Eat

¢–$$ ✕ **Blue Goose.** Here you'll find four-egg omelets for breakfast; later, in-dulge in Granny Smith chicken salad, veal parmigiana, or a big steak-and-lobster dinner. Casual and friendly, it's just off Wine Country Road in downtown Prosser. There's a small menu for kids. ✉ *306 7th St.* ☎ *509/786–1774* ⊟ *AE, MC, V.*

$$ ✕⊡ **Vintners Inn.** This 1905 Queen Anne at the Hinzerling Winery was remodeled as a farmhouse-style B&B in 2001. Five-course prix-fixe dinners ($$$–$$$$ by reservation only) are served boarding-house style on Friday and Saturday nights. ✉ *1520 Sheridan Ave., 99350* ☎ *509/786–2163 or 800/727–6702* ⊕ *www.hinzerling.com* ⇆ *2 rooms* ⌂ *Din-ing room, wine bar, some pets allowed (fee); no room phones, no room TVs, no kids, no smoking* ⊟ *AE, MC, V* ⅋ *BP.*

$–$$ ⊡ **Inn at Horse Heaven.** Just off I–82 beneath its namesake hills, this hand-some property has a lobby where you can choose a book from a small library and relax beside the fireplace. All the rooms here are no-smok-ing. Smokers are accommodated next door at the Best Western Prosser Inn, which shares the same ownership and has an outdoor pool. ✉ *259 Merlot Dr. 99350* ☎ *509/786–7090 or 866/749–6127* 🖷 *509/786–2148* ⊕ *www.innathorseheaven.com* ⇆ *35 rooms* ⌂ *In-room data ports, some in-room hot tubs, 1 kitchen, microwaves, refrigerators, cable TV, indoor pool, exercise equipment, hot tub, laundry facilities; no smoking* ⊟ *AE, D, DC, MC, V.* ⅋ *CP.*

Benton City

❽ *16 mi east of Prosser.*

The Yakima River zigzags north, making a giant bend around Red Mountain and the West Richland district before pouring into the Columbia River. Benton City—which, with a mere 3,000 residents, is hardly a city—is on a bluff west of the river and facing vineyard-cloaked Red Mountain. High-carbonate soil, a location in a unique high-pres-sure pocket, and geographical anomalies have led to this district being given its own appellation. You can access the wineries from Route 224.

★ **Blackwood Canyon Vintners** winemaker Michael Taylor Moore freely admits he's pushing the edge. Meticulously crafting wines by hand, he shuns modern filters, pumps, and even sulfites, and carefully avoids pes-ticides. Chardonnays, sémillons, merlots, cabernets, and late-harvest wines age *sur lies* (on their sediment), for as many as eight years before re-lease. ✉ *53258 N. Sunset Rd.* ☎ *509/588–6249* ⊕ *www.blackwoodwine.com* ⊙ *Daily 10–6.*

★ Robust reds aged in French oak are the specialty of **Hedges Cellars,** whose spectacular hillside château dominates upper Red Mountain. White wines aren't made here, but the cabernet sauvignon, cabernet franc, merlot, syrah, and reserve blends are superb. ✉ *53511 N. Sunset Rd.* ☎ *509/588–3155* ⊕ *www.hedgescellars.com* ⊙ *Apr.–Dec., Fri.–Sun. 11–5.*

John Williams of **Kiona Vineyards Winery** planted the first grapes on Red Mountain in 1975, made his first wines in 1980, and produced the first commercial lemberger, a light German red, in the United States. Today

Kiona also produces premium Riesling, chenin blanc, chardonnay, cabernet sauvignon, merlot, syrah, sangiovese, and dessert wines. ⊠ *44612 Sunset Rd.* ☎ *509/588–6716* ☉ *Daily noon–5.*

Tiny **Oakwood Cellars** produces lemberger, merlot, cabernet sauvignon, chardonnay, and Riesling. The boutique winery is on the west slope of Red Mountain overlooking the Yakima River. ⊠ *40504 N. Demoss Rd.* ☎ *509/588–5332* ☉ *Mar.–Nov., weekends noon–5.*

Picnickers enjoy the grounds at **Seth Ryan Winery** on lower Red Mountain. The boutique winery produces German-style gewürztraminer and rieslings, plus chardonnay, merlot, and cabernets sauvignon and franc. ⊠ *35306 Sunset Rd.* ☎ *509/588–6780* ⊕ *www.sethryan.com* ☉ *Late Feb.–mid-Nov., Thurs.–Mon. 10–6; late Nov.–mid-Feb., Fri.–Sun. noon–5.*

Named for the calcium carbonate in its soil, **Terra Blanca**, "white earth" in Latin, nonetheless is a specialist in red wines. Specialties are syrah, merlot, cabernet sauvignon, and chardonnay. ⊠ *34715 N. Demoss Rd.* ☎ *509/588–6082* ⊕ *www.terrablanca.com* ☉ *Mid-Feb.–Dec., daily 11–6.*

Yakima River Valley A to Z

AIR TRAVEL
Although major airlines serve the region's two airports, most people fly into Seattle or Portland, Oregon, and drive to the area.

AIRPORTS & TRANSFERS Yakima Air Terminal is 4 mi southeast of downtown Yakima. Tri-Cities Airport is more convenient to the lower Yakima Valley. Taxis and public transit are available at both airports. (In Yakima, Valley Cab or Yakima City Transit can provide transportation to hotels.) The Central Washington Airporter offers shuttle services between Sea-Tac airport between Seattle and Tacoma) and Yakima ($35 one-way) four times a day with stops in downtown Seattle, Cle Elum ($25), and Ellensburg ($30).
🛪 Airports **Tri-Cities Airport** ⊠ 3601 N. 20th Ave., Pasco ☎ 509/547-6352. **Yakima Air Terminal** ⊠ 2300 W. Washington Ave. ☎ 509/575-6150.
🛪 Transfer Information **Central Washington Airporter** ☎ 360/380-2859. **Valley Cab** ☎ 509/469-2029. **Yakima City Transit** ☎ 509/575-6175.

CARRIERS Horizon Airlines has eight nonstops daily between Sea-Tac and Yakima, a 45-minute flight. Tri-Cities Airport has a similar schedule from Seattle, a 60-minute trip, with additional nonstop connections to Denver, Portland, and Salt Lake City. It's served by Delta and United as well as Horizon.
🛪 Airlines **Delta** ☎ 800/221-1212 ⊕ www.delta.com. **Horizon Air** ☎ 800/547-9308 ⊕ www.horizonair.com. **United** ☎ 800/241-6522 ⊕ www.ual.com.

BUS TRAVEL
Greyhound Lines runs to and from Seattle on several routes. Its I–90 route passes through Ellensburg ($38 round-trip) three times daily from Seattle en route to Spokane and points east. It also travels along Route 97 south from Ellensburg through Yakima ($47) and Toppenish ($60) once a day before cutting away from the Yakima Valley. Its I–82 route offers two more daily trips to Ellensburg, Yakima, and Toppenish, proceeding through Sunnyside ($60) and Prosser ($66) en route to the Tri-Cities.

Yakima is the only city in the region with a public transportation system. Yakima City Transit buses operate weekdays 6 AM to 6:45 PM and Saturday from 8:45 to 6:45 at half-hour intervals on nine routes. The fare is 50¢.
🚌 Bus Information **Greyhound Lines** ☎ 800/229-9424 ⊕ www.greyhound.com. **Yakima City Transit** ☎ 509/575-6175 ⊕ www.ci.yakima.wa.us/services/transit.

CAR RENTAL

Local Agencies Savemore Auto Rentals ✉ 225 S. 2nd Ave., Yakima ☎ 509/575-5400. **U Save Auto Rental** ✉ 615 S. 1st St., Yakima ☎ 509/452-5555.

CAR TRAVEL

The region has a single interstate, though it has two different numbers. I–90 links Seattle to Cle Elum and Ellensburg before heading east toward Spokane. I–82 branches south off I–90 just east of Ellensburg, and runs through the Yakima Valley to the so-called Tri-Cities (Richland, Pasco, and Kennewick). Route 97 is the primary link from Ellensburg north (Wenatchee, Canada's Okanagan Valley) and from Yakima south toward central Oregon).

From just north of Yakima, Route 410 passes Mt. Rainer on the north, connecting with Route 164 and I–5 south of Seattle; Route 12 passes Mt. Rainer on the south. Both routes offer spectacular alpine scenery but occasionally hazardous driving conditions. A major section of Route 410 is closed by winter snow.

If you're touring wineries, be sure to stop at the Yakima Valley Visitor Information Center (Exit 34 off I–82) to pick up a wine tour brochure and map of more than 30 wineries. Most are within a few miles of the freeway and there are directional signs.

The Yakima Valley Highway is a reliable, off-the-beaten-track alternative to I–82 for wine-country visits; but it can be slow, especially through towns, or if farm machinery is on the road. Because of unmarked turns and other potential hazards, it's wise to stick to the freeway after dark. Gas stations in towns, and at major freeway intersections, are typically open well after dark.

EMERGENCIES

Doctors & Dentists Chalet Dental Clinic ✉ 6006 Summitview Ave., Yakima ☎ 509/965-0080. **Lake Aspen Urgent Care Center** ✉ 1420 N. 16th Ave., Yakima ☎ 509/452-2706.

Hospitals Providence Yakima Medical Center ✉ 110 S. 9th Ave., Yakima ☎ 509/575-5000. **Yakima Valley Memorial Hospital** ✉ 2811 Tieton Dr., Yakima ☎ 509/249-5219.

MAIL & SHIPPING

Post Offices Ellensburg ✉ 100 E. 3rd Ave. ☎ 509/962-4360. **Sunnyside** ✉ 713 E. Edison Ave. ☎ 509/837-5039. **Yakima Central** ✉ 112 S. 3rd St. ☎ 509/225-1389. **Yakima Main** ✉ 205 W. Washington Ave. ☎ 509/225-1389.

Overnight Services Federal Express ✉ 3102 W. Washington Ave., Yakima ☎ 800/463-3339. **UPS** ✉ 106 S. 3rd St., Yakima ☎ 509/248-0200.

MONEY MATTERS

Major banks—including Bank of America, Key Bank, and Washington Mutual Bank—are generally open Monday–Thursday 10–5, Friday 10–6, and Saturday 10–1. ATMs are widely available.

Banks Bank of America ☎ 800/642-9855 ⊕ www.bankofamerica.com. **Key Bank** ☎ 206/447-5767 ⊕ www.keybank.com. **US Bank** ☎ 800/872-2657 ⊕ www.usbank.com. **Washington Mutual** ☎ 800/756-8000 ⊕ www.wamu.com.

TOURS

Lifelong residents run Yakima Valley Tours's custom agricultural, historical, wine-tasting, and adventure-sports tours. Accent! Tours has informative trips to area wineries. Winery Excursions personalizes winery tours for two to six guests. Bus companies such as A & A Motorcoach, and limo services, including Moonlit Rides, conduct charter tours of the Yakima area.

🎫 **A & A Motorcoach** ✉ 2410 S. 26th Ave., Yakima ☎ 509/575-3676 ⊕ www. aamotorcoach.com. **Accent! Tours** ✉ 1001 W. Yakima Ave., Yakima ☎ 509/575-3949 ⊕ www.accenttours.com. **Moonlit Rides** ✉ 3908 River Rd., Yakima ☎ 509/575-6846. **Winery Excursions** ✉ Yakima ☎ 509/952-1813. **Yakima Valley Tours** ✉ 551 N. Holt Rd., Mabton ☎ 509/894-5449 ⊕ www.yakimavalleytours.com.

VISITOR INFORMATION

🎫 Tourist Information **Cle Elum/Roslyn Chamber of Commerce** ✉ 401 W. 1st St., Cle Elum ☎ 509/674-5958 ⊕ www.cleelumroslyn.org. **Ellensburg Chamber of Commerce** ✉ 609 N. Main St. ☎ 509/925-2002 or 888/925-2204 ⊕ ellensburg-chamber. com. **Prosser Chamber of Commerce** ✉ 1230 Bennett Ave. ☎ 509/786-3177 or 800/ 408-1517 ⊕ www.prosserchamber.org. **Sunnyside Chamber of Commerce** ✉ 520 S. 7th St. ☎ 509/837-5939 or 800/457-8089 ⊕ www.sunnysidechamber.com. **Toppenish Chamber of Commerce** ✉ 5A S. Toppenish Ave. ☎ 509/865-3262 or 800/569-3982 **Yakima Valley Visitor Information Center** ✉ 101 Fair Ave., Exit 34 off I-82 ☎ 509/ 573-3388 or 800/221-0751 ⊕ www.visityakima.com. **Yakima Valley Winery Association** ☎ 800/258-7270 ⊕ www.yakimavalleywine.com.

EASTERN WASHINGTON

Updated by
Shelley Arenas

Plateau was created by a series of lava flows that were later deeply cut by glacial floods. Because its soil is mostly made up of alluvial deposits and windblown silt (known to geologists as loess), it's very fertile. But little annual rainfall means that its vast central section—more than 30,000 square mi from the foothills of the Cascades and the northeastern mountains east to Idaho and south to Oregon—has no forests. In fact, except for a few scattered pine trees in the north, oaks in the southwest, and willows and cottonwoods along creeks and rivers, it has no trees.

This treeless expanse is part of an even larger steppe and desert region that runs north into Canada and south to California and the the Sea of Cortez. There is water, however, carried from the mountains by the great Columbia and Snake rivers and their tributaries. Irrigation provides the region's cities with shrubs, trees, and flowers, and its fields bear a great variety of crops: asparagus, potatoes, apples, peaches, alfalfa, sweet corn, wheat, lentils, and much more. This bounty of agriculture makes the region prosperous and provides funds for symphony halls and opera houses, theaters, art museums, and universities.

Southeast of the Columbia Plateau lies a region of rolling hills and fields. Farmers of the Palouse region and of the foothills of the Blue Mountains don't need to irrigate their fields, as rain here produces record crops of wheat, lentils, and peas. It's a blessed landscape, flowing green and golden under the sun in waves of loam. The region is not only fertile, it is historically significant as well. The Lewis and Clark expedition passed through the Palouse in 1805, and Walla Walla was one of the earliest settlements in the inland Northwest.

The northeastern mountains, from the Okanogan to the Pend Oreille Valley, consist of granite peaks, glaciated cliffs, grassy uplands, and sunlit forests. Few Washingtonians seem to know about this region's attractions, however. Even at the height of the summer its roads and trails are rarely crowded.

The hidden jewel of these mountains is the Sanpoil River Valley, which is a miniature Yosemite Valley with vertical rock walls rising 2,000–3,000 feet straight from the river, their height accentuated by the narrowness of the canyon. The valley has no amenities and is still in the possession of its original owners, the Indians of the Colville Reservation, who have preserved its beauty. These wild highlands have few visitor facilities. Towns in the Okanogan Valley and the regional metropolis of Spokane, on the fringes of the region, offer more services.

Richland

❶ *202 mi southeast of Seattle, 145 mi southwest of Spokane.*

Richland is the northernmost of the three municipalities along the banks of the Columbia River known as the Tri-Cities (the others are Pasco and Kennewick). Founded in the 1880s, Richland was a pleasant farming village until 1942, when the federal government built a nuclear reactor on the nearby Hanford Nuclear Reservation. The Hanford site was instrumental in the building of the Tri-Cities and still plays a major role in the area's economy. In recent years, this has also become a major wine producing area. You can find more than 60 wineries within a 50-mi radius, many with tasting rooms.

The **Barnard Griffin Winery and Tasting Room** is next to Route 182. Rob and Deborah Griffin offer a variety of fine wines, including excellent merlot and cabernet. ⊠ *878 Tulip La.* ☎ *509/627-7776* ⊕ *www. barnardgriffin.com* ⊗ *May–Oct., daily 10–6; Nov.–Apr., call for hrs.*

Next door to Barnard Griffin Winery and Tasting Room, **Bookwalter Winery** produces six varieties, from sweet Johannesburg Riesling to a classic merlot. ⊠ *894 Tulip La.* ☎ *509/627-5000* ⊗ *Daily 10–6.*

The **CREHST Museum** (CREHST stands for the Columbia River Exhibition of History, Science, and Technology) has educational exhibits, some of which are hands-on. Displays show the area's development from prehistoric times to the to the nuclear age. ⊠ *95 Lee Blvd.* ☎ *509/943-9000* ⊕ *www.crehst.org* ⊠ *$3.50* ⊗ *Mon.–Sat. 10–5, Sun. noon–5.*

Where to Stay & Eat

$–$$$ ✕ **Sundance Grill.** Candlelight and live piano music make this restaurant an intimate, romantic spot for dinner; there are nice river views from the patio. The menu features prime beef, pasta, and fresh seafood. Lunch centers around sandwiches and salads. The wine list is one of the largest in the area. ⊠ *450 Columbia Point Dr.* ☎ *509/942-7120* ⊟ *AE, D, MC, V.*

$–$$ ✕ **Monterosso's Restaurant.** In a refurbished railroad dining car, this small and charming Italian restaurant is fun for the whole family, but it's also suitable for a romantic meal. It's known for its tortellini and manicotti; also try the homemade tiramisu and cheesecake. ⊠ *1026 Lee Blvd.* ☎ *509/946-4525* ⊟ *AE, D, MC, V.*

¢–$$$ ✕ **Atomic Ale Brewpub and Eatery.** The staff is friendly at this small, casual brewpub, which serves only house-brewed beers. The delicious pizzas are cooked in a wood-fired oven; soups, sandwiches, and salads are also fine. ⊠ *1015 Lee Blvd.* ☎ *509/946-5465* ⊟ *AE, MC, V.*

¢–$$ ✕ **Rattlesnake Mountain Brewing Company.** The spacious deck of this pub and family restaurant has wonderful views of the Columbia. Serving a variety of chicken, steak, pasta, and shrimp dishes, the eatery is famous for its buffalo wings and its seven home-brewed beers. There's also a kids' menu. ⊠ *2696 N. Columbia Center Blvd.* ☎ *509/783-5661* ⊟ *AE, D, DC, MC, V.*

¢–$ ✕ **Emerald of Siam.** This small storefront restaurant has long had the best Asian food in eastern Washington. That's because owner-chef (as well as poet and cookbook author) Ravadi Quinn has an uncommon understanding of food and its basic ingredients, and can coax the most flavor from any dish. Try the pad thai and the curried dishes. ✉ *1314 Jadwin Ave.* ☎ *509/946–9328* ▭ *AE, D, MC, V* ☺ *Closed Sun. No lunch Sat.*

¢–$ ✕ **Mandarin House.** Among the favorite dishes at this popular downtown eatery are the Mongolian beef and the garlic chicken. The interior is decorated in a familiar Chinese theme. ✉ *1035 Lee Blvd.* ☎ *509/943–6843* ▭ *MC, V.*

¢–$ ✕▥ **Shilo Inn Rivershore.** Bordering the Columbia River above the mouth of the Yakima, the Shilo Inn has easy access to riverside trails and parks. Rooms have coffeemakers, irons, and ironing boards. In O'Callahan's Restaurant and Lounge ($–$$), enjoy the view from inside or out on the deck as you indulge in aged beef, Southern fried catfish, pastas, or salads. ✉ *50 Comstock St., 99352* ☎ *509/946–4661* 🖷 *509/943–6741* ⊕ *www.shiloinns.com/Washington/richland.html* ⇋ *151 rooms, 13 suites* ⌂ *Restaurant, room service, some kitchenettes, some refrigerators, cable TV, pool, wading pool, gym, hot tub, bar, laundry facilities, business services, airport shuttle, free parking, some pets allowed (fee)* ▭ *AE, D, DC, MC, V* ☥ *BP.*

¢–$ ▥ **Red Lion Hotel Richland Hanford House.** Richland's Red Lion overlooks the Columbia River and is near many major Hanford contractors and government facilities. The hotel borders a greenbelt riverfront park and has easy access to trails along the levee; ask for a room with a river view. A private boat dock offers poolside food and drink service. ✉ *802 George Washington Way, 99352* ☎ *509/946–7611* 🖷 *509/943–8564* ⊕ *www.redlion.com* ⇋ *149 rooms* ⌂ *Restaurant, room service, in-room data ports, pool, gym, outdoor hot tub, bar, laundry service, business services, airport shuttle, free parking, some pets allowed* ▭ *AE, D, DC, MC, V.*

¢ ▥ **Hampton Inn Richland.** This enormous chain hotel stretches along the west shore of the Columbia River adjacent to a park and a riverfront promenade. Many of the rooms have spectacular views of the river; some have balconies. ✉ *486 Bradley Blvd., 99352* ☎ *509/943–4400 or 800/426–7866* 🖷 *509/943–1797* ⊕ *www.northwestinns.com/richland.html* ⇋ *130 rooms* ⌂ *Microwaves, refrigerators, cable TV, indoor pool, gym, in-room hot tubs, laundry service, Internet, business services, airport shuttle* ▭ *AE, D, DC, MC, V* ☥ *CP.*

¢ ▥ **Holiday Inn Express & Suites.** One of the area's newest hotels, the Holiday Inn is next door to the Columbia Center Mall, in the heart of Richland's shopping and business district. It is also just a mile from the convention center. ✉ *1970 Center Pkwy., 99352* ☎ *509/737–8000 or 800/465–4329* 🖷 *509/737–8002* ⊕ *www.ichotelsgroup.com/h/d/hi/1/en/hd/rlwwa* ⇋ *62 rooms, 20 suites* ⌂ *Microwaves, refrigerators, cable TV, in-room VCRs, 2 pools (1 indoor), gym, hot tub, laundry facilities, Internet, business services, meeting rooms* ▭ *AE, D, DC, MC, V* ☥ *CP.*

Pasco

❷ *10 mi east of Richland.*

Tree-shaded Pasco, a college town and the Franklin County seat, is an oasis of green on the Columbia River near a site where the Lewis and Clark expedition made camp in 1805. The city began as a railroad switchyard and now has a busy container port. The neoclassic Franklin County Courthouse (1907) is worth a visit for its fine marble interior.

The Pasco Basin has first-rate vineyards and wineries and some of the state's most fertile land. You can purchase the regional bounty at the farmers' market, held downtown every Wednesday and Saturday morning during the growing season.

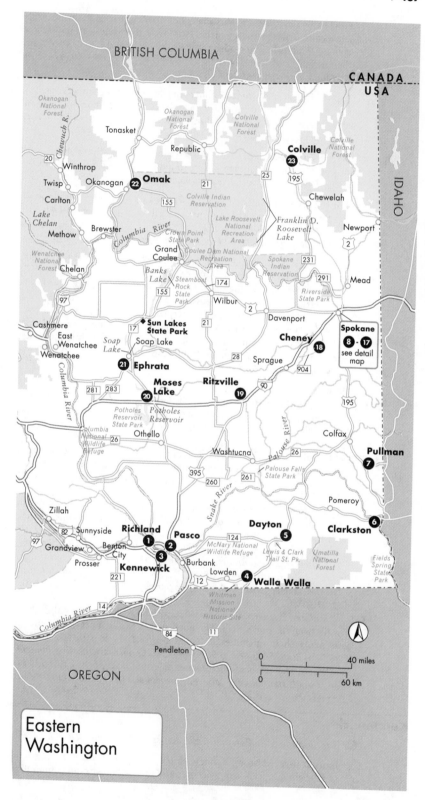

Eastern
Washington

Franklin County Historical Museum is home to numerous items illustrating local history, including artifacts from Native American tribes. Revolving exhibits have included those on the Lewis and Clark expedition, the railroad, and World War II. ⊠ *305 N. 4th Ave.* ☎ *509/547–3714* ⌨ *Donations accepted* ☉ *Tues.–Sat. noon–4.*

Just off Route 182, **Gordon Brothers Family Vineyards** produces some of the region's most acclaimed wines. Try the chardonnay, merlot, or cabernet sauvignon. ⊠ *5960 Burden Blvd.* ☎ *509/547–6331* ⊕ *www. gordonwines.com* ⌨ *Free* ☉ *Daily 10–6.*

Preston Estate Vineyards is one of the Pasco Basin's oldest wineries. The tasting room has great views of surrounding fields. ⊠ *502 E. Vineyard Dr.* ☎ *509/545–1990* ⊕ *www.prestonwines.com* ⌨ *Free* ☉ *Daily 10–5:30.*

For those who prefer beer to wine, 7,000-square-foot **Ice Harbor Brewing Company** has a tasting room as well as a gift shop. ⊠ *415 W. Columbia St.* ☎ *509/545–0927 or 888/701–2350* 🖨 *509/545–0571* ⊕ *www.iceharbor.com* ⌨ *Free* ☉ *Weekdays noon–6, Sat. 9–4.*

Sacajawea State Park, at the confluence of the Snake and Columbia rivers, occupies the site of Ainsworth, a railroad town that flourished from 1879 to 1884. It's named for the Shoshoni Indian woman who guided the Lewis and Clark expedition over the Rocky Mountains and down the Snake River. The 284-acre park has an interpretive center and a large display of Native American tools. A beach, boat launch, picnic area, and children's playground round out the facilities; sand dunes, marshes, and ponds are great for watching wildlife. ⊠ *Off U.S. 12, 5 mi southeast of Pasco* ☎ *509/545–2361* ⌨ *$5* ☉ *Apr.–Sept., 6:30 AM–sunset.*

Where to Stay & Eat

$$–$$$ ✕ **Vineyard Steak House at the Doubletree Inn.** Locals come to this formal dining room to celebrate special occasions and to dine on fresh seafood and well-aged beef. ⊠ *2525 N. 20th St.* ☎ *509/547–0701* ⊟ *AE, D, DC, MC, V.*

¢–$$$ ✕ **Fiesta! Mexican Restaurant.** This family-friendly authentic Mexican restaurant specializes in seafood. Almost every entrée comes with homemade corn tortillas fresh off the grill. ⊠ *510 Lewis St.* ☎ *509/543–6884* ⊟ *MC, V.*

¢–$ 🏨 **Red Lion Hotel Pasco.** This large, full-service hotel is loaded with amenities, including in-room coffeemakers, irons, and ironing boards. It's just four blocks from the airport. ⊠ *2525 N. 20th St., 99301* ☎ *509/547–0701* 🖨 *509/547–4278* ⊕ *www.redlion.com* ↩ *279 rooms, 10 suites* ♨ *2 restaurants, coffee shop, room service, in-room data ports, some refrigerators, cable TV, pool, gym, hot tub, bar, Internet, business services, airport shuttle, free parking, some pets allowed* ⊟ *AE, D, DC, MC, V.*

¢–$ 🏨 **Tri-Cities Sleep Inn.** Right off I–182 at Exit 7, this hotel is only a short walk from the outlet mall. The hotel strives to add a personal touch to its many chain amenities. ⊠ *9930 Bedford St., 99301* ☎ *509/545–9554 or 800/753–3746* 🖨 *509/544–9548* ⊕ *www.tricitiessleepinn.com* ↩ *62 rooms* ♨ *Some microwaves, in-room data ports, cable TV, indoor pool, spa, laundry service, business services, no-smoking rooms* ⊟ *AE, D, MC, V* ⦿ *CP.*

Kennewick

❸ *3 mi southwest of Pasco, directly across the Columbia River.*

In its 100-year history, Kennewick (*ken*-uh-wick) evolved from a railroad town to a farm-supply center and then to a bedroom community for Hanford workers and a food-processing capital for the Columbia Basin. The name Kennewick translates as "grassy place," and Native Americans had winter villages here long before Lewis and Clark passed through. Arrowheads and other artifacts aside, the 9,000-year-old skeleton of Kennewick Man is being studied by scientists at the University of Washington to determine if its features are American Indian or, as some claim, Caucasian.

One of Washington's great parks, 3-mi-long, riverfront **Columbia Park** has boat ramps, a golf course, a picnic area, and tennis courts. In summer, hydroplane races are held here. ⊠ *Rte. 12 west to Lake Wallula* ☎ *509/783–3711.*

The entire entryway of the **East Benton County Historical Museum** is made of petrified wood. Photographs, agricultural displays, and a large collection of arrowheads interpret area history. ⊠ *205 Keewaydin Dr.* ☎ *509/582–7704* ⊕ *www.owt.com/ebchs* ⊠ *$2* ⊙ *Tues.–Sat. noon–4.*

Two Rivers Park is on the Columbia's west bank. The park has a boat ramp, swimming beach, and picnic tables. ⊠ *Rte. 397, left on Finley Rd.* ☎ *509/783–3118* ⊠ *Free* ⊙ *Daily sunrise–sunset.*

At 103 feet, the single-lift locks at the **Ice Harbor Lock and Dam**, located about 12 mi southeast of Kennewick, are among the world's highest. Cars can cross the dam on a narrow road. ⊠ *2339 Ice Harbor Dr., Burbank* ☎ *509/547–7781* ⊠ *Free* ⊙ *Apr.–Sept., daily 9–5.*

On a hill above Kennewick, **Badger Mountain Vineyard** offers a beautiful view of the valley and wine made without pesticides or preservatives. ⊠ *1106 S. Jurupa St.* ☎ *509/627–4986* ⊕ *www.badgermtnvineyard. com* ⊠ *Free* ⊙ *Daily 10–5.*

In winter, **McNary National Wildlife Refuge** is a resting and feeding area for up to 100,000 migrating Canada geese, mallards, and American wigeons. But its 3,629 acres of water and marsh, croplands, grasslands, trees, and shrubs are most enjoyable in spring and summer, when there is no hunting. A self-guided 2-mi trail winds through the marshes, and a cabinlike blind hidden in the reeds allows you to watch ducks, geese, grebes, and yellow-headed blackbirds up close. With luck you may also spot long-billed curlews and white pelicans. ⊠ *64 Maple Rd., Burbank, ¼ mi east of U.S. 12, south of Snake River Bridge* ☎ *509/547–4942* ⊠ *Free* ⊙ *Daily 24 hrs.*

Where to Stay & Eat

★ **$$$** ✕ **Blue Moon.** One of the Tri-Cities' highest-rated, most expensive, and most exclusive restaurants, the Blue Moon serves exotic seven-course dinners, with one seating on Friday night and another on Saturday night. The menu, which changes monthly, has included such entrées as wild boar chipotle and sauteed ostrich medallions with wild mushroom demi-glace. An extensive wine list includes many northwestern varieties. The dining room is intimate and tranquil, with a unique cobalt blue in which string has been woven into a pattern that creates the illusion of tiles. ⊠ *20 W. Canal Dr.* ☎ *509/582–6598* ⚑ *Reservations essential* ☰ *MC, V* ⊙ *Closed Sun.–Thurs. No lunch.*

$–$$$ ✕ **Cedar's Restaurant.** Right on the edge of the Columbia River, Cedar's has beautiful views and a 200-foot dock for boaters coming to dine. The menu includes top-quality steaks, pasta, poultry, and fresh salmon, and the extensive wine list features many local labels. ⊠ *355 Clover Island Dr.* ☎ *509/582–2143* ☰ *AE, V, D, DC, MC, V.*

¢–$ ✕ **Casa Chapala.** At this delightful, no-smoking family restaurant, the dishes are as authentic as Mexican fare gets hereabouts. It's known for an extensive menu, including *arroz con pollo* (chicken with rice), and there's a kids' menu, too. ⌧ *107 E. Columbia Dr.* ☎ *509/582–7848* ▭ *AE, D, DC, MC, V.*

¢–$ 🏨 **Red Lion Columbia Center.** Talk about convenience: It's next to a regional shopping mall and a block from the convention center. Enjoy dining in the skylight Cavanaugh's Landing restaurant, which offers an extensive Sunday buffet brunch, and visit the lounge for live music and dancing. ⌧ *1101 N. Columbia Center Blvd., 99336* ☎ *509/783–0611 or 800/733–5466* 🖷 *509/735–3087* ⊕ *www.redlion.com* ⇌ *154 rooms, 8 suites* ⟺ *Restaurant, room service, in-room data ports, cable TV, pool, gym, hot tub, lounge, business services, airport shuttle, some pets allowed (fee)* ▭ *AE, D, DC, MC, V.*

Walla Walla

❹ *52 mi southeast of Kennewick.*

Walla Walla, founded in the 1850s on the site of a Nez Perce village, was Washington's first metropolis. As late as the 1880s its population was larger than that of Seattle. Walla Walla occupies a lush green valley below the rugged Blue Mountains. Its beautiful downtown boasts old residences, green parks, and the campus of Whitman College, Washington's oldest institution of higher learning.

A successful downtown restoration has earned Walla Walla high praise. The heart of downtown, at Second and Main streets, looks as pretty as it did 50 years ago, with beautifully maintained old buildings and newer structures designed to fit in. Residents and visitors come here to visit shops, wineries, cafés, and restaurants.

West of town, the green Walla Walla Valley—famous for asparagus, sweet onions, cherries, and wheat—has emerged as Washington's premier viticultural region. Tall grain elevators mark Lowden, a few miles west of Walla Walla, a wheat hamlet that now has several wineries.

Planted with native and exotic flowers and trees, **Pioneer Park** (⌧ E. Alder St.) is a shady, turn-of-the-20th-century park with a fine aviary. It was originally landscaped by sons of Frederick Law Olmsted, who designed New York City's Central Park.

Large, tree-lined lawns surround the many beautiful 19th-century stone and brick structures of the **Whitman College** (⌧ 345 Boyer Ave. ☎ 509/ 527–5111) campus. The school began as a seminary in 1859 and became a college in 1883.

Waterbrook Winery hides in a converted warehouse just south of Lowden, but the tasting room of the Valley's largest winery is in downtown Walla Walla. Waterbrook is best known for chardonnay, sauvignon blanc, and viognier. ⌧ *31 E. Main St.* ☎ *509/522–1262* ⊕ *www. waterbrook.com* ⊘ *Tues.–Sat. 11–4:30.*

Canoe Ridge Vineyards, owned by the Chalone Wine Group, produces merlot, cabernet, chardonnay, and other wines. A tasting room and vineyard tours are offered. ⌧ *1102 W. Cherry St.* ☎ *509/527–0885* ⊕ *www. canoeridgevineyard.com* ⊘ *May–Sept., daily 11–5; Oct.–Apr., daily 11–4.*

At **Seven Hills Winery,** owner Casey McClellan makes well-balanced merlot, cabernet sauvignon, and syrah. ⌧ *212 N. 3rd Ave.* ☎ *509/529– 7198* ⊕ *www.sevenhillswinery.com* ⊘ *Daily 10:30–4:30.*

★ ☾ **Whitman Mission National Historic Site,** 7 mi west of Walla Walla, is a reconstruction of Waiilatpu Mission, a Presbyterian outpost established on Cayuse Indian lands in 1836. The park preserves the foundations of the mission buildings, a short segment of the Oregon Trail, and, on a nearby hill, the graveyard where the Native American victims of an 1847 measles epidemic and subsequent uprising are buried. ⊠ *328 Whitman Mission Rd.* ☎ *509/522–6360* ⊕ *www.nps.gov/whmi* ☜ *$3* ☉ *Daily sunrise–sunset.*

★ ☾ **Ft. Walla Walla Museum,** a few miles west of Walla Walla, occupies a museum building. Before the U.S. Army established Ft. Walla Walla at this site, five fur-trader forts bearing that name were built near Wallula, above the mouth of the Walla Walla River. All of them were destroyed by flood waters. ⊠ *755 Myra Rd. at Dalles Military Rd.* ☎ *509/525–7703* ⊕ *www. fortwallawallamuseum.org* ☜ *$3* ☉ *Apr.–Oct., Tues.–Sun. 10–5.*

Lovers of fine wines make pilgrimages to **Woodward Canyon Winery,** 12 mi west of Walla Walla, for the superb cabernet sauvignon, merlot, and chardonnay. The winery occasionally produces other varietals. ⊠ *11920 Rte. 12, Lowden* ☎ *509/525–4129* ⊕ *www.woodwardcanyon.com* ☉ *Mon.–Sat. 10–5, Sun. noon–4.*

A few blocks from Woodward Canyon Winery is **L'Ecole N. 41.** Housed in the lower floors of a former schoolhouse, the winery produces outstanding sémillon and merlot, among other wines. ⊠ *41 Lowden School Rd., Lowden* ☎ *509/525–0940* ⊕ *www.lecole.com* ☉ *Daily 11–4.*

About a mile east of L'Ecole N. 41 is **Three Rivers Winery.** Just off Route 12 and surrounded by vineyards, the winery is home to premium cabernet sauvignon, merlot, sangiovese, and syrah. It also has a nice tasting room, a gift shop, summer concerts, and a 3-hole golf course. ⊠ *5641 Rte. 12* ☎ *509/526–9463* ⊕ *www.threeriverswinery.com* ☉ *Daily 10–5.*

Where to Stay & Eat

★ **$–$$$** ✕ **Whitehouse-Crawford Restaurant.** In a former wood-planing mill, this restaurant has gained a reputation for quality and excellence. Local is the watchword here, where hamburgers are made with beef from the Thundering Hooves Farm in nearby Touchet. Try the smoked trout and spinach salad and save room for the twice-baked chocolate cake. The extensive wine list features many Walla Walla Valley winemakers. ⊠ *55 W. Cherry St.* ☎ *509/525–2222* ▤ *AE, MC, V* ☉ *Closed Mon. and Tues. No lunch.*

★ **$–$$** ✕ **Creektown Café.** About seven blocks off Main Street, the intimate Creektown Café is one of the town's hidden gems. The emphasis is on local ingredients, and the menu changes seasonally. The sweet onion soup is a favorite with locals. Try the desserts with fresh fruit from local growers. Patio seating is available in summer. ⊠ *1129 S. 2nd Ave.* ☎ *509/ 522–4777* ▤ *AE, D, MC, V* ☉ *Closed Sun. and Mon.*

¢–$ ✕ **Grapefields.** This popular café and wine shop with 12 tables is known for its homemade bread pudding and its quiche. There's a French-influenced lunch menu and a Northwest dinner menu that includes pasta, seafood, chicken, and beef (the flank steak is noteworthy). The extensive wine list includes 24 varieties that you can order by the glass. ⊠ *4 E. Main St.* ☎ *509/522–3993* ▤ *AE, MC, V* ☉ *Closed Mon. No dinner Sun.*

¢–$ ✕ **Merchants Ltd.** A local favorite since it opened in 1976, this classic deli-and-bakery serves excellent breakfasts and lunches six days a week, as well as a popular spaghetti dinner on Wednesday nights. ⊠ *21 E. Main St.* ☎ *509/525–0900* ▤ *AE, D, MC, V* ☉ *Closed Sun. No dinner Thurs.–Tues.*

$$–$$$ ▦ **Inn at Abeja.** Twenty-five acres of gardens and vineyards surround a turn-of-the-20th-century farm with guest cottages and suites. Each accommodation has board games, books, and magazines, binoculars (to

better enjoy the bucolic views), CD players, and hand-knit afghans. Breakfast can be delivered to your room or served in the small barn. It's a short drive to both downtown Walla Walla and valley wineries. ⊠ *2014 Mill Creek Rd., 99362* ☎ *509/526–7400* ⊕ *www.abeja.net/inn.htm* ⥅ *3 cottages, 2 suites* ⌂ *Kitchens, cable TV, in-room VCRs* ▭ *MC, V* ⎮◎⎮ *BP.*

$ ⊡ **Green Gables Inn.** One block from the Whitman Campus, this 1909 Arts and Crafts–style mansion sits among flowering plants and shrubs on a quaint, tree-lined street. Charming guest rooms, their names derived from Lucy Maud Montgomery's *Anne of Green Gables,* are individually decorated with Victorian antiques. The Idlewild contains a fireplace and private deck, while French doors in Dryad's Bubble lead to a small, private balcony. ⊠ *922 Bonsella St., 99362* ☎ *509/525–5501* ⊕ *www.greengablesinn.com* ⥅ *5 rooms* ⌂ *Some in-room hot tubs, refrigerators, cable TV, in-room VCRs; no smoking* ▭ *AE, D, MC, V* ⎮◎⎮ *BP.*

¢–$ ⊡ **Best Western Walla Walla Suites Inn.** The location 1 mi from wineries and from Whitman College makes this a convenient place to stay while touring the area. You'll be welcomed with fresh cookies in the evening, and the mini-suites are stocked with popcorn. ⊠ *7 E. Oak St., 99362* ☎ *509/525–4700* 🖷 *509/525–2457* ⊕ *www.bestwestern.com* ⥅ *78 suites* ⌂ *In-room data ports, microwaves, refrigerators, indoor pool, gym, hot tub, laundry facilities, laundry service, business services, some pets allowed (fee)* ▭ *AE, D, DC, MC, V* ⎮◎⎮ *CP.*

¢–$ ⊡ **Inn at Blackberry Creek.** Blackberry Creek runs through the backyard of this secluded but centrally located inn. Built in 1906, the Kentucky farmhouse–style home sits on a 1½-acre lot in a residential area near the city park. ⊠ *1126 Pleasant St., 99362* ☎ *509/522–5233 or 877/ 522–5233* ⊕ *www.innatblackberrycreek.com* ⥅ *3 rooms* ⌂ *Refrigerators, in-room VCRs, Internet, business services; no kids under 13* ▭ *AE, D, V, MC* ⎮◎⎮ *BP.*

¢–$ ⊡ **La Quinta Inn.** In downtown Walla Walla, next door to restaurants and shopping, this hotel is right off Route 12 at the 2nd Avenue exit. Hot cookies are served in the evenings. ⊠ *520 N. 2nd Ave., 99362* ☎ *509/ 525–2522* 🖷 *509/522–2565* ⊕ *www.lq.com* ⥅ *61 rooms* ⌂ *Some refrigerators, cable TV, indoor pool, gym, hot tub, Internet, business services, some pets allowed* ▭ *AE, D, DC, MC, V* ⎮◎⎮ *CP.*

¢ ⊡ **Howard Johnson.** This 1960s chain hotel on Main Street has quiet, well-maintained rooms, most of which open onto a courtyard with a pool. It's two blocks from Whitman College. ⊠ *325 E. Main St., 99362* ☎ *509/529–4360 or 800/634–7669 Ext. 25* 🖷 *509/529–7463* ⊕ *www. hojo.com* ⥅ *82 rooms, 3 suites* ⌂ *In-room data ports, some refrigerators, cable TV, pool, exercise equipment, hot tub, sauna, laundry facilities, some pets allowed, no smoking rooms* ▭ *AE, D, DC, MC, V* ⎮◎⎮ *CP.*

★ ¢ ⊡ **Marcus Whitman Hotel.** Since its restoration this 1928 hotel has become *the* landmark in downtown Walla Walla. The hotel has standard and deluxe rooms as well as two-room parlor suites. Most guest quarters, which are adorned with Renaissance-style Italian furnishings, have king beds. The Marc restaurant has fine dining, with views of the Blue Mountains and the valley. You can sample local wines at the Vineyard Wine Bar, and stop for coffee or a quick lunch at the Rose Street Café. ⊠ *6 W. Rose St., 99362* ☎ *509/525–2200 or 866/826–9422* 🖷 *509/ 529–9282* ⊕ *www.marcuswhitmanhotel.com* ⥅ *75 rooms, 16 suites* ⌂ *Restaurant, bar, shop, business services, convention center, airport shuttle* ▭ *MC, V.*

Dayton

⑤ *31 mi northeast of Walla Walla.*

The tree-shaded county seat of Columbia County is the kind of Currier & Ives place many people conjure up when they imagine the best qualities of rural America. This tidy town has 83 buildings listed on the National Register of Historic Places, including the state's oldest railroad depot and courthouse.

At Washington's oldest standing depot, the **Dayton Historical Depot Society** houses exhibits illustrating the history of Dayton and surrounding communities. ☒ *222 Commercial St.* ☎ *509/382–2026* ⊕ *www. daytondepot.org* ☒ *$3* ☉ *Tues.–Sat. 11–4.*

> **off the beaten path**

PALOUSE FALLS STATE PARK – Just north of its confluence with the Snake River, the Palouse River gushes over a basalt cliff higher than Niagara Falls and drops 198 feet into a steep-walled basin. Those who are sure-footed can hike to an overlook above the falls, which are at their fastest during spring runoff in March. Just downstream from the falls at the Marmes Rock Shelter, remains of the earliest-known inhabitants of North America, dating back 10,000 years, were discovered by archaeologists. The park has 10 primitive campsites. ☒ *Rte. 12, 50 mi north of Dayton* ☎ *360/902–8844 or 888/226–7688* ☒ *$5 per vehicle. Campsites $15–$21* ☉ *Park daily sunrise–sunset; campsites mid-Mar.–Sept.*

Where to Stay & Eat

★ **$$–$$$** ✕ **Patit Creek Restaurant.** The chef turns out inspired beef, lamb, and pork dishes at at this small café, which has been a favorite southeastern Washington eatery for some 20 years. Not only can the food be truly sublime, but the service is also excellent. The wine list is short but has some rare Walla Walla Valley vintages. ☒ *725 E. Dayton Ave.* ☎ *509/ 382–2625* ☰ *MC, V* ☉ *Closed Sun.–Tues. No lunch Sat.*

$$–$$$ ✕ **Weinhard Café.** The past seems to echo through this restaurant, which is near the Weinhard Hotel and in what was once a pharmacy. Try a panini sandwich for lunch; for dinner, homemade ravioli with Parmesan and potato stuffing—served with wilted greens and smoked bacon—is a good bet. ☒ *258 E. Main St.* ☎ *509/382–1681* ☰ *MC, V* ☉ *Closed Sun. and Mon.*

¢–$ ▥ **Purple House Bed and Breakfast.** This Italianate-style house was built in 1882 by a pioneer physician. Today European art and Chinese collectibles adorn the interior. Bedrooms are individually appointed with a tasteful selection of Victorian antiques. Afternoon pastries and tea are presented in the parlor. ☒ *415 Clay St., 99328* ☎ *509/382–3159* ⤴ *4 rooms* ☽ *Pool, some pets allowed; no kids under 16, no smoking* ☰ *MC, V* ⦿ *BP.*

¢–$ ▥ **Weinhard Hotel.** Step back into the Old West at this hotel, which was built as a saloon and lodge in the late 1800s by the nephew of beer baron Henry Weinhard. Rooms have modern amenities but period antiques; fruit baskets and bouquets of flowers are thoughtful touches. Enjoy sparkling cider and live music at weekend evening socials; catch a breeze in the pleasant rooftop garden. ☒ *235 E. Main St., 99328* ☎ *509/382–4032* 🖷 *509/382–2640* ⊕ *www.weinhard.com* ⤴ *15 rooms* ☽ *Dining room, fans, in-room data ports, cable TV, some pets allowed; no smoking* ☰ *D, MC, V* ⦿ *CP.*

Sports & the Outdoors

The **Bluewood** ski area is 22 mi south of Dayton in the Umatilla National Forest. Though small, with just three triple chairlifts and about two dozen runs, Bluewood is popular with both skiers and snowboarders because of its especially dry snow and high elevation. The resort also has 5 km of cross-country trails as well as a restaurant, a pub, a ski shop, and a gift shop. Lift tickets cost $32. ⊠ *4th St. and N. Touchet Rd.* ☎ *509/ 382–4725* ⊕ *www.bluewood.com* ☉ *Mid-Nov.–Apr., Wed.–Sun, 9–4.*

Clarkston

❻ *58 mi northeast of Dayton.*

This former ferry town was founded in 1862 as a way station for travelers heading to the Idaho goldfields. It is the twin city of Lewiston, Idaho, across the river. Clarkston is surrounded by grass-covered hills—green in spring and gold in summer. Along the river a pleasant walkway, the Greenbelt, and Swallows Park invite visitors to explore. You can walk all the way downriver to Asotin, about 5 mi south of town. Swallow Rock is dotted with the jug-shape mud nests of cliff swallows. Clarkston has a symphony orchestra, a civic theater, and art galleries.

Valley Art Center has rotating exhibits of watercolors, oils, and other media by local artists, and sells bronze castings, pottery, and woven willow furniture. ⊠ *842 6th St.* ☎ *509/758-8331* 🖅 *Free* ☉ *Weekdays 9–4.*

The small **Asotin County Museum,** in the county seat of Asotin, 5 mi south of Clarkston, preserves a few old buildings moved from nearby communities, including a log cabin with blacksmith's forge. The museum itself was the first funeral home in the city. There's a very good collection of local branding irons (a rustler's dream) and old carriages. ⊠ *215 Filmore St., Asotin* ☎ *509/243–4659* 🖅 *$2 suggested donation* ☉ *Tues.–Sat. 1–5 and by appointment.*

Fields Spring State Park is partially on Puffer Butte, 30 mi south of Clarkston and in the Blue Mountains. The views are great, and the bird-watching is rewarding year-round. In spring there are spectacular wildflower displays. Primitive camping is allowed. ⊠ *Rte. 129* ☎ *509/256–3332* ⊕ *www.parks.wa.gov* 🖅 *Free* ☉ *Daily sunrise–sunset.*

Where to Stay

¢ 🏨 **Cliff House Bed and Breakfast.** On a bluff above the Snake River 7 mi west of Clarkston, Cliff House has views up and down the river valley. Snag a hammock on one of the three decks surrounding the house and watch barges and ships pass by. A Native American motif dominates one room, while an imposing river view beautifies the other. ⊠ *1227 Westlake Dr., 99403* ☎ *509/758–1267* ⊕ *www.cliffhouseclarkston. com* 🛏 *2 rooms* ⚒ *Exercise equipment, hot tub, library; no room phones, no smoking* 🚫 *No credit cards* 🍽 *BP.*

¢ 🏨 **Quality Inn.** This hotel next to the convention center has a great view of the Snake River and the grass-covered hills of the southern Palouse. Riverboats dock adjacent to the hotel, and jetboat excursions take off regularly. Large picture windows in the two-level restaurant frame the putting course and the river. ⊠ *700 Port Dr., 99403* ☎ *509/758–9500* 🖨 *509/758-5580* ⊕ *www.qualityinns.com* 🛏 *75 rooms, 22 suites* ⚒ *Restaurant, room service, in-room data ports, some in-room hot tubs, some microwaves, some refrigerators, cable TV, pool, gym, bar, laundry facilities, business services, no-smoking rooms* 🚫 *AE, D, DC, MC, V.*

Pullman

❼ *33 mi northwest of Clarkston.*

This funky, liberal town—home of Washington State University—is in the heart of the rather conservative Palouse agricultural district. The town's freewheeling style can perhaps be explained by the fact that most of the students come from elsewhere in Washington.

The Palouse River, whose upper course flows though the town, is an exception among Washington rivers: because of the high erosion rate of the light Palouse loess soils it usually runs muddy, almost like a gruel during floods (most Washington Rivers run clear, even after major storms). The 198-foot-high Palouse Falls further downstream, near Washtucna, dramatically drop as a thin sheet of water into a steep box canyon.

Opened in 1892 as the state's agriculture school, **Washington State University** today sprawls almost all the way to the Idaho state line. To park on campus, pick up a parking pass in the Security Building on Wilson Road. ⊠ *1 SE Stadium Way* ☎ *509/335–4527* 🖶 *509/335–9113* ⊕ *www.wsu.edu* 🏷 *Free* ⊙ *Weekdays.*

On weekdays between 9:30 and 4:30, you can pop into **Ferdinand's** (⊠ S. Fairway La. ☎ 509/335–2141), a soda fountain–cheese shop in the food-science building, to buy Aged Cougar Gold, a cheddar-type cheese in a can. The small **Museum of Art** (⊠ WSU Fine Arts Center ☎ 509/335–1910 or 509/335–6607) has lectures as well as exhibitions that might include turned-wood art, Native American art, or landscaping displays. It's open weekdays 10–4 and weekends 1–5; admission is free. The **Charles R. Conner Museum of Zoology** (⊠ WSU Fine Arts Center ☎ 509/335–3515) has the finest collection of stuffed birds and mammals and preserved invertebrates in the Pacific Northwest. It's open daily 8–5, and there's no admission fee.

Steptoe Memorial State Park is named after an army officer who lost a battle in 1858 against Native Americans at nearby Rosalia. The lieutenant colonel and other survivors snuck away at night—a retreat historians think was permitted by the Indians. The park has picnic tables but no water. ⊠ *32 mi north of Pullman via Rte. 195* ☎ *360/902–8844* ⊕ *www.parks.wa.gov* 🏷 *$5 day use* ⊙ *Daily 6–6.*

Kamiak Butte County Park has a 3,360-foot-tall butte that's part of a mountain chain that was here long before the lava flows of the Columbia basin erupted millions of years ago. Ten miles north of Pullman, the park has great views of the Palouse hills and Idaho's snow-capped peaks to the east as well as nine primitive campsites, a picnic area, and a 1-mi trail to the top of the butte. ⊠ *Rte. 272 to Rd. 5100 to Rd. 6710* ☎ *509/397–6238* 🏷 *Free* ⊙ *Daily sunrise–sunset.*

Where to Stay & Eat

¢ ✕ **Basilio's Italian Café.** In the heart of downtown, Basilio's serves up such classics as pasta, lasagna, and chicken parmagiana in addition to an assortment of sandwiches. Gaze at scenic downtown from the sidewalk seating area. ⊠ *337 E. Main St.* ☎ *509/334–7663* ▭ *MC, V.*

¢ ✕ **Sella's Calzone and Pastas.** Made daily from scratch, the calzones are always fresh at this cozy storefront. The most popular is the Coug (pepperoni, mushrooms, and black olives), followed by the Frugal Gourmet (artichoke hearts, sun-dried tomatoes, pesto sauce, and mozzarella). Pizzas, sandwiches, pastas, and salads are also served. ⊠ *1115 E. Main St.* ☎ *509/334–1895* ▭ *AE, MC, V.*

¢–$$ ⊠ **Churchyard Inn.** Registered as a National and State historic site, this 1905 Flemish-style inn, 15 mi southeast of Pullman in Uniontown, was once a parish house for the adjacent church, and then a convent, before becoming a B&B in 1995. Ceiling fans whir above the period antiques that adorn each room. A 1,200-square-foot suite has a full kitchen and fireplace. ⊠ *206 St. Boniface St., Uniontown 99179* ☎ *509/229–3200 or 800/227–2804* ⊟ *509/229–3213* ⊕ *www.churchyardinn.com* ⇨ *7 rooms* ⚐ *Some in-room hot tubs; no a/c, no kids under 14, no smoking* ⊟ *D, MC, V* ⏹ *BP.*

¢ ⊠ **Country Bed and Breakfast.** About 5½ mi south of Pullman, this 1893 farmhouse is surrounded by junipers and flowering trees. The interior is modern and comfortable, and the owners hospitable. There's a playroom with free pinball, pool, and other games, and an outside patio with a fireplace. ⊠ *2701 Staley Rd., 99163* ☎ *509/334–4453* ⊟ *509/332–5163* ⇨ *7 rooms, 4 with bath* ⚐ *Hot tub, outdoor hot tub, some pets allowed; no a/c in some rooms, no room phones, no smoking* ⊟ *D, MC, V* ⏹ *CP.*

Spokane

❽–⓱ *75 mi north of Pullman, 282 mi east of Seattle.*

Washington's second largest city, Spokane (spo-*can*, not spo-*cane*) takes its name from the Spokan tribe of Salish Indians. It translates as "Children of the Sun," a fitting name for this sunny city. It's also a city of flowers and trees, public gardens, parks, and museums. Known as the "Capital of the Inland Empire," Spokane is the cultural and financial center of the inland Northwest.

Spokane began as a Native American village at a roaring waterfall where each autumn salmon ascended in great numbers. American settlers built a sawmill at the falls in 1873. Several railroads arrived after 1881, and Spokane soon became the transportation hub of eastern Washington. In 1885 Spokane built the first hydroelectric plant west of the Mississippi. Downtown boomed after the fire of 1889, as the city grew rich from mining ventures in Washington, Idaho, and Montana, and from shipping to the south the wheat grown on the Palouse hills.

Until they were cleared away for the 1974 World's Fair, bridges and railroad trestles hid Spokane's magnificent falls from view. Today they form the heart of downtown's Riverfront Park, and the city rises from the falls in a series of broad terraces to the valley's rim. Urban parks are among Spokane's assets. The dry, hot summers here make it easy to plan golf, fishing, and hiking excursions; long, snowy winters provide nearly six months to enjoy skiing, snowboarding, and sledding.

Numbers in the margin correspond to points of interest on the Spokane map.

a good tour

Begin your tour of Spokane west of downtown at the **Finch Arboretum** ❽ on Woodland Boulevard off Sunset Boulevard. From the arboretum, head east on Sunset Boulevard, left on Chestnut Street, and left on First Avenue to get to the **Northwest Museum of Arts and Culture** ❾. Riverside Avenue, a block north of First Avenue, leads east to **Riverfront Park** ❿. From here, you can see Spokane Falls. If you have kids in tow, make a stop before or after the park at the **Children's Museum of Spokane** ⓫. Across from Riverfront Park, check out the **Caterina Winery** ⓬. About 1 mi south of downtown off Grand Boulevard is the **Cathedral of St. John the Evangelist** ⓭, and the pleasant **Manito Park and Gardens** ⓮ are about six blocks south of here. If you have time to venture out of the city, head north on Division Street, which becomes Route 2 (Newport Highway) to **Cat Tales**

Zoological Park ⑮, about 13 mi from downtown. From here a 2-mi drive east will take you to **Townshend Cellar** ⑯, where you can sample Columbia Valley and huckleberry wines. Drive through the countryside another 10 mi south to reach **Arbor Crest Wine Cellars** ⑰ and its pleasant views of the Spokane River. From here, head north to I–90 for the 6-mi drive back to downtown.

TIMING You could easily drive the in-city route in an hour. Plan to spend a half day at Riverfront Park and two hours at the Northwest Museum of Arts and Culture, with at least a half an hour to an hour for stops at the other sights. For the destinations outside of the city, figure on driving about 1½ hours round-trip from downtown and making half-hour stops at each site.

What to See

⑰ **Arbor Crest Wine Cellars.** The eclectic mansion of Royal Riblet, the inventor of a square-wheel tractor and the poles that hold up ski lifts, was built in 1924. Sample complimentary Arbor Crest wines, enjoy the striking view of the Spokane River below, or meander through the impeccably kept grounds (the house isn't open to tours). Enjoy Sunday evening concerts (5:30 [pm]–sunset), most of them free, from July through September. ⊠ *4705 N. Fruithill Rd.* ☎ *509/927–9463* ⊕ *www.arborcrestwinery.com* ✉ *Free* ⊘ *Daily noon–5.*

⑫ **Caterina Winery.** Featuring wines that have won both national and international awards, this is also one of Washington's few downtown wineries. It's in the Broadview Building, formerly home to Carnation Dairy, across the river from Riverfront Park. ⊠ *905 N. Washington St.* ☎ *509/328–5069* ⊕ *www.caterina.com* ✉ *Free* ⊘ *Mon.–Sat. noon–5.*

⑬ **Cathedral of St. John the Evangelist.** An architectural masterpiece, the church was constructed with sandstone from Tacoma and Boise and limestone from Indiana. It's considered one of America's most important and beautiful Gothic cathedrals. The cathedral's renowned 49-bell carillon has attracted international guest musicians. Free concerts are held on Thursday evenings in July; bring a picnic to enjoy on the lawn. ⊠ *127 E. 12th Ave.* ☎ *509/838–4277* ⊕ *www.stjohns-cathedral.org* ✉ *Free* ⊘ *Tours Mon., Tues., and Thurs.–Sat. noon–3.*

☾ ⑮ **Cat Tales Zoological Park.** Among the large cats living at this zoo are lions, tigers, ligers (a combination of lion and tiger), leopards, puma, and lynx. Guided tours give background on the animals. There's also a petting zoo. ⊠ *N. 17020 Newport Hwy., 12 mi north of I–90 Mead* ☎ *509/238–4126* ⊕ *www.cattales.org* ✉ *$6* ⊘ *May–Sept., Tues.–Sun. 10–6; Oct.–Apr., Wed.–Sun. 10–4.*

☾ ⑪ **Children's Museum of Spokane.** Hands-on exhibits focus on building and construction, art, and bubbles. A Greek village allows children to dress in costume and play in a market, cottage, and kitchen. Infants and toddlers can explore the pint-sized garden exhibit, complete with a tree house. ⊠ *110 N. Post St.* ☎ *509/624–5437* ⊕ *www.childrensmuseum.net* ✉ *$3.75* ⊘ *Tues.–Sat. 10–5.*

⑧ **Finch Arboretum.** This mile-long green patch along Garden Springs Creek has an extensive botanical garden with more than 2,000 labeled trees, shrubs, and flowers. Follow the walking tour on well-manicured paths along the creek, or follow your whim—depending on the season— through flowering rhododendrons, hibiscus, magnolias, dogwoods, hydrangeas, and more. ⊠ *3404 W. Woodland Blvd., off Sunset Blvd.* ☎ *509/625–6657* ✉ *Free* ⊘ *Daily sunrise–sunset.*

Arbor Crest
Wine Cellars ...**17**

Caterina
Winery **12**

Cathedral of
St. John the
Evangelist **13**

Cat Tales
Zoological
Park **15**

Children's
Museum of
Spokane **11**

Finch
Arboretum **8**

Manito Park and
Gardens **14**

Northwest
Museum of Arts
and Culture **9**

Riverfront
Park **10**

Townshend
Cellar **16**

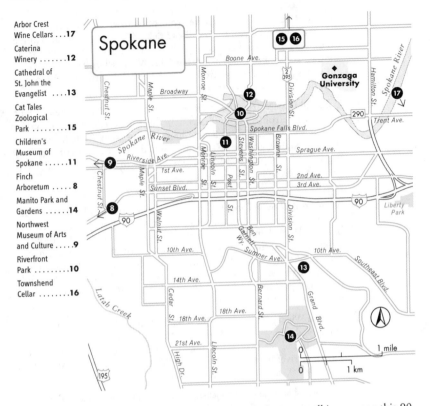

★ ☺ ⓮ **Manito Park and Gardens.** A pleasant place to stroll in summer, this 90-acre park has a formal Renaissance-style garden, conservatory, Japanese garden, duck pond, and rose and perennial gardens. Snowy winters find its hills full of sledders and its frozen pond packed with skaters. ⊠ *S. Grand Blvd. between 17th and 25th Aves.* ☎ *509/625–6622* 🎫 *Free* ☉ *Daily sunrise–sunset; Japanese garden Apr.–Oct., 8* AM *to ½-hr before sunset.*

★ ☺ ⓿ **Northwest Museum of Arts and Culture.** What is affectionately referred to as the MAC is in an impressive six-level glass-and-wood structure. The museum has an audiovisual display and artifacts that trace Spokane's history as well as a fine Native American collection that includes baskets and beadwork of the Plateau Indians. The MAC also hosts several traveling exhibits each year. Wander the adjacent Victorian, the Campbell House, to admire the interior or view mining-era exhibits; guided tours are available by reservation only. ⊠ *2316 W. 1st Ave.* ☎ *509/456–3931* ⊕ *www.northwestmuseum.org* 🎫 *$7* ☉ *Tues.–Sun. 11–5.*

★ ☺ ⓾ **Riverfront Park.** The 100-acre park is what remains of Spokane's Expo '74. Sprawling across several islands in the Spokane River, near the falls, the park was developed from old railroad yards. One of the modernist buildings houses an IMAX theater, a skating rink, and an exhibition space. The opera house occupies the former Washington State pavilion. The stone clock tower of the former Great Northern Railroad Station, built in 1902, stands in sharp architectural contrast to the Expo '74 building. A children's train chugs around the park in summer, and a 1909 carousel, hand-carved by master builder Charles I. D. Looff, is a local landmark. Another icon here is the giant red slide shaped like a Radio Flyer wagon. ⊠ *Riverfront Park, 507 N. Howard St.* ☎ *509/625–6600* ⊕ *www.spokaneriverfrontpark.com* 🎫 *Park: free. Summer day pass for* *most attractions: $11* ⊙ *Park: 4* AM–*midnight. Attractions: Apr.–Oct., hrs vary.*

🔟 **Townshend Cellar.** A drive to the Green Bluff countryside about 13 mi northeast of downtown leads wine lovers to this small winery and its tasting room. Open since 1998, it's already won awards for its cabernet sauvignon, and also makes merlot, chardonnay, syrah, port, and chenin blanc. Berries from nearby Idaho are used in huckleberry port, blush, and sparkling wine. ⊠ *16112 N. Greenbluff Rd., via N. Division and Rte. 2 north* ☎ *509/238-4346* ⊕ *www.townshendcellar.com* 🆓 *Free* ⊙ *Open Fri.–Sun. noon–5 and by appointment.*

Where to Eat

$$–$$$ ✕ **Milford's Fish House.** This brick and terra-cotta tile structure was built in 1925, and the terrazzo floor and tin ceiling are relics of that era. The interior's exposed brick walls and wood details, lit by candles, create a romantic environment in which to enjoy the wide array of seafood dishes and steaks. Everything is fresh here and it is hard to predict what the menu will include, but you might find such items as tuna, shark, cod, salmon, snapper, mahi mahi, clams, and prawns. ⊠ *719 N. Monroe St.* ☎ *509/326-7251* ▭ *D, MC, V* ⊙ *No lunch.*

$$ ✕ **Paprika.** Stuffed ahi tuna and stuffed poblano chiles are among the eclectic dishes served at this formal, intimate restaurant in the South Hill neighborhood across from St. John's Cathedral. ⊠ *1228 S. Grand Blvd.* ☎ *509/455-7545* ▭ *AE, D, MC, V* ⊙ *Closed Sun. and Mon. No lunch.*

★ **$–$$$** ✕ **Luna.** You'll find inventive approaches to classics here, including pork chops, salmon, lamb, and game hen. The menu highlights fresh ingredients grown in the restaurant's garden. Sunday brunch has such treats as scrambled egg salad with field greens and smoked bacon, tofu and veggie scramble, and French toast with caramelized bananas. Sunday night prix-fixe dinners ($20) feature ethnic cuisines. Luna is especially known for its extensive wine list, with more than 500 vintages. A terrace is open in summer. ⊠ *5620 S. Perry St.* ☎ *509/448-2383* ▭ *AE, DC, MC, V.*

$–$$$ ✕ **Niko's Greek Restaurant and Wine Bar.** Sunlight streaming through the large storefront windows renders the dining room bright and cheerful. Lamb is the specialty here, served in a variety of ways including curried, grilled with rosemary, and grilled on skewers in a marinade of lemon, garlic, and white wine. Vegetarian dishes are plentiful, as are the wines—there are over 900 choices on the wine list. ⊠ *725 W. Riverside Ave.* ☎ *509/624-7444* ▭ *AE, DC, MC, V* ⊙ *No lunch weekends.*

★ **$–$$** ✕ **Catacombs.** Catacombs wins accolades for its unique setting and menu. The underground restaurant is in the former boiler room of the Montvale Hotel. Modeling his creation on pubs and underground restaurants he's visited on his travels, owner Rob Brewster has incorporated stone walls, iron chandeliers, lots of brick, and wall tapestries. Try a thin-crust pizza or one of the European specialties, such as Hungarian goulash. For dessert, pretend you're camping and roast s'mores at your table. ⊠ *10 S. Monroe St.* ☎ *509/838-4610* ▭ *AE, D, MC, V* ⊙ *No lunch Sun.*

★ **$–$$** ✕ **Clinkerdagger's.** In a former flour mill with great views of the Spokane River, Clink's has been a Spokane institution since 1974. The seafood, steaks, and prime rib are excellent, and you don't have to pick just one: you can mix and match small portions of several entrées to make a full meal. ⊠ *621 W. Mallon Ave.* ☎ *509/328-5965* ▭ *AE, D, DC, MC, V* ⊙ *No lunch Sun.*

$–$$ ✕ **Europa Pizzeria and Bakery.** The name might fool you: pizza occupies only part of the menu, which also includes lots of homemade pastas, calzones, and salads. Candles on the tables, murals, exposed brick, and wood beams give a European flavor to the dining room and adjacent pub. ⊠ *125 S. Wall St.* ☎ *509/455–4051* ▭ *AE, D, MC, V.*

$–$$ ✕ **Rock City Grill.** This upbeat restaurant, which is close to Riverfront Park, has excellent pastas and gourmet wood-fired pizzas. Expect some kidding around from the outgoing staff, who will make sure your soft drinks and lemonades never go empty. Save room for such desserts as Snickers pie or tiramisu for two. If you love peanut sauce, take some home; it's available by the bottle. ⊠ *505 W. Riverside Ave.* ☎ *509/455– 4400* ▭ *AE, D, DC, MC, V.*

★ **$** ✕ **Mizuna Restaurant.** Fresh flowers and redbrick walls lend both color and charm to this downtown eatery. Local produce is the inspiration for such scrumptious vegetarian fare as Moroccan Portobello steak, white cheddar and apple salad, and ahi served with wilted spinach and sun-dried tomato vinaigrette. If you don't eat seafood, request tofu or wheat gluten in place of the ahi tuna. The wine bar has tastings, and highlights Northwest wines with a five-course winemakers' dinner several times a year. ⊠ *214 N. Howard St.* ☎ *509/747–2004* ▭ *AE, D, MC, V* ⊘ *No lunch weekends; no dinner Mon.*

¢–$$ ✕ **Onion.** Within a former drugstore and saloon, this restaurant evokes the past with a pressed tin ceiling, old photographs, and an ornate bar built in 1905. The restaurant has been serving pastas, salads, burgers, and steaks with enthusiasm and spirit since it opened in 1974. ⊠ *302 W. Riverside Ave.* ☎ *509/747–3852* ▭ *AE, D, DC, MC, V.*

¢–$$ ✕ **Steam Plant Grill.** Built in 1916 as a steam plant (it generated power for the downtown area for more than 70 years), this restaurant has several dining rooms. You can eat inside a boiler, inside a hot water tank, or on a balcony overlooking the entire complex. The menu options are equally broad; there is a coconut curry salad, a halibut fish taco, steak, and lamb chops. The most popular dish is fish-and-chips, fried in a batter made from beer brewed on the premises. ⊠ *159 S. Lincoln St.* ☎ *509/777–3900* ▭ *AE, D, MC, V.*

¢–$ ✕ **Elk Public House.** This eatery in the relaxed Browne's Addition neighborhood, west of downtown, serves upscale pub food such as lamb sandwiches, pastas, salads, and many vegetarian dishes, together with 18 microbrews, most from the Northwest. A copper bar stands along one wall, in front of a mirror, giving the interior a saloon-like appearance. ⊠ *1931 W. Pacific Ave.* ☎ *509/363–1973* ⌖ *Reservations not accepted* ▭ *MC, V.*

¢–$ ✕ **Frank's Diner.** Right off the Maple Street Bridge, this is the state's oldest railroad-car restaurant. Built as an observation car in 1906, it has original light fixtures, stained glass windows, and mahogany details. Breakfast is the specialty here, and portions are large; for dinner there's such comfort food as turkey with mashed potatoes. Everything is made from scratch. ⊠ *1516 W. 2nd Ave.* ☎ *509/747–8798* ▭ *D, MC, V.*

¢ ✕ **Mary Lou's Milk Bottle.** Built in 1933, this restaurant is shaped like a gigantic milk bottle. The focus is on burgers, though some Greek dishes are also served. Since 1978 the eatery has been selling homemade ice cream. ⊠ *802 W. Garland Ave.* ☎ *509/325–1772* ▭ *No credit cards.*

¢ ✕ **Rocky Rococo's Pizza Restaurant.** Housed in a Renaissance Revival–style building that was once a movie palace, this restaurant has extremely high ceilings with the original, theater fixtures. Pizza is the focus here, though there are also salads and pastas. ⊠ *520 W. Main St.* ☎ *509/747–1000* ▭ *AE, MC, V.*

Where to Stay

★ **$$–$$$$** ▦ **Coeur d'Alene Resort.** Each plush room at this lakeside high-rise, in Idaho and just 31 mi east of Spokane, has either a balcony with terrific views of the water or a fireplace. The lower-priced rooms are standard motel fare. The top-of-the-line restaurant, Beverly's, is known for its fine Northwest cuisine, superb wine cellar, and incomparable views. The golf course is famous for its unique floating green. ⊠ *2nd and Front Sts., Exit 11 off I–90, Coeur d'Alene, ID 83814* ☎ *208/765–4000 or 800/ 688–5253* 🖷 *208/667–2707* ⊕ *www.cdaresort.com* 🛏 *326 rooms, 11 suites* ♿ *4 restaurants, minibars, cable TV with video games and movies, 18-hole golf course, pro shop, pool, gym, spa, Internet, business services, meeting rooms, no-smoking rooms* ▤ *AE, D, DC, MC, V.*

★ **$$–$$$$** 🏨 **Hotel Lusso.** Italian-marble tile ornaments the floor, archways, and fountains of this hotel's elegant lobby. Guest rooms are appointed with European furnishings and many modern amenities. Each evening the hotel hosts a wine and cheese social. ⊠ *N. 1 Post St., 99201* ☎ *509/747– 9750* 🖷 *509/747–9751* ⊕ *www.hotellusso.com* 🛏 *36 rooms, 12 suites* ♿ *Restaurant, room service, in-room data ports, some in-room hot tubs, minibars, cable TV with movies, lounge, some pets allowed; no smoking* ▤ *AE, D, DC, MC, V* ⚭ *CP.*

★ **$$** 🏨 **Davenport Hotel.** Elegant rooms have hand-carved mahogany furniture and fine Irish linens as well as high-speed Internet access and flat-screen TVs. Though the sleeping areas are not huge, the marble bathrooms, with big soaking tubs and separate showers, are spacious and inviting. You can dine in the restaurant or in the Peacock Lounge, which serves light fare and has a cigar room. On the lobby level are an espresso bar, candy and flower shops, and an art gallery. ⊠ *10 S. Post St., 99201* ☎ *509/ 455–8888 or 800/899–1482* 🖷 *509/624–4455* ⊕ *www.davenporthotel. com* 🛏 *260 rooms, 24 suites* ♿ *Restaurant, in-room data ports, cable TV with movies and video games, indoor pool, hot tub, spa, lounge, shops, concierge, Internet, business services, convention center, some pets allowed (fee); no smoking* ▤ *AE, D, DC, MC, V.*

$ 🏨 **Doubletree Hotel Spokane City Center.** This chain property is convenient to Riverfront Park, RiverPark Square shopping, and downtown cultural facilities. You'll find standard decor and amenities in the comfortable rooms, as well as some extras like irons and ironing boards, coffeemakers, and Doubletree's signature warm chocolate chip cookies upon arrival. ⊠ *322 N. Spokane Falls Ct., 99201* ☎ *509/455–9600 or 800/222–TREE* 🖷 *509/455–6285* ⊕ *www.doubletree.com* 🛏 *375 rooms* ♿ *2 restaurants, room service, in-room data ports, minibars, cable TV with movies and video games, indoor pool, gym, sauna, lounge, laundry service, concierge, business services, meeting rooms, car rental, no-smoking rooms* ▤ *AE, D, DC, MC, V.*

$ 🏨 **Residence Inn.** About 12 mi east of Spokane, right off I–90, the Residence Inn is convenient to Coeur d'Alene, and 5 mi from two golf courses. It's also right across from the Spokane Valley Mall and numerous restaurants. A mile north is Sullivan Park, a stop on the 37-mi-long Centennial Trail. Spacious suites have full kitchens; some have fireplaces and separate bedrooms. You can fill up on free snacks and beverages during the evening hospitality hour and weekly barbecues. ⊠ *15915 E. Indiana Ave., 99207* ☎ *509/892–9300* 🖷 *509/892–9400* ⊕ *www. residenceinn.com* 🛏 *84 suites* ♿ *In-room data ports, kitchens, tennis court, pool, hot tub, laundry facilities, Internet, business services, concierge, some pets allowed (fee), no-smoking rooms* ▤ *AE, D, DC, MC, V* ⚭ *BP.*

$ 🏨 **WestCoast Ridpath Hotel.** Business and leisure travelers like the downtown Ridpath. Towering above the city, this older hotel has spacious, well-appointed rooms. Ankeny's Restaurant atop the hotel has a panoramic view of Spokane. Guests have access to a nearby full-service health club. ⊠ *515 W. Sprague Ave., 99201* ☎ *509/838–2711 or 800/ 426–0670* 🖷 *509/747–6970* ⊕ *www.westcoasthotels.com* 🛏 *342* rooms ♿ 2 restaurants, pool, gym, 2 bars, convention center, no smoking rooms = AE, D, DC, MC, V.

¢-$$ **Red Lion Hotel at the Park.** This hotel is adjacent to Riverfront Park and just a two-block walk from the downtown shopping district. All floors in the main building open onto an atrium lobby; more guest rooms are in two newer wings. In summer, cool off in the swimming lagoon's waterfalls and waterslide. ✉ *303 W. North River Dr., 99201* ☎ *509/326–8000 or 800/RED–LION* 🖪 *509/325–7329* ⓕ *www.redlion.com* 🗨 *375 rooms, 25 suites* ♿ *3 restaurants, room service, in-room data ports, minibars, cable TV with video games and movies, pool, indoor pool, hot tub, sauna, 2 lounges, concierge, convention center, airport shuttle, no-smoking rooms* = AE, D, DC, MC, V.

¢-$ **Angelica's Bed and Breakfast.** On a tree-lined residential street, this 1907 brick mansion is a paradigm of Victorian elegance, with polished wood floors, lace curtains, beautiful antique furniture, and period lighting. Each individually appointed room has its own charm: Yvonne, for example, has a tile fireplace and a canopy bed. ✉ *1321 W. 9th Ave., 99204* ☎ *509/624–5598 or 800/987–0053* ⓕ *www.angelicasbb.com* 🗨 *4 rooms* ♿ *Some in-room data ports; no room phones, no TV in some rooms, no kids under 12, no smoking* = AE, MC, V = BP.

¢-$ **Fotheringham House.** A comfortable B&B in historic Browne's Addition, this Queen Anne–style house was built in 1891 for the mayor of Spokane. Beautifully restored and preserved, it is filled with antiques. The immaculate gardens have a fountain and a birdbath; the lovely veranda has a porch swing, and there's a park across the street. ✉ *2128 W. 2nd Ave., 99204* ☎ *509/838–1891* 🖪 *509/838–1807* ⓕ *www. fotheringham.net* 🗨 *4 rooms (1 with shower only, 3 share bath)* ♿ *No room phones, no kids under 12, no smoking* = AE, MC, V ☀ *Closed Jan. and Dec. 23–26* = BP.

¢-$ **Marianna Stolz House.** Across from Gonzaga University on a tree-lined street, this B&B is an American foursquare home built in 1908. Listed on Spokane's historical register, it's decorated with leaded-glass china cabinets, Renaissance-revival armchairs, and original dark-fir woodwork. ✉ *427 E. Indiana Ave., 99207* ☎ *509/483–4316 or 800/978–6587* 🖪 *509/483–6773* ⓕ *www.mariannastoltzhouse.com* 🗨 *4 rooms, 2 with bath* ♿ *Cable TV, no-smoking rooms; no children under 7* = AE, D, DC, MC, V = BP.

¢-$ **Red Lion River Inn.** East of Riverfront Park in the heart of downtown, this hotel overlooks the Spokane River. The Inn strives for a resort-like atmosphere, with tennis, volleyball, and basketball courts, horseshoes, and two outdoor pools. In summer enjoy views of the river from the patio while eating at Ripples on the River restaurant. ✉ *N. 700 Division St., 99202* ☎ *509/326–5577 or 800/RED–LION* 🖪 *509/326–1120* ⓕ *www.redlion.com* 🗨 *245 rooms, 2 suites* ♿ *Restaurant, room service, in-room data ports, cable TV, tennis courts, 2 pools, wading pool, hot tub, sauna, bar, business services, airport shuttle, free parking, some pets allowed, no-smoking rooms* = AE, D, DC, MC, V = CP.

¢   **Best Western Pheasant Hill.** This Spokane Valley hotel is right off I–90 Exit 289, about 10 mi from downtown. It's convenient to the Spokane Valley Mall and across from the Spokane Valley Medical Center. Rooms are pleasant and spacious; the indoor pool is open 24 hours. Besides the full hot breakfast in the morning, you can chow down in the evening with complimentary fresh-made soups, peanut butter and jelly sandwiches, and fresh-baked cookies and milk, available 6–midnight. ✉ *12415 E. Mission Ave., 99216* ☎ *509/926–7432* 🖪 *509/892–1914* ⓕ *www. bestwestern.com/pheasanthill* 🗨 *105 rooms* ♿ *In-room data ports, microwaves, refrigerators, cable TV with movies, indoor pool, gym, hot* *tub, laundry facilities, laundry service, Internet, business services, no-smoking rooms* ▭ *AE, D, DC, MC, V* ⦿ *BP.*

Nightlife & the Arts

NIGHTLIFE Part of a national chain, the tropical-themed **Banana Joe's** (✉ 321 W. Sprague Ave. ☎ 509/624–4549), is a hip place to dance and mingle. The DJ plays sounds of the 1970s, '80s, and '90s for the dance-inclined, while pool tables and big-screen TVs draw the sporting crowd. At the **Blue Spark** (✉ 15 S. Howard St. ☎ 509/838–5787), the '80s are still trendy, as evidenced by the music and decor. It's known for great service, great drinks, and a party atmosphere. Check out Monday open-mike night. **B-Side** (✉ 230 W. Riverside Ave. ☎ 509/624–7638) is one of Spokane's favorite venues for live music, and diversity is the word here. Local acts perform punk, rock, jazz, funk, and hip-hop. You can catch a live show several nights a week, or visit Wednesday for DJ-hosted hip-hop.

Downstairs at **Dempsey's Brass Rail** (✉ 909 W. 1st St. ☎ 509/747–5362) is Spokane's most popular gay bar and restaurant; upstairs it's a dance club popular with the local college crowd, both gay and straight. There's a cover on weekends. **Mootsy's** (✉ 406 W. Sprague Ave. ☎ 509/838–1570) is a down-to-earth bar with a pool table, where you can get a microbrew and take in live music most weekends.

THE ARTS **Interplayers Ensemble** (✉ 174 S. Howard St. ☎ 509/455–7529) is a professional theater company whose season runs October–June. The 200-seat **Spokane Civic Theatre** (✉ 1020 N. Howard St. ☎ 509/325–2507) presents musicals and dramas on two stages September–June. The **Spokane Symphony** (✉ 601 W. Riverside Ave. ☎ 509/624–1200) plays classical and pops concerts from September to May in the opera house, as well as free outdoor concerts at city parks in summer and performs chamber music in the elegant Davenport Hotel. In 2000 the symphony purchased the landmark art deco–style Fox Theater, and began an ambitious renovation project. **Theatre Ballet of Spokane** (✉ 416 W. Sprague Ave. ☎ 509/455–6500) and various entertainers perform in the Metropolitan Performing Arts Center, a restored neoclassical structure built in 1915.

Sports & the Outdoors

CLIMBING You can get a taste of rock climbing on the indoor wall at **Mountain Gear** (✉ 2002 N. Division St. ☎ 509/325–9000 or 800/829–2009). A three-hour class costs $20; rent climbing shoes for $6 a day.

GOLF **Hangman Valley** (✉ 2210 E. Hangman Valley Rd. ☎ 509/448–1212), an 18-hole, par-72 course, has a greens fee of $22. **Indian Canyon** (✉ 4304 W. West Dr. ☎ 509/747–5353), an 18-hole course on the slope of a basalt canyon, has great views of North Spokane and Mt. Spokane. The greens fee is $25. **Liberty Lake** (✉ 24403 E. Sprague Ave., Liberty Lake ☎ 509/255–6233), is near MeadowWood, so avid golfers ★ can visit both and play 36 holes. The greens fee is $22. **MeadowWood** (✉24501 E. Valleyway Ave., Liberty Lake ☎509/255–9539) is Spokane's newest golf course. A Scottish-style course, it has been ranked in Washington's top 10. Greens fee is $22.

HIKING The hills around Spokane are laced with trails, almost all of which connect with 37-mi-long Centennial Trail, which winds along the Spokane River. Beginning in Nine Mile Falls, northwest of Spokane, the well-marked trail ends in Idaho. Maps are available at the visitor center at 201 W. Main Street. Northwest of downtown at Riverside State Park, a paved trail leads through a 17-million-year-old fossil forest in Deep Creek Canyon. From there it's easy to get to the western end of the Centennial Trail by crossing the suspension bridge at the day-use parking lot; trails heading both left and right will lead to the Centennial.

HOCKEY The Spokane Chiefs of the Western Hockey League play at the **Spokane Arena** (⊠ 720 W. Mallon Ave. ☎ 509/328–0450 ⊕ www. spokanechiefs.com).

SKIING **49° North** (⊠ Rte. 395, Chewelah ☎ 509/935–6649 ⊕ www.ski49n.com), an hour north of Spokane in the Colville National Forest, is a 1,200-acre family-oriented resort. Lift tickets cost $28–$34; snowboards and snowblade rentals are about $26. **Mt. Spokane** (⊠ 29500 N. Mt. Spokane Park Dr., Mead ☎ 509/238–2220 ⊕ www.mtspokane.com), 23 mi northeast of Spokane, is a modest downhill resort with a 2,000-foot drop and 10 mi of groomed cross-country ski trails. Snowshoeing is also an option. There's night skiing Wednesday–Saturday. Lift tickets cost $24–$31. A state Sno-Park permit, available at the resort, is required.

Shopping

When the **Flour Mill** (⊠ W. 621 Mallon Ave. ⊕ www.spokaneflourmill. com) was built in 1895, it was a huge technical innovation. Today it's home to shops, restaurants, and offices. The mill sits virtually atop the falls, north of the river. At the north end of Spokane, **Northtown Mall** (⊠ 4750 N. Division Ave. ⊕ www.shopnorthtownmall.com) is anchored by Bon-Macy's, Sears Roebuck, JCPenney, and Mervyn California. Dozens of smaller shops line the three levels of this big mall.

Upscale **RiverPark Square** (⊠ 808 W. Main St. ⊕ www.riverparksquare. com) has Nordstrom, Talbots, Williams-Sonoma, Restoration Hardware, Pottery Barn, and other national retailers—more than 30 stores in all. Several restaurants are here or nearby, and there's a 20-screen movie theater. The two-story **Spokane Valley Mall** (⊠ 14700 E. Indiana Ave. ⊕ www. spokanevalleymall.com), about 12 mi east of downtown in the newly incorporated city of Spokane Valley, is anchored by Bon-Macy's, Sears Roebuck, and JCPenney. It also has a movie theater and many restaurants.

Cheney

🔞 *16 mi southwest of Spokane.*

As you walk the tree-shaded streets of this small, quiet college town, it's hard to believe that Cheney once competed with Spokane for regional dominance. Most of the buildings on the Eastern Washington University campus date from the post–World War II education boom, but a few older structures have aged gracefully.

The **Cheney Historical Museum** has artifacts of local and regional historic importance, including a 1935 fire truck. ⊠ *614 3rd St.* ☎ *509/235–4343 or 509/235–4466* ⊠ *Free* ⊙ *Mar.–Oct., Tues. and Sat. 1–3; Nov.–Mar., by appointment.*

Tree-shaded **Eastern Washington University** (⊠ 526 5th St. ☎ 509/359–2397 ⊕ www.ewu.edu) has six original buildings on the National Register of Historic Places, but most of the 300-acre campus consists of post–World War II concrete-and-glass structures. From late July to late August you can watch the Seattle Seahawks football team practice here. The **Gallery of Art** (☎ 509/359–2493) has changing exhibits of works by local and nationally known artists throughout the school year. It's open weekdays 9–5; admission is free.

At the **Turnbull National Wildlife Refuge,** a 17,000-acre preserve of rolling hills, pine woods, lakes, and marshes 5 mi south of Cheney, look for ducks and geese, hawks, falcons, and songbirds. It has Washington's only known nesting site of the endangered trumpeter swan. ⊠ *Cheney–Plaza Rd.* ☎ *509/235–4723* ⊕ *turnbull.fws.gov* ⊠ *$3 Mar.–Oct., free rest of year* ⊙ *Daily sunrise–sunset.*

Where to Stay & Eat

$ ✕ **Willow Springs Station.** This restaurant occupies an old railroad station whose original details—like the tin ceiling—have been retained. Railroad memorabilia and equipment adorn the walls. Popular dishes include liver and onions, meat loaf, and biscuits and gravy. Breakfast is also served. ✉ *809 1st St.* ☎ *509/235–4420* ▤ *AE, D, MC, V.*

¢ ▥ **Willow Springs Motel.** This small motel is in a quiet neighborhood close to Eastern Washington University and 12 mi from Spokane. ✉ *5 B St., 99004* ☎ *509/235–5138* 🖷 *509/235–4528* 📞 *43 rooms* ♘ *Room service, some kitchenettes, cable TV, laundry facilities, some pets allowed (fee)* ▤ *AE, D, DC, MC, V.*

Ritzville

19 *50 mi southwest of Cheney.*

In the heart of the wheat country at the junction of two major highways, I-90 and Route 395, the Adams county seat has long occupied a position of importance in eastern Washington, despite its small size. Its old downtown has several interesting buildings, most notably the eclectic house built by Dr. Frank R. Burroughs in 1889, now the county historical society's museum. The town made headline news in 1980 when it received more than its share of Mt. St. Helen's ash.

The **Dr. Frank Burroughs House** is furnished with period pieces and historic objects, including the doctor's medical tools and records, and clothes and household items from the 1890s to the 1920s. ✉ *408 W. Main St.* ☎ *509/659–1936* ⊕ *www.ritzville.com* ▨ *Free* ☉ *Memorial Day–Labor Day, weekdays 1–4; otherwise by appointment.*

The **Railroad Depot Museum** highlights the history of rail travel in this town, where trains used to stop 8–10 times a day. Railroad equipment, a working telegraph machine, and a horse-drawn hearse are on display. ✉ *Railroad Ave. and Washington St.* ☎ *509/659–1936* ▨ *Free* ☉ *Memorial Day–Labor Day, weekdays 1–4; otherwise by appointment.*

Where to Stay & Eat

$-$$ ✕ **Circle T Restaurant.** This steak-and-seafood house is a favorite hangout of local farmers. Specialties include New York steak and grilled oysters. You can also get breakfast. ✉ *214 W. Main St., 99169* ☎ *509/659–0922* ▤ *MC, V.*

¢-$ ✕ **Jake's Café.** This quintessential roadside diner—adjacent to a gas station off I-90—is open 24 hours a day. All menu items are available at any time. Typical fare includes steaks, burgers, and sandwiches. ✉ *1500 W. 1st Ave.* ☎ *509/659–1961* ▤ *AE, D, MC, V.*

¢-$ ▥ **The Portico.** Built in 1902 in a variety of styles (Queen Anne, Classical Revival, and Craftsman), this B&B has been beautifully maintained and appointed by its owners. The parquet floor in the entrance hall, with its pattern of light and dark oak bordered with serpentine work in maple, is a perfect example. Rooms are furnished with antiques, such as a carved walnut canopy bed with a mermaid at its head and an angel at its foot. ✉ *502 S. Adams St., 99169* ☎ *509/659–0800* 📞 *4 rooms* ♘ *Cable TV; no smoking* ▤ *AE, D, MC, V* ▮◐▮ *BP.*

¢ ▥ **Best Western Bronco Inn.** This bright inn opened in 2003, so expect modern amenities and decor. It's centrally located and convenient to Ritzville's historical buildings and City Park, which has an outdoor pool with waterslide, barbecues, basketball court, bandstand, and gazebo. ✉ *105 W. Galbreath Way, 99169* ☎ *509/659–5000* 🖷 *509/659–5002* ⊕ *www.bestwestern.com* 📞 *63 rooms* ♘ *In-room data ports, some microwaves, some refrigerators, indoor pool, gym, hot tub, laundry facil-*

ities, Internet, business services, some pets allowed (fee), no-smoking rooms ▭ *AE, D, DC, MC, V* ⊙I *CP.*

Moses Lake

20 *45 mi west of Ritzville.*

The natural lake from which this sprawling town takes its name seems to be an anomaly in the dry landscape of east-central Washington. But ever since the Columbia Basin Project took shape, there's been water everywhere. Approaching Moses Lake from the west on I–90 you'll pass lushly green irrigated fields; to the east lie vast stretches of wheat. The lakes of this region have more shorebirds than Washington's ocean beaches. Potholes Reservoir is an artificial lake that supports as much wildlife as does the Columbia Wildlife Refuge. The Winchester Wasteway, west of Moses Lake, is a great place to paddle a kayak or canoe and watch birds as you glide along the reedy banks. The airfield north of town was once a major air force base and now serves as a training facility for airline pilots.

Claw-shaped, 38-foot-deep, 18-mi-long **Moses Lake** is filled by Crab Creek—which originates in the hills west of Spokane—with three side branches known as Parker Horn, Lewis Horn, and Pelican Horn. The city sprawls over the peninsulas formed by these "horns" and can therefore be a bit difficult to get around. This is the state's second largest lake. ⊠ *Rte. 17, off Rte. I–90.*

Fossils collected all over North America, including prehistoric land and marine animals, are exhibited at the **Moses Lake Museum and Art Center.** One gallery also has visual arts displays. ⊠ *228 W. 3rd Ave.* ☎ *509/ 766–9395* ◻ *Free* ⊙ *Tues.–Sat. 11–5.*

★ ℭ Cool off from the hot central Washington sunshine at the **Moses Lake Family Aquatic Center.** In addition to the Olympic-sized pool, there are two 200-foot water slides, a tube slide, a "baby octopus" slide, and diving boards. ⊠ *McCosh Park, 4th and Cedar* ☎ *509/766–9246* ◻ *$5* ⊙ *July–Labor Day, daily 11:30–8; Memorial Day–June, weekends 11:30–8, weekdays 4–8.*

Cascade Park has a beach on the east shore of Moses Lake where in summer the water gets warm enough for swimming. The park is popular for camping and boating, and can be quite noisy with water-skiers. ⊠ *Valley Rd. and Cascade Valley* ☎ *509/766–9240* ◻ *Free* ⊙ *Daily sunrise–10 PM.*

Across the water from the town of Moses Lake, **Moses Lake Community Park** is a great place to picnic and fish for trout, bluegill, crappie, and catfish. It's 5 mi from downtown. ⊠ *West side of lake off I–90* ☎ *509/ 765–5852* ◻ *Free* ⊙ *Daily sunrise–10 PM.*

Reed-lined **Winchester Wasteway,** a slough west of Moses Lake and off I–90, carries excess irrigation waters south toward the Columbia. It's a good place for watching waterfowl, rails, songbirds, muskrats, and beavers. ⊠ *Dodson Rd. S* ☎ *509/765–7888* ◻ *Free* ⊙ *Daily 24 hrs.*

Potholes Reservoir is an artificial lake in a natural depression carved by the huge Spokane Floods. Its waters are contained by O'Sullivan Dam, one of the country's largest earth-filled dams. ⊠ *Rte. 17 to Rte. 170* ☎ *509/754–4624* ⊙ *Daily sunrise–sunset.*

Potholes State Park is 20 mi southwest of Moses Lake on the west side of O'Sullivan Dam. Camping and boating, as well as fishing for trout, perch, and walleye, are popular diversions. ⊠ *Rte. 17 to Rte. 170*

☎ *360/902–8844 or 888/226–7688* ⊕ *www.parks.wa.gov* ☒ *$5 for day use, $10–$22 for camping* ☉ *Daily sunrise–sunset.*

Columbia National Wildlife Refuge attracts a great number of birds: hawks, falcons, golden eagles, ducks, sandhill cranes, herons, American avocets, black-necked stilts, and yellow-headed and red-winged blackbirds. The refuge is also home to beavers, muskrats, badgers, and coyotes. It's 8 mi northwest of the town of Othello, about 20 mi southeast of Moses Lake. ☒ *Refuge headquarters at 735 E. Main St., Othello* ☎ *509/488–2668* ⊕ *www.r1.fws.gov* ☒ *Free* ☉ *Daily sunrise–sunset; office open Mon.–Thurs. 7–4:30, Fri. 7–3:30.*

Shopping
Vendors come to the **Columbia Basin Farmers' Market** each Saturday and Wednesday in summer and early fall to sell fresh produce and handmade arts and crafts. ☒ *Civic Center Park, 5th and Balsam Sts.* ☎ *509/762–5500* ☉ *Mid-June–mid-Oct., Wed. 3–7, Sat. 7:30–1.*

Ephrata

㉑ *20 mi northwest of Moses Lake.*

Ephrata (e-*fray*-tuh), a pleasant small farm town and the Grant County seat, is in the exact center of Washington. It was settled quite early because its abundant natural springs made it an oasis in the dry steppe country of the Columbia Basin. Native Americans visited the springs, as did cattle drovers after American ranchers stocked the open range. Ephrata began to grow after the Great Northern Railroad established a terminal here in 1892. At the time thousands of wild horses roamed the range.

Cattlemen took advantage of the railroad to round up and ship out thousands of wild horses. The last great roundup was held in 1906, when the last 2,400 horses of a herd that once numbered some 25,000 were corralled and shipped out by rail.

Built in the 1920s, the redbrick **Grant County Courthouse** has a facade framed by white columns and a majestic set of stairs. Although it may seem antique from the exterior, the building has a unique and progressive feature: it's heated by thermal springs. ☒ *35 C St. NW* ☎ *509/754–2011 Ext. 628* ☉ *Weekdays 8–5.*

The **Grant County Historical Museum and Village** consists of more than 30 pioneer-era buildings brought here from other parts of Grant County. They include a blacksmith forge, saloon, barbershop, and printing office. ☒ *742 Basin St. N* ☎ *509/754–3334* ☒ *$3* ☉ *May–Sept., Mon.–Tues. and Thurs.–Sat. 10–5, Sun. 1–4.*

Soap Lake, 6 mi north of Ephrata, has water high in dissolved carbonates, sulfates, and chlorides. Even though the lake has long been famous for its mineral waters and therapeutic mud baths, the eponymous small town has never quite succeeded as a resort—perhaps because the miraculous waters have been heavily diluted by irrigation waters. But agriculture is much more profitable anyway, and many other beautiful recreation areas are nearby.

Where to Stay & Eat
¢–$ ✕ **Country Deli.** In the center of town, this popular eatery serves burgers, salads, and pastas in a comfortable, low-key dining room. A gazebo in the front of the restaurant provides outdoor dining during warmer months. You can also get breakfast here. ☒ *245 Basin St. NW* ☎ *509/754–3143* ▤ *AE, MC, V* ☉ *No dinner Sun. and Mon.*

¢–$ 🏨 **Inn at Soap Lake.** Built in 1905 as a stable and blacksmith shop, this beachside structure was converted to an inn in 1915. Each room contains a soaking tub in which to enjoy Soap Lake's natural mineral water. Floral patterns dominate most rooms, which are appointed with contemporary furnishings and modern amenities. ✉ *226 Main Ave. E, Soap Lake 98851* ☎ *509/246–1132 or 800/557–8514* 📠 *509/246– 1132* ⊕ *www.innsoaplake.com* ⇨ *20 rooms, 8 cottages* ♿ *Picnic area, in-room hot tubs, kitchenettes, microwaves, refrigerators, cable TV, massage, beach; no smoking* ⊟ *AE, D, MC, V.*

¢–$ 🏨 **Ivy Chapel Inn Bed and Breakfast.** Occupying a brick church from the '40s, this B&B has a unique structure. The chapel, with its cathedral ceilings and large stained-glass windows, is used for weddings and meetings. All rooms have high-speed Internet access. ⇨ *6 rooms* ♿ *In-room data ports, cable TV, hot tub, library, Internet; no smoking* ✉ *164 D St. SW, 98823* ☎ *509/754–0629* 📠 *509/754–0791* ⊕ *www. ivychapelinn.com* ⊟ *AE, D, DC, MC, V* ⏵⏴ *BP.*

¢–$ 🏨 **Notaras Lodge.** The rooms at this three-building lodge on the shores of Soap Lake are individually decorated. Water from the lake is piped into the bathrooms (bring lots of room freshener), though you can choose to have regular water instead. ✉ *13 Canna St., 98851* ☎ *509/246– 0462* 📠 *509/246–1054* ⊕ *www.notaraslodge.com* ⇨ *15 rooms* ♿ *Restaurant, picnic area, some in-room hot tubs, microwaves, refrigerators, cable TV, some pets allowed (fee), no-smoking rooms* ⊟ *MC, V.*

Coulee Dam National Recreation Area

60 mi northeast of Ephrata, 239 mi northeast of Seattle, 87 mi northwest of Spokane.

Grand Coulee Dam is the world's largest concrete structure. At almost a mile long, it justly deserves the moniker of Eighth Technological Wonder of the World. Beginning in 1932, 9,000 men excavated 45 million cubic yards of rock and soil and dammed the Grand Coulee, a gorge created by the Columbia River, with 12 million cubic yards of concrete— enough to build a sidewalk the length of the equator. By the time the dam was completed in 1941, 77 men had perished and 11 towns were submerged under the newly formed Roosevelt Lake. The waters backed up behind the dam turned eastern Washington's arid soil into fertile farming land, but not without consequence: Salmon fishing stations that were a source of food and spiritual identity for Native Americans were destroyed. Half the dam was built on the Colville Indian Reservation on the north shore of the Columbia; the Colville tribes later received restitution in excess of $75 million from the U.S. government.

In 1946 most of Roosevelt Lake and the grassy and pine woodland hills surrounding it were designated the Coulee Dam National Recreation Area. Crown Point Vista, about 5 mi west of Grand Coulee on Route 174, may have the best vantage for photographs of the dam, Roosevelt Lake, Rufus Woods Lake (below the dam), and the town of Coulee Dam.

After nightfall from Memorial Day through September, the dam is transformed into an unlikely entertainment complex by an extravagant, free laser-light show. With 300-foot eagles flying across the white water that flows over the dam, the show is spectacular, if hokey. The audio portion is broadcast on 90.1 FM. Show up early to get a good seat.

The **Coulee Dam National Recreation Area Visitors Arrival Center** has colorful displays about the dam, a 13-minute film on the site's geology and the dam's construction, and information about the laser-light show. The U.S. Bureau of Reclamation, which oversees operation and maintenance of the dam, conducts tours year-round, weather and maintenance schedules permitting. You can also pick up a self-guided historical walking tour that will take you from the visitors center through the old part of town, across the bridge, and into the old engineers' town. ✉ *Rte. 155 north of Grand Coulee* ☎ *509/633–9265, 509/633–3074, or 509/633– 3838 to the dam* ⊕ *www.grandcouleedam.org* ✉ *Free* ☉ *Late May–July, daily 8:30 AM–11 PM; Aug., daily 8:30 AM–10:30 PM; Sept., daily 8:30 AM–9:30 PM; Oct. and Nov., and Feb.–late May, weekdays 9–5.*

The **Lake Roosevelt National Recreation Area** contains the 150-mi-long lake created by the Columbia River when it was backed up by Grand Coulee Dam. Several Native American villages, historic sites, and towns lie beneath the waters. ✉ *1008 Crest Dr., headquarters address* ☎ *509/633– 9441* ⊕ *www.nps.gov/laro* ✉ *Free day use; camping $10 May–Sept, $5 Oct.–Apr.* ☉ *Daily sunrise–sunset.*

At **Steamboat Rock State Park** a 2,200-foot-high flat-topped lava butte rises 1,000 feet above Banks Lake, the 31-mi-long irrigation reservoir filled with water from Lake Roosevelt by giant pumps and siphons. Water is distributed from the south end of the lake throughout the Columbia Basin. The state park has campsites and is popular with boaters and anglers. ✉ *Rte. 155, 16 mi north of Coulee City* ☎ *360/902–8844 or 888/ 226–7688* ⊕ *www.parks.wa.gov* ✉ *$5 day use, camping $10–$22* ☉ *Daily 6:30 AM–sunset.*

Sun Lakes State Park is a high point in the coulee. Campgrounds, picnic areas, and a state-run golf course attract visitors year-round; in summer the lakes bristle with boaters. From the bluffs on Route 2, west of the dam, you can get a great view over this enormous canyon. To the north, the banks of the lake are hemmed in by cliffs. At Dry Falls, the upstream erosion of the canyon caused by the floods stops. Below Dry Falls, steep, barren cliffs—some 1,000 feet tall—rise from green meadows, marshes, and blue lakes bordered by trees. Most of the water is irrigation water seeping through the porous rock, but the effect is no less spectacular. Eagles and ravens soar along the cliffs while songbirds, ducks, and geese hang out in the bottomlands.

South of the Sun Lakes, the landscape turns even wilder. The coulee narrows and the cliffs often look like they are on fire, an illusion created by the bold patterns of orange and yellow lichens. The waters of the lakes change, too. The deep blue waters of the small lakes below Dry Falls are replaced by lapis lazuli in the Sun Lakes and turn milky farther south. Presentations at the park's interpretive center at Dry Falls survey the area's geology, and an excellent film describes the great floods. ✉ *From Grand Coulee Dam take Rte. 155 south, Rte. 2 east, and Rte. 17 south* ☎ *360/902–8844 or 888/226–7688* ⊕ *www.parks. wa.gov* ✉ *$5 day use, $10–$22 camping* ☉ *Daily 6:30 AM–sunset.*

Route 155 passes through the **Colville Indian Reservation,** one of the largest reservations in Washington, with about 7,700 enrolled members of the Colville Confederated Tribes. This was the final home for Chief Joseph and the Nez Perce, who fought a series of fierce battles with the U.S. Army in the 1870s after the U.S. government enforced a treaty that many present-day historians agree was fraudulent. Chief Joseph lived on the Colville reservation until his death in 1904. There's a memorial to him off Route 155 east of the town of Nespelem, 17 mi north of the dam; four blocks away (two east and two north) is his grave. You can drive through the reservation's undeveloped landscape, and except for a few highway signs you'll feel like you've time-traveled to pioneer days. For a better understanding of frontier history, visit the **Colville Confederated**

Tribes Museum and Gift Shop (⊠ 512 Mead Way Coulee Dam ☎ 509/ 633–0751), ½ mi north of Grand Coulee Dam via Route 155.

Where to Stay & Eat

¢–$ ✕ **Flo's Cafe.** One mile south of the dam, this diner dishes up heaps of local color along with loggers' food: biscuits and gravy, corned-beef hash, hamburgers, chicken-fried steak, and chef's salads. Flo's is open for breakfast but closes at 2 PM daily. ⊠ *316 Spokane Way, Grand Coulee* ☎ *509/ 633–3216* ▭ *No credit cards* ⊘ *No dinner.*

¢–$ ✕ **Melody Restaurant.** This casual, family-friendly spot with excellent views of Grand Coulee Dam prepares sandwiches, steaks, seafood, and pasta and is open for breakfast. ⊠ *512 River Dr., Coulee Dam* ☎ *509/ 633–1151* ▭ *AE, D, MC, V.*

¢–$ ▦ **Coulee House Motel.** This motel with "the best dam view in town" (someone had to say it) has modern rooms decorated in earth tones. ⊠ *110 Roosevelt Ave., Coulee Dam 99116* ☎ *509/633–1101 or 800/ 715–7767* ⎙ *509/633–1416* ⊕ *www.couleehouse.com* ⇘ *61 rooms* ♨ *Some refrigerators, some kitchens, cable TV, pool, 2 hot tubs, laundry facilities, some pets allowed (fee), no-smoking rooms* ▭ *AE, D, DC, MC, V.*

¢ ▦ **Columbia River Inn.** The spacious, brightly colored rooms all have private decks at this inn across the street from Grand Coulee Dam, with easy access to hiking trails and fishing. ⊠ *10 Lincoln St., Coulee Dam 99116* ☎ *509/633–2100 or 800/633–6421* ⎙ *509/633–2633* ⊕ *www. columbiariverinn.com* ⇘ *35 rooms* ♨ *In-room data ports, some in-room hot tubs, some microwaves, some refrigerators, cable TV, pool, business services, airport shuttle; no smoking* ▭ *AE, D, MC, V.*

¢ ▦ **Gold House Inn Bed and Breakfast.** Some of the rooms at this big, golden-color contemporary B&B on a hilltop have breathtaking views of Grand Coulee Dam. ⊠ *411 Partello Park, Grand Coulee 99133* ☎ *509/633– 3276 or 800/835–9369* ⎙ *509/633–1298* ⊕ *www.grandcouleedam. com/gold* ⇘ *7 rooms, 5 with private bath* ♨ *Some cable TV, hot tub; no smoking* ▭ *AE, D, MC, V* ⊙❘ *BP.*

Omak

❷ *52 mi northwest of Grand Coulee Dam.*

Omak is a small mill and orchard town in the beautifully rustic Okanogan Valley of north-central Washington. Lake Omak to the southeast, on the Colville Reservation, is part of an ancient channel of the Columbia River, which ran north prior to the last Ice Age before turning south at Omak in what is now the lower Okanogan Valley.

In recent years, Omak has been criticized by animal lovers for its mid-August Omak Stampede and Suicide Race. During the annual event, wild horses race down a steep bluff and across the Okanogan River. Some horses have been killed and riders seriously injured. Most of the riders are from the Colville Reservation, and elders defend the race as part of Indian culture. Despite the detractors, more spectators attend the event each year.

At the **Okanogan County Historical Museum** you'll find displays of Okanogan pioneer life and a replica of an Old West town. Outside is Okanogan's oldest building, a 19th-century log cabin, and antique farm equipment. ⊠ *1410 2nd Ave. N* ☎ *509/422–4272* ⊠ *$2* ⊘ *Memorial Day weekend–Labor Day, daily 10–4; otherwise by appointment.*

The **Okanogan National Forest** is a region of open woods, meadows, and pastoral river valleys in the Okanogan highlands. There's lots of wildlife: deer, black bear, coyotes, badgers, bobcats, cougars, grouse, hawks, and golden eagles. Campgrounds are scattered throughout the region. There are six snow parks with groomed trails for snowmobilers, and open areas for cross-country skiing. Ski areas are at Loup Loup Pass (Nordic and alpine) and Sitzmark (alpine only). ✉ *1240 2nd Ave. S (office)* ☎ *509/826–3275* ⊕ *www.fs.fed.us/r6/oka* ✉ *Free* ⊙ *Office: weekdays 7:45–4:30.*

Where to Stay & Eat

★ **$–$$** ✕ **Breadline Cafe.** For more than 20 years Breadline has been a top destination for dinner and entertainment in the Okanogan Valley. A varied menu highlights local organic produce, certified Angus beef, crepes, and seafood. You'll find Cajun items such as jambalaya, as well as an around-the-world assortment of cuisines, including Thai, Italian, and Greek. ✉ *102 S. Ash St.* ☎ *509/826–5836* ▤ *MC, V* ⊙ *Closed Sun.*

¢ ▥ **Omak Inn.** Just off I–97, this motel is close to restaurants and shopping. A small patio and expansive lawn behind the pool allow for relaxing in the summer heat. ✉ *912 Koala Dr., 98841* ☎ *509/826–3822 or 800/204–4800* ▤ *509/826–2980* ⊕ *www.omakinn.com* ↝ *49 rooms* ⌂ *Restaurant, in-room data ports, some in-room hot tubs, some microwaves, some refrigerators, cable TV, pool, gym, hot tub, laundry facilities, business services, some pets allowed (fee), no-smoking rooms* ▤ *AE, D, MC, V* ⦿ *CP.*

¢ ▥ **Rodeway Inn.** The closest motel to the Omak Stampede grounds is within walking distance of several restaurants. Suites have whirlpool tubs or fireplaces. ✉ *122 N. Main St.* ☎ *509/826–0400* ▤ *509/826–5635* ↝ *50 rooms, 11 suites* ⌂ *In-room data ports, some in-room hot tubs, some kitchens, microwaves, refrigerators, cable TV, pool, some pets (fee), no-smoking rooms* ▤ *AE, D, DC, MC, V* ⦿ *BP.*

Colville

㉓ *115 mi east of Omak.*

This small town, the seat of Stevens County, sits in a valley surrounded by lakes, forests, and mountains. The town has many well-maintained old houses and a pleasant, well-to-do atmosphere. Colville became regionally famous in 1983 when Mike Hale opened Hale's Microbrewery—which has moved to the Seattle area.

At the **Keller Heritage Center** you can see a farmstead, lookout tower, trappers' cabins, blacksmith shop, sawmill, and museum. ✉ *700 N. Wynne St.* ☎ *509/684–5968* ⊙ *May and Sept., daily 1–4; June–Aug., Mon.–Thurs. 11–5, Fri.–Sun. 2–5; otherwise by appointment.*

Colville National Forest is a vast region encompassing mountain, forests, and meadows in the state's northeast corner. Here the desert area ends, and three mountain ranges (Selkirks, Kettle River, and Okanogan)—considered foothills of the Rocky Mountains—traverse the forest from north to south. It's a beautiful, wild area, where only the river bottoms are dotted with widely spaced settlements and where the mountains (whose average height is about 4,500 feet) are largely pristine. The streams abound with trout, and the forests with deer and black bear. This is perfect backpacking country, with many trails to remote mountain lakes. ✉ *765 S. Main St.* ☎ *509/684–7000* ⊕ *www.fs.fed.us/r6/colville/* ✉ *$5* ⊙ *Daily sunrise–sunset.*

Where to Stay & Eat

¢–$ ✕ **Café Italiano.** The chef embellishes the predominately French and northern Italian menu with Greek, Arabic, and Indian dishes, resulting in about 125 choices. When you enter the dining room, it is like entering an Italian villa. The ceiling is painted the color of a bright blue sky with passing clouds. A rose garden with water fountain provides outdoor dining during the warmer months. ⊠ *153 W. 2nd Ave.* ☎ *509/ 684–5957* ⌷ *Reservations essential* ▤ *MC, V* ⊘ *No lunch weekends.*

¢ ▨ **Benny's Colville Inn.** This is a comfortable family motel nestled in a pristine valley between the Kettle and Selkirk mountain ranges. ⊠ *915 S. Main St.* ☎ *509/684–2517 or 800/680–2517* ⨴ *509/684–2546* ⊕ *www. colvilleinn.com* ⇅ *105 rooms* ⌂ *Restaurant, pool, some in-room hot tubs, gym, hot tub, some pets allowed, no-smoking rooms* ▤ *AE, D, MC, V.*

¢ ▨ **Comfort Inn.** The backdrop of this chain hotel is majestic mountains; you can't forget you are near the forest with the enormous amount of wildlife in the area. ⊠ *166 NE Canning Dr., 99114* ☎ *509/684–2010 or 800/ 228–5150* ⨴ *509/684–1918* ⊕ *www.choicehotels.com* ⇅ *53 rooms* ⌂ *In-room data ports, cable TV, indoor pool, hot tub, laundry service, some pets allowed, no-smoking rooms* ▤ *AE, D, DC, MC, V* ⦿ *CP.*

Eastern Washington A to Z

AIR TRAVEL

Spokane International Airport is the main hub for air travel in eastern Washington. Smaller airports include Pullman, Tri-Cities, Walla Walla, and Lewiston, Idaho (across the border from Clarkston).

AIRPORTS & TRANSFERS Many hotels offer a free airport shuttle service. Spokane Transit runs about hourly, 6–6 daily, and costs $1. Wheatland Express has shuttle service between the Spokane Airport and Pullman and Moscow, Idaho. Reservations are recommended; the cost is $34 one-way.

Anytime Anywhere Taxi and Yellow Cab are two companies that serve the Spokane area. Metered fares run $1.80 a mile. A taxi ride from the Spokane airport to downtown costs about $15.

🖪 Airports **Lewiston-Nez Perce County Airport** ⊠ 406 Burrell Ave., Lewiston ☎ 208/ 746–7962 ⊕ www.lcairport.net. **Pullman-Moscow Regional Airport** ⊠ 3200 Airport Complex N, Pullman ☎ 509/338–3223 ⊕ www.ci.pullman.wa.us/Airport.htm. **Spokane International Airport** ⊠ 9000 W. Airport Dr., Spokane ☎ 509/455–6455 ⊕ www. spokaneairports.net. **Tri-Cities Airport** ⊠ 3601 N. 20th, Pasco ☎ 509/547–6352 ⊕ www.portofpasco.org/aphome.htm. **Walla Walla Regional Airport** ⊠ 45 Terminal Loop Rd., Walla Walla ☎ 509/525–3100.

🖪 Transfer Information **Anytime Anywhere Taxi** ☎ 509/536–1666. **Spokane Transit Authority** ☎ 509/334–2200 or 800/334–2207. **Wheatland Express** ☎ 509/334–2200 or 800/334–2207. **Yellow Cab** ☎ 509/624–4321.

CARRIERS Spokane International Airport is served by the airlines listed below, including Horizon, which also serves the smaller regional airports. Tri-Cities is served by Delta and United Express.

🖪 Airlines **Air Canada** ☎ 800/776–3000 ⊕ www.aircanada.ca. **Alaska Airlines** ☎ 800/426–0333 ⊕ www.alaskair.com. **America West** ☎ 800/235–9292 ⊕ www. americawest.com. **Big Sky** ☎ 800/237–7788 ⊕ www.bigskyair.com. **Delta** ☎ 800/ 221–1212 ⊕ www.delta.com. **Horizon** ☎ 800/547–9308 ⊕ www.horizonair.com. **Northwest** ☎ 800/225–2525 ⊕ www.nwa.com. **Southwest** ☎ 800/435–9792 ⊕ www. iflyswa.com. **United** ☎ 800/241–6522 ⊕ www.ual.com.

BUS TRAVEL

Greyhound Lines runs daily to Spokane from Seattle (5–6½ hrs) and Portland (8–13 hrs). The line serves Cheney, Ephrata, Moses Lake, Omak, Pasco, Pullman, Richland, and Walla Walla. Spokane has an extensive local bus system. The fare is $1; exact change or a token is required. Pick up schedules, maps, and tokens at the bus depot or the Plaza, the major downtown transfer point.

🖪 Bus Information **The Plaza** ⊠ 701 W. Riverside Ave. ☎ 509/328–7433 ⊕ www. spokanetransit.com. **Greyhound Lines** ⊠ W. 221 1st Ave., in the Amtrak station ☎ 509/ 624–5251 ⊕ www.greyhound.com.

CAR TRAVEL

Spokane can be reached by I–90 from the east or west. Route 395 runs north from Spokane to Colville and the Canadian border. Route 195 traverses southeastern Washington to Pullman. Leave Route 195 at Colfax, heading southwest on Route 26 and then 127, and finally Route 12 to Dayton and Walla Walla. South of I–90, Route 395 leads to the Tri-Cities from the east; the Tri-Cities can also be accessed via I–82 from the west. Gas stations along the main highways cater to truckers and some are open 24 hours.

Downtown Spokane is laid out along a true grid: Streets run north–south, avenues east–west; many are one-way. Spokane's heaviest traffic is on I–90 between Spokane and Spokane Valley on weekday evenings. Metered parking is available on city streets; there are also several downtown lots.

EMERGENCIES

🖪 Doctors & Dentists **Spokane Medical Society** ☎ 509/325-5010 referrals
🖪 Hospitals **Deaconess Medical Center** ⊠ 800 W. 5th Ave., Spokane ☎ 509/458-5800. **Kennewick General Hospital** ⊠ 900 South Auburn St., Kennewick ☎ 509/586-6111. **Pullman Memorial Hospital** ⊠ 1125 NE Washington Ave., Pullman ☎ 509/332-2541. **Samaritan Hospital** ⊠ 801 E. Wheeler Rd., Moses Lake ☎ 509/765-5606. **Sacred Heart Medical Center** ⊠ 101 W. 8th Ave., Spokane ☎ 509/474-3131. **Walla Walla General Hospital** ⊠ 1025 S. 2nd Ave., Walla Walla ☎ 509/525-0480.

MAIL & SHIPPING

🖪 Post Offices **Ephrata** ⊠ 119 1st Ave. NW ☎ 509/754-8990. **Moses Lake** ⊠ 223 W. 3rd Ave. ☎ 509/764-5507. **Pullman** ⊠ 1135 S. Grand Ave. ☎ 509/334-3093. **Richland** ⊠ 815 Jadwin Ave. ☎ 509/943-2044. **Spokane** ⊠ 904 W. Riverside Ave. ☎ 509/252-2337. **Walla Walla** ⊠ 128 N. 2nd Ave. ☎ 509/526-9793.

MONEY MATTERS

ATMs are easy to find in most towns, at banks, grocery stores, shopping centers, and airports. Bank of America, US Bank, and Washington Mutual are among the region's better-known banks. In larger towns many grocery stores have bank branches.
🖪 Banks **Bank of America** ☎ 800/642-9855 ⊕ www.bankofamerica.com. **US Bank** ☎ 800/872-2657 ⊕ www.usbank.com. **Washington Mutual** ☎ 800/756-8000 ⊕ www.wamu.com.

TOURS

Columbia River Journeys conducts cruises on the Snake River and tours through the region's wineries by bus.
🖪 Tour-Operator **Columbia River Journeys** ⊠ 1229 Columbia Park Trail, Richland ☎ 509/734-9941 or 888/486-9119.

TRAIN TRAVEL

Amtrak's *Empire Builder* runs daily between Spokane and Seattle and between Spokane and Portland, stopping at points in between (including Ephrata and Pasco). Reservations are recommended. Round-trip fares vary depending on season; $65 is a typical fare between Seattle and Spokane.
🖪 Train Information **Amtrak** ☎ 800/872-7245 ⊕ www.amtrak.com.

VISITOR INFORMATION

🖪 Tourist Information **Clarkston Chamber of Commerce** ⊠ 502 Bridge St. ☎ 800/933-2128 ⊕ clarkstonchamber.org. **Colville Chamber of Commerce** ⊠ 121 E. Astor Ave. ☎ 509/684-5973 ⊕ www.colville.com. **Ephrata Chamber of Commerce** ⊠ 90 Alder St. ☎ 509/754-4656 ⊕ www.ephratachamber.com. **Grand Coulee Dam Area Chamber of Commerce** ⊠ 306 Midway, Grand Coulee ☎ 800/268-5532 or 509/268-5332

⊕ www.grandcouleedam.org. **Moses Lake Area Chamber of Commerce** ⊠ 324 S. Pioneer Way, Moses Lake ☏ 509/765-7888 or 800/992-6234 ⊕ www.moseslake.com. **Omak Visitor Information Center** ⊠ 401 Omak Ave. ☏ 509/826-4218 or 800/225-6625 ⊕ www.omakchronicle.com//omakvic. **Pullman Chamber of Commerce** ⊠ 415 N. Grande Ave. ☏ 509/334-3565 or 800/365-6948 ⊕ www.pullmanchamber.com. **Ritzville Area Chamber of Commerce** ⊠ 201 W. Railroad Ave. ☏ 509/659-1936 ⊕ www. ritzville.com. **Spokane Area Visitors Information** ⊠ 801 W. Riverside Ave. ☏ 509/624-1341 ⊕ www.visitspokane.com. **Tri-Cities Visitor and Convention Bureau** ⊠ 6951 W. Grandridge Blvd., Kennewick ☏ 800/254-5824 ⊕ www.visittri-cities.com. **Walla Walla Valley Chamber of Commerce** ⊠ 29 E. Sumach St. ☏ 509/525-0850 or 877/998-4748 ⊕ www.wwchamber.com. **West Plains Chamber of Commerce** ⊠ 201 1st St., Cheney 99004 ☏ 509/235-8480 ⊕ westplainschamber.org.

WASHINGTON A TO Z

Updated by
Holly S. Smith

To research prices, get advice from other travelers, and book travel arrangements, visit www.fodors.com.

AIR TRAVEL

AIRPORTS Sea-Tac International Airport, 15 mi south of Seattle, is the state's main gateway. Bellingham International is a hub for northwestern Washington and Canada. Port Angeles's Fairchild International, on the Olympic Peninsula, is a gateway between the United States and Canada via Vancouver Island. Spokane International, 6 mi south of that city, is the main eastern Washington airport. If you're planning to visit the Long Beach Peninsula, Mt. St. Helens National Volcanic Monument, and places near the Columbia River Gorge, you're better off flying into the Portland International Airport in Oregon, 10 mi south of Vancouver, Washington. ⚑ Airport Information **Bellingham International** ☏ 360/671-5674 ⊕ www. portofbellingham.com. **Fairchild International** ⊠ Port Angeles ☏ 360/457-1138 ⊕ www.portofpa.com/airport. **Portland International Airport** ⊠ Portland, OR ☏ 877/ 739-4636 ⊕ www.portlandairportpdx.com. **Seattle-Tacoma International Airport** ⊠ Seattle ☏ 206/431-4444 ⊕ www.seatac.org. **Spokane International Airport** ⊠ Spokane ☏ 509/455-6455 ⊕ www.spokaneairports.net.

BOAT & FERRY TRAVEL

Several ferries carry cars and passengers between ports in Washington and Canada. Washington State Ferries depart for the San Juan Islands and Sidney, British Columbia from Anacortes, about 90 minutes north of Seattle. Bellingham is the southern terminus of the Alaska Marine Highway System, providing vehicle and passenger transportation to Alaska's Inside Passage. Victoria/San Juan Cruises operates passenger-only service between Bellingham and Victoria, British Columbia, from May through October.

You can also reach Victoria, B.C. from the Olympic Peninsula. Hop on the *Victoria Express* passenger ferry, which makes the one-hour trip from Port Angeles ($25) twice daily from mid-May to mid-October. Or take your car on the M.V. *Coho*, operated by Black Ball Transport, which makes the 1½-hour crossing four times daily from mid-May through mid-October and twice daily the rest of the year (except when it's docked for maintenance, from mid-January through mid-March). Rates are $33 per car and driver, $8.50 per passenger, and $3.75 for a bike. The *Victoria Express* departs from the Landing Mall terminal; the *Coho* leaves from the ferry terminal at the foot of Laurel Street.

Cruise ships depart from Seattle. Norwegian Cruise Lines (Bell Street Pier Cruise Terminal at Pier 66), make seven-day Alaska cruises in summer and five-day Los Angeles–Vancouver cruises that stop in Seattle. Both Holland America and Princess Cruises lines make seven-day Alaska trips and dock at the Terminal 30 facility south of Downtown.

🚢 Boat & Ferry Information **Alaska Marine Highway System** ☎ 800/642-0066 ⊕ www.state.ak.us/ferry. **Black Ball Transport** ☎ 360/457-4491 in Port Angeles, 250/386-2202 in Victoria ⊕ www.cohoferry.com. **Port of Seattle** ☎ 800/426-7817 ⊕ www.portseattle.org. ***Victoria Express*** ☎360/452-8088 or 800/633-1589 ⊕www.victoriaexpress.com.**Victoria/San Juan Cruises** ☎ 800/443-4552 ⊕ www.whales.com. **Washington State Ferries** ☎ 206/464-6400 or 888/808-7977 ⊕ www.wsdot.wa.gov/ferries. 🚢 Cruise Lines **Holland America** ☎ 877/932-4259 ⊕ www.hollandamerica.com. **Norwegian Cruise Lines** ☎800/327-7030 ⊕www.norwegiancruiselines.com. **Princess Cruises** ☎ 800/421-1700 ⊕ www.princess.com.

BUS TRAVEL

Greyhound Lines and Northwest Trailways run throughout Washington and the Pacific Northwest. From Seattle, Greyhound serves San Francisco (20–25 hours, $66.75) and Los Angeles (26–29 hours, $86). Fares are slightly less on weekdays than on weekends. Ask about companion rates, advance purchase savings, and seasonal discounts.

🚌 Bus Information **Greyhound Lines** ✉ 811 Stewart St., Seattle ☎ 206/628-5526 or 800/231-2222 ⊕ www.greyhound.com ✉ 221 W. 1st Ave., Spokane ☎ 509/624-5251. **Northwest Trailways** ✉ 811 Stewart St., Seattle ☎ 800/366-3830 ⊕ www.northwesttrailways.com ✉ 221 W. 1st Ave., Spokane ☎ 509/624-5251.

CAR TRAVEL

Interstate 5, the main north–south route through western Washington, runs from the Canadian border through Seattle to Oregon. Interstate 90 meanders east from Seattle through the Cascades to Idaho and Montana. Interstate 82 heads southeast from I–90 near Ellensburg and connects with I–84 in northern Oregon. Route 2 goes east from Everett, traversing the mountains before wending its way to Spokane, where it joins I–90. Route 20 is another beautiful east–west route that cuts through the North Cascades. Route 12 slices east–west through southern Washington, passing Mt. Rainier and then serving as the main Yakima Valley route. Route 101 hugs the Olympic Peninsula and continues down the Pacific coast all the way to Southern California.

EMERGENCY SERVICES
Washington police and state troopers patrol the main highways, and you'll find call boxes, rest areas with phones, or gas stations every few miles. The Washington State Patrol Web site lists the address and phone number of each district office in the state.

🚓 **Washington State Patrol Emergency Hotline** ☎ 911 ⊕ www.wsp.wa.gov.

ROAD CONDITIONS
In-town roads and lesser highways usually have four lanes; interstates have six or eight. Gas is most expensive in Seattle, on the islands, along backroads, and near the Canadian border. Major roads in Washington are well-maintained, but ongoing construction creates delays and detours. Traffic is abominable in Downtown Seattle any time of day; count on weekday traffic jams around Tacoma, Olympia, Puyallup, Everett, Spokane, and the Seattle suburbs. During peak traffic hours take a ferry from Seattle to Port Orchard, Bremerton, or Bainbridge Island to avoid congested Route 16. Note that traffic jams occur near ferry-departure points on weekdays, holidays, and summer weekends.

In winter, snow and ice often close mountain roads and passes. Tire chains, studs, or snow tires are essential during winter; add blankets, shovels, flares, a cell phone, and nourishment if you're going off the main roads. After the first snowfall, Cayuse Pass on Route 123, Chinook Pass on Route 410, and the North Cascades Highway (Route 20 from Newhalem to Mazama) are closed for the winter. Contact the Department of Transportation or AAA highway hotline for weather updates.

📆 **AAA Highway Hotline** ☎ 206/646-2190. **Mountain Pass Report** ☎ 206/368-4499 or 888/766-4636 ⊕ www.traffic.wsdot.wa.gov/sno-info. **Washington State Department of Transportation** ☎ 360/705-7000 ⊕ www.wsdot.wa.gov.

RULES OF THE ROAD   Right turns on red are permitted unless otherwise indicated. Seat belts are mandatory for drivers and passengers. Children under age 4 and/or 40 pounds must be strapped into approved safety seats; children over these limits but under age 8 and 80 pounds need an approved booster seat. Motorcyclists *and* bicyclists must wear helmets.

The speed limit on most highways is 55 mph. State troopers make their presence felt along the interstates and rural roads, with even greater numbers patrolling on holiday weekends and during late hours.

📆 **Traffic Safety Commission** ☎ 360/753-6197.

EMERGENCIES

The Coast Guard provides boating safety advice and emergency services for vessels. Use VHF-FM radio, Channel 16 (156.8 MHz) if you have an emergency.

📆 Emergency Services **Coast Guard** ☎ 800/992-8813. **General Emergency Number** ☎ 911.

MEDIA

NEWSPAPERS & MAGAZINES   Seattle has two daily morning newspapers, the *Seattle Post-Intelligencer* and *Seattle Times. The Tacoma Tribune* and the *Olympian* cover the South Sound. In eastern Washington, the *Spokane Valley News Herald* and the *Yakima Herald* are the major regional papers. Two glossy magazines, *Seattle* and *Northwest Life,* have in-depth articles about Washington people, places, and events.

RADIO & TELEVISION   Throughout Puget Sound, KUOW (94.9 FM) and KPLU (88.5 FM) are the National Public Radio affiliates. Other FM stations include KMPS (94.1), country; KING (98.1), classical; KEZX (98.9), smooth jazz; KZOK (102.5), classic rock; KCMS (105.3), Christian pop; and KNDD (107.7), modern alternative rock. AM stations KIRO (710), KNWX (770), and KOMO (1000) are all news, talk, and traffic. Around Spokane, turn to KAGU (88.7 FM) for classical music, KEZE (96.9 FM) for '80s hits, KISC (98.1 FM) and KZZU (92.9 FM) for Top 40 hits, and KGA (1510 AM) for news and talk radio.

SPORTS & THE OUTDOORS

Contact the Washington State Parks Department or the National Parks Service for information about camping, boating, and mountain activities.

📆 **National Parks Service** ☎ 206/470-4060. **Washington State Parks Department** ☎ 360/586-6645 for winter sports, 360/586-6590 for boating information, 888/226-7688 for tent camping and RV details.

BICYCLING & HORSEBACK RIDING   Seattle-based Cascade Bicycle Club makes trips throughout the state. Backcountry Bicycle Trails Club leads state-wide trips and races. The Backcountry Horsemen of Washington has information on horseback trails throughout the state.

📆 Bicycling & Riding Contacts **Backcountry Bicycle Trails** ☎ 206/283-2995 ⊕ www.bbtc.org. **Backcountry Horsemen** ✉ 5747 78th Ave. NE, Olympia 98516 ☎ 360/956-0928 ⊕ www.bchw.org. **Cascade Bicycle Club** ✉ 7400 Sand Point Way NE, Bldg. 138, Seattle 98115 ☎ 206/522-3222 ⊕ www.cascade.org.

CLIMBING   The Seattle Mountaineers Club is a statewide organization for outdoor adventures. REI leads classes and trips around the state. Boeing Alpine

Society, a climbing club, leads backpacking and mountain adventure activities. Contact the folks at Rainier Mountaineering, Inc., at the base of Mt. Rainier, before climbing to the peak.

Rockclimbers can practice at Vertical World gyms around Puget Sound, then put their skills to use on climbs recommended in the Inland Northwest Rockclimb—a guide to more than 600 climbing routes in eastern Washington. The Cascade Orienteering Club can help you navigate the Washington wilderness.

🗂 Climbing Contacts **Boeing Alpine Society** ⊕ www.boealps.org. **Cascade Orienteering Club** ✉ 10559 41st Pl. NE, Seattle 98125 ☎ 206/399-1724 ⊕ www.cascadeoc. org. **Inland Northwest Rockclimb** ⊕ www.inlandnwclimb.com. **REI** ☎ 800/426-4840 ⊕ www.rei.com. **Rainier Mountaineering, Inc.** ☎ 888/892-5462 ⊕ www.rmiguides. com. **Seattle Mountaineers Club** ✉ 300 W. 3rd Ave., Seattle 98119 ☎ 206/284-8484 ⊕ www.mountaineers.org. **Vertical World** ✉ 2123 W. Elmore St., Seattle 98199 ☎ 206/ 283-4497 ⊕ www.verticalworld.com.

SNOWMOBILING The Washington State Snowmobile Association can hook you up with events in various communities.

🗂 Snowmobile Contact **Washington State Snowmobile Association** ☎ 800/783-WSSA ⊕ www.wssaonline.com.

WATER SPORTS Contact top-rated Adventure Raft Company about white-water trips and the Washington Kayak Club about kayak outings. The 5th Dimension Dive Club conducts scuba classes, rents gear, and arranges cold-water trips throughout the state; the Washington Scuba Alliance is another information source for divers. The Washington Fly Fishing Club is a good resource for trips to Washington rivers. For more information on fishing in general, contact the Department of Fish and Wildlife.

🗂 **Adventure Raft Company** ☎ 360/757-4212 ⊕ www.raftarc.com. **Department of Fish and Wildlife** ☎ 360/902-2700. **5th Dimension** ✉ Gilman Village, 375 NW Gilman Rd., Issaquah 98027 ☎ 425/427-1282 ⊕ www.islanddive.com. **Washington Fly Fishing Club** ✉ Garfield High School, 23rd Ave. and Cherry St., Seattle 98122 ☎ 206/938-3300 ⊕ www.wffc.com. **Washington Kayak Club** ☎ 206/433-1983 ⊕ www. washingtonkayakclub.org. **Washington Scuba Alliance** ✉ 120 State Ave., #18, Olympia 98501 ☎ 206/463-2497.

TOURS

Carlson Wagon-Lit is an excellent travel agency with branches throughout the state. Doug Fox Travel is in Seattle, Olympia, and other major cities. Susan Parr Travel runs tours from Port Angeles. Cascade Travel is based in Wenatchee. American Express has a travel office in Spokane.

Deli Llama High Country Adventure organizes trekking adventures with pack llamas on the Olympic Peninsula and the North Cascades. Hesselgrave International operates a variety of tours and trips in the Northwest. San Juan Islands Shuttle Express operates whale-watching trips. Victoria San Juan Cruises operates all-day nature cruises through the San Juan Islands to Victoria. Western Prince Cruises charters boats for half-day whale-watching cruises during summer; in spring and fall, bird-watching and scuba-diving tours are offered.

🗂 **Carlson Wagon-Lit** ✉ 207 N. Washington St., Spokane 99201 ☎ 509/455-4523 ✉ 2631 12th Ct. SW, Olympia 98502 ☎ 360/943-0711 ✉ 1201 Pacific Ave., Tacoma 98402 ☎ 253/ 383-8000. **Cascade Travel** ✉ 127½ Methow St., Wenatchee 98801 ☎ 509/662-7775. **Deli Llamas** ✉ 17045 Llama La., Bow 98232 ☎ 360/757-4212. **Doug Fox Travel** ✉ 310 Capital Mall, Olympia 98501 ☎ 360/943-6666. **Hesselgrave International** ✉ 1268 Mt. Baker Hwy., Bellingham 98228 ☎ 360/734-3570. **San Juan Islands Shuttle Express** ✉ Alaska Ferry Terminal, 355 Harris Ave., Bellingham 98225 ☎ 360/671-1137. **Susan Parr Travel** ✉ 1234 E. Front St., Port Angeles 98362 ☎ 360/452-2188 or 800/455-7177

⊕ www.susanparrtravel.com. **Victoria San Juan Cruises** ⊠ Alaska Ferry Terminal, 355 Harris Ave., Bellingham 98225 ☎ 800/443-4552. **Western Prince Cruises** ⊠ Friday Harbor, San Juan Island 98250 ☎ 360/378-5315.

TRAIN TRAVEL
Amtrak's *Empire Builder* runs daily between Seattle and Chicago, stopping in Spokane. The scenic *Coast Starlight* runs daily along the Pacific Ocean between Seattle and San Francisco, stopping in Tacoma, Olympia, and Portland. The *Mt. Baker International* is another beautiful coastal route run daily from Seattle to Vancouver. Regular and business-class cars are available, as are private bedrooms for multiday trips. Custom Class cars have free snacks and extra legroom. Reservations are necessary, major credit cards are accepted, and deep discounts are often available.

🚆 Train Information **Amtrak** ⊠ King St. Station, 303 S. Jackson St., International District, Seattle ☎ 206/382-4125 or 800/872-7245 ⊕ www.amtrak.com.

VISITOR INFORMATION
🚆 Tourist Information **Washington Tourism Development Division** ☎ 360/725-5050 ⊕ www.tourism.wa.gov.

VANCOUVER & VICTORIA

INCLUDING VANCOUVER ISLAND & SOUTHERN BRITISH COLUMBIA

5

FODOR'S CHOICE

C Restaurant, *Downtown Vancouver*

Dr. Sun Yat-Sen Garden, *Chinatown, Vancouver*

Fairmont Château Whistler Resort, *Whistler*

Granville Island Public Market, *Granville Island, Vancouver*

Hastings House, *hotel on Salt Spring Island*

Liliget Feast House, *Native American restaurant in Vancouver*

Mahle House, *contemporary restaurant in Nanaimo*

Pacific Rim National Park Reserve

Pan Pacific Hotel, *Downtown Vancouver*

Royal British Columbia Museum, *Downtown Victoria*

Sooke Harbour House, *hotel in Sooke*

Stanley Park, *Vancouver*

The Wickaninnish Inn, *hotel in Tofino*

Updated by
Sue Kernaghan

MOST OF BRITISH COLUMBIA'S POPULATION CLUSTERS in two coastal cities. Vancouver is an international city whose relaxed lifestyle is spiced by a varied cultural scene embracing large ethnic communities. Victoria, the provincial capital on Vancouver Island, is a smaller, more subdued town of 19th-century brick and well-tended gardens. Rich cultural sights and excellent restaurants fill both cities, making a welcome stop to complement your Pacific Northwest adventure. If you want to experience some of British Columbia's natural beauty, add a side trip to one or two of the nearby destinations on Vancouver Island and Southern British Columbia.

About the Restaurants

A diverse gastronomic experience awaits you in Vancouver. A wave of Asian immigration and tourism has brought a proliferation of upscale Asian eateries. Cutting-edge restaurants currently perfecting and defining Pacific Northwest fare—including such homegrown regional favorites as salmon and oysters, accompanied by British Columbia wines—have become some of the city's leading attractions. In Victoria, "fresh, local, organic" has become a mantra for many chefs. Wild salmon, locally made cheeses, Pacific oysters, forest-foraged mushrooms, organic vegetables in season, local microbrews, and even wines from Vancouver Island's few family-run wineries can all be sampled here. Although Vancouver and Victoria have British Columbia's most varied and cosmopolitan cuisine, smaller communities, particularly Whistler, and several fine inns have defined an excellence in local cuisine. Regional fare includes seafood, lamb, organic produce, and increasingly good wine.

Dining is fairly informal. Casual but neat dress is appropriate everywhere. A 15% tip is expected. Smoking is banned in nearly all public places, including restaurants and bars.

About the Hotels

Accommodations in Vancouver and Victoria range from luxurious waterfront hotels to neighborhood bed-and-breakfasts and basic European-style pensions. Many of the best choices are in the downtown core, either in the central business district or in the West End near Stanley Park. Victoria in particular has a great selection of English-style B&Bs. Accommodations on Vancouver Island and Southern British Columbia range from bed-and-breakfasts and country inns to rustic cabins and deluxe chain hotels.

Most small inns and B&Bs on the island ban smoking indoors, and virtually all hotels in the area have no-smoking rooms. Most accommodations in the region lack air-conditioning, as it rarely gets hot enough to need it. Advance reservations are always a good idea, especially in July and August, and in some of the more isolated towns.

WHAT IT COSTS in Canadian dollars				
	$$$$	$$$	$$	$	¢
RESTAURANTS	over $30	$20–$30	$12–$20	$8–$12	under $8
HOTELS	over $250	$175–$250	$125–$175	$75–$125	under $75

Restaurant prices are for a main course at dinner, not including 7% GST and 10% liquor tax. Hotel prices are for two people in a standard double room in high season, excluding 10% provincial accommodation tax, service charge, and 7% GST.

If you have 1 to 3 days For a short trip, Vancouver is a fine place to begin. There's plenty to explore, from Stanley Park and Granville Island to museums and attractions downtown. Spend some time meandering through the trendy shops on Robson Street and taking in the eclectic dining scene. On Day 3, take the ferry to Victoria. Here, you can explore the flower-fringed Inner Harbour and the museums and attractions nearby to Market Square and the shops and restaurants of Chinatown. If you want to extend your stay, stay overnight and spend a day in world-famous Butchart Gardens, only half an hour away by car.

If you have 4 to 6 days A brief stay in Vancouver can be followed by a tour of Victoria. Follow the itinerary above, heading to Sooke on day 4. Day 5 allows time to see the Quw'utsun' Cultural and Conference Centre in Duncanand the murals and restored Victorian buildings of Chemainus. On Day 6, one alternative is to trek across the island to the scenic west coast to visit Ucluelet and Tofino(pick one for your overnight) and spend some time whale-watching or hiking around Pacific Rim National Park Reserve.

VANCOUVER

By Sue Kernaghan

Vancouver is a young city, even by North American standards. Founded in 1886, it was not yet a town in 1871, when British Columbia became part of the Canadian confederation. Still, Vancouver's history, such as it is, remains visible to the naked eye: eras are stacked east to west along the waterfront like some century-old archaeological dig—from cobblestone late-Victorian Gastown to shiny postmodern glass cathedrals of commerce.

Today, Vancouver has a cosmopolitan population of about 2 million. The mild climate, exquisite natural scenery, and relaxed outdoor lifestyle continually attract new residents, and the number of visitors is increasing for the same reasons. People often get their first glimpse of Vancouver when catching an Alaskan cruise, and many return at some point to spend more time here.

Exploring Vancouver

There is much to see and do in Vancouver, but when time is limited (as it usually is for cruise-ship passengers), the most popular options are a walking tour of Gastown and Chinatown, a visit to Granville Island, and a driving or biking tour of Stanley Park, one of two 1,000-acre wilderness parks within the city limits (the other, Pacific Spirit Park, lies near the University of British Columbia). The heart of Vancouver—which includes the downtown area, Stanley Park, and the West End high-rise residential neighborhood—sits on this peninsula hemmed in by English Bay and the Pacific Ocean to the west; by False Creek, the inlet home to Granville Island, to the south; and by Burrard Inlet, the working port of the city, to the north, past which loom the North Shore mountains.

Numbers in the text correspond to numbers in the margin and on the Downtown Vancouver, Stanley Park, and Granville Island maps.

Downtown Vancouver & Gastown

Most cruise ships visiting Vancouver dock at **Canada Place ❶** ▶, where you can stroll around the cruise-ship-style decks for great ocean and mountain views or catch a film at the IMAX theater. Across Canada Place Way (next to the Fairmont Waterfront Hotel) you'll find the Vancouver Tourist InfoCentre. A short stroll up Howe Street will take you to **Sinclair Centre ❷**, a magnificently restored complex of government buildings that houses offices and retail shops. If you go to Sinclair Centre's upper mall level and leave by the Granville Street exit, you'll come out onto a pedestrian overpass. A left turn will take you to Granville Square, which has great views of the Coast Mountains and Vancouver's working harbor. The redbrick building behind you is **Waterfront Station ❸**, Vancouver's original train terminal. You can enter the station from Granville Square and leave by the main, Cordova Street exit. Across Cordova, between Seymour and Richards streets, is the entrance to the **Vancouver Lookout! Harbour Centre Tower ❹**, where you can take in panoramic views of the city.

From the lookout, return to Cordova Street and continue east along Water Street into Gastown. Named for saloon keeper "Gassy" Jack Deighton, this is Vancouver's oldest neighborhood. The first stop, at the corner of Water and Richards streets, is the **Landing,** a 1905 warehouse that now houses shops and a brewpub. At the window at the rear of the lobby, you can take in scenic views of Burrard Inlet and the North Shore mountains. A block east, at the corner of Water and Cambie streets, you can see and hear the world's first **steam clock ❺** (it chimes on the quarter hour). Just past the steam clock is the entrance to **Storyeum ❻**, a multimedia historical attraction set to open in 2004. About 1½ blocks east, you'll pass **Gaoler's Mews ❼**, a courtyard tucked behind 12 Water Street.

Next to Gaoler's Mews at the corner of Water and Carrall streets is the Byrnes Block. Vancouver's oldest brick building, it was built on the site of Gassy Jack Deighton's second saloon after the 1886 Great Fire, which wiped out most of the fledgling settlement of Vancouver. At Powell and Alexander streets is the Hotel Europe, Vancouver's first reinforced concrete structure. Once billed as the best hotel in the city, this 1908 flatiron building is one of the world's best examples of this style of triangular architecture. The glass tiles in the sidewalk on Alexander Street once provided light for an underground saloon. A statue of Gassy Jack stands on the west side of Maple Tree Square, at the intersection of Water, Powell, Alexander, and Carrall streets, where he built his first saloon.

TIMING The walk itself will take less than half an hour each way; allow about 30 minutes for the Vancouver Lookout and at least 90 minutes for Storyeum. Note that the area just to the south of Gastown (roughly east of Cambie and south of Cordova) is one of Vancouver's roughest neighborhoods. Although Gastown itself (along Water Street) is busy with tourists and quite safe during the day, you may want to avoid walking through the area after dark.

What to See

▶ ❶ **Canada Place.** When Vancouver hosted the Expo '86 world's fair, this former cargo pier was transformed into the Canadian pavilion. The complex, which now encompasses the luxurious **Pan Pacific Hotel,** the **Vancouver Convention and Exhibition Centre,** the **World Trade Centre,** and the city's main cruise-ship terminal, mimics the style and size of a luxury ocean liner. You can stroll its exterior promenade and admire views of Burrard Inlet, Stanley Park, and the North Shore mountains. The **CN IMAX Theatre** (☎ 604/682–4629 ✉ C$11) shows films on a five-story-high screen. The roof, shaped like five sails, has become a Van-

5

First Nations Culture

Interest in the British Columbia's Native culture is enjoying a renaissance. First Nations groups such as the Kwakwaka'wakw, Haida, Nisga'a and Coast Salish have occupied the land for some 12,000 years, and you can see their rich heritage throughout the region in art galleries, restaurants, and cultural centers as well as at ceremonial potlances and in re-created villages. Northern B.C. and the Queen Charlotte Islands have the best examples, including totems, ancient villages, and museum collections of some of the province's finest First Nations artifacts.

The Great Outdoors

Nature has truly blessed Vancouver and Victoria, surrounding it with verdant forests, towering mountains, coves, inlets, rivers, and the wide sea. Diving, biking, hiking, skiing, snowboarding, and sailing are among the many outdoor activities possible in or near the city. Whether you prefer to relax on a beach by yourself or join a kayaking tour with an outfitter, Vancouver and Victoria have plenty to offer.

Skiing & Snowboarding

With more than half the province higher than 4,200 feet above sea level, more than 60 resorts have downhill skiing and snowboarding facilities. Most of them also offer groomed cross-country (Nordic) ski trails, and many of the provincial parks have cross-country trails as well. The resorts are easy to get to, as several have shuttles from the nearest airport.

Whale-Watching

About 200 resident and nearly as many transient orcas, or killer whales, as well as humpback whales, minke whales, and other marine mammals travel the island's eastern coastal waters. These, and the gray whales that migrate along the west coast, are the primary focus of the many whale-watching boat tours leaving Victoria, Campbell River, Telegraph Cove, Ucluelet, Bamfield, and Tofino in spring and summer months. July, August, and September are the best months to see orcas; in March and April thousands of migrating gray whales pass close to the west coast of Vancouver Island on their way from Baja California to Alaska. Harbor seals, sea lions, porpoises, and marine-bird sightings are a safe bet anytime.

---

couver skyline landmark. ✉ *999 Canada Place Way, Downtown* ☎ *604/ 647–7390 or 604/775–7200* ⊕ *www.canadaplace.ca.*

❼ Gaoler's Mews. The brick-paved courtyard and the mews leading off it resemble a hidden slice of Victorian England. Once the site of the city's first civic buildings—the constable's cabin, customhouse, and a two-cell log jail—the mews today are home to architectural offices, two courtyard cafés, and an Irish pub. ✉ *Behind 12 Water St., Gastown.*

❷ Sinclair Centre. Vancouver architect Richard Henriquez knitted four government office buildings into Sinclair Centre, an office-retail complex that takes up an entire city block between Cordova and Hastings, Howe and Granville streets. Inside are designer clothing shops, federal government offices, and fast-food outlets. The two Hastings Street buildings—the 1910 **Post Office,** which has an elegant clock tower, and the 1911 **Winch Building**—are linked with the 1937 **Post Office Extension**

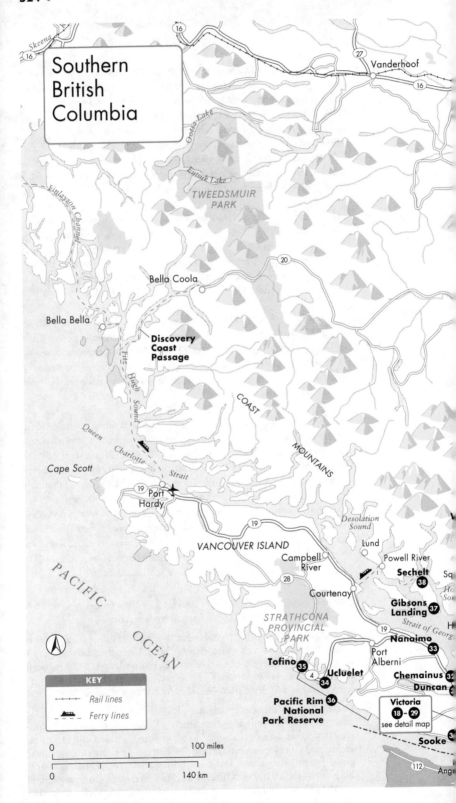

Southern
British
Columbia

Vanderhoof

Bella Coola

Bella Bella

**Discovery
Coast
Passage**

Cape Scott

TWEEDSMUIR
PARK

COAST

MOUNTAINS

Desolation
Sound

Lund

Powell River

Sechelt
38

Port
Hardy

VANCOUVER ISLAND

Campbell
River

Courtenay

STRATHCONA
PROVINCIAL
PARK

**Gibsons
Landing**
37

Nanaimo
33

Port
Alberni

Tofino **35**

Chemainus
Duncan

Ulcuelet
34

Victoria
18-**29**
see detail map

PACIFIC

OCEAN

**Pacific Rim
National
Park Reserve**
36

Sooke

KEY

Rail lines

Ferry lines

0   100 miles

0   140 km

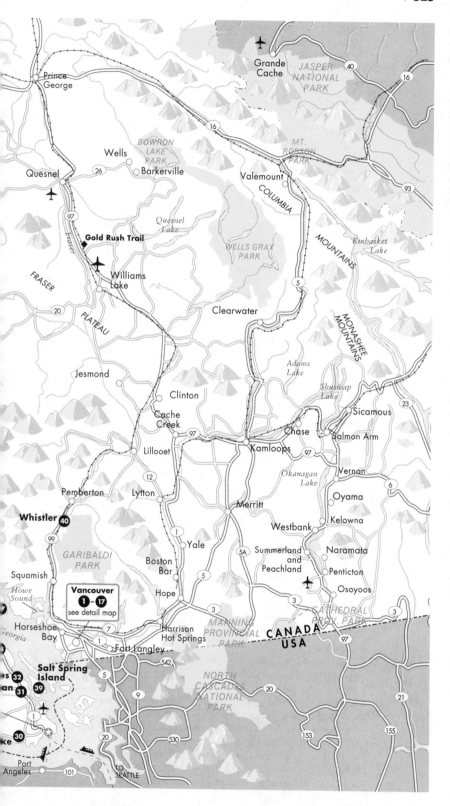

and the 1913 **Customs Examining Warehouse** to the north. In 1986 a meticulous restoration involved moving the post office facade to the Granville Street side of the complex. The original clockwork from the old clock tower is now on display inside on the upper level of the arcade. ⊠ *757 W. Hastings St., Downtown.*

❺ **Steam clock.** The world's first steam clock, built by Ray Saunders of **Landmark Clocks** (⊠ 123 Cambie St., Gastown ☎ 604/669–3525), is powered by the same underground steam system that heats many Vancouver buildings. On the quarter hour a whistle blows; on the hour a huge cloud of steam spews from the clock. ⊠ *Corner of Cambie and Water Sts., Gastown.*

❻ **Storyeum.** Set to open in spring 2004, this major new attraction will bring western Canada's history to life through multimedia presentations, live theater, and life-size sets. At this writing, the 75- to 80-minute walk-through was slated to start with a two-story descent in a massive cylindrical elevator. Visitors will then move through an interpretation of an aboriginal creation myth; a look at First Nations culture at its artistic peak; and performances about the fur trade, the gold rush, the coming of the railway, and modern-day immigration. Book ahead, as numbers are limited for each show. ⊠ *142 Water St., Gastown* ☎ *888/786–7938* ⊕ *www.storyeum.com* 🖃 *May–Oct. C$22, Nov.–Apr. C$20* ☉ *May–Oct., daily 9–7, tours every ½ hr; Nov.–Apr., daily 10–6, tours every hr.*

❹ **Vancouver Lookout! Harbour Centre Tower.** The lookout looks like a flying saucer stuck atop a high-rise. At 553 feet high, it affords one of the best views of Vancouver. A glass elevator whizzes you up 50 stories to the circular observation deck, where knowledgeable guides point out the sights and give a tour every hour on the hour. On a clear day you can see Vancouver Island and Mount Baker in Washington State. The top-floor restaurant makes one complete revolution per hour; the elevator ride up is free for diners. Tickets are good all day, so you can visit in daytime and return for another look after dark. ⊠ *555 W. Hastings St., Downtown* ☎ *604/689–0421* ⊕ *www.vancouverlookout.com* 🖃 *C$10* ☉ *May–mid-Oct., daily 8:30 AM–10:30 PM; mid-Oct.–Apr., daily 9–9.*

❸ **Waterfront Station.** This former Canadian Pacific Railway passenger terminal was built between 1912 and 1914 as the western terminus for Canada's transcontinental railway. After Canada's railways merged, the station became obsolete, but a 1978 renovation transformed it into an office-retail complex and depot for SkyTrain, SeaBus, and West Coast Express passengers. In the main concourse, panels near the ceiling depict the scenery travelers once saw on journeys across Canada. Here you can catch a 13-minute SeaBus trip across the harbor to the waterfront public market at Lonsdale Quay in North Vancouver. ⊠ *601 W. Cordova St., Downtown* ☎ *604/953–3333 SeaBus and SkyTrain, 604/683–7245 West Coast Express.*

Chinatown

a good
walk

Vancouver's Chinatown, declared a historic district in 1971, is one of the oldest and largest such areas in North America. Chinese immigrants were among the first to recognize the possibilities of Vancouver's setting and have played an important role here since the 18th century. Many came to British Columbia during the 1850s seeking their fortunes in the Cariboo gold rush. Thousands more arrived in the 1880s, recruited as laborers to build the Canadian Pacific Railway. Though much of Vancouver's Chinese community has now moved to suburban Richmond, Chinatown is still a vital neighborhood. The style of architecture in Vancouver's Chinatown is patterned on that of Guangzhou (Canton).

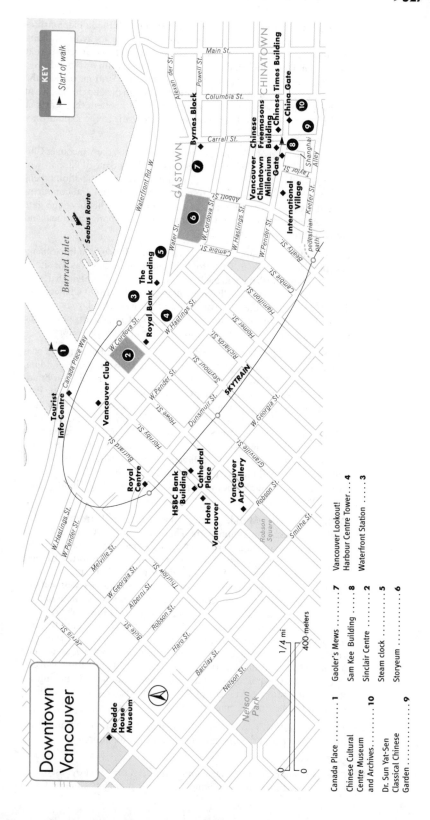

Downtown Vancouver

KEY

▲ Start of walk

Burrard Inlet

Seabus Route

Tourist Info Centre

Canada Place Way

Vancouver Club

Royal Bank

The Landing

GASTOWN

Byrnes Block

Gaoler's Mews

CHINATOWN

Chinese Freemasons Building

Chinese Times Building

China Gate

Vancouver Chinatown Millenium Gate

Sam Kee Building

International Village

Shanghai Alley

pedestrian path

Main St.

Alexander St.

Powell St.

Columbia St.

Carrall St.

Abbott St.

Cambie St.

Water St.

W. Cordova St.

W. Hastings St.

W. Pender St.

Keefer St.

Taylor St.

Beatty St.

Hamilton St.

Homer St.

Richards St.

Seymour St.

Dunsmuir St.

SKYTRAIN

W. Georgia St.

Waterfront Rd. W.

W. Cordova St.

W. Hastings St.

W. Pender St.

Howe St.

Hornby St.

Burrard St.

Royal Centre

HSBC Bank Building

Cathedral Place

Hotel Vancouver

Vancouver Art Gallery

Robson Square

Granville St.

Robson St.

Smithe St.

W. Georgia St.

Melville St.

W. Hastings St.

W. Pender St.

Thurlow St.

Bute St.

Jervis St.

Alberni St.

Robson St.

Haro St.

Barclay St.

Nelson St.

Nelson Park

Roedde House Museum

0 ——— 1/4 mi
0 ——— 400 meters

Canada Place 1
Chinese Cultural Centre Museum and Archives 10
Dr. Sun Yat-Sen Classical Chinese Garden 9
Gaoler's Mews 7
Sam Kee Building 8
Sinclair Centre 2
Steam clock 5
Storyeum 6
Vancouver Lookout! 1
Harbour Centre Tower . . . 4
Waterfront Station 3

Although Chinatown is less than a mile from the Canada Place cruise-ship terminal, it's best to get there by cab or bus to avoid walking through the city's rough skid-row neighborhood. You can get a taxi at the stand in front of Canada Place, catch a No. 3 Main or No. 8 Fraser bus from Cordova and Seymour near Waterfront Station, or take the SkyTrain to Stadium station. Alternatively, you can pick up the Silk Road Walking Tour, a self-guided route marked with banners that starts at the Vancouver Public Library downtown and leads to the main attractions in Chinatown.

At the intersection of West Pender and Taylor streets, the Vancouver Chinatown Millennium Gate marks the western boundary of Chinatown. This four-pillar, three-story-high, brightly painted arch spanning Pender Street was erected in 2002 to mark the millennium and commemorate the Chinese community's role in Vancouver's history. The gate incorporates both Eastern and Western symbols and both traditional and modern Chinese themes.

Just east of the Millennium Gate, a right turn will take you into Shanghai Alley. Also known as Chinatown Heritage Alley, this was the site of the first Chinese settlement in the Vancouver area. By 1890, Shanghai Alley and neighboring Canton Alley were home to about 1,000 Chinese residents. At the end of the alley is a replica of the West Han Dynasty Bell, a gift to Vancouver from the city of Guangzhou, China. Surrounding the bell are a series of panels relaying some of the area's early history.

If you return to Pender Street and turn right, the first building you pass is the **Sam Kee Building** ❽ ▶, the world's narrowest office building. Across Pender at 3 West Pender Street is the Chinese Freemasons Building, notable for its two completely different facades. The side facing Pender represents a fine example of Cantonese recessed balconies. The Carrall Street side displays the Victorian style common throughout the British Empire. Dr. Sun Yat-Sen hid for months in this building from agents of the Manchu dynasty while he raised funds for its overthrow, which he accomplished in 1911. Directly across Carrall Street is the 1902 Chinese Times Building, at 1 East Pender, where in the early 20th century illicit mah-jongg games were played in the building's hidden mezzanine floor.

On the south side of Pender Street, just east of Carrall Street, is another brightly painted, four-column gate. This one, called the China Gate, was built by a group of Beijing artisans for the Chinese Pavilion at Expo '86; the gate (and some dragons) now guards the entrance to the Chinese Cultural Centre complex. Step through the gate and into the courtyard behind. To your right is the entrance to the **Dr. Sun Yat-Sen Classical Chinese Garden** ❾, the first authentic classical Chinese garden built outside China. Straight ahead is the entrance to Dr. Sun Yat-Sen Park, a free public park also built in a classical Chinese style. A short path through the park will take you out to Columbia Street, where, to your left, you'll find the entrance to the **Chinese Cultural Centre Museum and Archives** ❿, a museum and art gallery celebrating Chinese-Canadian culture. Finish up by poking around in the open-front markets and import shops that line several blocks of Pender and Keefer streets (one block south of Pender Street), running east.

TIMING   The walk itself will take about 20 minutes. Allow about an hour each for the garden and the museum and extra time for shopping.

What to See

❿ **Chinese Cultural Centre Museum and Archives.** This Ming dynasty–style facility is dedicated to promoting an understanding of Chinese-Canadian history and culture. The art gallery on the first floor hosts traveling exhibits by Chinese and Canadian artists. A compelling permanent exhibit traces the history of Chinese Canadians in British Columbia. A Chinese-Canadian military museum is also on-site. ⊠ *555 Columbia St., Chinatown* ☎ *604/658–8880* ⊕ *www.cccvan.com* ⊠ *C$4, free Tues.* ⊙ *Tues.–Sun. 11–5.*

❾ Dr. Sun Yat-Sen Classical Chinese Garden. The first authentic Ming dynasty–style garden constructed outside of China, this garden was built in 1986 by 52 artisans from Suzhou, China. It incorporates design elements and traditional materials from several of Suzhou's centuries-old private gardens. As you walk along the paths, remember that no power tools, screws, or nails were used in the construction. Guided tours, which are helpful in understanding the symbolism involved in the garden, are included in the price of admission. They're conducted on the hour between mid-June and the end of August (call for times the rest of the year). A concert series, including classical, Asian, world, jazz, and sacred music, plays on Friday evenings in July and August. The free public Dr. Sun Yat-Sen Park, next door, is also in the style of a traditional Chinese garden. ⊠ *578 Carrall St., Chinatown* ☎ *604/662–3207* ⊕ *www. vancouverchinesegarden.com* ⊠*C$8.25* ⊙ *May–mid-June and Sept., daily 10–6; mid-June–Aug., daily 9:30–7; Oct.–Apr., Tues.–Sun. 10–4:30.*

Fodor's Choice
★

▶ **❽ Sam Kee Building.** *Ripley's Believe It or Not!* recognizes this structure, dating from about 1913, as the narrowest office building in the world. In 1913, when the city confiscated most of merchant Chang Toy's land to widen Pender Street, he built in protest on what he had left—just 6 feet. These days the building houses an insurance agency whose employees make do with the 4-foot-10-inch-wide interior. ⊠ *8 W. Pender St., Chinatown.*

Stanley Park

a good tour

A morning or afternoon in Stanley Park gives you a capsule tour of Vancouver that includes beaches, the ocean, Douglas fir and cedar forests, and a view of the North Shore mountains. One of the most popular ways to see the park is to walk, rollerblade, or cycle along Vancouver's famous Seawall Walk, a 9-km (5½-mi) seaside pathway around the park's circumference. The seawall extends an additional mile to just west of the cruise-ship terminal at **Canada Place,** so you can start your ride from there. Alternatively, rent a bike on Denman Street near the park entrance and start your ride at the foot of Alberni Street next to Lost Lagoon. Go through the underpass, veer right, and follow the cycle-path markings to the seawall. Cyclists must ride in a counterclockwise direction, wear a helmet, and stay on their side of the path.

Fodor's Choice
★

It's also possible to see the park by car, entering at the foot of Georgia Street and driving counterclockwise around the one-way Stanley Park Drive. An even better option is to take the free Stanley Park Shuttle, which provides frequent transportation between the park entrance and all the major sights daily from mid-June to mid-September. To get to the park by transit, take any bus marked Stanley Park from the corner of Pender and Granville, downtown. Another option is the Stanley Park Horse-Drawn Tours (⇨ Tours *in* Vancouver and Victoria A to Z), which includes a free bus ride from the Canada Place cruise-ship terminal to Stanley Park.

Whether you're driving, cycling, or rollerblading, the first sight you'll pass on your right is the Tudor-style Vancouver Rowing Club, a private athletic club established in 1903. Watch for the information booth on the left, and the turnoff to the renowned **Vancouver Aquarium Marine Sci-**

ence Centre ⑪ ▸, the **Miniature Railway and Children's Farmyard** ⑫, and Painters' Corner, where artists sell their work. Also near the information booth, a salmon demonstration stream has information about the life cycle of this important resource. As you continue along the main road or the seawall, the next thing you'll pass is the Royal Vancouver Yacht Club. About ½ km (¼ mi) farther is the causeway to Deadman's Island, a former burial ground for the local Salish people and now a small naval training base that is not open to the public. The site of the **totem poles** ⑬, a bit farther down the road and on your left, is a popular photo stop. Ahead at the water's edge, just past the sign for Hallelujah Point, is the Nine O'Clock Gun. This cannon, originally intended to alert fishermen to the close of the day's fishing, has been fired at the stroke of nine almost every night since 1894. To the north is Brockton Point and its small lighthouse and foghorn.

Inland on your left is Brockton Oval, where you can catch a rugby game in winter or a cricket match in summer. Next, on the water side, watch for the *Girl in a Wetsuit*, a sculpture on a rock just offshore that resembles Copenhagen's *Little Mermaid*. A little farther along the seashore is a replica of the dragon-shape figurehead from the SS *Empress of Japan,* which plied these waters between 1891 and 1922.

At Km 3 (Mi 2) is Lumberman's Arch, a log archway dedicated to workers in Vancouver's first industry. The Children's Water Park across the road is also popular throughout the summer. About 2 km (1 mi) farther is the Lions Gate Bridge—the halfway point of the seawall. Just past the bridge is Prospect Point, at 211 feet the highest point in the park. The top has breathtaking views of the North Shore and Burrard Inlet as well as a snack bar, restaurant, and gift shop. From the seawall you can see where cormorants nest in the cliffs. Continuing around the seawall or the drive, you'll come to the English Bay side and the beginning of sandy beaches. The imposing rock just offshore is **Siwash Rock** ⑭, the focus of a native legend. If you're driving, watch for a sign for the Hollow Tree. This 56-foot-wide stump gives an idea of how large some of the old-growth trees were. Continue along to reach the swimming area and snack bar at Third Beach.

The road and the seawall pass the large, heated pool at **Second Beach** ⑮. If you're walking or cycling, you can take a shortcut from here back to Lost Lagoon by taking the pathway behind the pool that cuts into the park. Either of the footbridges ahead leads to a path along the south side of the lagoon that takes you back to your starting point at the foot of Alberni or Georgia Street. If you continue along the seawall from Second Beach, you will emerge from the park into a high-rise residential neighborhood, the West End. Here are plenty of places to stop for coffee, ice cream, or a drink along Denman, Davie, or Robson streets.

TIMING A driving tour, with time out for stops and photos, will take about an hour. You'll find pay parking lots near most of the sights in the park; a C$4 ticket (C$3 between October and March) allows you to park all day and to move between lots. A biking tour will take several hours. Add at least two hours to tour the aquarium thoroughly, and you've filled a half- to full-day tour.

What to See

🕑 ⑫ **Miniature Railway and Children's Farmyard.** A child-size steam train takes youngsters and adults on a ride through the woods of Stanley Park. Just next door is a farmyard full of tame, pettable critters, including goats, rabbits, and guinea pigs. ✉ *Off Pipeline Rd., Stanley Park* ☎ 604/ 257–8531 🎟 *Each site C$5, adults accompanying children C$2.50.*

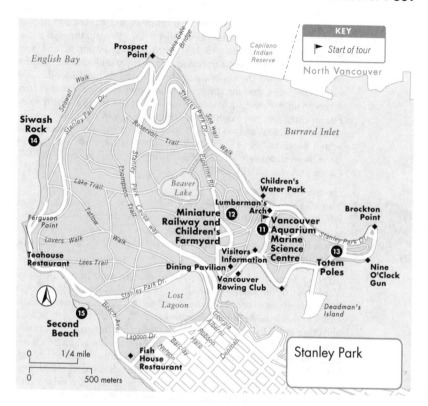

Stanley Park

English Bay

Prospect Point ◆

Siwash Rock ⑭

Burrard Inlet

Children's Water Park

Lumberman's Arch ◆

Miniature Railway and Children's Farmyard ⑫

Vancouver Aquarium Marine Science Centre ⑪

Brockton Point

Beaver Lake

Visitors Information ◆

Dining Pavilion ◆

Totem Poles ⑬

Nine O'Clock Gun ◆

Vancouver Rowing Club ◆

Ferguson Point

Teahouse Restaurant

Lost Lagoon

Deadman's Island

Second Beach ⑮

Fish House Restaurant ◆

KEY

▶ Start of tour

North Vancouver

Capilano Indian Reserve

0 — 1/4 mile

0 — 500 meters

🕐 *June–early Sept., daily 11–5; Oct., daily 6 PM–10 PM; Dec., daily 3 PM–10 PM; Sept., and Jan.–May, weekends 11–4, weather permitting.*

🅒 ⑮ **Second Beach.** In summer the main draw is the 50-meter pool with water slides and lifeguards. The shallow end fills up on hot days, but the lap-swimming section is usually deserted. Nearby you'll also find a sandy beach, a playground, and covered picnic sites. ⊠ *Stanley Park Dr., Stanley Park* ☎ *604/257–8371 pool, summer only* ⊕ *www.city.vancouver. bc.ca/parks* ⊡ *Beach free, pool C$4.25* 🕐 *Pool mid-May–mid-June, week-days noon–8:45, weekends 10–8:45; mid-June–Labor Day, daily 10–8:45.*

⑭ **Siwash Rock.** Legend tells of a young First Nations man who, about to become a father, bathed persistently to wash his sins away so that his son could be born pure. For his devotion he was blessed by the gods and immortalized in the shape of Siwash Rock. The rock is visible from the seawall; however, if you're driving you'll need to park and take a short path through the woods. A sign marks the trail.

⑬ **Totem poles.** Totem poles are an important art form among native peoples along British Columbia's coast. These eight poles, all carved in the latter half of the 20th century, include replicas of poles originally brought to the park from the north coast in the 1920s, as well as poles carved specifically for the park by First Nations artists. The several styles of poles represent a cross section of B.C. native groups, including the Kwakwaka'wakw, Haida, and Nisga'a. The combination of carved animals, fish, birds, and mythological creatures represents clan history. An information center near the site has a snack bar, a gift shop, and information about British Columbia's First Nations.

★ 🅒 ▶ ⑪ **Vancouver Aquarium Marine Science Centre.** Pools with windows below the water level let you come face to face with beluga whales, dolphins, sea otters, sea lions, and harbor seals at this research and educational facility. In the Amazon rain-forest gallery you can walk through a jungle setting populated with piranhas, sloths, tortoises, caimans, and tropical birds and vegetation. Other displays, many with hands-on features for children, show the underwater life of coastal British Columbia, the Canadian Arctic, and the tropics. Whale shows and dive shows (where divers swim with the aquatic life—including the sharks) are held daily. For an extra fee, you can help the trainers feed and train otters, seals, dolphins, belugas, and sea lions. Be prepared for lines on weekends and school holidays. ✉ *845 Avison Way, Stanley Park* ☎ *604/659–3474* ⊕ *www.vanaqua.org* 💲 *C$15.95* ⏱ *July–Labor Day, daily 9:30–7; Labor Day–June, daily 10–5:30.*

Granville Island

a good walk

This 35-acre peninsula in False Creek, just south of downtown Vancouver, is home to one of North America's most successful urban-redevelopment schemes. Once a derelict industrial site, Granville Island is now a vibrant urban park, with a bustling public market, several theaters, galleries, crafts shops, and artisans' studios.

To reach Granville Island, make the 15-minute walk from downtown Vancouver to the south end of Hornby Street. Aquabus Ferries depart from here about every five minutes and deliver passengers across False Creek at the **Granville Island Public Market** ⑯ ▶, which has a slew of food and other stalls. False Creek ferries leave every five minutes for Granville Island from a dock behind the Vancouver Aquatic Centre, on Beach Avenue, and deliver passengers between the Bridges pub and the Public Market. Still another option is to take a 20-minute ride on a TransLink bus; from Waterfront Station or stops on Granville Street, take False Creek South Bus 50 to the edge of the island. Buses 4 UBC and 7 Dunbar will also take you within a few minutes' walk of the island. On summer weekend afternoons, you can hop the **Downtown Historic Railway** (⇨ Train Travel in Vancouver and Victoria A to Z), a tram line that runs to the island from stops around False Creek. The market is a short walk from the bus, ferry, or tram stop. If you drive, parking is free for up to three hours, and paid parking is available in garages on the island.

From the market walk south on Johnston Street or take the waterside boardwalk that runs behind the Arts Club Theatre and around the Creekhouse building. Either way, just past the shops of the Creekhouse building is **Ocean Art Works**, an longhouse-style space where you can watch artists at work. Continue south to the **Emily Carr Institute of Art and Design,** the province's leading art college. Just to the right of the main entrance is the **Charles H. Scott Gallery**, which hosts contemporary exhibitions in various media. From the gallery, turn left and follow a covered walkway along the south side of the art school to **Sea Village,** one of the only houseboat communities in Vancouver. Then take the boardwalk that starts at the houseboats and continues partway around the island.

Turn right in front of the Granville Island Hotel (the large white building), right again onto Cartwright Street, and take the right fork into Railspur Alley. This part of the island has a mix of crafts galleries, studios, and workshops and is a great place to watch artisans at work. You can see wooden boats being built at the Alder Bay Boat Company at 1247 Cartwright Street, and you can watch glassblowers at work in the New Small Sterling Glass Studio, which is around the corner at 1440 Old Bridge Street. The Federation of Canadian Artists Gallery, the Crafts Association of B.C. Crafthouse, and the Gallery of B.C. Ceramics all showcase local works.

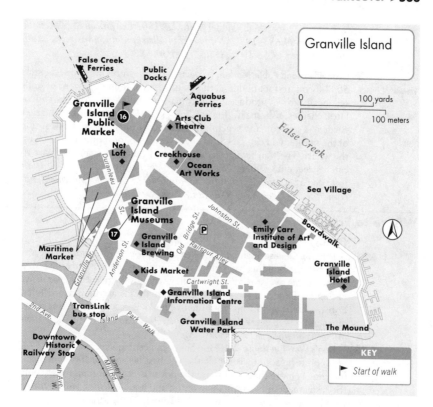

Back on Cartwright Street, you can pick up maps and find out about special events, including the festivals, outdoor concerts, and dance performances often held on the island at the **Granville Island Information Centre** (open daily 9–5). Just behind the information center the free water slides and sprinklers at the **Granville Island Water Park** are open in the summer. A little farther along the street, the **Kids Market** is full of toy and other kid-focused stores. At **Granville Island Brewing,** across the street from the Kids Market, you can take a brewery tour.

Cross Anderson Street and walk north on Duranleau Street. The **Granville Island Museums** ⑰ are on your left. The sea-oriented shops of the **Maritime Market** are next. The upscale **Net Loft** shopping arcade is the last place to explore. Once you have come full circle, you can either take the ferry back to downtown Vancouver or stay for dinner and catch a play at one of the theaters on the island (⇨ Nightlife and the Arts).

TIMING If your schedule is tight, you can tour Granville Island in three to four hours. If you like to shop or if a festival is in progress, you'll likely need a full day.

What to See

⑰ **Granville Island Museums.** Here you'll find three museums under one roof. The **Sport Fishing Museum** houses the world's largest collection of angling artifacts, including examples of tied flies, and a mounted replica of the largest salmon ever caught with a rod and reel. The collection of the **Model Ships Museum** includes exquisitely detailed replicas of early-20th-century military and working vessels and an excellent collection of model submarines. The **Model Trains Museum** has the world's largest toy-train collection on public display, including a diorama of the Fraser Canyon and the Kettle Valley that involves 1,000 feet of track and some large-scale (3-foot-high) model trains. ⊠ *1502 Duranleau St., Granville Island* ☏ *604/683–1939* ⊕ *www.granvilleislandmuseums.com* ✉ *All three museums C$6.50* ⊙ *Daily 10–5:30.*

▶ ⑯ **Granville Island Public Market.** Because no chain stores are allowed in this 50,000-square-foot building, each outlet here is unique. Dozens of stalls sell locally grown produce direct from the farm; others sell crafts, chocolates, cheeses, fish, meat, flowers, and exotic foods. In summer, market gardeners sell fruit and vegetables from trucks outside. On the west side of the market you can pick up a snack, espresso, or fixings for lunch on the wharf. The Market Courtyard, on the water side, is a good place to catch street entertainers. Weekends can get madly busy here. ⊠ *1689 Johnston St., Granville Island* ☏ *604/666–6477* ⊕ *www.granvilleisland. com* ⊙ *Feb.–Dec., daily 9–6; Jan., Tues.–Sun. 9–6.*

FodorsChoice ★

Where to Eat

Chinese

$–$$$$ ✕ **Imperial Chinese Seafood.** This elegant Cantonese restaurant in the art-deco Marine Building, two blocks west of the Canada Place cruise-ship terminal, has two-story, floor-to-ceiling windows with spectacular views of Stanley Park and the North Shore mountains across Burrard Inlet. Lobster, crab, or shrimp from the live tanks is recommended, as is the dim sum, served every day from 11 to 2:30. ⊠ *355 Burrard St., Downtown* ☏ *604/688–8191* ▭ *DC, MC, V.*

¢–$$ ✕ **Hon's Wun-Tun House.** Mr. Hon has been keeping Vancouverites in Chinese comfort food since the 1970s. The best bets on the 300-item menu (nothing is more than C$15) are the pot stickers (dumplings that come fried, steamed, or in soup), the wonton and noodle dishes, and anything with barbecued meat. The shiny Robson Street location has a separate kitchen for vegetarians and an army of fast-moving waitresses who keep your tea topped up. The older Chinatown outlet is atmospherically steamy and crowded. ⊠ *1339 Robson St., Downtown* ☏ *604/685– 0871* ⊠ *268 Keefer St., Chinatown* ☏ *604/688–0871* ⌖ *Reservations not accepted* ▭ *MC, V at Robson St.; no credit cards at Keefer St.*

Contemporary

$$$–$$$$ ✕ **Five Sails.** A special-occasion restaurant at the Pan Pacific Hotel, Five Sails has a stunning panoramic view of Canada Place, Lions Gate Bridge, and the lights of the North Shore across the inlet. The white-tablecloth and candlelight decor doesn't attempt to compete with the view. The broad-reaching, seasonally changing menu takes its inspiration from both Europe and the Pacific Rim. Highlights have included slow-roasted B. C. salmon, date-crusted venison loin, and seared ahi tuna with foie gras and trumpet mushrooms. ⊠ *Pan Pacific Hotel, 300–999 Canada Pl., Downtown* ☏ *604/891–2892* ▭ *AE, DC, MC, V* ⊙ *No lunch.*

$$–$$$ ✕ **Aqua Riva.** This lofty, lively modern room just yards from the Canada Place cruise-ship terminal affords striking views over the harbor and the North Shore mountains. Food from the wood-fire oven, rotisserie, and grill includes thin-crust pizzas with innovative toppings, grilled salmon, and spit-roasted chicken. Lunch brings a good selection of salads, sandwiches, and salmon dishes. A microbrew and martini list rounds out the menu. Brunch is served Sunday between May and October. ⊠ *200 Granville St., Downtown* ☏ *604/683–5599* ▭ *AE, DC, MC, V* ⊙ *No lunch weekends.*

$$–$$$ ✕ **Teahouse Restaurant.** This former officers' mess in Stanley Park is perfectly poised for watching sunsets over the water. The West Coast Continental menu includes such specialties as roasted pear salad and lobster ravioli as well as seasonally changing treatments of duck breast, B.C.

salmon, and rack of lamb. In summer you can dine on the patio. Afternoon tapas are served year-round. ✉ *7501 Stanley Park Dr., at Ferguson Point, Stanley Park* ☎ *604/669–3281* ▤ *AE, MC, V.*

$$–$$$ ✕ **Water Street Café.** The tables at this popular Gastown café spill out onto the sidewalk for front-row views of the steam clock across the street. Inside, the café is chic but casual, with slate-blue-and-white decor and tall windows overlooking bustling Water Street. It's tempting to pick one of the dozen or so varieties of pasta, but the crab chowder, West Coast crab cakes, and Fanny Bay oysters are also good choices. The breads are baked fresh daily. ✉ *300 Water St., Gastown* ☎ *604/689–2832* ▤ *AE, MC, V.*

Italian

$$–$$$ ✕ **Umberto Borgo Antico Al Porto.** Terra-cotta tiles and graceful archways give this spacious room a classical feel; upstairs, tall windows look out toward the harbor. Just a few blocks from the Canada Place cruise-ship dock, Borgo Antico serves such Tuscan dishes as grilled calamari salad, gnocchi with artichokes and sun-dried tomatoes, veal medallions with lemon and capers, and osso buco with risotto. The wine cellar has more than 300 selections. ✉ *321 Water St., Gastown* ☎ *604/683–8376* ▤ *AE, DC, MC, V* ☉ *Closed Sun. No lunch Sat.*

Pacific Northwest

$$–$$$ ✕ **Liliget Feast House.** This intimate downstairs room resembles the interior of a longhouse, with wooden walkways across pebble floors,
Fodor'sChoice contemporary First Nations art on the walls, and cedar-plank tables with
★ tatami-style benches. It's one of the few places in the world serving the original Northwest Coast First Nations cuisine. A feast platter lets you try most of the fare, which includes bannock bread, baked sweet potato with hazelnuts, alder-grilled salmon, buffalo smokies, duck breast, venison strips, oysters, mussels, and steamed fern shoots. ✉ *1724 Davie St., West End* ☎ *604/681–7044* ⊕ *www.liliget.com* ▤ *AE, DC, MC, V* ☉ *Closed Mon. and Tues. Oct.–Feb. No lunch.*

Pizza

$ ✕ **Incendio.** The hand-flipped thin-crust pizzas, with innovative toppings including Asiago cheese, prosciutto, roasted garlic, and sun-dried tomatoes, and the mix-and-match pastas and sauces (try the hot smoked-duck sausage, artichoke, and tomato combination, or the mango-basil-butter sauce) draw crowds to this Gastown eatery. The room, in a circa-1900 heritage building, with exposed brick, local artwork, and big curved windows, has plenty of atmosphere. ✉ *103 Columbia St., Gastown* ☎ *604/688–8694* ▤ *AE, MC, V* ☉ *No lunch weekends.*

Seafood

$$$–$$$$ ✕ **C Restaurant.** Dishes such as lightly smoked Skeena wild salmon and
Fodor'sChoice octopus-bacon-wrapped scallops have established C as Vancouver's
★ most innovative seafood restaurant. Start with shucked oysters from the raw bar or try C's Taster Box, in which several morsels are served dramatically on a four-tier display. An eight-course tasting menu highlights local and exotic seafood. Both the chic, ultramodern interior and the waterside patio overlook False Creek. ✉ *2–1600 Howe St., Downtown* ☎ *604/681–1164* ⊕ *www.crestaurant.com* ▤ *AE, DC, MC, V* ☉ *No lunch weekends or Oct.–mid-Dec. and Jan.–Apr.*

Where to Stay

$$$$ ▥ **Pan Pacific Hotel.** Most cruise ships calling at Vancouver arrive at
Fodor'sChoice Canada Place, a striking waterfront facility shaped like an ocean liner,
★ which is also home to this luxurious 23-story hotel. A dramatic water-

fall graces the three-story atrium lobby, and the rooms are spacious and modern, with light woods, travertine vanities, Italian linens, and stunning ocean, mountain, or skyline views. The restaurants and health-club facilities are among the city's finest. ⊠ *300–999 Canada Pl., Downtown, V6C 3B5* ☎ *604/662–8111, 800/663–1515 in Canada, 800/937–1515 in U.S.* ⊟ *604/685–8690* ⊕ *www.panpacific.com* ⇆ *465 rooms, 39 suites* ⚫ *3 restaurants, room service, in-room data ports, some in-room faxes, in-room safes, some kitchens, minibars, cable TV with movies and video games, pool, gym, hair salon, hot tub, outdoor hot tub, sauna, spa, steam room, racquetball, squash, lobby lounge, shops, baby-sitting, dry cleaning, laundry service, concierge, Internet, business services, parking (fee), some pets allowed, no-smoking floors* ☰ *AE, DC, MC, V.*

$$$–$$$$ 🏨 **Fairmont Waterfront.** An underground walkway leads from this striking 23-story glass hotel to Vancouver's cruise-ship terminal. Views from the lobby and from 60% of the guest rooms are of Burrard Inlet, Stanley Park, and the North Shore Mountains. Other rooms look onto the city skyline and a terraced herb garden. The spacious rooms have big picture windows and are attractively furnished with blond-wood furniture and contemporary Canadian artwork. Large corner rooms have the best views. Rooms on the Fairmont Gold floor have extra amenities, including a private lounge and a concierge. ⊠ *900 Canada Place Way, Downtown, V6C 3L5* ☎ *604/691–1991* ⊟ *604/691–1828* ⊕ *www. fairmont.com* ⇆ *489 rooms, 29 suites* ⚫ *Restaurant, room service, in-room data ports, in-room safes, some kitchenettes, minibars, cable TV with movies and video games, pool, gym, hot tub, massage, steam room, lounge, dry cleaning, laundry service, concierge, concierge floor, Internet, business services, meeting rooms, parking (fee), some pets allowed (fee), no-smoking floors* ☰ *AE, D, DC, MC, V.*

$$$–$$$$ 🏨 **O Canada House.** This beautifully restored 1897 Victorian, within walking distance of downtown, is where the first version of "O Canada," the
★ national anthem, was written in 1909. Each spacious bedroom is appointed with late-Victorian antiques. The top-floor room is enormous, with two king beds and a private sitting area. A separate one-room coach house in the garden is a romantic option. Breakfast, served in the dining room, is a lavish affair. ⊠ *1114 Barclay St., West End, V6E 1H1* ☎ *604/688– 0555 or 877/688–1114* ⊟ *604/488–0556* ⊕ *www.ocanadahouse.com* ⇆ *7 rooms* ⚫ *Refrigerators, cable TV, in-room VCRs, concierge, free parking; no a/c, no kids under 12, no smoking* ☰ *MC, V* ⊗ *BP.*

$$–$$$ 🏨 **Days Inn.** Two blocks from the Canada Place cruise-ship terminal, this moderately priced hotel operates a free shuttle bus to Vancouver's train and bus station and to both cruise-ship terminals. Rooms in this 1920 six-story building are small but cheerful, with modern pine furniture and floral bedspreads. The two-bedroom, one-bathroom units are a good value for groups and families. ⊠ *921 W. Pender St., Downtown, V6C 1M2* ☎ *604/681–4335 or 877/681–4335* ⊟ *604/681–7808* ⊕ *www. daysinnvancouver.com* ⇆ *80 rooms, 5 suites* ⚫ *Restaurant, in-room data ports, in-room safes, some microwaves, refrigerators, cable TV with movies, lounge, pub, baby-sitting, dry cleaning, laundry facilities, laundry service, parking (fee), no-smoking floors* ☰ *AE, D, DC, MC, V.*

$–$$ 🏨 **Sylvia Hotel.** To stay here from June through August you'll need to book six months to a year ahead. This Virginia-creeper-covered 1912 building is so popular because of its low rates and near-perfect location, about 25 feet from the beach on scenic English Bay, 200 feet from Stanley Park, and a 20-minute walk from Robson Street. The rooms and apartment-style suites vary from tiny to spacious. Many are large enough to sleep four and all have windows that open. Contemporary beds, linens, and sofas come in a dark green-and-cream color scheme. ⊠ *1154 Gilford St., West End, V6G 2P6* ☎ *604/681–9321* ⊟ *604/682–3551*

⊕ *www.sylviahotel.com* ⌁ *97 rooms, 22 suites ⧖ Restaurant, room service, in-room data ports, some kitchens, cable TV, lounge, dry cleaning, laundry service, parking (fee), some pets allowed, no-smoking floors; no a/c ⊟ AE, DC, MC, V.*

Nightlife & the Arts

For information on events, pick up a free copy of the *Georgia Straight*, available at cafés and bookstores around town, or look in the entertainment section of the *Vancouver Sun* (Thursday's paper has listings in the "Queue" section). For tickets, book through **Ticketmaster** (☎ 604/280–4444 ⊕ www.ticketmaster.ca). You can pick up half-price tickets on the day of the event, as well as full-price advance tickets, at **Tickets Tonight** (⊠ 200 Burrard St., Downtown ☎ 604/684–2787 ⊕ www.ticketstonight.ca), at the Vancouver Tourist Info Centre.

Nightlife

BARS, PUBS &
LOUNGES

A massive deck with expansive False Creek views is the big draw at **Bridges** (⊠ 1696 Duranleau St., Granville Island ☎ 604/687–4400), near the Public Market. There's a cozy pub and a restaurant at the same site. Near Stanley Park and attached to Cardero's Restaurant, **Cardero's Pub** (⊠ 1583 Coal Harbour Quay, West End ☎ 604/669–7666) has deep leather couches, marina views, and recycled ship timbers as well as other nautical touches; the pub grub is top-notch. **Cloud 9** (⊠ 1400 Robson St., West End ☎ 604/687–0511), a revolving lounge and restaurant on the 42nd floor of the Empire Landmark Hotel, takes in 360-degree views of Stanley Park, English Bay, and the downtown core.

A seaside patio, casual Pacific Northwest restaurant, and house-brewed German-style beer make the **Dockside Brewing Company** (⊠ Granville Island Hotel, 1253 Johnston St., Granville Island ☎ 604/685–7070) a popular hangout. For a pint of properly poured Guinness and live traditional Irish music try the **Irish Heather** (⊠ 217 Carrall St., Gastown ☎ 604/688–9779). Upstairs is a restaurant, and out back, in an atmospheric coach house, a **Shebeen,** or whiskey house, serves about 130 whiskies. Though technically a seafood restaurant, the massive three-level **Sand Bar** (⊠ 1535 Johnson St., Granville Island ☎ 604/669–9030) has a party atmosphere most nights and dancing on weekends. The sushi bar downstairs is a sedate hideaway, and the covered rooftop patio has dramatic views over False Creek.

Harbor views, pub food, and traditionally brewed beer are the draws at **Steamworks** (⊠ 375 Water St., Gastown ☎ 604/689–2739), a multilevel, wood-paneled brewpub on the edge of Gastown. The **Yaletown Brewing Company** (⊠ 1111 Mainland St., Yaletown ☎ 604/681–2739) is housed in a renovated warehouse with a glassed-in brewery, turning out eight tasty beers. It also has a lively singles-scene pub, a patio, and a restaurant.

COMEDY

The **Vancouver International Comedy Festival** (☎ 604/683–0883 ⊕ www.comedyfest.com), held in late July and early August, brings an international collection of improv, stand-up, circus, and other acts to Granville Island. The **Vancouver TheatreSports League** (☎ 604/738–7013), a hilarious improv troupe, performs at the New Revue Stage on Granville Island.

DANCE CLUBS

A smartly dressed crowd flocks to dance and celebrity-spot at upscale **Au Bar** (⊠ 674 Seymour St., Downtown ☎ 604/648–2227 ⊕ www.aubarnightclub.com). The **Commodore Ballroom** (⊠ 868 Granville St., Downtown ☎ 604/739–7469), a 1929 art-deco dance hall with a massive sprung dance floor, hosts bands six nights a week; Tuesday is DJ night. You can dance under the stars at **Skybar** (⊠ 670 Smithe St.,

Downtown ☎ 604/697–9199 ⊕ www.skybarvancouver.com), a chic three-level club with a rooftop patio. The fashionable **Voda** (⊠ 783 Homer St., Downtown ☎ 604/684–3003), in the Westin Grand Hotel, is one of the few places for which Vancouverites dress up. The intimate club draws a thirtysomething professional crowd to its weekend Top 40 and house nights and a younger crowd for midweek hip-hop.

The Arts

MUSIC   The Jazz Hotline of the **Coastal Jazz and Blues Society** (☎ 604/872–5200 ⊕ www.coastaljazz.ca) has information about concerts and clubs. The society also runs the **Vancouver International Jazz Festival,** which lights up 40 venues around town every June. **Festival Vancouver** (☎ 604/688–1152 ⊕ www.festivalvancouver.bc.ca) is Vancouver's biggest music event, with more than 50 performances of orchestral, chamber, choral, world music, opera, and jazz in venues around the city in early August. The **Vancouver Symphony Orchestra** (☎ 604/876–3434 ⊠ 601 Smithe St., Downtown) is the resident company at the **Orpheum Theatre.**

THEATER   The **Arts Club Theatre Company** (⊠ 1585 Johnston St., Granville Island ☎ 604/687–1644 ⊕ www.artsclub.com) operates two theaters. The **Arts Club Granville Island Stage** is an intimate venue that showcases works by local playwrights. The **Stanley Theatre** at 2750 Granville Street is a lavish former movie palace staging works by such perennial favorites as William Shakespeare and Noël Coward. Both operate year-round. **Bard on the Beach** (☎ 604/739–0559 or 877/739–0559 ⊕ www.bardonthebeach.org) is a summer series of Shakespeare's plays performed in tents on the beach at Vanier Park. Big international shows, from Broadway musicals to Chinese dance productions, play at the **Centre in Vancouver for the Performing Arts** (⊠ 777 Homer St., Downtown ☎ 604/602–0616 ⊕ www.centreinvancouver.com). The **Queen Elizabeth Theatre** (⊠ 600 Hamilton St., Downtown ☎ 604/665–3050) is a major venue for ballet, opera, and other events. **Theatre Under the Stars** (☎ 604/687–0174) performs such popular family-friendly musicals as *The Sound of Music* and *Kiss Me Kate* at Malkin Bowl, an outdoor amphitheater in Stanley Park, during July and August. Small theater troupes from around the world perform at the **Vancouver Fringe Festival** (☎ 604/257–0350 ⊕ www.vancouverfringe.com), staged in early September at various venues on and around Granville Island. The **Vancouver Playhouse** (⊠ 649 Cambie St., Downtown ☎ 604/665–3050 ⊕ www.vancouverplayhouse.com), in the same complex as the Queen Elizabeth Theatre, is the leading venue in Vancouver for mainstream theatrical shows.

Shopping

Vancouver is full of individual boutiques and specialty shops. Store hours are generally 9:30–6 Monday, Tuesday, Wednesday, and Saturday; 9:30–9 Thursday and Friday; and 10–5 Sunday. You'll pay both 7.5% Provincial Sales Tax (PST) and 7% Goods and Services Tax (GST) on most purchases. Non-Canadian residents can reclaim the GST paid on most purchases. You can pick up refund forms at many shops and at the airport. For an instant refund, see **Global Refund** (⊠ 900 W. Georgia St. ☎ 604/893–8478) on the lower level of the Fairmont Hotel Vancouver.

Department Stores

The **Bay** (⊠ 674 Granville St., at Georgia St., Downtown ☎ 604/681–6211), founded as part of the fur trade in the 17th century, is now a midprice department store downtown. Modeled on Paris's Colette store, **Bruce** (⊠ 1038 Alberni St., Downtown ☎ 604/688–8802) is Vancouver's first "lifestyle" department store, with the latest in designer fashion, home decor, and eyewear. **Holt Renfrew** (✉ 633 Granville St., Downtown ☎ 604/681–3121) focuses on high fashion for men and women.

Shopping Districts & Malls

About two dozen high-end art galleries, antiques shops, and Oriental-rug emporiums are packed end to end between 5th and 15th avenues on Granville Street, in an area known as **Gallery Row.** As you continue south along Granville Street, **Granville Rise,** between Broadway and 16th Avenue, is lined with chic fashion, home decor, and specialty food shops. **Pacific Centre Mall** (✉ 700 W. Georgia St., Downtown ☎ 604/688–7236), on two levels and mostly underground, takes up three city blocks in the heart of downtown. Midpriced, mainstream clothing shops predominate on the lower level; the upper floor houses designer boutiques. **Robson Street** stretching from Burrard to Bute is the city's main fashion-shopping and people-watching artery. Gap and Banana Republic have their flagship stores here, as do Canadian fashion outlets Club Monaco and Roots. Souvenir shops and cafés, Asian food shops, video outlets, and cheap noodle bars abound. Shops in and near **Sinclair Centre** (✉ 757 W. Hastings St., Downtown) cater to sophisticated and pricey tastes.

Bustling **Chinatown**—centered on Pender and Main streets—is full of restaurants and markets. It's most lively on weekend evenings in summer, when the Chinatown Night Market, an Asian-style outdoor street market, sets up along Keefer and Pender streets. **Commercial Drive,** north of East 1st Avenue, is the heart of Vancouver's Italian and Latin American communities. It's lined with cappuccino bars, Latin cafés, and imported-food shops. **Granville Island** (⇨ Exploring Vancouver) has a lively public market and a wealth of galleries, crafts shops, and artisans' studios. Treasure hunters enjoy the 300 block of **West Cordova Street,** near Gastown, where offbeat shops sell curios, vintage clothing, and locally designed fashions.

Specialty Stores

ANTIQUES   Three key antiques-hunting grounds are Gallery Row on Granville Street; the stretch of antiques stores along Main Street from 25th to 30th Avenue; and along Front Street, between 6th and Begbie streets near New Westminster Quay in New Westminster.

The **Vancouver Antique Centre** (✉ 422 Richards St., Downtown ☎ 604/669–7444) has about a dozen antiques and collectibles dealers under one roof.

ART GALLERIES   Gallery Row along Granville Street between 5th and 15th avenues has about a dozen high-end contemporary art galleries. You'll also find a number of notable galleries on the downtown peninsula.

Buschlen Mowatt (✉ 1445 W. Georgia St., West End ☎ 604/682–1234) exhibits the works of contemporary Canadian and international artists. The **Diane Farris Gallery** (✉ 1590 W. 7th Ave., South Granville ☎ 604/737–2629) often showcases new Canadian and international artists. The **Douglas Reynolds Gallery** (✉ 2335 Granville St., South Granville ☎ 604/731–9292) displays one of the city's finest collections of Northwest Coast First Nations art and specializes in woodwork and jewelry. The **Inuit Gallery of Vancouver** (✉ 206 Cambie St., Gastown ☎ 604/688–7323 or 888/615–8399) exhibits Northwest Coast and Inuit art. The **Marion Scott Gallery** (✉ 481 Howe St., Downtown ☎ 604/685–1934) specializes in Inuit art.

BOOKS   The serene **Banyen Books** (✉ 3608 W. 4th Ave. ☎ 604/732–7912) is Vancouver's best source for new age, philosophy, and alternative health titles. Vancouver's two **Chapters** (✉ 788 Robson St., Downtown ☎ 604/

682–4066 ✉ 2505 Granville St., at Broadway, South Granville ☎ 604/731–7822) are enormous, with a café in each location. The stores stock a vast selection of popular books and CDs and often discounted best-sellers. **Duthie Books** (✉ 2239 W. 4th Ave., Kitsilano ☎ 604/732–5344) is a long-established homegrown general-interest bookshop. **MacLeod's Books** (✉ 455 W. Pender St., Downtown ☎ 604/681–7654) is one of the city's best antiquarian- and used-book stores. **Wanderlust** (✉ 1929 W. 4th Ave., Kitsilano ☎ 604/739–2182) carries thousands of travel books and maps as well as luggage and travel accessories.

CLOTHES **Dream** (✉ 311 W. Cordova St., Gastown ☎ 604/683–7326) is where up-and-coming local designers sell their wares. Men's and women's fashions by Versace, Yves Saint Laurent Rive Gauche, Dior, Prada, and others are available at **Leone** (✉ 757 W. Hastings St., Downtown ☎ 604/683–1133) in Sinclair Centre. You'll find more affordable, locally made fashions—and an Italian café—at **A-Wear** (✉ 350 Howe St., Downtown ☎ 604/685–9327) on Leone's lower floor.

For outdoorsy clothes that double as souvenirs (many sport maple-leaf logos), check out the sweatshirts, leather jackets, and other cozy casuals at **Roots** (✉ 1001 Robson St., West End ☎ 604/683–4305), outfitter to the Canadian Olympic team. Globe trotters like the practical, hard wearing, Canadian-made travel clothing available at **Tilley Endurables** (✉ 2401 Granville St., South Granville ☎ 604/732–4287).

GIFTS Museum and gallery gift shops are among the best places to buy high-quality souvenirs—West Coast native art, books, music, jewelry, and other items.

The **Clamshell Gift Shop** (✉ Vancouver Aquarium Marine Science Centre, 845 Avison Way, Stanley Park ☎ 604/659–3413 or 800/663–0562) sells souvenir clothing and aquatic-theme toys and gifts. The **Gallery Store** (✉ 750 Hornby St., Downtown ☎ 604/662–4706), in the Vancouver Art Gallery, sells a good selection of art books and locally designed jewelry. **Hill's Native Art** (✉ 165 Water St., Gastown ☎ 604/685–4249) has Vancouver's largest selection of First Nations art. **Lattimer Gallery** (✉ 1590 W. 2nd Ave., False Creek ☎ 604/732–4556), near Granville Island, is full of native arts and crafts in all price ranges.

The **Museum of Anthropology Gift Shop** (✉ 6393 N.W. Marine Dr., University of British Columbia campus ☎ 604/822–5087) stocks Northwest Coast jewelry, carvings, and prints as well as a collection of books on First Nations history and culture. At the **Salmon Shop** (✉ 1689 Johnston St., Granville Island ☎ 604/669–3474), in the Public Market, you can pick up fresh or smoked salmon wrapped for travel. **Salmon Village** (✉ 779 Thurlow St., West End ☎ 604/685–3378), just off Robson Street's main shopping strip, has all manner of travel-ready Canadian delicacies, from maple syrup to salmon.

JEWELRY **Birks** (✉ 698 W. Hastings St., Downtown ☎ 604/669–3333) takes up the grand lower floor of a neoclassical building that was the former headquarters of the Canadian Imperial Bank of Commerce. **Cartier Jewellers** (✉ 408 Howe St., Downtown ☎ 604/683–6878) is the Vancouver outlet of the famous jewelry chain. **Palladio** (✉ 855 W. Hastings St., Downtown ☎ 604/685–3885) carries high-fashion jewelry in gold and platinum.

OUTDOOR EQUIPMENT **Coast Mountain Sports** (✉ 2201 W. 4th Ave., Kitsilano ☎ 604/731–6181 ✉ Park Royal Shopping Centre, Marine Dr., West Vancouver ☎ 604/922–3336 ✉ Metrotown Shopping Centre, Burnaby ☎ 604/434–9397 ✉ Coquitlam Shopping Centre, Coquitlam ☎ 604/945–9511) sells high-performance (and high-fashion) gear. The massive **Mountain Equip-**

ment **Co-op** (✉ 130 W. Broadway, Fairview ☎ 604/872–7858) is a local institution with a good selection of high-performance and midprice clothing and equipment. A onetime $5 membership is required.

Vancouver A to Z

To research prices, get advice from other travelers, and book travel arrangements, visit www.fodors.com.

AIR TRAVEL TO & FROM VANCOUVER

Air Canada, Air Canada Jazz, and WestJet Airlines serve destinations around Western Canada. West Coast Air and Harbour Air Seaplanes operate 35-minute harbor-to-harbor service (downtown Vancouver to downtown Victoria) several times a day. Planes leave from near the Pan Pacific Hotel at 300–999 Canada Place. Helijet International has helicopter service from downtown Vancouver and the Vancouver airport to Seattle and Victoria. The heliport is near Vancouver's Pan Pacific Hotel.

🛫 Airlines & Contacts **Air Canada** ☎ 888/247-2262 ⊕ www.aircanada.ca. **Air Canada Jazz** ☎ 888/247-2262 ⊕ www.flyjazz.ca. **Harbour Air** ☎ 604/274-1277 or 800/665-0212 ⊕ www.harbour-air.com. **Helijet International** ☎ 800/665-4354 or 604/273-1414 ⊕ www.helijet.com. **West Coast Air** ☎ 604/606-6888 or 800/347-2222 ⊕ www.westcoastair.com. **WestJet Airlines** ☎ 800/538-5696 ⊕ www.westjet.com.

AIRPORTS & TRANSFERS

Vancouver International Airport is on Sea Island, about 23 km (14 mi) south of downtown off Highway 99. An airport-improvement fee is assessed on all flight departures: C$5 for flights within British Columbia or the Yukon; C$10 for other flights within North America; C$15 for overseas flights. Major credit cards and Canadian and United States currencies are accepted. Alaska, American, British Airways, Continental, Northwest, Qantas, and United serve the airport. The two major domestic carriers are Air Canada and WestJet.

🛬 Airport Information **Vancouver International Airport** ✉ Grant McConachie Way, Richmond ☎ 604/207-7077 ⊕ www.yvr.ca.

AIRPORT TRANSFER The drive from the airport to downtown takes 20 to 45 minutes, depending on the time of day. Airport hotels provide shuttle service to and from the airport. The Vancouver Airporter Service bus leaves the international- and domestic-arrivals levels of the terminal building approximately every half hour, stopping at major downtown hotels. The first bus arrives at the airport at 6:10 AM, and the service runs until 11:30 PM. The fare is C$12 one-way and C$18 round-trip.

Taxi stands are in front of the terminal building on domestic- and international-arrivals levels. The taxi fare to downtown is about C$25. Area cab companies include Black Top and Yellow. Limousine service from LimoJet Gold costs about C$34 one-way.

To travel downtown by public transit, take any TransLink bus marked Airport Station; then transfer at Airport Station to a No. 98 Burrard Station bus. To return to the airport, take a No. 98 Richmond Centre bus and transfer at Airport Station.

🚕 Taxis & Shuttles **Black Top Cabs** ☎ 604/681-2181. **LimoJet Gold** ☎ 604/273-1331 or 800/278-8742. **TransLink** ☎ 604/953-3333 ⊕ www.translink.bc.ca. **Vancouver Airporter Service** ☎ 604/946-8866 or 800/668-3141. **Yellow Cab** ☎ 604/681-1111.

BOAT & FERRY TRAVEL

BC Ferries operates two major ferry terminals outside Vancouver. From Tsawwassen to the south (an hour's drive from downtown), ferries sail to Swartz Bay near Victoria, to Nanaimo on Vancouver Island, and to the Gulf Islands (the small islands between the mainland and Vancouver Island). From Horseshoe Bay (45 minutes north of downtown), ferries sail to the Sunshine Coast and to Nanaimo on Vancouver Island.

At press time, HarbourLynx planned to start direct, high-speed, foot-passenger-only service between downtown Vancouver and downtown Nanaimo on Vancouver Island. The trip will take about an hour and costs C$22.

The SeaBus is a 400-passenger commuter ferry that crosses Burrard Inlet from Waterfront Station downtown to the foot of Lonsdale Avenue in North Vancouver. Leaving every 15 to 30 minutes, the bus takes 13 minutes and costs the same as the TransLink bus. With a transfer, connection can be made to any TransLink bus or SkyTrain.

Aquabus Ferries connect several stations on False Creek, including Science World, Granville Island, Stamp's Landing, Yaletown, and the Hornby Street dock. Some Aquabus ferries take bicycles, and the company also operates two historic wooden boats on some runs. False Creek Ferries provides foot-passenger service between the Aquatic Centre on Beach Avenue, Granville Island, Science World, Stamp's Landing, and Vanier Park. False Creek and Aquabus ferries are not part of the TransLink system, so bus transfers aren't accepted.

FARES & SCHEDULES   Vehicle reservations on Vancouver to Victoria and Nanaimo routes are optional and cost C$15 in addition to the fare. There's no extra charge for reservations on Gulf Island routes.

🚢 **Boat & Ferry Information** **Aquabus Ferries** ☎ 604/689-5858 ⊕ www.aquabus. bc.ca. **BC Ferries** ☎ 250/386-3431, 888/223-3779 in British Columbia ⊕ www.bcferries. com. **False Creek Ferries** ☎ 604/684-7781 ⊕ www.granvilleislandferries.bc.ca. **HarbourLynx** ☎ 866/206-5969 or 250/753-4443 in Nanaimo, 604/688-5465 in Vancouver ⊕ www.harbourlynx.com. **SeaBus** ☎ 604/953-3333 ⊕ www.translink.bc.ca.

BUS & RAPID TRANSIT TRAVEL

Vancouver's TransLink system, comprising buses, the SeaBus, and the SkyTrain (an elevated train that runs underground through the downtown core), can get you just about anywhere you need to go. Exact change (C$2 in Vancouver, C$3–C$4 to the suburbs) or a FareSaver ticket (available from convenience stores) is required. Day passes, good for unlimited travel all day, cost C$8. B.C. Transit runs an extensive service in Victoria and the surrounding areas, including service to the B. C. Ferries terminal at Swartz Bay. An all-day pass costs C$5.50. Double-decker buses run on some routes. Pacific Coach Lines operates daily connecting service between Victoria and Vancouver on B.C. Ferries.

🚌 **B.C. Transit** ☎ 250/382-6161 ⊕ www.bctransit.com. **Pacific Coach Lines** ☎ 604/ 662-8074 or 800/661-1725 ⊕ www.pacificcoach.com. **TransLink** ☎ 604/953-3333 ⊕ www.translink.bc.ca.

CAR TRAVEL

Interstate 5 in Washington State becomes Highway 99 at the U.S.–Canada border. Vancouver is a three-hour drive (226 km [140 mi]) from Seattle. A car can be handy for touring areas outside the city center, but it isn't essential. On the compact downtown peninsula, however, it's generally easier to get around on foot or by public transport, especially in light of the congestion, limited parking, and many one-way streets.

Vancouver's rush-hour traffic, about 7–9 weekday mornings and starting at 3 PM weekday afternoons, can be horrendous. The worst bottlenecks outside the city center are the North Shore bridges (especially the Lions Gate Bridge), the George Massey Tunnel on Highway 99 south of Vancouver, and Highway 1 through Coquitlam and Surrey.

EMERGENCIES

🆘 Emergency Services **Ambulance, fire, police** ☎ 911.

LODGING

Hello BC, operated by the provincial Ministry of Tourism, can book accommodations anywhere in British Columbia. Town & Country Bed and Breakfast Reservation Service specializes in B&Bs.

🆘 Reservation Services **Super, Natural BC** ☎ 604/663-6000 or 800/435-5622 ⊕ www.hellobc.com. **Town & Country Bed and Breakfast Reservation Service** ✉ 2803 W. 4th Ave., Kitsilano ✉ Box 74542, Vancouver V6K 1K2 ☎📠 604/731-5942 ⊕ www.townandcountrybedandbreakfast.com.

MONEY MATTERS

Most merchants in Vancouver will accept U.S. dollars, though if you exchange your money, you'll probably get a better rate at a bank. ATMs are easy to find: most bank branches and many convenience stores have them.

TAXIS

It's difficult to hail a cab in Vancouver. Unless you're near a hotel, you'll have better luck calling a taxi service. Try Black Top or Yellow.

🆘 Taxi Companies **Black Top** ☎ 604/681-2181. **Yellow** ☎ 604/681-1111.

TOURS

Gray Line, the largest tour operator, leads orientation tours of Vancouver. The Vancouver Trolley Company runs turn-of-the-20th-century-style trolleys through Vancouver on a two-hour narrated tour of the major sights, including Gastown, Chinatown, Granville Island, and Stanley Park. A day pass (C$25) allows you to complete one full circuit, getting off and on as often as you like. Stanley Park Horse-Drawn Tours runs horse and carriage tours of Stanley Park between March 15 and October 31; the C$20.55 fare includes a shuttle-bus ride to the park from downtown.

🆘 **Gray Line** ☎ 604/879-3363, 800/667-0882 in Vancouver, 250/388-5248, 800/663-8390 in Victoria ⊕ www.grayline.ca. **Stanley Park Horse-Drawn Tours** ☎ 604/681-5115 ⊕ www.stanleyparktours.com. **Vancouver Trolley Company** ☎ 604/801-5515 or 888/451-5581 ⊕ www.vancouvertrolley.com.

TRAIN TRAVEL

The Pacific Central Station, at Main Street and Terminal Avenue, near the Main Street SkyTrain station, is the hub for rail service. Amtrak has daily service between Seattle and Vancouver. VIA Rail provides transcontinental service through Jasper to Toronto three times a week.

The volunteer-run Downtown Historic Railway operates two restored electric trams (built in 1905 and 1913) along a 5-km (3-mi) track between Science World and Granville Island. The trams, which also stop at 1st Avenue and Ontario Street and at Leg-in-Boot Square, near 6th Avenue and Moberly Street, operate every half hour between 12:30 PM and 5 PM weekends and holidays from mid-May to mid-October. The adult fare is C$2.

🆘 **Amtrak** ☎ 800/872-7245 ⊕ www.amtrak.com. **Downtown Historic Railway** ☎ 604/665-3903 ⊕ www.trams.bc.ca. **Pacific Central Station** ✉ 1150 Station St., Downtown ☎ No phone. **VIA Rail** ☎ 800/561-8630 in Canada, 800/561-3949 in U.S. ⊕ www.viarail.ca.

VISITOR INFORMATION

Easily spotted on Vancouver streets in their red uniforms, Downtown Ambassadors, sponsored by the Downtown Vancouver Business Improvement Association, provide information, directions, safe walks, and emergency assistance to anyone visiting Vancouver's central business district.

🚶 **Downtown Ambassadors** ☎ 604/689-4357 ⊕ www.downtownvancouver.net. **Granville Island Information Centre** ✉ 1398 Cartwright St., Granville Island ☎ 604/666-5784 ⊕ www.granvilleisland.com. **Hello B.C.** ☎ 800/435-5622 ⊕ www.hellobc.com. **Vancouver Tourist Info Centre** ✉ 200 Burrard St., Downtown ☎ 604/683-2000 ⊕ www.tourismvancouver.com.

VICTORIA

By Sue Kernaghan

The capital of British Columbia, Victoria is the oldest city (founded 1843) on Canada's west coast and the first European settlement on Vancouver Island. It was chosen to be the westernmost trading outpost of the British-owned Hudson's Bay Company in 1843 and became the capital of British Columbia in 1868. Victoria has since evolved into a walkable, livable seaside town of gardens, waterfront pathways, and restored 19th-century architecture. Often described as the country's most British city, Victoria is these days—except for the odd red phone box, good beer, and well-mannered drivers—working to change that image, preferring to celebrate its combined native, Asian, and European heritage. Though it's quite touristy during the summer, it's also at its prettiest then, with flowers hanging from 19th-century lampposts and strollers enjoying the beauty of Victoria's natural harbor.

Exploring Victoria

Great views, lush gardens, and fine museums are the highlights of a visit to Victoria's walkable downtown. A trip to popular Butchart Gardens is worthwhile if you've got the time.

Numbers in the text correspond to numbers in the margin and on the Downtown Victoria map.

a good tour

For some wonderful views, begin your tour of Victoria on the waterfront at the Tourism Victoria Visitor Information Centre. Just across the way is the **Fairmont Empress Hotel** 🔞 ▶, a majestic railway hotel that originally opened in 1908 (the public entrance is at the south end, off Belleville Street). A short walk around the harbor along the Inner Harbour Walk (take any of the staircases from Government Street down to the water level) will take you to the **Royal London Wax Museum.** Originally Victoria's steamship terminal, this colonnaded building now houses more than 300 wax figures. Floating in the harbor beside the wax museum are the Pacific Undersea Gardens, an underwater exhibit of local sea life. Across Belleville Street is the **Parliament Buildings** 🔞 complex, where British Columbia's provincial legislature sits. Cross Government Street to reach the **Royal British Columbia Museum** 🔞, where you can explore thousands of years of history. Just behind the museum and bordering Douglas Street are the totem poles and ceremonial longhouse of Thunderbird Park; **Helmcken House** 🔞, the oldest house in Victoria; and the tiny 19th-century **St. Ann's Schoolhouse.** A few blocks south on Douglas Street will take you to seaside Beacon Hill Park. A few blocks west of the park on Government Street is the **Emily Carr House,** the birthplace of one of British Columbia's best-known artists. From the park, go north on Blanshard Street to see the grounds and chapel of **St. Ann's Academy** 🔞. Then take Belleville Street west to Douglas Street and stop off at the glass-roof **Crystal Garden Conservation Centre** 🔞, where you can see endangered tropical birds and animals and hundreds of flowers.

For a different kind of wildlife exhibit, continue two blocks north (uphill) on Douglas and turn left at Courtney Street. Half a block in on your

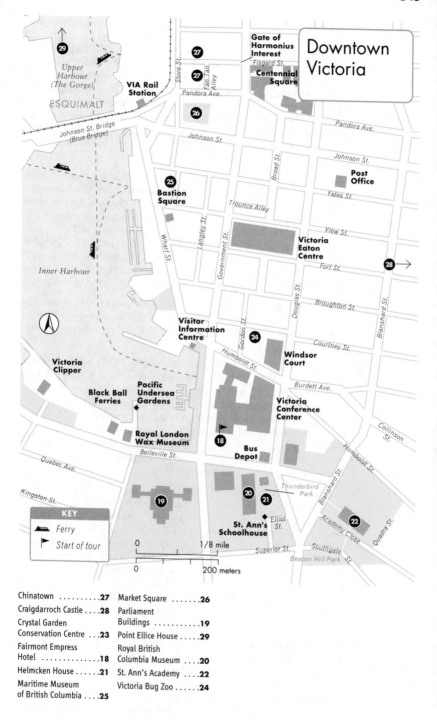

Downtown Victoria

Chinatown ....**27**   Market Square **26**

Craigdarroch Castle ....**28**   Parliament

Crystal Garden   Buildings **19**

Conservation Centre ...**23**   Point Ellice House **29**

Fairmont Empress   Royal British

Hotel ....**18**   Columbia Museum **20**

Helmcken House ......**21**   St. Ann's Academy **22**

Maritime Museum   Victoria Bug Zoo **24**

of British Columbia **25**

left you'll find the **Victoria Bug Zoo** ㉔, a creepy-crawly attraction popular with children. From the Bug Zoo, continue west on Courtney Street to Government Street, Victoria's main shopping thoroughfare. Head north about three blocks to Government and View streets, where you'll find the entrance to the cobblestone **Bastion Square,** the original site of Fort Victoria and the Hudson's Bay Company trading post, which now has restaurants and offices. Just north of Government and View, on the right-hand side of Government Street, is the entrance to Trounce Alley, a pretty pedestrian-only shopping arcade. Back at Bastion Square, you can stop in at the **Maritime Museum of British Columbia** ㉕ and learn about an important part of the province's history.

North of Bastion Square a few blocks, on Store Street between Johnson Street and Pandora Avenue, is **Market Square** ㉖, one of the most picturesque shopping districts in the city. Across Pandora Avenue is the entrance to the narrow, shop-lined Fan Tan Alley, which leads to Fisgard Street, the heart of **Chinatown** ㉗. A 15-minute walk or a short drive east on Fort Street will take you to Joan Crescent and lavish **Craigdarroch Castle** ㉘ and the nearby Art Gallery of Greater Victoria. In summer a ride on Harbour Ferries from the Inner Harbour will take you to **Point Ellice House** ㉙, a 19th-century waterside home and garden.

TIMING   Many of the sights are within easy walking distance of one another, and the tour could be covered in half a day. Allot a full day if you plan on visiting the Royal British Columbia Museum and the other museums.

What to See

㉗ **Chinatown.** Victoria's Chinatown, founded in 1858, is the oldest in Canada. If you enter Chinatown from Government Street, you'll walk under the elaborate **Gate of Harmonious Interest,** made from Taiwanese ceramic tiles and decorative panels. Along the street, merchants display fragile paper lanterns, wicker baskets, and exotic groceries. **Fan Tan Alley,** just off Fisgard Street, holds claim not only to being the narrowest street in Canada but also to having been the gambling and opium center of Chinatown, where games of mah-jongg, fan-tan, and dominoes were played. It's now lined with tiny shops.

㉘ **Craigdarroch Castle.** This lavish mansion was built as the home of British Columbia's first millionaire, coal baron Robert Dunsmuir. He died in 1889, just a few months before the castle's completion. Converted into a museum depicting turn-of-the-20th-century life, the castle has elaborately framed landscape paintings, stained-glass windows, carved woodwork—precut in Chicago for Dunsmuir and sent by rail—and a beautifully restored painted ceiling in the drawing room. From the tower, you can enjoy great views of Victoria and the Olympic Mountains. ⌂ *1050 Joan Crescent, Rockland* ☎ *250/592–5323* ⊕ *www.craigdarrochcastle.com* ▤ *C$10* ☺ *Mid-June–Labor Day, daily 9–7; Labor Day–mid-June, daily 10–4:30.*

㉓ **Crystal Garden Conservation Centre.** Opened in 1925 as the largest saltwater swimming pool in the British Empire, this glass-roof building now houses exotic flora and a variety of endangered tropical fauna, including flamingos, tortoises, macaws, lemurs, bats, and butterflies. ⌂ *713 Douglas St., Downtown Victoria* ☎ *250/953–8815* ⊕ *www.bcpcc. com/crystal* ▤ *C$9* ☺ *Mid-June–mid-Sept., daily 9–8; mid-Sept.–Oct. and mid-Mar.–mid-June, daily 9–6; Nov.–mid-Mar., daily 9–5.*

⑱ **The Fairmont Empress Hotel.** Opened in 1908 by the Canadian Pacific Railway, the Empress is one of the grand château-style hotels you'll find in many Canadian cities. Designed by Francis Rattenbury, who also designed the Parliament Buildings, the Empress, with its solid Edwardian grandeur, has become a symbol of the city. The ingredients that made the 472-room hotel a tourist attraction in the past—old-world architecture and ornate decor, a commanding view of the Inner Harbour—are still here. The archives, a historical photo and cartoon display on the lower level, are open to the public. Nonguests can also stop by the Empress for a traditional afternoon tea (reservations recommended), meet for a curry under the tiger skin in the Bengal Room, enjoy a treatment at the hotel's Willow Stream spa, sample the superb French-influence cuisine in the Empress Room restaurant, or check out the high-end shops and galleries in the hotel's arcade. **Miniature World** (☎ 250/385-9731), a display of doll-size dioramas, including one of the world's longest model railways, is on the Humboldt Street side of the complex. ⊠ *721 Government St., entrance at Belleville and Government, Downtown Victoria* ☎ *250/384-8111, 250/389-2727 tea reservations* ⊕ *www.fairmont.com/empress* ⊠ *Afternoon tea C\$50 in summer, C\$26–C\$35 in winter; Miniature World C\$9.*

㉑ Helmcken House. The oldest house in British Columbia was erected in 1852 for pioneer doctor and statesman John Sebastian Helmcken. It is a treasure trove of history, from the family's Victorian furnishings to the doctor's intriguing collection of 19th-century medical tools. Audio tours last 20 minutes. Beside Helmcken House is **Thunderbird Park,** with totem poles and a ceremonial longhouse constructed by Kwakiutl chief Mungo Martin. Next door is **St. Ann's Schoolhouse,** one of British Columbia's oldest schools (you can view the interior through the door). ⊠ *10 Elliot St., Downtown Victoria* ☎ *250/361-0021* ⊕ *www.heritage. gov.bc.ca* ⊠ *C\$5* ☉ *May–Oct., daily 10–5; Nov.–Apr., Thurs.–Mon. noon–4; some Christmas and Halloween programs.*

㉕ Maritime Museum of British Columbia. In Victoria's original courthouse, model ships, Royal Navy charts, photographs, uniforms, and ships' bells chronicle British Columbia's seafaring history. Among the hand-built boats on display is the Tilikum, a dugout canoe that sailed from Victoria to England between 1901 and 1904. An 1899 hand-operated cage lift, believed to be the oldest continuously operating elevator in North America, ascends to the third floor, where an 1888 Vice-Admiralty courtroom looks set for a court-martial. ⊠ *28 Bastion Sq., Old Town* ☎ *250/385-4222* ⊕ *www.mmbc.bc.ca* ⊠ *C\$6* ☉ *Daily 9:30–4:30.*

㉖ Market Square. During Victoria's late-19th-century heyday, this three-level square, originally the courtyard of an old inn, provided everything a sailor, miner, or up-country lumberjack could want. Now, beautifully restored to its original architectural, if not commercial, character, it's a traffic-free café- and boutique-lined hangout. ⊠ *560 Johnson St., Old Town* ☎ *250/386-2441.*

★ ⑲ Parliament Buildings. Designed by Francis Rattenbury, who also designed the Fairmont Empress Hotel, these massive stone structures, completed in 1898, dominate the Inner Harbour. Two statues flank the main doors: one of Sir James Douglas (1803–77), who chose the site where Victoria was built, and another of Sir Matthew Baille Begbie (1819–94), the man in charge of law and order during the gold rush. Atop the central dome is a gilded statue of Captain George Vancouver (1757–98), the first European to sail around Vancouver Island. A statue of Queen Victoria (1819–1901) stands in front of the complex. More than 3,000 lights outline the buildings at night. The interior is lavishly appointed with stained-glass windows and murals depicting scenes from the province's history. From the public gallery, when the legislature is in session you can watch British Columbian democracy at work; tradition has the opposing parties sitting 2½ sword lengths apart. Informative half-hour tours are free. ⊠ *501 Belleville St., Downtown Victoria* ☎ *250/387–3046* ⊕ *www.legis.gov.bc.ca* ⊠ *Free* ⊗ *Mid-May–Labor Day, daily 8:30–5; Sept.–mid-May, weekdays 8:30–5; last tour at 4 PM.*

㉙ Point Ellice House. This restored 1860s Italianate villa overlooking the Upper Harbour has the largest collection of Victorian furnishings in western Canada. Tea with home-baked goodies is served on the lawn. You can also take an audio tour of the house, stroll in the gardens, or try your hand at croquet. To get here, take a Harbour Ferries boat from the dock in front of the Empress Hotel. Reservations are recommended for tea. ⊠ *2616 Pleasant St., Upper Harbour* ☎ *250/380–6506* ⊕ *www. heritage.gov.bc.ca* ⊠ *C$7, C$20 with tea* ⊗ *Mid-May–mid-Sept., daily noon–5; tea daily noon–4; some Christmas and Halloween programs.*

㉛ Royal British Columbia Museum. This excellent museum, one of Victoria's leading attractions, traces several thousand years of British Columbian history. Exhibits include a genuine Kwakwaka'wakw longhouse (the builders retain rights to its ceremonial use) and an extensive collection of First Nations masks and other artifacts. The Natural History Gallery re-creates the sights and sounds of a rain forest, tidal wetlands, and other B.C. natural habitats, and the Open Ocean exhibit mimics a submarine journey. A replica of Captain Vancouver's ship, the HMCS *Discovery,* creaks convincingly, and a re-created frontier town comes complete with cobbled streets, silent movies, and the smells of home baking. Century Hall reviews British Columbia's 20th-century history, and an on-site IMAX theater shows *National Geographic* films on a six-story-high screen. ⊠ *675 Belleville St., Downtown Victoria* ☎ *250/356–7226 or 888/447–7977* ⊕ *www.royalbcmuseum.bc.ca* ⊠ *$10, IMAX theater $9.75, combination ticket $17.75* ⊗ *Museum daily 9–5; theater daily 9–8; call for show times.*

Fodor'sChoice ★

㉒ St. Ann's Academy. This former convent and school, founded in 1858, played a central role in British Columbia's pioneer life. The academy's chapel, the first Roman Catholic cathedral in Victoria, has been restored to look just as it did in the 1920s. The 6-acre grounds, with fruit trees and herb and flower gardens, are also being restored as historic landscapes. ⊠ *835 Humboldt St., Downtown Victoria* ☎ *250/953–8828* ⊕ *www.bcpcc.com/stanns* ⊠ *By donation* ⊗ *Gardens daily. Chapel mid-May–Labor Day, daily 10–4; Labor Day–mid-May, call for hrs.*

㉔ Victoria Bug Zoo. Kids of all ages are drawn to this offbeat, two-room mini-zoo. Many of the bugs—mostly large tropical varieties, such as stick insects, scorpions, and centipedes—can be held; staff members are on hand to dispense scientific information. ⊠ *631 Courtney St., Inner Harbour* ☎ *250/384–2847* ⊕ *www.bugzoo.bc.ca* ⊠ *C$6* ⊗ *July and Aug., daily 9–9; Sept.–June, Mon.–Sat. 9:30–5:30, Sun. 11–5:30.*

off the beaten path

BUTCHART GARDENS – This impressive 55-acre garden, 21 km (13 mi) north of downtown Victoria, on the way to the Swartz Bay ferry terminal, grows more than 700 varieties of flowers in its sunken, Italian, Japanese, and rose gardens. In summer, subtle lights illuminate the gardens at night, and fireworks light the sky over the gardens every Saturday night in July and August. Also on the premises are a seed and gift shop, two restaurants, and a coffee shop. Traditional English afternoon tea is served daily in the dining room. To get to the gardens by transit, take Bus 75 from downtown. ⊠ *800 Benvenuto Ave., Brentwood Bay* ☎ *250/652–5256 or 866/652–4422* ⊕ *www.butchartgardens.com* ⊠ *Mid-June–late Sept. C$20, discounted rates rest of yr* ⊗ *Mid-June–Aug., daily 9 AM–10:30 PM; Sept.–mid-June, daily 9 AM–dusk; call for precise times.*

Where to Eat

Cafés

¢–$ ╳ **Willie's Bakery.** This handsome Victorian building near Market Square is home to a bakery-café, serving wholesome breakfasts, rich soups, delicious sandwiches made with house-baked bread, tasty baked treats, and thin-crust pizzas. The brick patio with an outdoor fireplace and little fountain provides a pleasant spot to watch the world go by. ⊠ *537 Johnson St., Old Town* ☎ *250/381–8414* ⌂ *Reservations not accepted* ▭ *AE, DC, MC, V* ⊗ *No dinner Sept.–mid-May.*

Italian

$$–$$$$ ╳ **Il Terrazzo.** A charming redbrick terrace edged by potted greenery, lighted by flickering candles, and warmed by fireplaces and overhead heaters makes Il Terrazzo, tucked away off Waddington Alley and not visible from the street, the locals' choice for romantic alfresco dining in Victoria. Starters include mussels steamed with banana peppers, sun-dried tomatoes, cilantro, garlic, Asiago cheese, and cream. Main courses, such as the Dijon-encrusted rack of lamb and osso buco with porcini mushrooms, come piping hot from the restaurant's wood oven. ⊠ *555 Johnson St., off Waddington Alley, call for directions, Old Town* ☎ *250/ 361–0028* ▭ *AE, DC, MC, V* ⊗ *No lunch Sun., or Sat. Oct.–Apr.*

$$ ╳ **Zambri's.** The setting is a downtown strip mall, but inside is a lively trattoria worthy of a neighborhood in Rome. Lunch is casual. You order at the counter from a daily-changing roster of pastas, soups, and hot hearty sandwiches (such as the hot meatball or Italian sausage). Dinner brings table service and a weekly changing menu of such hearty fare as *tagliolini* (long, thin pasta) with veal, tomato, and artichoke and roasted pork loin with quince butter sauce and polenta. On Saturday night a five-course prix-fixe menu is served to a reservation-only crowd. ⊠ *110–911 Yates St., Downtown Victoria* ☎ *250/360–1171* ⌂ *Reservations not accepted* ▭ *AE, MC, V* ⊗ *Closed Sun.*

Pacific Northwest

★ $$–$$$ ╳ **Cafe Brio.** Lush Modigliani nudes and rich gold walls create a warm glow at this Italian-villa-style building. The menu, described by the owners as "West Coast contemporary with a Tuscan hint," changes seasonally and uses a wealth of local, organic ingredients. Appetizers might include smoked sablefish and potato ravioli or seared jumbo scallops with watercress. Main dishes could be Cowichan Bay duck breast; fusilli with roast mushrooms, arugula, and goat cheese; or wild sockeye salmon. The three-course tasting menus, including a vegetarian option, are popular choices. ⊠ *944 Fort St., Downtown Victoria* ☎ *250/383–0009* ▭ *AE, MC, V* ⊗ *No lunch.*

★ $$–$$$ ╳ **Herald Street Caffé.** Organic local ingredients—often prepared with Asian touches—good vegetarian selections, and house-made breads, pastas and desserts help make this lively art-filled bistro stand out among Victoria's Pacific Northwest restaurants. Try the steamed mussels in lemon Szechuan peppercorn sauce, the ginger-prawn spinach linguine, or the crab cakes with cilantro-lime pesto. Every evening between 5:30 and 6:30 you can have a three-course menu for less than $20. ⊠ *546 Herald St., Chinatown* ☎ *250/381–1441* ▭ *AE, DC, MC, V* ⊗ *No lunch Mon. or Tues.*

Seafood

$$$–$$$$ ╳ **The Blue Crab Bar and Grill.** Fresh seafood and expansive harbor views make this modern, airy restaurant a popular lunch and dinner spot. Signature dishes include Dungeness crab and shrimp cakes, and a scallop and jumbo prawn sautée, though the long list of daily specials is always tempt-

ing. In the attached lounge area, open nightly until 1 AM and with equally impressive views, you can choose from the dinner menu or opt for more casual, lower-priced fare. ✉ *146 Kingston St., in Coast Harbourside Hotel and Marina, James Bay* ☎ 250/480–1999 ▭ *AE, D, DC, MC, V.*

¢–$ ✕ **Barb's Place.** This funky, blue-painted take-out shack floats on the quay where the fishing boats dock, west of the Inner Harbour off Erie Street. Cod, lingcod, halibut, oysters, seafood burgers, chowder, and carrot cake are all prepared fresh on the premises. If you eat on the picnic tables on the wharf, you'll have a front-row view of the vessels such as paddle wheelers, houseboats, and vintage fishing boats that moor in the harbor. Ferries sail to Fisherman's Wharf from the Inner Harbor. ✉ *Fisherman's Wharf, Erie St., James Bay* ☎ *250/384–6515* ▭ *MC, V* ☺ *Closed Nov.–Feb.*

Vegetarian

$–$$ ✕ **Re-Bar Modern Food.** This bright and cheery café in Bastion Square is *the* place for vegetarians in Victoria, though the almond burgers, veggie enchiladas, decadent home-baked goodies, and big breakfasts will keep omnivores happy. An extensive tea and fresh-juice selection shares space with espresso, microbrews, and B.C. wines on the drinks list. ✉ *50 Bastion Sq., Old Town* ☎ *250/361–9223* ⊕ *www.rebarmodernfood.com* ▭ *AE, MC, V* ☺ *No dinner Sun.*

Afternoon Tea

Perhaps it's the city's British heritage, perhaps it's just a fun thing to do, but the tradition of afternoon tea lives on in Victoria. Many cafés will serve a tea, but the most popular and authentic places are clustered near the Inner Harbour and in the city's very British Oak Bay district, which you may hear described as being "behind the tweed curtain." A note about terminology: afternoon tea is a snack of tea, cakes, and sandwiches taken about 4 PM. High tea is a hot meal eaten at dinnertime. The following places serve afternoon tea.

Victoria's best-known, most elaborate, and most expensive afternoon tea is served, as it has been since 1908, on bone china at antique tables in the airy tea lobby of the **Fairmont Empress Hotel** (✉ 721 Government St., Downtown Victoria ☎ 250/389–2727). The tea is, of course, the hotel's own special blend, and the cakes, scones, tarts, and little crustless sandwiches are prepared by some of Victoria's finest pastry chefs. As you face the bill of $C50 per person in high season, remember that tea at the Empress is more than a snack. It was, historically, a way to keep civilization alive in this farthest outpost of the empire. Reservations are recommended.

Long-established and dripping with British memorabilia, the woodbeamed **Blethering Place** (✉ 2250 Oak Bay Ave., Oak Bay ☎ 250/598–1413) serves a tea of scones, Devonshire cream, fruit, sandwiches, cakes, tarts, and more between 11 AM and 7:30 PM. English breakfasts are available in the morning. The cozy, lace-curtained **James Bay Tea Room** (✉ 332 Menzies St. ☎ 250/382–8282) is a short walk from the Inner Harbour and serves full teas all day, starting at 7 AM. Breakfast and lunch are also available here.

Where to Stay

$$$$ ▦ **Delta Victoria Ocean Pointe Resort and Spa.** Across the "blue bridge" (Johnson Street Bridge) from downtown Victoria, the waterfront Delta Victoria has a resort's worth of facilities, including a full spa. You'll find expansive views of the Inner Harbour and the Parliament Buildings across

the water from the hotel's striking two-story-high lobby windows and half of the guest rooms. Modern rooms are comfortable and spacious, and the apartment-size suites have separate living and dining areas. An on-site adventure center can arrange fishing, kayaking, whale-watching, and more. ☒ *45 Songhees Rd., V9A 6T3* ☎ *250/360–2999 or 800/667–4677* 🖷 *250/360–1041* ⊕ *www.deltahotels.com* ⋙ *240 rooms, 6 suites* ♨ *2 restaurants, room service, in-room data ports, minibars, cable TV with movies and video games, 2 tennis courts, indoor pool, health club, hair salon, hot tub, sauna, bicycles, racquetball, squash, lounge, shop, baby-sitting, dry cleaning, laundry service, concierge, Internet, business services, meeting rooms, travel services, parking (fee), some pets allowed, no-smoking floors* ⊟ *AE, DC, MC, V.*

★ **$$$–$$$$** 🏨 **Abigail's Hotel.** A Tudor-style inn built in 1930, Abigail's is within walking distance of downtown. The guest rooms are attractively furnished in an English Arts and Crafts style, with whirlpool tubs and fireplaces in many rooms. Six large, luxurious rooms in the Coach House have whirlpool tubs, king-size four-poster beds, and wood-burning fireplaces. A lavish hot breakfast is included in the rate. ☒ *906 McClure St., Downtown Victoria, V8V 3E7* ☎ *250/388–5363 or 800/561–6565* 🖷 *250/388–7787* ⊕ *www.abigailshotel.com* ⋙ *23 rooms* ♨ *Some fans, in-room data ports, some refrigerators, cable TV, some in-room VCRs, shop, dry cleaning, laundry service, free parking; no a/c, no TV in some rooms, no kids under 10, no smoking* ⊟ *AE, MC, V* ⋈ *BP.*

★ **$$$–$$$$** 🏨 **Beaconsfield Inn.** This 1905 registered heritage building just four blocks from the Inner Harbour is one of Victoria's most faithfully restored Edwardian mansions. Antique furniture, mahogany floors, fireplaces, stained-glass windows, Ralph Lauren fabrics, and such period details as the Edwardian wooden canopied tub in one room render each room and suite unique. Lavish breakfasts and afternoon tea and sherry in the conservatory or around the library fire complete the Edwardian country-house ambience. ☒ *998 Humboldt St., Downtown Victoria, V8V 2Z8* ☎ *250/384–4044 or 888/884–4044* 🖷 *250/384–4052* ⊕ *www.beaconsfieldinn.com* ⋙ *5 rooms, 4 suites* ♨ *Library, free parking; no a/c, no room phones, no room TVs, no smoking* ⊟ *MC, V* ⋈ *BP.*

$$$–$$$$ 🏨 **The Fairmont Empress.** Opened in 1908, this harborside château and city landmark has aged gracefully. Its sympathetically restored Edwardian decor and top-notch service recall a more gracious age. Rooms vary in size and layout, but most are tastefully lush, with rich fabrics, buttery walls, and rosewood furniture. Many of those facing Government Street have front-row views of the Inner Harbour. ☒ *721 Government St., Downtown Victoria, V8W 1W5* ☎ *250/384–8111 or 800/441–1414* 🖷 *250/389–2747* ⊕ *www.fairmont.com/empress* ⋙ *436 rooms, 41 suites* ♨ *3 restaurants, room service, some fans, in-room data ports, some in-room safes, minibars, cable TV with movies and video games, indoor pool, gym, hot tub, sauna, spa, lounge, shops, baby-sitting, dry cleaning, laundry service, concierge, Internet, business services, convention center, meeting rooms, parking (fee), some pets allowed (fee), no-smoking floors; no a/c in some rooms* ⊟ *AE, D, DC, MC, V.*

$$–$$$ 🏨 **Swans Suite Hotel.** Across the road from the waterfront in Victoria's old town, this 1913 former warehouse is one of the city's most attractive boutique hotels. There's a brewery, restaurant, and pub on the first floor and a nightclub in the cellar. High-ceiling, apartmentlike suites, all decorated with Pacific Northwest art, fill the upper floors. The lavish penthouse suite has a private hot tub. ☒ *506 Pandora Ave., Old Town, V8W 1N6* ☎ *250/361–3310 or 800/668–7926* 🖷 *250/361–3491* ⊕ *www.swanshotel.com* ⋙ *30 suites* ♨ *Room service, fans, in-room data ports, kitchens, microwaves, cable TV, some in-room VCRs, wine* *shop, dry cleaning, laundry facilities, laundry service, business services, meeting rooms, parking (fee); no a/c, no smoking ⊟ AE, DC, MC, V.*

$ 🏠 **Craigmyle Guest House.** This Edwardian manor near Craigdarroch Castle, a mile from the city center, is Victoria's oldest bed-and-breakfast and one of its better values. The four-story guest house houses a variety of rooms, some with original furniture, claw-foot tubs, and offbeat combinations of patterned wallpaper and floral bedspreads. All have private baths, though a few are across the hall from the room. A small garden, a guest kitchen, a big comfy common room, and some units that sleep four make this a good choice for families. ⊠ *1037 Craigdarroch Rd., V8S 2A5* ☎ *250/595–5411 or 888/595–5411* 🖷 *250/370–5276* ⊕ *www. bctravel.com/craigmyle* ⇲ *16 rooms, 1 suite* ↻ *No room phones; no room TVs, no smoking* ⊟ *AE, MC, V* ⦿ *BP.*

Nightlife & the Arts

For entertainment listings, pick up a free copy of *Monday Magazine* (it comes out every Thursday) or call the Talking Super Pages at 250/ 953–9000.

Nightlife

BARS & CLUBS The **Snug Pub** (⊠ 1175 Beach Dr., Oak Bay ☎ 250/598–4556), about 10 minutes from downtown in the Oak Bay Beach Hotel, is the nearest thing to a traditional English pub in Victoria, with a cozy Tudor ambience and a waterside deck. The **Strathcona Hotel** (⊠ 919 Douglas St., Downtown Victoria ☎ 250/383–7137) is something of an entertainment complex, with a restaurant, a nightclub, and seven different bars, including a sports bar, a hillbilly-theme bar, and a rooftop patio where patrons play beach volleyball in summer. The **Saltaire Lounge** (⊠ 100–407 Swift St., Old Town ☎ 250/383–8439), a chic waterfront cocktail bar near Chinatown with a large patio overlooking the Gorge waterway, hosts live jazz on weekends.

BREWPUBS Pub culture is an important part of life in Victoria, and many of the city's most atmospheric pubs brew their own beer. The patio at the **Canoe Brewpub** (⊠ 450 Swift St., Old Town ☎ 250/361–1940) has views over the Gorge waterway. The former power station has a wide range of in-house brews, top-notch bar snacks, and a restaurant.

Chic and arty **Hugo's Brewhouse** (⊠ 625 Courtney St., Downtown Victoria ☎ 250/920–4844) serves lunch, dinner, and six of its own brews. This multipurpose nightspot is a pub by day, a lounge in the early evening, and a dance club at night. Across the Johnson Street Bridge, **Spinnakers Brew Pub** (⊠ 308 Catherine St., Vic West ☎ 250/386–2739), with a waterfront deck and cozy rooms filled with pub paraphernalia, pours Victoria's most extensive menu of microbrews. The excellent pub grub and in-house restaurant make this a popular eatery. **Swans Pub** (⊠ 1601 Store St., Downtown Victoria ☎ 250/361–3310), in a 1913 heritage building, serves its own microbrews in a room decorated with Pacific Northwest native art and has live music from Sunday through Thursday nights.

The Arts

MUSIC **Pacific Opera Victoria** (☎ 250/385–0222) performs three productions a year in the Royal Theatre (⊠ 805 Broughton St., Downtown Victoria ☎ 250/386–6121). The **Victoria Symphony** (☎ 250/385–6515) plays in the Royal Theatre (⊠ 805 Broughton St. ☎ 250/386–6121) and at the University Centre Auditorium (⊠ Finnerty Rd., University of Victoria campus ☎ 250/721–8480). The **TerrifVic Jazz Party** (☎ 250/953–2011) showcases internationally acclaimed musicians every April at seven venues around Victoria. The **Victoria Jazz Society** (☎ 250/388–4423) organizes an annual JazzFest International in late June and the Vancouver Island Blues Bash in Victoria every Labor Day weekend.

THEATER An old church houses the **Belfry Theatre** (✉ 1291 Gladstone Ave., Fernwood ☎ 250/385–6815), whose resident company specializes in contemporary Canadian dramas. **McPherson Playhouse** (✉ 3 Centennial Sq., Downtown Victoria ☎ 250/386–6121) hosts touring theater and dance companies.

Shopping

Shopping Districts & Malls

Victoria Eaton Centre (✉ 1 Victoria Eaton Centre, at Government and Fort Sts., Downtown Victoria ☎ 250/952–5680), a department store and mall, holds about 100 boutiques and restaurants. **Antique Row**, on Fort Street between Blanshard and Cook streets, has more than 60 antiques, curio, and collectibles shops. **Market Square** (✉ 560 Johnson St., Downtown Victoria ☎ 250/386–2441) has everything from toys and music to jewelry, local arts, and new-age accoutrements. High-end fashion boutiques, crafts shops, and galleries line **Trounce Alley**, a pedestrian-only lane north of View Street between Broad and Government streets.

Specialty Stores

Most of Victoria's specialty shops are on or near Government Street stretching north from the Empress Hotel.

At **Artina's** (✉ 1002 Government St., Downtown Victoria ☎ 250/386–7000 or 877/386–7700) you can find unusual Canadian art jewelry—mostly handmade, one-of-a-kind pieces. The **Cowichan Trading Co., Ltd** (✉ 1328 Government St., Downtown Victoria ☎ 250/383–0321) sells First Nations jewelry, art, moccasins, and Cowichan sweaters. The **Fran Willis Gallery** (✉ 1619 Store St., upstairs, Downtown Victoria ☎ 250/ 381–3422) shows contemporary Canadian paintings and sculpture. **Hill's Native Art** (✉ 1008 Government St., Downtown Victoria ☎ 250/ 385–3911) sells souvenirs and original West Coast First Nations art. **Irish Linen Stores** (✉ 1019 Government St., Downtown Victoria ☎ 250/383–6812) stocks fine linen, lace, and hand-embroidered items. **Munro's Books** (✉ 1108 Government St., Downtown Victoria ☎ 250/382–2464), in a restored 1909 building, sells a strong selection of local titles. Forty varieties of tea, plus coffees, tarts, and cakes, are available at **Murchie's** (✉ 1110 Government St., Downtown Victoria ☎ 250/383–3112). Handmade chocolates are displayed in antique cases at **Roger's Chocolates** (✉ 913 Government St. ☎ 250/384–7021). At **Starfish Glassworks** (✉ 630 Yates St., Downtown Victoria ☎ 250/388–7827) you can watch glassblowers create original works.

Victoria A to Z

To research prices, get advice from other travelers, and book travel arrangements, visit www.fodors.com.

AIR TRAVEL TO & FROM VICTORIA

Victoria International Airport is served by Horizon, Pacific Coastal, and WestJet airlines. Air Canada and its regional service, Air Canada Jazz, provide frequent airport-to-airport service from Vancouver to Victoria. Flights take about 35 minutes.

West Coast Air and Harbour Air provide 35-minute harbor-to-harbor service (between downtown Vancouver and downtown Victoria) several times a day. Kenmore Air Harbor operates direct daily floatplane service from Seattle to Victoria's Inner Harbour. Helijet International has helicopter service from downtown Vancouver, Vancouver International Airport, Abbotsford International Airport, and Boeing Field Seattle to downtown Victoria. The Vancouver heliport is near Vancouver's SeaBus terminal.

Air Canada ☎ 888/247-2262 ⊕ www.aircanada.ca. **Air Canada Jazz** ☎ 888/247-2262 ⊕ www.flyjazz.ca. **Harbour Air** ☎ 604/274-1277 or 800/665-0212 ⊕ www.harbour-air.com. **Helijet International** ☎ 800/665-4354, 604/273-1414, or 250/382-6222 ⊕ www.helijet.com. **Kenmore Air Harbor** ☎ 425/486-1257 or 800/543-9595 ⊕ www.kenmoreair.com. **West Coast Air** ☎ 604/606-6888 or 800/347-2222 ⊕ www.westcoastair.com. **WestJet Airlines** ☎ 800/538-5696 ⊕ www.westjet.com.

AIRPORTS & TRANSFERS

Victoria International Airport is 25 km (15 mi) north of downtown Victoria, off Highway 17.

Airport Information Abbotsford International Airport ✉ 30440 Liberator Ave., Abbotsford V2T 6H5 ☎ 604/855-1135. **Vancouver International Airport** ☎ 604/207-7077 ⊕ www.yvr.ca. **Victoria International Airport** ✉ 1640 Electra Blvd., off Hwy. 17, Sidney ☎ 250/953-7500 ⊕ www.victoriaairport.com.

AIRPORT
TRANSFER

To drive from the airport to downtown, take Highway 17 south. A taxi ride costs between C$35 and C$40, plus tip. The Airporter bus service drops off passengers at most major hotels. The fare is C$13 one-way, C$23 round-trip. There is no public transit available at Victoria International Airport, but the Airporter will take you to the nearest transit stop for C$2.

Shuttle Airporter ☎ 250/386-2525 ⊕ www.akalairporter.travel.bc.ca.

BOAT & FERRY TRAVEL

BC Ferries operates daily service between Vancouver and Victoria. Ferries arrive at and depart from the Swartz Bay Terminal at the end of Highway 17 (the Patricia Bay Highway), 32 km (20 mi) north of downtown Victoria. Sailing time is about 1½ hours. The *Victoria Clipper* runs daily year-round passenger-only service between Victoria and Seattle. The round-trip fare from mid-May to late September is C$100 to C$127, depending on the time of day; the rest of the year the round-trip is C$99; and advance purchase tickets can be as low as C$61.

Within Victoria, Victoria Harbour Ferries serve the Inner Harbour, with stops that include the Fairmont Empress, Chinatown, Point Ellice House, the Delta Victoria Ocean Pointe Resort, and Fisherman's Wharf.

Boat & Ferry Information BC Ferries ☎ 250/386-3431; 888/223-3779 in B.C.; 604/444-2890; 888/724-5223 in B.C. for vehicle reservations ⊕ www.bcferries.com. **Victoria Clipper** ☎ 206/448-5000 in Seattle; 800/888-2535 elsewhere ⊕www.victoriaclipper.com. **Victoria Harbour Ferries** ☎ 250/708-0201 ⊕ www.harbourferry.com.

BUS TRAVEL

Pacific Coach Lines operates daily, connecting service between Victoria and Vancouver using BC Ferries. BC Transit serves Victoria and the surrounding areas, including the Swartz Bay ferry terminal and Butchart Gardens. An all-day pass costs C$5.50.

Bus Information BC Transit ☎ 250/382-6161 ⊕ www.bctransit.com. **Pacific Coach Lines** ☎ 604/662-8074 in Vancouver; 250/385-4411 in Victoria; 800/661-1725 elsewhere ⊕ www.pacificcoach.com.

EMERGENCIES

Emergency Services Ambulance, fire, police ☎ 911.

TAXIS

Taxi Company Empress Taxi ☎ 250/381-2222.

TOURS

Gray Line double-decker bus tours visit the city center, Chinatown, Antique Row, Oak Bay, and Beacon Hill Park; a combination tour includes Butchart Gardens. Tally-Ho Sightseeing and Victoria Carriage Tours operate horse-drawn tours of the city. Both tours leave from the corner of Belleville and Menzies streets, near the Parliament buildings.

Fees & Schedules Gray Line ☎ 250/388-5248 or 800/663-8390 ⊕ www.grayline. ca/victoria. **Tally-Ho Sightseeing** ☎ 250/383-5067 or 866/383-5067 ⊕ www. tallyhotours.com. **Victoria Carriage Tours** ☎ 877/663-2207 or 250/383-2207 ⊕ www. victoriacarriage.com.

VISITOR INFORMATION

Tourist Information Hello B.C. ☎ 800/435-5622 ⊕ www.hellobc.com. **Tourism Victoria** ✉ 812 Wharf St. ☎ 250/953-2033 or 800/663-3883 ⊕ www.tourismvictoria.com.

VANCOUVER ISLAND

By Sue Kernaghan

The largest island on Canada's west coast, Vancouver Island stretches 564 km (350 mi) from Victoria in the south to Cape Scott in the north. A ridge of mountains, blanketed in spruce, cedar, and Douglas fir, crowns the island's center, providing opportunities for skiing, climbing, and hiking. Outside Victoria and Nanaimo, most towns on the island are so small as to be dwarfed by the surrounding wilderness. However, many have a unique charm, from pretty Victorian Chemainus to such isolated growing ecotourism centers as Tofino.

Sooke

30 *42 km (26 mi) west of Victoria on Hwy. 14.*

The village of Sooke provides a peaceful seaside escape, with rugged beaches, hiking trails through the surrounding rain forest, and views of Washington's Olympic Mountains across the Strait of Juan de Fuca. **East Sooke Regional Park**, 7 km (4 mi) east of Sooke on the south side of Sooke Harbour, has more than 3,500 acres of beaches, hiking trails, and wildflower-dotted meadows. A popular hiking and biking route, the **Galloping Goose Regional Trail** (☎ 250/478-3344) is a former railway line that runs all the way to Victoria. The **Sooke Potholes Provincial Park** (✉ End of Sooke River Rd., off Hwy. 14) has a series of swimming holes by the Sooke River. **Whiffen Spit,** a natural breakwater about a mile long, makes a scenic walk with great bird-watching. It's at the end of Whiffen Spit Road, west of the village.

The **Sooke Region Museum and Visitor Information Centre** (✉ 2070 Phillips Rd., off Hwy. 14 ☎ 250/642-6351) displays First Nations crafts and artifacts from 19th-century Sooke. It's open daily 9–6 in July and August, Tuesday–Sunday 9–5 the rest of the year. Donations are accepted.

Where to Stay & Eat

$-$$ ✕ **Seventeen Mile House.** This 1894 roadhouse is a study in island architecture at the end of the 19th century. It's a good place for pub fare, a beer, or fresh local seafood on the road between Sooke and Victoria. ✉ *5126 Sooke Rd.* ☎ 250/642-5942 ☰ *MC, V.*

$$$$ ✕🏠 **Sooke Harbour House.** This 1929 oceanfront inn is home to one of FodorśChoice Canada's finest dining rooms. The cuisine is organic and seasonal and ★ makes the most of the local bounty. The menu ($$$–$$$$) changes daily, the seafood is just-caught fresh, much of the produce is grown on the property, and the wine cellar is among the country's best. The guest rooms, each with a sitting area and fireplace, are individually decorated (some with bird or seaside themes); all but one have ocean views and private decks or patios. In summer and on weekends throughout the year rates include a picnic lunch. ⊠ *1528 Whiffen Spit Rd., V0S 1N0* ☎ *250/642–3421 or 800/889–9688* 🖶 *250/642–6988* ⊕ *www.sookeharbourhouse. com* 🛏 *28 rooms* ☖ *Restaurant, room service, some in-room hot tubs, refrigerators, massage, croquet, piano, shop, laundry service, Internet, business services, meeting rooms, some pets allowed (fee); no a/c, no room TVs, no smoking* ⊟ *DC, MC, V* ⧖ *BP; CP Sun.–Thurs. Nov.–Apr.*

$$–$$$ ✕🖾 **Point No Point Resort.** Here's a place for your inner Robinson Crusoe. Twenty-four cabins sit on the edge of a cliff overlooking a mile of private beach, Juan de Fuca Strait, and the Olympic Mountains. The one- and two-bedroom cabins, in single, duplex, and quad units, range from rustic to romantic. Every unit has a kitchen, a fireplace or wood-stove, and a deck. The lodge restaurant ($$$) serves lunch, afternoon tea, and dinner from a seafood-oriented menu. Each table has a pair of binoculars for spotting whales and ships at sea. ⊠ *1505 West Coast Rd., 24 km (15 mi) west of Sooke, V0S 1N0* ☎ *250/646–2020* 🖶 *250/646–2294* ⊕ *www.pointnopointresort.com* 🛏 *24 cabins* ☖ *Restaurant, some in-room hot tubs, hiking, some pets allowed (fee); no a/c, no room phones, no room TVs, no smoking* ⊟ *AE, MC, V* ⧖ *Restaurant: nodinner Mon. and Tues., and weekdays in Jan.*

Duncan

③① *60 km (37 mi) north of Victoria on the Trans-Canada Hwy., or Hwy. 1.*

Duncan is nicknamed the City of Totems for the many totem poles that dot the small community. Although Duncan looks a little drab from the highway, the surrounding Cowichan Valley is a bucolic region dotted with artists' studios and small wineries, many of which give tours, tastings, and entertainment. The **Duncan Visitor Infocentre** (⊠ 381 Trans-Canada Hwy. ☎888/303–3337 or 250/746–4636) has details about totem tours, winery tours, and other things to do in the area.

The **Cowichan Valley Museum** (⊠Canada Ave. ☎250/746–6612) has some interesting historic exhibits in a still-functioning 1912 train station. Between May and September, free walking tours of the totems leave hourly from the Cowichan Valley Museum.

☾ The **Quw'utsun' Cultural and Conference Centre,** covering 6 acres on the banks of the Cowichan River, is one of Canada's leading First Nations cultural and educational facilities. You can see the work of some of the Northwest's most renowned artists in a lofty longhouse-style gallery, learn about the history of the Cowichan people from a multimedia show, and sample traditional foods at the Riverwalk Café. You can also watch artisans at work in the world's largest carving house and even try your hand at carving on a visitors' pole. Crafts demonstrations and performances take place in summer. The gift shop sells, among other items, hand-knit Cowichan sweaters, for which the region is known. ⊠ *200 Cowichan Way* ☎ *250/746–8119 or 877/746–8119* ⊕ *www.quwutsun. ca* 🖾 *C$11* ⧖ *May–Sept., daily 9–6; Oct.–Apr., daily 10–5; café closed Nov.–Apr.*

The **British Columbia Forest Discovery Centre** spans some 100 acres, combining indoor and outdoor forestry-related exhibits, including a 1930s-era logging camp, and a historic train that takes visitors around the site. Interpretive trails through the forest lead to trees as much as 600 years old. ⊠ *2892 Drinkwater Rd. (Trans-Canada Hwy.)* ☎ *250/715–1113* ⊕ *www.bcforestmuseum.com* 🖾 *C$9* ⧖ *Easter–May and Sept.–mid-Oct., daily 10–4; June–Aug., daily, 10–6.*

off the beaten path	**COWICHAN BAY** – About 9 km (5 mi) southeast of Duncan (take Cowichan Bay Rd. off Highway 1), this funky little area, cafés, craft studios, and B&Bs line the waterfront. The **Cowichan Bay Maritime Centre** (☎ 250/746–4955) has old dive suits, model boats, and other maritime-related displays set up along a pier. There's also a First Nations art studio and boat-building workshop here.

Where to Eat

\$\$–\$\$\$ ✕ **Vinoteca on the Vineyard.** This 1903 farmhouse with its wide veranda is the centerpiece of the Vigneti Zanatta vineyard. Try the chef's Italian-influenced, locally sourced cuisine together with the vineyard's own wines. The menu changes frequently, but lunch might be an open-face smoked duck sandwich or chicken and porcini mushroom crepes; dinner could be tagliatelle with lemon basil cream sauce or chicken breast marinated in champagne. ⊠ *5039 Marshall Rd., 5 km (3 mi) from Duncan* ☎ *250/709–2279* ⌖ *Reservations essential* ▭ *MC, V* ⊘ *Closed Mon., Jan., and Feb.*

Chemainus

❸❷ *25 km (16 mi) north of Duncan.*

Chemainus is known for the bold epic murals that decorate its townscape, as well as for its beautifully restored Victorian homes. Once dependent on the lumber industry, the small community began to revitalize itself in the early 1980s when its mill closed down. Since then the town has brought in international artists to paint more than 30 murals depicting local historical events around town. Footprints on the sidewalk lead you on a self-guided tour of the murals. Restaurants, shops, tearooms, coffee bars, art galleries, horse-and-carriage tours, several B&Bs, and antiques dealers have helped to create one of the prettiest little towns on Vancouver Island. The **Chemainus Theatre** (⊠ 9737 Chemainus Rd. ☎ 250/246–9820 or 800/565–7738) presents family-oriented performances along with dinner.

Where to Stay & Eat

\$\$ ✕ **Hummingbird Restaurant.** A husband-and-wife team runs this little two-room café, which serves soup, salad, and sandwich lunches as well as more elaborate dinners, including a popular warm goat-cheese salad starter and a variety of seafood and pasta entrées. Personal touches, such as the organic flowers and home-grown herbs decorating each plate, make this a popular stop. ⊠ *9893 Maple St.* ☎ *250/246–2290* ▭ *AE, V* ⊘ *Closed Tues. No dinner Wed.*

\$\$ ✕ **The Waterford Restaurant.** White linen, fresh flowers, local art, and a wisteria-draped patio brighten this pretty Victorian building. French-trained chef Dwayne Maslen and his wife, Linda, welcome guests with such Pacific Northwest fare as salmon with a leek, caper, and white wine sauce; scallops and prawns Provençale; and rack of lamb with a rosemary mint demi-glace. At lunchtime try the seafood crepes. ⊠ *9875 Maple St.* ☎ *250/246–1046* ▭ *AE, MC, V* ⊘ *Closed Mon.; Oct.–Mar., call for hrs.*

★ **\$–\$\$** ▦ **Bird Song Cottage.** The whimsical white-and-lavender Victorian cottage, an easy walk from the beach and town, has been playfully decorated with antiques and collectibles, including a grand piano, a Celtic harp, and Victorian hats. A full breakfast (often with piano accompaniment) is served in a glassed-in sunporch. The Nightingale room has a private garden and a claw-foot tub, and the other two rooms have baths with showers; every room has a window seat. The innkeeper also runs the nearby **Castlebury Cottage** (⊠ 9910 Croft St. ☎ 250/246–9228

🖨 250/246–2909 ⊕ www.castleburycottage.com), a one-suite medieval-theme cottage with a kitchen (C$230–C$325). ✉ 9909 *Maple St.* 🖃 *Box 1432, V0R 1K0* ☎ *250/246–9910 or 866/246–9910* 🖨 *250/ 246–2909* ⊕ *www.birdsongcottage.com* 🗫 *3 rooms* ⚭ *Cable TV, in-room VCRs, piano, laundry service; no a/c, no kids under 8, no room phones, no TV in some rooms, no smoking* 🖃 *AE, MC, V* 🍴 *BP.*

Nanaimo

㉝ *25 km (16 mi) north of Chemainus, 110 km (68 mi) northwest of Victoria.*

Nanaimo, Vancouver Island's largest city after Victoria, is the primary commercial and transport link for the mid-island, with direct ferry service to the mainland. Though Nanaimo's many malls sprawl untidily to the north, the landscape to the south, in the regions of Cedar and Yellow Point and around the village of Ladysmith, remains pretty and rural.

Downtown Nanaimo's **Harbourside Walkway**, which starts at the foot of Bastion Street, is a pleasant shop- and café-lined stroll past visiting yachts and fishing boats. The round building overlooking the waterfront at the foot of Bastion Street is the **Bastion** (☎ 250/753–1821), an 1853 Hudson's Bay Company arsenal, one of the last of its kind in North America. The restored interior is open 10–4 daily, June 1 to Labor Day. Admission is C$1.

Re-created streets from Nanaimo's Old Town and Chinatown highlight the **Nanaimo District Museum** (✉ 100 Cameron Rd. ☎ 250/753–1821 ⊕ www.nanaimo.museum.bc.ca/ndm), which also has exhibits on the local First Nations' culture and the region's coal-mining history, and a variety of interesting temporary exhibits. You can pick up maps here for self-guided heritage walks around town. Mid-May to Labor Day the museum is open 10–5 daily; the rest of the year it's open Tuesday–Saturday 10–5. Admission is C$2.

Where to Stay & Eat

$$–$$$ ✕ **Mahle House.** Much of the innovative Pacific Northwest cuisine served
Fodor$Choice   at this cozy 1904 farmhouse is raised in the restaurant's organic garden
★   or in the neighborhood. The menu changes frequently, but highlights have included different versions of lamb, rabbit, venison, mussels, and salmon, as well as good vegetarian options. On Wednesday night, you can try the Adventure Dining Experience: for C$29 you get five courses chosen by the chef, and your dinner companions (up to a party of four) each get something different. Mahle House is about 12 km (7 mi) south of Nanaimo. ✉ 2104 Hemer Rd., at Cedar Rd. ☎ 250/722–3621 ⊕ www.mahlehouse.com 🖃 AE, MC, V ☉ Closed Mon., Tues., and 1st 2 wks in Jan. No lunch.

$$–$$$ ✕ **Milano Café and Grill.** Botticelli prints, arias on the CD player, and a fountain playing beside a flower-draped patio bring a little bit of the Italian Riviera to this 1892 downtown house. The seafood is local, the salmon is wild, and the pasta, sauces, breads, desserts, and even ice cream are made from scratch by the Lebanese-Italian team in the kitchen. ✉ 247 Milton St. ☎ 250/740–1000 🖃 AE, DC, MC, V ☉ Call for Sun. hrs.

$–$$ ✕ **Crow and Gate Neighbourhood Pub.** Set among lawns on a country road south of Nanaimo, this weathered building is probably the most authentic British-style pub in the province. Potpies, ploughmen's lunches, and roast beef with Yorkshire pudding appear on the menu, as do local oysters and both British and British Columbian brews. From Highway 1 between Ladysmith and Nanaimo, follow the signs for Yellow Point Lodge, then the signs for the pub. No one under 19 is admitted. ⊠ *2313 Yellow Point Rd., Ladysmith* ☎ *250/722–3731* ⌂ *Reservations not accepted* ⊟ *MC, V.*

$–$$$ 🏨 **Yellow Point Lodge.** Since the 1930s, this lodge, on 165 waterfront acres south of Nanaimo, has been a kind of adults-only summer camp. Everything's included, from the use of kayaks, bicycles, and tennis courts to the meals and snacks served communally in the dining room (rates are for two people). Accommodations range from comfortable lodge rooms to cozy cottages with bed frames made with logs. In addition, some summer-only cabins share a bathhouse and don't have running water. ⊠ *3700 Yellow Point Rd., Ladysmith V9G 1E8* ☎ *250/245–7422* 🖶 *250/245–7411* ⊕ *www.yellowpointlodge.com* ⇆ *9 lodge rooms, 25 rooms, 9 units in shared cabins, 12 private cabins* ⌂ *Dining room, some refrigerators, 2 tennis courts, saltwater pool, outdoor hot tub, massage, sauna, beach, boating, mountain bikes, badminton, boccie, croquet, hiking, horseshoes, Ping-Pong, volleyball, piano, meeting room; no a/c, no kids under 14, no room phones, no room TVs, no smoking* ⊟ *AE, MC, V* ⦿ *AP.*

Ucluelet

③④ *295 km (183 mi) northwest of Victoria.*

Ucluelet, which in the Nuu-chah-nulth First Nations language means "people with a safe landing place," is, along with Bamfield and Tofino, one of the towns serving the Pacific Rim National Park Reserve. Whale-watching is another main draw, though visitors also come in the off-season to watch the dramatic winter storms that pound the coast here.

Various charter companies take boats to greet the 20,000 gray whales that pass close to Ucluelet on their migration to the Bering Sea every March and April. Some gray whales remain in the area year-round. **Pacific Rim Whale Festival,** (☎ 250/726–7742 ⊕ www.island.net/~whalef), a two-week event (here and in Tofino), welcomes the whales each spring.

Ucluelet is the starting point for the **Wild Pacific Trail,** a path that winds along the coast and through the rain forest. Eventually it will link Ucluelet to the Pacific Rim National Park Reserve. At press time two sections were complete. A 2½-km (1½-mi) loop starts at **He-Tin-Kis Park** off Peninsula Road and can also be reached from the **Amphitrite Point Lighthouse** at the end of Coast Guard Road. Another 4-km (2½-mi) stretch starts at **Big Beach** at the end of Matterson Road.

Where to Stay & Eat

$–$$ ✕ **Matterson House.** In a tiny 1931 cottage with seven tables and an outdoor deck, husband-and-wife team Sandy and Jennifer Clark serve up generous portions of seafood, burgers, pasta, and filling standards such as prime rib and veal cutlets. It's simple food, prepared well with fresh local ingredients; everything, including soups, desserts, and the wonderful bread, is homemade. The wine list has local island wines unavailable elsewhere and worth trying. Matterson House is also a good breakfast stop. ⊠ *1682 Peninsula Rd.* ☎ *250/726–2200* ⊟ *MC, V.*

★ $$$–$$$$ ✕🏨 **Tauca Lea by the Sea.** This all-suites, family-friendly, waterfront resort of blue-stained cedar lodges combines a variety of facilities with a respect for the natural surroundings. The spa provides rain-forest-inspired pampering treatments, and the marina-view Boat Basin restaurant ($$–$$$$) serves Pacific Northwest fare with fresh, local ingredients—some of it straight from the fishing boats. Handcrafted furniture and terra-cotta tiles decorate the spacious suites, which also have fireplaces and ocean-view decks. A boardwalk around the property leads to a sheltered viewpoint for spotting wildlife across the inlet. Ask about kayaking and surfing packages. ⊠ *1971 Harbour Crescent* ⬦ *Box 1171, V0R 3A0* ☎ *250/726–4625 or 800/979–9303* 🖷 *250/726–4663* ⊕ *www.taucalearesort.com* ⇌ *65 suites* ⚒ *In-room data ports, kitchens, cable TV, some in-room VCRs, mountain bikes, lounge, shop, laundry facilities, meeting rooms, some pets allowed (fee); no a/c, no smoking* ⊟ *AE, DC, MC, V.*

$$$–$$$$ ⌂ **A Snug Harbour Inn.** Set on a cliff above the Pacific, this couples-oriented B&B has some of the most dramatic views anywhere. The rooms, all with fireplaces, private balconies or decks, and whirlpool baths, are decorated in a highly individual style. The Lighthouse room winds up three levels for great views, the Valhalla has a nautical theme, and the Atlantis room is dramatic, with a black Jacuzzi tub for two. Eagles nest nearby, and a staircase leads down to a rocky beach. Two rooms in a separate cottage have forest views, one of which is wheelchair accessible. ⊠ *460 Marine Dr.* ⬦ *Box 318, V0R 3A0* ☎ *250/726–2686 or 888/ 936–5222* 🖷 *250/726–2685* ⊕ *www.awesomeview.com* ⇌ *6 rooms* ⚒ *Outdoor hot tub, some pets allowed (fee); no a/c, no kids, no room phones, no room TVs, no smoking* ⊟ *MC, V* ⦿⍿ *BP.*

¢–$$$ ⌂ **Canadian Princess Resort.** You can book a cabin on this 1932 steam-powered survey ship moored at Ucluelet's marina. Though hardly opulent, the staterooms are comfortable, with one to four berths and shared bathrooms. The captain's cabin is a full suite with a private bath. The resort's shoreside rooms are bigger, if less atmospheric, with private entrances, contemporary furnishings, and patios or balconies; a few have fireplaces, and some are large enough to sleep six. Many guests come here to fish or whale-watch—the resort is home to one of the area's larger charter companies. ⊠ *1943 Peninsula Rd.* ⬦ *Box 939, V0R 3A0* ☎ *250/726–7771 or 800/663–7090* 🖷 *250/726–7121* ⊕ *www.obmg. com* ⇌ *40 shoreside rooms, 35 shipboard cabins without bath, 1 suite* ⚒ *Restaurant, pub, shop, meeting rooms; no a/c, no room phones, no TV in some rooms, no smoking* ⊟ *AE, DC, MC, V* ⦿ *Closed mid-Sept.–mid-Mar.*

Tofino

㉟ *42 km (26 mi) northwest of Ucluelet, 337 km (209 mi) northwest of Victoria.*

The end of the road makes a great stage—and Tofino is certainly that. On a narrow peninsula just beyond the north end of the Pacific Rim National Park Reserve, this is as far west as you can go on Vancouver Island by paved road. One look at the pounding Pacific surf at Chesterman Beach and the old-growth forest along the shoreline convinces many people that they've reached not just the end of the road but the end of the Earth.

Tofino's 1,400 or so permanent residents host about a million visitors every year, but they have made what could have been a tourist trap into a funky little town with several art galleries, good restaurants, and plenty of opportunity to get out to the surrounding wilds. Reservations are highly recommended any time of year.

Boats and floatplanes provide access to the surrounding roadless wilderness. The most popular day trip is to **Hot Springs Cove,** where you can soak in natural rock pools. On **Meares Island,** an easy 20-minute boardwalk trail leads to trees up to 1,600 years old. On **Flores Island,** a challenging five-hour hike called Walk on the Wild Side leads through the old growth.

At the **Tofino Botanical Gardens** (⊠ 1084 Pacific Rim Hwy. ☎ 250/725–1220 ⊕ www.tofinobotanicalgardens.com) trails wind through displays of indigenous plant life. The 12-acre waterfront site about 2 km (1 mi) south of the village on the Pacific Rim Highway is open 9 to dusk daily, and the C$10 admission is good for three days. The on-site **Café Pamplona** (open 8 AM–11 PM daily) serves organic produce grown in the gardens.

Where to Stay & Eat

$$–$$$ ✕ **RainCoast Café.** Minimalist and candlelit with peekaboo sea views, this tiny village-center restaurant shines with Asian takes on local seafood. For starters, consider the spinach salad with smoked ahi tuna and sugared pecans or the Vietnamese hot-and-sour seafood chowder. Main courses include wild salmon with almond-maple star anise butter and halibut with stir-fried vegetables in Thai green-curry coconut cream. Poultry and vegetarian dishes also appear. ⊠ 101–120 4th St. ☎ 250/725–2215 ⊟ AE, MC, V ⊗ No lunch.

$$–$$$ ✕ **The Schooner on Second.** You can't miss this 1940s red-clapboard building in central Tofino—it's the one with the schooner sticking out the back; the bow of the boat takes up a chunk of the cozy rooms. The seafood-oriented menu changes frequently, but try, if it's available, the halibut Bawden Bay, which is a halibut fillet stuffed with Brie, crab, and shrimp in an apple-brandy sauce. The Schooner is also popular with locals and tourists alike for its hearty breakfasts and its lunchtime sandwiches, burgers, and pastas. ⊠ 331 Campbell St. ☎ 250/725–3444 ⊟ AE, MC, V.

$$$$ ✕⊡ **The Wickaninnish Inn.** On a rocky promontory above Chesterman
Fodor'sChoice Beach, with open ocean on three sides and old-growth forest as a back-
★ drop, sits this cedar-sided inn. Every room has an ocean view, balcony, and fireplace; the Ancient Cedars Spa adds to the pampering. The glass-enclosed Pointe Restaurant ($$$$) has views of the crashing surf and is renowned for its Pacific Northwest cuisine; the kitchen makes the most of such local delicacies as oysters, gooseneck barnacles, wild mushrooms, Dungeness crab, and Pacific salmon. ⊠ Osprey La., at Chesterman Beach ⬡ Box 250, V0R 2Z0 ☎ 250/725–3100 or 800/333–4604 🖷 250/725–3110 ⊕ www.wickinn.com ☎ 65 rooms, 11 suites ♨ Restaurant, room service, in-room data ports, minibars, microwaves, cable TV, exercise equipment, steam room, beach, library, recreation room, lounge, Internet, business services, meeting rooms, some pets allowed (fee); no a/c, no smoking ⊟ AE, DC, MC, V.

★ $$$–$$$$ ✕⊡ **Long Beach Lodge Resort.** Dramatic First Nations art, a tall granite fireplace, and expansive views of the crashing surf define the striking great room at this luxury lodge, which overlooks the long stretch of sand at Cox Bay. Throughout the lodge and cabins are handcrafted furniture, exposed fir beams, soothing earth tones, and such artful details as hand-woven-kelp amenities baskets. Accommodations include comfortable lodge rooms and two-bedroom cabins. The chef uses fresh, local, organic ingredients for the daily multicourse menus ($$$), for the shared plates served in the great room, and even for the picnic lunches. ⊠ 1441 Pacific Rim Hwy. ⬡ Box 897, V0R 2Z0 ☎ 250/725–2442 or 877/844–7873 🖷 250/725–2402 ⊕ www.longbeachlodgeresort.com ☎ 43 rooms, 10 cottages ♨ Restaurant, in-room data ports, kitchens, minibars, cable TV, some in-room VCRs, lounge, meeting room, some pets allowed (fee); no a/c, no smoking ⊟ AE, MC, V ⊙⊡ CP.

$$ ✕⊡ **Inn at Tough City.** Vintage advertising paraphernalia and First Nations art create a fun and funky look at this harborside inn. The name is derived from Tofino's old nickname, from the days before roads, when life was rough here. It certainly isn't anymore: the guest rooms have bold

colors, stained-glass windows, hardwood floors, antiques, decks or balconies, and down duvets. Several have striking views over Tofino Harbour and Clayoquot Sound, fireplaces, and soaking tubs. The hotel's restaurant, Tough City Sushi ($$–$$$), uses fresh local seafood for its sushi and Pacific Northwest fare. ⊠ *350 Main St.* ⬛ *Box 8, V0R 2Z0* ☎ *250/725–2021 or 877/725–2021* 🖷 *250/725–2088* ⊕ *www.toughcity. com* ⌦ *8 rooms* ⚘ *Restaurant, cable TV, some pets allowed (fee); no a/c, no smoking* 🖃 *AE, MC, V.*

Sports & the Outdoors

WHALE-
WATCHING &
MARINE
EXCURSIONS

In March and April, gray whales migrate along the coast here; resident grays can be seen anytime between May and November. In addition, humpback whales, sea otters, orca, bears, and other wildlife are increasingly seen in the area. Most whale-watching operators lead excursions along the coast and to the region's outlying islands, including Meares Island, Flores Island, and Hot Springs Cove. Services range from no-frills water-taxi drop-off to tours with experienced guides.

Jamie's Whaling Station (⊠ 606 Campbell St. ☎ 250/725–3919; 800/667–9913 in Canada ⊕ www.jamies.com) runs whale-watching tours on both Zodiacs and more comfortable covered 65-foot boats. **Remote Passages Marine Excursions** (⊠ 71 Wharf St. ☎ 250/725–3330 or 800/666–9833 ⊕ www.remotepassages.com), a well-established operator, runs whale-watching, bear-watching, and other wildlife-viewing trips with an ecological and educational focus using both Zodiacs and covered boats. **Sea Trek Tours and Expeditions** (☎ 250/725–4412 or 800/811–9155 ⊕ www.seatrektours.bc.ca) operates whale- and bear-watching and harbor tours as well as day trips to Hot Springs Cove and Meares Island and glass-bottom-boat tours.

Pacific Rim National Park Reserve

36 *9 km (5 mi) south of Tofino.*

Fodor'sChoice
★

This national park has some of Canada's most stunning coastal and rainforest scenery, abundant wildlife, and a unique marine environment. It comprises three separate units—Long Beach, the Broken Group Islands, and the West Coast Trail—for a combined area of 123,431 acres, and stretches 130 km (81 mi) along Vancouver Island's west coast. The **Park Information Centre** (⊠ 2 km [1 mi] north of Tofino-Ucluelet junction on Hwy. 4 ☎ 250/726–4212) is open daily mid-June to mid-September, 9:30–5. Park-use fees apply in all sections of the park.

The **Long Beach** unit gets its name from a 16-km (10-mi) strip of hard-packed sand strewn with driftwood, shells, and the occasional Japanese glass fishing float. Long Beach is the most accessible part of the park and can get busy in summer. People come in the off-season to watch winter storms and to see migrating whales in early spring. A C$10 daily group pass, available from dispensers in the parking lots, is required for each private vehicle and includes admission to the Wickaninnish Interpretive Centre and all park interpretive programs, including shows at the Green Point campground theater. You can camp at Long Beach at the **Green Point Campground** (⊠ Off Hwy. 4 just north of Tofino-Ucluelet junction ☎ 800/689–9025 ⊕ www.discovercamping.ca) between mid-March and mid-October. Walk-in sites, in the woods and on the beach, are issued on a first-come, first-served basis and fill quickly. Drive-in sites (with no RV hook-ups) can be reserved by phone or through the Web site. A theater at the campground runs films and interpretive programs about park ecology and history; park information centers have schedules.

A first stop for many Pacific Rim National Park visitors, the **Wickaninnish Interpretive Centre** (✉ Hwy. 4 ☎ 250/726–4701 center; 250/726–7706 restaurant) is on the ocean's edge about 16 km (10 mi) north of Ucluelet. It's a great place to learn about the wilderness; theater programs and exhibits provide information about the park's marine ecology and rainforest environment. Open daily mid-March to mid-October 10:30–6, the center is also a good lunch stop—it was originally an inn, and its restaurant still serves up hearty seafood lunches and dinners. Park information is available here when the Park Information Centre is closed.

The 100-plus islands of the **Broken Group Islands** archipelago can be reached only by boat. The islands and their clear waters are alive with sea lions, seals, and whales. The inner waters are good for kayaking. Guided kayak and charter-boat tours are available from Ucluelet, Bamfield, and Port Alberni. Camping is limited to designated sites and costs C$8 per person per night. The sites are rustic and available on a first-come, first-served basis.

The third element of the park, the **West Coast Trail,** runs along the coast from Bamfield to Port Renfrew. This extremely rugged 75-km (47-mi) trail is for experienced hikers. It can be traveled only on foot, takes an average of six days to complete, and is open from May 1 to September 30. The park controls the number of people allowed on the trail, and reservations are highly recommended if you plan to hike between mid-June and mid-September; it's first-come, first-served the rest of the time. A number of fees apply: C$25 for a reservation, C$90 in park-use fees (including camping), and C$25 in ferry fares. Reservations can be made up to three months in advance via Hello B.C. (☎ 800/435–5622) from March through September. ⬧ *Box 280, Ucluelet V0R 3A0* ☎ *250/726–7721* 🖷 *250/726–4720* ⊕ *www.parkscanada.gc.ca/pacificrim.*

Vancouver Island A to Z

To research prices, get advice from other travelers, and book travel arrangements, visit www.fodors.com.

AIR TRAVEL

Air Canada Jazz serves the larger towns on Vancouver Island. Baxter Aviation links Vancouver to Nanaimo by seaplane. Kenmore Air Harbor runs daily direct seaplane flights from Seattle to Victoria year-round and has summer service from Seattle to Nanaimo. North Vancouver Air links Tofino with Vancouver and Seattle. Northwest Seaplanes operates summer floatplane service between Seattle and Nanaimo, Tofino, and other Vancouver Island destinations.

🛪 Airlines & Contacts **Air Canada Jazz** ☎ 888/247-2262 ⊕ www.flyjazz.ca. **Baxter Aviation** ☎ 250/754-1066 or 800/661-5599 ⊕ www.baxterair.com. **Kenmore Air Harbor** ☎ 425/486-1257 or 800/543-9595 ⊕ www.kenmoreair.com. **North Vancouver Air** ☎ 604/278-1608 or 800/228-6608 ⊕ www.northvanair.com. **Northwest Seaplanes** ☎ 425/277-1590 or 800/690-0086 ⊕ www.nwseaplanes.com.

AIRPORTS

Vancouver Island is served by Victoria International Airport. Otherwise, there are domestic airports in or near many towns on the island, including Nanaimo.

🛪 Airport Information **Nanaimo airport** ✉ 3350 Spitfire Rd., Cassidy ☎ 250/245-2157.

BOAT & FERRY TRAVEL

BC Ferries has frequent, year-round passenger and vehicle service to Vancouver Island. Vehicle reservations can be made for any of these routes; a C$15 reservation fee applies.

At press time HarbourLynx planned to start direct, high-speed, foot-passenger-only service between downtown Nanaimo and downtown Vancouver. The trip will take about an hour and cost C$22.

🚊 Boat & Ferry Information **BC Ferries** ☎ 250/386-3431; 888/223-3779 in B.C.; 604/444-2890 vehicle reservations; 888/724-5223 in B.C. ⊕ www.bcferries.com. **HarbourLynx** ☎ 866/206-5969 or 250/753-4443 in Nanaimo; 604/688-5465 in Vancouver ⊕ www.harbourlynx.com.

BUS TRAVEL

Gray Line of Victoria provides bus service to most towns on Vancouver Island. Long Beach Link runs a scheduled shuttle-bus service along the island's west coast, serving Ucluelet, Tofino, Tofino Airport, and the Pacific Rim National Park Reserve between May and September. From Vancouver, Greyhound serves Nanaimo and Pacific Coach Lines serves Victoria.

🚊 Bus Information **Gray Line of Victoria** ☎ 250/385-4411 or 800/318-0818 ⊕ www.grayline.ca/victoria. **Greyhound** ☎ 604/482-8747 or 800/661-8747 ⊕ www.greyhound.ca. **Long Beach Link** ☎ 250/726-7790 or 866/726-7790 ⊕ www.longbeachlink.com. **Pacific Coach Lines** ☎ 250/385-4411 or 800/661-1725 ⊕ www.pacificcoach.com.

CAR TRAVEL

Major roads on Vancouver Island, and most secondary roads, are paved and well engineered. Many wilderness and park-access roads are unpaved. Inquire locally about logging activity before using logging or forest-service roads. B.C. Highways has 24-hour highway reports; the toll call is 75¢ a minute.

The Trans-Canada Highway (Highway 1) runs from Victoria to Nanaimo. Highway 14 connects Victoria to Sooke on the west coast. Highway 4 crosses the island from Parksville to Tofino and Pacific Rim National Park Reserve.

🚊 **B.C. Highways** ☎ 900/565-4997 75¢ a minute.

EMERGENCIES

🚊 **Ambulance, fire, poison control, police** ☎ 911.

OUTDOORS & SPORTS

KAYAKING Several companies conduct multiday sea-kayaking trips to the coastal areas of Vancouver Island. Some of the excursions are suitable for beginners, and many trips provide an excellent chance to view orcas. Ecosummer Expeditions runs multiday paddles to Johnstone Strait. Gabriola Cycle and Kayak has sea-kayaking trips to the Broken Group Islands and other areas off the west coast of Vancouver Island, as well as to Johnstone Strait. Ocean West has three- to six-day paddling, camping, and orca-watching trips in Johnstone Strait. Majestic Ocean Kayaking offers guided half-day harbor tours, day trips, and multiday camping trips to the Broken Group Islands and other areas.

🚊 **Ecosummer Expeditions** ☎ 250/674-0102 or 800/465-8884 ⊕ www.ecosummer.com. **Gabriola Cycle and Kayak** ☎ 250/247-8277 ⊕ www.gck.ca. **Majestic Ocean Kayaking** ☎ 250/726-2868 or 800/889-7644 ⊕ www.oceankayaking.com. **Ocean West** ☎ 604/898-4979 or 800/660-0051 ⊕ www.ocean-west.com.

TRAIN TRAVEL

VIA Rail operates the Malahat service, a small-gauge train that runs daily between Victoria and Nanaimo.

🚊 Fees & Schedules **VIA Rail** ☎ 800/561-8630 in Canada; 800/561-3949 in U.S. ⊕ www.viarail.ca.

VISITOR INFORMATION

Ⅰ Tourist Information **Tofino Visitor Info Centre** ⊠ 1426 Pacific Rim Hwy. ☎ 250/725-3414 ⊕ www.tofinobc.org. **Tourism Nanaimo** ⊠ 2290 Bowen Rd., V9T 3K7 ☎ 250/756-0106 or 800/663-7337 ⊕ www.tourismnanaimo.com. **Tourism Vancouver Island** ⊠ 203-335 Wesley St., Nanaimo V9R 2T5 ☎ 250/754-3500 ⊕ www.islands.bc.ca.

SOUTHERN BRITISH COLUMBIA

By Chris
McBeath

With most of the population clustered in Vancouver and Victoria, those who venture farther afield have plenty of room to explore. Two hours north of Vancouver is the popular resort town of Whistler, with North America's two biggest ski mountains. Near Vancouver is the Sunshine Coast with its secluded fjords, and the Gulf Islands, both popular vacation spots for B.C. residents.

Gibsons Landing

㊲ *5 km (3 mi) plus 12 nautical mi northwest of Vancouver.*

The first stop on the Sunshine Coast, 5 km (3 mi) north of the Langdale ferry terminal, Gibsons Landing (often just called Gibsons) is an attractive seaside town that's best known as the location of *The Beachcombers,* a syndicated, long-running Canadian TV show about life on the B.C. coast. **Molly's Reach** (⊠ Molly's La. ☎ 604/886–9710), a waterfront café built as a set for the show, still serves fish-and-chips and TV memories.

The **Sunshine Coast Museum and Archives** (⊠ 716 Winn Rd. ☎ 604/886–8232 ⊕ www.gibsonslibrary.bc.ca) has an eclectic collection of pioneer artifacts, rare butterflies, and exhibits showcasing the region's seafaring history. It's open mid-June to Labor Day, Tuesday–Saturday 10:30–4:30, and Tuesday, Thursday, and Saturday 1:30–4:30 the rest of the year; donations are suggested.

Where to Stay & Eat

$$–$$$ ✕ **The Creekhouse.** The chef-owner at this wisteria-draped cottage in Roberts Creek serves classic French cuisine with a touch of Italian. The menu changes seasonally, but you can always find good lamb and local seafood options. Hardwood floors, white tablecloths, a fireplace, and outdoor patios create a casual, cozy ambience. ⊠ *1041 Roberts Creek Rd., Roberts Creek* ☎ *604/885–9321* ▭ *MC, V* ☺ *Closed Mon.–Thurs. No lunch.*

$–$$ ✕ **Gumboot Garden Café.** This funky, kid-friendly village-center café is such an area institution that the sign outside reads simply CAFÉ. The made-from-scratch soups, breads, sauces, and desserts feature, where possible, local and organic ingredients. There's a patio, woodstove, flower-stuffed gum boots (rubber boots) by the door, and a warm atmosphere that makes it tempting to just hang out. Try the eggs, sausage, and homemade granola breakfasts; the burritos, burgers, and soups at lunch; or the candlelight dinners of pizza, pasta, seafood, and vegetarian dishes. ⊠ *1057 Roberts Creek Rd., Roberts Creek* ☎ *604/885–4216* ▭ *MC, V* ☺ *No dinner Mon.–Wed. June–Sept. or Sun.–Wed. Oct.–May.*

$$–$$$ ✕▥ **Bonniebrook Lodge.** This seaside lodge, 5 km (3 mi) north of Gibsons, is a romantic spot. Rooms and suites in the original 1922 building and in the 1998 addition are attractive, with custom pine furniture, a woodsy green color scheme, fireplaces, and whirlpool tubs for two. Chez Philippe, a fine French restaurant ($$–$$$), is open to the public for dinner, serving such entrées as rack of lamb in a seven-grain crust, and grilled scallops with a saffron cream sauce. The C$30 four-course set menu is an excellent value. ✉ *1532 Oceanbeach Esplanade* 🏠 *R. R. 5, V0N 1V5* ☎ *604/886–2887 or 877/290–9916; 604/886–2188 dinner reservations* 🖂 *604/886–8853* ⊕ *www.bonnniebrook.com* 🛏 *5 rooms, 2 suites* 👌 *Fans, refrigerators, cable TV, in-room VCRs; no room phones, no smoking* ▭ *AE, DC, MC, V* ⊗ *Restaurant closed Tues.–Thurs. mid-Sept.–mid-May. No lunch. Lodge and restaurant closed Jan.* ⦿ BP.

Sechelt

🟤**38** *37 km (23 mi) plus 12 nautical mi northwest of Vancouver.*

Sechelt, the largest town on the lower Sunshine Coast, is home to many artists and writers as well as a strong First Nations community, the Sechelt Nation. If you're in Sechelt in mid-August, you can catch readings by internationally acclaimed Canadian writers at the **Sunshine Coast Festival of the Written Arts** (✉ 5511 Shorncliffe Ave., Sechelt V0N 3A1 ☎ 604/885–9631 or 800/565–9631 ⊕ www.writersfestival.ca), held at Sechelt's Rockwood Centre.

House of Hewhiwus (✉ 5555 Hwy. 101 ☎ 604/885–8991) includes a small First Nations museum and a gift shop–art gallery.**Porpoise Bay Provincial Park** (☎ 604/898–3678; 800/689–9025 camping reservations ⊕ www. discovercamping.ca or www.bcparks.ca), north of Sechelt on Sechelt Inlet, is a wonderful destination for summer fun, including hiking trails, and a sandy swimming beach.

The coast's best scenery is to the north of Sechelt, around and beyond the little marinas of Madiera Park, Garden Bay, and Irvine's Landing, collectively known as Pender Harbour. Here Highway 101 winds past forests, mountains, and a confusion of freshwater lakes and ocean inlets. In summer **Pender Harbour Ferries** (☎ 604/883–2561 Pender Harbour Info Centre) runs 1½-hour boat tours of the area.

A dramatic natural sight is at **Skookumchuk Narrows Provincial Park** (✉ Egmont Rd. off Hwy. 101 ☎ 604/898–3678), 5 km (3 mi) inland from the Earls Cove ferry terminal and 45 km (28 mi) northwest of Sechelt. You can walk through the forest for 4 km (2½ mi) to a viewpoint where, at the turn of the tide, seawater churning through the narrow channel creates thrilling tidal rapids. Tide tables are posted at the trailhead.

Princess Louisa Inlet is an 8-km (5-mi) long narrow fjord at the top of Jervis Inlet; more than 60 waterfalls tumble down its steep, rugged walls. The fjord is accessible only by boat or floatplane.

Where to Stay & Eat

$–$$ ╳ **The Old Boot Eatery.** Upbeat jazz, mismatched furniture, and a Wild West mural create a fun atmosphere at this town-center local favorite. Twenty different pastas range from simple spaghetti with meat sauce to elaborate creations such as linguine with tiger prawns and Italian sausage. The bread, pasta sauces, and thin-crust pizza are all made from scratch. Half orders and a kids' menu make this a good choice for families. ✉ 5530 Wharf St. Plaza, Sechelt ☎ 604/885–2727 ▭ AE, MC, V ⊗ Closed Sun.

$–$$ ╳▦ **Ruby Lake Resort.** The Cogrossi family from Milan chose this lakeside resort as the place to serve the area's best Italian home cooking ($–$$$$). Local seafood, house-smoked salmon, and homegrown organic produce highlight seafood, pasta, and vegetarian dishes, served in the woodsy restaurant or on the patio. A floating footbridge leads to five spacious duplex cottages, all with private entrances, pine furniture, and textured decor. They overlook a lagoon that is also a bird sanctuary. Two suites on the lake are especially romantic: each has a wood-stove, soaker tub, and a lakeside deck with sunset views. ⊠ *Hwy. 101* 🗗 *R.R. 1, Site 20, C25, Madeira Park V0N 2H0* ☎ *604/883–2269 or 800/717–6611* 🖷 *604/883–3602* ⊕ *www.rubylakeresort.com* ⇆ *10 cottages, 2 suites* ♿ *Restaurant, some kitchens, some kitchenettes, refrigerators, cable TV, lake, massage, dock, boating, hiking, bar, meeting room; no room phones, no smoking, no TV in some rooms* ⊟ *MC, V* ☺ *Closed Jan.–mid-Mar. and Oct.–May. Restaurant closed Mon.–Thurs. No lunch* ↿◉↾ *CP.*

Salt Spring Island

➌⓿ *28 nautical mi from Swartz Bay (32 km [20 mi] north of Victoria), 22 nautical mi from Tsawwassen (39 km [24 mi] south of Vancouver).*

Named for the saltwater springs at its north end, Salt Spring is the largest and most developed of the Gulf Islands. Among the first non-native settlers to arrive in the 1850s were African-Americans fleeing repression in California, seafarers from Hawaii, and a small group of Australians. The agrarian tradition they and other immigrants established remains strong (a Fall Fair has been held every September since 1896), but tourism and art now support the local economy. Many artists' studios are open to tour; watch for roadway signs or pick up a tour map at the visitor center in Ganges.

Ganges, a pedestrian-oriented seaside village about 6 km (4 mi) from the Long Harbour ferry terminal, is the main commercial center for Salt Spring Island's 10,000 residents. It has dozens of smart boutiques, galleries, and restaurants.

At the south end of Salt Spring Island, where the ferries from Victoria arrive, is the tiny village of **Fulford,** which has a café, a kayaking outlet, and several offbeat boutiques. Ferries from Crofton, on Vancouver Island, arrive on the west side of Salt Spring Island at **Vesuvius,** an even smaller community with a restaurant, an old-fashioned general store, a swimming beach, and crafts studios. The island's best sunset views are from the deck of the **Vesuvius Inn Neighbourhood Pub** (☎ 250/537–2312) at the end of Vesuvius Bay Road.

Near the center of Salt Spring Island, the summit of **Mt. Maxwell Provincial Park** (⊠ Mt. Maxwell Rd. off Fulford–Ganges Rd.) has spectacular views of south Salt Spring, Vancouver Island, and other Gulf Islands. The last portion of the drive is steep, winding, and unpaved.

Ruckle Provincial Park (⊠ Beaver Point Rd. ☎ 250/539–2115 or 877/559–2115 ⊕ www.discovercamping.ca or www.bcparks.ca) is the site of an 1872 homestead and extensive fields still farmed by the Ruckle family. The park also has picnic spots and seaside campsites, 11 km (7 mi) of coastline, and 8 km (5 mi) of trails leading to rocky headlands. Camping is free from November to mid-March on a first-come, first-served basis. Reservations are required for rest of the year

There's no public transportation on Salt Spring, so your land-travel options are cabs or rental cars. Several establishments also rent bikes and scooters. The tiny *Queen of de Nile* ferry runs from Moby's Marine Pub and Ganges Marina to Ganges town center. A water taxi runs to Mayne and Galiano islands.

Where to Stay & Eat

★ **$$$–$$$$** ✕ **House Piccolo.** Piccolo, the Finnish-born chef-owner of this tiny restaurant, serves beautifully prepared and presented European cuisine. Cre-

ations include Scandinavian-influenced dishes such as B.C. venison with a rowan- and juniper-berry scented demi-glace and broiled sea scallop brochettes. For dessert the vodka-moistened lingonberry crepes are hard to resist. The 250-item wine list includes many hard-to-find vintages. The indoor tables are cozy and candlelit; the outdoor patio is a pleasant summer dining spot. ⊠ *108 Hereford Ave., Ganges* ☎ *250/537–1844* ▱ *MC, V* ☽ *No lunch.*

$–$$ ✕ **The Oystercatcher Seafood Bar & Grill.** Panfried oysters and fresh salmon share menu space with burgers, pasta, cocktail snacks, and a kids' menu at this popular spot on Ganges's waterfront. Inside, the look is casual, nautical, and up-to-date, with a river-rock fireplace, rich colors, and a scull suspended from the ceiling. On the deck and patio, harbor views steal the scene. Open for breakfast in summer, the Oystercatcher serves food all day and morphs into a Bellini bar come sundown. ⊠ *104 Manson Rd., on waterfront, Ganges* ☎ *250/537–5041* ▱ *MC, V.*

$$$$ ✕▦ **Hastings House.** The centerpiece of this 25-acre seaside estate is
Fodor's Choice a 1930 country house, built in the style of an 16th-century Tudor-style
★ manor by Barbara Wedgwood, the British pottery heiress. Guest quarters, which are in the manor, in renovated historic outbuildings, and in a newer addition overlooking Ganges Harbour, are decorated in an English country style, with antiques, locally crafted woodwork, and fireplaces or woodstoves. Five-course prix-fixe dinners in the manor house are open to the public ($$$$; reservations essential, jacket required in main dining room). The excellent cuisine includes local lamb, seafood, and herbs and produce from the inn's gardens. The spa gives facials, manicures, and massages. ⊠ *160 Upper Ganges Rd., V8K 2S2* ☎ *250/537–2362 or 800/661–9255* ᐧ *250/537–5333* ⊕ *www. hastingshouse.com* ⇌ *3 rooms, 14 suites, 1 guest house* ⌂ *Restau-*

rant, in-room data ports, minibars, spa, bicycles, boccie, croquet, lounge, laundry service, business services, meeting rooms, no-smoking rooms; no kids under 16, no room TVs ▭ *AE, MC, V* ☺ *Closed mid-Nov.–mid-Mar.* ⦿| *BP.*

$$$ ⊡ **Apple Hill Farm.** Francophile Nancy France has filled this weathered hillside farmhouse with local art and whimsical treasures. The guest rooms (one with a sauna), the cozy common room with its big river-rock fireplace, and the nooks and crannies throughout are decorated in a singular European country style and have meadow and sea views. A wide deck, a rustic gazebo, and 43 acres of farmland provide plenty of opportunities for contemplation. Riding stables are next door. Expect breakfast to include organic eggs, fruit, and vegetables from the farm. ⊠ *201 Wright Rd., V8K 2H8* ☎ *250/537–9738* 🖷 *250/538–0217* ⊕ *www.applehillfarm.net* ⟿ *3 rooms* ⌂ *Refrigerators, tennis court, hot tub, massage, sauna, hiking, piano; no room phones, no room TVs, no smoking* ▭ *MC* ⦿| *BP.*

$$–$$$ ⊡ **Beddis House.** This 1900 waterfront farmhouse is home to a guest lounge, a sunlit breakfast room, and three guest rooms, all enriched with country pine and a sprinkling of antiques. The rooms have woodstoves, claw-foot tubs, and an ocean-view deck or balcony. The Rose Bower Room takes up most of the top floor and has a king-size four-poster bed as well as sea and garden views. You can stroll in the 1¼-acre garden or step down to the inn's white clamshell beach. Local outfitters will deliver kayaks to the property. ⊠ *131 Miles Ave., V8K 2E1* ☎ *250/537–1028 or 866/537–1028* ⊕ *www.beddishousebandb.com* ⟿ *3 rooms* ⌂ *Fans, beach, croquet, laundry service, Internet; no kids under 14, no room phones, no room TVs, no smoking* ▭ *MC, V* ☺ *Closed Dec. and Jan.* ⦿| *BP.*

Sports & the Outdoors

For information about hiking trails and beach access, pick up a copy of the "Salt Spring Out-of-Doors Map" at the visitors information centre.

BOATING, KAYAKING & SAILING **Island Escapades** (⊠ 163 Fulford-Ganges Rd., Ganges ☎ 250/537–2537 or 888/529–2567 ⊕ www.islandescapades.com) has guided kayaking (C$35–C$95 for two to six hours; the longer tour includes a three-course dinner on the beach) and sailing trips (C$40–C$75 per person for three or four hours).

Salt Spring Marine Rentals (⊠ On Ganges Harbour next to Moby's Marine Pub ☎ 250/537–9100 ⊕ www.saltspring.com/rentals) rents kayaks and powerboats. Kayaks cost C$45 a day or C$12 per hour; powerboats are C$110 a day. Here's where to arrange fishing, sailing, and sightseeing charters; buy fishing licenses; and rent scooters (C$70 a day).

Whistler

40 *120 km (74 mi) north of Vancouver.*

Whistler and Blackcomb mountains, part of Whistler Resort, are consistently ranked among North America's top ski destinations. Between them they have the largest ski area and two longest vertical drops on the continent, as well as one of the world's most advanced lift systems. The ski-in, ski-out village has enough shops, restaurants, nightlife, and other activities that it's easy to fill a vacation without ever hitting the slopes. In winter the resort buzzes with skiers and snowboarders from all over the world. In summer, the pace relaxes as the focus shifts to cycling, hiking, golfing, and boating around Whistler Valley, although heli-skiers will still find snow.

At the base of the mountains are Whistler Village, Village North (also called Marketplace), and Upper Village—a rapidly expanding, interconnected community of lodgings, restaurants, pubs, and boutiques. Locals refer to the entire area as Whistler Village. With dozens of hotels and condos within a five-minute walk of the mountains, the site is always bustling. Another village center, called Whistler Creek, is developing along Highway 99 a couple of miles to the south.

Whistler Village is a pedestrians-only community. Anywhere you want to go within the resort is within a few minutes' walk, and parking lots are just outside the village. The bases of Whistler and Blackcomb mountains are also just at the village edge; in fact, you can ski right into the lower level of the Fairmont Chateau Whistler Hotel.

Where to Stay & Eat

$$$–$$$$ ✕ **Val d'Isère.** Chef-owner Roland Pfaff satisfies a skier's craving for fine French food with traditional dishes from his native Alsace and with Gallic takes on Canadian produce. Some specialties served in this elegant room overlooking the Town Plaza are Dungeness crab ravioli with smoked-salmon cream sauce and veal tenderloin with Vancouver Island morel mushroom sauce. ⊠ *Bear Lodge, Town Plaza, 4314 Main St.* ☎ *604/932–4666* ▤ *AE, DC, MC, V* ⊘ *No lunch Nov.–May.*

★ **$$–$$$$** ✕ **Araxi.** Golden walls, terra-cotta tiles, and original artwork create a vibrant backdrop to the French-influenced Pacific Northwest cuisine here. Local farmers grow produce exclusively for Araxi's chef, who also make good use of cheese, game, and fish from the province. Breads and pastries are made in-house each morning. The menu changes seasonally, but dishes have included Fraser Valley rabbit and alder-smoked B. C. arctic char with saffron and oyster-mushroom sauce. Wine lovers, take note: there's a 13,000-bottle inventory and five sommeliers. A heated patio is open in summer, and the lounge, with a low-price bar menu ($), is a popular après-ski spot. ⊠ *4222 Village Sq.* ☎ *604/932– 4540* ▤ *AE, DC, MC, V* ⊘ *No lunch Oct.–May.*

$–$$ ✕ **Pasta Lupino.** Fresh pasta at tiny prices draws hungry skiers to this little Whistler Marketplace trattoria. You can mix and match from a choice of pastas of the day with homemade alfredo, Bolognese, or fresh basil and plum tomato sauce or dig into one of the house specialties: lasagna, ravioli, and spaghettini with meatballs. Vegetarian pastas, decadent desserts, beer, and wine are also available. The eight tables fill up quickly, but there's always takeout. ⊠ *121–4368 Main St., next to 7-11* ☎ *604/905–0400* ⬧ *Reservations not accepted* ▤ *MC, V.*

$$$$ 🏨 **Fairmont Château Whistler Resort.** This family-friendly fortress, just steps
Fodor'sChoice from the Blackcomb ski lifts, is a self-contained, ski-in, ski-out resort-
★ within-a-resort, with its own shopping arcade, golf course, and an impressive spa with exotic Asian and Ayurvedic treatments. The lobby is filled with rustic Canadiana, handmade Mennonite rugs, enticing overstuffed sofas, and a grand fireplace. Standard rooms are comfortably furnished and of average size, decorated in burgundies and turquoises, and most have mountain views. Rooms and suites on the Entrée Gold floors have fireplaces, whirlpool tubs, and their own concierge and private lounge. The resort's Wildflower Restaurant serves fine Pacific Northwest fare against stunning mountain views. ⊠ *4599 Château Blvd., V0N 1B4* ☎ *604/938–8000 or 800/606–8244* 🖷 *604/938–2099* ⊕ *www.fairmont.com* ⇨ *500 rooms, 56 suites* ⚭ *2 restaurants, room service, in-room safes, minibars, cable TV with movies and video games, 18-hole golf course, 3 tennis courts, 2 pools (1 indoor-outdoor), gym, 4 hot tubs (1 indoor and 3 outdoor), sauna, spa, steam room, ski shop,*

ski storage, lobby lounge, shops, baby-sitting, dry cleaning, laundry facilities, concierge, concierge floor, Internet, business services, convention center, parking (fee), some pets allowed (fee), no-smoking floors
≡ AE, D, DC, MC, V.

★ **$$$$** 🏨 **Westin Resort & Spa.** This luxury hotel has a prime location on the
edge of the village. Stone, slate, pine, and cedar are used throughout the
two-story lobby. The studio and one- and two-bedroom suites are chic
and cozy, with moss-green and rust color schemes, gas fireplaces, ex-
tradeep tubs, and exceptionally comfortable beds. The 1,400-square-
foot, split-level suites are great for families: each has a full kitchen and
a loft bedroom with a whirlpool tub. The spa, with 25 treatment rooms
and a mountain-view lounge, has facials, body wraps, and holistic ther-
apies such as herbology and acupuncture. ⊠ 4090 Whistler Way, V0N
1B4 ☎ 604/905–5000 or 888/634–5577 📠 604/905–5589 ⊕ www.
westinwhistler.net ⌧ 204 rooms, 215 suites ⌂ Restaurant, room service, in-room data ports, in-room safes, some kitchens, cable TV with
movies and video games, golf privileges, indoor-outdoor pool, health
club, hot tub, outdoor hot tub, massage, sauna, spa, steam room, ski
shop, ski storage, bar, shops, baby-sitting, children's programs (ages 18
months–12 years), dry cleaning, laundry facilities, laundry service, concierge, Internet, business services, meeting rooms, parking (fee); no
smoking ≡ AE, D, DC, MC, V.

★ **$$$–$$$$** 🏨 **Durlacher Hof.** Custom woodwork, exposed ceiling beams, a kache-
lofen (farmhouse fireplace-oven), and antler chandeliers hung over fir
benches and tables exemplify the rustic Tyrolean theme of this inn, a
few minutes' walk from the village. The bedrooms are adorned in Ralph
Lauren and have custom-crafted furniture; most have balconies. Two
top-floor rooms are very spacious and have such amenities as whirlpool
tubs; smaller rooms have showers rather than tubs. Rates include a hearty
European breakfast and afternoon tea; dinner is served occasionally.
⊠ 7055 Nesters Rd., V0N 1B7 ☎ 604/932–1924 or 877/932–1924
📠 604/938–1980 ⊕ www.durlacherhof.com ⌧ 8 rooms ⌂ Outdoor
hot tub, massage, sauna, ski storage, piano, free parking; no room
phones, no room TVs, no smoking ≡ MC, V ⍾ BP.

$$–$$$ 🏨 **Summit Lodge.** Service is gracious and attentive at this friendly bou-
tique hotel, which is also one of Whistler's best values. Tucked in a
quiet part of the village, the spacious rooms here are beautifully dec-
orated with soft neutrals, custom-made cherry-wood furnishings, orig-
inal art, granite countertops, and such details as aromatherapy toiletries.
All units have balconies and fireplaces. A shuttle whisks guests to the
nearby slopes. ⊠ 4359 Main St., V0N 1B4 ☎ 604/932–2778 or 888/
913–8811 📠 604/932–2716 ⊕ www.summitlodge.com ⌧ 75 rooms,
6 suites ⌂ In-room data ports, kitchenettes, cable TV, in-room VCRs,
pool, exercise equipment, outdoor hot tub, sauna, ski storage, dry clean-
ing, laundry facilities, laundry service, concierge, business services, meet-
ing rooms, parking (fee), some pets allowed (fee), no-smoking floors
≡ MC, V.

Nightlife

For a small mountain village, Whistler has a surprisingly good choice
of nightlife, most of it in the pedestrian-oriented village and within
walking distance of the hotels and ski slopes. Most of the pubs, clubs,
and bars are open year-round. Dance clubs are open until 2 AM Mon-
day–Saturday and until 1 AM on Sunday (be prepared to line up on week-
ends); pubs close around 1 AM, midnight on Sunday. Most nightspots
serve food, which is often good value compared with that of Whistler's
pricey restaurants, and many of them either ban smoking or have large

no-smoking areas. You have to be at least 19 to enter bars or nightclubs, though many pubs have separate restaurant sections open to all. For entertainment listings, pick up a free copy of Whistler's weekly news magazine, the *Pique*.

Sports & the Outdoors

The best first stop for any Whistler outdoor activity is the **Whistler Activity and Information Center** (✉ 4010 Whistler Way ☎ 604/932–2394 or 604/938–2769) in the conference center at the edge of the village, where you can book activities; pick up hiking, biking, and cross-country skiing trail maps; and find out about equipment rentals.

DOWNHILL
SKIING &
SNOWBOARDING

Blackcomb and Whistler mountains (☎ 604/932–3434 or 800/766–0449 ⊕ www.whistlerblackcomb.com) receive an average of 360 inches of snow a year. The regular season is the longest in Canada, with lifts operating from late November to early June. If that's not enough, Blackcomb's Horstman Glacier is open June to early August for summer glacier skiing. The mountains' statistics are impressive: the resort covers 7,071 acres of skiable terrain in 12 alpine bowls and on three glaciers; it has more than 200 marked trails and is served by the continent's most advanced high-speed lift system. Blackcomb has a 5,280-foot vertical drop, North America's longest, and a top elevation of 7,494 feet. Whistler's drop comes in second at 5,020 feet, and its top elevation is 7,160 feet.

For a primer on the ski facilities, drop by the resort's free Whistler Welcome Night, held at 6:30 every Sunday evening during ski season at the base of the village gondolas. First-timers at Whistler, whether beginners or experienced skiers or snowboarders, may want to try Ski or Ride Esprit. Run by the resort, these three- to four-day programs combine ski or snowboarding lessons, après-ski activities, and an insider's guide to the mountains.

The **Mountain Adventure Centre** (✉ Pan Pacific Lodge, 4320 Sundial Crescent ☎ 604/905–2295) rents high-performance gear and lets you swap equipment during the day. It also has two alpine locations, one in the Fairmont Chateau Whistler and another at Blackcomb Day Lodge. **Whistler/Blackcomb Ski and Snowboard School** (✉ 4545 Blackcomb Way ☎ 604/932–3434 or 800/766–0449) has lessons for skiers of all levels. Equipment rentals are available at the **Whistler/Blackcomb Hi Performance Rentals** (✉ 3434 Blackcomb Way ☎ 604/905–2252), at the Whistler gondola base, and at several outlets in the village.

Shopping

Whistler has almost 200 stores, including chain and designer outlets, art galleries, gift shops, and, of course, outdoor-clothing and ski shops. Most are clustered in the pedestrian-only Whistler Village Centre; more can be found a short stroll away in Village North, Upper Village, and in the shopping concourses of the major hotels. Many goods reflect the tastes (and budgets) of the international moneyed set that vacations here, though savvy shoppers can get good deals on ski gear in spring and on summer clothing in fall.

Almost anything you buy in British Columbia is subject to a Canada-wide 7% Goods and Services Tax (GST) and a 7.5% Provincial Sales Tax (PST), and these are added at the register. If you aren't a Canadian resident, you can reclaim the GST on goods you take out of the country. **Maple Leaf GST Refund Services** (✉ 4299 B Mountain Sq. ☎ 604/905–4977) can give you an immediate refund.

British Columbia A to Z

To research prices, get advice from other travelers, and book travel arrangements, visit www.fodors.com.

AIR TRAVEL

Air Canada subsidiaries and WestJet connect Vancouver with most major towns in the province. Amigo Airways flies from Vancouver to all the southern Gulf Islands. Harbour Air Seaplanes provides regular service from Victoria, Nanaimo, and Vancouver to the southern Gulf Islands. Pacific Spirit–Tofino Air has scheduled floatplane service from Vancouver International Airport to all southern Gulf Islands. Seair Seaplanes flies from Vancouver to Salt Spring Island.

🔄 Airlines & Contacts **Air Canada Jazz** ☎ 888/247-2262 ⊕ www.aircanada.ca. **Amigo Airways** ☎ 250/758-7450 or 866/692-6440 ⊕ www.amigoairways.ca. **Harbour Air Seaplanes** ☎ 604/274-1277 or 800/665-0212 southern routes; 250/627-1341 or 800/689-4234 Prince Rupert-Queen Charlotte Island routes (in B.C. only) ⊕ www.harbour-air.com. **Pacific Spirit/Tofino Air** ☎ 250/247-9992 or 800/665-2359 ⊕ www.tofinoair.ca. **Seair Seaplanes** ☎ 604/273-8900 or 800/447-3247 ⊕ www.seairseaplanes.com.

AIRPORTS

British Columbia is served by Vancouver International Airport. An alternative is Abbotsford International Airport, about a hour drive from Vancouver. Parking here is free. There are domestic airports in most cities.

🔄 Airport Information **Vancouver International Airport** ☎ 604/207-7077 ⊕ www.yvr.ca. **Abbotsford International Airport** ☎ 604/855-1135 ⊕ www.abbotsfordairport.ca.

AIRPORT TRANSFERS LimoJet Gold runs a limousine service from Vancouver International Airport to Whistler for C$275 per trip. Perimeter Whistler Express has daily service from Vancouver International Airport to Whistler (nine times a day in ski season, with slightly fewer trips in the summer).

🔄 Taxis & Shuttles **LimoJet Gold** ☎ 604/273-1331 or 800/278-8742 ⊕ www.limojetgold.com. **Perimeter Whistler Express** ☎ 604/266-5386 or 877/317-7788 ⊕ www.perimeterbus.com.

BOAT & FERRY TRAVEL

BC Ferries provides service to Salt Spring Island. On Salt Spring Island the *Queen of de Nile* runs from Moby's Marine Pub and Ganges Marina to Ganges town center.

🔄 Boat & Ferry Information **BC Ferries** ☎ 250/386-3431; 888/223-3779 in B.C. and Alberta ⊕ www.bcferries.com. *Queen of de Nile* ☎ 250/537-5252 Salt Spring Island Visitor Centre for details.

BUS TRAVEL

Greyhound Canada connects destinations throughout British Columbia with cities and towns all along the Pacific Northwest coast. The company has service to Whistler from the downtown Vancouver depot every few hours. Whistler transit operates a free public transit system that loops throughout the village, and paid public transit serves the whole valley.

🔄 Bus Information **Downtown Vancouver Depot** ✉ 1150 Station St. ☎ No phone. **Greyhound Canada** ☎ 604/482-8747 or 800/661-8747 ⊕ www.greyhound.com. **Whistler Transit** ☎ 604/932-4020.

CAR TRAVEL

Highway 99, also known as the Sea to Sky Highway, connects Vancouver to Whistler. Highway 101, the Pan-American Highway, serves the Sunshine Coast. Major roads, and most secondary roads, are paved and well engineered, although snow tires and chains are needed for winter travel.

🔄 **BC Highways** ☎ 900/565-4997 75¢ a minute.

EMERGENCIES

🚹 Ambulance, fire, police, poison control ☎ 911 or 0.

TAXIS

For a cab in Whistler call Sea to Sky Taxi. Sunshine Coast Cabs operates along the coast.

🚹 Taxi Companies **Sea to Sky Taxi** ☎ 604/932-3333. **Sunshine Coast Cabs** ☎ 604/886-7337.

VISITOR INFORMATION

Hello B.C, run by the provincial ministry of tourism, has information about the province.

🚹 Tourist Information **Hello B.C.** ☎ 888/435-5622 ⊕ www.hellobc.com. **Salt Spring Island Visitor Information Centre** ✉ 121 Lower Ganges Rd. ☎ 250/537-5252 or 866/216-2936 ⊕ www.saltspringtoday.com. **Sechelt Visitor Information Centre** ✉ 5790 Teredo St. ☎ 604/885-0662 or 877/633-2963 ⊕ www.secheltchamber.bc.ca. **Tourism Whistler** ✉ 4010 Whistler Way ☎ 604/932-4222 or 800/944-7853; 604/664-5625 in Vancouver ⊕ www.mywhistler.com. **Whistler Activity and Information Center** ✉ 4010 Whistler Way ☎ 604/932-2394.

INDEX

A

A.C. Gilbert's Discovery Village, *125*
Abacela Vineyards and Winery, *189*
Aberdeen, WA, *404–405*
Aberdeen Museum of History, *404*
Abigail's Hotel ⌂, *551*
Ace Hotel ⌂, *271*
Adler House II, *91*
Afternoon tea, *550*
Ahtanum Mission, *473*
Air Station Flying Museum, *345–346*
Air travel. ⇨ *See* Plane travel
Airports, *F29*
Albany Regional Museum, *128–129*
Alcohol, *F38*
Alexander Blockhouse, *356*
Alexander's Country Inn ✕⌂, *449*
Alexis Hotel ⌂, *F19, 265–266*
Alibi Room (bar), *278–279*
Alice's Restaurant ✕, *338*
Alsea Bay Bridge Interpretive Center, *97*
Alton Baker Park, *133*
Alvord Desert, *215–216*
American Advertising Museum, *12*
American Hop Museum, *477*
Amity Vineyards, *121–122*
Anacortes Historical Museum, *359*
Anderson House Museum, *149*
Ann Starrett Mansion ⌂, *F21, 433*
Anthony Lakes Ski Area, *206*
Antiques, *60–61, 295, 299, 300, 301, 303, 305–306, 539*
Apartment and house rentals, *F39–F40*
Aplets and Cotlets/Liberty Orchards Co., Inc., *378*
Appleton Pass Trail, *427–428*
Araxi ✕, *570*
Ark ✕, *F23, 447*
Arlington, WA, *345–346*
Art, shopping for, *61, 295–296, 301–302, 303, 539*
Arthur D. Feiro Marine Laboratory, *417*
Ashford, WA, *449–450*
Ashland, OR, *183–186*
Ashland Creek Inn ⌂, *185*
Asotin County Museum, *494*
Astoria, OR, *77, 81–82*
Astoria Column, *77, 81*
Astoria Riverfront Trolley, *82*

ATMs, *F42*
Auto racing, *F16, 59*
Avery Park, *129*
Ayer-Shea House, *15*
Azalea Park, *109*

B

Bada Lounge, *279*
Badger Mountain Vineyard, *489*
Bainbridge Island, WA, *315–316, 320*
Bainbridge Island Vineyard and Winery, *316*
Baker City, OR, *205–208*
Ballard Locks, *240–241*
Ballooning, *76, 118*
Baltic Club (dance club), *281*
Bandon, OR, *105–106*
Bandon Beach State Park, *105*
Bandon Historical Society Museum, *105*
Barnard Griffin Winery and Tasting Room, *485*
Baseball, *59, 136, 334*
Basketball, *59, 137, 287, 476*
Bastion, *558*
Battle Mountain Scenic Corridor, *196*
Bay View State Park, *361*
Bayfront (Newport), *93–94*
Beaches, *F17, 75, 84, 93, 95, 105, 109, 142, 287–289, 317, 330, 342, 398, 412, 413, 415–416, 425–426, 531, 562*
Beaches Restaurant ✕, *462*
Beacon Rock State Park, *146, 463*
Beaconsfield Inn ⌂, *551*
Beaverton, OR, *114–115*
Bed-and-breakfasts, *F40*
Beekman House, *182*
Bell tower (Port Townsend), *430*
Bellevue Botanical Gardens, *243*
Bellevue Club Hotel ⌂, *277–278*
Bellingham, WA, *362–366*
Bellingham Cruise Terminal, *363*
Bend, OR, *164–171*
Bend Public Library, *165*
Benson Hotel ⌂, *42*
Benton City, WA, *481–482*
Benton County Historical Museum, *129*
Bethany Lake Park, *114*
Beverly Beach State Park, *95*
Bicycling, *F45, 56–57, 75, 137, 170, 219, 289, 347, 354, 387, 392, 398, 426, 434–435, 446, 516*
Big Cedar, *413–414*

Big Cliff Dam, *154*
Big Summit Prairie Loop, *164*
Birchfield Manor ✕⌂, *F20, 475*
Bird Song Cottage ⌂, *557–558*
Bird-watching, *90, 91, 95–96, 100, 109, 111, 130, 216, 316, 361, 406–407, 447, 456, 489, 504, 506, 555*
Bis on Main ✕, *260*
Bistro ✕, *84*
Bite of Seattle (festival), *F15*
BJ's Garden Gate ⌂, *419*
Black Butte, *155*
Black Sheep ✕, *184–185*
Blackman's House Museum, *347*
Blackwood Canyon Vintners, *481*
Bloedel Donavan Park, *363*
Bloedel Reserve, *316*
Blue Basin, *210*
Blue Heron Bistro ✕, *104*
Blue Heron French Cheese Company, *88*
Blue Moon ✕, *489*
Blue River Dam and Lake, *131*
Boat travel. ⇨ *See* Ferry and boat travel
Boating, *F17, 75, 203, 289–291, 326–327, 354, 387, 392, 398, 426, 435, 438, 569*
Boeing Everett Facility, *344*
Bon Odori (festival), *F15*
Bonair Winery, *477*
Bonneville Dam, *145*
Bonneville Fish Hatchery, *145*
Book shops, *61–62, 296, 300, 302, 303, 394–305, 306, 539–540*
Bookwalter Winery, *485*
Bowman Museum, *162*
Brad's Swingside Cafe ✕, *261*
Brasa ✕, *252*
Breadline Cafe ✕, *511*
Bremerton, WA, *322–324*
Bremerton Marina, *322*
Brewpubs, brew theaters, and microbreweries
  Portland, 7, 50–51
  Seattle, 280
  Vancouver and Victoria, 537, 552
Brice Creek Trail, *137*
Bridge of the Gods, *145–146*
British Columbia. ⇨ *See* Southern British Columbia; Vancouver; Vancouver Island; Victoria
British Columbia Forest Discovery Centre, *556*
Britt Festivals, *F15*

Broadway Center for the Performing Arts, 328
Broken Group Islands, 563
Brookings, OR, 108–110
Brookings Azalea Festival, F14
Brownsville, OR, 130–131
Buckner Homestead, 375
Bullards Beach State Park, 105
Bumbershoot–The Seattle Arts Festival, F15
Burke-Gilman/Sammamish River Trail, 244
Burke Museum of Natural History and Culture, 239
Burns, OR, 212–213
Bus travel, F30
Oregon, 110, 139, 157, 172, 190, 217–219
Portland, 65–66
Seattle, 308
Vancouver and Victoria, 542, 554, 564, 573
Washington, 349, 382–383, 436, 465, 482, 512, 515
Bush Barn Art Center, 125–126
Bush House, 125–126
Bush's Pasture Park, 125–126
Business hours, F30, 65
Butchart Gardens, 548
Butte Creek Mill, 180

C

C and M Stables, 100
C Restaurant ✕, F22, 535
Cabins Creekside at Welches ⌂, 154
Cafe Juanita ✕, 260
Cafe Mozart ✕, 379
Cameras and photography, F31
Camp Sherman, OR, 156–157
Camp Six Logging Museum, 330
Campbell, 15
Camping, F40, 86, 97–98, 159, 204, 205, 372, 415, 420, 424–425, 455–456, 562
Canada Day, F15
Canada Place, F15, 522–523
Canadian International Dragon Boat Festival, F15
Cannon Beach, OR, 84–85
Cannon Beach Sand Castle Contest, F15
Canoe Ridge Vineyards, 490
Canoeing, 75, 100–101, 170
Canyon Life Museum, 154–155
Cape Alva Trail, 427
Cape Arago Lighthouse, 104
Cape Arago State Park, 103–104
Cape Blanco Lighthouse, 106
Cape Blanco State Park, 106

Cape Disappointment, 442
Cape Foulweather, 93
Cape Kiwanda State Natural Area, 89
Cape Lookout State Park, 89
Cape Meares Lighthouse, 89
Cape Meares State Park, 89
Cape Perpetua Interpretive Center, 98
Cape Sebastian State Park, 108
Caper's Fine Dining ✕, 375
Capitol Campus, 337
Capitol Lake, 337
Capriccio Ristorante ✕, 129
Car rental and travel, F31–F33
Oregon, 75, 110, 139, 157, 172–173, 190, 218, 219
Portland, 66–67
Seattle, 308
Vancouver and Victoria, 542, 564, 573
Washington, 349, 383, 400–401, 437, 465–466, 483, 513, 515–516
Carl G. Washburne Memorial, 100
Carol Ships (festival), F14
Carpenter House Museum, 468
Carrol Rim Trail, 211
Cascade Locks, OR, 144–145
Cascade Park, 506
Cascade Pass, 372
Cascade Room at Dolce Skamania Lodge ✕, 146
Cascades (OR). ⇨ See Columbia Gorge and the Cascades
Cascades Dining Room ✕, 151
Cashmere, WA, 378
Casinos, 90–91, 102, 158–159, 179, 334, 410–411, 430
Castle Rock, 460
Caswell's on the Bay B&B ⌂, 446
Cat Tales Zoological Park, 497
Caterina Winery, 497
Cathedral of St. John the Evangelist, 497
Caverns, 99, 167, 187–188
Celilo Park, 149
Cemeteries, F25, 182–183, 237, 339
Center for Wooden Boats, 290
Central Oregon, 158–173
children, attractions for, 158, 166, 167
lodging, 158–159, 161, 162, 163, 168–169, 172
nightlife and the arts, 169–170
parks, 159, 161, 162, 163–164, 166, 167
restaurants, 158–159, 161, 162, 163, 168, 171–172
shopping, 170–171, 172

sports and outdoor activities, 159, 164, 167, 170
transportation, 172–173
visitor information, 173
Central Library, 5–6
Central Washington Agriculture Museum, 473
Central Washington University, 469
Centralia, WA, 448–449
Century Ballroom, 282
Century Drive (Bend), 165–166
C'est Si Bon ✕, F22, 418
Champoeg State Park, 120–121
Chanticleer Inn ⌂, 433
Charles R. Conner Museum of Zoology, 495
Charleston Marina Complex, 103
Chateau Lorane Winery, 137
Chateau Ste. Michelle Winery, 244
Chateaulin ✕, 185
Cheese-making, 88, 479
Chehalis-Centralia Steam Train Ride, 448
Chelan, WA, 374–376
Chelan County Historical Society's Museum and Pioneer Village, 378
Chemainus, B.C., 557–558
Chemainus Theatre, 557
Cheney, WA, 504–505
Cheney Cowles Memorial Museum, 504
Chetco River, 109
Chetco River Inn ⌂, 109–110
Chetco Valley Historical Museum, 109
Children, traveling with, F33–F34
Children's Museum (Jacksonville), 182
Children's Museum (Portland), 17
Children's Museum (Seattle), 224
Children's Museum of Spokane, 497
Children's Museum of Tacoma, 328
Chimpanzee and Human Communication Institute, 469
China Beach Retreat ⌂, 443
Chinatown Gate, 12
Chinese Cultural Centre Museum and Archives, 528–529
Chinook, WA, 440, 442
Chinook Winds (casino), 90–91
Chinook Wines, 480
Christina's ✕, F22, 390
Chuckanut Drive (Bellingham), 363

Churches
Oregon, 150
Portland, 6, 8
Victoria, 548
Washington, 390, 473, 497
Cinco de Mayo Festival, F14, 6
Cinerama, 283–284
City Hall (Portland), 6
Claar Cellars, 477
Clallam Bay Spit, 415–416
Clallam County Historical
Museum, 417
Clarkston, WA, 494
Clarno, OR, 211–212
Cle Elum, WA, 468–469
Cle Elum Bakery, 468
Cle Elum Telephone Museum,
468
Clear Creek Distillery, 15–16
Cleawox Lake, 100
Climate, F13
Cline Falls State Park, 163
Clinkerdagger's ✕, 499
Clothing shops, 62, 296–297,
299, 300, 302, 304, 305,
306, 540
Cloudcap Overlook, 174
Clymer Museum of Art, 469,
471
CN IMAX Theatre, 522–523
Coffeehouses and teahouses,
F25, 51–52, 280–281
Coldwater Ridge Visitors
Center, 460
Colette's Bed & Breakfast 🏠,
F20, 419
Colleges and universities
Oregon, 111, 118, 121, 127,
129, 135, 149
Portland, 10, 11
Seattle, 239
Washington, 337, 362, 469,
490, 495, 504
Collier Memorial State Park
and Logging Museum, 179
Columbia Gorge (stern-
wheeler), 145
Columbia Gorge and the
Cascades, Oregon, 140–158
children, attractions for, 148
lodging, 142, 144, 145,
146–147, 148–149, 150,
151–152, 153–154, 155,
156–157
parks, 141, 142, 147, 149,
150–151, 155–156
restaurants, 141–142, 144, 145,
146, 148–149, 150, 151,
152, 153, 155, 156
sports and outdoor activities,
152, 153
transportation, 157
visitor information, 157–158
Columbia Gorge Discovery
Center-Wasco County
Historical Museum, 149
Columbia Gorge Interpretive
Center, F23, 146, 463

Columbia Gorge Sailpark, 147
Columbia National Wildlife
Refuge, 507
Columbia Park, 489
Columbia River Maritime
Museum, F23, 77
Columbia Waterfront
Renaissance Trail, 462
Columbia Winery, 244
Colville, WA, 511–512
Colville Confederated Tribe
Museum and Gift Shop,
509–510
Colville Indian Reservation,
509–510
Colville National Forest, 511
Commonwealth Lake Park,
114
Consulates, F34, 67
Consumer protection, F34
Cooks Butte Park, 115
Cooper Mountain Vineyards,
115
Coos Bay, OR, 103–104
Coos County Historical Society
Museum, 102
Copalis Beach, WA, 411–413
Coquille Lighthouse, 105
Coquille River Museum, 105
Cork ✕, F22, 168
Corvallis, OR, 129–130
Cottage Grove, OR, 137–138
Cottage Grove Lake, 138
Cottage Grove Museum, 138
Couer d'Alene Resort 🏠,
500–501
Cougar Dam and Lake, 131
Cougar Mountain Zoo, 244
Cougar Rock Campground,
455
Coulee Dam National
Recreation Area, 508–510
Country Museum (Hillsboro),
113
Country Museum/Restored
Train Station (Silverton),
124
Coupeville, WA, 356–358
Couvron ✕, 25
Cove Palisades State Park,
F26, 161
Covered bridges, 138
Cowichan Bay Maritime
Centre, 557
Cowichan Valley Museum, 556
Coxcomb Hill (Astoria), 77
Craigdarroch Castle, 546
Crater Lake Lodge, 174, 176
Crater Lake National Park,
173–174, 176–178
Crater Rock Museum, 180
Craterian Ginger Rogers
Theater, 180
Credit cards, F6, F42
Creektown Café ✕, 491
CREHST Museum, 485
Crook County Courthouse, 162
Crown Point State Park, 142

Cruises, F34–F35, 145, 435
Crystal Garden Conservation
Centre, 546
Crystal Mountain Ski Area,
F25, 458
Cuisine, F17, F38, 225
Currency, F42
Curry County Historical
Museum, 108
Customs and duties, F35–F36
Customs Examining
Warehouse, 526

D

D River, 90
Dabney State Park, 142
Dahlia Lounge ✕, F22, 245
Dalles, OR, 149–150
Dalles Dam and Reservoir,
150
Dams, 131, 145, 150, 154,
191–192, 377, 471, 489,
508–510
Dance clubs, 52, 281–282,
537–538
Darigold Dairy Fair (cheese
factory), 479
Darlingtona Botanical
Wayside, 99
Davenport Hotel 🏠, 501
David and Lee Manuel
Museum, 201
Day Building, 16
Dayton, WA, 493–494
Dayton Historical Depot
Society, 493
Deady Hall, 135
Dean Creek Elk Viewing Area,
101
Deception Pass State Park,
358
Deepwood Estate, 126
Delores Winningstad Theater,
10
Depoe Bay, OR, 92–93
Depoe Bay Park, 92
Depot Deli & Cafe ✕, 171
Deschutes Historical Museum,
166
Detroit, OR, 154–155
Detroit Dam, 154
Devil's Elbow State Park,
98–99
Devil's Lake State Park, 91
Devil's Punchbowl, 93
Devil's Punchbowl State
Natural Area, 95
Diamond, OR, 213–214
Diamond Craters, 213
Dick and Jane's Spot, 471
Dimitriou's Jazz Alley
(nightclub), 282
Dining, F17, F21–F23, F38.
⇨ Also Restaurants under
cities and areas
Fodor's choice, F21–F23
price categories, 24, 74, 245,
514, 520

Dining Room at Salishan ✕, 92
Disabilities and accessibility, F36–F37, 67–68
Discounts and deals, F37–F38, 68
Discovery Park, 241
Discovery Trail, 444
Dr. Frank Burroughs House, 505
Dr. Sun Yat-Sen Classical Chinese Garden, F24, 529
Dog racing, 59
Dolce Skamania Lodge ⌂, 146–147, 464
Domaine Serene (winery), 122
Dorena Lake, 138
Douglas County Coastal Visitors Center, 102
Douglas County Museum, 189
Downtown Bend, 166
Drain, OR, 138–139
Drain Castle, 138
Drake Park, 166
Drews Reservoir, 216
Drift Creek Wilderness, 97
Duck Pond Cellars, 119
Duck Soup Inn ✕, F22, 395
Duncan, B.C., 556–557
Dundee, OR, 119–120
Dungeness Crab and Seafood Festival, F16
Dungeness Lighthouse, 429
Dungeness Spit, 429
Dupuis Restaurant ✕, 418
Durlacher Hof ⌂, 571
Duties. ⇨ See Customs and duties
Dykstra House ✕, 479

E

Eagle Cap Wilderness, 199
Eagle Point Inn ⌂, F21, 414–415
Eagle's Nest ✕, 217
East Benton County Historical Museum, 489
East Linn Museum, 131
East Sooke Regional Park, 555
Eastern Oregon, 191–218
children, attractions for, 201
festivals and seasonal events, 194, 198
guided tours, 194
lodging, 192, 193, 197–198, 200, 201, 202–203, 204, 205, 207–208, 209, 210–211, 212–213, 214, 215, 217
parks, 191, 192, 196, 197, 199, 202, 204, 207, 208, 209–210, 212, 213, 216
restaurants, 192, 193, 194, 197, 199–200, 201, 202–203, 205, 207–209, 210, 211, 212, 214, 215, 217
shopping, 198, 215

sports and outdoor activities, 193, 197, 198, 203, 205, 206, 217
transportation, 217–218
visitor information, 218
Eastern Oregon Museum, 206
Eastern Washington, 484–514
children, attractions for, 490–491, 497, 498–499, 505, 506
emergencies, 513
guided tours, 513
lodging, 486, 488, 490, 491–492, 493, 494, 496, 500–503, 505–506, 508, 510, 511, 512
mail and shipping, 513
money matters, 513
nightlife, 503
parks and gardens, 488, 489, 490–491, 493, 494, 495, 497, 498–499, 504, 506–507, 508–511
restaurants, 485–486, 488, 489–490, 491, 493, 495, 499–500, 505, 507, 510, 511–512
shopping, 504, 507
sports and outdoor activities, 494, 503–504
transportation, 512–513
visitor information, 513–514
Eastern Washington University, 504
Eastsound, WA, 389
Eaton Hill Winery, 478
Ebey's Landing National Historic Reserve, 356
Echo, OR, 193
Ecola State Park, 84
Ediz Hook (sand spit), 417
Edmonds, WA, 342–343
Edmonds Art Festival, F15
Edmonds Historical Museum, 342
Edmonds Underwater Park, 343
El Camino ✕, 261
El Puerco Lloron ✕, 249
Elkhorn Drive, 206–207
Ellensburg, WA, 469, 471–472
Elliot Bay Antiques, 301
Elliot Bay Book Company, F25, 302
Elliot Grand Hyatt ⌂, 264
Elsinore Theatre, 126
Emergencies
Oregon, 219
Portland, 68
Seattle, 309
Vancouver and Victoria, 543, 554, 564, 574
Washington, 349, 383, 401, 437, 466, 483, 513, 516
Emigrant Springs State Heritage Area, 196
Emmanuel Church, 390

Enchanted Forest, 128
End of the Oregon Trail Interpretive Center, 116
Enterprise, OR, 200–201
Ephrata, WA, 507–508
Ermatinger House, 117
Etta's Seafood ✕, 252
Eugene, OR, 132–137
Eugene Saturday Market, 133
Everett, WA, 343–345
Evergreen Aviation Museum, F23, 121
Excelsior Café ✕, 135
Excelsior Inn ⌂, 136
Exhibit Center, 184
Experience Music Project, 228
Ezra Meeker Mansion, 335

F

Face Rock Wayside, 105
Fairhaven, WA, 363
Fairmont Château Whistler Resort ⌂, F19, 570–571
Fairmont Empress Hotel, 546–547
Fairmont Olympic Hotel ⌂, F19, 264–265
Fandango ✕, 251–252
Farewell Bend State Park, 208
Farmers Market (Silverton), 124
Favell Museum of Western Art and Native American Artifacts, 179
Federation Forest State Park, 336
Fenix (nightclub), 282
Ferndale, WA, 366
Fernhill Wetlands, 111
Ferry and boat travel, F29–F30
Oregon, 100
Seattle, 307
Vancouver and Victoria, 541–542, 554, 563–564, 566, 573
Washington, 349, 383, 374, 382, 400, 436, 514–515
Festivals and seasonal events, F14–F16. ⇨ Also under cities and areas
Fidalgo Island, WA, 358–359
Fields Spring State Park, 494
5th Avenue Theater (Seattle), 285
5th Street Public Market (Eugene), 133
Finch Arboretum, 497
Finley National Wildlife Refuge, 130
Firemen's Pond, 163
First Congregational Church, 6
First Nation sites. ⇨ See Native American sites
Fish House Inn Bed and Breakfast and RV Park ⌂, 210–212

Fishing, F17, F45, 57, 75, 198, 219–220, 291, 381, 392, 398, 415, 420, 426–427, 443, 517

Fitness clubs and spas, 291–292

Five Sea Suns Bed & Breakfast ☷, 419–420

Flaming Geyser State Park, 336

Flavel House, 81

Flerchinger Vineyards, 148

Florence, OR, 99–101

Flores Island, 560

Flying M Ranch ☷, F20, 119–120

Fodor's choice, F19–F26

Fogarty Creek State Park, 92

Foley Station ✕, 199–200

Football, 292

Forest Discovery Center Museum, 17

Forest Grove, OR, 111, 113

Forest Grove Educational Arboretum, 111

Forest Park, 17, 19

Forests, national, 130, 150–151, 163–164, 179–180, 181, 186–187, 207, 212, 216, 317, 367, 422–423, 462, 510–511

Foris Vineyards, 188

Forks, WA, 413–415

Ft. Borst, 448

Ft. Canby State Park, 442

Fort Casey State Park, 356

Fort Clatsop National Memorial, 81

Ft. Columbia State Park and Interpretive Center, 440, 442

Fort Dalles Museum, 149

Fort Ebey State Park, 356

Fort Flagler State Park, 431

Fort Klamath Museum and Park, 178–179

Fort Nisqually, 330

Ft. Simcoe Historical State Park, 477

Fort Stevens, 81

Fort Vancouver Days, F15

Ft. Vancouver National Historic Site, 462

Ft. Walla Walla Museum, 491

Fort Worden Accommodations ☷, 434

Fort Worden State Park, 431

Forts
Oregon, 81, 178–179
Washington, 330, 356, 431, 440, 442, 448, 462, 477, 491

42nd Street Cafe ✕, 444

Four Rivers Cultural Center and Museum, 208

Fox Island Historical Museum, 324

Franklin County Historical Museum, 488

Frazier's ✕, 214

Freeland, WA, 354

Fremont National Forest, 216

Fremont Street Fair, F15

Frenchglen, OR, 214–216

Frenchglen Mercantile, 215

Friday Harbor House ☷, 396

Fruit Loop, 147

Frye Art Museum, 233

Fullford, B.C., 567

Funhouse, 389

G

Gaches Mansion, 359

Gallery at Salishan, 91

Gallery I, 471

Galloping Goose Regional Trail, 555

Ganges, B.C., 567

Gaoler's Mews (Vancouver), 523

Gardens. ⇨ See Parks and gardens

Garibaldi, OR, 85

Gaslight Inn ☷, F21, 276

Gasworks Park, 242

Gay and lesbian clubs, 52, 281

Gay and lesbian travel, F38–F39

Geiser Grand Hotel ✕☷, 07–208

Genoa ✕, 36

George E. Owen Memorial Rose Garden, 133

George Fox College, 118

George Huesner House, 16

Giant Spruce Trail, 98

Gibsons Landing, B.C., 565–566

Gifford Pinchot National Forest, 462

Gift shops, 62–63, 297–298, 299, 300, 302, 304, 305, 306, 540

Gig Harbor, WA, 324–327

Gig Harbor Museum, 324

Ginko and Wanapum State Parks, 471

Glacier, WA, 366–367

Gleneden Beach, OR, 91–92

Goat Rocks Wilderness, 459

Gold Beach, OR, 107–108

Goldendale, WA, 464–465

Goldendale Observatory, 464

Golf, F18, 57–58, 75, 292–293, 381, 446, 476, 503

Gordon Brothers Family Vineyards, 488

Government Camp, OR, 152–153

Governor Hotel ☷, 39

Governor Tom McCall Waterfront Park, 6

Grand Ronde, OR, 123

Grant County Courthouse, 507

Grant County Historical Museum (John Day), 209

Grant County Historical Museum and Village (Ephrata), 507

Grant's Brewery Pub ✕, 475

Grants Pass, OR, 186–187

Grants Pass Museum of Art, 186

Granville Island, 532–534

Granville Island Museums, 533–534

Granville Island Public Market, F35, 534

Grays Harbor County courthouse, 403

Grays Harbor Lighthouse, 406

Grays Harbor National Wildlife Refuge, 406–407

Great Canadian Family Picnic, F15

Great Jones Home (shop), 295

Green Lake, 242

Green Point Campground, 562

Green River Gorge, 336

Greenbank, WA, 354, 356

Greenbank Farm, 354

Greenway Park, 114

Gresham, OR, 141–142

Gresham History Museum, 141

Griffiths-Priday Ocean State Park, 412

Grotto, 22

Grove of the Patriarchs, 454

Guest House Cottages ☷, 354, 356

H

Halfway, OR, 204–205

Harbor Walkway (Westport), 406

Harbour Pointe Golf Club, 293

Harbourside Walkway (Nanaimo), 558

Harney County Historical Museum, 212

Harris Beach State Park, 109

Harris Ranch Trail, 97

Hart Mountain National Antelope Refuge, 216

Hastings House ✕☷, F21, 568–569

Hatfield Library, 127

Hatfield Marine Science Center, 94

Haystack Rock, 84, 89

Heathman Hotel (Portland) ✕☷, F20, 25, 42–43

Heathman Lodge (Vancouver, WA) ✕☷, 462–463

Heceta Head Lighthouse, 98–99

Hedges Cellars, 481

Hellgate Jetboat Excursions, 186

Hells Canyon, OR, 203–204

Hells Canyon National Recreation Area, 204

Helmcken House, *547*
Hemlock Street (Cannon Beach), *84*
Hendricks Park, *133*
Hendrix, Jimi, *339*
Henry Art Gallery, *239*
Heritage Museum (Astoria), *81*
Hermiston, OR, *192–193*
Higgins ✕, *F22, 25*
High Desert Museum, *F23, 167*
Hiking, *F45, 75, 164, 203, 220, 372–373, 381, 427–428, 438, 457, 503*
Hillcrest Park, *361*
Hillsboro, OR, *113–114*
Hillsboro Saturday Market, *113*
Hing Loon ✕, *F23, 254*
Hinterland Ranch, *171*
Hinzerling Vineyards, *480*
Historic Columbia River Highway, *142*
Hockey, *59, 334, 504*
Hogue Cellars, *480*
Hoh River Rain Forest, *422–423*
Hoh Valley Trail, *427*
Holidays, *F39*
Holt Center for the Performing Arts, *133–134*
Home exchanges, *F40*
Honeyman Memorial State Park, *100*
Hong Kong Bar ✕, *184*
Hood River, OR, *147–149*
Hood River Valley Blossom Festival, *F14*
Hood River Vineyards, *148*
Hoover-Minthorne House, *118*
Hoquiam, WA, *406–407*
Horizon's Edge Winery, *478*
Horse racing, *59, 294, 334*
Horseback riding, *203, 217, 294, 347, 381, 392, 398, 446, 516*
Horsethief Lake State Park, *464*
Hostels, *F40–F41*
Hot Point Overlook, *204*
Hot Rock State Park, *191*
Hot springs, *422, 560*
Hot Springs Cove, *560*
Hotel Bellwether ☒, *364*
Hotel Diamond ☒, *214*
Hotel Lusso ☒, *501*
Hotel Monaco ☒, *265*
Hotels, *F41.* ⇨ *Also Lodging under cities and areas price categories, 39, 74, 264, 514, 520*
House of Hewhiwus, *566*
House Piccolo ✕, *567–568*
Houses, historic
Oregon, 81, 117, 118, 120, 125–127, 129, 130–131, 138, 174, 176, 182, 213
Portland, 15, 16, 17, 19–20

Vancouver and Victoria, 523, 526, 529, 546, 547, 548
Washington, 335, 347, 356, 359, 375, 430, 446, 462, 471, 477–478, 505
Hovander Homestead Park, *366*
Hoyt Arboretum, *19*
Humbug Mountain State Park, *107*
Hurricane Ridge, *422*
Hutson Museum, *147*
Hyatt Vineyards, *478*

I

Ice Harbor Brewing Company, *488*
Ice Harbor Lock and Dam, *489*
Icicle Junction, *379*
Ilwaco, WA, *442–443*
Ilwaco Heritage Museum, *442*
Index, WA, *347–348*
Index Town Wall, *347*
Indian Beach, *84*
Inn at Harbor Steps ☒, *F20, 267*
Inn at Langley ✕☒, *F19, 353*
Inn @ Northrup Station ☒, *47*
Inn at the Market ☒, *F19, 267*
Insurance, *F31, F39*
International Museum of Glass, *F23, 328*
International Pinot Noir Celebrations, *121*
International Rose Test Garden, *19*
Ira Keller Fountain, *7*
Island County Historical Museum, *356*
Island Grill ✕, *358*
Island in Time Trail, *210*
Issaquah Salmon Days, *F16*

J

Jackson Bottom Wetlands Preserve, *114*
Jackson F. Kimball State Park, *179*
Jackson Memorial Visitor Center of Paradise, *454*
Jacksonville, OR, *181–183*
Jacksonville Cemetery, *F25, 182–183*
Jacksonville Inn ✕☒, *183*
Jacksonville Museum, *182*
Jamestown S'Klallam Village, *428*
Japanese Garden (Olympia), *337*
Japanese Garden (Portland), *F24, 19*
Jason Lee House, *126–127*
Jazz festivals, *F14, F15*
Jean Vollum Natural Capital Center, *13*

Jefferson County Historical Museum (Port Townsend), *430–431*
Jefferson County Museum (Madras), *159*
Jersich Park, *324*
Jetboat excursions, *186*
Jewelry shops, *63, 540*
Jimi Hendrix grave site, *339*
John D. Boon Home, *126–127*
John Day Fossil Beds National Monument, *209–210*
John Inskeep Environmental Learning Center, *116*
Johnston Ridge Observatory, *460*
Joseph, OR, *201–203*
Joseph H. Stewart State Park, *181*
Josephson's (smokehouse), *81*
Justice Center (Portland), *6–7*

K

Kah-Nee-Ta Resort and Casino ✕☒, *158–159*
Kam Wah Chung & Co. Museum, *209*
Kamiak Butte County Park, *495*
Karpeles Manuscript Library Museum, *328*
Kayaking, *387, 393, 399, 435, 438, 517, 564, 569*
KC's Espresso & Deli ✕, *155*
Keller Auditorium, *7*
Keller Heritage Center, *511*
Kelsey Creek Farm and Park, *244*
Kennewick, WA, *488–490*
Kerbyville Museum, *188*
Kestrel Vintners, *480*
Khu Larb Thai ✕, *432*
Kiger Gorge, *214–215*
Kiger Mustang Lookout, *213–214*
King County Fair, *F15*
Kiona Vineyards Winery, *481–482*
Kite festival, *F16*
Kites, shopping for, *446*
Kitsap County Historical Society Museum, *323*
Kittitas County Museum, *471*
Klamath County Museum, *179*
Klamath Falls, OR, *178–180*
Kla-Mo-Ya Casino, *179*
Klickitat County Historical Museum, *464*
Klipsan Beach Cottages ☒, *446*
Klondike Gold Rush National Historical Park, *234*
Knight Library, *135*
KOIN Center, *8*
Kokanee Cafe ✕, *156*
Kopachuk State Park, *325*

L

La Conner, WA, *359–360*
La Grande, OR, *198–200*
La Push, WA, *414*
La Wis Wis Campground, *456*
Lady of the Lake Boat Company, *374*
Lady Washington (ship), *404*
Lake Chelan State Park, *374*
Lake County Museum, *216–217*
Lake Crescent, *422*
Lake Loop, *115*
Lake Oswego, OR, *115–116*
Lake Owyhee State Park, *208*
Lake Ozette, *422*
Lake Quinault, *423*
Lake Roosevelt National Recreation Area, *509*
Lake Terrell Wildlife Preserve, *366*
Lake Simtustus RV Park, *159, 161*
Lake Whatcom Railway, *369*
Lakecliff Bed & Breakfast 🏠, *149*
Lakeview, OR, *216–217*
Lakeview Cemetery, *237*
Lampreia ✕, *F22, 250*
Lane County Historical Museum, *134*
Langley, WA, *352–354*
Lara House Bed & Breakfast Inn 🏠, *F20, 169*
Larrabee State Park, *363*
Latimer Quilt and Textile Center, *87*
Laurelhurst Park, *22*
Lava Butte and Lava River Cave, *167*
Le Gourmand ✕, *262*
Le Pichet ✕, *F22, 248*
Leadbetter State Park, *447*
Leavenworth, WA, *379–381*
L'Ecole No. 41 (winery), *491*
Lenin, statue of, *242*
Les Amis (shop), *306*
Lewis & Clark College, *11*
Lewis & Clark Interpretive Center, *442*
Lewis Building, *430*
Lewis County Historical Museum, *448*
Liliget Feast House ✕, *F22, 535*
Lime Kiln Point State Park, *394*
Lincoln City, OR, *90–91*
Lincoln County Historical Society Museums, *95*
Linfield College, *121*
Linn County Historical Museum, *130*
Lion and the Rose 🏠, *F21, 45*
Lithia Park, *184*
Little Mountain Park, *361*
Little Red Schoolhouse, *389*

Lodging, *F18, F39–F41.*
⇨ *Also under cities and areas*
with children, F33
disabilities and accessibility, F36–F37
Fodor's choice, F19–F21
price categories, 39, 74, 264, 514, 520
Loeb State Park, *109*
Log Cabin Inn ✕🏠, *132*
Long Beach, WA, *444–446*
Long Beach Boardwalk, *444*
Long Beach Kites (shop), *446*
Long Beach Lodge Resort ✕🏠, *561*
Long Beach Peninsula, WA, *440–447*
Longmire Museum, *451, 454*
Longview, WA, *461*
Lonny's ✕, *F22, 431*
Lopez Island, WA, *385–388*
Lopez Island Historical Museum, *386*
Lopez Island Vineyard, *386*
Lost Lake, *148*
Lovers Lane Loop Trail, *427–428*
Lower Klamath National Wildlife Refuge, *179*
Luggage, *F43–F44*
Luna ✕, *499*
Lunar New Year, *F14*

M

MacMaster House 🏠, *47–48*
Madras, OR, *159, 161*
Mahle House ✕, *F22, 558*
Mail and shipping, *F41–F42, 69, 309, 384, 401, 437, 466, 483, 513*
Main City Park (Gresham), *141*
Maison de Padgett Winery, *478*
Makah Cultural and Research Center, *416*
Makah Maiden Café ✕, *416–417*
Makah National Fish Hatchery, *416*
Malheur National Forest, *212*
Malheur National Wildlife Refuge, *213*
Malls and department stores, *60, 297, 298, 302–303, 304, 305, ,538–539*
Manito Park and Gardens, *498*
Manzanita, OR, *86*
Marblemount, WA, *369*
Marco's Supper Club ✕, *F21, 251*
Marcus Whitman Hotel 🏠, *492*
Marinas, *387, 392*
Marine Discovery Tours, *94–95*

Marine Gardens, *93*
Marine Park, *383*
Mariner Square (Newport), *94*
Marion County Historical Society Museum, *126–127*
Marion Oliver McCaw Hall, *285*
Mario's of Seattle (shop), *297*
Maritime Heritage Park, *362*
Maritime Museum of British Columbia, *547*
Mark O. Hatfield U.S. Courthouse, *8*
Marlin Handbell Ringers, *379*
Marriott Sea-Tac 🏠, *273*
Marriott Waterfront 🏠, *266*
Mary Smith House, *16*
Maryhill Museum of Art, *F23–F24, 464*
Mattey House Bed & Breakfast 🏠, *F21, 122–123*
Matthews Beach Park, *288–289*
Maude Kerns Art Center, *134*
Maxwell Sliding Railroad Display, *193*
Mayer State Park, *150*
Mazama Village, OR, *176*
Mazatlan Mexican Restaurant ✕, *114*
McAllister Museum of Aviation, *473*
McKay Creek National Wildlife Refuge, *196*
McKenzie Bridge, OR, *131*
McKenzie Pass, *132*
McKenzie River Highway, *132*
McLoughlin House National Historic Site, *117*
McMenamins Edgefield 🏠, *F21, 142*
McMenamins Kennedy School 🏠, *46*
McMinnville, OR, *121–123*
McNary Lock and Dam, *191–192*
McNary National Wildlife Refuge, *489*
Meal plans *F7, F39*
Meares Island, *560*
Medford, OR, *180–181*
Media, *69, 516*
Meerkerk Rhododendron Gardens, *354*
Merenda ✕, *F22, 168*
Methodist Parsonage, *126–127*
Metolius Recreation Area, *155–156*
Metolius River, *155*
Metolius River Resort 🏠, *F19, 156–157*
Microbreweries. ⇨ *See* Brew pubs, brew theaters, and microbreweries
Mill Casino-Hotel, *102*
Mill Ends Park, *11*

Millennium Plaza Park, 115
Millersylvania State Park, 337
Milo McIver State Park, 117
Miniature Railway and
   Children's Farmyard,
   530–531
Miniature World, 547
Mission Mill Village, 126–127
Mitchell, OR, 211
Moclips, WA, 412
Model Ships Museum,
   533–534
Model Trains Museum,
   533–534
Molly's Reach (café), 565
Molson Indy Formula, F16
Money matters, F42, 309,
   349–350, 384, 401–402,
   437, 466, 483, 513, 543
Monorail travel, 309
Monsoon ✕, 257
Montage ✕, F23, 34
Monteith House Museum, 129
Montesano, WA, 403
Mopeds, 392, 398
Moran State Park, 390
Morrison Riverfront Park
   Walk, 404
Moses Lake, WA, 506–507
Moses Lake Community Park,
   506
Moses Lake Family Aquatic
   Center, 506
Moses Lake Museum and Art
   Center, 506
Mt. Adams, 464
Mount Angel Abbey, 127
Mt. Ashland Inn 🏠, 185
Mt. Ashland Ski Area, 184
Mt. Bachelor Ski Area, 167
Mount Baker-Snoqualmie
   National Forest, 367
Mt. Higgins House 🏠, 346
Mt. Hood, 150–152
Mount Hood Jazz Festival, F15
Mt. Hood National Forest,
   150–151
Mount Hood Scenic Railroad
   and Dinner Train, 148
Mt. Hood Visitors Center, 153
Mt. Jefferson, 155–156
Mt. Maxwell Provincial Park,
   567
Mt. Rainier National Park,
   F24, F26, 450–459
Mt. Rainier Scenic Railroad,
   449
Mount St. Helens, 459–460
Mt. Tabor Park, 22
Mount Vernon, WA, 360–362
Mountain climbing, F17, F45,
   219, 366, 426, 457–458,
   516–517
Mowich Lake Campground,
   456
Moyer House, 130–131
Mud Mountain, 336
Mugg Estuarine Park, 90

Multnomah Falls Lodge ✕,
   144
Museum at Warm Springs,
   158
Museum of Art, 495
Museum of Flight (Seattle),
   234
Museum of Flight Restoration
   Center (Everett), 344
Museum of History & Industry,
   239
Museum of Northwest Art,
   359
Museum of the North Beach,
   412
Museum of the Oregon
   Territory, 117
Museums, F23–F24. ⇨ Also
   specific museums
Music, shopping for, 63–64,
   300, 302, 303, 304–305,
   306

N

Nahcotta, WA, 446–447
Nanaimo, B.C., 558–559
Nanaimo District Museum, 558
Nathan Loeb House, 16
National Fish Hatchery, 379
National Historic Oregon Trail
   Interpretive Center, 206
National Park Inn ✕🏠, 455
Native American sites
   Oregon, 196
   Vancouver and Victoria, 531,
   523, 556, 557
   Washington, 335–336, 344,
   416, 428, 477, 498, 509–510
Nature Conservancy Cascade
   Head Trail, 90
Naval Undersea Museum,
   323
Neah Bay, 416
Neahkahnie Mountain, 84, 85
Nehalem Bay Winery, 86
Neptune State Park, 97
Newberg, OR, 118
Newberry Volcanic National
   Monument, 167
Newell House Museum, 120
Newmark Theater, 10
Newport, OR, 93–96
Newport Belle Bed & Breakfast
   🏠, F20, 96
Nicholas' Restaurant ✕, 37
Nick's Italian Cafe ✕, 122
Nightlife and the arts. ⇨ See
   under cities and areas
NikeTown, 8
99W Drive-in, 118
Nordic Heritage Museum,
   242–243
North Bend, OR, 102–103
North Bend, WA, 340–341
North Cascades Highway,
   F26, 370
North Cascades Institute,
   367

North Cascades National Park,
   369–373
North Cascades National Park
   Headquarters, 367
North Cascades Visitor Center,
   370, 372
North Central Washington
   Museum, 376–377
North Clackamas Aquatic
   Park, 22
North Head Lighthouse, 443
Northwest Actors Studio,
   286
Northwest Alpacas Ranch, 23
Northwest Festival of Jazz and
   Wine, F15
Northwest Folklife Festival,
   F14
Northwest Museum of Arts
   and Culture, 498
Northwest Trek, 336
Northwestern Washington,
   350–385
   children, attractions for, 356,
   358, 359, 362, 366
   emergencies, 383
   festivals and seasonal events,
   379
   guided tours, 284
   lodging, 353–354, 356,
   357–358, 360, 361–362,
   364–365, 367, 372, 373–374,
   375–376, 377–378, 380–381
   mail and shipping, 384
   money matters, 384
   nightlife and the arts, 365
   parks and gardens, 354, 356,
   358, 359, 361, 362, 363,
   366, 367, 369–373, 374–375,
   377
   restaurants, 352–353, 356–357,
   358, 359–360, 361, 363–364,
   369, 373, 374, 375–376,
   377, 379–380
   shopping, 354, 359, 366
   sports and outdoor activities,
   354, 366, 367, 372–373,
   376, 378, 381
   transportation, 382–383, 384
   visitor information, 384–385
Nutcracker Museum, 379
Nutty Narrows, 461
Nye Beach, 94

O

O Canada House 🏠, 536
Oak Harbor, WA, 358
Oaks Amusement Park, 23
Oakwood Cellars, 482
Ocean Park, WA, 446
Ocean Shores, WA, 407,
   410–411
Ocean Shores Interpretive
   Center, 410
Oceanaire ✕, F22, 249
Ochoco National Forest,
   163–164
Ochoco Viewpoint, 162

Odlin County Park, *386*
Odyssey Maritime Discovery Center, *228*
Of Sea and Shore Museum, *322*
Officers' Row, *462*
Ohanapecosh Campground, *456*
Ohanapecosh Visitors Center, *454*
Ohme Gardens, *377*
Okanagan County Historical Museum, *510*
Okanagan National Forest, *510–511*
Okanagan-Wenatchee National Forest, *377*
Oktoberfest, *F16*
Old Aurora Colony, *120–121*
Old Aurora Colony Museum, *124*
Old Church, *8*
Old Church Inn ☒ , *433*
Old Fort Townsend State Park, *431*
Old Perpetual (geyser), *216*
Old St. Peter's Landmark, *150*
Old Snohomish Village, *347*
Olmstead Place State Park, *471*
Olympia, WA, *336–339*
Olympic Beach, *342*
Olympic Game Farm, *428*
Olympic National Park, **420–428**
Olympic Park Institute, *421–422*
Olympic Peninsula, WA, *402–439*
children, attractions for, *405–406, 417, 428, 431*
emergencies, *437*
guided tours, *438*
lodging, *403, 405, 406, 407, 410–411, 412–413, 414–415, 416, 417, 419–420, 423–425, 429–430, 432–434*
mail and shipping, *437*
money matters, *437*
nightlife and the arts, *430, 434*
parks, *404, 406–407, 412, 415–416, 420–428, 429, 431*
restaurants, *403, 404–405, 406, 407, 410, 412–413, 414, 416–417, 418, 423–424, 429, 430, 431–432*
shopping, *420, 435*
sports and outdoor activities, *415, 420, 425–428, 434–435*
transportation, *436–437*
visitor information, *438–439*
Omak, WA, *510–511*
Ona Beach State Park, *95*
Oneonta Gorge, *144*
Ontario, OR, *208–209*
Ontario State Park, *208*
Orcas Island, WA, *389–393*

Oregon, *F11, 72–220.*
⇨ *Also* Central Oregon; Columbia Gorge and the Cascades; Eastern Oregon; Oregon Coast; Portland; Southern Oregon; Willamette Valley and the Wine Country
emergencies, *219*
itinerary recommendations, *73*
lodging, *74*
price categories, *74*
restaurants, *74*
sports and outdoor activities, *75–76, 219–220*
timing the visit, *76–77*
transportation, *218–219, 220*
visitor information, *220*
Oregon Bach Festival, *F15*
Oregon Brewer's Festival, *F15*
Oregon Capitol, *127*
Oregon Cascades. ⇨ *See* Columbia Gorge and the Cascades
Oregon Caves National Monument, *187–188*
Oregon City, OR, *116–118*
Oregon Coast, *77–110*
children, attractions for, *77, 81, 87, 94, 95, 99, 100, 101, 106, 109*
lodging, *82, 83, 84–85, 86, 87, 88, 90, 91, 92, 93, 96, 97–98, 99, 102, 104, 106, 107, 108, 109–110*
parks and gardens, *83, 84, 85, 89, 90, 91, 92, 95, 97–99, 100, 101, 102, 103–104, 105–106, 107, 108*
restaurants, *82, 83, 84, 86, 87, 88, 90, 91, 92, 93, 96, 98, 100, 101, 102–103, 104, 106, 108, 109*
shopping, *104*
sports and outdoor activities, *100–101*
transportation, *110*
visitor information, *110*
Oregon Coast Aquarium, *94*
Oregon Coast Music Festival, *F15*
Oregon Connection (shop), *104*
Oregon Dunes National Recreation Area, *100*
Oregon Dunes National Recreation Area Visitors Center, *101*
Oregon Garden, *124*
Oregon History Center, *8*
Oregon Islands National Wildlife Refuge, *104*
Oregon Maritime Center and Museum, *13*
Oregon Museum of Science and Industry (OMSI), *23*
Oregon Shakespeare Festival, *F14*

Oregon State Fair, *F15*
Oregon State University, *129*
Oregon Trail Regional Museum, *206*
Oregon Vortex Location of the House of Mystery, *182*
Oregon Wine Tasting Room and the Bellevue Market, *122*
Oregon Zoo, *19*
Oregon's International Museum of Carousel Art, *148*
Osborn Aquatic Center, *129*
Oswald West State Park, *85*
Otter Crest Loop, *93*
Out N' About ☒ , *188*
Outdoor wear and equipment stores, *64, 298–299, 540–541*
Owen Beach, *330*
Owens Meats (smokehouse), *468*
Oyster Bar ✕ , *363–364*
Oysterville, WA, *447*

P

Pacific Beach State Park, *412*
Pacific City, OR, *89–90*
Pacific County Historical Society Museum, *447*
Pacific Crest Trail, *146*
Pacific National Exhibition, *F16*
Pacific Northwest Arts Fair, *F15*
Pacific Rim National Park Reserve, *F24, 562-563*
Pacific Rim Whale Festival, *F14, 559*
Pacific Science Center, *228*
Pacific University, *111*
Packing for the trip, *F43–F44*
Packwood, WA, *459*
Padilla Bay National Estuarine Reserve, *361*
Painted Hills, OR, *211*
Paisley, OR, *216*
Paley's Place ✕ , *F22, 32*
Palisades, *212*
Palouse Falls State Park, *493*
Pambiche ✕ , *35*
Pan Pacific Hotel ☒ , *F19, 522–523, 535–536*
Panacea Bed and Breakfast ☒ , *F21, 396*
Panama Hotel ☒ , *272*
Pantages (theater), *328*
Paradise Inn ✕☒ , *455*
Paradise Ski Area, *458*
Paradisos del Sol (winery), *478*
Parkdale, OR, *147*
Parker House ☒ , *F21, 197*
Parks and gardens, *F24, F26, F42–F43.* ⇨ *Also under* cities and areas

Parliament Buildings (Victoria), 547–548
Pasco, WA, 486, 488
Pass Creek Covered Bridge, 138
Passports and visas, F44
Patit Creek Restaurant ✕, 493
Pearson Air Museum, 462
Pelindaba Lavender Farm, 395
Pender Harbour Ferries, 566
Pendleton, OR, 194, 196–198
Pendleton Round-Up (rodeo), 194, 198
Pendleton Woolen Mills, 196
Perfume shops, 64
Petals Garden Café ✕, 429
Peter Skene Ogden Wayside, 163
Petersen's Rock Gardens, 163
Pettygrove House, 17
Phone Company ✕, 207
Pike Place Market, F25, 228–229, 298
Pike Place Market Festival, F14
Pine Mountain Observatory, 167
Pine Ridge Inn 🏨, 168
Pine Valley Lodge ✕🏨, 205
Pinnacles Overlook, 176
Pioneer Farm Museum and Ohop Indian Village, 335–336
Pioneer Mother's Memorial Log Cabin, 120
Pioneer Museum, 87
Pioneer Park (Ferndale), 366
Pioneer Park (Walla Walla), 490
Pittock Mansion, 19–20
Plane travel, F27–F29
with children, F33
luggage, F43–F44
Oregon, 110, 139, 218
Portland, 64–65
Seattle, 307
Vancouver and Victoria, 541, 553–554, 563, 573
Washington, 348–349, 382, 399–400, 436, 465, 482, 512, 514
Planetarium (Eugene), 134
Point Defiance Park, 329–330
Point Defiance Zoo and Aquarium, 329
Point Ellice House, 548
Polar Bear Swim, F14
Police Museum, 6–7
Polson Museum, 407
Pontin del Roza (winery), 480
Ponzi Vineyards, 115
Porpoise Bay Provincial Park, 566
Port Angeles, WA, 417–420
Port Angeles Fine Arts Center, 417–418

Port Gamble Historic Museum, 322
Port Orford, OR, 106–107
Port Townsend, WA, 430–435
Portland, OR, F11, 2–70
addresses, 64
Ankeny Square, 14
business hours, 65
children, attractions for, 13, 17, 19, 22, 23, 67
Chapman Square, 6
consulates, 67
disabilities and accessibility, 67–68
discounts and deals, 68
Downtown, 4–11, 24–25, 28–30, 39, 42–45, 50, 51
East of the Willamette River, 20–23, 33–38, 45–47
East Portland, 50, 51–52
emergencies, 68
festivals and seasonal events, 6
fountains, 6, 7, 14
Glazed Terra-Cotta National Historic District, 6
guided tours, 69–70
Hawthorne District, 20, 22
itinerary recommendations, 3–4
Japanese-American Historical Plaza, 12
lodging, 39–49, 68–69
Lownsdale Square, 6
mail and shipping, 69
media, 69
nightlife and the arts, 49–56
Nob Hill and vicinity, 14–17, 32–33, 50, 51
Northeast Alberta Street, 22
parks and gardens, 6, 11, 13, 17, 19, 22
Pearl District, Old Town/ Chinatown, 11–14, 30–31
Pioneer Courthouse Square, 8, 10
Portland International Airport area, 48–49
price categories, 24, 39
restaurants, 8, 13, 16, 20, 23–39
Sellwood District, 23
shopping, 59–64
sports and outdoor activities, 7, 56–59
telephones, 69
Terry Schrunk Plaza, 11
timing the visit, 5
transportation, 64–67, 69, 70
visitor information, 70
Washington Park and Forest Park, 17–20
West of Downtown, 38–39, 47–48
Yamhill National Historic District, 11
Portland Art Museum, 10
Portland Building, 10
Portland Center for the Performing Arts, 10

Portland Classical Chinese Garden, F24, 13
Portland Institute for Contemporary Art (PICA), 13
Portland/Oregon Visitors Association, 10
Portland Rose Festival, F15
Portland Saturday Market, F25, 13–14
Portland State University, 10
Portteus Vineyards, 478
Potholes Reservoir, 506
Potholes State Park, 506–507
Poulsbo, WA, 320, 322
Poulsbo Marine Science Center, F24, 320
Powell's City of Books (shop), F25, 14
Prehistoric Gardens, 106
Preston Estate Vineyards, 488
Price categories
dining, 24, 74, 245, 514, 520
lodging, 39, 74, 264, 514, 520
Princess Louisa Inlet, 566
Prineville, OR, 161–162
Prineville Reservoir State Park, 162
Prosser, WA, 480
Pullman, WA, 495–496
Purple Point Information Center, 375
Puyallup, WA, 335–336
Puyallup Fair, F16

Q
Quinault Beach Resort & Casino 🏨, 410–411
Quinault Pride Fish House, 412
Quw'utsun' Cultural and Conference Centre, 556

R
Rafting, 75, 203, 376, 381, 517
Rail passes, F47–F48
Railroad Depot Museum, 505
Railroads. ⇨ Also Train travel
Oregon, 148, 193, 207
Seattle, 244
Vancouver, 530–531
Washington, 339, 341, 369, 448, 449
Rainbow Falls State Park, 448
Rainier Mountain Festival, F16
Rainy Day Gallery, 446
Raphael's ✕, 197
Ray's Boathouse ✕, 264
Recreational Equipment, Inc., F25, 299
Red Agave ✕, F23, 135
Redhook Brewery, 280
Redmond, OR, 162–163
Reedsport, OR, 101–102
Renton, WA, 339–340

Renton Historical Museum, *339*
Restaurant Osterreich ✕, *379*
Restaurant Zoë ✕, *F23*, *251*
Restaurants, *F17*, *F21–F23*,
   F38. ⇨ *Also under cities*
   and areas
Fodor's choice, F21–F23
price categories, 24, 74, 245,
   514, 520
Rhododendron Species
   Botanical Garden, *329*
Rice Northwest Museum of
   Rocks and Minerals, *113*
Richardson's Recreational
   Ranch, *161*
Richland, WA, *485–486*
Rim Visitor Center, *176*
Ripley's Believe It or Not
   (museum), *94*
Ritzville, WA, *505–506*
Riverfest, *F14*
Riverfront Park, *498–499*
Robert Straub State Park, *89*
Roche Harbor, *394–395*
Rockaway Beach, OR, *86–87*
Rock-climbing, *294*, *366*,
   503, *516–517*
Rockhounding, *76*
Rocky Reach Dam, *377*
Rodeos, *193*, *194*, *198*
Rogue River, *107–108*
Rogue River National Forest,
   181
Rogue River Views, *190*
Rood Bridge Park, *114*
Rooster Rock State Park, *142*
Roozengaarde (commercial
   garden), *359*
Rosalie Whyel Museum of Doll
   Art, *245*
Rose Farm, *117*
Roseburg, OR, *188–190*
Roslyn, WA, *468*
Ross Ragland Theater, *179*
Rothschild House, *430*
Round Barn, *213*
Round-Up Hall of Fame
   Museum, *194*
Rover's ✕, *256*
Row River Trail, *138*
Royal British Columbia
   Museum, *F24*, *548*
Ruby Beach, *413*
Ruckle Provincial Park, *567*
Run of the River 🖫, *380*
Running and jogging, *137*
Rutherglen Mansion ✕🖫, *461*

S

Sacajawea State Park, *488*
Saddle Mountain State Park,
   83
Sagelands Vineyard, *473*
Sailboarding, *76*
Sailing, *289–291*, *326–327*,
   387, *392*, *569*
St. Ann's Academy, *548*
Salem, OR, *125–128*

Salem Art Fair and Festival,
   F15
Salish Lodge ✕🖫, *F19*, *341*
Salishan (resort), *91*
Salmon Harbor, *101*
Salmon Street Fountain, *6*
Salt Spring Island, B.C.,
   567–569
Salumi ✕, *F23*, *255*
Sam Kee Building, *529*
Samuel H. Boardman State
   Park, *108*
San Juan Center for Art &
   Nature, *394*
San Juan County Fair, *F16*
San Juan Historical Museum,
   394
San Juan Island, WA, *393–399*
San Juan Island National
   Historic Park, *394*
San Juan Islands, WA,
   385–402
children, attractions for, 386,
   389, 394
emergencies, 401
guided tours, 402
lodging, 386–387, 390–392,
   396–397
mail and shipping, 401
money matters, 401–402
parks, 386, 390, 394
restaurants, 386, 390, 395–396
shopping, 388, 393, 399
sports and outdoor activities,
   387, 392–393, 398–399
transportation, 399–401
visitor information, 402
Sanctuary ✕, *442*
Sand Point Magnuson Park,
   289
Santiago's ✕, *475*
Sarah Spurgeon Art Gallery,
   469
Schminck Memorial Museum,
   216
Schneider Museum of Art, *184*
Schreiner's Iris Gardens, *127*
Schurman Rock, *294*
Science Factory (museum),
   134
Science Fiction Experience,
   228
Scoggin Valley Park and
   Henry Higgins Lake, *111*
Scuba diving, *327*, *334*, *343*,
   393, *399*, *435*, *438*, *517*
Sea Gulch, *95*
Sea Lion Caves, *99*
Sea Rose (shop), *97*
Seafair, *F15*
Seashells, shopping for, *97*
Seaside, OR, *82–84*
Seaside Aquarium, *83*
Seattle, WA, *F11–F12*,
   222–311
Ballard, 263–264
Belltown, 224, 228–232,
   250–252, 264–272, 299

Broadway shopping district,
   235, 237
Capitol Hill, 235–238,
   255–257, 274, 276–277,
   303–304
children, attractions for, 224,
   228–229, 232, 233–234, 237,
   238, 239, 240–241, 242–243,
   244, 245
Downtown, 224, 228–232,
   245, 248–250, 264–272,
   295–299
Eastside, 243–245, 260–261,
   277–278
emergencies, 309
First Hill, 273
Fremont Center, 241–242,
   262–262, 273, 305–306
Green Lake and Phinney, 262
guided tours, 310–311
International District, 254–255,
   272, 300–301
itinerary recommendations, 223
lodging, 264–278
mail and shipping, 309
money matters, 309
nightlife and the arts, 225,
   278–286
North and West of Downtown,
   239–243
parks and gardens, 234,
   237–238, 241, 242, 243,
   244, 287–289
Pike-Pine Corridor, 237
Pioneer Square, F25, 234,
   254–255, 272, 301–303
price categories, 245, 264
Queen Anne, 224, 228–232,
   252–254, 273, 299–300
restaurants, 225, 245–264
Seattle-Tacoma International
   Airport area, 273–274
shopping, 225, 228–229, 235,
   237, 295–306
South and East of Downtown,
   232–234
sports and outdoor activities,
   286–294
transportation, 307–308,
   309–310, 311
University District, 238–239,
   257, 259–260, 276–277,
   304–305
visitor information, 311
Seattle Aquarium, *229*
Seattle Art Museum, *229*
Seattle Asian Art Museum,
   F24, *237*
Seattle Center, *232*
Seattle Cherry Blossom
   Festival, *F14*
Seattle environs, *314–350*
children, attractions for, 320,
   322–323, 334, 328, 329–330,
   334, 335–336, 337, 341,
   342, 344
emergencies, 349
guided tours, 350

lodging, 316, 320, 322, 323–324, 326, 332–333, 336, 338–339, 340–342, 343, 345, 346, 347, 348
money matters, 349–350
nightlife and the arts, 326, 333–334, 342
parks and gardens, 316, 324, 325, 329–330, 331, 336, 337, 338, 342
restaurants, 316, 320, 323, 325–326, 331–332, 336, 338, 339, 340, 341–342, 343, 344–345, 346
shopping, 335, 347
sports and outdoor activities, 326–327, 334, 342, 343, 347
transportation, 348–349, 350
visitor information, 350
Seattle IMAX Dome Theater, 232
Seattle International Children's Festival, F14
Seattle International Film Festival, F14
Seattle Mariners' Opening Day, F14
Seattle Symphony, 284
Seaview, WA, 443–444
Sechelt, B.C., 566–567
Second Beach, 531
Sedro-Woolley, WA, 367, 369
Sedro-Woolley Museum, 369
Sehome Hill Arboretum, 362
Sekiu, WA, 415–416
Senator George Baldwin Hotel Museum, 179
Senior-citizen travel, F44
Sequim, WA, 428–430
Sequim Bay State Park, 429
Sequim-Dungeness Museum, 428
Seth Ryan Winery, 482
Seven Hills Winery, 490
Shadywood Park, 114
Shark Reef, 386
Shaw Island, WA, 388–389
Shaw Island Historical Museum, 389
Sheep Rock, OR, 210–211
Shelburne Inn ✕☾, F21, 444
Shopping, F25–F26. ⇨ Also under cities and areas
Shore Acres State Park, 103
Siltcoos River Canoe Trail, 100–101
Silver Falls State Park, 124–125
SilverLake at Roza Hills (winery), 478
Silverton, OR, 123–124
Sinclair Centre, 523, 526
Siskiyou National Forest, 186–187
Sisters, OR, 171–172
Siuslaw National Forest, 130
Siuslaw Pioneer Museum, 100

Siwash Rock, 531
Skagit County Historical Museum, 359
Skagit Festival of Family Farms, F16
Skagit River Loop, 373
Skagit Valley Tulip Festival, F14
Skating, 58
Skidmore Fountain, 14
Skiing, F18, F25, F45, 58, 76, 137, 152, 153, 156, 164, 167, 170, 184, 186, 206, 217, 220, 342, 347, 367, 378, 381, 428, 458–459, 476, 494, 504, 523, 572
Skinner Butte Park, 134
Skookumchuck Narrows Provincial Park, 566
Skykomish, WA, 348
Smith Rock State Park, F26, 163
Snake River, 203–204
Snohomish, WA, 346–347
Snohomish County Children's Museum, 344
Snohomish County Historic Museum, 344
Snoqualmie, WA, 341–342
Snoqualmie Valley Historical Museum, 340
Snoqualmie Valley Railroad, 341
Snowboarding, 217, 494, 523, 572
Snowmobiling, 517
Snowshoeing, 428, 459
Soap Lake, 507
Sokol Blosser (winery), 119
Sol Duc Hot Springs, 422
Sol Duc Trail, 427–428
Sooke, B.C., 555–556
Sooke Harbour House ✕☾, F19, 555–556
Sooke Potholes Provincial Park, 555
Sooke Regional Museum and Visitor Information Centre, 555
Sorrento ☾, 273
South Beach State Park, 95
South Bend, WA, 447–448
South Slough National Estuarine Research Reserve, 104
South Whidbey Historical Museum, 352
Southern British Columbia, 565–574
emergencies, 574
festivals and seasonal events, 566
guided tours, 566
lodging, 565–567, 568–569, 570–571
nightlife, 571–572
parks, 566, 567

price categories, 520
restaurants, 565–569, 570
shopping, 572
sports and outdoor activities, 569
transportation, 566, 573, 574
visitor information, 574
Southern Oregon, 173–190
children, attractions for, 182, 184, 189
festivals and seasonal events, 183, 185–186
lodging, 178, 180, 181, 183, 185, 187, 188, 189–190
nightlife and the arts, 183, 185–186
parks, 173–174, 176, 178–180, 181, 184, 186–187
restaurants, 178, 180, 181, 183, 184–185, 187, 188, 189–190
sports and outdoor activities, 184, 186
transportation, 190
visitor information, 190
Southern Oregon History Center, 181
Southwestern Washington, 439–467
children, attractions for, 440, 442, 444, 445, 446, 447, 448, 449, 451, 454, 459–460, 462, 463, 464
emergencies, 466
guided tours, 466
lodging, 443, 444, 445, 446, 448, 449–450, 454–456, 459, 461, 462–463, 464, 465
mail and shipping, 466
money matters, 466
parks, 440, 442, 447, 448, 450–459, 462, 463, 464
restaurants, 442, 443, 444–445, 447, 448–449, 454–455, 461, 462–463, 464
shopping, 446
sports and outdoor activities, 443, 446, 456–459
transportation, 465–466
visitor information, 467
Space Needle, F25, 232
Spencer Butte, 134
Spencer Spit State Park, 386
Spirit of Washington Dinner Train ✕, 244, 339
Spokane, WA, 496–504
Spokane Interstate Fair, F16
Sports and outdoor activities, F17–F18, F45. ⇨ Also under cities and areas
Sport Fishing Museum, 533–534
Spout Springs (ski area), 197
Spring Bay Inn ☾, F19, 391
Springwater Trail Corridor, 141
Squalicum Harbor Marina, 362

Stadium Historic District (Tacoma), 330
Stang Manor Bed and Breakfast ⛅, 200
Stanley Park, F24, 529–532
Star Bistro ✕, 352
State Capitol Museum (Olympia), 337
State of Oregon Sports Hall of Fame, 11
Steam clock, 526
Steam trains. ⇨ See Railroads
Steamboat Inn ✕⛅, F20, 189–190
Steamboat Rock State Park, 509
Steel Information Center, 176
Steens Mountain, 214–215
Stehekin, WA, 375
Stephanie Inn ✕⛅, 84
Steptoe Memorial State Park, 495
Stevens Crawford Heritage House, 117
Stevenson, WA, 145–147, 463–464
Stonington Gallery, F25, 302
Storyeum, 526
Streetcar travel, 309–310
Student travel, F45
Summit at Snoqualmie Pass (ski resort), F25, 342
Sun Lakes State Park, 509
Sun Mountain Lodge, ✕⛅, 373
Sun Notch, 176
Sunnyside, WA, 479–480
Sunrise Visitor Center, 454
Sunriver Resort ⛅, F19, 168–169
Sunset Bay State Park, 103
Sunshine Coast Festival of the Written Arts, 566
Sunshine Coast Museum and Archives, 565
Sur La Table (shop), F25, 298
Sweet Home, OR, 131
Swimming, 58
Sumpter Valley Railroad, 207
Sunbathing, 58
Suttle Lake Resort and Marina ✕⛅, 156
Symbols, F7

T

Tacoma, WA, 327–335
Tacoma Art Museum, 330
Tacoma Narrows Bridge, 330
Tacoma Nature Center at Snake Lake, 330
Tamastslikt Cultural Institute, 196
Tanglewood Island, 324
Tauca Lea by the Sea ✕⛅, 559–560
Taxes, F45–F46

Taxis
Portland, 69
Seattle, 310
Vancouver and Victoria, 543, 554
Taylor Hotel, 446
Teapot Dome, 477–478
Tefft Cellars, 478
Telephones, F46, 69
Temple Beth Israel, 17
Tennant Lake Natural History Interpretive Center, 366
Tennis, 58
Terminal Gravity Brew Pub ✕, 201
Terra Blanca (winery), 482
TerrifVic Jazz Party, F14
Thanksgiving Day Parade, F16
Theatre on the Square, 328
Theatre West, 91
Thomas Kay Woolen Mill Museum, 126–127
Three Capes Loop, 89
Three Doors Down ✕, 36
Three Rivers Winery, 491
Thurston County Fair, F15
Thurston Wolfe (winery), 480
Tillamook, OR, 87–88
Tillamook Bay, 85
Tillamook County Creamery, 87–88
Tillamook Head, 83
Tillamook Naval Air Station Museum, 88
Tillamook Rock Light Station, 83
Tillicum Beach Campground, 97–98
Timberline Lodge ⛅, F20, 151–152
Time, F46
Timing the visit, F13–F16
Tina's ✕, F22, 119
Tipping, F46
Tofino, B.C., 560–562
Tofino Botanical Gardens, 561
Toppenish, WA, 477
Totem poles, 531, 556
Tou Velle State Park, 181
Touch of Europe Bed & Breakfast Inn ✕⛅, 475
Tours and packages, F38, F46–F47
Townshend Cellar, 499
Toy shops, 64
Tradewinds (whale-watching cruises), 92
Trail of the Cedars, 373
Train travel, F47–F48. ⇨ Also Railroads
Oregon, 220
Portland, 70
Seattle, 311
Vancouver and Victoria, 542, 543, 564
Washington, 350, 384, 513, 518

Travel agencies, F48
disabilities and accessibility, F37
tours and packages, F46–F47
Trevett-Nunn House, 17
Trolley cars, 10, 70, 82, 115–116, 473
Troutdale, OR, 142, 144
Tu Tú Tun Lodge ⛅, F20, 108
Tualatin Hills Nature Park, 114
Tucker Cellars, 479
Tulalip Museum, 344
Tumwater Falls Park, 337
Tumwater Historical Park, 338
Turnbull National Wildlife Refuge, 504
Turtles Bar & Grill ✕, 135
1200 Bistro and Lounge ✕, 256
Twenty-Five Mile Creek State Park, 374
Two Rivers Park, 489

U

U.S. Bank, 206
U.S. Coast Guard Station Cape Disappointment, 442
Ucluelet, B.C., 559–560
Ukiah-Dale Forest State Park, 197
Umatilla, OR, 191–192
Umatilla County Historical Society Museum, 194
Umatilla Indian Reservation, 196
Umatilla Marina Park, 192
Umatilla National Forest, 197
Umatilla National Wildlife Refuge, 192
Umpqua Discovery Center, 101
Umpqua Lighthouse Park, 102
Umpqua River Lighthouse, 102
Under the Greenwood Tree ⛅, F20, 181
Underground (guided tour), F25, 194
Undersea Gardens, 94
Union Hotel ⛅, F21, 200
Union County Museum, 199
Union Station (Portland), 14
Union Station (Tacoma), 330–331
Union's National Historic District, 199
Unity Lake State Park, 207
University District Street Fair, F14
University of Oregon, 135
University of Oregon Museum of Art, 135
University of Oregon Museum of Natural History, 135
University of Washington, 239
Uppertown Firefighters Museum, 81–82
USS *Turner Joy* (navy destroyer), 322–323
Uwajimaya (market), F26, 300–301

V

Valley Art Center, *494*
Valley Bronze of Oregon,
    201–202
Valley Cafe ✕, *471*
Valley of the Rogue State
    Park, *F24, 187*
Valley River Inn ✕▥ , *136*
Valley View Vineyard, *182*
Valleyfest, *F16*
Vancouver, B.C., *F12,
    521–544*
*children, attractions for,
    530–532*
Chinatown, 526, 528–529
Downtown, 522–523, 526
emergencies, 543
Gastown, 522–523, 526
Granville Island, 532–534
guided tours, 543
lodging, 520, 535–537, 543
money matters, 543
nightlife and the arts, 537–538
parks and gardens, 529–532
price categories, 520
restaurants, 520, 534–535
shopping, 534, 538–541
Stanley Park, F24, 529–532
transportation, 541–543
visitor information, 543–544
Vancouver, WA, *461–463*
Vancouver Aquarium Marine
    Science Centre, *531–532*
Vancouver Convention and
    Exhibition Centre, *522–523*
Vancouver Island, B.C.,
    555–565
children, attractions for, 556
emergencies, 564
*festivals and seasonal events,
    559*
*lodging, 555–556, 557–558,
    559–560, 561–562*
*parks and gardens, 555, 556,
    559, 561, 562–563*
*restaurants, 555–556, 557,
    558–560, 561–562*
*sports and outdoor activities,
    562, 564*
transportation, 563–564
visitor information, 565
Vancouver Lookout! Harbour
    Centre Tower, *526*
Vancouver Sea Festival, *F15*
Vesuvius, B.C., *567*
Victoria, B.C., *F12, 544–555*
*children, attractions for, 546,
    547, 548*
Chinatown, 546
emergencies, 554
guided tours, 555
lodging, 520, 550–552
Market Square, 547
nightlife and the arts, 552–553
parks and gardens, 546, 548
price categories, 520
restaurants, 520, 549–550
shopping, 553

transportation, 553–554
visitor information, 555
Victoria Bug Zoo, *548*
Views, *F26*
Viking Fest, *F14*
VineHeart (winery), *480*
Vintage Inn ▥ , *F21, 463*
Visas. ⇨ *See* Passports and
    visas
Visitor information, *F48.*
    ⇨ *Also under cities and
    areas*
Vivace Roasteria
    (coffeehouse), *F25,
    280–281*
Volcanoes, *167, 450,
    459–460*
Volunteer Fireman's Museum,
    359
Volunteer Park, *237–238*

W

W. W. Seymour Botanical
    Conservatory, *331*
Waiting for the Interurban
    (statue), *242*
Waldo Lake, *137*
Waldport, OR, *96–97*
Walking, *347, 438*
Walla Walla, WA, *490–492*
Waller Hall, *127*
Wallowa County Museum, *202*
Wallowa Lake Lodge ✕▥ ,
    202–203
Wallowa Lake State Recreation
    Park, *202*
Wallowa Lake Tramway, *202*
Wallowa Mountain Loop, *203*
Wallowa Mountains, *199*
Wallowa-Whitman National
    Forest, *207*
Wanapum Dam Visitor Center,
    471
Wanapum State Park, *471*
Warm Springs, OR, *158–159*
Wasco County Courthouse,
    149
Washington, *F12, 313–518.*
    ⇨ *Also* Eastern
    Washington; Northwestern
    Washington; Olympic
    Peninsula; San Juan
    Islands; Seattle; Seattle
    environs; Southwestern
    Washington; Yakima River
    Valley
emergencies, 516
guided tours, 517–518
itinerary recommendations, 315
lodging, 314
media, 516
price categories, 314
restaurants, 313–314
*sports and outdoor activities,
    317, 516–517*
timing the visit, 314
transportation, 514–516, 518
visitor information, 518

Washington Hills Cellar, *479*
Washington Park (Fidalgo
    Island), *359*
Washington Park (Portland),
    17–20
Washington Park Arboretum
    (Seattle), *238*
Washington State Apple
    Festival, *F16*
Washington State History
    Museum, *331*
Washington State International
    Kite Festival, *F16*
Washington State University,
    495
Washington's Fruit Place
    Visitor Center, *473*
Water sports, *517*
Waterbrook Winery, *490*
Waterfall Gardens ▥ , *316,
    320*
Waterfront Seafood Grill ✕ ,
    252
Waterfront Station, *526*
Watertown Hotel ▥ ,
    276–277
Wax Works, *94*
Weather information, *F13*
Web sites, *F48*
Welches, OR, *153–154*
Wellspring ▥ , *450*
Wenatchee, WA, *376–378*
West Coast Game Park,
    105–106
West Coast Trail, *563*
West Valley Veterans
    Memorial, *123*
Western Washington
    University, *362*
Westin Resort & Spa ▥ , *571*
Westport Aquarium, *405–406*
Westport Maritime Museum,
    406
Westward Ho! Sternwheeler,
    100
Weyerhauser/Hoffstadt Bluff
    Visitors Center, *460*
Whale Museum, *394*
Whale-watching, *92, 94–95,
    98, 366, 393, 399, 443,
    523, 562*
Whatcom Falls Park, *362*
Whatcom Museum of History
    and Art, *362*
Whidbey Island, WA,
    351–358
Whiffen Spit, *555*
Whispering Spruce Trail, *98*
Whistler, B.C., *569–572*
Whistler Summer Festivals,
    F15
White Pass Village (ski area),
    458–459
Whitehouse-Crawford
    Restaurant ✕ , *491*
Whitman College, *490*
Whitman Mission National
    Historic Site, *490–491*

Wickaninnish Inn ✕⌖, *F19, 561*

Wickaninnish Interpretive Centre, *563*

Wild and Scenic Snake River Corridor, *204*

Wildlife preserves

Oregon, 90, 93, 95–96, 104, 109, 130, 179, 192, 196, 213, 216

Vancouver and Victoria, 562–563

Washington, 337, 361, 366, 406–407, 447, 489, 504, 507

Wildlife Safari, *189*

Wildlife viewing, *F18, 76, 91, 100, 101, 105–106, 107, 114, 189, 213–214, 428, 459*

Willamette Falls Locks, *117*

Willamette Mission State Park, *127*

Willamette Shore Trolley, *115–116*

Willamette University, *127*

Willamette Valley and the Wine Country, Oregon, *111–140*

children, attractions for, 113, 128, 134

festivals and seasonal events, 121, 136

lodging, 113, 116, 117–118, 119–120, 122–123, 124, 128, 130, 131, 132, 136

nightlife and the arts, 136

parks and gardens, 111, 114, 115, 117, 120–121, 124–126, 127, 129, 130, 133, 134, 138

restaurants, 113, 114, 115, 116, 117, 119, 121, 122, 123, 124, 128, 129, 130, 131, 132, 135–136, 138–139

shopping, 113, 124, 133, 137

sports and outdoor activities, 118, 136–137

transportation, 139

visitor information, 139–140

William M. Tugman State Park, *101*

Willow Crest Winery, *480–481*

Willows Lodge ⌖ , *277*

Winchester Bay's Salmon Harbor, *102*

Winchester Wasteway, *506*

Wine festivals, *F15*

Wineglass Cellars, *478*

Winema National Forest, *179–180*

Wineries

Oregon, 76, 86, 115, 119, 121–122, 137, 148, 182, 188, 189

Seattle, 244

Washington, 316, 386, 473, 477, 478, 479, 480–482, 485, 488, 489, 490, 491, 497, 499

Wing Luke Museum, *F24, 234*

Winthrop, WA, *373–374*

Wizard Island, *176*

Wolfhaven International (wolf sanctuary), *337*

Wonderland Trail, *F26, 457*

Wooden Boat Festival, *F16*

Woodland Park Zoo, *243*

Woodmark Hotel ⌖ , *278*

Woodward Canyon Winery, *491*

World Championship Cypress Tree, *109*

World Kite Museum and Hall of Fame, *444*

World Trade Center (Portland), *11*

World Trade Center (Vancouver), *522–523*

Wright Park, *331*

WSeattle ⌖ , *F20, 266*

Yachats, OR, *97–98*

Yachats Ocean Road State Recreation Area, *98*

Yakima, WA, *472–473, 475–477*

Yakima Area Arboretum, *473*

Yakima Cellars, *473*

Yakima Electronic Railway Museum, *473*

Yakima Nation Cultural Center, *477*

Yakima River Valley, WA, *467–484*

children, attractions for, 471, 473, 476, 477, 479

emergencies, 483

guided tours, 483–484

lodging, 468–469, 472, 475–476, 479, 480, 481

mail and shipping, 483

money matters, 483

parks, 471, 477

restaurants, 468, 472–472, 473, 475–476, 478–480, 481

shopping, 476–477

sports and outdoor activities, 476

transportation, 482–483

visitor information, 484

Yakima River Winery, *481*

Yakima Valley Museum, *473*

Yamhill, OR, *119–120*

Yaquina Bay Bridge, *94*

Yaquina Bay Lighthouse, *93*

Yaquina Bay State Park, *95*

Yaquina Head, *93*

Yaquina Head Lighthouse, *95*

Yaquina Head Outstanding Natural Area, *95–96*

Z

Zigzag, OR, *153–154*

Zillah, WA, *477–479*

Zoos

Portland, 19

Seattle, 243, 244

Victoria, 548

Washington, 329, 428, 497

NOTES

NOTES

FODOR'S KEY TO THE GUIDES

America's guidebook leader publishes guides for every kind of traveler.
Check out our many series and find your perfect match.

FODOR'S GOLD GUIDES
America's favorite travel-guide series offers the most detailed insider reviews of hotels, restaurants, and attractions in all price ranges, plus great background information, smart tips, and useful maps.

COMPASS AMERICAN GUIDES
Stunning guides from top local writers and photographers, with gorgeous photos, literary excerpts, and colorful anecdotes. A must-have for culture mavens, history buffs, and new residents.

FODOR'S CITYPACKS
Concise city coverage in a guide plus a foldout map. The right choice for urban travelers who want everything under one cover.

FODOR'S EXPLORING GUIDES
Hundreds of color photos bring your destination to life. Lively stories lend insight into the culture, history, and people.

FODOR'S TRAVEL HISTORIC AMERICA
For travelers who want to experience history firsthand, this series gives in-depth coverage of historic sights, plus nearby restaurants and hotels. Themes include the Thirteen Colonies, the Old West, and the Lewis and Clark Trail.

FODOR'S POCKET GUIDES
For travelers who need only the essentials. The best of Fodor's in pocket-size packages for just $9.95.

FODOR'S FLASHMAPS
Every resident's map guide, with dozens of easy-to-follow maps of public transit, restaurants, shopping, museums, and more.

FODOR'S CITYGUIDES
Sourcebooks for living in the city: thousands of in-the-know listings for restaurants, shops, sports, nightlife, and other city resources.

FODOR'S AROUND THE CITY WITH KIDS
Up to 68 great ideas for family days, recommended by resident parents. Perfect for exploring in your own backyard or on the road.

FODOR'S HOW TO GUIDES
Get tips from the pros on planning the perfect trip. Learn how to pack, fly hassle-free, plan a honeymoon or cruise, stay healthy on the road, and travel with your baby.

FODOR'S LANGUAGES FOR TRAVELERS
Practice the local language before you hit the road. Available in phrase books, cassette sets, and CD sets.

KAREN BROWN'S GUIDES
Engaging guides—many with easy-to-follow inn-to-inn itineraries—to the most charming inns and B&Bs in the U.S.A. and Europe.

BAEDEKER'S GUIDES
Comprehensive guides, trusted since 1829, packed with A–Z reviews and star ratings.

OTHER GREAT TITLES FROM FODOR'S
Baseball Vacations, The Complete Guide to the National Parks, Family Vacations, Golf Digest's Places to Play, Great American Drives of the East, Great American Drives of the West, Great American Vacations, Healthy Escapes, National Parks of the West, Skiing USA.